Internet links

There are lots of useful websites where you can find out more about science. We have created links to some of the best sites on the Usborne Quicklinks Website. To visit the sites, go to **www.usborne-quicklinks.com** and type the keywords "science dictionary". Here are some of the things you can do on the internet:

Try online puzzles, games and quizzes
Email your questions to online science experts
Take part in interactive experiments

Internet safety

The websites recommended in Usborne Quicklinks are regularly reviewed. However, the content of a website may change at any time and Usborne Publishing is not responsible for the content of websites other than its own. We recommend that children are supervised while on the internet.

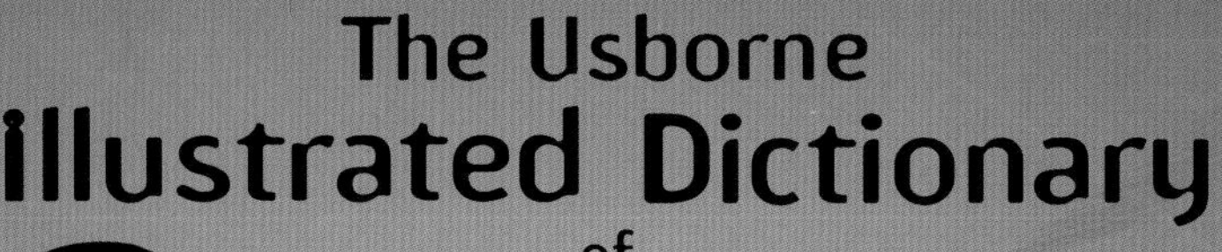

The Usborne Illustrated Dictionary of SCIENCE

Corinne Stockley,
Chris Oxlade and Jane Wertheim
Revision editor: Kirsteen Rogers

Designers: Karen Tomlins and Verinder Bhachu
Digital illustrator: Fiona Johnson
Illustrators: Kuo Kang Chen and Guy Smith

Scientific advisors:
Dr. Tom Petersen, John Hawkins, Dr. John Durell and Jerry McCoy (Physics) Dr. John Waterhouse, Nick Christou, John Raffan, Rae Michaelis, Alan Alder and Dr. Larry Scroggins (Chemistry) Dr. Margaret Rostron, Dr. John Rostron and Dr. Jan Mercer (Biology)

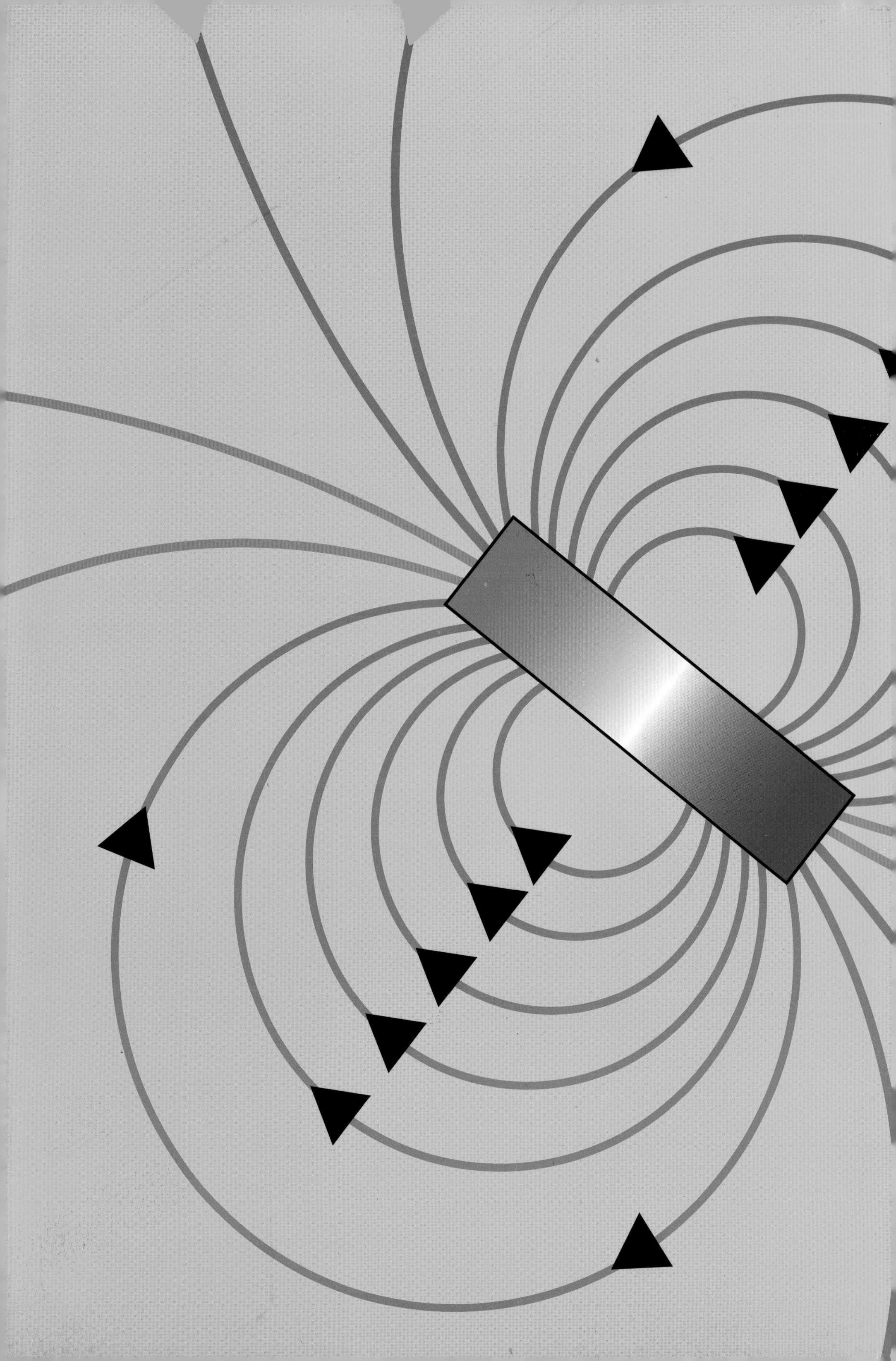

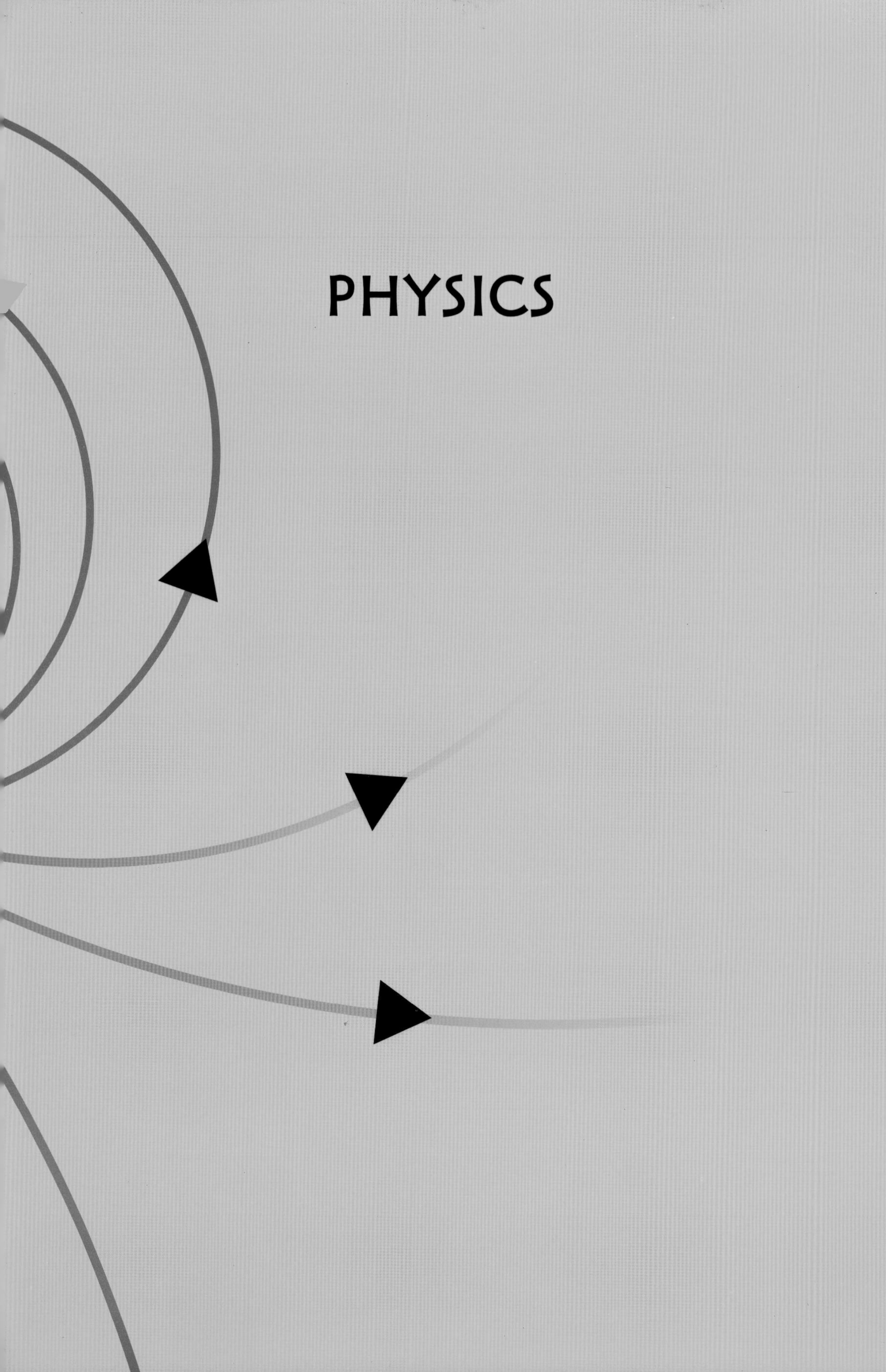
PHYSICS

ABOUT PHYSICS

Physics is the study of the properties and nature of matter, the different forms of energy and the ways in which matter and energy, interact in the world around us. In this book, physics is divided into six colour-coded sections. The areas covered by these sections are explained below.

Mechanics and general physics

Covers the main concepts of physics, e.g. forces, energy and the properties of matter.

Electricity and magnetism

Explains the forms, uses and behaviour of these two linked phenomena.

Heat

Explains heat energy in terms of its measurement and the effects of its presence and transference. Includes the gas laws.

Atomic and nuclear physics

Examines atomic and nuclear structure and energy, radioactivity, fission and fusion.

Waves

Looks at the properties and effects of wave energy and examines sound, electromagnetic and light waves in detail.

General physics information

General material – charts and tables, also information on the treatment of experimental results.

CONTENTS

Mechanics and general physics

Heat

Waves

Electricity and magnetism

Atomic and nuclear physics

General physics information

ATOMS AND MOLECULES

The Ancient Greeks believed that all matter was made up of tiny particles which they called **atoms**. This idea has since been expanded and theories such as the **kinetic theory** have been developed which can be used to explain the physical nature and behavior of substances in much greater detail. Matter can exist in three different **physical states**. The state of a substance depends on the nature of the substance, its temperature and the pressure exerted on it. Changes between states are caused by changes in the pressure or temperature (see **changes of state**, page 30).

Atom

Table tennis ball

Earth

If atoms were the size of table tennis balls, by the same scale, table tennis balls would be as big as the Earth.

Atom

The smallest part of a substance which can exist and still retain the properties of the substance. The internal structure of the atom is explained on pages 82-83. Atoms are extremely small, having radii of about 10^{-10}m and masses of about 10^{-25}kg. They can form **ions*** (electrically charged particles) by the loss or gain of **electrons*** (see **ionization**, page 88).

Diagram showing relative sizes of some atoms

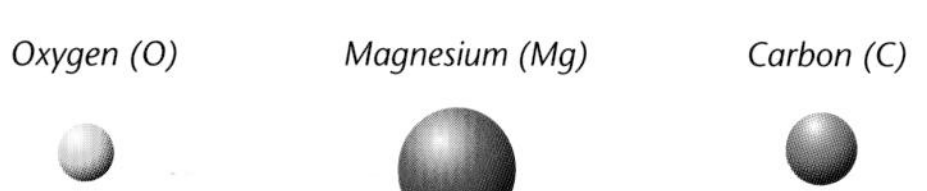
Oxygen (O)
Magnesium (Mg)
Carbon (C)

Molecule

The smallest naturally-occurring particle of a substance. Molecules can consist of any number of **atoms**, from one (e.g. neon) to many thousands (e.g. proteins), all held together by **electromagnetic forces***. All the molecules of a pure sample of a substance contain the same atoms in the same arrangement.

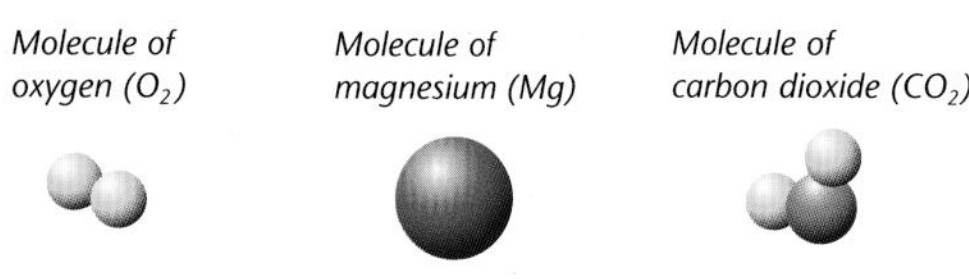
Molecule of oxygen (O_2)
Molecule of magnesium (Mg)
Molecule of carbon dioxide (CO_2)

Note that many substances do not have **molecules**, for example:

Ionic compound* *of* ***anions**** *and* ***cations****.

***Atomic lattice** of **atoms** all bonded together.*

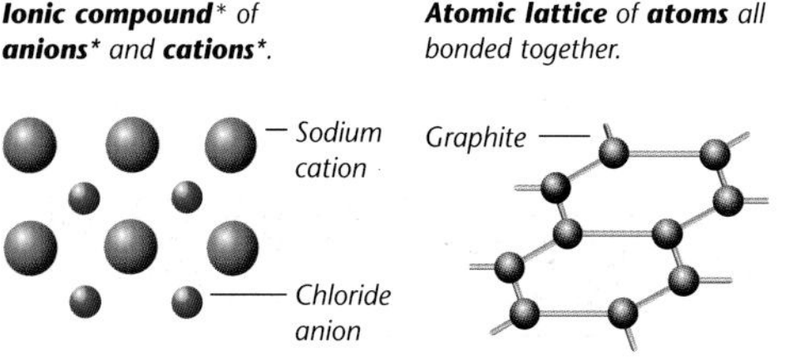
Sodium cation
Chloride anion
Graphite

Element

A substance which cannot be split into simpler substances by a chemical reaction. All **atoms** of the same element have the same number of **protons*** in their **nuclei*** (see **atomic number**, page 82).

Compound

A substance whose **molecules** contain the **atoms** of two or more **elements**, chemically bonded together, and which can thus be split into simpler substances. A **mixture** has no chemical bonding and is therefore not a compound.

***Element** 1*

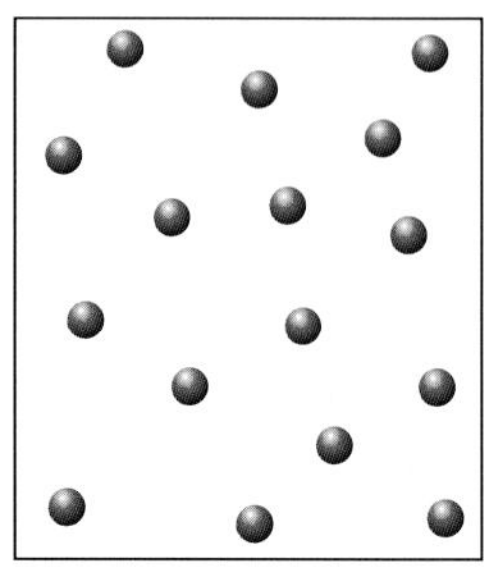

***Element** 2*

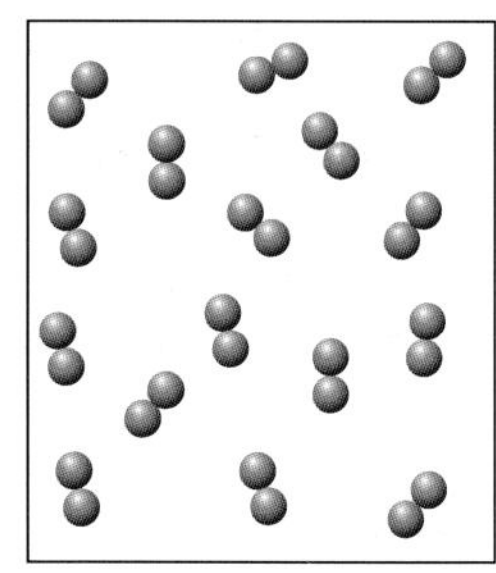

***Compound** of elements 1 and 2 – elements bonded together.*

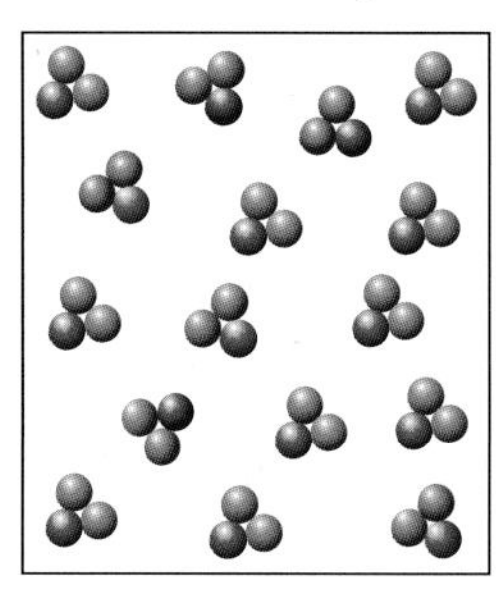

***Mixture** of elements 1 and 2 – no chemical bonding.*

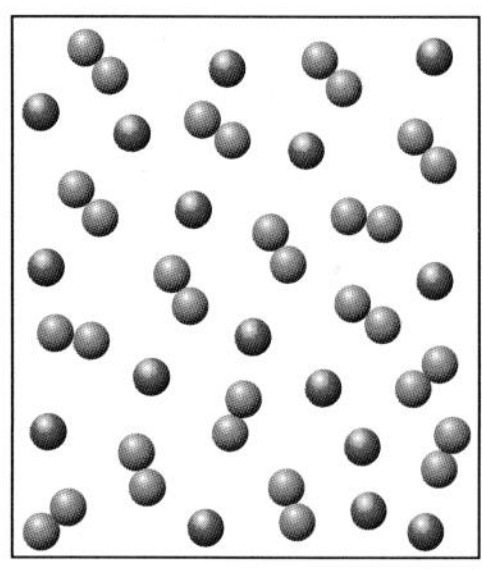

* **Anions, Cations**, 88 (**Ionization**); **Electromagnetic force**, 6; **Electrons**, 83; **Ionic compound**, 131; **Ions**, 88 (**Ionization**); **Nucleus, Protons**, 82.

Physical states

Solid state

A **state** in which a substance has a definite volume and shape and resists forces which try to change these.

Liquid state

A **state** in which a substance flows and takes up the shape of its containing vessel. It is between the **solid** and **gaseous** states.

Gaseous state

A **state** in which a substance expands to fill its containing vessel. Substances in this state have a relatively low density.

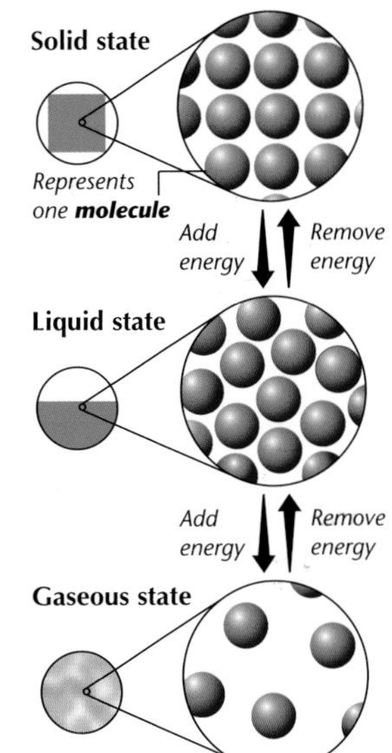
Solid state
Represents one **molecule**
Add energy
Remove energy
Liquid state
Add energy
Remove energy
Gaseous state

__Molecules__ vibrate about mean positions, having __molecular potential energy__ and __vibrational kinetic energy__*.*

Average energy of molecule much less than that needed by it to break free from other molecules.

Energy added breaks down regular pattern – molecules can move around and thus have both __translational__ and __rotational kinetic energy__.*

Average energy of molecule is just enough for it to break free from neighboring molecules, only to be captured by the next ones along.

Molecules have very large separation – they move virtually independently of each other – __intermolecular forces__ can be ignored.*

Average energy of molecule much greater than needed to break free from other molecules.

Gas

A substance in the **gaseous state** which is above its **critical temperature** and so cannot be turned into a liquid just by increasing the pressure – the temperature must be lowered first, to create a **vapor**.

Vapor

A substance in the **gaseous state** which is below its **critical temperature** (see **gas**) and so can be turned into a liquid by an increase in pressure alone – no lowering of temperature is required.

The kinetic theory

The **kinetic theory** explains the behavior of the different physical states in terms of the motion of **molecules**. In brief, it states that the molecules of **solids** are closest together, have least energy and so move the least, those of **liquids** are further apart with more energy, and those of **gases** are furthest apart with most energy. See above right.

Brownian motion

The observed random motion of small particles in water or air. It supports the kinetic theory, as it could be said to be due to impact with water or air **molecules**.

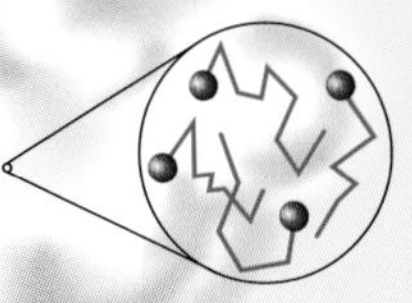

***Brownian motion** of smoke particles as they are hit by **molecules** in the air.*

Diffusion

The mixing of two **gases**, **vapors** or **liquids** over a period of time. It supports the kinetic theory, since the particles must be moving to mix, and gases can be seen to diffuse faster than liquids.

***Molecules** of two **gases** diffuse together over time.*

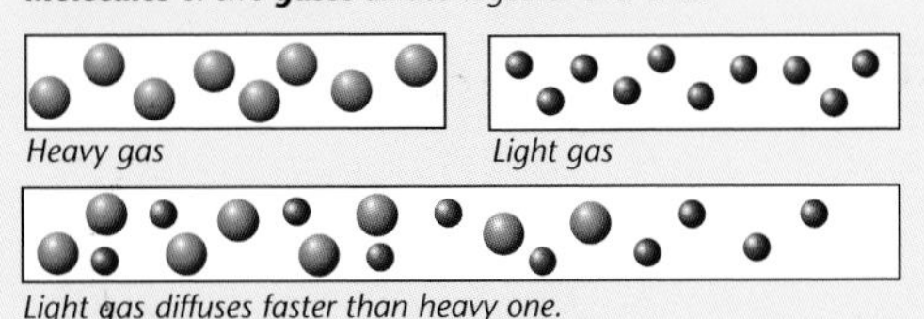
Heavy gas
Light gas

Light gas diffuses faster than heavy one.

Graham's law of diffusion

States that, at constant temperature and pressure, the rate of **diffusion** of a **gas** is inversely proportional to the square root of its density.

$$\text{Rate of diffusion} \propto \sqrt{\frac{1}{\text{density of gas}}}$$

* **Intermolecular forces**, 7; **Molecular potential energy**, 8; **Rotational**, **Translational** and **Vibrational kinetic energy**, 9 (**Kinetic energy**).

FORCES

A **force** influences the shape and motion of an object. A single force will change its velocity (i.e. **accelerate*** it) and possibly its shape. Two equal and opposite forces may change its shape or size. It is a **vector quantity***, having both magnitude and direction, and is measured in **newtons**. The main types of force are **gravitational**, **magnetic**, **electric** and **strong nuclear**. See pages 104-107 for a comparison of the first three of these.

*The Earth's **gravitational force** makes seeds fall to the ground.*

Showing forces in diagrams

***Forces** are shown by arrowed lines (the length represents magnitude and the arrow represents direction).*

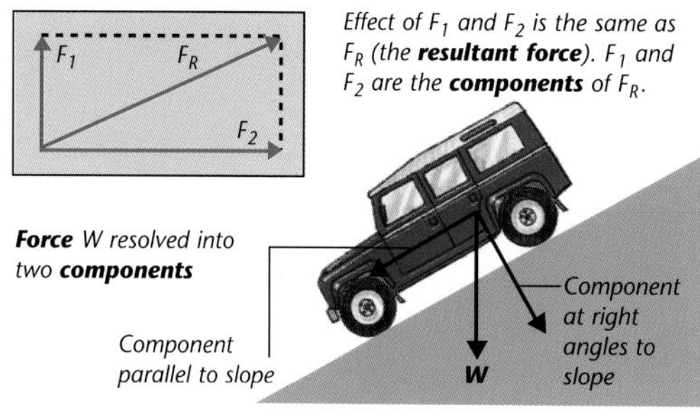
F_1
F_R
F_2
Effect of F_1 and F_2 is the same as F_R (the resultant force). F_1 and F_2 are the components of F_R.
Force W resolved into two components
Component parallel to slope
W
Component at right angles to slope

Newton (N)

The **SI unit*** of force. One newton is the force needed to accelerate a mass of 1kg by 1m s^{-2}.

Force field

The region in which a force has an effect. The maximum distance over which a force has an effect is the **range** of the force. Force fields are represented by lines with arrows, called **field lines**, to show their strength and direction (see also pages 58 and 72).

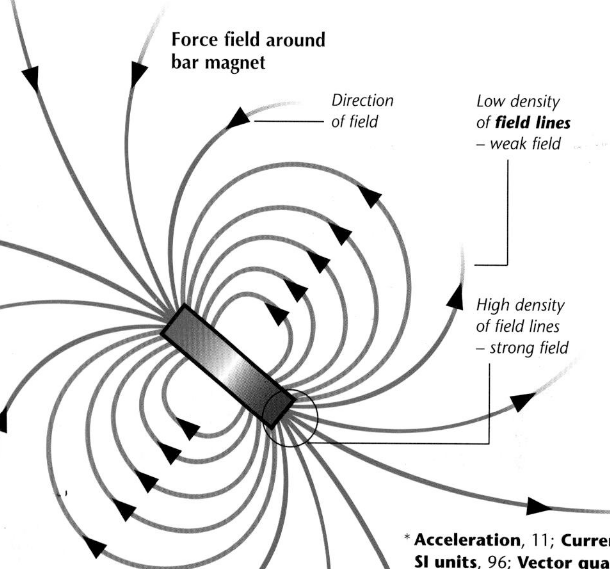
Force field around bar magnet
Direction of field
Low density of field lines – weak field
High density of field lines – strong field

Gravitational force or gravity

The force of attraction between any two objects which have mass (see also pages 18-19). It is very small unless one of the objects is very massive.

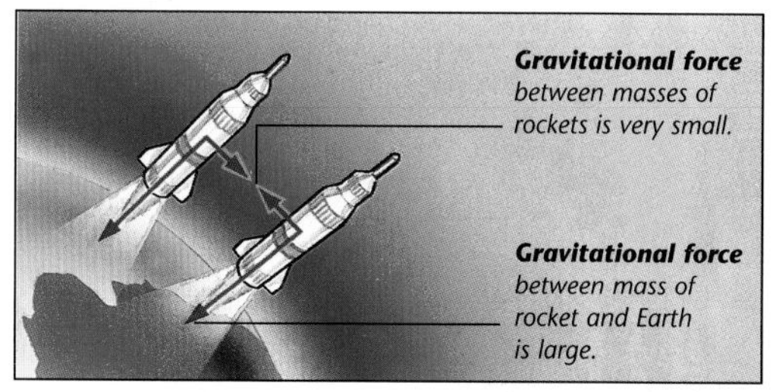
Gravitational force between masses of rockets is very small.
Gravitational force between mass of rocket and Earth is large.

Electromagnetic force

A combination of the **electric** and **magnetic forces**, which are closely related and difficult to separate.

Electric or electrostatic force

The force between two electrically-charged particles (see also page 56). It is repulsive if the charges are the same, but attractive if they are opposite.

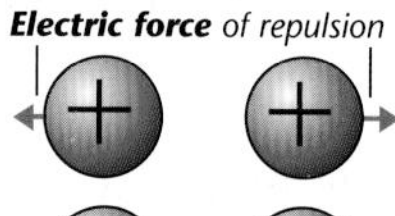
Electric force of repulsion

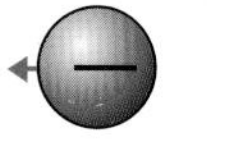
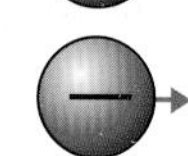
Electric force of attraction

Magnetic force

A force between two moving charges. These moving charges can be electric **currents*** (see also page 60) or **electrons*** moving around in their **electron shells***.

Magnetic forces in electric wires

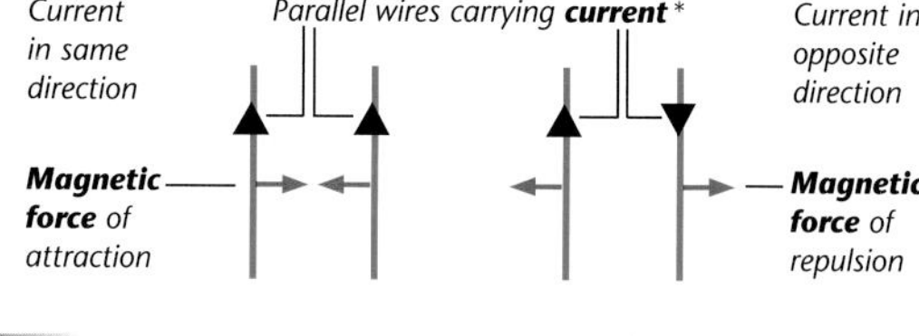
Current in same direction
Parallel wires carrying current*
Current in opposite direction
Magnetic force of attraction
Magnetic force of repulsion

* **Acceleration**, 11; **Current**, 60; **Electrons**, **Electron shells**, 83; **SI units**, 96; **Vector quantity**, 108.

Intermolecular forces

The **electromagnetic forces** between two molecules. The strength and direction of the forces vary with the separation of the molecules (see diagram below).

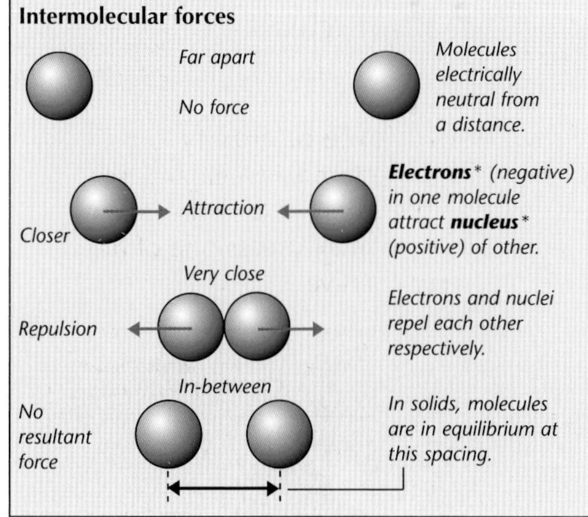
Intermolecular forces
Far apart
No force
Molecules electrically neutral from a distance.
Closer
Attraction
Electrons* (negative) in one molecule attract **nucleus*** (positive) of other.
Very close
Repulsion
Electrons and nuclei repel each other respectively.
In-between
No resultant force
In solids, molecules are in equilibrium at this spacing.

Tension

Equal and opposite forces which, when applied to the ends of an object, increase its length. They are resisted by the **intermolecular force** of attraction.

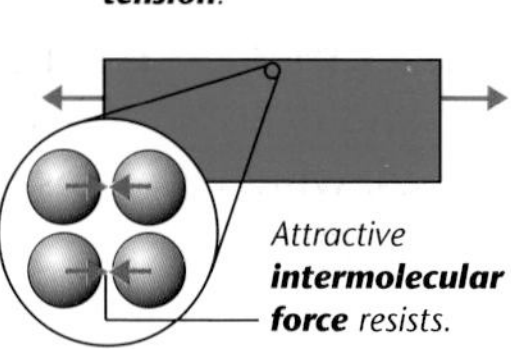
Molecules pulled apart by **tension**.
Attractive **intermolecular force** resists.

Compression

Equal and opposite forces which decrease the length of an object. They are opposed by the **intermolecular force** of repulsion.

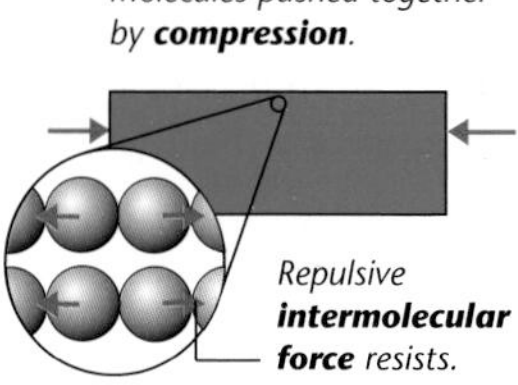
Molecules pushed together by **compression**.
Repulsive **intermolecular force** resists.

Contact force

The **intermolecular force** of repulsion between the molecules of two objects when they touch.

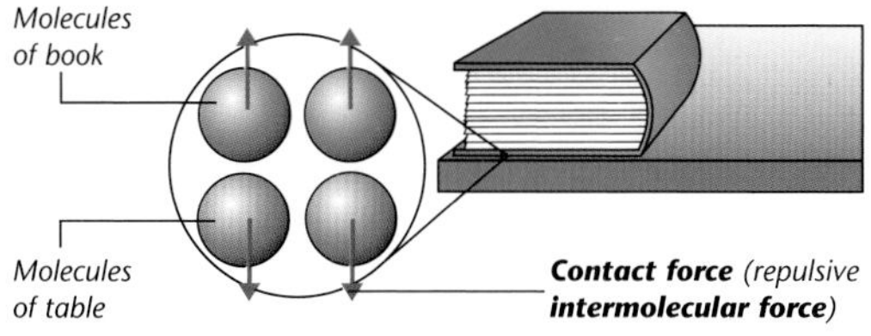
Molecules of book
Molecules of table
Contact force (repulsive **intermolecular force**)

Strong nuclear force

The force of attraction between all the particles of an atomic **nucleus*** (the **protons*** and **neutrons***). It prevents the **electric force** of repulsion between the protons from pushing the nucleus apart (see also page 84).

*Particles in an atomic nucleus are held together by the **nuclear force**.*

Frictional force or friction

The force which acts to oppose the motion of two touching surfaces over each other, caused by the **intermolecular force** of attraction between the molecules of the surfaces. There are two types, the **static** and the **kinetic frictional force**.

Static frictional force

The **frictional force** between two touching surfaces when a force is applied to one of them but they are not moving. The maximum value of the static frictional force occurs when they are on the point of sliding over each other. This is called the **limiting force**.

Kinetic frictional force or sliding frictional force

The **frictional force** when one surface is sliding over another at constant speed. It is slightly less than the **limiting force** (the maximum **static frictional force**).

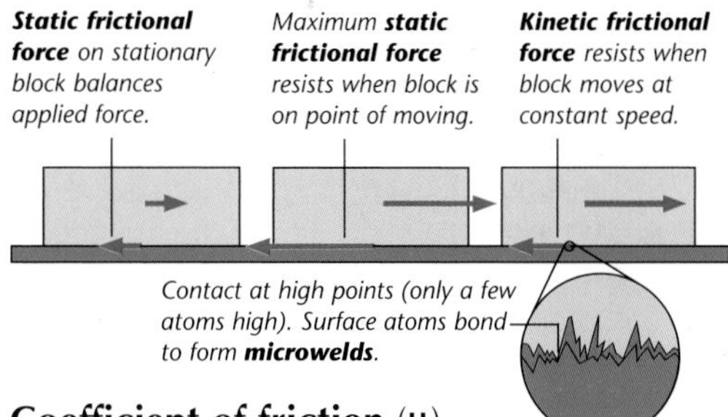
Static frictional force on stationary block balances applied force.
Maximum **static frictional force** resists when block is on point of moving.
Kinetic frictional force resists when block moves at constant speed.
Contact at high points (only a few atoms high). Surface atoms bond to form **microwelds**.

Coefficient of friction (μ)

The ratio of the **frictional force** between two surfaces to that pushing them together (the **normal contact force**). There are two values, the **coefficient of static friction** and the **coefficient of kinetic friction**.

Coefficient of friction $\mu = \dfrac{\text{frictional force (F)}}{\text{normal contact force (R)}}$

* **Electrons**, 83; **Neutrons**, **Nucleus**, **Protons**, 82.

ENERGY

Work is done when a force moves an object. **Energy** is the capacity to do work. When work is done on or by an object, it gains or loses energy respectively. Energy exists in many different forms and can change between them (energy **conversion** or **transformation**), but cannot be created or destroyed (**law of conservation of energy**). The **SI unit*** of energy and work is the **joule** (**J**).

The energy from the Sun is the equivalent of that supplied by one million million million power stations.

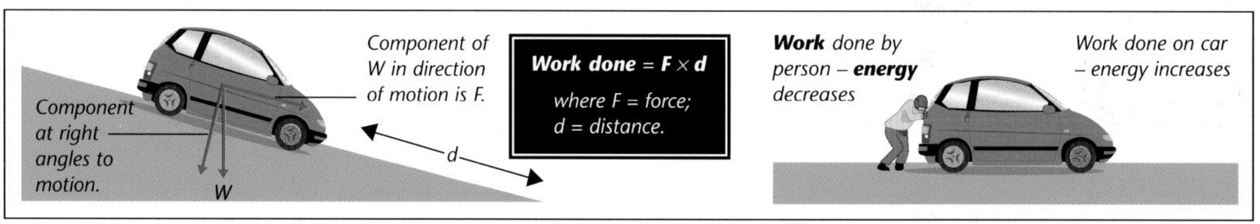

Component at right angles to motion.
W
Component of W in direction of motion is F.
d
Work done = **F × d**
where F = force;
d = distance.
Work done by person – **energy** decreases
Work done on car – energy increases

Potential energy (P.E.)

The energy of an object due to its position in a **force field***, which it has because work has been done to put it in that position. The energy has been "stored up". The three forms of potential energy are **gravitational potential energy**, **electromagnetic potential energy** and **nuclear potential energy** (depending on the force involved).

Gravitational potential energy

The **potential energy** associated with the position of an object relative to a mass which exerts a **gravitational force*** on it. If the object is moved further from the mass (e.g. an object being lifted on Earth), work is done on the body and its gravitational potential energy is raised.

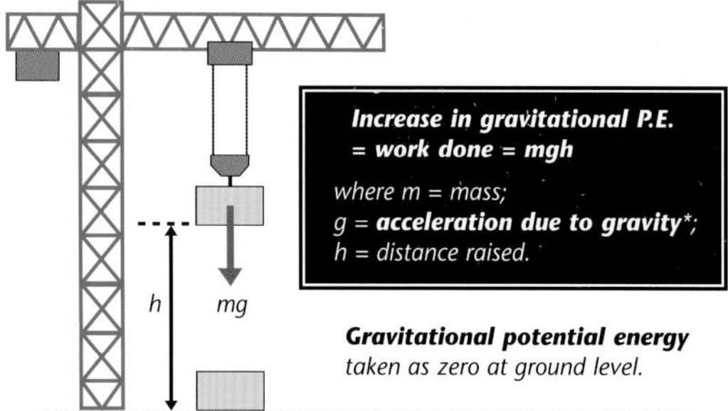

h
mg
Increase in gravitational P.E. = work done = mgh
where m = mass;
g = **acceleration due to gravity***;
h = distance raised.

Gravitational potential energy *taken as zero at ground level.*

Nuclear potential energy

The **potential energy** stored in an atomic **nucleus***. Some nuclear potential energy is released during **radioactive decay***.

Electromagnetic potential energy

The **potential energy** associated with the position of a body in a **force field*** created by an **electromagnetic force***.

Molecular potential energy

The **electromagnetic potential energy** associated with the position of molecules relative to one another. It is increased when work is done against the **intermolecular force***.

Elastic potential energy or strain energy

An example of the **molecular potential energy**, stored as a result of stretching or compressing an object. It is the work done against the **intermolecular force***.

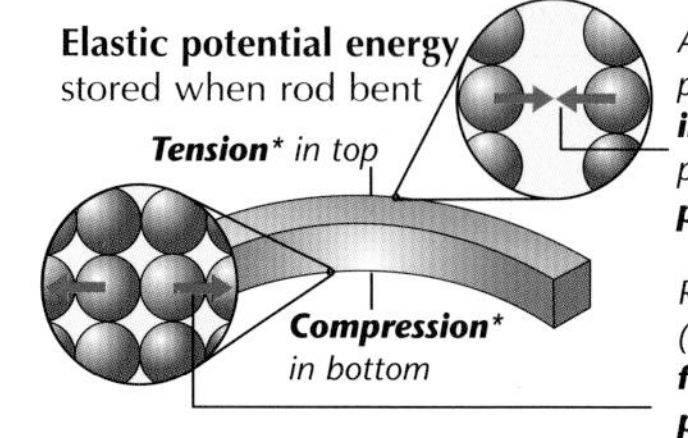

Elastic potential energy stored when rod bent
Tension* in top
Compression* in bottom
Attraction between particles (see **intermolecular forces**, page 7). **Molecular potential energy** stored.
Repulsion between particles (see **intermolecular forces**, page 7). **Molecular potential energy** stored.

Chemical energy

Energy stored in substances such as fuels, food, and chemicals in batteries. It is released during chemical reactions, e.g. as heat when a fuel burns, when the **electromagnetic potential energy** of the atoms and molecules changes.

Plants convert energy from sunlight into food – a store of ***chemical energy****.*

* **Acceleration due to gravity**, 18; **Compression**, 7; **Electromagnetic force**, **Force field**, **Gravitational force**, 6; **Intermolecular forces**, 7; **Nucleus**, 82; **Radioactive decay**, 87; **SI units**, 96; **Tension**, 7.

Kinetic energy (K.E.)

The energy associated with movement. It takes the form of **translational**, **rotational** and **vibrational energy**.

Kinetic energy of two objects linked by a spring

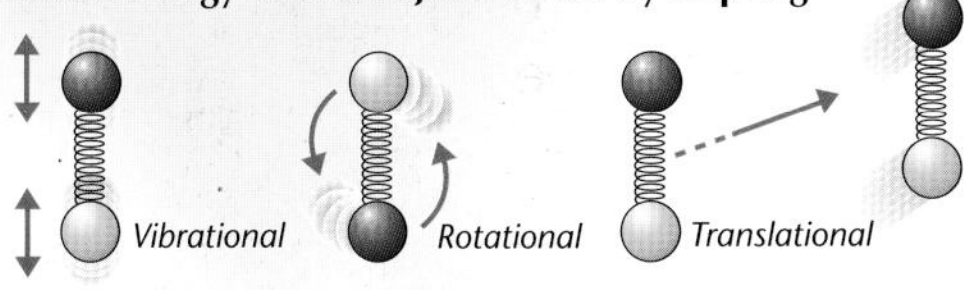
Vibrational
Rotational
Translational

K.E. = ½ mv² *where m = mass; v = velocity.*

Mechanical energy

The sum of the **kinetic energy** and **gravitational potential energy** of an object.

*The **mechanical energy** of a pendulum is constant (if resistive forces are neglected).*

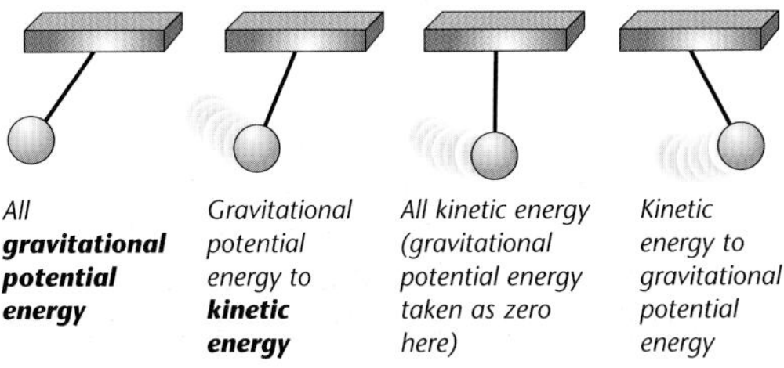
All gravitational potential energy
Gravitational potential energy to kinetic energy
All kinetic energy (gravitational potential energy taken as zero here)
Kinetic energy to gravitational potential energy

Internal or thermal energy

The sum of the **kinetic energy** and the **molecular potential energy** of the molecules in an object. If the temperature of an object increases, so does its internal energy.

Internal energy and temperature

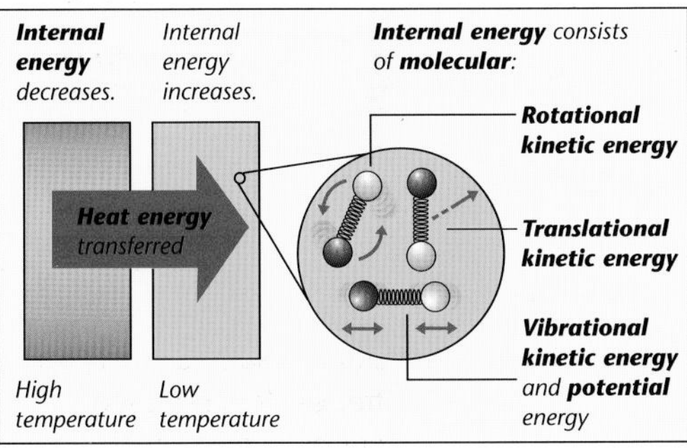
Internal energy decreases.
Internal energy increases.
Internal energy consists of molecular:
Rotational kinetic energy
Heat energy transferred
Translational kinetic energy
Vibrational kinetic energy and potential energy
High temperature
Low temperature

Heat energy or heat

The energy which flows from one place to another because of a difference in temperature (see pages 28-33). When **heat energy** is absorbed by an object, its **internal energy** increases (see diagram above).

Wave energy

The energy associated with wave action. For example, the energy of a water wave consists of the **gravitational potential energy** and **kinetic energy** of the water molecules.

Electric and magnetic energy

The types of energy associated with electric charge and moving electric charge (current). They are collectively referred to as **electromagnetic energy**.

Radiation

Any energy in the form of **electromagnetic waves*** or streams of particles. See also pages 29 and 86-87.

Power

The rate of doing work or the rate of change of energy. The **SI unit*** of power is the **watt** (**W**), which is equal to 1 joule per second.

Energy conversion in a power station

*Coal is the fossilized remains of plants that grew long ago (see also **fuel**, page 208). It is a store of **chemical energy** that came from the Sun.*

*Furnace in power station burns fuel and boils water. Here, **chemical energy** is converted to **internal energy** of steam.*

*Steam turns turbines. Internal energy of steam is converted to **rotational kinetic energy** of the turbine.*

*Generator converts kinetic energy to **electric energy**.*

*Appliances such as heaters, lamps and audio equipment convert electric energy into **heat energy**, light (**wave energy**) and sound (wave energy).*

* **Electromagnetic waves**, 44; **SI units**, 96.

MOTION

Motion is the change in position and orientation of an object. The motion of a **rigid** object (one which does not change shape) is made up of **translational motion**, or **translation**, i.e. movement of the **center of mass** from one place to another, and **rotational motion**, or **rotation**, i.e. movement around its center of mass. The study of the motion of points is called **kinematics**.

*A satellite spinning in orbit displays **rotational motion** (1) and **translational motion** (2).*

Linear motion

Linear or **rectilinear motion** is movement in a straight line and is the simplest form of **translational motion** (see introduction). The linear motion of any rigid object is described as the motion of its **center of mass**.

Center of mass

The point which acts as though the total mass of the object were at that point. The center of mass of a **rigid** object (see introduction) is in the same position as its **center of gravity** (the point through which the Earth's gravitational force acts on the object).

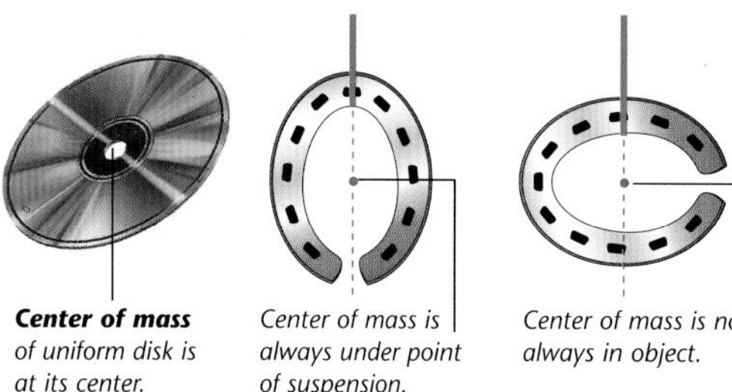

***Center of mass** of uniform disk is at its center.*

Center of mass is always under point of suspension.

Center of mass is not always in object.

Displacement

The distance and direction of an object from a fixed reference point. It is a **vector quantity***. The position of an object can be expressed by its displacement from a specified point.

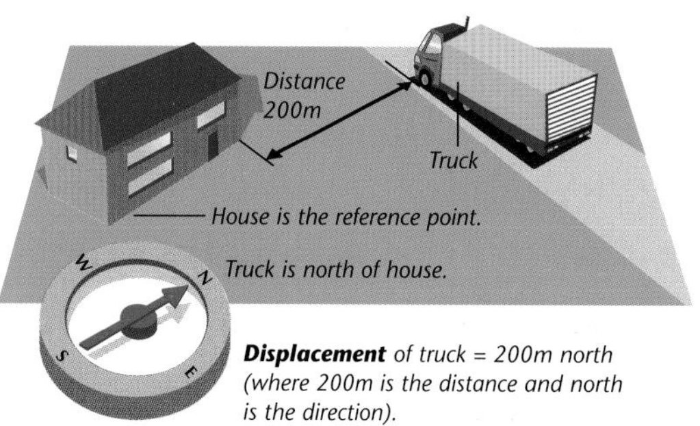
Distance
200m
Truck
House is the reference point.
Truck is north of house.
N
E
S
W

***Displacement** of truck = 200m north (where 200m is the distance and north is the direction).*

Speed

The ratio of the distance traveled by an object to the time taken. If the speed of an object is constant, it is said to be moving with **uniform speed**. The **average speed** of an object over a time interval is the distance traveled by the object divided by the time interval. The **instantaneous speed** is the speed at any given moment.

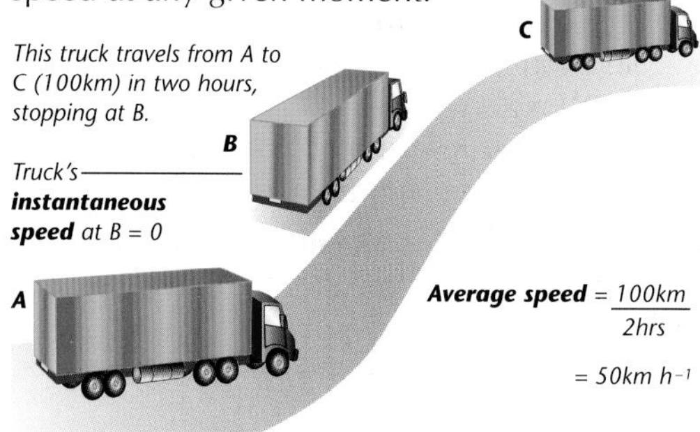
A
B
C
Truck's **instantaneous speed** at B = 0

This truck travels from A to C (100km) in two hours, stopping at B.

Average speed $= \frac{100km}{2hrs}$

$= 50km\ h^{-1}$

Velocity

The **speed** and direction of an object (i.e. its **displacement** in a given time). It is a **vector quantity***. **Uniform velocity**, **average velocity** and **instantaneous velocity** are all defined in a similar way to **uniform speed** etc. (see **speed**).

A displacement-time graph for an object which moves in a straight line from A to B and back to A (showing velocity calculation)

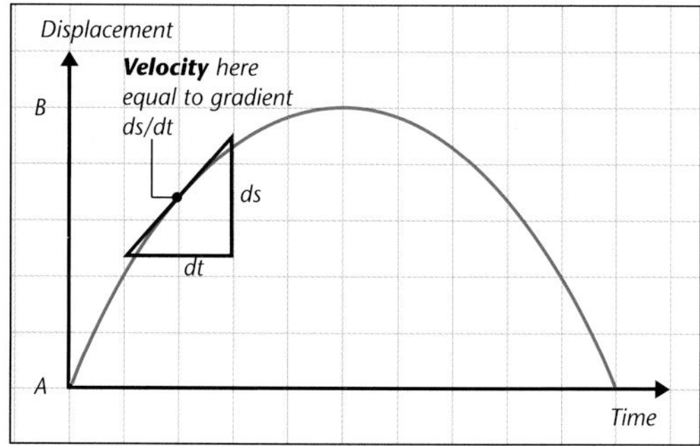
Displacement
Velocity here equal to gradient ds/dt
B
ds
dt
A
Time

* **Vector quantity**, 108.

Relative velocity

The **velocity** which an object appears to have when seen by an observer who may be moving. This is known as the velocity of the object relative to the observer.

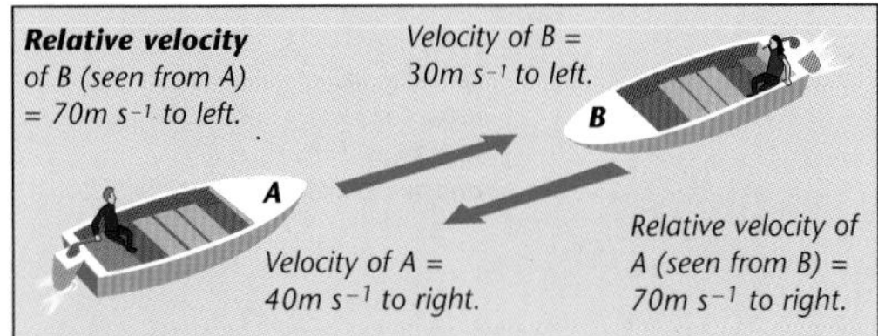

Relative velocity of B (seen from A) = 70m s⁻¹ to left.
Velocity of B = 30m s⁻¹ to left.
B
A
Velocity of A = 40m s⁻¹ to right.
Relative velocity of A (seen from B) = 70m s⁻¹ to right.

Acceleration

The ratio of the change in **velocity** of an object to the time taken. It is a **vector quantity***. An object accelerates if its **speed** changes (the usual case in **linear motion**) or its direction of travel changes (the usual case in **circular motion***). **Deceleration** in one direction is acceleration in the opposite direction (negative acceleration). An object whose velocity is changing the same amount in equal amounts of time is moving with **uniform acceleration**.

Graphs of velocity versus time showing acceleration

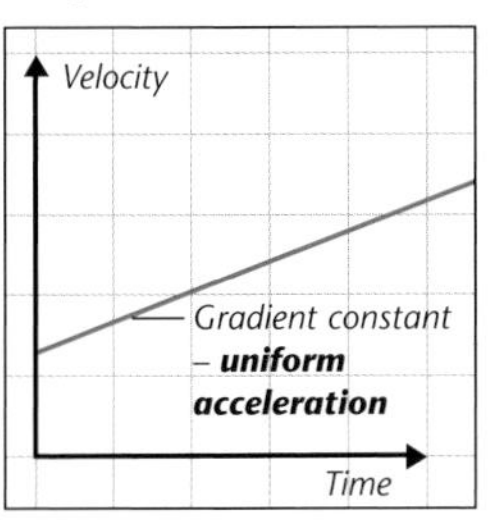

Velocity
Gradient constant – **uniform acceleration**
Time

Distance traveled in equal time intervals increases.

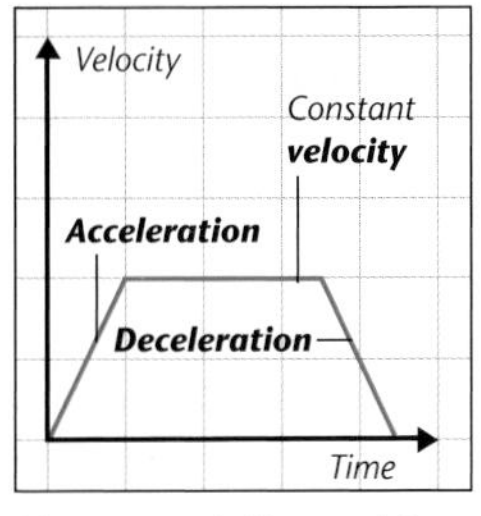

Velocity
Constant **velocity**
Acceleration
Deceleration
Time

Distance traveled in equal time intervals increases, remains constant, then decreases.

Rotational motion

The movement of an object about its **center of mass**. In rotational motion, each part of the object moves along a different path, so that the object cannot be considered as a whole in calculations. It must be split into small pieces and the **circular motion*** of each piece must be considered separately. From this, the overall motion of the object can be seen.

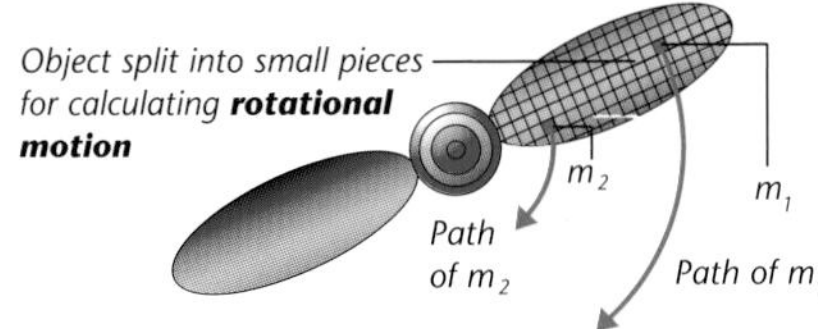

Object split into small pieces for calculating **rotational motion**
m_2
m_1
Path of m_2
Path of m_1

Equations of uniformly accelerated motion

Equations which are used in calculations involving **linear motion** with **uniform acceleration**. A **sign convention** must be used (see below). The equations use **displacement**, not distance, so changes of direction must be considered.

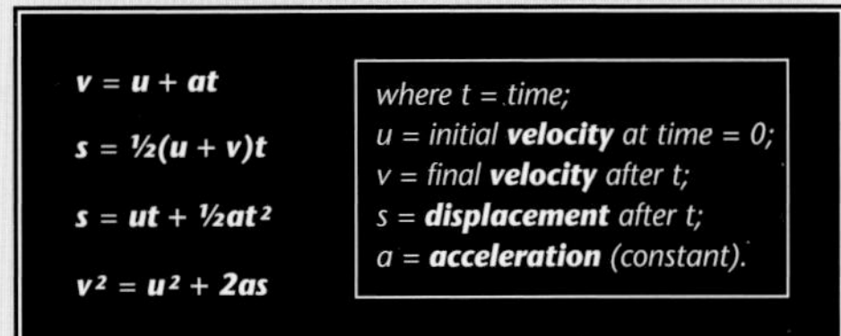

$$v = u + at$$

$$s = \tfrac{1}{2}(u + v)t$$

$$s = ut + \tfrac{1}{2}at^2$$

$$v^2 = u^2 + 2as$$

where t = time;
u = initial **velocity** at time = 0;
v = final **velocity** after t;
s = **displacement** after t;
a = **acceleration** (constant).

Sign convention

A method used to distinguish between motion in opposite directions. One direction is chosen as positive, and the other is then negative. The sign convention must be used when using the equations of motion (see above).

Sign convention

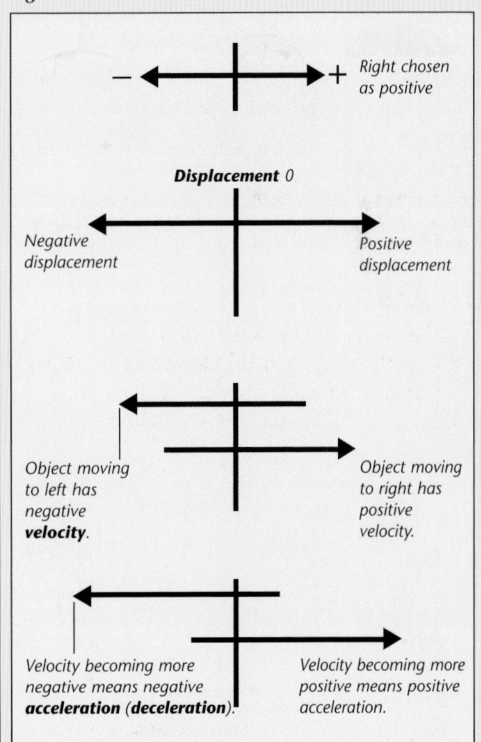

–
+
Right chosen as positive
Displacement 0
Negative displacement
Positive displacement
Object moving to left has negative **velocity**.
Object moving to right has positive velocity.
Velocity becoming more negative means negative **acceleration** (**deceleration**).
Velocity becoming more positive means positive acceleration.

* **Circular motion**, 17; **Vector quantity**, 108.

DYNAMICS

Dynamics is the study of the relationship between the motion of an object and the forces acting on it. A single force on an object causes it to change speed and/or direction (i.e. **accelerate***). If two or more forces act and there is no resultant force, the object does not accelerate, but may change shape.

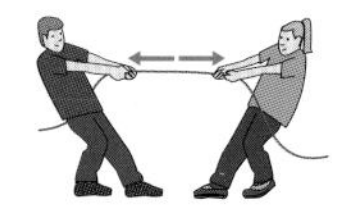

Two equal but opposite forces. No resultant force – no acceleration, but rope stretches.

Forces not equal. Rope still stretches, but also accelerates to left due to resultant force.

Mass

A measurement of the **inertia** of an object. The force needed to accelerate an object by a given amount depends on its mass – a larger mass needs a larger force.

Momentum

The **mass** of an object multiplied by its **velocity***. Since velocity is a **vector quantity***, so is momentum. See also **law of conservation of linear momentum**.

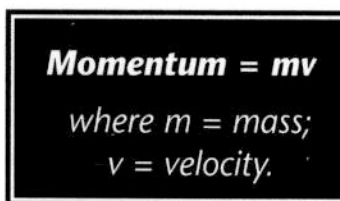

Momentum = mv

where m = mass;
v = velocity.

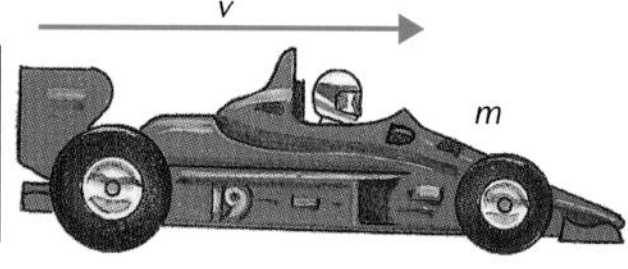
v
m

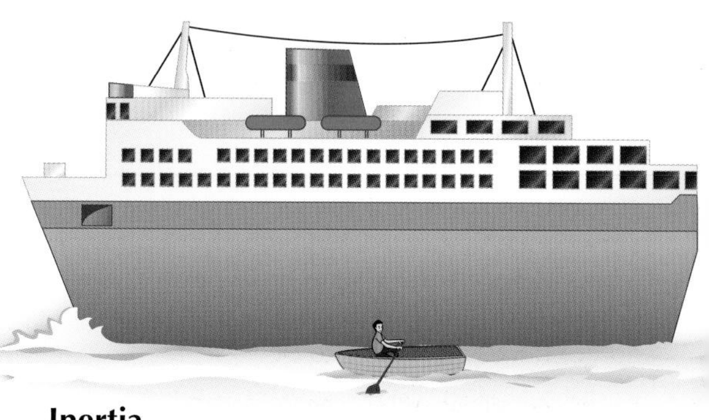

Inertia

The tendency of an object to resist a change of **velocity*** (i.e. to resist a force trying to **accelerate*** it). It is measured as **mass**.

*The large ship has much greater **inertia** (and therefore **mass**) than the little boat – a much larger force is needed to **accelerate*** it.*

Impulse

The force acting on an object multiplied by the time for which the force acts. From **Newton's second law**, impulse is equal to the change in **momentum** of an object. An equal change in momentum can be achieved by a small force for a long time or a large force for a short time.

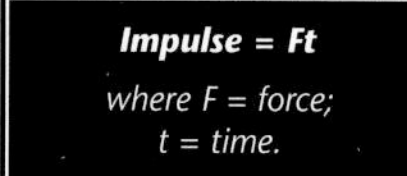

Impulse = Ft

where F = force;
t = time.

*"Crumple zone" in the front of a car increases **collision** time – this makes force smaller.*

Crumple zone

*Since force is rate of change of **momentum** (see **Newton's second law**) then:*

Impulse = change in momentum

Newton's laws of motion

Three laws formulated by Newton in the late 1670s which relate force and motion.

Newton's first law

An object will remain at rest or in uniform motion unless acted upon by a force.

Forces on the object below are equal – no resultant force, so no acceleration.

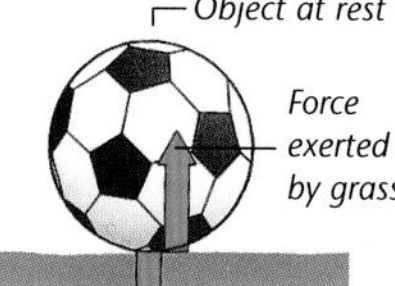
Object at rest
Force exerted by grass
Force due to gravity (weight)

Newton's second law

If the **momentum** of an object changes, i.e. if it **accelerates***, then there must be a resultant force acting on it. Normally, the **mass** of the object is constant, and the force is thus proportional to the acceleration of the object. The direction of the acceleration is the same as the direction of the force.

$$\text{Force} = \frac{\text{change in momentum}}{\text{time}}$$

*If **mass** remains constant, then:*

$$\text{Force} = \text{mass} \times \text{acceleration}$$

* **Acceleration**, 11; **Vector quantity**, 108; **Velocity**, 10.

Collision

An occurrence which results in two or more objects exerting relatively large forces on each other over a relatively short time. This is not the everyday idea of a collision, because the objects do not necessarily have to be in contact.

Example of collision without contact

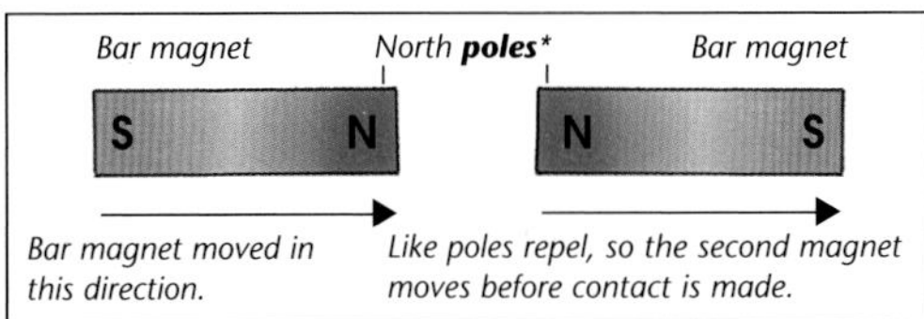

Bar magnet
North **poles***
Bar magnet
S
N
N
S
Bar magnet moved in this direction.
Like poles repel, so the second magnet moves before contact is made.

Law of conservation of linear momentum

If there is no external force on an object, then its linear **momentum** remains constant. If the system is considered just before and just after the **collision**, forces such as friction can be ignored.

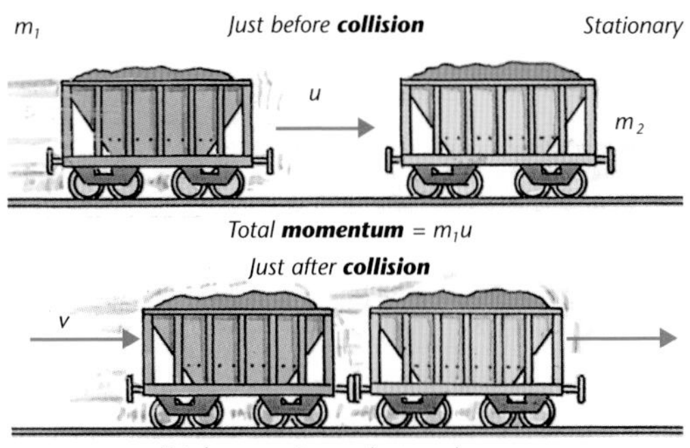

m_1
Just before **collision**
Stationary
u
m_2
Total **momentum** = m_1u
Just after **collision**
v
Total **momentum** = $(m_1 + m_2)v = m_1u$

Mass** increases – **velocity decreases to conserve momentum.*

Rocket engine

An engine which produces a high **velocity*** stream of gas through a nozzle by burning fuel held on board. The **mass** of gas is small, but its high velocity means it has a high **momentum**. The rocket gains an equal amount of momentum in the opposite direction (see **law of conservation of linear momentum**). Rocket engines are used in space because other engines require air.

Rocket engine

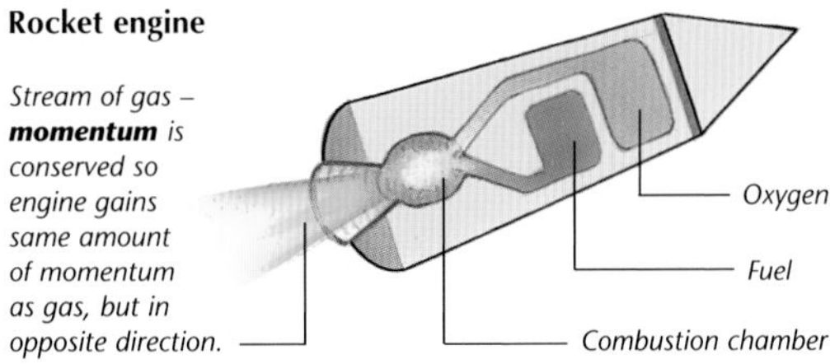

Stream of gas – **momentum** is conserved so engine gains same amount of momentum as gas, but in opposite direction.
Oxygen
Fuel
Combustion chamber

Jet engine

An engine in which air is drawn in at the front to burn fuel, producing a high **velocity*** jet of gas. The principle is the same as that for the rocket engine, except that the gas is produced differently and the engine cannot be used in space because it requires air.

Jet engine

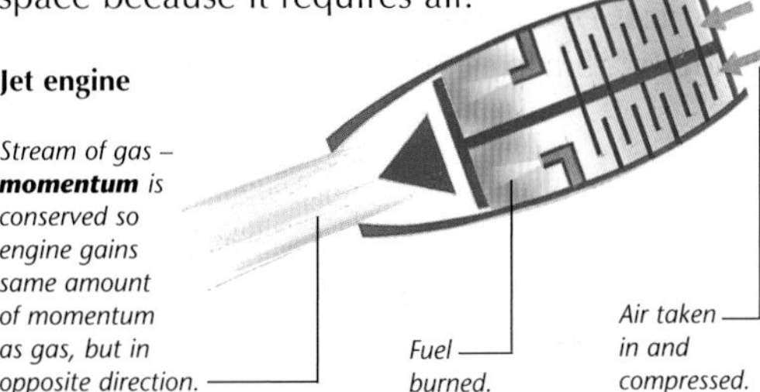

Stream of gas – **momentum** is conserved so engine gains same amount of momentum as gas, but in opposite direction.
Fuel burned.
Air taken in and compressed.

Example of Newton's second law

*A tennis ball hit by a racket undergoes a change of **momentum**.*

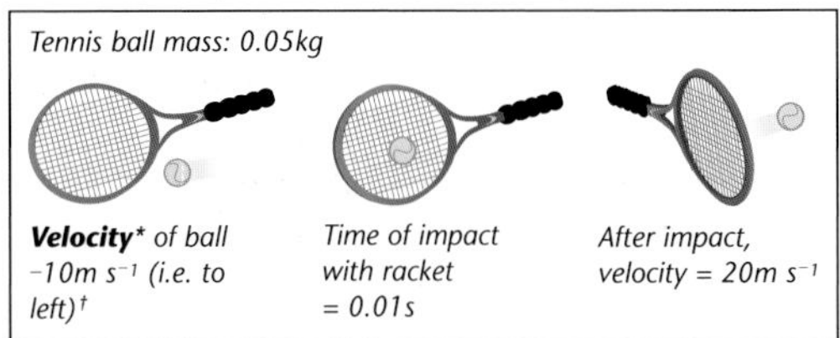

Tennis ball mass: 0.05kg
Velocity* of ball $-10m\ s^{-1}$ (i.e. to left)†
Time of impact with racket = 0.01s
After impact, velocity = $20m\ s^{-1}$

Resultant force found as follows:

$$\text{Force at impact} = \frac{\text{change in momentum}}{\text{time}} = \frac{(0.05 \times 20) - (0.05 \times -10)}{0.01} = 150N$$

Or:

$$\text{Force} = \text{mass} \times \text{acceleration} = \frac{\text{mass} \times \text{change in velocity}}{\text{time}}$$

$$= \frac{0.05 \times 30}{0.01} = 150N$$

Newton's third law

Forces always occur in equal and opposite pairs. Thus if object A exerts a force on object B, object B exerts an equal but opposite force on A. These forces do not cancel each other out, as they act on different objects.

Example of Newton's third law

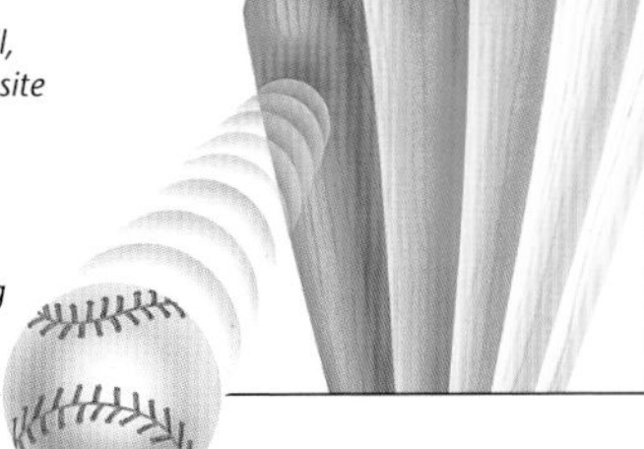

Bat exerts force on ball, accelerating it in opposite direction.

Ball exerts equal and opposite force on bat (felt as sudden slowing down of bat).

* **Pole**, 70; **Velocity**, 10.

† *Movement to right considered as positive (see **sign convention**, page 11).*

TURNING FORCES

A single force produces an **acceleration*** (see **dynamics**, page 12). In **linear motion***, it is a **linear acceleration**. In **rotational motion***, **angular acceleration*** (spinning faster or slower) is caused by a turning force or **moment** acting about the axis of rotation (the **fulcrum**).

*The rear rotor blades of a helicopter apply a **moment** to the helicopter which prevents it from spinning.*

Moment or torque

A measure of the ability of a force to rotate an object about an axis (the **fulcrum**). It is the size of the force multiplied by the perpendicular distance from the axis to the line along which the force acts (see diagram below). The **SI unit*** of moment is the **Newton meter** (**Nm**).

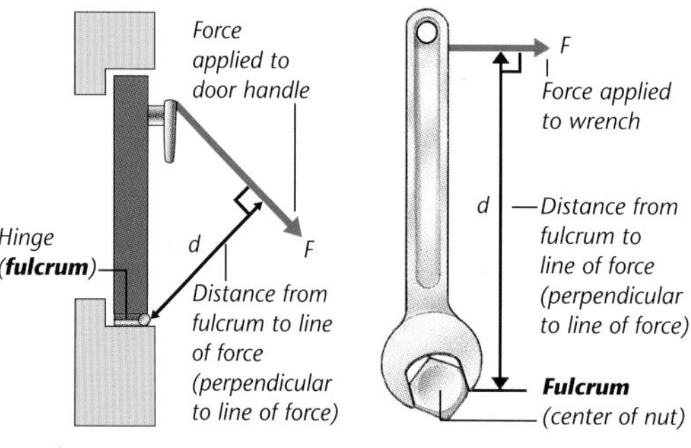

Force applied to door handle
Hinge (fulcrum)
d
F
Distance from fulcrum to line of force (perpendicular to line of force)
F
Force applied to wrench
d
Distance from fulcrum to line of force (perpendicular to line of force)
Fulcrum (center of nut)

In each case:

Moment = Fd

When considering moments, the axis about which they are taken must be stated and a **sign convention*** must be used to distinguish between clockwise and counterclockwise moments. The **resultant moment** is the single moment which has the same effect as all the individual moments acting together.

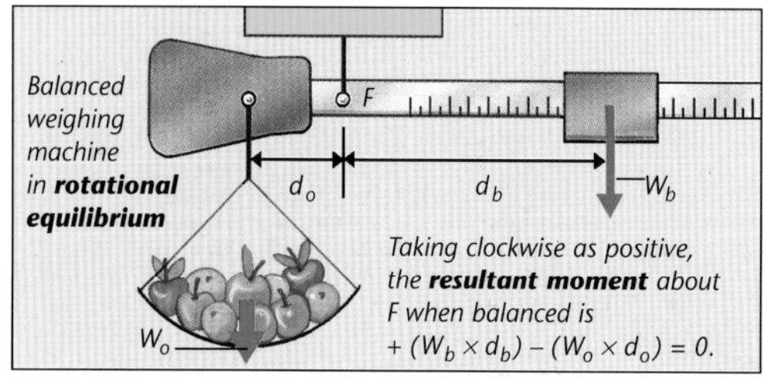

Balanced weighing machine in rotational equilibrium
F
d_o
d_b
W_b
W_o
Taking clockwise as positive, the resultant moment about F when balanced is $+(W_b \times d_b) - (W_o \times d_o) = 0$.

Couple

Two parallel forces which are equal and opposite but do not act along the same line. They produce a turning effect only, with no resultant acceleration of the **center of mass***. The **resultant moment** produced by a couple is the sum of the moments produced, and equals the perpendicular distance between the lines along which the forces act, multiplied by the size of one force.

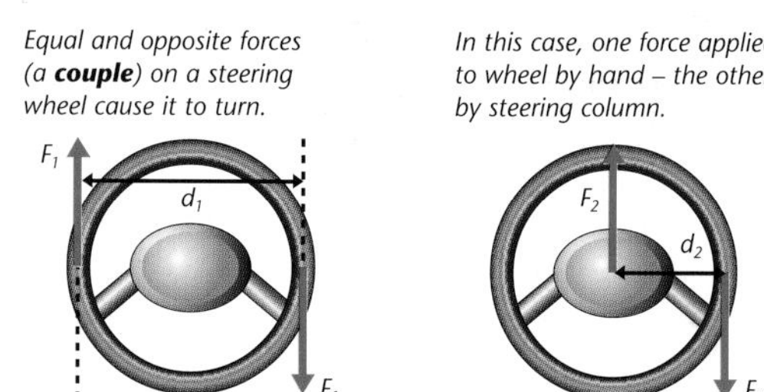

Equal and opposite forces (a couple) on a steering wheel cause it to turn.
F_1
d_1
F_1
In this case, one force applied to wheel by hand – the other by steering column.
F_2
d_2
F_2
Moment of couple = $F_1 \times d_1$
Moment of couple = $F_2 \times d_2$

Toppling

A condition which occurs if the vertical line through the **center of mass*** of an object does not pass through the base of the object. If this occurs, a **couple** of the weight and the **normal contact force*** rotates the object further over.

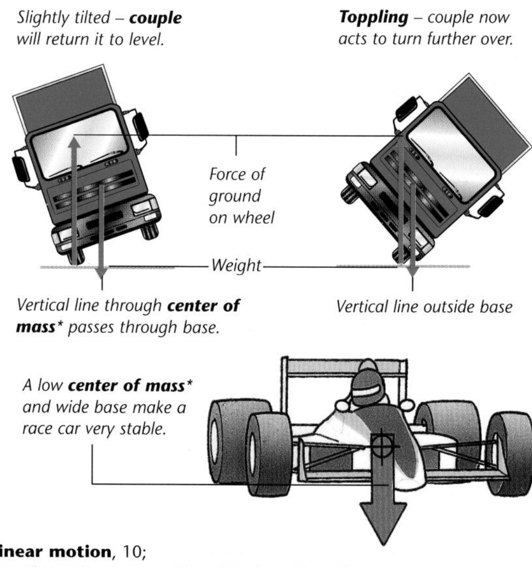

Slightly tilted – couple will return it to level.
Toppling – couple now acts to turn further over.
Force of ground on wheel
Weight
Vertical line through center of mass* passes through base.
Vertical line outside base
A low center of mass* and wide base make a race car very stable.

* **Acceleration**, 11; **Angular acceleration**, 17; **Center of mass**, **Linear motion**, 10; **Normal contact force**, 7 (**Coefficient of friction**); **Rotational motion**, **Sign convention**, 11; **SI units**, 96.

Equilibrium

When an object is not accelerating, it is said to be in **equilibrium**. It can be in **linear equilibrium** (i.e. the **center of mass*** is not accelerating) and/or **rotational equilibrium** (i.e. not accelerating about the center of mass). In addition, both cases of equilibrium are either **static** (not moving) or **dynamic** (moving).

Linear equilibrium

The state of an object when there is no acceleration of its **center of mass***, i.e. its speed and direction of motion do not change. The resultant force on the object when it is in linear equilibrium must be zero.

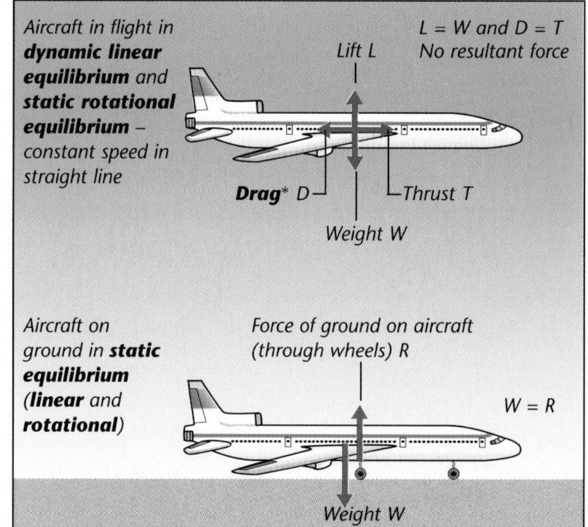
Aircraft in flight in **dynamic linear equilibrium** and **static rotational equilibrium** – constant speed in straight line
L = W and D = T
No resultant force
Lift L
Drag* D
Thrust T
Weight W
Aircraft on ground in **static equilibrium** (**linear** and **rotational**)
Force of ground on aircraft (through wheels) R
W = R
Weight W

Rotational equilibrium

The state of an object when there is no **angular acceleration***, i.e. it spins at constant **angular velocity***. If an object is in rotational equilibrium, the **resultant moment** (see **moment**) about any axis is zero.

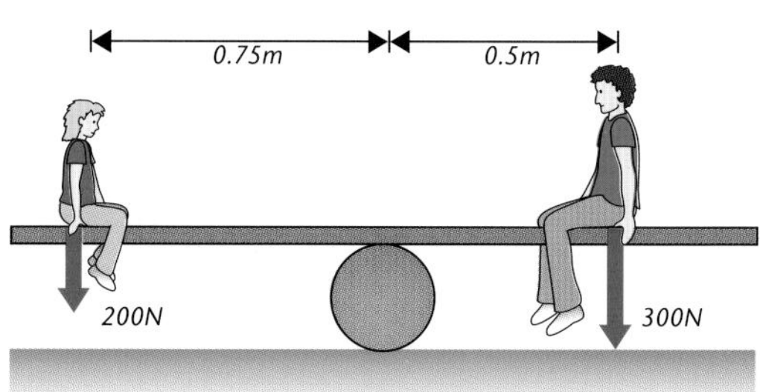
0.75m
0.5m
200N
300N

*Beam in **static rotational equilibrium**, since 200 × 0.75 = 300 × 0.5*

Stable equilibrium

A state in which an object moved a small distance from its equilibrium position returns to that position. This happens if the **center of mass*** is raised when the object is moved.

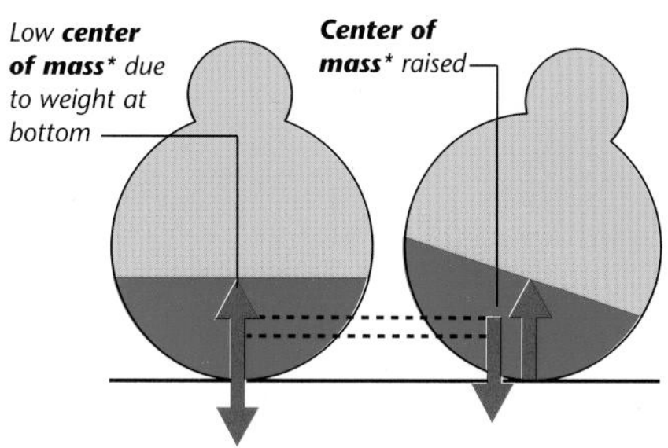
Low **center of mass*** due to weight at bottom
Center of mass* raised

*Weight and force from ground form **couple** to turn toy upright.*

Unstable equilibrium

A state in which an object moved a small distance from its equilibrium position moves further from that position. This happens if the **center of mass*** is lowered when the object is moved.

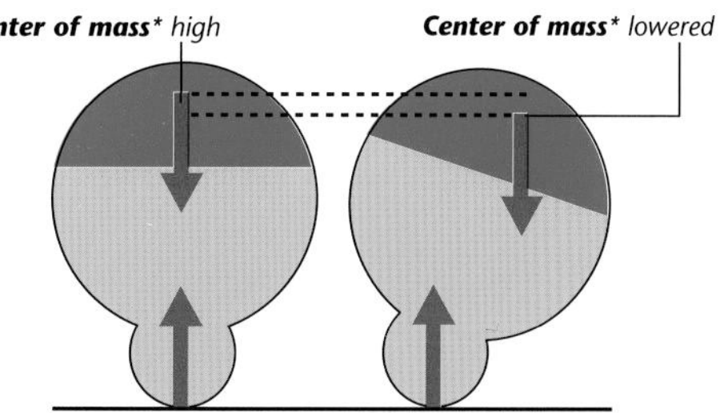
Center of mass* high
Center of mass* lowered

*Weight and force form **couple** which turns toy further over.*

Neutral equilibrium

A state in which an object moved a small distance from its equilibrium position remains in the new position. This happens if the **center of mass*** remains at the same height.

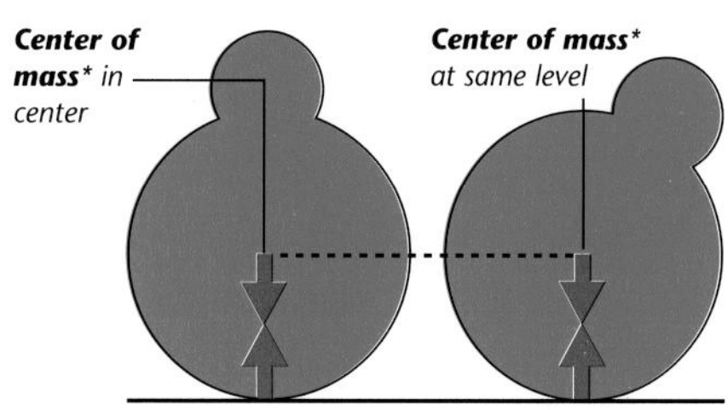
Center of mass* in center
Center of mass* at same level

*Weight and force on same line – no **couple** so toy stays in new position.*

* **Angular acceleration**, **Angular velocity**, 17; **Center of mass**, 10; **Drag**, 19 (**Terminal velocity**).

PERIODIC MOTION

Periodic motion is any motion which repeats itself exactly at regular intervals. Examples of periodic motion are objects moving in a circle (**circular motion**), the swing of a pendulum and the vibration of molecules. **Wave motion*** consists of the periodic motion of particles or fields.

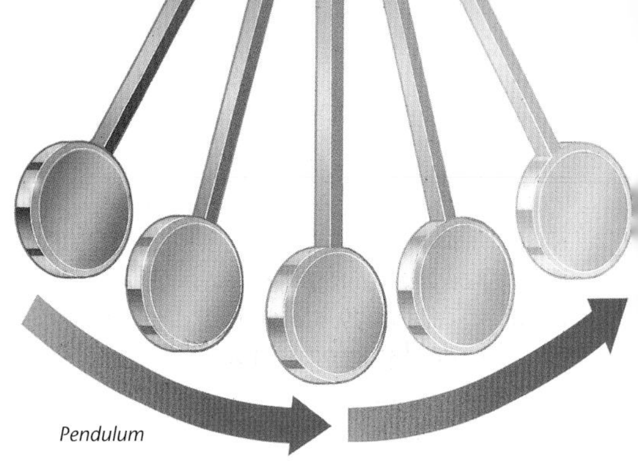
Pendulum

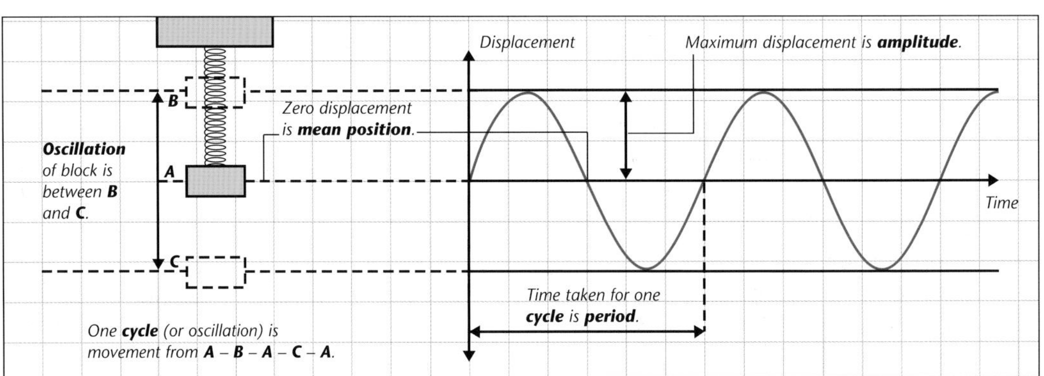
Displacement
Maximum displacement is **amplitude**.
B
Zero displacement
is **mean position**.
Oscillation of block is between **B** and **C**.
A
Time
C
Time taken for one
cycle is **period**.
One **cycle** (or oscillation) is
movement from **A – B – A – C – A**.

Cycle

The movement between a point during a motion and the same point when the motion repeats. For example, one rotation of a spinning object.

Oscillation

Periodic motion between two extremes, e.g. a mass moving up and down on the end of a spring. In an oscillating system, there is a continuous change between **kinetic energy*** and **potential energy***. The total energy of a system (sum of its kinetic and potential energy) remains constant if there is no **damping**.

Period (T)

The time taken to complete one **cycle** of a motion, e.g. the period of rotation of the Earth about its axis is 24 hours.

Frequency (f)

The number of **cycles** of a particular motion in one second. The **SI unit*** of frequency is the **Hertz** (**Hz**), which is equal to one cycle per second.

$f = \frac{1}{T}$ where f = **frequency**; T = **period**.

Mean position

The position about which an object **oscillates**, and at which it comes to rest after oscillating, e.g. the mean position of a pendulum is when it is vertical. The position of zero displacement of an oscillating particle is usually taken as this point.

Amplitude

The maximum displacement of an **oscillating particle** from its **mean position**.

Damping

The process whereby **oscillations** die down due to a loss of energy, e.g. shock absorbers in cars cause oscillations to die down after a car has gone over a bump in the road.

Damping in an oscillating system

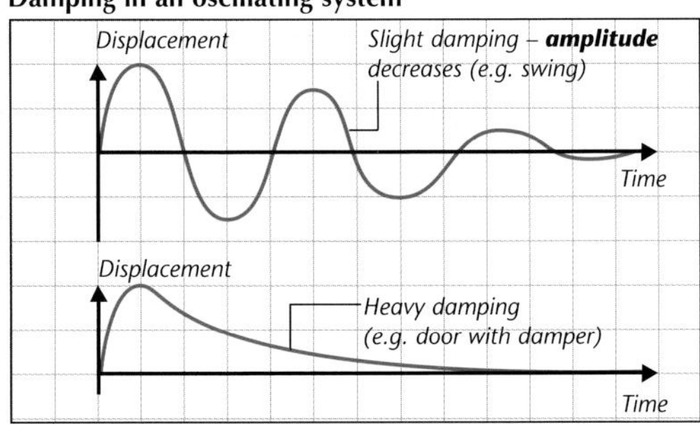
Displacement
Slight damping – **amplitude** decreases (e.g. swing)
Time
Displacement
Heavy damping
(e.g. door with damper)
Time

* **Kinetic energy**, 9; **Potential energy**, 8;
SI units, 96; **Wave motion**, 34.

Natural or **free oscillation**

The **oscillation** of a system when left after being started. The **period** and **frequency** of the system are called the **natural period** and **natural frequency** (these remain the same as long as the **damping** is not too great).

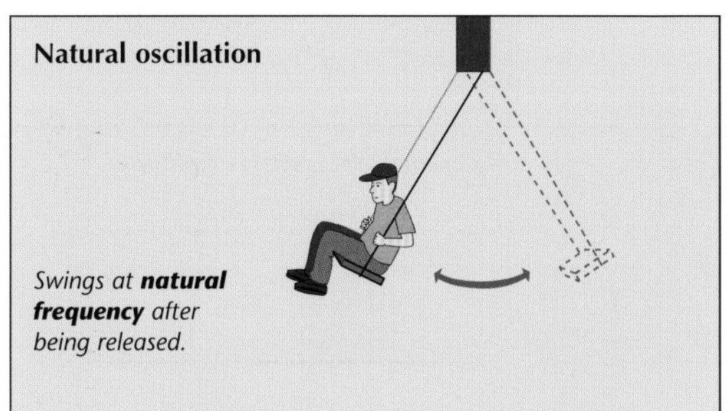
Natural oscillation
Swings at ***natural frequency*** after being released.

Forced oscillation

The **oscillation** of a system when given a repeated driving force (a force applied to the system) at regular intervals. The system is made to oscillate at the **frequency** of the driving force, irrespective of its **natural frequency**.

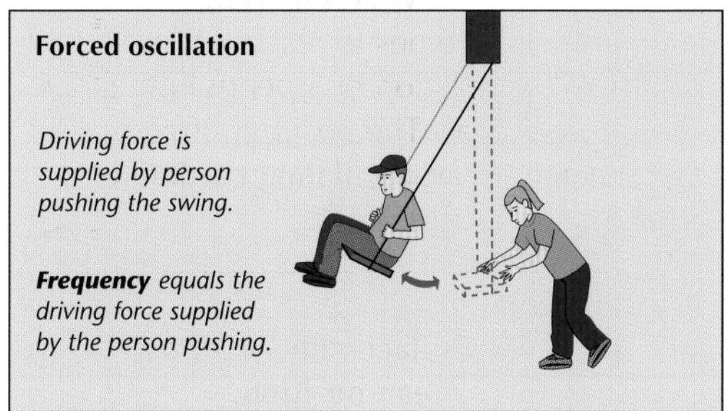
Forced oscillation
Driving force is supplied by person pushing the swing.
Frequency equals the driving force supplied by the person pushing.

Resonance

The effect exhibited by a system in which the **frequency** of the driving force (a force applied to the system) is about the same as the **natural frequency** of the system. The system then has a large **amplitude**.

Resonance
Driving force at end of each swing – at ***natural frequency*** of swing.
Amplitude increases – ***resonance*** occurs.

Circular motion

Uniform circular motion

The motion of an object in a circle at constant speed. Since the direction (and therefore the **velocity***) changes, the object is constantly **accelerating*** toward the center (**centripetal acceleration**), and so there is a force acting toward the center. Circular motion can be considered in terms of **angular velocity**.

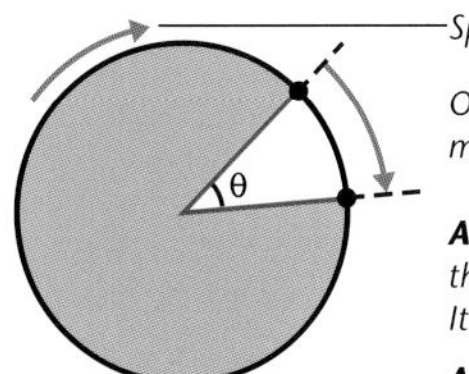
θ
Speed around circle is constant.
Object takes time t to move through angle θ.
Angular velocity is a measure of the angle moved through per second. It is measured in radians per second.
Angular velocity = θ/t rad s⁻¹

Centripetal acceleration (a)

The **acceleration*** of an object in circular motion (see above) acting toward the center of the circle.

Centripetal force

The force which acts on an object toward the center of a circle to produce **centripetal acceleration**, and so keeps the object moving in a circle.

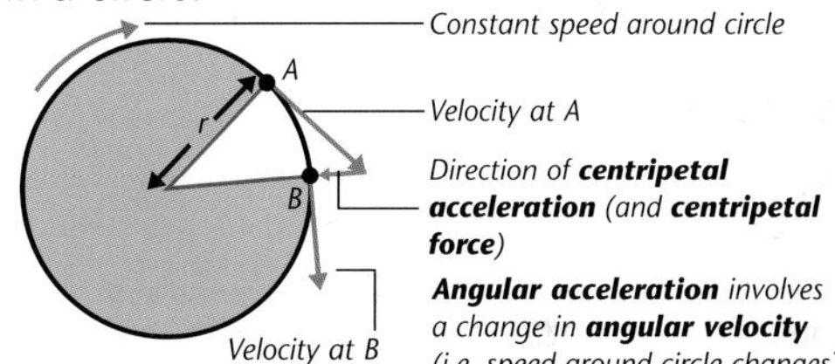
Constant speed around circle
A
r
B
Velocity at A
Direction of ***centripetal acceleration*** (and ***centripetal force***)
Angular acceleration involves a change in ***angular velocity*** (i.e. speed around circle changes).
Velocity at B

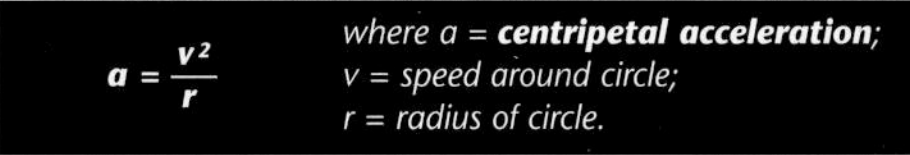

$$a = \frac{v^2}{r}$$

*where a = **centripetal acceleration**; v = speed around circle; r = radius of circle.*

Centripetal force has an equal and opposite reaction (see **Newton's second law**, page 12), called **centrifugal force**. It does not act on the object moving in the circle so is not considered in forces calculations.

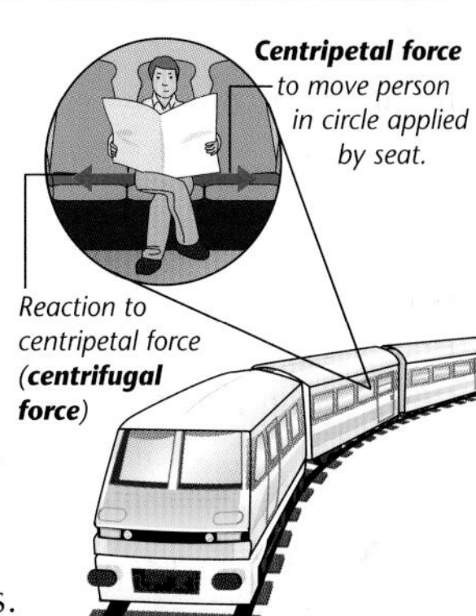
Centripetal force to move person in circle applied by seat.
Reaction to centripetal force (***centrifugal force***)

* **Acceleration**, 11; **Velocity**, 10.

GRAVITATION

Gravitation is the effect of the **gravitational force*** of attraction (see also page 104) which acts between all objects in the universe. It is noticed with massive objects like the planets, which remain in orbit because of it. The gravitational force between an object and a planet, which pulls the object downward, is called the **weight** of the object.

F

Mass M

d

Saturn with Tethys, one of the 18 moons that orbit it.

F

Mass m

The gravitational force between two objects can be calculated from their masses (M and m) and the distance between them (d).

Newton's law of gravitation

States that there is a gravitational force of attraction between any two objects with mass which depends on the masses of the objects and the distance between them. The **gravitational constant** (**G**) has a value of $6.7 \times 10^{-11} Nm^2 kg^{-2}$, and its small value means that gravitational forces are negligible unless one of the masses is very large.

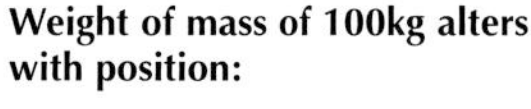

$$F = G\frac{Mm}{d^2}$$ where G = ***gravitational constant***.

Weight

The gravitational pull of a massive object (e.g. a planet) on another object. The weight of an object is not constant, but depends on the distance from, and mass of the planet. Hence, although the mass of an object is independent of its position, its weight is not.

Weight of mass of 100kg alters with position:

Weighing scales measure the force exerted on them. At the surface of the Earth, the weight of mass 100kg is 980N.

On surface of Moon (smaller than Earth), weight of mass 100kg is 160N.

At 10,000km above surface of Earth, weight of mass 100kg is 150N.

Acceleration due to gravity (g)

The **acceleration*** produced by the gravitational force of attraction. Its value is the same for any mass at a given place. It is about $9.8 m s^{-2}$ on the Earth's surface, and decreases above the surface according to **Newton's law of gravitation**. The value of $9.8 m s^{-2}$ is used as a unit of acceleration (the **g-force**).

Object
(mass m)
Planet (mass M)

*From **Newton's law of gravitation** and **Newton's second law***:*

Force on mass (= mg)

$$= G\frac{Mm}{d^2}$$

*So **acceleration due to gravity (g)**:*

$$g = G\frac{M}{d^2}$$

*During tight turns, pilots experience high **g-forces** (e.g. 5g – five times the normal) which can lead to blackout.*

*__Acceleration__, 11; **Gravitational force**, 6; **Newton's second law**, 12.

Terminal velocity

The maximum, constant **velocity*** reached by an object falling through a gas or liquid. As the velocity increases, the resistance due to the air or liquid (**drag**) increases. Eventually, the drag becomes equal to the **weight** of the object, and its velocity does not increase any more.

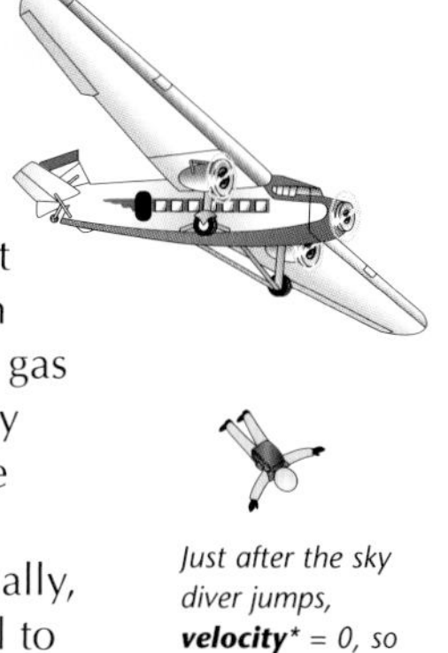

*Just after the sky diver jumps, **velocity*** = 0, so **drag** = 0 and **acceleration*** = g.*

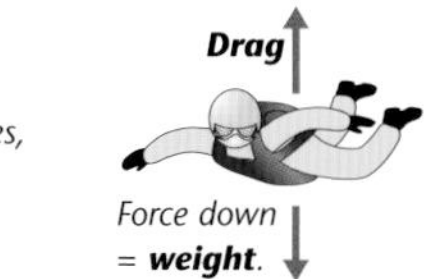
Drag
Force down = weight.

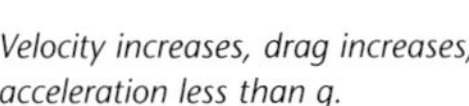

Velocity increases, drag increases, acceleration less than g.

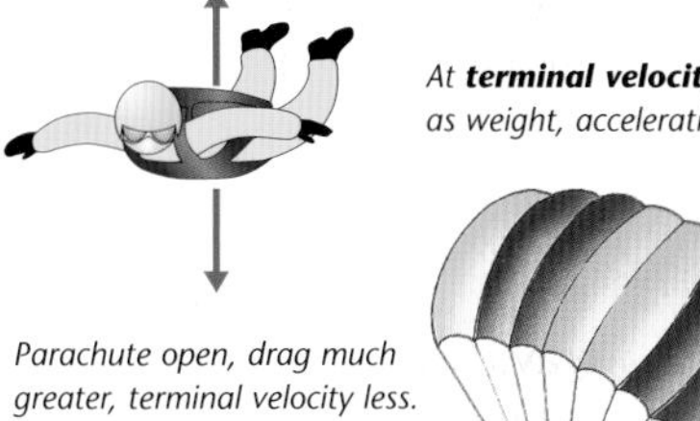

*At **terminal velocity**, drag same as weight, acceleration = 0.*

Parachute open, drag much greater, terminal velocity less.

Escape velocity

The minimum **velocity*** at which an object must travel in order to escape the gravitational pull of a planet without further propulsion. It is about 40,000km h^{-1} on Earth.

Free fall

The unrestricted motion of an object when it is acted upon only by the gravitational force (i.e. when there are no resistive or other forces acting, e.g. air resistance).

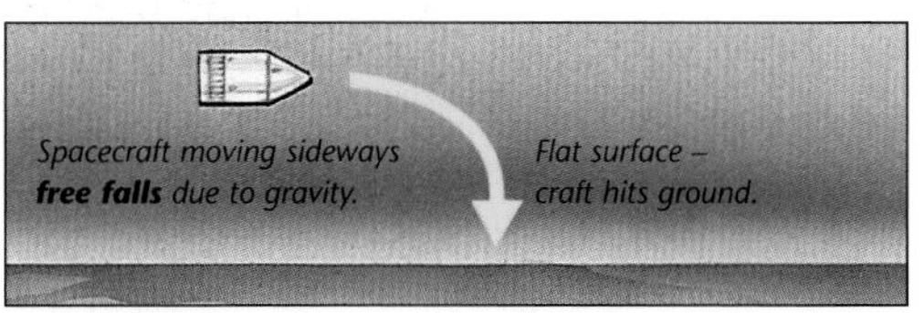
Spacecraft moving sideways free falls due to gravity.
Flat surface – craft hits ground.

Surface is curved.
Planet's surface falls away as quickly as spacecraft free falls.
Spacecraft gets no nearer to planet and therefore orbits.

* **Acceleration**, 11; **Period**, 16; **Velocity**, 10.

Weightlessness

The state in which an object does not exert any force on its surroundings.

True weightlessness

Weightlessness due to an object being in a gravity-free region.

Apparent weightlessness

The state of an object when it is as if there were no gravitational forces acting. This occurs if two objects **accelerate*** independently in the same way.

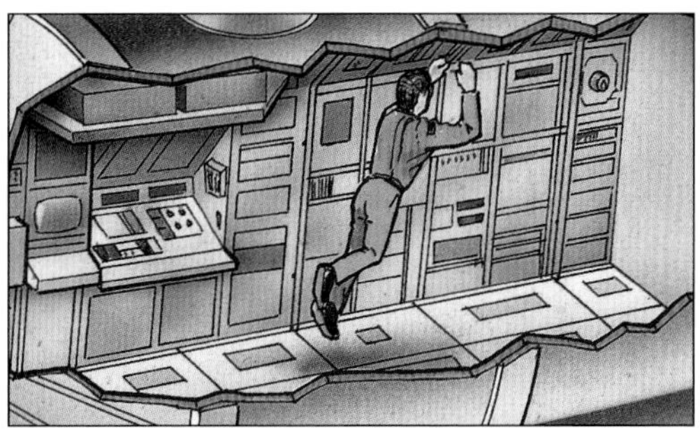

*Astronaut inside an orbiting spacecraft **free falls** in same way as spacecraft and is therefore **apparently weightless** inside it.*

Geo-stationary or parking orbit

The path of a satellite which orbits the Earth in the same direction as the rotation of the Earth so that it stays above the same place on the surface all the time. The satellite has a **period*** of 24 hours.

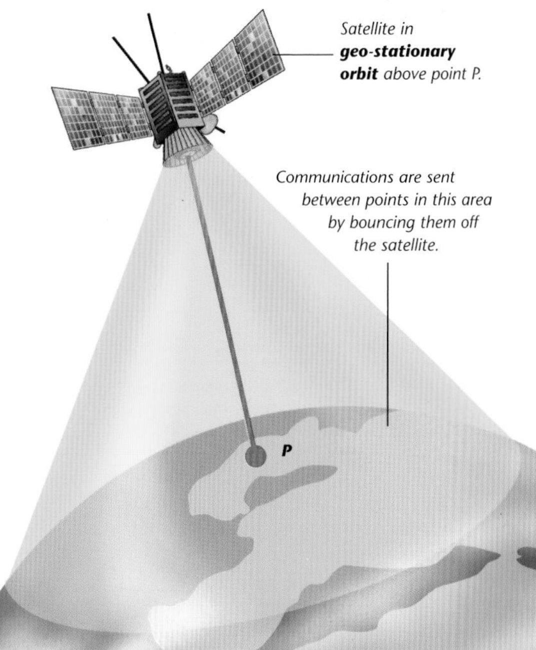
Satellite in geo-stationary orbit above point P.
Communications are sent between points in this area by bouncing them off the satellite.
P

MACHINES

A **machine** is a device which is used to overcome a force called the **load**. This force is applied at one point and the machine works by the application of another force called the **effort** at a different point. For example, a small effort exerted on the rope of a **pulley** overcomes the weight of the object being raised by the pulley.

A hydraulic machine helps to power this robot arm.

Pulley system – an example of a machine

(See also page 21.)

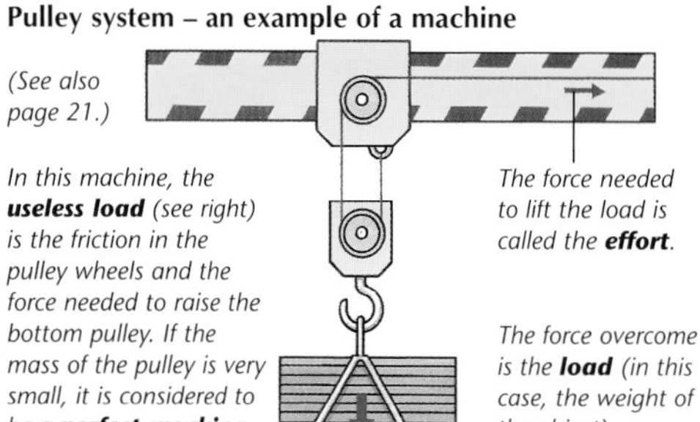

*In this machine, the **useless load** (see right) is the friction in the pulley wheels and the force needed to raise the bottom pulley. If the mass of the pulley is very small, it is considered to be a **perfect machine**.*

*The force needed to lift the load is called the **effort**.*

*The force overcome is the **load** (in this case, the weight of the object).*

Useless load

The force needed to overcome the **frictional forces*** between the moving parts of a machine and to raise any of its moving parts.

Perfect machine

A theoretical machine, with a **useless load** of zero. Machines in which the useless load is negligible compared to the load can be considered as perfect machines.

Mechanical advantage (M.A.)

The load (L) divided by the effort (E). A mechanical advantage greater than one means that the load overcome is greater than the effort. The mechanical advantage of any given **perfect machine** remains the same as the load increases. The mechanical advantage of any given real machine increases slightly with load because **useless load** becomes less significant as the load increases.

$$M.A. = \frac{L}{E}$$

Diagram of screwjack showing effort, load and work done

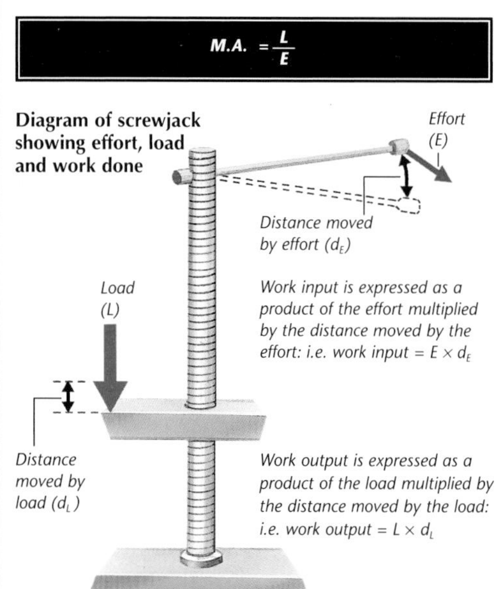
Effort (E)
Distance moved by effort (d_E)
Load (L)
Distance moved by load (d_L)

Work input is expressed as a product of the effort multiplied by the distance moved by the effort: i.e. work input = $E \times d_E$

Work output is expressed as a product of the load multiplied by the distance moved by the load: i.e. work output = $L \times d_L$

Efficiency

The **work** done (force × distance – see page 8) on the load (work output) divided by the work done by the effort (work input), expressed as a percentage. All real machines have an efficiency of less than 100% due to **useless load**. **Perfect machines** are 100% efficient.

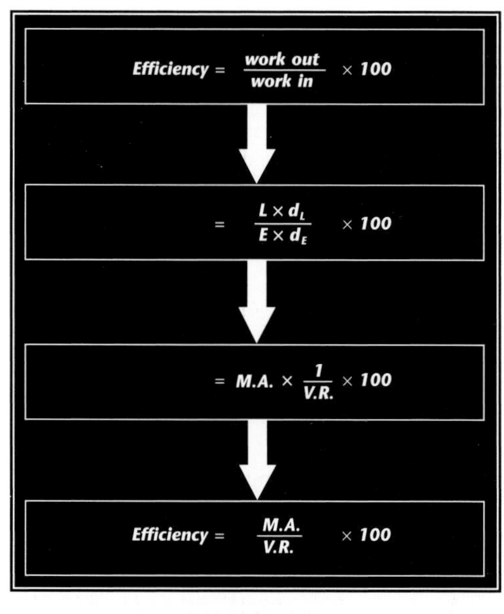
$Efficiency = \frac{\text{work out}}{\text{work in}} \times 100$
$= \frac{L \times d_L}{E \times d_E} \times 100$
$= M.A. \times \frac{1}{V.R.} \times 100$
$Efficiency = \frac{M.A.}{V.R.} \times 100$

*In a **perfect machine** (100% efficiency):* **M.A. = V.R.**

* **Frictional force**, 7.

Examples of machines

Hydraulic press

A large and small cylinder connected by a pipe and filled with fluid, used to produce large forces.

Hydraulic press

Volume of liquid moved $= a \times d_E = A \times d_L$ *so* **V.R.**$(d_E / d_L) = A / a$

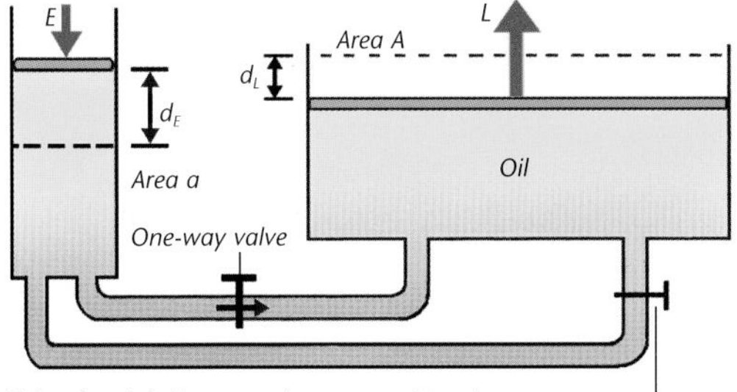

E
L
Area A
d_L
d_E
Area a
Oil
One-way valve

Valve closed during operation – opened to release pressure

Pulley system

A wheel (or combination of wheels) and a rope, belt or chain which transmits motion.

Pulley system on a crane

Pulley systems

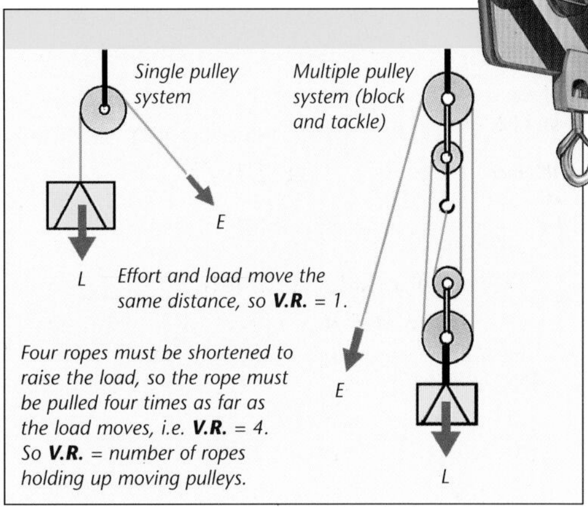

Single pulley system
Multiple pulley system (block and tackle)
E
L
Effort and load move the same distance, so V.R. = 1.
Four ropes must be shortened to raise the load, so the rope must be pulled four times as far as the load moves, i.e. V.R. = 4.
So V.R. = number of ropes holding up moving pulleys.
E
L

Lever

Any rigid object which is pivoted about an axis called the **fulcrum** (**F**). The load and effort can be applied on either or the same side. There are three classes of lever, shown below.

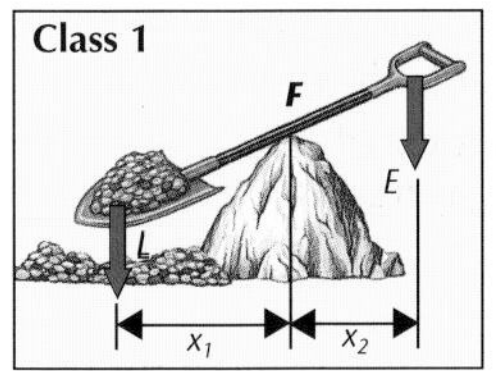

Class 1
F
E
L
x_1
x_2

Fulcrum between effort and load.

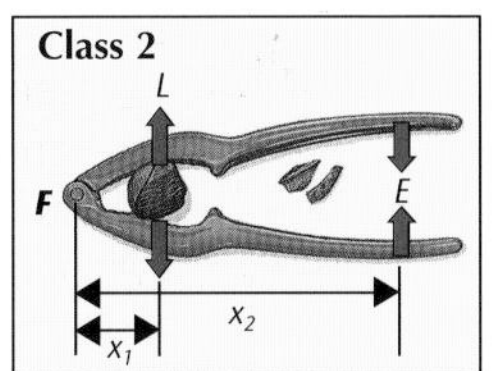

Class 2
L
F
E
x_1
x_2

Load between effort and fulcrum.

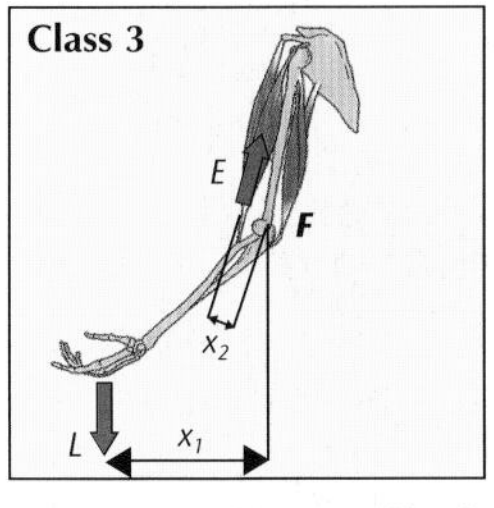

Class 3
E
F
x_2
L
x_1

Effort between fulcrum and load.

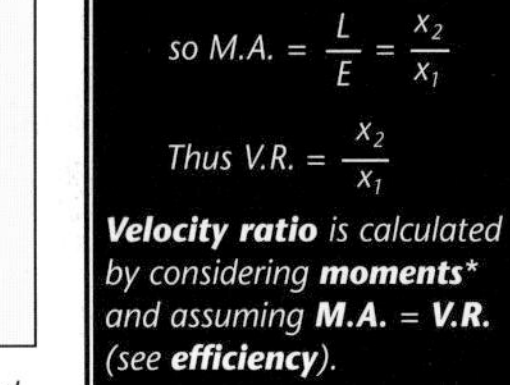

For ***equilibrium*****:*

$L \times x_1 = E \times x_2$

so $M.A. = \frac{L}{E} = \frac{x_2}{x_1}$

Thus $V.R. = \frac{x_2}{x_1}$

Velocity ratio *is calculated by considering* ***moments***** and assuming* ***M.A. = V.R.*** *(see* ***efficiency****).*

Inclined plane

A plane surface at an angle to the horizontal. It is easier to move an object up an inclined plane than to move it vertically upwards.

Inclined plane

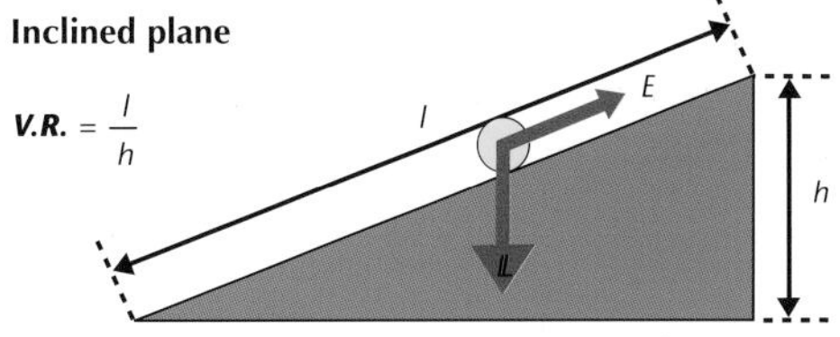

V.R. = l / h
l
E
L
h

Gear

A combination of toothed wheels used to transmit motion between rotating shafts.

Twice as many teeth on the driven wheel means that the driving wheel must rotate twice as many times.

So ***V.R.*** *= number of teeth on driven wheel divided by number of teeth on driving wheel.*

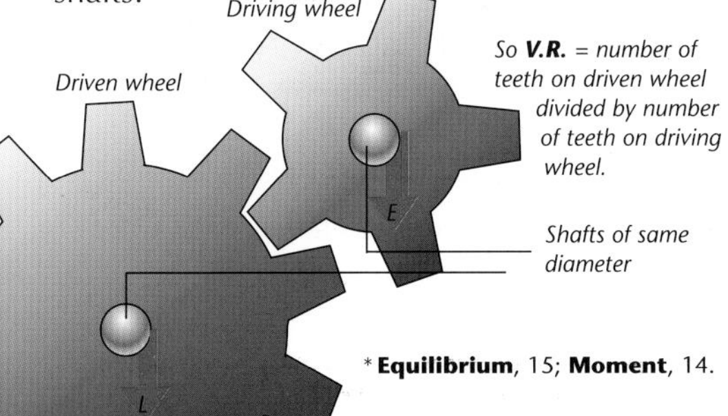

Driving wheel
Driven wheel
E
L
Shafts of same diameter

Screw jack

A system in which a screw thread is turned to raise a load (e.g. a car jack). The **pitch** is the distance between each thread on the screw.

Screw jack

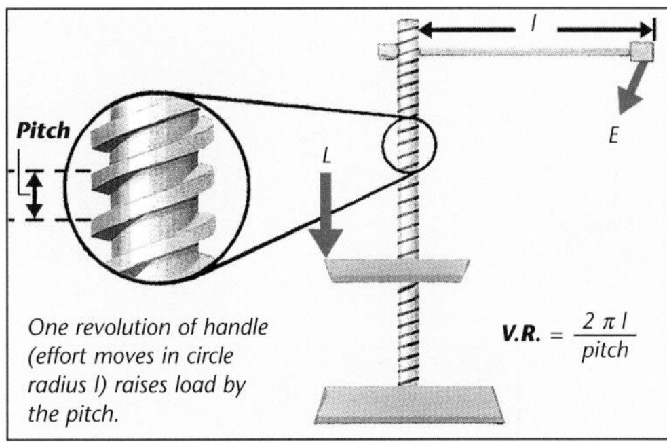

l
Pitch
L
E
One revolution of handle (effort moves in circle radius l) raises load by the pitch.
V.R. = 2 π l / pitch

* **Equilibrium**, 15; **Moment**, 14.

MOLECULAR PROPERTIES

There are a number of properties of matter which can be explained in terms of the behavior of molecules, in particular their behavior due to the action of the forces between them (**intermolecular forces***). Among these properties, and explained on this double page, are **elasticity**, **surface tension** and **viscosity**. See also pages 4-5 and 24-25.

Elasticity

The ability of a material to return to its original shape and size after distorting forces (i.e. **tension*** or **compression***) have been removed. Materials which have this ability are **elastic**; those which do not are **plastic**.

*Cool wax is **plastic** (the seal leaves a permanent impression in the wax).*

Elasticity is a result of **intermolecular forces*** – if an object is stretched or compressed, its molecules move further apart or closer together respectively. This results in a force of attraction (in the first case) or repulsion (in the second), so the molecules return to their average separation when the distorting force is removed. This always happens while the size of the force is below a certain level (different for each material), but all elastic materials finally become plastic if the force exceeds this level (see **elastic limit** and **yield point**).

*Balloons are **elastic** – they return to their original shape after stretching.*

Hooke's law

States that,
when a distorting force is applied to an object, the **strain** is proportional to the **stress**. As the size of the force increases, though, the **limit of proportionality** (or **proportional limit**) is reached, after which Hooke's law is no longer true (see graph, page 23).

Strain and stress in a stretched wire

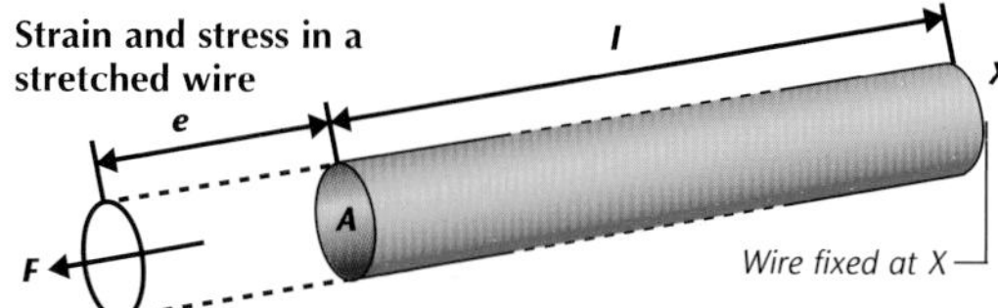

l
X
e
A
F
Wire fixed at X

***Strain** is stated as change in length per unit length.*

$$\text{Strain} = \frac{e}{l}$$ where e = change in length; l = original length.

***Stress** is stated as force applied per unit area.*

$$\text{Stress} = \frac{F}{A}$$ where F = force applied; A = cross-sectional area.

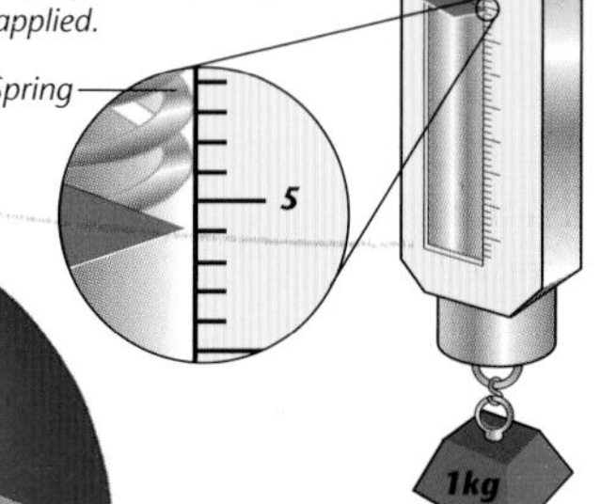

Spring
5
1kg

***Spring balance** uses **Hooke's law** to measure force. Spring is extended in proportion to force applied.*

*Scale **calibrated*** so that length of spring gives size of force in **newtons***.*

*For an object in **tension*** or **compression**, **stress** divided by **strain** (see above) is always same figure for a given material (**Young's modulus** – see page 112) until **limit of proportionality** is reached.*

Elastic limit

The point, just after the **limit of proportionality** (see **Hooke's law**), beyond which an object ceases to be **elastic**, in the sense that it does not return to its original shape and size when the distorting force is removed. It does return to a similar shape and size, but has suffered a permanent strain (it will continue to return to this new form if forces are applied, i.e. it stays elastic in this sense).

* **Calibration**, 344; **Compression**, **Intermolecular forces**, 7; **Newton**, 6; **Tension**, 7.

Yield point

The point, just after the **elastic limit**, at which a distorting force causes a major change in a material. In a **ductile*** material, the internal structure changes – bonds between molecular layers break and the layers flow over each other. This change is called **plastic deformation** (the material becomes **plastic**). It continues as the force increases, and the material will eventually break. A **brittle** material, by contrast, will break at its yield point. The **yield stress** of a material is the value of the **stress** at its yield point. See graph below.

Stress/strain graph for a ductile* material

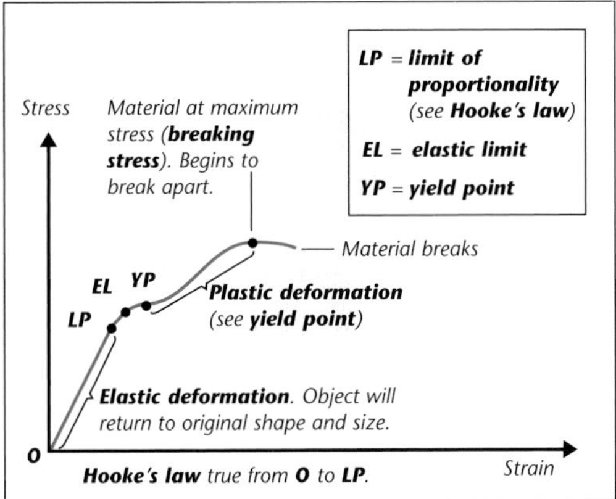
LP = limit of proportionality (see Hooke's law)
EL = elastic limit
YP = yield point
Stress
Material at maximum stress (breaking stress). Begins to break apart.
Material breaks
EL
YP
LP
Plastic deformation (see yield point)
Elastic deformation. Object will return to original shape and size.
O
Strain
Hooke's law true from O to LP.

Viscosity

The ease of flow of a fluid. It depends on the size of the **frictional force*** between different layers of molecules as they slide over each other.

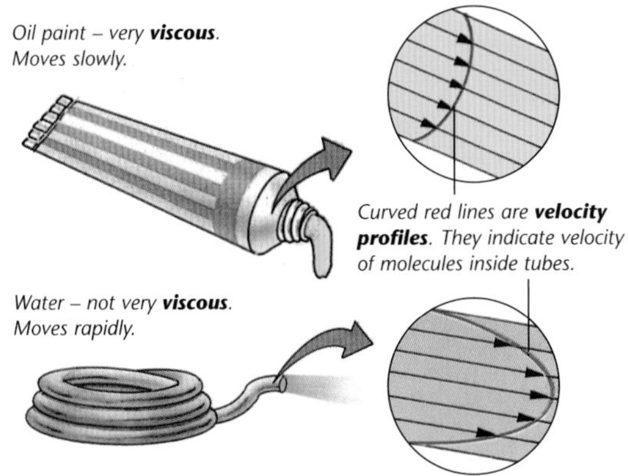
Oil paint – very viscous. Moves slowly.
Curved red lines are velocity profiles. They indicate velocity of molecules inside tubes.
Water – not very viscous. Moves rapidly.

*Outer layers of fluid slowed by **frictional force*** between them and sides of container. Working inwards, friction gradually loses effect. Effect lost much faster in water than oil paint.*

Surface tension

The skin-like property of a liquid surface resulting from **intermolecular forces*** which cause it to contract to the smallest possible area.

Two examples of surface tension

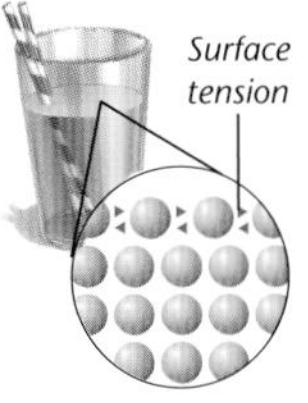
Surface tension

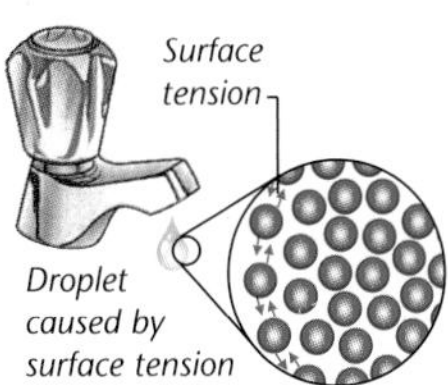
Surface tension
Droplet caused by surface tension

At the surface, the molecules are slightly further apart than the inner ones, and at a separation such that they attract each other (see **intermolecular forces**, page 7). The molecules cannot move closer because of equal forces on either side. The surface molecules are therefore in a constant state of tension, giving the surface elastic properties.

Water bug on water's surface

Adhesion

An **intermolecular force*** of attraction between molecules of different substances.

***Capillary action** or **capillarity** is a result of **adhesion** or **cohesion**.*

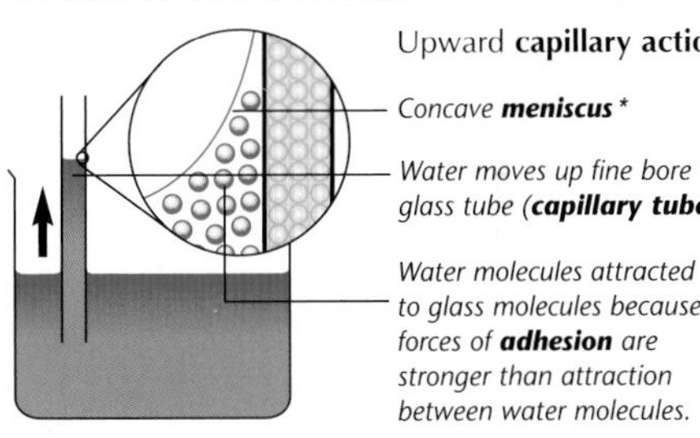
Upward capillary action
Concave meniscus *
Water moves up fine bore glass tube (capillary tube).
Water molecules attracted to glass molecules because forces of adhesion are stronger than attraction between water molecules.

Cohesion

An **intermolecular force*** of attraction between molecules of the same substance.

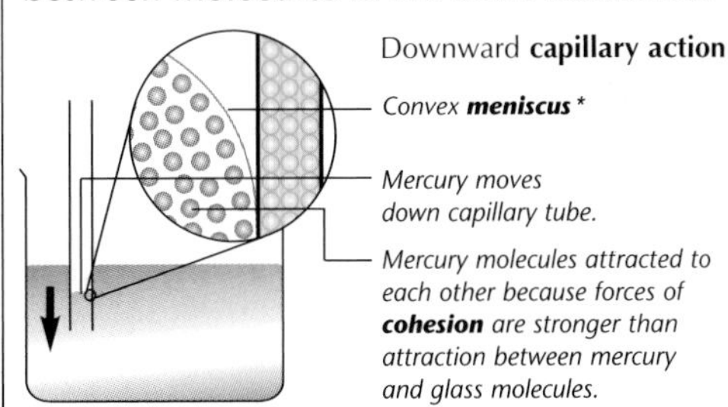
Downward capillary action
Convex meniscus *
Mercury moves down capillary tube.
Mercury molecules attracted to each other because forces of cohesion are stronger than attraction between mercury and glass molecules.

* **Ductile**, 344; **Frictional force**, **Intermolecular forces**, 7; **Meniscus**, 345.

DENSITY AND PRESSURE

The **density** (ρ) of an object depends on both the mass of its molecules and its volume (see formula, right). For example, if one substance has a higher density than another, then the same volumes of the substances have different masses (the first mass being greater than the second). Similarly, the same masses have different volumes.

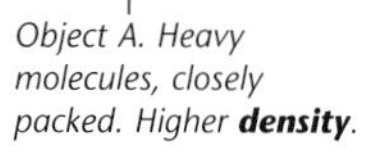

*Object A. Heavy molecules, closely packed. Higher **density**.*

Object B. Light molecules, widely spaced. Lower density.

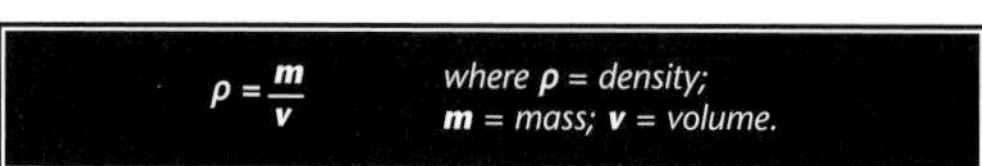

$\rho = \frac{m}{v}$ where ρ = density; m = mass; v = volume.

Hence $m = \rho \times v$

v is the same for objects A and B, so object A has greater mass.

*The **SI unit*** of density is the kg m^{-3}.*

Relative density or specific gravity

The density of a substance relative to the density of water (which is 1,000kg m^{-3}). It indicates how much more or less dense than water a substance is, so the figures need no units, e.g. 1.5 (one and a half times as dense). It is found by dividing the mass of any volume of a substance by the mass of an equal volume of water.

Eureka can

A can used to measure the volume of a solid object with an irregular shape, in order to calculate its density. The volume of water displaced is equal to the volume of the object. The density of the object is its mass divided by this volume.

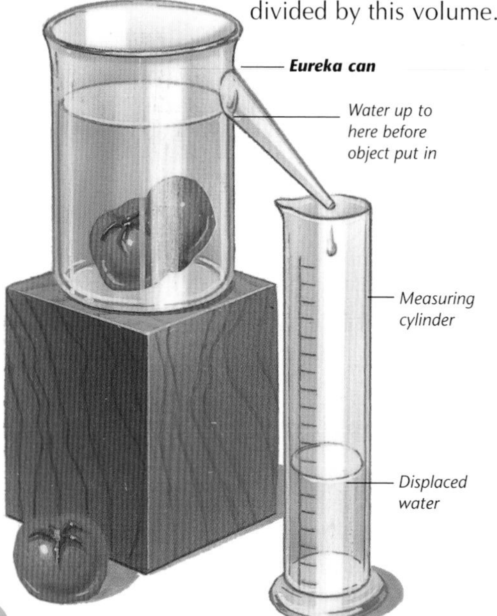

Eureka can
Water up to here before object put in
Measuring cylinder
Displaced water

Density bottle

A container which, when completely full, holds a precisely measured volume of liquid (at constant temperature). It is used to measure the density of liquids (by measuring the mass of the bottle and liquid, subtracting the mass of the bottle and dividing by the volume of liquid).

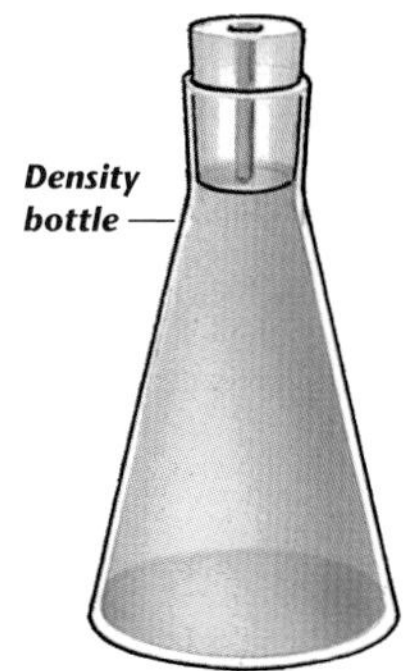

Density bottle

*Fine bore tube (**capillary tube**) in glass stopper. Bottle filled, stopper inserted, excess liquid rises through tube and runs out – ensures same volume each time.*

Hydrometer or aerometer

An instrument which measures the density of a liquid by the level at which it floats in that liquid. If the liquid is very dense, the hydrometer floats near the surface, as only a small volume of liquid needs to be displaced to equal the weight of the hydrometer.

Hydrometer

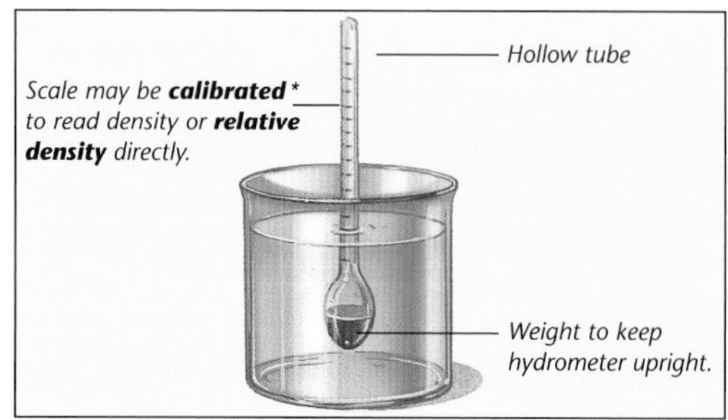

Hollow tube
Scale may be calibrated* to read density or relative density directly.
Weight to keep hydrometer upright.

* **Calibration**, 344; **SI units**, 96.

Pressure

Pressure is the force, acting at right angles, exerted by a solid, liquid or gas on a unit area of a substance (solid, liquid or gas).

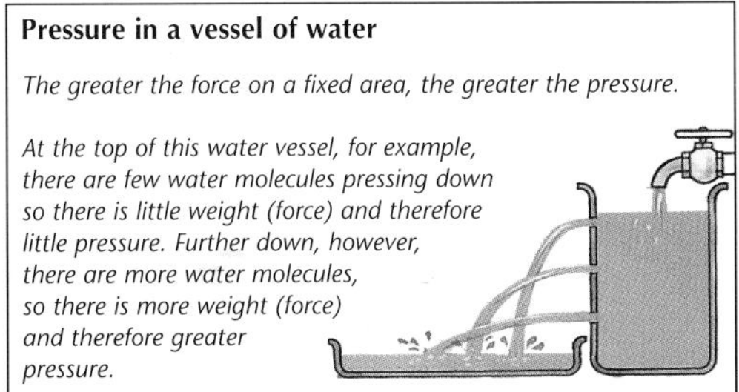

Pressure in a vessel of water

The greater the force on a fixed area, the greater the pressure.

At the top of this water vessel, for example, there are few water molecules pressing down so there is little weight (force) and therefore little pressure. Further down, however, there are more water molecules, so there is more weight (force) and therefore greater pressure.

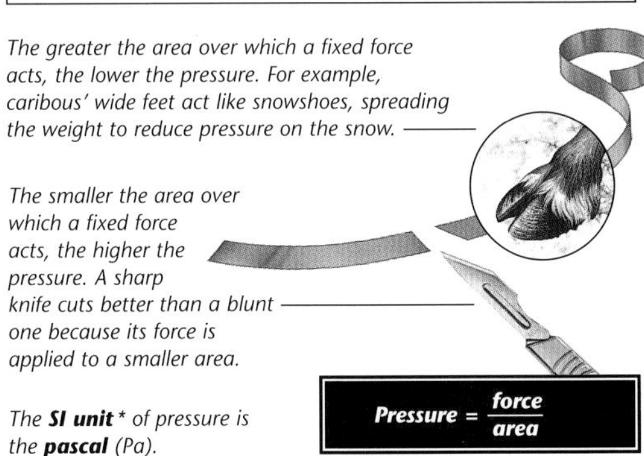

The greater the area over which a fixed force acts, the lower the pressure. For example, caribous' wide feet act like snowshoes, spreading the weight to reduce pressure on the snow.

The smaller the area over which a fixed force acts, the higher the pressure. A sharp knife cuts better than a blunt one because its force is applied to a smaller area.

*The **SI unit*** of pressure is the **pascal** (Pa).*

$$\textbf{Pressure} = \frac{\textbf{force}}{\textbf{area}}$$

Barometer

An instrument used to measure **atmospheric pressure** – the pressure caused by the weight of air molecules above the Earth. There are several common types.

*A **barometer** for the home gives **pressure** readings and brief weather descriptions.*

Simple barometer

Atmospheric pressure = *760mm of mercury*

Torricellian vacuum *(no pressure acting down)*

Atmospheric pressure

Mercury

Fixed diameter tube

Manometer

A U-shaped tube containing a liquid. It is used to measure difference in fluid pressures.

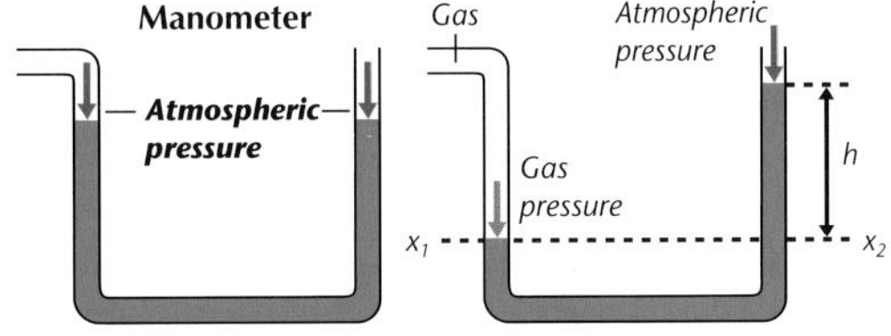
Manometer
Atmospheric pressure
Gas
Atmospheric pressure
Gas pressure
h
x_1
x_2

Pressures at x_1 and x_2 (same level) must be the same.
So pressure of gas = pressure at x_2
= atmospheric pressure + pressure of height (h) of liquid.

Objects in fluids

An object in a fluid experiences an upward force called the **buoyant force**. According to **Archimedes' principle**, this is equal to the weight of the fluid displaced by the object. The **principle of flotation** further states that, if the object is floating, the weight of displaced fluid (buoyant force) is equal to its own weight. It can be shown (see below) that whether an object sinks, rises or floats in a fluid depends entirely on density.

Archimedes' principle

Buoyant force = weight of fluid displaced

Principle of flotation

For a floating object: ***U = W*** — *where **U** = buoyant force; **W** = weight of object.*

Weight = mass (m) × acceleration due to gravity (g)
*Mass = density (**ρ**) × volume (v)*
*So weight (of object or fluid displaced) = **ρ**vg*

*Submarines demonstrate **Archimedes' principle** and the **principle of flotation**. Altering air/water mix in ballast tanks alters density.*

*Submarine has two forces acting on it – its own weight and the **buoyant force**.*

1. *If U = W, sub remains at a given depth.*

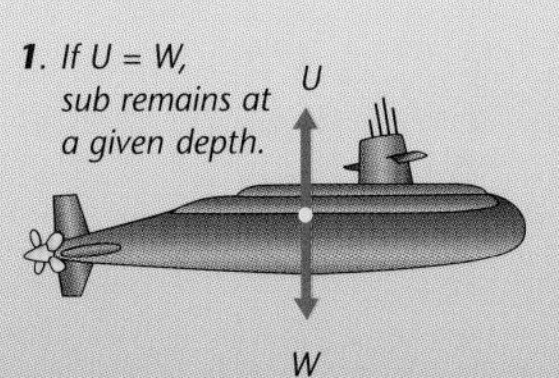
U
W

2. *If U > W, sub starts to rise.*

Sub breaks surface and floats. U = W, though density still less than that of water (see below), because now volume of water displaced is less.

3. *If **U** < W, sub starts to sink.*

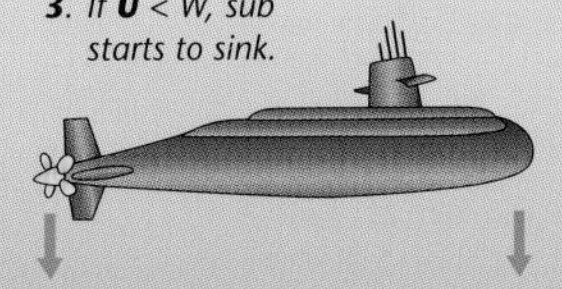

*Both W and U = **ρ**vg (see above). v and g are the same for both, and density (**ρ**) of water is constant. So 1, 2 and 3 can be brought about by altering the density of the sub. In 1, the sub's density is the same as that of water, in 2 it is less and in 3 it is greater.*

* **SI units**, 96.

TEMPERATURE

The **temperature** of an object is a measurement of how hot the object is. It is measured using **thermometers** which can be **calibrated*** to show a number of different temperature scales. The internationally accepted scales are the **absolute temperature scale** and the **Celsius scale**.

*On Venus, the **temperature** is approximately 480°C, or 753K. This is because thick clouds trap the Sun's radiation and prevent the heat from escaping.*

Thermometer

An instrument used to measure temperature. There are many different types and they all work by measuring a **thermometric property** – a property which changes with temperature. **Liquid-in-glass thermometers**, for example, measure the volume of a liquid (they are **calibrated*** so that increases in volume mark rises in temperature).

Liquid-in-glass thermometer

A common type of **thermometer** which measures temperature by the expansion of a liquid in a fine bore glass tube (**capillary tube**). A glass bulb holds a reservoir of the liquid, which is usually either mercury or colored alcohol. These substances are very responsive to temperature change – mercury is used for higher temperature ranges and alcohol for lower ones.

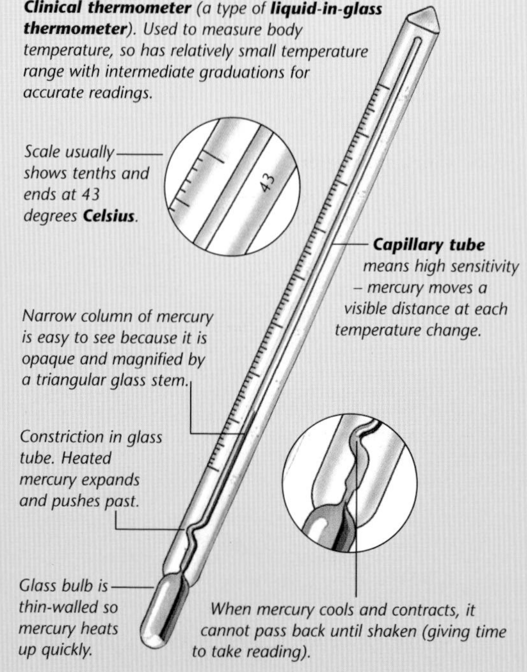

Clinical thermometer (a type of **liquid-in-glass thermometer**). Used to measure body temperature, so has relatively small temperature range with intermediate graduations for accurate readings.
Scale usually shows tenths and ends at 43 degrees **Celsius**.
43
Capillary tube means high sensitivity – mercury moves a visible distance at each temperature change.
Narrow column of mercury is easy to see because it is opaque and magnified by a triangular glass stem.
Constriction in glass tube. Heated mercury expands and pushes past.
Glass bulb is thin-walled so mercury heats up quickly.

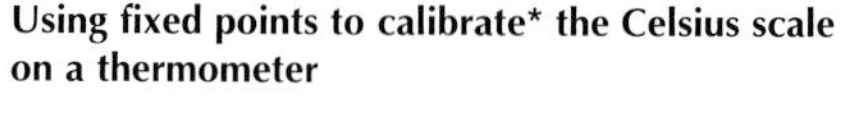

When mercury cools and contracts, it cannot pass back until shaken (giving time to take reading).

Temperature scales

Fixed point

A temperature at which certain recognizable changes always take place (under given conditions), and which can thus be given a value against which all other temperatures can be measured. Examples are the **ice point** (the temperature at which pure ice melts) and the **steam point** (the temperature of steam above water boiling under **atmospheric pressure***). Two fixed points are used to **calibrate*** a thermometer – a **lower** and an **upper fixed point**. The distance between these points is known as the **fundamental interval**.

Using fixed points to calibrate* the Celsius scale on a thermometer

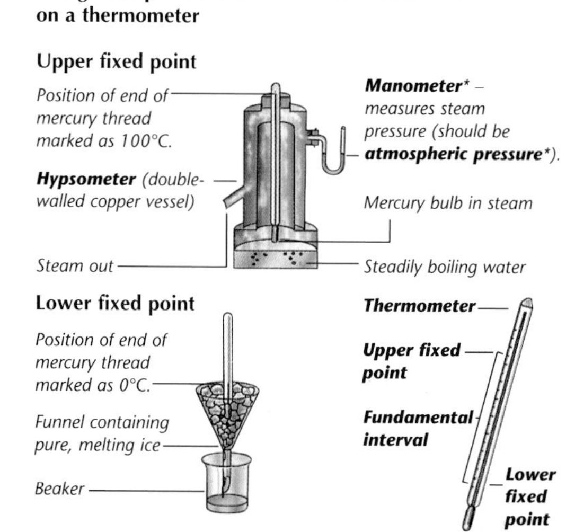

Upper fixed point
Position of end of mercury thread marked as 100°C.
Hypsometer (double-walled copper vessel)
Steam out
Manometer* – measures steam pressure (should be **atmospheric pressure***).
Mercury bulb in steam
Steadily boiling water
Lower fixed point
Position of end of mercury thread marked as 0°C.
Funnel containing pure, melting ice
Beaker
Thermometer
Upper fixed point
Fundamental interval
Lower fixed point

* **Atmospheric pressure**, 25 (**Barometer**); **Calibration**, 344; **Manometer**, 25.

Maximum and **minimum thermometers**

Special **liquid-in-glass thermometers** which record the maximum or minimum temperature reached over a period of time. They contain a metal and glass **index** (see picture below) which is pushed up or pulled down (respectively) by the liquid **meniscus***. The index stays at the maximum or minimum position it reaches during the time the thermometer is left. It is reset using a magnet.

Maximum thermometer

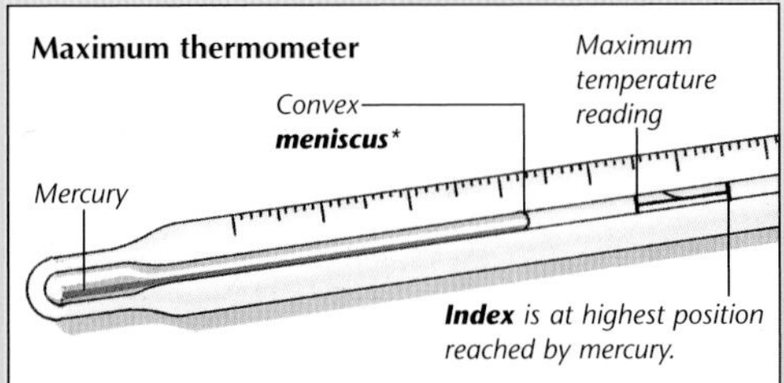
Maximum temperature reading
Convex meniscus*
Mercury
Index is at highest position reached by mercury.

Minimum thermometer

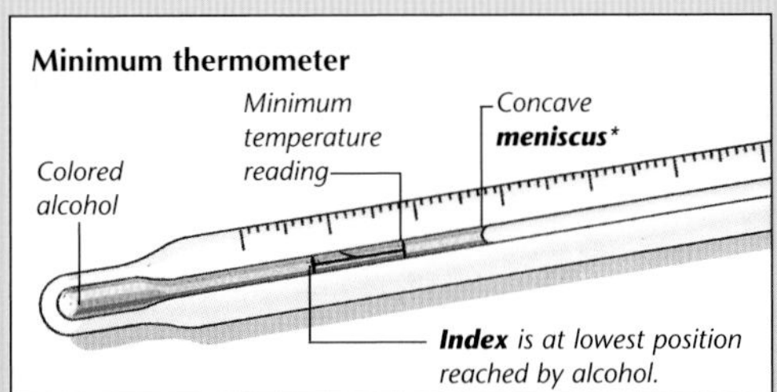
Minimum temperature reading
Concave meniscus*
Colored alcohol
Index is at lowest position reached by alcohol.

Other types of thermometer

Resistance thermometer

Measures temperature from change in **resistance*** it causes in a coil of wire. Similar devices, e.g. under aircraft wings, use resistance change in **thermistors***.

*Aircraft have **thermistors*** under their wing surfaces to measure the air temperature.*

Liquid crystal thermometer

A thermometer containing liquid crystals that change color when they are heated.

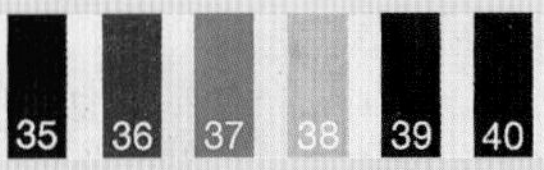
35
36
37
38
39
40

*A **liquid crystal thermometer** on the skin shows its temperature.*

Digital thermometer

A thermometer with a heat-sensitive electric component.

Digital display shows temperature.

Thermocouple

A device which uses the **e.m.f.*** produced across metal junctions to measure temperature difference.

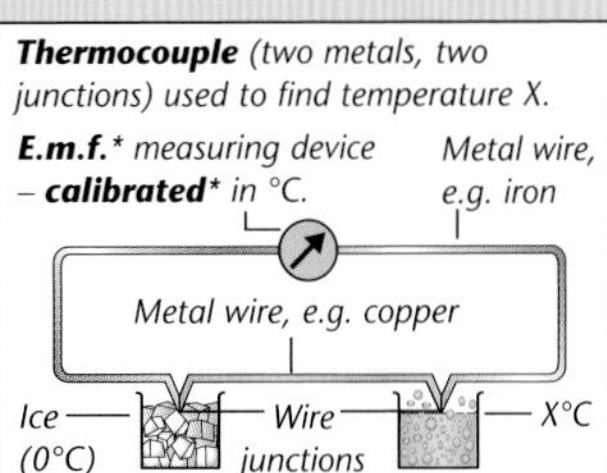
E.m.f.* measuring device – calibrated* in °C.
Metal wire, e.g. iron
Metal wire, e.g. copper
Ice (0°C)
Wire junctions
X°C

***Thermocouple** (two metals, two junctions) used to find temperature X.*

Absolute or **thermodynamic temperature scale**

A standard temperature scale, using units called **kelvins** (**K**). The zero value is given to the lowest possible temperature theoretically achievable, called **absolute zero**. It is impossible to have a lower temperature, as this would require a negative volume (see graph, right) which cannot exist.

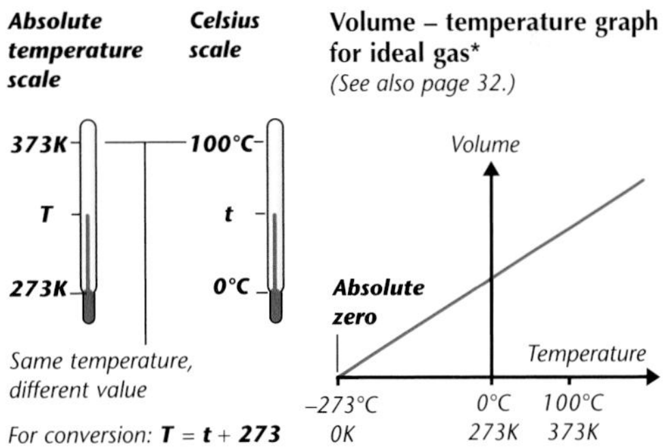
Absolute temperature scale
Celsius scale
373K
100°C
T
t
273K
0°C
Same temperature, different value
For conversion: T = t + 273
Volume – temperature graph for ideal gas*
(See also page 32.)
Volume
Absolute zero
Temperature
–273°C
0K
0°C
273K
100°C
373K

Celsius scale (°C)

A standard temperature scale identical in graduations to the **absolute temperature scale**, but with the zero and one hundred degree values given to the **ice point** and **steam point** respectively (see **fixed point**).

Fahrenheit scale (°F)

An old scale with the values 32°F and 212°F given to the **ice point** and **steam point** respectively (see **fixed point**). It is rarely used in scientific work.

* **Calibration**, 344; **Electromotive force (e.m.f.)**, 60; **Ideal gas**, 33; **Meniscus**, 345; **Resistance**, 62; **Thermistor**, 65.

TRANSFER OF HEAT

Whenever there is a temperature difference, **heat energy** (see page 9) is transferred by **conduction**, **convection** or **radiation** from the hotter to the cooler place. This increases the **internal energy*** of the cooler atoms, raising their temperature, and decreases the energy of the hotter atoms, lowering theirs. It continues until the temperature is the same across the region – a state called **thermal equilibrium**.

*Gliders are lifted up by **convection currents** of warm air (see bottom of page).*

Conduction or thermal conduction

The way in which heat energy is transferred in solids (and also, to a much lesser extent, in liquids and gases). In good **conductors** the energy transfer is rapid, occurring mainly by the movement of free **electrons*** (electrons which can move about), although also by the vibration of atoms – see **insulators** (bad conductors), below.

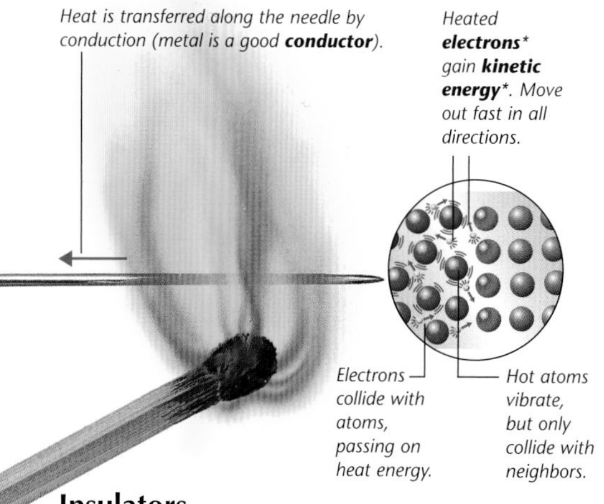
Heat is transferred along the needle by conduction (metal is a good conductor).
Heated electrons* gain kinetic energy*. Move out fast in all directions.
Electrons collide with atoms, passing on heat energy.
Hot atoms vibrate, but only collide with neighbors.

Insulators

Materials such as wood and most liquids and gases, in which the process of **conduction** is very slow (they are bad **conductors**). As they do not have free **electrons***, heat energy is only transferred by conduction by the vibration and collision of neighboring atoms.

Conductivity or thermal conductivity

A measure of how good a heat **conductor** a material is (see also page 112). The rate of heat energy transfer per unit area through an object depends on the conductivity of the material and the **temperature gradient**. This is the temperature change with distance along the material. The higher the conductivity and the steeper the gradient, the faster the energy transfer that takes place.

Metal pan – high conductivity (good conductor)
Plastic handle – low conductivity (bad conductor)
1
x
2
Flow of heat energy

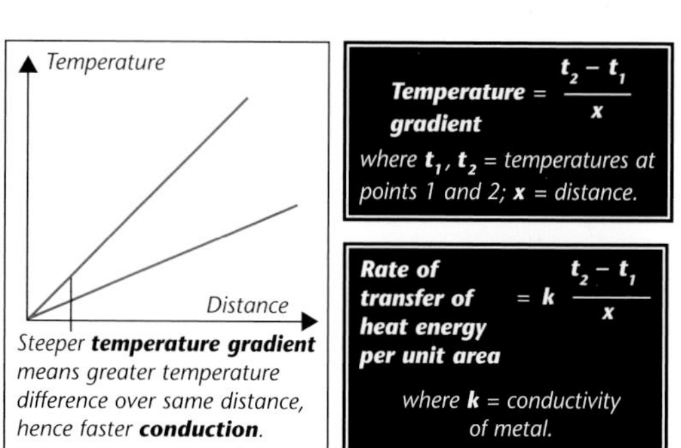
Temperature
Distance
Steeper temperature gradient means greater temperature difference over same distance, hence faster conduction.
Temperature gradient = $\frac{t_2 - t_1}{x}$
where t_1, t_2 = temperatures at points 1 and 2; x = distance.
Rate of transfer of heat energy per unit area = $k\frac{t_2 - t_1}{x}$
where k = conductivity of metal.

Convection

A way in which heat energy is transferred in liquids and gases. If a liquid or gas is heated, it expands, becomes less dense and rises. Cooler, denser liquid or gas then sinks to take its place. Thus a **convection current** is set up. The picture on the right shows how convection currents cause daytime coastal breezes, a process which is reversed at night.

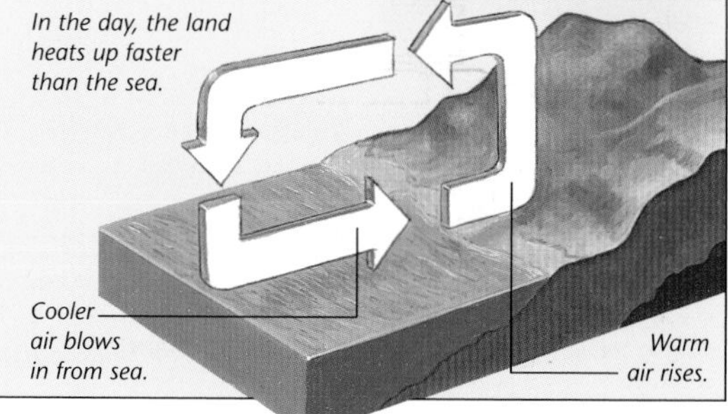
In the day, the land heats up faster than the sea.
Cooler air blows in from sea.
Warm air rises.

* **Electrons**, 83; **Internal energy**, **Kinetic energy**, 9.

Radiation

A way in which heat energy is transferred from a hotter to a cooler place without the **medium*** taking part in the process. This can occur though a vacuum, unlike **conduction** and **convection**. The term radiation is also often used to refer to the heat energy itself, otherwise known as **radiant heat energy**. This takes the form of **electromagnetic waves***, mainly **infra-red radiation***. When these waves fall on an object, some of their energy is absorbed, increasing the object's **internal energy*** and hence its temperature. See also **Leslie's cube**, right.

Use of radiation to supply hot water

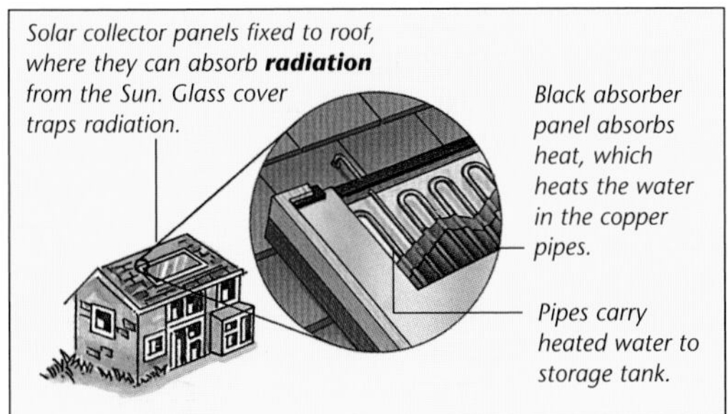
Solar collector panels fixed to roof, where they can absorb **radiation** from the Sun. Glass cover traps radiation.
Black absorber panel absorbs heat, which heats the water in the copper pipes.
Pipes carry heated water to storage tank.

Thermopile

A device for measuring **radiation** levels. It consists of two or more **thermocouples*** (normally over 50) joined end to end. Radiation falls on the metal junctions on one side and the temperature difference between these hot junctions and the cold ones on the other side produces **e.m.f.*** across the thermopile, the size of which indicates how much radiation has been absorbed.

Thermopile

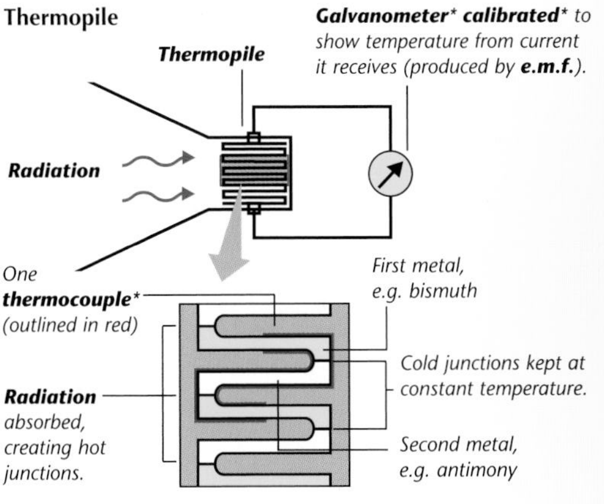
Thermopile
Galvanometer* calibrated* to show temperature from current it receives (produced by e.m.f.).
Radiation
One thermocouple* (outlined in red)
First metal, e.g. bismuth
Cold junctions kept at constant temperature.
Radiation absorbed, creating hot junctions.
Second metal, e.g. antimony

Leslie's cube

A thin-walled, hollow cube (good **conductor**) with different outside surfaces. It is used to show that surfaces vary in their ability to **radiate** and absorb heat energy. Their powers of doing so are compared with an ideal called a **black body**, which absorbs all radiation that falls on it, and is also the best radiator.

Leslie's cube *used to compare powers of* ***radiation*** *– numbers show best (1) to worst (4) surface.*

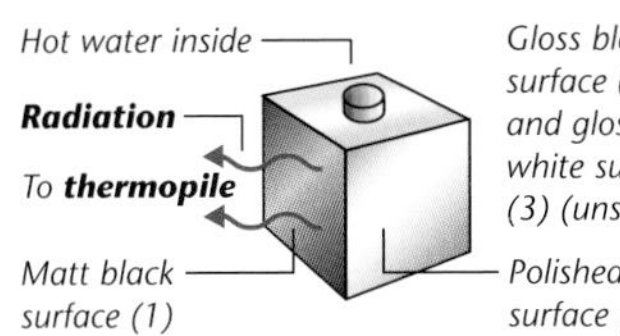
Hot water inside
Radiation
To thermopile
Matt black surface (1)
Gloss black surface (2) and gloss white surface (3) (unseen)
Polished metal surface (4)

Vacuum flask

A flask which keeps its contents at constant temperature. It consists of a double-walled glass container, with a vacuum between the walls (stopping heat energy transfer by **conduction** and **convection**) and shiny surfaces (minimizing transfer by **radiation**).

Vacuum flask

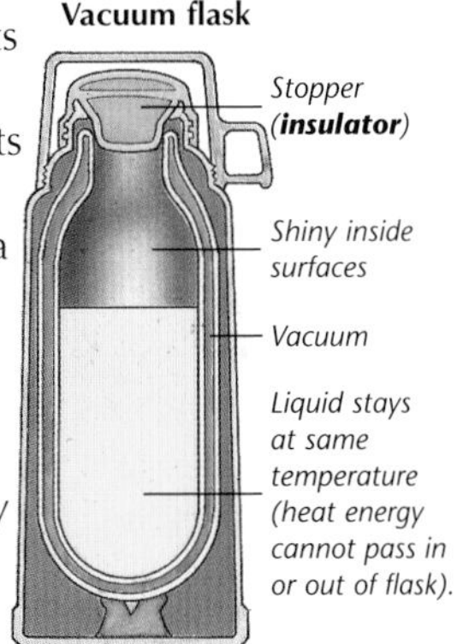
Stopper (insulator)
Shiny inside surfaces
Vacuum
Liquid stays at same temperature (heat energy cannot pass in or out of flask).

Greenhouse effect

The warming effect produced when **radiation** is trapped in a closed area, e.g. a greenhouse. The objects inside absorb the Sun's radiation and re-emit lower energy radiation which cannot pass back through the glass. Carbon dioxide in the atmosphere forms a similar barrier, and its level is increasing, hence the Earth is slowly getting warmer.

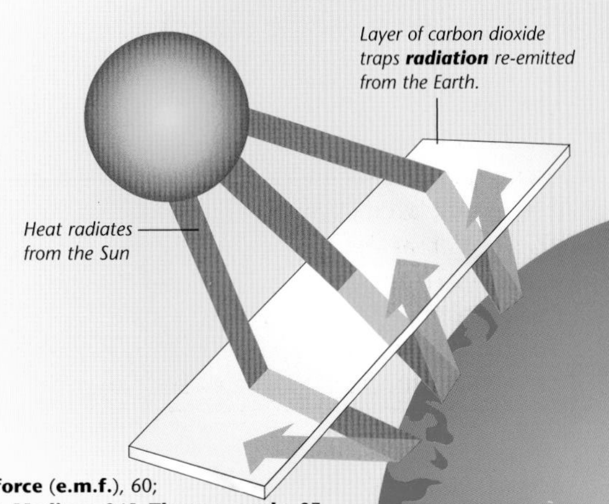
Layer of carbon dioxide traps radiation re-emitted from the Earth.
Heat radiates from the Sun

* **Calibration**, 344; **Electromagnetic waves**, 44; **Electromotive force (e.m.f.)**, 60; **Galvanometer**, 77; **Infra-red radiation**, 45; **Internal energy**, 9; **Medium**, 345; **Thermocouple**, 27.

EFFECTS OF HEAT TRANSFER

When an object absorbs or loses **heat energy** (see pages 28-29), its **internal energy*** increases or decreases. This results in either a rise or fall in temperature (the amount of which depends on the **heat capacity** of the object) or a **change of state**.

During evaporation, molecules escape from the surface of a liquid.

Changes of state

A **change of state** is a change from one **physical state** (the solid, liquid or gaseous state) to another (for more about **physical states**, see page 5). While a change of state is happening, there is no change in temperature. Instead, all the energy taken in or given out is used to make or break molecular bonds. This is called **latent heat** (**L**) – see graphs, page 31. The **specific latent heat** (**l**) of a substance is a set value, i.e. the heat energy taken in or given out when 1kg of the substance changes state.

Evaporation

The conversion of a liquid to a vapor by the escape of molecules from its surface. It takes place at all temperatures, the rate increasing with any one or a combination of the following: increase in temperature, increase in surface area or decrease in pressure. It is also increased if the vapor is immediately removed from above the liquid by a flow of air. The **latent heat** (see above) needed for evaporation is taken from the liquid itself which cools and in turn cools its surroundings.

Vaporization

The change of state from liquid to gaseous at a temperature called the **boiling point** (when the liquid is said to be **boiling**). The term is also used more generally for any change resulting in a gas or vapor, i.e. including also **evaporation** and **sublimation**.

Condensation

The change of state from gas or vapor to liquid.

Melting

The change of state from solid to liquid at a temperature called the **melting point** of the solid.

Freezing

The change of state from liquid to solid at the **freezing point** (the same temperature as the **melting point** of the solid).

Sublimation

The conversion of a substance from a solid directly to a gas, or vice-versa, without passing through the liquid state. Iodine and carbon dioxide are two substances that **sublime**.

Changes of state
Temperature remains constant (see graphs, page 31).

Changes due to heating

*Heat energy taken in, which would have raised the temperature, used instead (as **latent heat**) to break bonds.*

Changes due to cooling

*Heat energy which would have been lost (lowering temperature) used instead (as **latent heat**) to make bonds between molecules.*

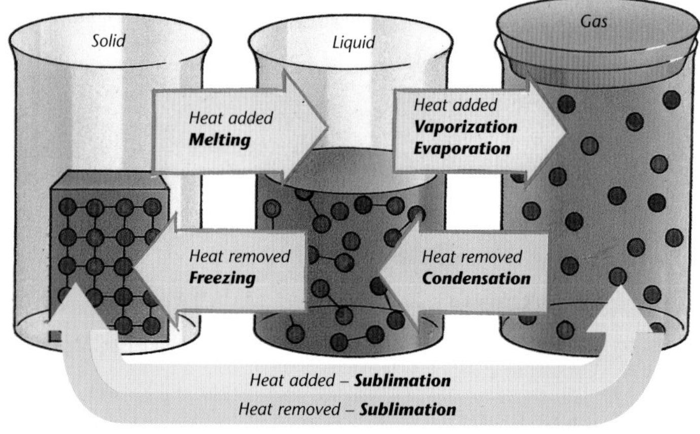
Solid
Liquid
Gas
Heat added
Melting
Heat added
Vaporization
Evaporation
Heat removed
Freezing
Heat removed
Condensation
Heat added – Sublimation
Heat removed – Sublimation

* **Internal energy**, 9.

Graph showing increase of temperature with heat added

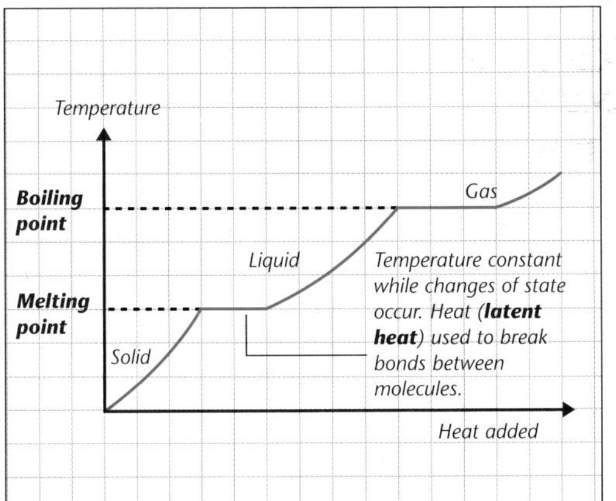
Temperature
Boiling point
Melting point
Gas
Liquid
Solid
Temperature constant while changes of state occur. Heat (**latent heat**) used to break bonds between molecules.
Heat added

Graph showing decrease of temperature as object cools

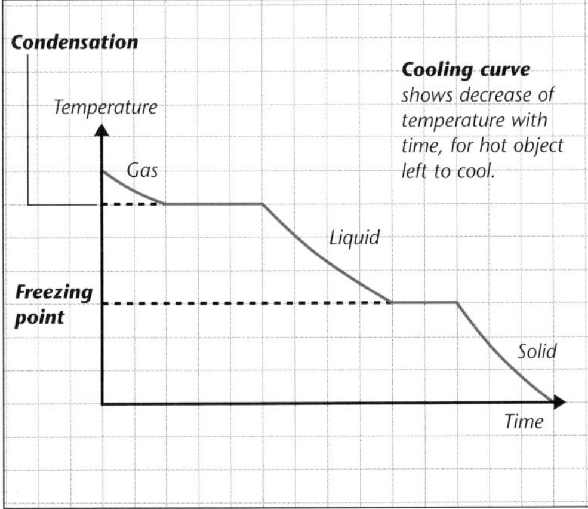
Condensation
Temperature
Gas
Cooling curve shows decrease of temperature with time, for hot object left to cool.
Liquid
Freezing point
Solid
Time

Specific latent heat of vaporization

The heat energy taken in when 1kg of a substance changes from a liquid to a gas at its **boiling point**. It is the same as the heat given out when the process is reversed

Specific latent heat of fusion

The heat energy taken in when 1kg of a substance changes from a solid to a liquid at its **melting point**. It is the same as the heat given out when the process is reversed. See also page 112.

$Q = ml$ *where Q = heat energy lost or gained by object; m = mass; l = **specific latent heat**.*

*The **SI unit*** of **specific latent heat** is the joule per kilogram (J kg⁻¹).*

Heat capacity (C)

The heat energy taken in or given out by an object per temperature change by 1K. It is a property of the object and depends on both its mass and the material(s) of which it is made (as well as the temperature and pressure), hence its value is different for every object.

$Q = C(t_2 - t_1)$ *where Q = heat energy lost or gained; C = heat capacity; t_1 and t_2 = initial and final temperatures respectively.*

*The **SI unit*** of **heat capacity** is the joule per kelvin ($J\ K^{-1}$).*

Specific heat capacity (c)

The heat energy taken in or given out per unit mass per unit temperature change. It is a property of the substance alone, i.e. there is a set value for each substance (though this changes with temperature and pressure). See also page 112.

$Q = mc(t_2 - t_1)$ *where m = mass; c = **specific heat capacity**; Q, t_1, t_2 as above.*

*The **SI unit*** of **specific heat capacity** is the joule per kilogram per kelvin ($J\ kg^{-1}\ K^{-1}$).*

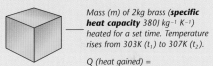

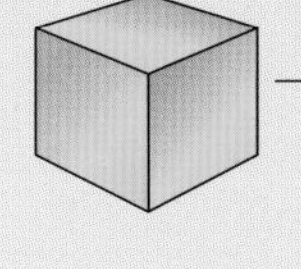

*Mass (m) of 2kg brass (**specific heat capacity** 380J $kg^{-1}\ K^{-1}$) heated for a set time. Temperature rises from 303K (t_1) to 307K (t_2).*

Q (heat gained) = 2 × 380 × (307–303)J

So Q = 3,040J

Thus same amount of heat energy taken in by 16kg of brass would raise temperature by 0.5K.

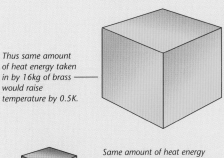

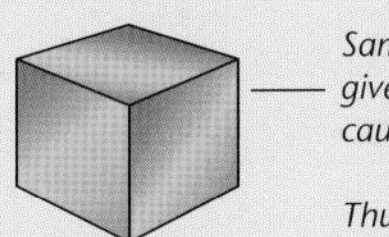

Same amount of heat energy given to mass of 2kg of copper causes temperature rise of 3.8K.

*Thus **specific heat capacity** of copper is 400J $kg^{-1}\ K^{-1}$.*

* **SI units**, 96.

EXPANSION DUE TO HEATING

Most substances expand when heated – their molecules move faster and further apart. The extent of this expansion (**expansivity**) depends on **intermolecular forces***. For the same amount of heat applied (at constant pressure), solids expand least, as their molecules are closest together and so have the strongest forces between them. Liquids expand more, and gases the most.

Expansion of solids on heating must be taken into account in building work.

Rubberized compound put between paving stones

Bimetallic strip

A device which shows the expansion of solids due to heating. It is made up of two different strips of metal, joined along their (equal) length. When heated or cooled, both metals expand or contract (respectively), but at different rates, so the strip bends. Such strips are used in **thermostats**.

Thermostat (temperature regulator)

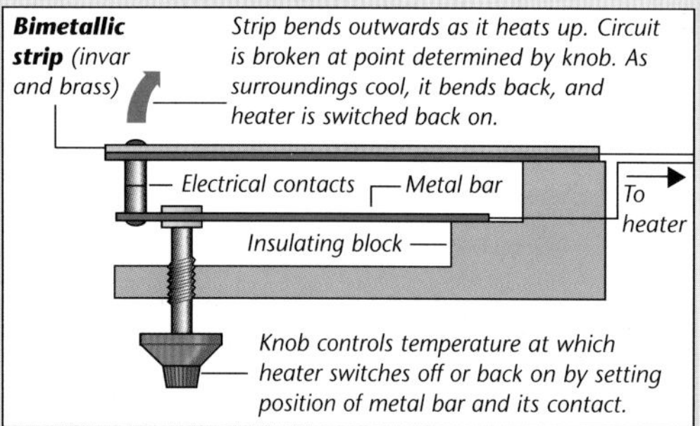

Bimetallic strip (invar and brass)
Strip bends outwards as it heats up. Circuit is broken at point determined by knob. As surroundings cool, it bends back, and heater is switched back on.
Electrical contacts
Metal bar
To heater
Insulating block
Knob controls temperature at which heater switches off or back on by setting position of metal bar and its contact.

Linear coefficient of expansion (α)

A measurement of the fraction of its original length by which a solid expands for a temperature rise of 1K.

Areal coefficient of expansion (β)

A measurement of the fraction of its original area by which a solid expands for a temperature rise of 1K.

For solids or liquids:

$$\text{Expansivity (linear, superficial or cubic)} = \frac{\text{change in (length, area or volume)}}{\text{original (length, area or volume)} \times \text{temperature rise}}$$

*Note the only relevant measurement for liquids is **cubic expansivity**. It is either **real** or **apparent** (see right), therefore so also is the change in volume in formula.*

For gases:

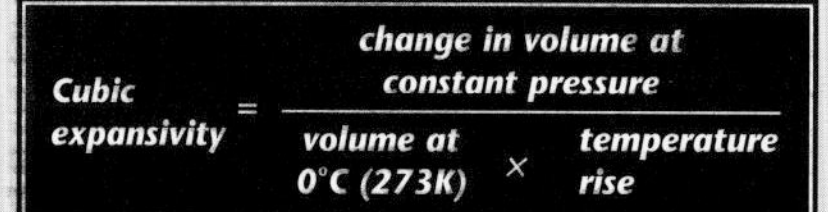

$$\text{Cubic expansivity} = \frac{\text{change in volume at constant pressure}}{\text{volume at 0°C (273K)} \times \text{temperature rise}}$$

Volume coefficient of expansion (γ)

A measurement of the fraction of its original volume by which a substance expands for a temperature rise of 1K. It is the same for all gases (at constant pressure) when they are assumed to behave as **ideal gases**. Since gases expand by very large amounts, the original volume is always taken at 0°C so that proper comparisons can be made (this is not necessary with solids or liquids as the changes are so small).

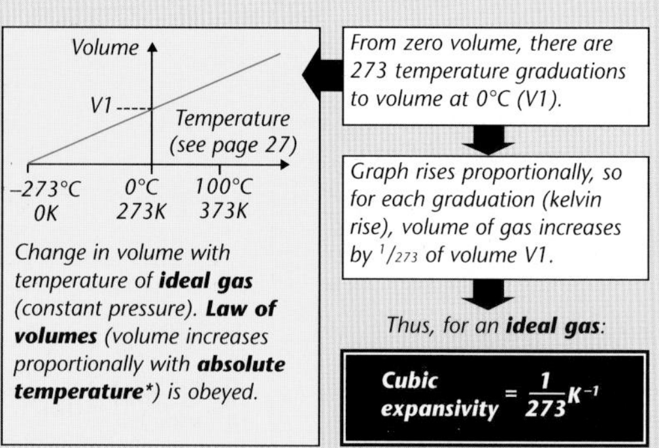

Volume
V1
Temperature (see page 27)
–273°C
0K
0°C
273K
100°C
373K
From zero volume, there are 273 temperature graduations to volume at 0°C (V1).
Graph rises proportionally, so for each graduation (kelvin rise), volume of gas increases by 1/273 of volume V1.
Thus, for an ideal gas:
Cubic expansivity = 1/273 K⁻¹

*Change in volume with temperature of **ideal gas** (constant pressure). **Law of volumes** (volume increases proportionally with **absolute temperature***) is obeyed.*

Real or absolute cubic expansivity

An accurate measurement of the fraction of its volume by which a liquid expands for a temperature rise of 1K.

Apparent cubic expansivity

A measurement of the fraction of its volume by which a liquid apparently expands for a temperature rise of 1K. In fact, the heat applied also causes very slight expansion of the container, so its calibrated measurements are no longer valid.

Anomalous expansion

The phenomenon whereby some liquids contract instead of expanding when the temperature rises within a certain range (e.g. water between 0°C and 4°C).

* **Absolute temperature scale**, 27; **Intermolecular forces**, 7.

Behavior of gases

All gases behave in a similar way, and there are several **gas laws** which describe their behavior (see below and right). An **ideal gas** is a theoretical gas which, by definition, exactly obeys **Boyle's law** at all temperatures and pressures, but in fact also obeys the two other laws as well. When real gases are at normal temperatures and pressures, they show approximately ideal behavior (the higher the temperature and the lower the pressure, the better the approximation), hence the laws may be generally applied.

Boyle's law

The volume of a fixed mass of gas at constant temperature is inversely proportional to the pressure. For example, if the pressure on the gas increases, the volume decreases proportionally – the molecules move closer together. Note that the pressure exerted by the gas increases (the molecules hit the container walls more often).

Boyle's law

$$V \propto \frac{1}{P} \quad \text{or} \quad PV = \text{constant}$$

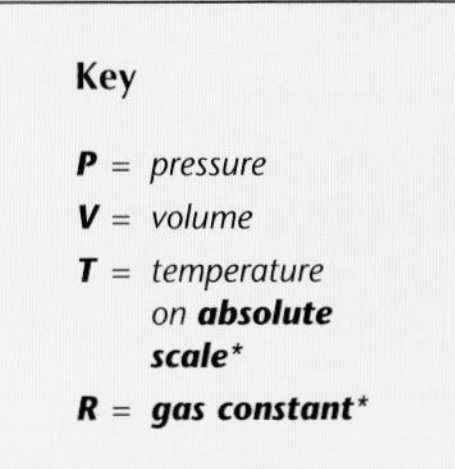
Key
P = pressure
V = volume
T = temperature on absolute scale*
R = gas constant*

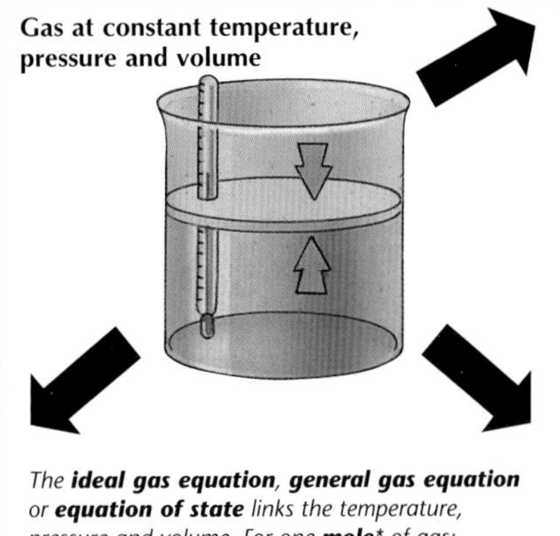
Gas at constant temperature, pressure and volume

*The **ideal gas equation**, **general gas equation** or **equation of state** links the temperature, pressure and volume. For one **mole*** of gas:*

$$\frac{PV}{T} = R \quad \text{or} \quad PV = RT$$

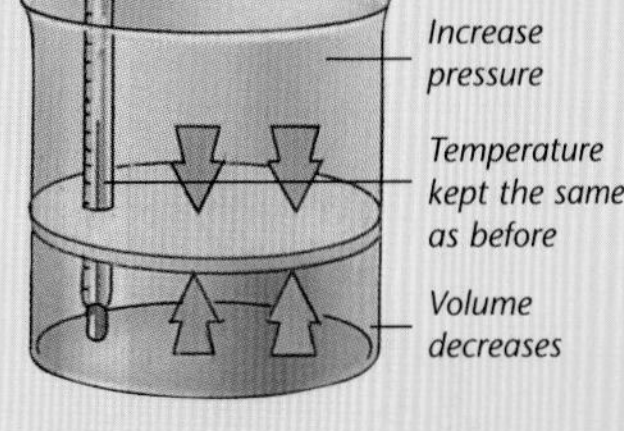
Increase pressure
Temperature kept the same as before
Volume decreases

Pressure law

The pressure of a fixed mass of gas at constant volume is proportional to the temperature on the **absolute scale***. For example, if the temperature increases but the volume is kept the same, the pressure inside the gas increases proportionally – the molecules move faster, and hit the container walls more often. Note that the pressure exerted on the gas to keep the volume constant must increase.

Pressure law

$$P \propto T \quad \text{or} \quad \frac{P}{T} = \text{constant}$$

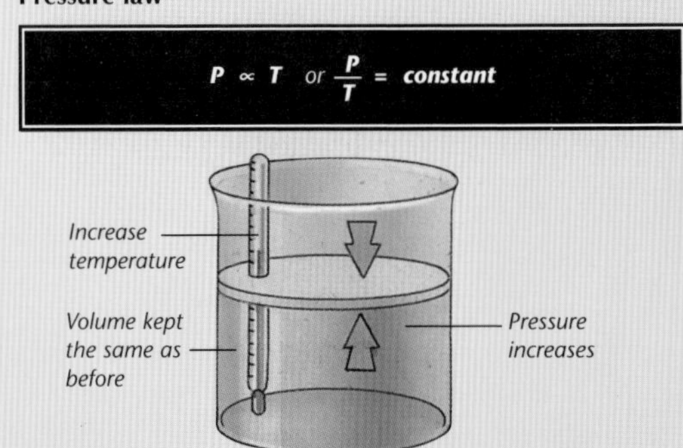
Increase temperature
Volume kept the same as before
Pressure increases

Law of volumes

The volume of a fixed mass of gas at constant pressure is proportional to the temperature on the **absolute scale***. For example, if the temperature increases and the pressure is kept the same, the volume increases proportionally (given an expandable container) – the molecules move faster and further apart. Note that the pressure exerted by the gas remains constant (the molecules hit the walls at the same frequency – they have more space, but greater energy).

Law of volumes

$$V \propto T \quad \text{or} \quad \frac{V}{T} = \text{constant}$$

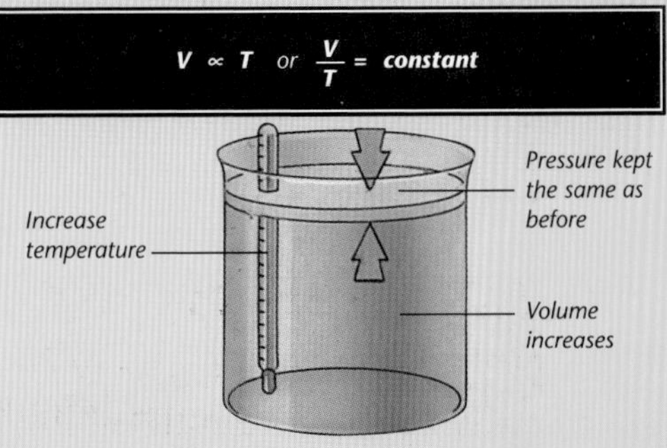
Increase temperature
Pressure kept the same as before
Volume increases

* **Absolute temperature scale**, 27; **Gas constant**, 113; **Mole**, 96.

WAVES

All **waves** transport energy without permanently displacing the **medium*** through which they travel. They are also called **traveling waves**, as the energy travels from a source to surrounding points (but see also **stationary wave**, page 43). There are two main types – **mechanical waves**, such as sound waves, and **electromagnetic waves** (see page 44). In all cases, the **wave motion** is regular and repetitive (i.e. **periodic motion** – see page 16) in the form of **oscillations** – regular changes between two extremes. In mechanical waves it is particles (molecules) that oscillate, and in electromagnetic waves it is electric and magnetic fields.

Mechanical wave *(**transverse wave**) passes along string.*

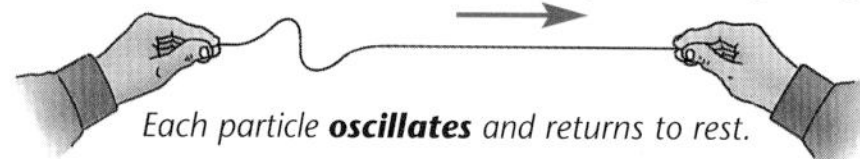
Each particle **oscillates** and returns to rest.

Displacement/time graph for oscillation of one particle

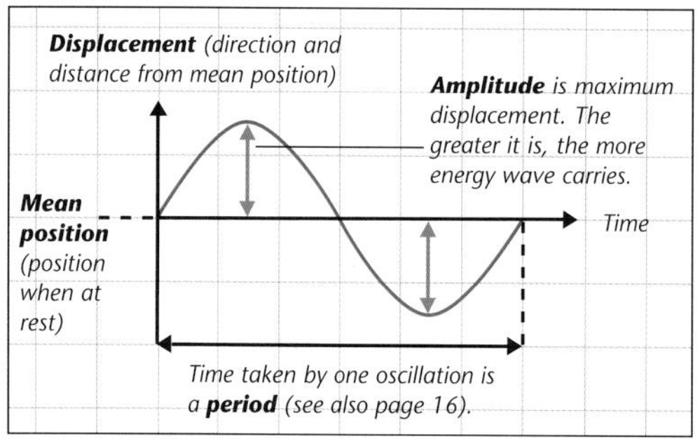
Displacement (direction and distance from mean position)
Amplitude is maximum displacement. The greater it is, the more energy wave carries.
Mean position (position when at rest)
Time
Time taken by one oscillation is a **period** (see also page 16).

Transverse waves

Waves in which the oscillations are at right angles to the direction of energy (wave) movement, e.g. water waves (oscillation of particles) and all **electromagnetic waves*** (oscillation of fields – see introduction).

Crests or peaks

Points where a wave causes maximum positive displacement of the **medium***. The crests of some waves, e.g. water waves, can be seen as they travel.

Troughs

Points where a wave causes maximum negative displacement of the **medium***. The troughs of some waves, e.g. water waves, can be seen as they travel.

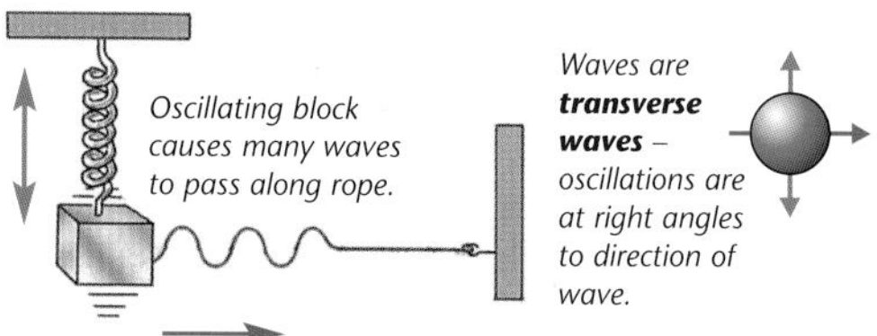
Oscillating block causes many waves to pass along rope.
Waves are **transverse waves** – oscillations are at right angles to direction of wave.

Displacement/distance graph for particles of section of rope at two "frozen" moments

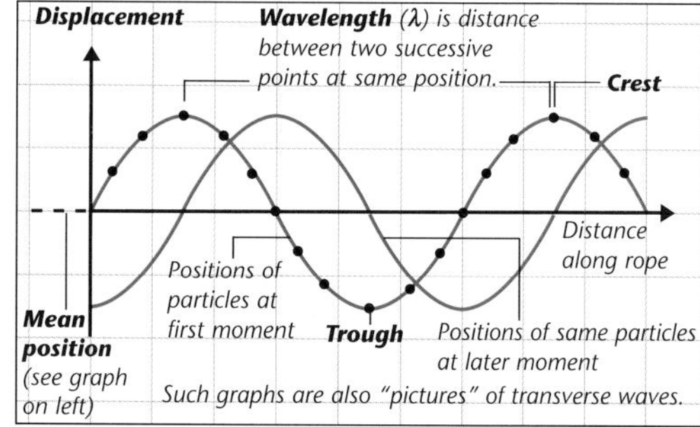
Displacement
Wavelength (λ) is distance between two successive points at same position.
Crest
Distance along rope
Positions of particles at first moment
Trough
Positions of same particles at later moment
Mean position (see graph on left)
Such graphs are also "pictures" of transverse waves.

Wavefront

Any line or section taken through an advancing wave which joins all points that are in the same position in their oscillations. Wavefronts are usually at right angles to the direction of the waves and can have any shape, e.g. **circular** and **straight wavefronts**.

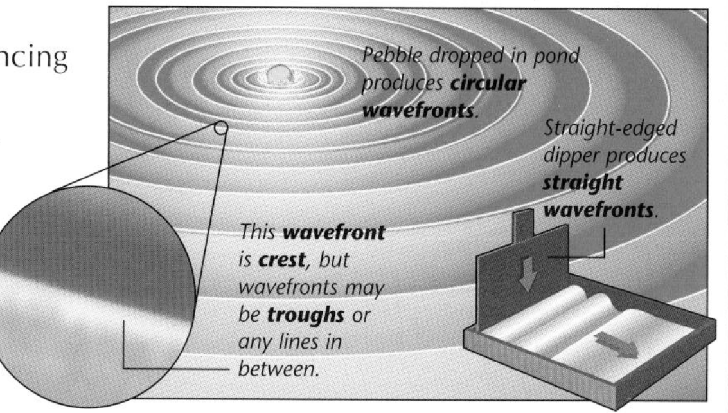
Pebble dropped in pond produces **circular wavefronts**.
Straight-edged dipper produces **straight wavefronts**.
This **wavefront** is **crest**, but wavefronts may be **troughs** or any lines in between.

* **Electromagnetic waves**, 44; **Medium**, 345.

Longitudinal waves

Waves in which the oscillations are along the line of the direction of wave movement, e.g. sound waves. They are all **mechanical waves** (see introduction), i.e. it is particles which oscillate.

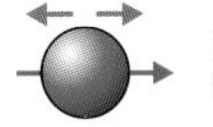

*In **longitudinal waves**, particles oscillate along line of wave direction.*

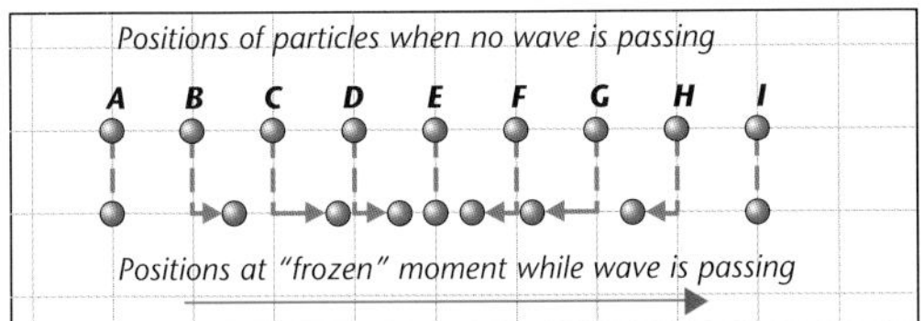

Positions of particles when no wave is passing
A
B
C
D
E
F
G
H
I
Positions at "frozen" moment while wave is passing

Graph of particles above at "frozen" moment
Graph not in this case "picture" of wave (see second graph, page 34).

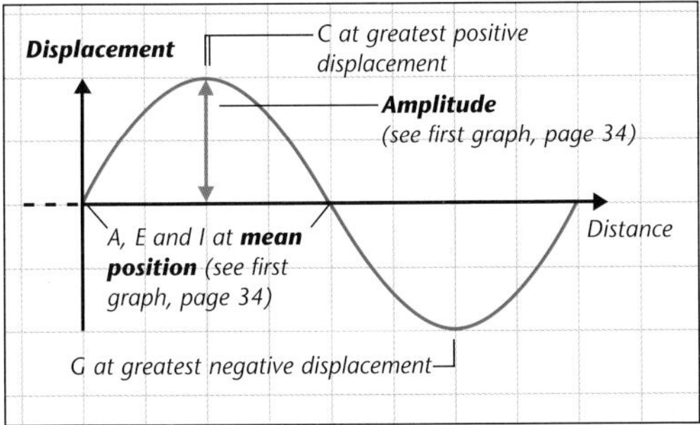

Displacement
C at greatest positive displacement
Amplitude
(see first graph, page 34)
Distance
A, E and I at mean position (see first graph, page 34)
G at greatest negative displacement

Compressions

Regions along a **longitudinal wave** where the pressure and density of the molecules are higher than when no wave is passing.

Rarefactions

Regions along a **longitudinal wave** where the pressure and density of the molecules are lower than when no wave is passing.

Graph of pressure or density versus distance for longitudinal wave shows compressions and rarefactions.

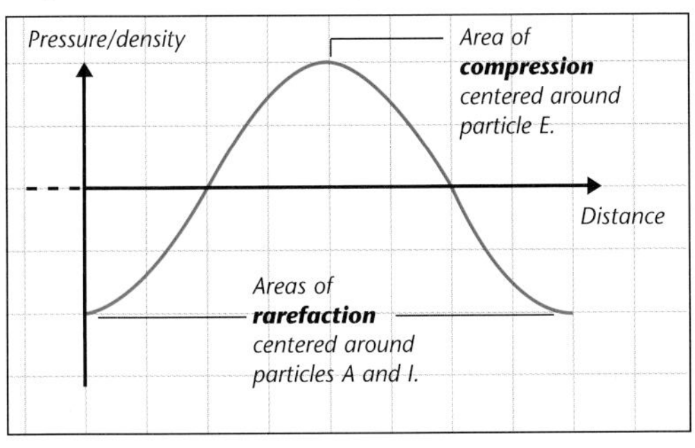

Pressure/density
Area of compression centered around particle E.
Distance
Areas of rarefaction centered around particles A and I.

Wave speed

The distance moved by a wave per unit of time. It depends on the **medium*** through which the wave is traveling.

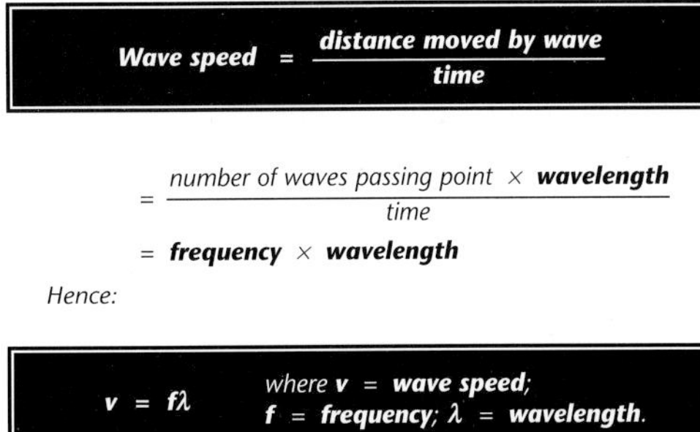

$$\text{Wave speed} = \frac{\text{distance moved by wave}}{\text{time}}$$

$$= \frac{\text{number of waves passing point} \times \text{wavelength}}{\text{time}}$$

$$= \text{frequency} \times \text{wavelength}$$

Hence:

$$v = f\lambda$$

where v = **wave speed**; f = **frequency**; λ = **wavelength**.

Frequency (f)

The number of oscillations which occur in one second when waves pass a given point (see also page 16). It is equal to the number of **wavelengths** (see second graph, page 34) per second.

Attenuation

The gradual decrease in **amplitude** (see first graph, page 34) of a wave as it passes through matter and loses energy. The amplitudes of oscillations occurring further from the source are less than those of oscillations nearer to it. This can be seen as an overall **damping***.

Graph showing attenuated wave

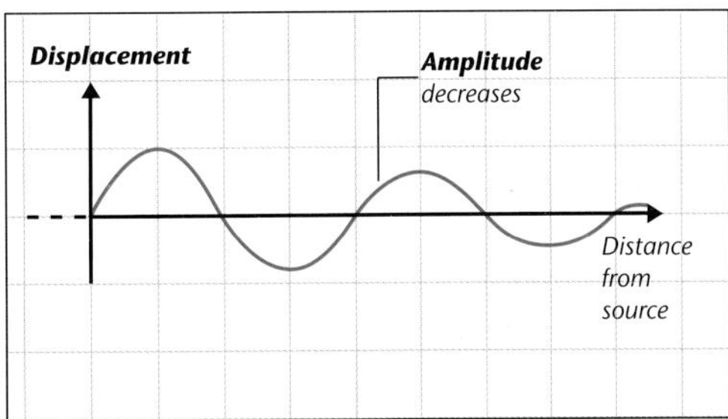

Displacement
Amplitude decreases
Distance from source

Wave intensity

A measurement of the energy carried by a wave. It is worked out as the amount of energy falling on unit area per second. It depends on the **frequency** and **amplitude** of the wave, and also on the **wave speed**.

* **Damping**, 16; **Medium**, 345.

REFLECTION, REFRACTION AND DIFFRACTION

An obstacle or a change of **medium*** causes a wave to undergo **reflection**, **refraction** or **diffraction**. These are different types of change in wave direction and often also result in changes in the shape of the **wavefronts***. For more about the reflection and refraction of light waves, see pages 47-53.

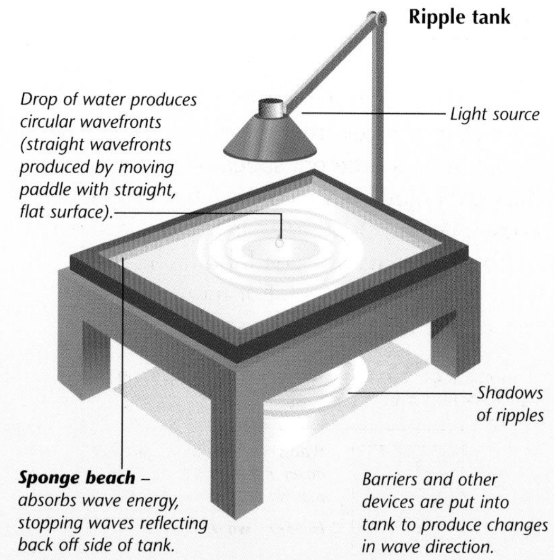

Ripple tank
Drop of water produces circular wavefronts (straight wavefronts produced by moving paddle with straight, flat surface).
Light source
Shadows of ripples
Sponge beach – absorbs wave energy, stopping waves reflecting back off side of tank.
Barriers and other devices are put into tank to produce changes in wave direction.

Ripple tank

A tank of water used to demonstrate the properties of water waves (see right).

Reflection

The change in direction of a wave due to its bouncing off a boundary between two **media***. A wave that has undergone reflection is called a **reflected wave**. The shape of its wavefronts depends on the shape of the **incident wavefronts** and the shape of the boundary. For more about the reflection of light waves, see pages 47-49.

Incident wave

A wave that is traveling toward a boundary between two **media***. Its wavefronts are called **incident wavefronts**.

Circular wavefronts hitting concave boundary produce straight wavefronts in this case (i.e. with ship at this distance).

Ship's horn produces sound waves.
Circular wavefronts (**incident waves**)
Straight wavefronts (**reflected waves**)

Examples of reflected wave shapes

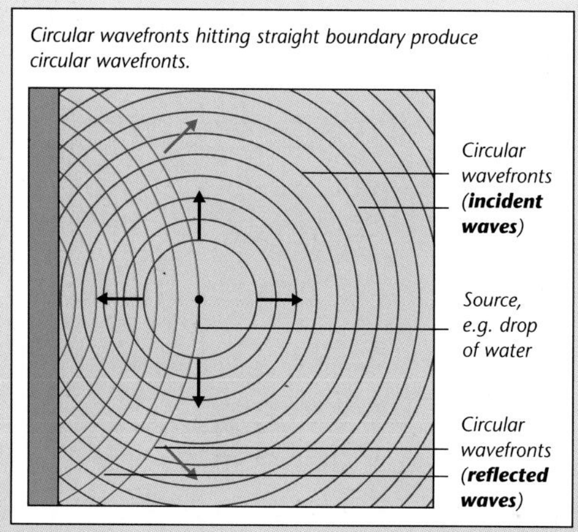

Circular wavefronts hitting straight boundary produce circular wavefronts.
Circular wavefronts (**incident waves**)
Source, e.g. drop of water
Circular wavefronts (**reflected waves**)

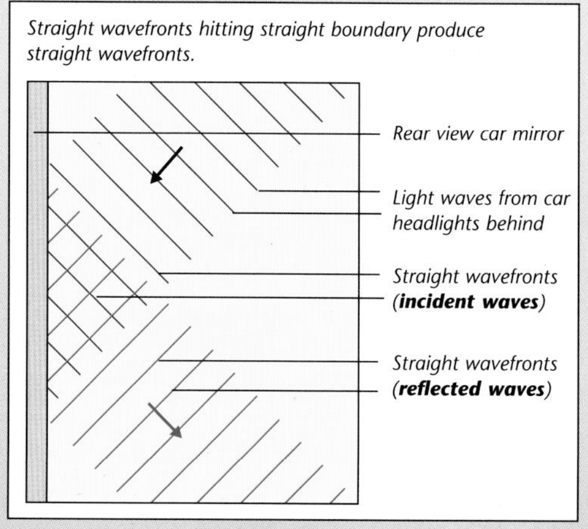

Straight wavefronts hitting straight boundary produce straight wavefronts.
Rear view car mirror
Light waves from car headlights behind
Straight wavefronts (**incident waves**)
Straight wavefronts (**reflected waves**)

* **Medium**, 345; **Wavefront**, 34.

Refraction

The change in direction of a wave when it moves into a new **medium*** which causes it to travel at a different speed. A wave which has undergone refraction is called a **refracted wave**. Its **wavelength*** increases or decreases with the change in speed, but there is no change in **frequency***. For more about the refraction of light waves, see pages 50-53.

Examples of refraction of waves in a ripple tank when moving into a new medium

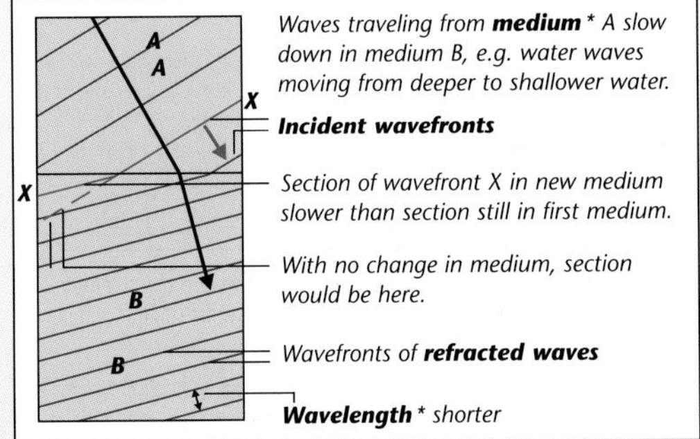
A
A
X
X
B
B
Waves traveling from **medium** * A slow down in medium B, e.g. water waves moving from deeper to shallower water.
Incident wavefronts
Section of wavefront X in new medium slower than section still in first medium.
With no change in medium, section would be here.
Wavefronts of **refracted waves**
Wavelength * shorter

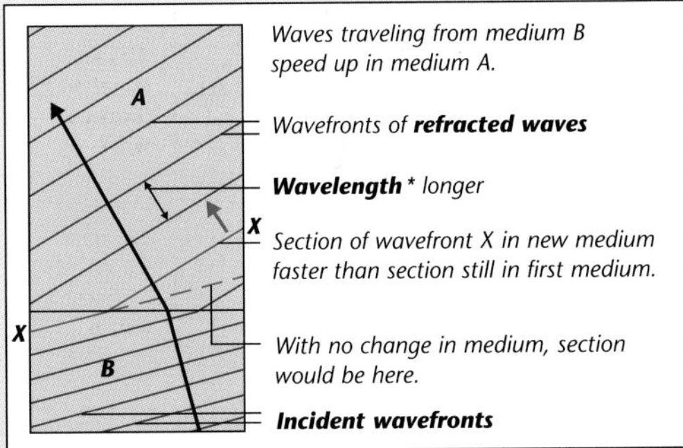
A
X
X
B
Waves traveling from medium B speed up in medium A.
Wavefronts of **refracted waves**
Wavelength * longer
Section of wavefront X in new medium faster than section still in first medium.
With no change in medium, section would be here.
Incident wavefronts

Other examples:

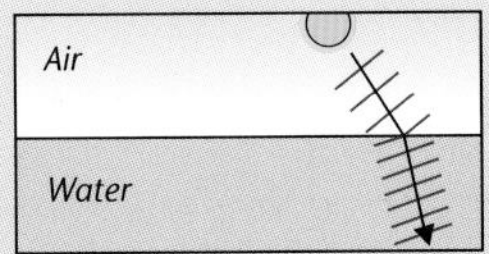
Air
Water

Waves slow down on entering a denser medium.

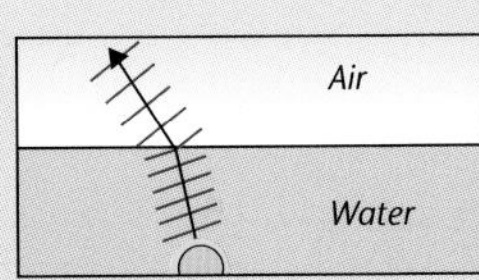
Air
Water

They speed up on entering a less dense medium.

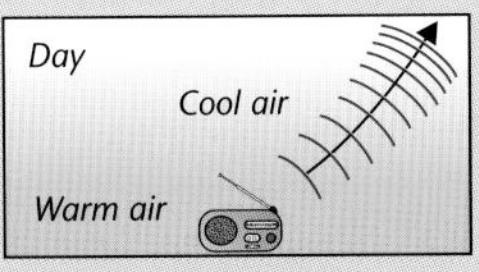
Day
Cool air
Warm air

Sound waves slow down on entering a cooler medium (cooler means denser).

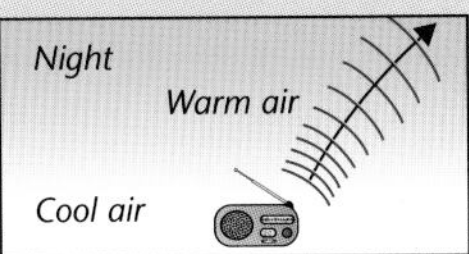
Night
Warm air
Cool air

They speed up on entering a warmer medium (warmer means less dense).

Refractive index (n)

A number which indicates the power of refraction of a given **medium*** relative to a previous medium. It is found by dividing the speed of the **incident wave** in the first medium by the speed of the **refracted wave** in the given medium (subscript numbers are used – see formula). The **absolute refractive index** of a medium is the speed of light in a vacuum (or, generally, in air) divided by the speed of light in that medium†.

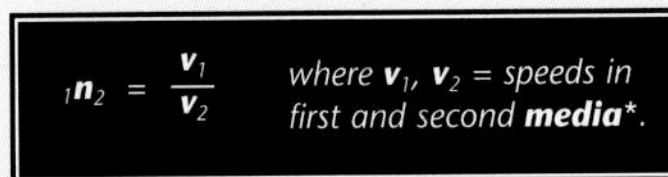
$_1n_2 = \frac{v_1}{v_2}$
where v_1, v_2 = speeds in first and second **media***.

*This means **refractive index** of **medium*** 2 relative to medium 1.*

Diffraction

The bending effect which occurs when a wave meets an obstacle or passes through an aperture. The amount the wave bends depends on the size of the obstacle or aperture compared to the **wavelength*** of the wave. The smaller the obstacle or aperture by comparison, the more the wave bends.

Diffraction of waves (sound waves) around obstacle

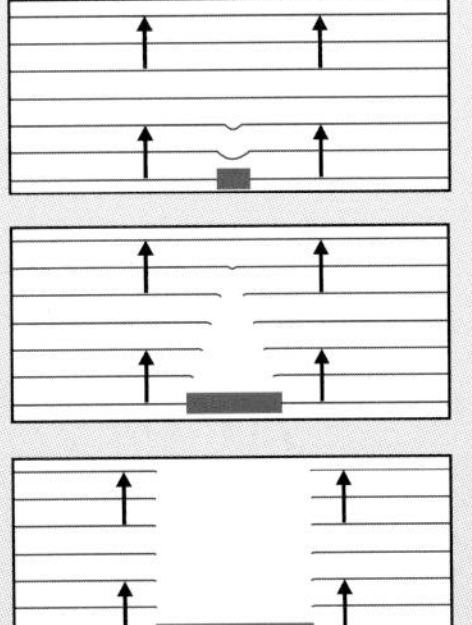

*Obstacle small compared to **wavelength*** (wavelength of sound is about 2m) – a lot of diffraction, so no "shadow" formed.*

Obstacle about same size as wavelength – some diffraction, so small "shadow" formed, i.e. area through which no waves pass.

Obstacle large compared to wavelength – almost no diffraction, so large "shadow" formed.

Diffraction of water waves passing through aperture (slit)

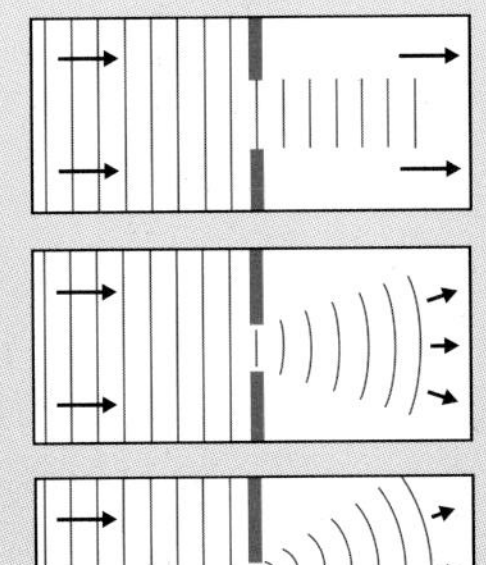

*Aperture wide compared to **wavelength*** – little diffraction.*

Aperture about same size as wavelength – some diffraction.

Aperture narrow compared to wavelength – a lot of diffraction.

* **Frequency**, 35; **Medium**, 345; **Wavelength**, 34.
† *For more about **refractive index** and light, see page 50.*

WAVE INTERFERENCE

When two or more waves travel in the same or different directions in a given space, variations in the size of the resulting disturbance occur at points where they meet (see **principle of superposition**). This effect is called **interference**. When interference is demonstrated, e.g. in a **ripple tank***, sources which produce **coherent waves** are always used, i.e. waves with the same wavelength and frequency, and either **in phase** or with a constant **phase difference** (see **phase**). This ensures that the interference produces a regular, identifiable **interference pattern** of disturbance (see picture, page 39). The use of non-coherent waves would result only in a constantly-changing confusion of waves.

Phase

Two waves are **in phase** if they are of the same frequency and corresponding points are at the same place in their oscillations (e.g. both at **crests***) at the same instant. They are **out of phase** if this is not the case, and exactly out of phase if their displacements are exactly opposite (e.g. a crest and a **trough***). The **phase difference** between two waves is the amount, measured as an angle, by which a point on one wave is ahead of or behind the corresponding point on the other. For waves exactly out of phase, the phase difference is 180°; for waves in phase, it is 0°.

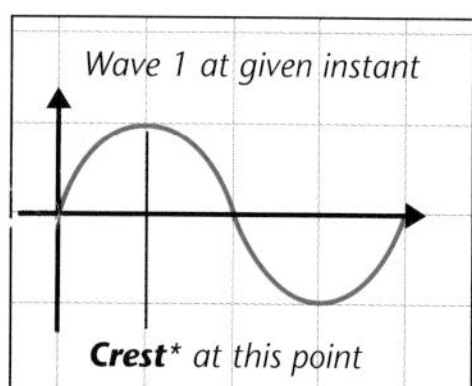

Wave 1 at given instant
Crest* at this point

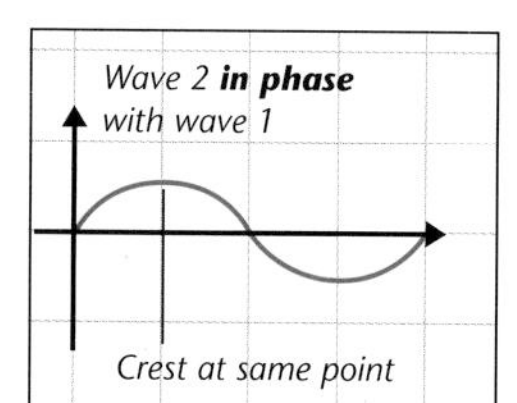

Wave 2 in phase with wave 1
Crest at same point

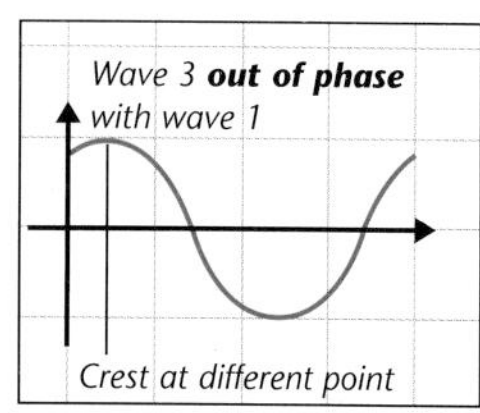

Wave 3 out of phase with wave 1
Crest at different point

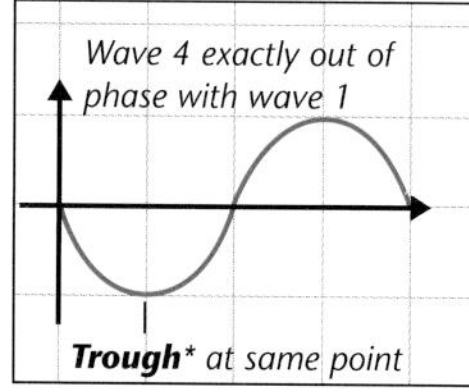

Wave 4 exactly out of phase with wave 1
Trough* at same point

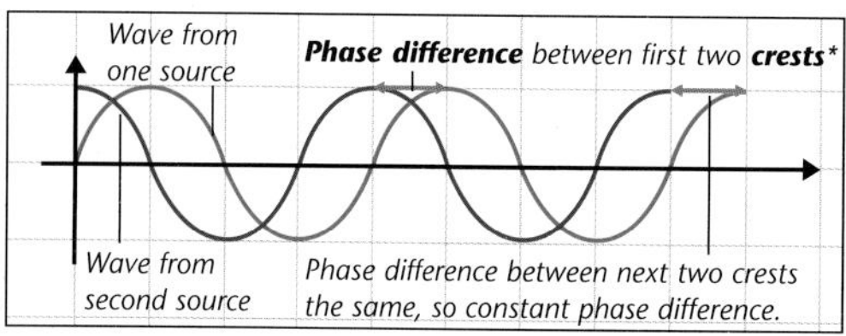

Wave from one source
Phase difference between first two crests*
Wave from second source
Phase difference between next two crests the same, so constant phase difference.

Young's slits

An arrangement of narrow, parallel slits, used to create two sources of **coherent** light (see introduction). They are needed because coherent light waves cannot be produced (for studying interference) as easily as other coherent waves, as light wave emission is usually random. The interference of the light **diffracted*** through the slits is seen on a screen as light and dark bands called **interference fringes**.

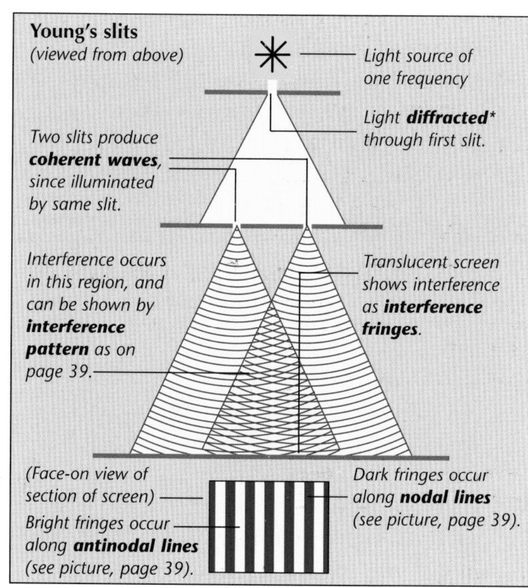

Young's slits
(viewed from above)
Light source of one frequency
Light diffracted* through first slit.
Two slits produce coherent waves, since illuminated by same slit.
Interference occurs in this region, and can be shown by interference pattern as on page 39.
Translucent screen shows interference as interference fringes.
(Face-on view of section of screen)
Bright fringes occur along antinodal lines (see picture, page 39).
Dark fringes occur along nodal lines (see picture, page 39).

Principle of superposition

States that when the **superposition** of two or more waves occurs at a point (i.e. two or more waves come together), the resultant displacement is equal to the sum of the displacements (positive or negative) of the individual waves.

* **Crests**, 34; **Diffraction**, 37; **Ripple tank**, 36; **Troughs**, 34.

Constructive interference

The increase in disturbance (reinforcement) which results from the **superposition** of two waves which are **in phase** (see **phase**).

Destructive interference

The decrease in disturbance which results from the **superposition** of two waves which are **out of phase**.

Constructive interference

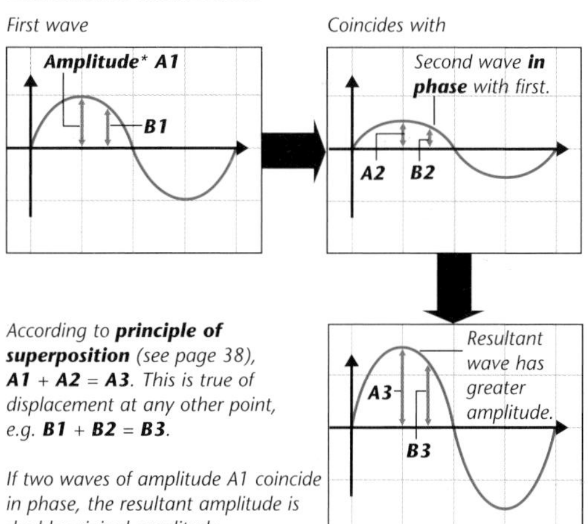
First wave
Amplitude* A1
B1
Coincides with
Second wave in phase with first.
A2
B2
Resultant wave has greater amplitude.
A3
B3

*According to **principle of superposition** (see page 38), **A1** + **A2** = **A3**. This is true of displacement at any other point, e.g. **B1** + **B2** = **B3**.*

If two waves of amplitude A1 coincide in phase, the resultant amplitude is double original amplitude.

Destructive interference

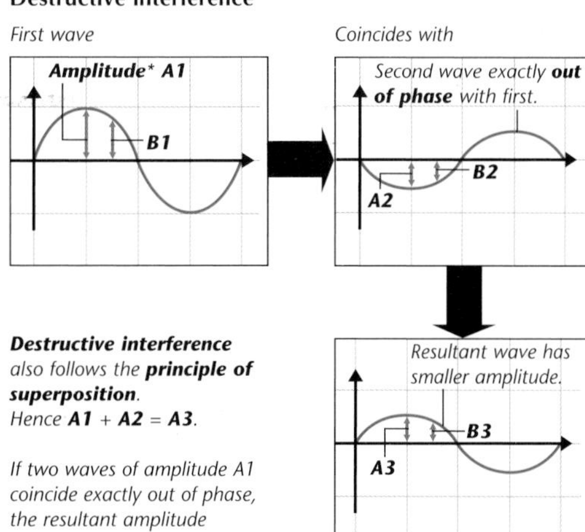
First wave
Amplitude* A1
B1
Coincides with
Second wave exactly out of phase with first.
A2
B2
Resultant wave has smaller amplitude.
A3
B3

***Destructive interference** also follows the **principle of superposition**. Hence **A1** + **A2** = **A3**.*

If two waves of amplitude A1 coincide exactly out of phase, the resultant amplitude is zero.

Nodes or nodal points

Points at which destructive interference is continually occurring, and which are consequently regularly points of minimum disturbance, i.e. points where **crest*** meets **trough*** or **compression*** meets **rarefaction***. A **nodal line** is a line consisting entirely of nodes. Depending on waves, nodal lines may indicate, for example, calm water, soft sound or darkness (see also **Young's slits** picture, page 38).

Antinodes or antinodal points

Points at which **constructive interference** is continually occurring, and which are consequently regularly points of maximum disturbance, i.e. points where two **crests***, **troughs***, **compressions*** or **rarefactions*** meet. An **antinodal line** is a line consisting entirely of antinodes. Depending on waves, antinodal lines may indicate, for example, areas of rough water, loud sound or bright light (see also **Young's slits** picture).

Interference pattern at "frozen" moment
(not all antinodal/nodal lines shown).

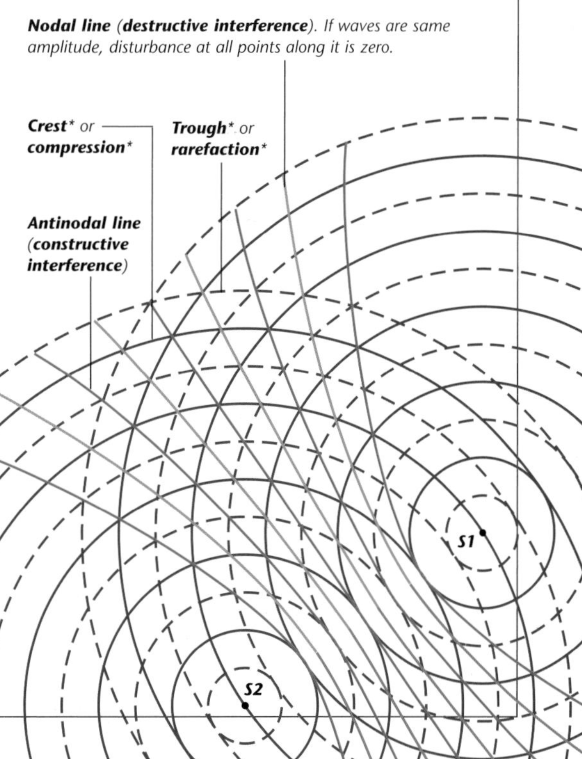
Two sources (S1 and S2) produce coherent waves, in this case in phase.
Nodal line (destructive interference). If waves are same amplitude, disturbance at all points along it is zero.
Crest* or compression*
Trough* or rarefaction*
Antinodal line (constructive interference)
S1
S2

* **Amplitude**, 34; **Compressions**, 35; **Crests**, 34; **Rarefactions**, 35; **Troughs**, 34.

SOUND WAVES

Bats emit **ultrasonic waves** to locate objects.

Sound waves, also called **acoustic waves**, are **longitudinal waves*** – waves which consist of particles oscillating along the same line as the waves travel, creating areas of high and low pressure (**compressions*** and **rarefactions***). They can travel through solids, liquids and gases and have a wide range of **frequencies***. Those with frequencies between about 20 and 20,000 **Hertz*** (the **sonic range**) can be detected by the human ear and are what is commonly referred to as sound (for more about perception of sound, see pages 42-43). Others, with higher and lower frequencies, are known as **ultrasound** and **infrasound**. The study of the behavior of sound waves is called **acoustics**.

Ultrasound

Sound composed of **ultrasonic waves** – waves with **frequencies*** above the range of the human ear, i.e. above 20,000 **Hertz***. Ultrasound has a number of uses.

Ultrasound *is used in* ***ultrasound scanning*** *of the human body (it uses* ***echoes*** *– see page 41).*

Bone, fat and muscle all reflect ***ultrasonic waves*** *differently. Reflected waves (****echoes****), e.g. from an unborn baby, are converted into electrical pulses which form an image (****scan****) on a screen.*

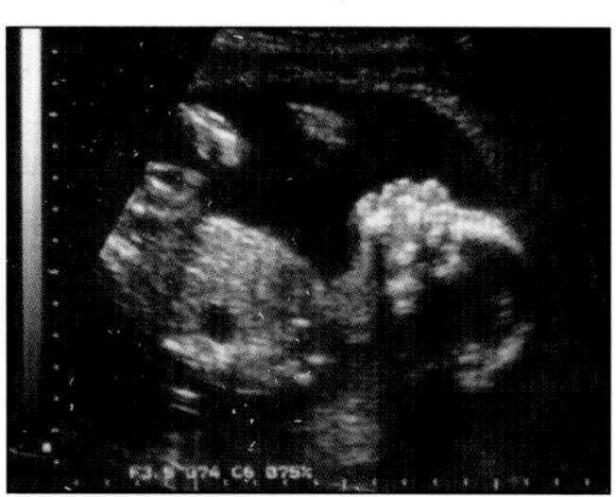

Scan of baby in mother's womb at 20 weeks

Infrasound

Sound composed of **infrasonic waves** – waves with **frequencies*** below the range of the human ear, i.e. below 20 **Hertz***. At present infrasound has few technical uses, as it can cause uncomfortable sensations in humans.

Sonic boom

A loud bang heard when a **shock wave** produced by an aircraft moving at **supersonic speed** passes a listener.

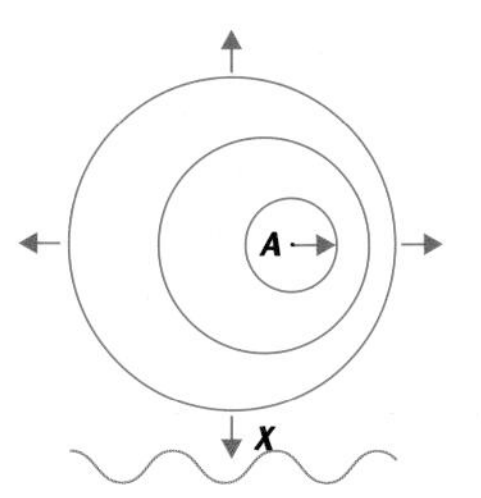
A
X

As aircraft (A) travels forward, it creates ***longitudinal waves**** *in air, i.e. areas of high and low pressure (****compressions**** *and* ***rarefactions****).*

Wavefronts* *can "get away" from aircraft and begin to disperse.*

Listener at X will hear waves as sound (a "whoosh" of air – as well as separate sound of engines).

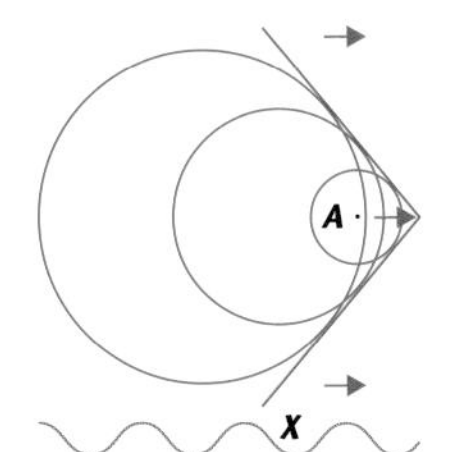
A
X

Supersonic *aircraft (A) overtakes its wavefronts while creating more, so they overlap.*

*Causes large build up of pressure (****shock wave****) pushed in front of aircraft and unable to "get away". It is like bow wave of ship (if ship moving faster than water waves it creates).*

Listener at X will hear wave as sudden loud ***sonic boom****.*

Behavior of sound waves

Speed of sound

The speed at which sound waves move. It depends on the type and temperature of the **medium*** through which the sound waves travel. The speed of sound waves as they travel through dry air at 0°C is $331 m s^{-1}$, but this increases if the air temperature increases, or decreases if the air temperature goes down.

Subsonic speed

A speed below the **speed of sound** in the same **medium*** and under the same conditions.

Supersonic speed

A speed above the **speed of sound** in the same **medium*** and under the same conditions.

A supersonic passenger jet

* **Compressions**, **Frequency**, 35; **Hertz**, 16 (**Frequency**); **Longitudinal waves**, 35; **Medium**, 345; **Rarefactions**, 35; **Wavefront**, 34.

The **ultrasonic waves** emitted by a bat bounce back, telling it the distance and size of the object. This technique is called **echolocation**.

Echo

A sound wave which has been reflected off a surface, and is heard after the original sound. Echoes, normally those of **ultrasonic waves**, are often used to locate objects and determine their exact position (by measuring the time the echo takes to return to the source). This technique has a number of names, each normally used in a slightly different context, though the distinctions between them are unclear. **Ultrasound scanning** is one example. Others are **echo-sounding** and **sonar**, both of which have marine connotations (echo-sounding normally refers to using echoes to measure the depth of water below a ship, sonar to using them to detect objects under water). **Echolocation** usually describes the way animals use echoes to find prey or avoid obstacles in the dark.

Sonar (derived from **so**und **na**vigation and **r**anging)

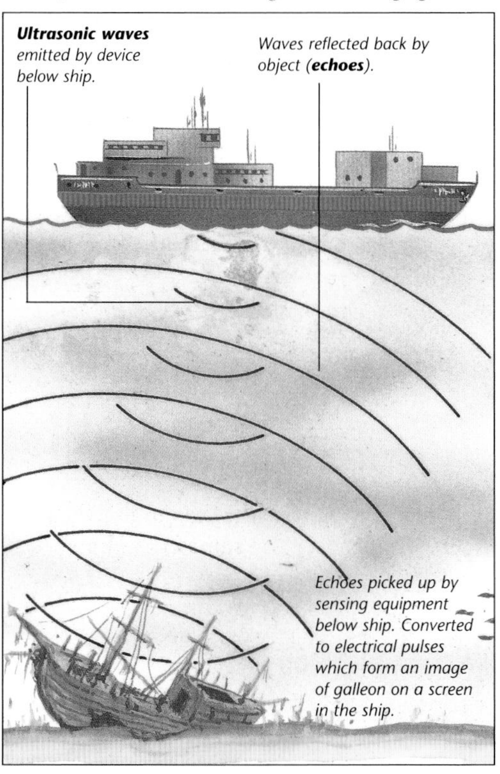
Ultrasonic waves emitted by device below ship.
Waves reflected back by object (**echoes**).
Echoes picked up by sensing equipment below ship. Converted to electrical pulses which form an image of galleon on a screen in the ship.

Reverberation

The effect whereby a sound seems to persist for longer than it actually took to produce. It occurs when the time taken for the **echo** to return to the source is so short that the original and reflected waves cannot be distinguished. If the wave is reflected off many surfaces, then the sound is enhanced further.

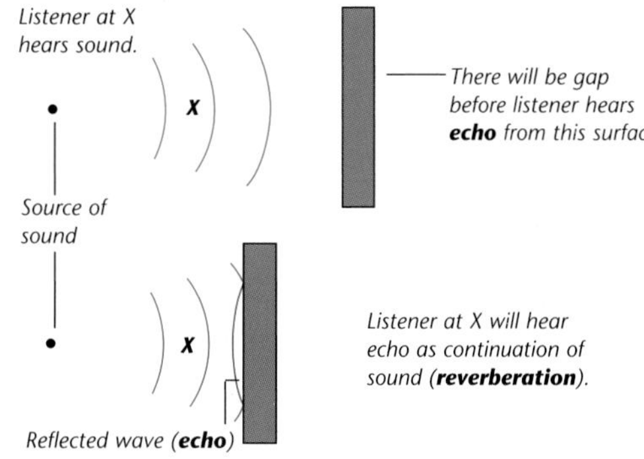
Listener at X hears sound.
X
There will be gap before listener hears **echo** from this surface.
Source of sound
X
Listener at X will hear echo as continuation of sound (**reverberation**).
Reflected wave (**echo**)

Doppler effect

The change in **frequency*** of the sound heard when either the listener or the source moves relative to the other. If the distance between them is decreasing, a higher frequency sound is heard than that actually produced. If it is increasing, a lower frequency sound is heard.

Doppler effect

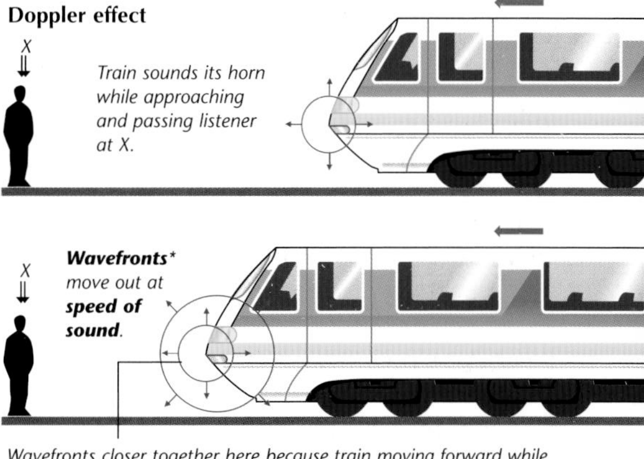
X
Train sounds its horn while approaching and passing listener at X.
X
Wavefronts* move out at **speed of sound**.

Wavefronts closer together here because train moving forward while producing sound waves. Heard at X as sound of higher **frequency***. Lower frequency sound will be heard when train has passed.

X

* **Frequency**, 35; **Wavefront**, 34.

PERCEPTION OF SOUND

Sounds heard by the ear can be pleasant or unpleasant. When the waveform of a **sound wave** (see pages 40-41) repeats itself regularly, the sound is usually judged to be pleasant. However, when the waveform is unrepeated and irregular, the sound is thought of as a **noise**. Every sound has a particular **loudness** and **pitch** and many, especially musical sounds, are produced by **stationary waves**.

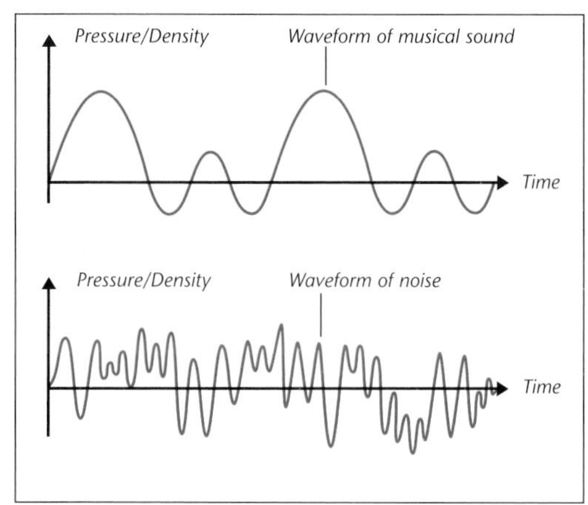
Pressure/Density
Waveform of musical sound
Time
Pressure/Density
Waveform of noise
Time

Loudness

The size of the sensation produced when sound waves fall on the ear. It is subjective, depending on the sensitivity of the ear, but is directly related to the **wave intensity*** of the waves. It is most often measured in **decibels** (**dB**), but also, more accurately, in **phons** (these take into account the fact that the ear is not equally sensitive to sounds of all **frequencies***).

*Aircraft taking off measures 110**dB**.*

Pitch

The perceived **frequency*** of a sound wave, i.e. the frequency heard as sound. A high pitched sound has a high frequency and a low pitched sound has a low frequency.

*The sound of a bird's song is high **pitched**. It has a high **frequency***.*

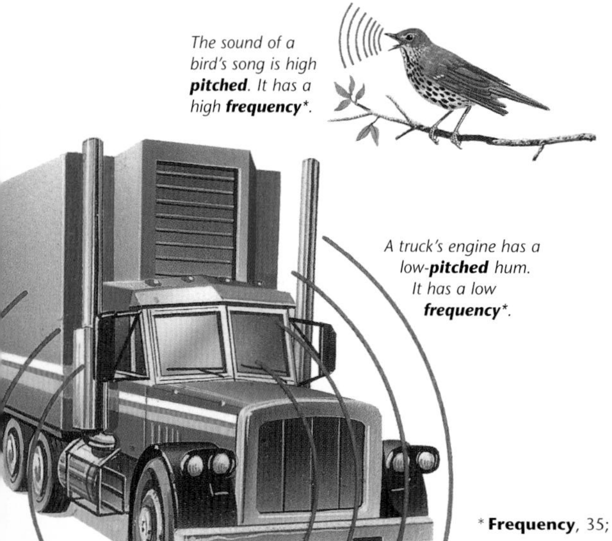

*A truck's engine has a low-**pitched** hum. It has a low **frequency***.*

Beats

The regular variation in **loudness** with time which is heard when two sounds of slightly different **frequency*** are heard together. This is the result of **interference*** between the two waves. The **beat frequency** is equal to the difference in frequency between the two sounds (see diagram below). The closer together the frequency of the sounds, the slower the beats.

Beat frequency

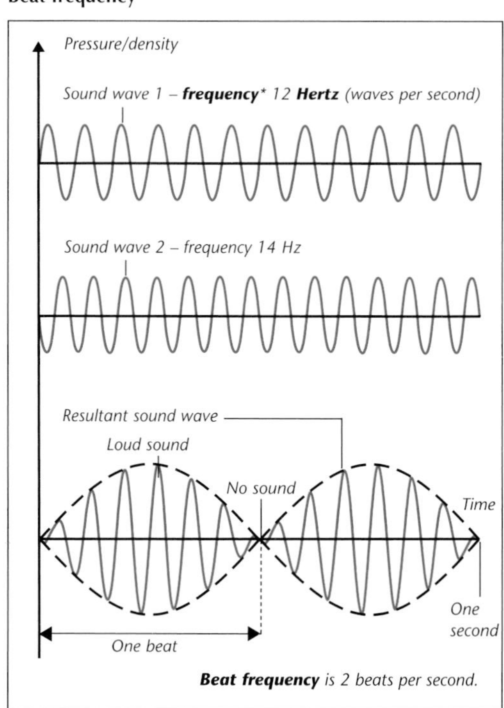
Pressure/density
Sound wave 1 – **frequency*** 12 **Hertz** (waves per second)
Sound wave 2 – frequency 14 Hz
Resultant sound wave
Loud sound
No sound
Time
One beat
One second

***Beat frequency** is 2 beats per second.*

* **Frequency**, 35; **Interference**, 38; **Wave intensity**, 35.

Stationary or **standing wave**

A wave that does not appear to move. It is not in fact a true wave, but is instead made up of two waves of the same velocity and **frequency*** continuously moving in opposite directions between two fixed points (most commonly the ends of a plucked string or wire). The repeated crossing of the waves results in **interference*** – when the waves are **in phase***, the resultant **amplitude*** is large, and when they are **out of phase***, it is small or zero. At certain points (the **nodes**), it is always zero. The amplitude and frequency of a stationary wave in a string or wire determines those of the sound waves it produces in the air – the length and tension of the string or wire determine the range of frequencies, and hence the pitch of the sound produced.

Sonometer

*Apparatus used to demonstrate **stationary waves**. When plucked, wire vibrates and sound box amplifies sound caused by vibration.*

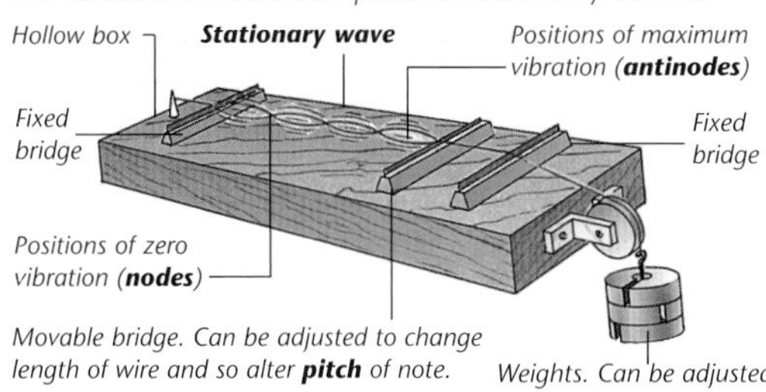
Hollow box
Stationary wave
Positions of maximum vibration (antinodes)
Fixed bridge
Fixed bridge
Positions of zero vibration (nodes)

*Movable bridge. Can be adjusted to change length of wire and so alter **pitch** of note.*

Weights. Can be adjusted to change tension of wire and so alter pitch of note.

Formation of stationary wave

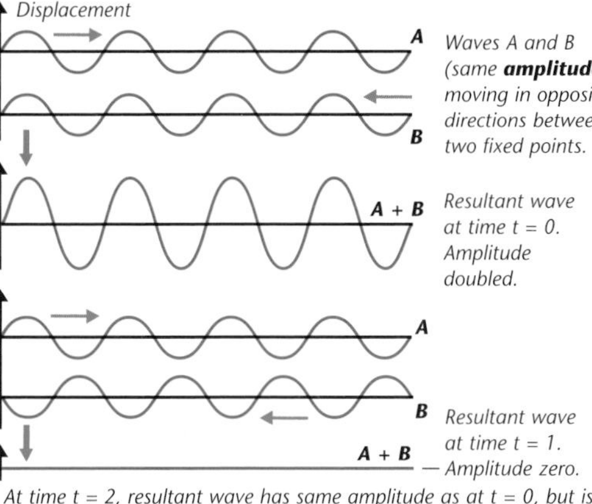
Displacement
A
B
A + B
A
B
A + B

*Waves A and B (same **amplitude***) moving in opposite directions between two fixed points.*

Resultant wave at time t = 0. Amplitude doubled.

Resultant wave at time t = 1. Amplitude zero.

*At time t = 2, resultant wave has same amplitude as at t = 0, but is transposed, i.e. **crests*** where there were **troughs*** and vice versa.*

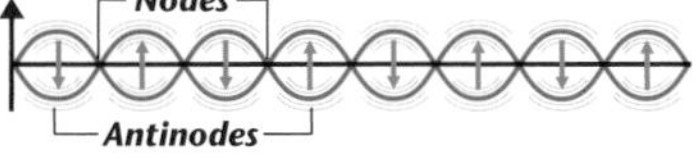
Nodes
Antinodes

Resultant wave moves rapidly between position held at t = 0 and that held at t = 2. Wave observed appears stationary.

Musical sounds

All music is based on some kind of **musical scale**. This is a series of **notes** (sounds of specific **pitch**), arranged from low to high pitch with certain **intervals** between them (a musical interval is a spacing in **frequency***, rather than time). The notes are arranged so that pleasant sounds can be obtained. What is regarded as a pleasant sound depends on the culture of the listener.

*Western **musical scale** is based on **diatonic scale** – consists of 8 **notes** (white notes on piano) ranging from lower to upper C.*

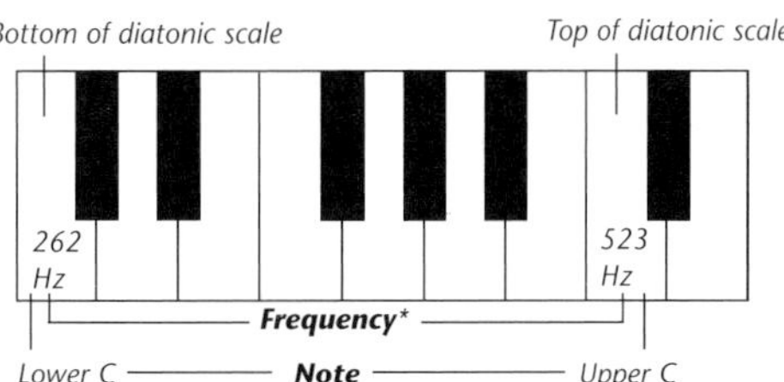
Bottom of diatonic scale
Top of diatonic scale
262 Hz
523 Hz
Frequency*
Lower C
Note
Upper C

*Black notes have **frequencies*** between those of notes on **diatonic scale**. Together with these, they form **chromatic scale**.*

Modes of vibration

The same note played on different instruments, although recognizable as the same, has a distinct sound quality (**timbre**) characteristic to the instrument. This is because, although the strongest vibration is the same for each note whatever the instrument (its **frequency*** is the **fundamental frequency**), vibrations at other frequencies (**overtones**) are produced at the same time. The set of vibrations specific to an instrument are its modes of vibration.

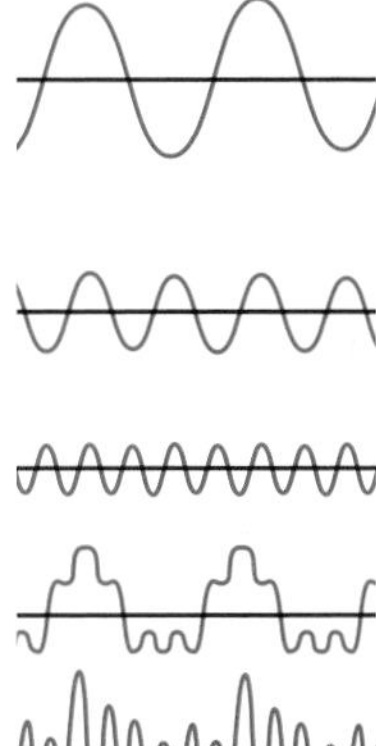

*Lowest **mode of vibration** (**fundamental frequency**) of note on given instrument. If frequencies of **overtones** are simple multiples of fundamental frequency, they are also called **harmonics**.*

1st overtone (2nd harmonic, i.e. frequency doubled. Fundamental frequency is 1st harmonic).

2nd overtone. This is 4th harmonic. In this case there is no 3rd harmonic.

Combined modes of vibration (i.e. all three together). Characteristic waveform of note for this instrument.

Same note played on different instrument may look like this.

* **Amplitude**, **Crests**, 34; **Frequency**, 35; **In phase**, 38 (**Phase**); **Interference**, 38; **Out of phase**, 38 (**Phase**); **Troughs**, 34.

ELECTROMAGNETIC WAVES

Electromagnetic waves are **transverse waves***, consisting of oscillating **electric** and **magnetic fields***. They have a wide range of **frequencies***, can travel through most **media***, including vacuums, and, when absorbed, cause a rise in temperature (see **infra-red radiation**). **Radio waves** and some **X-rays** are emitted when free **electrons*** are accelerated or decelerated, e.g. as a result of a collision. All other types occur when molecules change energy states (see page 84) and occur as pulses called **photons** (see **quantum theory**, page 84), rather than a continuous stream. For the wavelengths and frequencies of the different types of waves (the **electromagnetic spectrum**), see the table on page 113.

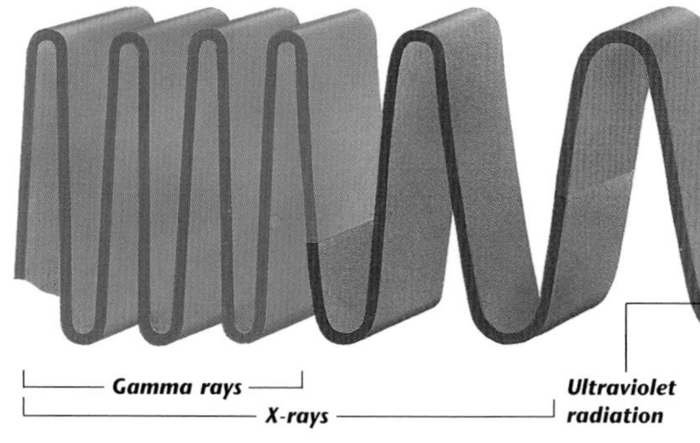
Gamma rays
X-rays
Ultraviolet radiation

Electromagnetic spectrum *(range of electromagnetic waves) shown above. It is made up of* ***wavebands****, i.e. particular ranges of* ***frequencies**** *and* ***wavelengths**** *within which the waves all have the same characteristic properties.*

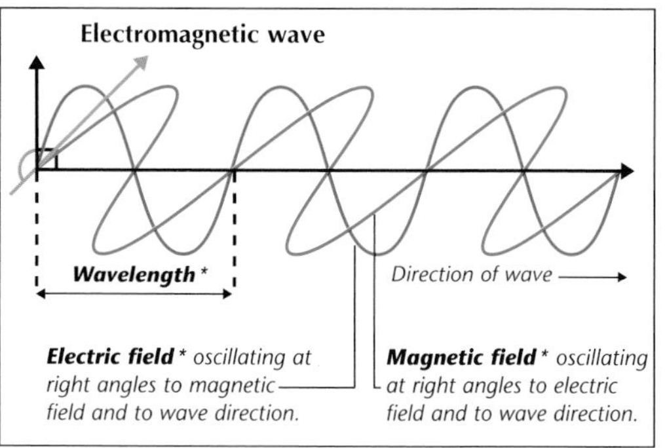
Electromagnetic wave
Wavelength *
Direction of wave
Electric field * oscillating at right angles to magnetic field and to wave direction.
Magnetic field * oscillating at right angles to electric field and to wave direction.

Gamma rays (γ-rays)

Electromagnetic waves emitted by **radioactive*** substances (see also page 86). They are in the same **waveband** and have the same properties as **X-rays**, but are produced in a different way, and are at the top end of the band with regard to energy.

X-rays

Electromagnetic waves which **ionize*** gases they pass through, cause **phosphorescence** and bring about chemical changes on photographic plates. They are produced in **X-ray tubes*** and have many applications.

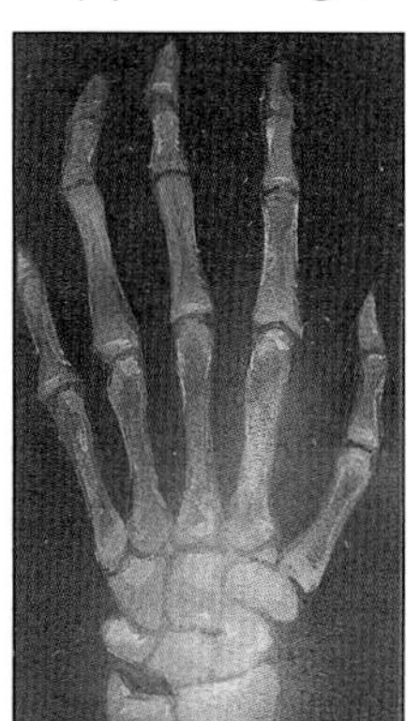

X-radiography *produces pictures (****radiographs****) of inside of body.* ***X-rays*** *pass through tissue but are absorbed by denser bones, so bones appear opaque.*

X-rays were passed through this hand to project a clear image of the bones onto a photographic plate.

Ultraviolet radiation (UV radiation)

Electromagnetic waves produced, for example, when an electric current is passed through **ionized*** gas between two **electrodes***. They are also emitted by the Sun, but only small quantities reach the Earth's surface. These small quantities are vital to life, playing the key part in **photosynthesis***, but larger amounts are dangerous. Ultraviolet radiation causes **fluorescence**, e.g. when produced in **fluorescent tubes***, and also a variety of chemical reactions, e.g. tanning of the skin.

Phosphorescence

A phenomenon shown by certain substances (**phosphors**) when they are hit by short **wavelength*** electromagnetic waves, e.g. **gamma rays** or **X-rays**. The phosphors absorb the waves and emit visible light, i.e. waves of longer wavelength. This emission may continue after the gamma or X-rays have stopped. If it only occurs briefly afterwards in rapid flashes, these are called **scintillations** (see also **scintillation counter**, page 90).

* **Electric field**, 58; **Electrode**, 66; **Electrons**, 83; **Fluorescent tube**, 80 (**Discharge tube**); **Frequency**, 35; **Ionization**, 88; **Magnetic field**, 72; **Medium**, 345; **Photosynthesis**, 254; **Radioactivity**, 86; **Transverse waves**, **Wavelength**, 34; **X-ray tube**, 80.

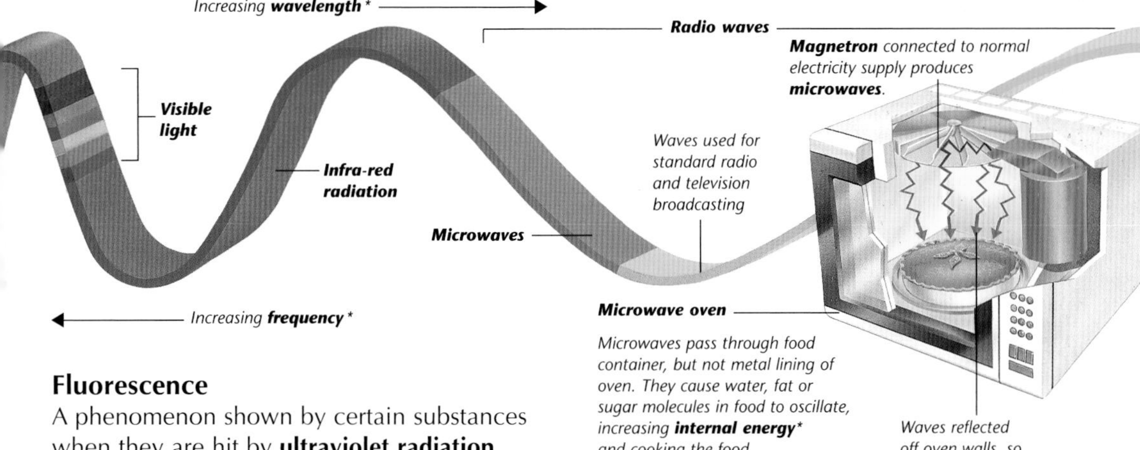
Increasing wavelength*
Radio waves
Magnetron connected to normal electricity supply produces microwaves.
Visible light
Waves used for standard radio and television broadcasting
Infra-red radiation
Microwaves
Increasing frequency*
Microwave oven
Microwaves pass through food container, but not metal lining of oven. They cause water, fat or sugar molecules in food to oscillate, increasing internal energy* and cooking the food.
Waves reflected off oven walls, so food cooks evenly.

Fluorescence

A phenomenon shown by certain substances when they are hit by **ultraviolet radiation**. They absorb the ultraviolet radiation and emit **visible light**, i.e. light waves of a longer **wavelength***. This emission stops as soon as the ultraviolet radiation stops.

Visible light

Electromagnetic waves which the eye can detect. They are produced by the Sun, by **discharge tubes*** and by any substance heated until it glows (emission of light due to heating is called **incandescence**). They cause chemical changes, e.g. on photographic film, and the different **wavelengths*** in the **waveband** are seen as different colors (see page 54).

Infra-red radiation (IR radiation)

The electromagnetic waves most commonly produced by hot objects and therefore those which are most frequently the cause of temperature rises (see introduction and **radiation**, page 29). They can be used to form **thermal images** on special infra-red sensitive film, which is exposed by heat, rather than light.

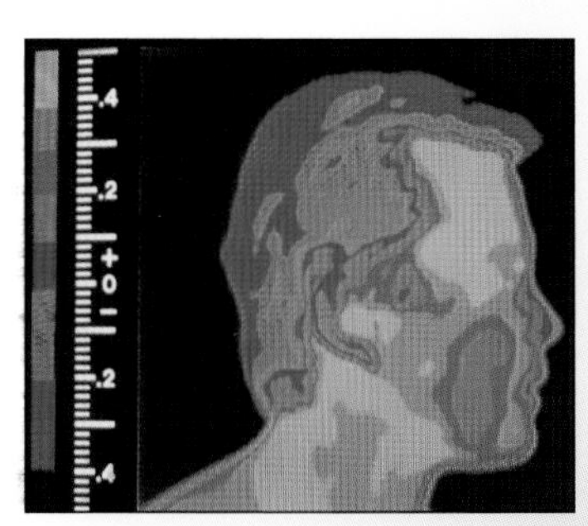

Thermal image *of a man's head*

Each different color represents a temperature difference of 0.1°C (see scale on left of picture).

The blue areas of the head are colder, and the yellow areas are hotter.

Microwaves

Very short **radiowaves** used in **radar** (**ra**dio **d**etection **a**nd **r**anging) to determine the position of an object by the time it takes for a reflected wave to return to the source (see also **sonar**, page 41 (**Echo**)). **Microwave ovens** use microwaves to cook food rapidly.

Radio waves

Electromagnetic waves produced when free **electrons*** in radio antennae are made to oscillate (and are hence accelerated) by an **electric field***. The fact that the frequency of the oscillations is imposed by the field means that the waves occur as a regular stream, rather than randomly.

How radio waves are used to communicate over long distances

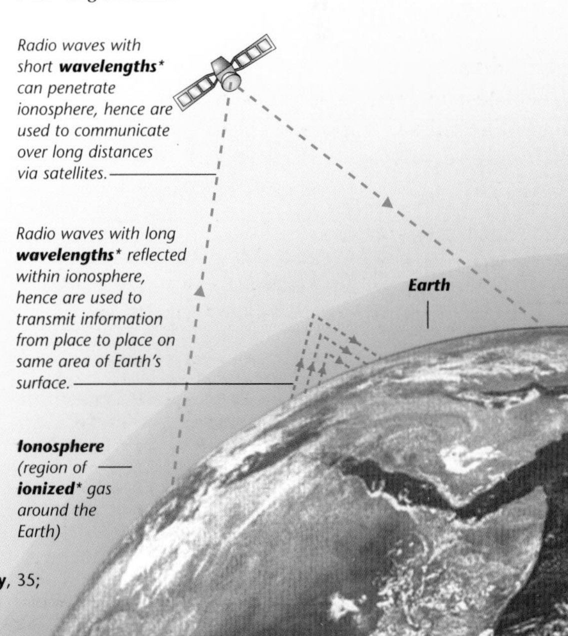
Radio waves with short wavelengths* can penetrate ionosphere, hence are used to communicate over long distances via satellites.
Radio waves with long wavelengths* reflected within ionosphere, hence are used to transmit information from place to place on same area of Earth's surface.
Earth
Ionosphere (region of ionized* gas around the Earth)

* **Discharge tube**, 80; **Electric field**, 58; **Electrons**, 83; **Frequency**, 35; **Internal energy**, 9; **Ionization**, 88; **Nuclear power station**, 94; **Wavelength**, 34.

LIGHT

Light consists of **electromagnetic waves*** of particular **frequencies*** and **wavelengths*** (see pages 44-45), but is commonly referred to and diagrammatically represented as **rays**. Such a ray is actually a line (arrow) which indicates the path taken by the light waves, i.e. the direction in which the energy is being carried.

Shadow

An area which light rays cannot reach due to an obstacle in their path. If the rays come from a point they are stopped by the obstacle, creating a complete shadow called an **umbra**.

Casting an umbra

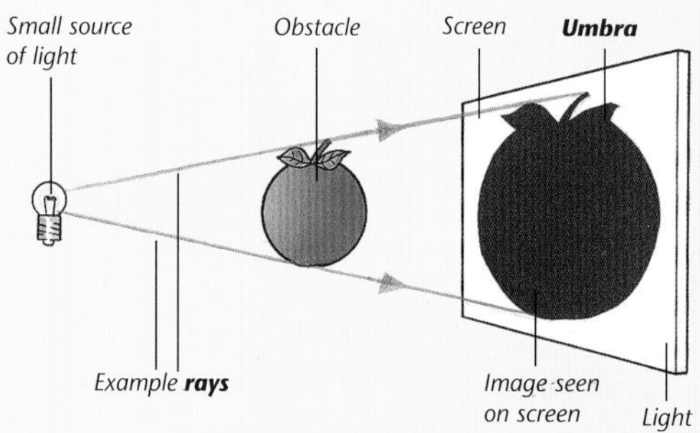

Small source of light
Obstacle
Screen
Umbra
Example rays
Image seen on screen
Light

If the light rays come from an extended source, a semi-shadow area called a **penumbra** is formed around the umbra.

Casting a penumbra

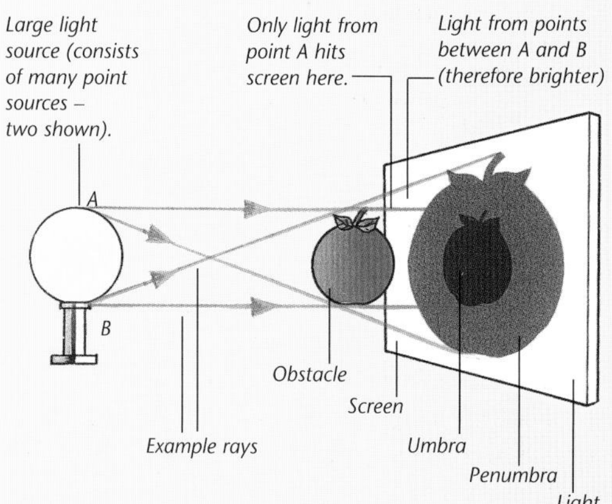

Large light source (consists of many point sources – two shown).
Only light from point A hits screen here.
Light from points between A and B (therefore brighter)
A
B
Obstacle
Screen
Example rays
Umbra
Penumbra
Light

Eclipse

The total or partial "blocking off" of light from a source. This occurs when an object casts a **shadow** by passing between the source and an observer. A **solar eclipse** is seen from the Earth when the Moon passes between the Earth and the Sun, and a **lunar eclipse** is seen when the Earth is between the Sun and the Moon.

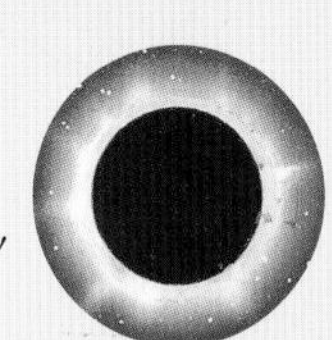

Moon blocking out Sun's light in an annular solar eclipse

Solar eclipse

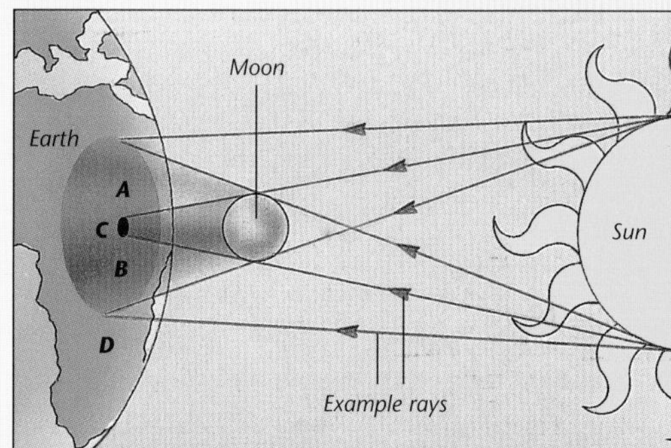

Moon
Earth
A
C
B
D
Sun
Example rays

The eclipse, as seen from positions A, B, C and D.

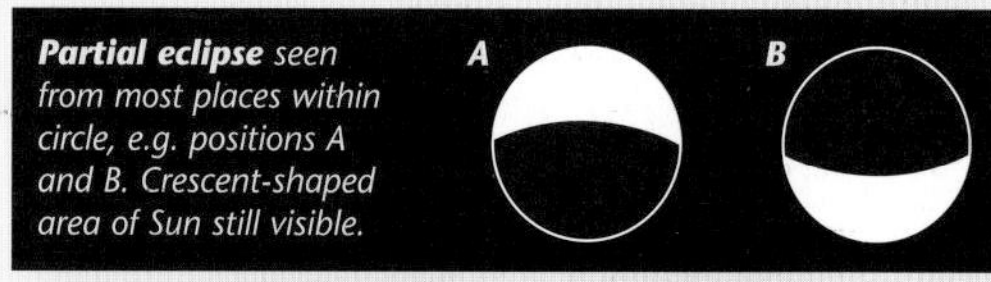

Partial eclipse seen from most places within circle, e.g. positions A and B. Crescent-shaped area of Sun still visible.
A
B

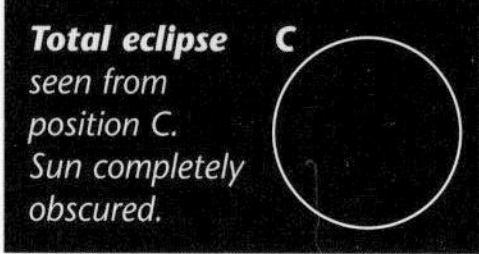

Total eclipse seen from position C. Sun completely obscured.
C

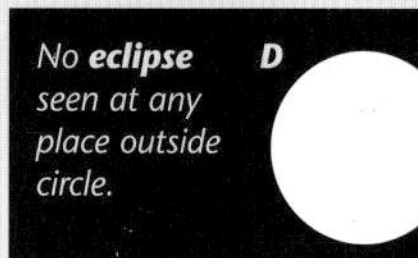

No eclipse seen at any place outside circle.
D

Annular eclipse

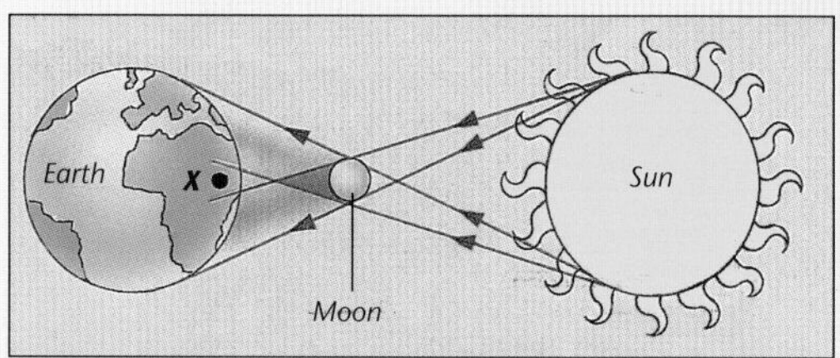

Earth
X
Sun
Moon

The eclipse, as seen from position X.

*An **annular eclipse** is a special **eclipse** which consists of a bright ring around a black area. It occurs when the Moon, Earth and Sun are particular distances apart.* **X**

* **Electromagnetic waves**, 44; **Frequency**, 35; **Wavelength**, 34.

REFLECTION OF LIGHT

Reflection is the change in direction of a wave when it bounces off a boundary (see page 36). Mirrors are usually used to show the reflection of light (see below and also pages 48-49). It must be noted that when an object and its image are drawn in mirror (and **lens***) diagrams, the object is assumed to be producing light rays itself. In fact the rays come from a source, e.g. the Sun, and are reflected off the object.

Laws of reflection of light

1. The **reflected ray** lies in the same plane as the **incident ray** and the **normal** at the **point of incidence**.
2. The **angle of incidence** (**i**) = the **angle of reflection** (**r**).

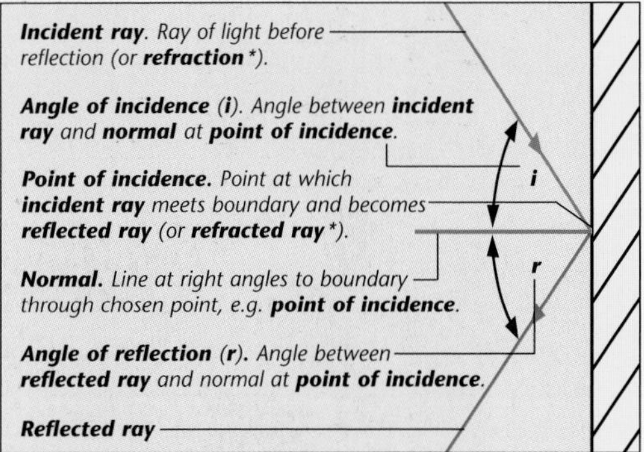

Incident ray. Ray of light before reflection (or refraction*).
Angle of incidence (i). Angle between incident ray and normal at point of incidence.
Point of incidence. Point at which incident ray meets boundary and becomes reflected ray (or refracted ray*).
Normal. Line at right angles to boundary through chosen point, e.g. point of incidence.
Angle of reflection (r). Angle between reflected ray and normal at point of incidence.
Reflected ray
i
r

Regular reflection

The reflection of parallel **incident rays** (see above) off a flat surface such that all the **reflected rays** are also parallel. This occurs when surfaces are very smooth, e.g. highly polished surfaces such as mirrors.

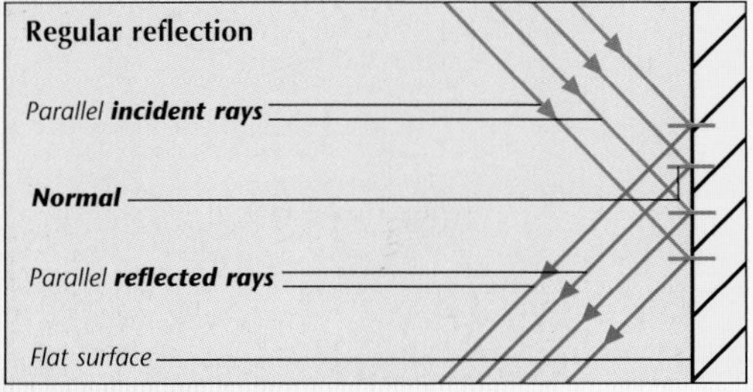

Regular reflection
Parallel incident rays
Normal
Parallel reflected rays
Flat surface

Diffuse reflection

The reflection of parallel **incident rays** (see left) off a rough surface such that the **reflected rays** travel in different directions and the light is scattered. This is the most common type of reflection as most surfaces are irregular when considered on a scale comparable to that of the **wavelength*** of light (see page 113).

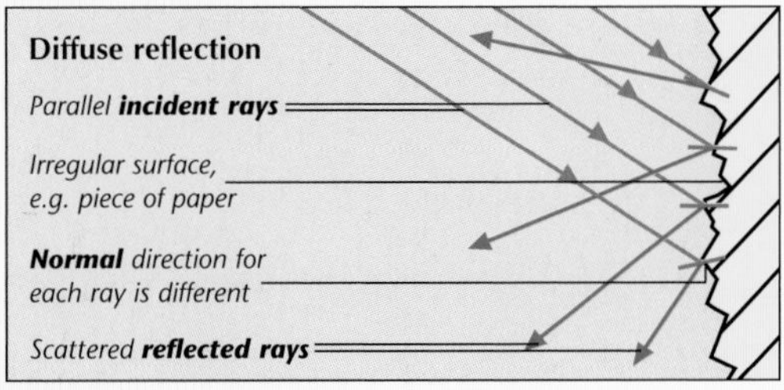

Diffuse reflection
Parallel incident rays
Irregular surface, e.g. piece of paper
Normal direction for each ray is different
Scattered reflected rays

Plane mirror

A mirror with a flat surface (see also **curved mirrors**, pages 48-49). The image it forms is the same size as the object, the same distance behind ("inside") the mirror as the object is in front, and **laterally inverted** (the left and right sides have swapped around).

Reflection in plane mirror

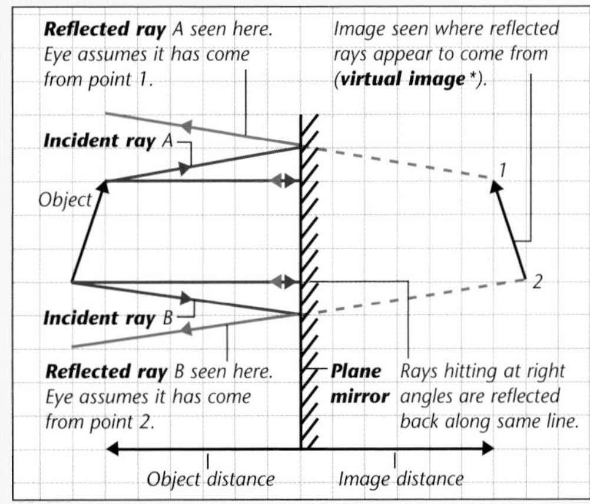

Reflected ray A seen here. Eye assumes it has come from point 1.
Image seen where reflected rays appear to come from (virtual image*).
Incident ray A
Object
1
2
Incident ray B
Reflected ray B seen here. Eye assumes it has come from point 2.
Plane mirror
Rays hitting at right angles are reflected back along same line.
Object distance
Image distance

Parallax

The apparent displacement of an observed object due to the difference between two points of view. For example, an object which is observed first with the left eye, and then with the right eye, appears to have moved. The first point of view is the left eye, and the second is the right eye. (See also **parallax error**, page 102.)

* **Lenses**, 52; **Refracted ray**, **Refraction**, 50; **Virtual image**, 49 (**Image**); **Wavelength**, 34.

Reflection of light (continued)

Light rays are reflected from curved surfaces, as from flat surfaces, according to the **laws of reflection of light** (see page 47). The images formed by reflection from **curved mirrors** are particularly easily observed. There are two types of curved mirror – **concave** and **convex mirrors**. For all diagrams showing reflection of light, the object is assumed to be the source of the light (see **reflection of light**, page 47) and certain points (see below), together with known facts about light rays passing through them, are used to construct the paths of the reflected rays.

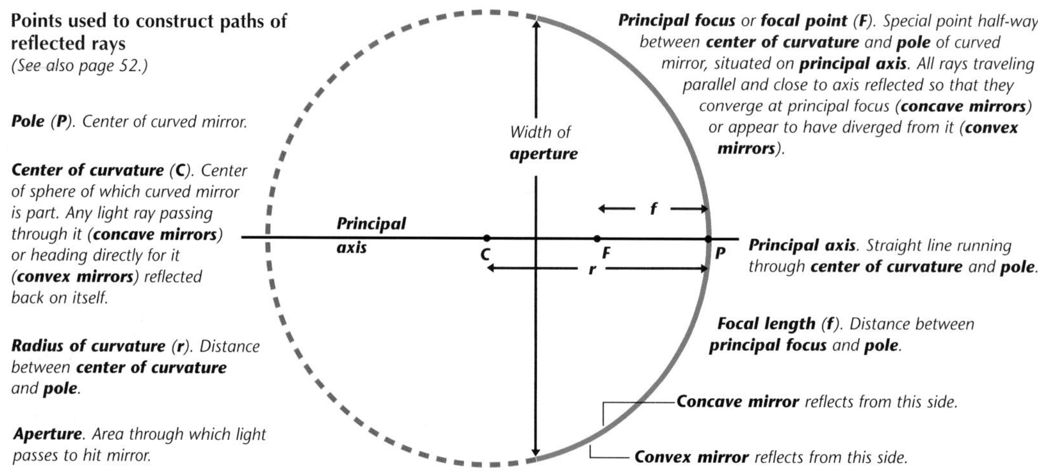

Points used to construct paths of reflected rays
(See also page 52.)
Pole (P). Center of curved mirror.
Center of curvature (C). Center of sphere of which curved mirror is part. Any light ray passing through it (concave mirrors) or heading directly for it (convex mirrors) reflected back on itself.
Radius of curvature (r). Distance between center of curvature and pole.
Aperture. Area through which light passes to hit mirror.
Width of aperture
Principal axis
C
F
P
f
r
Principal focus or focal point (F). Special point half-way between center of curvature and pole of curved mirror, situated on principal axis. All rays traveling parallel and close to axis reflected so that they converge at principal focus (concave mirrors) or appear to have diverged from it (convex mirrors).
Principal axis. Straight line running through center of curvature and pole.
Focal length (f). Distance between principal focus and pole.
Concave mirror reflects from this side.
Convex mirror reflects from this side.

Concave or **converging mirror**

A mirror with a reflecting surface which curves inward (part of the inside of a sphere). When light rays parallel to the **principal axis** fall on such a mirror, they are reflected so that they converge at the **principal focus** in front of the mirror. The size, position and type of **image** formed depends on how far the object is from the mirror.

Convex or **diverging mirror**

A mirror with a reflecting surface which curves outwards (part of the outside of a sphere). When light rays parallel to the **principal axis** fall on such a mirror, they are reflected so that they appear to diverge from the **principal focus** behind ("inside") the mirror. The **images** formed are always upright and reduced, and **virtual images** (see **image**).

Concave mirror

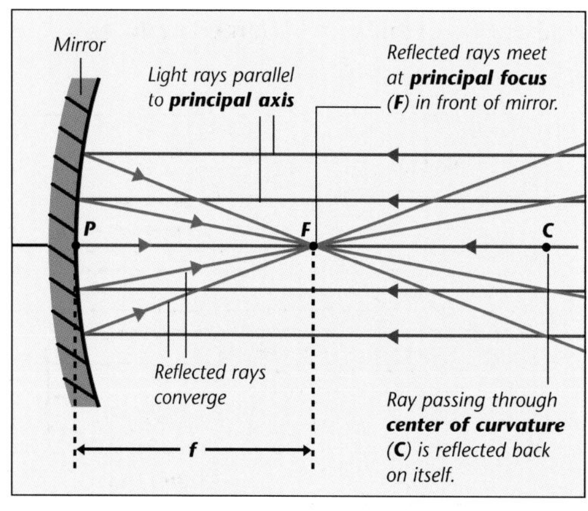

Mirror
Light rays parallel to principal axis
Reflected rays meet at principal focus (F) in front of mirror.
P
F
C
Reflected rays converge
Ray passing through center of curvature (C) is reflected back on itself.
f

Convex mirror

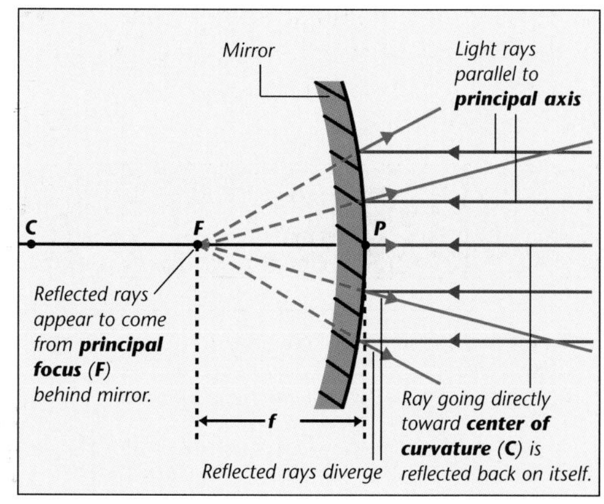

Mirror
Light rays parallel to principal axis
C
F
P
Reflected rays appear to come from principal focus (F) behind mirror.
f
Reflected rays diverge
Ray going directly toward center of curvature (C) is reflected back on itself.

Image

A view of an object as seen in a mirror. Just as an object is only seen because of light rays coming from it (see **reflection of light**, page 47), so too an image is seen where reflected rays (originally from the object) actually diverge from (**real image**), or appear to diverge from (**virtual image**).

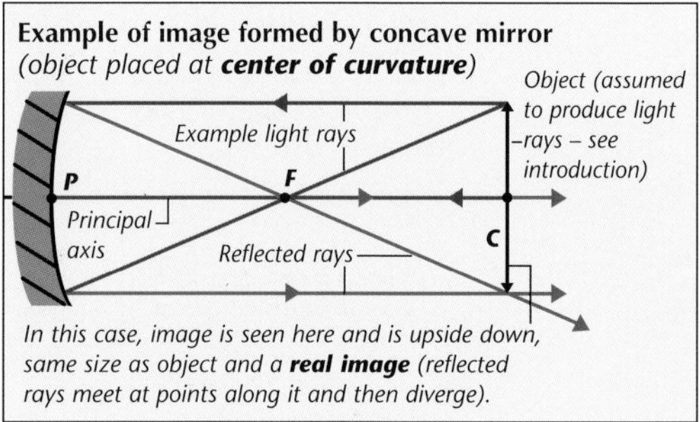

Example light rays
P
F
Principal axis
Reflected rays
C
Object (assumed to produce light rays – see introduction)

Example of image formed by concave mirror *(object placed at **center of curvature**)*

*In this case, image is seen here and is upside down, same size as object and a **real image** (reflected rays meet at points along it and then diverge).*

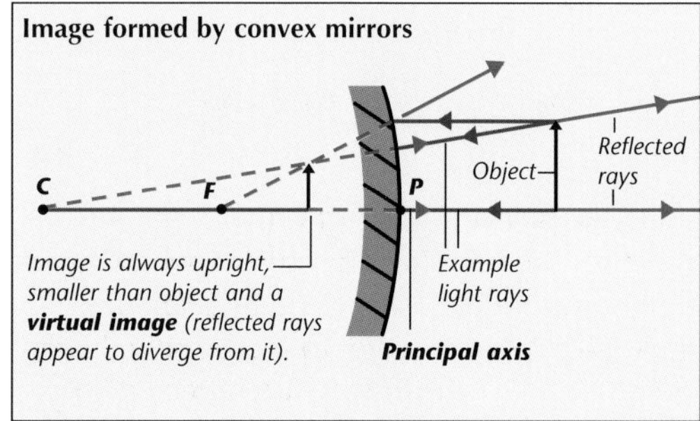

C
F
P
Object
Reflected rays
Example light rays
Principal axis

Image formed by convex mirrors

*Image is always upright, smaller than object and a **virtual image** (reflected rays appear to diverge from it).*

Mirror or lens formula

Gives the relationship between the distance of an object from the center of a curved mirror or **lens***, the distance of its **image** from the same point and the **focal length** of the mirror or lens. An image may be formed either side of a mirror or lens, so a **sign convention*** is used to give position.

Mirror formula: $\frac{1}{f} = \frac{1}{v} + \frac{1}{u}$ where f = ***focal length***; v = ***image*** distance (from ***pole***); u = object distance (from pole).

Real is positive sign convention for mirrors and lenses

1. *All distances are measured from the mirror as origin.*
2. *Distances of objects and **real images** are positive.*
3. *Distances of **virtual images** are negative.*
4. *The **focal lengths** of **convex mirrors** and **lenses*** are positive. The focal lengths of **concave mirrors** and lenses are negative.*

Linear magnification

The ratio of the height of the image formed by a mirror or **lens*** to the object height.

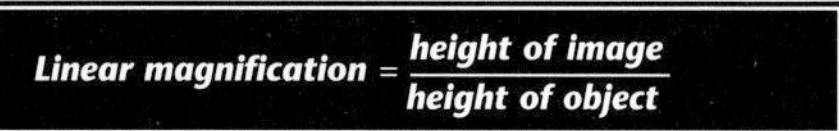

$$\textit{Linear magnification} = \frac{\textit{height of image}}{\textit{height of object}}$$

Example of linear magnification

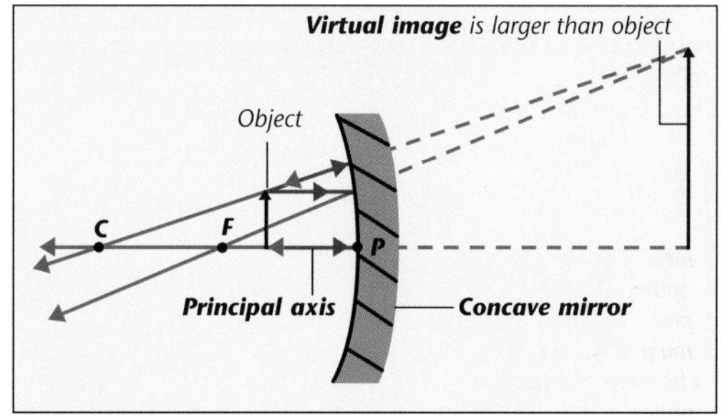

Virtual image is larger than object
Object
C
F
P
Principal axis
Concave mirror

Principle of reversibility of light

States that, for a ray of light on a given path due to reflection, **refraction*** or **diffraction***, a ray of light in the opposite direction in the same conditions will follow the same path. Light rays parallel to the **principal axis**, for example, are reflected by a **concave mirror** to meet at the **principal focus**. If a point source of light is placed at the principal focus, the rays are reflected parallel to the axis.

Spherical aberration

An effect seen when rays parallel to the **principal axis** (and different distances from it), hit a curved mirror and are reflected so that they intersect at different points along the axis, forming a **caustic curve**. The larger the **aperture**, the more this effect is seen. It is also seen in **lenses*** with large apertures.

Spherical aberration

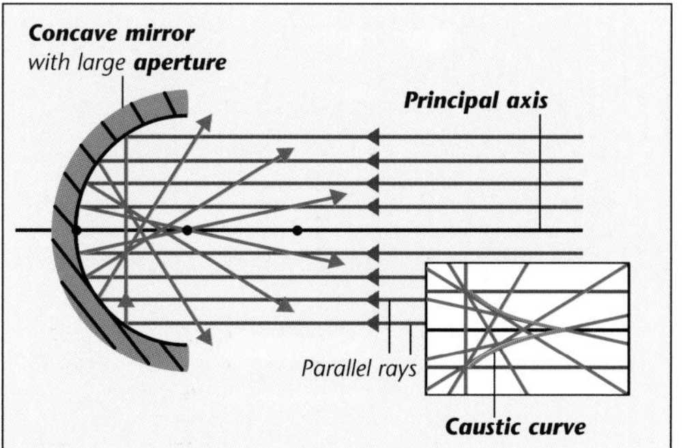

Concave mirror with large aperture
Principal axis
Parallel rays
Caustic curve

* **Diffraction**, 37; **Lens**, 52; **Refraction**, 37; **Sign convention**, 11.

REFRACTION OF LIGHT

Refraction is the change in direction of any wave as a result of its velocity changing when it moves from one **medium*** into another (see also page 37). When light rays (see page 46) move into a new medium, they are refracted according to the **laws of refraction of light**. The direction in which they are refracted depends on whether they move into a denser or less dense medium and are consequently slowed down or speeded up (see diagram below).

Refraction *makes the end of this straw appear bent in the drink.*

Refraction at boundary between two media *

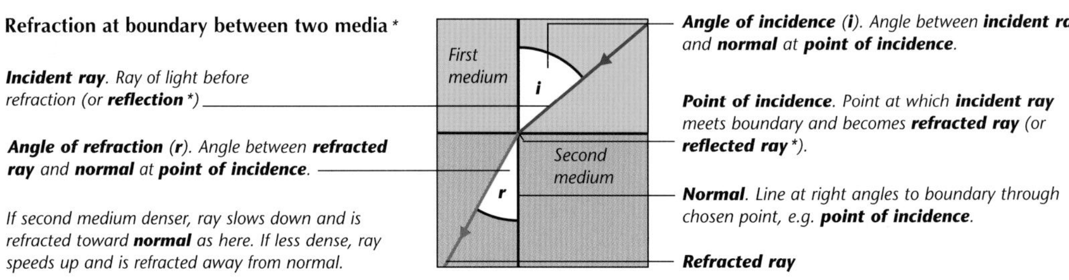

Incident ray. *Ray of light before refraction (or* ***reflection*** *)*
Angle of refraction (r). *Angle between* ***refracted ray*** *and* ***normal*** *at* ***point of incidence***.
If second medium denser, ray slows down and is refracted toward ***normal*** *as here. If less dense, ray speeds up and is refracted away from normal.*
First medium
i
Second medium
r
Angle of incidence (i). *Angle between* ***incident ray*** *and* ***normal*** *at* ***point of incidence***.
Point of incidence. *Point at which* ***incident ray*** *meets boundary and becomes* ***refracted ray*** *(or* ***reflected ray*** **).*
Normal. *Line at right angles to boundary through chosen point, e.g.* ***point of incidence***.
Refracted ray

Laws of refraction of light

1. The **refracted ray** lies in the same plane as the **incident ray** and **normal** at the **point of incidence**.

2. (**Snell's law**). The ratio of the **sine*** of the **angle of incidence** to the sine of the **angle of refraction** is a constant for two given **media***.

This constant is the **refractive index** (**n** – see page 37). When referring to light, this is also known as the **optical density** and, as with refractive index in other cases, can also be calculated by dividing the velocity of light in one medium by its velocity in the second medium. See also **apparent depth** picture.

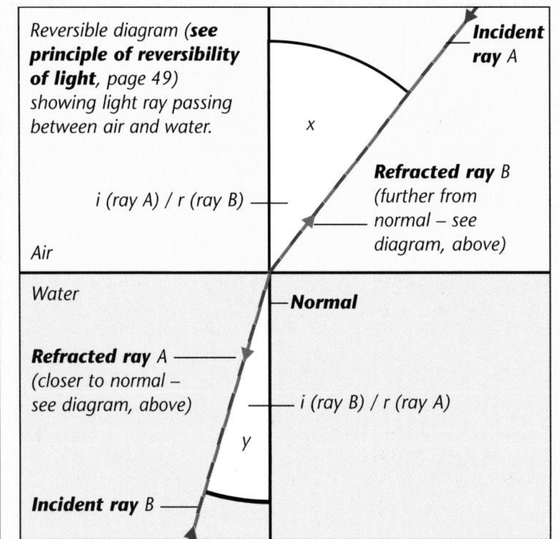

*Reversible diagram (****see principle of reversibility of light****, page 49) showing light ray passing between air and water.*
Incident ray *A*
x
Refracted ray *B (further from normal – see diagram, above)*
i (ray A) / r (ray B)
Air
Water
Normal
Refracted ray *A (closer to normal – see diagram, above)*
i (ray B) / r (ray A)
y
Incident ray *B*

For either direction, ***refractive index*** ** of second* ***medium*** ** relative to first is written* $_1n_2$.

According to ***Snell's law***:

$$_1n_2 = \frac{\sin i}{\sin r}$$

Media may also be specified by subscript letters – $_an_w$ *means refractive index of water relative to air and* $_wn_a$ *means that of air relative to water.*

$$_an_w = \frac{\sin i \text{ (ray A)}}{\sin r \text{ (ray B)}} = \frac{\sin x}{\sin y}$$

$$_wn_a = \frac{\sin i \text{ (ray B)}}{\sin r \text{ (ray B)}} = \frac{\sin y}{\sin x}$$

$$\text{Thus } _an_w = \frac{1}{_wn_a}$$

If no subscripts are given, the value is the ***absolute refractive index*** **.*

* **Absolute refractive index**, 37 (**Refractive index**); **Medium**, 345; **Reflected ray**, **Reflection**, 47; **Sine**, 345.

Apparent depth

The position at which an object in one **medium*** appears to be when viewed from another medium. The brain assumes the light rays have traveled in a straight line, but in fact they have changed direction as a result of refraction. Hence the object is not actually where it appears to be.

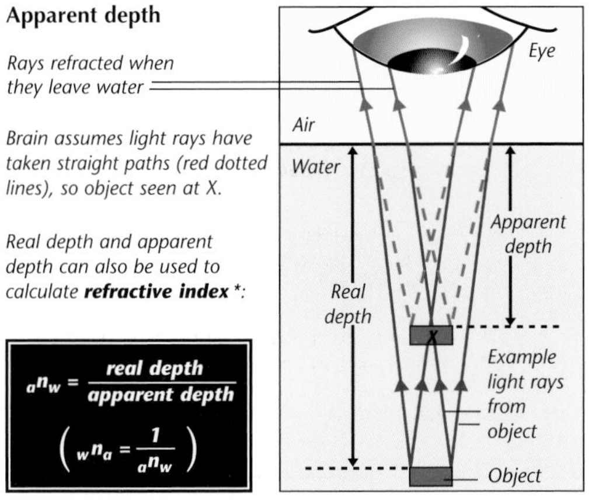

Apparent depth
Rays refracted when they leave water
Brain assumes light rays have taken straight paths (red dotted lines), so object seen at X.
Real depth and apparent depth can also be used to calculate refractive index *:
$_an_w = \frac{\text{real depth}}{\text{apparent depth}}$
$\left(_wn_a = \frac{1}{_an_w} \right)$
Eye
Air
Water
Apparent depth
Real depth
X
Example light rays from object
Object

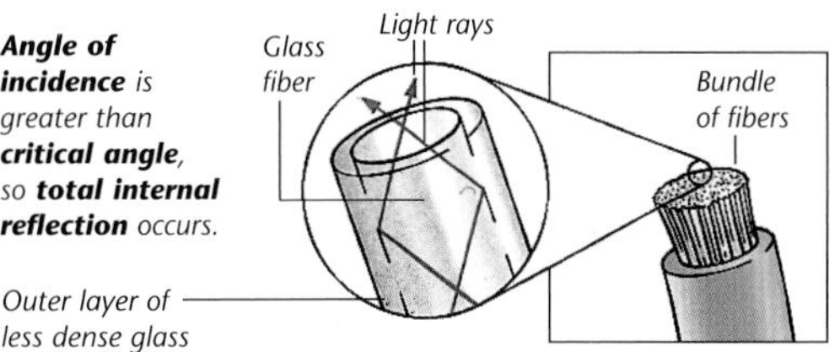

Angle of incidence is greater than critical angle, so total internal reflection occurs.
Glass fiber
Light rays
Bundle of fibers
Outer layer of less dense glass

Critical angle (c)

The particular **angle of incidence** of a ray hitting a less dense **medium*** which results in it being refracted at 90° to the **normal**. This means that the refracted ray (**critical ray**) travels along the boundary, and does not enter the second medium.

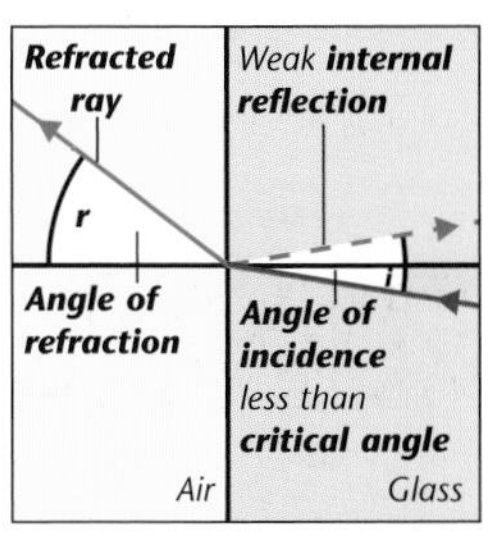

Refracted ray
Weak internal reflection
r
i
Angle of refraction
Angle of incidence less than critical angle
Air
Glass

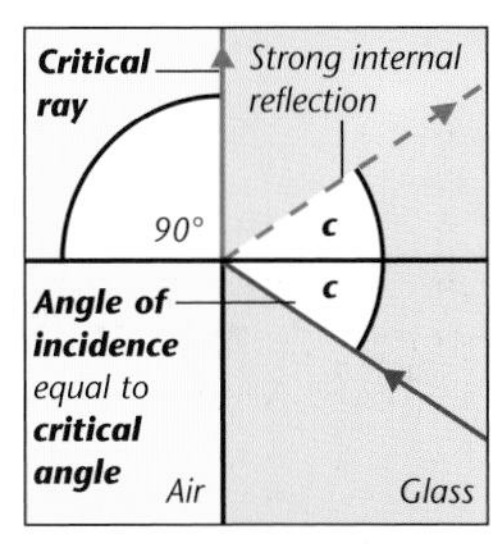

Critical ray
Strong internal reflection
90°
c
c
Angle of incidence equal to critical angle
Air
Glass

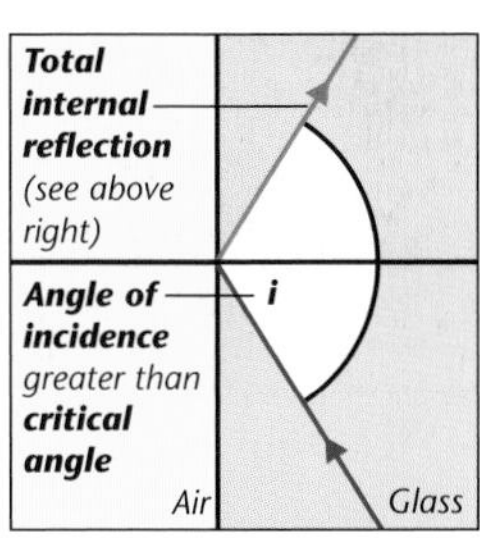

Total internal reflection (see above right)
Angle of incidence greater than critical angle
i
Air
Glass

Critical angle *can also be used to calculate* ***refractive index*** **:*

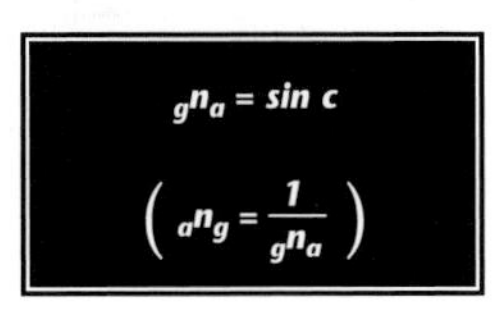

$$_gn_a = \sin c$$

$$\left(_an_g = \frac{1}{_gn_a} \right)$$

(Note: sine of 90° is 1.)

Rainbows form when light is ***refracted*** *through tiny drops of rain present in the air after rain. Each drop acts like a* ***prism***, ***dispersing**** *light into the colors of the* ***visible light spectrum****.

Total internal reflection

When light traveling from a dense to a less dense **medium*** hits the boundary between them, some degree of reflection back into the denser medium always accompanies refraction. When the **angle of incidence** is greater than the **critical angle**, total internal reflection occurs, i.e. all the light is internally reflected.

Optical fibers *transmit light by* ***total internal reflection***. *Bundles of such fibers have a number of uses, e.g. in communications and in medicine (e.g. in* ***endoscopes***, *used by doctors to see inside the body).*

Prism

A transparent solid which has two plane refracting surfaces at an angle to each other. Prisms are used to produce **dispersion*** and change the path of light by refraction and **total internal reflection.**

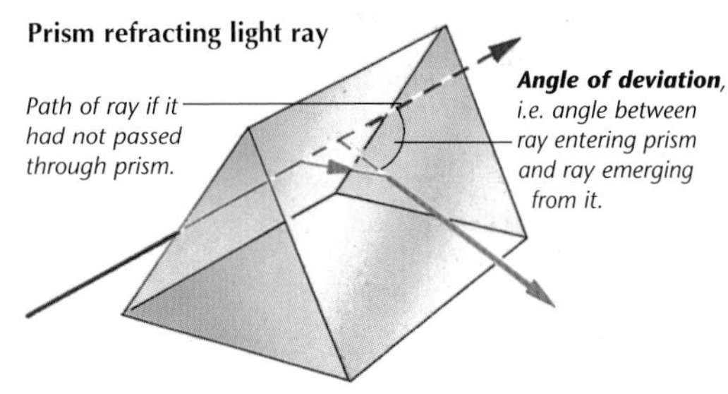

Prism refracting light ray
Path of ray if it had not passed through prism.
Angle of deviation, i.e. angle between ray entering prism and ray emerging from it.

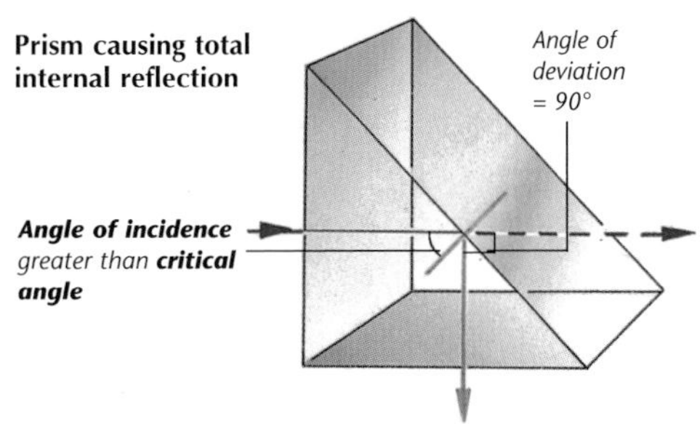

Prism causing total internal reflection
Angle of deviation = 90°
Angle of incidence greater than critical angle

* **Dispersion**, 54 (**Color**); **Medium**, 345;
Refractive index, 37; **Visible light spectrum**, 54.

Refraction of light (continued)

Light rays are refracted at curved surfaces, e.g. **lenses**, as at flat surfaces, according to the **laws of refraction of light** (see page 50). Unlike with flat surfaces, though, images are formed. There are two basic types of lens, **concave** and **convex lenses**, which can act as **diverging** or **converging lenses** depending on their **refractive index*** relative to the surrounding **medium***. For all diagrams showing image production by refraction, the object is assumed to be the light source (see **reflection of light**, page 47), and certain points (see below), together with known facts about light rays passing through them, are used to construct the paths of the refracted rays. The positions of objects and images can be determined using the **mirror** (**lens**) **formula***.

*A magnifying glass is a **converging lens** used so that objects are made to look bigger than they really are.*

Points used to construct paths of refracted rays
(See also page 48.)

*All the lenses shown are considered to be thin lenses (i.e. the thickness of the lens is small compared to the **focal length**). Although light rays bend both on entering the lens and emerging from it, they are drawn as bending only once, at a vertical line running through **optical center** of the lens.*

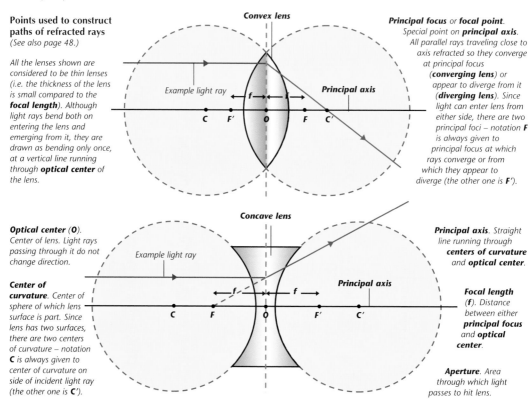

Convex lens

Example light ray

Principal axis

C F′ O F C′

f f

***Principal focus** or **focal point**. Special point on **principal axis**. All parallel rays traveling close to axis refracted so they converge at principal focus (**converging lens**) or appear to diverge from it (**diverging lens**). Since light can enter lens from either side, there are two principal foci – notation **F** is always given to principal focus at which rays converge or from which they appear to diverge (the other one is **F′**).*

Concave lens

Example light ray

Principal axis

C F O F′ C′

f f

***Optical center** (**O**). Center of lens. Light rays passing through it do not change direction.*

***Center of curvature**. Center of sphere of which lens surface is part. Since lens has two surfaces, there are two centers of curvature – notation **C** is always given to center of curvature on side of incident light ray (the other one is **C′**).*

***Principal axis**. Straight line running through **centers of curvature** and **optical center**.*

***Focal length** (**f**). Distance between either **principal focus** and **optical center**.*

***Aperture**. Area through which light passes to hit lens.*

Converging lens

A lens which causes parallel rays falling on it to converge on the **principal focus** on the other side of the lens. Both **concave** and **convex lenses** can act as **converging lenses**, depending on the **refractive index*** of the lens relative to the surrounding **medium***. A glass convex lens in air acts as a converging lens, as shown in the diagram on the right.

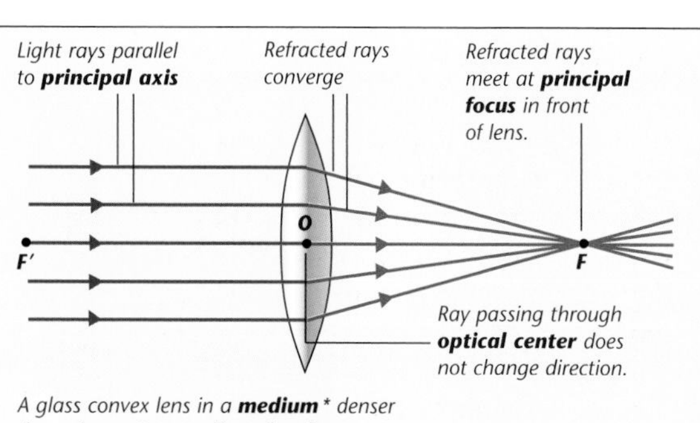

Light rays parallel to principal axis
Refracted rays converge
Refracted rays meet at principal focus in front of lens.
O
F′
F
Ray passing through optical center does not change direction.

*A glass convex lens in a **medium*** denser than glass acts as a **diverging lens**.*

* **Medium**, 345; **Mirror formula**, 49; **Refractive index**, 37.

Power (P)

A measure of the ability of a lens to converge or diverge light rays, given in **diopters** (when **focal length** is measured in meters). The shorter the focal length, the more powerful the lens.

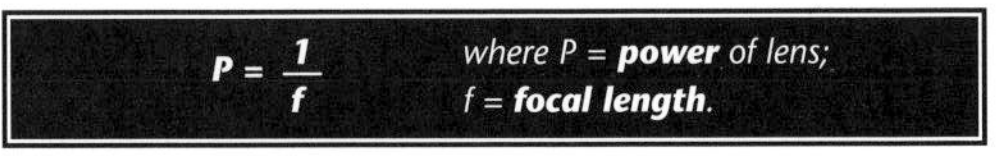

$$P = \frac{1}{f}$$ *where P = **power** of lens; f = **focal length**.*

Binoculars use lenses to magnify objects.

Convex lens

A lens with at least one surface curving outwards. A lens with one surface curving inwards and one outwards is convex if its middle is thicker than its outer edges (it is a **convex meniscus**). A glass convex lens in air acts as a **converging lens**. The size, position and type of image it forms (**real*** or **virtual***) depends on how far it is from the object.

Types of convex lens

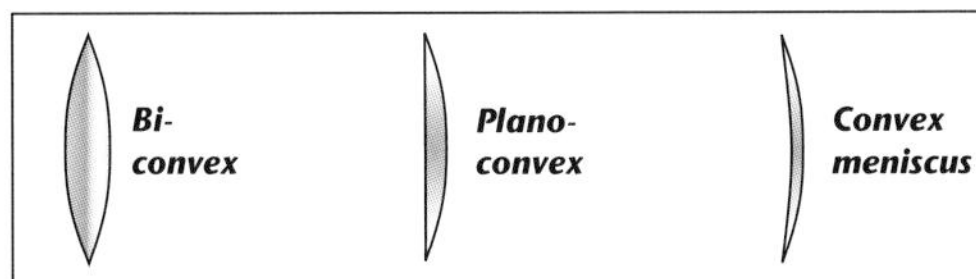
Bi-convex
Plano-convex
Convex meniscus

Convex lens

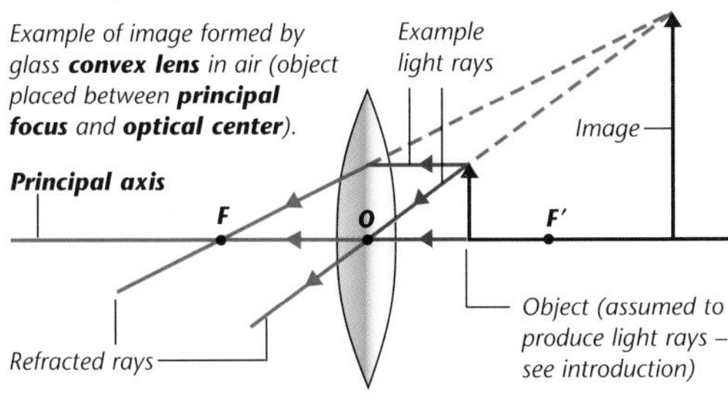
Example of image formed by glass convex lens in air (object placed between principal focus and optical center).
Example light rays
Image
Principal axis
F
O
F′
Refracted rays
Object (assumed to produce light rays – see introduction)

*In this case, image is seen behind the object and is upright, larger than object and a **virtual image***.*

Concave lens

A lens which has at least one surface curving inwards. A lens with one surface curving inwards and one outwards is concave if its middle is thinner than its outer edges (it is a **concave meniscus**). A glass concave lens in air acts as a **diverging lens**. The position of the object in relation to the lens may vary, but the image is always of the same type.

Types of concave lens

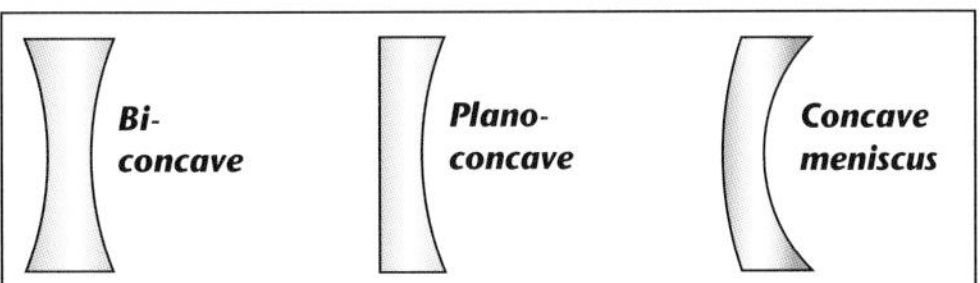
Bi-concave
Plano-concave
Concave meniscus

Concave lens

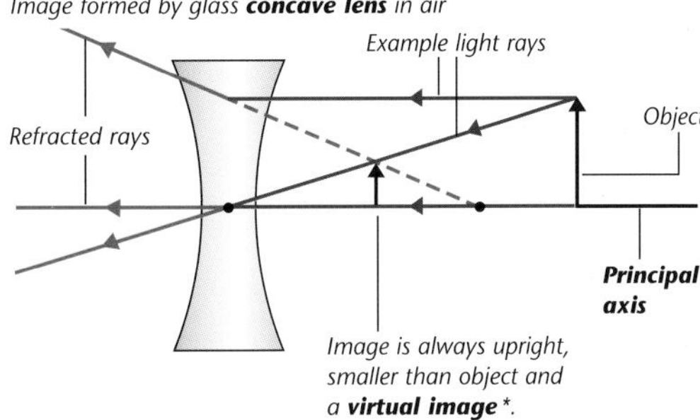
Image formed by glass concave lens in air
Example light rays
Refracted rays
Object
Principal axis

*Image is always upright, smaller than object and a **virtual image***.*

Diverging lens

A lens which causes parallel rays falling on it to diverge so that they appear to have come from the **principal focus** on the same side as the rays enter. Both **concave** and **convex lenses** can act as diverging lenses, depending on the **refractive index*** of the lens relative to the surrounding **medium***. A glass concave lens in air acts as a diverging lens, as shown in the diagram on the right.

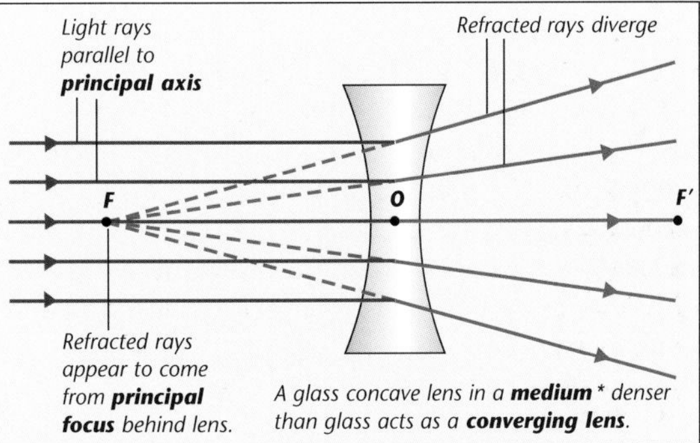
Light rays parallel to principal axis
Refracted rays diverge
F
O
F′
Refracted rays appear to come from principal focus behind lens.

*A glass concave lens in a **medium*** denser than glass acts as a **converging lens**.*

* **Medium**, 345; **Real image**, 49 (**Image**); **Refractive index**, 37; **Virtual image**, 49 (**Image**).

OPTICAL INSTRUMENTS

An **optical instrument** is one which acts on light, using one or more **lenses*** or **curved mirrors*** to produce a required type of image. Listed below are some of the more common optical instruments.

Camera

An optical instrument that is used to form and record an image of an object on film. The image is inverted and a **real image***.

Camera (reflex)

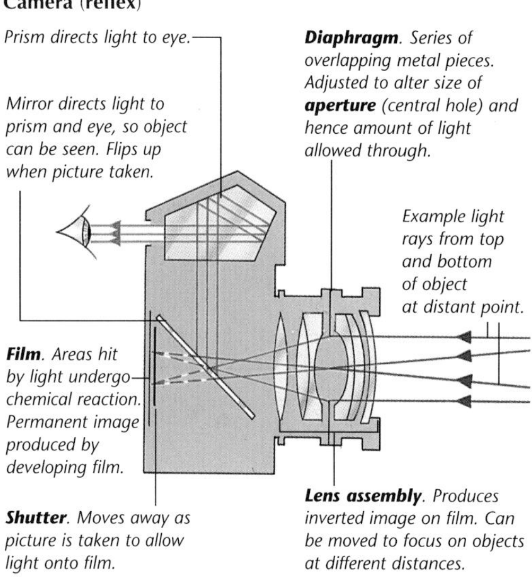

Prism directs light to eye.
Mirror directs light to prism and eye, so object can be seen. Flips up when picture taken.
Diaphragm. Series of overlapping metal pieces. Adjusted to alter size of *aperture* (central hole) and hence amount of light allowed through.
Example light rays from top and bottom of object at distant point.
Film. Areas hit by light undergo chemical reaction. Permanent image produced by developing film.
Shutter. Moves away as picture is taken to allow light onto film.
Lens assembly. Produces inverted image on film. Can be moved to focus on objects at different distances.

As before (see page 52), refraction by lenses shown as one change of direction only, this time on line through optical center of whole lens assembly.

Microscope

An optical instrument which magnifies very small objects. If it has only one **lens***, it is a **simple microscope** or **magnifying glass**. If it has more, it is a **compound microscope**.

Compound microscope

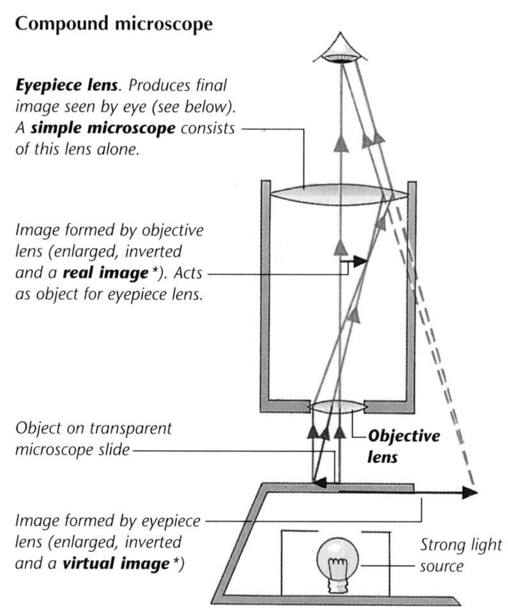

Eyepiece lens. Produces final image seen by eye (see below). A *simple microscope* consists of this lens alone.
Image formed by objective lens (enlarged, inverted and a *real image* *). Acts as object for eyepiece lens.
Object on transparent microscope slide
Objective lens
Image formed by eyepiece lens (enlarged, inverted and a *virtual image* *)
Strong light source

Color

When all the different **wavelengths*** of **visible light** (see page 45) fall on the eye at the same time, white light is seen. However, white light can also undergo **dispersion**, whereby it is split into the **visible light spectrum** (i.e. its different wavelengths) by **refraction***. This may occur accidentally (see **chromatic aberration**), or it may be produced on purpose, e.g. with a **spectrometer**.

White light enters *prism**.

Inside a spectrometer

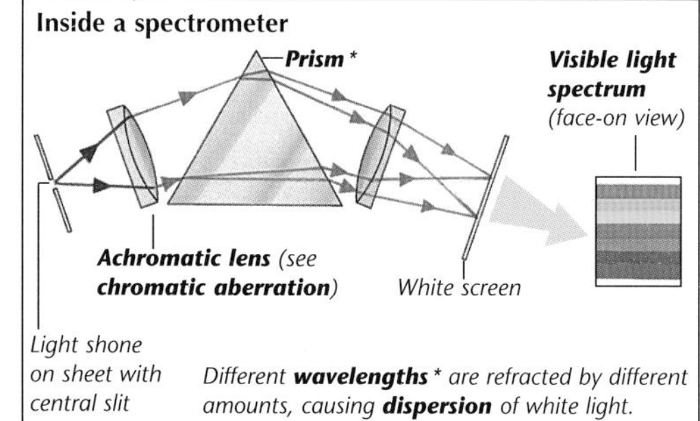

Prism *
Visible light spectrum (face-on view)
Achromatic lens (see *chromatic aberration*)
White screen
Light shone on sheet with central slit
Different *wavelengths* * are refracted by different amounts, causing *dispersion* of white light.

Visible light spectrum

A display of the colors that make up a beam of white light. Each color band represents a very small range of **wavelengths*** – see **visible light**, page 45.

Light **refracted** by **prism*** to form a color spectrum.

Slide projector

An optical instrument which produces a magnified image of a slide.

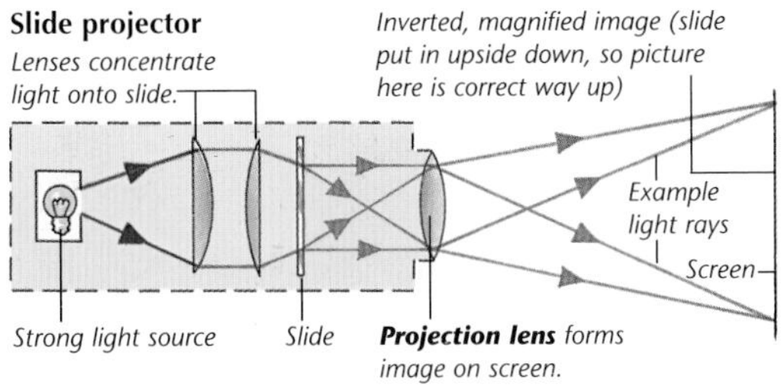
Slide projector
Lenses concentrate light onto slide.
Inverted, magnified image (slide put in upside down, so picture here is correct way up)
Example light rays
Screen
Strong light source
Slide
Projection lens forms image on screen.

Telescope

An optical instrument used to make very distant (and therefore apparently very small) objects appear larger.

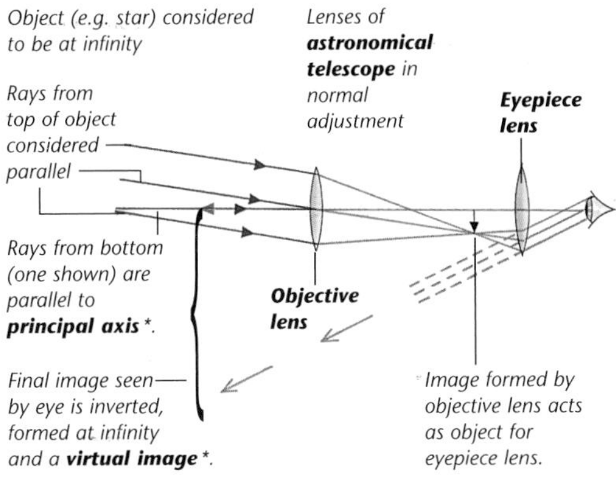
Telescope
Object (e.g. star) considered to be at infinity
Lenses of astronomical telescope in normal adjustment
Rays from top of object considered parallel
Eyepiece lens
Rays from bottom (one shown) are parallel to principal axis*.
Objective lens
Final image seen by eye is inverted, formed at infinity and a virtual image*.
Image formed by objective lens acts as object for eyepiece lens.

Visual angle

The angle, at the eye, of the rays coming from the top and bottom of an object or its image. The greater it is, the larger the object or image appears. Optical instruments which produce magnification, e.g. **microscopes**, do so by creating an image whose visual angle is greater than that of the object seen by the unaided eye. The **angular magnification** or **magnifying power** (see below) of such an instrument is a measurement of the amount by which it does so.

$$\text{Angular magnification} = \frac{\text{visual angle of image}}{\text{visual angle of object}}$$

Chromatic aberration or chromatism

The halo of colors (the **visible light spectrum** – see below, left) sometimes seen around images viewed through lenses. It results from **dispersion** (see **color**). To avoid this, good quality optical instruments contain one or more **achromatic lenses** – each consisting of two lenses combined so that any dispersion produced by one is corrected by the other.

Achromatic lenses in compound microscopes minimize chromatic aberration.

Primary colors

Red, blue and green light – colors that cannot be made by combining other colored light. Mixed equally, they give white light. By mixing them in the right proportions, every color in the **visible light spectrum** can be produced. Note that these are the pure primary colors – those referred to in art (red, blue and yellow) only act as primary colors because the paints are impure.

Primary colors

Green, Blue, Red, △Cyan, △Yellow, △Magenta

***Complementary** colors are any two that produce white light when mixed, e.g. red and cyan.*

*△ = **secondary colors** (combinations of primary colors)*

Color mixing

If white light is shone onto a pure colored filter, only light of the same color (range of **wavelengths***) as the filter passes through (the other colors are absorbed). This is **subtractive mixing** or **color mixing by subtraction**. If light of two different colors, filtered out in this way, is shone onto a white surface, a third color (a mixture of the two) is seen by the eye. This is **additive mixing** or **color mixing by addition**.

This light bulb looks blue because it only lets through blue light (all other colors have been absorbed by the blue coating).

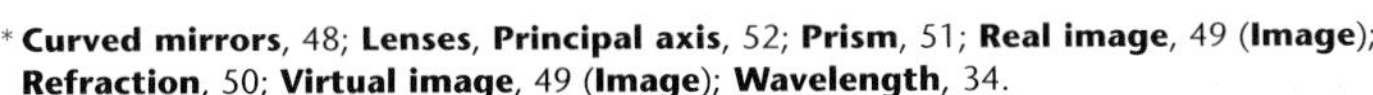
* **Curved mirrors**, 48; **Lenses**, **Principal axis**, 52; **Prism**, 51; **Real image**, 49 (**Image**); **Refraction**, 50; **Virtual image**, 49 (**Image**); **Wavelength**, 34.

STATIC ELECTRICITY

Electricity is the phenomenon caused by the presence or movement of charges (**electrons*** or **ions***) which exert an **electric force***. A material is said to have a negative electric charge if it has a surplus of electrons, and a positive electric charge if it has a deficit of electrons. An electric **current** (see page 60) is the movement of a charge through materials. (In a metal it is the electrons that move.) This can be contrasted with **static electricity**, which can be said to be electricity "held" by a material with electric charge.

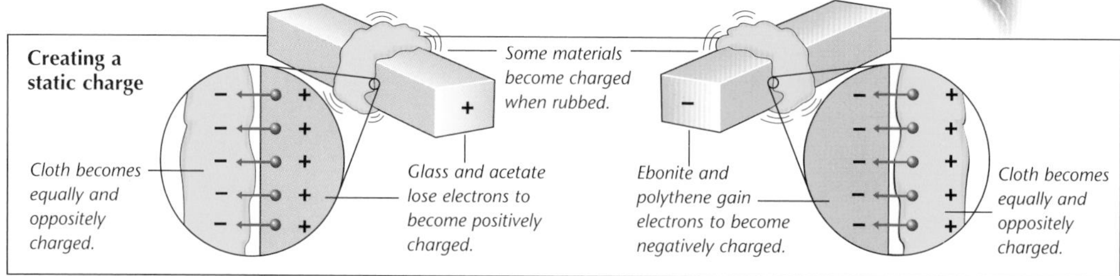

Creating a static charge
Some materials become charged when rubbed.
Cloth becomes equally and oppositely charged.
Glass and acetate lose electrons to become positively charged.
Ebonite and polythene gain electrons to become negatively charged.
Cloth becomes equally and oppositely charged.

First law of electrostatics

Like charges repel each other and unlike charges attract. A charged particle always attracts an uncharged **conductor** by **induction**.

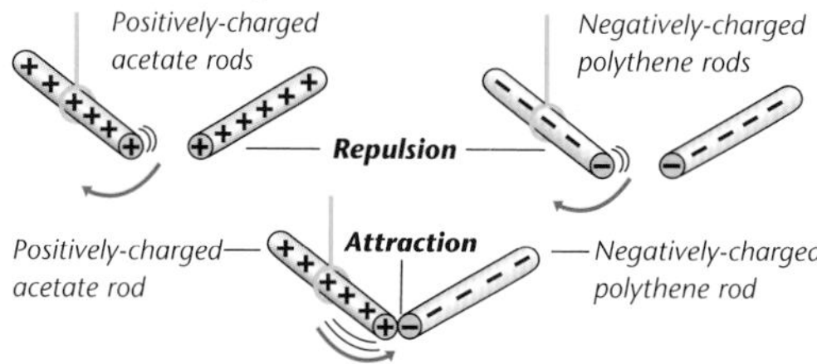

Attraction and repulsion
Positively-charged acetate rods
Negatively-charged polythene rods
Repulsion
Positively-charged acetate rod
Attraction
Negatively-charged polythene rod

Conductor

A material containing a large number of charges (e.g. electrons) which are free to move (see also **conductivity**, page 63). It can therefore **conduct** electricity (carry an electric **current** – see introduction). Metals, e.g. copper, aluminum and gold, are good conductors because they contain large numbers of electrons which are free to move.

Insulator

A material with very few or no charges (e.g. electrons) free to move (i.e. a bad **conductor**). Some insulators become electrically charged when rubbed. This is because electrons from the surface atoms are transferred from one substance to the next, but the charge remains on the surface.

Electroscope

An instrument for detecting small amounts of electric charge. A **gold leaf electroscope** is the most common type. When the leaf and rod become charged, they repel and the leaf diverges from the rod. The greater the charges, the larger the divergence of the leaf. A **condensing electroscope** contains a **capacitor*** between the cap and the case which increases the sensitivity.

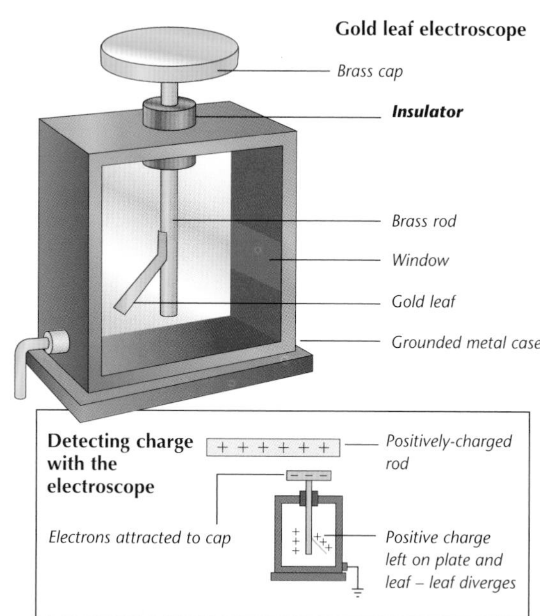

Gold leaf electroscope
Brass cap
Insulator
Brass rod
Window
Gold leaf
Grounded metal case
Detecting charge with the electroscope
Positively-charged rod
Electrons attracted to cap
Positive charge left on plate and leaf – leaf diverges

* **Capacitor**, 59; **Electric force**, 6; **Electrons**, 83; **Ions**, 88 (**Ionization**).

Induction or **electrostatic induction**

A process by which a **conductor** becomes charged with the use of another charge but without contact. Generally charges are induced in different parts of an object because of repulsion and attraction. By removing one type of charge the object is left permanently charged.

Charging a conductor by induction

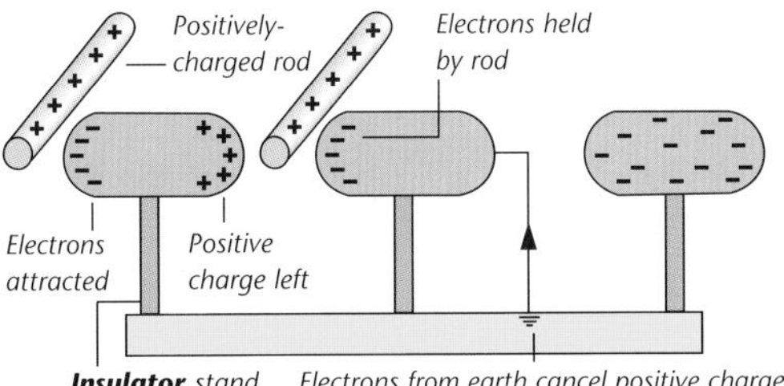

Positively-charged rod
Electrons held by rod
Electrons attracted
Positive charge left
Insulator stand
Electrons from earth cancel positive charge

Proof plane

A small disk made of a **conductor** mounted on a handle made of an **insulator**. It is used to transfer charge between objects.

Surface density of charge

The amount of charge per unit area on the surface of an object. It is greater where the surface is more curved, which leads to charge being concentrated at sharp points (see **point action**). Only a sphere has constant surface density of charge.

Variations in surface density of charge

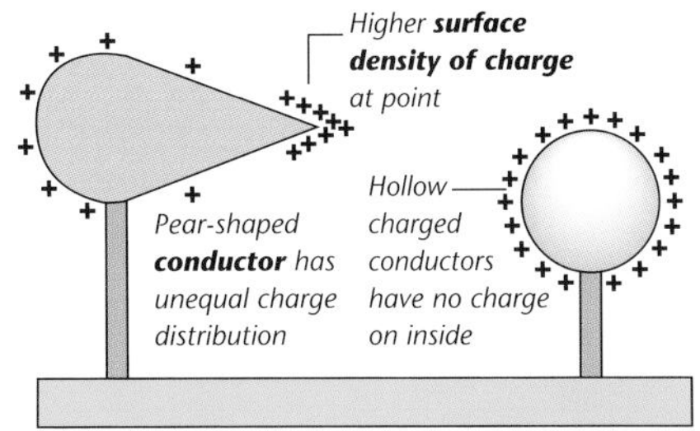

Higher surface density of charge at point
Hollow charged conductors have no charge on inside
Pear-shaped conductor has unequal charge distribution

Point action

The action which occurs around a sharp point on the surface of a positively-charged object. Positive ions in the air are repelled by the large charge at the point (see **surface density of charge**). These collide with air molecules and knock off electrons to produce more positive ions which are also repelled. The result is an **electric wind** of air molecules.

Lightning

The sudden flow of electricity from a cloud which has become charged due to the rubbing together of different particles, e.g. water droplets. A **lightning conductor** is used to help cancel the charge on the cloud by **point action** and to conduct the electricity down to earth so that it does not flow through buildings. The lightning strike is like the effect in a **discharge tube***.

Action of lightning conductor

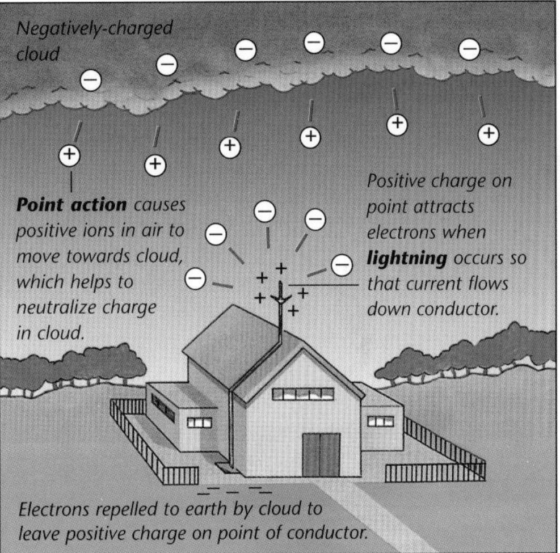

Negatively-charged cloud
Point action causes positive ions in air to move towards cloud, which helps to neutralize charge in cloud.
Positive charge on point attracts electrons when lightning occurs so that current flows down conductor.
Electrons repelled to earth by cloud to leave positive charge on point of conductor.

Van de Graaff generator

A machine in which positive charge from a point is transferred (by **point action**) to a moving band, collected by another point and deposited on a sphere-shaped conductor.

Van de Graaff generator

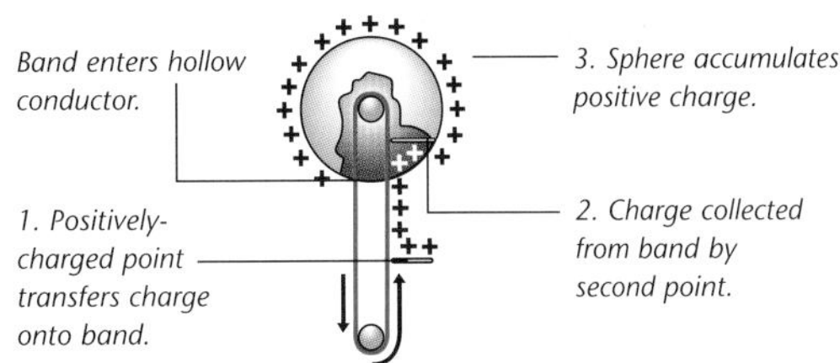

Band enters hollow conductor.
3. Sphere accumulates positive charge.
1. Positively-charged point transfers charge onto band.
2. Charge collected from band by second point.

Electrophorus

An instrument consisting of a negatively-charged **insulator** and a brass plate attached to an insulating handle. It is used to produce a number of positive charges from one negative charge.

* **Discharge tube**, 80; **Mechanical energy**, 9.

POTENTIAL AND CAPACITANCE

A charge or collection of charges causes an **electric field**, i.e. a **force field*** in which charged particles experience an **electric force***. The intensity of an electric field at a point is the force per unit positive charge at that point, and the direction is the direction of the force on a positive charge at that point (see also pages 104-107). Charged objects in an electric field have **potential energy*** because of their charge and position. **Potential** itself is a property of the field (see below).

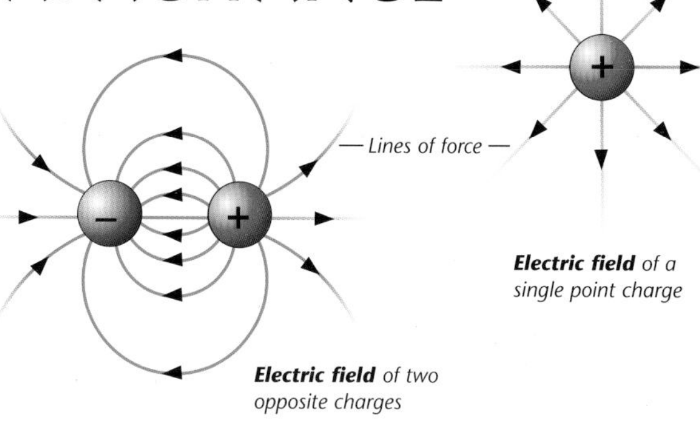

— Lines of force —

***Electric field** of a single point charge*

***Electric field** of two opposite charges*

$$F \propto \frac{q_1 q_2}{d^2}$$

*where F = **electric force***;*
q_1, q_2 = size of charges;
d = separation.

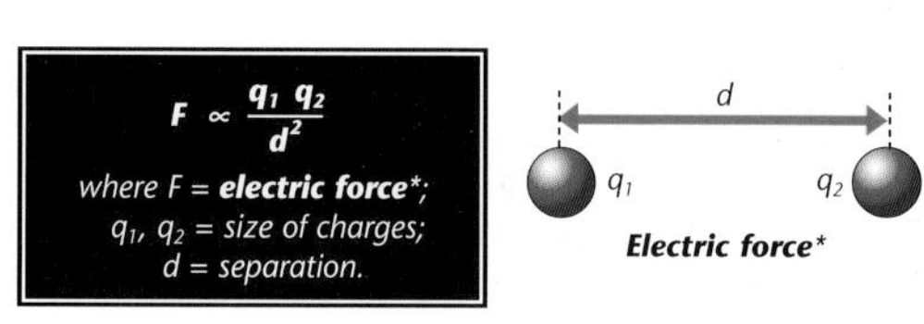

d
q_1
q_2

Electric force*

Potential

The **potential energy*** per unit charge at a point in an electric field, i.e. the work done in moving a unit positive charge to this point. The potential energy of a charge depends on the potential of its position and on its size. A positive charge tends to move towards points of lower potential. This is moving down the **potential gradient**. Potential cannot be measured, but the **potential difference** between two points can.

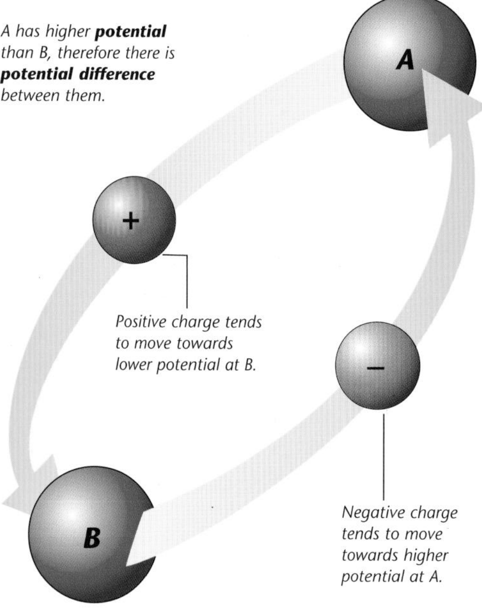

A has higher **potential** than B, therefore there is **potential difference** between them.
A
B
+
–
Positive charge tends to move towards lower potential at B.
Negative charge tends to move towards higher potential at A.

Potential difference

A difference in **potential** between two points, equal to the energy change when a unit positive charge moves from one place to another in an electric field. The unit of potential difference is the **volt** (potential difference is sometimes called **voltage**). There is an energy change of one joule if a charge of one **coulomb*** moves through one volt. A reference point (usually a connection to earth) is chosen and given a potential of zero.

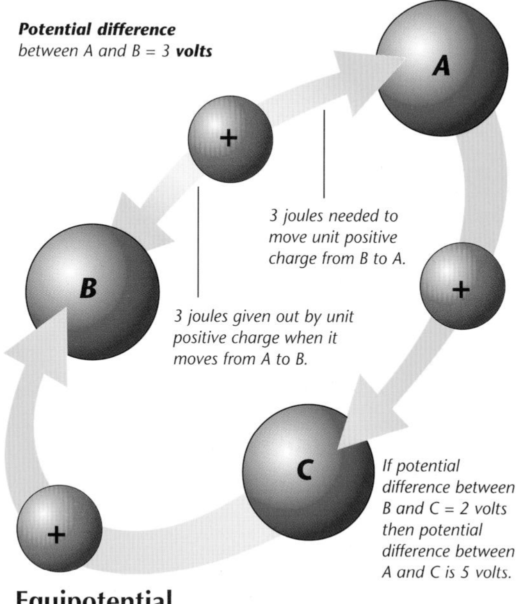

Potential difference between A and B = 3 **volts**
A
B
C
+
+
+
3 joules needed to move unit positive charge from B to A.
3 joules given out by unit positive charge when it moves from A to B.
If potential difference between B and C = 2 volts then potential difference between A and C is 5 volts.

Equipotential

A surface over which the **potential** is constant.

* **Coulomb**, 60; **Electric force**, **Force field**, 6; **Potential energy**, 8.

Capacitance

When a **conductor*** is given a charge it undergoes a change in **potential**. **Capacitance** is the ratio of the charge gained by an object to its increase in potential. An object with a higher capacitance requires a larger charge to change its potential by the same amount as an object with a smaller capacitance.

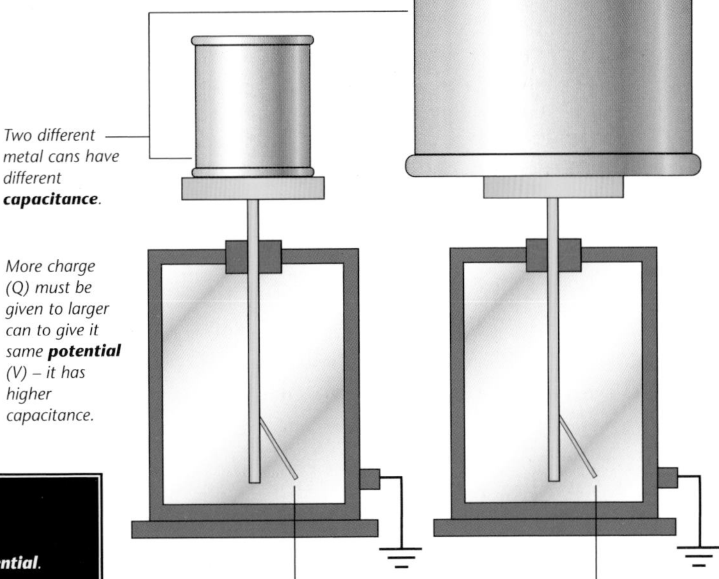

Two different metal cans have different **capacitance**.
More charge (Q) must be given to larger can to give it same **potential** (V) – it has higher capacitance.
Same leaf divergence shows same potential.

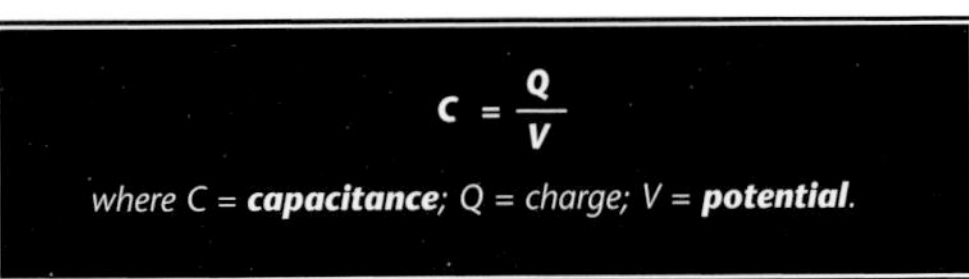

$$C = \frac{Q}{V}$$

*where C = **capacitance**; Q = charge; V = **potential**.*

Farad

The unit of capacitance. It is the capacitance of an object whose **potential** is increased by one **volt** when given a charge of one **coulomb***.

Capacitor

A device for storing electric charge, consisting of two parallel metal plates separated by an insulating material called a **dielectric**. The capacitance of a capacitor depends on the dielectric used, so a dielectric is chosen to suit the capacitance needed and the physical size required.

Capacitor

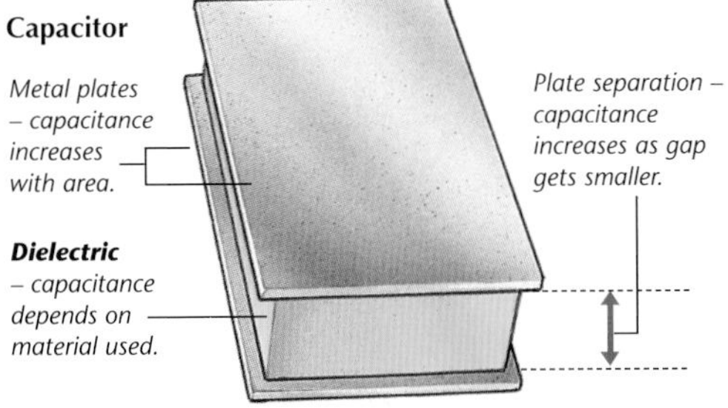

Metal plates – capacitance increases with area.
Dielectric – capacitance depends on material used.
Plate separation – capacitance increases as gap gets smaller.

Dielectric constant

The ratio of the capacitance of a **capacitor** with a given **dielectric** to the capacitance of the same capacitor with a vacuum between the plates. The value is thus the factor by which the capacitance is increased by using the given dielectric instead of a vacuum. (Note that measuring the dielectric against air would produce a very similar result.)

Electrolytic capacitor

A **capacitor** with a paste or jelly **dielectric** which gives it a very high capacitance in a small volume. Due to the nature of the dielectric, it must be connected correctly to the electricity supply.

Variable capacitor

A **capacitor** consisting of two sets of interlocking vanes, often with an air **dielectric**. The size of the interlocking area is altered to change the capacitance.

Variable capacitor

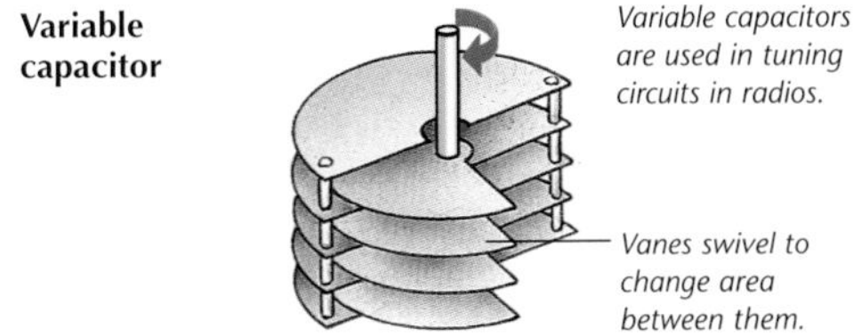

Variable capacitors are used in tuning circuits in radios.
Vanes swivel to change area between them.

Leyden jar

A **capacitor** consisting of a glass jar with foil linings inside and out. It was one of the first capacitors invented.

Paper capacitor

A **capacitor** made with two long foil plates separated by a thin waxed paper **dielectric**. **Polyester capacitors** are made in a similar way.

Paper capacitor

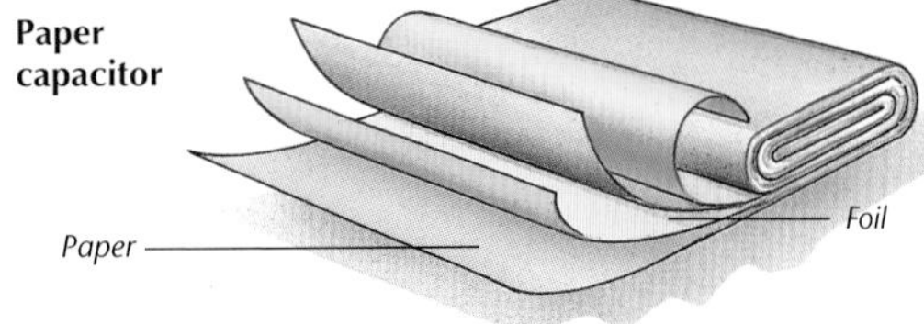

Paper
Foil

* **Conductor**, 56; **Coulomb**, 60.

ELECTRIC CURRENT

An electric **current** (**I**) is the rate of flow of electric charge. In metal conductors, the charge which flows consists of electrons (negatively charged particles – see page 83), and these flow because in an **electric field*** there is a difference in **potential*** between two places. Therefore a **potential difference*** is needed to produce an electric current. A **circuit** is a closed loop, consisting of a source of potential difference and one or more components, around which the current flows.

This battery (current source), wires and light bulb form a circuit.

Electromotive force (e.m.f.)

The **potential difference*** produced by a **cell***, **battery*** or **generator***, which causes current to flow in a circuit. A source of e.m.f. has two **terminals** (where wires are connected), between which it maintains a potential difference. A **back e.m.f.** is an e.m.f. produced by a component in the circuit which opposes the main e.m.f.

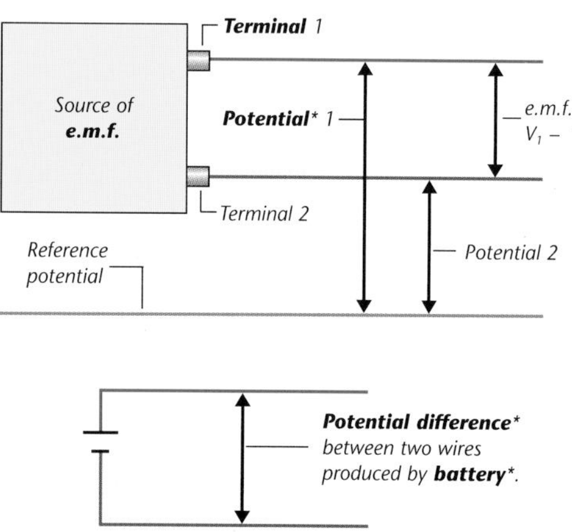

Terminal 1
Source of e.m.f.
Potential* 1
e.m.f. = $V_1 - V_2$
Terminal 2
Potential 2
Reference potential
Potential difference* between two wires produced by battery*.

*One **terminal** connected to reference **potential****

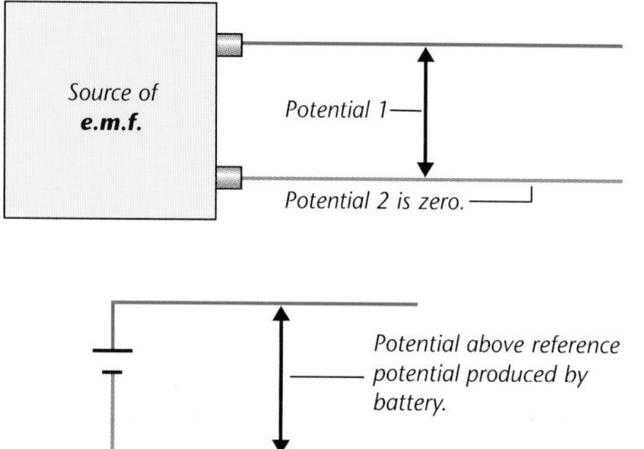

Source of e.m.f.
Potential 1
Potential 2 is zero.
Potential above reference potential produced by battery.

Ampere or amp (A)

The **SI unit*** of current (see also page 96). One ampere is the current which, when flowing through two infinitely long wires one meter apart in a vacuum, produces a force of 2×10^{-7} newtons per meter of wire. Current is accurately measured by a **current balance**, which, by adapting the theory above, measures the force between two coils of wire through which current is flowing. **Ammeters*** are **calibrated*** using current balances.

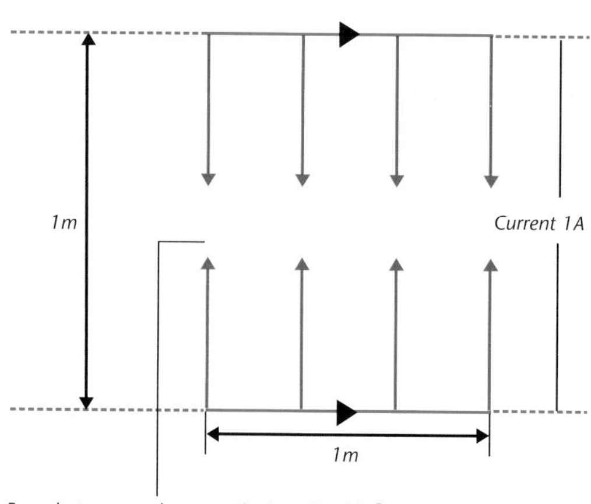

1m
Current 1A
1m

Force between each meter of wire = 2×10^{-7}N

Coulomb

The **SI unit*** of electric charge. It is equal to the amount of charge which passes a point in a conductor if one **ampere** flows through the conductor for one second.

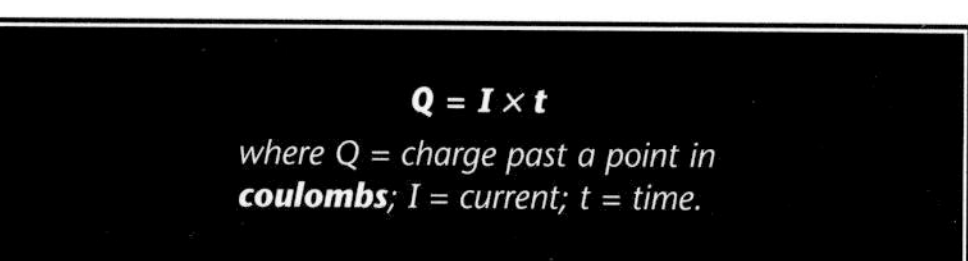

$Q = I \times t$
where Q = charge past a point in coulombs; I = current; t = time.

* **Ammeter**, 77; **Battery**, 68; **Calibration**, 344; **Cell**, 68; **Electric field**, 58; **Generator**, 78; **Potential**, **Potential difference**, 58; **SI units**, 96.

Direct current (d.c.)

Current which flows in one direction only. Originally current was assumed to flow from a point with higher **potential*** to a point with lower potential. Electrons actually flow the other way, but the convention has been kept.

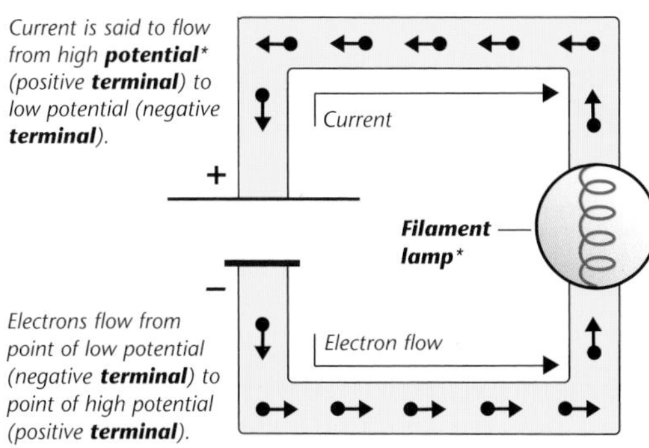
Current is said to flow from high **potential*** (positive **terminal**) to low potential (negative **terminal**).
Current
+
–
Filament lamp*
Electrons flow from point of low potential (negative **terminal**) to point of high potential (positive **terminal**).
Electron flow

Alternating current (a.c.)

Current whose direction in a circuit changes at regular intervals. It is caused by an alternating **electromotive force**. Plotting a graph of current versus time gives the waveform of the current. Alternating currents and electromotive forces are generally expressed as their **root mean square** values (see picture, below).

Electrons flow alternately one way then the other.

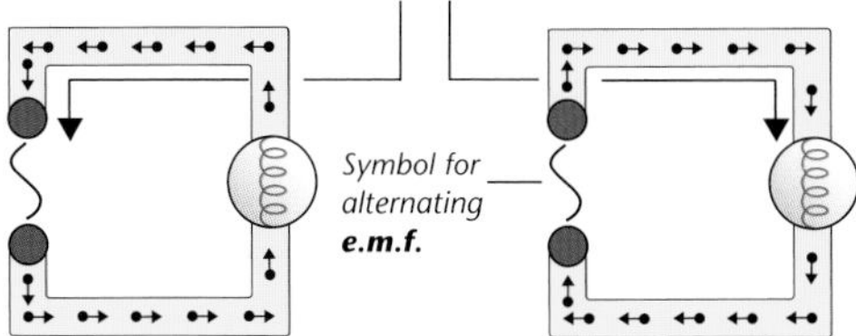
Symbol for alternating **e.m.f.**

Graph of current versus time

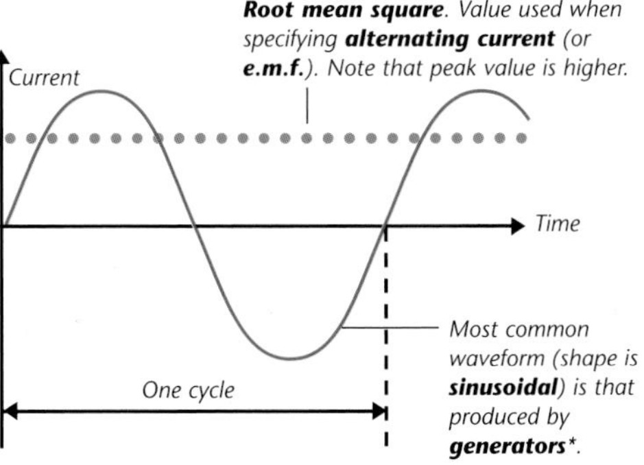
Root mean square. Value used when specifying **alternating current** (or **e.m.f.**). Note that peak value is higher.
Current
Time
One cycle
Most common waveform (shape is **sinusoidal**) is that produced by **generators***.

Electricity supply

Electricity for domestic and industrial use is produced at power stations by large **generators***. These produce **alternating current** at a frequency of 60Hz. Alternating current, unlike **direct current**, can be easily transformed (see **transformer**, page 79) to produce larger or smaller **potential differences***. This means that high voltages and thus low currents can be used for transmission, which considerably reduces power losses in the transmission cables.

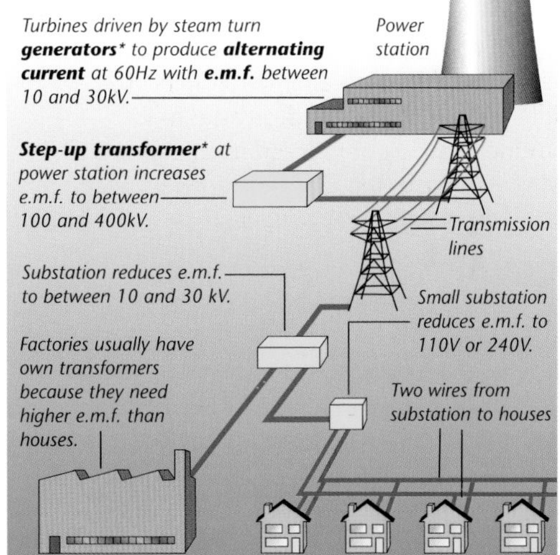
Turbines driven by steam turn **generators*** to produce **alternating current** at 60Hz with **e.m.f.** between 10 and 30kV.
Power station
Step-up transformer* at power station increases e.m.f. to between 100 and 400kV.
Transmission lines
Substation reduces e.m.f. to between 10 and 30 kV.
Small substation reduces e.m.f. to 110V or 240V.
Factories usually have own transformers because they need higher e.m.f. than houses.
Two wires from substation to houses

All domestic electricity supplies consist of at least two wires from a substation along which **alternating current** flows. In some cases, one of the wires is connected to ground so that the **potential*** of the other alternates above and below ground. In some countries there is an additional wire connected to ground as a safety measure.

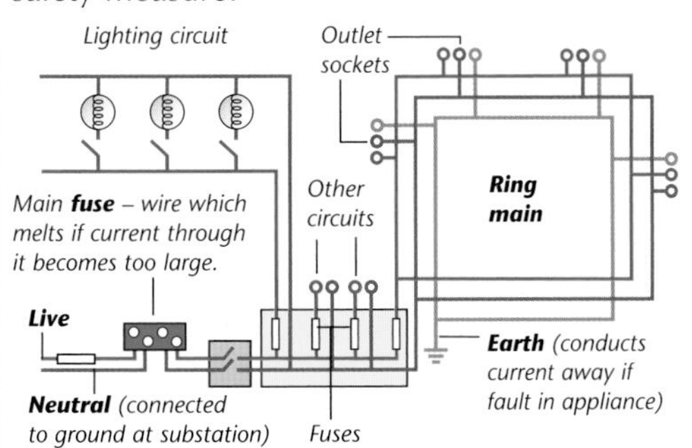
Lighting circuit
Outlet sockets
Other circuits
Ring main
Main **fuse** – wire which melts if current through it becomes too large.
Live
Neutral (connected to ground at substation)
Fuses
Earth (conducts current away if fault in appliance)

* **Filament lamp**, 64; **Generator**, 78; **Potential**, 58; **Potential difference**, 58; **Step-up transformer**, 79.

CONTROLLING CURRENT

The strength of a current flowing in a circuit depends on the nature of the components in the circuit as well as the **electromotive force***. The **resistance** of the components and the magnetic and electric fields they set up all affect the current in them.

Ohm's law

The current in an object at constant temperature is proportional to the **potential difference*** across its ends. The ratio of the potential difference to the current is the **resistance** of the object. The object must be at constant temperature for the law to apply since a current will heat it up and this will change its resistance (see also **filament lamp**, page 64). Ohm's law does not apply to some materials, e.g. **semiconductors***.

***Ohm's law** states:*

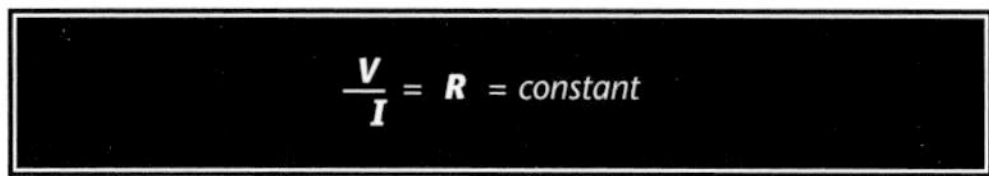
$\frac{V}{I} = R = \text{constant}$

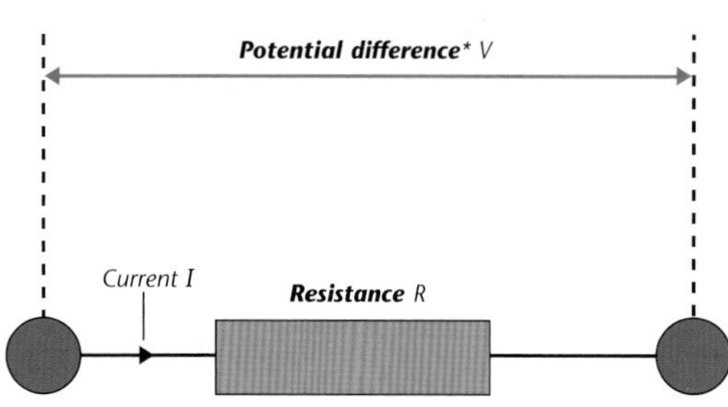
Potential difference* V
Current I
Resistance R

Example:

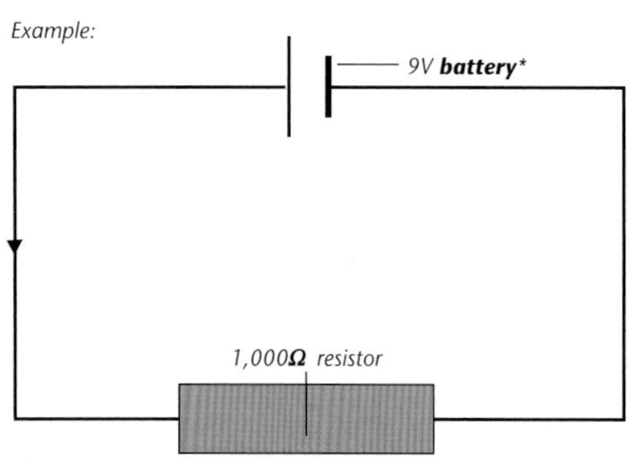
9V battery*
1,000Ω resistor

*Current I through **resistor** R* $= \frac{V}{R} = \frac{9}{1,000} = 0.009A = 9mA$

Resistance (R)

The ability of an object to resist the flow of current. The value depends on the **resistivity** of the substance from which the object is made, its shape and its size. The unit of resistance is the **ohm** (**Ω**). Electrons moving in the object hit atoms and give them energy, heating the object and using up energy from the source of **electromotive force***.

*The rate at which electrical energy is changed, because of **resistance**, to heat energy (i.e. the **power***) can be calculated thus:*

Power $= IV = I^2R$
where I = current;
*V = **potential difference****
across resistance; R = resistance.

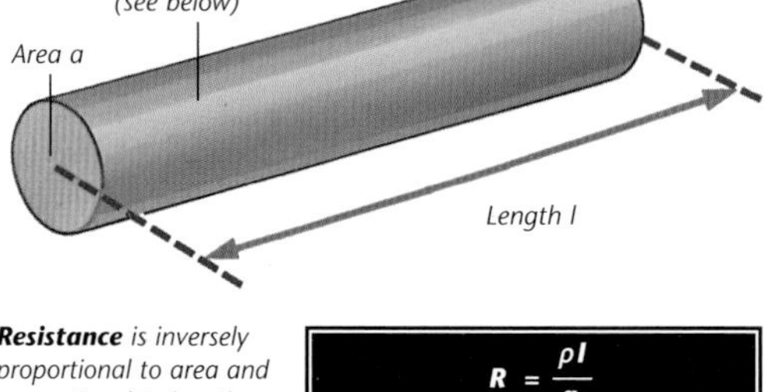
Material of resistivity ρ
(see below)
Area a
Length l

***Resistance** is inversely proportional to area and proportional to length.*

$$R = \frac{\rho l}{a}$$

Resistivity (ρ)

The ability of a substance to resist current. Good **conductors*** have a low resistivity and **insulators*** have a high resistivity. It is the **reciprocal*** of the **conductivity** of the substance and depends on temperature. See also page 112.

Resistor

A device with a particular **resistance** value. Resistors can have values from less than one **ohm** up to many millions of ohms. The most common type is the **carbon resistor**, made from compressed carbon of known **resistivity**.

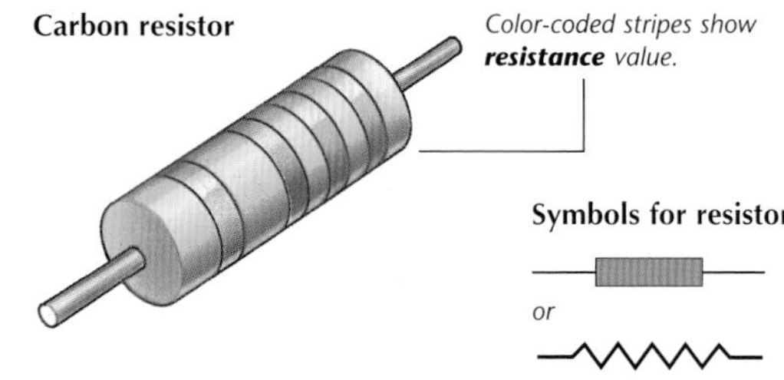
Carbon resistor
Color-coded stripes show resistance value.
Symbols for resistor
or

* **Battery**, 68; **Conductor**, 56; **Electromotive force (e.m.f.)**, 60; **Insulator**, 56; **Potential difference**, 58; **Power**, 9; **Reciprocal**, 345; **Semiconductors**, 65.

Conductivity

The ability of a substance to allow the flow of current (see also **conductor** and **insulator**, page 56). It is the inverse of the **resistivity**.

Internal resistance (r)

The **resistance** of a **cell*** or **battery*** to the current it causes. It is the resistance of the connections in the cell and some chemical effects (e.g. **polarization***). The current in a circuit may therefore be less than expected.

***Internal resistance** is part of **resistance** of circuit.*

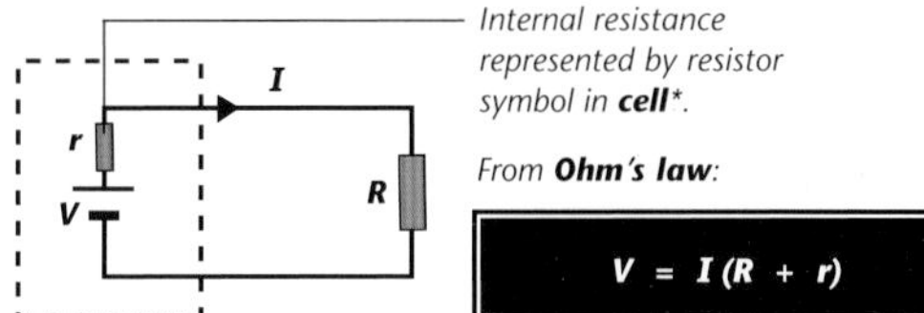
I
r
V
R
Internal resistance represented by resistor symbol in cell*.
From Ohm's law:
V = I(R + r)

Variable resistor

A device whose **resistance** can be changed mechanically. It is either a coil of wire of a particular **resistivity** around a drum along which a contact moves (for high currents) or a carbon track with a moving contact. A variable resistor can be used as a **potential divider** if an extra contact is added. It is then a **potentiometer**.

Types of variable resistor

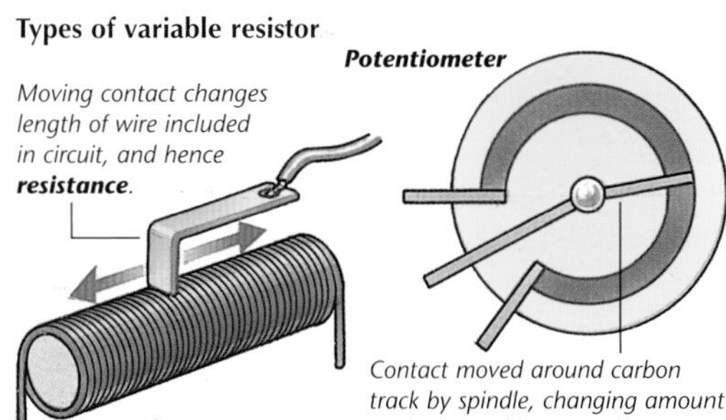
Potentiometer
Moving contact changes length of wire included in circuit, and hence resistance.
Rheostat
Contact moved around carbon track by spindle, changing amount in circuit, and hence resistance.

Potential divider or voltage divider

A device used to produce a **potential difference*** from another, higher potential difference.

Circuit diagram of potential divider

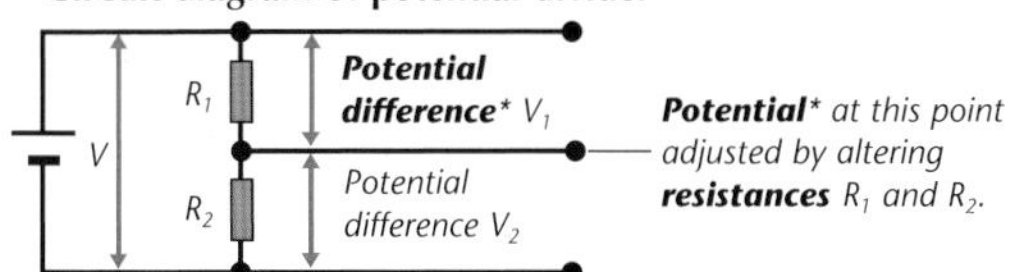
R1
R2
V
Potential difference* V1
Potential difference V2
Potential* at this point adjusted by altering resistances R1 and R2.

Wheatstone bridge

A circuit used to measure an unknown **resistance** (see diagram). When the **galvanometer*** indicates no current, the unknown value of one **resistor** can be calculated from the other three. The **meter bridge** is a version of the wheatstone bridge in which two of the resistors are replaced by a meter of wire with a high resistance. The position of the contact from the galvanometer on the wire gives the ratio R_3/R_4 in the circuit shown below.

Wheatstone bridge

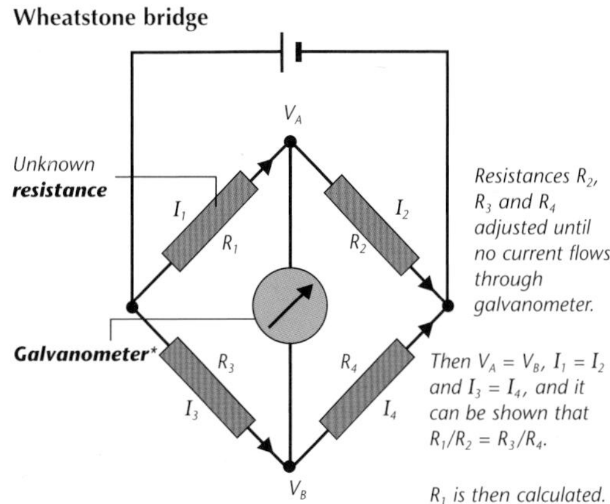
VA
Unknown resistance
I1
R1
I2
R2
Resistances R2, R3 and R4 adjusted until no current flows through galvanometer.
Galvanometer*
R3
I3
R4
I4
Then VA = VB, I1 = I2 and I3 = I4, and it can be shown that R1/R2 = R3/R4.
VB
R1 is then calculated.

Kirchhoff's laws

Two laws which summarize conditions for the flow of current at an instant. The first states that the total current flowing towards a junction is equal to the total current flowing away from the junction. The second states that the sum of the **potential differences*** around a circuit, which for each **resistor** is the product of the current and the **resistance**, is equal to the **electromotive force*** applied to the circuit.

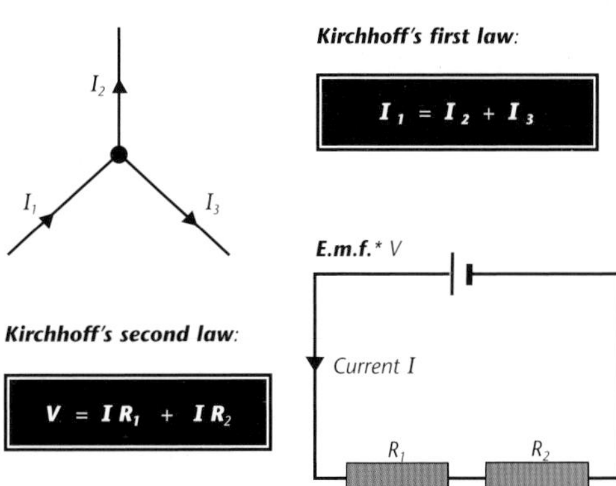
I2
I1
I3
Kirchhoff's first law:
I1 = I2 + I3
E.m.f.* V
Current I
R1
R2
Kirchhoff's second law:
V = IR1 + IR2

* **Battery**, **Cell**, 68; **Electromotive force (e.m.f.)**, 60; **Galvanometer**, 77; **Polarization**, 68; **Potential**, **Potential difference**, 58.

Controlling current (continued)

Series

An arrangement of components in which all of the current passes through them one after the other.

Resistors* in **series**

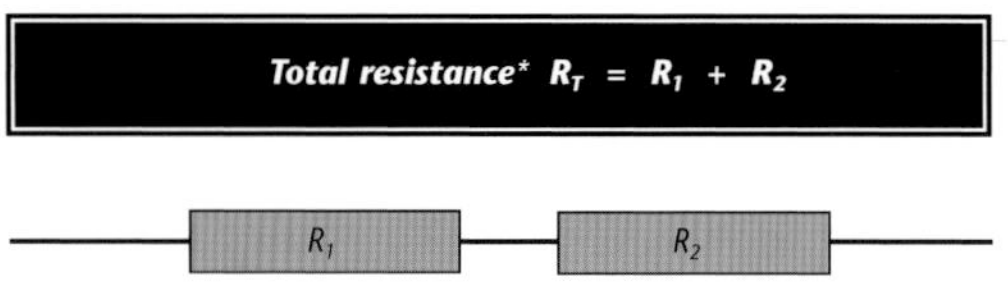
Total resistance* $R_T = R_1 + R_2$
R_1
R_2

Capacitors* in **series**

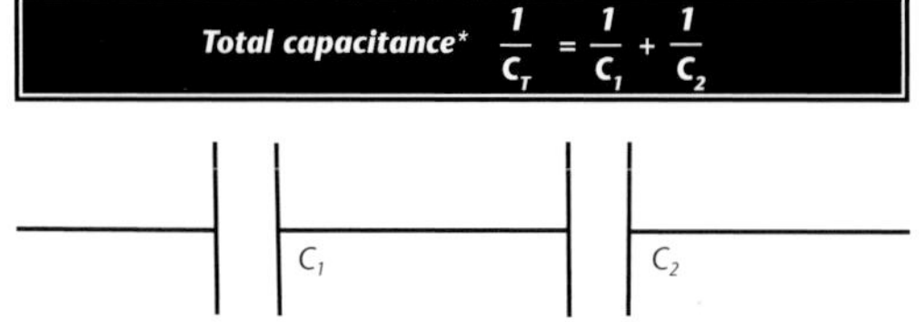
Total capacitance* $\frac{1}{C_T} = \frac{1}{C_1} + \frac{1}{C_2}$
C_1
C_2

Parallel

An arrangement of components in which current divides to pass through all at once.

Resistors* in parallel

Capacitors* in parallel

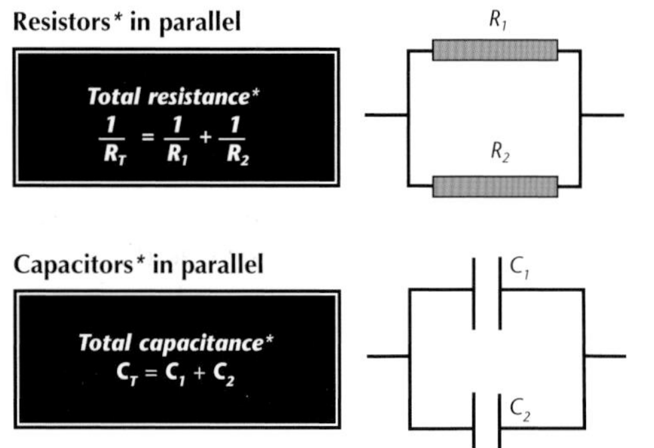
Total resistance* $\frac{1}{R_T} = \frac{1}{R_1} + \frac{1}{R_2}$
R_1
R_2
Total capacitance* $C_T = C_1 + C_2$
C_1
C_2

Filament lamp

A lamp consisting of a coil of tungsten wire (the **filament**) inside a glass bulb containing argon or nitrogen gas at low pressure. When current flows through the coil, it heats up rapidly and gives out light. Tungsten is used because it has a very high melting point and the bulb is gas-filled to reduce evaporation of the tungsten.

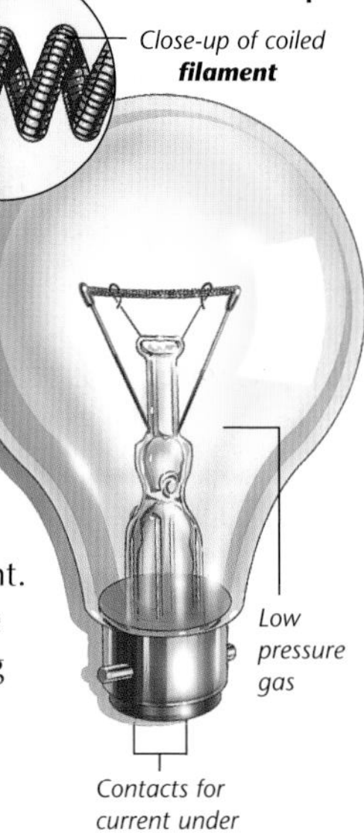
Filament lamp
Close-up of coiled filament
Low pressure gas
Contacts for current under base of bulb

Switch

A device, normally mechanical (but see also **transistor**), which is used to make or break a circuit. A **relay*** is used when a small current is required to switch a larger current on and off.

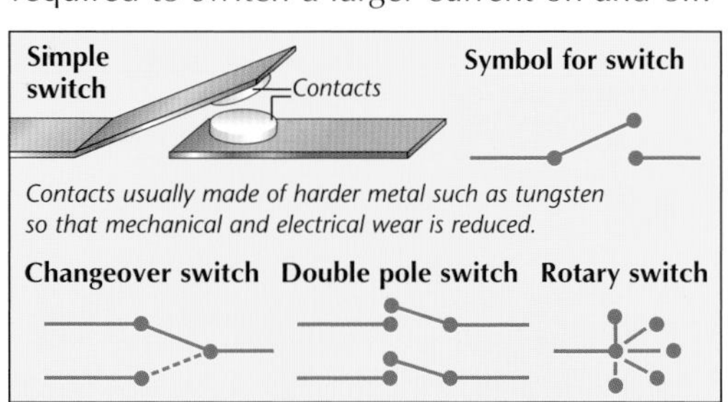
Simple switch
Contacts
Symbol for switch
Contacts usually made of harder metal such as tungsten so that mechanical and electrical wear is reduced.
Changeover switch
Double pole switch
Rotary switch

Impedance

The ratio of the **potential difference*** applied to a circuit to the **alternating current*** which flows in it. It is due to two things, the **resistance*** of the circuit and the **reactance**. The effect of impedance is that the **e.m.f.*** and current can be out of phase.

Reactance

The "active" part of **impedance** to **alternating current***. It is caused by **capacitance*** and **inductance** in a circuit which alter the **electromotive forces*** as the current changes.

Inductance

The part of the **impedance** of a circuit due to changing current affecting the **e.m.f.*** (see also **electromagnetic induction**, page 78). This happens in a device called an **inductor**.

Alternating potential difference*

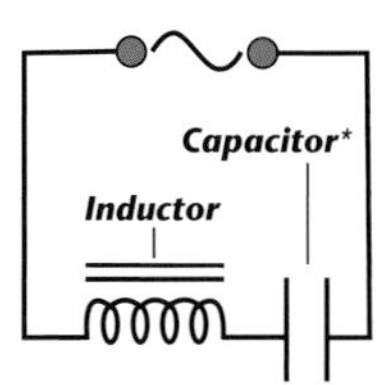
Capacitor*
Inductor

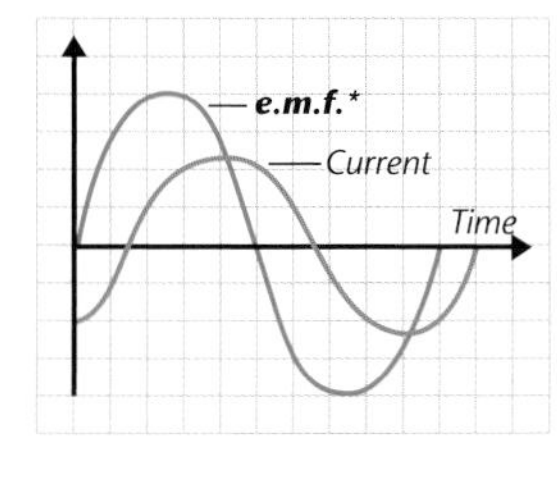
e.m.f.*
Current
Time

* **Alternating current**, 61; **Capacitance**, **Capacitor**, 59; **Electromotive force** (**e.m.f.**), 60; **Potential difference**, 58; **Relay**, 75; **Resistance**, **Resistor**, 62.

SEMICONDUCTORS

Semiconductors are materials whose **resistivity*** is between that of a **conductor** and an **insulator** (see page 56) and decreases with increasing temperature or increasing amounts of impurities (see **doping**, below). They are widely used in electronic circuits (see also page 111).

Doping

The introduction of a small amount of impurity into a semiconductor. Depending on the impurity used, the semiconductor is known as either a **p-type** or **n-type**. Combinations of these types are used to make **diodes** and **transistors**.

Diode

A device made from one piece of **p-type** semiconductor (see **doping**) and one piece of **n-type** semiconductor joined together. It has a very low **resistance*** in one direction (when it is said to be **forward biased**) and a very high resistance in the other direction (**reverse biased**).

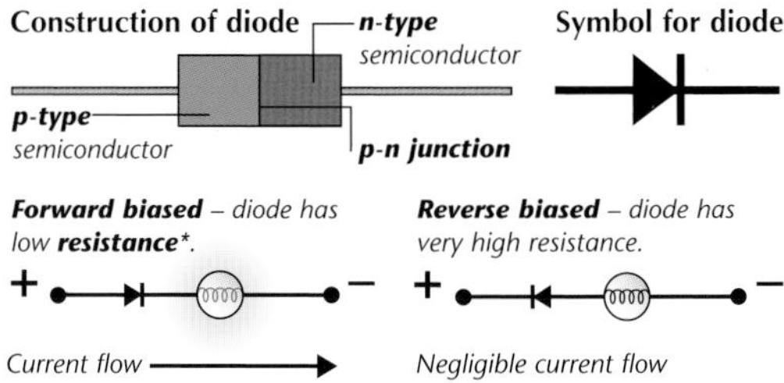
Construction of diode
n-type semiconductor
p-type semiconductor
p-n junction
Symbol for diode
Forward biased – diode has low resistance*.
Reverse biased – diode has very high resistance.
Current flow
Negligible current flow

Half-wave rectification

The use of a **diode** to remove all the current flowing in one direction from **alternating current***. Current only flows one way around the circuit.

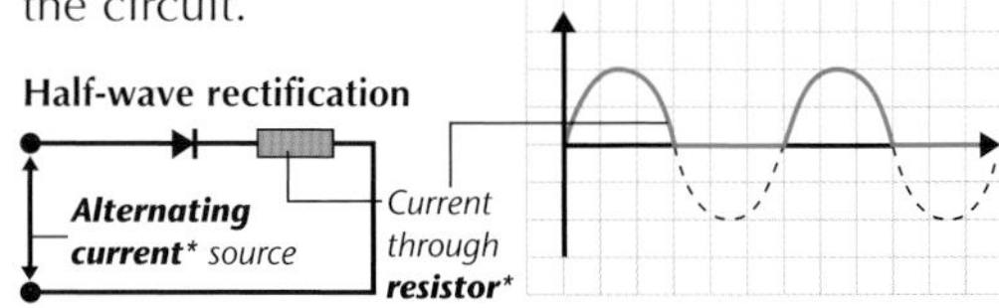
Half-wave rectification
Alternating current* source
Current through resistor*

Full-wave rectification

The conversion of **alternating current*** to **direct current***. It is used when direct current is required from alternating current.

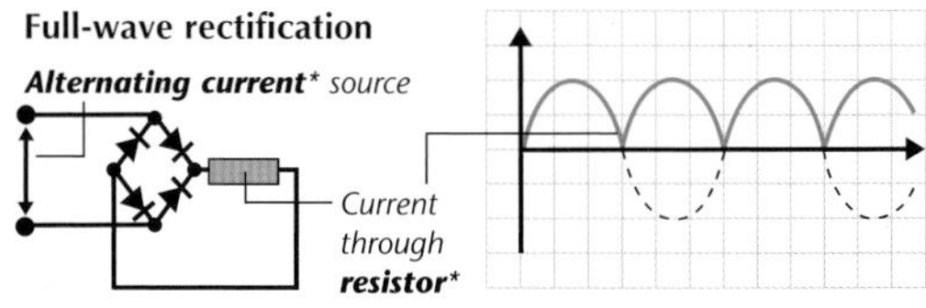
Full-wave rectification
Alternating current* source
Current through resistor*

Light emitting diode (LED)

A **diode** with a higher **resistance*** than normal, in which light is produced instead of heat.

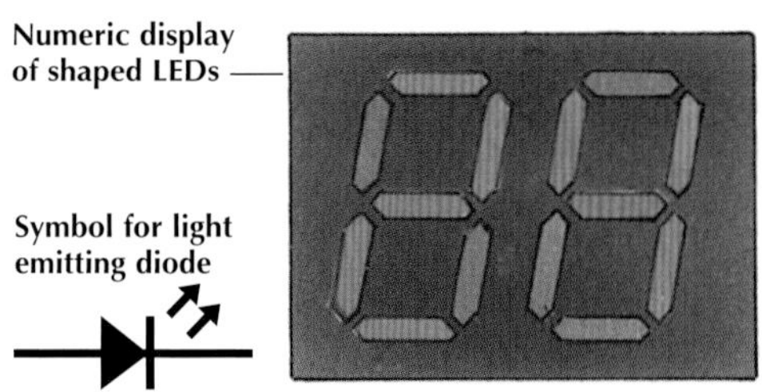
Numeric display of shaped LEDs
Symbol for light emitting diode

Thermistor

A semiconductor device whose **resistance*** varies with temperature, used in electronic circuits to detect temperature changes.

Transistor

A semiconductor, normally made from a combination of the two types of semiconductor. There are three connections, the **base**, **collector** and **emitter** (see diagrams below). The **resistance*** between the collector and emitter changes from very high to very low when a small current flows into the base. This small base current can therefore be used to control a much larger collector to emitter current.

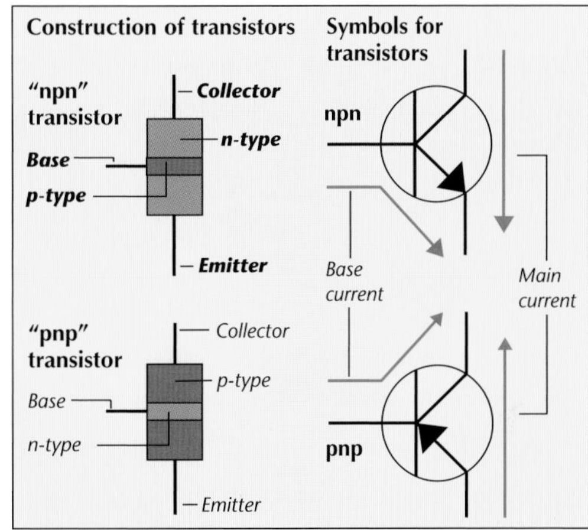
Construction of transistors
Symbols for transistors
"npn" transistor
Collector
n-type
Base
p-type
Emitter
npn
Base current
Main current
"pnp" transistor
Collector
p-type
Base
n-type
Emitter
pnp

* **Alternating current**, 61; **Direct current**, 61; **Resistance**, **Resistivity**, **Resistor**, 62.

ELECTROLYSIS

Electrolysis is the process whereby electric current flows through a liquid containing **ions*** (atoms which have gained or lost an **electron*** to become charged) and the liquid is broken down as a result. The current is conducted by the movement of ions in the liquid, and chemicals are deposited at the points where the current enters or leaves the liquid. There are a number of industrial applications.

Electrolyte

A compound which conducts electricity when either molten or dissolved in water. All compounds made from ions or which split into ions when dissolved (**ionization***) are electrolytes. The concentration of ions in an electrolyte determines how well it conducts electricity.

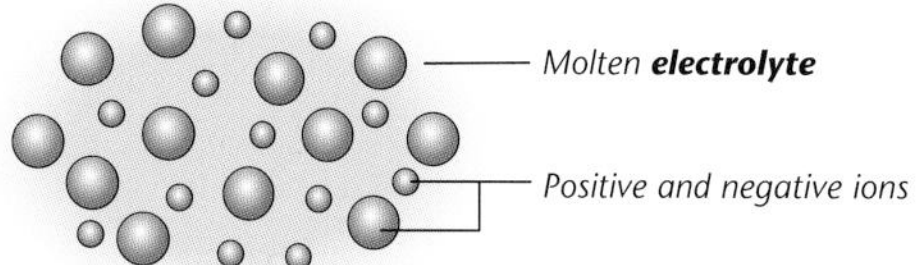

Molten electrolyte
Positive and negative ions

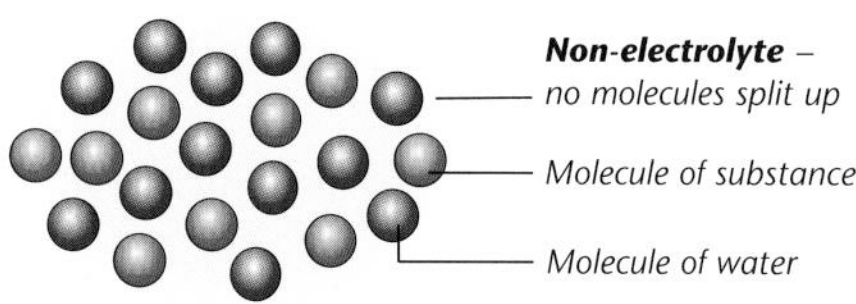

Non-electrolyte – no molecules split up
Molecule of substance
Molecule of water

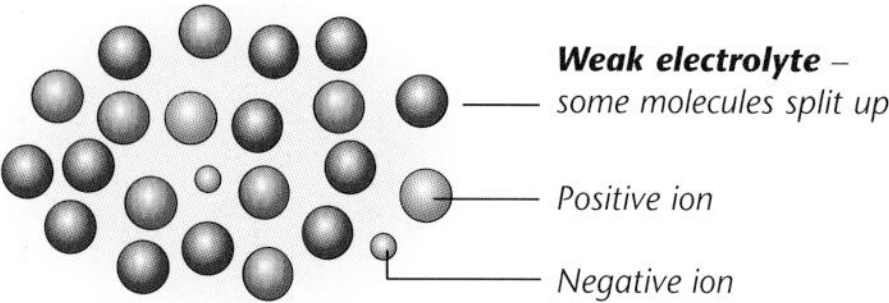

Weak electrolyte – some molecules split up
Positive ion
Negative ion

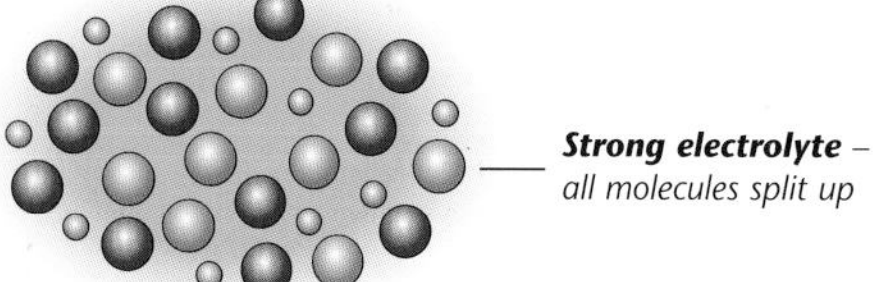

Strong electrolyte – all molecules split up

Electrode

A piece of metal or carbon placed in an **electrolyte** through which electric current enters or leaves during electrolysis. Two are needed – the **anode** (positive electrode) and the **cathode** (negative electrode). An **active electrode** is one which is chemically changed by electrolysis; an **inert electrode** is one which is not changed.

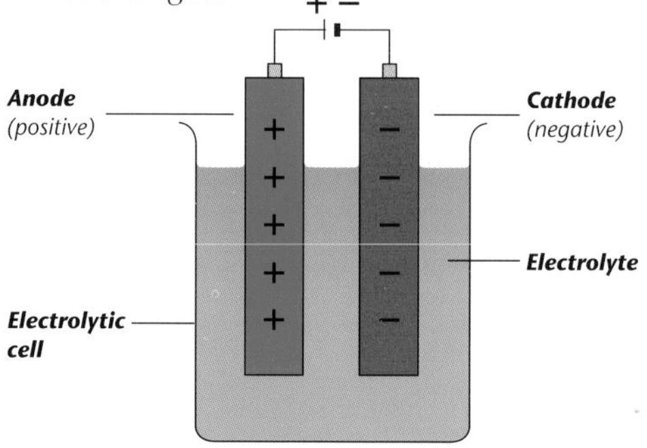

+ –
Anode (positive)
Cathode (negative)
Electrolyte
Electrolytic cell

Electrolytic cell

A vessel in which electrolysis takes place. It contains the **electrolyte** and the **electrodes**.

Ionic theory of electrolysis

A theory which attempts to explain what happens in the **electrolyte** and at the **electrodes** during electrolysis. It states that the **cations** (positive ions) are attracted towards the **cathode** and the **anions** (negative ions) towards the **anode**. There they gain or lose electrons respectively to form atoms (they are then said to be **discharged**). If there are two or more different anions, then one of them will be discharged in preference to the others. This is called **preferential discharge**.

Electrolysis of copper sulphate solution

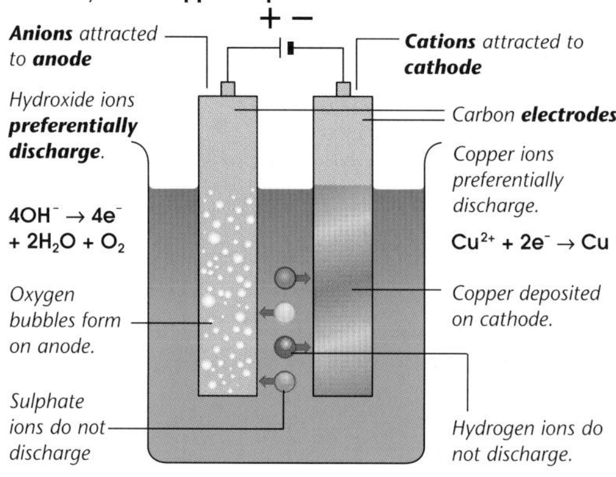

+ –
Anions attracted to anode
Cations attracted to cathode
Hydroxide ions preferentially discharge.
Carbon electrodes
Copper ions preferentially discharge.
$4OH^- \rightarrow 4e^- + 2H_2O + O_2$
$Cu^{2+} + 2e^- \rightarrow Cu$
Oxygen bubbles form on anode.
Copper deposited on cathode.
Sulphate ions do not discharge
Hydrogen ions do not discharge.

* **Electrons**, 83; **Ions**, 88 (**Ionization**).

Faraday's laws of electrolysis

Two laws which relate the quantity of electricity which passes through an **electrolyte** to the masses of the substances which are deposited. **Faraday's first law** states that the mass of the substance deposited is proportional to the quantity of electricity (the **electrochemical equivalent** of a substance is the mass liberated by one ampere flowing for one second). **Faraday's second law** states that the mass of the substance deposited is inversely proportional to the size of the charge on its ion.

Electrolysis of copper sulphate solution with copper electrodes (copper voltameter)

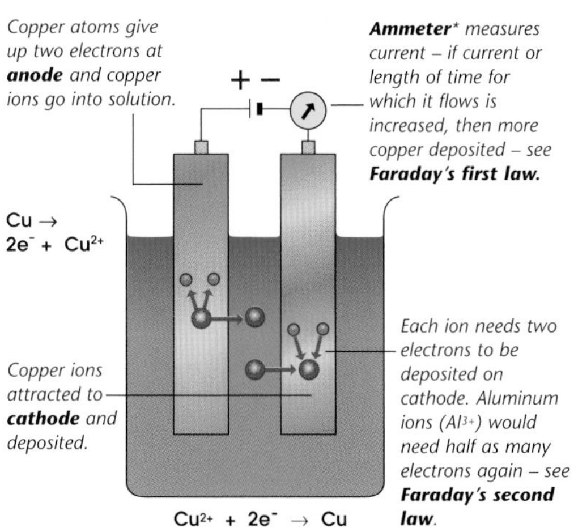

Copper atoms give up two electrons at **anode** and copper ions go into solution.
+ –
Ammeter* measures current – if current or length of time for which it flows is increased, then more copper deposited – see **Faraday's first law.**
$Cu \rightarrow 2e^- + Cu^{2+}$
Each ion needs two electrons to be deposited on cathode. Aluminum ions (Al^{3+}) would need half as many electrons again – see **Faraday's second law**.
Copper ions attracted to **cathode** and deposited.
$Cu^{2+} + 2e^- \rightarrow Cu$

Voltameter or coulometer

An **electrolytic cell** used for investigating the relationships between the amount of substance produced at the **electrodes** and the current which passes through the cell. For example, the **copper voltameter** (see below left) contains copper sulphate and copper electrodes.

Hoffmann voltameter

A type of **voltameter** used for collecting and measuring the volumes (and hence the masses) of gases liberated during electrolysis. For example, electrolysis of acidified water produces hydrogen and oxygen in a two to one ratio (note that this also indicates the chemical composition of water, i.e. H_2O).

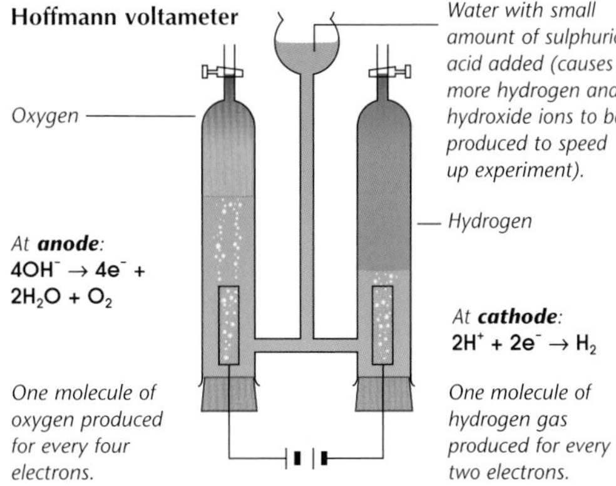

Hoffmann voltameter
Water with small amount of sulphuric acid added (causes more hydrogen and hydroxide ions to be produced to speed up experiment).
Oxygen
Hydrogen
At **anode**: $4OH^- \rightarrow 4e^- + 2H_2O + O_2$
At **cathode**: $2H^+ + 2e^- \rightarrow H_2$
One molecule of oxygen produced for every four electrons.
One molecule of hydrogen gas produced for every two electrons.

Uses of electrolysis

Electroplating or electrodeposition

The coating of a metal object with a thin layer of another metal by electrolysis. The object forms the **cathode**, and ions of the coating metal are in the **electrolyte**.

*Steel is cheap but **corrodes*** easily, so steel food cans are plated with a very fine layer of tin (which is less reactive) to prevent corrosion.*

Electro-refining

A method of purifying metals by electrolysis. Impure metal forms the **anode**, from which metal ions move to the **cathode** and form pure metal. The impurities fall to the bottom of the vessel.

Metal extraction

A process which produces metals from their molten ores by electrolysis. Very reactive metals are obtained by this process, e.g. sodium and aluminum.

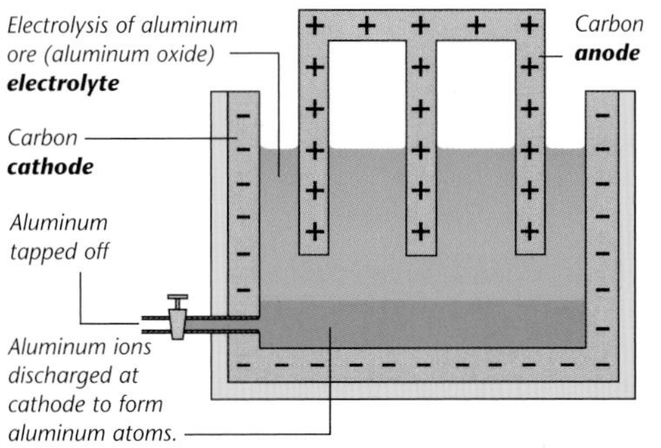

Electrolysis of aluminum ore (aluminum oxide) **electrolyte**
Carbon **anode**
Carbon **cathode**
Aluminum tapped off
Aluminum ions discharged at cathode to form aluminum atoms.

* **Ammeter**, 77; **Corrosion**, 209.

CELLS AND BATTERIES

The Italian scientist Volta first showed that a **potential difference*** exists between two different metals when they are placed in certain liquids (**electrolytes***) and therefore that a **direct current*** can be produced from chemical energy. This arrangement is called a **cell**, **electrochemical** or **voltaic cell**. The potential difference (caused by chemical changes in the cell) is called an **electromotive force*** and its size depends on the metals used. A **battery** is two or more connected cells.

G F M D D C C

Engraving showing an experiment with frog's legs

*Early experiments showed that fluids in a dead frog act as an **electrolyte*** and carry current between two pieces of metal.*

Voltaic pile

The first battery made, consisting of a pile of silver and zinc disks separated by cardboard or cloth soaked in salt water. This arrangement is the same as a number of **simple cells** linked together.

Close-up of a Voltaic pile

Volta's battery, known as a Voltaic pile

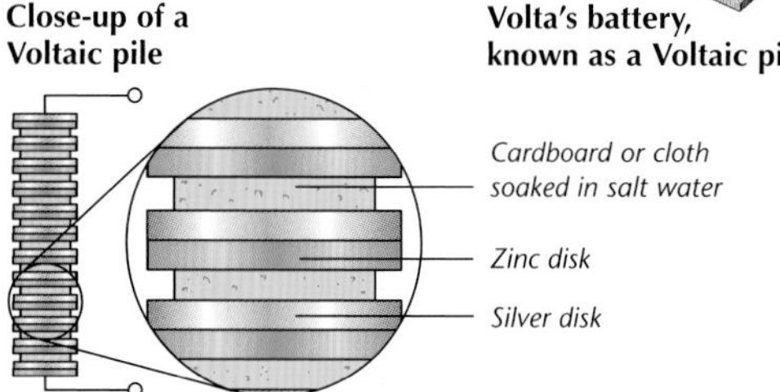
Cardboard or cloth soaked in salt water
Zinc disk
Silver disk

Simple cell

Two plates of different metals separated by a salt or acid solution **electrolyte*** (normally copper and zinc plates and dilute sulphuric acid). The simple cell only produces an **electromotive force*** for a short time before **polarization** and **local action** have an effect.

Action of simple cell

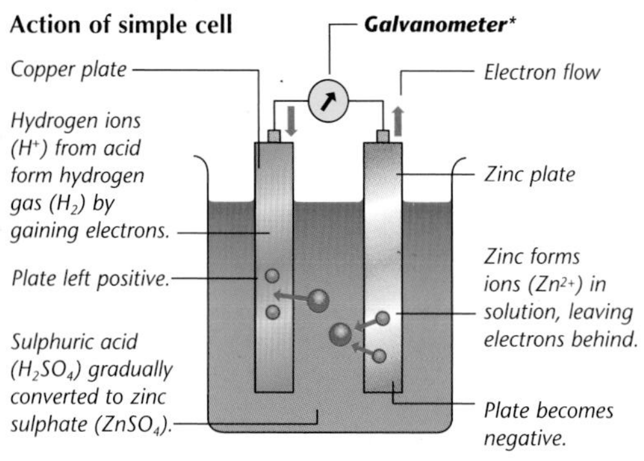
*Galvanometer**
Copper plate
Electron flow
Hydrogen ions (H^+) from acid form hydrogen gas (H_2) by gaining electrons.
Zinc plate
Plate left positive.
Zinc forms ions (Zn^{2+}) in solution, leaving electrons behind.
Sulphuric acid (H_2SO_4) gradually converted to zinc sulphate ($ZnSO_4$).
Plate becomes negative.

Polarization

The formation of bubbles of hydrogen on the copper plate in a **simple cell**. This reduces the **electromotive force*** of the cell, both because the bubbles insulate the plate and also because a **back e.m.f.*** is set up. Polarization can be eliminated by adding a **depolarizing agent**, which reacts with the hydrogen to form water.

Polarization and local action in a simple cell

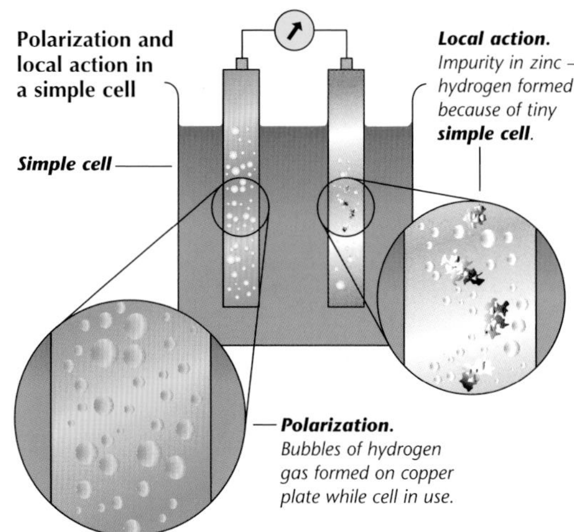
Local action. *Impurity in zinc – hydrogen formed because of tiny **simple cell**.*
Simple cell
Polarization. *Bubbles of hydrogen gas formed on copper plate while cell in use.*

Local action

The production of hydrogen at the zinc plate in a **simple cell**. Impurities (traces of other metals) in the zinc plate mean that tiny simple cells are formed which produce hydrogen due to **polarization**. Hydrogen is also produced as the zinc dissolves in the acid (even when the cell is not working). Local action can be prevented by coating the plate with an **amalgam***.

* **Amalgam**, 344; **Back e.m.f.**, 60 (**Electromotive force**); **Direct current**, 61; **Electrolyte**, 66; **Galvanometer**, 77; **Potential difference**, 58.

Capacity
The ability of a cell to produce current over a period of time. It is measured in **ampere hours**. For example, a 10 ampere-hour cell should produce one ampere for 10 hours.

Leclanché cell
A cell in which **polarization** is overcome by manganese dioxide (a **depolarizing agent**). This removes hydrogen more slowly than it is formed, but continues working to remove excess hydrogen when the cell is not in use. The cell provides an **electromotive force*** of 1.5V.

Leclanché cell

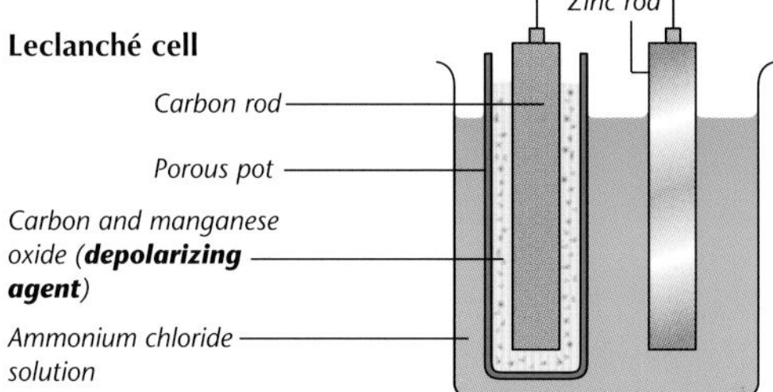
Zinc rod
Carbon rod
Porous pot
Carbon and manganese oxide (**depolarizing agent**)
Ammonium chloride solution

Dry cell
A version of the **Leclanché cell** in which the ammonium chloride solution is replaced by paste containing ammonium chloride, meaning that it is portable. The cell provides an **electromotive force*** of 1.5V. Dry cells deteriorate slowly due to **local action**, but still have a life of many months.

Dry cell

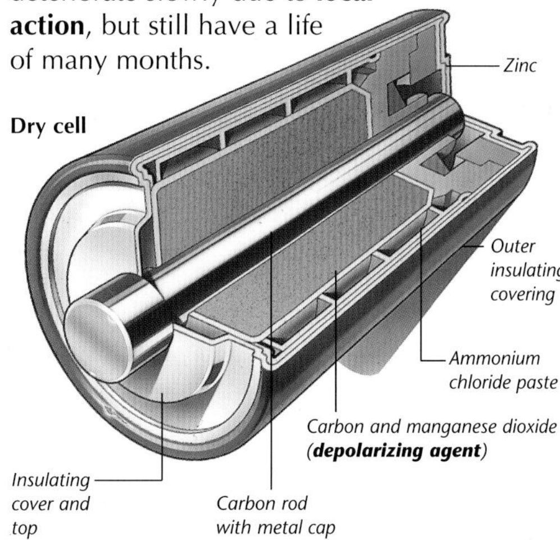
Zinc
Outer insulating covering
Ammonium chloride paste
Carbon and manganese dioxide (**depolarizing agent**)
Insulating cover and top
Carbon rod with metal cap

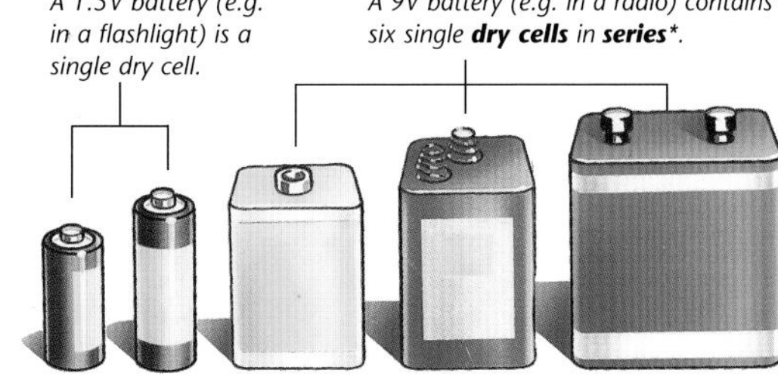
A 1.5V battery (e.g. in a flashlight) is a single dry cell.
A 9V battery (e.g. in a radio) contains six single **dry cells** in **series***.

Standard cell
A cell which produces an accurately known and constant **electromotive force***. It is used in laboratories for experimental work.

Primary cell
Any cell which has a limited life because the chemicals inside it are eventually used up and cannot be replaced easily.

Secondary cell
Also known as an **accumulator** or **storage cell**. A cell which can be recharged by connection to another source of electricity. The main types are the **lead-acid accumulator** and the **nickel-cadmiun alkaline cell**.

Alkaline cell
A secondary cell containing an **electrolyte*** of potassium hydroxide solution. The plates are normally made of nickel and cadmium compounds (it is then called a **nickel-cadmium cell**). Alkaline cells may be left for months in a discharged condition without ill-effect.

Lead-acid accumulator
A **secondary cell** containing a dilute sulphuric acid **electrolyte***, and plates made from lead and lead compounds. The cell can give out a very large current because it has a low **internal resistance***. It is mainly used in vehicles for starting and lighting.

Battery consisting of lead-acid accumulators

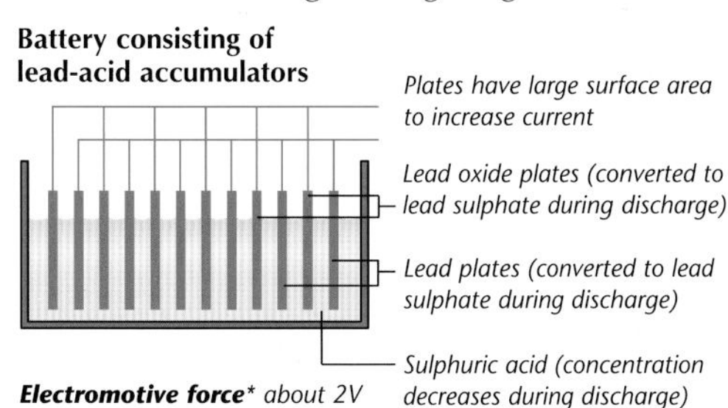
Plates have large surface area to increase current
Lead oxide plates (converted to lead sulphate during discharge)
Lead plates (converted to lead sulphate during discharge)
Sulphuric acid (concentration decreases during discharge)
Electromotive force* about 2V

* **Electromotive force (e.m.f.)**, 60; **Electrolyte**, 66; **Internal resistance**, 63; **Series**, 64.

MAGNETS

All **magnets** have a **magnetic field*** around them, and a **magnetic force*** exists between two magnets due to the interaction of their fields. Any material which is capable of being **magnetized** (can become a magnet) is described as **magnetic** (see **ferromagnetic**, below) and becomes magnetized when placed in a magnetic field. The movement of charge (normally **electrons***) also causes a magnetic field (see **electromagnetism**, pages 74-76).

These paper clips have been temporarily ***magnetized****.*

Pole

A point in a magnet at which its **magnetic force*** appears to be concentrated. There are two types of pole – the **north** or **north seeking pole** and the **south** or **south seeking pole** (identified by allowing the magnet to line up with the Earth's **magnetic field***). All magnets have an equal number of each type of pole. The **first law of magnetism** states that unlike poles attract and like poles repel.

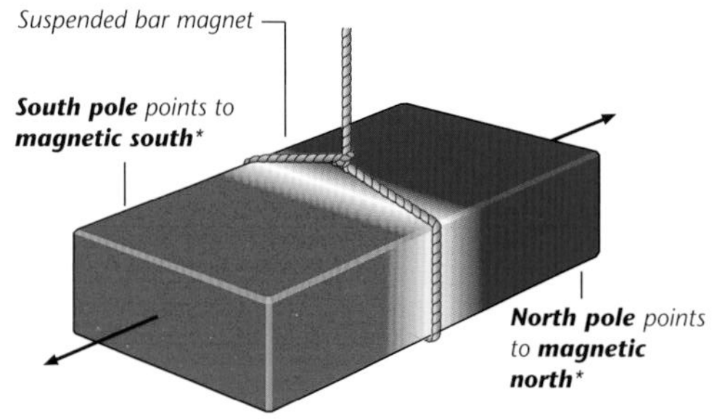

Suspended bar magnet
South pole points to magnetic south*
North pole points to magnetic north*

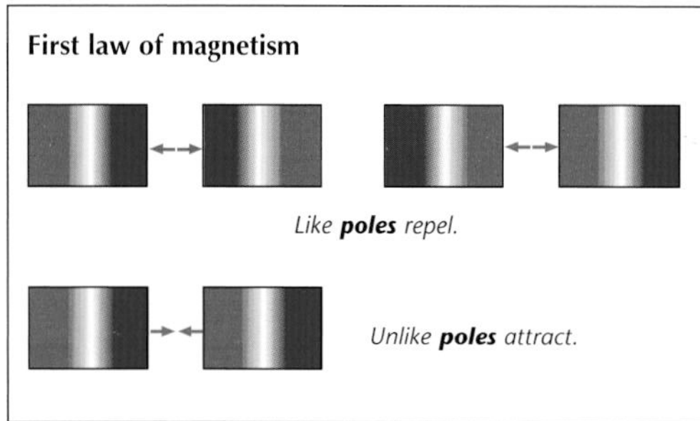

First law of magnetism
Like poles repel.
Unlike poles attract.

Magnetic axis

An imaginary line about which the **magnetic field*** of a magnet is symmetrical.

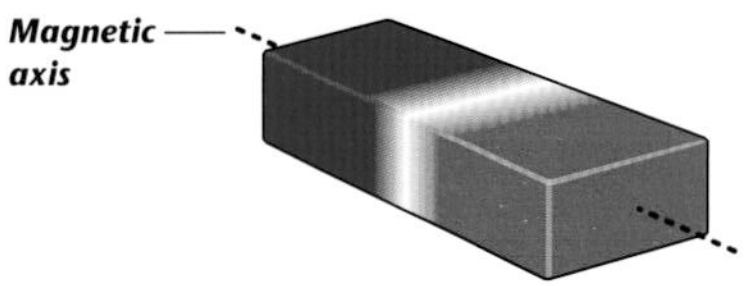

Magnetic axis

Ferromagnetic

Describes a material which is strongly magnetic (i.e. is magnetized easily). Iron, nickel, cobalt and alloys of these are ferromagnetic, and are described as either **hard** or **soft**. **Sintered** materials (made by converting various mixtures of powders of the above metals into solids by heat and pressure) can be made magnetically very hard or soft by changing the metals used.

Hard

Describes a **ferromagnetic** material which does not easily lose its magnetism after being magnetized, e.g. steel. Magnets made from these materials are called **permanent magnets**.

Hard ferromagnetic *materials are used as* ***permanent magnets****, e.g. as compass needles.*

Soft

Describes a **ferromagnetic** material which does not retain its magnetism after being magnetized, e.g. iron. Magnets made from these materials are called **temporary magnets**. **Residual magnetism** is the small amount of magnetism which can be left in magnetically soft materials.

Soft ferromagnetic *materials are used as* ***cores**** *in* ***electromagnets****.*

Susceptibility

A measurement of the ability of a substance to become magnetized. **Ferromagnetic** materials have a high susceptibility.

* **Core**, **Electromagnet**, 74; **Electrons**, 83; **Magnetic field**, 72; **Magnetic force**, 6; **Magnetic north**, **Magnetic south**, 73.

Domain theory of magnetism

States that **ferromagnetic** materials consist of **dipoles** or **molecular magnets**, which interact with each other. These are all arranged in areas called **domains**, in which they all point in the same direction. A ferromagnetic material becomes magnetized when the domains become **ordered** (i.e. aligned).

*In a non-magnetized state, **domains** are jumbled. The overall effect is that the domains cancel each other out.*

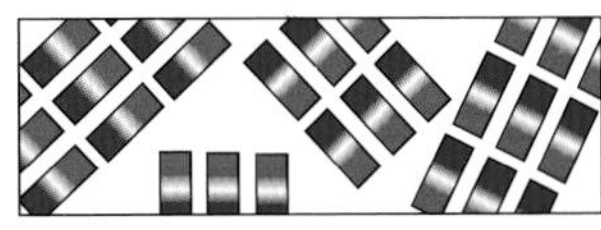

*In a magnetized state, **domains** are ordered. If ordered completely (as here) magnet is **saturated** – cannot become stronger.*

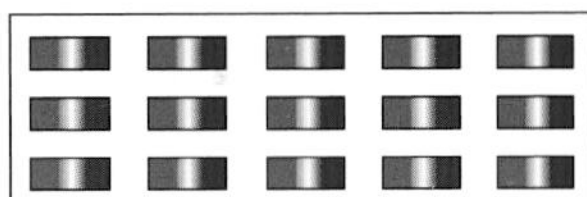

Magnetization

When an object is magnetized, all the **dipoles** become aligned (see **domain theory**). This only happens when an object is in a **magnetic field*** and is called **induced magnetism**.

Induced magnetism

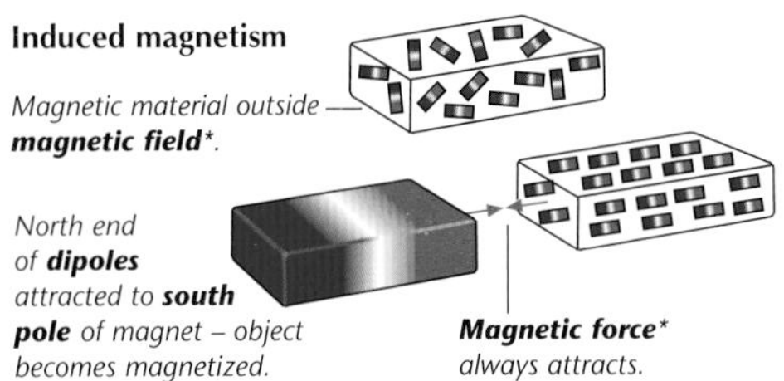
Magnetic material outside magnetic field*.
North end of dipoles attracted to south pole of magnet – object becomes magnetized.
Magnetic force* always attracts.

Single touch

A method of magnetizing an object by stroking it repeatedly with the **pole** of a **permanent magnet** (see **hard**). Magnetism is induced in the object from the **magnetic field*** of the magnet.

Magnetism induced by single touch

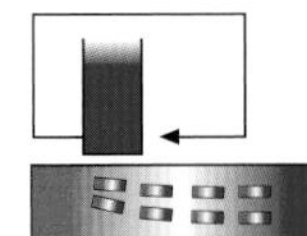

Divided touch

A method of magnetizing an object by stroking it repeatedly from the center out with the opposite **poles** of two **permanent magnets** (see **hard**). Magnetism is induced in the object from the **magnetic field*** of the magnets.

Magnetism induced by divided touch

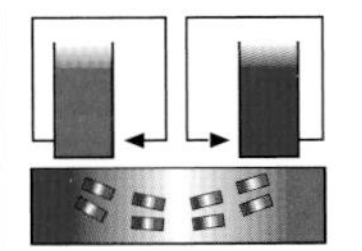

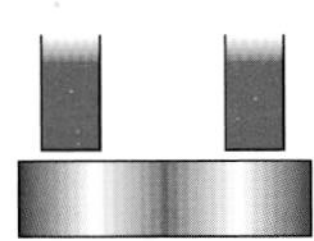

*Consequent poles are produced when like poles are used in **divided touch**.*

Demagnetization

The removal of magnetism from an object. This can be achieved by placing the object in a changing **magnetic field***, such as that created by a coil carrying **alternating current***. Alternatively, the **dipoles** (see **domain theory**, above) can be excited to point in random directions by hammering randomly or by heating above 700°C.

Self-demagnetization

Loss of magnetism by a magnet because of the attraction of the **dipoles** (see **domain theory**) for the opposite **poles** of the magnet. It is reduced using pieces of soft iron (called **keepers**) arranged to form a closed loop of poles.

Self-demagnetization of bar magnet

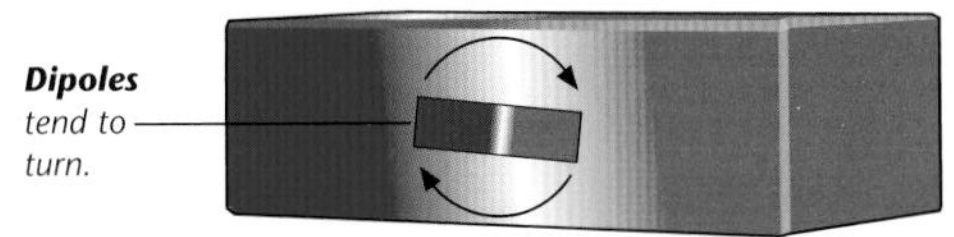
Dipoles tend to turn.

Reducing self-demagnetization

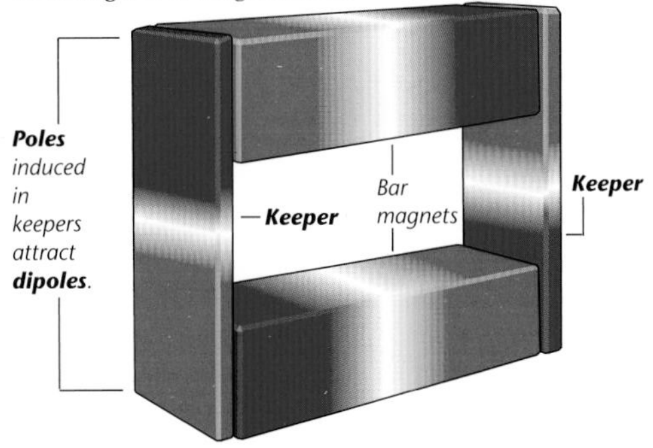
Poles induced in keepers attract dipoles.
Keeper
Bar magnets
Keeper

* **Alternating current**, 61; **Magnetic field**, 72; **Magnetic force**, 6.

MAGNETIC FIELDS

A **magnetic field** is a region around a **magnet** (see page 70) in which objects are affected by the **magnetic force***. The strength and direction of the magnetic field are shown by **magnetic field lines**.

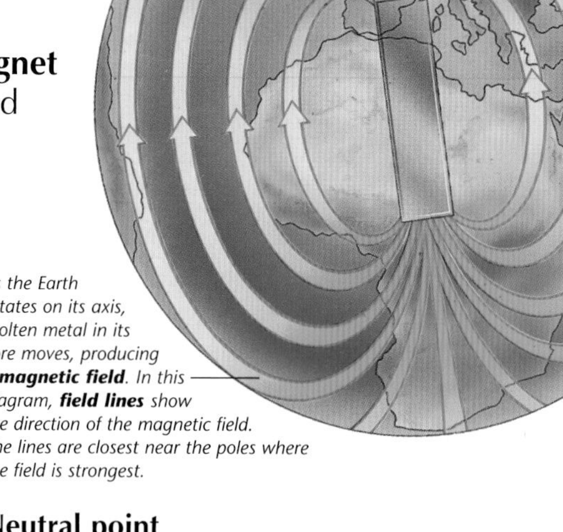

*As the Earth rotates on its axis, molten metal in its core moves, producing a **magnetic field**. In this diagram, **field lines** show the direction of the magnetic field. The lines are closest near the poles where the field is strongest.*

Magnetic field lines or flux lines

Lines which indicate the direction of the magnetic field around a magnet. They also show the strength of the field (see **magnetic flux density**, below). The direction of the field is the direction of the force on a **north pole***. Magnetic field lines are plotted by sprinkling iron filings around a magnet or by recording the direction of a **plotting compass** (a small compass with no directions marked on it) at various points.

Result of sprinkling iron filings around a magnet

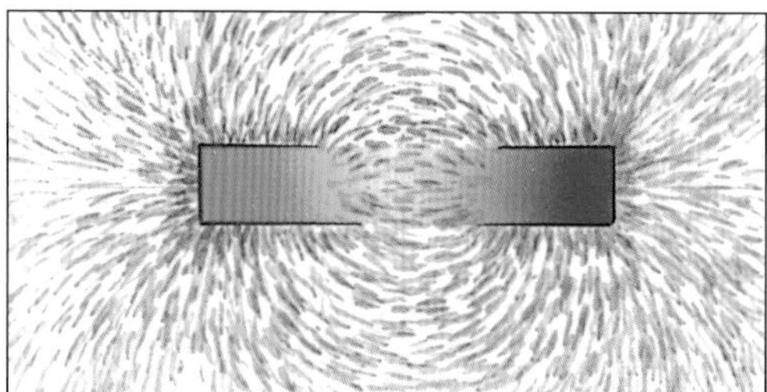

*Iron filings line up due to **induced magnetism****.

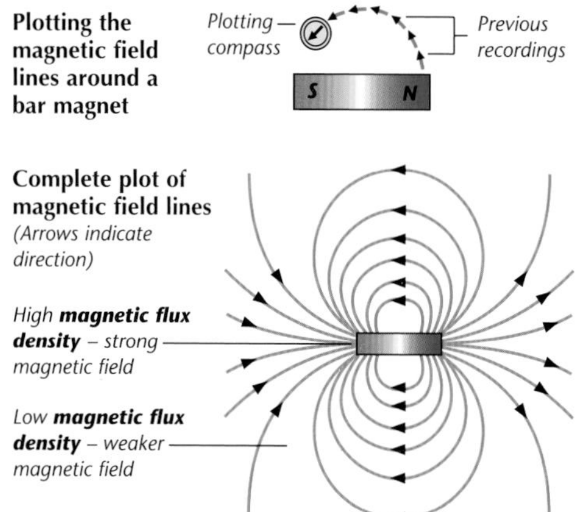
Plotting the magnetic field lines around a bar magnet
Plotting compass
Previous recordings
S
N
Complete plot of magnetic field lines
(Arrows indicate direction)
High magnetic flux density – strong magnetic field
Low magnetic flux density – weaker magnetic field

Magnetic flux density

A measurement of the strength of a magnetic field at a point. This is shown by the closeness of the **magnetic field lines** to each other. Magnetic flux density is normally highest around the **poles***.

Neutral point

A point of zero magnetism (the **magnetic flux density** is zero). It occurs where two or more magnetic fields interact with an equal but opposite effect. A bar magnet positioned along the **magnetic meridian**, with the **south pole*** pointing to the north, has two neutral points in line with its **magnetic axis***.

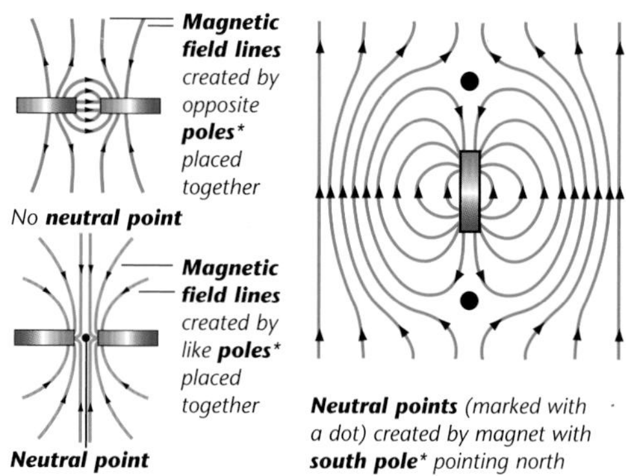
Magnetic field lines created by opposite poles* placed together
No neutral point
Magnetic field lines created by like poles* placed together
Neutral point

Neutral points** (marked with a dot) created by magnet with **south pole pointing north*

Diamagnetism

Magnetism displayed by some substances when placed in a strong magnetic field. A piece of diamagnetic material tends to spread **magnetic field lines** out and lines up with its long side perpendicular to them.

Paramagnetism

Magnetism displayed by some substances when placed in a strong magnetic field. A piece of paramagnetic material tends to concentrate **magnetic field lines** through it and lines up with its long side parallel to them. It is caused by **dipoles*** moving slightly towards alignment.

* **Dipole**, 71 (**Domain theory of magnetism**); **Electrons**, 83; **Induced magnetism**, 71; **Magnetic force**, 6; **Magnetic axis**, **Pole**, 70.

The Earth's magnetism

The Earth has a magnetic field which acts as though there were a giant bar magnet in its center, lined up approximately between its geographic north and south poles, although the angle is constantly changing. The north pole of a compass points towards a point called **magnetic north**, its south pole to **magnetic south**.

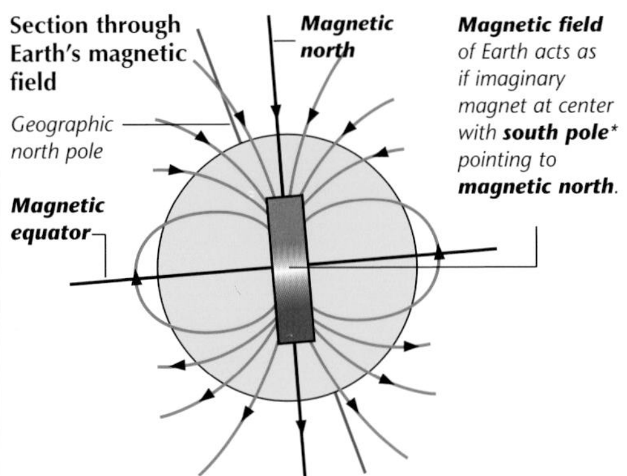
Section through Earth's magnetic field
Magnetic north
Magnetic field of Earth acts as if imaginary magnet at center with south pole* pointing to magnetic north.
Geographic north pole
Magnetic equator

Magnetic meridian

The vertical plane containing the **magnetic axis*** of a magnet suspended in the Earth's magnetic field (i.e. with its **north pole*** pointing to **magnetic north**).

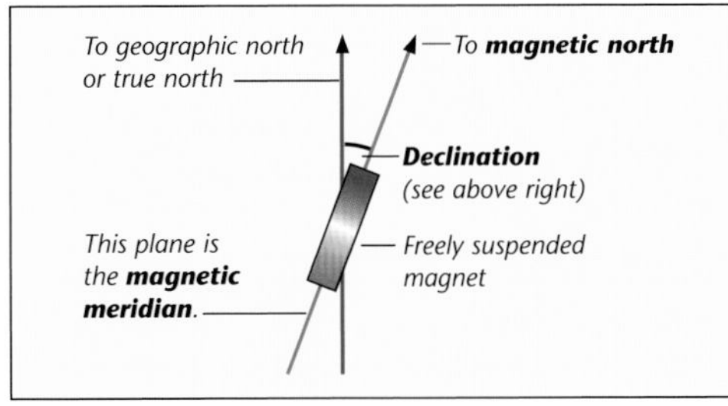
To geographic north or true north
To magnetic north
Declination (see above right)
This plane is the magnetic meridian.
Freely suspended magnet

Declination

The angle between a line taken to true north (the geographic north pole) and one taken along the **magnetic meridian** (towards **magnetic north**) at a point. The position of magnetic north is gradually changing and so the declination alters slowly with time.

This migrating tern may use the Earth's magnetic field to guide it.

Isogonal lines

Lines joining places with equal **declination**. These are redrawn from time to time because of the changing direction of the Earth's magnetic field.

Inclination or dip

The angle between a horizontal line on the Earth's surface and the direction of the Earth's magnetic field at a point. It is measured using a **dip circle** (see picture, below).

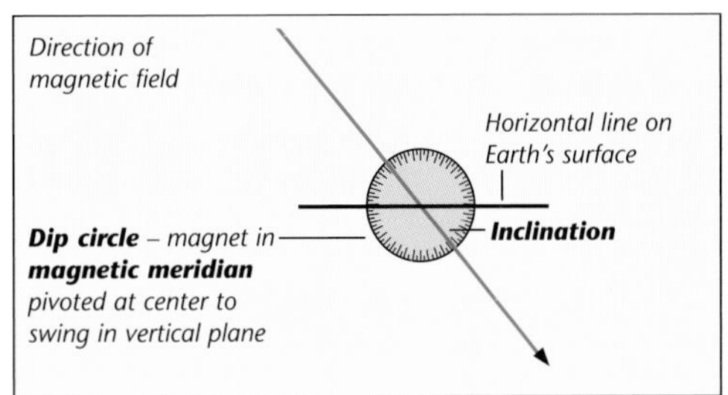
Direction of magnetic field
Horizontal line on Earth's surface
Dip circle – magnet in magnetic meridian pivoted at center to swing in vertical plane
Inclination

Isoclinal line

A line linking places with the same **inclination**.

Permeability

A measure of the ability of a substance to "conduct" a magnetic field. Soft iron is much more permeable than air, so the magnetic field tends to be concentrated through it.

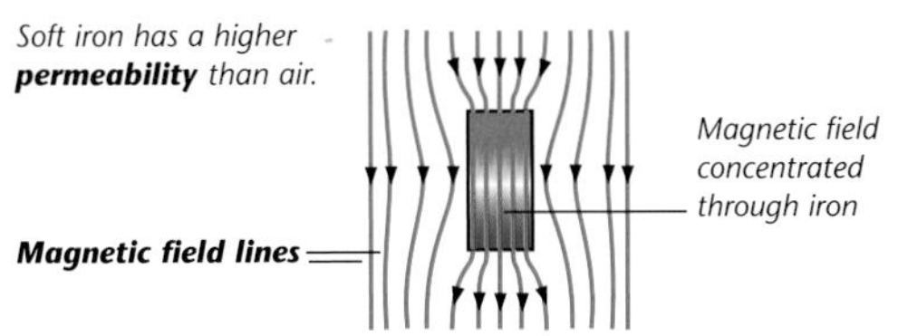
Soft iron has a higher permeability than air.
Magnetic field concentrated through iron
Magnetic field lines

Shielding or screening

The use of soft magnetic material to stop a magnetic field from reaching a point, effectively by "conducting" the field away. This is used in sensitive instruments, e.g. oscilloscopes.

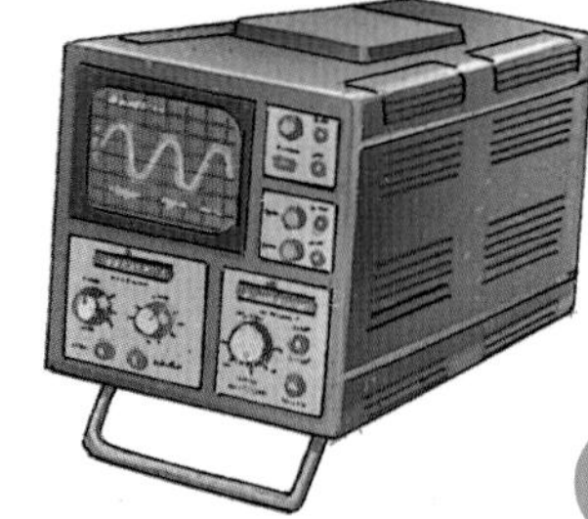

*Oscilloscope beams are **shielded** from unwanted magnetic fields by **mumetal**, a special alloy with a very high **permeability**.*

* **Magnetic axis**, **Pole**, 70.

ELECTROMAGNETISM

An electric current flowing through a wire produces a **magnetic field** (see pages 72-73) around the wire, the shape of which depends on the shape of the wire and the current flowing. These magnetic fields can be plotted in the same way as for **permanent magnets***. This effect, called **electromagnetism**, is used in very powerful magnets and also to produce motion from an electric current.

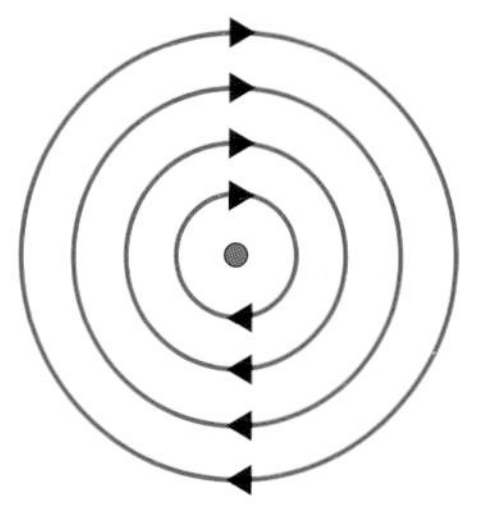

*Cross-section of the **magnetic field** which would exist if there was a wire (shown in green) carrying current directly into the page.*

Maxwell's screw rule

States that the direction of the magnetic field around a current-carrying wire is the way a screw turns when being screwed in the direction of the current.

Maxwell's screw rule

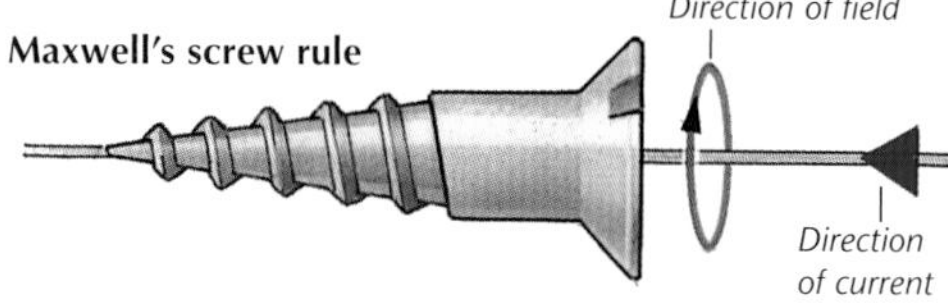
Direction of field
Direction of current

Right-hand grip rule

States that the direction of a magnetic field around a wire is that from the base to the tips of the fingers if the wire is gripped by the right hand with the thumb pointing in the direction of the current.

Right-hand grip rule

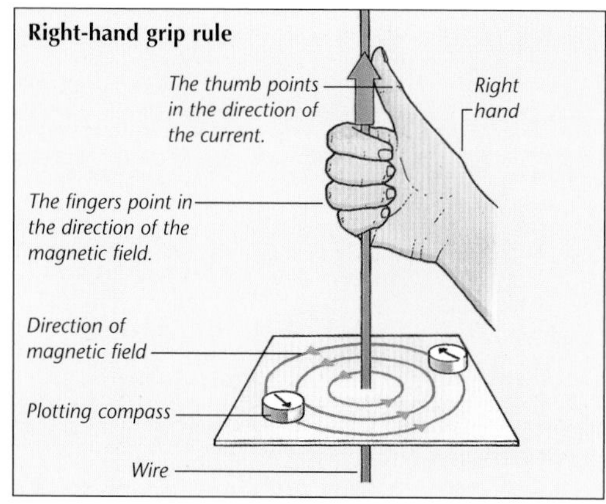
The thumb points in the direction of the current.
Right hand
The fingers point in the direction of the magnetic field.
Direction of magnetic field
Plotting compass
Wire

Coil

A number of turns of current-carrying wire, produced by wrapping the wire around a shaped piece of material (a **former**). Examples are a **flat coil** and a **solenoid**.

Flat coil or plane coil

A **coil** of wire whose length is small in comparison with its diameter.

Solenoid

A **coil** whose length is large in comparison with its diameter. The magnetic field produced by a solenoid is similar to that produced by a bar magnet. The position of the **poles*** depends on the current direction.

Solenoid

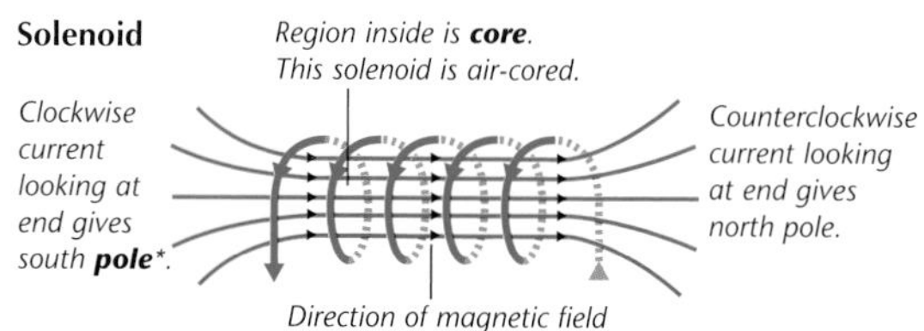
Region inside is **core**. This solenoid is air-cored.
Clockwise current looking at end gives south **pole***.
Counterclockwise current looking at end gives north pole.
Direction of magnetic field

S

Arrowheads on an S point in a clockwise direction (clockwise current = south pole).

Arrowheads on an N point in an counterclockwise direction (counterclockwise current = north pole).

Core

The material in the center of a **coil** which dictates the strength of the field. Soft **ferromagnetic*** materials, most commonly soft iron, create the strongest magnetic field and are used in **electromagnets**.

Electromagnet

A **solenoid** with a **core** of soft, strongly **ferromagnetic*** material. This forms a magnet which can be switched on and off simply by turning the current on and off. Practical electromagnets are constructed so that two opposite **poles*** are close to each other, producing a strong magnetic field.

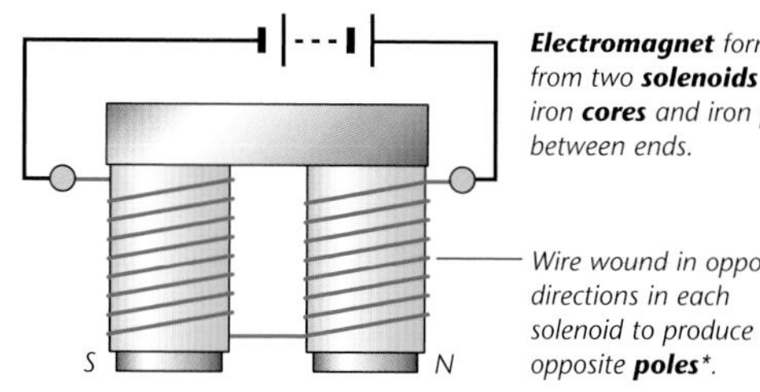
S
N
Wire wound in opposite directions in each solenoid to produce opposite **poles***.

***Electromagnet** formed from two **solenoids** with iron **cores** and iron piece between ends.*

* **Ferromagnetic**, 70; **Permanent magnets**, 70 (**Hard**); **Pole**, 70.

Applications of electromagnets

Electromagnets have a large number of applications, all of which use the fact that they attract metals when they are switched on and therefore convert **electric energy*** to **mechanical energy***. In two of the following examples, sound energy is produced from the mechanical energy.

Electric buzzer

A device which produces a buzzing noise from **direct current***. A metal arm is attracted by an **electromagnet**, moves towards it, and in doing so breaks the circuit carrying current to the electromagnet. The arm is thus released and the process is repeated. The resulting vibration of the arm produces a buzzing noise. In the **electric bell**, a hammer attached to the arm repeatedly strikes a bell.

Electric bell

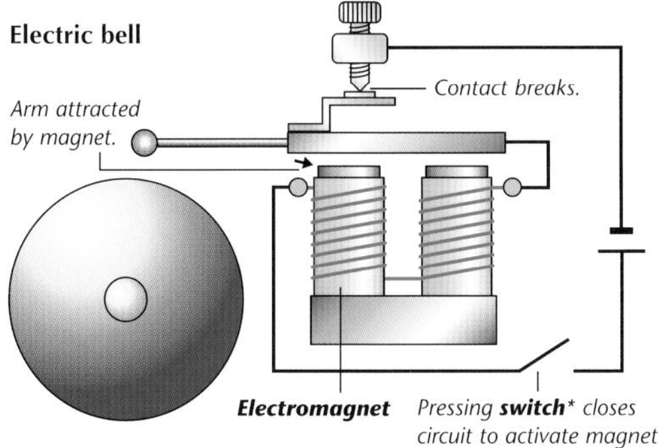
Contact breaks.
Arm attracted by magnet.
Electromagnet
Pressing switch* closes circuit to activate magnet.

Earphone

A device used to transform electrical signals to sound waves. The **permanent magnet*** attracts the metal diaphragm, but the strength of this attraction is changed as changing current (the incoming signals) flows through the coils of the **electromagnet**. The diaphragm thus vibrates to produce sound waves.

Earphone

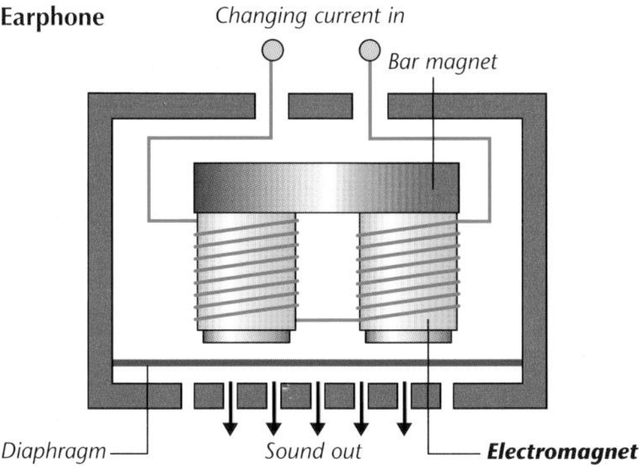
Changing current in
Bar magnet
Diaphragm
Sound out
Electromagnet

Lifting magnets

Large **electromagnets** which are used in steelworks to lift heavy loads. The activated electromagnet attracts steel, enabling it to be moved. The load is released when the current is switched off.

Lifting magnet *used to move scrap metal from one place to another.*

Relay

A device in which a **switch*** is closed by the action of an **electromagnet**. A relatively small current in the **coil** of the electromagnet can be used to switch on a large current without the circuits being electrically linked.

Relay

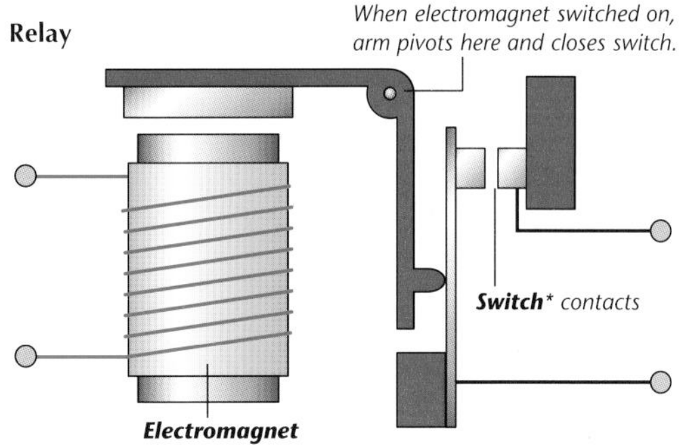
When electromagnet switched on, arm pivots here and closes switch.
Switch* contacts
Electromagnet

"Maglev" train

A train with **electromagnets** attached underneath, which runs on tracks with electromagnets on them. The magnets repel each other, so the train hovers just above the track. The reduced friction between the train and the track means that the train can travel faster.

Japanese "maglev" train

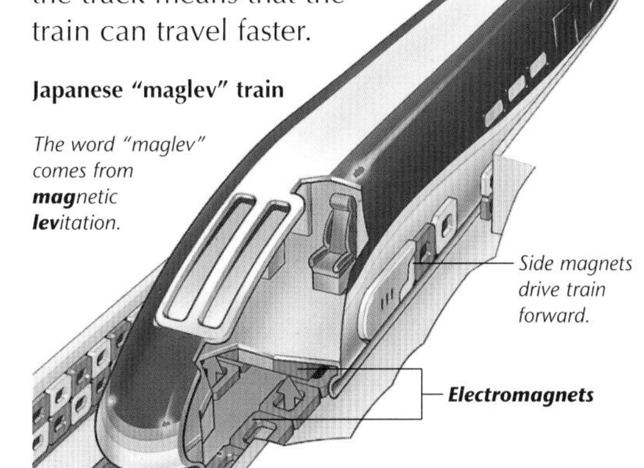
The word "maglev" comes from magnetic levitation.
Side magnets drive train forward.
Electromagnets

* **Direct current**, 61; **Electric energy**, 9; **Ferromagnetic**, 70; **Mechanical energy**, 9; **Permanent magnets**, 70 (**Hard**); **Pole**, 70; **Switch**, 64.

Electromagnets continued – the Lorentz force

The **Lorentz force** occurs when a current-carrying wire goes through a magnetic field. A force acts on the wire which can produce movement. This effect is used in **electric motors**, where **mechanical energy*** is produced from **electric energy***. The effect can also be used to measure current (see page 77), since the force depends on its magnitude.

Fleming's left-hand rule. See diagram, right. A right-hand rule can also be used. The thumb indicates force, but the meaning of the index and first fingers is reversed.

Fleming's left-hand rule

Points in direction of force

Points in direction of field

Points in direction of current

Electric motor

A device which uses the **Lorentz force** to transform **electric energy*** to **mechanical energy***. The simplest motor consists of a current-carrying, square-shaped **flat coil***, free to rotate in a magnetic field (see diagram below). Motors produce a **back e.m.f.*** opposing the e.m.f. which drives them. This is produced because once the motor starts, it acts as a **generator*** (i.e. the movement of the coil in the field produces an opposing current).

Simple electric motor

Commutator. *A ring split into two or more pieces, via which current enters and leaves the **coil*** of an **electric motor**. It ensures that the current enters the coil in the correct direction to make the motor rotate in one direction continuously.*

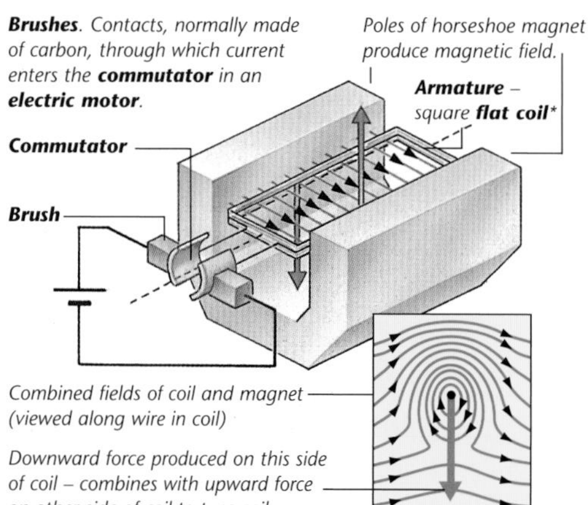

Brushes. Contacts, normally made of carbon, through which current enters the commutator in an electric motor.
Poles of horseshoe magnet produce magnetic field.
Armature – square flat coil*
Commutator
Brush
Combined fields of coil and magnet (viewed along wire in coil)
Downward force produced on this side of coil – combines with upward force on other side of coil to turn coil.

Exploded view of a powerful electric motor

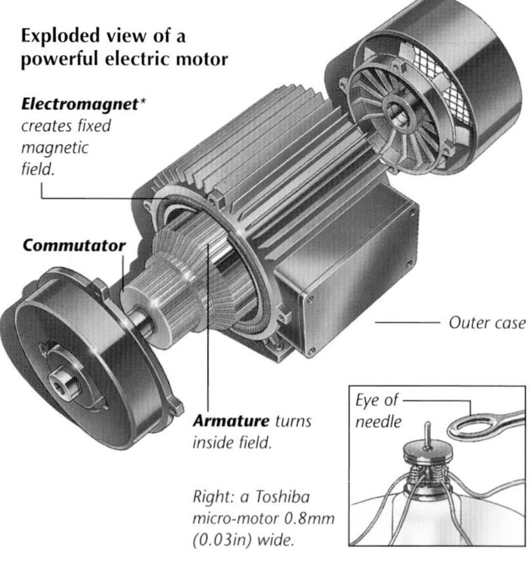

Electromagnet* creates fixed magnetic field.
Commutator
Outer case
Armature turns inside field.
Eye of needle
Right: a Toshiba micro-motor 0.8mm (0.03in) wide.

Field windings

Sets of **coils*** around the outside of an **electric motor**, which take the place of a permanent magnet to produce a stronger magnetic field. This increases the power of the motor.

Loudspeaker

A device which uses the **Lorentz force** to transform electrical signals into **sound waves***. It consists of a **coil*** in a **radial magnetic field** (the direction of the field at any point is along a radius of this coil). As the current changes, the coil, which is attached to a paper cone, moves in and out of the field (see diagram). The paper cone vibrates the air, producing sound waves which depend on the strength and frequency of the current.

Loudspeaker

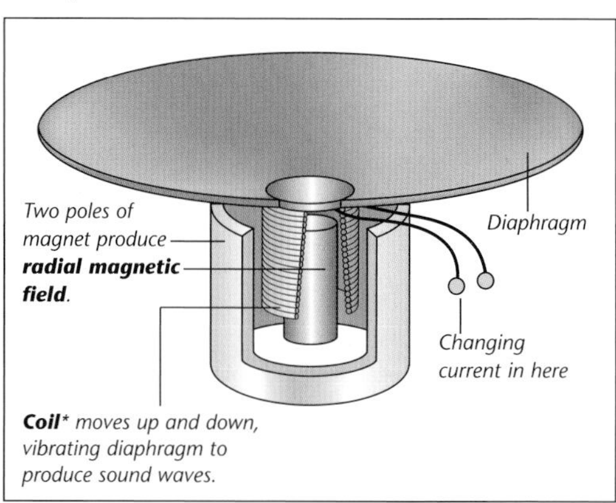

Two poles of magnet produce radial magnetic field.
Diaphragm
Changing current in here
Coil* moves up and down, vibrating diaphragm to produce sound waves.

* **Back e.m.f.**, 60 (**Electromotive force**); **Coil**, 74; **Electric energy**, 9; **Electromagnet**, **Flat coil**, 74; **Generator**, 78; **Mechanical energy**, 9; **Sound waves**, 40.

ELECTRIC METERS

Current can be detected by placing a suspended magnet near a wire and observing its deflection. This idea can be extended to produce a device (a **meter**) in which the deflection indicates on a scale the strength of the current. The current measuring device can then be adapted to measure **potential difference***.

Galvanometer

Any device used to detect a **direct current*** by registering its magnetic effect. The simplest is a compass placed near a wire to show whether a current is present. The **moving coil galvanometer** uses the **Lorentz force** to show a deflection on a scale (see diagram).

Moving coil galvanometer

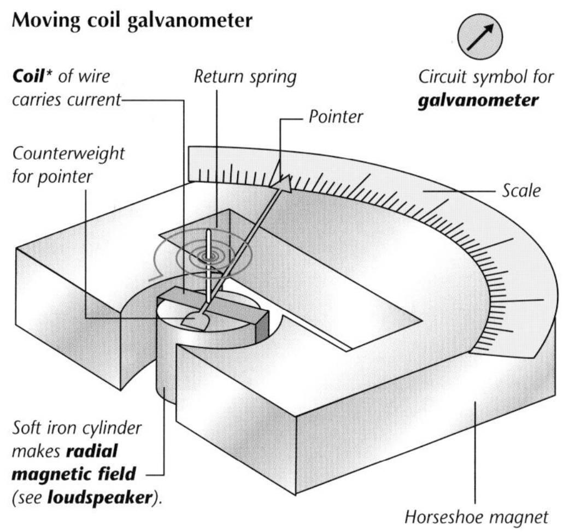

Coil* of wire carries current
Return spring
Pointer
Circuit symbol for **galvanometer**
Counterweight for pointer
Scale
Soft iron cylinder makes **radial magnetic field** (see **loudspeaker**).
Horseshoe magnet

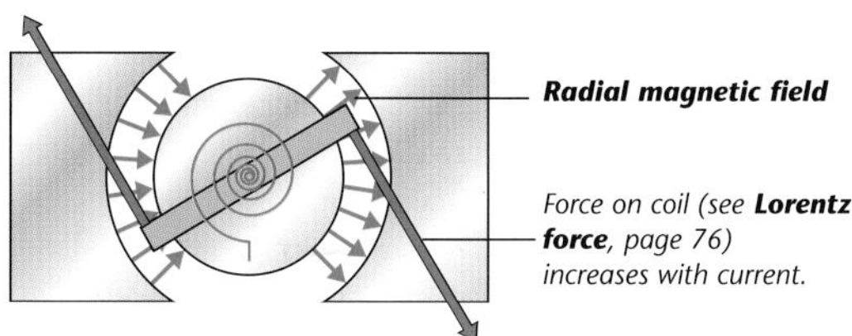

Radial magnetic field
Force on coil (see **Lorentz force**, page 76) increases with current.

Moving iron meter

A **meter** in which the current to be measured induces magnetism in two pieces of iron which attract or repel each other to produce a deflection.

Ammeter

A device used to measure current. It is a version of the **moving coil galvanometer**, designed so that a certain current produces a **full scale deflection**, i.e. the pointer moves to its maximum position. To measure higher currents, a **shunt** is added (see diagram below). A larger current now produces full scale deflection on the new scale.

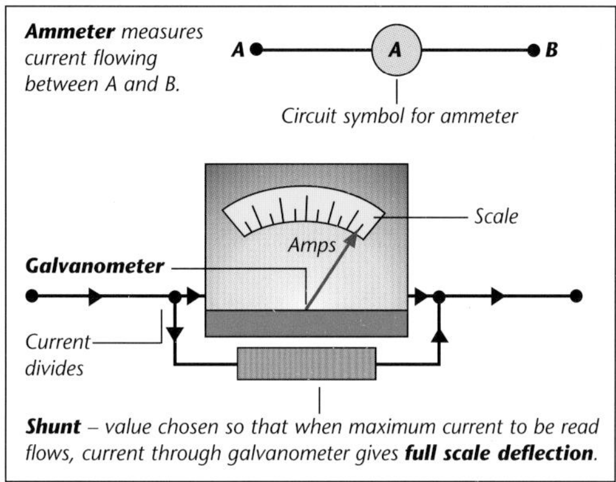

Ammeter measures current flowing between A and B.
A
A
B
Circuit symbol for ammeter
Scale
Amps
Galvanometer
Current divides
Shunt – value chosen so that when maximum current to be read flows, current through galvanometer gives **full scale deflection**.

Voltmeter

A device used to measure the **potential difference*** between two points. It is a **galvanometer** between the two points with a high **resistance*** in **series***. A certain potential difference produces the current for a **full scale deflection** (see **ammeter**). To measure higher potential differences, a **multiplier** is added (see diagram below).

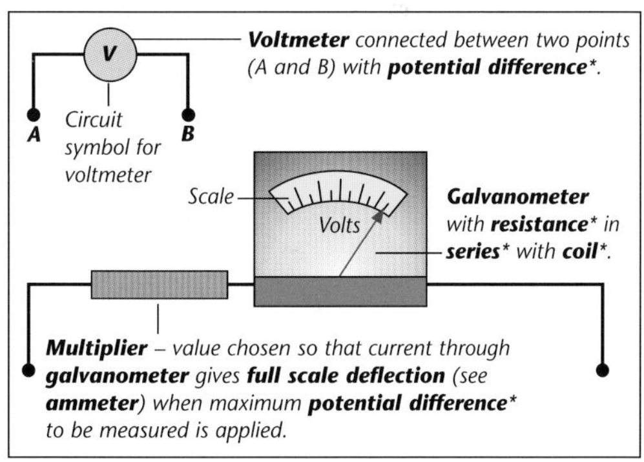

V
Voltmeter connected between two points (A and B) with **potential difference***.
A
Circuit symbol for voltmeter
B
Scale
Volts
Galvanometer with **resistance*** in **series*** with **coil***.
Multiplier – value chosen so that current through **galvanometer** gives **full scale deflection** (see **ammeter**) when maximum **potential difference*** to be measured is applied.

Multimeter

A **galvanometer** combined with the **shunts** (see **ammeter**) and **multipliers** (see **voltmeter**) necessary to measure currents and **potential differences***.

* **Coil**, 74; **Direct current**, 61; **Potential difference**, 58; **Resistance**, 62; **Series**, 64.

ELECTROMAGNETIC INDUCTION

Michael Faraday found that, as well as a current passing through a magnetic field producing movement (see **motor effect**, page 76), movement of a **conductor*** in a magnetic field produces an **electromotive force*** in the conductor. This effect, called **electromagnetic induction**, happens whenever a conductor is placed in a changing magnetic field.

*Faraday induced an electromotive force by rotating a disk (the **conductor***) near a magnet, using this device called a disk **dynamo**.*

Faraday's law of induction

States that the size of an induced electromotive force in a **conductor*** is proportional to the rate at which the magnetic field changes.

Lenz's law

States that an induced electromotive force always acts to oppose the cause of it, e.g. in an **electric motor***, the e.m.f. produced because it acts as a **generator** opposes the e.m.f. driving the motor.

Fleming's right-hand rule or dynamo rule

The direction of an induced current can be worked out from the direction of the magnetic field and the movement by using the right hand (see diagram).

Fleming's right-hand rule

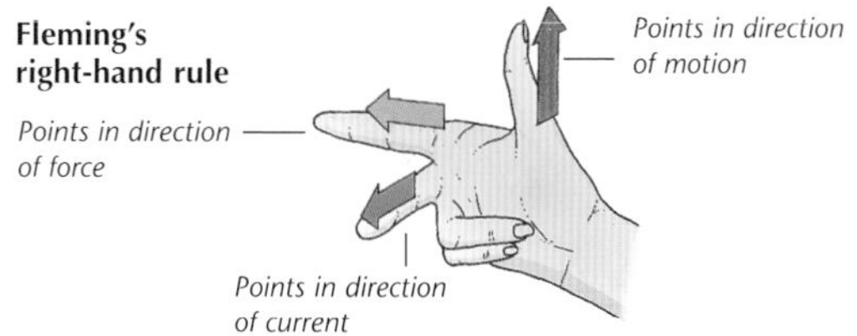
Points in direction of motion
Points in direction of force
Points in direction of current

Generator or dynamo

A device used to produce electric current from **mechanical energy***. In the simplest generator (see diagram, right), an alternating electromotive force is induced in a **coil*** as it rotates in a magnetic field. A generator for **direct currents*** has a **commutator***, as on an **electric motor***, which means the current always flows in the same direction.

Simple generator

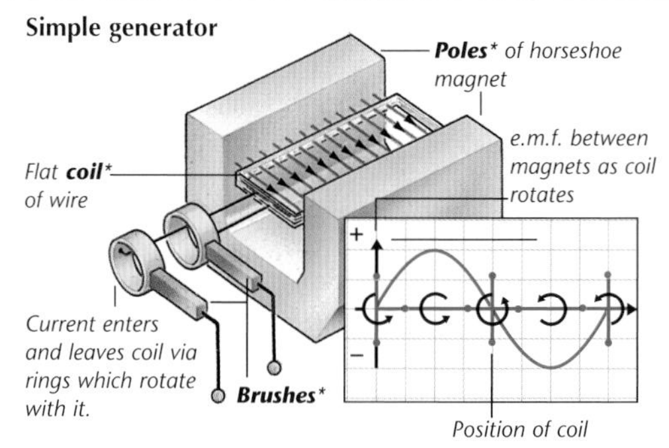
Poles* of horseshoe magnet
e.m.f. between magnets as coil rotates
Flat coil* of wire
Current enters and leaves coil via rings which rotate with it.
Brushes*
Position of coil
+
–

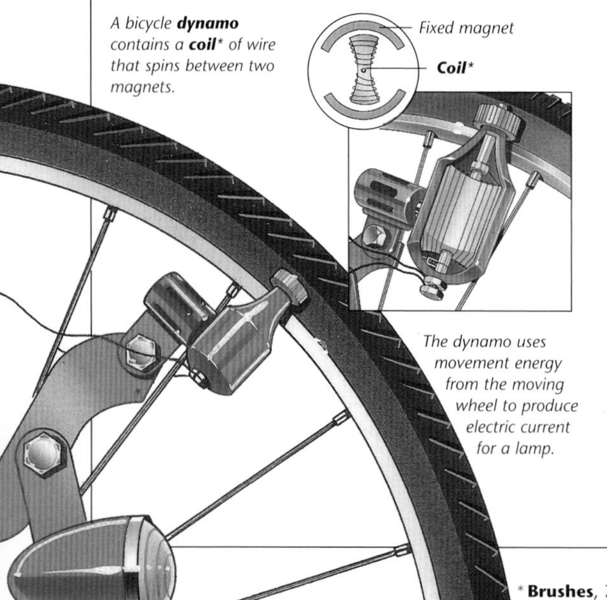
Fixed magnet
Coil*

*A bicycle **dynamo** contains a **coil*** of wire that spins between two magnets.*

The dynamo uses movement energy from the moving wheel to produce electric current for a lamp.

Mutual induction

The induction of an electromotive force in a **coil*** of wire by changing the current in a different coil. The changing current produces a changing magnetic field which induces a current in any other coil in the field. This was first demonstrated with **Faraday's iron ring**.

Faraday's iron ring

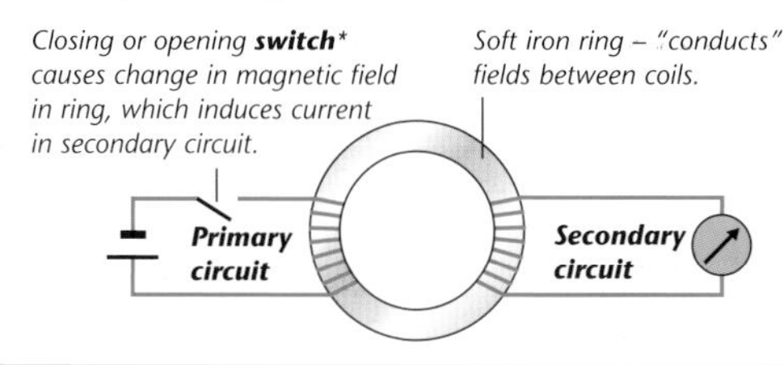
Closing or opening switch* causes change in magnetic field in ring, which induces current in secondary circuit.
Soft iron ring – "conducts" fields between coils.
Primary circuit
Secondary circuit

* **Brushes**, 76; **Coil**, 74; **Commutator**, 76; **Conductor**, 56; **Direct current**, 61; **Electric motor**, 76; **Electromotive force (e.m.f.)**, 60; **Mechanical energy**, 9; **Pole**, 70; **Switch**, 64.

Self-induction

The induction of an electromotive force in a **coil*** of wire due to the current inside it changing. For example, if the current in a coil is switched off, the resulting change in the magnetic field produces an electromotive force across the coil, in some cases much higher than that of the original.

Eddy current

A current set up in a piece of metal when a magnetic field around it changes, even though the metal may not be part of a circuit. Eddy currents can cause unwanted heat energy, e.g. in the iron core of a **transformer**. This can be prevented by laminating the iron core (see **transformers**, below).

Transformers

A **transformer** consists of two **coils*** of wire wound onto the same **core*** of soft **ferromagnetic*** material. It is used to change an alternating electromotive force in one of the coils to a different e.m.f. in the other coil, e.g. in electricity supply, see page 61. Hardly any energy is lost between the two circuits in a well-designed transformer.

Simple transformer

*Soft iron core – normally laminated to reduce **eddy currents** which cause energy loss in the form of heat.*

***Primary coil** – e.m.f. applied here*

***Secondary coil** – e.m.f. induced here*

Primary coil

The **coil*** in a transformer to which an alternating electromotive force is applied in order to produce an electromotive force in the **secondary coil**.

Secondary coil

The **coil*** in a transformer in which an alternating electromotive force is induced by the electromotive force applied to the **primary coil**. Some transformers have two or more secondary coils.

Turns ratio

The ratio of the number of turns in the **secondary coil** in a **transformer** to the number of turns in the **primary coil**. The turns ratio is also the ratio of the electromotive force in the secondary coil to that in the primary coil.

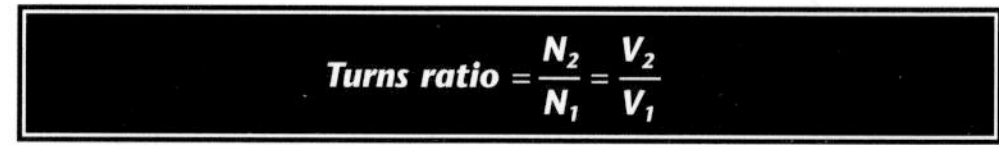
$$\text{Turns ratio} = \frac{N_2}{N_1} = \frac{V_2}{V_1}$$

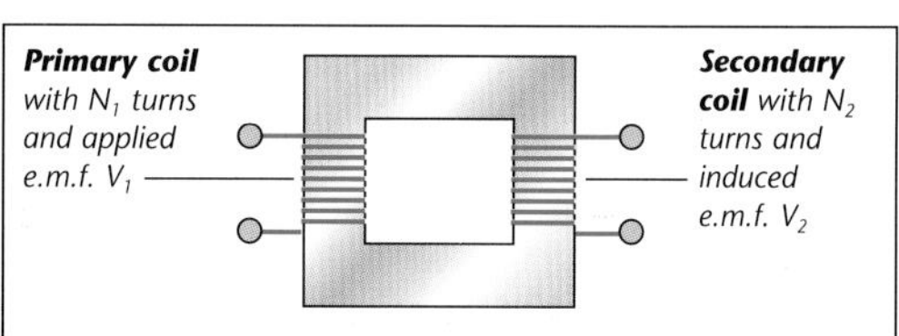
Primary coil with N_1 turns and applied e.m.f. V_1
Secondary coil with N_2 turns and induced e.m.f. V_2

Step-up transformer

A **transformer** in which the electromotive force in the **secondary coil** is greater than that in the **primary coil**. The **turns ratio** is greater than one.

Step-up transformer

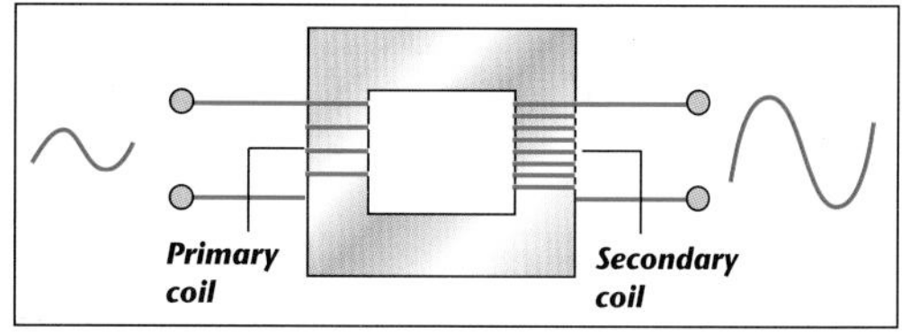
Primary coil
Secondary coil

Step-down transformer

A **transformer** in which the electromotive force in the **secondary coil** is less than that in the **primary coil**. The **turns ratio** is less than one.

Step-down transformer

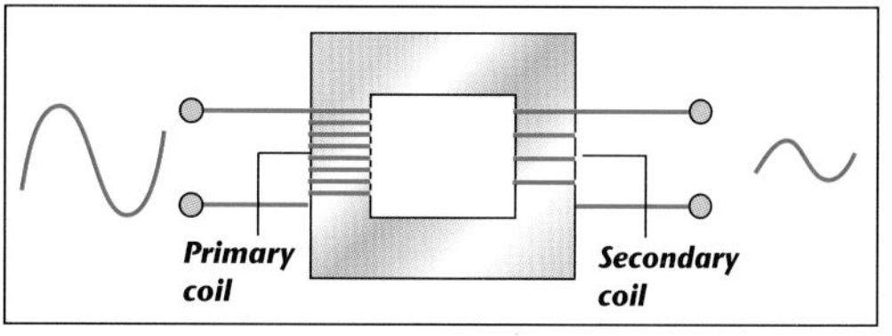
Primary coil
Secondary coil

* **Coil**, **Core**, 74; **Ferromagnetic**, 70.

CATHODE RAYS

A **cathode ray** is a continuous stream of **electrons** (negatively-charged particles – see page 83) traveling through a low pressure gas or a vacuum. It is produced when electrons are freed from a metal **cathode*** and attracted to an **anode***. Cathode rays have a number of applications, from the production of **X-rays*** to **television**. All of these involve the use of a shaped glass tube (called an **electron tube**) containing a low pressure gas or a vacuum for the rays to travel in. The rays are normally produced by an **electron gun**, which forms part of the tube.

Electron gun

A device which produces a continuous stream of electrons (a cathode ray). It consists of a heated **cathode*** which gives off electrons (this is called **thermionic emission**) and an **anode*** which attracts them to form a stream.

Typical experimental electron tube

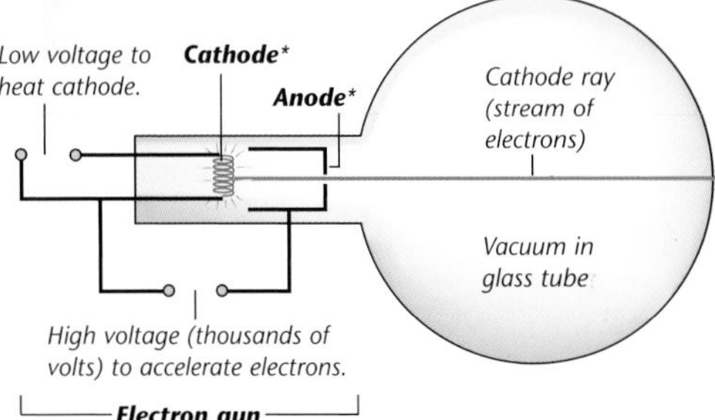
Low voltage to heat cathode.
Cathode*
Anode*
Cathode ray (stream of electrons)
Vacuum in glass tube
High voltage (thousands of volts) to accelerate electrons.
Electron gun

Maltese cross tube

An **electron tube** in which the cathode ray is interrupted by a cross which casts a "shadow" on a **fluorescent*** screen at the end of the tube. This shows that the electrons are moving in straight lines.

Maltese cross tube

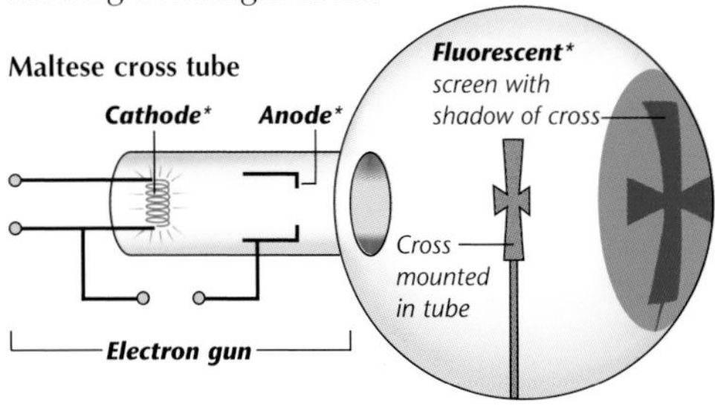
Cathode*
Anode*
Fluorescent* screen with shadow of cross
Cross mounted in tube
Electron gun

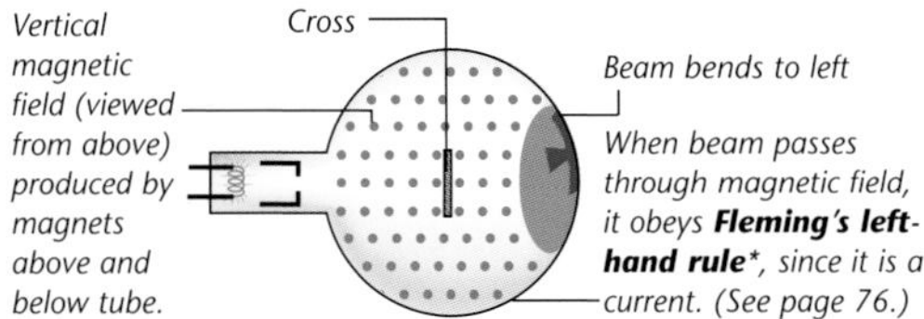
Vertical magnetic field (viewed from above) produced by magnets above and below tube.
Cross
Beam bends to left
When beam passes through magnetic field, it obeys Fleming's left-hand rule*, since it is a current. (See page 76.)

Discharge tube

A gas-filled glass tube in which **ions*** and electrons are attracted by the **electrodes*** and move towards them at high speed. As they do so, they collide with gas atoms, causing these atoms to split into more ions and electrons, and emit light at the same time. The color of the light depends on the gas used, e.g. neon produces orange light (used in advertising displays) and mercury vapor produces blue-green light (used for street lighting). Discharge tubes use up to five times less electricity than other lighting. A **fluorescent tube** is a discharge tube filled with mercury vapor, which emits **ultraviolet radiation***. This hits the inside of the tube, causing its coating of special powder to give out **visible light*** (see **fluorescence**, page 45).

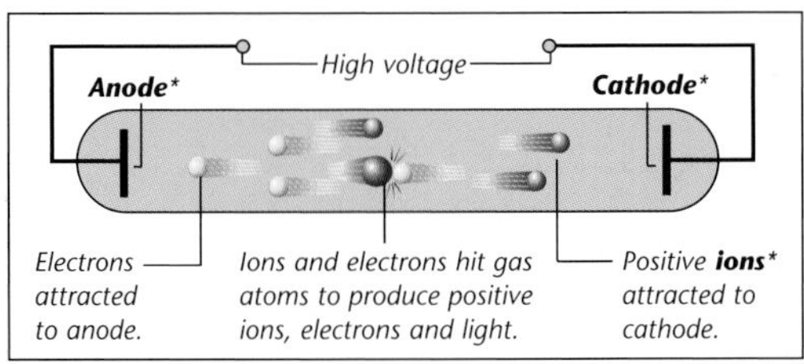
High voltage
Anode*
Cathode*
Electrons attracted to anode.
Ions and electrons hit gas atoms to produce positive ions, electrons and light.
Positive ions* attracted to cathode.

X-ray tube

A special electron tube used to produce a beam of **X-rays***. A cathode ray hits a tungsten target which stops the electrons suddenly. This causes X-rays to be emitted.

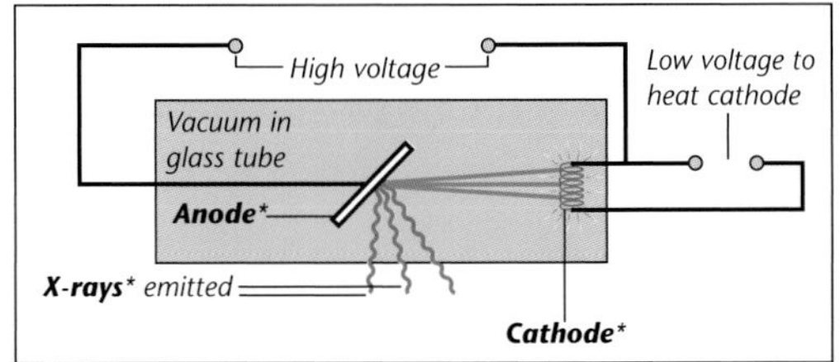
High voltage
Low voltage to heat cathode
Vacuum in glass tube
Anode*
X-rays* emitted
Cathode*

* **Anode**, **Cathode**, 66 (**Electrode**); **Fleming's left-hand rule** 76; **Fluorescence**, 45; **Ions**, 88 (**Ionization**); **Ultraviolet radiation**, 44; **Visible light**, 45; **X-rays**, 44.

The cathode ray oscilloscope

The **cathode ray oscilloscope** (**CRO**) is an instrument used to study currents and **potential differences***. A cathode ray from an **electron gun** produces a spot on a **fluorescent*** screen. In normal use, the ray is repeatedly swept across the back of the screen at a selected speed and so produces a visible trace across the front. If a signal is fed into the oscilloscope, the vertical position of the beam will change according to the strength of the signal, and the trace on the screen then shows this change over time.

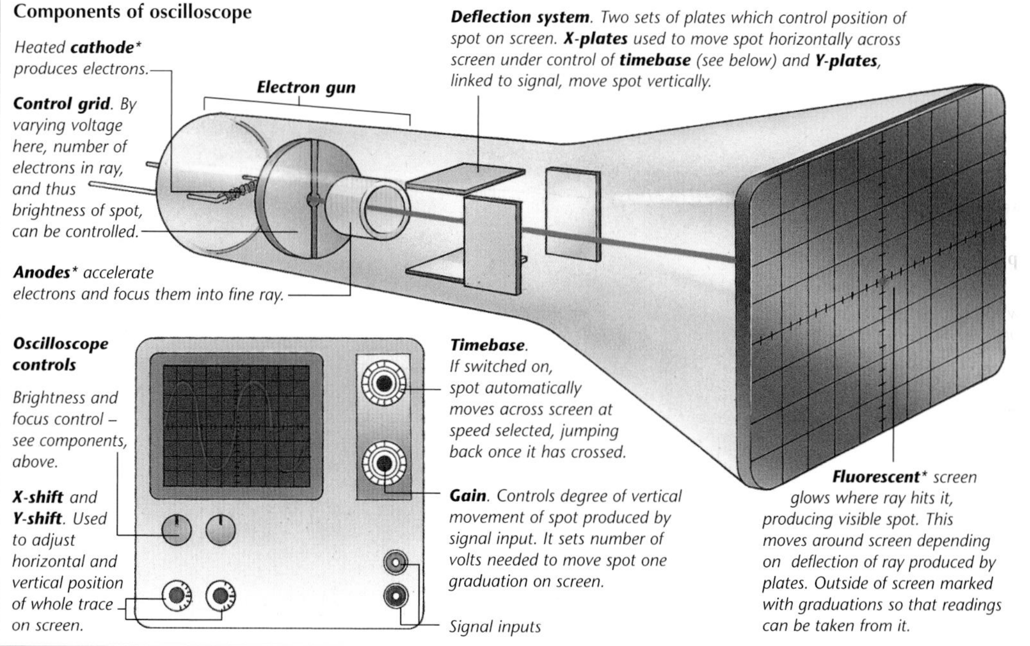

Components of oscilloscope
Heated **cathode*** produces electrons.
Electron gun
Control grid. By varying voltage here, number of electrons in ray, and thus brightness of spot, can be controlled.
Anodes* accelerate electrons and focus them into fine ray.
Deflection system. Two sets of plates which control position of spot on screen. **X-plates** used to move spot horizontally across screen under control of **timebase** (see below) and **Y-plates**, linked to signal, move spot vertically.
Fluorescent* screen glows where ray hits it, producing visible spot. This moves around screen depending on deflection of ray produced by plates. Outside of screen marked with graduations so that readings can be taken from it.
Oscilloscope controls
Brightness and focus control – see components, above.
X-shift and **Y-shift**. Used to adjust horizontal and vertical position of whole trace on screen.
Timebase. If switched on, spot automatically moves across screen at speed selected, jumping back once it has crossed.
Gain. Controls degree of vertical movement of spot produced by signal input. It sets number of volts needed to move spot one graduation on screen.
Signal inputs

Television

Television pictures are reproduced by using an **electron tube** in which the cathode ray scans across the screen varying in strength according to the signal. Different levels of light, according to the strength of the ray, are given off from different parts of the screen to produce a picture (see diagram on right).

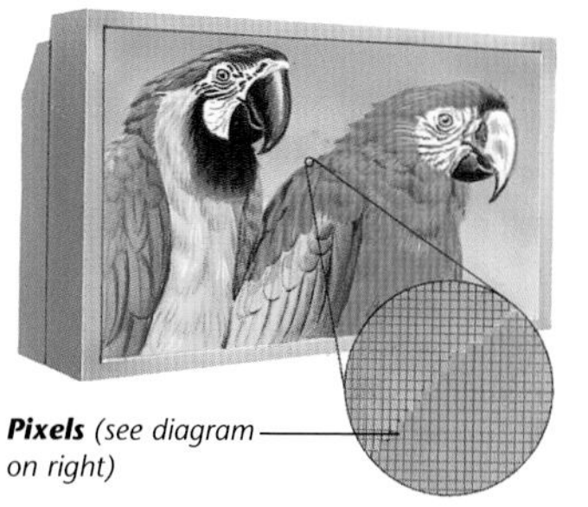

Pixels (see diagram on right)

*Extra large high-definition televisions (HTDVs) have more **pixels** than ordinary TVs (see right), so the picture is sharper.*

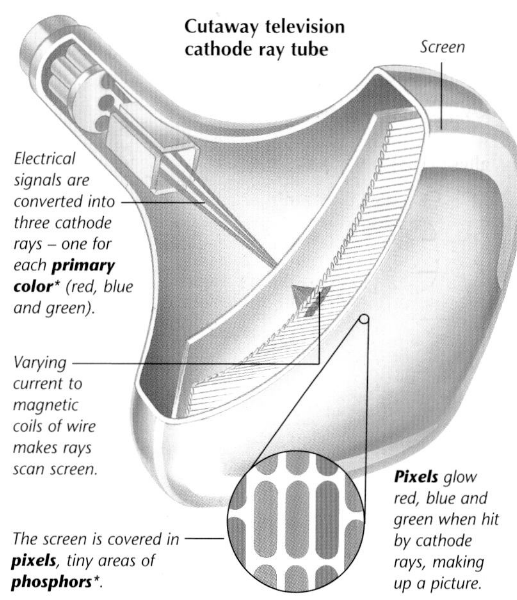

Cutaway television cathode ray tube
Screen
Electrical signals are converted into three cathode rays – one for each **primary color*** (red, blue and green).
Varying current to magnetic coils of wire makes rays scan screen.
The screen is covered in **pixels**, tiny areas of **phosphors***.
Pixels glow red, blue and green when hit by cathode rays, making up a picture.

* **Anode**, **Cathode**, 66 (**Electrode**); **Fluorescence**, 45; **Phosphors**, 44 (**Phosphorescence**); **Potential difference**, 58; **Primary colors**, 55.

ATOMIC STRUCTURE

A great deal has been learned about the physical nature of atoms (see also page 4) since Greek philosophers first proposed that all matter was made of basic indivisible "building blocks". It is now known that an atom is not indivisible, but has a complex internal structure, consisting of many different smaller particles (**subatomic particles**) and a lot of empty space.

Orbital *model of an atom (see page 83)*

Rutherford-Bohr atom

A "solar system" representation of an atom, devised by Ernest Rutherford and Niels Bohr in 1911. It is now known to be incorrect (**electrons** have no regular "orbits" – see **electron shells**).

Rutherford-Bohr atom model

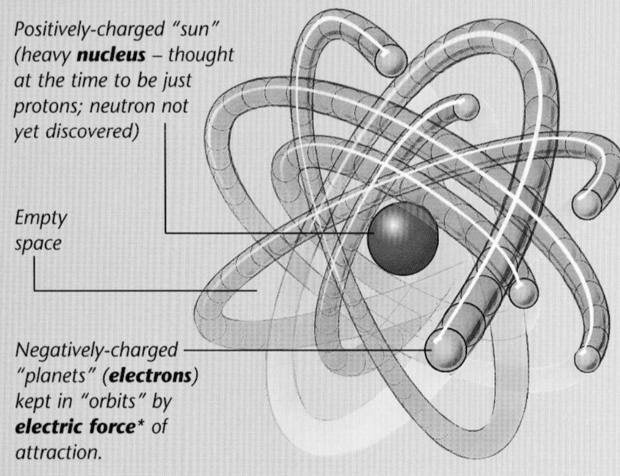
Positively-charged "sun" (heavy nucleus – thought at the time to be just protons; neutron not yet discovered)
Empty space
Negatively-charged "planets" (electrons) kept in "orbits" by electric force* of attraction.

Nucleus (pl. nuclei) or atomic nucleus

The central core of an atom, consisting of closely-packed **nucleons** (**protons** and **neutrons**).

Nucleus – (almost all the mass of the atom, but very tiny – its radius is approximately $^1/_{10{,}000}$*th that of the atom)*

Neutron *(mass approximately 1,840 times that of an* ***electron****)*

Proton *(mass approximately 1,836 times that of an* ***electron****)*

Protons

Positively-charged particles in the **nucleus**. The number of protons (**atomic number**) identifies the element and equals the number of **electrons**, so atoms are electrically neutral.

Neutrons

Electrically neutral particles in the **nucleus**. The number of neutrons in atoms of the same element can vary (see **isotope**).

Mass number (A)

The number of **protons** and **neutrons** (**nucleons**) in a **nucleus**. It is the whole number nearest to the **relative atomic mass** of the atom, and is important in identifying **isotopes**.

Atomic number (Z)

The number of **protons** in a **nucleus** (hence also the number of **electrons** around it). All atoms with the same atomic number are of the same element (see also **isotope**).

Neutron number (N)

The number of **neutrons** in a **nucleus**, calculated by subtracting the atomic number from the mass number. See also graph, page 87.

The ***mass*** *and* ***atomic numbers*** *are often written with the symbol of an element:*

$^{12}_{6}\mathrm{C}$

Mass number (A) *shows nucleus has 12* ***nucleons****.*

Atomic number (Z) *shows that six of these are* ***protons****.*

Neutron number (N) *= A – Z*
So N = 6 ▶

$^{23}_{11}\mathrm{Na}$

Mass number (A) *shows nucleus has 23* ***nucleons****.*

Atomic number (Z) *shows that 11 of these are* ***protons****.*

Neutron number (N) *= A – Z*
So N = 12 ▶

* **Electric force**, 6.

Electrons

Particles with a negative charge and very small mass. They move around the **nucleus** in **electron shells**. See also **protons**.

Electron shells

Regions of space around a **nucleus** containing moving **electrons**. An atom can have up to seven (from the inside, called the **K**, **L**, **M**, **N**, **O**, **P** and **Q shells**). Each can hold up to a certain number of electrons (the first four, from the inside, can take up to 2, 8, 18 and 32 electrons respectively).

The further away the shell is from the nucleus, the higher the energy of its electrons (the shell has a given **energy level**). The **outer shell** is the last shell with electrons in it. If this is full or has an **octet** (8 electrons), the atom is very stable (see page 85).

The positions of electrons in their shells cannot be exactly determined at any one time, but each shell consists of **orbitals**, or **probability clouds**. Each of these is a region in which one or two electrons are likely to be found at any time (see also illustration on page 82).

Modern model (simplified), carbon-12 isotope

*First **electron shell (K shell)** has two **electrons**.*

Nucleus

***Outer shell (L shell)** has four **electrons**.*

Five more possible shells

Modern model (complex), carbon-12 isotope

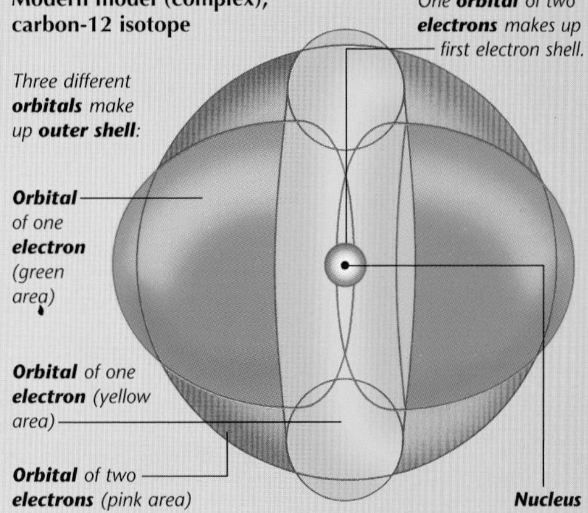
One orbital of two electrons makes up first electron shell.
Three different orbitals make up outer shell:
Orbital of one electron (green area)
Orbital of one electron (yellow area)
Orbital of two electrons (pink area)
Nucleus

Isotopes

Different forms of the same element, with the same atomic number, but different **neutron numbers** and hence different **mass numbers**. There are isotopes of every element, since even if only one natural form exists (i.e. the element is **monoisotopic**), others can be made artificially (see **radioisotope**, page 86).

__Mass numbers__ are used with names or symbols when __isotopes__ are being specified:

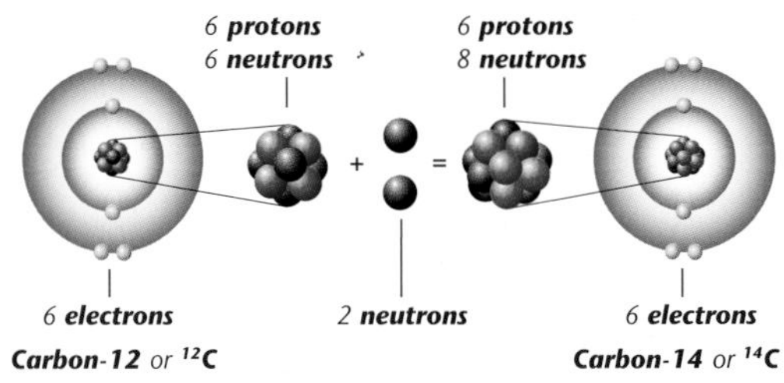
6 protons
6 neutrons
6 protons
8 neutrons
+
=
6 electrons
2 neutrons
6 electrons
Carbon-12 or ¹²C
Carbon-14 or ¹⁴C

Relative atomic mass

Also called **atomic mass** or **atomic weight**. The mass of an atom in **unified atomic mass units** (**u**). Each of these is equal to $^1/_{12}$ of the mass of a carbon-12 atom (**isotope**). The relative atomic mass of a carbon-12 atom is thus 12u, but no other values are whole numbers, e.g. the relative atomic mass of aluminum is 26.9815u.

The relative atomic mass takes into account the various isotopes of the element, if these occur in a natural sample. Natural chlorine, for example, has three chlorine-35 atoms to every one of chlorine-37, and the relative atomic mass of chlorine (35.453u) is a proportional average of the two different masses of these isotopes.

ATOMIC AND NUCLEAR ENERGY

All things, whether large objects or minute particles, have a particular **energy state**, or level of **potential energy*** ("stored" energy). Moreover, they will always try to find their lowest possible energy state, called the **ground state**, which is the state of the greatest stability. In most cases, this involves recombining in some way, i.e. adding or losing constituents. In all cases it results in the release of the "excess" energy – in large amounts if the particles are atoms, and vast amounts if they are nuclei. The greater the **binding energy** of an atom or nucleus, the greater its stability, i.e. the less likely it is to undergo any change.

Binding energy (B.E.)

The energy input needed to split a given atom or nucleus into its constituent parts (see pages 82-83). The **potential energy*** of an atom or nucleus is less than the total potential energy of its parts when these are apart. This is because, when they came together, the parts found a lower (collective) **energy state** (see introduction and **nuclear force**), and so lost energy. The binding energy is a measure of this difference in potential energy – it is the energy needed to "go back the other way" – so the greater it is, the lower the potential energy of an atom or nucleus and the greater its stability. Binding energy varies from atom to atom and nucleus to nucleus.

Nuclear force

The strong force which holds the parts of a nucleus (**nucleons***) together and overcomes the **electric force*** of repulsion between the **protons***. Its effect varies according to the size of the nucleus (see graph, opposite) as the force only acts between immediately adjacent nucleons. The greater the attractive effect of the nuclear force, the higher the **binding energy** of the nucleus (i.e. the more energy was lost when the parts came together).

Quantum theory

States that energy takes the form of minute, separate pulses called **quanta** (sing. **quantum**), rather than a steady stream. The theory was originally limited to energy emitted by bodies (i.e. **electromagnetic wave*** energy), though all other kinds of energy (see pages 8-9) are now generally included. Electromagnetic quanta are now specified as **photons**. The theory further states that the amount of energy carried by a photon is proportional to the **frequency*** of the emitted electromagnetic radiation (see pages 44-45).

*Energy carried by **quantum (photon)**:*

$$E = hf$$

*where E = energy in joules; h = **Planck's constant** (6.63×10^{-34} J s^{-1}); f = **frequency*** in Hertz.*

Electron volt (eV)**. Unit of atomic energy, equal to energy gained by one electron moved through **potential difference of 1V.*

$$1eV = 1.6 \times 10^{-19} J$$

***Megaelectron volt (MeV)**. Unit of nuclear energy, equal to 1 million eV.*

$$1MeV = 1.6 \times 10^{-13} J$$

Mass defect

The mass of an atom or nucleus is less than the sum of the masses of its parts when these are apart. The difference is the mass defect. It is the mass of the **potential energy*** lost when the parts came together (see **binding energy**, above, and formula, right).

*Einstein showed that energy has mass. Hence any loss of **potential energy*** also results in a loss of mass – the mass of the energy itself. **Einstein's mass-energy formula**:*

$$E = mc^2$$

where E = energy in joules; m = mass in kilograms; c = 3×10^8 (numerical value of speed of light in m s^{-1}).

* **Electric force**, 6; **Electromagnetic waves**, 44; **Frequency**, 35; **Nucleons**, 82 (**Nucleus**); **Potential difference**, 58; **Potential energy**, 8; **Protons**, 82.

Levels of nuclear stability

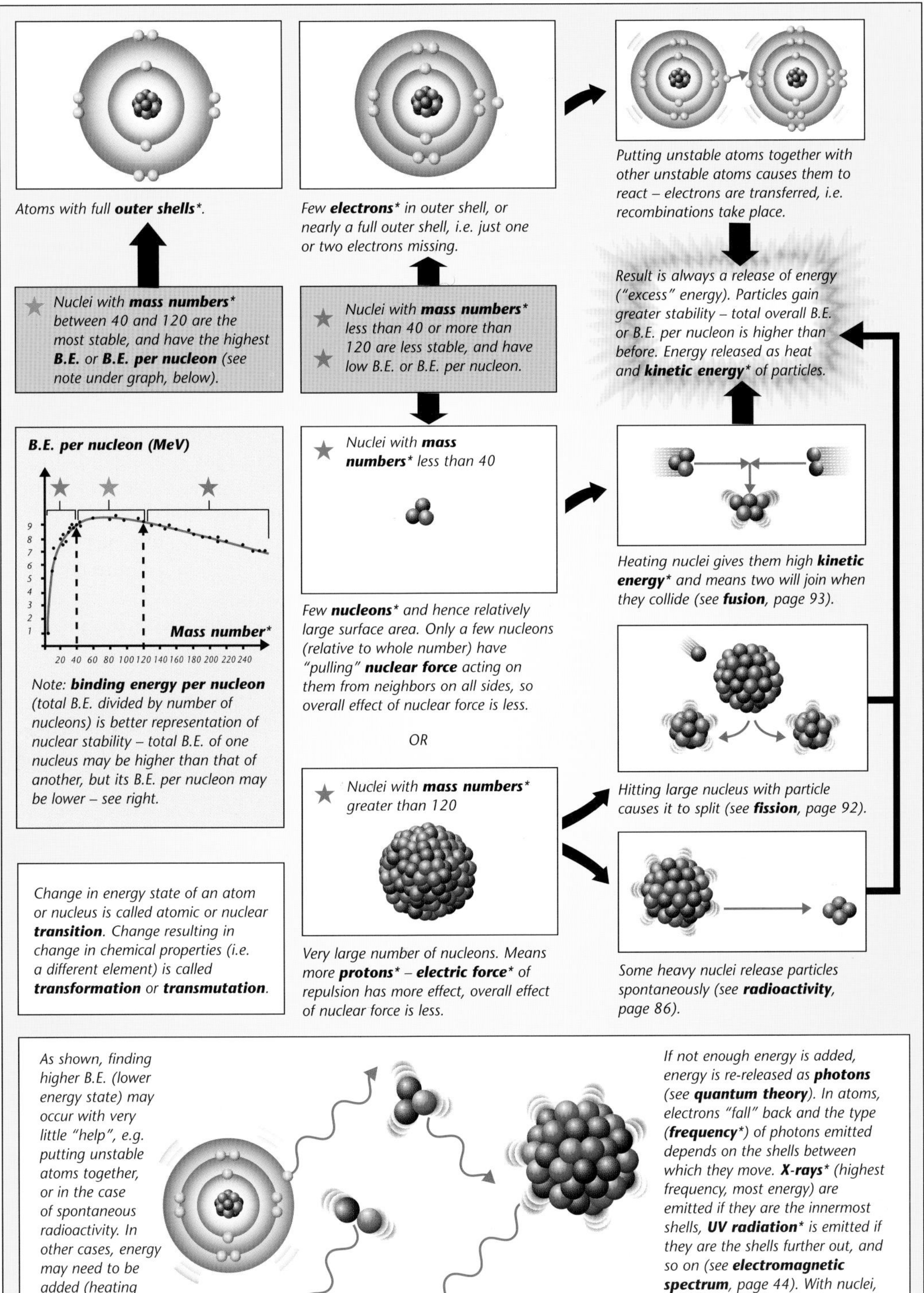

Atoms with full **outer shells***.
Few **electrons*** in outer shell, or nearly a full outer shell, i.e. just one or two electrons missing.
Putting unstable atoms together with other unstable atoms causes them to react – electrons are transferred, i.e. recombinations take place.
Nuclei with **mass numbers*** between 40 and 120 are the most stable, and have the highest **B.E.** or **B.E. per nucleon** (see note under graph, below).
Nuclei with **mass numbers*** less than 40 or more than 120 are less stable, and have low B.E. or B.E. per nucleon.
Result is always a release of energy ("excess" energy). Particles gain greater stability – total overall B.E. or B.E. per nucleon is higher than before. Energy released as heat and **kinetic energy*** of particles.
B.E. per nucleon (MeV)
1 2 3 4 5 6 7 8 9
Mass number*
20 40 60 80 100 120 140 160 180 200 220 240
Note: **binding energy per nucleon** (total B.E. divided by number of nucleons) is better representation of nuclear stability – total B.E. of one nucleus may be higher than that of another, but its B.E. per nucleon may be lower – see right.
Nuclei with **mass numbers*** less than 40
Few **nucleons*** and hence relatively large surface area. Only a few nucleons (relative to whole number) have "pulling" **nuclear force** acting on them from neighbors on all sides, so overall effect of nuclear force is less.
OR
Nuclei with **mass numbers*** greater than 120
Very large number of nucleons. Means more **protons*** – **electric force*** of repulsion has more effect, overall effect of nuclear force is less.
Heating nuclei gives them high **kinetic energy*** and means two will join when they collide (see **fusion**, page 93).
Hitting large nucleus with particle causes it to split (see **fission**, page 92).
Some heavy nuclei release particles spontaneously (see **radioactivity**, page 86).
Change in energy state of an atom or nucleus is called atomic or nuclear **transition**. Change resulting in change in chemical properties (i.e. a different element) is called **transformation** or **transmutation**.
As shown, finding higher B.E. (lower energy state) may occur with very little "help", e.g. putting unstable atoms together, or in the case of spontaneous radioactivity. In other cases, energy may need to be added (heating atoms, nuclei or particles).
If not enough energy is added, energy is re-released as **photons** (see **quantum theory**). In atoms, electrons "fall" back and the type (**frequency***) of photons emitted depends on the shells between which they move. **X-rays*** (highest frequency, most energy) are emitted if they are the innermost shells, **UV radiation*** is emitted if they are the shells further out, and so on (see **electromagnetic spectrum**, page 44). With nuclei, **γ-rays*** are always emitted (more energy is involved).

* **Electric force**, 6; **Electrons**, 83; **Frequency**, 35; **Kinetic energy**, 9; **Mass number**, 82; **Nucleons**, 82 (**Nucleus**); **Outer shell**, 83 (**Electron shells**); **Protons**, 82; **Ultraviolet** (**UV**) **radiation**, **X-rays**, 44; **Gamma** (γ) **rays**, 44, 86.

RADIOACTIVITY

Radioactivity is a property of some unstable **nuclei** (see pages 82 and 84), whereby they break up spontaneously into nuclei of other elements and emit **radiation***, a process known as **radioactive decay**. There are three types of radiation emitted by radioactive elements: streams of **alpha particles** (called **alpha rays**); streams of **beta particles** (**beta rays**) and **gamma rays**. For more about the detection and uses of radiation, see pages 88-91.

Radioisotope or radioactive isotope

Any radioactive substance (all substances are effectively isotopes – see page 83). There are several naturally-occurring radioisotopes, most of which still exist because they have very long **half-lives** (e.g. uranium-238), though one, carbon-14, is continually produced by **cosmic rays** (see **background radiation**, page 88). Other radioisotopes are produced by **nuclear fission***, and more still are produced in research centers, where nuclei are hit by fast particles (e.g. **protons*** and **neutrons***). These are speeded up in **particle accelerators**, e.g. **cyclotrons** (see picture below).

Cut-away diagram of vacuum chamber (central part of cyclotron)

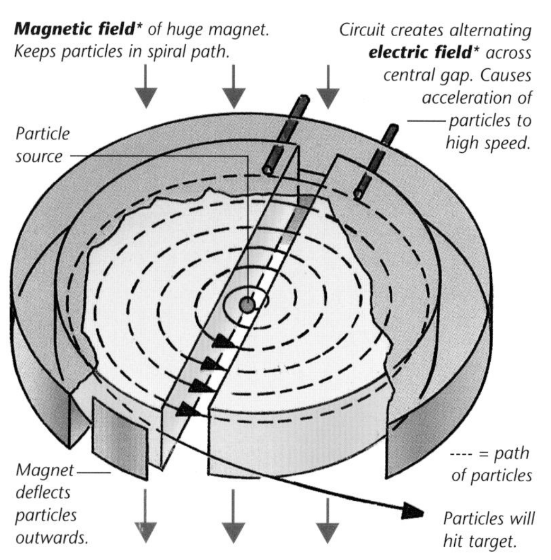
Magnetic field* of huge magnet. Keeps particles in spiral path.
Circuit creates alternating ***electric field**** across central gap. Causes acceleration of particles to high speed.
Particle source
Magnet deflects particles outwards.
---- = path of particles
Particles will hit target.

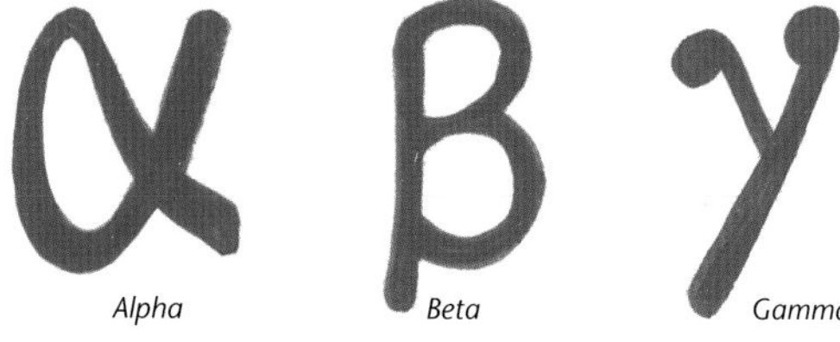
Alpha
Beta
Gamma

The Greek letters used for the three types of radiation*

Alpha particles (α-particles)

Positively-charged particles ejected from some radioactive nuclei (see **alpha decay**). They are relatively heavy (two **protons*** and two **neutrons***), move relatively slowly and have a low penetrating power.

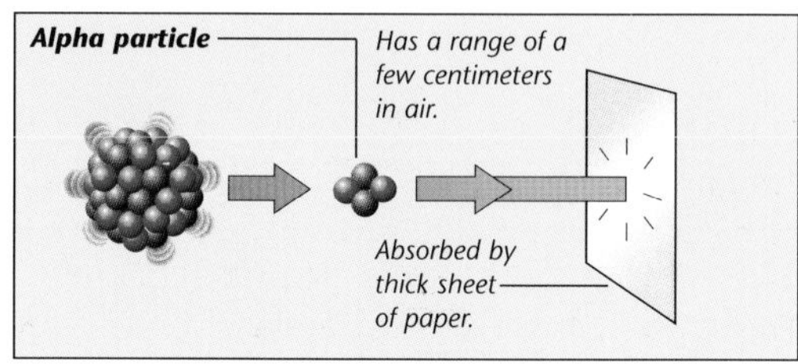
Alpha particle
Has a range of a few centimeters in air.
Absorbed by thick sheet of paper.

Beta particles (β-particles)

Particles ejected from some radioactive nuclei at about the speed of light. There are two types – **electrons*** and **positrons**, which have the same mass as electrons, but a positive charge. See **beta decay**, page 87.

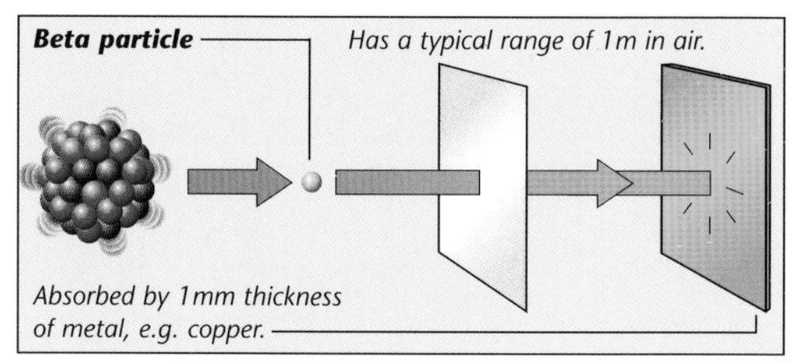
Beta particle
Has a typical range of 1m in air.
Absorbed by 1mm thickness of metal, e.g. copper.

Gamma rays (γ-rays)

Invisible **electromagnetic waves** (see also page 44). They have the highest penetrating power and are generally, though not always, emitted from a radioactive nucleus after an **alpha** or **beta particle**.

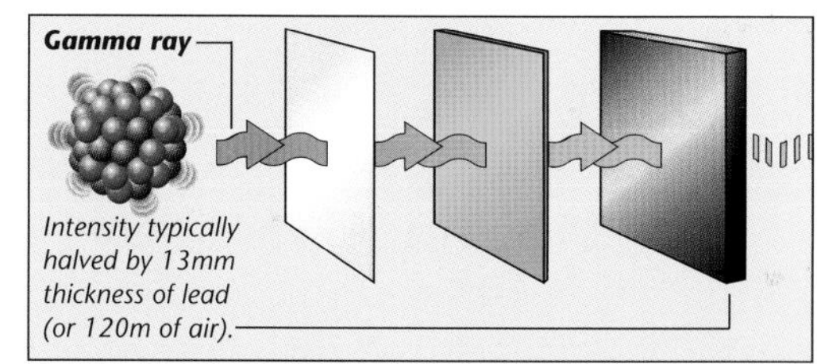
Gamma ray
Intensity typically halved by 13mm thickness of lead (or 120m of air).

* **Electric field**, 58; **Electrons**, 83; **Magnetic field**, 72; **Neutrons**, 82; **Nuclear fission**, 92; **Protons**, 82; **Radiation**, 9.

Radioactive decay

The spontaneous splitting up of a radioactive nucleus, which results in the ejection of **alpha** or **beta particles**, often followed by **gamma rays**. When a nucleus ejects such a particle, i.e. undergoes a nuclear **disintegration**, energy is released (see page 84), and a different nucleus (and atom) is formed. If this is also radioactive, the decay process continues until a stable (non-radioactive) atom is reached. Such a series of disintegrations is called a **decay series, decay chain, radioactive series** or **transformation series**.

Half-life (T½)

The time it takes for half the atoms on average in a sample to undergo **radioactive decay**, and hence for the radiation emitted to be halved. This is all that can be accurately predicted – it is impossible to predict the decay of any single atom, since they decay individually and randomly. The range of half-lives is vast, e.g. the half-life of strontium-90 is 28 years; that of uranium-238 is 4.5×10^9 years.

Alpha decay (α-decay)

The loss of an **alpha particle** by a radioactive nucleus. This decreases the **atomic number*** by two and the **mass number*** by four, and so a new nucleus is formed.

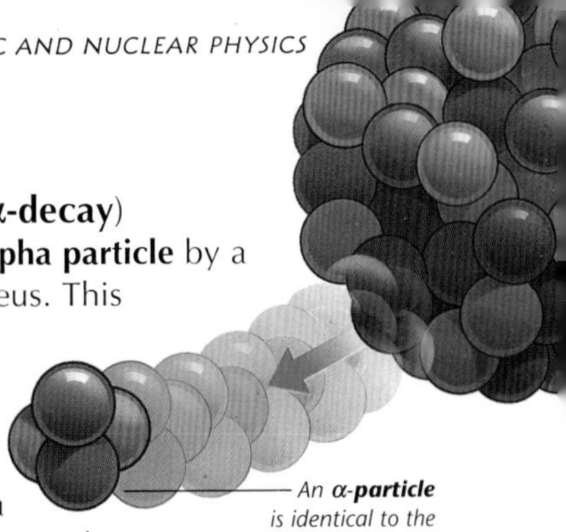

An *α-particle* is identical to the nucleus of a helium atom.

Beta decay (β-decay)

The loss of either kind of **beta particle** by a radioactive nucleus. The electron (**β**⁻ or **e**⁻) is ejected (with another particle called an **antineutrino**) when a **neutron*** decays into a **proton***. The positron (**β**⁺ or **e**⁺) is ejected (with another particle called a **neutrino**) when a proton decays into a neutron. Beta decay thus increases or decreases the **atomic number*** by one (the **mass number*** stays the same).

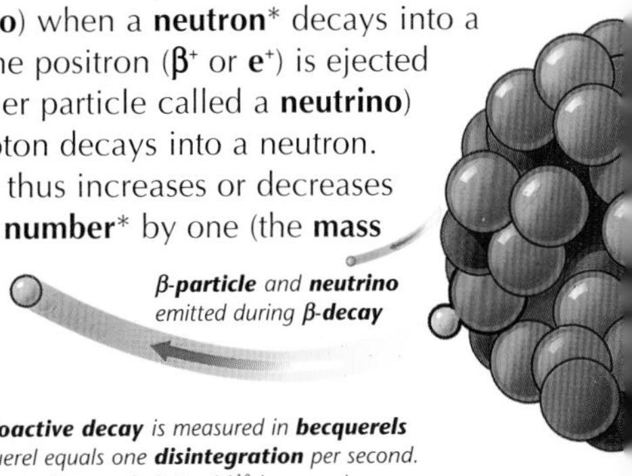

β-particle and **neutrino** emitted during *β-decay*

*The rate of **radioactive decay** is measured in **becquerels** (**Bq**). One becquerel equals one **disintegration** per second. An older unit, the **curie**, equals 3.7×10^{10} becquerels.*

Decay series, showing radioactive decay of thorium-232 to stable lead-208

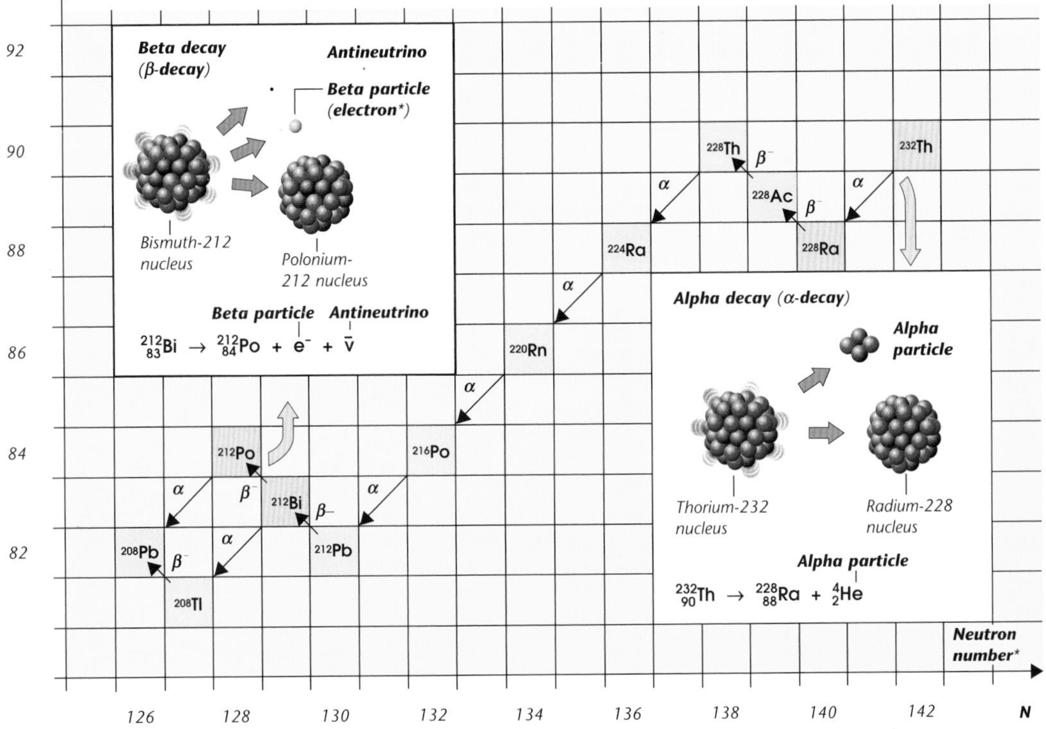

Z
Atomic number*
92
90
88
86
84
82
^{232}Th
α
^{228}Ra
β⁻
^{228}Ac
β⁻
^{228}Th
α
^{224}Ra
α
^{220}Rn
α
^{216}Po
α
^{212}Pb
β⁻
^{212}Bi
β⁻
^{212}Po
α
α
^{208}Tl
β⁻
^{208}Pb
126
128
130
132
134
136
138
140
142
N
Neutron number*

Beta decay (β-decay)
Antineutrino
Beta particle (electron*)
Bismuth-212 nucleus
Polonium-212 nucleus
Beta particle
Antineutrino

$$^{212}_{83}\text{Bi} \rightarrow {}^{212}_{84}\text{Po} + e^- + \bar{\nu}$$

Alpha decay (α-decay)
Alpha particle
Thorium-232 nucleus
Radium-228 nucleus
Alpha particle

$$^{232}_{90}\text{Th} \rightarrow {}^{228}_{88}\text{Ra} + {}^{4}_{2}\text{He}$$

* **Atomic number**, 82; **Electrons**, 83; **Mass number**, **Neutron number**, **Neutrons**, **Protons**, 82.

DETECTING AND MEASURING RADIOACTIVITY

There are a number of devices which detect and measure the radiation emitted by radioactive substances (**radioisotopes***). Some are used mainly in laboratories (to study artificially produced radioisotopes); others have a wider range of uses (e.g. as monitoring devices for safety purposes) and can also be used to detect **background radiation**. Most of the devices detect and measure the radiation by monitoring the **ionization** it causes – see **Geiger counter** and **pulse electroscope**, right, and **cloud** and **bubble chambers**, page 90.

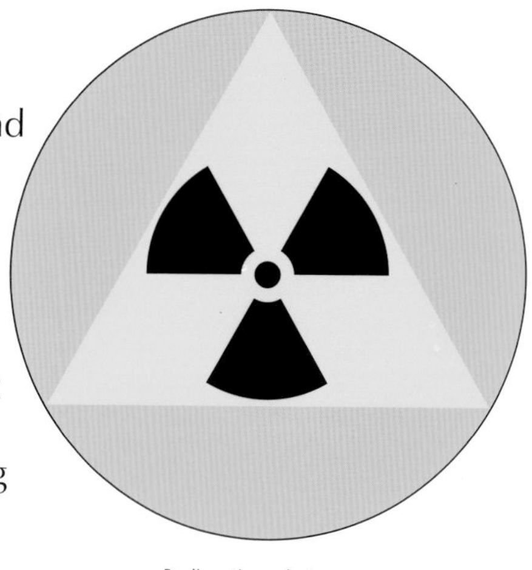

*Radioactive substances (**radioisotopes***) have special hazard warning labels.*

Background radiation
Radiation present on Earth (in relatively small amounts), originating both from natural and unnatural sources. One notable natural source is carbon-14, which is taken in by plants and animals. This is constantly being produced from stable nitrogen-14 due to bombardment by **cosmic rays** (**cosmic radiation**) entering the atmosphere from outer space. These are streams of particles of enormously high energy. Unnatural sources of radiation include industry, medicine and weapons testing. The **background count** is a measure of the background radiation.

Plants, rocks and animals contain carbon-14, a natural source of radiation.

*A **Geiger counter**, used for measuring the **background count**.*

Ionization

The creation of **ions** (electrically-charged particles), which occurs when atoms (which are electrically neutral) lose or gain **electrons***, creating **cations** (positive ions) or **anions** (negative ions) respectively.

Ionization

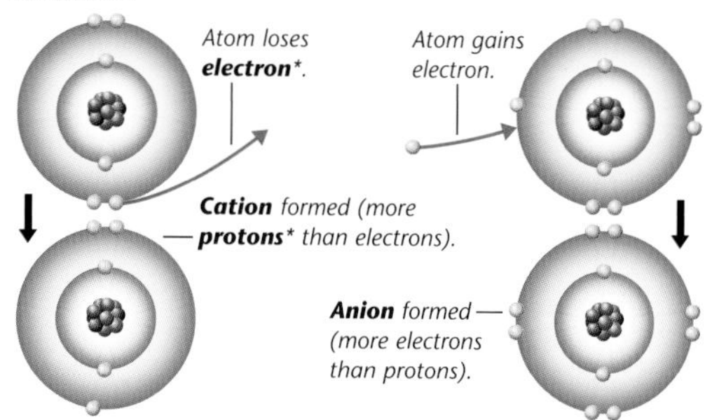
Atom loses **electron***.
Atom gains electron.
Cation formed (more **protons*** than electrons).
Anion formed (more electrons than protons).

In the case of radiation, **alpha** and **beta particles*** ionize the atoms of substances they pass through, usually creating cations. This is because their energy is so high that they cause one or more electrons to be "knocked out". For more about ions and ionization, see pages 130-131.

Ionization due to radiation

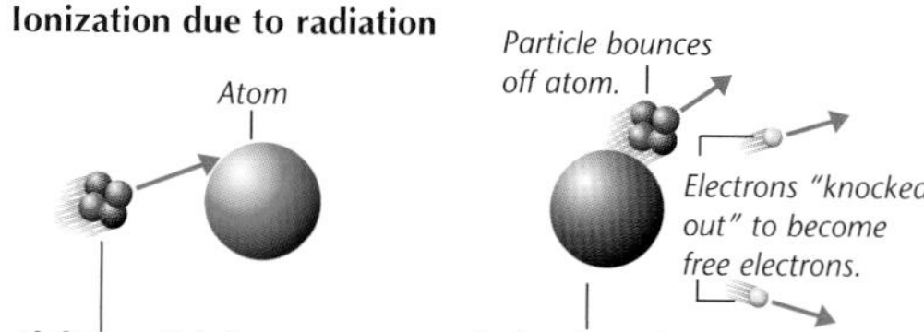
Atom
Alpha particle*
Particle bounces off atom.
Electrons "knocked out" to become free electrons.
Cation formed

* **Alpha particles**, **Beta particles**, 86; **Electrons**, 83; **Protons**, 82; **Radioisotope**, 86.

Detection devices

Dosimeter or **film badge**

A device worn by all who work with radioactive material. It contains photographic film (which radiation will darken). This is developed regularly and the amount of darkening shows the **dose** of radiation the wearer has been exposed to.

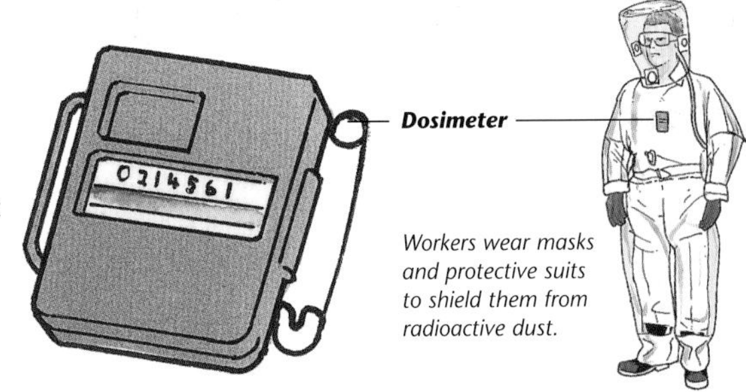
0214561
Dosimeter
Workers wear masks and protective suits to shield them from radioactive dust.

Geiger counter

A piece of apparatus (see picture, page 88) consisting of a **Geiger-Müller tube**, a **scaler** and/or **ratemeter** and often a loudspeaker. The tube is a gas-filled cylinder with two **electrodes*** – its walls act as the **cathode***, and it has a central wire **anode***. The whole apparatus indicates the presence of radiation by registering pulses of current between the electrodes. These pulses result from the **ionization** the radiation causes in the gas (normally low pressure argon, plus a trace of bromine). A scaler is an electronic counter which counts the pulses and a ratemeter measures the count rate – the average rate of pulses in counts per second.

Geiger counter

1. Radiation enters via thin window.

*2. Each particle or ray **ionizes** several gas atoms.*

*3. Ions attracted to cathode, **electrons*** to anode.*

*4. Other atoms are hit on the way, creating **avalanche** of more ions and electrons.*

5. Electrons taken in at anode and "pulled" from cathode (to turn ions back into atoms).

6. Pulse of current (amplified because of avalanche) flows round circuit for each original particle or ray.

+

–

Radioactive source

*Wire **anode****

*Cylinder walls form **cathode****.

Resistor*

Amplifier

*To loudspeaker. Clicks with each pulse (irregular intervals show randomness of **radioactive decay****).*

Enhances each pulse further

*To **scaler** and/or **ratemeter***

Pulse (**Wulf**) **electroscope**

A type of **gold-leaf electroscope***. The walls of a chamber of air around the cap form the **cathode***, and a side **anode*** is placed close to the leaf. This attracts **electrons*** down from the cap, leaving it positively charged (the leaf moves away from the rod, as they are both negatively charged, but not enough to touch the anode before the radioactive source is introduced). The leaf indicates the presence of radiation by beating forward and back for each **ionization** it causes.

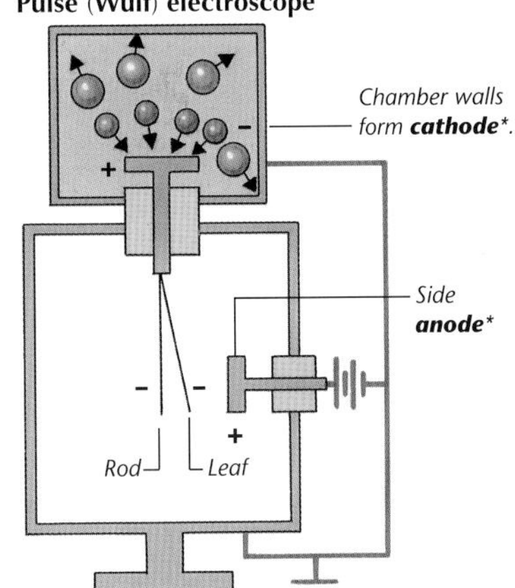
Pulse (Wulf) electroscope
Chamber walls form cathode*.
+
–
Side anode*
–
–
+
Rod
Leaf

*1. Radiation from radioactive source **ionizes** air in chamber.*

*2. **Avalanche** of ions and **electrons*** formed (see **Geiger counter**).*

3. Ions move to cathode, electrons enter cap and are pulled down leaf by anode.

*4. Leaf moves over to touch anode and pulse of current flows (see **Geiger counter**).*

5. Leaf becomes neutral and moves back to rod, aided by spring. Process starts again.

* **Anode**, **Cathode**, 66 (**Electrode**); **Electrons**, 83;
Gold-leaf electroscope, 56 (**Electroscope**); **Radioactive decay**, 87; **Resistor**, 62.

Detection devices (continued)

Cloud chamber

A device in which the paths taken by **alpha** and **beta particles*** show up as tracks. This happens when the vapor in the chamber (alcohol or water vapor) is turned into **supersaturated** vapor by cooling (in one of two different ways – see below). A supersaturated vapor is vapor below the temperature at which it should condense, but which does not condense because there are no dust or other particles present for droplets to form around.

Wilson cloud chamber
Vapor cooled by sudden increase in volume (withdrawal of piston).

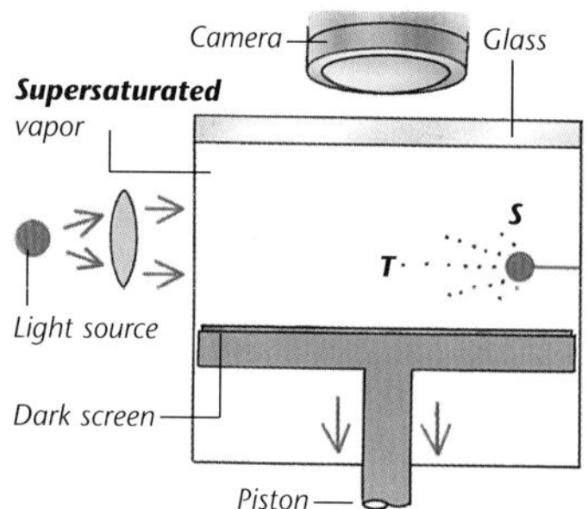

Camera
Glass
Supersaturated vapor
S
T
Light source
Dark screen
Piston

1. *Radiation from source (**S**) causes **ionization*** of vapor.*

2. *Ions formed act like dust particles, i.e. vapor condenses on them.*

3. *Tracks of liquid droplets (**T**) left where vapor has condensed (visible long enough to be photographed).*

Diffusion cloud chamber
*Vapor cooled by a base of dry ice (solid carbon dioxide). Vapor **diffuses*** downwards.*

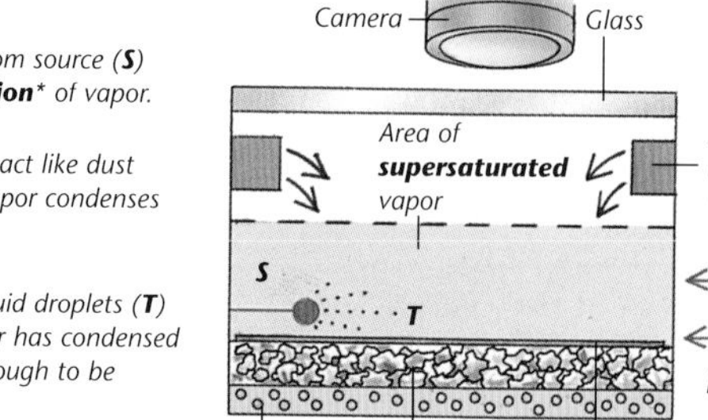

Camera
Glass
Area of supersaturated vapor
Felt pad soaked in alcohol/ water
S
T
Light source
Sponge
Dry ice
Dark screen

Cloud chamber** tracks (right) are produced at irregular intervals, showing random nature of **radioactive decay.*

*Tracks made by heavy **α-particles*** are short, straight and thick.*

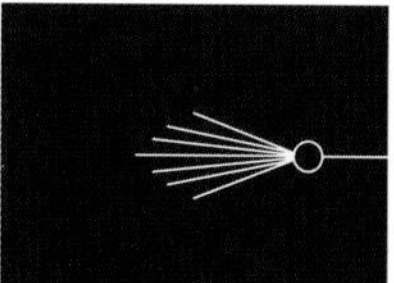

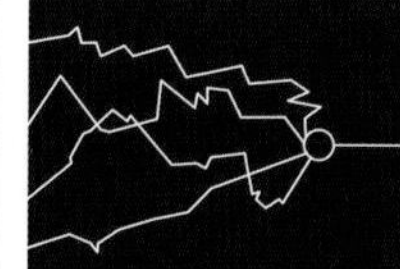

*Tracks made by light **β-particles*** are long, straggly and thin.*

Gamma rays do not create tracks themselves, but can knock **electrons*** out of single atoms. These then speed away and create tracks like β-particle tracks (see left).*

Bubble chamber

A device which, like a cloud chamber, shows particle tracks. It contains **superheated** liquid (usually hydrogen or helium) – liquid heated to above its boiling point, but not actually boiling because it is under pressure. After the pressure is suddenly lowered, nuclear particles entering the chamber cause **ionization*** of the liquid atoms. Wherever this occurs, the energy released makes the liquid boil, producing tracks of bubbles.

***Bubble chamber** tracks, showing paths taken by nuclear particles.*

Bubble tracks are generally curved, because a magnetic field is set up to deflect particles. (This leads to better identification.)

Scintillation counter

A device which detects **gamma rays***. It consists of a **scintillation crystal** and a **photomultiplier** tube. The crystal is made of a **phosphor*** (e.g. sodium iodide). Phosphors emit light flashes (**scintillations**) when hit by radiation.

Scintillation counter

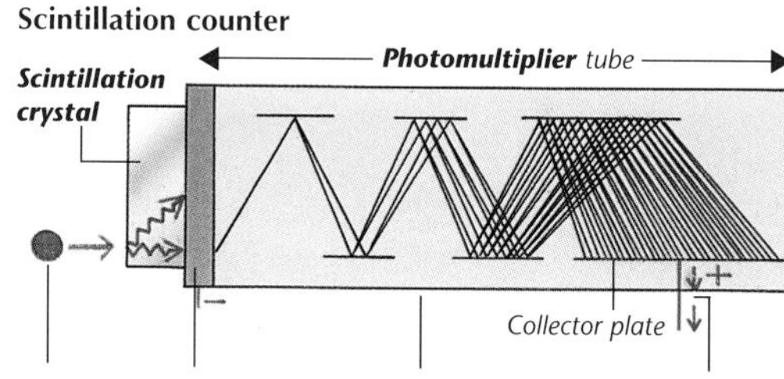

Scintillation crystal
Photomultiplier tube
Collector plate
–
+

1. *Radiation from source makes crystal emit light*

2. *Photosensitive material with negative charge. Emits **electrons*** when hit by light flashes.*

3. *Main part of tube (**electron multiplier**). Electrons accelerated to far end by electric field, hitting metal plates and releasing more electrons.*

4. *Strong pulse of current hence produced for each original **gamma ray***. This is shown on **scaler** and/or **ratemeter** (see **Geiger counter**, page 89).*

* **Alpha particles**, **Beta particles**, 86; **Diffusion**, 5; **Electrons**, 83; **Gamma rays**, 86; **Ionization**, 88; **Phosphors**, 44 (**Phosphorescence**); **Radioactive decay**, 87.

USES OF RADIOACTIVITY

The radiation emitted by **radioisotopes*** (radioactive substances) can be put to a wide variety of uses, particularly in the fields of medicine, industry and archaeological research.

Radiology
The study of radioactivity and **X-rays***, especially with regard to their use in medicine.

Radiotherapy
The use of the radiation emitted by **radioisotopes*** to treat disease. All living cells are susceptible to radiation, so it is possible to destroy malignant (cancer) cells by using carefully controlled doses of radiation.

Robots are often used in industry to handle dangerous radioactive substances.

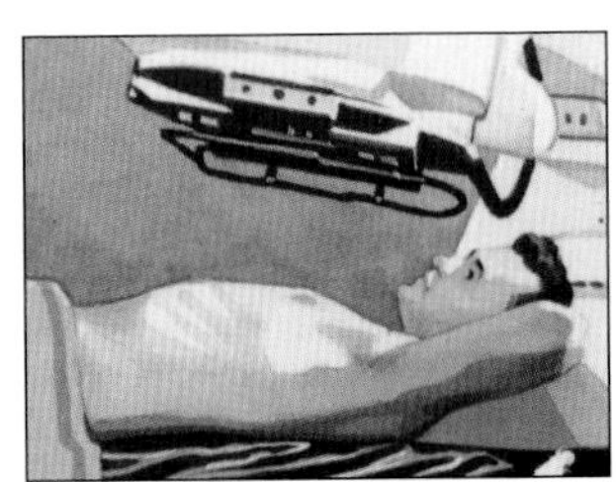

*This patient is undergoing **external beam radiotherapy**, where the radiation is emitted from a machine outside the body. Some types of cancer can be treated by **radioactive implants** inserted into the body.*

Radioactive tracing
A method of following the path of a substance through an object, and detecting its concentration as it moves. This is done by introducing a **radioisotope*** into the substance and tracking the radiation it emits. The radioisotope used is called a **tracer**, and the substance is said to be **labeled**. In medical diagnosis, for example, high levels of the radioisotope in an organ may indicate the presence of malignant (cancer) cells. The radioisotopes used always have short **half-lives*** and decay into harmless substances.

Irradiation
Food, such as fruit and meat can be **irradiated** with **gamma rays***. The radiation delays ripening in fruit and vegetables, and destroys bacteria in meat, enabling it to keep fresh for longer.

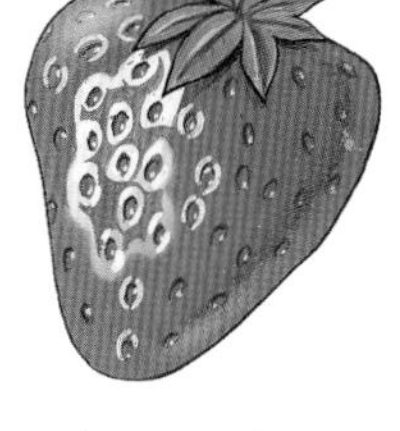

*After two weeks, this **irradiated** strawberry is still firm and fresh.*

Gamma radiography (γ-radiography)
The production of a **radiograph** (similar to a photograph) by the use of **gamma rays*** (see also **X-radiography**, page 44). This has many uses, including quality control in industry.

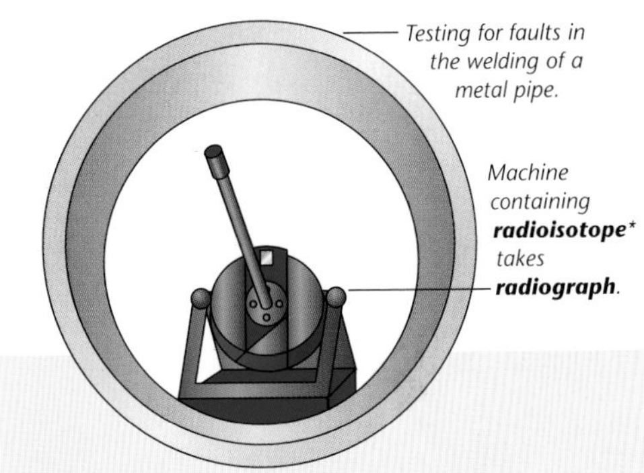
Testing for faults in the welding of a metal pipe.
Machine containing ***radioisotope**** takes ***radiograph***.

Radiocarbon dating or carbon dating
A way of calculating the time elapsed since living matter died. All living things contain a small amount of carbon-14 (a **radioisotope*** absorbed from the atmosphere), which continues to emit radiation after death. This emission gradually decreases (carbon-14 has a **half-life*** of 5,700 years), so the age of the remains can be calculated from its strength.

__Radiocarbon dating__ showed that this insect trapped in amber is 5,000 years old.

* **Gamma rays**, 86; **Half-life**, 87; **Radioisotope**, 86; **X-rays**, 44.

NUCLEAR FISSION AND FUSION

The central **nucleus** of an atom (see page 82) holds vast amounts of "stored" energy (see pages 84-85). **Nuclear fission** and **nuclear fusion** are both ways in which this energy can be released. They are both **nuclear reactions** (reactions which bring about a change in the nucleus).

Mushroom-shaped cloud from the explosion of a ***fission bomb****.*

Nuclear fission

The process in which a heavy, unstable nucleus splits into two (or more) lighter nuclei, roughly equal in size, with the release of two or three **neutrons*** (**fission neutrons**) and a large amount of energy (see also page 84). The two lighter nuclei are called **fission products** or **fission fragments** and many of them are **radioactive***. Fission is made to happen (see **induced fission**) in **fission reactors*** to produce heat energy. It does not often occur naturally (**spontaneous fission**).

Induced fission of uranium-235

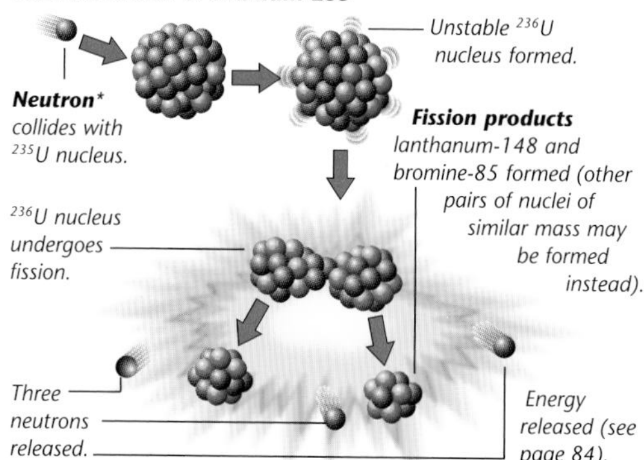

Unstable ^{236}U nucleus formed.
Neutron* collides with ^{235}U nucleus.
Fission products lanthanum-148 and bromine-85 formed (other pairs of nuclei of similar mass may be formed instead).
^{236}U nucleus undergoes fission.
Three neutrons released.
Energy released (see page 84).

Nuclear equation *for reaction, above (see* ***mass*** *and* ***atomic numbers****, page 82):*

$$^{235}_{92}U + ^{1}_{0}n \rightarrow ^{236}_{92}U \rightarrow ^{148}_{57}La + ^{85}_{35}Br + 3^{1}_{0}n + \text{energy}$$

Spontaneous fission

Nuclear fission which occurs naturally, i.e. without assistance from an outside agency. This may happen to a nucleus of a heavy element, e.g. the **isotope*** uranium-238, but the probability is very low compared to that of a simpler process like **alpha decay*** occurring instead.

Induced fission

Nuclear fission of a nucleus made unstable by artificial means, i.e. by being hit by a particle (often a **neutron***), which it then absorbs. Not all nuclei can be induced to fission in this way; those which can, e.g. those of the **isotopes*** uranium-235 and plutonium-239, are described as **fissile**. If there are lots of fissile nuclei in a substance (see also **thermal** and **fast reactor**, page 95), the neutrons released by induced fissions will cause more fissions (and neutrons), and so on. This is known as a **chain reaction**. A well-controlled chain reaction is allowed to occur in a **fission reactor***, but that occurring in a **fission bomb** is uncontrolled and extremely explosive.

Induced fission causing a chain reaction

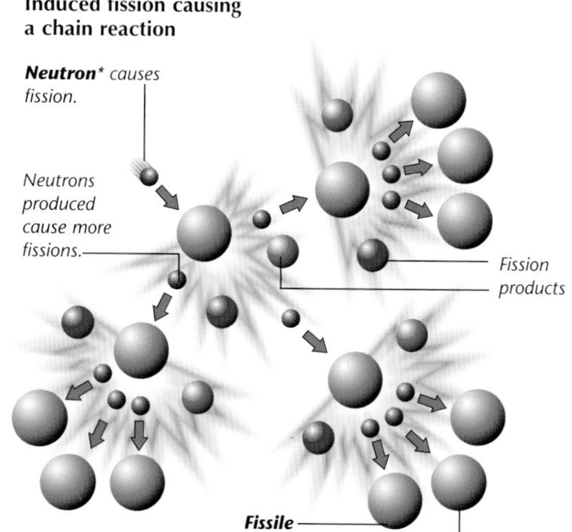

Neutron* causes fission.
Neutrons produced cause more fissions.
Fission products
Fissile nuclei

* **Alpha decay**, 87; **Fission reactor**, 94; **Isotopes**, 83; **Neutrons**, 82; **Radioactivity**, 86.

Critical mass

The minimum mass of a **fissile** substance needed to sustain a **chain reaction** (see **induced fission**). In smaller **subcritical masses**, the surface area to volume ratio is too high, and too many of the **neutrons*** produced by the first fissions escape into the atmosphere. Nuclear fuel is kept in subcritical masses.

Fission bomb or atom bomb (A-bomb)

A bomb in which two **subcritical masses** (see above) are brought together by a trigger explosion. The resulting **chain reaction** (see **induced fission**) releases huge amounts of energy.

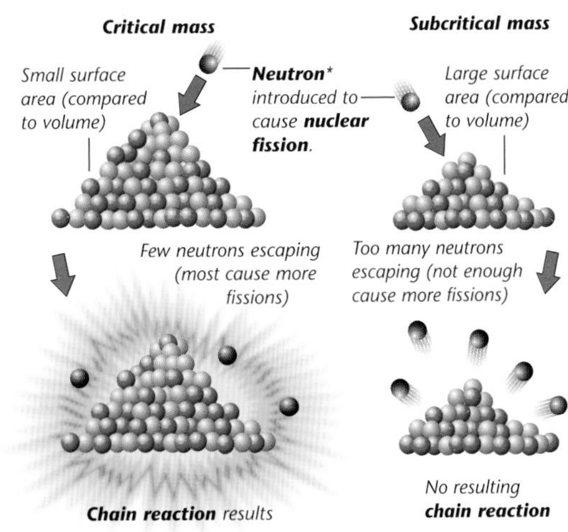
Critical mass
Subcritical mass
Small surface area (compared to volume)
Neutron* introduced to cause nuclear fission.
Large surface area (compared to volume)
Few neutrons escaping (most cause more fissions)
Too many neutrons escaping (not enough cause more fissions)
Chain reaction results
No resulting chain reaction

Nuclear fusion

The collision and combination of two light nuclei to form a heavier, more stable nucleus, with the release of large amounts of energy (see also page 84). Unlike **nuclear fission**, it does not leave **radioactive*** products. Nuclear fusion requires temperatures of millions of degrees Celsius, to give the nuclei enough **kinetic energy*** for them to fuse when they collide. (Because of the high temperatures, fusion reactions are also called **thermonuclear reactions**.) It therefore only occurs naturally in the Sun (and stars like it), but research is being carried out with the aim of achieving controlled, induced fusion in **fusion reactors***.

Example of nuclear fusion
*(**D-T reaction** – see also **fusion reactor**, page 94.)*

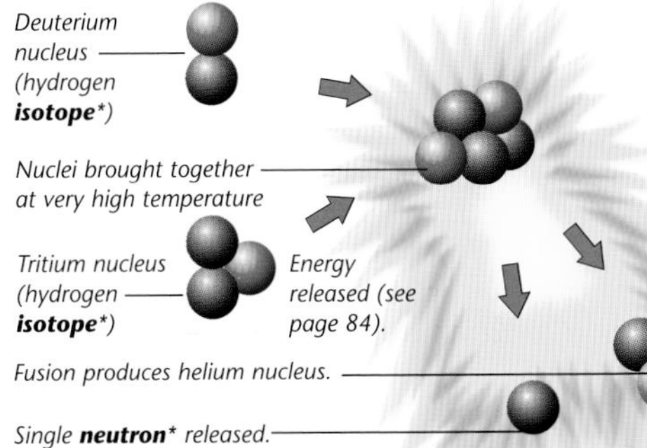
Deuterium nucleus (hydrogen isotope*)
Nuclei brought together at very high temperature
Tritium nucleus (hydrogen isotope*)
Energy released (see page 84).
Fusion produces helium nucleus.
Single neutron* released.

***Nuclear equation** for reaction above (see **mass and atomic numbers**, page 82):*

$$^{2}_{1}H + ^{3}_{1}H \rightarrow ^{4}_{2}He + ^{1}_{0}n + \text{energy}$$

Fusion bomb or hydrogen bomb (H-bomb)

A bomb in which uncontrolled **nuclear fusion** occurs in a mixture of tritium and deuterium (hydrogen **isotopes***). A trigger **fission bomb** creates the high temperature needed (fusion bombs are also called **fission-fusion bombs**). The energy released is about 30 times that released from a fission bomb of the same size.

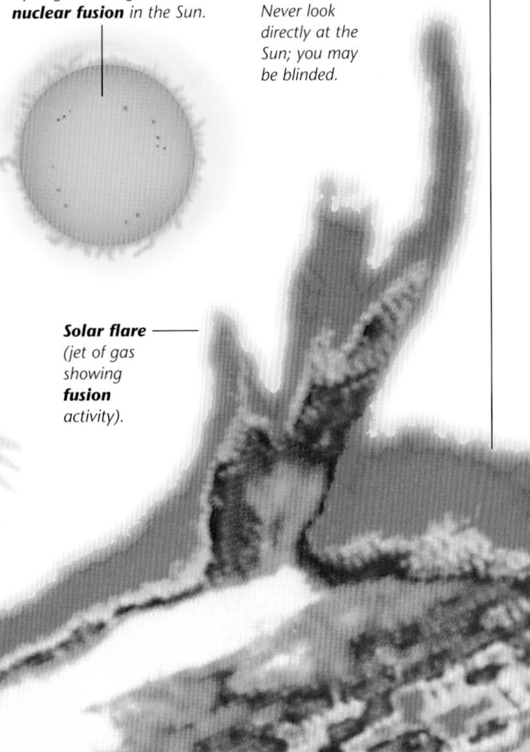
Hydrogen undergoes nuclear fusion in the Sun.
WARNING: Never look directly at the Sun; you may be blinded.
Solar flare (jet of gas showing fusion activity).

* **Fusion reactor**, 94; **Isotopes**, 83; **Kinetic energy**, 9; **Neutrons**, 82; **Radioactivity**, 86.

POWER FROM NUCLEAR REACTIONS

A **nuclear reactor** is a structure inside which nuclear reactions produce vast amounts of heat. There are potentially two main types of reactor – **fission reactors** and **fusion reactors**, though the latter are still being researched. All present-day **nuclear power stations** are built around a central fission reactor and each generates, per unit mass of fuel, far larger amounts of power (electricity) than any other type of power station.

Fission reactor

A **nuclear reactor** in which the heat is produced by **nuclear fission***. There are two main types in use in nuclear power stations – **thermal reactors** and **fast reactors** or **fast breeder reactors** (see page opposite), both of which use uranium as their main fuel.

The uranium is held in long cylinders packed in the **core** (center of the reactor). The rate of the **chain reaction*** (and hence the rate of power production) is closely controlled by **control rods**. The diagram below shows how a fission reactor can be used to generate power.

Schematic diagram of fission reactor and power station complex

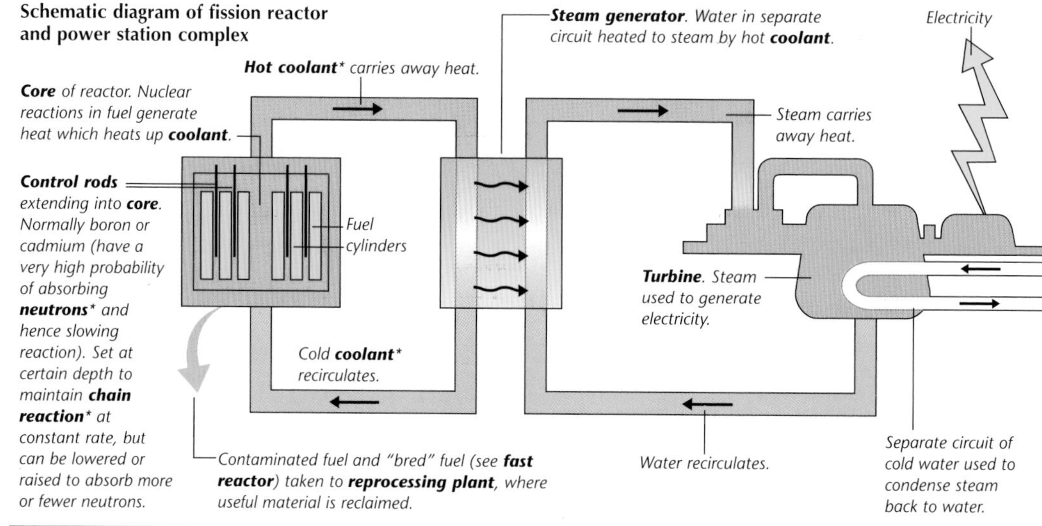

Hot coolant* carries away heat.
***Core** of reactor. Nuclear reactions in fuel generate heat which heats up **coolant**.*
Control rods *extending into **core**. Normally boron or cadmium (have a very high probability of absorbing **neutrons*** and hence slowing reaction). Set at certain depth to maintain **chain reaction*** at constant rate, but can be lowered or raised to absorb more or fewer neutrons.*
Fuel cylinders
*Cold **coolant*** recirculates.*
*Contaminated fuel and "bred" fuel (see **fast reactor**) taken to **reprocessing plant**, where useful material is reclaimed.*
***Steam generator**. Water in separate circuit heated to steam by hot **coolant**.*
Steam carries away heat.
Electricity
***Turbine**. Steam used to generate electricity.*
Water recirculates.
Separate circuit of cold water used to condense steam back to water.

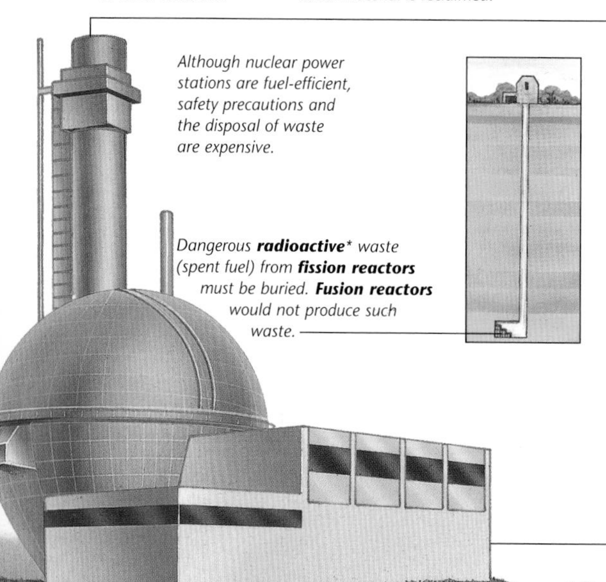

Although nuclear power stations are fuel-efficient, safety precautions and the disposal of waste are expensive.
*Dangerous **radioactive*** waste (spent fuel) from **fission reactors** must be buried. **Fusion reactors** would not produce such waste.*

Fusion reactor

A type of **nuclear reactor**, being researched but as yet undeveloped, in which the heat would be produced by **nuclear fusion***. This would probably be the fusion of the nuclei of the hydrogen **isotopes*** deuterium and tritium – known as the **D-T reaction** (see picture, page 93). There are several major problems to be overcome before a fusion reactor becomes a reality, but it would produce about four times as much energy per unit mass of fuel as a **fission reactor**. Also, hydrogen is abundant, whereas uranium is scarce, and dangerous and expensive to mine.

* **Chain reaction**, 92 (**Induced fission**); **Coolant**, 344; **Isotopes**, 83; **Neutrons**, 82; **Nuclear fission**, 92; **Nuclear fusion**, 93; **Radioactivity**, 86.

Types of fission reactor

Thermal reactor

A **fission reactor** containing a **moderator** around the fuel cylinders. This is a substance with light nuclei, such as graphite or water. It is used to slow down the fast **neutrons*** produced by the first fissions in the uranium fuel – the neutrons bounce off the light nuclei (which themselves are unlikely to absorb neutrons) and eventually slow down to about 2,200m s^{-1}. Slowing the neutrons improves their chances of causing further fissions (and continuing the **chain reaction***). Faster neutrons are likely to be "captured" by the most abundant nuclei – those of the **isotope*** uranium-238 (see **fast reactor**), whereas slow neutrons can travel on until they find uranium-235 nuclei. These will undergo fission when hit by neutrons of any speed, but make up a smaller percentage of the fuel (despite the fact that it is now often enriched with extra atoms of ^{235}U).

Types of thermal reactor

Pressurized water reactor (PWR)

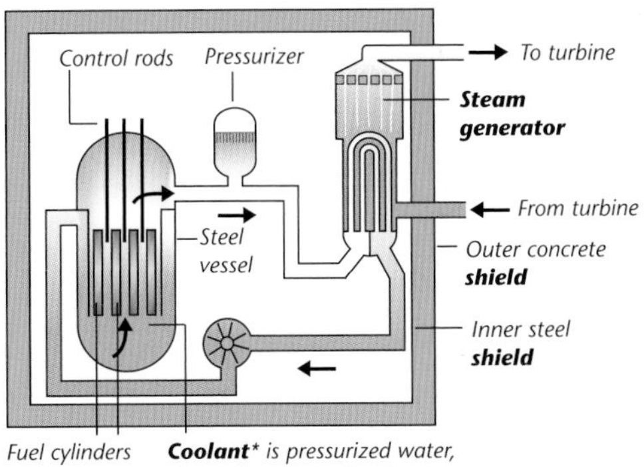
Control rods
Pressurizer
To turbine
Steam generator
From turbine
Steel vessel
Outer concrete shield
Inner steel shield
Fuel cylinders
Coolant* is pressurized water, also acting as moderator.

Advanced gas-cooled reactor (AGR)

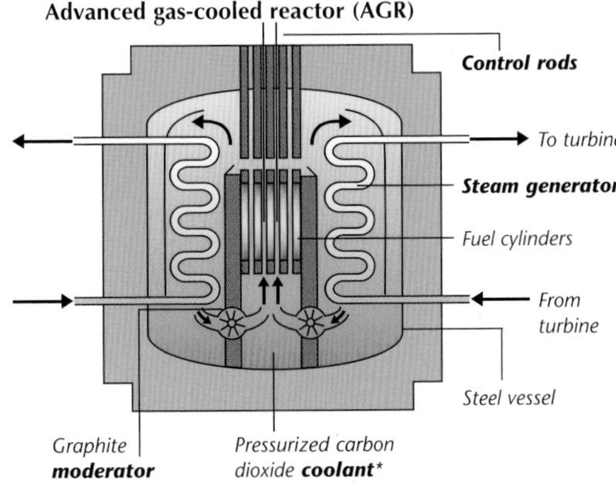
Control rods
To turbine
Steam generator
Fuel cylinders
From turbine
Steel vessel
Graphite moderator
Pressurized carbon dioxide coolant*

Fast reactor or fast breeder reactor (FBR)

A **fission reactor**, inside which the **neutrons*** which cause the fission are allowed to remain as fast neutrons (traveling at about 2 × 10^7m s^{-1}). The fuel used is always enriched with extra nuclei of uranium-235 (see **thermal reactor**) and plutonium-239. Both of these will fission easily when hit by fast neutrons, unlike uranium-238, which is far more likely to "capture" the neutrons (becoming ^{239}U) and undergo **radioactive decay***. The final product of this decay, however, is ^{239}Pu. Fast reactors are also called "breeders" because this decay process of ^{239}U to ^{239}Pu is allowed to happen in a blanket of ^{238}U around the main fuel. Hence more fuel is created and can be stored. Fast reactors have a more compact core and run at higher temperatures than thermal reactors. They are also more efficient, using up a much greater proportion of their fuel before it becomes contaminated.

Fast reactor

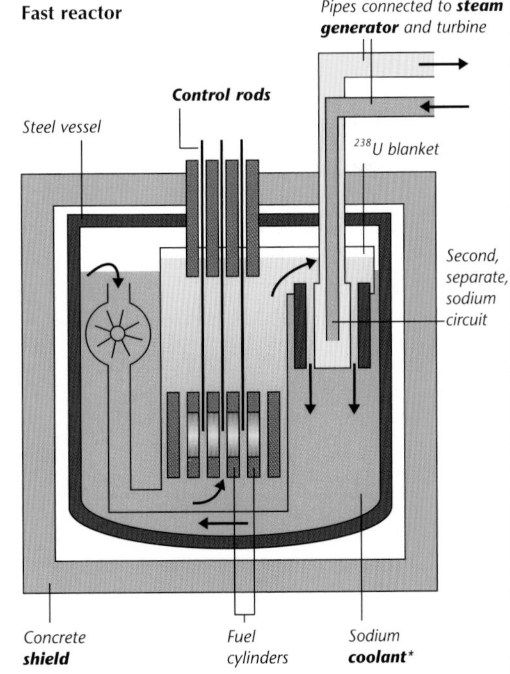
Pipes connected to steam generator and turbine
Control rods
Steel vessel
^{238}U blanket
Second, separate, sodium circuit
Concrete shield
Fuel cylinders
Sodium coolant*

* **Chain reaction**, 92 (**Induced fission**); **Coolant**, 344; **Isotopes**, 83; **Neutrons**, 82; **Radioactive decay**, 87.

QUANTITIES AND UNITS

Physical quantities are such things as **mass***, **force*** and **current***, which are used in the physical sciences. They all have to be measured in some way and each therefore has its own **unit**. These are chosen by international agreement and are called **International System** or **SI units** – abbreviated from the French Système International d'Unités. All quantities are classified as either **basic quantities** or **derived quantities**.

Basic quantities

A set of quantities from which all other quantities (see **derived quantities**) can be defined (see table, below). Each basic quantity has its **basic SI unit**, in terms of which any other SI unit can be defined.

Basic quantity	Symbol	Basic SI unit	Abbreviation
Mass	*m*	*kilogram*	*kg*
Time	*t*	*second*	*s*
Length	*l*	*meter*	*m*
Current	*I*	*ampere*	*A*
Temperature	*T*	*kelvin*	*K*
Quantity of substance	–	*mole*	*mol*
Luminous intensity	–	*candela*	*cd*

Prefixes

A given SI unit may sometimes be too large or small for convenience, e.g. the meter is too large for measuring the thickness of a piece of paper. Standard fractions and multiples of the SI units are therefore used and written by placing a prefix before the unit (see table below). For example, the millimeter (mm) is equal to one thousandth of a meter.

Fractions and multiples in use

Fraction or multiple	Prefix	Symbol
10^{-9}	*nano-*	*n*
10^{-6}	*micro-*	*μ*
10^{-3}	*milli-*	*m*
10^{-2}	*centi-*	*c*
10^{-1}	*deci-*	*d*
10^{1}	*deca-*	*dc*
10^{2}	*hecto-*	*h*
10^{3}	*kilo-*	*k*
10^{6}	*mega-*	*M*
10^{9}	*giga-*	*G*

Basic SI units

Kilogram (kg)

The SI unit of mass. It is equal to the mass of an international prototype metal cylinder kept at Sèvres, near Paris.

Second (s)

The SI unit of time. It is equal to the duration of 9,192,631,770 **periods*** of a certain type of radiation emitted by the cesium-133 atom.

Meter (m)

The SI unit of length. It is equal to the distance light travels in a vacuum in $^1/_{299,792,458}$ of a second.

Ampere (A)

The SI unit of electric current (see also page 60). It is equal to the size of a current flowing through parallel, infinitely long, straight wires in a vacuum that produces a force between the wires of 2 x 10^{-7}N every meter.

Kelvin (K)

The SI unit of temperature. It is equal to $^1/_{273.16}$ of the temperature of the **triple point** of water (the point at which ice, water and steam can all exist at the same time) on the **absolute temperature scale***.

Mole (mol)

The SI unit of the quantity of a substance (note that this is different from mass because it is the number of particles of a substance). It is equal to the amount of substance which contains 6.023 x 10^{23} (this is **Avogadro's number**) particles (e.g. atoms or molecules).

Candela (cd)

The SI unit of intensity of light. It is equal to the strength of light from $^1/_{600,000}$ square meters of a **black body*** at the temperature of freezing platinum and at a pressure of 101,325N m^{-2}.

* **Absolute temperature scale**, 27; **Black body**, 29 (**Leslie's cube**); **Current**, 60; **Force**, 6; **Mass**, 12; **Period**, 16.

Derived quantities

Quantities other than **basic quantities** which are defined in terms of these or in terms of other derived quantities. The derived quantities have **derived SI units** which are defined in terms of the **basic SI units** or other derived units. They are determined from the defining equation for the quantity and are sometimes given special names.

Derived quantity	Symbol	Defining equation	Derived SI unit	Name of unit	Abbreviation
Velocity	*v*	$v = \frac{\text{change in displacement}}{\text{time}}$	$m\ s^{-1}$	–	–
Acceleration	*a*	$a = \frac{\text{change in velocity}}{\text{time}}$	$m\ s^{-2}$	–	–
Force	*F*	*F* = *mass* × *acceleration*	$kg\ m\ s^{-2}$	*newton*	*N*
Work	*W*	*W* = *force* × *distance*	*N m*	*joule*	*J*
Energy	*E*	*Capacity to do work*	*J*	–	–
Power	*P*	$P = \frac{\text{work done}}{\text{time}}$	$J\ s^{-1}$	*watt*	*W*
Area	*A*	*Depends on shape (see page 101)*	m^2	–	–
Volume	*V*	*Depends on shape (see page 101)*	m^3	–	–
Density	*ρ*	$\rho = \frac{\text{mass}}{\text{volume}}$	$kg\ m^{-3}$	–	–
Pressure	*P*	$P = \frac{\text{force}}{\text{area}}$	$N\ m^{-2}$	*pascal*	*Pa*
Period	*T*	*Time for one cycle*	*s*	–	–
Frequency	*f*	*Number of cycles per second*	s^{-1}	*hertz*	*Hz*
Impulse	–	*Impulse* = *force* × *time*	*N s*	–	–
Momentum	–	*Momentum* = *mass* × *velocity*	$kg\ m\ s^{-1}$	–	–
Electric charge	*Q*	*Q* = *current* × *time*	*A s*	*coulomb*	*C*
Potential difference	*V*	$V = \frac{\text{energy transferred}}{\text{charge}}$	$J\ C^{-1}$	*volt*	*V*
Capacitance	*C*	$C = \frac{\text{charge}}{\text{potential difference}}$	$C\ V^{-1}$	*farad*	*F*
Resistance	*R*	$R = \frac{\text{potential difference}}{\text{current}}$	$V\ A^{-1}$	*ohm*	*Ω*

EQUATIONS, SYMBOLS AND GRAPHS

All **physical quantities** (see pages 96-97) and their units can be represented by **symbols** and are normally dependent in some way on other quantities. There is therefore a relationship between them which can be expressed as an **equation** and shown on a **graph**.

Equations

An **equation** represents the relationship between two or more physical quantities. This relationship can be expressed as a **word equation** or as an equation relating **symbols** which represent the quantities. The latter is used when a number of quantities are involved, since it is then easier to manipulate. Note that the meaning of the symbols must be stated.

Word equation

$$\text{Density} = \frac{\text{mass}}{\text{volume}}$$

Symbol equation

$$Q = m \times c \times (t_2 - t_1) \text{ or } Q = mc(t_2 - t_1)$$

where Q = heat energy lost or gained; m = mass; c = specific heat capacity; t_1 and t_2 = temperatures.

Graphs

A **graph** is a visual representation of the relationship between two quantities. It shows how one quantity depends on another. Points on a graph are plotted using the values for the quantities obtained during an experiment or by using the equation for the relationship if it is known. The two quantities plotted are called the **variables**.

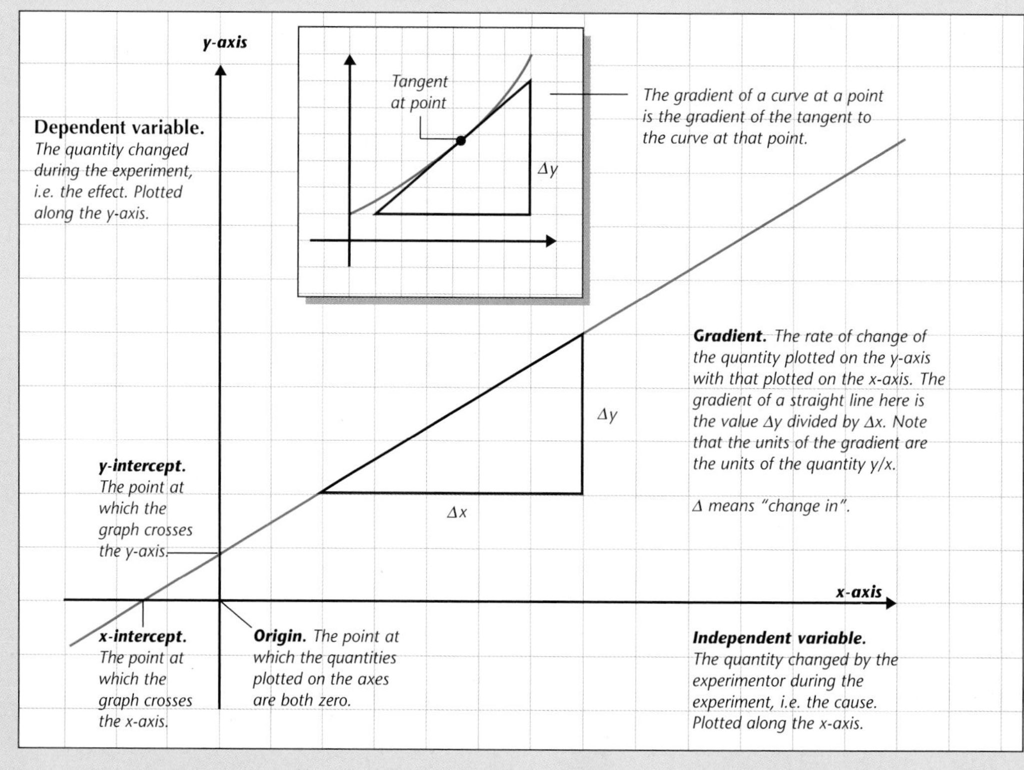
y-axis
Tangent at point
Δy
The gradient of a curve at a point is the gradient of the tangent to the curve at that point.
Dependent variable. The quantity changed during the experiment, i.e. the effect. Plotted along the y-axis.
Gradient. The rate of change of the quantity plotted on the y-axis with that plotted on the x-axis. The gradient of a straight line here is the value Δy divided by Δx. Note that the units of the gradient are the units of the quantity y/x.
Δ means "change in".
Δy
Δx
y-intercept. The point at which the graph crosses the y-axis.
x-axis
x-intercept. The point at which the graph crosses the x-axis.
Origin. The point at which the quantities plotted on the axes are both zero.
Independent variable. The quantity changed by the experimentor during the experiment, i.e. the cause. Plotted along the x-axis.

Symbols

Symbols are used to represent **physical quantities**. The value of a physical quantity consists of a numerical value and its unit. Therefore any symbol represents both a number and a unit.

Symbols represent number and unit, e.g. m = 2.1kg, or s = 400J kg^{-1} K^{-1}.

"Current through resistor = I" (i.e. it is not necessary to say I amps since the unit is included).

Note that a symbol divided by a unit is a pure number, e.g. m = 2.1kg means that m/kg = 2.1.

This notation is used in tables and to label graph axes.

Any number in this column is a length in meters.

Any number in this column is a time squared measured in seconds squared.

l/m	t^2/s^2
0.9	3.6
1.0	4.0
1.1	4.4
1.2	4.8

Any number on this scale is a force in newtons.

Any number on this scale is a length in millimeters.

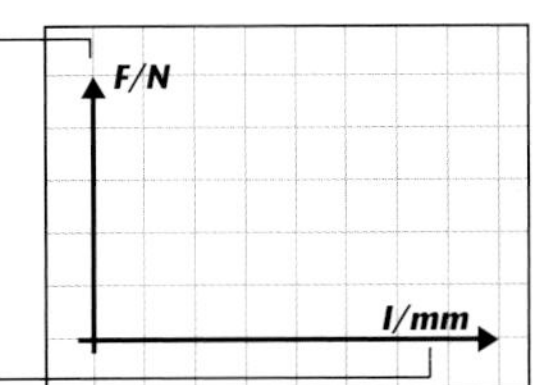
F/N
l/mm

Plotting graphs

1. The quantity controlled during an experiment should be plotted along the x-axis, and the quantity which changes as a result along the y-axis.

2. Scales on the axes should have values that are easy to find. (Avoid squares representing multiples of three.)

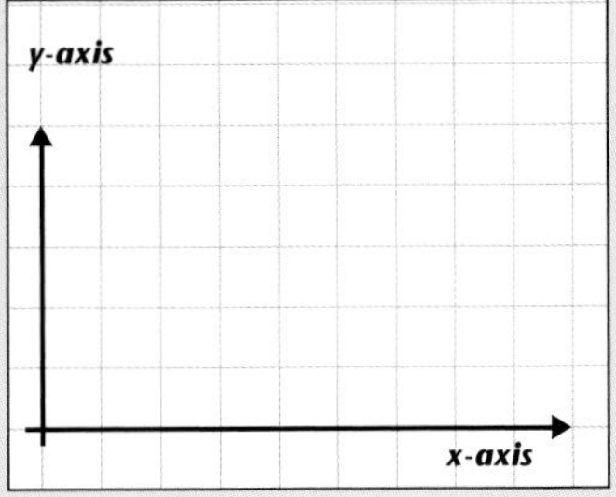
y-axis
x-axis

3. The axes should be labeled by the symbol representing the quantity (or name of the quantity) and its unit, e.g. length/mm.

4. Points on the graph should be marked in pencil with a × or a ⊙.

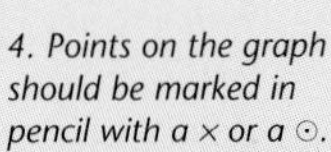

Velocity/m s^{-1}

Time/s

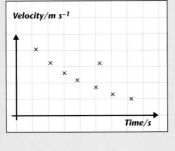

5. A smooth curve or straight line should be drawn which best fits the points (this is because physical quantities are normally related in some definite way). Note that joining the points up will not often produce a smooth curve. This is due to experimental errors.

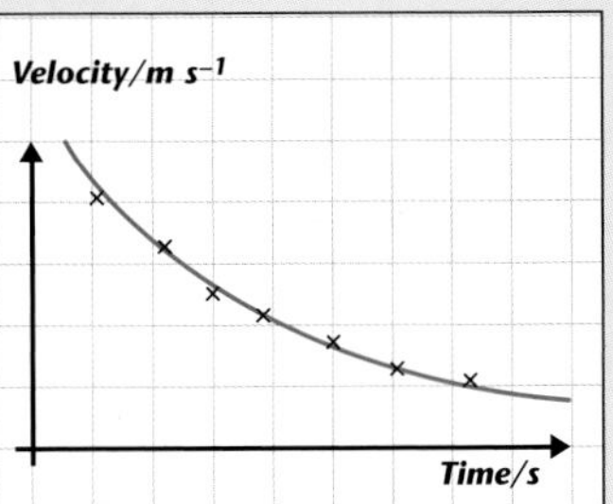
Velocity/m s⁻¹
Time/s

Information from graphs

A straight line graph which passes through the origin shows that the quantities plotted on the axes are proportional to each other (i.e. if one is doubled then so is the other).

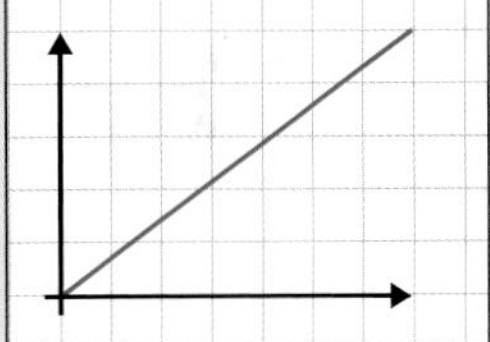

A straight line portion of a graph shows the region in which the relationship between two quantities is linear (i.e. one always changes by the same amount for a fixed change in the other).

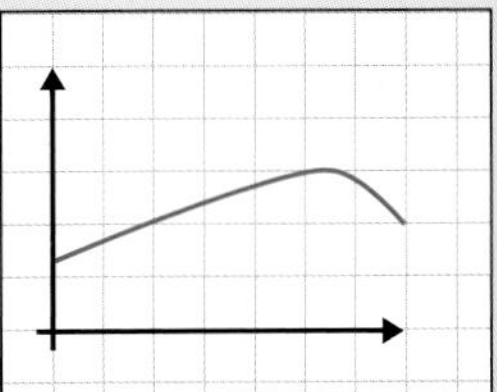

The amount of scatter of the points about the smooth curve gives an indication of the errors in the data due to inaccuracies in the procedure, the equipment and the measuring (this happens in any experiment).

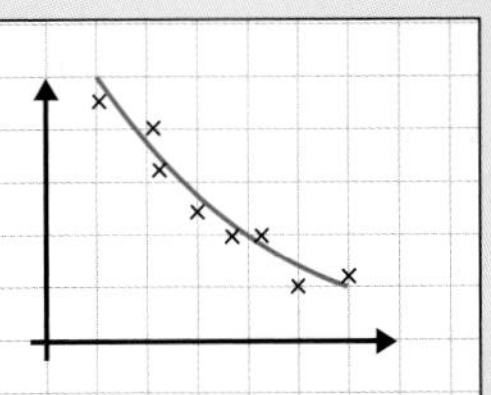

Individual points a long way from the curve are probably due to an error in measuring that piece of data in the experiment. However, the point should not be ignored – it should be checked and remeasured if possible.

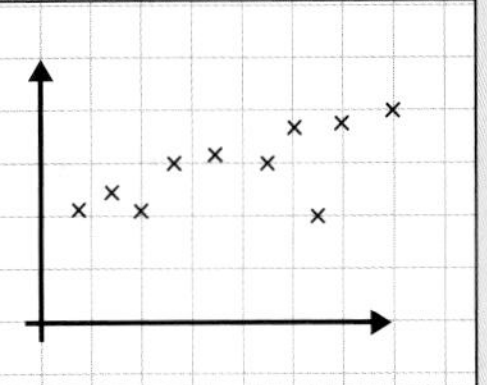

MEASUREMENTS

Measurement of length

The method used to measure a length depends on the magnitude of the length. A meter ruler is used for lengths of 50mm or more. The smallest division is normally 1mm and so lengths can be estimated to the nearest 0.5mm. For lengths less than 50mm, the error involved would be unacceptable (see also **reading error**, page 103). A **vernier scale** is therefore used. For the measurement of very small lengths (to 0.01mm) a **micrometer screw gauge** is used (see opposite).

Vernier scale

A short scale which slides along a fixed scale. The position on the fixed scale of the zero line of the vernier scale can be found accurately. It is used in measuring devices such as the **vernier slide callipers**.

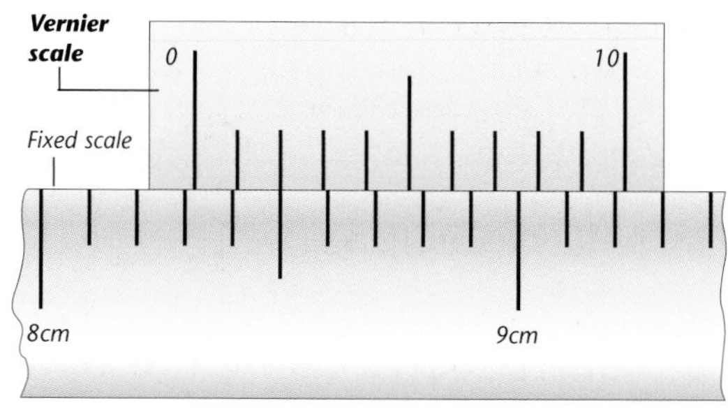

Vernier scale
Fixed scale
0
10
8cm
9cm

Method of reading position of zero line on vernier scale:

1. Read the position of the zero line approximately – in this case 8.3cm.

2. Find the position on the vernier scale where the marks coincide – in this case 2.

3. Add this to the previous figure – the accurate reading is 8.32cm.

Vernier slide callipers

An instrument containing a **vernier scale**, used to measure lengths in the range 10 to 100mm.

Method of measurement:

1. Close the jaws and check that the zero on the **vernier scale** coincides with the zero on the fixed scale. If not, note the reading (this is the **zero error***).

2. Close or open the jaws onto the object to be measured.

3. Lock the sliding jaw into position.

4. Record the reading on the scale.

5. Add or subtract the zero error (see 1) to get the correct reading.

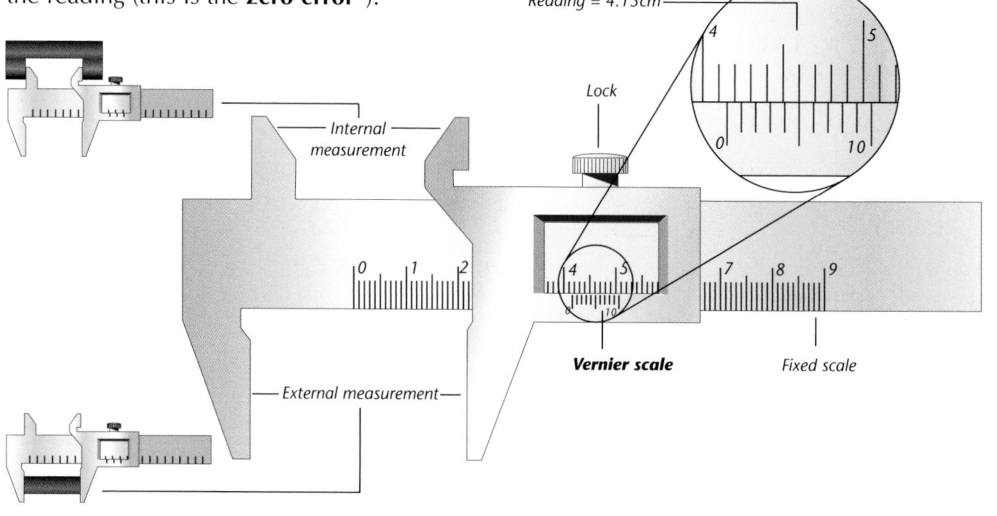

Reading = 4.15cm
Lock
Internal measurement
External measurement
Vernier scale
Fixed scale

* **Zero error**, 102.

Micrometer screw gauge

An instrument used for accurate measurements up to about 30mm.

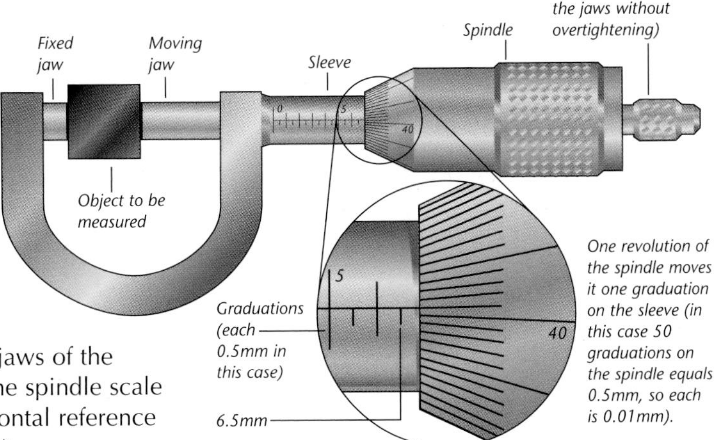
Fixed jaw
Moving jaw
Object to be measured
Sleeve
Spindle
Ratchet (used to close the jaws without overtightening)
Graduations (each 0.5mm in this case)
6.5mm
5
40
One revolution of the spindle moves it one graduation on the sleeve (in this case 50 graduations on the spindle equals 0.5mm, so each is 0.01mm).

Method of measurement:

1. Determine the value of a division on the spindle scale (see diagram).

2. Using the ratchet, close the jaws of the instrument fully. The zero on the spindle scale should coincide with the horizontal reference line. If not, note the **zero error***.

3. Using the ratchet, close the jaws on the object to be measured until it is gripped.

4. Note the reading of the highest visible mark on the sleeve scale (in this case 6.5mm).

5. Note the division on the spindle scale which coincides with the horizontal reference line (in this case 0.41mm).

6. Add the two readings and add or subtract the zero error (see 2) to get the correct reading (in this case 6.91mm).

Measurement of area and volume

The volume of a liquid is calculated from the space it takes up in its containing vessel. The internal volume of the containing vessel is called its **capacity**. The **SI unit*** of capacity is the **liter** (**l**), equal to $10^{-3}m^3$. Note that $1ml = 1cm^3$. The volume of a liquid is measured using a graduated vessel.

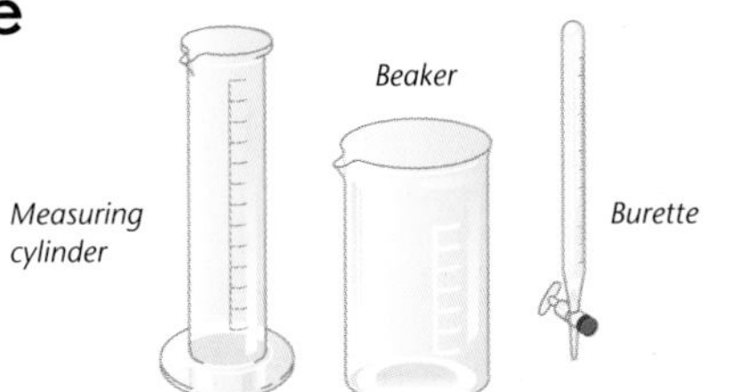
Measuring cylinder
Beaker
Burette

Examples of graduated vessels for measuring volume

The surface area and volume of a solid of regular shape are calculated from length measurements of the object (see below).

For solids of irregular shape, see **eureka can**, page 24.

Regular shaped solid	*Rectangular bar*	*Sphere*	*Cylinder*
*Measurements made using **vernier slide callipers** or **micrometer screw gauge***	*h = height* *w = width* *l = length*	*r = radius*	*r = radius* *l = length*
Volume V of solid calculated from	$V = lwh$	$V = \frac{4}{3}\pi r^3$	$V = \pi r^2 l$
Surface area A calculated from	$A = 2wl + 2hl + 2hw$ *(2wl: Top; 2hl: Sides; 2hw: Ends)*	$A = 4\pi r^2$	$A = 2\pi rl + 2\pi r^2$ *(2πrl: Curved surface; 2πr²: Ends)*

* **SI units**, 96; **Zero error**, 102.

ACCURACY AND ERRORS

All experimental measurements are subject to some errors, other than those caused by carelessness (like misreading a scale). The most common errors which occur are **parallax errors**, **zero errors** and **reading errors**. When stating a reading, therefore, a number of **significant figures** should be quoted which give an estimate of the accuracy of the readings.

Parallax error

The error which occurs when the eye is not placed directly opposite a scale when a reading is being taken.

Parallax error reading a meter ruler

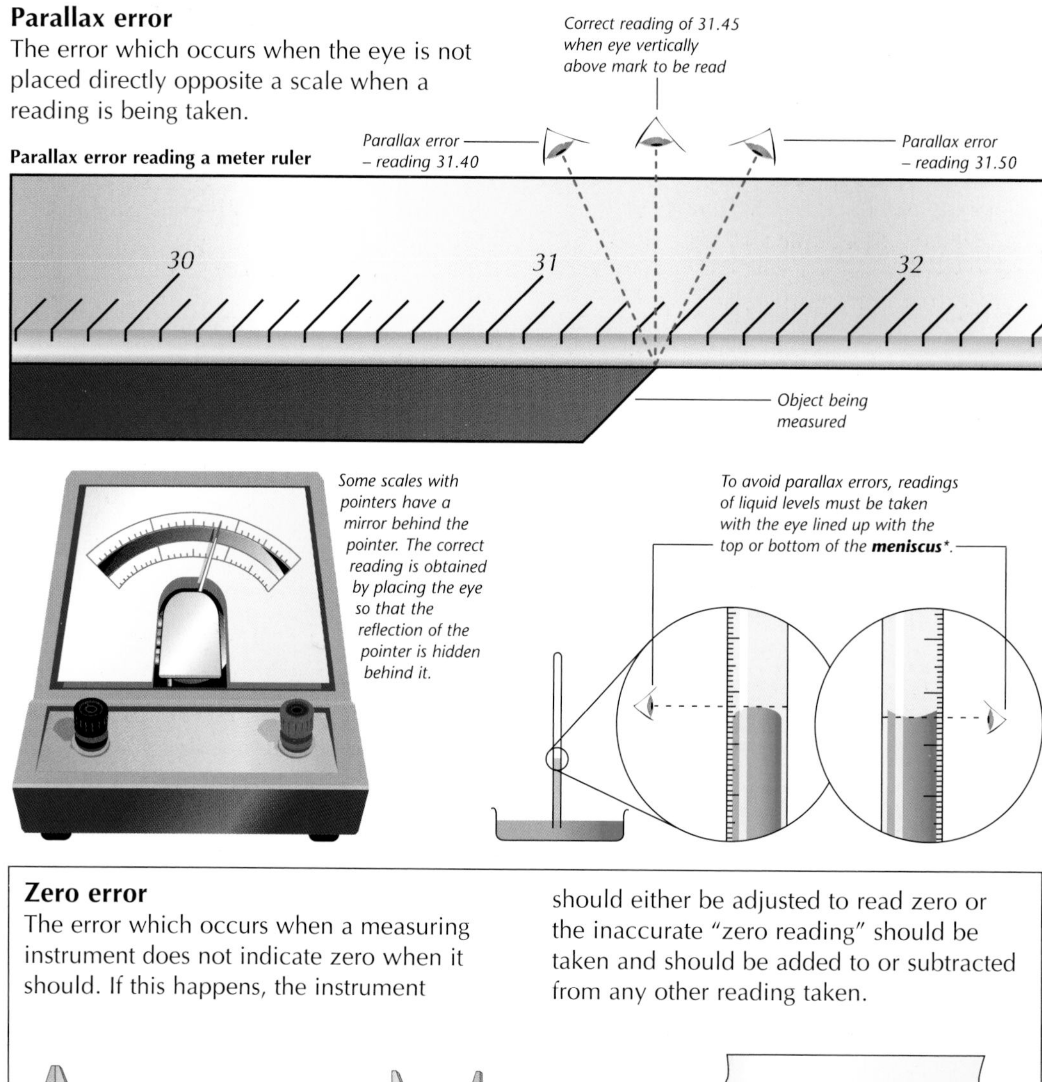

Correct reading of 31.45 when eye vertically above mark to be read
Parallax error – reading 31.40
Parallax error – reading 31.50
30
31
32
Object being measured
Some scales with pointers have a mirror behind the pointer. The correct reading is obtained by placing the eye so that the reflection of the pointer is hidden behind it.
To avoid parallax errors, readings of liquid levels must be taken with the eye lined up with the top or bottom of the **meniscus***.

Zero error

The error which occurs when a measuring instrument does not indicate zero when it should. If this happens, the instrument should either be adjusted to read zero or the inaccurate "zero reading" should be taken and should be added to or subtracted from any other reading taken.

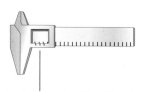

*Reading on **vernier slide callipers*** when closed (i.e. should read zero) is 0.2mm. This is **zero error**.*

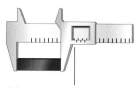

0.2mm must be subtracted from any reading (in this case, apparent reading is 53.9 but actual length is 53.9 – 0.2, i.e. 53.7mm).

10
20
30
40
50

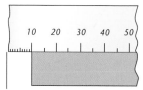

Zero error on meter ruler may be due to worn end. Should be solved by measuring from 10mm line and subtracting 10mm from all readings.

* **Meniscus**, 345; **Vernier slide callipers**, 100.

Reading error

The error due to the guesswork involved in taking a reading from a scale when the reading lies between the scale divisions.

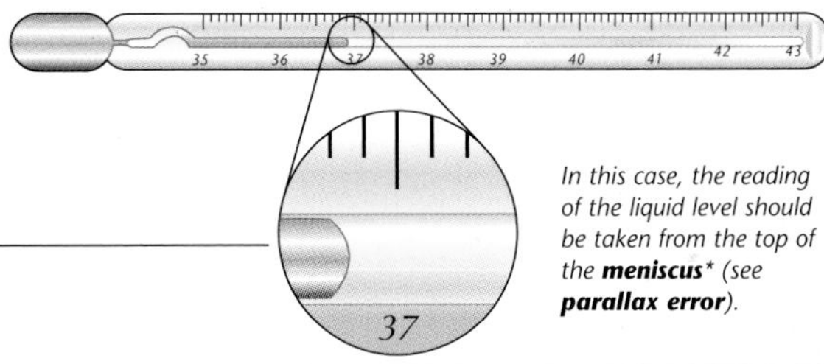
35
36
37
38
39
40
41
42
43
37

Reading on thermometer is between 36.8°C and 36.9°C. Best estimate of next figure is half a division to give a reading of 36.85°C.

*In this case, the reading of the liquid level should be taken from the top of the **meniscus*** (see **parallax error**).*

Significant figures

The number of **significant figures** in a value is the number of figures in that value ignoring leading or trailing zeros (but see below) and disregarding the position of the decimal point. They give an indication of the accuracy of a reading.

*A reading of 3704mm has four **significant figures**. It can be written as:*

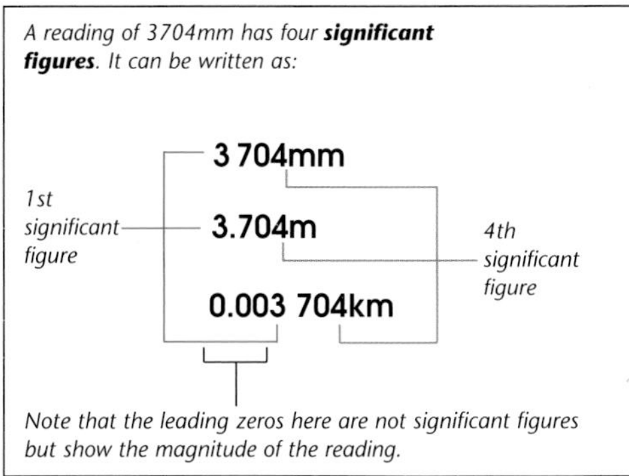
3 704mm
3.704m
0.003 704km
1st significant figure
4th significant figure

Note that the leading zeros here are not significant figures but show the magnitude of the reading.

The number of significant figures quoted is an indication of the accuracy of a reading or result.

Smallest division on ammeter scale = 0.1A

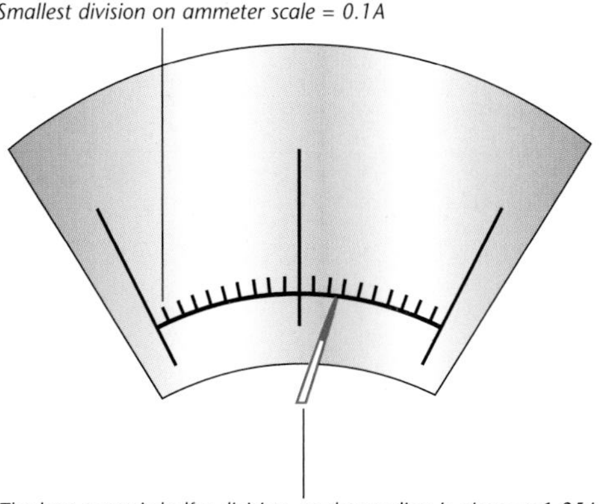

The best guess is half a division, so the reading is given as 1.25A. Three significant figures indicate that the reading is accurate to about 0.05A.

A reading with more figures, e.g. 1.2518A, implies more accuracy than is possible on this scale.

Rounding

The process of reducing the number of figures quoted. The last significant figure is dropped and the new last figure changed depending on the one dropped.

7.3925	*(quoted to 5 significant figures)*
= 7.393	*(rounded to 4 significant figures)*
= 7.39	*(rounded to 3 significant figures)*
= 7.4	*(rounded to 2 significant figures)*
= 7	*(rounded to 1 significant figure)*

0.08873	*(quoted to 4 significant figures)*
= 0.0887	*(rounded to 3 significant figures)*
= 0.089	*(rounded to 2 significant figures)*
= 0.09	*(rounded to 1 significant figure)*

Note that

29.000	*is quoted to 5 significant figures*
= 29.0	*(to 3 significant figures)*
= 29	*(to 2 significant figures)*
= 30	*(to 1 significant figure)*

In the last case here, the 0 is not a significant figure but must be included (see below).

For large numbers like 283,000 it is impossible to say how many of the figures are significant (the first three must be) because the zeros have to be included to show the magnitude. This ambiguity is removed by using the **exponential notation** (see page 109).

* **Meniscus**, 345.

FIELDS AND FORCES

This table is a comparison of the three forces normally encountered in physics (excluding the **nuclear force**). In fact, most of the forces dealt with in physics, e.g. the **contact force** between two objects, are examples of the **electromagnetic force** which is a combination of the **magnetic** and **electric forces**. For more about these and all other forces, see pages 6-7.

Gravitational force

(see also pages 6 and 18)

Type of force

Note that a force can only exist between two masses, charges or currents, and that the size of the force is the same on both of them (see also **Newton's third law**, page 13). Note also that the forces only act between objects which are the same, e.g. there is a force between two masses, but not between a mass and a current.

Force acts between two objects with mass. It is always attractive.

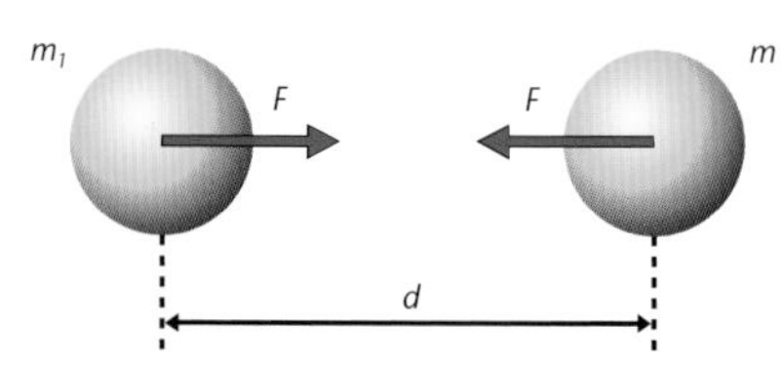

m_1
m
F
F
d

$$F = G\frac{m_1 m}{d^2}$$

$G = 6.7 \times 10^{-11} Nm^2\ kg^{-2}$

G is the **gravitational constant***. Its very small value means that the gravitational force is only noticeable when one of the objects is very large (e.g. a planet).

Description of force in terms of force field

The **force field** is the region around an object (mass, charge or current) in which its effects (gravitational, electric or magnetic) can be detected – see also page 6.

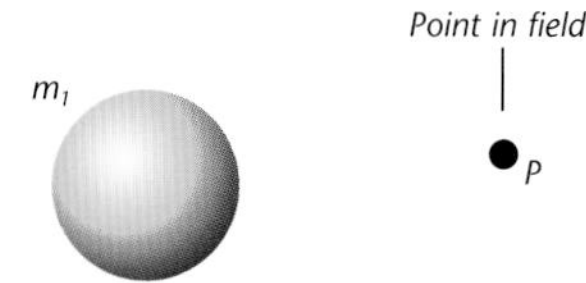

Point in field
m_1
P

Mass m_1 produces a **gravitational field** in the space around it (see **field intensity**, page 106).

A second mass experiences a gravitational force when placed at any point (e.g. P) in the gravitational field of m_1.

A mass thus produces a gravitational field and is acted upon by a gravitational field.

Field direction

This is found by observing the effect of the force field on an object (mass, charge or current) placed in it.

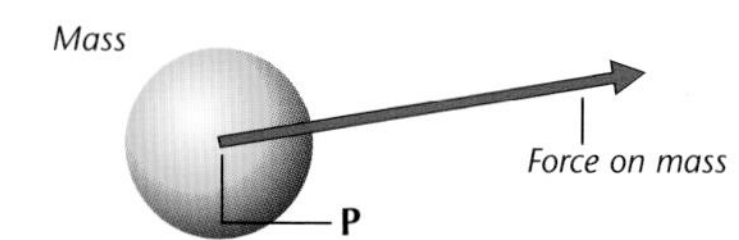

Mass
Force on mass
P

The direction of a gravitational field at a point P is the direction of the force on a mass placed at P.

* **Gravitational constant**, 18 (**Newton's law of gravitation**).

<table>
<tr>
<th>Electric force
(see also pages 6 and 58)</th>
<th>Magnetic force
(see also pages 6 and 70)</th>
</tr>
<tr>
<td>
Force is between two charges. It is attractive if the charges are of the opposite sign, i.e. one negative and one positive, and repulsive if the charges are of the same sign.

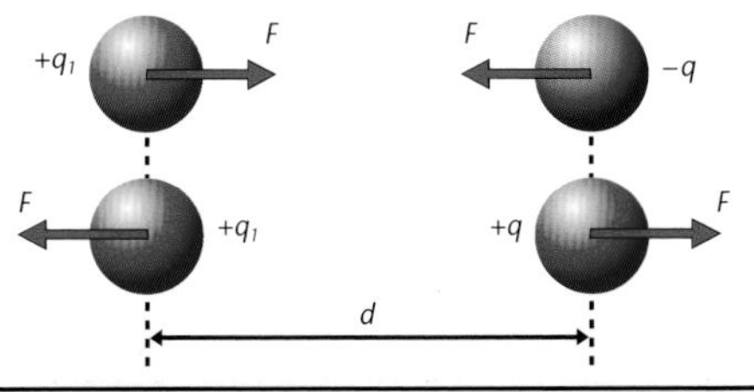
+q1
F
F
−q
F
+q1
+q
F
d

$$F = K_E \frac{q_1 q}{d^2}$$

In air $K_E = 9 \times 10^9 Nm^2 \, C^{-2}$

This very large value means it is difficult to separate opposite charges.
</td>
<td>
Force is between two objects in which current is flowing. If the currents flow in the same direction, the force is attractive. If the currents flow in opposite directions, the force is repulsive.

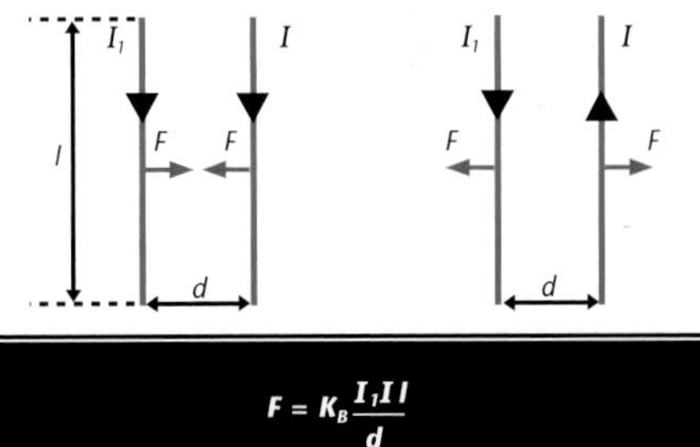
I1
I
l
F
F
d
I1
I
F
F
d

$$F = K_B \frac{I_1 I l}{d}$$

In air $K_B = 2.7 \times 10^{-7} N \, A^{-2}$

This small value indicates that the magnetic force is very small in comparison to the electric force.
</td>
</tr>
<tr>
<td>

q1
q1
Point in field
P

Charge q_1 produces an **electric field*** in the space around it (see **field intensity**, page 106).

A second charge experiences an electric force when placed at any point (e.g. P) in the electric field of q_1.

A charge thus produces an electric field and is acted upon by an electric field.
</td>
<td>

I1
Point in field
P

Current I_1 produces a **magnetic field*** in the space around it (see **field intensity**, page 106).

A second current experiences a magnetic force when placed at any point P in the magnetic field of I_1.

A current thus produces a magnetic field and is acted upon by a magnetic field.
</td>
</tr>
<tr>
<td>
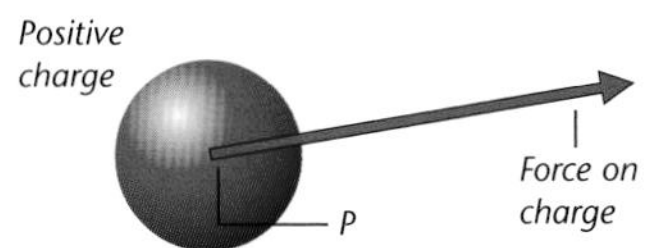
Positive charge
P
Force on charge

The direction of an electric field at a point P is the direction of the force on a positive charge placed at P.
</td>
<td>
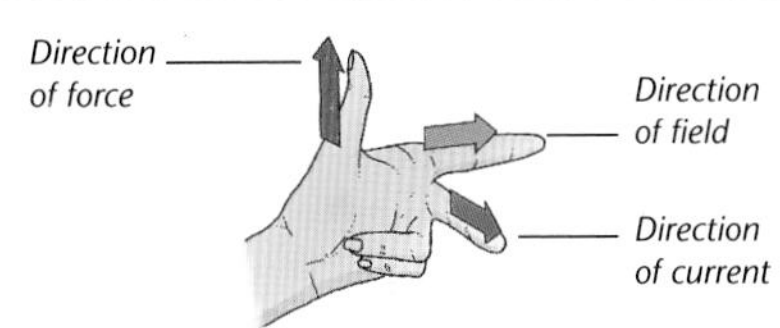
Direction of force
Direction of field
Direction of current

The direction of a magnetic field at a point P is given by **Fleming's left hand rule***.
</td>
</tr>
</table>

* **Electric field**, 58; **Fleming's left hand rule**, 76; **Magnetic field**, 72.

Fields and forces (continued)

Gravitational force

Field intensity
This is found by measuring the effect of the force field on an object (mass, charge or current) placed in it.

To measure the field intensity g of a gravitational field due to a mass m_1 at a point P, a test mass m is placed at P and the gravitational force F on it is measured. Then:

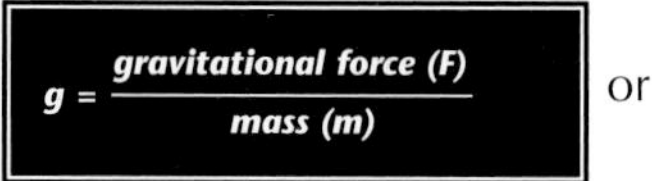

$$g = \frac{\text{gravitational force } (F)}{\text{mass } (m)}$$

or:

$$F = mg$$

By comparison with the equation above for the gravitational force, the field intensity g at a distance d from a mass m_1 is:

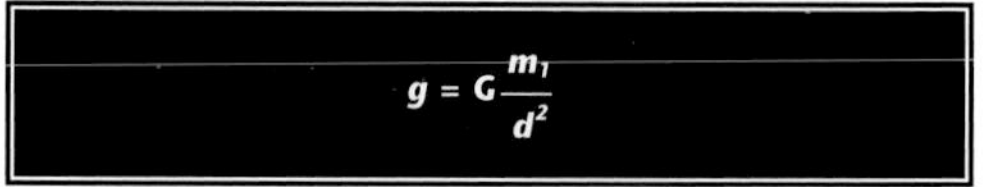

$$g = G\frac{m_1}{d^2}$$

Representation by field lines
Field lines (or **flux lines** or **lines of force** or **flux**) are used in all cases to represent the strength and direction of fields and to visualize them (see panel at bottom of page). Field lines never cross since the field would then have different directions at one point.

Gravitational field lines always end at a mass.

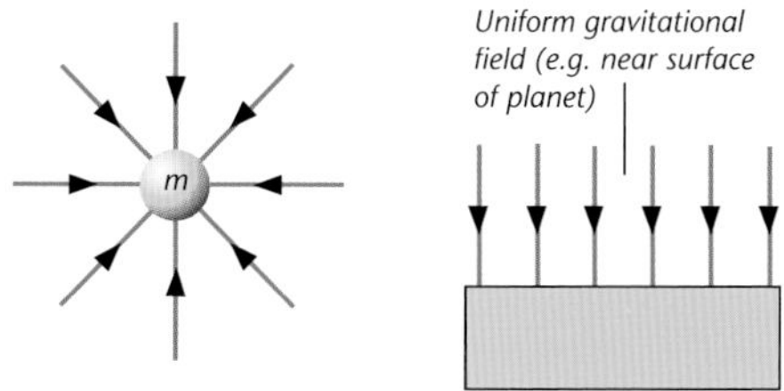
m
Uniform gravitational field (e.g. near surface of planet)

Potential energy (see also page 8)
This depends on **field intensity** and the object (its mass in a **gravitational field** or its charge in an **electric field***). The **potential*** at a point in a field is the energy per unit (of mass or charge) and depends upon the field only. Usually the only concern is the difference in potential, or **potential difference***, between two points. Potential can be defined by choosing a reference. The potential at a point is then the potential difference between the point and the reference point.

The gravitational potential difference between two points in a gravitational field is the work done against the forces of the field in moving a unit mass between the points.

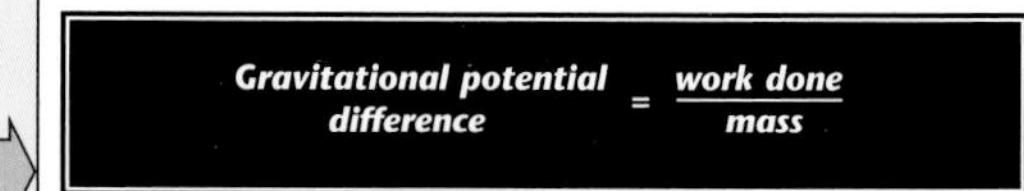

$$\text{Gravitational potential difference} = \frac{\text{work done}}{\text{mass}}$$

Gravitational potential decreases as point moves along field line in direction of field (in direction of arrow).

Gravitational potential higher at P_1 than P_2.

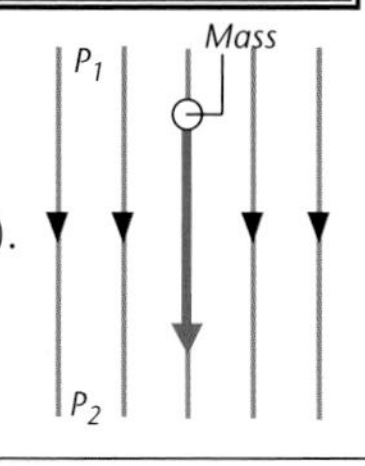
Mass
P_1
P_2

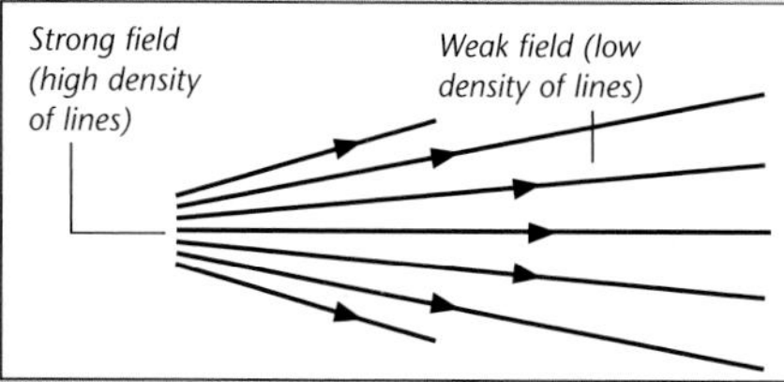
Strong field (high density of lines)
Weak field (low density of lines)

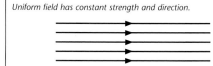

Uniform field has constant strength and direction.

* **Electric field**, **Potential**, **Potential difference**, 58.

Electric force

To measure the field intensity E of an electric field at a point P due to a charge q_1, a test positive charge q is placed at P and the electric force F on it is measured. Then:

$$E = \frac{\text{electric force (F)}}{\text{charge (q)}}$$

or:

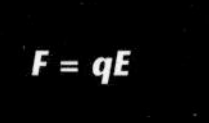
$$F = qE$$

By comparison with the equation above for the electric force, the field intensity E at a distance d from a charge q_1 is:

$$E = K_E \frac{q_1}{d^2}$$

Electric field lines always begin at a positive charge and end at an equal negative charge.

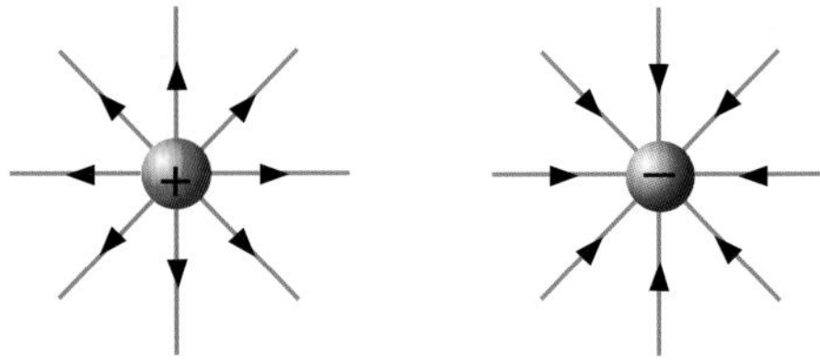

The electric potential difference between two points in an electric field is the work done against the forces of the field in moving a unit positive charge between them.

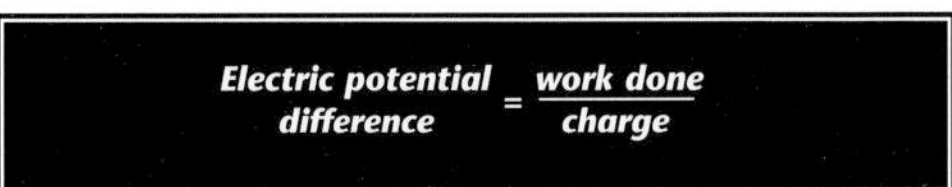
$$\text{Electric potential difference} = \frac{\text{work done}}{\text{charge}}$$

Electric potential decreases in direction of field (in direction of arrow).

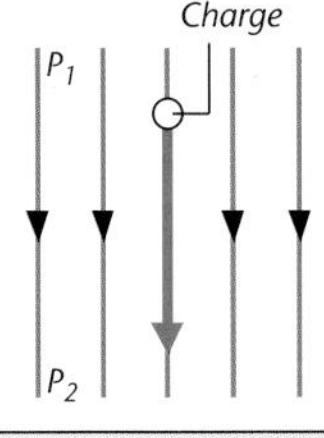
Charge
P_1
P_2

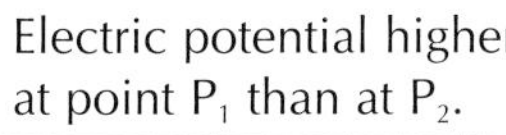
Electric potential higher at point P_1 than at P_2.

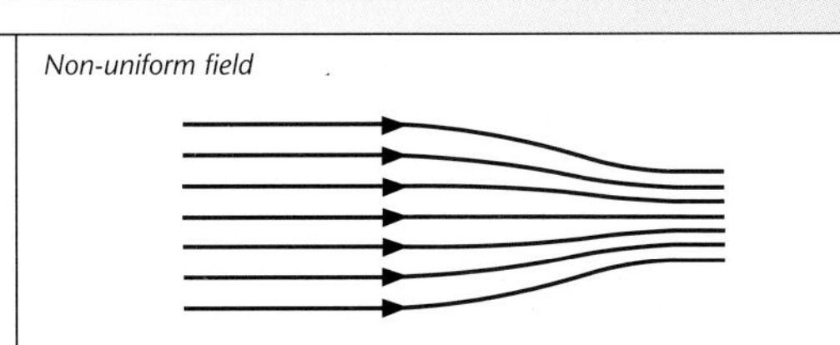
Non-uniform field

Magnetic force

To measure the field intensity B of a magnetic field due to I_1 at a point P, a conductor of length l carrying a current I is placed at P and the magnetic force F is measured. Then:

$$B = \frac{\text{magnetic force (F)}}{\text{current (I)} \times \text{length (l)}}$$

or:

$$F = BIl$$

By comparison with the equation above for the magnetic force, the field intensity B at a distance d from a current I_1 is:

$$B = K_B \frac{I_1}{d}$$

Magnetic field lines* have no beginning or end, but are always closed loops. This is because single north or south poles cannot exist. This is a fundamental difference compared to gravitational and electric fields.

Circular magnetic field lines around current-carrying wire.

Magnetic potential is much more difficult to define than for gravitational or electric fields because the field lines are circular. Note that if a point moves around a circular line in the diagram above, it returns to the same point, which must have the same potential, although it has moved along a field line. This means that magnetic potential is complicated to calculate.

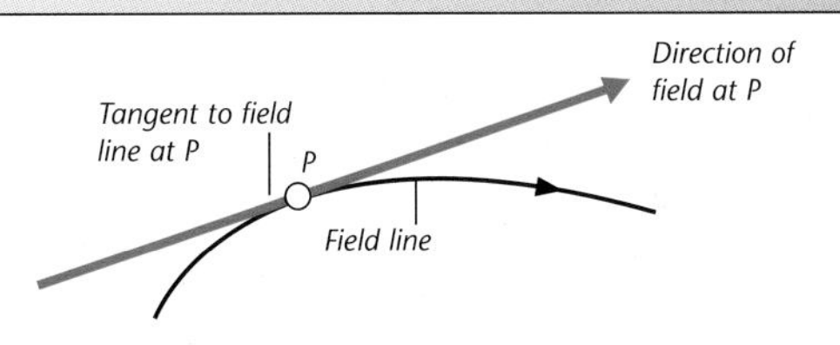
Direction of field at P
Tangent to field line at P
P
Field line

* **Magnetic field lines**, 72.

VECTORS AND SCALARS

All quantities in physics are either **scalar** or **vector quantities**, depending on whether the quantity has direction as well as magnitude.

Scalar quantity

Any quantity which has magnitude only, e.g. mass, time, energy, density.

Vector quantity

Any quantity which has both magnitude and direction, e.g. force, displacement, velocity and acceleration. When giving a value to a vector quantity, the direction must be given in some way as well as the magnitude. Usually, the quantity is represented graphically by an arrowed line. The length of the line indicates the magnitude of the quantity (on some chosen scale) and the direction of the arrow indicates the direction of the quantity.

*Arrows represent forces (**vector quantities**). Length indicates magnitude of force.*

30N

3cm

Scale is 1cm = 10 newtons

Forces act in opposite directions.

21N

2.1cm

Parallelogram rule

A rule used when adding together two **vector quantities**. The two vectors are drawn from one point to form two sides of a parallelogram which is then completed. The diagonal from the original common point gives the sum of the two vectors (the **resultant**).

The parallelogram rule is used to help navigation at sea. The direction and speed of the tide must be taken into account as the second vector quantity to be added to the direction and speed of the boat.

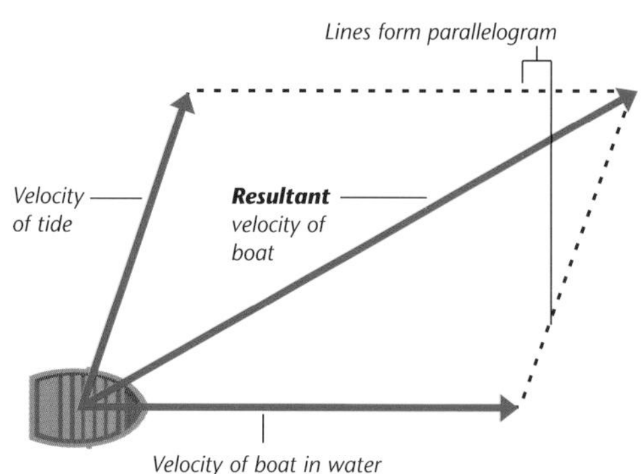
Lines form parallelogram
Velocity of tide
Resultant velocity of boat
Velocity of boat in water

Resolution

The process of splitting one **vector quantity** into two other vectors called its **components**. Normally, the two components are perpendicular to each other. Each component then represents the total effect of the vector in that direction.

Lift (**vector quantity**) from rotor of helicopter can be **resolved** into two **components**. The first acts upwards, in order to keep it airborne, and the second acts forwards, to move it along.

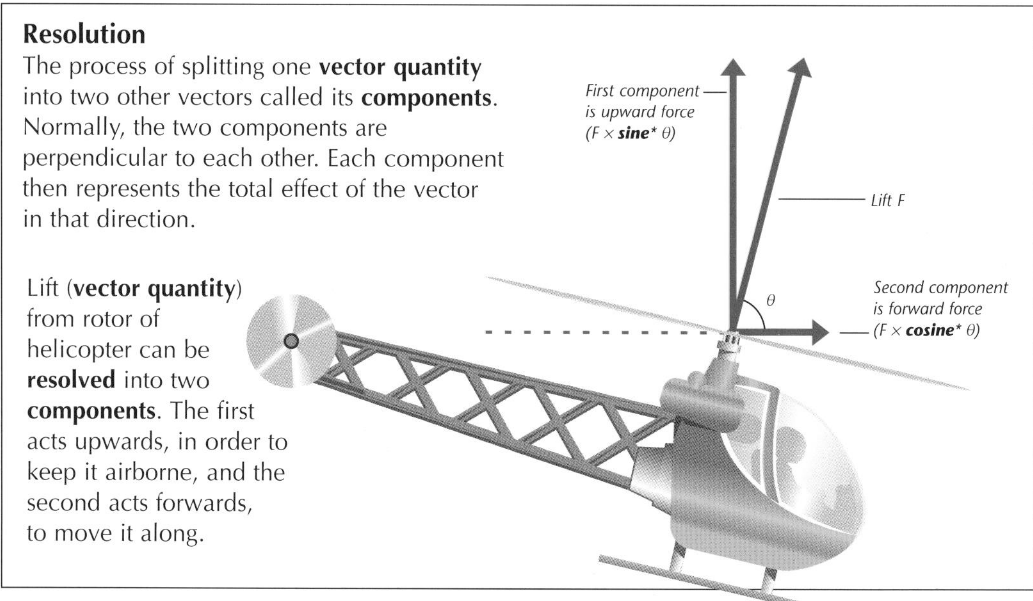
First component is upward force ($F \times$ **sine*** θ)
Lift F
θ
Second component is forward force ($F \times$ **cosine*** θ)

* **Cosine**, 344; **Sine**, 345.

NUMBERS

Very large or very small numbers (e.g. 10 000 000 or 0.000 001) take a long time to write out and are difficult to read. The **exponential notation** is therefore used. In this notation, the position of the decimal point is shown by writing the power ten is raised to.

1 000 000	$= 10^6$	*or "ten to the six"*
100 000	$= 10^5$	*or "ten to the five"*
10 000	$= 10^4$	*or "ten to the four"*
1 000	$= 10^3$	*or "ten to the three"*
100	$= 10^2$	*or "ten to the two"*
10	$= 10^1$	*or "ten to the one"*
1	$= 10^0$	*any number "to the nought" equals one*
0.1	$= 10^{-1}$	*or "ten to the minus one"*
0.01	$= 10^{-2}$	*or "ten to the minus two"*
0.001	$= 10^{-3}$	*or "ten to the minus three"*
0.0001	$= 10^{-4}$	*or "ten to the minus four"*
0.000 01	$= 10^{-5}$	*or "ten to the minus five"*
0.000 001	$= 10^{-6}$	*or "ten to the minus six"*

Note that a negative exponent means "one over" so that $10^{-3} = {}^1/_{10^3} = {}^1/_{1\,000}$. This also applies to units, e.g. kg m^{-3} means kg/m^3 or kg per m^3.

Exponents are added when multiplying numbers, e.g. $10^5 \times 10^{-3}$ ($= 100\,000 \times {}^1/_{1\,000}$) $= 10^{5-3} = 10^2 = 100$.

Scientific notation

A form of expressing numbers in which the number always has one digit before the decimal point and is followed by a power of ten in **exponential notation** to show its magnitude (see also **significant figures**, page 103).

Examples of numbers written in scientific notation†

56 342	5.6342×10^4
4 000	4×10^3 *(assuming 0s are not significant)*
569	5.69×10^2
23.3	2.33×10^1
0.98	9.8×10^{-1}
0.00211	2.11×10^{-3}

Order of magnitude

A value which is accurate to within a factor of ten or so. It is important to have an idea of the order of magnitude of some physical quantities so that a figure which has been calculated can be judged. For example, the mass of a person is about 60kg. Therefore a calculated result of 50kg or 70kg is quite reasonable, but a result of 6kg or 600kg is obviously not correct.

Typical orders of magnitude

Item	Mass/kg
Earth	6×10^{24}
Car	5×10^3
Human	5×10^1
Bag of sugar	1
Orange	2×10^{-1}
Golf ball	5×10^{-2}
Table tennis ball	2×10^{-3}
Proton	2×10^{-27}
Electron	10^{-30}

Item	Length/m
Radius of Milky Way galaxy	10^{19}
Radius of Solar System	10^{11}
Radius of Earth	5×10^6
Height of Mount Everest	10^4
Height of human	2
Thickness of paper	10^{-4}
Wavelength of light	5×10^{-7}
Radius of atom	10^{-10}
Radius of nucleus	10^{-14}

Item	Time/s
Age of Earth	2×10^{17}
Time since emergence of man	10^{13}
Human life time	2×10^9
Time span of year	3×10^7
Time span of day	9×10^4
Time between heart beats	1
Camera shutter speed	10^{-2}
Half-life of polonium-214	1.5×10^{-4}
Time for light to travel 1m	3×10^{-9}

Item	Energy/J
Energy given out by Sun per second	10^{26}
Energy released by San Francisco earthquake (1906)	3×10^{17}
Energy released by fission of 1g of uranium	10^{11}
Energy of lightning discharge	10^9
Energy of 1kW fire per hour	4×10^6
Kinetic energy of golf ball	20

† In scientific work, the convention is to print numbers up to 9999 closed up and without a comma. In numbers above this, small spaces are used to make the numbers easier to read at a glance. In non-technical writing, the convention is to add commas to numbers with four or more figures. The latter style is predominantly used in this book.

CIRCUIT SYMBOLS

This table shows the main symbols used to represent the various components used in electric circuits (see also pages 60-65).

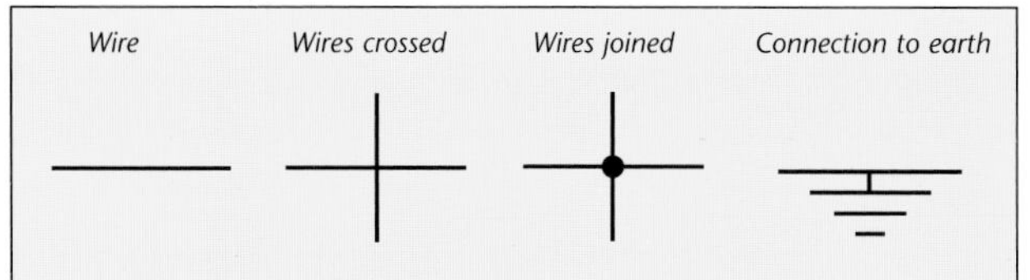
Wire
Wires crossed
Wires joined
Connection to earth

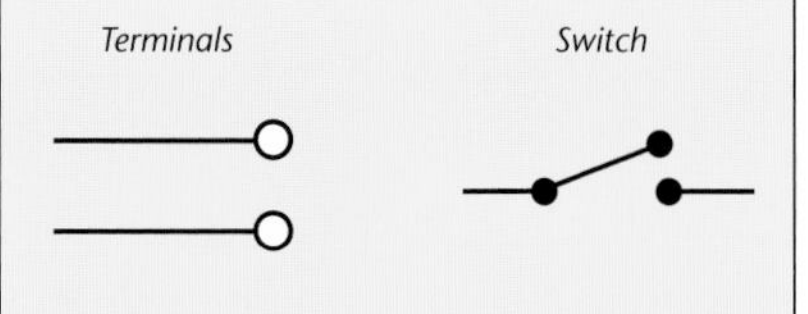
Terminals
Switch

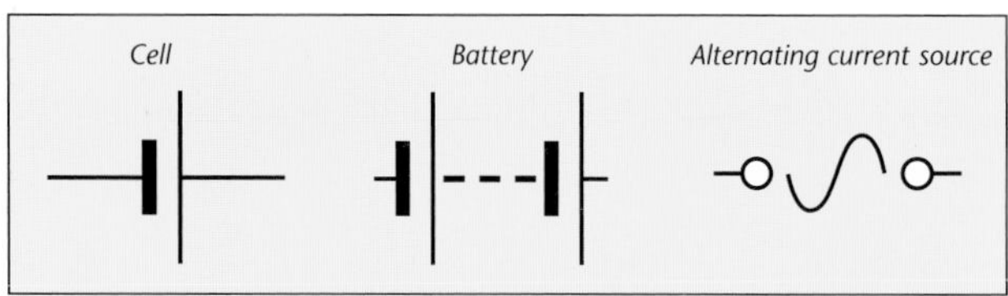
Cell
Battery
Alternating current source

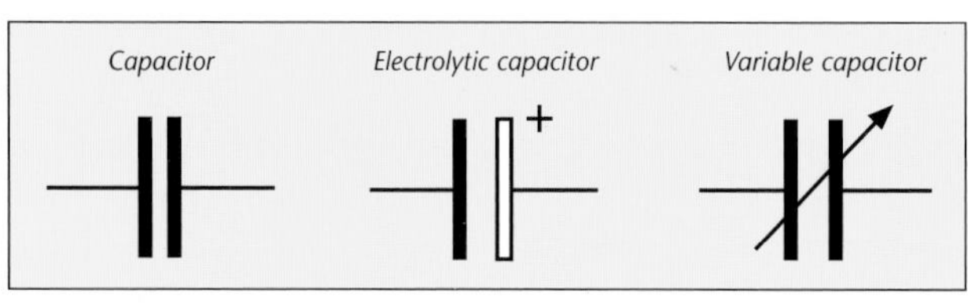
Capacitor
Electrolytic capacitor
+
Variable capacitor

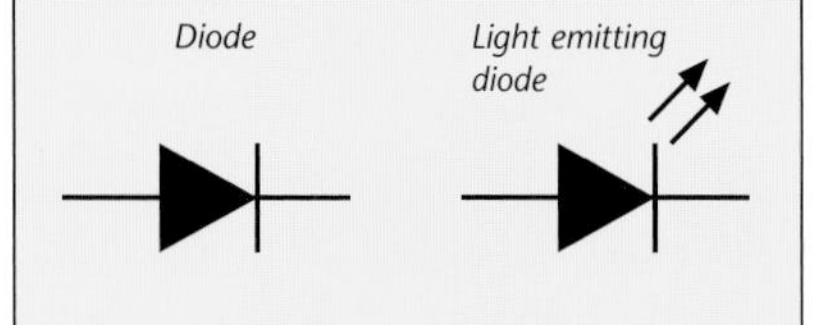
Diode
Light emitting diode

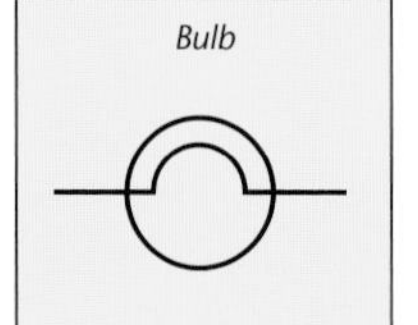
Bulb

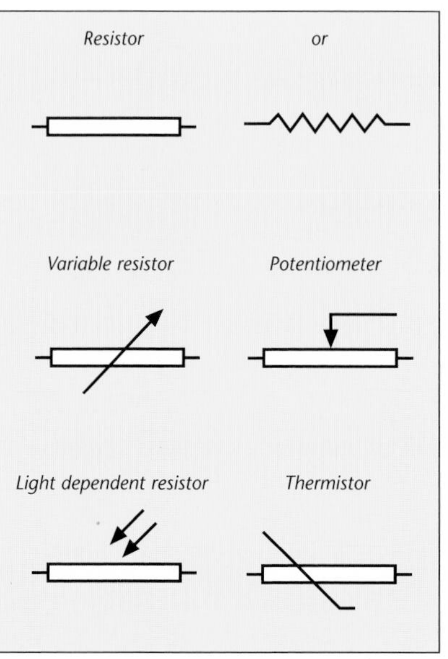
Resistor
or
Variable resistor
Potentiometer
Light dependent resistor
Thermistor

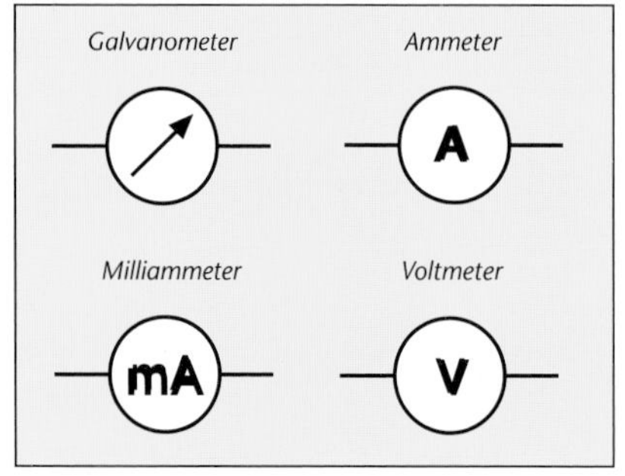
Galvanometer
Ammeter
A
Milliammeter
mA
Voltmeter
V

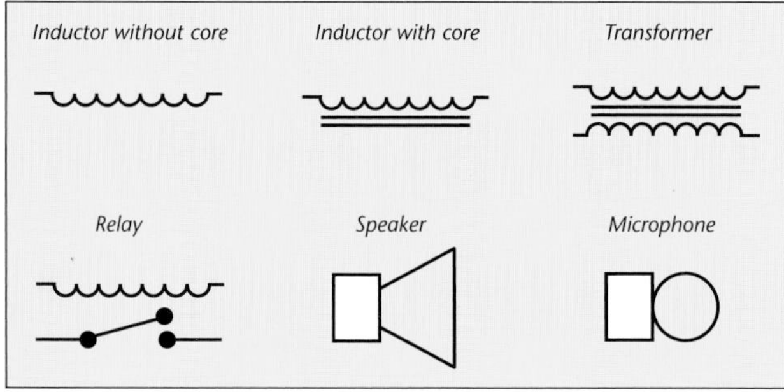
Inductor without core
Inductor with core
Transformer
Relay
Speaker
Microphone

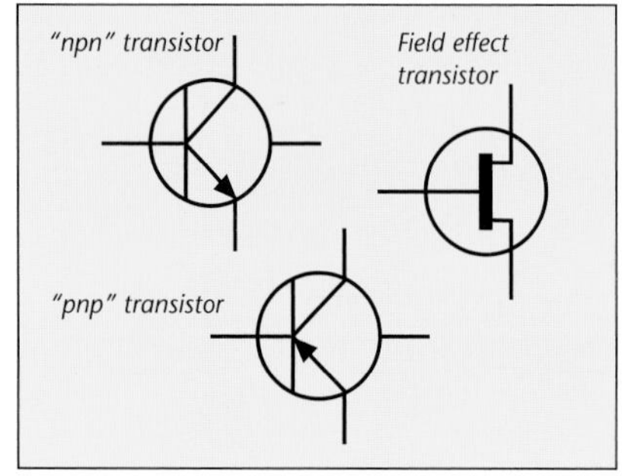
"npn" transistor
Field effect transistor
"pnp" transistor

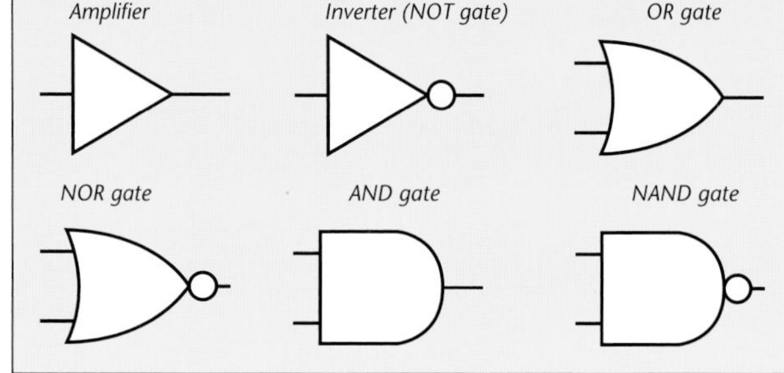
Amplifier
Inverter (NOT gate)
OR gate
NOR gate
AND gate
NAND gate

TRANSISTORS AND GATES

Transistors* can be used to amplify electrical signals, such as those from a microphone, and are also used as electronic switches. This has led to their use in complex circuits such as computers. They have replaced the much larger and slower valves and **relays***.

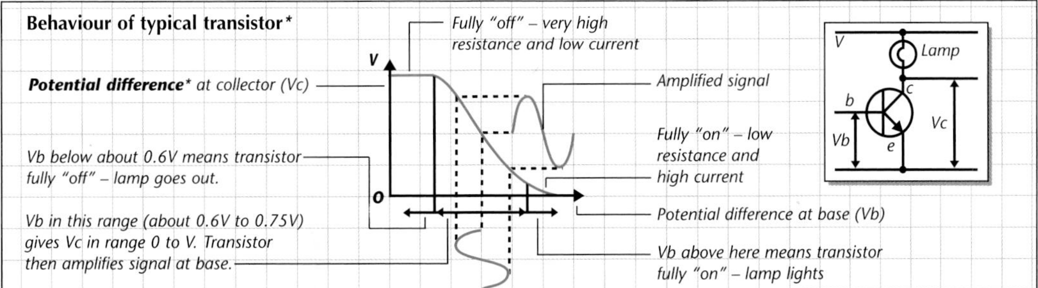
Behaviour of typical transistor*
Fully "off" – very high resistance and low current
V
Potential difference* at collector (Vc)
Amplified signal
Fully "on" – low resistance and high current
Vb below about 0.6V means transistor fully "off" – lamp goes out.
O
Potential difference at base (Vb)
Vb in this range (about 0.6V to 0.75V) gives Vc in range 0 to V. Transistor then amplifies signal at base.
Vb above here means transistor fully "on" – lamp lights
V
Lamp
b
c
Vc
Vb
e

Logic gates

The on and off states of a transistor are used to indicate the numbers 1 and 0, respectively. The circuits are therefore known as **digital** (other circuits are called **analogue**). Combinations of transistors with other components are used to make circuits which carry out logical operations.

Truth tables for basic logical operations

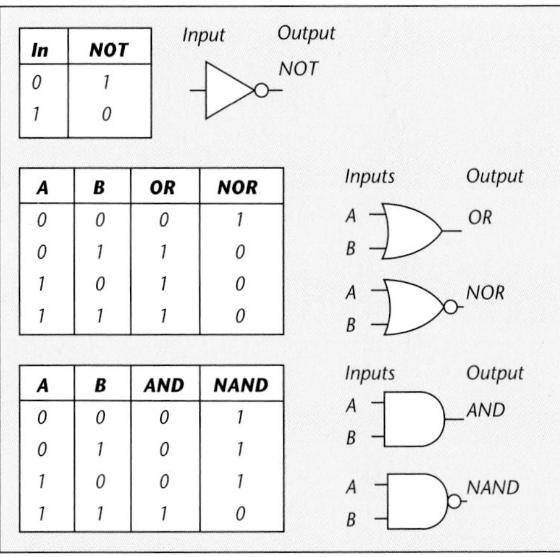

In	NOT
0	1
1	0

A	B	OR	NOR
0	0	0	1
0	1	1	0
1	0	1	0
1	1	1	0

A	B	AND	NAND
0	0	0	1
0	1	0	1
1	0	0	1
1	1	1	0

Input
Output
NOT
Inputs
Output
A
B
OR
A
B
NOR
Inputs
Output
A
B
AND
A
B
NAND

Combinations of these gates and other transistor circuits are used to make complex circuits which can perform mathematical operations, e.g. addition. These are called **integrated circuits**, and may contain many thousands of such components and connections, yet be built into a single slice of silicon.

Computers

Integrated circuits mean that many thousands of logic gates can be put onto a single tiny component called a microchip. The CPU of a computer (see below) can be put on one chip.

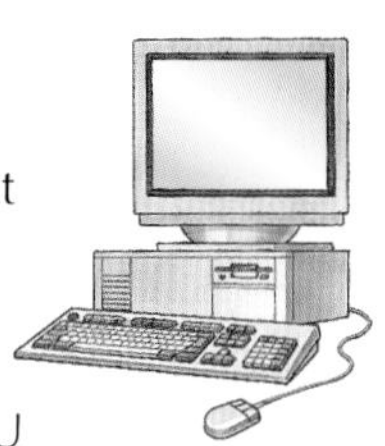

A personal computer with a CPU, monitor, keyboard and mouse

Typical computer system

*Disk and CD drives are examples of **input** and **output** devices. The disks can store many times more data than the **memory**, and also retain it when the computer is turned off (the information in the **read only memory** is lost).*

*Devices such as keyboard, mouse and screen are also **input** and **output** devices, from which data is put into the computer and to which it is sent. They are ways for the computer to link with the outside world.*

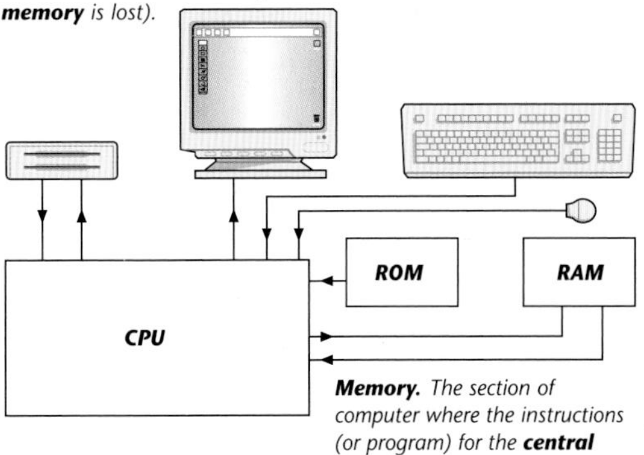
ROM
RAM
CPU

***Central processing unit (CPU).** The centre of the computer. It takes data from **memory** and **input** devices, performs operations on it (it can do this millions of times per second) and sends the results to memory or **output** devices.*

***Memory.** The section of computer where the instructions (or program) for the **central processing unit** and the data are held. There are two types, **random access memory (RAM)**, where data can be stored (written) and retrieved (read), and **read only memory (ROM)**, from which "prerecorded" data can only be read.*

* **Potential difference**, 58; **Relay**, 75; **Transistor**, 65.

PROPERTIES OF SUBSTANCES

Substance	Density† / 10^3kg m^{-3}	Young's modulus / 10^{10}N m^{-2}	Specific heat capacity† / J kg^{-1} K^{-1}	Specific latent heat of fusion / 10^4J kg^{-1}	Linear co-efficient of expansion / $10^{-6}K^{-1}$	Thermal conductivity / W m^{-1} K^{-1}	Resistivity† / 10^{-8} ρ m
Aluminum	*2.70*	*7.0*	*908*	*40.0*	*25*	*242*	*2.67*
Antimony	*6.62*	*7.8*	*210*	*16.5*	*11*	*19*	*44*
Arsenic	*5.73*	–	*335*	–	*6.0*	–	*33.3*
Bismuth	*9.78*	*3.2*	*112*	*5.5*	*14*	*9*	*117*
Brass	*8.6 (approx)*	*9.0*	*389*	–	*19*	*109*	*8 (approx)*
Cadmium	*8.65*	*5.0*	*230*	*5.5*	*30*	*96*	–
Cobalt	*8.70*	–	*435*	*24.0*	*12*	*93*	*6.4*
Constantan	*8.90*	–	*420*	–	*16*	*23*	*49*
Copper	*8.89*	*11.0*	*385*	*20.0*	*16*	*383*	*1.72*
Gallium	*5.93*	–	*377*	–	*19*	*34*	*17.4*
Germanium	*5.40*	–	*324*	–	*5.7*	*59*	*4.6 x 10^7*
Gold	*19.3*	*8.0*	*128*	*6.7*	*14*	*300*	*2.20*
Iridium	*22.4*	–	*135*	–	*6.5*	*59*	*5.2*
Iron (cast)	*7.60*	*11.0*	*460*	*21.0*	*12*	*71*	*10.3*
Iron (wrought)	*7.85*	*21.0*	*460*	*21.0*	*12*	*71*	*10.3*
Lead	*11.3*	*1.6*	*127*	*2.5*	*29*	*36*	*20.6*
Magnesium	*1.74*	*4.1*	*1,030*	*30.0*	*26*	*154*	*4.24*
Mercury	*13.6*	–	*139*	*1.2*	*12*	*9*	*95.9*
Molybdenum	*10.1*	–	*301*	–	*5.0*	*142*	*5.7*
Nickel	*8.80*	*21.0*	*456*	*29.0*	*13*	*59*	*6.94*
Palladium	*12.2*	–	*247*	*15.0*	*12*	*74*	*10.7*
Platinum	*21.5*	*17.0*	*135*	*11.5*	*9.0*	*71*	*10.5*
Selenium	*4.79*	–	*324*	*35.0*	*26*	*0.24*	*10^{12} (approx)*
Silicon (amorphous)	*2.35*	*11.3*	*706*	–	*2.5*	*175*	*10^{10} (approx)*
Silver	*10.5*	*7.7*	*234*	*10.5*	*19*	*414*	*1.63*
Steel (mild)	*7.80*	*22.0*	*450*	–	*12*	*46*	*15 (approx)*
Tantalum	*16.6*	*19.0*	*151*	–	*6.5*	*56*	*13.4*
Tellurium	*6.2*	–	*201*	–	*17*	*50*	*1.6 x 10^5*
Tin	*7.3*	*5.3*	*225*	*5.8*	*23*	*63*	*11.4*
Tungsten	*19.3*	*39.0*	*142*	–	*4.3*	*185*	*5.5*
Water	*1.00*	–	*4,200*	*33.4*	*33.4*	*0.2*	–
Zinc	*7.10*	*8.0*	*387*	*10.5*	*11*	*111*	*5.92*

† Density, specific heat capacity and resistivity all change with temperature. Values quoted here are for room temperature, i.e. 18-22°C.

Useful constants

Quantity	Symbol	Value
Speed of light in vacuum	c	2.998×10^{8}m s^{-1}
Charge on electron	e	1.602×10^{-19}C
Mass of electron	m_e	9.109×10^{-31}kg
Mass of proton	m_p	1.673×10^{-27}kg
Mass of neutron	m_n	1.675×10^{-27}kg
Avogadro's number	N_A	6.023×10^{23}mol^{-1}
Faraday's constant	F	9.65×10^{4}C mol^{-1}
Gravitational constant	G	6.670×10^{-11}N m^{2} kg^{-2}
Gas constant	R	8.314J mol^{-1} K^{-1}

Values of common quantities

Quantity	Value
Acceleration due to gravity g (gravitational field strength)	9.81m s^{-2}
Density of water	1.00×10^{3}kg m^{-3}
Density of mercury	13.6×10^{3}kg m^{-3}
Ice point (standard temperature)	273K
Steam point	373K
Standard atmospheric pressure	1.01×10^{5}Pa
Length of Earth day	8.64×10^{4}s

The electromagnetic spectrum*

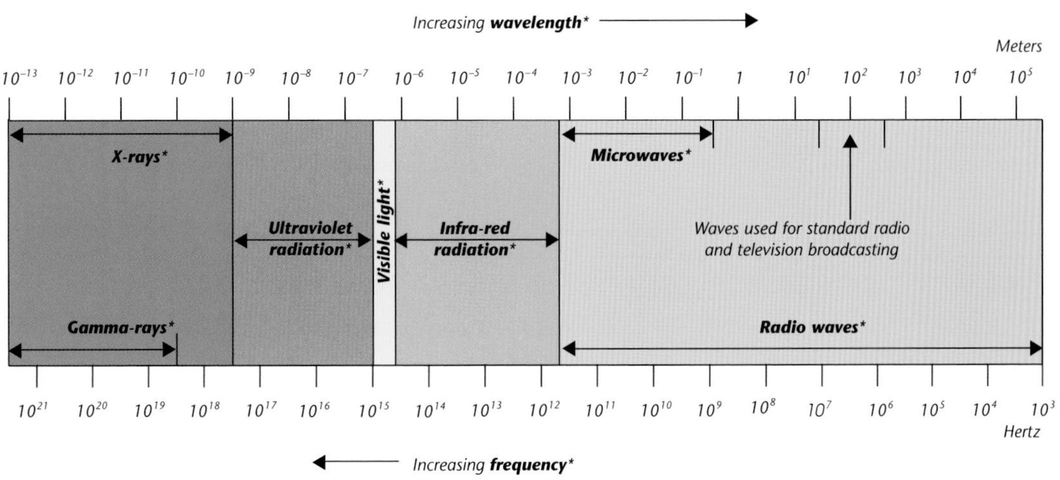
Increasing **wavelength***
Meters
10^{-13} 10^{-12} 10^{-11} 10^{-10} 10^{-9} 10^{-8} 10^{-7} 10^{-6} 10^{-5} 10^{-4} 10^{-3} 10^{-2} 10^{-1} 1 10^{1} 10^{2} 10^{3} 10^{4} 10^{5}
X-rays*
Microwaves*
Ultraviolet radiation*
Visible light*
Infra-red radiation*
Waves used for standard radio and television broadcasting
Gamma-rays*
Radio waves*
10^{21} 10^{20} 10^{19} 10^{18} 10^{17} 10^{16} 10^{15} 10^{14} 10^{13} 10^{12} 10^{11} 10^{10} 10^{9} 10^{8} 10^{7} 10^{6} 10^{5} 10^{4} 10^{3}
Hertz
Increasing **frequency***

* **Electromagnetic spectrum**, 44; **Frequency**, 35; **Gamma rays**, 44; **Infra-red radiation**, 45; **Microwaves**, **Radio waves**, 45; **Ultraviolet radiation**, 44; **Visible light**, 45; **Wavelength**, 34; **X-rays**, 44.

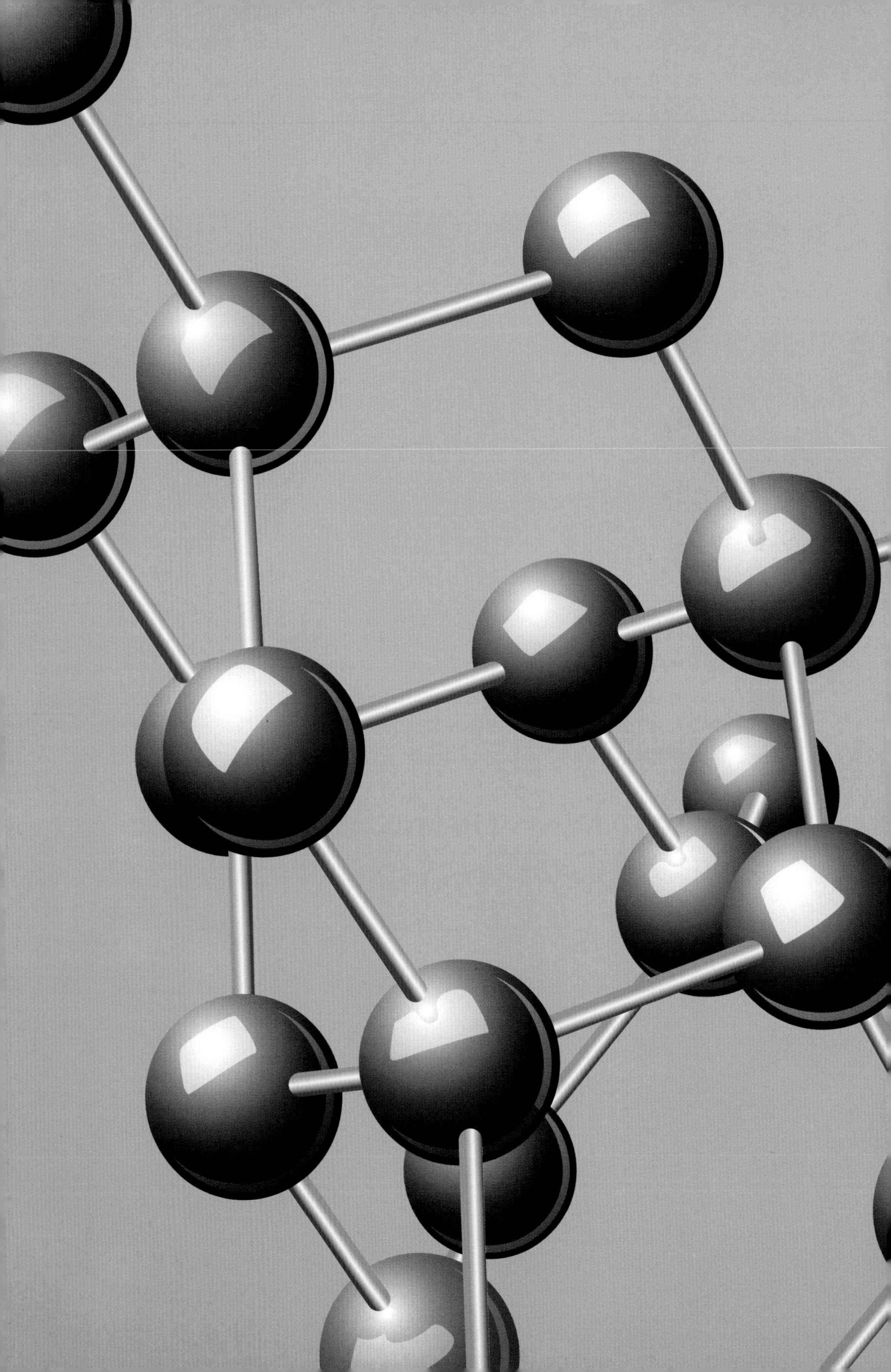

CHEMISTRY

ABOUT CHEMISTRY

Chemistry is the study of the elements which form all existing substances. It covers their structure, how they combine to create other substances and how they react under various conditions. In this book, chemistry is divided into five color-coded sections. The areas covered by these sections are explained below.

Physical chemistry

Covers the structures, properties and behavior of substances. Includes the basic laws of chemistry.

Organic chemistry

Covers the carbon-chain compounds. Examines their structures and the various groups into which they fall.

Inorganic chemistry

Looks at the groups of elements in the periodic table, their properties, uses and compounds (except carbon compounds).

Environmental chemistry

Explains the interaction of naturally-occurring chemicals, and the effect of pollution.

General chemistry information

Charts and tables of properties, symbols and means of identification, plus information on apparatus, preparations, tests and forms of chemical analysis.

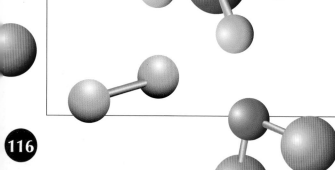

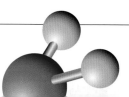

CONTENTS

Physical chemistry

Inorganic chemistry

Organic chemistry

Environmental chemistry

General chemistry information

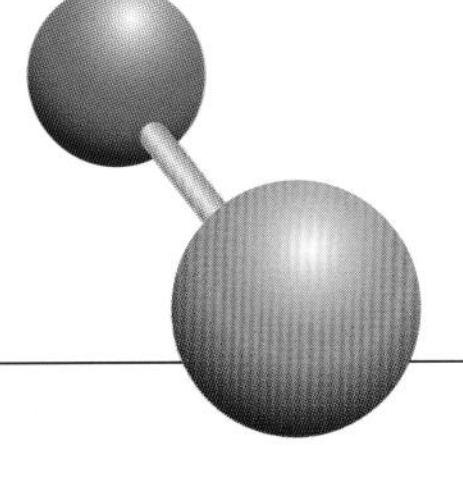

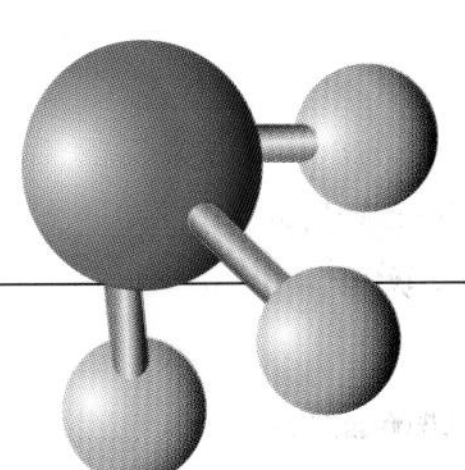

PHYSICAL CHEMISTRY

Physical chemistry is the study of the patterns of chemical behavior in **chemical reactions** under various conditions, which result from the **chemical** and **physical properties** of substances. Much of physical chemistry involves measurements of some kind. In the physical chemistry section of this book you can find out about the following areas:

1. Solids, liquids and gases, the changes between these states and the reasons for these changes in relation to the structure of a substance. (See **states of matter**, pages 120-121, **kinetic theory**, page 123 and **gas laws**, pages 142-143.)

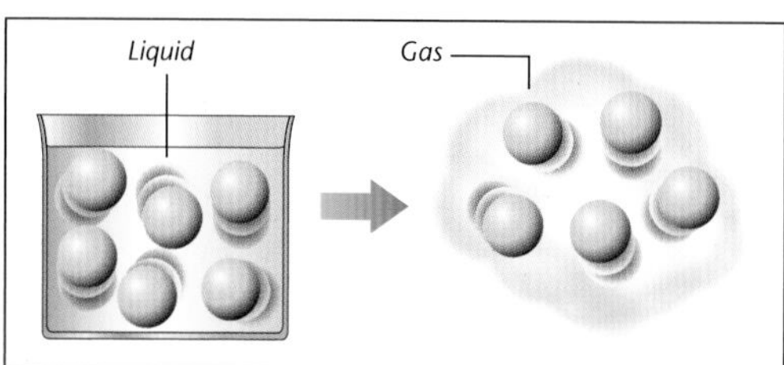
Liquid
Gas

2. The physical and chemical composition of substances – their particles and bonding. (See **elements**, **compounds and mixtures**, pages 122-123, **atoms and molecules**, pages 124-125, **bonding**, pages 130-134 and **crystals**, pages 135-137.)

Sulfur crystals occur in two shapes.

3. The structure of the atom and its importance in the structure of substances (see **atomic structure** and **radioactivity**, pages 126-129).

Structure of a sodium atom

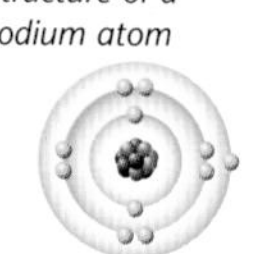

4. The measurement of quantities and the relationship between amounts of gases, liquids and solids (see **measuring atoms**, pages 138-139).

Measuring relative atomic mass

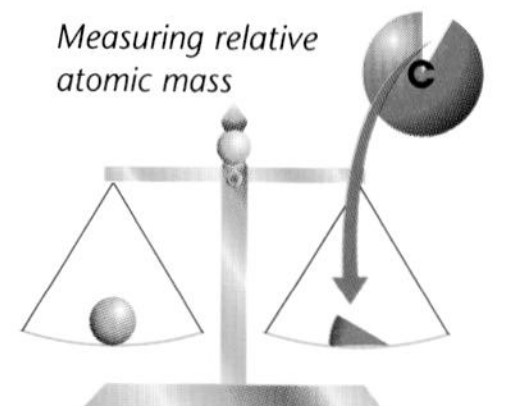
C

Chemical reactions in the cells of many deep-sea fish produce light, making the fish glow.

Luminous cells

5. Representing chemicals and chemical reactions (see **representing chemicals**, pages 140-141).

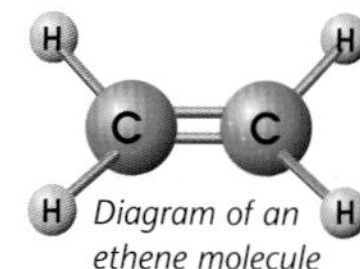
H
H
C
C
H
H

Diagram of an ethene molecule

Both these ways of representing an ethene molecule show that there are two carbon atoms and four hydrogen atoms.

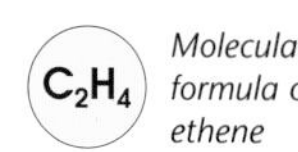
C_2H_4

Molecular formula of ethene

6. How substances mix (see **solutions and solubility**, pages 144-145).

Salt

Salt is soluble – it dissolves in water to leave a clear solution.

7. Changes during chemical reactions (see **energy and chemical reactions**, pages 146-147 and **rates of reaction**, pages 160-161) and special reactions (see **oxidation and reduction**, pages 148-149 and **reversible reactions**, pages 162-163).

Chemicals on a match burn when they react with phosphorus on the box.

8. Special types of chemical behavior (see **acids and bases**, pages 150-152 and **salts**, pages 153-155).

*Hydrochloric acid and sodium hydroxide (an alkaline solution) react together to form sodium chloride, a salt. The solutions have been colored with **litmus*** to show whether they are acidic, alkaline, or neutral.*

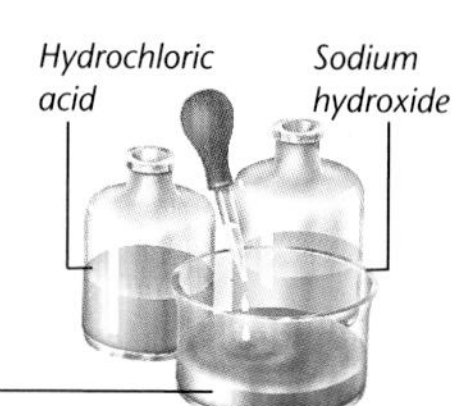
Hydrochloric acid
Sodium hydroxide
Sodium chloride

9. The action of electricity on substances and the production of electricity from reactions (see **electrolysis**, pages 156-157 and **reactivity**, pages 158-159).

Electrolysis of copper

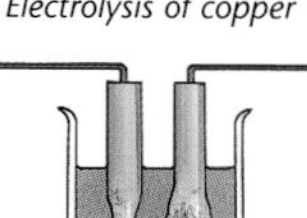

10. The different levels of reactivity shown by substances and the reasons for this (see **reactivity**, pages 158-159).

Stalagmites and stalactites form gradually as a result of a slow chemical reaction between calcium carbonate in limestone and carbonic acid in rainwater.

* **Litmus**, 152.

PROPERTIES AND CHANGES

Physical properties

All the properties of a substance except those which affect its behavior in **chemical reactions**. There are two main types – **qualitative properties** and **quantitative properties**.

Qualitative properties

Descriptive properties of a substance which cannot be given a mathematical value. They are such things as smell, taste and color.

Some qualitative properties used to describe substances

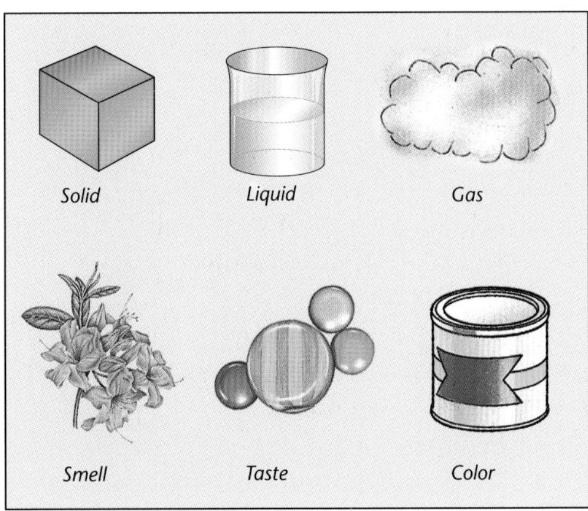
Solid
Liquid
Gas
Smell
Taste
Color

Quantitative properties

Properties which can be measured and given a specific mathematical value, e.g. melting point, boiling point, **mass***, **solubility*** and **density***. Other examples are shown below.

Some quantitative properties used to describe substances

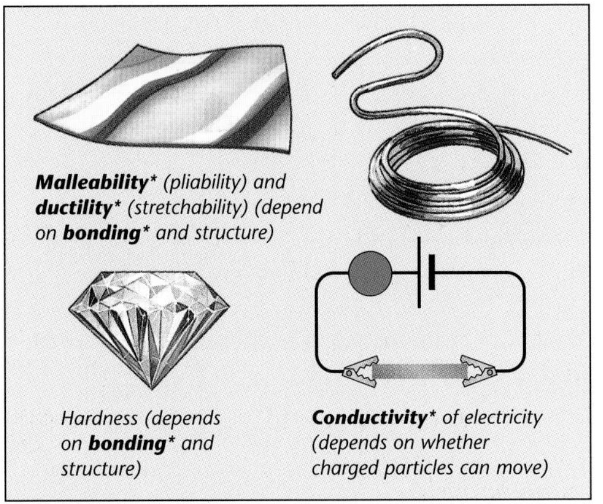
Malleability (pliability) and **ductility*** (stretchability) (depend on **bonding*** and structure)*
*Hardness (depends on **bonding*** and structure)*
Conductivity of electricity (depends on whether charged particles can move)*

Physical change

A change which occurs when one or more of the **physical properties** of a substance is changed. It is usually easily reversed.

*A **physical change** from solid to liquid is caused by adding energy to the particles of the substance (see **kinetic theory**, page 123).*

Ice cream melts from a solid to a liquid in the heat of the Sun.

Chemical properties

Properties which cause specific behavior of substances during **chemical reactions**.

Chemical properties** depend on **electron configuration, **bonding***, structure and energy changes.*

Chemical reaction

Any change which alters the **chemical properties** of a substance or which forms a new substance. During a chemical reaction, **products** are formed from **reactants**.

Reactants

The substances present at the beginning of a **chemical reaction**.

Products

The substances formed in a **chemical reaction**.

*The **rusting*** of iron is a chemical reaction. The reaction is quite slow – many reactions are much faster.*

*Iron, water and oxygen from the air are the **reactants**.*

Rust is the **product**.*

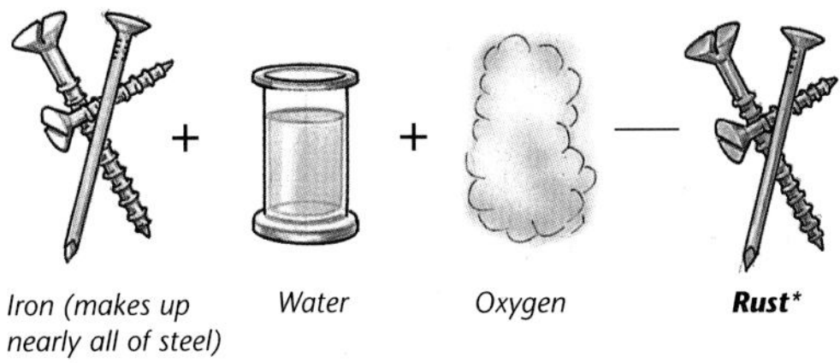
+
+
Iron (makes up nearly all of steel)
Water
Oxygen
Rust*

Reagent

A substance used to start a **chemical reaction**. It is also one of the **reactants**. Common reagents in the laboratory are hydrochloric acid, sulfuric acid and sodium hydroxide.

* **Bonding**, 130; **Conductivity**, 63; **Density**, 24; **Ductility**, 344 (**Ductile**); **Electron configuration**, 127; **Malleability**, 345 (**Malleable**); **Mass**, 12; **Rust**, 174; **Rusting**, 209 (**Corrosion**); **Solubility**, 145.

STATES OF MATTER

A substance can be **solid**, **liquid** or **gaseous**. These are the **physical states** or **states of matter** (normally shortened to **states**). Substances can change between states, normally when heated or cooled to increase or decrease the energy of the particles (see **kinetic theory**, page 123).

Crystals of ice – the ***solid*** *form of water*

Solid state

A state in which a substance has a definite volume and shape.

Solid state *– volume and shape stay the same.*

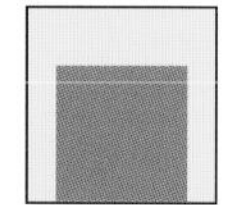

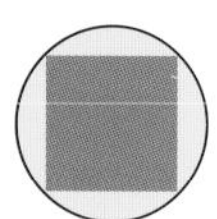

Liquid state

A state in which a substance has a definite volume, but can change shape.

Liquid state *– volume stays the same, but shape alters.*

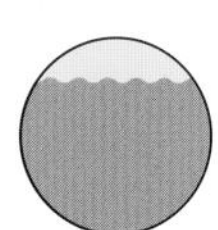

Gaseous state

A state in which a substance has no definite volume or shape. It is either a **vapor** or a **gas**. A vapor can be changed into a liquid by applying pressure alone; a gas must first be turned into a vapor by reducing its temperature to below a level called its **critical temperature**.

Gaseous state *– volume and shape will alter.*

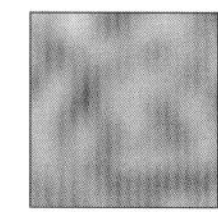

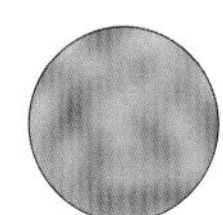

Phase

A separate part of a mixture of substances with different physical and chemical properties. A mixture of sand and water contains two phases, as does a mixture of oil and water.

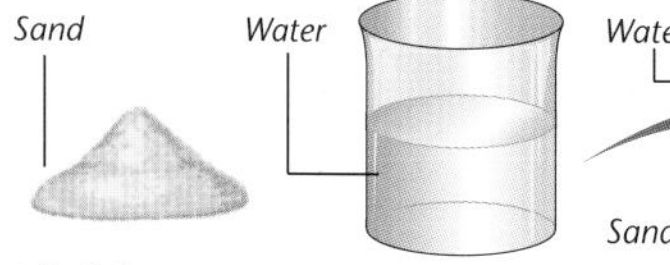
Sand
Water
Water
Sand

Fluid

A substance that will flow, i.e. is in either the **gaseous** or **liquid state**.

Changes of state

A **change of state** is a **physical change*** of a substance from one state to another. It normally occurs because of a change in the energy of the particles, caused by heating or cooling (see **kinetic theory**, page 123).

Molten

Describes the **liquid** state of a substance which is a **solid** at room temperature.

Solid *wax becomes* ***molten*** *when heated.*

Solidification

The change of state from **liquid** to **solid** of a substance which is a solid at room temperature and atmospheric pressure.

Melting

The change of state from **solid** to **liquid**, usually caused by heating. The temperature at which a solid melts is called its **melting point** (see also pages 212-213), which is the same temperature as its **freezing point** (see **freezing**). At the melting point, both solid and liquid states are present. An increase in pressure increases the melting point. All pure samples of a substance at the same pressure have the same melting point.

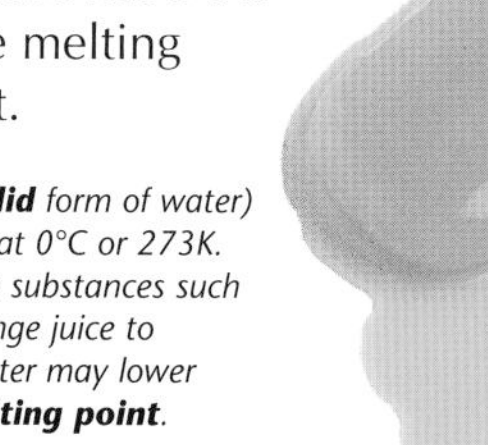

*Ice (****solid*** *form of water)* ***melts*** *at 0°C or 273K. Adding substances such as orange juice to the water may lower its* ***melting point****.*

* **Physical change**, 119.

Freezing

The change of state from **liquid** to **solid**, caused by cooling a liquid. The temperature at which a substance freezes is the **freezing point**, which is the same temperature as the **melting point** (see **melting**).

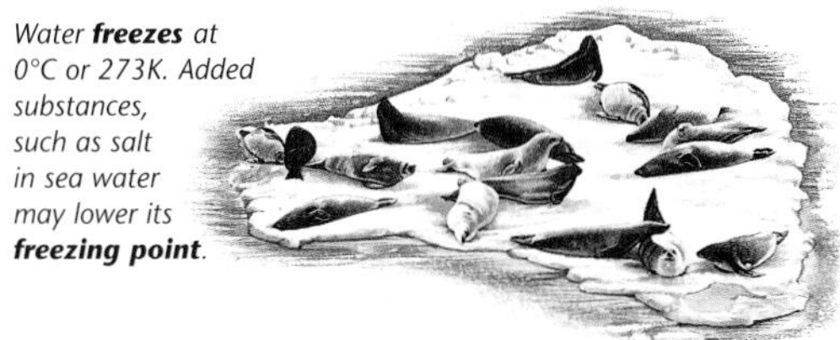

*Water **freezes** at 0°C or 273K. Added substances, such as salt in sea water may lower its **freezing point**.*

Fusion

The change of state from **solid** to **liquid** of a substance which is solid at room temperature and pressure. The substance is described as **fused** (or **molten**). A solid that has been fused and then solidified into a different form is also described as fused.

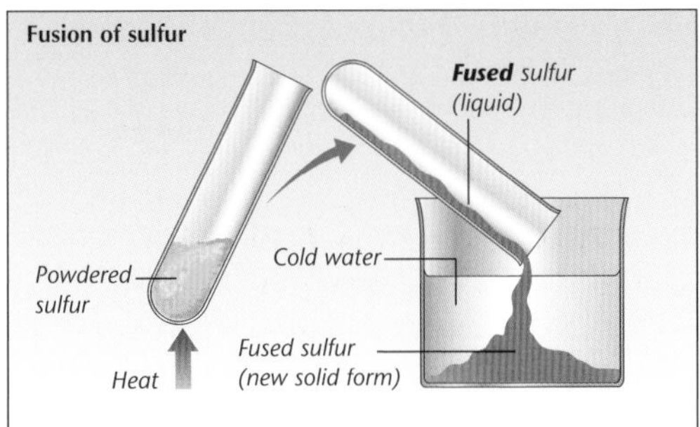
Fusion of sulfur
Fused sulfur (liquid)
Cold water
Powdered sulfur
Heat
Fused sulfur (new solid form)

Boiling

A change of state from **liquid** to **gaseous** (**vapor**) at a temperature called the **boiling point** (see also pages 212-213). It occurs by the formation of bubbles throughout the liquid. All pure samples of the same liquid at the same pressure have the same boiling point. An increase in pressure increases the boiling point. A decrease in pressure decreases the boiling point.

100°C

Water boils at 100°C or 373K.

Evaporation

A change of state from **liquid** to **gaseous** (**vapor**), due to the escape of molecules from the surface. (For more about this, see page 30.) A liquid which readily evaporates is described as **volatile***.

In rainforests where it is warm, raindrops quickly evaporate to form water vapor in the air.

Liquefaction

A change of state from **gaseous** (**gas**) to **liquid**, of a substance which is a gas at room temperature and pressure. It is caused by cooling (to form a **vapor**) and increasing pressure.

*Some **gases** are **liquefied** for transport.*

Condensation

A change of state from **gaseous** (**gas** or **vapor**) to **liquid**, of a substance which is a liquid at room temperature and pressure. It is normally caused by cooling.

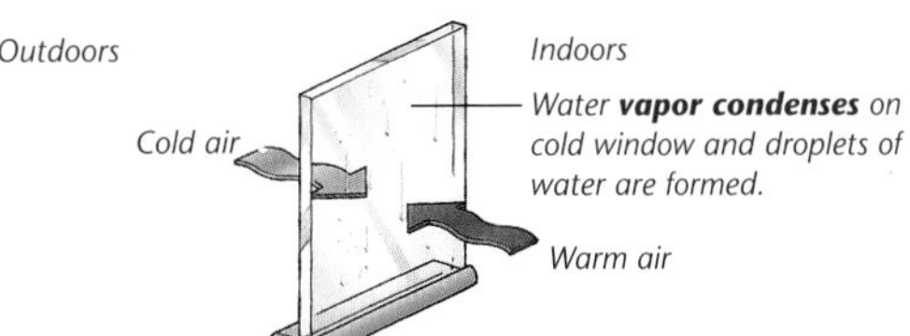
Outdoors
Indoors
Cold air
Warm air

*Water **vapor condenses** on cold window and droplets of water are formed.*

Sublimation

The change of state from **solid** to **gaseous** (**gas**, via **vapor**) on heating, and from gaseous directly to solid on cooling. At no stage is a liquid formed. See picture, page 162.

Vaporization

Any change resulting in a **gaseous state**, i.e. **boiling**, **evaporation** or **sublimation**.

* **Volatile**, 345.

ELEMENTS, COMPOUNDS AND MIXTURES

Elements, **compounds** and **mixtures** are the three main types of chemical substance. Most natural substances are made up of several compounds.

Element

A substance which cannot be split into a simpler substance by a chemical reaction. There are just over 100 known elements, classified in the **periodic table***, and most are solids or gases at room temperature. All atoms of the same element have the same number of **protons*** in their **nuclei*** (see **atomic number**, page 127).

*Iron and sulfur are **elements** – they cannot be broken down into simpler substances.*

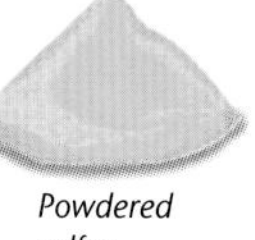

Powdered sulfur

Iron filings

Compound

A combination of two or more **elements**, bonded together in some way. It has different physical and chemical properties from the elements it is made of. The proportion of each element in a compound is constant, e.g. water is always formed from two parts hydrogen and one part oxygen. This is shown by its chemical **formula***, H_2O. Compounds are often difficult to split into their elements and can only be separated by chemical reactions or **electrolysis***, a process in which an electric current is used to cause a chemical change.

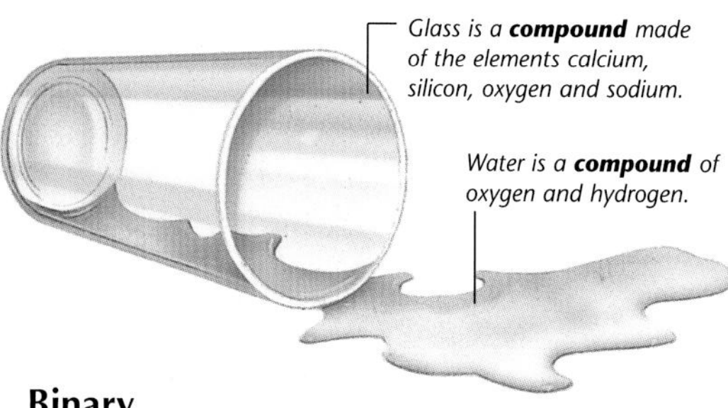

*Glass is a **compound** made of the elements calcium, silicon, oxygen and sodium.*

*Water is a **compound** of oxygen and hydrogen.*

Binary

Describes a **compound** composed of two **elements** only, e.g. carbon monoxide, which contains only carbon and oxygen.

Synthesis

The process by which a **compound** is built up from its **elements** or from simpler compounds by a sequence of chemical reactions, e.g. iron(III) chloride is made by passing chlorine gas over heated iron.

*Quartz is a **compound** of silicon and oxygen. The temperature and pressure at which **synthesis** takes place affects the structure of the mineral formed.*

Mixture

A blend of two or more **elements** and/or **compounds** which are not chemically combined. The proportions of each element or compound are not fixed, and each keeps its own properties. A mixture can usually be separated into its elements or compounds fairly easily by physical means.

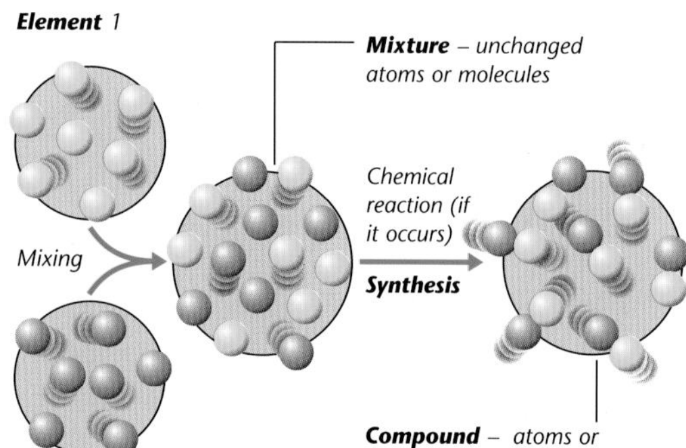

Element 1
Mixing
Element 2
***Mixture** – unchanged atoms or molecules*
Chemical reaction (if it occurs)
Synthesis
***Compound** – atoms or molecules in new combinations (see **bonding**, pages 130-134).*

Chemical symbol

A shorthand way of representing an **element** in **formulas** and **equations** (see pages 140-141). It represents one atom and usually consists of the first one or two letters of the name of the element, occasionally the Greek or Latin name. See pages 212-213 for a list of elements and their symbols, and pages 226-227 to match symbols to elements.

Sulfur

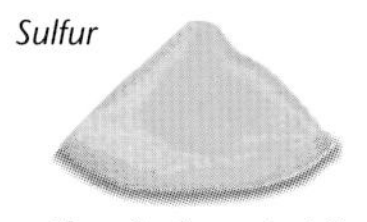

***Chemical symbol** S*

Iron

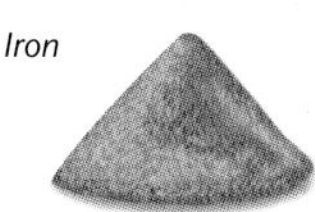

***Chemical symbol** Fe – ferrum is Latin for iron.*

* **Electrolysis**, 156; **Formulas**, 140; **Nucleus**, 126; **Periodic table**, 164; **Proton**, 126.

Homogeneous

Describes a substance where all the particles are in the same **phase***, e.g. **solutions*** (the physical and chemical properties throughout are the same).

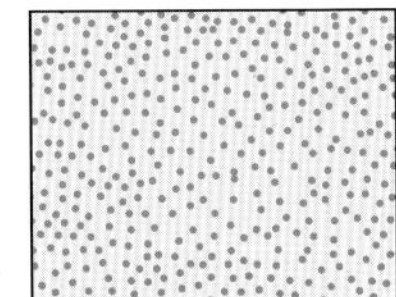

Homogeneous

*All particles are in the same **phase****.

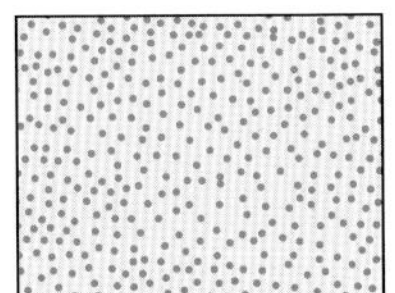

*The sand on the seashore is a **heterogeneous** mixture of tiny particles of quartz, seashell and organic matter.*

Heterogeneous

Describes a substance where the particles are in more than one **phase***, e.g. **suspensions*** (the properties of the solid particles are different from those of the liquid).

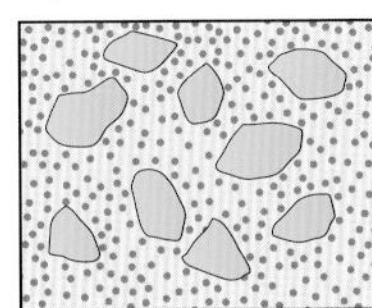

Heterogeneous

*Particles are in different **phases****.

Pure

Describes a sample of a substance which consists only of one **element** or **compound**. It does not contain any other substance in any proportions. If the substance does contain traces of another element or compound, then it is described as **impure** and the other substance is called an **impurity**.

Kinetic theory

The **kinetic theory** explains the behavior of solids, liquids and gases, and **changes of state*** between them, in terms of the movement of the particles of which they are made (see diagram below).

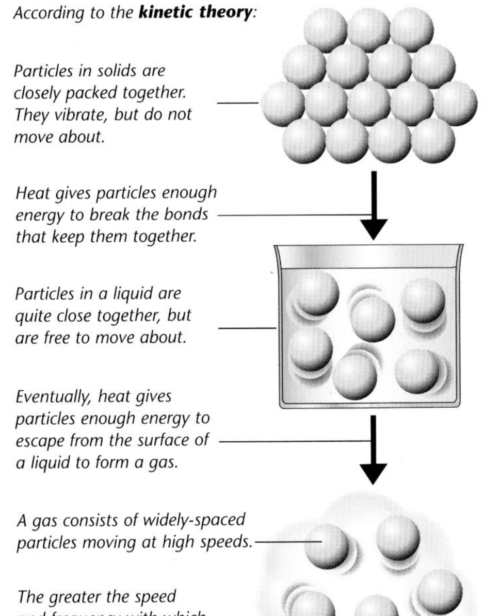

According to the kinetic theory:
Particles in solids are closely packed together. They vibrate, but do not move about.
Heat gives particles enough energy to break the bonds that keep them together.
Particles in a liquid are quite close together, but are free to move about.
Eventually, heat gives particles enough energy to escape from the surface of a liquid to form a gas.
A gas consists of widely-spaced particles moving at high speeds.
The greater the speed and frequency with which molecules of a gas hit surfaces or each other, the higher its pressure.

Brownian motion

The random motion of small particles in water or air. It supports the kinetic theory, as it is clearly due to unseen impact with the water or air molecules.

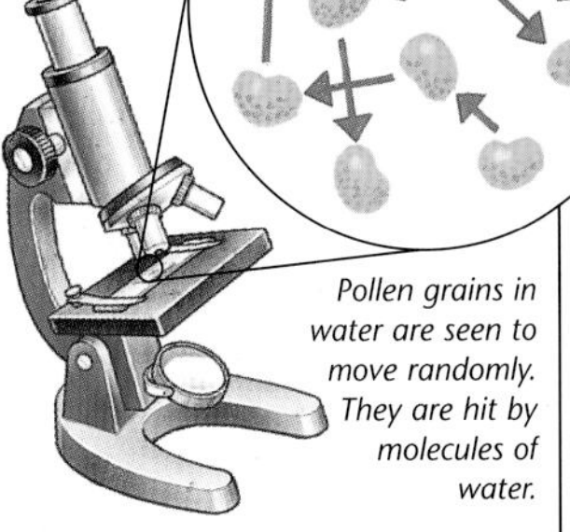

Pollen grains in water are seen to move randomly. They are hit by molecules of water.

Diffusion

The process by which two **fluids*** mix without mechanical help. The process supports the kinetic theory, since the particles must be moving to mix, and visible gases, such as bromine vapour (below), can be seen to diffuse faster than liquids. Only **miscible*** liquids diffuse.

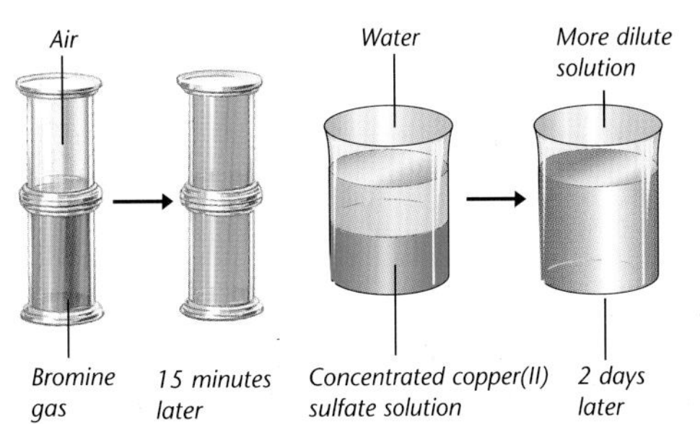

Air
Water
More dilute solution
Bromine gas
15 minutes later
Concentrated copper(II) sulfate solution
2 days later

* **Change of state**, **Fluid**, 120; **Miscible**, 145; **Phase**, 120; **Solution**, 144; **Suspension**, 145.

ATOMS AND MOLECULES

Over 2,000 years ago, the Greeks decided that all substances consisted of small particles which they called **atoms**. Later theories extended this idea to include **molecules** – atoms joined together. **Inorganic*** molecules generally only contain a few atoms, but **organic*** molecules can contain hundreds of atoms.

Atom

The smallest particle of an element that retains the chemical properties of that element. The atoms of many elements are bonded together in groups to form particles called **molecules** (see also **covalent bonding**, page 132). Atoms consist of three main types of smaller particles – see **atomic structure**, page 126.

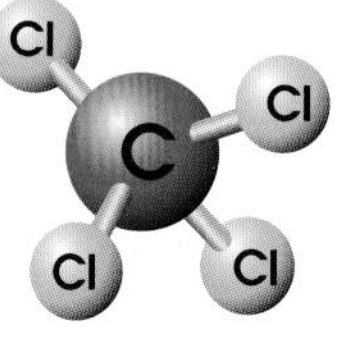

Cl
Cl
C
Cl
Cl

Tetrachloromethane (CCl_4) ***molecules*** *consist of one carbon and four chlorine* ***atoms****.*

Molecule

The smallest particle of an element or compound that normally exists on its own and still retains its properties. Molecules normally consist of two or more **atoms** bonded together – some have thousands of atoms. **Ionic compounds*** consist of **ions*** (electrically charged particles) and do not have molecules.

Ne

Neon ***molecules*** *consist of a single neon* ***atom****.*

Atomicity

The number of **atoms** in a **molecule**, calculated from the **molecular formula*** of the compound.

A ***molecule*** *with an* ***atomicity*** *of one is described as* ***monatomic****.*

He

Helium

A ***molecule*** *with an* ***atomicity*** *of two is described as* ***diatomic****.*

Hydrogen

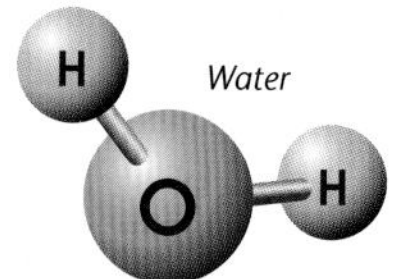

H
O
H

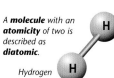

Water

A ***molecule*** *with an* ***atomicity*** *of three is described as* ***triatomic****.*

A ***molecule*** *with an* ***atomicity*** *of over three is described as* ***polyatomic****.*

Dalton's atomic theory

John Dalton's theory, published in 1808, attempts to explain how **atoms** behave. It is still generally valid. It states that:

1. All matter is made up of tiny particles called **atoms**.

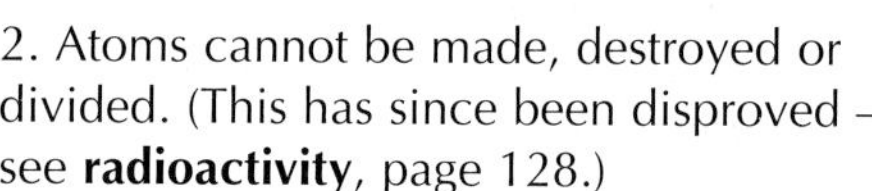

2. Atoms cannot be made, destroyed or divided. (This has since been disproved – see **radioactivity**, page 128.)

3. All atoms of the same element have the same properties and the same mass. (This has since been disproved – see **isotope**, page 127.)

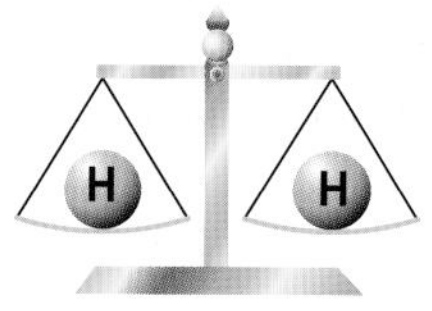

H
H

4. **Atoms** of different elements have different properties and different masses.

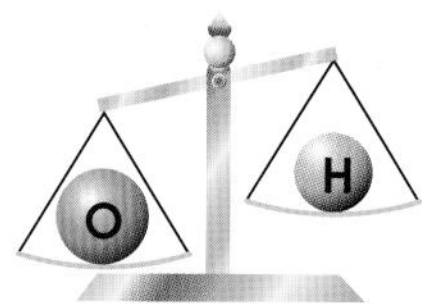

O
H

5. When compounds form, the **atoms** of the elements involved combine in simple whole numbers. (We now know, however, that large **organic*** molecules do not always combine in whole number ratios.)

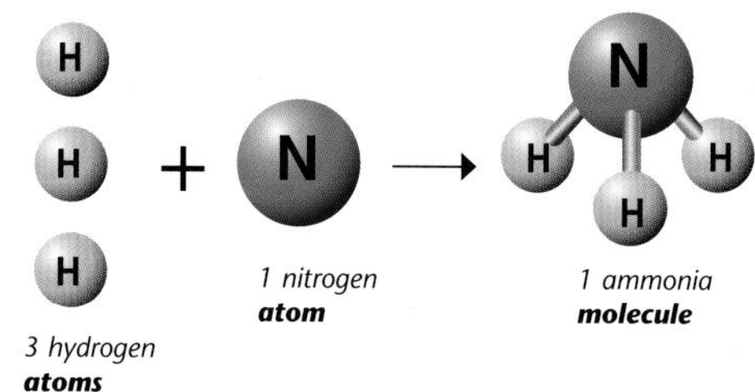

H
H
H
N
N
H
H
H

3 hydrogen ***atoms*** + *1 nitrogen* ***atom*** → *1 ammonia* ***molecule***

* **Inorganic chemistry**, 166; **Ion**, 130; **Ionic compound**, 131; **Molecular formula**, 140; **Organic chemistry**, 190.

Dimer
A substance with **molecules** formed from the combination of two molecules of a **monomer*** (a relatively small molecule).

*Nitrogen dioxide (**monomer***) combines to form dinitrogen tetraoxide (**dimer**).*

$NO_2(g)$	+	$NO_2(g)$	→	$N_2O_4(g)$
Nitrogen dioxide		*Nitrogen dioxide*		*Dinitrogen tetraoxide*

Trimer
A substance with **molecules** formed from the combination of three molecules of a **monomer***.

Macromolecule
A **molecule** consisting of a large number of **atoms**. It is normally an **organic*** molecule with a very high **relative molecular mass***.

Basic laws of chemistry

Three laws of chemistry were put forward in the late eighteenth and early nineteenth centuries. Two pre-date **Dalton's atomic theory** and the third (the **law of multiple proportions**) was developed from it. These laws were of great importance in the development of the atomic theory.

Law of constant composition
States that all pure samples of the same chemical compound contain the same elements combined in the same proportions by mass. It was developed by a Frenchman, Joseph Proust, in 1799.

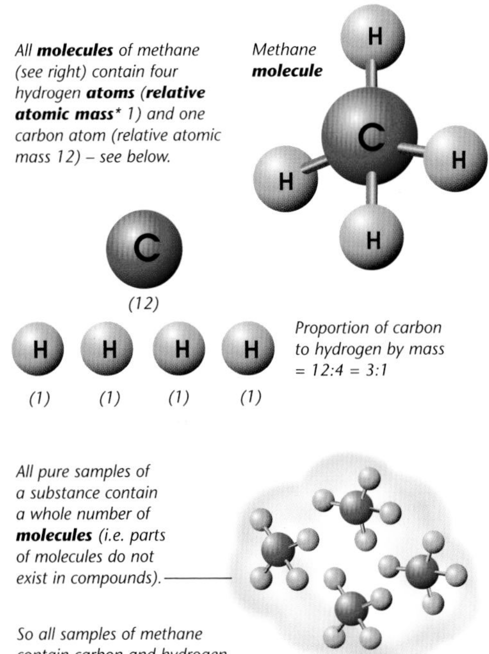
Methane
molecule
H
C
H
H
H
C
(12)
H
H
H
H
(1)
(1)
(1)
(1)

*All **molecules** of methane (see right) contain four hydrogen **atoms** (**relative atomic mass*** 1) and one carbon atom (relative atomic mass 12) – see below.*

Proportion of carbon to hydrogen by mass = 12:4 = 3:1

*All pure samples of a substance contain a whole number of **molecules** (i.e. parts of molecules do not exist in compounds).*

So all samples of methane contain carbon and hydrogen in the ratio 3:1 by mass.

Law of conservation of mass
States that matter can neither be created nor destroyed during a chemical reaction. It was developed by a Frenchman, Antoine Lavoisier, in 1774.

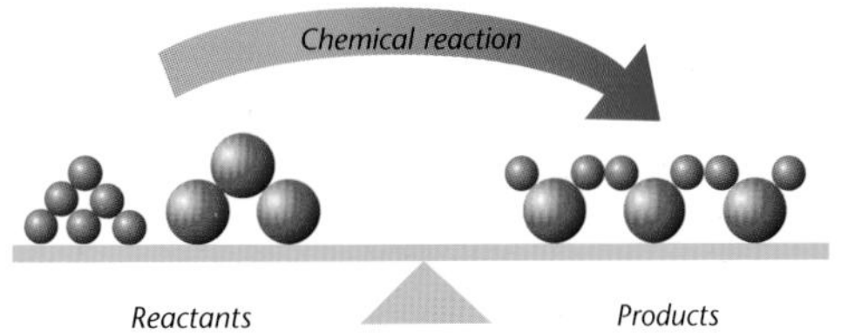
Chemical reaction
Reactants
Products

Law of multiple proportions
States that if two elements, A and B, can combine to form more than one compound, then the different masses of A which combine with a fixed mass of B in each compound are in a simple ratio. It is an extension of **Dalton's atomic theory**.

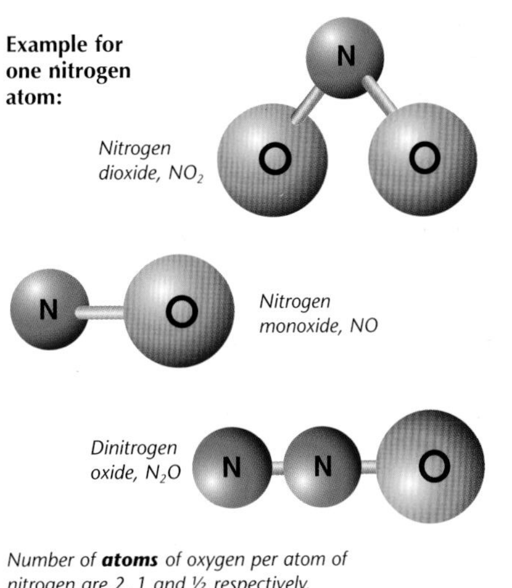
Example for one nitrogen atom:
Nitrogen dioxide, NO_2
N
O
O
N
O
Nitrogen monoxide, NO
Dinitrogen oxide, N_2O
N
N
O

*Number of **atoms** of oxygen per atom of nitrogen are 2, 1 and ½ respectively.*

Masses of oxygen in ratio 4:2:1

* **Monomers**, 200; **Organic chemistry**, 190;
Relative atomic mass, **Relative molecular mass**, 138.

ATOMIC STRUCTURE

Dalton's atomic theory (see page 124) states that the atom is the smallest possible particle. However, experiments have proved that it contains smaller particles, or **subatomic particles**. The three main subatomic particles are **protons** and **neutrons**, which make up the **nucleus**, and **electrons**, which are arranged around the nucleus.

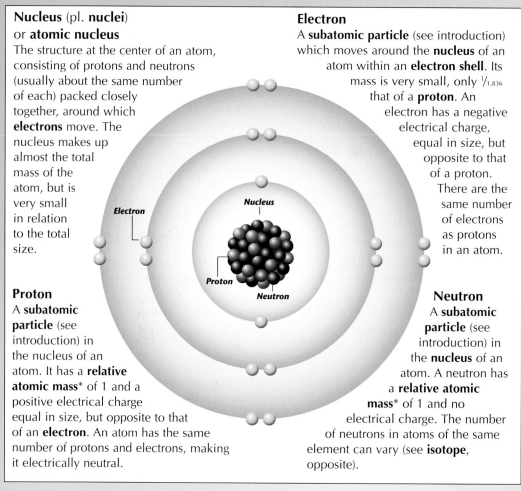

Nucleus (pl. **nuclei**) or **atomic nucleus**
The structure at the center of an atom, consisting of protons and neutrons (usually about the same number of each) packed closely together, around which **electrons** move. The nucleus makes up almost the total mass of the atom, but is very small in relation to the total size.

Electron
A **subatomic particle** (see introduction) which moves around the **nucleus** of an atom within an **electron shell**. Its mass is very small, only 1/1,836 that of a **proton**. An electron has a negative electrical charge, equal in size, but opposite to that of a proton. There are the same number of electrons as protons in an atom.

Proton
A **subatomic particle** (see introduction) in the nucleus of an atom. It has a **relative atomic mass*** of 1 and a positive electrical charge equal in size, but opposite to that of an **electron**. An atom has the same number of protons and electrons, making it electrically neutral.

Neutron
A **subatomic particle** (see introduction) in the **nucleus** of an atom. A neutron has a **relative atomic mass*** of 1 and no electrical charge. The number of neutrons in atoms of the same element can vary (see **isotope**, opposite).

Electron shell or **shell**
A region of space in which the **electrons** move around the **nucleus** of an atom. An atom can have up to seven shells, increasing in radius with distance from the nucleus, and each can hold up to a certain number of electrons. The model on the right is a simplified one – in fact, the exact positions of electrons cannot be determined at any one time, and each shell consists of **orbitals**.

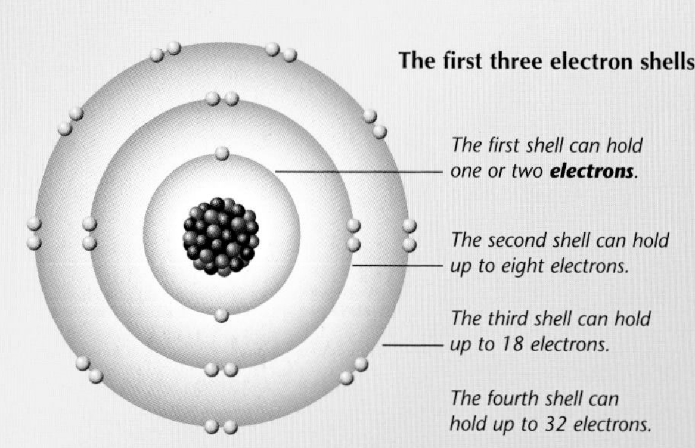
The first three electron shells
The first shell can hold one or two **electrons**.
The second shell can hold up to eight electrons.
The third shell can hold up to 18 electrons.
The fourth shell can hold up to 32 electrons.

* **Relative atomic mass**, 138.

Orbital

A region in which there can be either one or two **electrons**. Each **electron shell** consists of one or more orbitals of varying shapes.

Outer shell

The last **electron shell** in which there are **electrons**. The number of electrons in the outer shell influences how the element reacts and which **group** it is in (see **periodic table**, pages 164-165).

Electron configuration

A group of numbers which shows the arrangement of the **electrons** in an atom. The numbers are the numbers of electrons in each **electron shell**, starting with the innermost.

A sodium atom – electron configuration 2.8.1

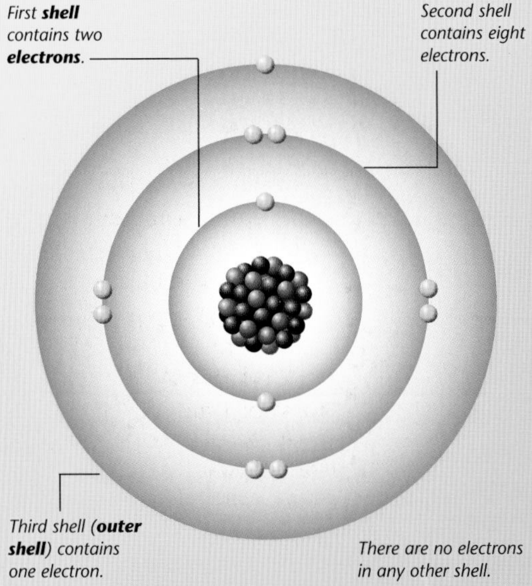

First ***shell*** *contains two* ***electrons****.*
Second shell contains eight electrons.
*Third shell (****outer shell****) contains one electron.*
There are no electrons in any other shell.

Octet

A group of eight **electrons** in a single **electron shell**. Atoms with an octet for the **outer shell** are very stable and unreactive. All **noble gases*** (except helium) have an octet. Other atoms can achieve a stable octet (and thus have an electron configuration similar to that of the nearest noble gas), either by sharing electrons with other atoms (see **covalent bonding**, page 132) or by gaining or losing electrons (see **ionic bonding**, page 131).

Atomic number

The number of **protons** in the **nucleus** of an atom. The atomic number determines what the element is, e.g. any atom with six protons is carbon, regardless of the number of **neutrons** and **electrons**.

Mass number

The total number of **protons** and **neutrons** in one atom of an element. The mass number of an element can vary because the number of neutrons can change (see **isotope**, below). The mass number is usually about twice the **atomic number**.

The ***atomic number*** *and* ***mass number*** *are often written with the symbol for the element.*

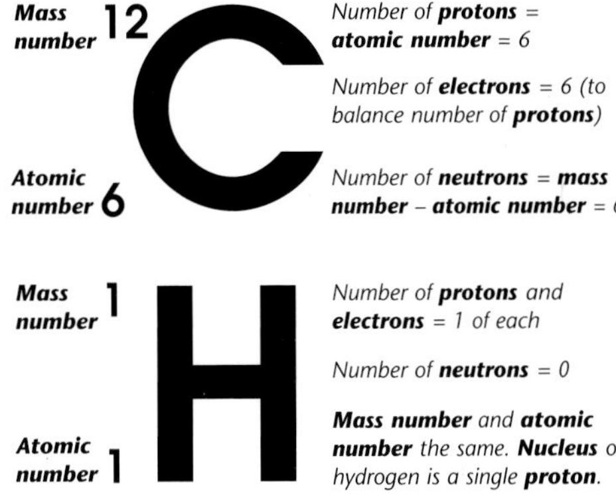

Mass number 12
C
Atomic number 6
Number of ***protons*** *=* ***atomic number*** *= 6*
Number of ***electrons*** *= 6 (to balance number of* ***protons****)*
Number of ***neutrons*** *=* ***mass number*** *–* ***atomic number*** *= 6*
Mass number 1
H
Atomic number 1
Number of ***protons*** *and* ***electrons*** *= 1 of each*
Number of ***neutrons*** *= 0*
Mass number *and* ***atomic number*** *the same.* ***Nucleus*** *of hydrogen is a single* ***proton****.*

Isotope

An atom of an element in which the number of **neutrons** is different from that in another atom of the same element. Isotopes of an element have the same **atomic number** but different **mass numbers**. Isotopes are distinguished by writing the mass number by the name or symbol of the element.

The three isotopes of carbon

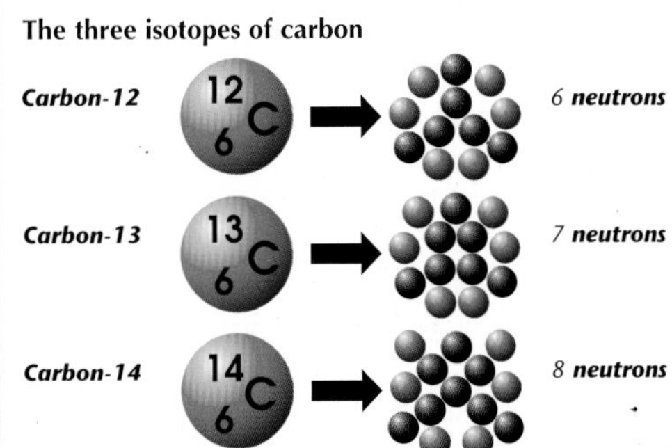

Carbon-12
12
6 C
6 ***neutrons***
Carbon-13
13
6 C
7 ***neutrons***
Carbon-14
14
6 C
8 ***neutrons***

*** Noble gases**, 189.

RADIOACTIVITY

Radioactivity is a property of unstable **nuclei*** (for more about the reasons for their instability, see pages 84-85). It involves the nuclei breaking up spontaneously into nuclei of other elements and emitting rays or particles (**radiation**), a process known as **radioactive decay**. A radioactive element is one whose nuclei are gradually splitting up in this way.

Nucleus* *emitting* ***gamma rays*** *– very high energy* ***electromagnetic**** *rays.*

Radioisotope or radioactive isotope

The general term for a radioactive substance, since all are **isotopes***. There are several naturally-occurring radioisotopes, such as carbon-14 and uranium-238, others are formed in a variety of ways. For more about this, see page 86.

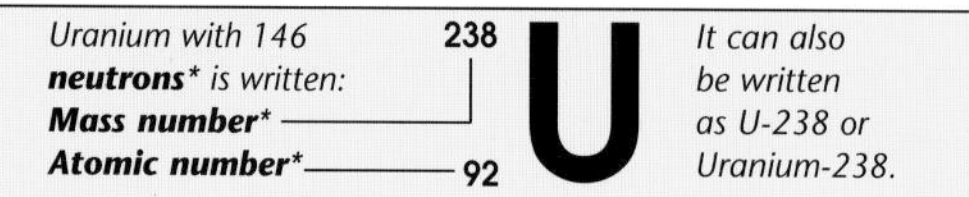

Uranium with 146 neutrons* is written:
Mass number*
Atomic number*
$^{238}_{92}U$
It can also be written as U-238 or Uranium-238.

Alpha particle (α-particle)

One type of particle emitted from the **nucleus*** of a radioactive atom. It is like a helium nucleus, consisting of two **protons*** and two **neutrons***, has a **relative atomic mass*** of 4 and a charge of plus 2. It moves slowly and has a low penetrating power.

Beta particle (β-particle)

A fast-moving particle emitted from a radioactive **nucleus***. There are two different types of beta particle (for more about this, see page 86). They can penetrate objects which have a low density and/or thickness, such as paper.

Gamma rays (γ-rays)

Rays generally emitted after an **alpha** or **beta particle** from a radioactive **nucleus***. They take the form of waves (like light and X-rays) and have a high penetrating power, going through aluminum sheeting. They can be stopped by a thick block of lead.

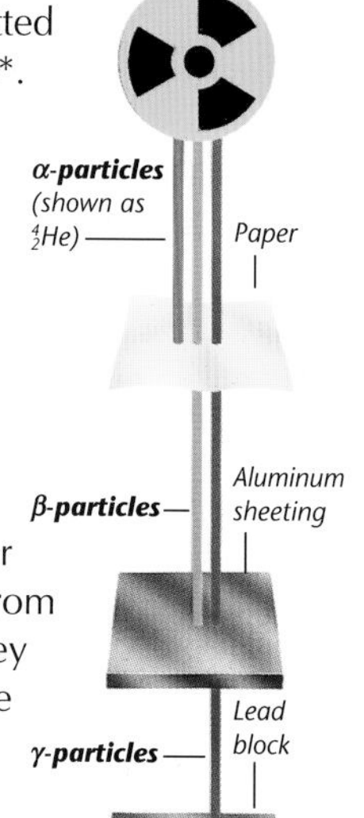

Source of radiation
α-particles (shown as $^{4}_{2}He$)
Paper
β-particles
Aluminum sheeting
γ-particles
Lead block

Radioactive decay

The process whereby the **nuclei*** of a radioactive element undergo a series of **disintegrations** (a **decay series**) to become stable. For more about the different types of decay, see page 87.

Disintegration

The splitting of an unstable **nucleus*** into two parts, usually another nucleus and an **alpha** or **beta particle**. The **atomic number*** changes, so an atom of a new element is produced. If this is a stable atom, then no further disintegrations occur. If it is unstable, it disintegrates in turn and the process continues as a **decay series** until a stable atom is formed.

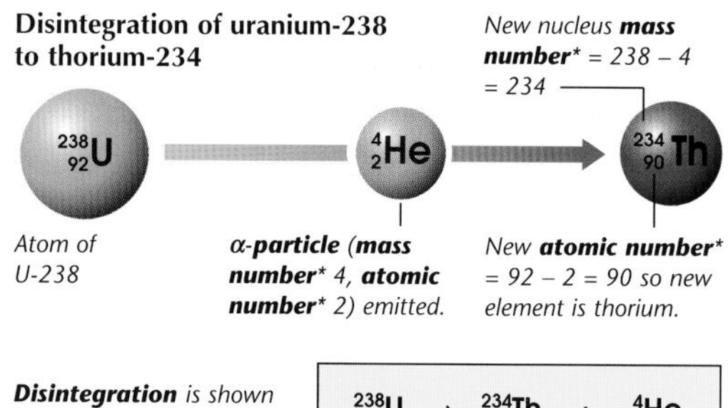

Disintegration of uranium-238 to thorium-234
New nucleus mass number* = 238 – 4 = 234
$^{238}_{92}U$
$^{4}_{2}He$
$^{234}_{90}Th$
Atom of U-238
α-particle (mass number* 4, atomic number* 2) emitted.
New atomic number* = 92 – 2 = 90 so new element is thorium.

Disintegration *is shown by a* ***nuclear equation.***

$$^{238}_{92}U \rightarrow \, ^{234}_{90}Th + \, ^{4}_{2}He$$

Decay series or radioactive series

The series of **disintegrations** involved when a radioactive element decays, producing various elements until one with stable atoms is formed.

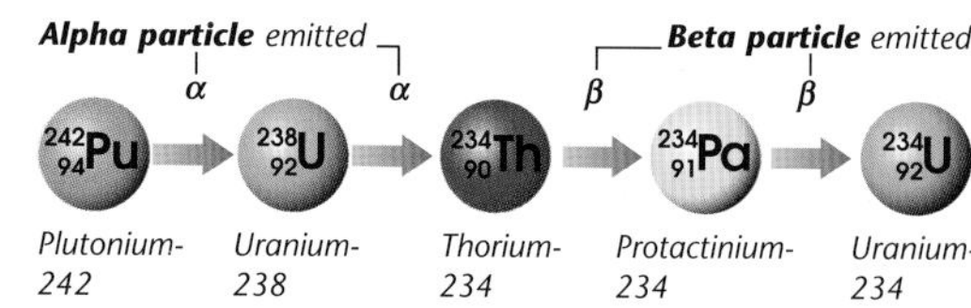

Decay series for plutonium-242 to uranium-234
For another example, see page 87.
Alpha particle emitted
Beta particle emitted
α
α
β
β
$^{242}_{94}Pu$
$^{238}_{92}U$
$^{234}_{90}Th$
$^{234}_{91}Pa$
$^{234}_{92}U$
Plutonium-242
Uranium-238
Thorium-234
Protactinium-234
Uranium-234

* **Atomic number**, 127; **Electromagnetic waves**, 44; **Isotope**, **Mass number**, 127; **Neutron**, **Nucleus**, **Proton**, 126; **Relative atomic mass**, 138.

Becquerel

A unit of **radioactive decay**. One becquerel is equal to one nuclear **disintegration** per second. A **curie** equals 3.7×10^{10} becquerels.

Half-life

The time taken for half of the atoms in a sample of a radioactive element to undergo **radioactive decay**. The amount of radiation emitted is halved. The half-life varies widely, e.g. the half-life of uranium-238 is 4.5 thousand million years, but that of radium-221 is only 30 seconds.

Radioactive decay curve

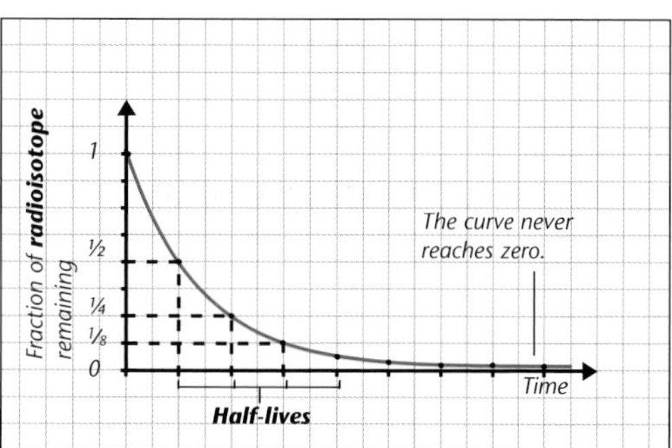

Fraction of radioisotope remaining
1
½
¼
⅛
0
The curve never reaches zero.
Time
Half-lives

Uses of radioactivity

Nuclear fission

The division of a **nucleus***, caused by bombardment with a **neutron***. The nucleus splits, forming neutrons and nuclei of other elements, and releasing huge amounts of energy. The release of neutrons also causes the fission of other atoms, which in turn produces more neutrons – a **chain reaction**. An element which can undergo fission is described as **fissile**. Controlled nuclear fission is used in **nuclear power stations***, but uncontrolled fission, e.g. in **fission bombs***, is very explosive.

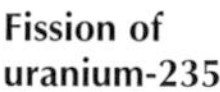
Fission of uranium-235

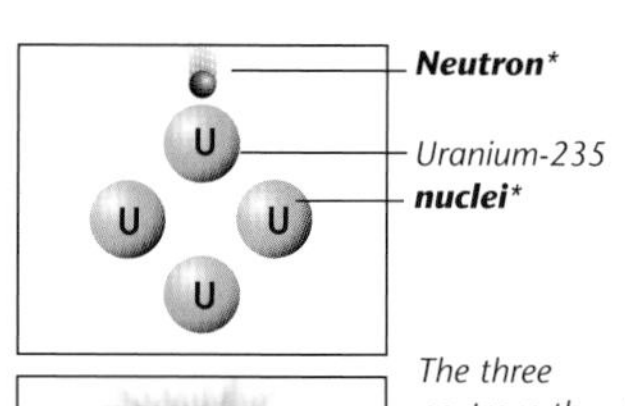

Neutron*
U
U
U
U
Uranium-235 nuclei*

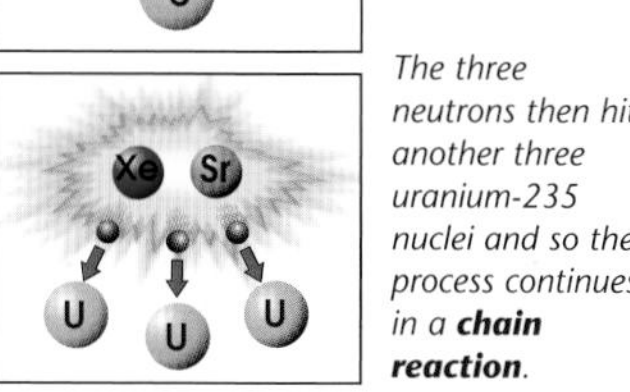

Xe
Sr
U
U
U

*When hit by a **neutron***, the nucleus splits up to form two other elements, strontium and xenon, and three neutrons.*

*The three neutrons then hit another three uranium-235 nuclei and so the process continues in a **chain reaction**.*

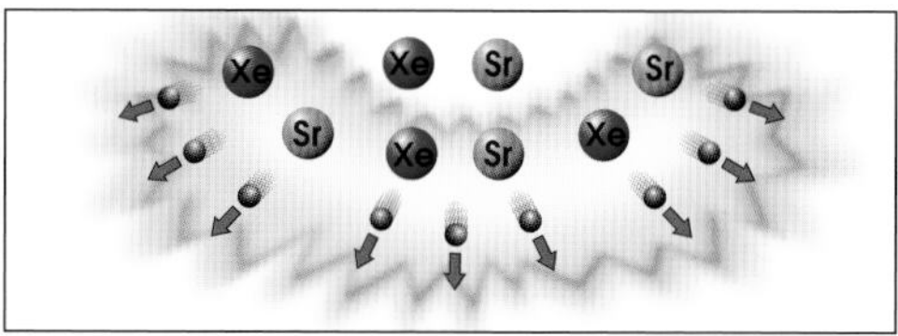

Xe
Xe
Sr
Sr
Sr
Xe
Sr
Xe

$$^{235}_{95}U + ^{1}_{0}n \rightarrow ^{90}_{38}Sr + ^{143}_{54}Xe + 3^{1}_{0}n$$

*A **neutron*** (**mass number*** 1, **atomic number*** 0)*

Nuclear fusion

The combination of two **nuclei*** to form a larger one. It will only take place at extremely high temperatures and releases huge amounts of energy. Nuclear fusion takes place in the **fusion bomb***.

Radioactive tracing

A method of following a substance as it moves by tracking radiation from a **radioisotope** introduced into it. The radioisotope used is called a **tracer** and the substance is said to be **labeled**.

Radiocarbon dating or carbon dating

A method used to calculate the time elapsed since a living organism died by measuring the radiation it gives off. All living things contain a small amount of carbon-14 (a **radioisotope**) which gradually decreases after death.

Radiology

The study of radioactivity, especially with regard to its use in medicine (**radiotherapy**). Cancer cells are susceptible to radiation, so cancer can be treated by small doses.

Irradiation

The treating of food, such as fruit, with **gamma rays** to keep it fresh.

Untreated strawberry

***Irradiated** strawberry after two weeks*

* **Atomic number**, 127; **Fission bomb**, **Fusion bomb**, 93; **Mass number**, 127; **Neutron**, 126; **Nuclear power station**, 94; **Nucleus**, 126.

BONDING

When substances react together, the tendency is always for their atoms to gain, lose or share **electrons*** so that they each acquire a stable (full) **outer shell*** of electrons. In doing so, these atoms develop some kind of attraction, or **bonding**, between them (they are held together by **bonds**). The three main types of bonding are **ionic bonding**, **covalent bonding** (see pages 132-133) and **metallic bonding** (see page 134). See also **intermolecular forces**, page 134.

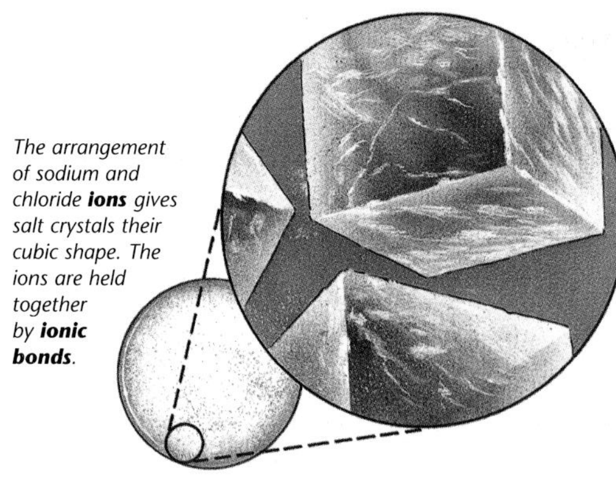

*The arrangement of sodium and chloride **ions** gives salt crystals their cubic shape. The ions are held together by **ionic bonds**.*

Valency electron

An electron, always in the **outer shell*** of an atom, used in forming a bond. It is lost by atoms in **ionic bonding** and **metallic bonding***, but shared with other atoms in **covalent bonding***.

Ions

An **ion** is an electrically charged particle, formed when an atom loses or gains one or more electrons to form a stable **outer shell***. All ions are either **cations** or **anions**.

Cation

An **ion** with a positive charge, formed when an atom loses electrons in a reaction (it now has more **protons*** than electrons). Hydrogen and metals tend to form cations. Their atoms have one, two or three electrons in their **outer shells***, and it is easier for them to lose electrons (leaving a stable shell underneath) than to gain at least five more.

*A magnesium atom has two electrons in its **outer shell***. These are lost to form an **ion** (**cation**) with a charge of +2. A magnesium ion (**cation**) is written Mg^{2+}.*

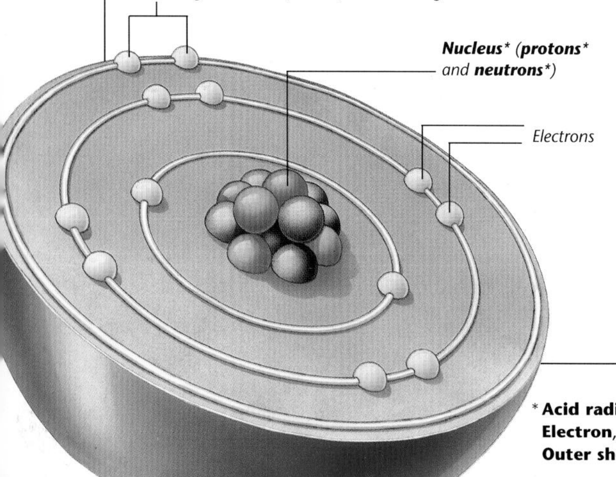

Nucleus* (protons* and neutrons*)
Electrons

Anion

An **ion** with a negative charge, formed when an atom gains electrons in a reaction (it now has more electrons than **protons***). Non-metals tend to form anions. Their atoms have five, six or seven electrons in their **outer shells***, and it is easier for them to gain electrons (to acquire a stable shell) than to lose at least five. Some anions are formed by groups of atoms gaining electrons, e.g. **acid radicals***.

*A fluorine atom has seven electrons in its **outer shell***, so it gains one to form an **ion** (**anion**) with a charge of –1. A fluoride ion (**anion**) is written F^-.*

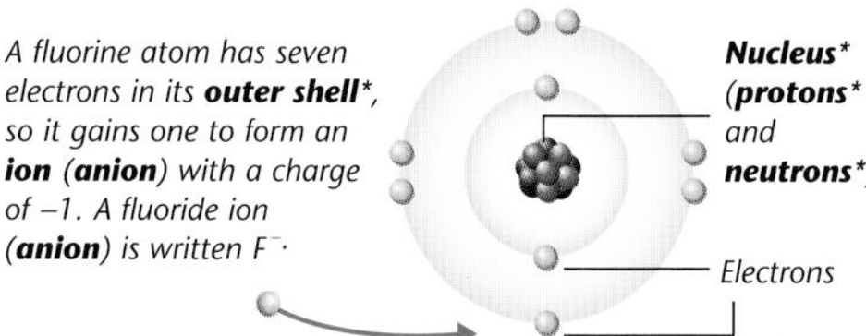

Nucleus* (protons* and neutrons*)
Electrons

Ionization

The process of forming **ions**. This either happens when atoms lose or gain electrons or when a compound splits up into ions, e.g. hydrogen chloride forming a solution.

***Ionization** of hydrogen chloride in water, forming hydrogen ions and chloride ions.*

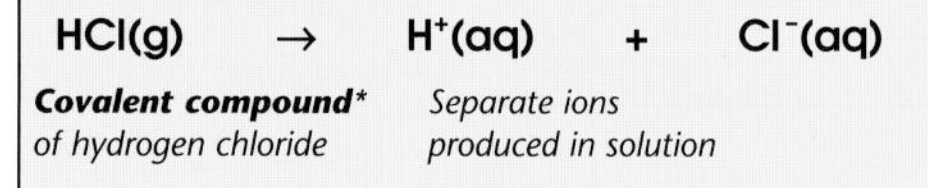

$HCl(g)$	$\rightarrow$	$H^+(aq)$	+	$Cl^-(aq)$
Covalent compound* of hydrogen chloride		Separate ions produced in solution		

* **Acid radical**, 153; **Covalent bonding**, **Covalent compounds**, 132; **Electron**, 126; **Metallic bonding**, 134; **Neutron**, **Nucleus**, 126; **Outer shell**, 127; **Proton**, 126.

Ionic bonding

When two elements react together to form **ions**, the resulting **cations** and **anions**, which have opposite electrical charges, attract each other. They stay together because of this attraction. This type of bonding is known as **ionic bonding** and the electrostatic bonds are called **ionic bonds**. Elements far apart in the **periodic table*** tend to exhibit this kind of bonding, coming together to form **ionic compounds**, e.g. sodium and chlorine (sodium chloride) and magnesium and oxygen (magnesium oxide).

Ionic compound

A compound whose components are held together by **ionic bonding**. It has no molecules, instead the **cations** and **anions** attract each other to form a **giant ionic lattice***. Ionic compounds have high melting and boiling points (the bonds are strong and hence large amounts of energy are needed to break them). They conduct electricity when **molten*** or in **aqueous solution*** because they contain charged particles (ions) which are free to move.

*Sodium and chlorine react to form sodium chloride, an **ionic compound**.*

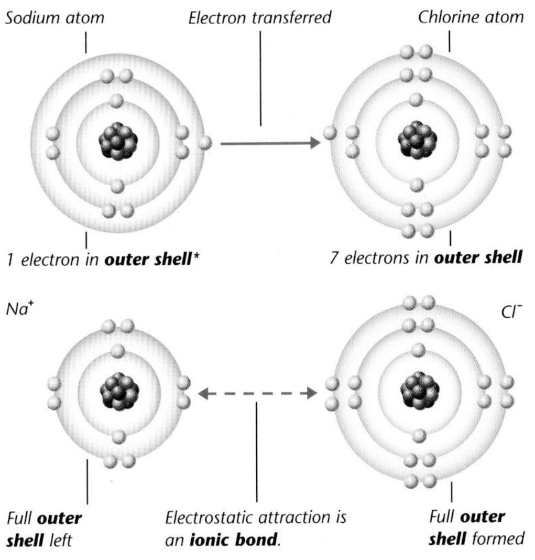
Sodium atom
Electron transferred
Chlorine atom
1 electron in outer shell*
7 electrons in outer shell
Na^+
Cl^-
Full outer shell left
Electrostatic attraction is an ionic bond.
Full outer shell formed

Formula of sodium chloride is NaCl or Na^+Cl^-.

Model showing part of the giant ionic lattice of sodium chloride

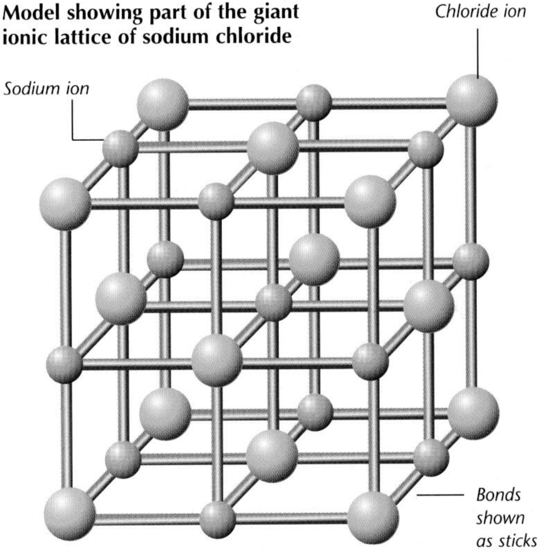
Chloride ion
Sodium ion
Bonds shown as sticks

*Note that there are no molecules – the formula gives the relative numbers of each type of ion in the **giant ionic lattice***. In this case, the formula NaCl indicates that the relative numbers of sodium and chloride ions are one to one.*

Electrovalency

The power of an **ion** to combine with another in **ionic bonding**. It is equal to the size of the charge on the ion. The ions combine in such proportions that the total charge of the compound is zero.

*Elements in Group 1 and Group 7 of the **periodic table*** are **monovalent** (have an **electrovalency** of one). Their ions each have a charge of +1 or –1.*

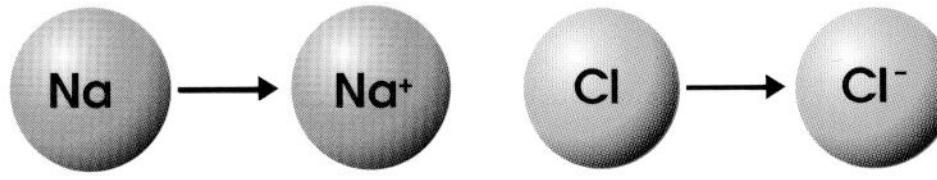
Na
Na^+
Cl
Cl^-

*Group 2 and Group 6 elements are **divalent** (have an **electrovalency** of two). Their ions each have a charge of +2 or –2.*

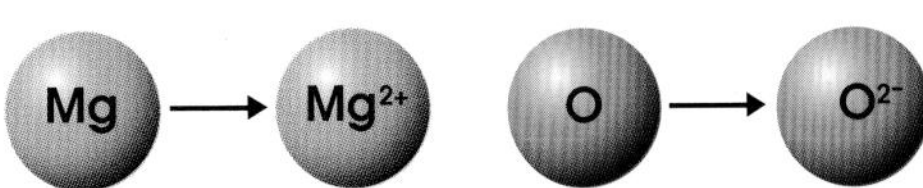
Mg
Mg^{2+}
O
O^{2-}

*Some Group 3 and Group 5 elements are **trivalent** (have an **electrovalency** of three). Their ions each have a charge of +3 or –3.*

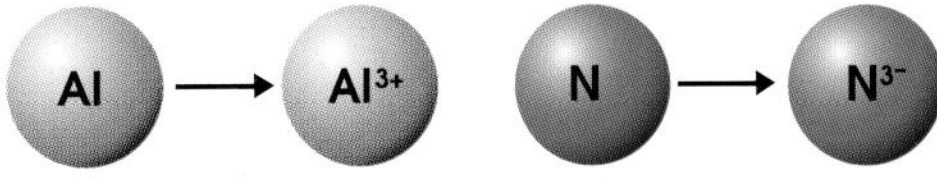
Al
Al^{3+}
N
N^{3-}

* **Aqueous solution**, 144; **Giant ionic lattice**, 137; **Molten**, 120; **Outer shell**, 127; **Periodic table**, 164.

Covalent bonding

Covalent bonding is the sharing of electrons between atoms in a molecule so that each atom acquires a stable **outer shell***. Electrons are shared in pairs called **electron pairs** (one pair being a **covalent bond**). Covalent bonds within a molecule are strong. **Covalent compounds** (compounds whose molecules have internal covalent bonds) are not normally so strongly held together. They are usually liquids or gases at room temperature because the forces between their molecules are **van der Waals' forces***. These weak forces need little energy to overcome them, so most covalent compounds have low melting and boiling points. They do not conduct electricity because there are no **ions*** present.

Single bond

A covalent bond that is formed when one pair of electrons is shared between two atoms.

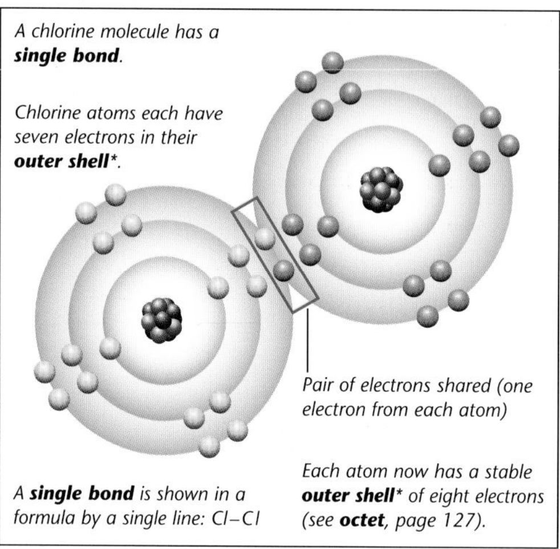
A chlorine molecule has a **single bond**.
Chlorine atoms each have seven electrons in their **outer shell***.
Pair of electrons shared (one electron from each atom)
A **single bond** is shown in a formula by a single line: Cl–Cl
Each atom now has a stable **outer shell*** of eight electrons (see **octet**, page 127).

Double bond

A covalent bond that is formed when two pairs of electrons are shared between two atoms.

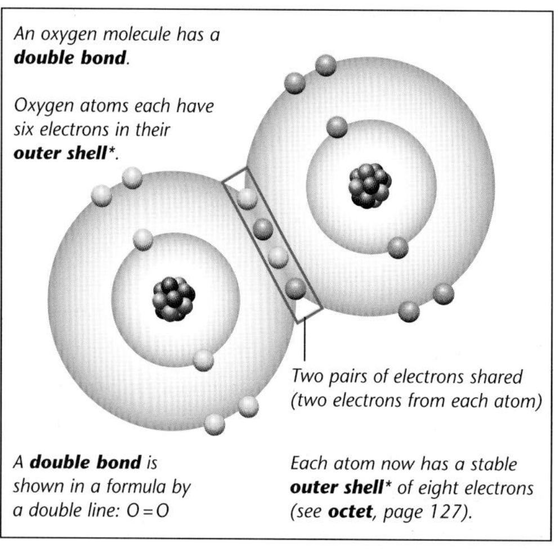
An oxygen molecule has a **double bond**.
Oxygen atoms each have six electrons in their **outer shell***.
Two pairs of electrons shared (two electrons from each atom)
A **double bond** is shown in a formula by a double line: O=O
Each atom now has a stable **outer shell*** of eight electrons (see **octet**, page 127).

Triple bond

A covalent bond that is formed when three pairs of electrons are shared between two atoms.

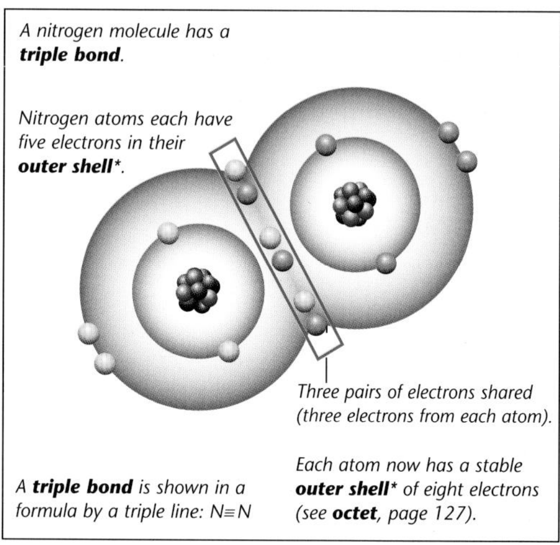
A nitrogen molecule has a **triple bond**.
Nitrogen atoms each have five electrons in their **outer shell***.
Three pairs of electrons shared (three electrons from each atom).
A **triple bond** is shown in a formula by a triple line: N≡N
Each atom now has a stable **outer shell*** of eight electrons (see **octet**, page 127).

Dative covalent bond or coordinate bond

A covalent bond in which both electrons in the bond are provided by the same atom. It donates a **lone pair**.

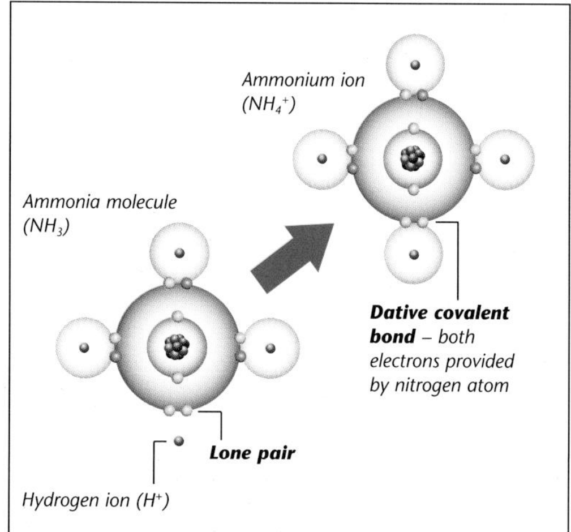
Ammonium ion (NH_4^+)
Ammonia molecule (NH_3)
Dative covalent bond – both electrons provided by nitrogen atom
Lone pair
Hydrogen ion (H^+)

* **Ions**, 130; **Outer shell**, 127; **van der Waals' forces**, 134.

Covalency

The maximum number of covalent bonds an atom can form. It is equal to the number of hydrogen atoms which will combine with the atom. The covalency of most elements is constant, but that of **transition metals*** varies.

Hydrogen chloride (HCl)

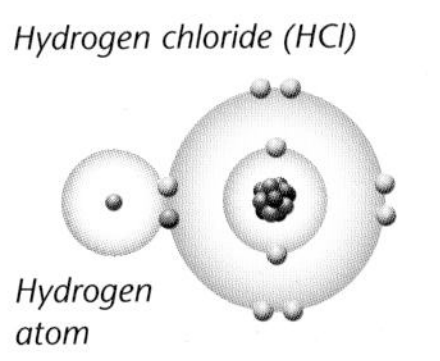
Hydrogen atom

Monovalent *elements have either one or seven electrons in the* ***outer shell****, e.g. hydrogen.*

Water (H_2O)

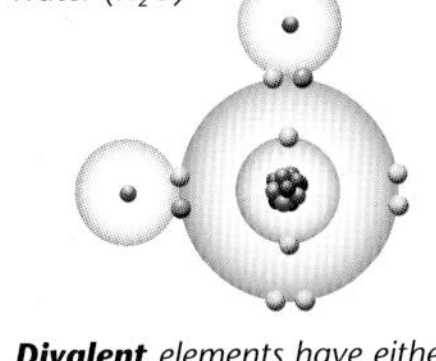

Divalent *elements have either two or six electrons in the* ***outer shell****, e.g. oxygen.*

Ammonia (NH_3)

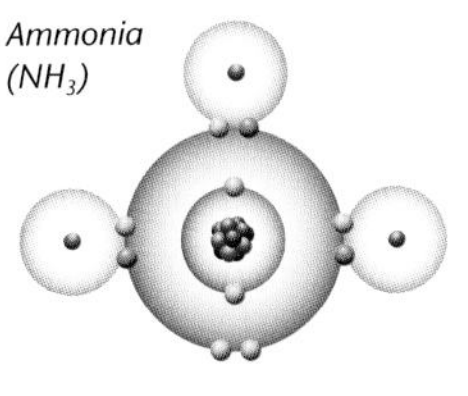

Trivalent *elements have either three or five electrons in the* ***outer shell****, e.g. nitrogen.*

Methane (CH_4)

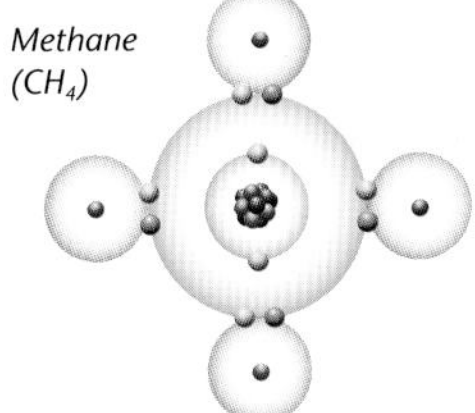

Tetravalent *elements have four electrons in the* ***outer shell****, e.g. carbon.*

Lone pair

A pair of electrons in the **outer shell*** of an atom which is not part of a covalent bond (see ammonia picture on previous page).

Electronegativity

The power of an atom to attract electrons to itself in a molecule. If two atoms with different electronegativities are joined, a **polar bond** is formed. Weakly electronegative atoms are sometimes called **electropositive** (e.g. sodium), as they form positive ions fairly easily.

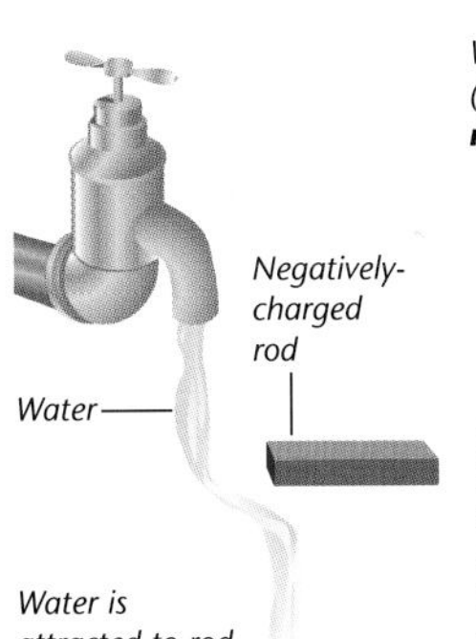
Negatively-charged rod
Water
Water is attracted to rod.

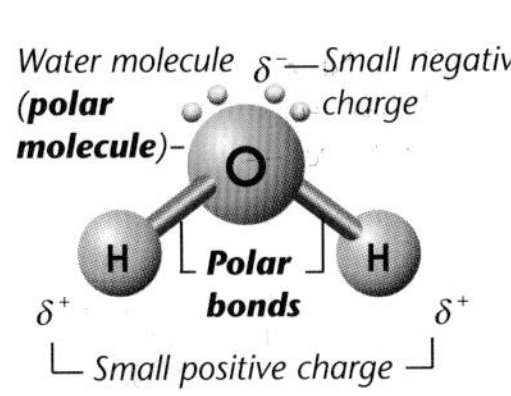
Water molecule (polar molecule)
δ⁻ Small negative charge
O
H
H
Polar bonds
δ⁺
δ⁺
Small positive charge

The difference in ***electronegativity*** *between oxygen (high) and hydrogen (low) causes water molecules to be* ***polar molecules****. The positive end of each water molecule is attracted to the charged rod, so the water "bends" toward it.*

Polar bond

A covalent bond in which the electrons spend a greater amount of time around one atom's **nucleus*** than the other. This effect is called **polarization**. It is caused by a difference in **electronegativity** between the atoms, the electrons being more attracted to one than the other.

Polar molecule

A molecule with a difference in electric charge between its ends, caused by an uneven distribution of **polar bonds**, and sometimes by **lone pairs**. Liquids with polar molecules may be **polar solvents*** and may dissolve **ionic compounds***. A **non-polar molecule** has no difference in charge at its ends.

Shapes of some simple polar and non-polar molecules

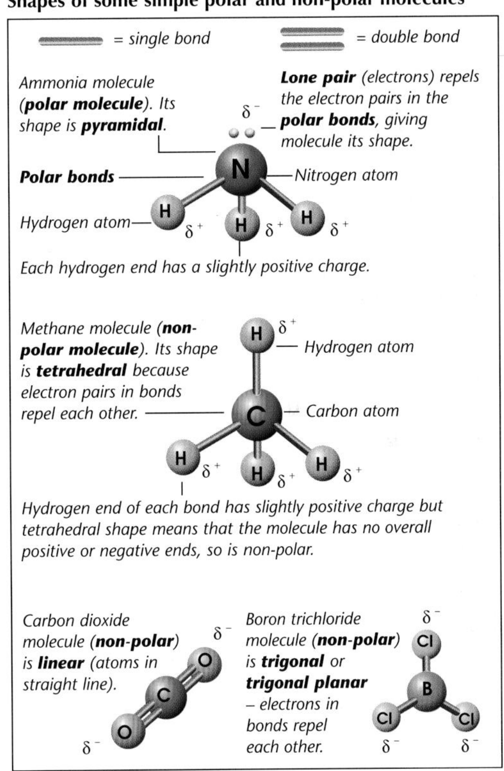
= single bond
= double bond
Ammonia molecule (polar molecule). Its shape is pyramidal.
Lone pair (electrons) repels the electron pairs in the polar bonds, giving molecule its shape.
Polar bonds
Nitrogen atom
Hydrogen atom
N
H
δ⁻
δ⁺
Each hydrogen end has a slightly positive charge.
Methane molecule (non-polar molecule). Its shape is tetrahedral because electron pairs in bonds repel each other.
Hydrogen atom
Carbon atom
C
Hydrogen end of each bond has slightly positive charge but tetrahedral shape means that the molecule has no overall positive or negative ends, so is non-polar.
Carbon dioxide molecule (non-polar) is linear (atoms in straight line).
O
Boron trichloride molecule (non-polar) is trigonal or trigonal planar – electrons in bonds repel each other.
B
Cl

Isomerism

The occurrence of the same atoms forming different arrangements in different molecules. The arrangements are **isomers***. They have the same **molecular formula*** but their other formulas may differ (see page 140).

* **Ionic compound**, 131; **Isomers**, 191; **Molecular formula**, 140; **Nucleus**, 126; **Outer shell**, 127; **Polar solvent**, 144; **Transition metals**, 172.

Metallic bonding

Metallic bonding is the attraction between particles in a **giant metallic lattice*** (i.e. in metals). The lattice consists of positive **ions*** of the metal with **valency electrons*** free to move between them. The free or **delocalized** electrons form the bonds between the ions and, because they can move, heat and electricity can be conducted through the metal. The forces between the electrons and ions are strong. This gives metals high melting and boiling points, since relatively large amounts of energy are needed to overcome them. For more about other types of bonding, see pages 130-133.

Delocalization

The sharing of **valency electrons*** by all the atoms in a molecule or **giant metallic lattice***. Delocalized electrons can belong to any of the atoms in the lattice and are able to move through the lattice, so the metal can conduct electricity and heat.

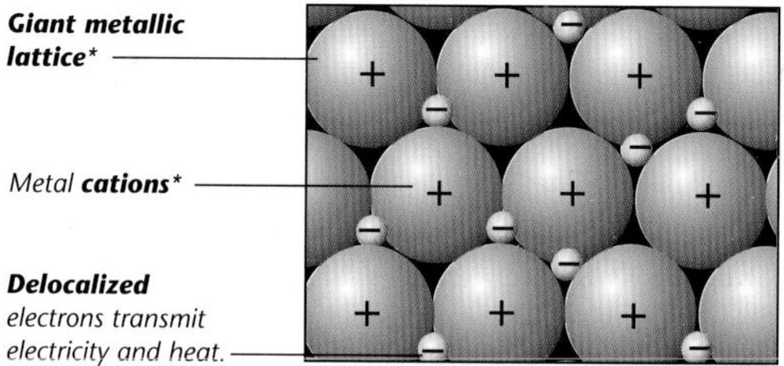
Giant metallic lattice*
*Metal **cations****
***Delocalized** electrons transmit electricity and heat.*

Intermolecular forces

van der Waals' forces

Weak attractive forces between molecules (**intermolecular forces***) caused by the uneven distribution and movement of electrons in the atoms of the molecules. The attractive force is approximately twenty times less than in **ionic bonding***. It is the force which holds **molecular lattices*** together, e.g. iodine, and solid carbon dioxide.

*Weak **van der Waals'** forces hold together this **molecular lattice*** of iodine.*

*Atoms of iodine held together in molecules by **covalent bonding****.

Hydrogen bond

An attraction between a **polar molecule*** containing hydrogen and a **lone pair*** of electrons in another molecule. The **polar bonds*** mean that each hydrogen atom has a slightly positive charge and is therefore attracted to the electrons. Hydrogen bonding accounts for high melting and boiling points in water in relation to other substances with small, but **non-polar molecules***. Both the hydrogen bonds and the **van der Waals' forces** must be overcome to separate the molecules.

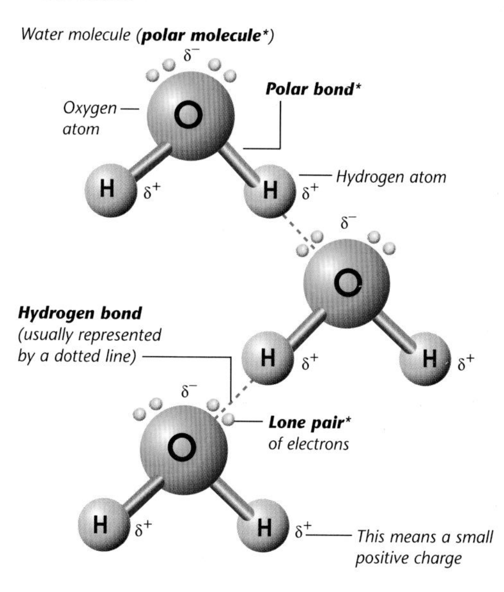
*Water molecule (**polar molecule***)*
δ^-
Oxygen atom
O
Polar bond*
H
δ^+
Hydrogen atom
***Hydrogen bond** (usually represented by a dotted line)*
Lone pair of electrons*
This means a small positive charge

* **Cation**, 130; **Covalent bonding**, 132; **Giant metallic lattice**, 137; **Intermolecular force**, 7; **Ion**, 130; **Ionic bonding**, 131; **Lone pair**, 133; **Molecular lattice**, 137; **Non-polar molecule**, 133 (**Polar molecule**); **Polar bond**, 133; **Valency electron**, 130.

CRYSTALS

Crystals are solids with regular geometric shapes, formed from regular arrangements of particles. The particles can be atoms, **ions*** or molecules and the bonding between them can be of any type or mixture of types. The edges of crystals are straight and the surfaces flat. Substances that form crystals are described as **crystalline**. Solids without a regular shape (i.e. those which do not form crystals) are described as **amorphous**.

*Gemstones are crystals that have been cut along their **cleavage planes****.*

Crystallization

The process of forming crystals. It can happen in a number of ways, e.g. cooling **molten*** solids, **subliming*** solids (solid to gas and back), placing a **seed crystal** (see right) in a **supersaturated*** solution or placing a seed crystal in a **saturated*** solution and cooling or evaporating the solution. The last method is the most common. Either cooling or evaporating means that the amount of soluble **solute*** decreases, so particles come out of the solution and bond to the seed crystal, which is suspended in the solution. Crystallization can be used to purify substances – see page 221.

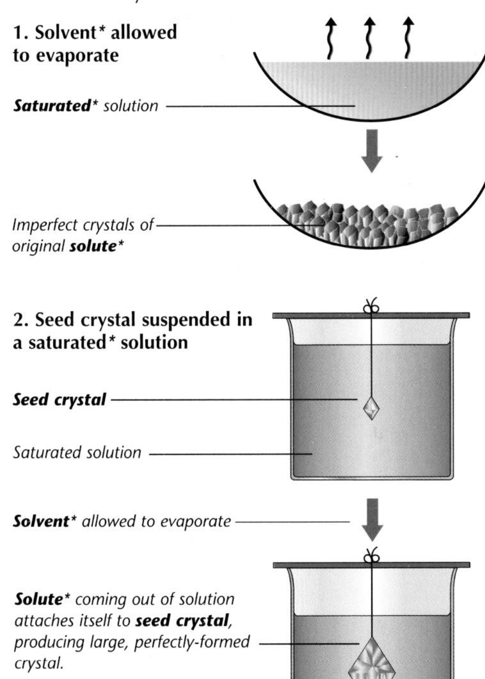
Methods of crystallization
1. Solvent* allowed to evaporate
Saturated* solution
Imperfect crystals of original solute*
2. Seed crystal suspended in a saturated* solution
Seed crystal
Saturated solution
Solvent* allowed to evaporate
Solute* coming out of solution attaches itself to seed crystal, producing large, perfectly-formed crystal.
Mother liquid

Seed crystal

A small crystal of a substance placed in a solution of the same substance. It acts as a base on which crystals form during **crystallization**. The crystal which grows will take on the same shape as the seed crystal.

Mother liquid

The solution left after **crystallization** has taken place in a solution.

Water of crystallization

Water contained in crystals of certain **salts***. The number of molecules of water combined with each pair of **ions*** is usually constant and is often written in the chemical **formula*** for the salt. The water can be driven off by heating. Crystals which contain water of crystallization are **hydrated***.

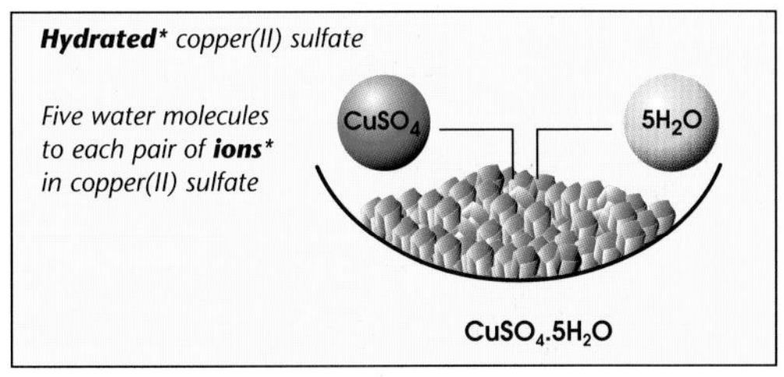
Hydrated* copper(II) sulfate
Five water molecules to each pair of ions* in copper(II) sulfate
$CuSO_4$
$5H_2O$
$CuSO_4.5H_2O$

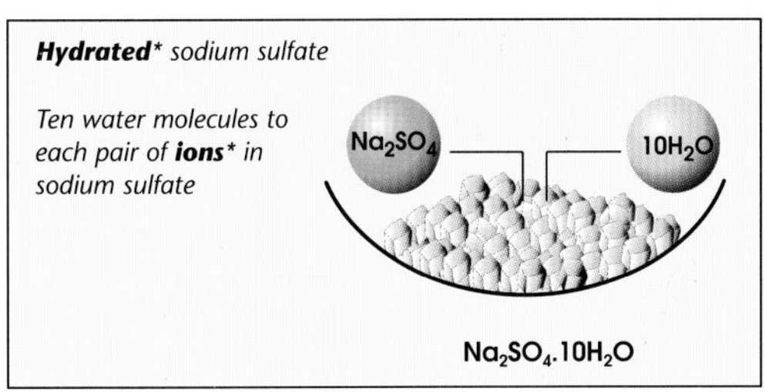
Hydrated* sodium sulfate
Ten water molecules to each pair of ions* in sodium sulfate
Na_2SO_4
$10H_2O$
$Na_2SO_4.10H_2O$

* **Cleavage plane**, 136; **Formulas**, 140; **Hydrated**, 154 (**Hydrate**); **Ion**, 130; **Molten**, 120; **Salts**, 153; **Saturated**, 145; **Solute**, **Solvent**, 144; **Sublimation**, 121; **Supersaturated**, 145.

Crystals continued – shapes and structures

Crystals (see page 135) exist in many different shapes and sizes. This is due to the different arrangement and bonding of the particles (atoms, molecules or **ions***). The arrangement in space of the particles and the way in which they are joined is called a **crystal lattice**. Different types of crystal lattice are shown on the opposite page. The shape of a particular crystal depends on its crystal lattice and how this lattice can be split along **cleavage planes**. The main crystal shapes are shown on the right – these are the basic shapes from which large crystals are built. A substance may have more than one crystalline form – see **polymorphism**, below.

Basic crystal shapes

Cubic

Tetragonal

Monoclinic

Triclinic or *rhombohedral*

Hexagonal

Polymorphism
The occurrence of two or more different crystals of the same substance, differing in shape and appearance. It is caused by different arrangements in the separate types. Changes between types often take place at a certain temperature called the **transition temperature**. Polymorphism in elements is called **allotropy**.

Allotropy
The occurrence of certain elements in more than one crystalline form. It is a specific type of **polymorphism**. The different forms are called **allotropes** and are caused by a change in arrangement of atoms in the crystals.

Monotropy
Polymorphism in which there is only one stable form. The other forms are unstable and there is no **transition temperature**.

Enantiotropy
Polymorphism in which there are two stable forms of a substance, one above its **transition temperature**, and one below.

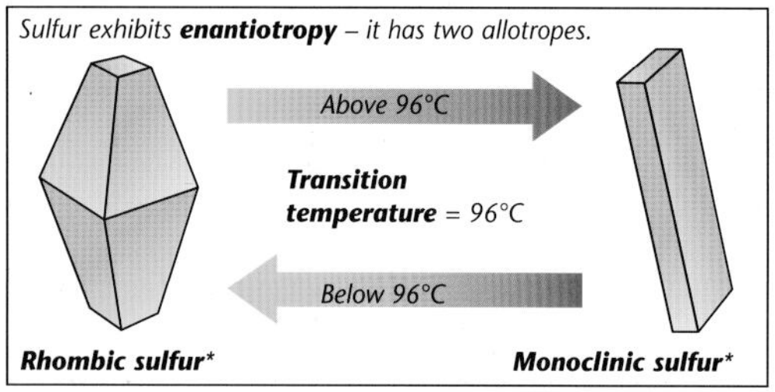
Sulfur exhibits **enantiotropy** – it has two allotropes.
Above 96°C
Transition temperature = 96°C
Below 96°C
Rhombic sulfur*
Monoclinic sulfur*

Transition temperature
The temperature at which a substance exhibiting **enantiotropy** changes from one form to another.

Isomorphism
The existence of two or more different substances with the same crystal structure and shape. They are described as **isomorphic**.

Cleavage plane
A plane of particles along which a crystal can be split, leaving a flat surface. If a crystal is not split along the cleavage plane, it shatters.

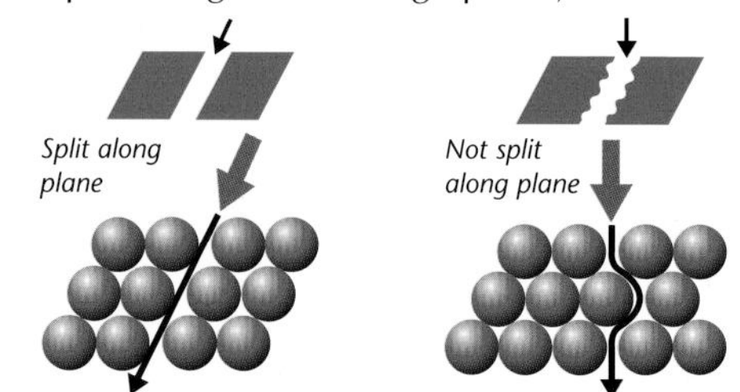
Split along plane
Not split along plane

X-ray crystallography
The use of X-rays to work out crystal structure. Deflected X-rays produce a **diffraction pattern** from which the structure is worked out (see below).

X-ray crystallography

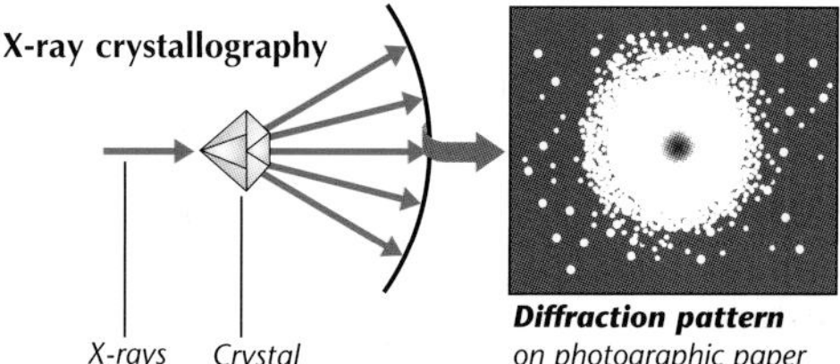
X-rays
Crystal
Diffraction pattern on photographic paper

* **Ions**, 130; **Monoclinic sulfur**, **Rhombic sulfur**, 184.

Crystal lattices

Giant atomic lattice

A **crystal lattice** consisting of atoms held together by **covalent bonding***, e.g. diamond. Substances with giant atomic lattices are extremely strong and have very high melting and boiling points.

Giant atomic lattice of diamond
(See also page 178.)

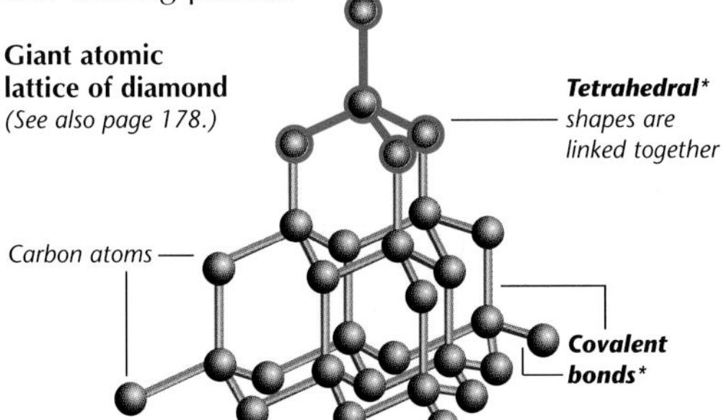
Tetrahedral* shapes are linked together
Carbon atoms
Covalent bonds*

Giant ionic lattice

A **crystal lattice** consisting of **ions*** held together by **ionic bonding***, e.g. sodium chloride. The ionic bonds are strong, which means that the substance has high melting and boiling points.

Giant ionic lattice of sodium chloride

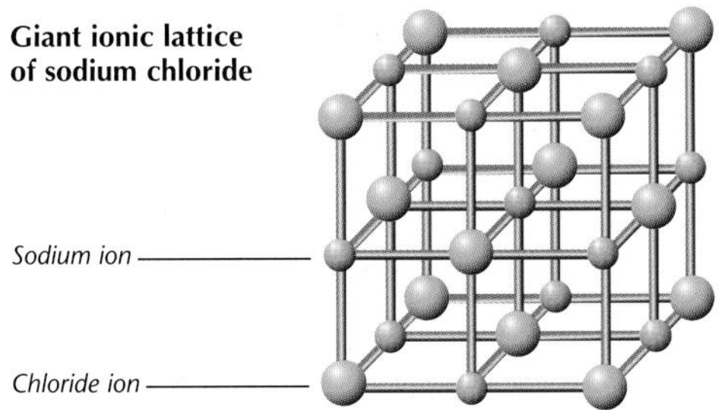
Sodium ion
Chloride ion

Giant metallic lattice

A **crystal lattice** consisting of metal atoms held together by **metallic bonding***, e.g. zinc. The **delocalized*** electrons are free to move about, making a metal a good conductor of heat and electricity. The layers of atoms can slide over one another, making metals **malleable*** and **ductile***.

Giant metallic lattice of zinc

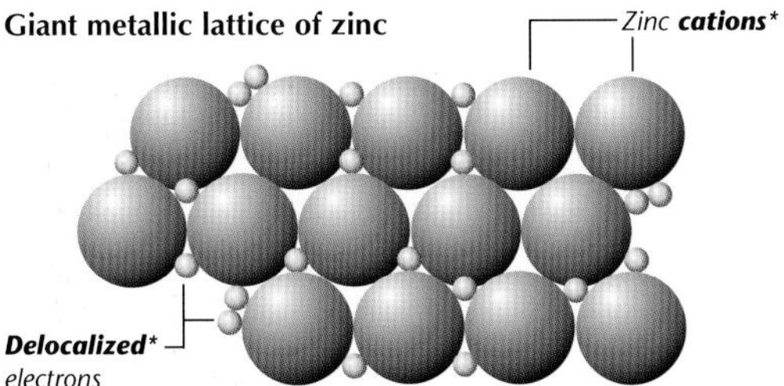
Zinc cations*
Delocalized* electrons

Molecular lattice

A **crystal lattice** consisting of molecules bonded together by **intermolecular forces** (see page 134), e.g. iodine. These forces are weak, so the crystal has low melting and boiling points compared with **ionic compounds*** and is easily broken. The **covalent bonds*** within the molecules themselves are stronger and break less easily.

Molecular lattice of solid iodine

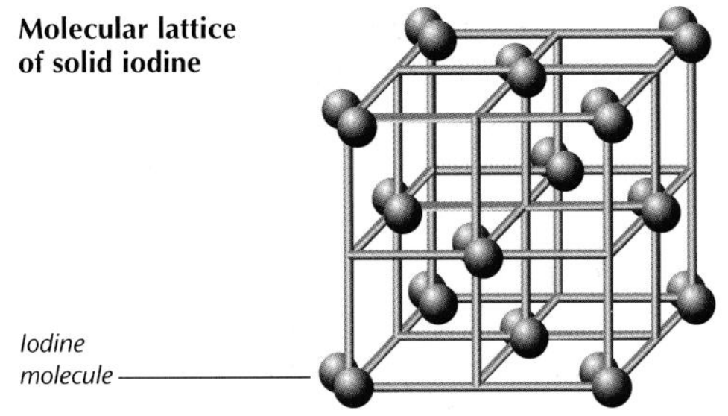
Iodine molecule

In crystals where the particles are all the same size, e.g. in a **giant metallic lattice**, various arrangements of the particles are possible. The most common are shown below.

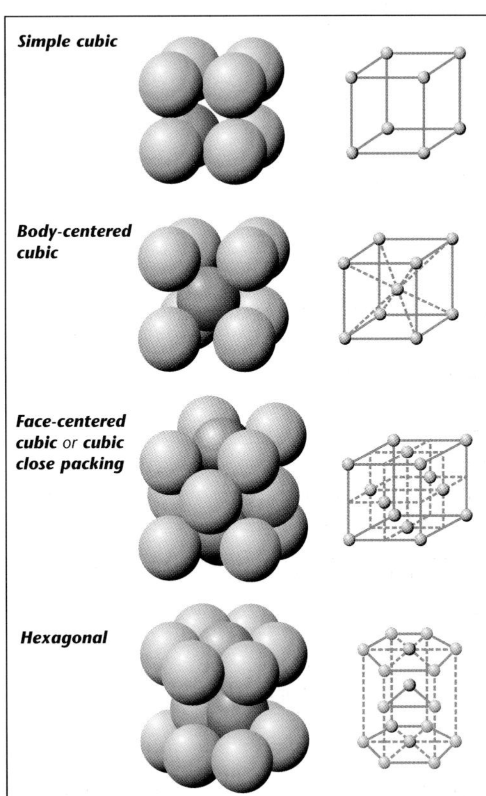
Simple cubic
Body-centered cubic
Face-centered cubic or cubic close packing
Hexagonal

* **Cation**, 130; **Covalent bonding**, 132; **Delocalization**, 134; **Ductile**, 344; **Ion**, 130; **Ionic bonding**, **Ionic compound**, 131; **Malleable**, 345; **Metallic bonding**, 134; **Tetrahedral**, 133.

MEASURING ATOMS

With a diameter of about 10^{-7} millimeters and a mass of about 10^{-22} grams, atoms are so small that they are extremely difficult to measure. Their masses are therefore measured in relation to an agreed mass to give them a manageable value. Because there are many millions of atoms in a very small sample of a substance, the **mole** is used for measuring quantities of particles. The masses of atoms and molecules are measured using a machine called a **mass spectrometer**.

Relative atomic mass or atomic weight

The average mass (i.e. taking into account **relative isotopic mass** and **isotopic ratio**) of one atom of a substance divided by one twelfth the mass of a carbon-12 atom (see **isotope**, page 127). See page 83 for more about its units, and pages 212-213 for a table of relative atomic masses.

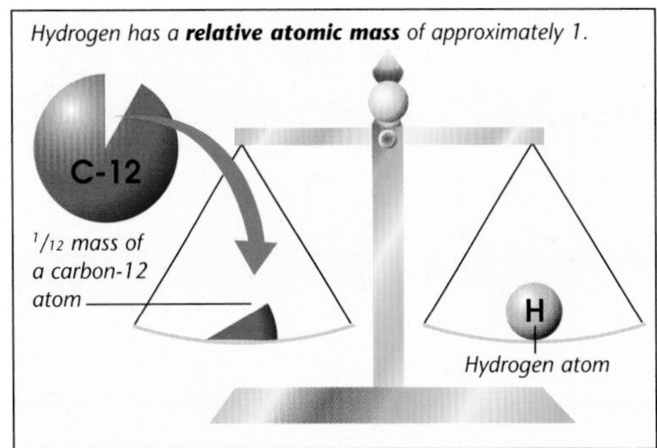

C-12
1/12 mass of a carbon-12 atom
H
Hydrogen atom

Hydrogen has a ***relative atomic mass*** *of approximately 1.*

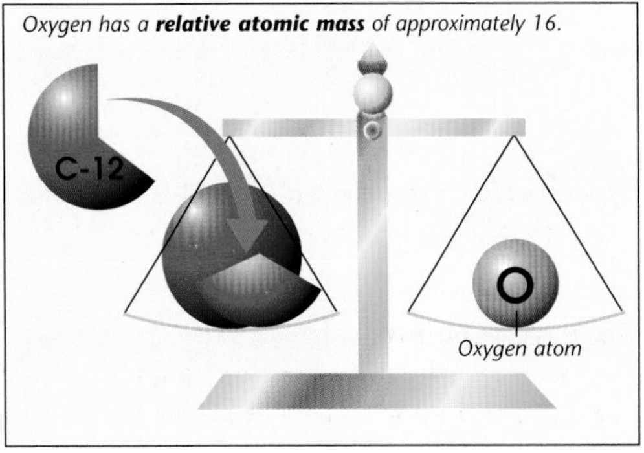

C-12
O
Oxygen atom

Oxygen has a ***relative atomic mass*** *of approximately 16.*

Relative molecular mass

Also called **molecular weight**, **relative formula mass** or **formula weight**. The mass of a molecule of an element or compound divided by one twelfth the mass of a carbon-12 atom (see **isotope**, page 127). It is the sum of the **relative atomic masses** of the atoms in the molecule.

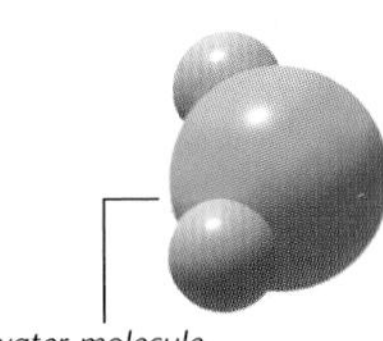
A water molecule contains one oxygen atom and two hydrogen atoms.

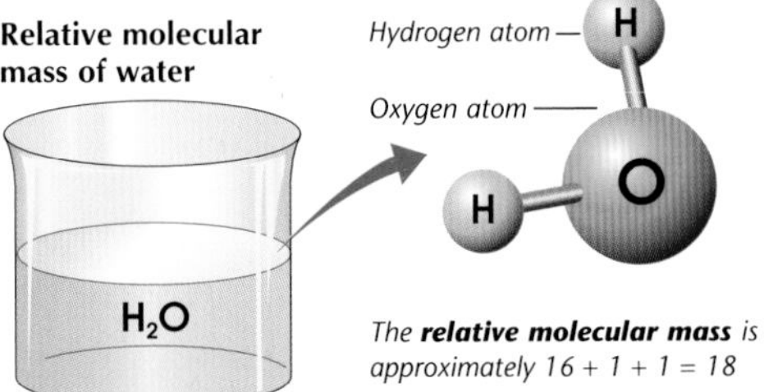

Relative molecular mass of water
Hydrogen atom
Oxygen atom
H
O
H
H_2O

The ***relative molecular mass*** *is approximately 16 + 1 + 1 = 18*

Relative molecular mass *also applies to* ***ionic compounds*****, even though they do not have molecules.*

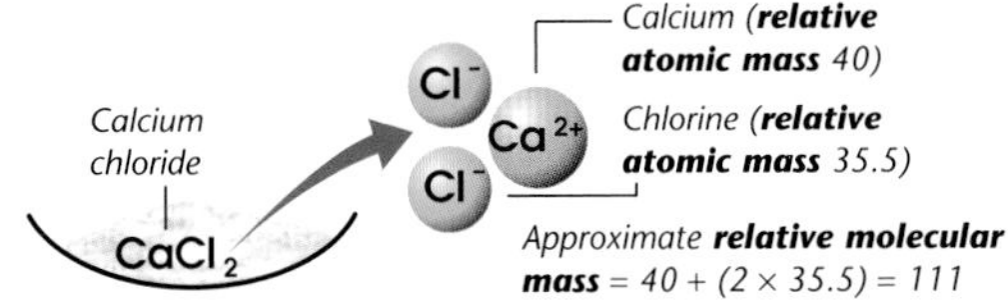

Calcium chloride
$CaCl_2$
Cl^-
Ca^{2+}
Cl^-
Calcium (relative atomic mass 40)
Chlorine (relative atomic mass 35.5)

Approximate ***relative molecular mass*** *= 40 + (2 × 35.5) = 111*

Relative isotopic mass

The mass of an atom of a specific **isotope*** divided by one twelfth the mass of a carbon-12 atom. It is nearly exactly the same as the **mass number*** of the isotope.

Isotopic ratio

The ratio of the number of atoms of each **isotope*** in a sample of an element. It is used with **relative isotopic masses** to calculate the **relative atomic mass** of an element.

Natural sample of chlorine contains about three times as many atoms of Cl-35 as Cl-37.

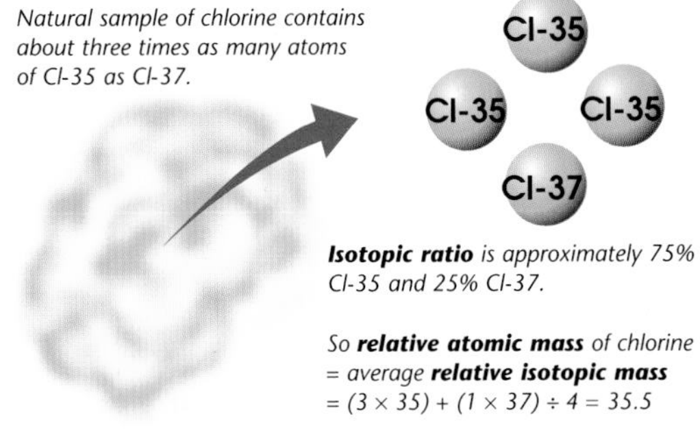

Cl-35
Cl-35
Cl-35
Cl-37

Isotopic ratio *is approximately 75% Cl-35 and 25% Cl-37.*

So ***relative atomic mass*** *of chlorine = average* ***relative isotopic mass*** *= (3 × 35) + (1 × 37) ÷ 4 = 35.5*

* **Ionic compound**, 131; **Isotope**, **Mass number**, 127.

Mole (mol)

The **SI unit*** of the amount of a substance. (See also page 96.) One mole contains the same number of particles as there are atoms in 12 grams of the carbon-12 **isotope***.

Avogadro's number

The number of particles per **mole**, equal to $6.023 \times 10^{23} mol^{-1}$.

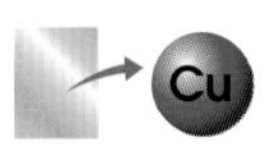
Cu

Each ***mole*** *of copper contains* ***Avogadro's number*** *of atoms.*

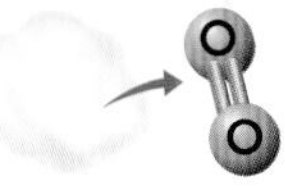

Each ***mole*** *of oxygen contains* ***Avogadro's number*** *of molecules.*

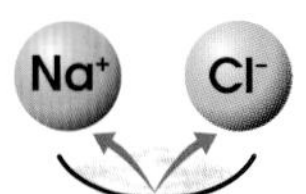
Na+
Cl-

A ***mole*** *of sodium chloride contains 1****mol*** *Na^+ ions and 1mol Cl^- ions.*

Molar mass

The mass of one **mole** of a given substance. It is the **relative atomic** or **molecular mass** of a substance expressed in grams.

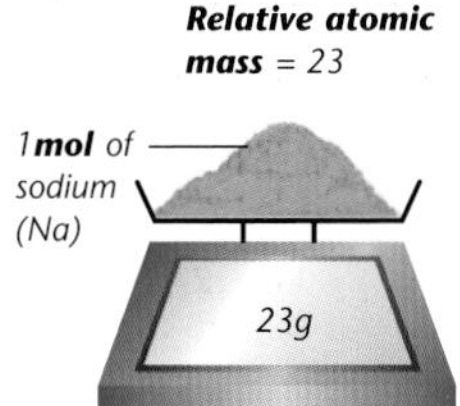
Relative atomic mass = 23
1mol of sodium (Na)
23g

Molar mass *23g*

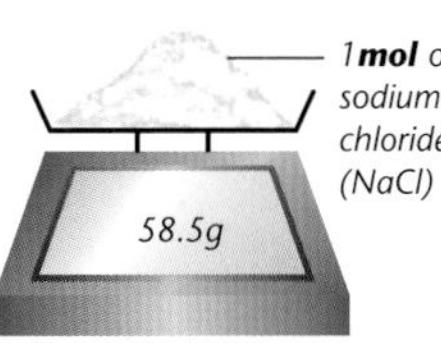
Relative molecular mass = 23 + 35.5
1mol of sodium chloride (NaCl)
58.5g

Molar mass *58.5g*

Molar volume

The volume of one **mole** of any substance, measured in cubic liters. Molar volumes of solids and liquids vary, but all gases under the same conditions have the same molar volume. The molar volume of any gas at **s.t.p.*** is 22.4 liters and at **r.t.p.** (**room temperature and pressure**, i.e. 20°C and 101,325 **pascals***) it is $24dm^3$.

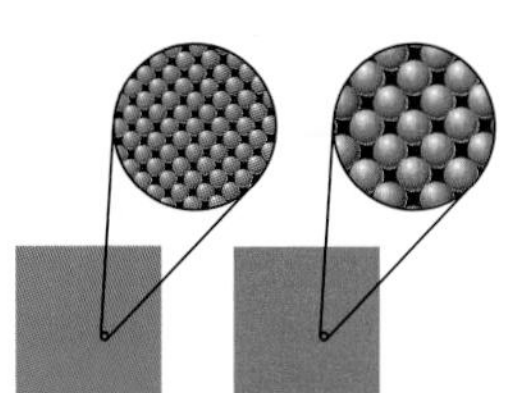

In solids and liquids, ***molar volume*** *depends on size and arrangement of particles.*

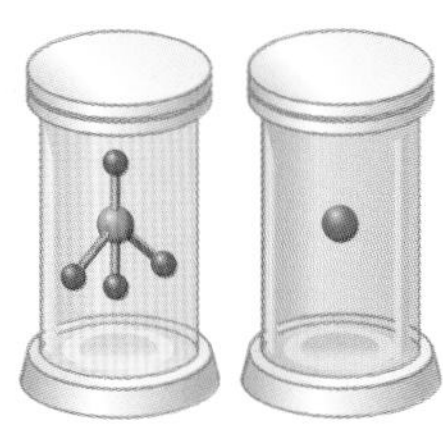

All gases (at same temperature and pressure) have same ***molar volume.*** *Their particles are not bonded together.*

Concentration

A measurement of the amount of a **solute*** dissolved in a **solvent***, expressed in **moles** per liter. **Mass concentration** is the mass of solute per unit volume, e.g. grams per liter.

Concentration *is the number of* ***moles*** *of* ***solute**** *dissolved in each liter of* ***solvent****.

4mol of solute*
2 liters of solvent*

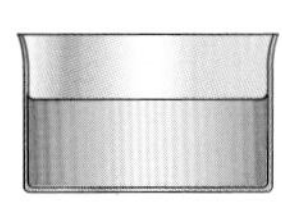

Concentration *of 2 moles per liter*

Molarity

A term sometimes used to describe the **concentration** when expressed in **moles** of **solute*** per liter of **solvent***. The molarity is also expressed as the **M-value**, e.g. a solution with a concentration of 3 moles per liter has a molarity of 3 and is described as a 3**M** solution.

*A 2****M*** *copper(II) sulfate solution contains 2****mol*** *of copper(II) sulfate in each liter.*

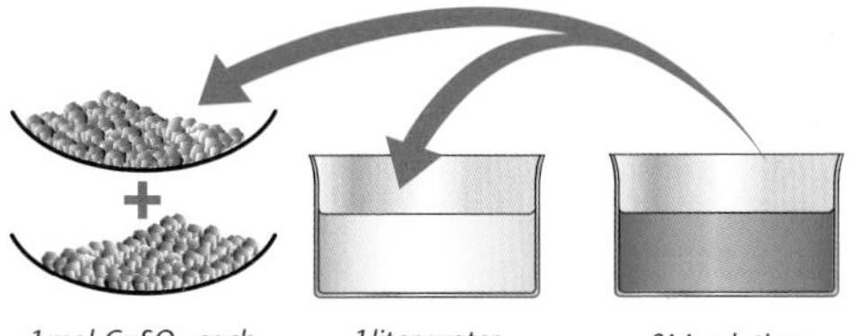
1mol $CuSO_4$ each
1liter water
2M solution

Molar solution

A solution that contains one **mole** of a substance dissolved in every liter of solution. It is therefore a 1M solution (see **molarity**).

A ***molar solution*** *(or 1M solution) of copper(II) sulfate contains 1****mol*** *of copper(II) sulfate in each liter.*

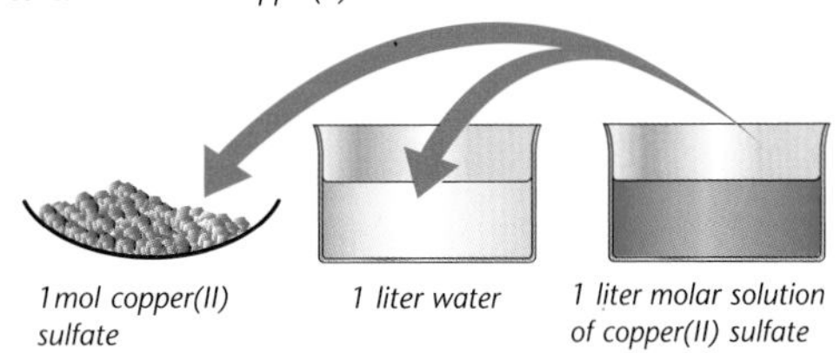
1mol copper(II) sulfate
1 liter water
1 liter molar solution of copper(II) sulfate

Standard solution

A solution of which the **concentration** is known. It is used for **volumetric analysis***.

* **Isotope**, 127; **Pascal**, 97; **SI units**, 96; **Solute**, **Solvent**, 144; **s.t.p.**, 143; **Volumetric analysis**, 222.

REPRESENTING CHEMICALS

Most chemicals are named according to the predominant elements they contain. Information about the chemical composition and structure of a compound is given by a **formula** (pl. **formulas**), in which the **chemical symbols*** for the elements are used. A chemical **equation** shows the reactants and products of a chemical reaction and gives information about how the reaction happens.

Formulas

Empirical formula

A formula showing the simplest ratio of the atoms of each element in a compound. It does not show the total number of atoms of each element in a **covalent compound***, or the **bonding** in the compound (see pages 130-134).

Displayed formula or full structural formula

A formula which shows the arrangement of the atoms in relation to each other in a molecule. All the bonds in the molecule are shown. In a displayed formula, single bonds are represented by a single line, double bonds by a double line, and so on.

Molecular formula

A formula representing one molecule of an element or compound. It shows which elements the molecule contains and the number of atoms of each in the molecule, but not the **bonding** of the molecule (see pages 130-134).

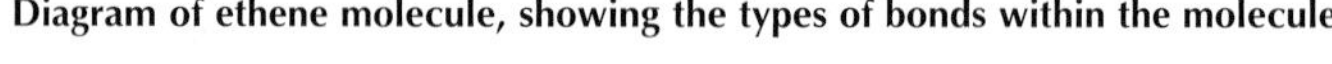
Diagram of ethene molecule, showing the types of bonds within the molecule

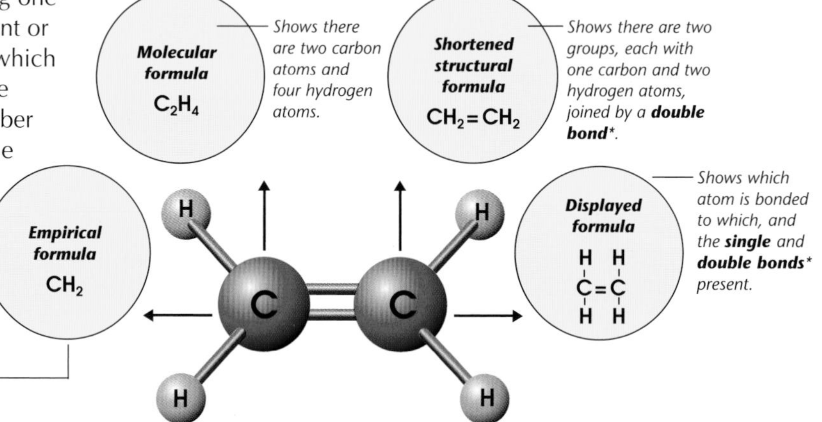

Molecular formula
C_2H_4
Shows there are two carbon atoms and four hydrogen atoms.
Shortened structural formula
$CH_2=CH_2$
*Shows there are two groups, each with one carbon and two hydrogen atoms, joined by a **double bond***.*
Empirical formula
CH_2
Shows there are two hydrogen atoms to every carbon atom.
Displayed formula
H H
C=C
H H
*Shows which atom is bonded to which, and the **single** and **double bonds*** present.*
H
C
C
H
H
H

Shortened structural formula

A formula which shows the sequence of groups of atoms (e.g. a **carboxyl group***) in a molecule and the **bonding** (see pages 130-134) between the groups of atoms (shown as lines).

Stereochemical formula or 3-dimensional structural formula

A formula which uses symbols to show the 3-dimensional arrangement of the atoms and **bonds*** in a molecule. See **stereochemistry**, page 191, for the stereochemical formula of methane.

Percentage composition

The composition of a compound expressed in terms of the percentage of its mass taken up by each element.

Percentage composition *of carbon dioxide (CO_2)*

One carbon atom. ***Relative atomic mass**** *= 12*

Two oxygen atoms. ***Relative atomic mass*** *= 2 × 16 = 32*

Relative molecular mass* *of compound =*

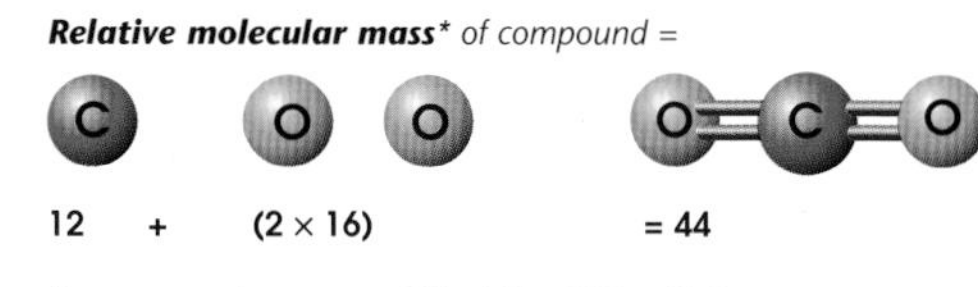

C
O
O
O C O
12 + (2 × 16) = 44

Percentage of oxygen = (32 ÷ 44) × 100 = 73%

Percentage of carbon = (12 ÷ 44) × 100 = 27%

Therefore, the ***percentage composition*** *of carbon dioxide = 27% carbon, 73% oxygen.*

* **Bonds**, 130; **Carboxyl group**, 195 (**Carboxylic acids**); **Chemical symbol**, 122; **Covalent compounds**, **Double bond**, 132; **Relative atomic mass**, **Relative molecular mass**, 138; **Single bond**, 132.

Names

Trivial name
An everyday name given to a compound. It does not usually give any information about the composition or structure of the compound, e.g. salt (sodium chloride), chalk (calcium carbonate).

Traditional name
A name which gives the predominant elements of a substance, without necessarily giving their quantities or showing the structure of the substance. Some traditional names are **systematic names**.

***Trivial name**: Green vitriol*
***Traditional name**: Ferrous sulfate*

Iron sulfate ($FeSO_4$)

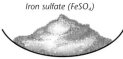

Systematic name
Iron(II) tetraoxosulfate(VI)

Oxidation state* *of iron, i.e. Fe^{2+}*

Oxidation state* *of sulfur is +6*

This name is normally simplified to iron(II) sulfate.

Systematic name
A name which shows the elements a compound contains, the ratio of numbers of atoms of each element and the **oxidation number*** of elements with variable **oxidation states***. The **bonding** (see pages 130-134) can also be worked out from the name. In some cases the systematic name is simplified. Some systematic names are the same as **traditional names**. See also **naming simple organic compounds**, page 214.

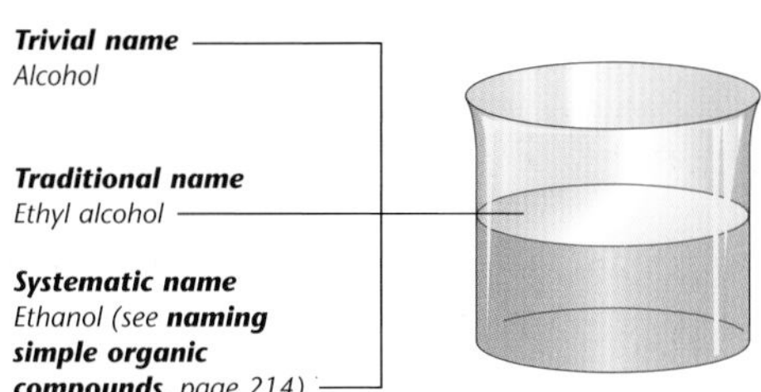
Trivial name
Alcohol
Traditional name
Ethyl alcohol
Systematic name
Ethanol (see naming simple organic compounds, page 214)

Equations

Word equation
An equation in which the substances involved in a reaction are indicated by their names, e.g:

Sodium + Water → Sodium hydroxide + Hydrogen

However, the names may be replaced by the **formulas** of the substances (see opposite page).

$$Na + H_2O \rightarrow NaOH + H_2$$

Balanced equation
An equation in which the number of atoms of each element involved in the reaction is the same on each side of the equation (i.e. it obeys the **law of conservation of mass***). The numbers of molecules of each substance are shown by the number in front of their **formula**, e.g:

$$2Na + 2H_2O \rightarrow 2NaOH + H_2$$

Ionic equation
An equation which only shows changes which occur to the ions in a reaction. (See example at bottom of page.)

State symbols
Letters written after the **formula** of a substance which show its **physical state*** in a reaction.

$$2Na(s) + 2H_2O(l) \rightarrow 2NaOH(aq) + H_2(g)$$

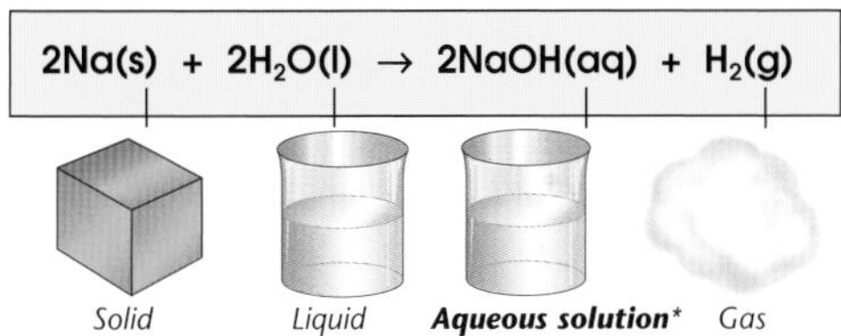
Solid
Liquid
Aqueous solution*
Gas

Spectator ion
An ion which remains the same after a chemical reaction.

*In the reaction below, Na^+, OH^-, H^+, Cl^- are all ions. Na^+, Cl^- appear on both sides of the equation – on this occasion they are **spectator ions**. Spectator ions are omitted from **ionic equations**.*

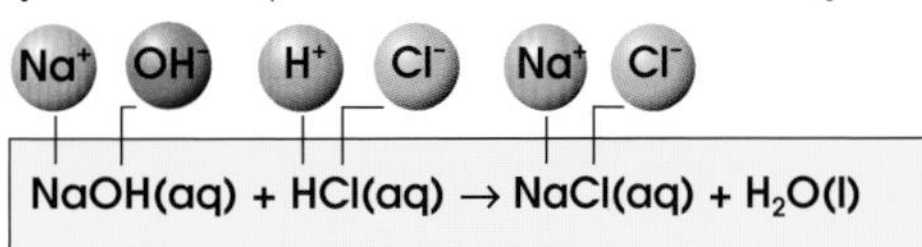
Na+
OH-
H+
Cl-
Na+
Cl-

$$NaOH(aq) + HCl(aq) \rightarrow NaCl(aq) + H_2O(l)$$

***Ionic equation** is:* $OH^-(aq) + H^+(aq) \rightarrow H_2O(l)$

* **Aqueous solution**, 144; **Law of conservation of mass**, 125; **Oxidation number**, **Oxidation state**, 149; **Physical states**, 120.

GAS LAWS

The molecules in a gas are widely spaced and move about in a rapid, chaotic manner (see **kinetic theory***). The combined volume of the gas molecules is much smaller than the volume the gas occupies, and the forces of attraction between the molecules are very weak. This is true for all gases, so they all behave in a similar way. Several **gas laws** describe this common behavior (see below).

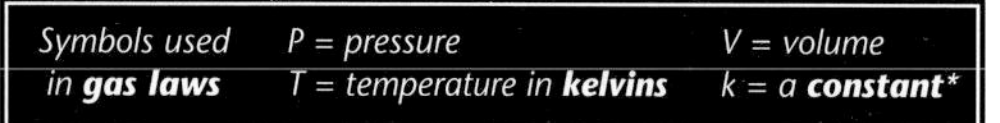

Symbols used in **gas laws**	P = pressure	V = volume
	T = temperature in **kelvins**	k = a **constant***

Gas at constant temperature, pressure and volume

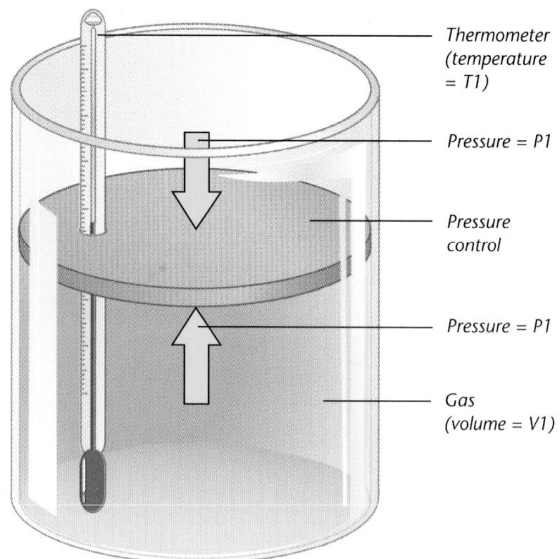

Thermometer (temperature = T1)
Pressure = P1
Pressure control
Pressure = P1
Gas (volume = V1)

Boyle's law

At constant temperature, the volume of a gas is inversely proportional to the pressure (the volume decreases as the pressure increases).

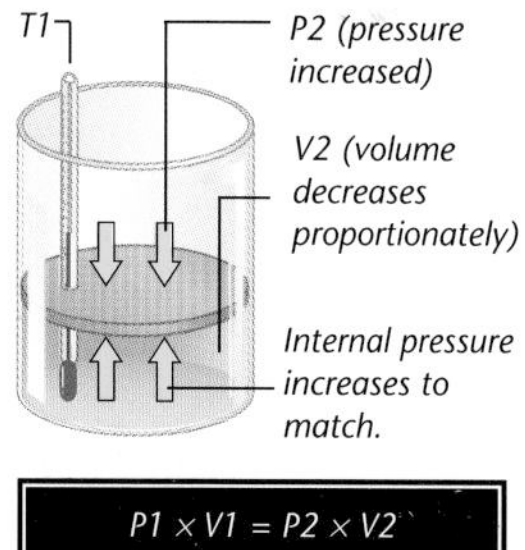

T1
P2 (pressure increased)
V2 (volume decreases proportionately)
Internal pressure increases to match.

$P1 \times V1 = P2 \times V2$
or $PV = k$

Law of volumes

At constant pressure, the volume is directly proportional to the temperature on the **absolute temperature scale** (the gas expands as the temperature increases).

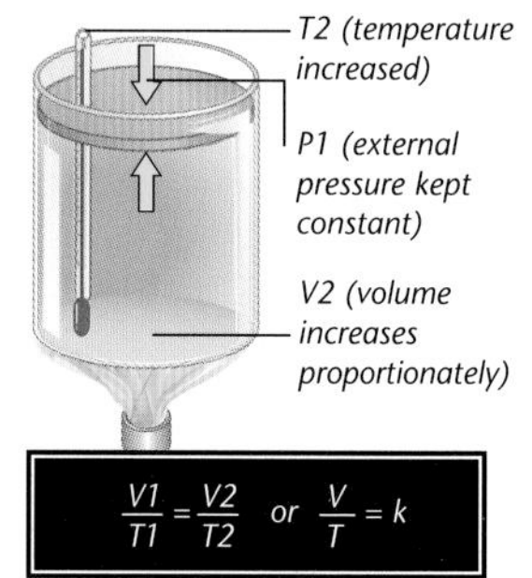

T2 (temperature increased)
P1 (external pressure kept constant)
V2 (volume increases proportionately)

$\frac{V1}{T1} = \frac{V2}{T2}$ or $\frac{V}{T} = k$

Pressure law or Third gas law

At constant volume, the pressure is directly proportional to the temperature on the **absolute temperature scale** (the pressure increases with the temperature).

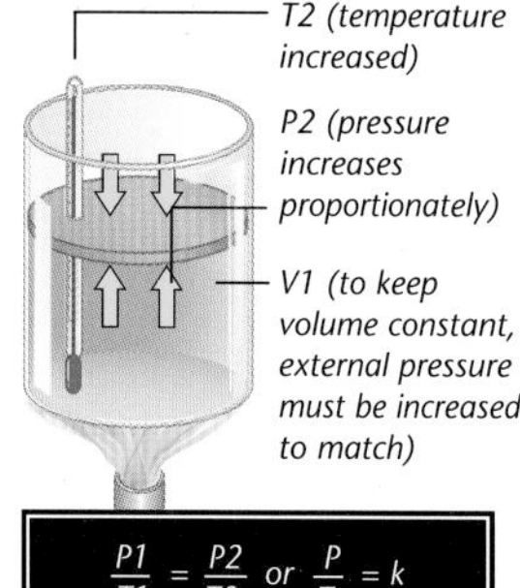

T2 (temperature increased)
P2 (pressure increases proportionately)
V1 (to keep volume constant, external pressure must be increased to match)

$\frac{P1}{T1} = \frac{P2}{T2}$ or $\frac{P}{T} = k$

Ideal gas equation or General gas equation

An equation that shows the relationship between the pressure, volume and temperature of a fixed mass of gas.

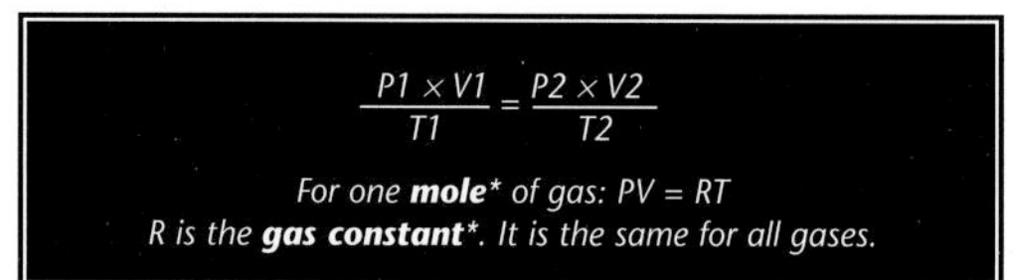

$$\frac{P1 \times V1}{T1} = \frac{P2 \times V2}{T2}$$

*For one **mole*** of gas: $PV = RT$*

*R is the **gas constant***. It is the same for all gases.*

Ideal gas

A theoretical gas that behaves in an "ideal" way. Its molecules have no volume, do not attract each other, move rapidly in straight lines and lose no energy when they collide. Many real gases behave in approximately the same way as ideal gases when the molecules are small and widely spaced.

Small, widely-spaced molecules

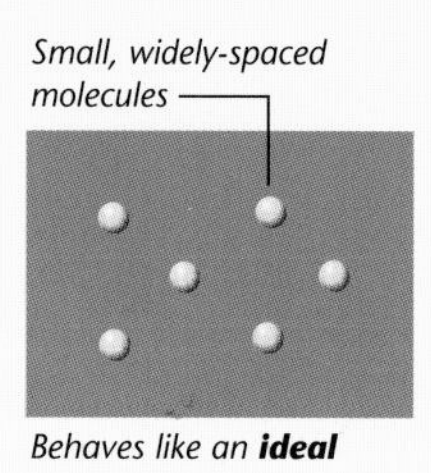

*Behaves like an **ideal gas**.*

Large molecules close together

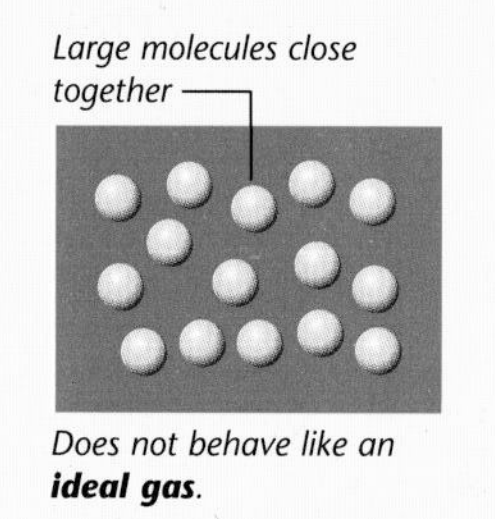

*Does not behave like an **ideal gas**.*

* **Constant**, 344; **Gas constant**, 113; **Kinetic theory**, 123; **Mole**, 139.

Partial pressure

The pressure that each gas in a **mixture*** of gases would exert if it alone filled the volume occupied by the mixture.

Dalton's law of partial pressures

The total pressure exerted by a **mixture*** of gases (which do not react together) is equal to the sum of the **partial pressure** of each gas in the mixture.

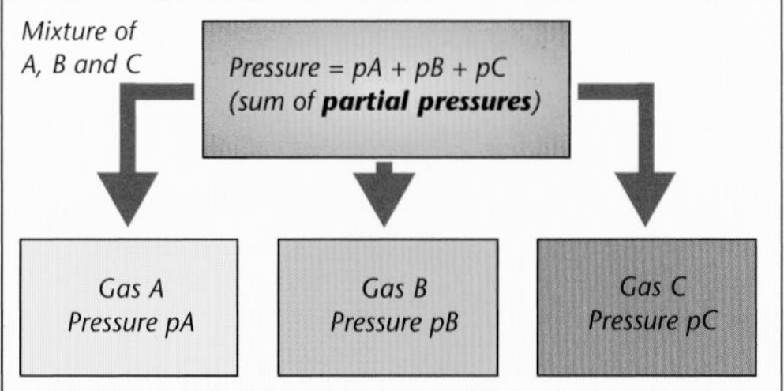
Mixture of
A, B and C
Pressure = pA + pB + pC
(sum of **partial pressures**)
Gas A
Pressure pA
Gas B
Pressure pB
Gas C
Pressure pC

Graham's law of diffusion

If the temperature and pressure are constant, the rate of **diffusion*** of a gas is inversely proportional to the square root of its density. The density of a gas is high if its molecules are heavy, and low if its molecules are light. Light molecules move faster than heavy molecules, so a gas with a high density diffuses more slowly than a gas with a low density.

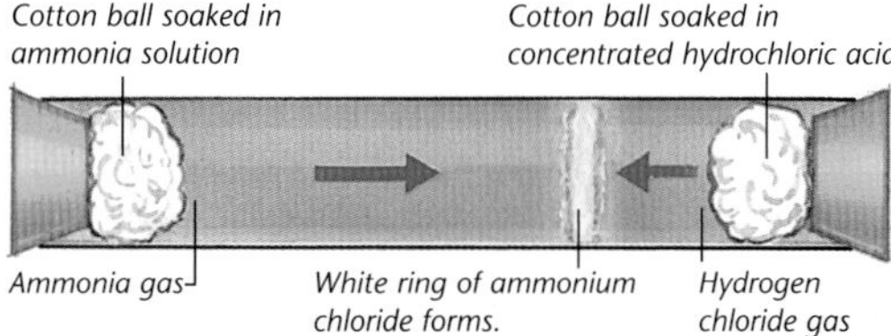
Cotton ball soaked in
ammonia solution
Cotton ball soaked in
concentrated hydrochloric acid
Ammonia gas
White ring of ammonium
chloride forms.
Hydrogen
chloride gas

*Light ammonia molecules **diffuse*** faster than hydrogen chloride molecules. The two gases meet nearer to the right-hand end of the tube.*

$$\text{Rate of diffusion} \propto \frac{1}{\sqrt{\text{density of gas}}}$$

(proportional)

Relative vapor density

The density of a gas relative to the density of hydrogen. It is calculated by dividing the density of a gas by the density of hydrogen. Relative vapor density is a ratio and has no units.

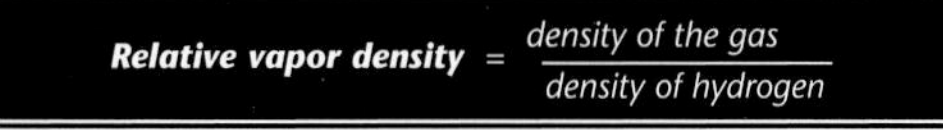

$$\text{Relative vapor density} = \frac{\text{density of the gas}}{\text{density of hydrogen}}$$

Gay-Lussac's law

When gases react together to produce other gases and all the volumes are measured at the same temperature and pressure, the volumes of the reactants and products are in a ratio of simple whole numbers.

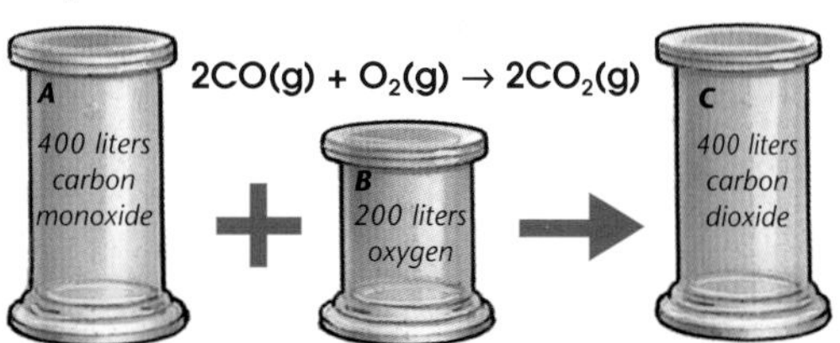
$2CO(g) + O_2(g) \rightarrow 2CO_2(g)$
A
400 liters
carbon
monoxide
B
200 liters
oxygen
C
400 liters
carbon
dioxide

*According to **Avogadro's law** (below), jars A and C above contain the same number of molecules.*

Avogadro's law or Avogadro's hypothesis

Equal volumes of all gases at the same temperature and pressure contain the same number of molecules.

s.t.p.

An abbreviation for **standard temperature and pressure**. These are internationally agreed standard conditions under which properties such as volume and density of gases are usually measured.

***s.t.p.** = temperature: 0°C or 273K (**kelvins**)*
*pressure: 101,325 **pascals****

Absolute temperature scale

A standard temperature scale, using units called **kelvins** (**K**). A kelvin is the same size as one degree **Celsius***, but the lowest point on the scale, zero kelvins or **absolute zero**, is equal to –273 degrees Celsius, a theoretical point where an **ideal gas** would occupy zero volume.

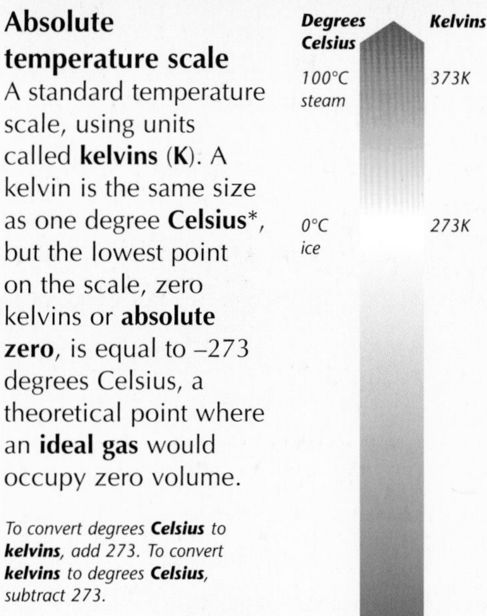
Degrees
Celsius
Kelvins
100°C
steam
373K
0°C
ice
273K
Absolute zero — –273°C
0K

*To convert degrees **Celsius** to **kelvins**, add 273. To convert **kelvins** to degrees **Celsius**, subtract 273.*

* **Celsius scale**, 27; **Diffusion**, 123; **Mixture**, 122; **Pascal**, 97.

SOLUTIONS AND SOLUBILITY

When a substance is added to a liquid, several things can happen. If the atoms, molecules or ions of the substance become evenly dispersed (**dissolve**), the **mixture*** is a **solution**. If they do not, the mixture is either a **colloid**, a **suspension**, or a **precipitate**. How well a substance dissolves depends on its properties, those of the liquid, and other factors such as temperature and pressure.

Solvent
The substance in which the **solute** dissolves to form a solution.

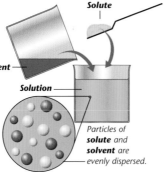

Solute
The substance which dissolves in the **solvent** to form a solution.

Solute

Solvent

Solution

*Particles of **solute** and **solvent** are evenly dispersed.*

Solvation
The process of **solvent** molecules combining with **solute** molecules as the solute dissolves. When the solvent is water, the process is called **hydration**. Whether or not solvation takes place depends on how much the molecules of the solvent and solute attract each other, and how strong the **bonds*** in the solute are.

Polar solvent
A liquid with **polar molecules***. Polar solvents generally dissolve **ionic compounds***. **Solvation** occurs because the charged ends of the solvent molecules attract the ions of the **giant ionic lattice***. Water is the most common polar solvent.

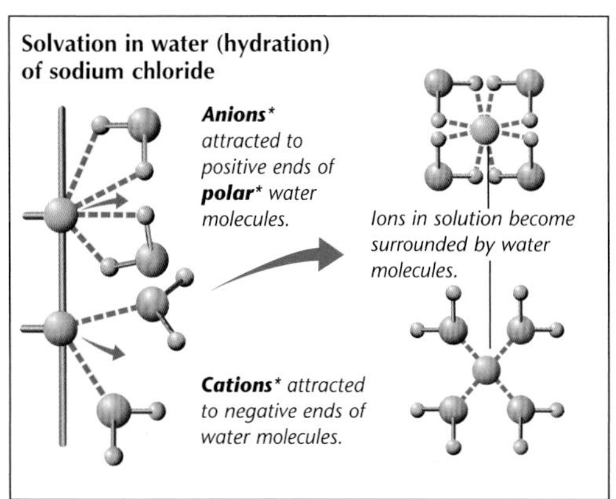

Solvation in water (hydration) of sodium chloride
Anions* attracted to positive ends of polar* water molecules.
Ions in solution become surrounded by water molecules.
Cations* attracted to negative ends of water molecules.

Non-polar solvent
A liquid with **non-polar molecules***. Non-polar solvents dissolve **covalent compounds***. The **solute** molecules are pulled from the **molecular lattice*** by the solvent molecules and **diffuse*** through the solvent. Many organic liquids are non-polar solvents.

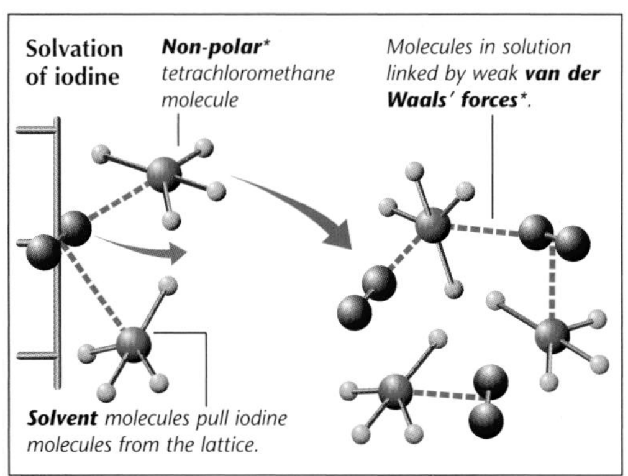

Solvation of iodine
Non-polar* tetrachloromethane molecule
Molecules in solution linked by weak van der Waals' forces*.
Solvent molecules pull iodine molecules from the lattice.

Aqueous solvent
A **solvent** containing water. Water molecules are **polar***, so aqueous solvents are **polar solvents**.

Aqueous solution
A solution formed from an **aqueous solvent**. Aqueous solvents are **polar solvents** and form aqueous solutions. **Non-polar solvents** are **non-aqueous solvents** and form **non-aqueous solutions**.

Dilute
Describes a solution with a low **concentration*** of **solute**.

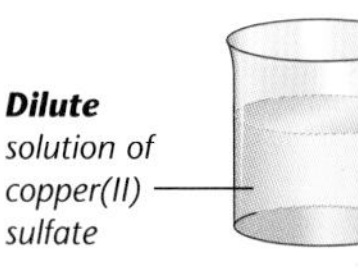

Dilute *solution of copper(II) sulfate*

Concentrated
Describes a solution with a high **concentration*** of **solute**.

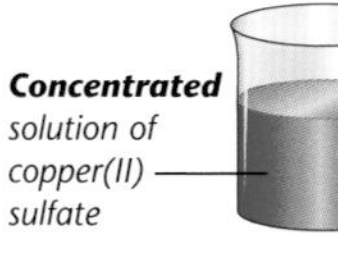

Concentrated *solution of copper(II) sulfate*

* **Anion**, **Bonding**, **Cation**, 130; **Concentration**, 139; **Covalent compounds**, 132; **Diffusion**, 123; **Giant ionic lattice**, 137; **Ionic compound**, 131; **Mixture**, 122; **Molecular lattice**, 137; **Non-polar molecule**, 133 (**Polar molecule**); **van der Waals' forces**, 134.

Saturated

Describes a solution that will not dissolve any more **solute** at a given temperature (any more solute will remain as crystals). If the temperature is raised, more solute may dissolve until the solution becomes saturated again.

Supersaturated

Describes a solution with more dissolved **solute** than a **saturated** solution at the same temperature. It is formed when a solution is cooled below the temperature at which it would be saturated, and there are no particles for the solute to **crystallize*** around, so the "extra" solute remains dissolved. The solution is unstable – if crystals are added or dust enters, the "extra" solute forms crystals.

Soluble

Describes a **solute** which dissolves easily in a **solvent**. The opposite of soluble is **insoluble**.

Solubility

The amount of a **solute** which dissolves in a particular amount of **solvent** at a known temperature.

*The **solubility** of a **solute** at a particular temperature is:*

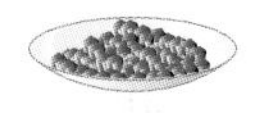

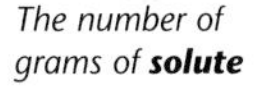

*The number of grams of **solute***

*which must be added to 100g of **solvent***

*to produce a **saturated** solution.*

The solubility of a solid usually increases with temperature, while the solubility of a gas decreases.

Sugar dissolves better in hot tea than in cold water.

Warm soft drinks have more bubbles than cold ones.

The change of solubility with temperature is shown by a **solubility curve**.

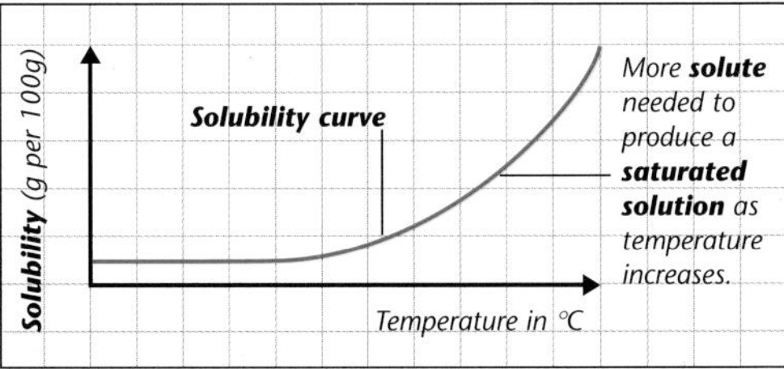
Solubility (g per 100g)
Solubility curve
More **solute** needed to produce a **saturated solution** as temperature increases.
Temperature in °C

Precipitate

An **insoluble** solid (see **soluble**) formed when a reaction occurs in a solution.

***Precipitates** are named according to their appearance.*

Flocculent

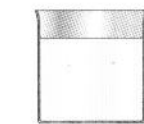

Milky

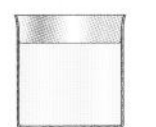

Creamy

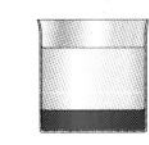

Heavy

*The reaction below forms a dense white **precipitate** of silver chloride.*

*Dense **precipitate** of silver chloride*

$$AgNO_3(aq) + NaCl(aq) \rightarrow AgCl(\downarrow) + NaNO_3(aq)$$

Silver nitrate — *Sodium chloride* — *This symbol ($\downarrow$) means **precipitate***

Miscible

Describes two or more liquids which **diffuse*** together. The opposite is **immiscible**.

Suspension

Fine particles of a solid (groups of atoms, molecules or ions) suspended in a liquid in which the solid does not dissolve.

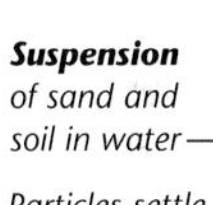

***Suspension** of sand and soil in water*

Particles settle to the bottom.

OR

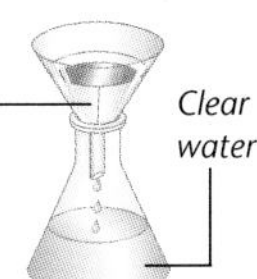

Particles can be filtered out.

Clear water

Colloid

A **mixture*** of extremely small particles of a substance dispersed in another in which it does not dissolve. The particles (groups of atoms, molecules or ions) are smaller than in a **suspension**.

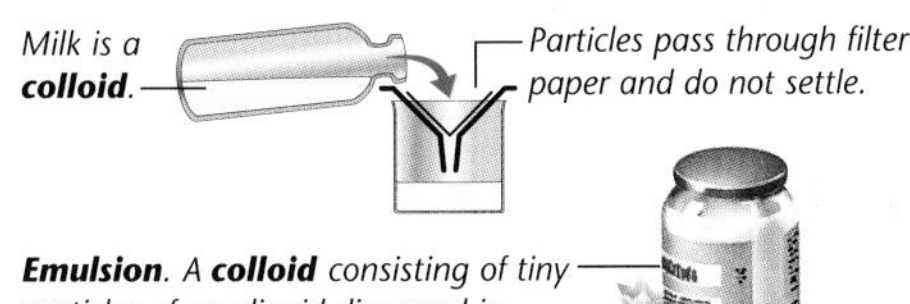

*Milk is a **colloid**.*

Particles pass through filter paper and do not settle.

***Emulsion**. A **colloid** consisting of tiny particles of one liquid dispersed in another liquid, e.g. mayonnaise.*

***Foam**. A **colloid** of small bubbles of gas dispersed in a liquid.*

***Mist**. A **colloid** consisting of tiny particles of a liquid dispersed in a gas.*

***Smoke**. A **colloid** consisting of tiny particles of a solid dispersed in a gas.*

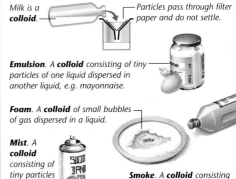

* **Crystallization**, 135; **Diffusion**, 123; **Mixture**, 122.

ENERGY AND CHEMICAL REACTIONS

Nearly all chemical reactions involve a change in energy. Some reactions involve electrical energy or light energy, but almost all involve heat energy. The change in energy in a reaction results from the different amounts of energy involved when bonds are broken and formed. The study of heat energy in chemical reactions is called **thermochemistry**.

Enthalpy (H)

The amount of energy that a substance contains. It is impossible to measure directly, but its change during a reaction can be measured.

Enthalpy change of reaction or heat of reaction (ΔH)

The amount of heat energy given out or absorbed during a chemical reaction. If the reaction is a **change of state***, this amount is also known, particularly in physics, as the **latent heat** (see page 30). Hence the **molar enthalpy changes of fusion** and **vaporization** on page 147 are closely allied to the **specific latent heats** on page 31, though the quantities are different (each being more relevant to its science).

Enthalpy change	=	*total* ***enthalpy*** *of products*	–	*total* ***enthalpy*** *of reactants*

Enthalpy change of reaction of hydrogen and oxygen

$$2H_2(g) + O_2(g) \rightarrow 2H_2O(g) \quad \Delta H = -488kJ$$

Heat is given out, so it is an ***exothermic reaction****.*

The value of ***ΔH*** *is only true for the number of* ***moles**** *and the* ***physical states**** *of the chemicals in the equation.*

J *stands for* ***joule*****, a unit of energy.* ***kJ*** *stands for* ***kilojoule*** *(1,000* ***joules****).*

Energy level diagram

A diagram which shows the **enthalpy change of reaction** for a reaction.

Energy level diagram for above reaction of hydrogen and oxygen

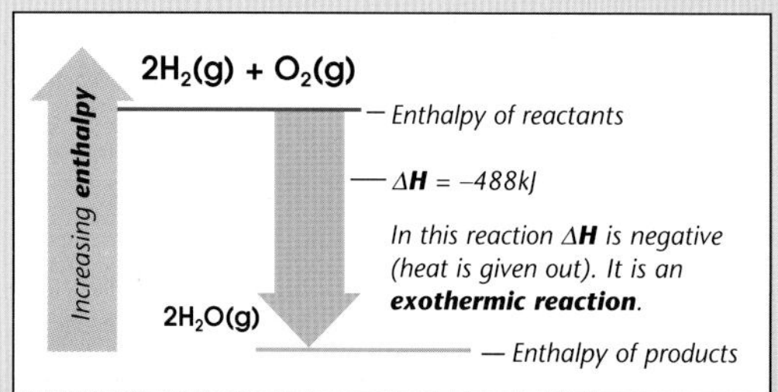
Increasing enthalpy
$2H_2(g) + O_2(g)$
Enthalpy of reactants
ΔH = –488kJ
In this reaction ΔH is negative (heat is given out). It is an exothermic reaction.
$2H_2O(g)$
Enthalpy of products

Standard enthalpy change of reaction ($\Delta H^{\ominus}$)

An **enthalpy change of reaction** measured at room temperature and pressure (**r.t.p.***). If solutions are used, their **concentration*** is 1**M***.

Exothermic reaction

A chemical reaction during which heat is transferred to the surroundings.

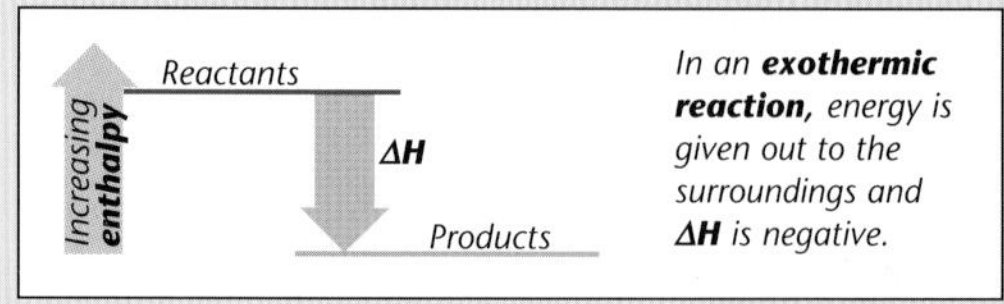
Increasing enthalpy
Reactants
ΔH
Products
In an exothermic reaction, energy is given out to the surroundings and ΔH is negative.

Endothermic reaction

A chemical reaction during which heat is absorbed from the surroundings.

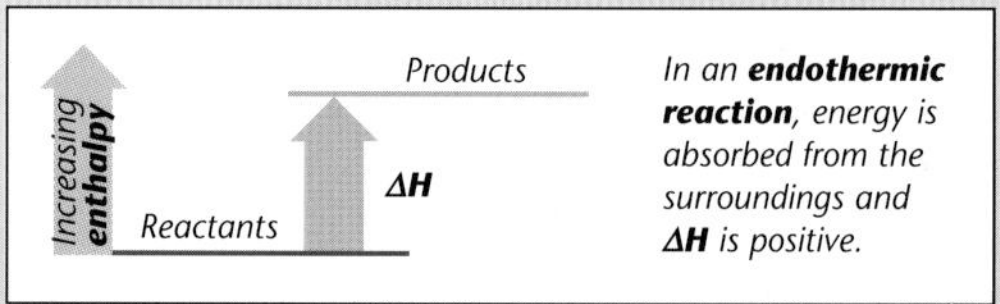
Increasing enthalpy
Products
ΔH
Reactants
In an endothermic reaction, energy is absorbed from the surroundings and ΔH is positive.

Bond energy

A measure of the strength of a **covalent bond*** formed between two atoms. Energy must be supplied to break bonds and is given out when bonds are formed. A difference in these energies produces a change in energy during a reaction.

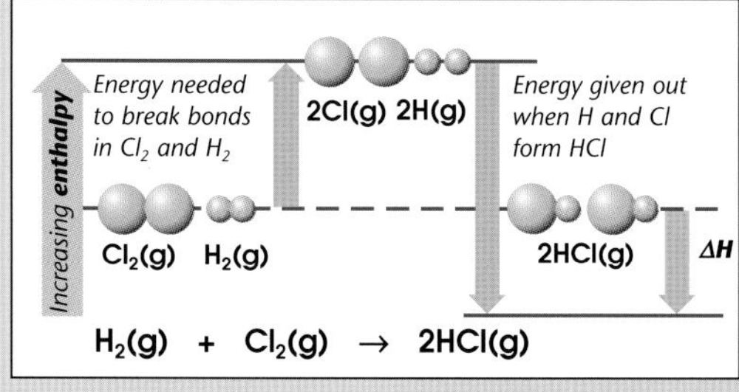
Increasing enthalpy
Energy needed to break bonds in Cl_2 and H_2
2Cl(g) 2H(g)
Energy given out when H and Cl form HCl
$Cl_2(g)$ $H_2(g)$
2HCl(g)
ΔH
$H_2(g) + Cl_2(g) \rightarrow 2HCl(g)$

Law of conservation of energy

During a chemical reaction, energy cannot be created or destroyed. In a **closed system*** the amount of energy is constant.

* **Change of state**, 120; **Closed system**, 162; **Concentration**, 139; **Covalent bond**, 132; **Joule**, 97; **M-value**, 139 (**Molarity**); **Mole**, 139; **Physical states**, 120; **r.t.p.**, 139 (**Molar volume**).

Hess's law

States that the **enthalpy change of reaction** that occurs during a particular chemical reaction is always the same, no matter what route is taken in going from the reactants to the products. The law can be illustrated by an **energy cycle** (see right). Hess's law is used to find enthalpy changes of reaction which cannot be measured directly, e.g. the **enthalpy change of formation** of methane.

Energy cycle

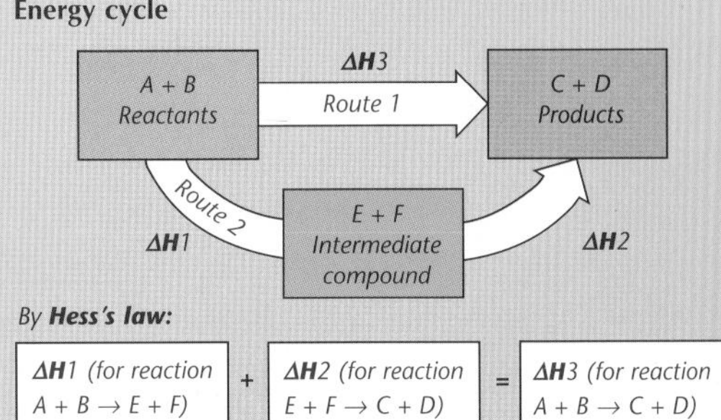
A + B
Reactants
ΔH3
Route 1
C + D
Products
Route 2
ΔH1
E + F
Intermediate
compound
ΔH2

*By **Hess's law:***

ΔH1 (for reaction A + B → E + F) + **ΔH2** (for reaction E + F → C + D) = **ΔH3** (for reaction A + B → C + D)

Special enthalpy changes

Enthalpy change of combustion or heat of combustion

The amount of heat energy given out when one **mole*** of a substance is completely burned in oxygen. The heat of combustion for a substance is measured using a **bomb calorimeter**.

Bomb calorimeter

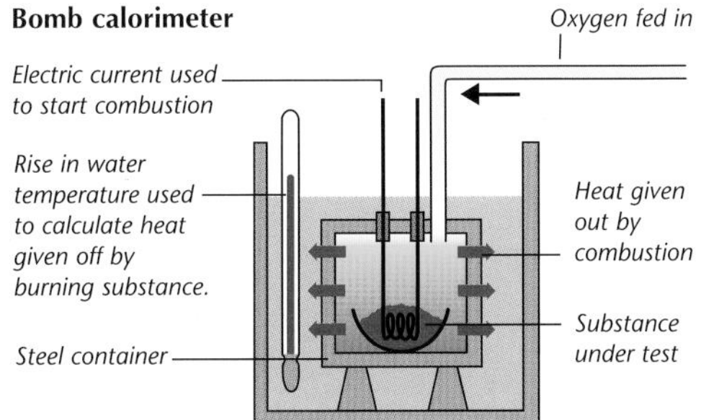
Oxygen fed in
Electric current used to start combustion
Rise in water temperature used to calculate heat given off by burning substance.
Steel container
Heat given out by combustion
Substance under test

Enthalpy change of neutralization or heat of neutralization

The amount of heat energy given out when one **mole*** of hydrogen ions (H^+) is **neutralized*** by one mole of hydroxide ions (OH^-). If the acid and alkali are fully **ionized***, the heat of neutralization is always –57kJ. The **ionic equation*** for neutralization is:

$$H^+(aq) + OH^-(aq) \rightarrow H_2O(l) \quad \Delta H = -57kJ$$

Hydrogen ion — *Hydroxide ion* — *Water molecule*

When a **weak acid*** or a **weak base*** is involved, the heat produced is less. Some energy must be supplied to ionize the acid fully.

Enthalpy change of solution or heat of solution

The amount of heat energy given out or taken in when one **mole*** of a substance dissolves in such a large volume of **solvent*** that further dilution produces no heat change.

Molar enthalpy change of fusion or molar heat of fusion

The amount of heat energy required to change one **mole*** of a solid into a liquid at its melting point. Energy must be supplied to break the bonds in the **crystal lattice*** of the solid.

Ice at 0°C
Water at 0°C
ΔH = +6.0kJ mol⁻¹
Mol⁻¹ means "for each mole*".

Molar enthalpy change of vaporization or molar heat of vaporization

The heat energy needed to change one **mole*** of a liquid into a vapor at its boiling point.

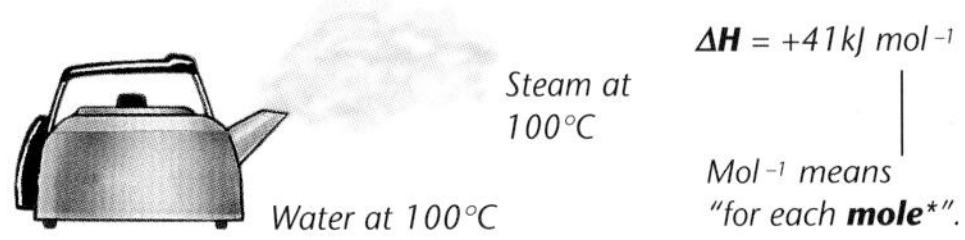
Steam at 100°C
Water at 100°C
ΔH = +41kJ mol⁻¹
Mol⁻¹ means "for each mole*".

Enthalpy change of formation or heat of formation

The heat energy given out or taken in when one **mole*** of a compound is formed from elements. For example:

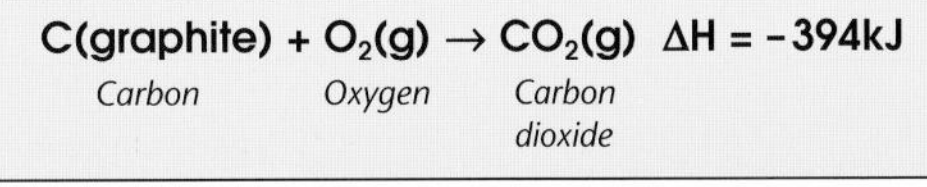

$$C(graphite) + O_2(g) \rightarrow CO_2(g) \quad \Delta H = -394kJ$$

Carbon — *Oxygen* — *Carbon dioxide*

* **Crystal lattice**, 136; **Ionic equation**, 141; **Ionization**, 130; **Mole**, 139; **Neutralization**, 151; **Solvent**, 144; **Weak acid**, **Weak base**, 152.

OXIDATION AND REDUCTION

The terms **oxidation** and **reduction** originally referred to the gain and loss of oxygen by a substance. They have now been extended to include the gain and loss of hydrogen and electrons. There is always a transfer of electrons in reactions involving oxidation and reduction, that is, the **oxidation state** of one or more of the elements is always changed.

Oxidation

A chemical reaction in which one of the following occurs:

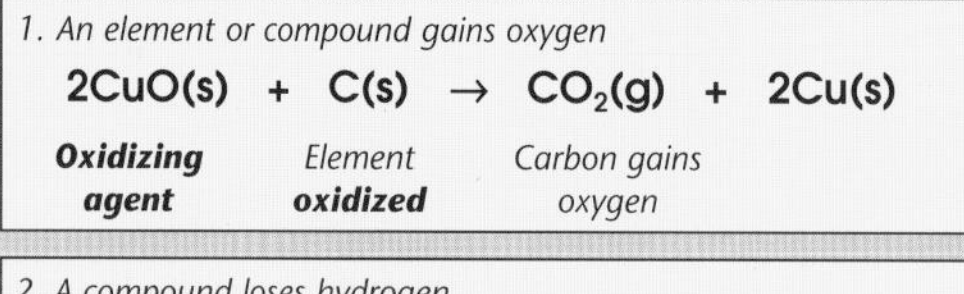

1. An element or compound gains oxygen

$$2CuO(s) + C(s) \rightarrow CO_2(g) + 2Cu(s)$$

Oxidizing agent — *Element* ***oxidized*** — *Carbon gains oxygen*

2. A compound loses hydrogen

$$Cl_2(g) + H_2S(g) \rightarrow 2HCl(g) + S(s)$$

Oxidizing agent — *Compound* ***oxidized*** — *Hydrogen sulfide loses hydrogen*

3. An atom or ion loses electrons

$$Cl_2(g) + 2Na(s) \rightarrow 2Na^+Cl^-(s)$$

Oxidizing agent — *Atom* ***oxidized*** — *Sodium loses electrons*

A substance that undergoes oxidation is said to be **oxidized**, and its **oxidation state** is increased. Oxidation is the opposite of **reduction**.

Oxidizing agent

A substance which accepts electrons, and so causes the **oxidation** of another substance. The **oxidizing agent** is always **reduced** in a reaction.

Reduction

A chemical reaction in which one of the following occurs:

1. A compound loses oxygen

$$2CuO(s) + C(s) \rightarrow CO_2(g) + 2Cu(s)$$

Compound ***reduced*** — ***Reducing agent*** — *Copper(II) oxide loses oxygen*

2. A compound or element gains hydrogen

$$Cl_2(g) + H_2S(g) \rightarrow 2HCl(g) + S(s)$$

Element ***reduced*** — ***Reducing agent*** — *Chlorine gains hydrogen*

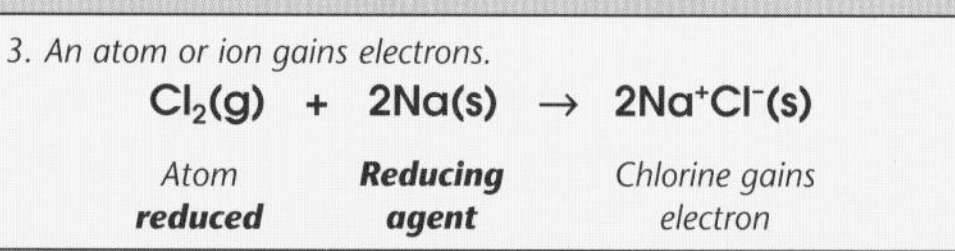

3. An atom or ion gains electrons.

$$Cl_2(g) + 2Na(s) \rightarrow 2Na^+Cl^-(s)$$

Atom ***reduced*** — ***Reducing agent*** — *Chlorine gains electron*

A substance that undergoes reduction is said to be **reduced**, and its **oxidation state** is decreased. Reduction is the opposite of **oxidation**.

Reducing agent

A substance which donates electrons, and so causes the **reduction** of another substance. The reducing agent is always **oxidized** in a reaction.

Redox

Describes a chemical reaction involving **oxidation** and **reduction**. The two processes always occur together because an **oxidizing agent** is always reduced during oxidation, and a **reducing agent** is always oxidized during reduction. In the example on the right, magnesium and chlorine undergo a redox reaction to form magnesium chloride.

$$Mg(s) + Cl_2(g) \rightarrow Mg^{2+} + 2Cl^-(s)$$

The simultaneous **oxidation** and **reduction** of the same element in a reaction is called **disproportionation**.

Redox reaction of magnesium and chlorine

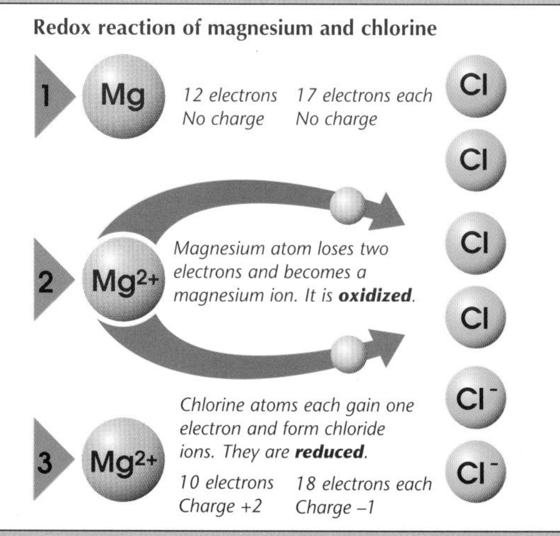

1
Mg
12 electrons
No charge
17 electrons each
No charge
Cl
Cl
2
Mg2+
Magnesium atom loses two electrons and becomes a magnesium ion. It is oxidized.
Cl
Cl
3
Mg2+
Chlorine atoms each gain one electron and form chloride ions. They are reduced.
10 electrons
Charge +2
18 electrons each
Charge –1
Cl-
Cl-

Oxidation state

The number of electrons which have been removed from, or added to, an atom when it forms a compound. The oxidation state of an element is usually equal to the charge on its ion. An element's oxidation state increases when it is **oxidized** and decreases when it is **reduced**.

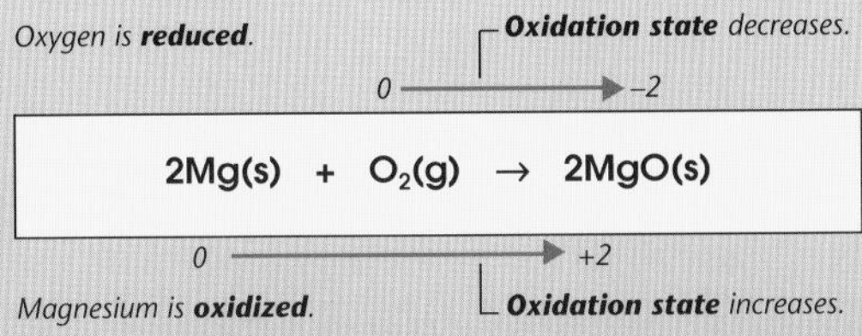

Oxygen is **reduced**.
Oxidation state decreases.
0 → −2
$2Mg(s) + O_2(g) \rightarrow 2MgO(s)$
0 → +2
Magnesium is **oxidized**.
Oxidation state increases.

The rules below help to work out the oxidation state of an element:

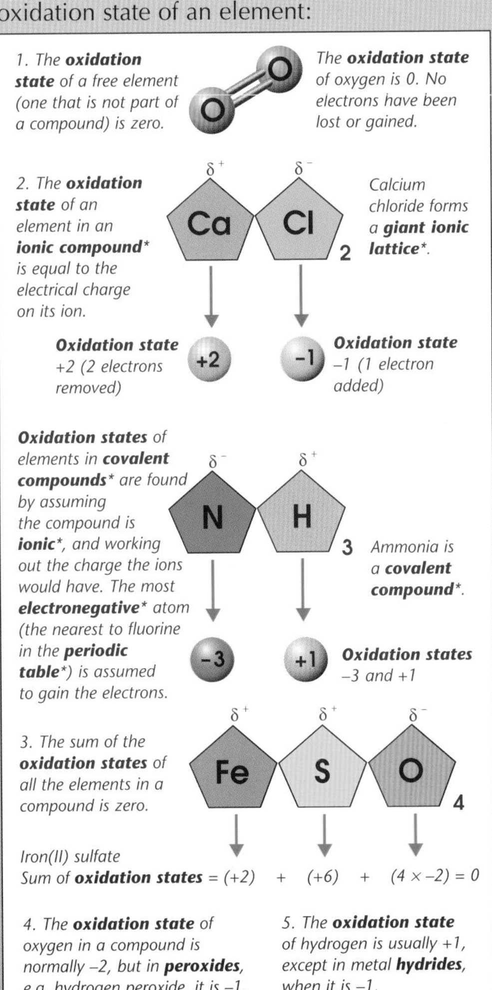

1. The **oxidation state** of a free element (one that is not part of a compound) is zero.
O
O
The **oxidation state** of oxygen is 0. No electrons have been lost or gained.
2. The **oxidation state** of an element in an **ionic compound*** is equal to the electrical charge on its ion.
δ+
δ−
Ca
Cl
2
Calcium chloride forms a **giant ionic lattice***.
Oxidation state +2 (2 electrons removed)
+2
−1
Oxidation state −1 (1 electron added)
Oxidation states of elements in **covalent compounds*** are found by assuming the compound is **ionic***, and working out the charge the ions would have. The most **electronegative*** atom (the nearest to fluorine in the **periodic table***) is assumed to gain the electrons.
δ−
δ+
N
H
3
Ammonia is a **covalent compound***.
−3
+1
Oxidation states −3 and +1
3. The sum of the **oxidation states** of all the elements in a compound is zero.
δ+
δ+
δ−
Fe
S
O
4
Iron(II) sulfate
Sum of **oxidation states** = (+2) + (+6) + (4 × −2) = 0
4. The **oxidation state** of oxygen in a compound is normally −2, but in **peroxides**, e.g. hydrogen peroxide, it is −1.
5. The **oxidation state** of hydrogen is usually +1, except in metal **hydrides**, when it is −1.

Oxidation number

A number that shows the **oxidation state** of an element in a compound. It is written in Roman numerals and placed in brackets after the name of the element. It is only included in the name of a compound when the element has more than one oxidation state.

Iron(III) chloride

Oxidation number of 3 and **oxidation state** of +3

Lead(IV) oxide

Oxidation number of 4 and **oxidation state** of +4

Redox potential

A measurement of the power of a substance to gain electrons in solution. A strong **reducing agent**, which readily loses electrons (which it can give to another substance), will have a high negative redox potential. A strong **oxidizing agent**, which easily gains electrons, will have a high positive redox potential. Redox potential is the same as **electrode potential***.

Redox series

A list of substances arranged in order of their **redox potentials**, the substance with the most negative redox potential being placed at the top. A substance usually **oxidizes** any substance above it in the series and **reduces** any substance below it. The further apart substances are in the series, the more easily they oxidize or reduce each other. The redox series is an extended version of the **electrochemical series***.

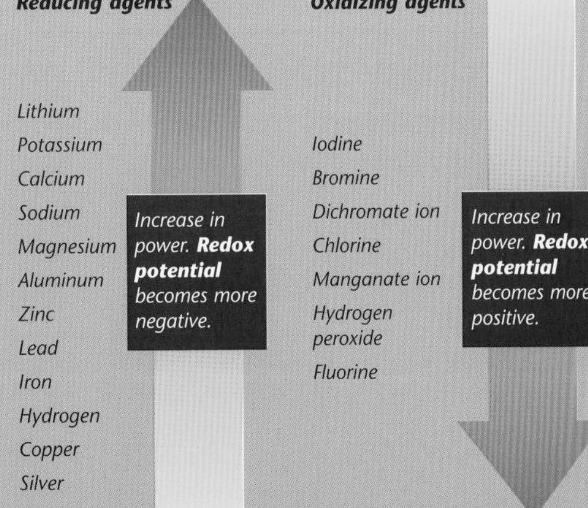

Reducing agents
Lithium
Potassium
Calcium
Sodium
Magnesium
Aluminum
Zinc
Lead
Iron
Hydrogen
Copper
Silver
Increase in power. **Redox potential** becomes more negative.
Oxidizing agents
Iodine
Bromine
Dichromate ion
Chlorine
Manganate ion
Hydrogen peroxide
Fluorine
Increase in power. **Redox potential** becomes more positive.

* **Covalent compounds**, 132; **Electrochemical series**, 159; **Electrode potential**, 158; **Electronegativity**, 133; **Giant ionic lattice**, 137; **Ionic compound**, 131, **Periodic table**, 164.

ACIDS AND BASES

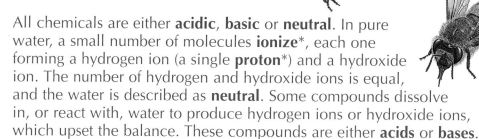

All chemicals are either **acidic**, **basic** or **neutral**. In pure water, a small number of molecules **ionize***, each one forming a hydrogen ion (a single **proton***) and a hydroxide ion. The number of hydrogen and hydroxide ions is equal, and the water is described as **neutral**. Some compounds dissolve in, or react with, water to produce hydrogen ions or hydroxide ions, which upset the balance. These compounds are either **acids** or **bases**.

The poison in a bee's sting is an ***acid****.*

Acid

A compound containing hydrogen which dissolves in water to produce hydrogen ions (H^+ – **protons***) in the solution. Hydrogen ions do not exist on their own in the solution, but join with water molecules to produce **hydronium ions**. These ions can only exist in solution, so an acid will only display its properties when it dissolves.

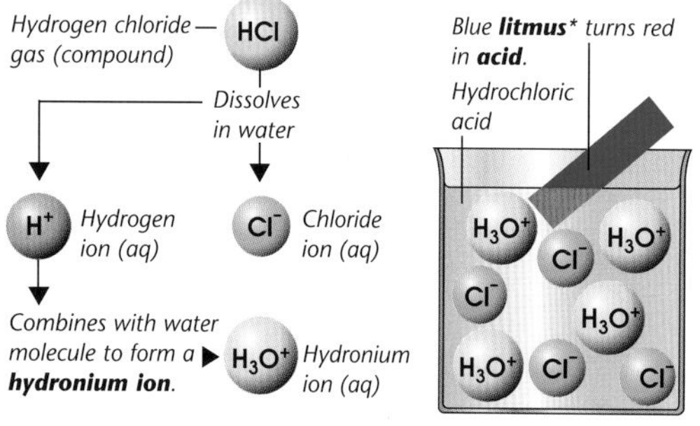

Hydrogen chloride gas (compound)
HCl
Dissolves in water
H+
Hydrogen ion (aq)
Cl-
Chloride ion (aq)
Combines with water molecule to form a hydronium ion.
H3O+
Hydronium ion (aq)
Blue litmus* turns red in acid.
Hydrochloric acid

Types of acid

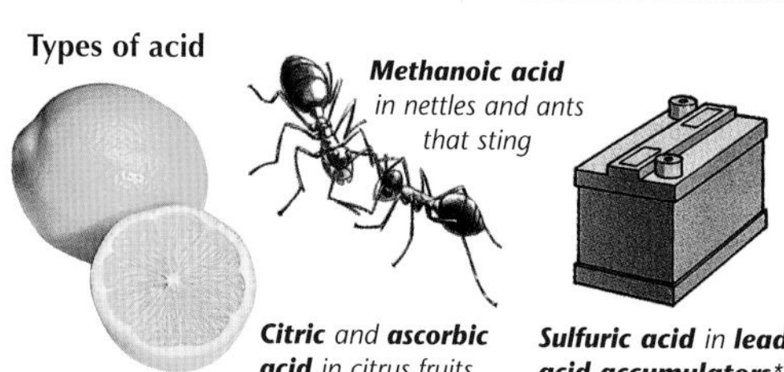

Methanoic acid in nettles and ants that sting
Citric and ascorbic acid in citrus fruits
Sulfuric acid in lead-acid accumulators*

Dilute acids have a sour taste, a **pH*** of less than 7 and turn blue **litmus*** red. They react with metals that are above hydrogen in the **electrochemical series*** to produce hydrogen gas.

$$H_2SO_4(aq) + Mg(s) \rightarrow MgSO_4(aq) + H_2(g)$$

Acid	Metal	Salt*	Hydrogen

Dilute **strong acids*** react with carbonates or hydrogencarbonates to produce carbon dioxide gas and are **neutralized** by **bases**.

Acidic

Describes any compound with the properties of an **acid**.

Some ***acids*** *are corrosive and may have warning labels.*

Hydronium ion (H_3O^+) or oxonium ion

An ion formed when a hydrogen ion attaches itself to a water molecule (see **acid**). When a reaction takes place in a solution containing hydronium ions, only the hydrogen ion takes part. Hence usually the hydronium ion can be considered to be a hydrogen ion.

Formation of hydronium ion (H_3O^+)

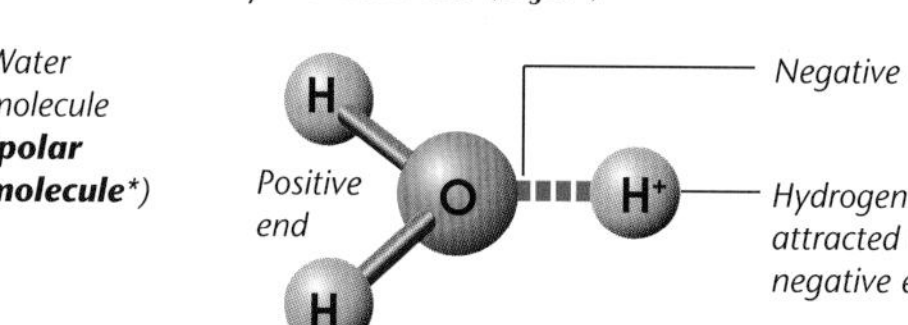

Water molecule (polar molecule*)
Positive end
Negative end
H
O
H
H+
Hydrogen ion attracted to negative end.

Mineral acid

An acid which is produced chemically from a mineral, e.g. hydrochloric acid is produced from sodium chloride, and sulfuric acid is produced from sulfur.

Mineral acid	Formula
Hydrochloric	HCl
Sulfuric	H_2SO_4
Sulfurous	H_2SO_3
Nitric	HNO_3
Nitrous	HNO_2
Phosphoric	H_3PO_4

Organic acid	Formula
Ethanedioic (Oxalic)	$(COOH)_2$
Methanoic (Formic)	$HCOOH$
Ethanoic (Acetic)	CH_3COOH

Organic acid

An **organic compound*** that is **acidic**. The most common ones are **carboxylic acids***.

When leaves die and decompose, they form an ***organic acid*** *called humic acid.*

* **Carboxylic acids**, 195; **Electrochemical series**, 159; **Ionization**, 130; **Lead-acid accumulator**, 159; **Litmus**, 152; **Organic compounds**, 190; **pH**, 152; **Polar molecule**, 133; **Proton**, 126; **Salts**, 153; **Strong acid**, 152.

Base

A substance that will **neutralize** an **acid** by accepting hydrogen ions. It is the chemical opposite of an acid. Bases are usually metal oxides and hydroxides, although ammonia is also a base. A substance with the properties of a base is described as **basic**. A base which dissolves in water is an **alkali**. Ammonia is produced when a base is heated with an ammonium **salt***.

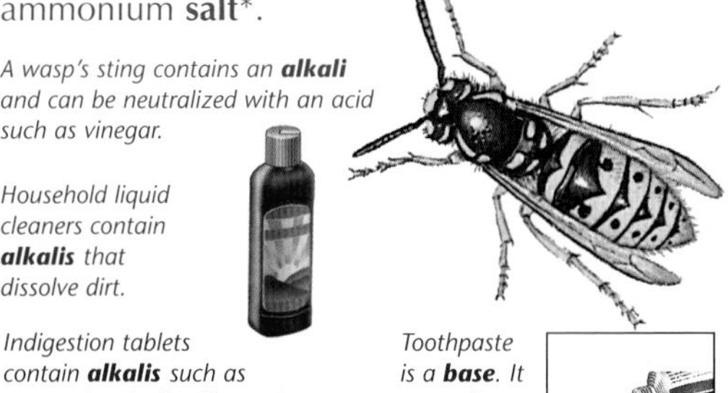

*A wasp's sting contains an **alkali** and can be neutralized with an acid such as vinegar.*

*Household liquid cleaners contain **alkalis** that dissolve dirt.*

*Indigestion tablets contain **alkalis** such as magnesium hydroxide which **neutralize** the acid produced by indigestion.*

*Toothpaste is a **base**. It neutralizes acids made in your mouth.*

Alkali

A **base**, normally a hydroxide of a metal in Group 1 or Group 2 of the **periodic table***, which is soluble in water and produces hydroxide ions (OH^-) in solution. These make a solution **alkaline**.

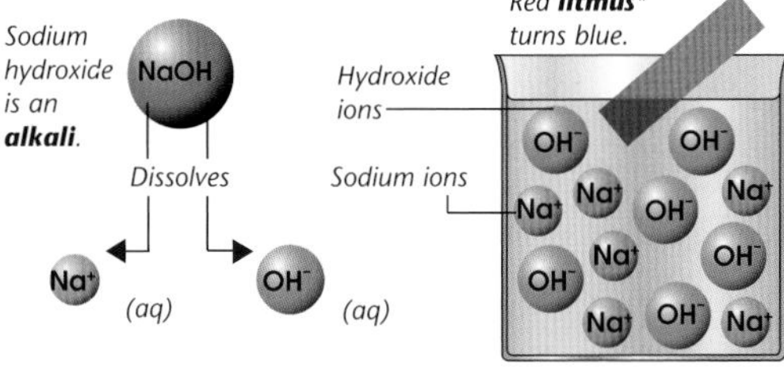

Sodium hydroxide is an alkali.
NaOH
Dissolves
Na+
(aq)
OH-
(aq)
Hydroxide ions
Sodium ions
Red litmus* turns blue.
OH-
Na+

Alkaline

Describes a solution formed when a **base** dissolves in water to form a solution which contains more hydroxide ions than hydrogen ions. Alkaline solutions have a **pH*** of more than 7, turn red **litmus*** blue, and feel soapy because they react with the skin. Alkaline solutions produced from **strong bases*** react with a few metals, e.g. zinc and aluminium, to give off hydrogen gas.

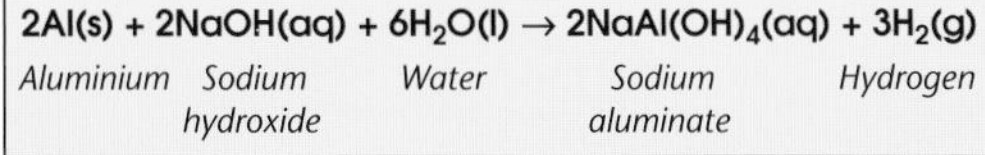

$2Al(s) + 2NaOH(aq) + 6H_2O(l) \rightarrow 2NaAl(OH)_4(aq) + 3H_2(g)$

Aluminium | Sodium hydroxide | Water | Sodium aluminate | Hydrogen

Amphoteric

Describes a substance that acts as an **acid** in one reaction, but as a **base** in another, e.g. zinc hydroxide.

Anhydride

A substance that reacts with water to form either an **acidic** or an **alkaline** solution (see **hydrolysis**, page 154). It is usually an oxide.

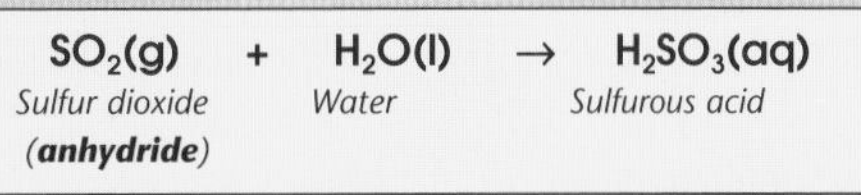

$SO_2(g) + H_2O(l) \rightarrow H_2SO_3(aq)$

*Sulfur dioxide (**anhydride**)* | *Water* | *Sulfurous acid*

Neutral

Describes a substance that does not have the properties of an **acid** or **base**. A neutral solution has an equal number of hydrogen and hydroxide ions. It has a **pH*** of 7 and does not change the color of **litmus***.

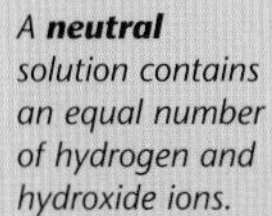
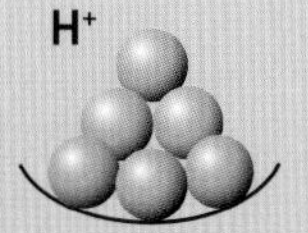
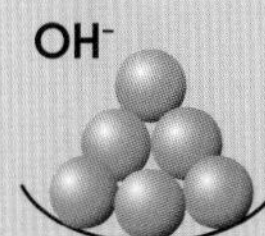

H^+
OH^-

*A **neutral** solution contains an equal number of hydrogen and hydroxide ions.*

Neutralization

The reaction between an **acid** and a **base** to produce a **salt*** and water only. An equal number of hydrogen and hydroxide ions react together to form a **neutral** solution. The **acid radical*** from the acid and **cation*** from the base form a salt.

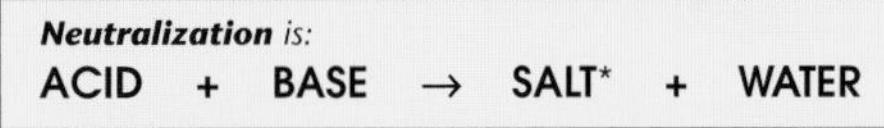

***Neutralization** is:*

ACID + BASE → SALT* + WATER

Bronsted-Lowry theory

Another way of describing **acids** and **bases**. It defines an acid as a substance which donates **protons***, and a base as one which accepts them.

*Ethanoic acid donates a **proton*** – it is an **acid**.*
*Water accepts a **proton*** – it is a **base**.*

$CH_3COOH(aq) + H_2O(l) \rightleftharpoons H_3O^+(aq) + CH_3COO^-(aq)$

*This sign means **reversible reaction****

Hydronium ion** donates **proton – it is an **acid**.*
*Ethanoate ion accepts **proton*** – it is a **base**.*

* **Acid radical**, 153; **Antacid**, 344; **Cation**, 130; **Litmus**, 152; **Periodic table**, 164; **pH**, 152; **Proton**, 126; **Reversible reaction**, 162; **Salts**, 153; **Strong base**, 152.

Acids and bases continued - strength and concentration

The **concentration*** of **acids** and **bases** (see previous two pages) depends on how many **moles*** of the acid or base are in a solution, but the strength depends on the proportion of their molecules which **ionize*** to produce **hydronium ions*** or hydroxide ions. A dilute **strong acid** can produce more hydrogen ions than a concentrated **weak acid**.

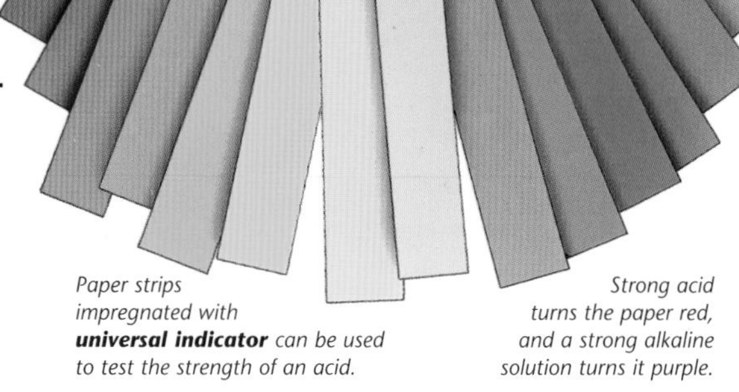

*Paper strips impregnated with **universal indicator** can be used to test the strength of an acid.*

Strong acid turns the paper red, and a strong alkaline solution turns it purple.

Strong acid

An acid that completely **ionizes*** in water, producing a large number of hydrogen ions in solution.

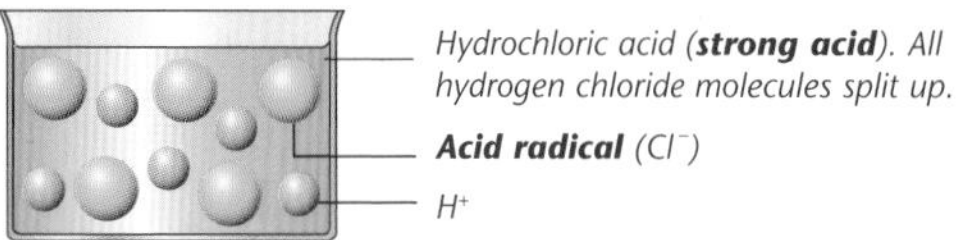
Hydrochloric acid (**strong acid**). All hydrogen chloride molecules split up.
Acid radical (Cl^-)
H^+

Weak acid

An acid that only partially **ionizes*** in water, i.e. only a small percentage of its molecules split into hydrogen ions and **acid radicals**.

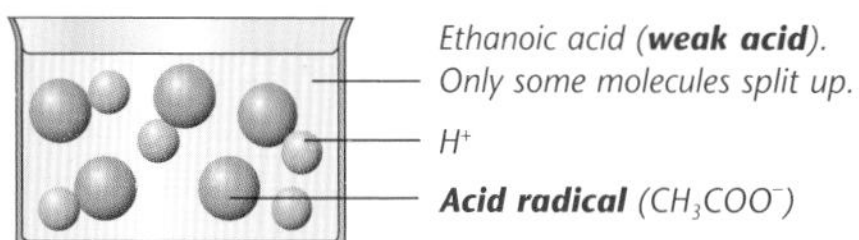
Ethanoic acid (**weak acid**). Only some molecules split up.
H^+
Acid radical (CH_3COO^-)

Strong base

A base that is completely **ionized*** in water. A large number of hydroxide ions are released to give a strongly alkaline solution.

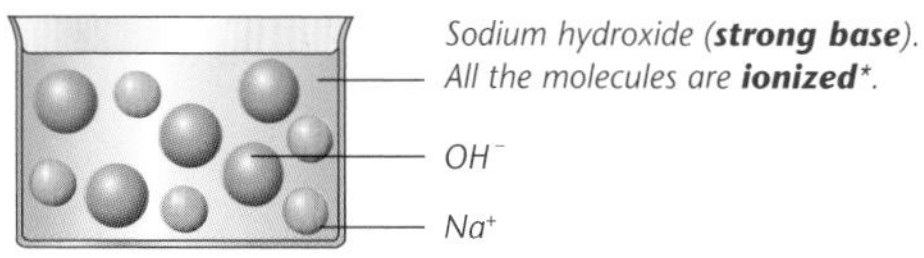
Sodium hydroxide (**strong base**). All the molecules are **ionized***.
OH^-
Na^+

Weak base

A base that is only partially **ionized*** in water. Only some molecules turn into hydroxide ions, giving a weakly alkaline solution.

Ammonia reacts slightly with water to give a low concentration of hydroxide ions:

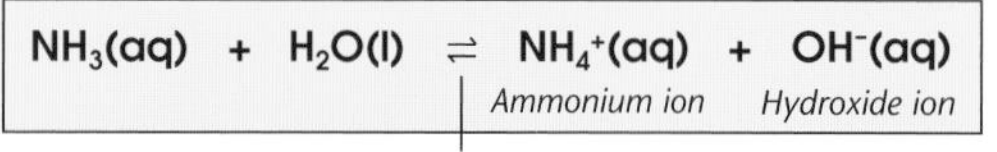

$$NH_3(aq) + H_2O(l) \rightleftharpoons NH_4^+(aq) + OH^-(aq)$$

Ammonium ion
Hydroxide ion

*This sign means **reversible reaction****

pH

Stands for **power of hydrogen**, a measure of hydrogen ion **concentration*** in a solution.

The pH scale

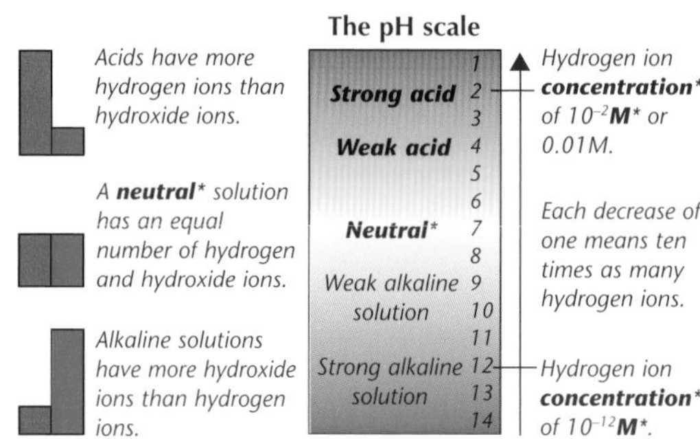
Acids have more hydrogen ions than hydroxide ions.
A **neutral*** solution has an equal number of hydrogen and hydroxide ions.
Alkaline solutions have more hydroxide ions than hydrogen ions.
1
Strong acid 2
3
Weak acid 4
5
6
Neutral* 7
8
Weak alkaline solution 9
10
11
Strong alkaline solution 12
13
14
Hydrogen ion **concentration*** of 10^{-2}**M*** or 0.01M.
Each decrease of one means ten times as many hydrogen ions.
Hydrogen ion **concentration*** of 10^{-12}**M***.

Indicator

A substance whose color depends on the **pH** of the solution it is in. Indicators can be used in solid or liquid form. Some common ones are shown at the bottom of this page.

Litmus

An **indicator** which shows whether a solution is acidic or alkaline. Acid turns blue litmus paper red, and alkaline solutions turn red litmus paper blue.

Blue litmus paper
Red litmus paper
Part dipped in acidic solution
Part dipped in alkaline solution

Universal indicator

An **indicator**, either in the form of paper or in solution, which shows the **pH** of a solution with a range of colors.

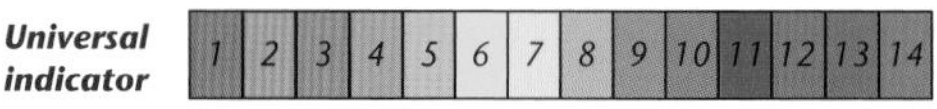
More acidic ◄ **Neutral*** ► More alkaline
Universal indicator
1 2 3 4 5 6 7 8 9 10 11 12 13 14

Some other indicators

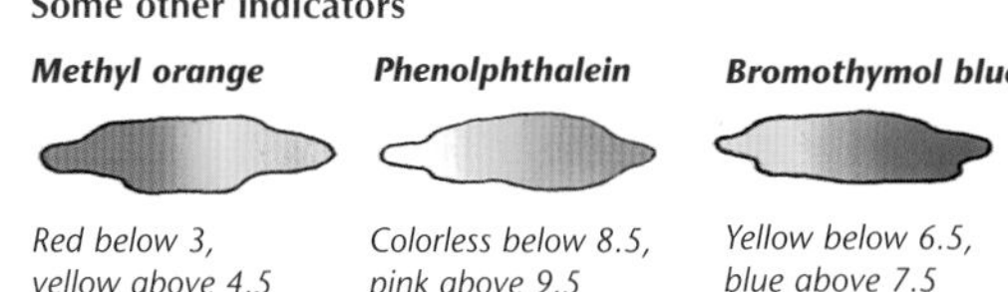
Methyl orange
Phenolphthalein
Bromothymol blue

Red below 3, yellow above 4.5

Colorless below 8.5, pink above 9.5

Yellow below 6.5, blue above 7.5

* **Concentration**, 139; **Hydronium ion**, 150; **Ionization**, 130; **M-value**, 139 (**Molarity**); **Mole**, 139; **Neutral**, 151; **Reversible reaction**, 162.

SALTS

All **salts** are **ionic compounds*** which contain at least one **cation*** and one **anion*** (called the **acid radical**). Theoretically, they can all be formed by replacing one or more of the hydrogen ions in an acid by one or more other cations, e.g. metal ions (see below) or ammonium ions. Salts have many industrial and domestic uses.

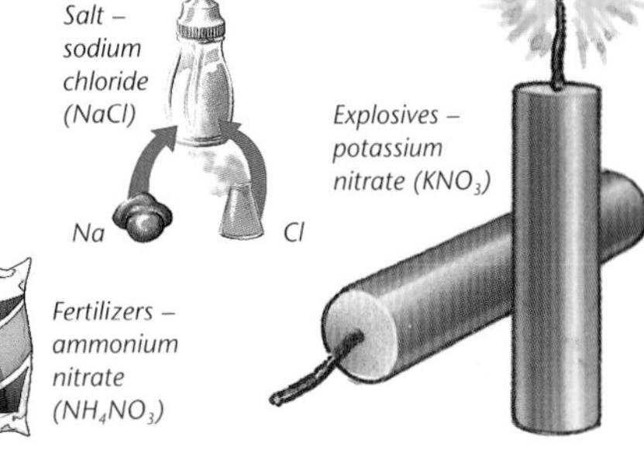
Salt – sodium chloride (NaCl)
Na
Cl
Explosives – potassium nitrate (KNO_3)
Fertilizers – ammonium nitrate (NH_4NO_3)

Metal + [Hydrogen (cation*) | Acid radical (anion*)] → [Metal (cation*) | Acid radical (anion*)] + Hydrogen

Acid *Salt*

Acid radical

The **anion*** left after the hydrogen ions have been removed from an acid. See table below.

Acid	Radical	Radical name
Hydrochloric	Cl^-	Chloride
Sulfuric	SO_4^{2-}	Sulfate
Sulfurous	SO_3^{2-}	Sulfite
Nitric	NO_3^-	Nitrate
Nitrous	NO_2^-	Nitrite
Carbonic	CO_3^{2-}	Carbonate
Ethanoic	CH_3COO^-	Ethanoate
Phosphoric	PO_4^{3-}	Phosphate

The radical name identifies the salt.

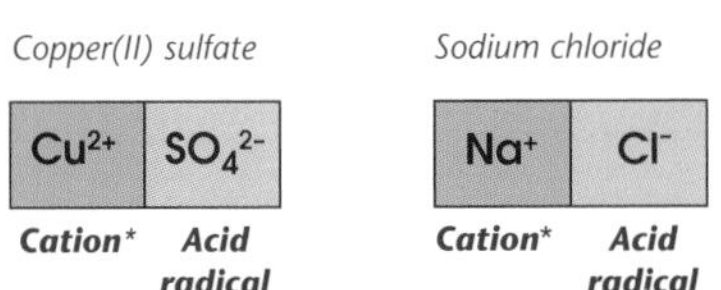
Copper(II) sulfate
Cu^{2+} SO_4^{2-}
Cation* Acid radical
Sodium chloride
Na^+ Cl^-
Cation* Acid radical

Basicity

The number of hydrogen ions in an acid that can be replaced to form a salt. Not all the hydrogen ions are necessarily replaced.

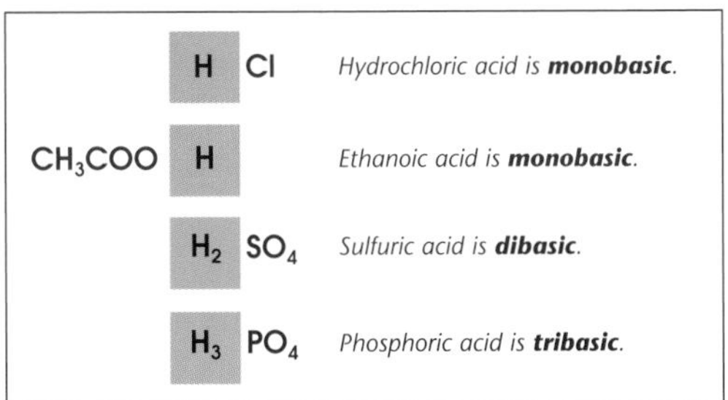
H Cl
Hydrochloric acid is **monobasic**.
CH_3COO H
Ethanoic acid is **monobasic**.
H_2 SO_4
Sulfuric acid is **dibasic**.
H_3 PO_4
Phosphoric acid is **tribasic**.

Normal salt

A salt containing only metal ions (or ammonium ions) and the **acid radical**, formed when all the hydrogen ions in an acid are replaced by metal ions (or ammonium ions).

Copper(II) sulfate and ammonium chloride (normal salts)

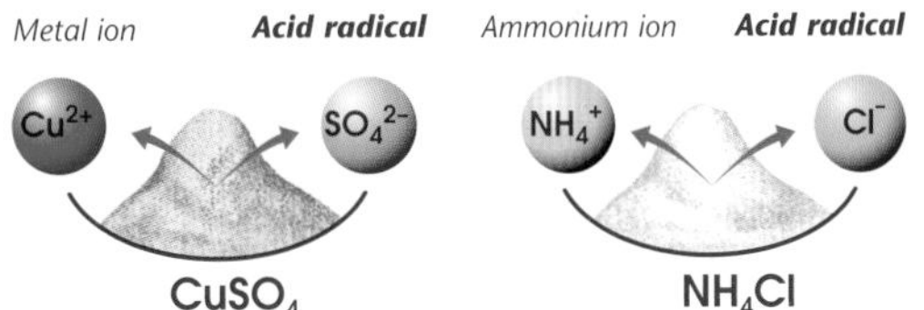
Metal ion
Acid radical
Ammonium ion
Acid radical
Cu^{2+}
SO_4^{2-}
NH_4^+
Cl^-
$CuSO_4$
NH_4Cl

Acid salt

A salt containing hydrogen ions as well as metal ions (or ammonium ions) and the **acid radical**, formed when only some hydrogen ions in an acid are replaced by metal ions (or ammonium ions). Only acids with a **basicity** of two or more can form acid salts. Most acid salts are acidic, but some form alkaline solutions.

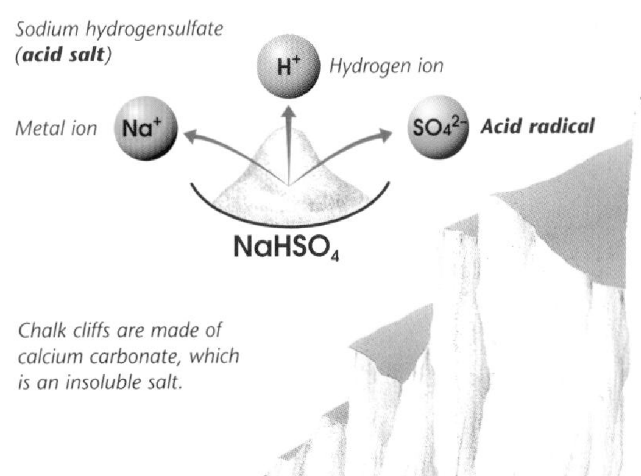
Sodium hydrogensulfate (**acid salt**)
H^+ Hydrogen ion
Metal ion Na^+
SO_4^{2-} Acid radical
$NaHSO_4$

Chalk cliffs are made of calcium carbonate, which is an insoluble salt.

* **Anion**, **Cation**, 130;
Ionic compound, 131.

Basic salt

A salt containing a metal oxide or hydroxide, metal ions and an **acid radical***. It is formed when a **base*** is not completely **neutralized*** by an acid.

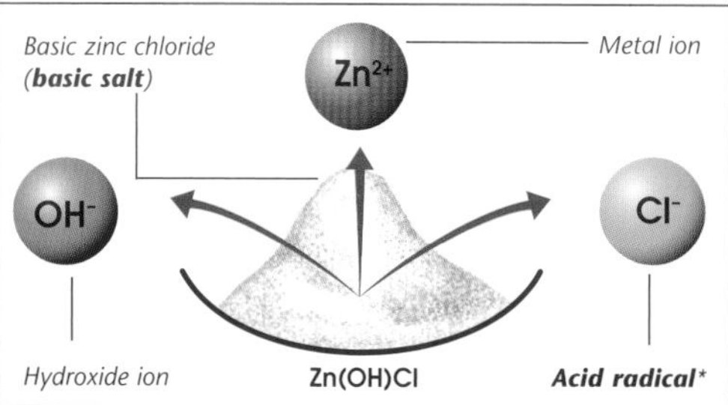

Basic zinc chloride (**basic salt**)
Zn^{2+}
Metal ion
OH^-
Cl^-
Hydroxide ion
Zn(OH)Cl
Acid radical*

Double salt

A salt formed when solutions of two **normal salts*** react together. It contains two different **cations*** (either two different metal ions or a metal ion and an ammonium ion) and one or more **acid radicals***.

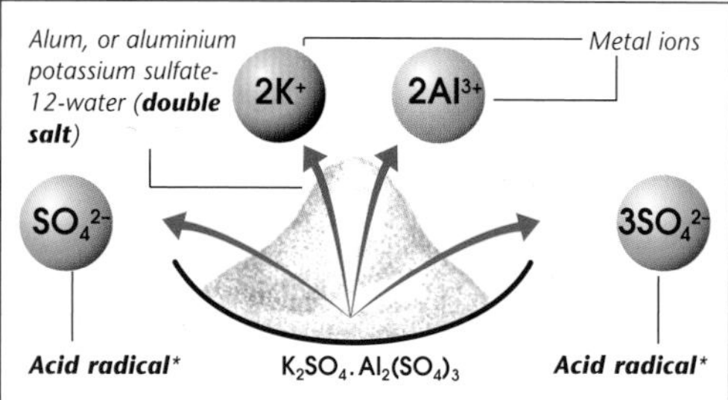

Alum, or aluminium potassium sulfate-12-water (**double salt**)
$2K^+$
$2Al^{3+}$
Metal ions
SO_4^{2-}
$3SO_4^{2-}$
Acid radical*
$K_2SO_4.Al_2(SO_4)_3$
Acid radical*

Complex salt

A salt in which one of the ions is a **complex ion**. This is made up of a central **cation*** linked (frequently by **dative covalent bonds***) to several small molecules (usually **polar molecules***) or ions.

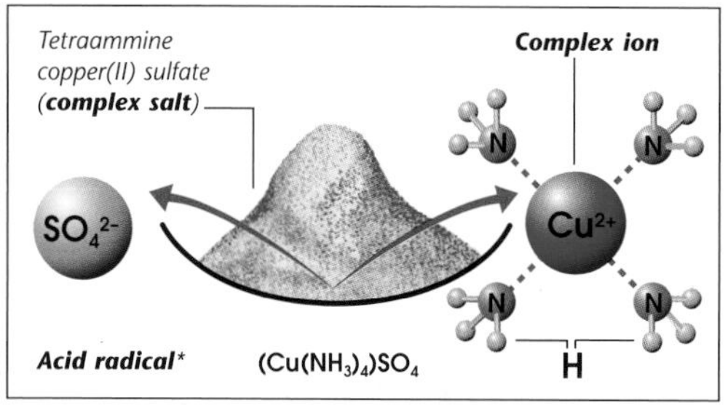

Tetraammine copper(II) sulfate (**complex salt**)
Complex ion
SO_4^{2-}
Cu^{2+}
N
N
N
N
H
Acid radical*
$(Cu(NH_3)_4)SO_4$

Anhydrate

A salt that does not contain **water of crystallization*** (it is **anhydrous**). The salt becomes a **hydrate** if it absorbs water.

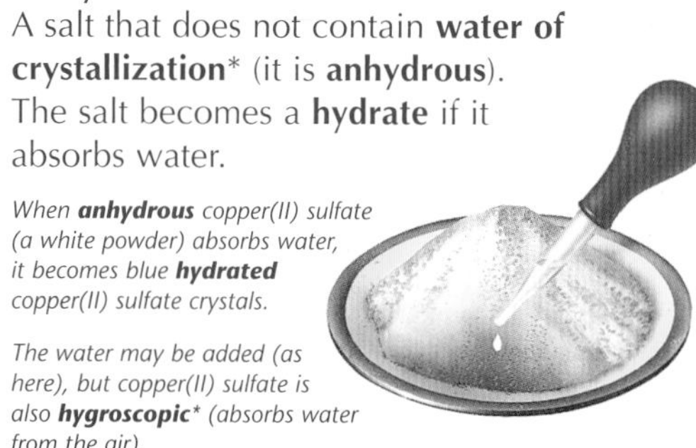

*When **anhydrous** copper(II) sulfate (a white powder) absorbs water, it becomes blue **hydrated** copper(II) sulfate crystals.*

*The water may be added (as here), but copper(II) sulfate is also **hygroscopic*** (absorbs water from the air).*

Hydrate

A salt that contains **water of crystallization*** (it is **hydrated**). The salt becomes an **anhydrate** if the water is removed.

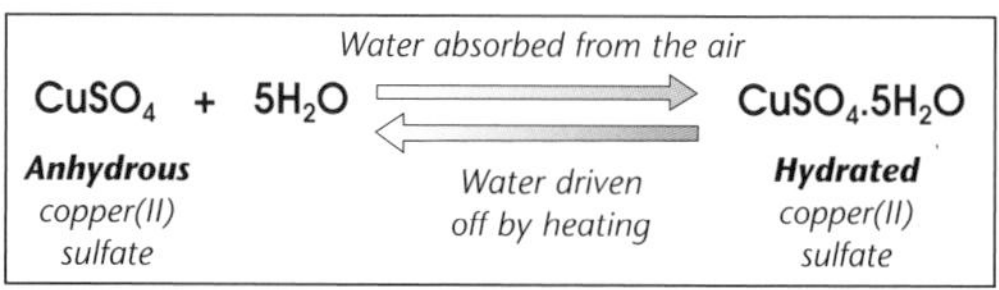

Water absorbed from the air
$CuSO_4 + 5H_2O \rightleftharpoons CuSO_4.5H_2O$
Anhydrous copper(II) sulfate
Water driven off by heating
Hydrated copper(II) sulfate

Dehydration

The removal of water from a substance. It is either removal of hydrogen and oxygen in the correct ratio to give water, or removal of water from a **hydrate** to give an **anhydrate**.

Hydrolysis

The chemical reaction of a compound with water to form another compound. When a salt reacts with water, the ions of the salt react with water molecules. This upsets the balance of hydrogen and hydroxide ions, and so gives an acidic or alkaline solution. A salt which has been made from the reaction between a **weak acid*** and a **strong base*** dissolves to give an alkaline solution. One which has been made from the reaction between a **strong acid*** and a **weak base*** dissolves to give an acidic solution.

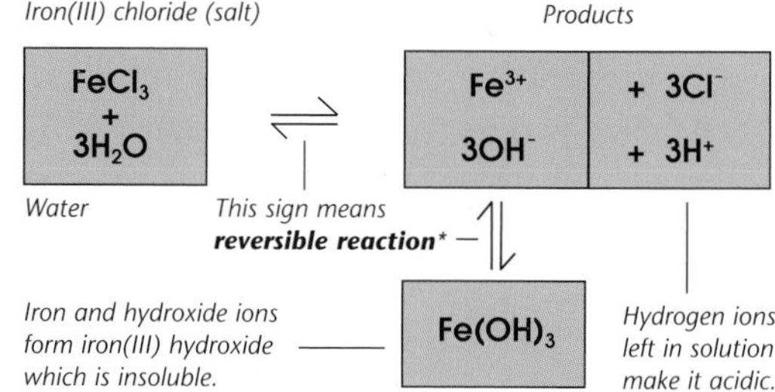

Iron(III) chloride (salt)
Products
$FeCl_3$ + $3H_2O$
Fe^{3+}
$+ 3Cl^-$
$3OH^-$
$+ 3H^+$
Water
This sign means **reversible reaction***
Iron and hydroxide ions form iron(III) hydroxide which is insoluble.
$Fe(OH)_3$
Hydrogen ions left in solution make it acidic.

* **Acid radical**, 153; **Base**, 151; **Cation**, 130; **Dative covalent bond**, 132; **Hygroscopic**, 206; **Neutralization**, 151; **Normal salt**, 153; **Polar molecule**, 133; **Reversible reaction**, 162; **Strong acid**, **Strong base**, 152; **Water of crystallization**, 135; **Weak acid**, **Weak base**, 152.

Preparation of salts

Salts can be made in a number of ways, the method depending on whether a salt is soluble or insoluble in water (see table below). Soluble salts are **crystallized*** from solutions of the salts (obtained in various ways – see below) and insoluble salts are obtained in the form of **precipitates***.

Solubility* of salts

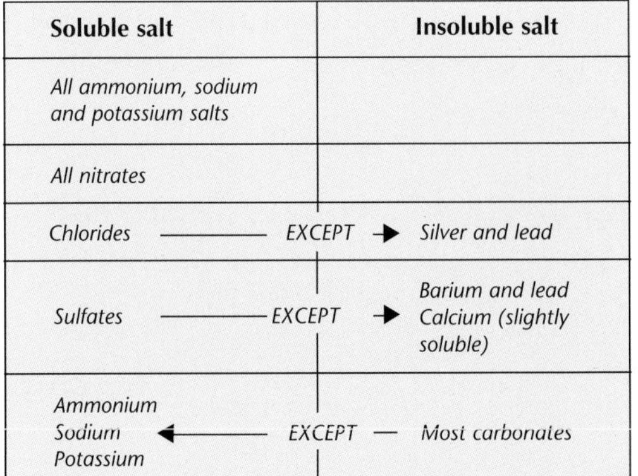

Soluble salt	Insoluble salt
All ammonium, sodium and potassium salts	
All nitrates	
Chlorides —— *EXCEPT* →	*Silver and lead*
Sulfates —— *EXCEPT* →	*Barium and lead* *Calcium (slightly soluble)*
Ammonium *Sodium* *Potassium* ← *EXCEPT* —	*Most carbonates*

Soluble salts can be made by the following methods, which all produce a solution of the salt. This is partly evaporated and left to **crystallize***.

1. **Neutralization***, in which an acid is neutralized by an alkali.

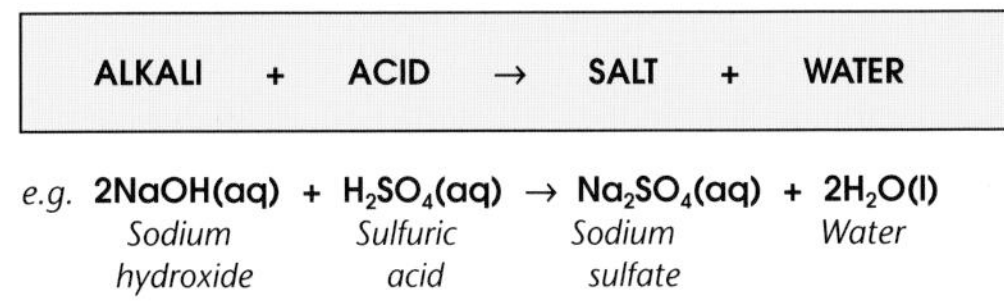

ALKALI + ACID → SALT + WATER

e.g. $2NaOH(aq) + H_2SO_4(aq) \rightarrow Na_2SO_4(aq) + 2H_2O(l)$

Sodium hydroxide, *Sulfuric acid*, *Sodium sulfate*, *Water*

2. The action of an acid on an insoluble carbonate.

INSOLUBLE CARBONATE + ACID → SALT + WATER + CARBON DIOXIDE

e.g. $MgCO_3(s) + 2HCl(aq) \rightarrow MgCl_2(aq) + H_2O(l) + CO_2(g)$

Magnesium carbonate, *Hydrochloric acid*, *Magnesium chloride*, *Water*, *Carbon dioxide*

3. The action of an acid on an insoluble **base***.

INSOLUBLE BASE* + ACID → SALT + WATER

e.g. $CuO(s) + H_2SO_4(aq) \rightarrow CuSO_4(aq) + H_2O(l)$

Copper(II) oxide, *Sulfuric acid*, *Copper(II) sulfate*, *Water*

Double decomposition

A chemical reaction between the solutions of two or more **ionic compounds*** in which ions are exchanged. One of the new compounds formed is an insoluble salt, which forms a **precipitate***. Most insoluble salts and hydroxides are made by this method – the precipitate is filtered out and washed.

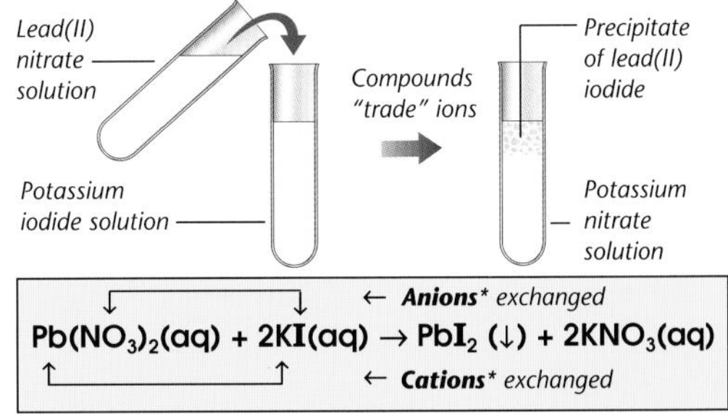

Lead(II) nitrate solution
Potassium iodide solution
Compounds "trade" ions
Precipitate of lead(II) iodide
Potassium nitrate solution
← Anions* exchanged
Pb(NO3)2(aq) + 2KI(aq) → PbI2 (↓) + 2KNO3(aq)
← Cations* exchanged

Direct synthesis

A chemical reaction in which a salt is made directly from its elements. This method is used to make salts which react with water and therefore cannot be made by using solutions.

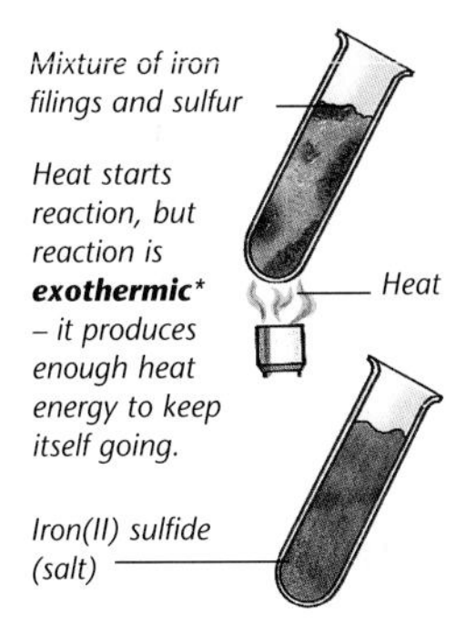

Mixture of iron filings and sulfur
Heat starts reaction, but reaction is exothermic* – it produces enough heat energy to keep itself going.
Heat
Iron(II) sulfide (salt)

$Fe(s) + S(s) \rightarrow FeS(s)$

Direct replacement

A reaction in which all or some of the hydrogen in an acid is replaced by another element, usually a metal. It is used to prepare soluble salts, except salts of sodium or potassium, both of which react too violently with the acid.

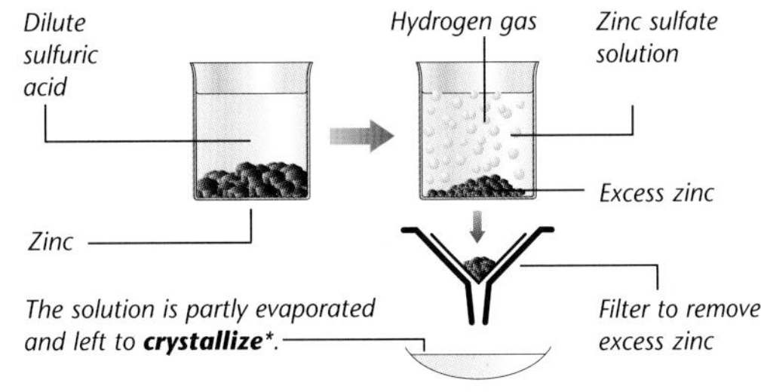

Dilute sulfuric acid
Zinc
Hydrogen gas
Zinc sulfate solution
Excess zinc
The solution is partly evaporated and left to crystallize*.
Filter to remove excess zinc

$Zn(s) + H_2SO_4(aq) \rightarrow ZnSO_4(aq) + H_2(g)$

* **Anion**, 130; **Base**, 151; **Cation**, 130; **Crystallization**, 135; **Exothermic reaction**, 146; **Ionic compound**, 131; **Neutralization**, 151; **Precipitate**, **Solubility**, 145.

ELECTROLYSIS

Electrolysis is a term describing the chemical changes which occur when an electric **current*** is passed through a liquid containing ions. Metals and graphite conduct electric current because some electrons are free to move through the **crystal lattice***, but **molten*** **ionic compounds*** or compounds which **ionize*** in solution conduct electric current by the movement of ions.

Electrolyte

A compound which conducts electricity when **molten*** or in **aqueous solution***, and decomposes during electrolysis. All **ionic compounds*** are electrolytes. They conduct electricity because when molten or in solution their ions are free to move. **Cations*** carry a positive charge and **anions*** a negative one. The number of ions in an electrolyte determines how well it conducts electricity.

Molten* *sodium chloride*

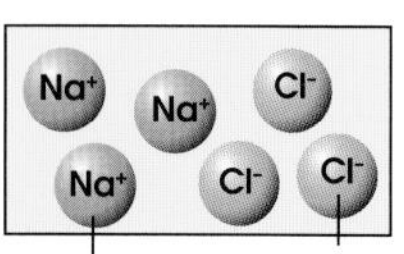

Na^+
Na^+
Cl^-
Na^+
Cl^-
Cl^-
Sodium cation*
Chloride anion*

Copper(II) sulfate solution (an ***aqueous solution****)*

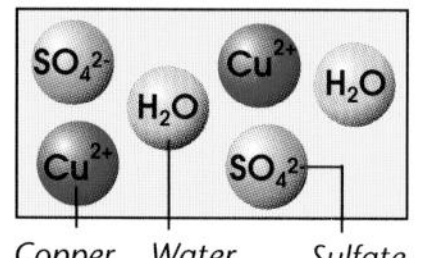

SO_4^{2-}
Cu^{2+}
H_2O
H_2O
Cu^{2+}
SO_4^{2-}
Copper cation*
Water molecule
Sulfate anion*

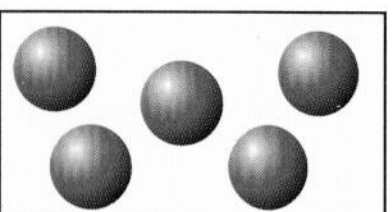

Non-electrolyte *– a compound which does not* ***ionize****.*

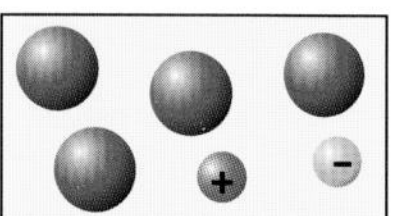

Weak electrolyte *– an* ***electrolyte*** *which is only partially* ***ionized****.*

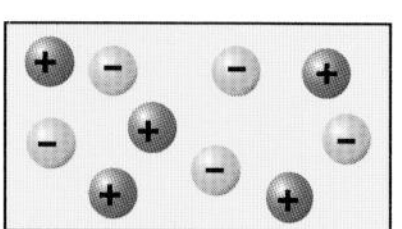

Strong electrolyte *– an* ***electrolyte*** *which is* ***ionized**** *completely.*

Electrode

A piece of metal or graphite placed in an **electrolyte** via which **current*** enters or leaves. There are two electrodes, the **anode** and **cathode**.

Inert electrode

An **electrode** that does not change during electrolysis, e.g. platinum. Some inert electrodes do react with the substances liberated.

Active electrode

An **electrode**, usually a metal, which undergoes chemical change during electrolysis.

Electrolytic cell

A vessel containing the **electrolyte** (either **molten*** or in **aqueous solution***) and the **electrodes**.

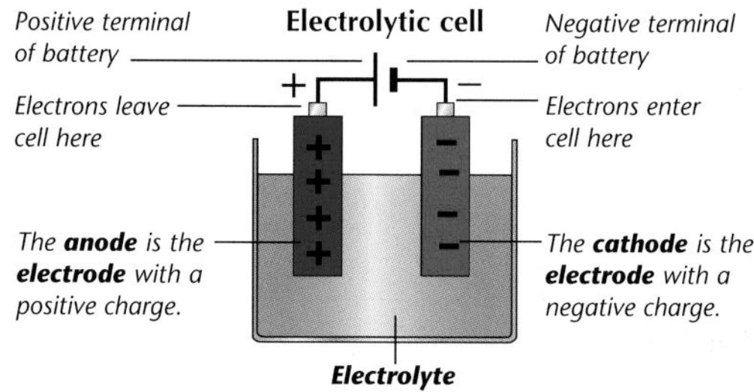

Electrolytic cell
Positive terminal of battery
Negative terminal of battery
Electrons leave cell here
Electrons enter cell here
The anode is the electrode with a positive charge.
The cathode is the electrode with a negative charge.
Electrolyte

Ionic theory of electrolysis

A theory which attempts to explain what happens in an **electrolytic cell** when it is connected to a supply of electricity. It states that **anions*** in the electrolyte are attracted to the **anode** (see **electrode**) where they lose electrons. The **cations*** are attracted to the **cathode** where they gain electrons. The ions which react at the electrodes are **discharged**. Electrons flow from the anode to the battery and from the battery to the cathode.

Electrolysis of molten* sodium chloride

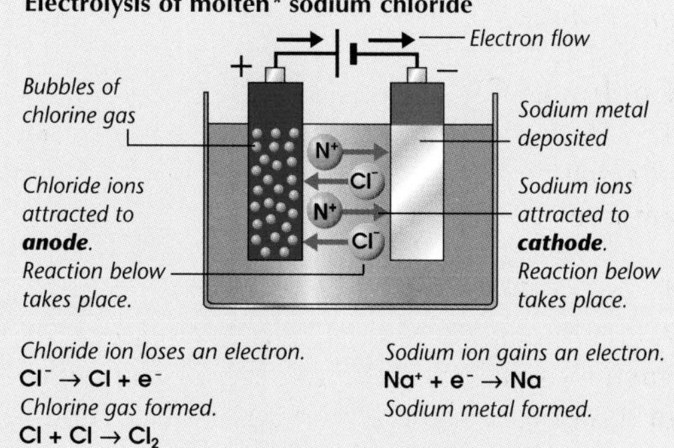

Electron flow
Bubbles of chlorine gas
Sodium metal deposited
Chloride ions attracted to anode.
Reaction below takes place.
Sodium ions attracted to cathode.
Reaction below takes place.
N^+
Cl^-
N^+
Cl^-

Chloride ion loses an electron.
$Cl^- \rightarrow Cl + e^-$
Chlorine gas formed.
$Cl + Cl \rightarrow Cl_2$

Sodium ion gains an electron.
$Na^+ + e^- \rightarrow Na$
Sodium metal formed.

* **Anion**, 130; **Aqueous solution**, 144; **Cation**, 130; **Crystal lattice**, 136; **Current**, 159; **Ionic compound**, 131; **Ionization**, 130; **Molten**, 120.

Faraday's first law of electrolysis

The mass of a substance produced by chemical reactions at the **electrodes** during electrolysis is proportional to the amount of electricity passed through the **electrolyte**.

Amount of electricity = current × time

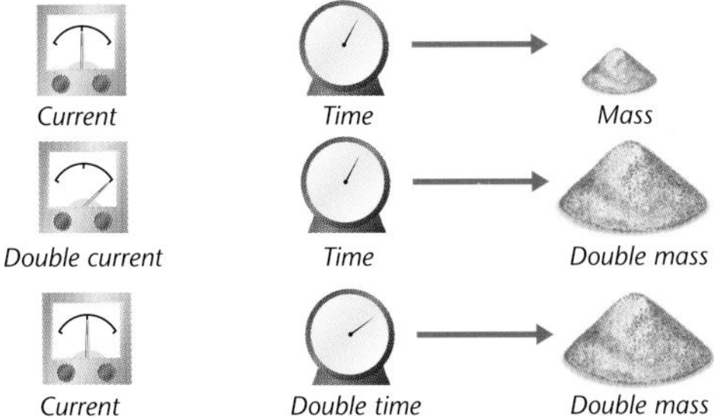
Current
Time
Mass
Double current
Time
Double mass
Current
Double time
Double mass

Faraday's second law of electrolysis

When the same amount of electricity is passed through different **electrolytes**, the number of **moles*** of each element deposited at the **electrodes** is inversely proportional to the size of the charge on its ion.

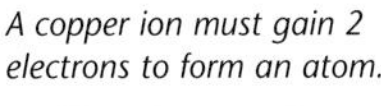

A copper ion must gain 2 electrons to form an atom.

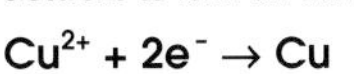

$Cu^{2+} + 2e^- \rightarrow Cu$

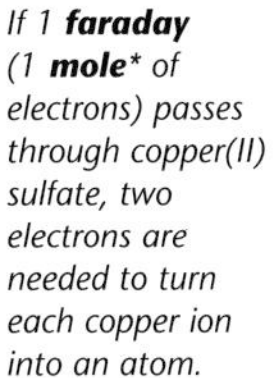

*If 1 **faraday** (1 **mole*** of electrons) passes through copper(II) sulfate, two electrons are needed to turn each copper ion into an atom.*

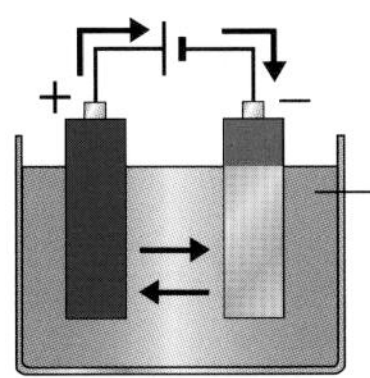

*Hence 1 **faraday** causes ½ **mole** of copper ions to be produced from atoms and deposited on the **cathode**. ½ is inversely proportional to 2 – the charge on a copper ion.*

Other examples:

*1**F** produces one **mole*** sodium atoms from sodium ions (Na^+).*

*1**F** produces $^1/_3$ **mole*** aluminum atoms from its ions (Al^{3+}).*

Voltameter or coulometer

A type of **electrolytic cell** used to measure the amount of a substance liberated during electrolysis.

Coulomb (C)

The **SI unit*** of electric charge. One coulomb of electricity passes a point when one **ampere*** flows for one second.

Faraday (F)

A unit of electric charge equal to 96,500 **coulombs**. It consists of the flow of one **mole*** of electrons and therefore liberates one mole of atoms from singly-charged ions.

Electrolysis in industry

Electro-refining

A method of purifying metals by electrolysis. Only the metal ions take part in electrolysis, the impurities are lost.

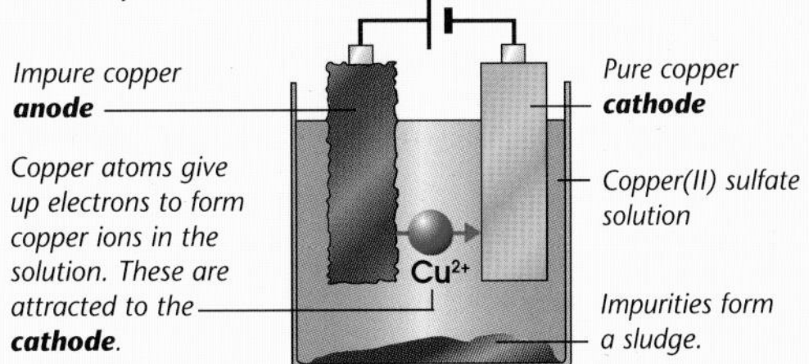
Impure copper
anode
Pure copper
cathode
Copper atoms give up electrons to form copper ions in the solution. These are attracted to the **cathode**.
Cu^{2+}
Copper(II) sulfate solution
Impurities form a sludge.

Metal extraction

A process which produces metals from their **molten*** ores by electrolysis. Metals at the top of the **reactivity series*** are obtained in this way (see **aluminum**, page 176 and **sodium**, page 168).

Anodizing

The coating of a metal object with a thin layer of its oxide. Hydroxide ions are **oxidized*** at the metal **anode** in the electrolysis of dilute sulfuric acid, forming water and oxygen, which oxidizes the metal.

*These aluminum camping flasks have been **anodized** with aluminum oxide to prevent them from corroding.*

Electroplating

The coating of a metal object with a thin layer of another metal by electrolysis. The object forms the **cathode**, onto which metal ions in the **electrolyte** are deposited.

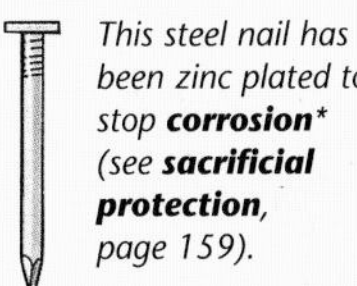

*This steel nail has been zinc plated to stop **corrosion*** (see **sacrificial protection**, page 159).*

DOBRO

The metal front of this guitar has been plated with chrome by electrolysis.

* **Ampere**, 60; **Corrosion**, 209; **Mole**, 139; **Molten**, 120; **Oxidation**, 148; **Reactivity series**, 158; **SI units**, 96.

REACTIVITY

The **reactivity** of an element depends on its ability to gain or lose the electrons which are used for **bonding** (see pages 130-134). The more reactive an element, the more easily it will combine with others. Some elements are very reactive, others very unreactive. This difference can be used to produce electricity and protect metals from **corrosion***.

Displacement

A reaction in which one element replaces another in a compound. An element will only displace another lower than itself in the **reactivity series** (see right).

*Zinc **displaces** copper from copper(II) sulfate solution.*

$$CuSO_4(aq) + Zn(s) \rightarrow ZnSO_4(aq) + Cu(s)$$

Reactivity series or activity series

A list of elements (usually metals), placed in order of their reactivity. The series is constructed by comparing the reactions of the metals with other substances, e.g. acids and oxygen (for a summary of reactions, see page 211).

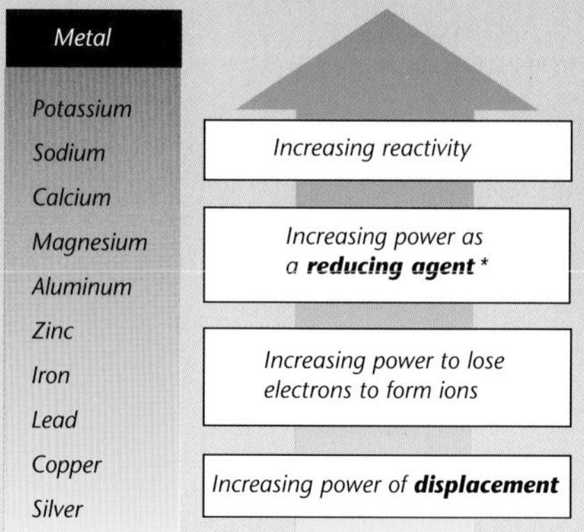

Metal
Potassium
Sodium
Calcium
Magnesium
Aluminum
Zinc
Iron
Lead
Copper
Silver
Increasing reactivity
Increasing power as a reducing agent*
Increasing power to lose electrons to form ions
Increasing power of displacement

Half cell

An element in contact with water or an **aqueous solution*** of one of its compounds. Atoms on the surface form **cations***, which are released into the solution, leaving electrons behind. The solution has a positive charge and the metal a negative charge, so there is a **potential difference** between them.

Electrode potential (E)

The **potential difference** in a **half cell**. It is impossible to measure directly, so is measured relative to that of another half cell, normally a **hydrogen electrode** (see diagram). Electrode potentials show the ability to **ionize*** in **aqueous solution*** and are used to construct the **electrochemical series**.

Measuring the electrode potential of a metal

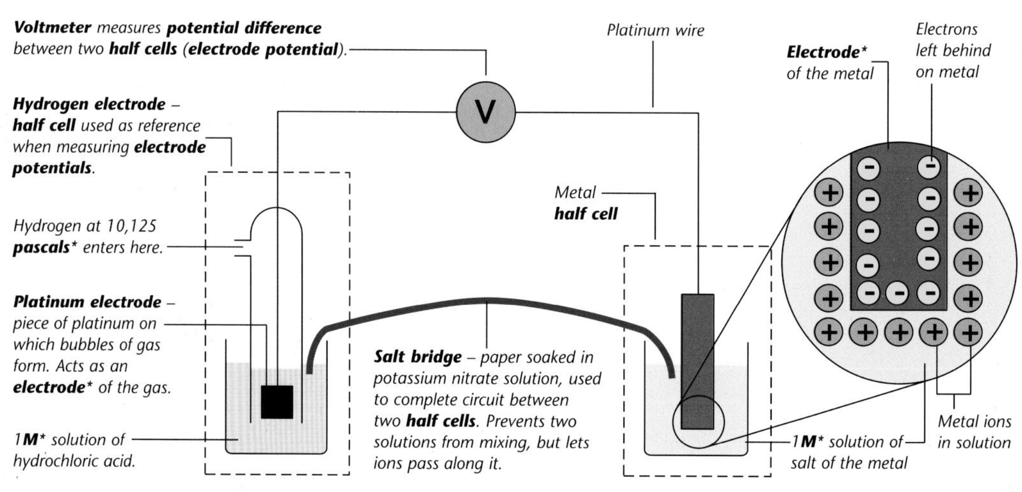

Voltmeter measures potential difference between two half cells (electrode potential).
V
Hydrogen electrode – half cell used as reference when measuring electrode potentials.
Hydrogen at 10,125 pascals* enters here.
Platinum electrode – piece of platinum on which bubbles of gas form. Acts as an electrode* of the gas.
1M* solution of hydrochloric acid.
Salt bridge – paper soaked in potassium nitrate solution, used to complete circuit between two half cells. Prevents two solutions from mixing, but lets ions pass along it.
Platinum wire
Metal half cell
Electrode* of the metal
Electrons left behind on metal
Metal ions in solution
1M* solution of salt of the metal

* **Aqueous solution**, 144; **Cation**, 130; **Corrosion**, 209; **Electrode**, 156; **Ionization**, 130; **M-value**, 139 (**Molarity**); **Pascal**, 97; **Reducing agent**, 148.

Electrochemical series

A list of the elements in order of their **electrode potentials**. The element with the most negative electrode potential is placed at the top. The position of an element in the series shows how readily it forms ions in **aqueous solution***, and is thus an indication of how reactive it is likely to be.

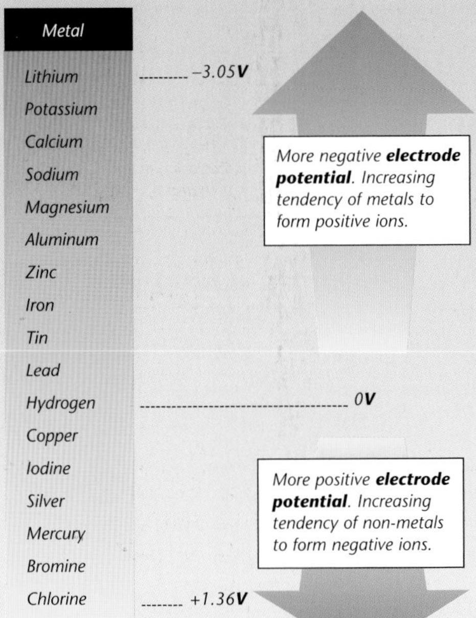
Metal
Lithium
−3.05V
Potassium
Calcium
Sodium
Magnesium
Aluminum
Zinc
Iron
Tin
Lead
Hydrogen
0V
Copper
Iodine
Silver
Mercury
Bromine
Chlorine
+1.36V
More negative electrode potential. Increasing tendency of metals to form positive ions.
More positive electrode potential. Increasing tendency of non-metals to form negative ions.

Cell or electrochemical cell

An arrangement of two **half cells** of different elements. The half cell with the most negative **electrode potential** forms the **negative terminal** and the other forms the **positive terminal**. When these are connected, a **current** flows between them. There are two types of cell – **primary cells**, which cannot be recharged, and **secondary cells**, which can be recharged. A **battery** is a number of linked cells.

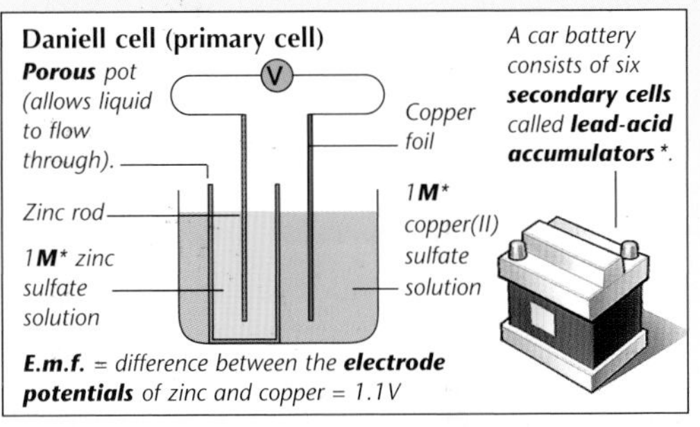
Daniell cell (primary cell)
Porous pot (allows liquid to flow through).
V
Copper foil
Zinc rod
1M* zinc sulfate solution
1M* copper(II) sulfate solution
A car battery consists of six secondary cells called lead-acid accumulators*.
E.m.f. = difference between the electrode potentials of zinc and copper = 1.1V

Potential difference or voltage

A difference in electric charge between two points, measured in **volts** (**V**) by an instrument called a **voltmeter**. If two points with a potential difference are joined, an electric **current**, proportional to the potential difference, flows between them.

Current

A flow of electrons (negatively-charged particles) through a material. The **SI unit*** of current is the **ampere*** (**A**), and current is measured using an **ammeter**. A current will flow in a loop, or **circuit**, between two points if there is a **potential difference** between them.

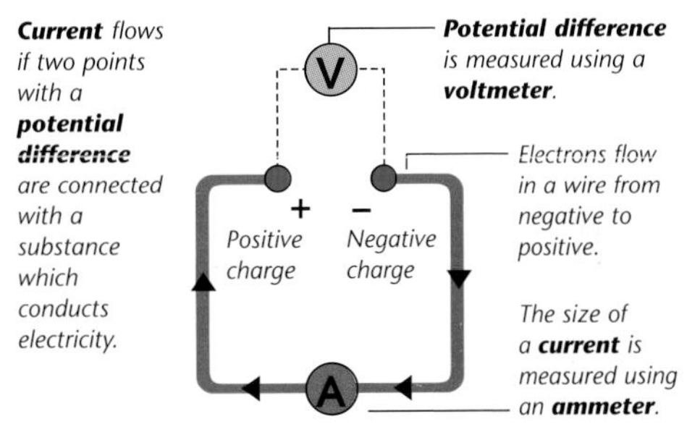
Current flows if two points with a potential difference are connected with a substance which conducts electricity.
Potential difference is measured using a voltmeter.
V
+
−
Positive charge
Negative charge
Electrons flow in a wire from negative to positive.
A
The size of a current is measured using an ammeter.

Electromotive force (e.m.f.)

The name given to the **potential difference** between the two terminals of a **cell** (i.e. the difference between the **electrode potentials** of the two **half cells**).

Sacrificial protection

Also known as **cathodic protection** or **electrical protection**. A method of preventing iron from **rusting*** by attaching a metal higher in the **electrochemical series** to it, which rusts instead.

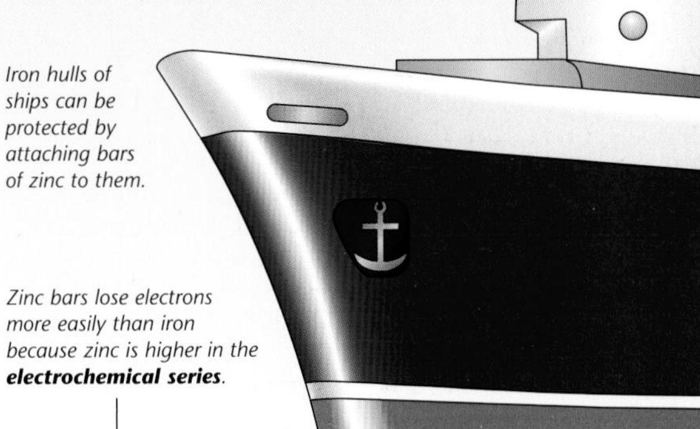
Iron hulls of ships can be protected by attaching bars of zinc to them.
Zinc bars lose electrons more easily than iron because zinc is higher in the electrochemical series.

* **Ampere**, 60; **Aqueous solution**, 144; **Lead-acid accumulator**, 69; **M-value**, 139 (**Molarity**); **Rusting**, 209 (**Corrosion**); **SI units**, 96.

RATES OF REACTION

The time it takes for a chemical reaction to finish varies from less than one millionth of a second to weeks or even years. It is possible to predict how long a particular reaction will take and how to speed it up or slow it down by altering the conditions under which it takes place. The efficiency of many industrial processes is improved by increasing the **rate of reaction**, e.g. by using high temperature and pressure, or a **catalyst**.

Rate of reaction

A measurement of the speed of a reaction. It is calculated by measuring how quickly reactants are used up or products are formed. The experimental method used to measure the rate of reaction depends on the **physical states*** of the reactants and products, and the data from such an experiment is plotted on a **rate curve**. The speed of a reaction varies as it proceeds. The rate at any time during the reaction is the **instantaneous rate**. The instantaneous rate at the start of the reaction is the **initial rate**. The **average rate** is calculated by dividing the total change in the amount of products or reactants by the time the reaction took to finish.

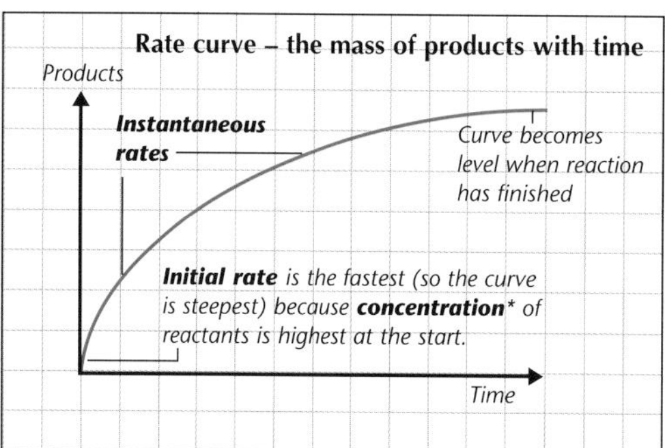
Rate curve – the mass of products with time
Products
Instantaneous rates
Curve becomes level when reaction has finished
Initial rate is the fastest (so the curve is steepest) because concentration* of reactants is highest at the start.
Time

Collision theory

Explains why altering the conditions under which a reaction takes place affects its rate. For a reaction to take place between two particles, they must collide, so if more collisions occur, the **rate of reaction** increases. However, only some collisions cause a reaction, since not all particles have enough energy to react (see **activation energy**, right).

Photochemical reaction

A reaction whose speed is affected by the intensity of light, e.g. **photosynthesis***. Light gives reacting particles more energy and so increases the **rate of reaction**.

Photosynthesis* *– the process by which plants make their food – is a* ***photochemical reaction****.*

Photochemical reactions *occur in photography.*

Silver crystals form where light falls on the film, recording the picture.

$$2AgCl(s) \rightarrow 2Ag(s) + Cl_2(g)$$

Activation energy (E)

The minimum energy that the particles of reactants must have for them to react when they collide (see **collision theory**). The **rate of reaction** depends on how many reacting particles have this minimum energy. In many reactions, the particles already have this energy and react immediately. In others, energy has to be supplied for the particles to reach the activation energy.

Friction produces heat, giving ***activation energy*** *to the particles in the match.*

* **Concentration**, 139; **Physical states**, 120; **Photosynthesis**, 209.

Changing rates of reaction

The **rate of reaction** will increase if the temperature is increased. The heat energy gives more particles an energy greater than the **activation energy**.

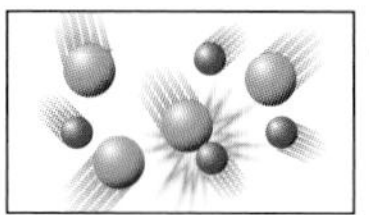

Heat added

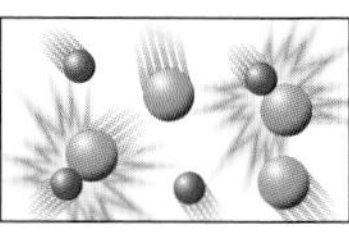

Heated particles collide with greater energy, so more react.

For reactions involving gases, the **rate of reaction** will increase if the pressure is increased. An increase in the pressure of a gas increases the temperature and decreases the volume (i.e. increases the **concentration*** – see also **gas laws**, page 142). The particles collide more often and with greater energy.

The **rate of reaction** will increase if the **concentration*** of one or more of the reactants is increased.

More molecules in the same space means more collisions.

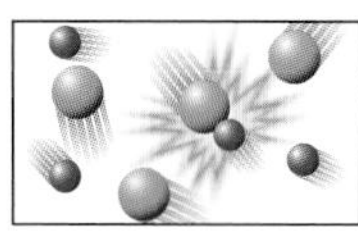

Low **concentration***

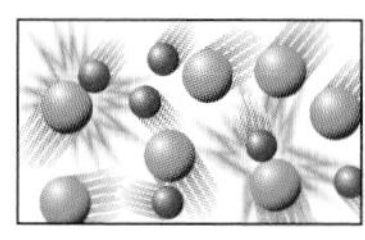

High **concentration***

The **rate of reaction** will increase if the surface area of a solid reactant is increased. Reactions in which one reactant is a solid can only take place at the surface of the solid.

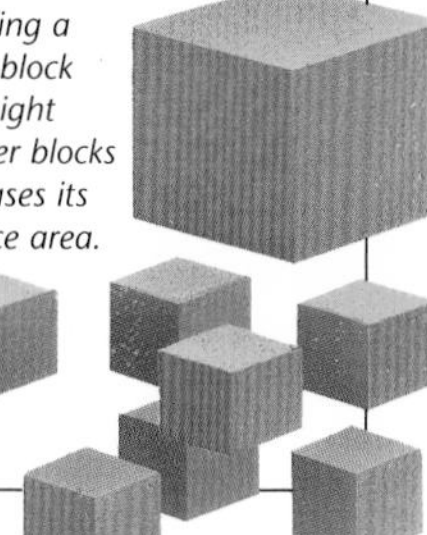

Breaking a large block into eight smaller blocks increases its surface area.

Catalyst

A substance that increases the rate of a chemical reaction, but is chemically unchanged itself at the end of the reaction. This process is known as **catalysis**. Catalysts work by lowering the **activation energy** of a reaction. The catalyst used in a reaction is written over the arrow in the equation (see page 182). A catalyst which increases the rate of one reaction may have no effect on another.

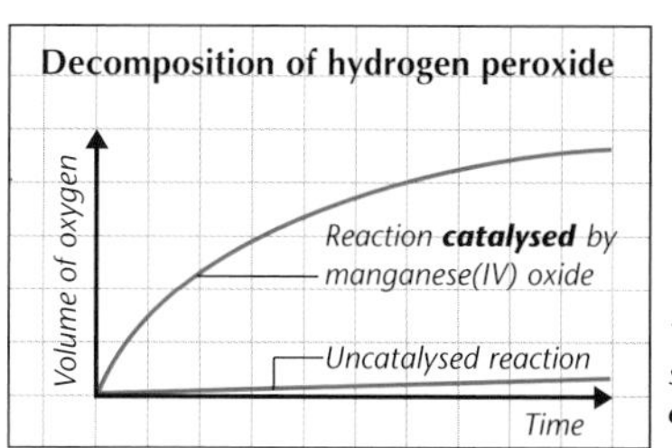

Decomposition of hydrogen peroxide
Volume of oxygen
Time
Reaction catalysed by manganese(IV) oxide
Uncatalysed reaction

Hydrogen peroxide decomposes to form oxygen and water.

*The reaction speeds up when a **catalyst** is used.*

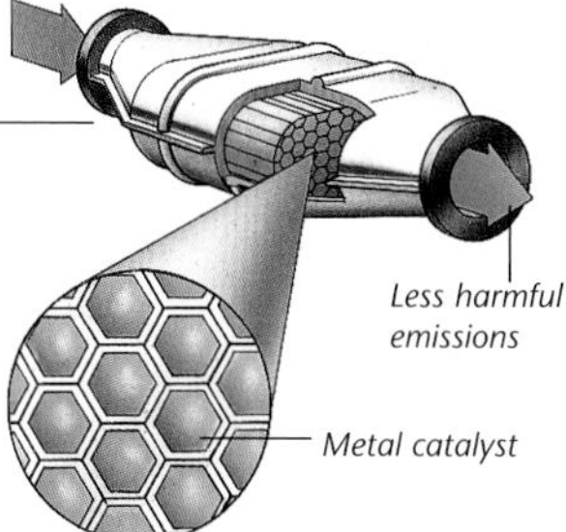

Less harmful emissions
Metal catalyst

*A catalytic converter in a car's exhaust system contains two metals, platinum and rhodium, which act as **catalysts**.*

Toxic carbon monoxide and hydrocarbons cling to the metals and react together to form carbon dioxide and water.

Autocatalysis

A process in which one of the products of a reaction acts as a **catalyst** for the reaction.

Surface catalyst

A **catalyst** which attracts the reactants to itself. It holds them close to each other on its surface, so they react easily.

Homogenous catalyst

A **catalyst** in the same **physical state*** as the reactants.

Heterogenous catalyst

A **catalyst** in a different **physical state*** from that of the reactants.

Promoter

A substance which increases the power of a **catalyst**, so speeding up the reaction.

Inhibitor

A substance that slows a reaction. Some work by reducing the power of a **catalyst**.

Enzyme

A **catalyst** found in living things which increases the **rate of reaction** in a natural chemical process. For more about enzymes, see page 333.

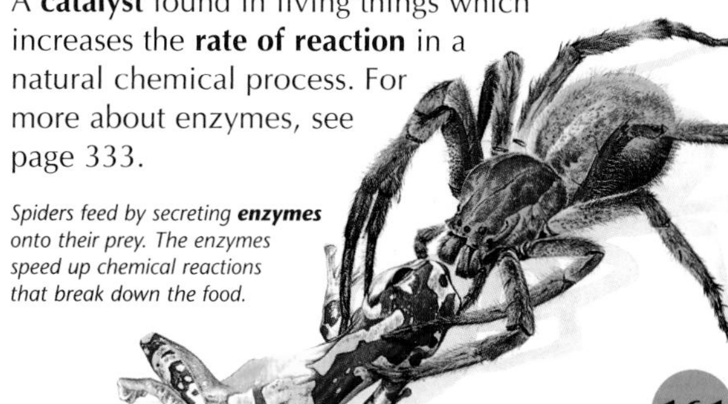

*Spiders feed by secreting **enzymes** onto their prey. The enzymes speed up chemical reactions that break down the food.*

* **Concentration**, 139; **Physical states**, 120.

REVERSIBLE REACTIONS

Many chemical reactions continue until one or all of the reactants are used up, and their products do not react together. When a reaction reaches this stage, it is said to have come to **completion**. Other reactions, however, never reach this stage. They are known as **reversible reactions**.

Reversible reaction

A chemical reaction in which the products react together to form the original reactants. These react again to form the products, and so on. The two reactions are simultaneous, and the process will not come to **completion** (see introduction) if it takes place in a **closed system**. At some stage during a reversible reaction, **chemical equilibrium** is reached.

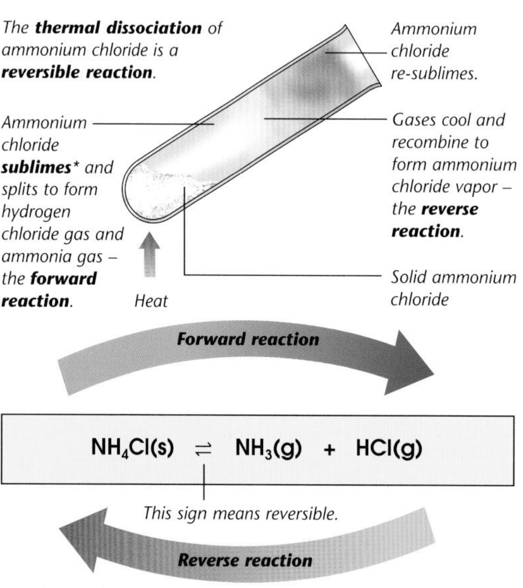

*The **thermal dissociation** of ammonium chloride is a **reversible reaction**.*
Ammonium chloride re-sublimes.
*Ammonium chloride **sublimes*** and splits to form hydrogen chloride gas and ammonia gas – the **forward reaction**.*
*Gases cool and recombine to form ammonium chloride vapor – the **reverse reaction**.*
Heat
Solid ammonium chloride
Forward reaction
$NH_4Cl(s) \rightleftharpoons NH_3(g) + HCl(g)$
This sign means reversible.
Reverse reaction

Forward reaction

The reaction in which products are formed from the original reactants in a **reversible reaction**. It goes from left to right in the equation.

Reverse reaction or backward reaction

The reaction in which the original reactants are reformed from their products in a **reversible reaction**. It goes from right to left in the equation.

*This tug of war represents a chemical reaction. The blue team are the reactants and the red team the products. If the red team wins, the reaction is a **forward reaction**. If the blue team wins, it is a **reverse reaction**.*

Dissociation

A type of **reversible reaction** in which a compound is divided into other compounds or elements. **Thermal dissociation** is dissociation caused by heating (the products formed recombine when cooled). Dissociation should not be confused with **decomposition**, in which a compound is irreversibly split up.

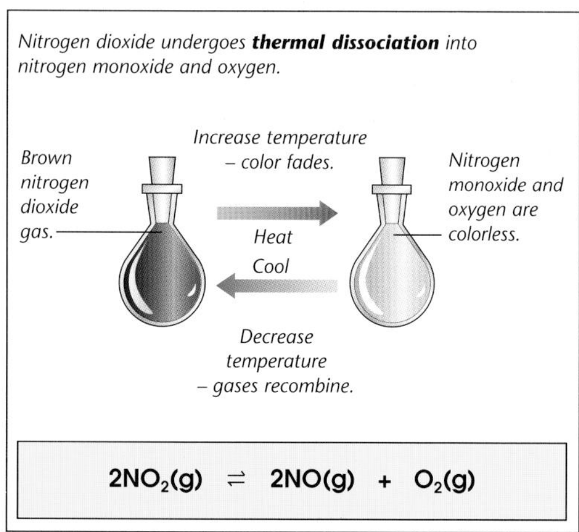

*Nitrogen dioxide undergoes **thermal dissociation** into nitrogen monoxide and oxygen.*
Brown nitrogen dioxide gas.
Increase temperature – color fades.
Heat
Cool
Nitrogen monoxide and oxygen are colorless.
Decrease temperature – gases recombine.
$2NO_2(g) \rightleftharpoons 2NO(g) + O_2(g)$

Closed system

A **system*** in which no chemicals can escape or enter. If a product of a **reversible reaction** escapes, for example into the atmosphere, the reaction can no longer move back the other way. A system from which chemicals can escape is an **open system**.

Equilibrium

The canceling out of two equal but opposite movements. For instance, a person walking up an escalator at the same speed as the escalator is moving down is in equilibrium. **Chemical equilibrium** is an example of equilibrium – it occurs when the **forward** and **reverse reactions** are taking place, but are canceling each other out.

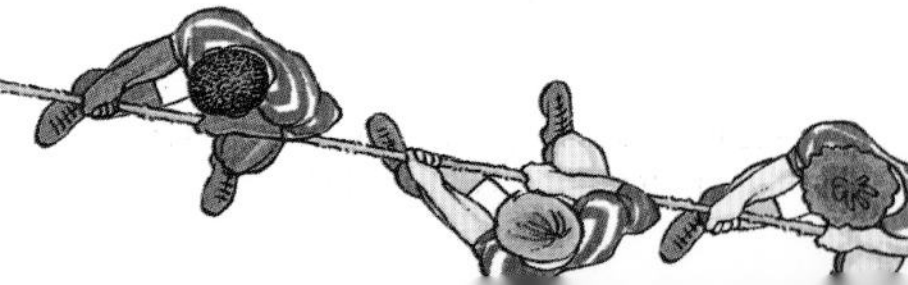

* **Sublimation**, 121; **System**, 345.

Chemical equilibrium

A stage reached in a **reversible reaction** in a **closed system** when the **forward** and **reverse reactions** take place at the same rate. Their effects cancel each other out, and the **concentrations*** of the reactants and products no longer change. Chemical equilibrium is a form of **equilibrium**.

*At start of reaction, higher **concentration*** of products than reactants.*

Fast **forward reaction**

Reactants  Products

Slow **reverse reaction**

*At **chemical equilibrium**, products and reactants formed at same rate.*

Reactants  Products

The position of chemical equilibrium

Any change of conditions (temperature, **concentration*** or pressure) during a **reversible reaction** alters the rate of either the **forward** or **reverse reaction**, destroying the **chemical equilibrium**. This is eventually restored, but with a different proportion of reactants and products. The **equilibrium position** is said to have changed.

*First **equilibrium position***

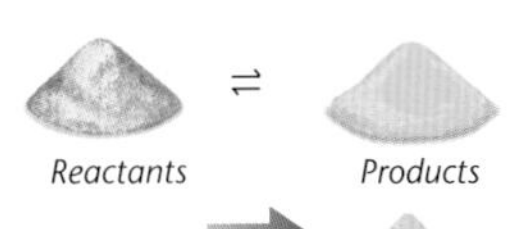

Reactants Products

*Alter conditions to favor **forward reaction** – **equilibrium position** is said to move right.*

More products formed.

*Alter conditions to favor **reverse reaction** – **equilibrium position** is said to move left.*

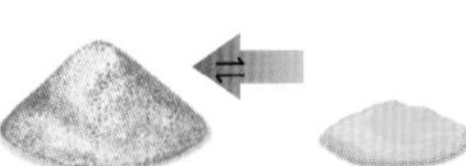

More reactants formed.

Le Chatelier's principle

A law stating that if changes are made to a **system*** in **equilibrium**, the system adjusts itself to reduce the effects of the change.

1. Changing the pressure in **reversible reactions** involving gases may alter the **equilibrium position**.

In the reaction $A(g) + B(g) \rightleftharpoons AB(g)$:

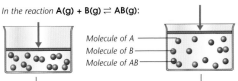

Molecule of A
Molecule of B
Molecule of AB

Raise pressure – position moves right – more AB formed – i.e. number of molecules decreases to lower pressure again.

Lower pressure – position moves left – more A and B formed – i.e. number of molecules increases to raise pressure again.

2. Changing the temperature in a **reversible reaction** also alters the **equilibrium position**. This depends on whether the reaction is **exothermic*** or **endothermic***. A reversible reaction which is exothermic in one direction is endothermic in the other.

*Ammonia is made by the **Haber process****.

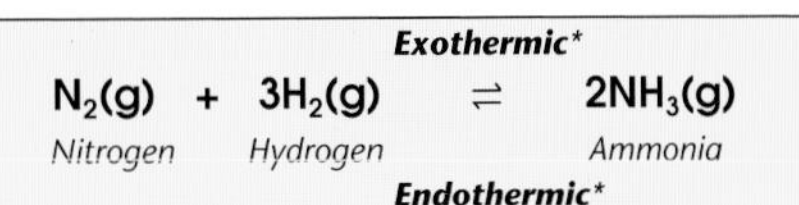
Exothermic*
N2(g) + 3H2(g) ⇌ 2NH3(g)
Nitrogen
Hydrogen
Ammonia
Endothermic*

N2
H2
NH3

*Temperature rises – rate of **endothermic* reverse reaction** increases to absorb heat. Less ammonia formed – position moves left.*

N2
H2
NH3

*Temperature falls – rate of **exothermic* forward reaction** increases, giving out more heat energy. More ammonia produced – position moves right.*

3. Changing the **concentration*** of the reactants or products in a **reversible reaction** also changes the equilibrium position.

*Raise **concentration*** of reactants – rate of **forward reaction** increased.* OR *Lower **concentration** of products – rate of **reverse reaction** decreased.*

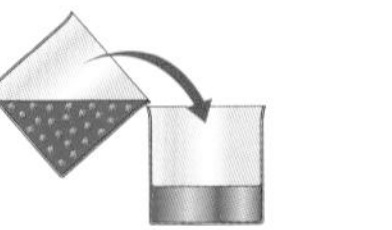

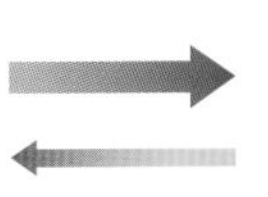

***Equilibrium position** moves right.*

*Lower **concentration** of reactants – rate of **forward reaction** decreased.* OR *Raise **concentration** of products – rate of **reverse reaction** increased.*

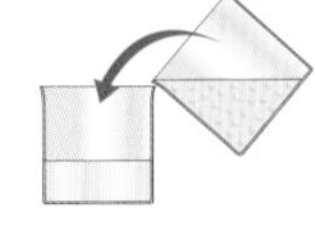

***Equilibrium position** moves left.*

* **Concentration**, 139; **Endothermic reaction**, **Exothermic reaction**, 146; **Haber process**, 180; **System**, 345.

THE PERIODIC TABLE

During the nineteenth century, many chemists tried to arrange the elements in an order which related to the size of their atoms and also showed regular repeating patterns in their behavior or properties. The most successful attempt was published by the Russian, Dimitri Mendeléev, in 1869, and still forms the basis of the modern **periodic table**.

Periodic table

An arrangement of the elements in order of their **atomic numbers***. Both the physical properties and chemical properties of an element and its compounds are related to the position of the element in the periodic table. This relationship has led to the table being divided into **groups** and **periods**. The arrangement of the elements starts on the left of period 1 with hydrogen and moves in order of increasing atomic number from left to right across each period in turn (see picture on the right).

Period

A horizontal row of elements in the **periodic table**. There are seven periods in all. Period 1 has only two elements – hydrogen and helium. Periods 2 and 3 each contain eight elements and are called the **short periods**. Periods 4, 5, 6 and 7 each contain between 18 and 32 elements. They are called the **long periods**. Moving from left to right across a period, the **atomic number*** increases by one from one element to the next. Each successive element has one more electron in the **outer shell*** of its atoms. All elements in the same period have the same number of shells, and the regular change in the number of electrons from one element to the next leads to a fairly regular pattern of change in the chemical properties of the elements across a period. For an example of such a gradual change in property, see below.

Periodic table

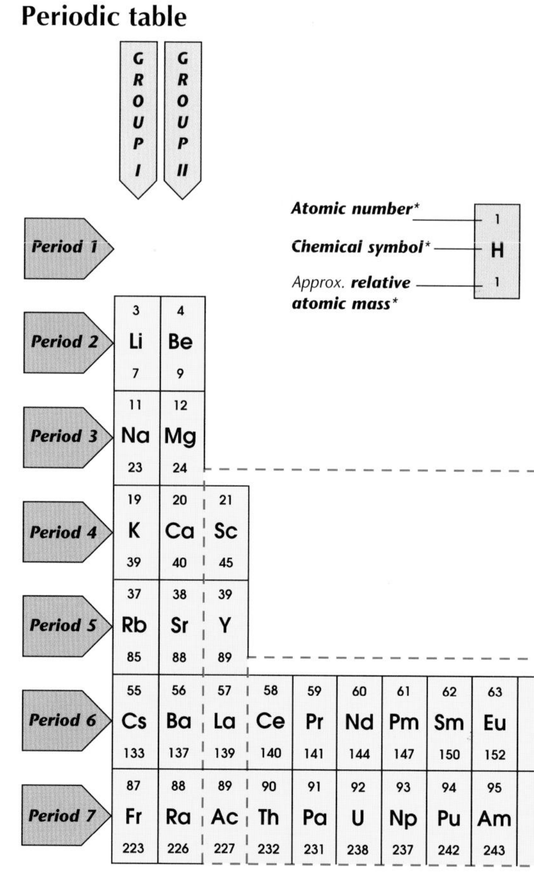

GROUP I
GROUP II
Atomic number*
Chemical symbol*
Approx. relative atomic mass*
1 H 1
Period 1
Period 2
Period 3
Period 4
Period 5
Period 6
Period 7
3 Li 7
4 Be 9
11 Na 23
12 Mg 24
19 K 39
20 Ca 40
21 Sc 45
37 Rb 85
38 Sr 88
39 Y 89
55 Cs 133
56 Ba 137
57 La 139
58 Ce 140
59 Pr 141
60 Nd 144
61 Pm 147
62 Sm 150
63 Eu 152
87 Fr 223
88 Ra 226
89 Ac 227
90 Th 232
91 Pa 231
92 U 238
93 Np 237
94 Pu 242
95 Am 243

Electron configuration* of elements across Period 2

All elements have the same ***outer shell****, but each successive element, going from left to right, has one more electron added to that shell.*

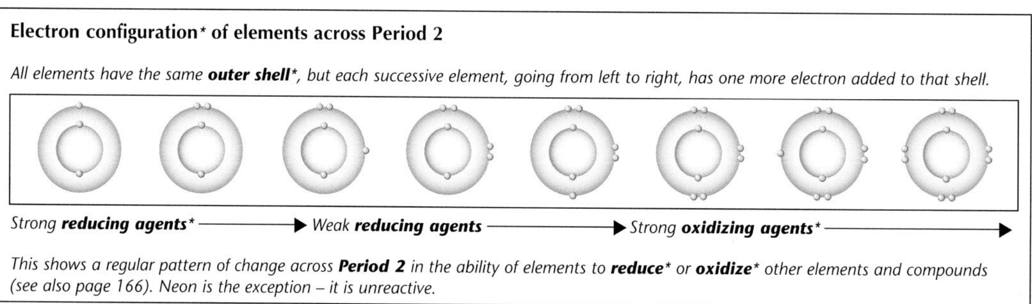

Strong reducing agents*
Weak reducing agents
Strong oxidizing agents*

This shows a regular pattern of change across ***Period 2*** *in the ability of elements to* ***reduce**** *or* ***oxidize**** *other elements and compounds (see also page 166). Neon is the exception – it is unreactive.*

* **Atomic number**, 127; **Chemical symbol**, 122; **Electron configuration**, **Outer shell**, 127; **Oxidation**, **Oxidizing agent**, **Reducing agent**, **Reduction**, 148; **Relative atomic mass**, 138.

Group

A vertical column of elements in the **periodic table**. All groups are numbered (except for **transition metal*** groups) using Roman numerals, and some have names. Elements in the same group have the same number of electrons in their **outer shell***, and so have similar chemical properties.

Groups with alternative names

Group number	***Group name***
Group I	*The **alkali metals** (see pages 168-169)*
Group II	*The **alkaline-earth metals** (see pages 170-171)*
Group VII	*The **halogens** (see pages 186-188)*
Group VIII *(or **Group 0**)*	*The **noble gases** (see page 189)*

Color-coding used in table

Metals ***Metalloids*** ***Non-metals***

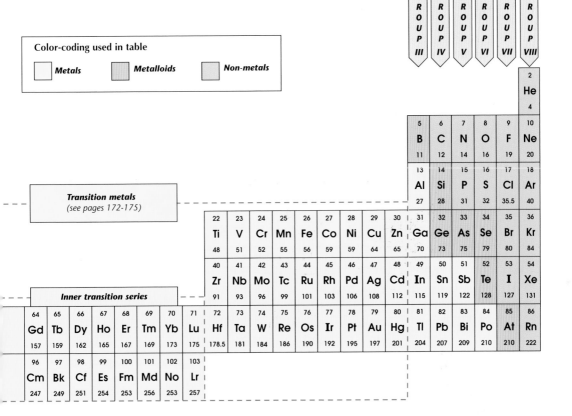

Transition metals
(see pages 172-175)

Inner transition series

																	GROUP III	GROUP IV	GROUP V	GROUP VI	GROUP VII	GROUP VIII
																						2 He 4
																	5 B 11	6 C 12	7 N 14	8 O 16	9 F 19	10 Ne 20
																	13 Al 27	14 Si 28	15 P 31	16 S 32	17 Cl 35.5	18 Ar 40
								22 Ti 48	23 V 51	24 Cr 52	25 Mn 55	26 Fe 56	27 Co 59	28 Ni 59	29 Cu 64	30 Zn 65	31 Ga 70	32 Ge 73	33 As 75	34 Se 79	35 Br 80	36 Kr 84
								40 Zr 91	41 Nb 93	42 Mo 96	43 Tc 99	44 Ru 101	45 Rh 103	46 Pd 106	47 Ag 108	48 Cd 112	49 In 115	50 Sn 119	51 Sb 122	52 Te 128	53 I 127	54 Xe 131
64 Gd 157	65 Tb 159	66 Dy 162	67 Ho 165	68 Er 167	69 Tm 169	70 Yb 173	71 Lu 175	72 Hf 178.5	73 Ta 181	74 W 184	75 Re 186	76 Os 190	77 Ir 192	78 Pt 195	79 Au 197	80 Hg 201	81 Tl 204	82 Pb 207	83 Bi 209	84 Po 210	85 At 210	86 Rn 222
96 Cm 247	97 Bk 249	98 Cf 251	99 Es 254	100 Fm 253	101 Md 256	102 No 253	103 Lr 257															

Metals and non-metals

Metal

An element with characteristic physical properties that distinguish it from a **non-metal**. Elements on the left of a **period** have metallic properties. Moving to the right, the elements gradually become less metallic. Elements that are not distinctly metal or non-metal, but have a mixture of properties, are called **metalloids**. Elements to the right of metalloids are non-metals.

Property	Metal	Non-metal
Physical state*	*Solids (except mercury)*	*Solid, liquid or gas (bromine is the only liquid).*
Appearance	*Shiny*	*Mainly non-shiny (iodine is one of the exceptions).*
Conductivity*	*Good*	*Poor (except graphite)*
Malleability*	*Good*	*Poor*
Ductility*	*Good*	*Poor*
Melting point	*Generally high*	*Generally low (except carbon)*
Boiling point	*Generally high*	*Generally low*

* **Conductivity**, 28, 63; **Ductility**, 344 (**Ductile**); **Malleability**, 345 (**Malleable**); **Outer shell**, 127; **Physical states**, 120; **Transition metals**, 172.

INORGANIC CHEMISTRY

Inorganic chemistry is the study of all the elements and their compounds except those compounds made of chains of carbon atoms (see **organic chemistry**, pages 190-205). The properties and reactions of inorganic elements and compounds follow certain patterns, or **trends**, in the **periodic table***. By looking up and down **groups*** and across **periods*** of the table, it is possible to predict the reactions of elements.

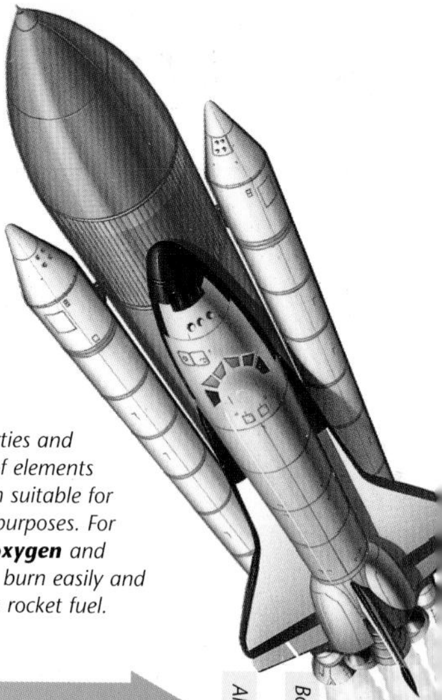

The properties and reactions of elements make them suitable for particular purposes. For example, ***oxygen*** *and* ***hydrogen*** *burn easily and are used in rocket fuel.*

Major periodic table trends

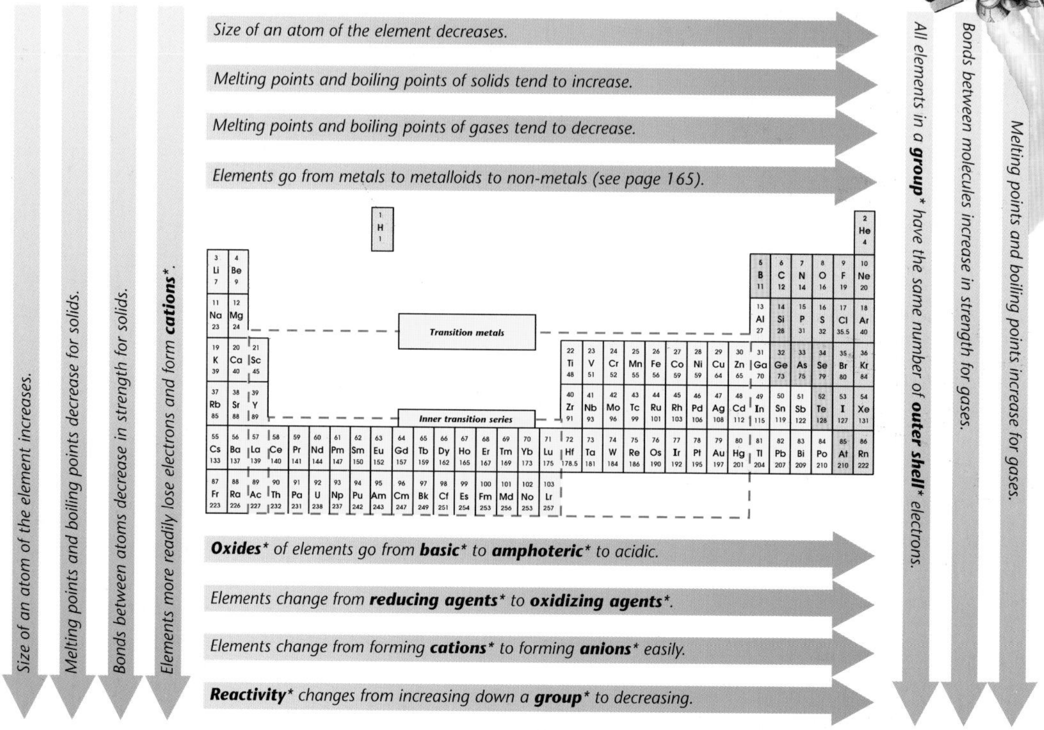

Size of an atom of the element decreases.

Melting points and boiling points of solids tend to increase.

Melting points and boiling points of gases tend to decrease.

Elements go from metals to metalloids to non-metals (see page 165).

Size of an atom of the element increases.

Melting points and boiling points decrease for solids.

Bonds between atoms decrease in strength for solids.

Elements more readily lose electrons and form ***cations****.*

								1 H 1																							2 He 4
3 Li 7	4 Be 9																									5 B 11	6 C 12	7 N 14	8 O 16	9 F 19	10 Ne 20
11 Na 23	12 Mg 24																									13 Al 27	14 Si 28	15 P 31	16 S 32	17 Cl 35.5	18 Ar 40
19 K 39	20 Ca 40	21 Sc 45															22 Ti 48	23 V 51	24 Cr 52	25 Mn 55	26 Fe 56	27 Co 59	28 Ni 59	29 Cu 64	30 Zn 65	31 Ga 70	32 Ge 73	33 As 75	34 Se 79	35 Br 80	36 Kr 84
37 Rb 85	38 Sr 88	39 Y 89															40 Zr 91	41 Nb 93	42 Mo 96	43 Tc 99	44 Ru 101	45 Rh 103	46 Pd 106	47 Ag 108	48 Cd 112	49 In 115	50 Sn 119	51 Sb 122	52 Te 128	53 I 127	54 Xe 131
55 Cs 133	56 Ba 137	57 La 139	58 Ce 140	59 Pr 141	60 Nd 144	61 Pm 147	62 Sm 150	63 Eu 152	64 Gd 157	65 Tb 159	66 Dy 162	67 Ho 165	68 Er 167	69 Tm 169	70 Yb 173	71 Lu 175	72 Hf 178.5	73 Ta 181	74 W 184	75 Re 186	76 Os 190	77 Ir 192	78 Pt 195	79 Au 197	80 Hg 201	81 Tl 204	82 Pb 207	83 Bi 209	84 Po 210	85 At 210	86 Rn 222
87 Fr 223	88 Ra 226	89 Ac 227	90 Th 232	91 Pa 231	92 U 238	93 Np 237	94 Pu 242	95 Am 243	96 Cm 247	97 Bk 249	98 Cf 251	99 Es 254	100 Fm 253	101 Md 256	102 No 253	103 Lr 257															

Transition metals

Inner transition series

Oxides* *of elements go from* ***basic**** *to* ***amphoteric**** *to acidic.*

Elements change from ***reducing agents**** *to* ***oxidizing agents****.*

Elements change from forming ***cations**** *to forming* ***anions**** *easily.*

Reactivity* *changes from increasing down a* ***group**** *to decreasing.*

All elements in a ***group**** *have the same number of* ***outer shell**** *electrons.*

Bonds between molecules increase in strength for gases.

Melting points and boiling points increase for gases.

Predicting reactions

Throughout the inorganic section of this book, each **group*** of elements has an introduction and chart which summarize some of the properties of the group's elements. Below the charts are blue boxes which highlight trends going down the group. After the introduction, more common group members are defined. Information on the other members of the group can often be determined from trends in **reactivity*** going down the group.

The following steps show how to predict the **reactivity*** of cesium with cold water. Cesium is in Group I (see pages 168-169).

1. The chart introducing Group I shows that the reactivity of the elements increases going down the group.

2. From the definitions of lithium, sodium and potassium, it is found that all three elements react with water with increasing violence going down the group – lithium reacts gently, sodium reacts violently and potassium reacts very violently.

It is predicted that cesium, as it comes after potassium going down the group, will react extremely violently with water.

* **Amphoteric**, 151; **Anion**, 130; **Basic**, 151 (**Base**); **Cation**, 130; **Group**, 165; **Outer shell**, 127; **Oxides**, 183; **Oxidizing agent**, 148; **Period**, 164; **Periodic table**, 164; **Reactivity**, 158; **Reducing agent**, 148.

HYDROGEN

Hydrogen (**H_2**), with an **atomic number*** of one, is the first and lightest element in the **periodic table***, and the most common in the universe. It is a **diatomic***, odourless, inflammable gas which only occurs naturally on Earth in compounds. It is made by the reaction of natural gas and steam at high temperatures, or the reaction of **water gas*** and steam over a **catalyst***. It is a **reducing agent***, burns in air with a light blue flame and, when heated, reacts with many substances, e.g. with sodium to form sodium hydride (all compounds of hydrogen and one other element are **hydrides**). Hydrogen is used, for example, to make margarines (see **hydrogenation**, page 193) and ammonia (see **Haber process**, page 180), and as a rocket fuel. See also pages 217 and 218.

Sucrose ($C_{12}H_{22}O_{11}$), the sugar in sweets, is a compound of carbon, hydrogen and oxygen.

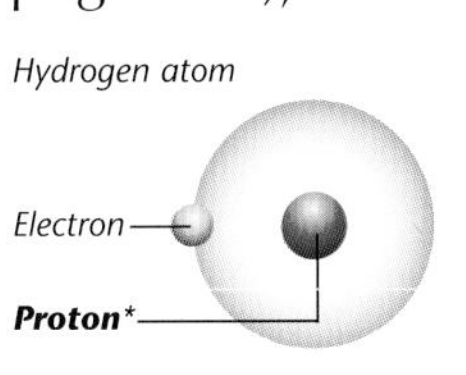
Hydrogen atom
Electron
Proton*

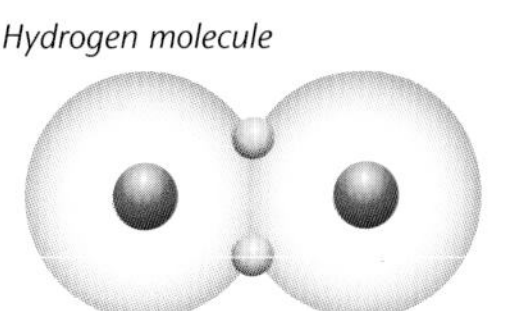
Hydrogen molecule

*Consists of two hydrogen atoms joined by a **covalent bond***.*

Hydrogen ion** (**H^+**). Consists of only one **proton (no electron). Formed when a hydrogen atom loses its electron. Hydrogen ions combine with water molecules to form **hydronium ions***. Excess hydronium ions in a solution make it acidic.*

Hydrogen reacts with sodium to make sodium hydride.

$$2Na(s) + H_2(g) \rightarrow 2NaH(s)$$

Sodium — Hydrogen — Sodium hydride

*Hydrogen is a **reducing agent***.*

$$CuO(s) + H_2(g) \rightarrow Cu(s) + H_2O(l)$$

Copper(II) oxide — Hydrogen — Copper — Water

Deuterium (D or ^2_1H)

An **isotope*** of hydrogen with one **proton*** and one **neutron***. It makes up 0.0156% of natural hydrogen. Water molecules containing deuterium are called **deuterium oxide** (**D_2O**) or **heavy water** molecules. Heavy water is used in nuclear reactors to slow the fast moving neutrons.

Tritium (T or ^3_1H)

An **isotope*** of hydrogen with one **proton*** and two **neutrons***. It is rare but is produced by nuclear reactors. It is **radioactive***, emitting **beta particles***. **Tritiated water** contains some water molecules in which a hydrogen atom has been replaced by a **tritium** atom. It is used by doctors to find how much fluid a patient passes.

Hydrogen peroxide (H_2O_2)

A syrupy liquid. It is an oxide of hydrogen and a strong **oxidizing agent***. It is sold in solution as disinfectant and bleach.

Water (H_2O)

An oxide of hydrogen and one of the most common compounds on Earth. It is a colorless, odorless liquid which freezes at 0°C, boils at 100°C, has its greatest density (1g cm^{-3}) at 4°C and is the best solvent known. It is made of **polar molecules*** linked by **hydrogen bonds*** and is formed when hydrogen burns in oxygen. See also pages 206 and 218.

Hydrogen atom

Covalent bonds*

Hydrogen atom

Oxygen atom

*Diagram of a **water** molecule (**polar molecule***)*

Hydroxide

A compound made of a **hydroxide ion** (**OH^-**) and a **cation***. Solutions containing more OH^- ions than H^+ ions are alkaline. Many hydroxides are not water-soluble, e.g. **lead(II) hydroxide** (**$Pb(OH)_2$**). However, the hydroxides of Group I elements and some others are water-soluble.

* **Atomic number**, 127; **Beta particle**, 128; **Catalyst**, 161; **Cation**, 130; **Covalent bond**, 132; **Diatomic**, 124; **Hydrogen bond**, 134; **Hydronium ion**, 150; **Isotope**, 127; **Neutron**, 126; **Oxidizing agent**, 148; **Periodic table**, 164; **Polar molecule**, 133; **Proton**, 126; **Radioactivity**, 128; **Reducing agent**, 148; **Water gas**, 179 (**Carbon monoxide**).

GROUP I, THE ALKALI METALS

The elements in **Group I** of the **periodic table*** are called **alkali metals** as they are all metals which react with water to form alkaline solutions. They all have similar chemical properties and their physical properties follow certain patterns. The chart below shows some of their properties.

Some properties of Group I elements

Name of element	Chemical symbol	Relative atomic mass*	Electron configuration*	Reactivity	Appearance	Uses
Lithium	Li	6.94	2,1	INCREASING ↓	Silver-white metal	See below.
Sodium	Na	22.99	2,8,1		Soft, silver-white metal	See below.
Potassium	K	39.10	2,8,8,1		Soft, silver-white metal	See page 169.
Rubidium	Rb	85.47	Complex configuration but still one outer electron,		Soft, silver-white metal	To make special glass
Cesium	Cs	132.90			Soft metal with gold sheen	In photocells* and as a catalyst*
Francium	Fr	No known stable isotope*				

*The atoms of all Group I elements have one electron in their **outer shell***, hence the elements are powerful **reducing agents*** because this electron is easily lost in reactions. The resulting ion has a charge of +1 and is more stable because its new outer shell is complete (see **octet**, page 127). All Group I elements react in this way to form **ionic compounds***.*

*Going down the group, the reaction of the elements with water gets more violent, each forming an alkaline solution and hydrogen gas. The first three members tarnish in air and **rubidium** and **caesium** catch fire. All Group I elements are stored under oil because of their reactivity. They are soft enough to be cut easily with a knife.*

These two pages contain more information on **lithium**, **sodium**, **potassium** and their compounds. They are typical Group I elements.

Lithium (Li)

The least reactive element in Group I of the periodic table and the lightest solid element. Lithium is rare and is only found in a few compounds, from which it is extracted by **electrolysis***. It burns in air with a crimson flame. Lithium reacts vigorously with chlorine to form **lithium chloride** (**LiCl**) which is used in welding flux and air conditioners. A piece of lithium placed in water glides across the surface, fizzing gently.

$$2Li(s) + 2H_2O(l) \rightarrow 2LiOH(aq) + H_2(g)$$

Lithium — *Water* — *Lithium hydroxide* — *Hydrogen*

*After the reaction, the solution is strongly alkaline, due to the **lithium hydroxide** formed.*

Sodium (Na)

A member of Group I of the periodic table, found in many compounds. Its main ore is **rock salt** (containing **sodium chloride** – see also **potassium**). It is extracted from molten sodium chloride by **electrolysis***, using a **Downs' cell**. Sodium burns in air with an orange-yellow flame and reacts violently with non-metals and water (see equation for **lithium** and water, and substitute Na for Li). It is used in sodium vapor lamps and as a coolant in nuclear power stations.

Downs' cell (used to extract sodium from molten sodium chloride by electrolysis*)

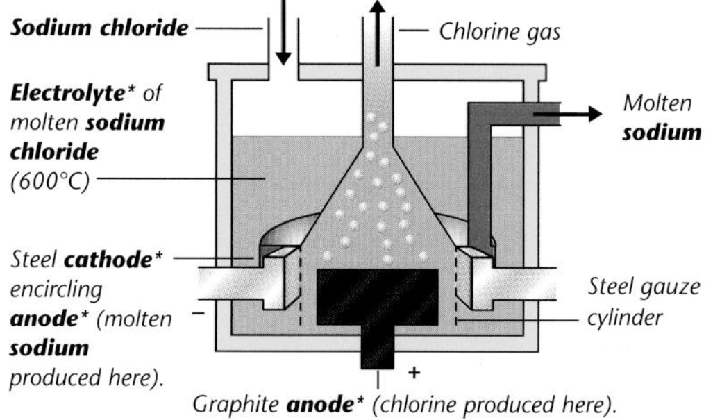

Sodium chloride
Chlorine gas
Electrolyte* of molten sodium chloride (600°C)
Molten sodium
Steel cathode* encircling anode* (molten sodium produced here).
Steel gauze cylinder
Graphite anode* (chlorine produced here).

* **Anode**, 156 (**Electrode**); **Catalyst**, 161; **Cathode**, 156 (**Electrode**); **Electrolysis**, **Electrolyte**, 156; **Electron configuration**, 127; **Ionic compound**, 131; **Isotope**, **Outer shell**, 127; **Periodic table**, 164; **Photocell**, 345; **Reducing agent**, 148; **Relative atomic mass**, 138.

Sodium hydroxide ($NaOH$) or caustic soda

A white, **deliquescent*** solid, produced by **electrolysis*** of **brine** (see **sodium chloride**). A **strong base***, it reacts with acids to form a sodium **salt*** and water. It is used to make soaps and paper.

Sodium carbonate (Na_2CO_3)

A white solid that dissolves in water to form an alkaline solution. Its **hydrate***, called **washing soda** ($Na_2CO_3.10H_2O$ – see also page 207), has white, **efflorescent*** crystals and is made when ammonia, water and **sodium chloride** react with carbon dioxide in the **Solvay process**.

*__Washing soda__ is used in the making of glass, as a __water softener*__ and in bath crystals.*

Sodium bicarbonate ($NaHCO_3$)

Also called **sodium hydrogencarbonate** or **bicarbonate of soda**. A white solid made by the **Solvay process** (see **sodium carbonate**). In water it forms a weak alkaline solution.

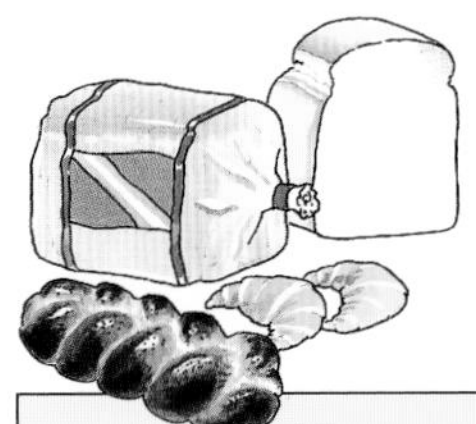

*__Sodium bicarbonate__ is used in baking. The carbon dioxide gas it gives off when heated makes dough rise. It is also used as an __antacid*__ to relieve indigestion.*

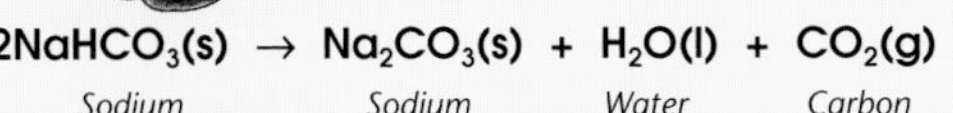

$$2NaHCO_3(s) \rightarrow Na_2CO_3(s) + H_2O(l) + CO_2(g)$$

Sodium bicarbonate → Sodium carbonate + Water + Carbon dioxide

Sodium chloride ($NaCl$) or salt

A white solid which occurs in sea water and **rock salt** (see **sodium**). It forms **brine** when dissolved in water and is used to make **sodium hydroxide** and **sodium carbonate**.

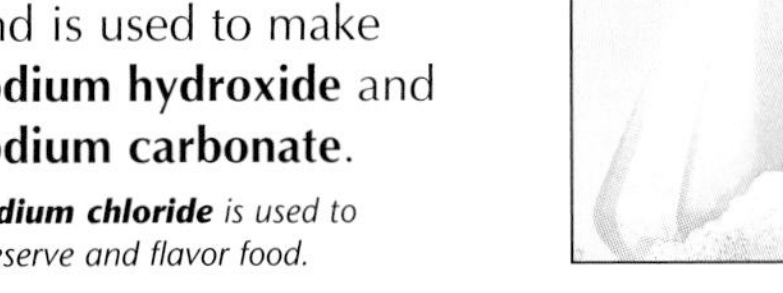

__Sodium chloride__ is used to preserve and flavor food.

Sodium nitrate ($NaNO_3$) or Chile saltpeter

A white solid used as a fertilizer and also to preserve meat.

Potassium (K)

A member of Group I of the periodic table. Potassium compounds are found in sea water and **rock salt** (containing **potassium chloride** – see also **sodium**). Potassium is extracted from molten potassium chloride by **electrolysis***. It is very reactive, reacting violently with chlorine and also with water (see equation for **lithium**, and substitute K for Li). It has few uses, but some of its compounds are important.

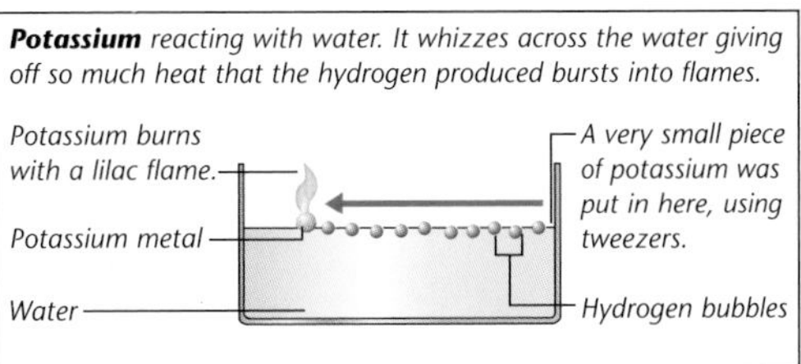
Potassium burns with a lilac flame.
Potassium metal
Water
A very small piece of potassium was put in here, using tweezers.
Hydrogen bubbles

__Potassium__ reacting with water. It whizzes across the water giving off so much heat that the hydrogen produced bursts into flames.

Potassium hydroxide (KOH) or caustic potash

A white, **deliquescent*** solid. It is a **strong base*** which reacts with acids to form a potassium **salt*** and water. It is used to make soap (see page 202).

Soap

Potassium carbonate (K_2CO_3)

A white solid which is very water-soluble, forming an alkaline solution. It is used to make glass, dyes and soap.

Potassium chloride (KCl)

A white, water-soluble solid. Large amounts are found in sea water and **rock salt** (see **potassium**). It is used in fertilizers and to produce **potassium hydroxide**.

Potassium nitrate (KNO_3) or saltpeter

A white solid which dissolves in water to form a **neutral*** solution. It is used in fertilizers, explosives and to preserve meat.

Gunpowder and some types of dynamite contain __potassium nitrate__.

Potassium sulfate (K_2SO_4)

A white solid, forming a **neutral*** solution in water. It is an important fertilizer.

* **Antacid**, 344; **Deliquescent**, **Efflorescent**, 206; **Electrolysis**, 156; **Hydrate**, 154; **Neutral**, 151; **Salts**, 153; **Strong base**, 152; **Water softeners**, 207.

GROUP II, THE ALKALINE-EARTH METALS

The elements in **Group II** of the **periodic table*** are called the **alkaline-earth metals**. The physical properties of the members of Group II follow certain trends, and, except **beryllium**, they all have similar chemical properties. They are very reactive, though less reactive than Group I elements. The chart below shows some of their properties. These two pages contain more information on **magnesium**, **calcium** and their compounds. Magnesium and calcium are typical Group II elements.

Some properties of Group II elements

Name of element	Chemical symbol	Relative atomic mass*	Electron configuration*	Reactivity	Appearance	Uses
Beryllium	Be	9.01	2,2	INCREASING ↓	Hard, white metal	In light, corrosion-resistant alloys*
Magnesium	Mg	24.31	2,8,2		Silver-white metal	See below.
Calcium	Ca	40.31	2,8,8,2		Soft, silver-white metal	See right.
Strontium	Sr	87.62	Complex configuration, but still 2 outer electrons		Soft, silver-white metal	In fireworks
Barium	Ba	137.34			Soft, silver-white metal	In fireworks and medicine
Radium	Ra	Rare radioactive* metal			Soft, silver-white metal	An isotope* is used to treat cancer.

*The atoms of all Group II elements have two electrons in their **outer shell***, hence the elements are good **reducing agents*** because these electrons are fairly easily lost in reactions. Each resulting ion has a charge of +2 and is more stable because its new outer shell is complete (see **octet**, page 127). All Group II elements react this way to form **ionic compounds***, though some **beryllium** compounds have **covalent*** properties.*

*Going down the group, elements react more readily with both water and oxygen (see **magnesium** and **calcium**). They all **tarnish*** in air, but **barium** reacts so violently with both water and oxygen that it is stored under oil.*

Magnesium (Mg)

A member of Group II of the periodic table. It only occurs naturally in compounds, mainly in either **dolomite** (**$CaCO_3.MgCO_3$** – a rock made of magnesium and **calcium carbonate**) or in **magnesium chloride** (**$MgCl_2$**), found in sea water. Magnesium is produced by the **electrolysis*** of molten magnesium chloride. It burns in air with a bright white flame.

$$2Mg(s) + O_2(g) \rightarrow 2MgO(s)$$
Magnesium + Oxygen → Magnesium oxide

***Magnesium** reacts rapidly with dilute acids:*

$$Mg(s) + 2HCl(aq) \rightarrow MgCl_2(aq) + H_2(g)$$
Magnesium + Hydrochloric acid → Magnesium chloride + Hydrogen

$$Mg(s) + Cl_2(g) \rightarrow MgCl_2(s)$$
Magnesium + Chlorine → Magnesium chloride

Magnesium burns vigorously in chlorine (see above), reacts slowly with cold water and rapidly with steam (see below).

$$Mg(s) + H_2O(g) \rightarrow MgO(s) + H_2(g)$$
Magnesium + Steam → Magnesium oxide + Hydrogen

Magnesium** is used to make **alloys, e.g. for building aircraft. It is also needed for plant **photosynthesis*** (it is found in **chlorophyll*** – the leaf pigment which absorbs light energy).*

* **Alloy**, 344; **Chlorophyll**, 255; **Covalent compounds**, 132; **Electrolysis**, 156; **Electron configuration**, 127; **Ionic compound**, 131; **Isotope**, **Outer shell**, 127; **Photosynthesis**, 254; **Periodic table**, 164; **Radioactivity**, 128; **Reducing agent**, 148; **Relative atomic mass**, 138; **Tarnish**, 345.

Magnesium hydroxide ($Mg(OH)_2$)

A white solid that is only slightly soluble in water. It is a **base*** and therefore **neutralizes*** acids.

Magnesium hydroxide *is used in* ***antacids**** *for treating stomach upsets, particularly indigestion.*

Magnesium sulfate ($MgSO_4$)

A white solid used in medicines for treating constipation, in leather processing and in fire-proofing.

Magnesium oxide (MgO)

A white solid which is slightly water-soluble. It is a **base***, forming magnesium **salts*** when it reacts with acids. It has a very high melting point and is used to line some furnaces.

$MgO(s)$	+	$2HCl(aq)$	$\rightarrow$	$MgCl_2(aq)$	+	$H_2O(l)$
Magnesium oxide		*Hydrochloric acid*		*Magnesium chloride*		*Water*

Calcium (Ca)

A member of Group II of the periodic table. It occurs naturally in many compounds, e.g. those found in milk, bones and in the Earth's crust. Calcium is extracted from its compounds by **electrolysis***. It burns in oxygen with a red flame and reacts readily with cold water and very rapidly with dilute acids (for equations see **magnesium** and substitute Ca for Mg). Calcium is used to make high-grade steel and in the production of uranium.

Calcium *compounds are found in bones and teeth.*

Calcium hydroxide ($Ca(OH)_2$) or slaked lime

A white solid which dissolves slightly in water to form **limewater**. This is weakly alkaline and is used to test for carbon dioxide (see page 218). Calcium hydroxide is used in mortars and to remove excess acidity in soils.

Calcium sulfate

A white solid that occurs both as **anhydrite calcium sulfate** ($CaSO_4$) and **gypsum** ($CaSO_4.2H_2O$). When heated, gypsum forms plaster of Paris.

Plaster of Paris used to make a cast of an animal track

Calcium oxide (CaO) or quicklime

A white solid. It is a **base*** which is made by heating **calcium carbonate** in a lime kiln.

$CaCO_3(s)$	$\rightleftharpoons$	$CaO(s)$	+	$CO_2(g)$
Calcium carbonate	***Reversible reaction****	*Calcium oxide*		*Carbon dioxide*

Calcium oxide, calcium carbonate *and* ***calcium hydroxide*** *are used to remove excess soil acidity.*

Calcium carbonate ($CaCO_3$)

A white, insoluble solid that occurs naturally as **limestone**, **chalk**, **marble** and **calcite**. It dissolves in dilute acids. Calcium carbonate is used to obtain **calcium oxide**, make cement and as building stone.

Limestone *rock is corroded because rainwater containing dissolved carbon dioxide reacts with the limestone to form* ***calcium bicarbonate*** *(which itself dissolves slightly in water).*

The ***calcium bicarbonate*** *formed when* ***limestone*** *dissolves in water causes* ***temporary hardness****.

$CaCO_3(s)$	+	$H_2O(l)$	+	$CO_2(g)$	$\rightarrow$	$Ca(HCO_3)_2(aq)$
Calcium carbonate		*Water*		*Carbon dioxide*		*Calcium hydrogencarbonate*

Calcium chloride ($CaCl_2$)

A white, **deliquescent***, water-soluble solid which is used as a **drying agent***.

* **Antacid**, 344; **Base**, 151; **Deliquescent**, 206; **Drying agent**, 344; **Electrolysis**, 156; **Neutralization**, 151; **Reversible reaction**, 162; **Salts**, 153; **Temporary hardness**, 207.

TRANSITION METALS

Transition metals have certain properties in common – they are hard, tough, shiny, **malleable*** and **ductile***. They **conduct*** heat and electricity, and have high melting points, boiling points and densities. Transition metals form **complex ions*** which are colored in solution. They also have more than one possible charge, e.g. Fe^{2+} and Fe^{3+}. Transition metals have many uses, some of which are shown on these two pages. (Information on iron, copper and zinc can be found on pages 174-175.) The members of the **inner transition series** (see page 165) are not shown here, as they are very rare and often unstable.

21 Sc Scandium 45	22 Ti Titanium 48	23 V Vanadium 51	24 Cr Chromium 52	25 Mn Manganese 55	26 Fe Iron 56	27 Co Cobalt 59	28 Ni Nickel 59	29 Cu Copper 64	30 Zn Zinc 65
39 Y Yttrium 89	40 Zr Zirconium 91	41 Nb Niobium 93	42 Mo Molybdenum 96	43 Tc Technetium 99	44 Ru Ruthenium 101	45 Rh Rhodium 103	46 Pd Palladium 106	47 Ag Silver 108	48 Cd Cadmium 112
57 La Lanthanum 139	72 Hf Hafnium 178.5	73 Ta Tantalum 181	74 W Tungsten 184	75 Re Rhenium 186	76 Os Osmium 190	77 Ir Iridium 192	78 Pt Platinum 195	79 Au Gold 197	80 Hg Mercury 201

Sc ***Scandium***
A very rare, light, silvery-white metal.

Ti ***Titanium***
*A metal used to make strong, light, corrosion-resistant **alloys*** with high melting points, e.g. those used in aircraft wings, artificial hips, heart pacemakers, golf clubs and jewelry.*

V ***Vanadium***
*A rare, hard, white metal that is used to increase the strength and hardness of steel **alloys*** such as those used to make tools. **Vanadium pentoxide** (V_2O_5) is the **catalyst*** used in the **contact process*** to make sulfuric acid.*

Cr ***Chromium***
*A hard, white metal found as **chrome iron ore**. It is used as a corrosion-resistant coating on steel objects and in stainless steel. Chromium plating is used on car parts, bicycle handlebars and cutlery.*

Mn ***Manganese***
*A hard, brittle, reddish-white metal. It is found as **pyrolusite** (MnO_2) and is used in many **alloys***, such as steels and bronzes.*

Fe ***Iron***
Has various uses, some of which are described on page 174.

Co ***Cobalt***
*A hard, silvery-white, magnetic metal found combined with sulfur and arsenic. It is used in **alloys***, e.g. with **iron** to make magnets. Its **radioisotope*** is used to treat cancer. **Cobalt(II) chloride** ($CoCl_2$) is used to test for water (see page 218). Cobalt produces a blue color in glass and ceramics.*

Ni ***Nickel***
*A magnetic metal that is found as **nickel sulfide** (NiS). It is used as a **catalyst***, in **alloys***, in **electroplating*** and in rechargeable batteries. An **alloy*** of nickel is used in coins and stainless steel.*

Cu ***Copper***
Has various uses, some of which are described on page 175.

Zn ***Zinc***
Has various uses, some of which are described on page 175.

* **Alloy**, 344; **Catalyst**, 161; **Complex ion**, 154 (**Complex salt**); **Conductivity**, 28, 63; **Contact process**, 185; **Ductile**, 344; **Electroplating**, 157; **Malleable**, 345; **Radioisotope**, 128.

Y ***Yttrium***
A metal used in crystals for lasers, and added to aluminum high-voltage electricity transmission lines to increase ***conductivity****.*

Zr ***Zirconium***
A rare metal used in ***alloys****,* ***abrasives****, flame-proofing compounds and to absorb* ***neutrons**** *in nuclear reactors.*

Nb ***Niobium***
A rare, gray metal. Small quantities of it are used in some stainless steel to make it resistant to corrosion at high temperatures. Its ***alloys**** *are used in jet engines and rockets.*

Mo ***Molybdenum***
A hard, white metal that is used in ***alloys****, e.g. special steels. It is used to make ball bearings and lamp filaments.*

Tc ***Technetium***
A metal which only occurs as an unstable ***isotope**** *formed by uranium* ***fission****. It is used in medicine to locate tumors.*

Ru ***Ruthenium***
A hard, brittle metal. It is used in ***alloys**** *and as a* ***catalyst****.*

Rh ***Rhodium***
A hard, silvery-white metal found with ***platinum****. It is used as a* ***catalyst****, in* ***alloys**** *and in thin films to make high quality mirrors.*

Pd ***Palladium***
A silvery-white metal used in ***alloys****, telephone relays and high-grade surgical instruments.* ***Catalysts**** *made of palladium and* ***platinum*** *reduce the carbon monoxide and* ***hydrocarbons**** *in car exhaust.*

Ag ***Silver***
A soft, white metal sometimes found combined with other elements, e.g. sulfur. It is used, often in ***alloys****, in jewelry and coinage and is also* ***electroplated**** *onto objects. Silver* ***halides**** *are used in photography.*

Cd ***Cadmium***
A soft, silvery-white metal found with ***zinc*** *and used to make* ***alloys**** *with low melting points. It is used in* ***control rods**** *in nuclear reactors and also in nickel-cadmium rechargeable batteries. Cadmium compounds are used as yellow, orange and red pigments in plastics, paints and ceramics.*

La ***Lanthanum***
*Similar in properties to aluminum, this is one of a group of rare metallic elements (****lanthanides****) with* ***atomic numbers**** *57-71. Camera lenses contain* ***lanthanum oxide*** *(****La_2O_3****).*

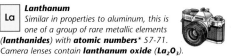

Hf ***Hafnium***
A metal used in ***control rods**** *in nuclear reactors to absorb* ***neutrons****, and in* ***alloys**** *to make cutting tools.*

Ta ***Tantalum***
A rare, pale gray metal used in electric lamp filaments and ***alloys****. Tantalum is also used in surgery to replace parts of the body, e.g. in skull plates and wire connecting the ends of nerves.*

W ***Tungsten***
A hard, gray metal that is resistant to corrosion. It is used in ***alloys**** *to make tools and lamp filaments.*

Re ***Rhenium***
A hard, heavy, gray metal used in ***thermocouples**** *and* ***catalysts****. It is used to make low-lead and lead-free* ***gasoline**** *with a high* ***octane rating****. An* ***alloy**** *of rhenium and* ***tungsten*** *is used in flash bulbs.*

Os ***Osmium***
A hard, white, crystalline metal, the densest element known. It is found with ***platinum*** *and used in* ***alloys**** *with platinum and* ***iridium****, e.g. in electrical contacts.* ***Osmium tetroxide*** *(****OsO_4****) is used to treat inflammatory arthritis.*

Ir ***Iridium***
A rare, hard, unreactive metal that looks like ***platinum*** *and is found with it. It is used in medicine in* ***radioactive**** *implants to control tumors and (with platinum) in heart pace-makers. It is also found in an* ***alloy**** *used for fountain pen nib-tips.*

Pt ***Platinum***
A hard, silvery-white metal used as a ***catalyst**** *and to make electrical contacts, jewelry, and various pin, plate and hinge devices for securing human bones. It is also used (with* ***iridium****) in wire* ***electrodes**** *in heart pacemakers.*

Au ***Gold***
A soft, shiny, yellow metal. It is very unreactive and usually found uncombined. South Africa and Russia have the most important gold deposits. Gold only reacts with very vigorous ***oxidizing agents**** *(such as chlorine) and certain combinations of acids. It is often used in* ***alloys**** *with* ***silver*** *or* ***copper*** *to give it more strength. These alloys are used in jewelry, coins and dentistry. Pure gold (24 carat gold) is also used in jewelry.*

Hg ***Mercury*** *or* ***quicksilver***
A poisonous, silvery-white, liquid metal mainly found as ***cinnabar*** *(HgS). It is used in thermometers, barometers, lamps and also in* ***amalgams**** *used by dentists.*

* **Abrasive**, **Alloy**, **Amalgam**, 344; **Atomic number**, 127; **Catalyst**, 161; **Conductivity**, 28, 63; **Control rods**, 94; **Electrode**, 156; **Electroplating**, 157; **Fission (nuclear)**, 129; **Gasoline**, 199; **Halides**, 186; **Hydrocarbons**, 190; **Isotope**, 127; **Neutron**, 126; **Octane rating**, 199; **Oxidizing agent**, 148; **Radioactivity**, 128; **Thermocouple**, 27.

IRON, COPPER AND ZINC

Iron (Fe)

A **transition metal*** in Period 4 of the **periodic table***. It is a fairly soft, white, magnetic metal which only occurs naturally in compounds. One of its main ores is **haematite (Fe_2O_3)**, or **iron(III) oxide**, from which it is extracted in a **blast furnace**. Iron reacts to form both **ionic** and **covalent compounds*** and reacts with moist air to form **rust**. It burns in air when cut very finely into iron filings and also reacts with dilute acids. It is above hydrogen in the **electrochemical series***.

Extracting iron using a blast furnace

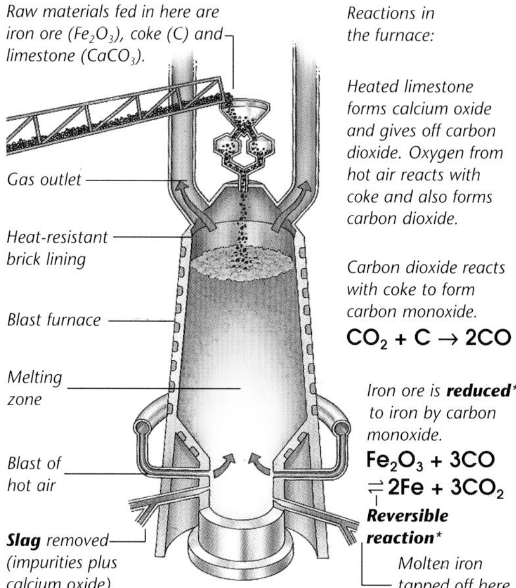

Raw materials fed in here are iron ore (Fe_2O_3), coke (C) and limestone ($CaCO_3$).
Gas outlet
Heat-resistant brick lining
Blast furnace
Melting zone
Blast of hot air
Slag removed (impurities plus calcium oxide).
Reactions in the furnace:
Heated limestone forms calcium oxide and gives off carbon dioxide. Oxygen from hot air reacts with coke and also forms carbon dioxide.
Carbon dioxide reacts with coke to form carbon monoxide.
$CO_2 + C \rightarrow 2CO$
Iron ore is **reduced*** to iron by carbon monoxide.
$Fe_2O_3 + 3CO \rightleftharpoons 2Fe + 3CO_2$
Reversible reaction*
Molten iron tapped off here.

Iron made in the blast furnace is called **pig iron**. It contains about 5% carbon and 4% other impurities, such as sulfur. Most pig iron is converted to **steel**, although some is converted to **wrought iron** (by **oxidizing*** impurities) and some is melted down again along with scrap steel to make **cast iron**. Iron is a vital mineral in the human diet, as it is needed to make **haemoglobin***.

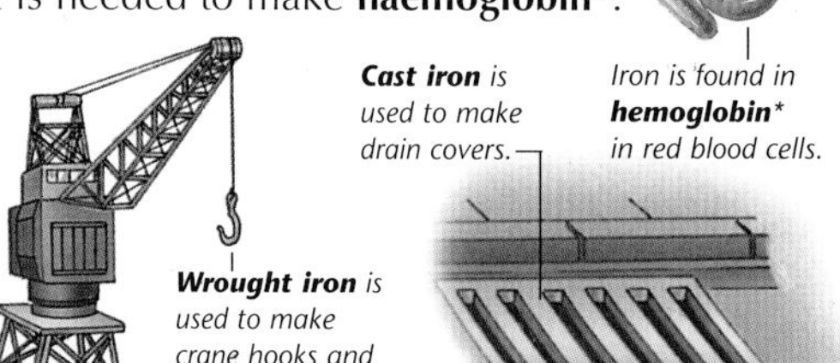

***Wrought iron** is used to make crane hooks and anchor chains.*

***Cast iron** is used to make drain covers.*

*Iron is found in **hemoglobin*** in red blood cells.*

Steel

An **alloy*** of **iron** and carbon which usually contains below 1.5% carbon. The carbon gives the alloy strength and hardness but reduces **malleability*** and **ductility***. Measured amounts of one or more **transition metals*** are often added to steel to give it specific properties, such as corrosion resistance in the case of **stainless steel** (which contains 11-14% chromium). Steel is often made by the **basic oxygen process**. Scrap steel, molten iron and lime are put into a furnace, and oxygen is blasted onto the metal to **oxidize*** impurities.

***Steel** is used to make many objects. These steel paper clips contain about 0.08% carbon.*

Iron(II) or ferrous compounds

Iron compounds containing Fe^{2+} ions, e.g. **iron(II) chloride ($FeCl_2$)**. Their solutions are green.

Iron(III) or ferric compounds

Iron compounds containing Fe^{3+} ions, e.g. **iron(III) chloride ($FeCl_3$)**. Their solutions are yellow or orange.

Rust ($Fe_2O_3.xH_2O$) or hydrated iron(III) oxide

A brown solid formed when **iron**, water and air react together (see **corrosion**, page 209). The "x" in the formula shows that the number of water molecules varies. Iron and **steel** can be protected from rust by **galvanizing** – coating with a layer of **zinc** (see also **sacrificial protection**, page 159). The surface zinc **oxidizes*** in air, stopping the zinc and iron below from being oxidized. Galvanized cars remain rust-free longer than others.

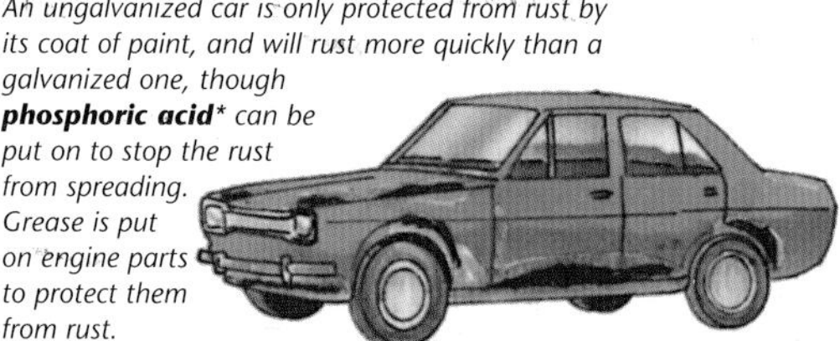

*An ungalvanized car is only protected from rust by its coat of paint, and will rust more quickly than a galvanized one, though **phosphoric acid*** can be put on to stop the rust from spreading. Grease is put on engine parts to protect them from rust.*

* **Alloy**, 344; **Covalent compounds**, 132; **Ductility**, 344 (**Ductile**); **Electrochemical series**, 159; **Hemoglobin**, 286 (**Red blood cells**); **Ionic compound**, 131; **Malleability**, 345 (**Malleable**); **Oxidation**, 148; **Periodic table**, 164; **Phosphoric acid**, 182 (**Phosphorus pentoxide**); **Reduction**, 148; **Reversible reaction**, 162; **Transition metals**, 172.

Copper (Cu)

A **transition metal*** in Period 4 of the **periodic table***. It is a red-brown, soft but tough metal found naturally in certain rocks. Its compounds are found in several ores, e.g. **copper pyrites** (**($CuFe)S_2$**) and **malachite** (**$CuCO_3.Cu(OH)_2$**). Copper is extracted from the former by crushing and removing sand and then roasting in a limited supply of air with silica. The iron combines with silica and forms **slag**. The sulfur is removed by burning to form sulfur dioxide. The copper produced is purified further by **electro-refining***. It is an unreactive metal and only **tarnishes*** very slowly in air to form a thin, green surface film of **basic copper sulfate** (**$CuSO_4.3Cu(OH)_2$**). Copper is below hydrogen in the **electrochemical series***. It does not react with water, dilute acids or alkalis. However, it does react with concentrated nitric or concentrated sulfuric acid. (See also page 219.)

__Copper__ is a very good conductor of electricity (although silver is better), so it is used to make wires for electric circuits. Because it is soft but tough, it is also used to make pipes for plumbing and central-heating systems.

*It is used in __alloys*__ such as __brass__ (copper plus __zinc__) and __bronze__ (copper plus tin) to make "copper" coins, and in __cupronickel__ (copper plus nickel) to make "silver" coins.*

*An __alloy*__ of copper and gold is used to make jewelry. The greater the amount of copper, the less the number of carats the gold will be, i.e. less than 24 carats (pure gold).*

Copper(I) or cuprous compounds

Compounds containing Cu^+ ions, e.g. **copper(I) oxide** and **copper(I) chloride** (**CuCl**). **Copper(I)** compounds do not dissolve in water.

__Copper(I) oxide (Cu_2O)__ is used to make glass and paint.

Copper(II) or cupric compounds

Compounds that contain Cu^{2+} ions, e.g. **copper(II) sulfate** and **copper(II) chloride**. Copper(II) compounds dissolve in water to form light blue solutions, and are much more common than **copper(I) compounds**. **Copper(II) sulfate** (**$CuSO_4$**) has many uses, e.g. in dyeing and **electroplating***. It is also used in **Bordeaux mixture**, which kills molds growing on fruit and vegetables. (See also test for water, page 218.) **Copper(II) chloride** (**$CuCl_2$**) is used to remove sulfur from **petroleum***.

__Copper(II) chloride__ is used in fireworks to give a green color.

Zinc (Zn)

An element in Period 4 of the **periodic table***. It is a silvery, soft metal which **tarnishes*** in air. It is too reactive to occur naturally, and its main ores are **zinc blende** (**ZnS**), **calamine** (**$ZnCO_3$**) and **zincite** (**ZnO**). The zinc is extracted by roasting the ore to form **zinc oxide** (**ZnO**) and then **reducing*** it by heating it with coke. Zinc is above hydrogen in the **electrochemical series***. It reacts with oxygen, with steam when red-hot, and with acids. It is used to coat iron and steel to prevent **rust** (**galvanizing** – see also page 174 and **sacrificial protection**, page 159). It is also used in **alloys***, particularly **brass** (copper and zinc).

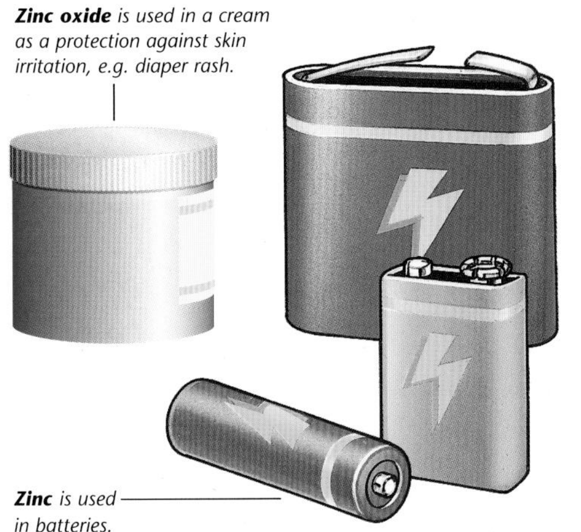

__Zinc oxide__ is used in a cream as a protection against skin irritation, e.g. diaper rash.

__Zinc__ is used in batteries.

* **Alloy**, 344; **Electrochemical series**, 159; **Electroplating**, **Electro-refining**, 157; **Petroleum**, 198; **Periodic table**, 164; **Reduction**, 148; **Tarnish**, 345; **Transition metals**, 172.

GROUP III ELEMENTS

The elements in **Group III** of the **periodic table*** are generally not as reactive as the elements in Groups I and II. Unlike those elements they show no overall trend in reactivity, and the first member of the group is a non-metal. The chart below shows some of their properties. More information on **aluminum** and its compounds can be found below the chart. Aluminum is the most widely used member of this group.

Some properties of Group III elements						
Name of element	**Chemical symbol**	**Relative atomic mass***	**Electron configuration***	**Reactivity**	**Appearance**	**Uses**
Boron	**B**	10.81	2,3	NO TREND	Brown powder or yellow crystals	In **control rods***, glass and to harden steel
Aluminum	**Al**	26.98	2,8,3		White metal	See below.
Gallium	**Ga**	69.72	Complex configuration but still three outer electrons		Silver-white metal	In **semiconductors***
Indium	**In**	114.82			Soft, silver-white metal	In **control rods*** and transparent electrodes
Thallium	**Tl**	204.37			Soft, silver-white metal	In rat poison

*Although all atoms of Group III elements have three outer electrons, they react to form different types of compound. Those of **boron**, and some of **aluminum**, are **covalent***. Other members of the group form mostly **ionic compounds***.*

Aluminum (Al)

A member of Group III of the periodic table. It is the most common metal found on Earth, and occurs naturally in many compounds, e.g. **bauxite** (see **aluminum oxide**) from which it is extracted by **electrolysis***. It is hard, light, **ductile***, **malleable*** and a good conductor of heat and electricity. It reacts with the oxygen in air to form a surface layer of **aluminum oxide** which stops further corrosion. It also reacts with chlorine, dilute acids and alkalis.

Some uses of aluminum and its alloys*

Thin sheets of aluminum are used to wrap food, e.g. chocolate bars. It is also used to make soda cans.

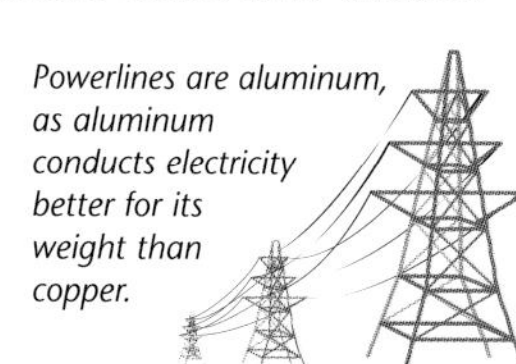

Powerlines are aluminum, as aluminum conducts electricity better for its weight than copper.

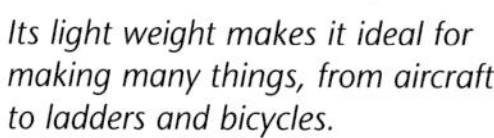

Its light weight makes it ideal for making many things, from aircraft to ladders and bicycles.

Aluminum oxide (Al_2O_3) or alumina

An **amphoteric***, white solid that is almost insoluble in water. It occurs naturally as **bauxite** (**$Al_2O_3.2H_2O$** – see also **aluminum**) and as **corundum** (**Al_2O_3**) – an extremely hard crystalline solid. It is used in some cements and to line furnaces.

The extraction by electrolysis* of aluminum from bauxite

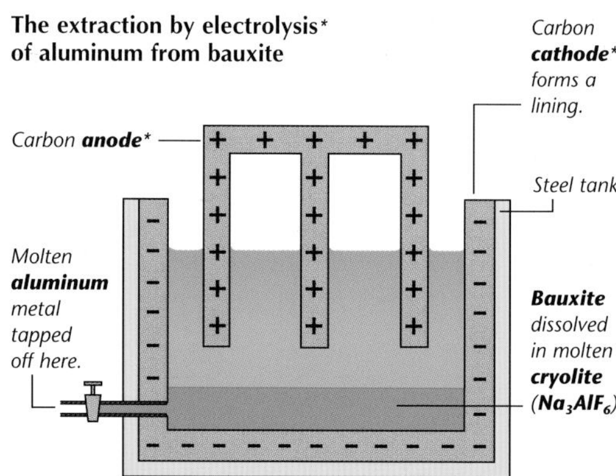
Carbon **cathode*** forms a lining.
Carbon **anode***
Steel tank
Molten **aluminum** metal tapped off here.
Bauxite dissolved in molten **cryolite** (**Na_3AlF_6**)

Aluminum hydroxide ($Al(OH)_3$)

A white, slightly water-soluble, **amphoteric*** solid, which is used in dyeing cloth, to make ceramics and as an **antacid***.

Aluminum sulfate ($Al_2(SO_4)_3$)

A white, water-soluble, crystalline solid used to purify water and make paper.

* **Alloy**, 344; **Amphoteric**, 151; **Anode**, 156 (**Electrode**); **Antacid**, 344; **Cathode**, 156 (**Electrode**); **Control rods**, 94; **Covalent compounds**, 132; **Ductile**, 344; **Electrolysis**, 156; **Electron configuration**, 127; **Ionic compound**, 131; **Malleable**, 345; **Periodic table**, 164; **Relative atomic mass**, 138; **Semiconductor**, 65.

GROUP IV ELEMENTS

The elements in **Group IV** of the **periodic table*** are generally not very reactive and the members show increasingly metallic properties going down the group. For more about the properties of these elements, see the chart below, **silicon** and **lead** (this page) and **carbon**, pages 178-179.

Some properties of Group IV elements

Name of element	Chemical symbol	Relative atomic mass*	Electron configuration*	Reactivity	Appearance	Uses
Carbon	C	12.01	2,4	NO TREND ↓	Solid non-metal (see page 178)	See page 178.
Silicon	Si	20.09	2,8,4		Shiny, gray **metalloid*** solid	See below.
Germanium	Ge	72.59	Complex configuration but still four outer electrons		Grayish-white **metalloid*** solid	In transistors
Tin	Sn	118.69			Soft, silver-white metal	Tin plating, e.g. food containers
Lead	Pb	207.19			Soft, silver-gray metal	See below.

*Although all atoms of Group IV elements have four outer electrons, they react to form different compound types. They all form **covalent compounds****, but **tin** and **lead** form **ionic compounds*** as well.*

Silicon (Si)

A member of Group IV of the periodic table. It is a hard, shiny, gray **metalloid*** with a high melting point. Silicon is the second most common element in the Earth's crust – it is found in sand and rocks as **silicon dioxide** and **silicates**. When it is ground into a powder it reacts with some alkalis and elements, otherwise it is generally unreactive.

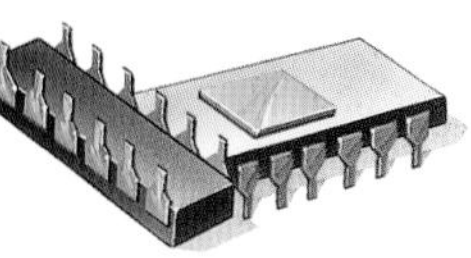

Silicon** is a **semiconductor and is used to make silicon chips – complete microelectronic circuits.*

Silicon dioxide (SiO_2)

Also called **silicon(IV) oxide**, or **silica**. An insoluble, white, crystalline solid. It occurs in many forms, such as **flint** and **quartz**. It is acidic and reacts with concentrated alkalis. **Silicon dioxide** has many uses, e.g. in the making of glass and ceramics.

***Sand** is impure **quartz**. Quartz crystals are used in watches.*

Silicates

Silicon compounds that also contain a metal and oxygen, e.g. **calcium metasilicate** ($CaSiO_3$), and make up most of the Earth's crust. They are used to make glass and ceramics.

Silicones

Complex, man-made compounds containing very long chains of **silicon** and oxygen atoms.

***Silicones** are used in high-performance oils and greases and for non-stick surfaces. They are also used in waxes, polishes and varnishes, as they are water-repellant.*

Lead (Pb)

A member of Group IV of the periodic table. A soft, **malleable*** metal extracted from **galena** (**lead(II) sulfide**). It is not very reactive, though it **tarnishes*** in air, reacts slightly with **soft water*** and slowly with chlorine and nitric acid. It forms **ionic compounds*** called **lead(II)** or **plumbous compounds**, e.g. **lead(II) oxide** (**PbO**), and **covalent compounds*** called **lead(IV)** or **plumbic compounds**, e.g. **lead(IV) oxide** (**PbO_2**). Lead has many uses, e.g. in car batteries and roofing. It is used in hospitals to protect people from the harmful effects of X-rays.

Car battery

Lead** and **lead(IV) oxide electrodes*

* **Covalent compounds**, 132; **Electron configuration**, 127; **Electrode**, 156; **Ionic compound**, 131; **Malleable**, 345; **Metalloids**, 165 (**Metal**); **Periodic table**, 164; **Relative atomic mass**, 138; **Semiconductor**, 65; **Soft water**, 207 (**Hard water**); **Tarnish**, 345.

CARBON

Carbon (**C**) is a member of **Group IV** of the **periodic table*** (see also chart, page 177). It is a non-metal and has several **allotropes***, including **diamond**, **graphite** and **buckminsterfullerene**, and an **amorphous*** (unstructured) form – **charcoal**. Carbon is not very reactive. It only reacts with steam when heated, and with hot, **concentrated*** sulfuric or nitric acids (see equation below). Carbon atoms can bond with up to four other atoms, including other carbon atoms. As a result, there are a vast number of carbon-based compounds (**organic compounds** – see page 190). Living tissue is made of carbon compounds, and animals break down these compounds to liberate energy (see **carbon cycle**, page 209).

Animal and plant proteins are compounds of carbon, oxygen, hydrogen and nitrogen.

Equation for the reaction of carbon and nitric acid:

C	+	$4HNO_3$	→	CO_2	+	$4NO_2$	+	$2H_2O$
Carbon		*Nitric acid*		*Carbon dioxide*		*Nitrogen dioxide*		*Water*

Carbon will burn in air when heated, to form carbon dioxide.

$C(s)$	+	$O_2(g)$	→	$CO_2(g)$
Carbon		*Oxygen*		*Carbon dioxide*

If burned in a limited supply of air, ***carbon monoxide*** *forms.*

$2C(s)$	+	$O_2(g)$	→	$2CO(g)$
Carbon		*Oxygen*		*Carbon monoxide*

Carbon is a ***reducing agent****. It reduces the* ***oxides**** *of any metal below zinc in the* ***reactivity series**** *of metals:*

C	+	$2PbO$	→	CO_2	+	$2Pb$
Carbon		*Lead(II) oxide*		*Carbon dioxide*		*Lead*

Carbon is used in industry to reduce metal oxide ores to metals (see ***iron****, page 174).*

Diamond *is found in a rock called* ***kimberlite****. Rough diamonds are dull but can be cut to make glittering gems.*

Diamond

A crystalline, transparent form of carbon. It is the hardest naturally occurring substance. All the carbon atoms are joined by strong **covalent bonds*** – accounting for its hardness and high melting point (3,750°C). Diamonds are used as **abrasives***, glass cutters, jewelry and on drill bits. **Synthetic diamonds** are made by subjecting **graphite** to high pressure and temperature, a very costly process.

The crystal structure of diamond

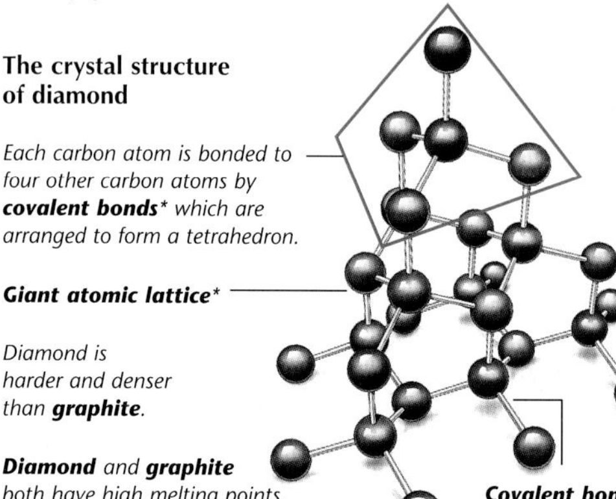
Each carbon atom is bonded to four other carbon atoms by covalent bonds* which are arranged to form a tetrahedron.
Giant atomic lattice*
Diamond is harder and denser than graphite.
Diamond and graphite both have high melting points.
Covalent bond*

Graphite

A gray, crystalline form of carbon. The atoms in each layer are joined by strong **covalent bonds***, but the layers are only linked by weak **van der Waals' forces*** which allow them to slide over each other, making graphite soft and flaky. Graphite is the only non-metal to conduct electricity well. It also conducts heat. It is used as a lubricant, in **electrolysis*** (as **inert electrodes***), as contacts in electric motors, and in pencil leads.

The crystal structure of graphite

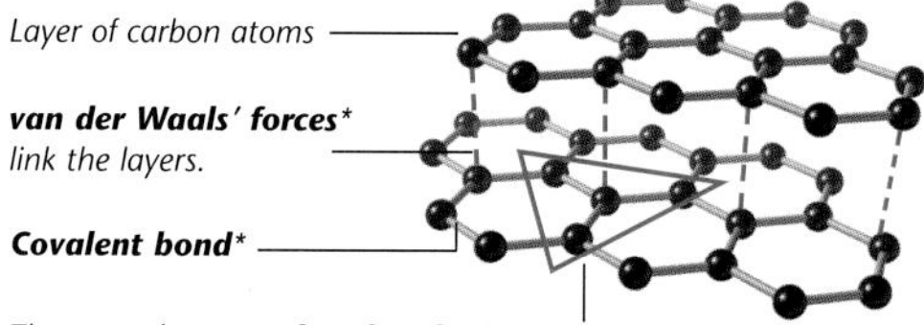
Layer of carbon atoms
van der Waals' forces* link the layers.
Covalent bond*

There are three ***covalent bonds**** *from every carbon atom to other carbon atoms in the same layer.*

* **Abrasive**, 344; **Allotropes**, 136 (**Allotropy**); **Amorphous**, 135; **Concentrated**, 144; **Covalent bond**, 132; **Electrolysis**, 156; **Giant atomic lattice**, 137; **Inert electrode**, 156; **Oxides**, 183; **Periodic table**, 164; **Reactivity series**, 158; **Reducing agent**, 148; **van der Waals' forces**, 134.

Buckminsterfullerene

A member of the family of **fullerenes** – spherical crystalline forms of carbon made by condensing vaporized **graphite** in helium. Buckminsterfullerene also occurs naturally in dust between stars and in some carbon-rich rocks. Each molecule has 60 atoms arranged in hexagons and pentagons. Double **covalent bonds*** join hexagons to hexagons. (Other fullerenes contain between 30 and 960 carbon atoms.) Buckminsterfullerene is an **insulator***, but some of its compounds are **superconductors** (substances which have no electrical **resistance***).

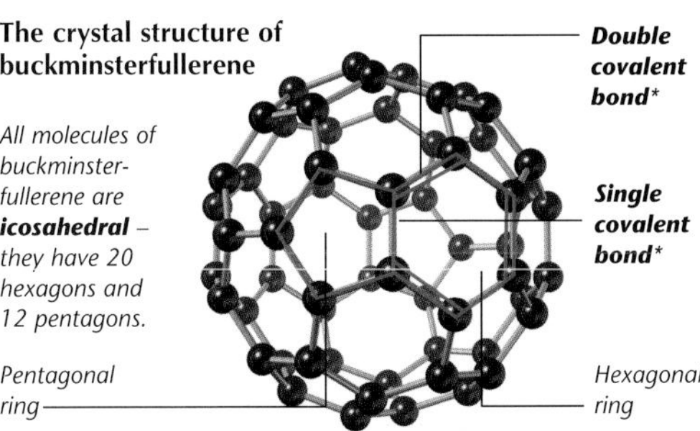
Double covalent bond*
Single covalent bond*
Pentagonal ring
Hexagonal ring

The crystal structure of buckminsterfullerene

*All molecules of buckminsterfullerene are **icosahedral** – they have 20 hexagons and 12 pentagons.*

Coal

A hard, black solid formed over millions of years from the fossilized remains of plant material. It is mainly carbon but contains hydrogen, oxygen, nitrogen and sulfur as well. Three types of coal exist – **lignite**, **anthracite** and **bituminous coal**. Coal is used as a fuel in power stations, industry and homes. It was once an important source of chemicals (now mostly produced from **petroleum***). Heating coal in the absence of air (**destructive distillation**) produces **coal gas**, **coal tar** and **coke**, as well as ammonia, benzene and sulfur. Coke, which is brittle and porous, contains over 80% carbon and is used as a smokeless fuel (as is **charcoal**, another impure form of carbon).

Carbon fibers

Black, silky threads of pure carbon made from organic textile fibres. They are stronger and stiffer than other materials of the same weight, and are used to make light boats.

Carbon dioxide (CO_2)

A colorless, odorless gas found in the atmosphere (see **carbon cycle**, page 209). It is made industrially by heating calcium carbonate in a lime kiln (see also page 216 for laboratory preparation). It dissolves in water to form **carbonic acid** (H_2CO_3).

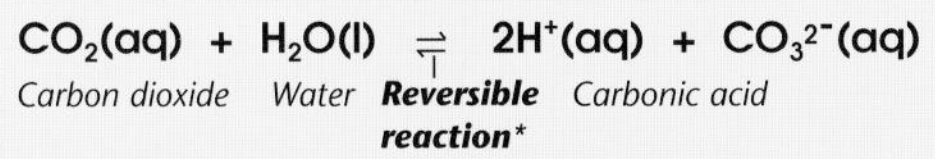

$$CO_2(aq) + H_2O(l) \rightleftharpoons 2H^+(aq) + CO_3^{2-}(aq)$$

Carbon dioxide | Water | **Reversible reaction*** | Carbonic acid

Carbon dioxide is not very reactive, though it reacts with both sodium and calcium hydroxide solutions (see page 218) and magnesium ribbon burns in it.

__Carbon dioxide__ has many uses. It is used to make drinks fizzy. Carbon dioxide escapes when the bottle or can is opened, as the pressure is released.

It is used in fire extinguishers. It is denser than air, so forms a blanket over the flames and does not allow air to reach the fire.

Carbon monoxide (CO)

A poisonous, colorless, odorless gas, made by passing **carbon dioxide** over hot carbon, and also by burning carbon fuels in a limited supply of air. It is not water-soluble, burns with a blue flame and is a **reducing agent*** (used to reduce metal oxide ores to metal – see **iron**, page 174). It is also used, mixed with other gases, in fuels, e.g. mixed with hydrogen in **water gas**, with nitrogen in **producer gas**, and with hydrogen (50%), methane and other gases in **coal gas**.

If there is not enough oxygen, the __carbon monoxide__ produced when fuel is burned is not changed to __carbon dioxide__. When a car engine runs in a closed garage, carbon monoxide accumulates.

Carbonates

Compounds made of a metal **cation*** and a **carbonate anion*** (CO_3^{2-}), e.g. **calcium carbonate** ($CaCO_3$). Except Group I carbonates, they are insoluble in water and decompose upon heating. They all react with acids to give off **carbon dioxide**.

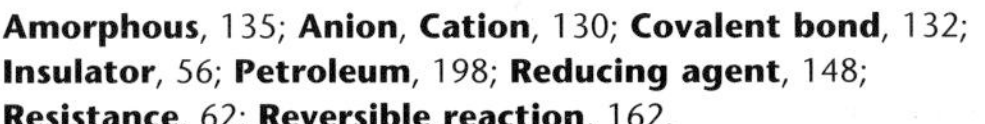

* **Amorphous**, 135; **Anion**, **Cation**, 130; **Covalent bond**, 132; **Insulator**, 56; **Petroleum**, 198; **Reducing agent**, 148; **Resistance**, 62; **Reversible reaction**, 162.

GROUP V ELEMENTS

The elements in **Group V** of the **periodic table*** become increasingly metallic going down the group (see chart below).

Some properties of Group V elements						
Name of element	**Chemical symbol**	**Relative atomic mass***	**Electron configuration***	**Reactivity**	**Appearance**	**Uses**
Nitrogen	**N**	14.00	2,5	INCREASING ↓	Colorless gas	See below.
Phosphorus	**P**	30.97	2,8,5		Non-metallic solid (see page 182)	See page 182.
Arsenic	**As**	74.92	Complex configuration but still five outer electrons		Three **allotropes*** (one is metallic)	In **semiconductors*** and **alloys***
Antimony	**Sb**	121.75			Silver-white metal	In type metal and other alloys
Bismuth	**Bi**	208.98			White metal with reddish tinge	In low melting point alloys and medicines

*All the atoms of Group V elements have five electrons in their **outer shell***. They all react to form **covalent compounds*** in which they share three of these electrons with three from another atom, or atoms (see **octet**, page 127). Antimony, bismuth and nitrogen also form **ionic compounds***.*

More information on **nitrogen**, **phosphorus** and their compounds can be found below and on pages 181-182. They are the two most abundant members of the group.

Nitrogen (N_2)

A member of Group V of the periodic table. A colorless, odorless, **diatomic*** gas that makes up 78% of the atmosphere. It can be produced by **fractional distillation of liquid air*** (but see also page 217). Its **oxidation state*** in compounds varies from –3 to +5. It reacts with a few reactive materials to form **nitrides**.

$$6Li(s) + N_2(g) \rightarrow 2Li_3N(s)$$

Lithium · *Nitrogen* · *Lithium nitride*

Nitrogen is essential for all organisms as it is found in molecules in living cells, e.g. proteins (see also **nitrogen cycle**, page 209). It is used in the manufacture of ammonia (see **Haber process**, right) and nitric acid. **Liquid nitrogen**, which exists below –196°C, has many uses, including freezing food.

*Packages of chips are filled with **nitrogen** gas to keep them fresh longer (when air is left in the package, the chips go stale). The gas in the package also cushions the chips against damage during transportation.*

Haber process

This process is used to make **ammonia** from **nitrogen** and hydrogen which are reacted in a ratio of 1:3. Ammonia is produced as fast and economically as possible by using a suitable temperature, pressure and **catalyst*** (see below). The reaction is **exothermic*** and **reversible***.

$$N_2(g) + 3H_2(g) \rightleftharpoons 2NH_3(g)$$

Nitrogen · *Hydrogen* · *Ammonia*

*Iron **catalyst***, 400°C, 250 atmospheres*

*(Under these conditions 15% of the reactants combine to form **ammonia**.)*

Haber process

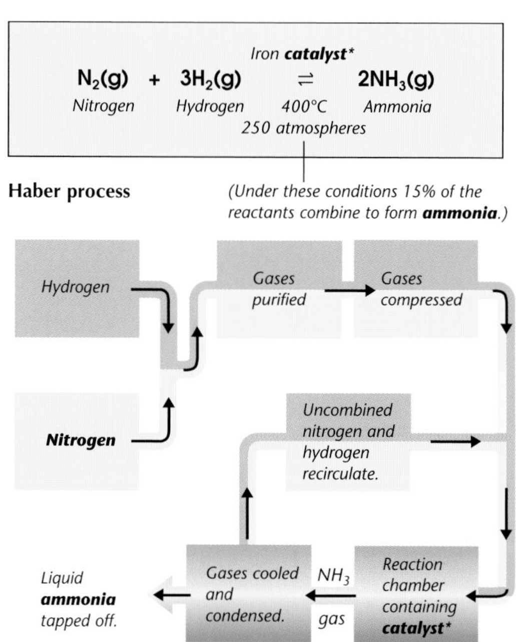

Hydrogen
Gases purified
Gases compressed
Nitrogen
Uncombined nitrogen and hydrogen recirculate.
Reaction chamber containing catalyst*
NH_3 gas
Gases cooled and condensed.
Liquid ammonia tapped off.

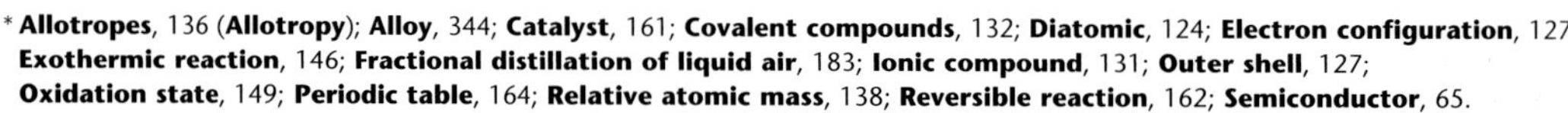
* **Allotropes**, 136 (**Allotropy**); **Alloy**, 344; **Catalyst**, 161; **Covalent compounds**, 132; **Diatomic**, 124; **Electron configuration**, 127; **Exothermic reaction**, 146; **Fractional distillation of liquid air**, 183; **Ionic compound**, 131; **Outer shell**, 127; **Oxidation state**, 149; **Periodic table**, 164; **Relative atomic mass**, 138; **Reversible reaction**, 162; **Semiconductor**, 65.

Ammonia (NH_3)

A colorless, strong-smelling gas that is less dense than air and is a **covalent compound*** made by the **Haber process**. It is a **reducing agent*** and the only common gas to form an alkaline solution in water. This solution is known as **ammonia solution** (NH_4OH) or **ammonium hydroxide**. Ammonia burns in pure oxygen to give nitrogen and water, and reacts with chlorine to give **ammonium chloride**.

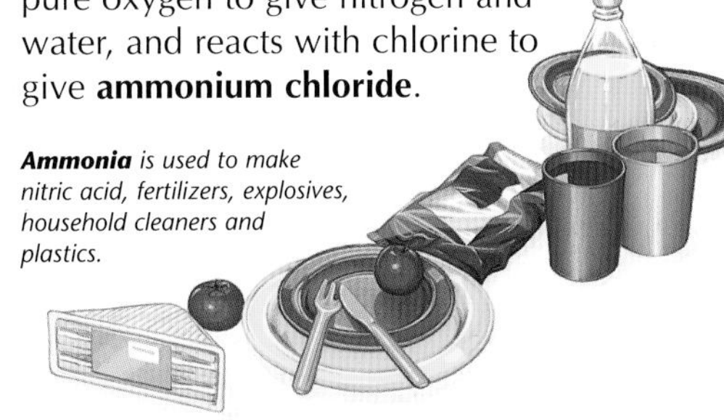

Ammonia *is used to make nitric acid, fertilizers, explosives, household cleaners and plastics.*

Ammonium chloride (NH_4Cl) or sal ammoniac

A white, water-soluble, crystalline solid made when **ammonia solution** (see **ammonia**) reacts with dilute hydrochloric acid. When heated it **sublimes*** and **dissociates*** (see equation below and page 162). It is used in the dry batteries which run many electrical appliances.

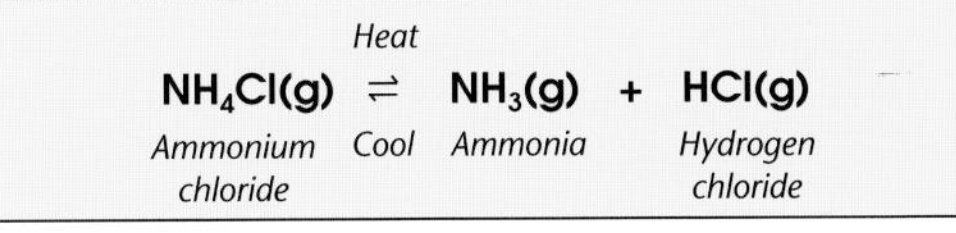

$$NH_4Cl(g) \underset{\text{Cool}}{\overset{\text{Heat}}{\rightleftharpoons}} NH_3(g) + HCl(g)$$

Ammonium chloride — Ammonia — Hydrogen chloride

Ammonium sulfate ($(NH_4)_2SO_4$)

A white, water-soluble, crystalline solid produced by the reaction of **ammonia** and sulfuric acid. It is a fertilizer.

Ammonium nitrate (NH_4NO_3)

A white, water-soluble, crystalline solid formed when **ammonia solution** (see **ammonia**) reacts with dilute nitric acid. It gives off **dinitrogen oxide** when heated.

Ammonium nitrate *is used in explosives and fertilizers. It is also found in mixtures used to feed potted plants.*

Dinitrogen oxide (N_2O)

Also called **nitrous oxide** or **laughing gas**. A colorless, slightly sweet-smelling, water-soluble gas. It is a **covalent compound*** formed by gently heating **ammonium nitrate**. It is used as an anaesthetic.

Dinitrogen oxide *supports the combustion of some reactive substances and relights a glowing splint.*

Nitrogen monoxide (NO)

Also called **nitric oxide** or **nitrogen oxide**. A colorless gas that is insoluble in water. It is a **covalent compound*** made when copper reacts with 50% concentrated nitric acid. It reacts with oxygen to form **nitrogen dioxide** and also supports the combustion of reactive elements.

Nitrogen dioxide (NO_2)

A very dark brown gas with a choking smell. It is a **covalent compound***.

$$Cu + 4HNO_3 \rightarrow Cu(NO_3)_2 + 2H_2O + 2NO_2$$

Copper — Concentrated nitric acid — Copper(II) nitrate — Water — Nitrogen dioxide

Nitrogen dioxide is made when copper reacts with concentrated nitric acid and when some **nitrates*** are heated. It supports combustion and dissolves in water to give a mixture of nitric acid and **nitrous acid** (HNO_2). It is used as an **oxidizing agent***.

Nitrogen dioxide dimerizes *(two molecules of the same substance bond together) below 21.5°C to form* ***dinitrogen tetraoxide (N_2O_4)****, a colorless gas.*

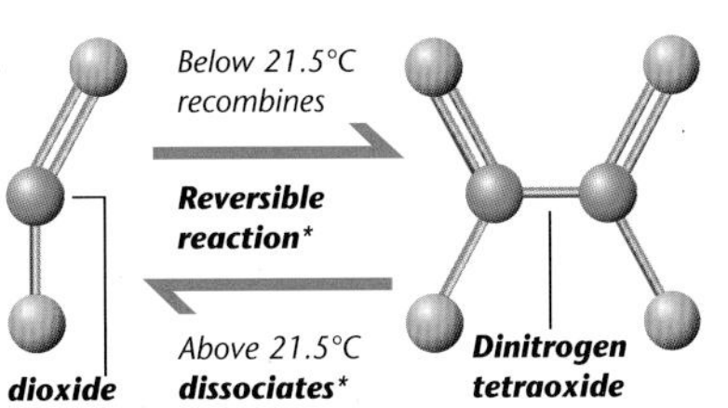
Below 21.5°C
recombines
+
Reversible reaction*
Above 21.5°C
dissociates*
Nitrogen dioxide
Dinitrogen tetraoxide

* **Covalent compounds**, 132; **Dissociation**, 162; **Nitrates**, 182; **Oxidizing agent**, 148; **Reducing agent**, 148; **Reversible reaction**, 162; **Sublimation**, 121.

Group V (continued)

Nitric acid (HNO_3) or nitric(V) acid

A light yellow, oily, water-soluble liquid. It is a **covalent compound*** containing nitrogen with an **oxidation state*** of +5. It is a very strong and corrosive acid which is made industrially by the three-stage **Ostwald process** (shown below).

Stage 1: Ammonia reacts with oxygen.

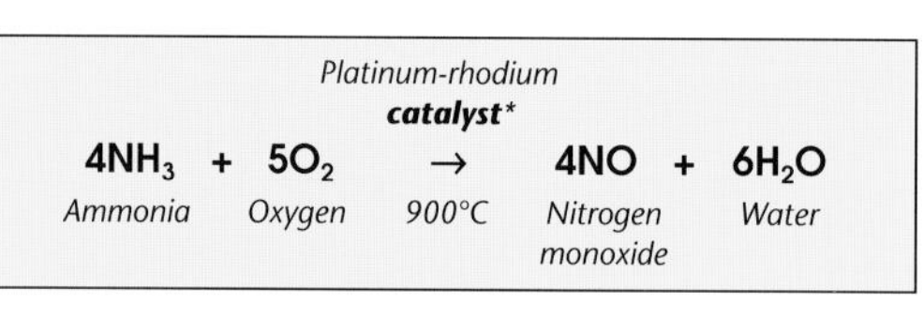
Platinum-rhodium
catalyst*
$4NH_3 + 5O_2 \rightarrow 4NO + 6H_2O$
Ammonia Oxygen 900°C Nitrogen monoxide Water

Stage 2: Nitrogen monoxide cools and reacts with more oxygen to give nitrogen dioxide.

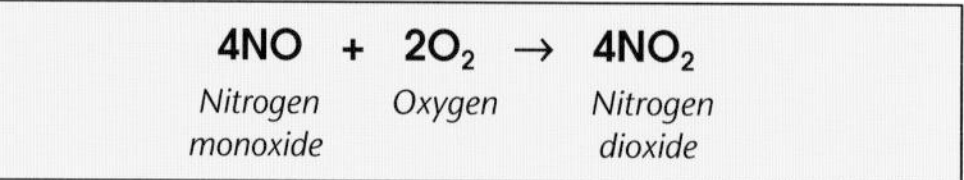
$4NO + 2O_2 \rightarrow 4NO_2$
Nitrogen monoxide Oxygen Nitrogen dioxide

*Stage 3: Nitrogen dioxide dissolves in water to form **nitric acid**.*

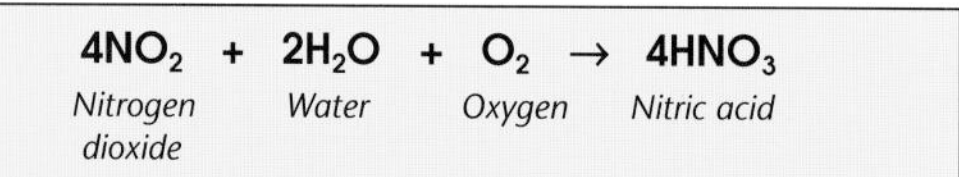
$4NO_2 + 2H_2O + O_2 \rightarrow 4HNO_3$
Nitrogen dioxide Water Oxygen Nitric acid

Concentrated nitric acid is a mixture of 70% nitric acid and 30% water. It is a powerful **oxidizing agent***. **Dilute nitric acid** is a solution of 10% nitric acid in water. It reacts with **bases*** to give **nitrate salts*** and water. Nitric acid is used to make fertilizers and explosives.

Nitrates or nitrate(V) compounds

Solid **ionic compounds*** containing the **nitrate anion*** (NO_3^-) and a metal **cation*** (see test for nitrate ion, page 218). Nitrogen in a nitrate ion has an **oxidation state*** of +5. Nitrates are **salts*** of **nitric acid** and are made by adding a metal oxide, hydroxide or carbonate to dilute nitric acid. All nitrates are water-soluble and most give off nitrogen dioxide and oxygen on heating (some exceptions are sodium, potassium and ammonium nitrates).

***Sodium nitrate** ($NaNO_3$) is used to make gunpowder.*

***Sodium** and **ammonium nitrates** are used as fertilizers.*

Nitrites or nitrate(III) compounds

Solid **ionic compounds*** that contain the **nitrite anion*** (NO_2^-) and a metal **cation***. They are usually **reducing agents***.

Phosphorus (P)

A non-metallic member of Group V (see chart, page 180). Phosphorus only occurs naturally in compounds. Its main ore is **apatite** ($3Ca_3(PO_4)_2.CaF_2$). It has two common forms. **White phosphorus**, the most reactive form, is a poisonous, waxy, white solid that bursts into flames in air. **Red phosphorus** is a dark red powder that is not poisonous and not very flammable.

*The minerals **apatite** (left) and turquoise (right) contain phosphorus.*

***Red phosphorus** on the tip of a match reacts when struck against the chemicals on a matchbox to produce a flame.*

Phosphorus pentoxide (P_2O_5)

A white solid and **dehydrating agent***, made by burning **phosphorus** in air. It reacts vigorously with water to form **phosphoric acid** (H_3PO_4) and is used to protect against **rust***.

*Living organisms such as plants contain **phosphorus** compounds which promote healthy growth.*

* **Anion**, 130; **Base**, 151; **Catalyst**, 161; **Cation**, 130; **Covalent compounds**, 132; **Dehydrating agent**, 344; **Ionic compound**, 131; **Oxidation state**, 149; **Oxidizing agent**, **Reducing agent**, 148; **Rust**, 174; **Salts**, 153.

GROUP VI ELEMENTS

The elements in **Group VI** of the **periodic table*** show increasing metallic properties and decreasing chemical reactivity going down the group. The chart below shows some of the properties of these elements.

Some properties of Group VI elements

Name of element	Chemical symbol	Relative atomic mass*	Electron configuration*	Reactivity	Appearance	Uses
Oxygen	O	15.99	2,6	DECREASING ↓	Colorless gas (see below)	See below.
Sulfur	S	32.06	2,8,6		Yellow, non-metallic solid (see page 184)	See page 184.
Selenium	Se	78.96	Complex configuration but still six outer electrons		Several forms, metallic and non-metallic	In **photocells***
Tellurium	Te	127.60			Silver-white **metalloid*** solid	In **alloys***, colored glass, **semiconductors***
Polonium	Po	**Radioactive*** element			Metal	

*The atoms of all the elements in Group VI have six electrons in their **outer shell***. They need two electrons to fill their outer shell (see **octet**, page 127) and react with other substances to form both **ionic** and **covalent compounds***. The elements with the smallest atoms are most reactive as the atoms produce the most powerful attraction for the two electrons.*

More information on **oxygen**, **sulfur** and their compounds can be found below and on pages 184-185. They are found widely and have many uses.

Oxygen (O_2)

A colorless, odorless, **diatomic*** gas that makes up 21% of the atmosphere. It is the most abundant element in the Earth's crust and is vital for life (see **internal respiration**, page 209). It supports combustion, dissolves in water to form a **neutral*** solution and is a very reactive **oxidizing agent***, e.g. it oxidizes iron to iron(III) oxide. Plants produce oxygen by **photosynthesis*** and it is obtained industrially by **fractional distillation of liquid air**. It has many uses, e.g. in hospitals and to break down sewage. See preparation of, and test for, oxygen, on pages 217 and 218.

Fractional distillation of liquid air (see also page 220)

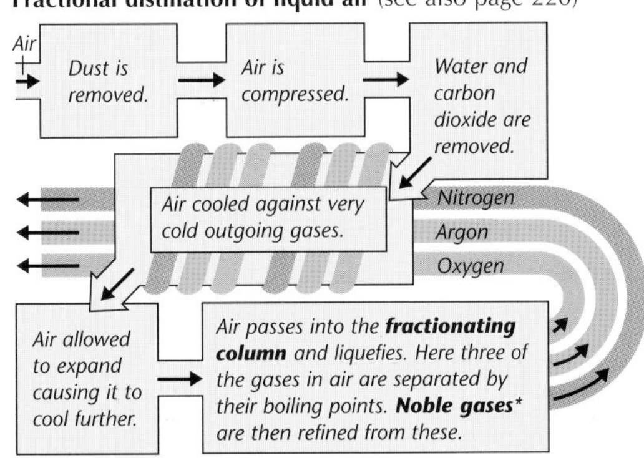
Air
Dust is removed.
Air is compressed.
Water and carbon dioxide are removed.
Air cooled against very cold outgoing gases.
Nitrogen
Argon
Oxygen
Air allowed to expand causing it to cool further.
Air passes into the ***fractionating column*** and liquefies. Here three of the gases in air are separated by their boiling points. ***Noble gases**** are then refined from these.

Ozone (O_3)

A poisonous, bluish gas made of molecules which contain three **oxygen** atoms. It is an **allotrope*** of oxygen found in the upper atmosphere where it absorbs most of the Sun's harmful ultraviolet radiation (but see **ozone depletion**, page 210). It is produced when electrical sparks pass through air, e.g. when lightning occurs. Ozone is a powerful **oxidizing agent*** and is sometimes used to sterilize water.

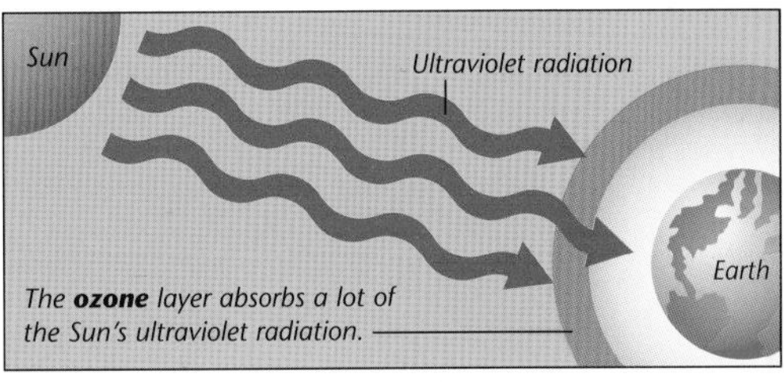
Sun
Ultraviolet radiation
Earth
The **ozone** layer absorbs a lot of the Sun's ultraviolet radiation.

Oxides

Compounds of **oxygen** and one other element. Metal oxides are mostly **ionic compounds*** and **bases***, e.g. **calcium oxide** (**CaO**). Some metal and **metalloid*** oxides are **amphoteric***, e.g. **aluminum oxide** (Al_2O_3). Non-metal oxides are **covalent*** and often **acidic***, e.g. **carbon dioxide** (CO_2).

* **Acidic**, 150; **Allotropes**, 136; **Alloy**, 344; **Amphoteric**, **Base**, 151; **Covalent compounds**, 132; **Diatomic**, 124; **Electron configuration**, 127; **Ionic compound**, 131; **Metalloids**, 165; **Neutral**, 151; **Noble gases**, 189; **Outer shell**, 127; **Oxidizing agent**, 148; **Periodic table**, 164; **Photocell**, 345; **Photosynthesis**, 254; **Radioactivity**, 128; **Relative atomic mass**, 138; **Semiconductor**, 65.

SULFUR

Sulfur (**S**) is a member of **Group VI** of the **periodic table*** (see chart, page 183). It is a yellow, non-metallic solid that is insoluble in water. It is **polymorphic*** and has two **allotropes*** – **rhombic** and **monoclinic sulfur**. Sulfur is found uncombined in underground deposits (see **Frasch process**) and is also extracted from **petroleum*** and metal **sulfides** (compounds of sulfur and another element), e.g. **iron(II) sulfide** (**FeS**). Sulfur burns in air with a blue flame to form **sulfur dioxide** and reacts with many metals to form sulfides. It is used to **vulcanize*** rubber, and to make **sulfuric acid**, medicines and **fungicides***.

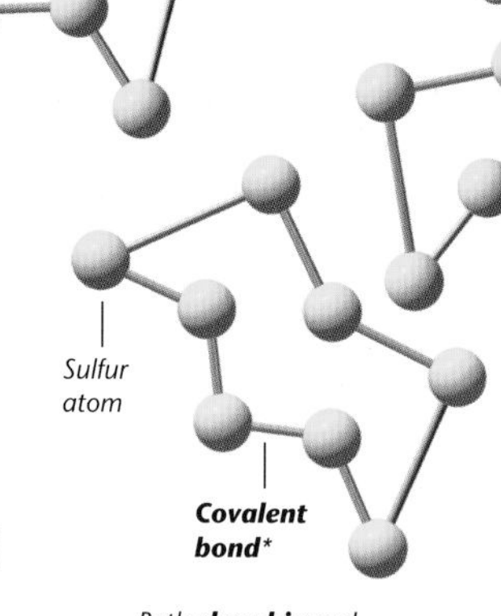
Sulfur atom
Covalent bond*

*Both **rhombic** and **monoclinic sulfur** are made of puckered rings of eight sulfur atoms.*

Rhombic sulfur

Also called **alpha sulfur** (**α-sulfur**) or **orthorhombic sulfur**. A pale yellow, crystalline **allotrope*** of sulfur, the most stable form at room temperature.

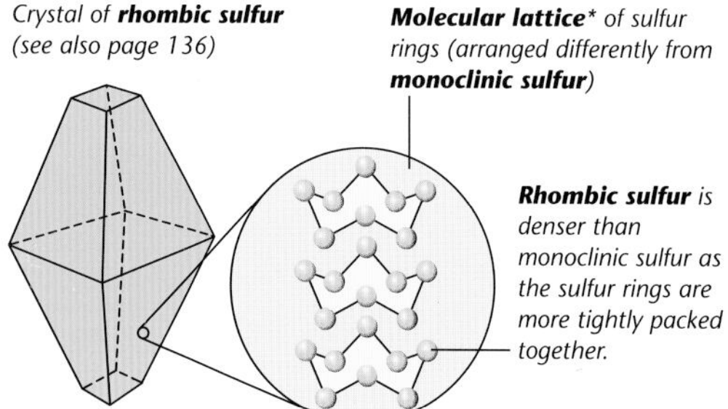

*Crystal of **rhombic sulfur** (see also page 136)*

Molecular lattice of sulfur rings (arranged differently from **monoclinic sulfur**)*

***Rhombic sulfur** is denser than monoclinic sulfur as the sulfur rings are more tightly packed together.*

Monoclinic sulfur or beta sulfur (β-sulfur)

A yellow, crystalline **allotrope*** of sulfur. It is more stable than **rhombic sulfur** at temperatures over 96°C.

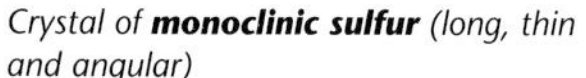

*Crystal of **monoclinic sulfur** (long, thin and angular)*

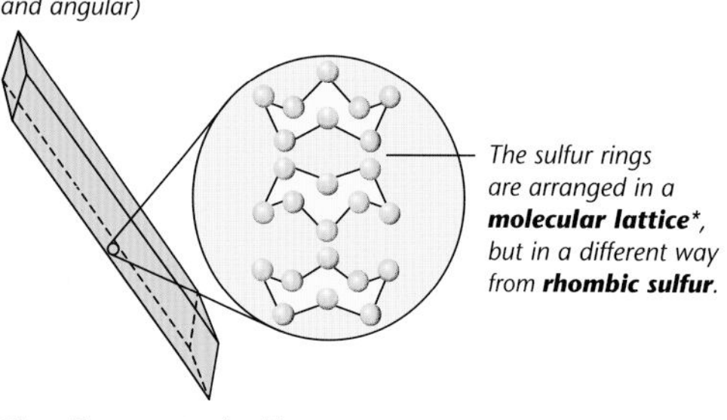

*The sulfur rings are arranged in a **molecular lattice***, but in a different way from **rhombic sulfur**.*

The allotropes* of sulfur

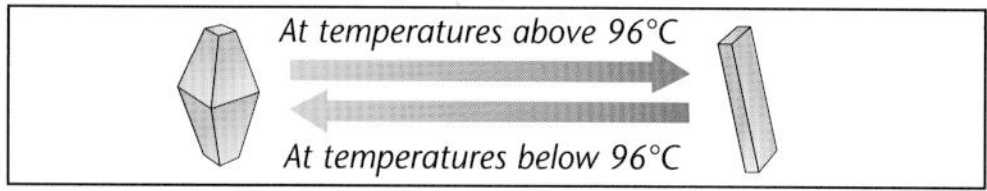
At temperatures above 96°C
At temperatures below 96°C

Plastic sulfur

A form of sulfur made when hot liquid sulfur is poured into water to cool it quickly. It can be kneaded and stretched into long fibers. It is not stable and hardens when rings of eight sulfur atoms reform (see above).

Flowers of sulfur

A fine, yellow powder formed when sulfur vapor is cooled quickly. The molecules are in rings of eight atoms.

Frasch process

The method used to extract sulfur from underground deposits by melting it. Sulfur produced this way is 99.5% pure.

Frasch process

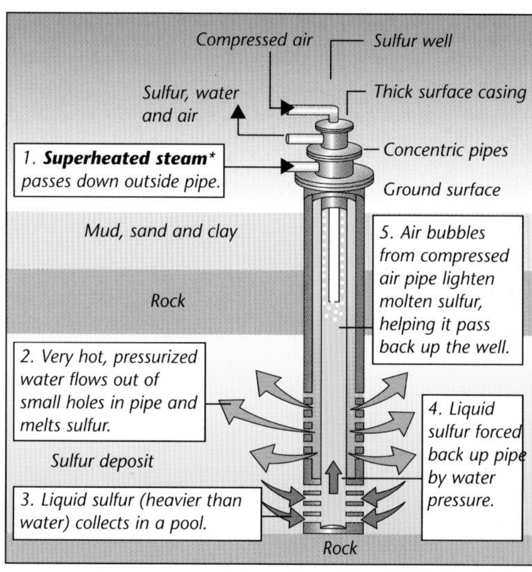
Compressed air
Sulfur well
Sulfur, water and air
Thick surface casing
1. Superheated steam* passes down outside pipe.
Concentric pipes
Ground surface
Mud, sand and clay
5. Air bubbles from compressed air pipe lighten molten sulfur, helping it pass back up the well.
Rock
2. Very hot, pressurized water flows out of small holes in pipe and melts sulfur.
4. Liquid sulfur forced back up pipe by water pressure.
Sulfur deposit
3. Liquid sulfur (heavier than water) collects in a pool.
Rock

* **Allotropes**, 136 (**Allotropy**); **Covalent bond**, 132; **Fungicide**, 344; **Molecular lattice**, 137; **Periodic table**, 164; **Petroleum**, 198; **Polymorphism**, 136; **Superheated steam**, **Vulcanization**, 345.

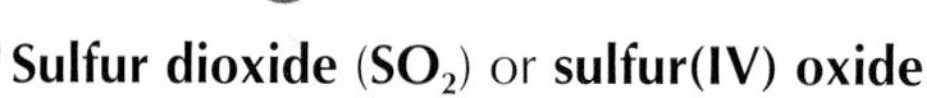

Sulfur dioxide (SO_2) or sulfur(IV) oxide

A poisonous, choking gas which forms **sulfurous acid** when dissolved in water. It is a **covalent compound*** made by burning sulfur in air or adding dilute acid to a **sulfite**. It usually acts as a **reducing agent***. It is used to make **sulfuric acid**, in **fumigation***, as a **bleach*** and as a preservative for fruit.

***Sulfur dioxide** is used as an insecticide.*

Sulfur trioxide (SO_3) or sulfur(VI) oxide

A white, **volatile*** solid that is formed by the **contact process** (see below, right). Sulfur trioxide reacts very vigorously with water to form **sulfuric acid**.

Sulfurous acid (H_2SO_3) or sulfuric(IV) acid

A colorless, **weak acid***, formed when **sulfur dioxide** dissolves in water.

Hydrogen sulfide (H_2S)

A colorless, poisonous gas, which smells like bad eggs. It dissolves in water to form a **weak acid***. It is given off when organic matter rots and when a dilute acid is added to a metal sulfide.

Sulfates or sulfate(VI) compounds

Solid **ionic compounds*** that contain a **sulfate ion** (SO_4^{2-}) and a **cation***. Many occur naturally, e.g. **calcium sulfate** ($CaSO_4$). They are **salts*** of **sulfuric acid**, made by adding **bases*** to dilute sulfuric acid.

***Sodium sulfate** solution is used to "fix" photographs. This process stops prints from going completely black when exposed to light.*

Sulfites or sulfate(IV) compounds

Ionic compounds* containing a **sulfite ion** (SO_3^{2-}) and a metal **cation*** e.g. **sodium sulfite** (Na_2SO_3). They are **salts*** of **sulfurous acid**, and react with dilute **strong acids***, giving off **sulfur dioxide**.

Sulfuric acid (H_2SO_4) or sulfuric(VI) acid

An oily, colorless, corrosive liquid. It is a **dibasic*** acid, made by the **contact process** (see below). **Concentrated sulfuric acid** contains about 2% water, is **hygroscopic*** and a powerful **oxidizing** and **dehydrating agent***. **Dilute sulfuric acid**, a **strong acid***, contains about 90% water. It reacts with metals above hydrogen in the **electrochemical series*** to give the metal **sulfate** and hydrogen.

Concentrated sulfuric acid** is an **oxidizing agent.*

$$Cu + 2H_2SO_4 \rightarrow CuSO_4 + SO_2 + 2H_2O$$

Copper + Concentrated sulfuric acid → Copper(II) sulfate + Sulfur dioxide + Water

Dilute sulfuric acid** reacts with a **base to give a **sulfate**.*

$$CuO(s) + H_2SO_4(aq) \rightarrow CuSO_4(aq) + H_2O(l)$$

Copper(II) oxide + Dilute sulfuric acid → Copper(II) sulphate + Water

***Sulfuric acid** is used to make many things e.g. fertilizers, man-made fibers, detergents and paints.*

*The reaction between **concentrated sulfuric acid** and water is very violent. To avoid accidents when the two are mixed, the acid is always added slowly to the water and not vice versa.*

Contact process

The industrial process used to make **sulfuric acid**.

Contact process

*Dry and pure **sulfur dioxide** and air are passed over a **catalyst*** of vanadium pentoxide at 450°C.*

$$2SO_2(g) + O_2(g) \rightarrow 2SO_3(g)$$

Sulfur dioxide + Oxygen → Sulfur trioxide

***Sulfur trioxide** is formed.*

***Sulfur trioxide** is absorbed by **concentrated sulfuric acid**, and **fuming sulfuric acid**, or **oleum**, is formed.*

$$SO_3 + H_2SO_4 \rightarrow H_2S_2O_7$$

Sulfur trioxide + Concentrated sulfuric acid → Fuming sulfuric acid

***Fuming sulfuric acid** is diluted to form **sulfuric acid**.*

$$H_2S_2O_7 + H_2O \rightarrow 2H_2SO_4$$

Fuming sulfuric acid + Water → Sulfuric acid

* **Base**, 151; **Bleach**, 344; **Catalyst**, 161; **Cation**, 130; **Covalent compounds**, 132; **Dehydrating agent**, 344; **Dibasic**, 153; **Electrochemical series**, 159; **Fumigation**, 344; **Hygroscopic**, 206; **Ionic compound**, 131; **Oxidizing agent**, **Reducing agent**, 148; **Salts**, 153; **Strong acid**, 152; **Volatile**, 345; **Weak acid**, 152.

GROUP VII, THE HALOGENS

The elements in **Group VII** of the **periodic table*** are called the **halogens**, and their compounds and ions are generally known as **halides**. Group VII members are all non-metals and their reactivity decreases going down the group – the chart below shows some of their properties. For further information on group members, see below and pages 187-188. The power of Group VII elements as **oxidizing agents*** decreases down the group. They can all oxidize the ions of any members below them in the group. For example, **chlorine** displaces both **bromide** and **iodide anions*** from solution by oxidizing them to **bromine** and **iodine** molecules respectively. Bromine only displaces iodide anions from solution, and iodine cannot displace any halide anions from solution.

$$2KI(aq) + Br_2(l) \rightarrow 2KBr(aq) + I_2(s)$$

Bromine *displaces* ***iodide anions**** *from potassium iodide. Each iodide anion loses an electron (is* ***oxidized****) when it is displaced by a* ***bromide anion****.*

Some properties of Group VII elements

Name of element	Chemical symbol	Relative atomic mass*	Electron configuration*	Oxidizing* power	Reactivity	Appearance
Fluorine	F	18.99	2,7	DECREASING ↓	DECREASING ↓	Pale yellow-green gas
Chlorine	Cl	35.45	2,8,7			Pale green-yellow gas
Bromine	Br	79.91	2,8,18,7			Dark-red fuming liquid
Iodine	I	126.90	2,8,18,18,7			Non-metallic black-gray solid
Astatine	At	No stable isotope*				

The atoms of all the elements in Group VII contain seven electrons in their ***outer shell**** *and they all react to form both* ***ionic*** *and* ***covalent compounds****. The elements at the top of the group form more ionic compounds than those further down the group.*

Fluorine *is never used in school laboratories as it is very poisonous and attacks glass containers.* ***Chlorine, bromine*** *and* ***iodine*** *do not react with glass, but chlorine is very poisonous, and so are the gases given off by the other two.*

Fluorine (F_2)

A member of Group VII of the periodic table. It is a **diatomic*** gas, extracted from **fluorospar** (**CaF_2**) and **cryolite** (**Na_3AlF_6**). It is the most reactive member of the group and is a very powerful **oxidizing agent***. It reacts with almost all elements. See pictures for some examples of its uses.

Fluorine *reacts to form useful, stable* ***organic compounds****, called* ***fluorocarbons****, e.g.* ***poly(tetrafluoroethene)****, or* ***PTFE*** *(see also page 195). Skis are coated with PTFE to reduce friction.*

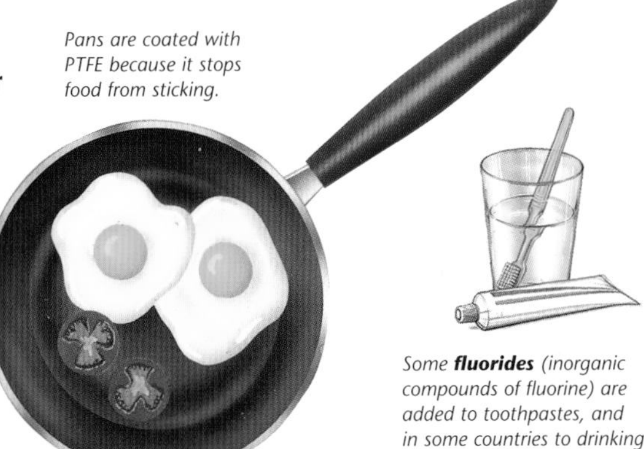

Pans are coated with PTFE because it stops food from sticking.

Some ***fluorides*** *(inorganic compounds of fluorine) are added to toothpastes, and in some countries to drinking water, to reduce tooth decay.*

* **Bromide anion**, 188 (**Bromides**); **Covalent compounds**, 132; **Diatomic**, 124; **Electron configuration**, 127; **Iodide anion**, 188 (**Iodides**); **Ionic compound**, 131; **Isotope**, 127; **Organic compounds**, 190; **Outer shell**, 127; **Oxidation**, **Oxidizing agent**, 148; **Periodic table**, 164; **Relative atomic mass**, 138.

Chlorine (Cl_2)

A member of Group VII of the periodic table. A poisonous, choking **diatomic*** gas which is very reactive and only occurs naturally in compounds. **Sodium chloride** (**NaCl**), its most important compound, is found in rock salt and brine. Chlorine is extracted from brine by **electrolysis***, using the **Downs' cell** (see **sodium**, page 168 and also **chlorine**, page 216). It is a very strong **oxidizing agent***. Many elements react with chlorine to form **chlorides** (see equation below).

*__Chlorine__ gas reacts with sodium to form __sodium chloride__ – common salt. Although chlorine gas is poisonous and sodium is extremely reactive, both chemicals lose these dangerous properties when they join together to form sodium chloride. In the laboratory, this reaction takes place inside a __fume cupboard*__, so the harmful gas does not escape.*

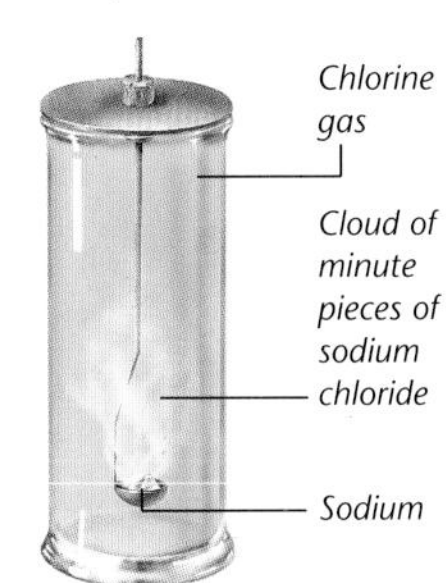
Chlorine gas
Cloud of minute pieces of sodium chloride
Sodium

$$2Na(s) + Cl_2(g) \rightarrow 2NaCl(s)$$

Hydrogen — Chlorine — Hydrogen chloride

*__Chlorine__ has many uses. It is used to make __hydrochloric acid__ (see __hydrogen chloride__), some organic solvents and also as a __germicide*__ in swimming pools. It is also used as a germicide in drinking water and disinfectants.*

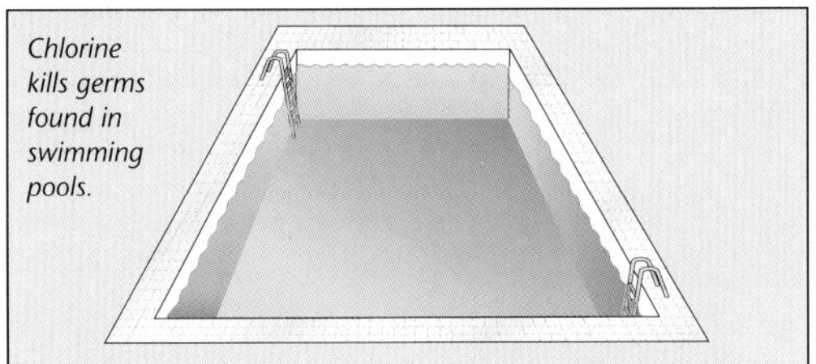

Chlorine kills germs found in swimming pools.

Chlorides

Compounds formed when **chlorine** combines with another element. Chlorides of non-metals (see **hydrogen chloride**) are **covalent compounds***, usually liquids or gases. Chlorides of metals, e.g. **sodium chloride** (**NaCl**), are usually solid, water-soluble, **ionic compounds*** made of a **chloride anion*** (**Cl^-**) and metal **cation***. See also page 218.

Hydrogen chloride (HCl)

A colorless, **covalent*** gas that forms ions when dissolved in a **polar solvent***. It is made by burning hydrogen in **chlorine**. It reacts with ammonia and dissolves in water to form **hydrochloric acid**, a **strong acid***. **Concentrated hydrochloric acid**, 35% hydrogen chloride and 65% water, is a fuming, corrosive and colorless solution. **Dilute hydrochloric acid**, about 7% hydrogen chloride and 93% water, is a colorless solution that reacts with **bases***, and with metals above hydrogen in the **electrochemical series***. Concentrated hydrochloric acid is used industrially to remove rust from steel sheets before they are **galvanized***.

__Concentrated hydrochloric acid__ is used to etch metals.

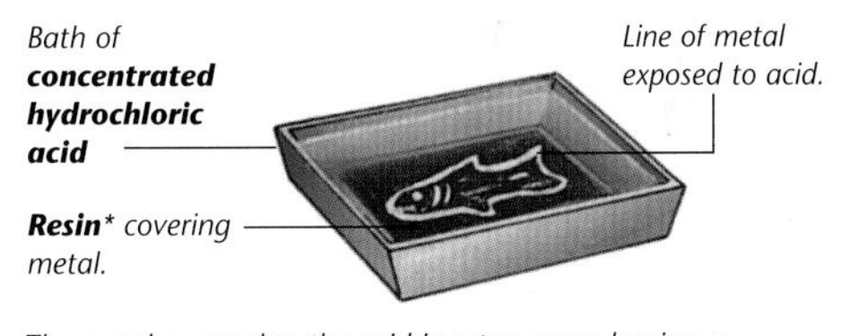
Bath of concentrated hydrochloric acid
Line of metal exposed to acid.
Resin* covering metal.

The metal exposed to the acid is eaten away, leaving a groove in the surface. When printing a picture, the groove is filled with ink.

Sodium hypochlorite (NaOCl) or sodium chlorate(I)

A crystalline, white solid, stored dissolved in water, and formed when **chlorine** is added to a cold, dilute sodium hydroxide solution. It is used in domestic **bleach*** and also to bleach paper pulp white for writing.

Bleached writing paper

Sodium chlorate ($NaClO_3$) or sodium chlorate(V)

A white, crystalline solid, formed when **chlorine** is added to warm concentrated sodium hydroxide, and also when **sodium hypochlorite** is warmed.

__Sodium chlorate__ kills weeds.

* **Anion**, 130; **Base**, 151; **Bleach**, 344; **Cation**, 130; **Covalent compounds**, 132; **Diatomic**, 124; **Electrochemical series**, 159; **Electrolysis**, 156; **Fume cupboard**, 224; **Galvanizing**, 174 (**Rust**); **Germicide**, 344; **Ionic compound**, 131; **Oxidizing agent**, 148; **Polar solvent**, 144; **Resins**, 345; **Strong acid**, 152.

Halogens (continued)

*Photographic film is coated with **silver bromide** which reacts with light to form a negative picture.*

Bromine (Br_2)

A member of **Group VII** of the **periodic table*** (the **halogens** – see chart, page 186). It is a **volatile***, **diatomic*** liquid that gives off a poisonous, choking vapor. It is very reactive and only occurs naturally in compounds, e.g. those found in marine organisms, rocks, sea water and some inland lakes. It is extracted from **sodium bromide** (**NaBr**) in sea water by adding chlorine. Bromine is a strong **oxidizing agent***. It reacts with most elements to form **bromides**, and dissolves slightly in water to give an orange solution of **bromine water**. Bromine compounds are used in medicine, photography, and disinfectants. It is used to make **1,2-dibromoethane** (**CH_2BrCH_2Br**) which is added to gasoline to stop lead from accumulating in engines.

Bromides

Compounds of **bromine** and one other element. Bromides of non-metals are **covalent compounds*** (see **hydrogen bromide**). Bromides of metals are usually **ionic compounds*** made of **bromide anions*** (**Br^-**) and metal **cations***. Excepting **silver bromide** (**AgBr**), they are all water-soluble. See also page 218.

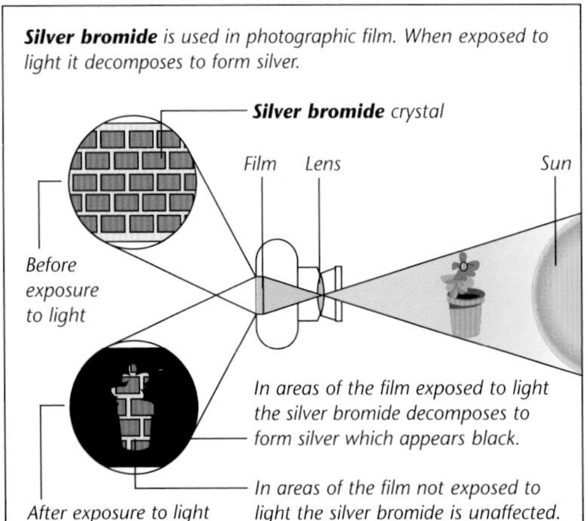

Silver bromide crystal
Film
Lens
Sun
Before exposure to light
In areas of the film exposed to light the silver bromide decomposes to form silver which appears black.
In areas of the film not exposed to light the silver bromide is unaffected.
After exposure to light

Silver bromide is used in photographic film. When exposed to light it decomposes to form silver.

Hydrogen bromide (HBr)

A colorless, pungent-smelling gas, made by the reaction of **bromine** with hydrogen. Its chemical properties are similar to those of hydrochloric acid.

Iodine (I_2)

A member of **Group VII** of the **periodic table*** (the **halogens** – see chart, page 186). A reactive, **diatomic***, crystalline solid. It is extracted from **sodium iodate** (**$NaIO_3$**) and seaweed. It is an **oxidizing agent*** and reacts with many elements to form **iodides**. When heated, it **sublimes***, giving off a purple vapor. Iodine is only slightly soluble in pure water, however, it dissolves well in **potassium iodide** (**KI**) solution and also in some organic solvents.

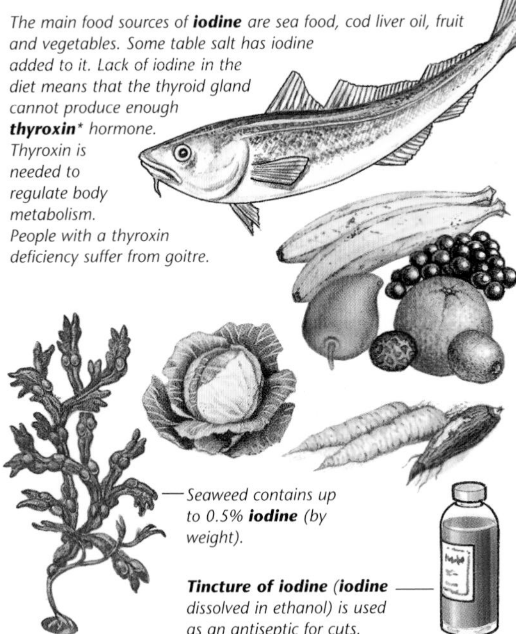

*The main food sources of **iodine** are sea food, cod liver oil, fruit and vegetables. Some table salt has iodine added to it. Lack of iodine in the diet means that the thyroid gland cannot produce enough **thyroxin*** hormone. Thyroxin is needed to regulate body metabolism. People with a thyroxin deficiency suffer from goitre.*

*Seaweed contains up to 0.5% **iodine** (by weight).*

***Tincture of iodine** (**iodine** dissolved in ethanol) is used as an antiseptic for cuts.*

Iodides

Compounds of **iodine** and one other element. Iodides of non-metals are **covalent compounds*** (see **hydrogen iodide**). Iodides of metals are usually **ionic***, made of **iodide anions*** (**I^-**) and metal **cations***. Except **silver iodide** (**AgI**), ionic iodides are water-soluble. See page 218.

Hydrogen iodide (HI)

A colorless gas with a pungent smell. It is a **covalent compound***, formed when hydrogen and **iodine** react. It dissolves in water to give a strongly **acidic*** solution called **hydroiodic acid** (its chemical properties are similar to those of hydrochloric acid).

* **Acidic**, 150; **Anion**, **Cation**, 130; **Covalent compounds**, 132; **Diatomic**, 124; **Ionic compound**, 131; **Periodic table**, 164; **Oxidizing agent**, 148; **Sublimation**, 121; **Thyroxin**, 336; **Volatile**, 345.

GROUP VIII, THE NOBLE GASES

The **noble gases**, also called **inert** or **rare gases**, make up **Group VIII** of the **periodic table***, **also called Group 0**. They are all **monatomic*** gases, obtained by the **fractional distillation of liquid air***. **Argon** forms 0.9% of the air and the other gases occur in even smaller amounts. They are all unreactive because their atoms' **electron configuration*** is very stable (they all have a full **outer shell***). The lighter members do not form any compounds, but the heavier members form a few.

Helium (He)
The first member of Group VIII of the periodic table. It is a colorless, odorless, **monatomic*** gas found in the atmosphere (one part in 200,000) and in some natural gases in the USA. It is obtained by the **fractional distillation of liquid air*** and is completely unreactive, having no known compounds. It is used in airships and balloons, as it is eight times less dense than air and not inflammable, and also by deep-sea divers to avoid "the bends".

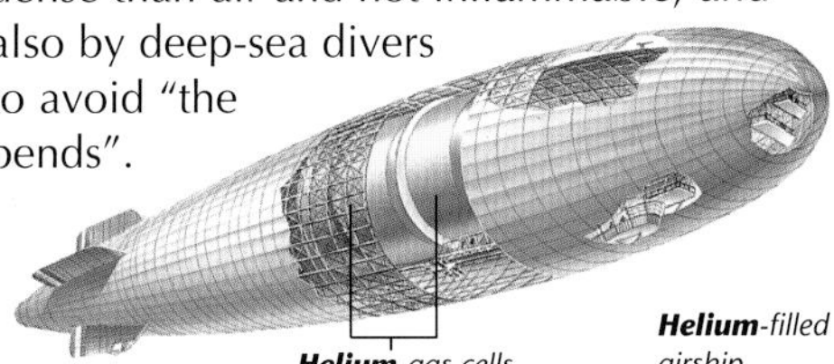
Helium gas cells

***Helium**-filled airship*

Neon (Ne)
A member of Group VIII of the periodic table. A colorless, odorless **monatomic*** gas found in the atmosphere (one part in 55,000). It is obtained by the **fractional distillation of liquid air*** and is totally unreactive, having no known compounds. It is used in neon signs and fluorescent lighting as it emits an orange-red glow when an electric discharge passes through it at low pressure.

***Neon** signs*

Radon (Rn)
The last member of Group VIII of the periodic table. It is **radioactive***, occurring as a result of the **radioactive decay*** of radium.

Argon (Ar)
The most abundant member of Group VIII of the periodic table. It is a colorless, odorless, **monatomic*** gas that makes up 0.9% of the air. Obtained by the **fractional distillation of liquid air***, it is totally unreactive, having no known compounds. It is used in electric light bulbs and fluorescent tubes.

Electric light bulb

Krypton (Kr)
A member of Group VIII of the periodic table. It is a colorless, odorless, **monatomic*** gas found in the atmosphere (one part in 670,000). It is obtained by the **fractional distillation of liquid air*** and is unreactive, only forming one known compound, **krypton fluoride (KrF_2)**. Krypton is used in some lasers and photographic flash lamps. It is also used in fluorescent tubes and in the stroboscopic lights which flank airport runways.

Xenon (Xe)
A member of Group VIII of the periodic table. A colorless, odorless **monatomic*** gas found in the atmosphere (0.006 parts per million). Obtained from the **fractional distillation of liquid air***, it is unreactive, forming only a very few compounds, e.g. **xenon tetrafluoride (XeF_4)**. It is used to fill fluorescent tubes and light bulbs.

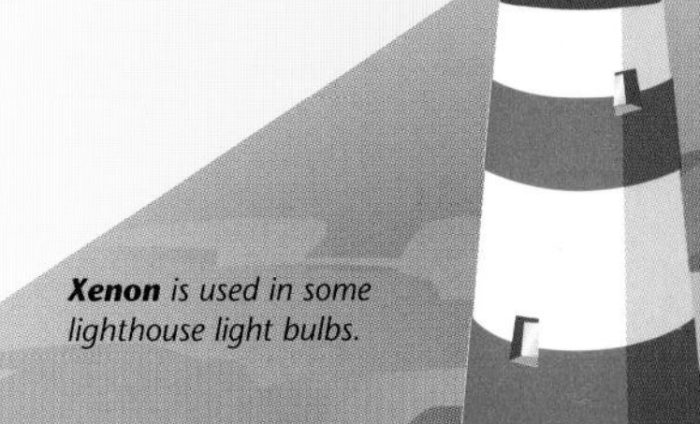

***Xenon** is used in some lighthouse light bulbs.*

* **Electron configuration**, 127; **Fractional distillation of liquid air**, 183; **Monatomic**, 124; **Outer shell**, 127; **Periodic table**, 164; **Radioactive decay**, **Radioactivity**, 128.

ORGANIC CHEMISTRY

Originally **organic chemistry** was the study of chemicals found in living organisms. However, it now refers to the study of all carbon-containing compounds, except the **carbonates*** and the **oxides*** of carbon. There are well over two million such compounds (**organic compounds**), more than all the other chemical compounds added together. This vast number of **covalent compounds*** is possible because carbon atoms can bond with each other to make a huge variety of **chains** and **rings**.

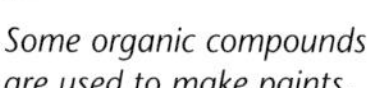

Some organic compounds are used to make paints.

Aliphatic compounds

Organic compounds whose molecules contain a **main chain** of carbon atoms. The chain may be **straight**, **branched** or even in **ring** form (though never a **benzene ring** – see **aromatic compounds**).

__Branched chain__ of carbon atoms in a 3-methyl pentane molecule. In a branched chain, a carbon atom may be bonded to more than two other carbon atoms.

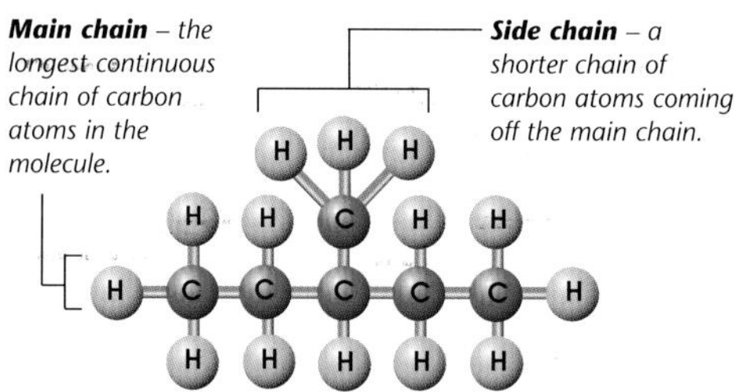
__Main chain__ – the longest continuous chain of carbon atoms in the molecule.
__Side chain__ – a shorter chain of carbon atoms coming off the main chain.

__Straight chain__ of carbon atoms in a butan-1-ol molecule. No carbon atom is bonded to more than two other carbons.

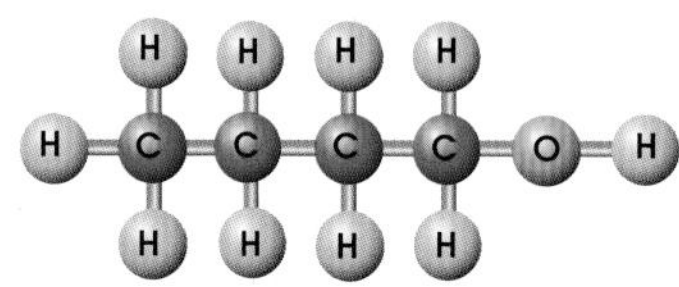

__Cyclohexane__ molecule. An example of a molecule containing a ring of carbon atoms.

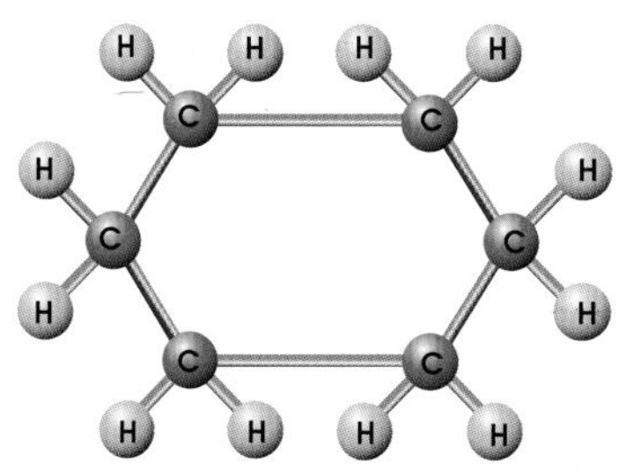

Aromatic compounds

Organic compounds whose molecules contain a **benzene ring**. A benzene ring has six carbon atoms but differs from an **aliphatic** ring because bonds between carbon atoms are neither **single** nor **double bonds*** but midway between, both in length and reactivity.

There are two possible ways of representing a __benzene ring__.

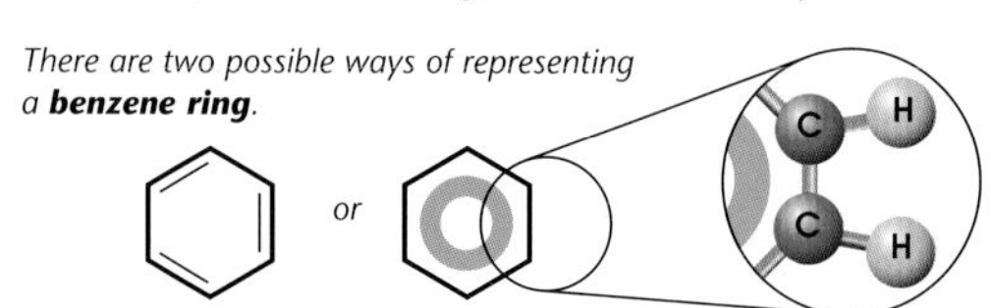
or

The bonds linking the carbon atoms are midway between __single__ and __double bonds__ because some electrons are free to move around the molecule.*

Hydrocarbons

Organic compounds that contain only carbon and hydrogen atoms.

Two examples of __hydrocarbon__ molecules:

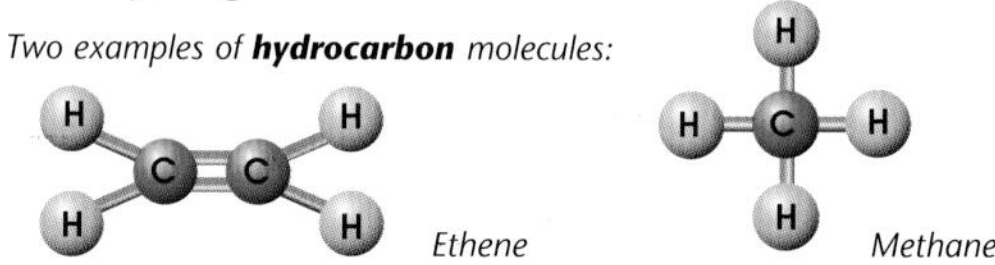
Ethene
Methane

Functional group

An atom or group of atoms that gives a molecule most of its chemical properties. Organic molecules can have several such groups (see also pages 194-195).

Most __functional groups__ contain at least one atom that is not carbon or hydrogen.

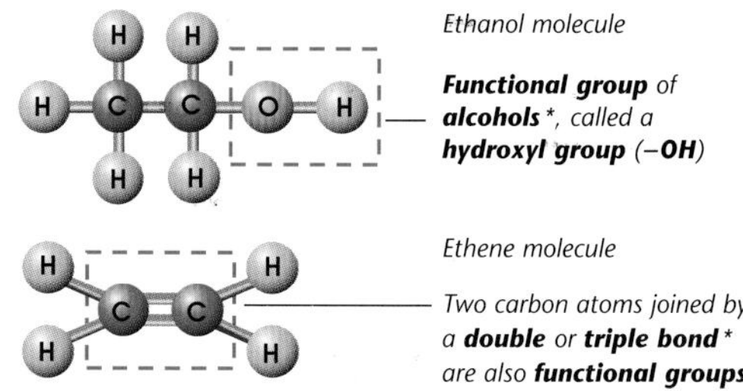
Ethanol molecule
__Functional group__ of __alcohols__, called a __hydroxyl group (–OH)__*
Ethene molecule
Two carbon atoms joined by a __double__ or __triple bond__ are also __functional groups__.*

* **Alcohols**, 196; **Carbonates**, 179; **Covalent compounds**, **Double bond**, 132; **Oxides**, 183; **Single bond**, **Triple bond**, 132.

Homologous series

A group of organic compounds which increase in size through the group by adding a $-CH_2-$ group each time. All series (except the **alkanes***) also have a **functional group**, e.g. the **alcohol*** **hydroxyl group** (**–OH**). Members of a series have similar chemical properties but their physical properties change as they get larger. A homologous series has a **general formula** for all its members.

The ***general formula*** *for* ***alcohols**** *is* $C_nH_{2n+1}OH$ *(where n stands for the number of carbon atoms).*

First two members of the homologous series of alcohols*

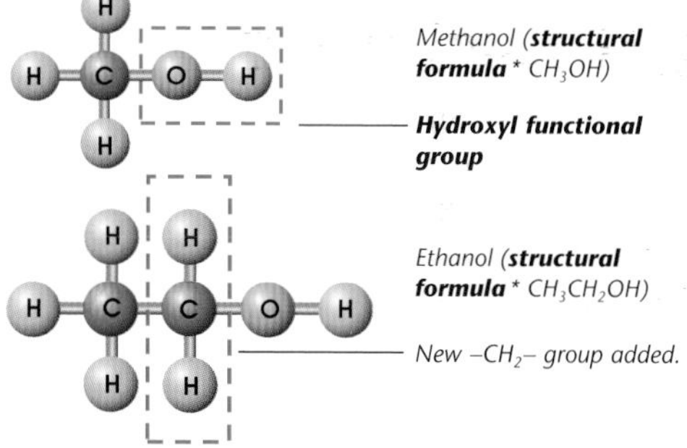

Methanol (structural formula* CH₃OH)
Hydroxyl functional group
Ethanol (structural formula* CH₃CH₂OH)
New –CH₂– group added.

Saturated compounds

Organic compounds whose molecules only have **single bonds*** between atoms.

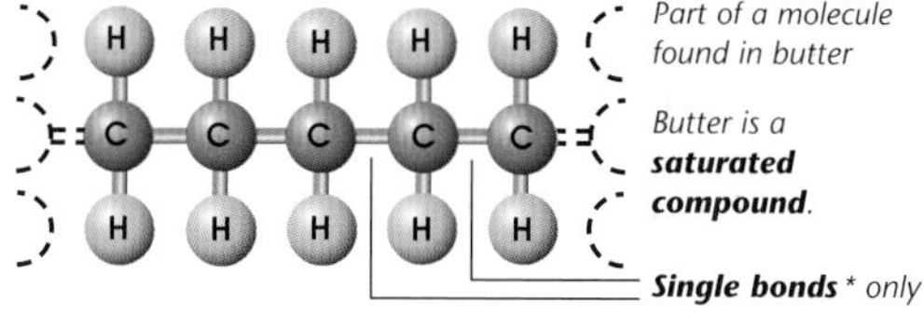

Part of a molecule found in butter
Butter is a saturated compound.
Single bonds* only

Unsaturated compounds

Organic compounds whose molecules have at least one **double** or **triple bond***.

Polyunsaturated compounds

A term used for compounds whose molecules have many **double** or **triple bonds***, e.g. those found in soft margarines.

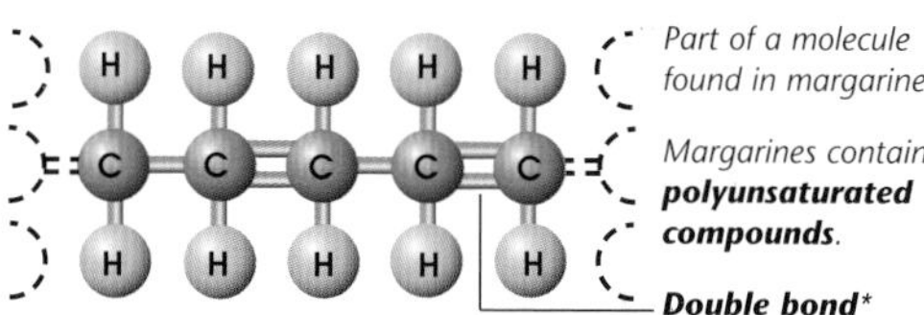

Part of a molecule found in margarine
Margarines contain polyunsaturated compounds.
Double bond*

Stereochemistry

The study of the 3-dimensional (3-D) structure of molecules. Comparing the 3-D structure of very similar organic molecules, e.g. **stereoisomers**, helps distinguish between them. The 3-D structure of a molecule is often shown by a **stereochemical formula*** – a diagram that shows how atoms are arranged in space.

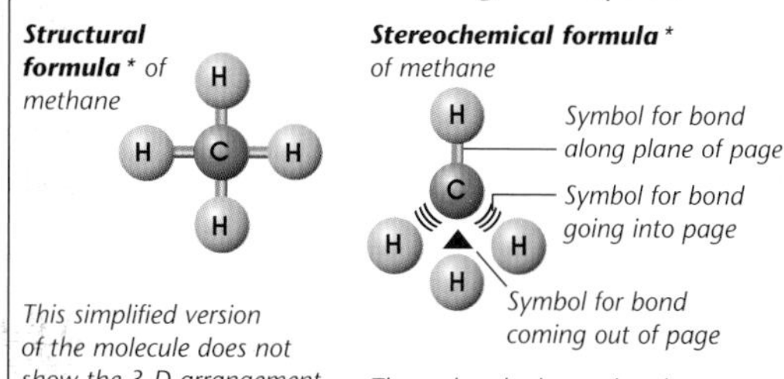

Structural formula* of methane
Stereochemical formula* of methane
Symbol for bond along plane of page
Symbol for bond going into page
Symbol for bond coming out of page
This simplified version of the molecule does not show the 3-D arrangement of the atoms.
The carbon-hydrogen bonds are arranged to form a tetrahedron.

Isomers

Two or more compounds with the same **molecular formula***, but different arrangements of atoms in their molecules. As a result, the compounds have different properties. There are two main types of isomer, **structural isomers** and **stereoisomers**.

Structural isomers

Compounds with the same **molecular formula***, but different **structural formulae***, i.e. the atoms are arranged in different ways.

The ***molecular formula**** C_2H_6O *has two different* ***structural formulae****.

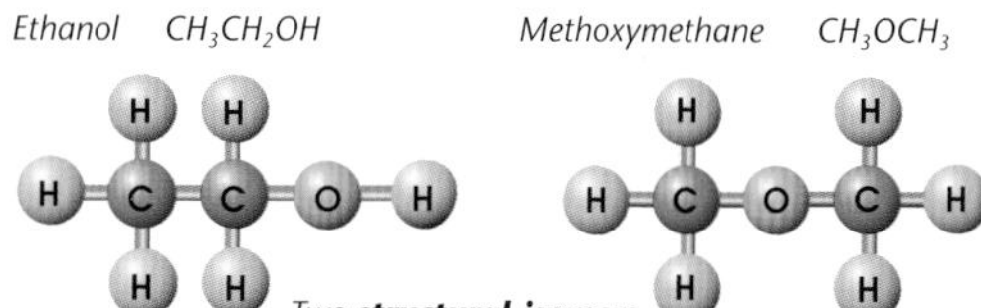

Ethanol CH₃CH₂OH
Methoxymethane CH₃OCH₃
Two structural isomers

Stereoisomers

Compounds with the same **molecular formula*** and grouping of atoms but a different 3-D appearance.

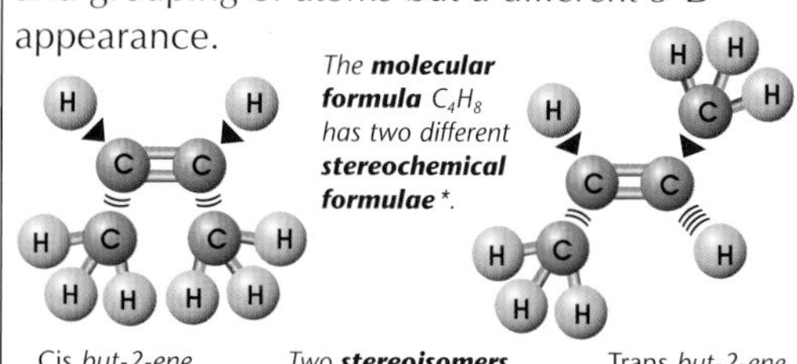

The molecular formula C₄H₈ has two different stereochemical formulae*.
Cis but-2-ene
Two stereoisomers
Trans but-2-ene

* **Alcohols**, 196; **Alkanes**, 192; **Double bond**, 132; **Molecular formula**, 140; **Single bond**, 132; **Stereochemical formula**, **Structural formula** (**shortened**), 140; **Triple bond**, 132.

ALKANES

Alkanes, or **paraffins**, are all **saturated*** **hydrocarbons*** and **aliphatic compounds***. They form a **homologous series*** which has a **general formula*** of C_nH_{2n+2}. As the molecules in the series increase in size, so the physical properties of the compounds change (see chart below). Alkanes are **non-polar molecules***. They burn in air to form carbon dioxide and water, and react with **halogens***, otherwise they are unreactive. Excepting **methane**, they are obtained from **petroleum***. They are used as fuels and to make other organic substances, e.g. plastics.

*The alkane **propane** is used as a fuel to heat the air in hot air balloons.*

Some properties of alkanes				
Name of compound	Molecular formula*	Structural formula*	Physical state at 25°C	Boiling point (°C)
Methane	CH_4	CH_4	Gas	−161.5
Ethane	C_2H_6	CH_3CH_3	Gas	−88.0
Propane	C_3H_8	$CH_3CH_2CH_3$	Gas	−42.2
Butane	C_4H_{10}	$CH_3CH_2CH_2CH_3$	Gas	−0.5
Pentane	C_5H_{12}	$CH_3CH_2CH_2CH_2CH_3$	Liquid	36.0
Hexane	C_6H_{14}	$CH_3CH_2CH_2CH_2CH_2CH_3$	Liquid	69.0

The first part of the name indicates the number of carbon atoms in the molecule. The -ane ending means the molecule is an alkane (see page 214).

The next molecule in the series is always one $-CH_2-$ group longer.

Gradual change of state as molecules get longer.

The boiling points of the alkanes increase regularly as the molecules get longer. Melting points and densities follow the same trend, getting higher as the molecules increase in size.

Methane (CH_4)
The simplest alkane. It is a colorless, odorless, inflammable gas, which reacts with **halogens*** (see equation, below right) and is a source of hydrogen. **Natural gas** contains 99% methane.

Ethane (C_2H_6)
A member of the alkanes. A gas found in small amounts in **natural gas** (see **methane**), but mostly obtained from **petroleum***. Its properties are similar to those of methane. It is used to make other organic chemicals.

Propane (C_3H_8)
A member of the alkanes. A gas that is usually obtained from **petroleum***. Its properties are similar to **ethane**. It is bottled and sold as fuel for cooking and heating.

*Alkanes are extracted from **petroleum*** and **natural gas** found deep under the ground.*

Cycloalkanes
Alkane molecules whose carbon atoms are joined in a ring, e.g. **cyclohexane** (see picture, page 190). Their properties are similar to those of other alkanes.

Substitution reaction
A reaction in which an atom or **functional group*** of a molecule is replaced by a different atom or functional group. The molecules of **saturated compounds***, e.g. alkanes, can undergo substitution reactions, but not **addition reactions** (see right).

Alkanes** react with **halogens by undergoing a **substitution reaction**. Here is an example:*

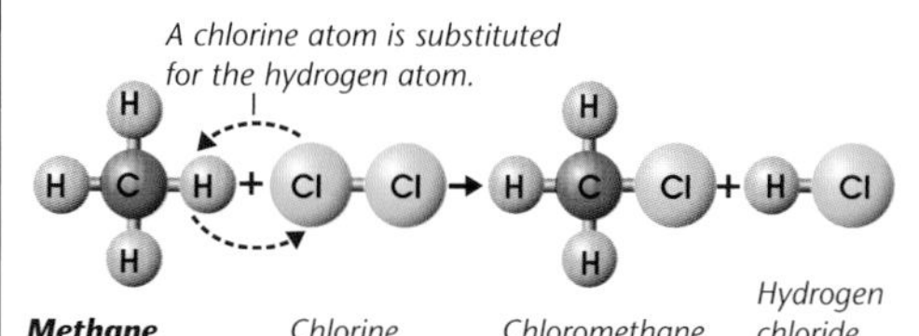
A chlorine atom is substituted for the hydrogen atom.
H
H C H + Cl Cl → H C Cl + H Cl
H
Methane
Chlorine
Chloromethane
Hydrogen chloride

* **Aliphatic compounds**, 190; **Functional group**, 190; **General formula**, 191 (**Homologous series**); **Halogens**, 186; **Hydrocarbons**, 190; **Molecular formula**, 140; **Non-polar molecule**, 133 (**Polar molecule**); **Petroleum**, 198; **Saturated compounds**, 191; **Structural formula (shortened)**, 140.

ALKENES

Alkenes, or **olefins**, are **unsaturated*** **hydrocarbons*** and **aliphatic compounds***. Alkene molecules contain one or more **double bonds*** between carbon atoms. Those with only one form a **homologous series*** with the **general formula*** C_nH_{2n}. As the molecules increase in size, their physical properties change gradually (see below). Alkenes are **non-polar molecules***. They burn with a smoky flame and in excess oxygen are completely **oxidized*** to carbon dioxide and water. Alkenes are more reactive than **alkanes**, because of their double bond – they undergo **addition reactions**, and some form **polymers***. Alkenes are made by **cracking*** alkanes and are used to make many products including plastics and antifreeze.

Some properties of alkenes				
Name of compound	Molecular formula*	Structural formula*	Physical state at 25°C	Boiling point (°C)
Ethene	C_2H_4	$CH_2{=}CH_2$	Gas	-104.0
Propene	C_3H_6	$CH_3CH{=}CH_2$	Gas	-47.0
But-1-ene	C_4H_8	$CH_3CH_2CH{=}CH_2$	Gas	-6.0
Pent-1-ene	C_5H_{10}	$CH_3CH_2CH_2CH{=}CH_2$	Liquid	30.0

*The number denotes the position of the **double bond*** in the molecule. Alkenes are named in the same way as **alkanes**, but end in -ene, not -ane (see page 214).*

*Each molecule is one $-CH_2-$ group longer. The position of the **double bond*** is shown.*

Gradual change from gases to liquids to solids as the molecules get longer.

As the molecules get longer, the boiling points of the alkenes increase regularly. Melting points and densities follow the same trend.

Ethene (C_2H_4) or ethylene

The simplest alkene (see chart above) – it is a colorless, sweet-smelling gas which undergoes **addition reactions** including **addition polymerization*** to form **poly(ethene)**, commonly known as **polythene**, (see **homopolymer**, page 200). Ethene is used to make plastics, and also ethanol and many other organic chemicals.

Propene (C_3H_6) or propylene

A member of the alkenes. It is a colorless gas used to make propanone (also known as **acetone** – see **ketones**, page 194) and **poly(propene)**, also called **polypropylene**.

*Some kitchen tools are made from **poly(propene)**, the **polymer*** of **propene**.*

Addition reaction

A reaction in which two molecules react together to produce a single larger molecule. One of the molecules must be **unsaturated*** (have a **double** or **triple bond***).

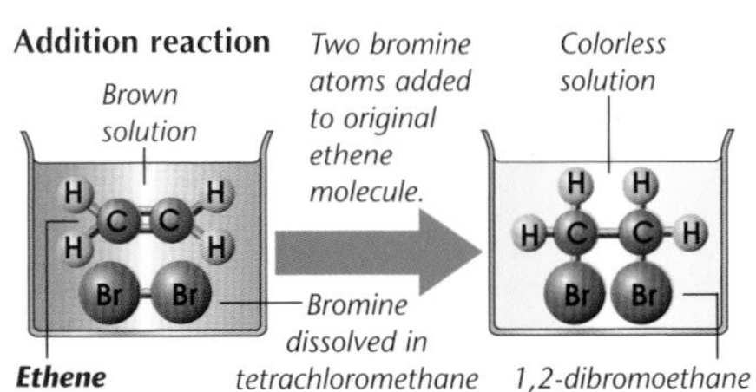
Addition reaction
Brown solution
Two bromine atoms added to original ethene molecule.
Colorless solution
H
C
Br
Bromine dissolved in tetrachloromethane
Ethene
1,2-dibromoethane

*The change of color is used as a test for **unsaturated compounds*** like alkenes.*

Hydrogenation

An **addition reaction** in which hydrogen atoms are added to an **unsaturated compound*** molecule.

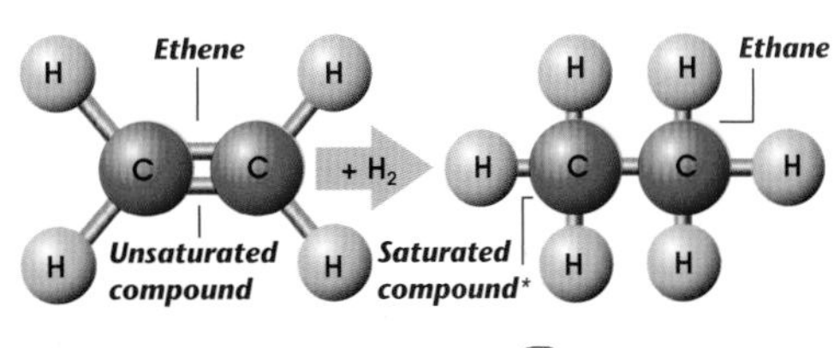
Ethene
H
C
+ H_2
Ethane
Unsaturated compound
Saturated compound*

*This type of reaction is used in the margarine industry to harden animal and vegetable oils. (These oils are **unsaturated compounds***, but not alkenes).*

Saturated
Unsaturated

* **Addition polymerization**, 200; **Aliphatic compounds**, 190; **Cracking**, 198; **Double bond**, 132; **General formula**, 191 (**Homologous series**); **Hydrocarbons**, 191; **Molecular formula**, 140; **Non-polar molecule**, 133 (**Polar molecule**); **Oxidation**, 148; **Polymers**, 200; **Saturated compounds**, 191; **Structural formula (shortened)**, 140; **Triple bond**, 132; **Unsaturated compounds**, 191.

ALKYNES

Alkynes, or **acetylenes**, are **unsaturated*** (each molecule has a carbon-carbon **triple bond***) and **aliphatic compounds***. They are **hydrocarbons*** and form a **homologous series*** with a **general formula*** C_nH_{2n-2}. Alkynes are named in the same way as **alkanes***, but end in -yne, not -ane (see page 214). They are **non-polar molecules*** with chemical properties similar to **alkenes***. They burn with a sooty flame in air, and a very hot flame in pure oxygen. Alkynes are produced by **cracking***. They are used to make plastics and solvents.

Structural formulae* of some alkynes	
Name of compound	Structural formula*
Ethyne	$CH \equiv CH$
Propyne	$CH_3C \equiv CH$
But-1-yne	$CH_3CH_2C \equiv CH$

Ethyne (C_2H_2) or acetylene

The simplest member of the alkynes. A colorless gas, less dense than air and with a slightly sweet smell. It is the only common alkyne. Ethyne undergoes the same reactions as the other alkynes but more vigorously, e.g. it reacts explosively with chlorine. It is used in oxy-acetylene welding torches as it burns with a very hot flame. Ethyne is made by **cracking*** and is used to make polyvinyl chloride (PVC) and other vinyl compounds.

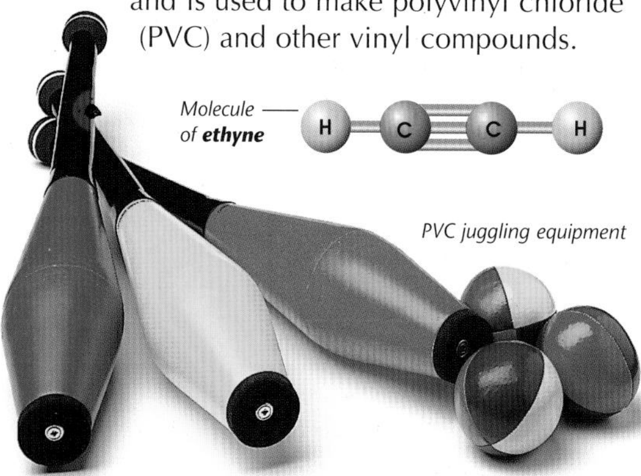
H
C
C
H
Molecule of **ethyne**

PVC juggling equipment

More homologous series

The following groups of organic compounds each form a **homologous series*** of **aliphatic compounds***. Each series has a particular **functional group*** and its members have similar chemical properties.

Aldehydes

Compounds that contain a **–CHO functional group***. They form a **homologous series*** with a **general formula*** $C_nH_{2n+1}CHO$, and are named like **alkanes*** but end in -al, not -ane (see page 215). They are colorless liquids (except **methanal**) and **reducing agents***, and undergo **addition***, **condensation*** and **polymerization reactions***. When **oxidized***, they form **carboxylic acids**.

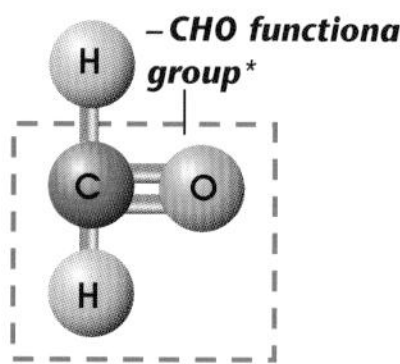
H
C
O
H
–CHO functional group*

*Molecule of **methanal** (**HCHO**) or **formaldehyde**, the simplest **aldehyde**. It is a colorless, poisonous gas with a strong smell. It dissolves in water to make **formalin** – used to preserve biological specimens. It is also used to make **polymers*** and adhesives.*

Ketones

Compounds that contain a **carbonyl group** (a **–CO– functional group***). Ketones form a **homologous series*** with a complex **general formula***. They are named like **alkanes*** but end in -one, not just -e. Most are colorless liquids. They have chemical properties similar to **aldehydes** but are not **reducing agents***.

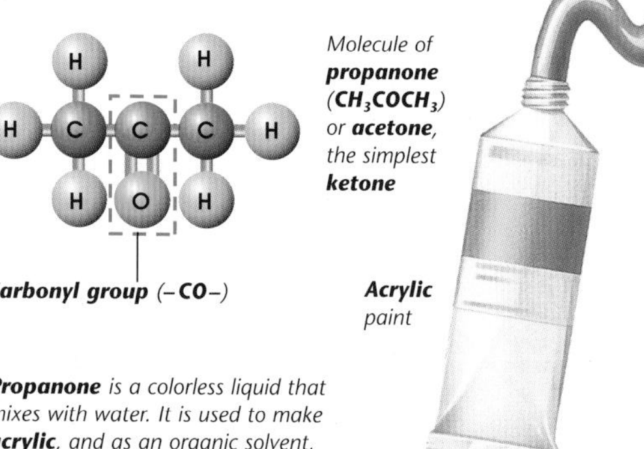
H
H
H
C
C
C
H
H
O
H
*Molecule of **propanone** (CH_3COCH_3) or **acetone**, the simplest **ketone***

***Carbonyl group** (–CO–)*

***Acrylic** paint*

***Propanone** is a colorless liquid that mixes with water. It is used to make **acrylic**, and as an organic solvent, e.g. as nail polish remover.*

* **Addition reaction**, 193; **Aliphatic compounds**, 190; **Alkanes**, 192; **Alkenes**, 193; **Condensation reaction**, 197; **Cracking**, 198; **Functional group**, 190; **General formula**, 191 (**Homologous series**); **Hydrocarbons**, 190; **Non-polar molecule**, 133; **Oxidation**, 148; **Polymerization, Polymers**, 200; **Reducing agent**, 148; **Structural formula**, 140; **Triple bond**, 132; **Unsaturated compounds**, 191.

Carboxylic acids

Compounds that contain a **carboxyl group** (a **–COOH functional group***) and form a **homologous series*** with a **general formula*** $C_nH_{2n+1}COOH$. Their names end in -oic acid (see page 215). Pungent, colorless **weak acids***, they react with **alcohols*** to give **esters** (see **condensation reaction**, page 197).

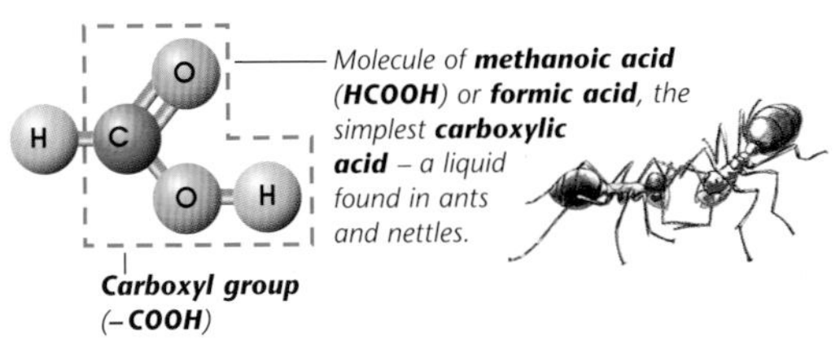

Molecule of ***methanoic acid*** *(**HCOOH**) or* ***formic acid****, the simplest* ***carboxylic acid*** *– a liquid found in ants and nettles.*

Carboxyl group *(**–COOH**)*

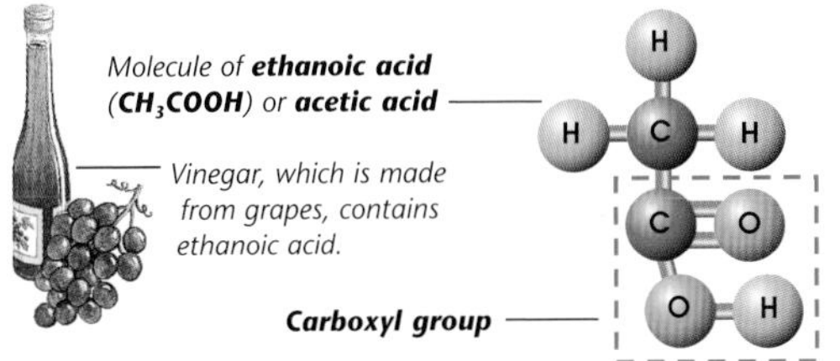

Molecule of ***ethanoic acid*** *(**CH_3COOH**) or* ***acetic acid***

Vinegar, which is made from grapes, contains ethanoic acid.

Carboxyl group

Dicarboxylic acids

Compounds that contain two **carboxyl groups** (see **carboxylic acids**) in each molecule.

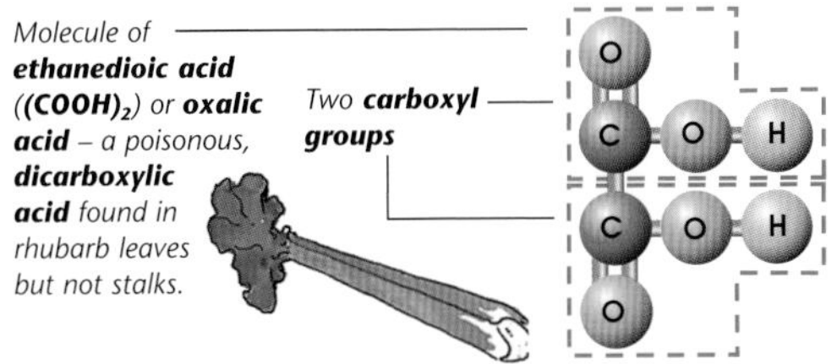

Molecule of ***ethanedioic acid*** *(**$(COOH)_2$**) or* ***oxalic acid*** *– a poisonous,* ***dicarboxylic acid*** *found in rhubarb leaves but not stalks.*

Two ***carboxyl groups***

Esters

A **homologous series*** of compounds containing a **–COO– functional group*** in every molecule. They are unreactive, colorless liquids made by reacting a **carboxylic acid** and **alcohol*** (see **condensation reaction**, page 197). Found in vegetable oils and animal fats, they give fruit and flowers their flavors and smells. They are used in perfumes and flavorings.

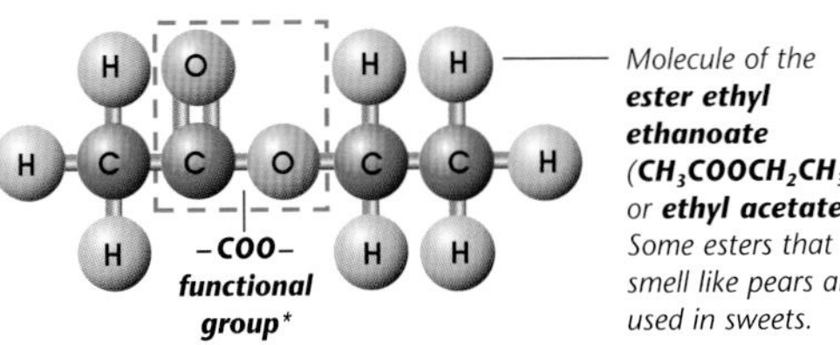

Molecule of the ***ester ethyl ethanoate*** *(**$CH_3COOCH_2CH_3$**) or* ***ethyl acetate****. Some esters that smell like pears are used in sweets.*

–COO– functional group*

Halogenoalkanes or alkyl halides

A **homologous series*** whose members contain one or more **halogen*** atoms (see also page 215). Most halogenoalkanes are colorless, **volatile*** liquids which do not mix with water. They will undergo **substitution reactions***. The most reactive contain iodine, and the least reactive contain fluorine.

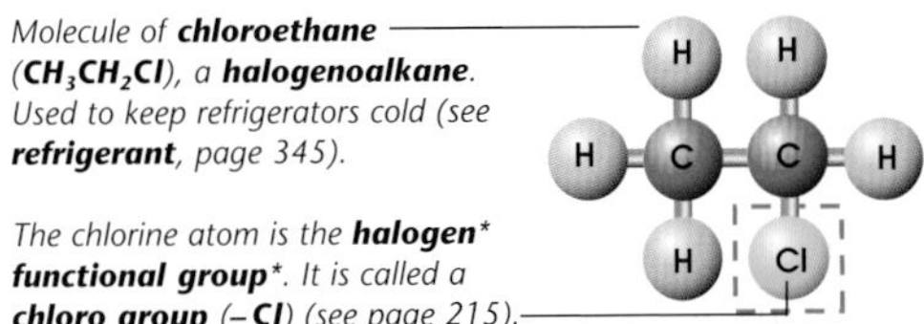

Molecule of ***chloroethane*** *(**CH_3CH_2Cl**), a* ***halogenoalkane****. Used to keep refrigerators cold (see* ***refrigerant****, page 345).*

The chlorine atom is the ***halogen* functional group****. It is called a* ***chloro group*** *(**–Cl**) (see page 215).*

Some important organic compounds have more than one **halogen*** atom in their molecules.

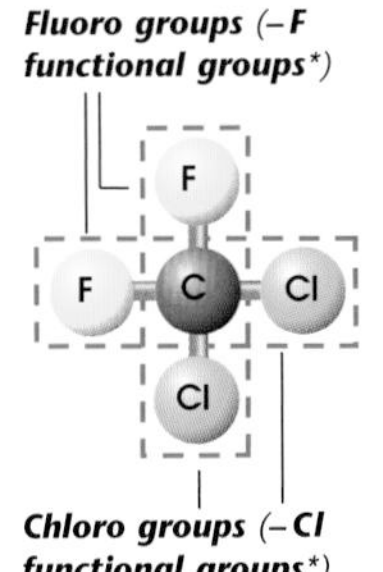

Fluoro groups *(**–F functional groups***)*

Chloro groups *(**–Cl functional groups***)*

Molecule of ***freon*** *(CCl_2F_2), a* ***chlorofluorocarbon*** *(a compound of chlorine, fluorine and carbon) once used as an aerosol propellant.*

The orange patch on this satellite image of the Earth's atmosphere shows the hole in the ***ozone**** *layer. Freon is believed to contribute to this damage, so other propellants are now used.*

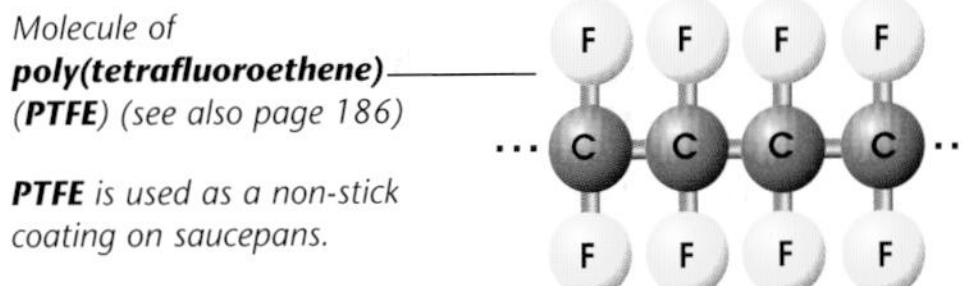

Molecule of ***poly(tetrafluoroethene)*** *(**PTFE**) (see also page 186)*

PTFE *is used as a non-stick coating on saucepans.*

Primary amines

Compounds that contain an **amino group** (**$-NH_2$ functional group***). They are **weak bases***, and have a fishy smell.

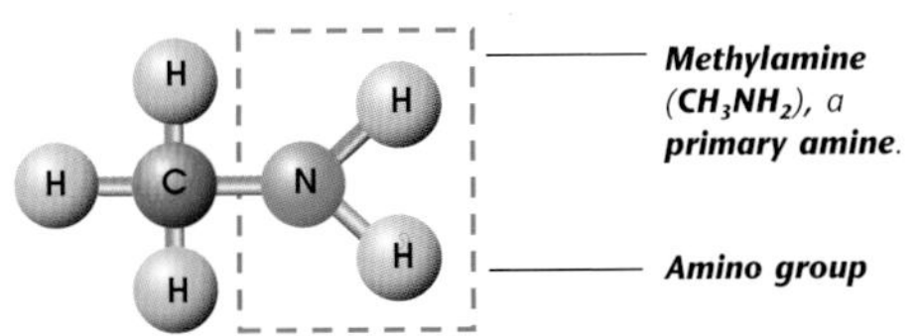

Methylamine *(**CH_3NH_2**), a* ***primary amine****.*

Amino group

Diamines

Compounds with two **amino groups** in each molecule.

* **Alcohols**, 196; **Functional group**, 191; **General formula**, 191 (**Homologous series**); **Halogens**, 186; **Ozone**, 210 (**Ozone depletion**); **Substitution reaction**, 192; **Volatile**, 345; **Weak acid**, **Weak base**, 152.

ALCOHOLS

Alcohols are organic compounds that contain one or more **hydroxyl groups** (**– OH functional groups***) in each molecule. The alcohols shown below in the chart are all members of a **homologous series*** of alcohols which are **aliphatic compounds*** with the **general formula*** $C_nH_{2n+1}OH$. As the molecules in the series increase in size, their physical properties change steadily. Some of the trends are shown in the chart below. As a result of their **hydroxyl groups**, alcohol molecules are **polar***, and have **hydrogen bonds***. Short-chain alcohols mix completely with water, but long-chain alcohols do not as their molecules have more $-CH_2-$ groups, making them less polar. Alcohols do not **ionize*** in water and are **neutral***. They burn, giving off carbon dioxide and water.

Some properties of alcohols

Name of compound	Structural formula*	Physical state at 25°C	Boiling point (°C)
Methanol	CH_3OH	Liquid	65.6
Ethanol	CH_3CH_2OH	Liquid	78.5
Propan-1-ol	$CH_3CH_2CH_2OH$	Liquid	97.2
Butan-1-ol	$CH_3CH_2CH_2CH_2OH$	Liquid	117.5

*Alcohols are named in the same way as **alkanes***, but end in -ol. The number in the name tells you which carbon atom the **hydroxyl group** is attached to (see opposite and page 214-215).*

The next member of the series (going down) is always a $-CH_2-$ group longer than the last.

The members gradually change to solids as the molecules get longer.

*Boiling points of alcohols increase as the molecules get longer. They have high boiling points in relation to their **relative molecular mass***, due to **hydrogen bonding***.*

Alcohols react with sodium:

$$2CH_3CH_2OH + 2Na \rightarrow 2CH_3CH_2ONa + H_2$$

Ethanol — Sodium — Sodium ethoxide — Hydrogen

Alcohols react with phosphorus halides to give **halogenoalkanes** (see page 195), and with **carboxylic acids*** to give **esters** (see **condensation reaction** and page 195).

Primary alcohols are **oxidized*** first to **aldehydes*** and then to **carboxylic acids***.

*Acidified potassium permanganate **catalyst****

$$CH_3CH_2CH_2OH \rightarrow CH_3CH_2CHO \rightarrow CH_3CH_2COOH$$

Propan-1-ol — Propanal — Propanoic acid

Secondary alcohols are **oxidized*** to **ketones** (see page 194).

*Acidified potassium permanganate **catalyst****

$$CH_3CHOHCH_3 \rightarrow CH_3COCH_3$$

Propan-2-ol — Propanone

Ethanol (CH_3CH_2OH, often written C_2H_5OH)

Also called **ethyl alcohol**, or **alcohol**. An alcohol which is a slightly sweet-smelling water-soluble liquid with a relatively high boiling point. It burns with an almost colorless flame and is made by ethene reacting with steam. It is also produced by **alcoholic fermentation**.

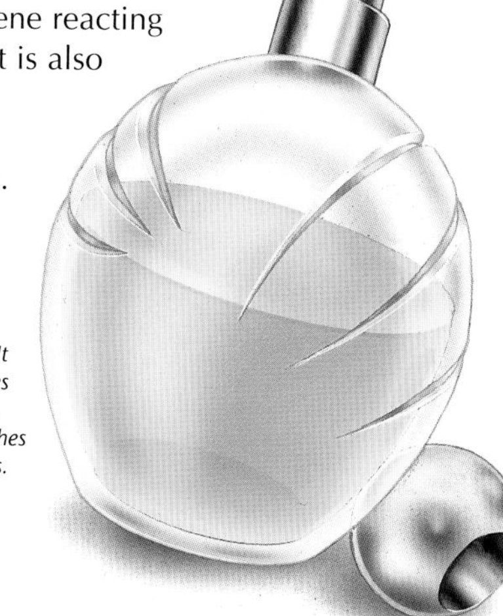

***Ethanol** is used as a solvent and in methylated spirits. It has many more uses including perfumes, paints, dyes, varnishes and alcoholic drinks.*

* **Aldehydes**, 194; **Aliphatic compounds**, 190; **Alkanes**, 192; **Carboxylic acids**, 195; **Catalyst**, 161; **Functional group**, 190; **General formula**, 191 (**Homologous series**); **Hydrogen bond**, 134; **Ionization**, 130; **Neutral**, 151; **Oxidation**, 148; **Polar molecule**, 133; **Relative molecular mass**, 138; **Structural formula** (**shortened**), 140.

Alcoholic fermentation

Glucose* in grapes is **fermented** to make wine.

The name of the process used to produce **ethanol** (the potent chemical in alcoholic drinks) from fruits or grain. **Glucose*** from fruit or grain is converted into ethanol by **enzymes*** (**catalysts*** of the reactions in living cells). Yeast is used in alcoholic fermentation because it has the enzyme **zymase** which catalyses the change of glucose to ethanol.

Laboratory fermentation

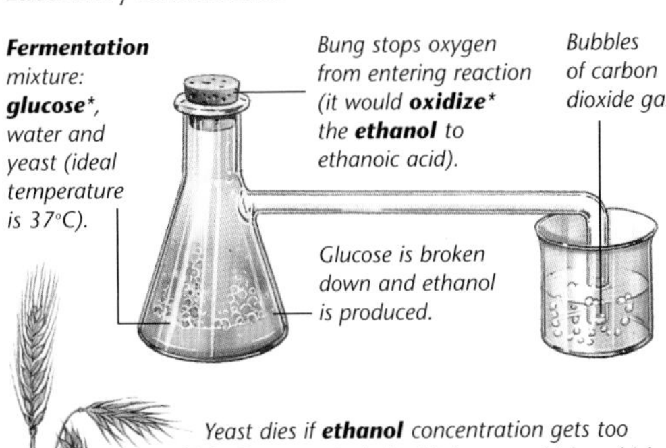

Fermentation *mixture:* ***glucose****, water and yeast (ideal temperature is 37°C).*
Bung stops oxygen from entering reaction (it would ***oxidize**** *the* ***ethanol*** *to ethanoic acid).*
Bubbles of carbon dioxide gas
Glucose is broken down and ethanol is produced.

Yeast dies if ***ethanol*** *concentration gets too high. Stronger alcoholic drinks, e.g. whisky, which is made from grains, are made by* ***distilling**** *the ethanol solution. This process separates the ethanol from the water, and the concentrated alcohol is used to make the drinks more potent.*

	Enzyme*			
$C_6H_{12}O_6$	$\rightarrow$	$2CH_3CH_2OH$	+	$2CO_2$
Glucose solution from fruit or barley		*Ethanol*		*Carbon dioxide*

Polyhydric alcohols

Alcohols whose molecules contain more than one **hydroxyl group** (see introduction).

Ethane-1,2-diol*, or* ***ethylene glycol*** *is a* ***diol*** *(contains two* ***hydroxyl groups****). Used as antifreeze.*

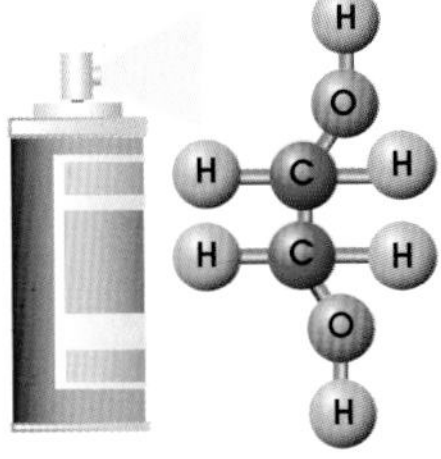

Propane-1,2,3-triol*,* ***glycerine****, or* ***glycerol****, is a* ***triol*** *(contains three* ***hydroxyl groups****). Used to make explosives.*

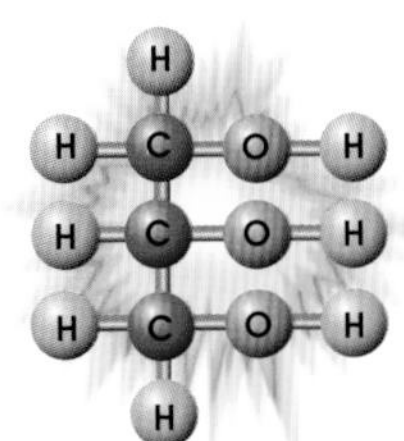

Condensation reaction

A type of reaction in which two molecules react together to form one, with the loss of a small molecule, e.g. water. (See also **condensation polymerization**, page 200.)

Example of a ***condensation reaction****:*

CH_3CH_2OH +	CH_3COOH $\rightarrow$	$CH_3COOCH_2CH_3$ +	H_2O
Ethanol	*Ethanoic acid*	*Ethyl ethanoate*	*Water molecule is lost*

This reaction is also an **esterification reaction** as the product ethyl ethanoate is an **ester***. An alcohol and an organic acid always react to form an ester.

Primary, secondary and tertiary alcohols

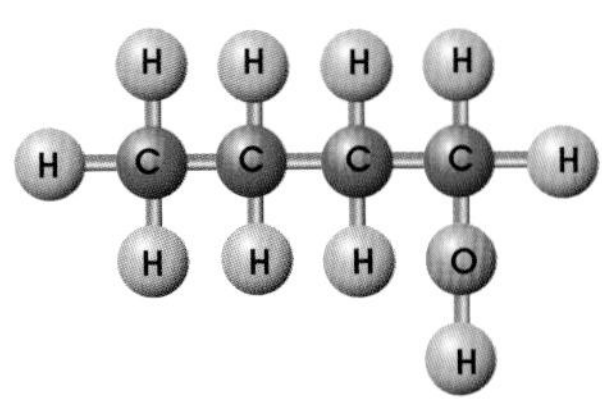

Molecule of ***butan-1-ol****, a* ***primary alcohol****. The carbon atom attached to the* ***hydroxyl group*** *(see introduction) has two hydrogen atoms attached to it.*

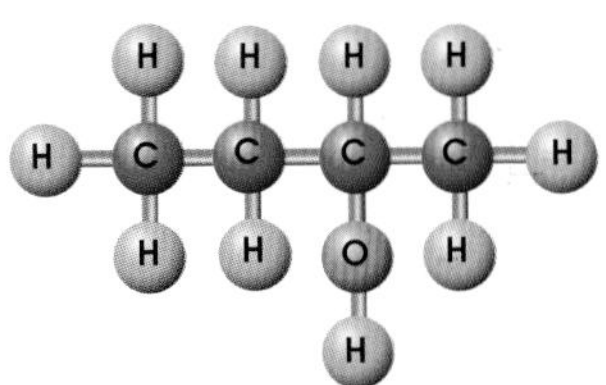

Molecule of ***butan-2-ol****, a* ***secondary alcohol****. The carbon atom attached to the hydroxyl group (see introduction) has one hydrogen atom attached to it.*

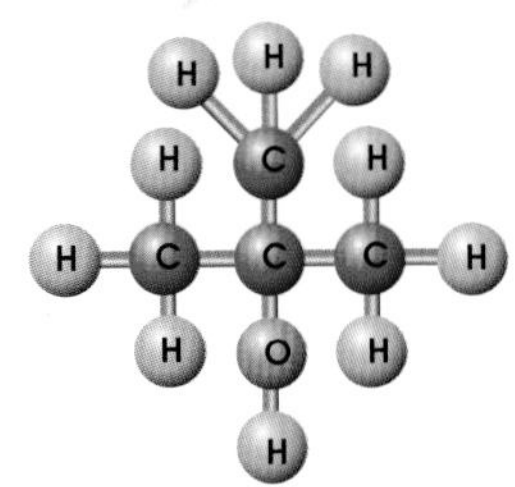

Molecule of ***2-methyl propan-2-ol****, a* ***tertiary alcohol****. The carbon atom attached to the hydroxyl group (see introduction) has no hydrogen atoms attached to it.*

The numbers in the names of the alcohols give the position of the carbon atom that the ***hydroxyl group*** *is bonded to. (See pages 214-215 for more information on naming alcohols.)*

* **Catalyst**, 161; **Distillation**, 220;
Enzyme, 161; **Esters**, 195;
Glucose, 204; **Oxidation**, 148.

PETROLEUM

Petroleum, or **crude oil**, is a dark, viscous liquid, usually found at great depths beneath the earth or sea-bed. It is often found with **natural gas***, which consists mainly of **methane***. Petroleum is formed over many thousands of years by the decomposition of animals and plants under pressure. It is a mixture of **alkanes*** which vary greatly in size and structure. Many useful products are formed by **refining** petroleum.

Refining

A set of processes which convert petroleum to more useful products. Refining consists of three main processes – **primary distillation**, **cracking** and **reforming**.

Primary distillation or fractional distillation of petroleum

A process used to separate petroleum into **fractions**, according to their boiling points (see also page 220). A **fractionating column** (see diagram) is kept very hot at the bottom, but it gets cooler towards the top. Boiled petroleum passes into the column as vapor, losing heat as it rises. When a fraction reaches a tray at a temperature just below its own boiling point, it condenses onto the tray. It is then drawn off along pipes. Fractions are distilled again to give better separations.

Fraction

A mixture of liquids with similar boiling points, obtained from **primary distillation**. **Light fractions** have low boiling points and short **hydrocarbon*** chains. **Heavy fractions** have higher boiling points and longer chains.

Cracking

A reaction which breaks large **alkanes*** into smaller alkanes and **alkenes***. The smaller alkanes are used as **gasoline**. Cracking occurs at high temperatures, or with a **catalyst*** (**catalytic cracking** or "**cat cracking**").

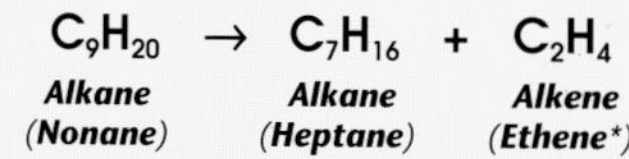
$C_9H_{20} \rightarrow C_7H_{16} + C_2H_4$
Alkane (Nonane)
Alkane (Heptane)
Alkene (Ethene*)

Reforming

A process which produces **gasoline** from lighter **fractions** by breaking up **straight chain*** **alkanes*** and reassembling them as **branched chain*** molecules.

Primary distillation
Bubble caps. Small domes which deflect the rising oil vapor down into the liquid on the tray. They improve the efficiency of the process.
Light fractions (least viscous) collected at top.
Fractionating column
Heavy fractions (most viscous) collected at bottom.

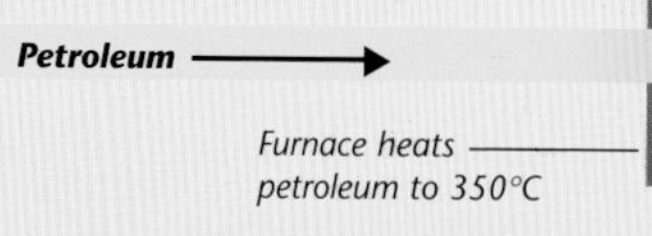
Petroleum
Furnace heats petroleum to 350°C

* **Alkanes**, 192; **Alkenes**, 193; **Branched chain**, 190; **Catalyst**, 161; **Ethene**, 193; **Hydrocarbons**, 190; **Natural gas**, 192 (**Methane**); **Straight chain**, 190.

Refinery gas

A gas which consists mainly of **methane***. Other **light fractions** contain **propane** and **butane** (both **alkanes***) and are made into **liquefied petroleum gas (LPG)**.

Liquefied petroleum gas *(see **refinery gas**) is used as bottled gas.*

Chemical feedstocks

Fractions of petroleum which are used in the production of organic chemicals. These fractions are mainly **refinery gas** and **naptha**, a part of the **gasoline** fraction.

Chemical feedstocks are used to make paint.

Refinery gas

Gasoline or petrol

A liquid **fraction** obtained from **primary distillation**. It consists of **alkanes*** with 5 to 12 carbon atoms in their molecules and has a boiling point range of 40-150°C. See also **cracking** and **reforming**.

Octane rating

A measure of how well **gasoline** burns, measured on a scale of 0 to 100. It can be increased by using an **anti-knock agent** such as methyl-tertiary-butyl-ether ($C_5H_{12}O$).

Gasoline *used in cars has an **octane rating** of over 90. It consists mainly of **branched chain* alkanes***.*

Gasoline

Kerosene or paraffin

A liquid **fraction** obtained from **primary distillation**. Kerosene consists of **alkanes*** with about 9-15 carbon atoms in their molecules. It has a boiling point range of 150-250°C.

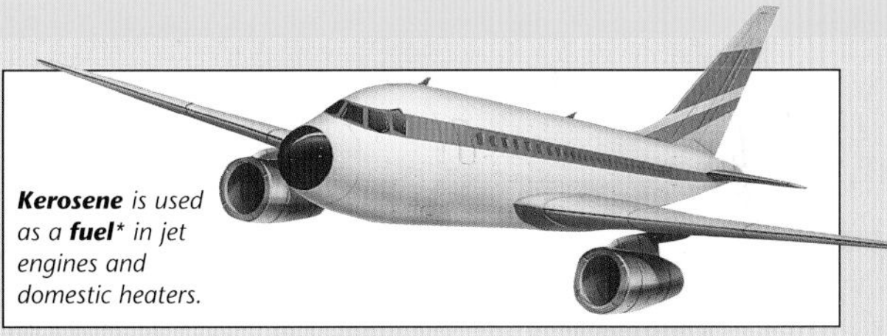

Kerosene *is used as a **fuel*** in jet engines and domestic heaters.*

Kerosene

Diesel oil or gas oil

A liquid **fraction** obtained from **primary distillation**. It consists of **alkanes*** with about 12-25 or more carbon atoms in their molecules. It has a boiling point of 250°C and above.

Diesel oil *is used as a **fuel*** in diesel engines.*

Diesel oil

Residue

The oil left after **primary distillation**. It consists of **hydrocarbons*** of very high **relative molecular masses***, their molecules containing up to 40 carbon atoms. Its boiling point is greater than 350°C. Some is used as **fuel oil**, which is used to heat homes and commercial buildings, as well as to generate electricity. The rest is re-distilled to form the substances on the right.

Lubricating oil

A mixture of non-**volatile*** liquids obtained from the distillation of **residue** in a vacuum.

Hydrocarbon waxes or paraffin waxes

Soft solids which are separated from **lubricating oil** after the distillation of **residue** in a vacuum.

Candles and polish

Bitumen or asphalt

A liquid left after the distillation of **residue** under vacuum. It is a tarry, black semi-solid at room temperature.

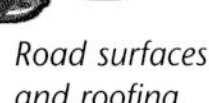

Road surfaces and roofing

Residue

* **Alkanes**, 192; **Branched chain**, 190; **Fuel**, 208; **Hydrocarbons**, 190; **Methane**, 192; **Relative molecular mass**, 138; **Volatile**, 345.

POLYMERS AND PLASTICS

Polymers are substances that consist of many **monomers** (small molecules) bonded together in a repeating sequence. They are very long molecules with a high **relative molecular mass***. Polymers occur naturally, e.g. **proteins***. There are also many **synthetic polymers**, e.g. **plastics**.

Monomers

Relatively small molecules that react to form polymers. For example, **ethene*** molecules are molecules which react together to form **polythene** (see also equation for **homopolymer**, below right).

Simplified picture of a polymerization reaction – a reaction in which monomers bond to form a polymer

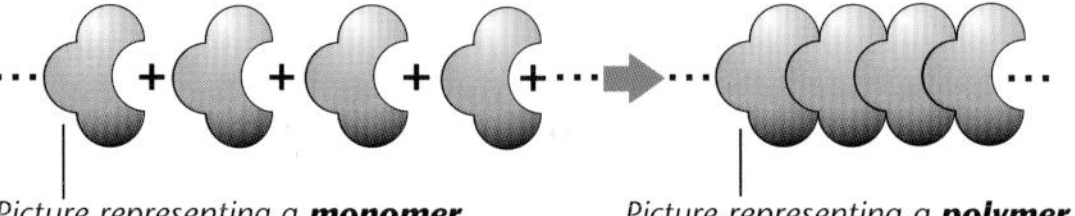

Picture representing a ***monomer***   *Picture representing a* ***polymer***

Synthetic polymers *such as* ***plastics*** *(see page 201) have many uses. Helmets for racing drivers are made of* ***thermosetting plastics*** *reinforced with synthetic fibers. Plastics used in the motorcycle bodywork reduce vehicle weight and help to save fuel.*

Addition polymerization

Polymerization reactions in which **monomers** bond to each other without losing any atoms. The polymer is the only product and has the same **empirical formula*** as the monomer. See also **addition reaction**, page 193.

Example of an addition polymerization reaction

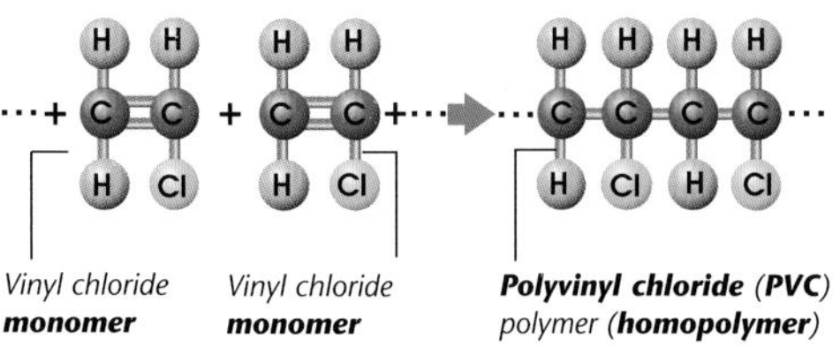

Vinyl chloride ***monomer***   *Vinyl chloride* ***monomer***   ***Polyvinyl chloride (PVC)*** *polymer (****homopolymer****)*

Condensation polymerization

Polymerization reactions in which **monomers** form a polymer with the loss of small molecules such as water. See **condensation reaction**, page 197.

Homopolymer

A polymer made from a single type of **monomer**.

Reaction to produce the homopolymer polythene

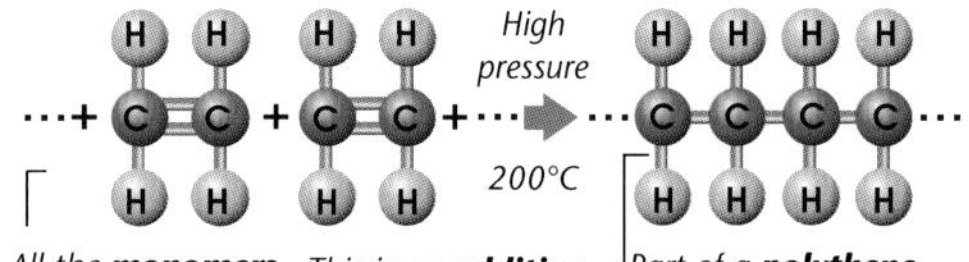
High pressure
200°C

All the ***monomers*** *are* ***ethene**** *molecules.*   *This is an* ***addition polymerization*** *reaction.*   *Part of a* ***polythene*** *molecule*

Copolymer

A polymer made from two or more different **monomers**. See **condensation polymerization** example below.

Depolymerization

The breakdown of a polymer into its original **monomers**. It occurs, for example, when **acrylic** is heated.

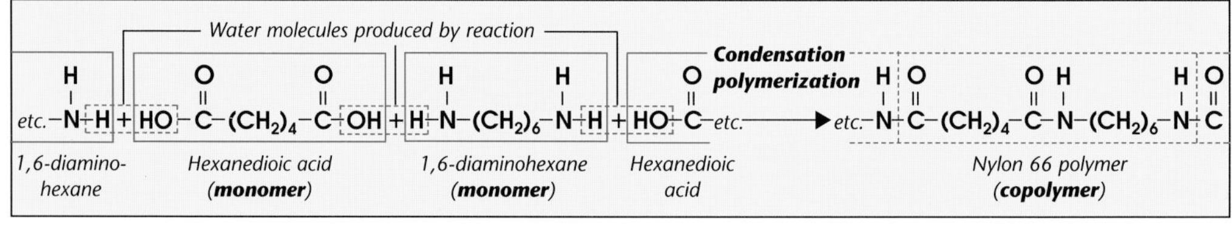
Water molecules produced by reaction
Condensation polymerization

1,6-diaminohexane   *Hexanedioic acid* ***(monomer)***   *1,6-diaminohexane* ***(monomer)***   *Hexanedioic acid*   *Nylon 66 polymer* ***(copolymer)***

* **Empirical formula**, 140; **Ethene**, 193; **Proteins**, 205; **Relative molecular mass**, 138.

Natural polymers or biopolymers

Polymers that occur naturally, e.g. **starch** and **rubber**. Starch is made from **monomers** of **glucose***. For a picture of the starch polymer, see **starch**, page 204.

Part of a rubber polymer

$$CH_3(CH_2)C{=}CH\text{–}CH_2\text{–}CH_2\text{–}C(CH_3){=}CH\text{–}CH_2\text{–}CH_2\text{–}C(CH_3){=}CH\text{–}CH_2$$

*Rubber is extracted from **latex*** tapped from the rubber tree. It is then **vulcanized*** to produce the rubber used in tires, hoses, etc.*

Synthetic or man-made polymers

Polymers prepared in the laboratory or in industry (not **natural polymers**), e.g. **nylons**.

Plastics

Synthetic polymers that are easily molded. They are made from chemicals derived from **petroleum*** and are usually durable, light solids which are thermal and electrical insulators. They are often not **biodegradable*** and give off poisonous fumes when burned. There are two types of plastic – **thermoplastics** which soften or melt on heating (e.g. **polythene**), and **thermosetting plastics** which harden upon heating and do not remelt (e.g. plastic used in worktops).

Polyesters

Copolymers, formed by the **condensation polymerization** of **diol*** and **dicarboxylic acid*** **monomers**. The monomers are linked by **–COO– functional groups***, as found in **esters***.

*Yachts have sails made of **polyesters**. Some **polyesters** are produced as fibers which are used in clothing and furnishing materials.*

Nylons

A family of **polyamides**. They are strong, hard-wearing polymers which stretch but do not absorb water or rot. They are used in fabrics, often mixed with other fibers. See **condensation polymerization** for the equation for the manufacture of nylon 66.

Polyamides

Copolymers formed by the **condensation polymerization** of a **dicarboxylic acid*** **monomer** with a **diamine*** **monomer**, e.g. **nylons**.

Polystyrene or poly(phenylethene)

A **homopolymer** formed by the **addition polymerization** of **styrene** (**phenylethene**).

***Polystyrene** is used to make disposable knives, forks and cups. Air-expanded sheets of polystyrene are used in packaging and insulation.*

Polythene

Also called **poly(ethene)** or **poly(ethylene)**. A **homopolymer** formed by the **addition polymerization** of **ethene*** (see **homopolymer**, page 200). Polythene is produced in two forms (depending on the method used) – a soft material of low density, and a hard, more rigid, material of high density. Polythene has a **relative molecular mass*** of between 10,000 and 40,000 and is used to make many things, e.g. polythene bags (soft type), bowls used for washing (harder type).

Acrylic

Also called **poly(methylmethacrylate)** or **poly((1-methoxycarbonyl)-1-methylethene)**. A **homopolymer** formed by **addition polymerization**. It is often used as a glass substitute.

Methyl methacrylate**, the acrylic **monomer

$$H_2C{=}C(CH_3)COOCH_3$$

***Acrylic** is used to make outdoor signs.*

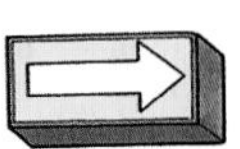

Polyvinyl chloride (PVC) or poly(chloroethene)

A hard-wearing **homopolymer** used to make many things, e.g. bottles and gloves. (See also **addition polymerization** picture, page 200).

*A **PVC** covering makes this underwater video camera waterproof.*

* **Biodegradable**, 210; **Carboxyl group**, 195 (**Carboxylic acids**); **Diamines**, 195; **Dicarboxylic acids**, 195; **Diols**, 197 (**Polyhydric alcohols**); **Esters**, 195; **Ethene**, 193; **Functional group**, 190; **Glucose**, 204; **Latex**, 345; **Petroleum**, 198; **Relative molecular mass**, 138; **Vulcanization**, 345.

DETERGENTS

Detergents are substances which, when added to water, enable it to remove dirt. They do this in three ways: by lowering the water's **surface tension*** so that it spreads evenly instead of forming droplets, by enabling grease molecules to dissolve in water, and also by keeping removed dirt suspended in the water. **Soap** is a type of detergent, but there are also many **soapless detergents**.

Detergent molecule

A large molecule consisting of a long **hydrocarbon*** chain with a **functional group*** at one end (making that end **polar***). The **non-polar*** chain is **hydrophobic** (repelled by water) and the polar end is **hydrophilic** (attracted to water). In water, these molecules group together to form **micelles**.

Simple representation of a detergent molecule

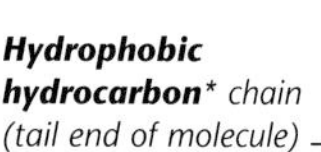

Hydrophobic hydrocarbon chain (tail end of molecule)*

Hydrophilic functional group (head end of molecule)*

Micelle

A spherical grouping of **detergent molecules** in water. Oils and greases dissolve in the **hydrophobic** center of the micelle. The picture below shows how micelles of dishwashing liquid remove grease.

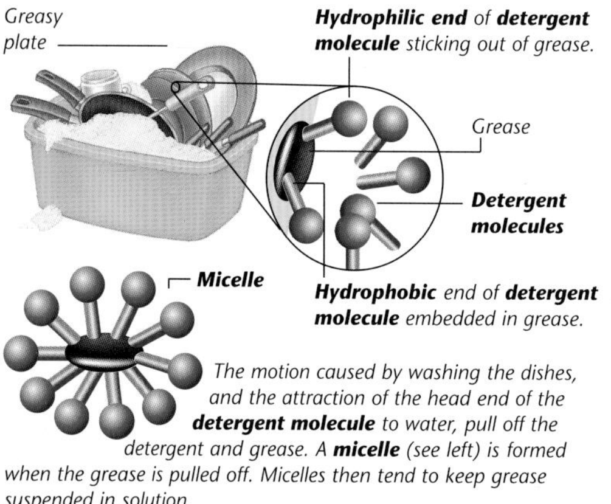
Greasy plate
Hydrophilic end of detergent molecule sticking out of grease.
Grease
Detergent molecules
Micelle
Hydrophobic end of detergent molecule embedded in grease.

*The motion caused by washing the dishes, and the attraction of the head end of the **detergent molecule** to water, pull off the detergent and grease. A **micelle** (see left) is formed when the grease is pulled off. Micelles then tend to keep grease suspended in solution.*

Soap

A type of detergent. It is the sodium or potassium **salt*** of a long-chain **carboxylic acid*** such as octadecanoic acid (see equation at bottom of page). It is made by reacting animal fats or vegetable oils (**esters***) with sodium hydroxide or potassium hydroxide solution (soap made with potassium hydroxide is softer). The process of making soap is **saponification**. Soap molecules form **micelles** in water. Soap produces a scum in **hard water*** whereas **soapless detergents** do not.

Saponification (soap-making)

Soap-making factory

*Measured amounts of **fats*** and sodium hydroxide or potassium hydroxide solutions are continuously fed into a large, hollow, column-like structure. The column is at high temperature and pressure.*

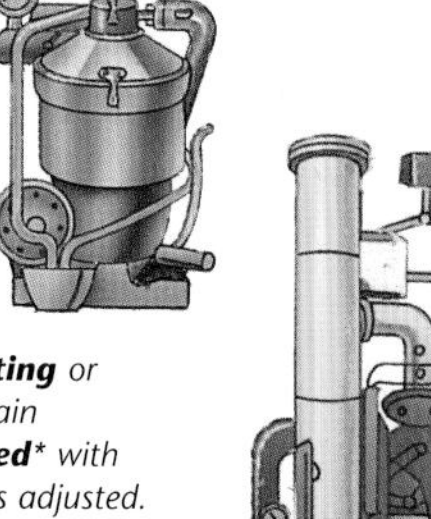

***Soap** and propane-1,2,3-triol are formed, and then the mixture is dissolved in salt water.*

*The final part of the process is **fitting** or **finishing**. Any unreacted long-chain **carboxylic acids*** are **neutralized*** with alkali and the salt concentration is adjusted. The mixture is then centrifuged to separate out the soap.*

Saponification equation

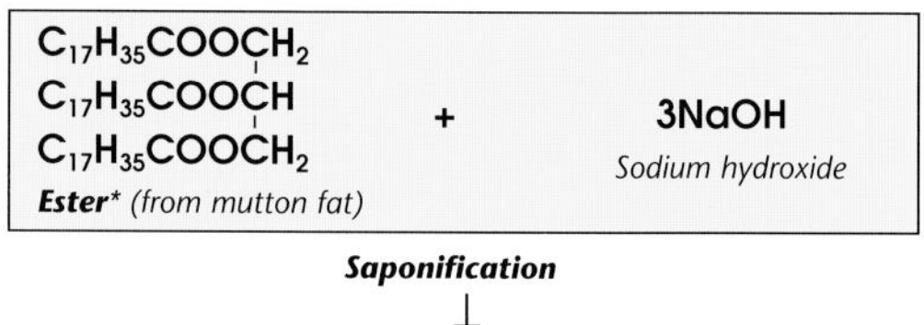

$$\begin{array}{l} C_{17}H_{35}COOCH_2 \\ C_{17}H_{35}COOCH \\ C_{17}H_{35}COOCH_2 \end{array} + 3NaOH$$

Ester (from mutton fat)* + *Sodium hydroxide*

Saponification ↓

$$3C_{17}H_{35}COO^-Na^+ + \begin{array}{l} CH_2OH \\ CHOH \\ CH_2OH \end{array}$$

Sodium octadecanoate (sodium stearate) – soap + *Propane-1,2,3-triol*

*All **soap** molecules are sodium or potassium **salts*** of long-chain **carboxylic acids***. In this example, the soap is a salt of **octadecanoic acid**.*

* **Carboxylic acids**, 195; **Esters**, 195; **Fats**, 205 (**Lipids**); **Functional group**, 190; **Hard water**, 207; **Hydrocarbons**, 190; **Neutralization**, 151; **Non-polar molecule**, 133 (**Polar molecule**); **Salts**, 153; **Surface tension**, 23.

Soapless detergents or **synthetic detergents**

Types of detergent made from by-products of **refining*** crude oil. They are used to make many products, including **laundry powders**, shampoos and hair conditioners, and are usually simply referred to as detergents. Soapless detergents do not form a scum in **hard water***, and lather better than **soaps**. If they are not **biodegradable** (see right), they pollute rivers.

*Example of a **soapless detergent** molecule that does not have an **ionic*** part – used in dish washing liquid.*

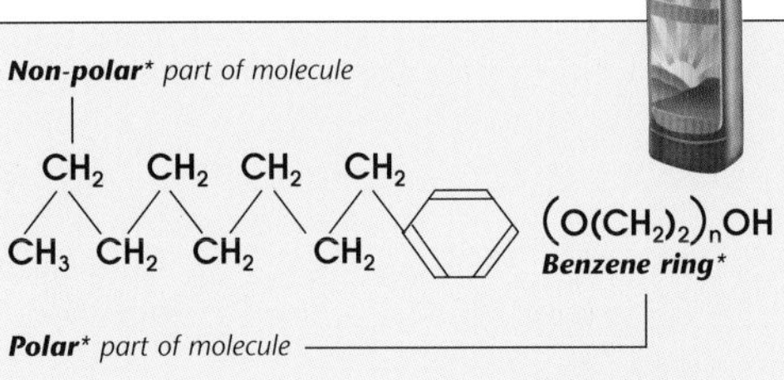

Non-polar* part of molecule
CH_2 CH_2 CH_2 CH_2
CH_3 CH_2 CH_2 CH_2
$(O(CH_2)_2)_nOH$
Benzene ring*
Polar* part of molecule

*Example of an **ionic*** **soapless detergent** molecule – used in kitchen (laundry) soap.*

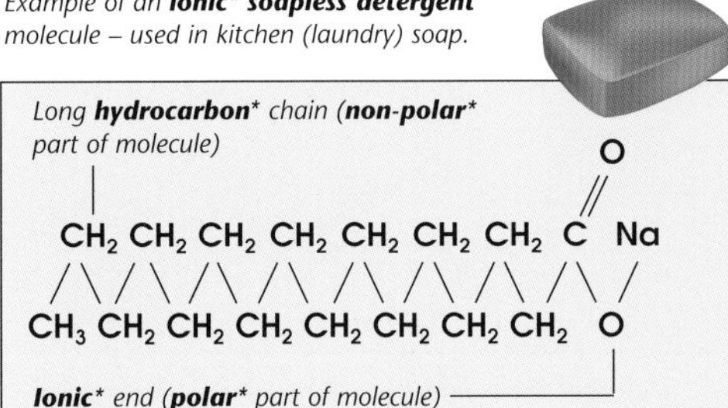

Long hydrocarbon* chain (non-polar* part of molecule)
O
CH_2 CH_2 CH_2 CH_2 CH_2 CH_2 CH_2 C Na
CH_3 CH_2 CH_2 CH_2 CH_2 CH_2 CH_2 CH_2 O
Ionic* end (polar* part of molecule)

Laundry powders

Soap or **soapless detergents** used to wash clothes. They are better for fabrics than water alone, as they make it easier to remove dirt. There are two main types of laundry powders – those used when hand-washing clothes (usually soap powders) and those used in washing machines. The latter are mostly soapless detergents with other substances added to keep the lather down and to brighten the appearance of the fabric. When they also contain **enzymes***, they are called **biological laundry powders**, or **enzyme detergents**. Enzymes help to break down **proteins*** and loosen dirt.

Biodegradable detergents

Soapless detergents that are broken down by bacteria (see **biodegradable**, page 210). Foams from **non-biodegradable detergents** cannot be broken down and cover the water, depriving life of oxygen.

***Non-biodegradable** detergents kill creatures living in water as they stop oxygen from dissolving in the water.*

Surfactants

Substances which lower the **surface tension*** of water. As a result of this property, detergents have many other uses, as well as removing dirt (see examples below).

*Lubricating greases use **surfactants** to make them gel better.*

*Paints contain **surfactants** to ensure that the pigment is evenly mixed in, and that the paint gives a smooth finish and does not drip.*

***Surfactants** are added to cosmetics to make face powder cover well and evenly. They also ensure that cosmetic creams mix well with water and thicken properly.*

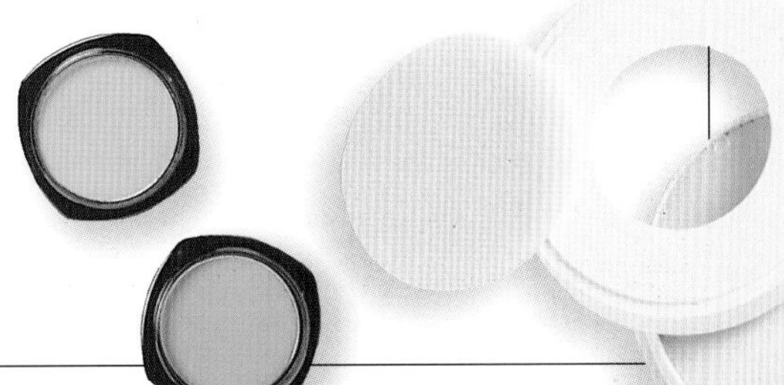

* **Benzene ring**, 190 (**Aromatic compounds**); **Enzyme**, 161; **Hard water**, 207; **Hydrocarbons**, 190; **Ionic compound**, 131; **Non-polar molecule**, 133 (**Polar molecule**); **Proteins**, 205; **Refining**, 198; **Surface tension**, 23.

FOOD

In order to survive and grow, living organisms need a number of different substances. These include the **nutrients** – **carbohydrates**, **proteins** and **fats** (see **lipids**) – which are all **organic compounds*** made by plant **photosynthesis*** and taken in by animals. Also important are the **accessory foods** – water and **minerals**, needed by both plants and animals, and **vitamins**, needed by animals only. **Roughage**, or **fiber**, is also needed by many animals to help move food through the gut. Different animals need different amounts of these substances for a healthy diet. For more about minerals and roughage, see page 331.

The human body needs a combination of nutrients to keep healthy.

Carbohydrates

Organic compounds* of varying complexity – the most complex, made of many individual units, being **polysaccharides** (see **starch**) and the simplest, made of just one unit, being **monosaccharides**. All have the **general formula*** $C_x(H_2O)_y$. Almost all living organisms use the monosaccharide **glucose** for energy.

Sugar

These foods contain ***carbohydrates****.*

Bread

Pasta

Chips

Glucose

A **monosaccharide** (see **carbohydrates**) with the **molecular formula*** $C_6H_{12}O_6$, the breakdown of which provides energy for plants and animals. Plants make their own by **photosynthesis***, storing it as **starch** until it is needed. Animals take in all forms of carbohydrate, break down the complex ones to glucose, and store this as the **polysaccharide** **glycogen**. For more about glucose, see pages 330-331, 334-335 and 338-339.

Simplified equation showing energy released when glucose is broken down in the body

$$C_6H_{12}O_6 + 6O_2 \rightarrow 6CO_2 + 6H_2O + \text{ENERGY}$$

Glucose	Oxygen taken in by respiration	Carbon dioxide	Water	(measured in kJ)

Sucrose

A **disaccharide**, i.e. a **carbohydrate**, composed of two **monosaccharide** units – in this case **glucose** and **fructose**. It is sweet-tasting, often used to sweeten food, and is commonly known as sugar. It has the **molecular formula*** $C_{12}H_{22}O_{11}$ and is obtained from sugar cane and sugar beet.

Starch

A **polysaccharide** (see **carbohydrates**) which is the storage form of **glucose** in plants. Like **glycogen** (see **glucose**), it is an example of a **natural polymer*** – the **monomers*** in this case being the glucose **monosaccharides**. Note that when these join, water molecules form at the links (see **condensation polymerization**, page 200).

Part of a starch molecule

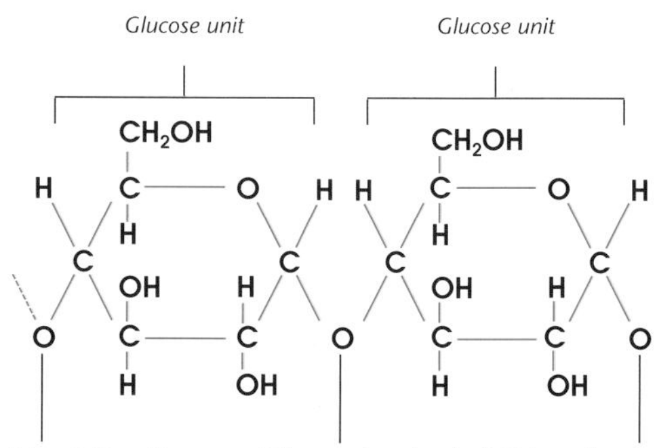
Glucose unit
Glucose unit
CH2OH
CH2OH
H
C
O
H
H
OH
OH

Before linking, these were OH on each molecule. H_2O formed and was "lost" into plant tissue.

* **General formula**, 191 (**Homologous series**); **Molecular formula**, 140; **Monomers**, 200; **Natural polymers**, 201; **Organic compounds**, 190; **Photosynthesis**, 209; **Polymer**, 200.

Amino acids

Compounds whose molecules contain a carbon atom joined to a **carboxyl group*** and an **amino group***. **Proteins** are made from amino acids. See also pages 328-329.

*There are about 20 different natural **amino acids**. They all contain an **amino group*** and a **carboxyl group***.*

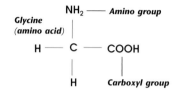

Glycine (amino acid)

$$NH_2\text{—}CH(H)\text{—}COOH$$

Amino group (NH_2); **Carboxyl group** (COOH)

How proteins are broken down in the body

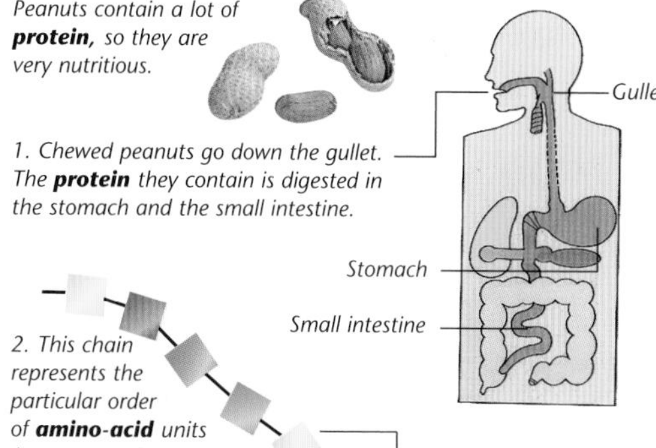

Gullet
Stomach
Small intestine

*Peanuts contain a lot of **protein**, so they are very nutritious.*

*1. Chewed peanuts go down the gullet. The **protein** they contain is digested in the stomach and the small intestine.*

*2. This chain represents the particular order of **amino-acid** units (**monomers***) in the protein found in peanuts. Each different protein has its amino acids in a different order.*

*Different colored squares represent different **amino acids**.*

*3. An **enzyme*** in the stomach breaks down the protein molecules (long chains called **polypeptides**) into shorter chains (still long enough to be called polypeptides).*

Enzymes are **catalysts*** that speed up reactions in the body.*

*4. An enzyme in the small intestine breaks the polypeptides into molecules made of two amino acids (**dipeptides**) or into single amino acids.*

5. Amino acid molecules can now be absorbed by the body.

6. In the body, certain enzymes make new proteins by joining amino acids together.

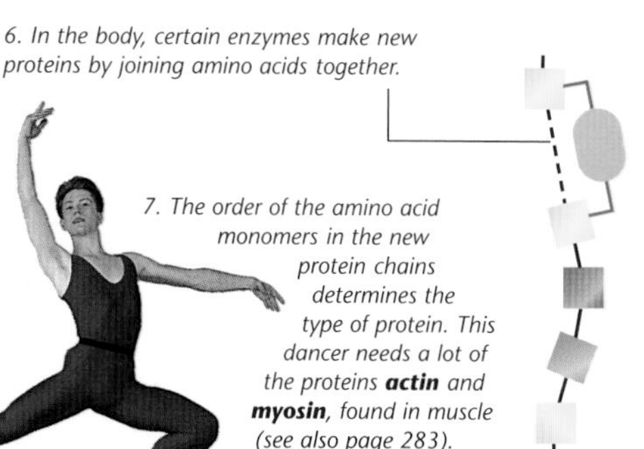

*7. The order of the amino acid monomers in the new protein chains determines the type of protein. This dancer needs a lot of the proteins **actin** and **myosin**, found in muscle (see also page 283).*

Proteins

Natural polymers* made from many **amino acid monomers*** joined together. The **relative molecular masses*** of proteins vary from 20,000 to several million. They are found mainly in meat, dairy food, nuts, cereal and beans. Animals need proteins for growth and repair of tissue. See also pages 330-331.

Vitamins

Organic compounds* found in small amounts in food. They are an essential part of the diet of animals. They are needed to help **enzymes*** **catalyse*** reactions in the body. See page 339 for a list of vitamins.

Example of a vitamin – vitamin C, also called ascorbic acid

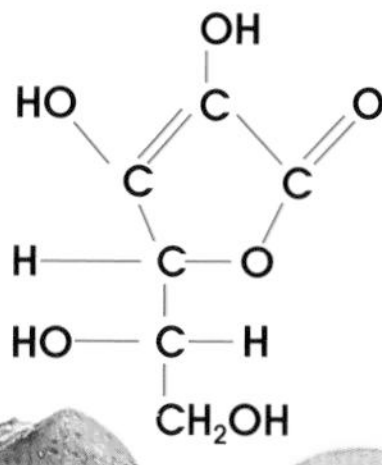

OH
HO
C
O
C
C
H
C
O
HO
C
H
CH₂OH

People who do not eat enough vitamin C get scurvy. Citrus fruits and vegetables are the main sources of this vitamin.

Lipids

A group of **esters***, including **fats** and waxes, found in living tissue (fats form a reserve energy source – see also pages 330-331). Insoluble in water but soluble in **organic solvents***, they are mostly solid or semi-solid and made of **saturated*** **carboxylic acids***, though a smaller group, the **oils**, are liquids and consist mainly of **unsaturated*** carboxylic acids.

Example of a reaction to make a fat

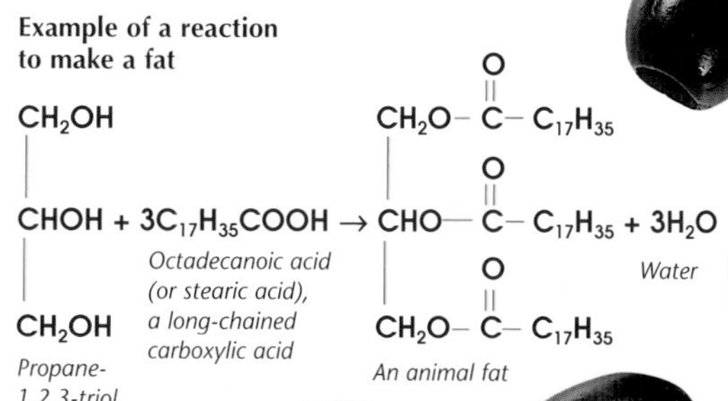

CH₂OH
CHOH + 3C₁₇H₃₅COOH → CHO—C—C₁₇H₃₅ + 3H₂O
CH₂OH
CH₂O—C—C₁₇H₃₅
CH₂O—C—C₁₇H₃₅
O
Propane-1,2,3-triol
Octadecanoic acid (or stearic acid), a long-chained carboxylic acid
An animal fat
Water

*Olives contain an **oil** which has a high proportion of **unsaturated*** fatty acids, such as oleic acid and linoleic acid. It is used in cooking.*

* **Amino group**, 195 (**Primary amines**); **Carboxyl group**, 195 (**Carboxylic acids**); **Catalysis**, 161 (**Catalyst**); **Enzyme**, 161; **Esters**, 195; **Monomers**, 200; **Natural polymers**, 201; **Organic solvent**, 345; **Relative molecular mass**, 138; **Saturated compounds**, **Unsaturated compounds**, 191.

WATER

Water (**H_2O**) is the most important compound on Earth. It is found on the surface and in the atmosphere, and is present in animals and plants. Vast amounts of water are used every day in the home and in industry, e.g. for manufacturing processes and the cooling of chemical plants. Water normally contains some dissolved gases, **salts*** and **pollutants***. See also page 167.

A molecule of water contains one oxygen atom and two hydrogen atoms.

*A water molecule is a **polar molecule***, which makes water a good **polar solvent***.*

H δ^+
δ^- O
H δ^+

Ice

The solid form of water. It has a **molecular lattice*** in which the molecules are further apart than in water. This is caused by **hydrogen bonds*** and means that ice is less dense than water, and that water expands when it freezes.

Cube of ice – the solid form of water

Water cycle

The constant circulation of water through the air, rivers and seas.

*Rainwater is relatively pure, but does contain some dissolved gases, e.g. carbon dioxide and sulfur dioxide (which produces **acid rain***).*

Rainwater runs off into rivers and flows back to the sea.

*Water vapor **condenses*** to form clouds.*

Water vapor

Waste water from houses is cleaned in sewage works.

*Combustion and **respiration****

Evaporation*

*River water is **hard water** if it contains certain **salts***.*

*Sea water contains about 4% dissolved **salts***.*

Transpiration (water evaporating from plants)*

Snow and ice on mountain tops melt.

Reservoir

Storage reservoir

Water from reservoirs is cleaned at waterworks.

Atmospheric water

Over 70% of the Earth's surface is covered with water.

Humidity

The amount of water vapor in the air. It depends on the temperature and is higher (up to 4% of the air) in warm air than cold air.

Hygroscopic

Describes a substance which can absorb up to 70% of its own mass of water vapor. Such a substance becomes damp, but does not dissolve. Sodium chloride is an example of a hygroscopic substance.

Deliquescent

Describes a substance which absorbs water vapor from the air and dissolves in it, forming a **concentrated*** solution.

*Calcium chloride left open to the air absorbs water vapor and forms a **concentrated*** solution.*

Efflorescent

Describes a crystal which loses part of its **water of crystallization*** to the air. A powdery coating is left on its surface.

A white powder forms on sodium carbonate crystals.

* **Acid rain**, 210; **Concentrated**, 144; **Condensation**, **Evaporation**, 121; **Hydrogen bond**, 134; **Molecular lattice**, 137; **Polar molecule**, 133; **Polar solvent**, 144; **Pollutants**, 210; **Respiration**, 298; **Salts**, 153; **Transpiration**, 252; **Water of crystallization**, 135.

Water supply

Distilled water

Water which has had **salts*** removed by **distillation***. It is very pure, but does contain some dissolved gases.

Desalination

The treatment of sea water to remove dissolved **salts***. It is done by **distillation*** or **ion exchange**.

Purification

The treatment of water to remove bacteria and other harmful substances, and produce water that is safe to drink.

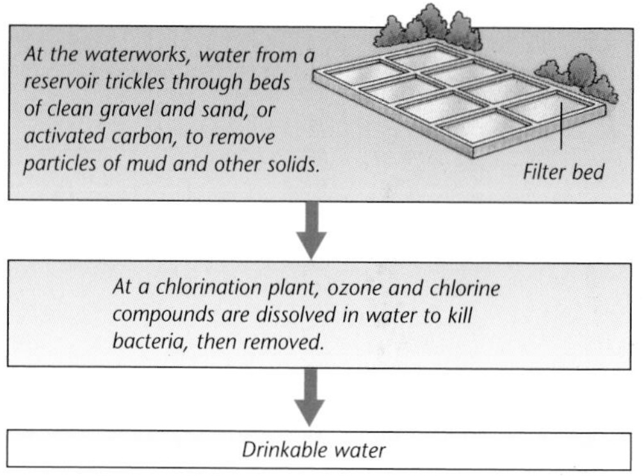

At the waterworks, water from a reservoir trickles through beds of clean gravel and sand, or activated carbon, to remove particles of mud and other solids.
Filter bed
At a chlorination plant, ozone and chlorine compounds are dissolved in water to kill bacteria, then removed.
Drinkable water

Hard water

Water which contains calcium and magnesium **salts*** that have dissolved from the rocks over which the water has flowed (see **calcium**, page 171). Water that does not contain these salts is called **soft water**. There are two types of hardness – **temporary hardness** (which can be removed relatively easily) and **permanent hardness** (which is more difficult to remove). Hard water does not lather with soap and forms a **scum**. Soft water lathers easily because it does not react with soap to form scum.

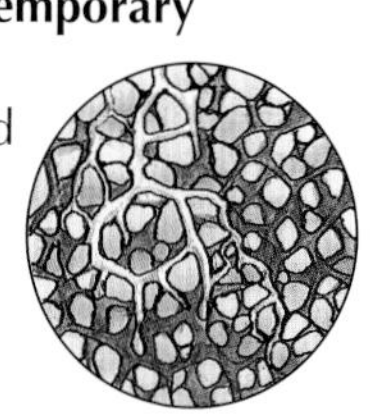

The types of mineral in water depend on the rocks it has flowed over.

Equation for the formation of scum

Calcium and magnesium ions (in hard water)	+	Soap (sodium stearate)	→	Scum (calcium and magnesium stearates)	+	Sodium ions

Temporary hardness

One type of water hardness, caused by the **salt*** calcium bicarbonate dissolved in the water. It can be removed by boiling, producing an insoluble white solid (calcium carbonate or "scale").

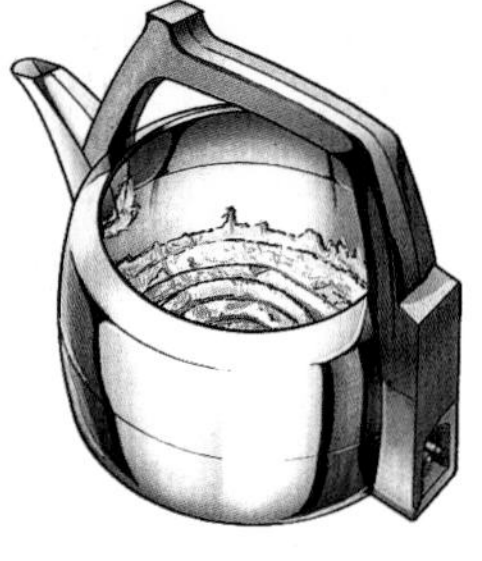

"Scale" forms in kettles which have been used to boil ***hard water****.*

Permanent hardness

The more severe type of water hardness, caused by calcium and magnesium **salts*** (sulfates and chlorides) dissolved in the water. It cannot be removed by boiling, but can be removed by **distillation*** (producing **distilled water**) or by **water softening** (**ion exchange** or use of **water softeners**).

Ion exchange

A method of **water softening** (see **permanent hardness**). Water is passed over a material such as **zeolite** (sodium aluminum silicate), which removes calcium and magnesium ions and replaces them with sodium ions. Some organic **polymers*** are also used as ion exchange materials.

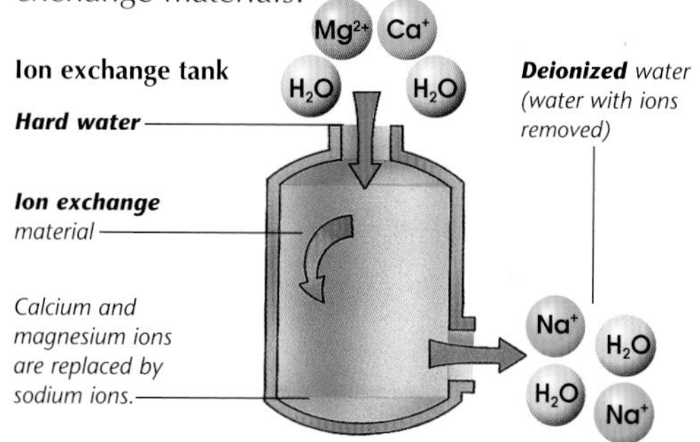

Ion exchange tank
Hard water
Ion exchange material
Calcium and magnesium ions are replaced by sodium ions.
Deionized water (water with ions removed)
Mg^{2+}
Ca^{+}
H_2O
H_2O
Na^{+}
H_2O
H_2O
Na^{+}

Water softeners

Substances used to remove **permanent hardness**. They react with the calcium and magnesium **salts*** to form compounds which do not react with soap.

Washing soda

The common name for the **hydrate*** of sodium carbonate (see also page 169). It is used as a **water softener** in the home.

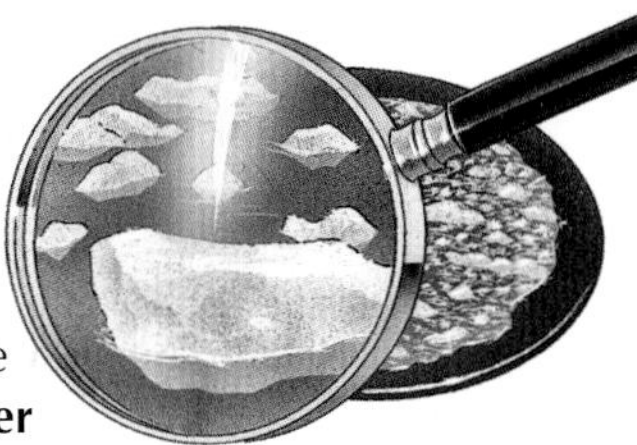

Crystals* *of washing soda*

* **Crystals**, 135; **Distillation**, 220; **Hydrate**, 154; **Polymers**, 200; **Salts**, 153.

AIR AND BURNING

Air is a mixture of gases, including oxygen, carbon dioxide and nitrogen, which surrounds the Earth and is essential for all forms of life. These gases can be separated by the **fractional distillation of liquid air***, and are used as raw materials in industry. Air also contains some water vapor and may contain **pollutants*** in some areas.

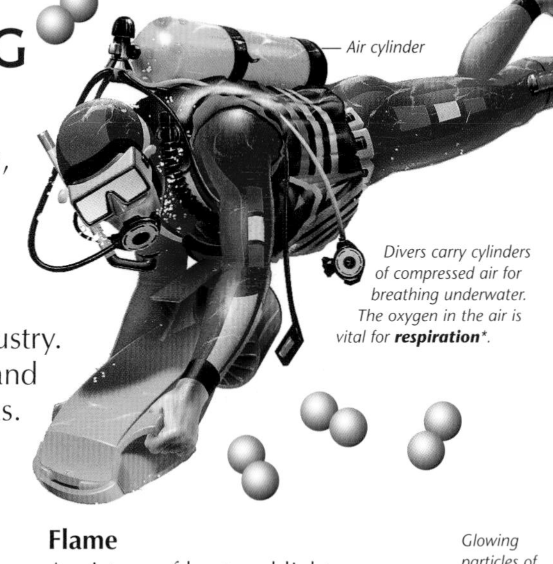
Air cylinder

Divers carry cylinders of compressed air for breathing underwater. The oxygen in the air is vital for ***respiration****.

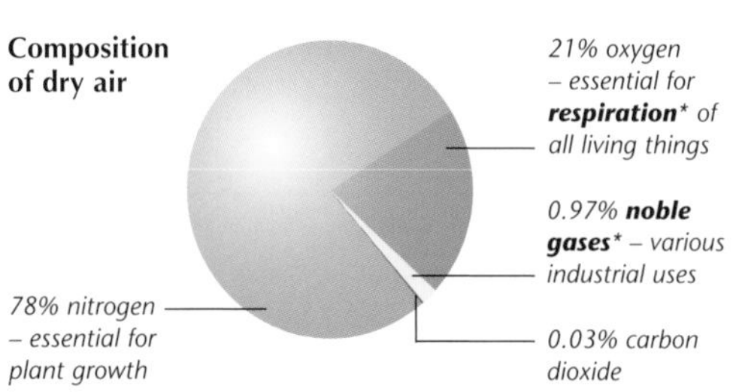
Composition of dry air
21% oxygen – essential for respiration* of all living things
0.97% noble gases* – various industrial uses
78% nitrogen – essential for plant growth
0.03% carbon dioxide

Combustion or burning

An **exothermic reaction*** between a substance and a gas. Combustion usually takes place in air, when the substance which burns combines with oxygen. Substances can also burn in other gases, though, e.g. chlorine. Combustion does not normally happen spontaneously. It has to be started by heating (see **activation energy**, page 160).

Natural gas* *(mainly* ***methane****) burns in gas cookers, producing heat for cooking.*

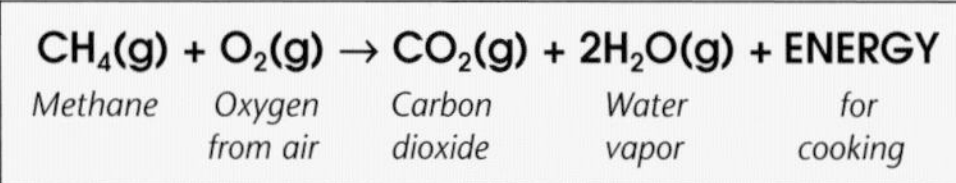
CH4(g) + O2(g) → CO2(g) + 2H2O(g) + ENERGY
Methane
Oxygen from air
Carbon dioxide
Water vapor
for cooking

$$CH_4(g) + O_2(g) \rightarrow CO_2(g) + 2H_2O(g) + \text{ENERGY}$$

Rapid combustion

Combustion in which a large amount of heat and light energy is given out.

Rapid combustion *can produce a large volume of gas as well as heat. This causes an explosion.*

Slow combustion

A form of **combustion** which takes place at low temperature. No **flames** occur. **Internal respiration** (see page 209) is a form of slow combustion.

Flame

A mixture of heat and light energy produced during **rapid combustion**.

Glowing particles of unburned carbon

A ***non-luminous flame*** *is produced when there is enough oxygen for all of the substance to burn.*

Unburned gas

A ***luminous flame*** *is produced when there is not enough oxygen for complete* ***combustion****.*

Air hole open

Air hole closed

Fuel

A substance which is burned to produce heat energy. Most fuels used today are **fossil fuels**, which were formed from the remains of prehistoric animal and plant life.

Wood is the oldest known ***fuel****.*

Fossil fuels*, such as* ***natural gas**** *and* ***petroleum**** *are extracted from deep under the ground.*

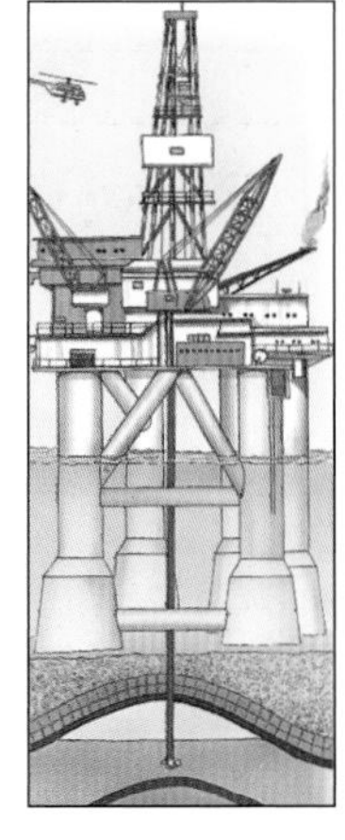

Calorific value

A measure of the amount of heat energy produced by a specific amount of a **fuel**. The table below shows the relative values for some common fuels.

Heat energy in ***kilojoules**** *per gram*

Fuel
Gasoline*
Natural gas*
Coal*
Coke*
Anthracite*
Wood

* **Anthracite**, 179 (**Coal**); **Coke**, 179 (**Coal**); **Exothermic reaction**, 146; **Fractional distillation of liquid air**, 183; **Gasoline**, 199; **Kilojoule**, 146; **Natural gas**, 192 (**Methane**); **Noble gases**, 189; **Petroleum**, 198; **Pollutants**, 210; **Respiration**, 298.

Corrosion

A reaction between a metal and the gases in air. The metal is **oxidized*** to form an oxide layer on the surface, usually weakening the metal, but sometimes forming a protective coat against further corrosion. Corrosion can be prevented by stopping oxygen from reaching the metal or by preventing electrons from leaving it (see **sacrificial protection**, page 159). The corrosion of iron is called **rusting** (see **rust**, page 174).

Internal respiration

A form of **slow combustion** in animals. It produces energy from the reaction of **glucose*** with oxygen. See also page 334 and **respiration**, page 298.

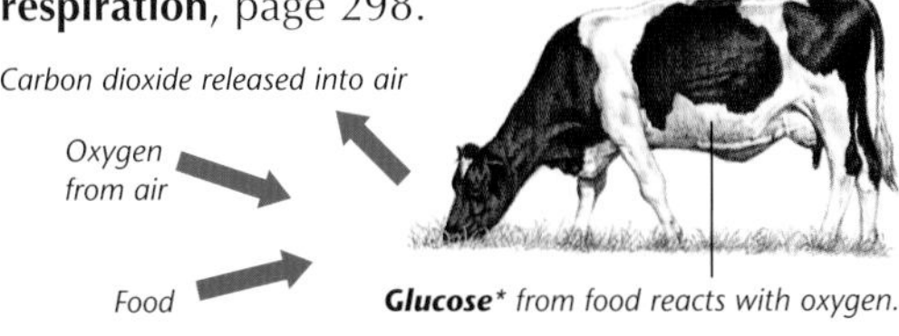
Carbon dioxide released into air
Oxygen from air
Food
Glucose* from food reacts with oxygen.

$$C_6H_{12}O_6 + 6O_2 \rightarrow 6CO_2 + 6H_2O + \text{ENERGY}$$

Energy produced by reaction of glucose and oxygen

Photosynthesis

A **photochemical reaction*** in green plants. It involves the production of **glucose*** from carbon dioxide and water, using the energy from sunlight. Photosynthesis is chemically the opposite of **internal respiration**. See also pages 254-255.

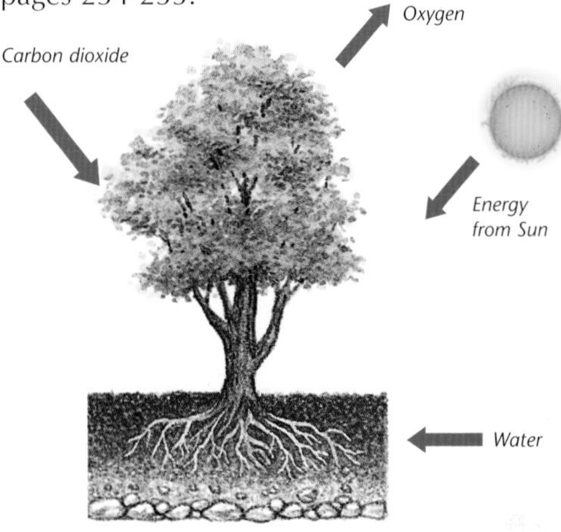
Oxygen
Carbon dioxide
Energy from Sun
Water

$$6CO_2 + 6H_2O \xrightarrow[\text{from Sun}]{\text{Energy}} C_6H_{12}O_6 + 6O_2$$

Carbon dioxide reacts with water, producing glucose.

Nitrogen cycle

The constant circulation of nitrogen through the air, animals, plants and the soil.

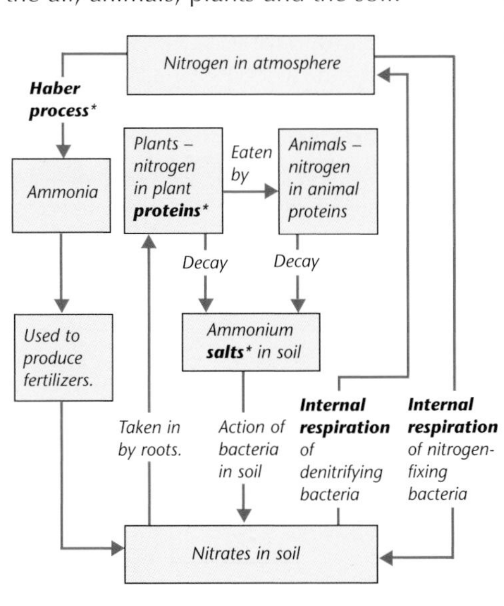
Nitrogen in atmosphere
Haber process*
Ammonia
Plants – nitrogen in plant proteins*
Eaten by
Animals – nitrogen in animal proteins
Decay
Decay
Used to produce fertilizers.
Ammonium salts* in soil
Taken in by roots.
Action of bacteria in soil
Internal respiration of denitrifying bacteria
Internal respiration of nitrogen-fixing bacteria
Nitrates in soil

Carbon cycle

The circulation of carbon through the air, animals, plants and the soil.

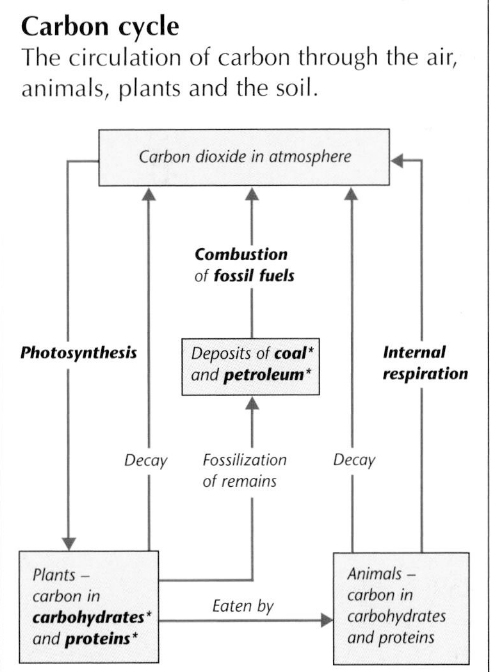
Carbon dioxide in atmosphere
Combustion of fossil fuels
Photosynthesis
Deposits of coal* and petroleum*
Internal respiration
Decay
Fossilization of remains
Decay
Plants – carbon in carbohydrates* and proteins*
Eaten by
Animals – carbon in carbohydrates and proteins

* **Carbohydrates**, 204; **Coal**, 179; **Glucose**, 204; **Haber process**, 180; **Oxidation**, 148; **Petroleum**, 198; **Photochemical reaction**, 160; **Proteins**, 205; **Salts**, 153.

POLLUTION

Pollution is the release into the land, atmosphere, rivers and oceans, of undesirable substances which upset the natural processes of the Earth. These substances are known as **pollutants**. The major sources and types of pollution are shown below.

Biodegradable

Describes a substance which is converted to simpler compounds by bacteria. Many plastics are not biodegradable (see also **biodegradable detergents**, page 203).

Smog

Fog mixed with dust and soot. It is acidic because of the sulfur dioxide produced when **fuels*** are burned in industrial cities.

*Sulfur dioxide, produced by impurities in **fuels***, is the major cause of **acid rain**.*

Acid rain

Rainwater which is more acidic than usual. Rainwater normally has a **pH*** of between 5 and 6, due to dissolved carbon dioxide forming dilute carbonic acid. Sulfur dioxide and oxides of nitrogen, products of the combustion of **fuels***, react with water in the atmosphere to produce sulfuric and nitric acids with a pH of about 3.

Greenhouse effect

The trapping of solar energy in the atmosphere by carbon dioxide, causing an increase in temperature. The burning of **fuels*** creates more carbon dioxide, making the problem worse. See also page 29.

Trapped solar energy

Ozone depletion

The thinning of the layer of **ozone*** gas in the upper atmosphere which protects the Earth from the Sun's harmful **ultraviolet radiation***. This effect is believed to be accelerated by chlorine acting as a **catalyst*** for the breakdown of oxygen to ozone. The chlorine comes from the decomposition of **chlorofluorocarbons*** (**CFCs**), chemicals used as a propellant in aerosols, as a coolant in refrigerators and in **polystyrene*** manufacture. International action is being taken to reduce the manufacture and use of CFCs, but many scientists believe that more could be done.

Thermal pollution

The effect of releasing warm water from factories and power stations into rivers and lakes. This causes a decrease in the oxygen dissolved in the water and affects aquatic life.

Eutrophication

An overgrowth of aquatic plants caused by an excess of nitrates, nitrites and phosphates from fertilizers in rivers. It results in a shortage of oxygen in the water, causing the death of fish and other water life.

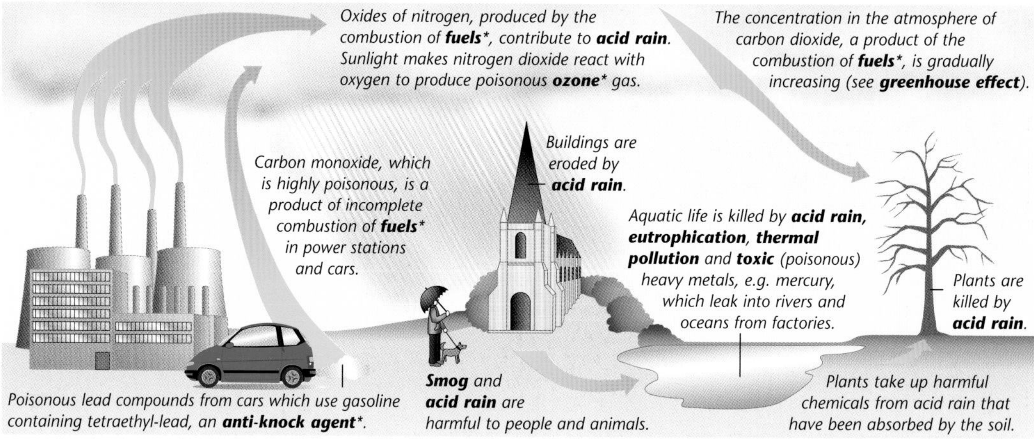
Oxides of nitrogen, produced by the combustion of fuels*, contribute to acid rain. Sunlight makes nitrogen dioxide react with oxygen to produce poisonous ozone* gas.
The concentration in the atmosphere of carbon dioxide, a product of the combustion of fuels*, is gradually increasing (see greenhouse effect).
Carbon monoxide, which is highly poisonous, is a product of incomplete combustion of fuels* in power stations and cars.
Buildings are eroded by acid rain.
Aquatic life is killed by acid rain, eutrophication, thermal pollution and toxic (poisonous) heavy metals, e.g. mercury, which leak into rivers and oceans from factories.
Plants are killed by acid rain.
Poisonous lead compounds from cars which use gasoline containing tetraethyl-lead, an anti-knock agent*.
Smog and acid rain are harmful to people and animals.
Plants take up harmful chemicals from acid rain that have been absorbed by the soil.

* **Anti-knock agent**, 199 (**Octane rating**); **Catalyst**, 161; **Chlorofluorocarbons**, 195; **Fuel**, 208; **Ozone**, 183; **Petroleum**, 198; **pH**, 152; **Polystyrene**, 201; **Purification**, 207; **Radioactivity**, 128; **Ultraviolet radiation**, 44.

THE REACTIVITY SERIES

(showing ten metals – see also page 158)

Metal	Symbol	Reaction with air	Reaction with water	Reaction with dilute strong acids*	Displacement* reactions	Reaction of carbon dioxide	Reaction of hydrogen with oxide	Action of heat on oxide	Action of heat on carbonate	Action of heat on nitrate	Symbol
Potassium	**K**	*Burn strongly to form oxides.*	*React with cold water to produce hydrogen gas and hydroxide. Hydroxide dissolves in water to form alkaline solution. React with decreasing vigor down the series.*	*Explosive reaction to give hydrogen gas and **salt*** solution.*	*All metals displace ions of metals below them from solution.*	*No reaction*	*No reaction*	*No reaction*	*No reaction*	*Decompose to form nitrite and oxygen.*	**K**
Sodium	**Na**										**Na**
Calcium	**Ca**	*Burn, when heated, to form oxides. Burn with decreasing vigor down the series.*		*React to give hydrogen gas and **salt*** solution with decreasing vigor down the series.*					*Decompose to form oxide and carbon dioxide with increasing ease down the series.*	*Decompose to form oxide, oxygen and nitrogen dioxide with increasing ease down the series.*	**Ca**
Magnesium	**Mg**										**Mg**
Aluminum	**Al**		*No reaction with cold water. React with steam to form hydrogen gas and oxide. React with decreasing vigor down the series.*								**Al**
Zinc	**Zn**					*Oxide **reduced*** to metal with increasing ease down the series. Carbon dioxide is formed.*					**Zn**
Iron	**Fe**										**Fe**
Lead	**Pb**	*Do not burn when heated, but form an oxide layer on surface.*	*No reaction*								**Pb**
Copper	**Cu**			*No reaction*			*Oxide **reduced*** to metal with increasing ease down the series. Water is formed.*				**Cu**
Silver	**Ag**	*No reaction*						*Decomposes to form metal and oxygen only.*	*and carbon dioxide.*	*and nitrogen dioxide.*	**Ag**

* **Displacement**, 158; **Reduction**, 148; **Salts**, 153; **Strong acid**, 152.

THE PROPERTIES OF THE ELEMENTS

Below is a chart giving information on the physical properties of the elements in the **periodic table** (see pages 164-165). The last eight elements (**atomic numbers*** 96-103 – see pages 165 and 226-227 for symbols and names) are not listed, as there is very little known about them – they all have to be made under special laboratory conditions and only exist for a fraction of a second. All the density measurements below are taken at room temperature except those of gases (marked with a †), which are measured at their boiling points. A dash (–) at any place on the chart indicates that there is no known value.

Element	Symbol	Atomic number*	Approximate relative atomic mass*	Density (g cm^{-3})	Melting point (°C) (brackets indicate approximations)	Boiling point (°C)
Actinium	***Ac***	*89*	*227*	*10.1*	*1,050*	*3,200*
Aluminum	***Al***	*13*	*27*	*2.7*	*660*	*2,470*
Americium	***Am***	*95*	*243*	*11.7*	*(1,200)*	*(2,600)*
Antimony	***Sb***	*51*	*122*	*6.62*	*630*	*1,380*
Argon	***Ar***	*18*	*40*	*1.4 †*	*–189*	*–186*
Arsenic	***As***	*33*	*75*	*5.73*	–	*613 (**sublimes***)*
Astatine	***At***	*85*	*210*	–	*(302)*	–
Barium	***Ba***	*56*	*137*	*3.51*	*714*	*1,640*
Beryllium	***Be***	*4*	*9*	*1.85*	*1,280*	*2,477*
Bismuth	***Bi***	*83*	*209*	*9.78*	*271*	*1,560*
Boron	***B***	*5*	*11*	*2.34*	*2,300*	*3,930*
Bromine	***Br***	*35*	*80*	*3.12*	*–7.2*	*58.8*
Cadmium	***Cd***	*48*	*112*	*8.65*	*321*	*765*
Calcium	***Ca***	*20*	*40*	*1.54*	*850*	*1,487*
Carbon	***C***	*6*	*12*	*2.25 (**graphite***)*	*3,730 (**sublimes***)*	*4,830*
				*3.51 (**diamond***)*	*3,750*	–
Cerium	***Ce***	*58*	*140*	*6.78*	*795*	*3,470*
Cesium	***Cs***	*55*	*133*	*1.9*	*28.7*	*690*
Chlorine	***Cl***	*17*	*35.5*	*1.56 †*	*–101*	*–34.7*
Chromium	***Cr***	*24*	*52*	*7.19*	*1,890*	*2,482*
Cobalt	***Co***	*27*	*59*	*8.7*	*1,492*	*2,900*
Copper	***Cu***	*29*	*64*	*8.89*	*1,083*	*2,595*
Dysprosium	***Dy***	*66*	*162*	*8.56*	*1,410*	*2,600*
Erbium	***Er***	*68*	*167*	*9.16*	*1,500*	*2,900*
Europium	***Eu***	*63*	*152*	*5.24*	*826*	*1,440*
Fluorine	***F***	*9*	*19*	*1.11 †*	*–220*	*–188*
Francium	***Fr***	*87*	*223*	–	*(27)*	–
Gadolinium	***Gd***	*64*	*157*	*7.95*	*1,310*	*3,000*
Gallium	***Ga***	*31*	*70*	*5.93*	*29.8*	*2,400*
Germanium	***Ge***	*32*	*73*	*5.4*	*937*	*2,830*
Gold	***Au***	*79*	*197*	*19.3*	*1,063*	*2,970*
Hafnium	***Hf***	*72*	*178.5*	*13.3*	*2,220*	*5,400*
Helium	***He***	*2*	*4*	*0.147 †*	*–270*	*–269*
Holmium	***Ho***	*67*	*165*	*8.8*	*1,460*	*2,600*
Hydrogen	***H***	*1*	*1*	*0.07 †*	*–259*	*–252*
Indium	***In***	*49*	*115*	*7.3*	*157*	*2,000*
Iodine	***I***	*53*	*127*	*4.93*	*114*	*184*
Iridium	***Ir***	*77*	*192*	*22.4*	*2,440*	*5,300*
Iron	***Fe***	*26*	*56*	*7.85*	*1,535*	*3,000*
Krypton	***Kr***	*36*	*84*	*2.16 †*	*–157*	*–152*
Lanthanum	***La***	*57*	*139*	*6.19*	*920*	*3,470*
Lead	***Pb***	*82*	*207*	*11.3*	*327*	*1,744*
Lithium	***Li***	*3*	*7*	*0.53*	*180*	*1,330*
Lutetium	***Lu***	*71*	*175*	*9.84*	*1,650*	*3,330*

* **Atomic number**, 127; **Diamond, Graphite**, 178; **Relative atomic mass**, 138; **Sublimation**, 121.

Element	Symbol	Atomic number*	Approximate relative atomic mass*	Density (g cm^{-3})	Melting point (°C) (brackets indicate approximations)	Boiling point (°C)
Magnesium	***Mg***	*12*	*24*	*1.74*	*650*	*1,100*
Manganese	***Mn***	*25*	*55*	*7.2*	*1,240*	*2,100*
Mercury	***Hg***	*80*	*201*	*13.6*	*–38.9*	*357*
Molybdenum	***Mo***	*42*	*96*	*10.1*	*2,610*	*5,560*
Neodymium	***Nd***	*60*	*144*	*7.0*	*1,020*	*3,030*
Neon	***Ne***	*10*	*20*	*1.2 †*	*–249*	*–246*
Neptunium	***Np***	*93*	*237*	*20.4*	*640*	–
Nickel	***Ni***	*28*	*59*	*8.8*	*1,453*	*2,730*
Niobium	***Nb***	*41*	*93*	*8.57*	*2,470*	*3,300*
Nitrogen	***N***	*7*	*14*	*0.808 †*	*–210*	*–196*
Osmium	***Os***	*76*	*190*	*22.5*	*3,000*	*5,000*
Oxygen	***O***	*8*	*16*	*1.15 †*	*–218*	*–183*
Palladium	***Pd***	*46*	*106*	*12.2*	*1,550*	*3,980*
Phosphorus	***P***	*15*	*31*	*1.82* (***white****)	*44.2* (***white***)	*280* (***white***)
				2.34 (***red****)	*590* (***red***)	–
Platinum	***Pt***	*78*	*195*	*21.5*	*1,769*	*4,530*
Plutonium	***Pu***	*94*	*242*	*19.8*	*640*	*3,240*
Polonium	***Po***	*84*	*210*	*9.4*	*254*	*960*
Potassium	***K***	*19*	*39*	*0.86*	*63.7*	*774*
Praseodymium	***Pr***	*59*	*141*	*6.78*	*935*	*3,130*
Promethium	***Pm***	*61*	*147*	–	*1,030*	*2,730*
Protactinium	***Pa***	*91*	*231*	*15.4*	*1,230*	–
Radium	***Ra***	*88*	*226*	*5*	*700*	*1,140*
Radon	***Rn***	*86*	*222*	*4.4 †*	*–71*	*–61.8*
Rhenium	***Re***	*75*	*186*	*20.5*	*3,180*	*5,630*
Rhodium	***Rh***	*45*	*103*	*12.4*	*1,970*	*4,500*
Rubidium	***Rb***	*37*	*85*	*1.53*	*38.9*	*688*
Ruthenium	***Ru***	*44*	*101*	*12.3*	*2,500*	*4,900*
Samarium	***Sm***	*62*	*150*	*7.54*	*1,070*	*1,900*
Scandium	***Sc***	*21*	*45*	*2.99*	*1,540*	*2,730*
Selenium	***Se***	*34*	*79*	*4.79*	*217*	*685*
Silicon	***Si***	*14*	*28*	*2.35*	*1,410*	*2,360*
Silver	***Ag***	*47*	*108*	*10.5*	*961*	*2,210*
Sodium	***Na***	*11*	*23*	*0.97*	*97.8*	*890*
Strontium	***Sr***	*38*	*88*	*2.62*	*768*	*1,380*
Sulfur	***S***	*16*	*32*	*2.07* (***rhombic****)	*113* (***rhombic***)	*444*
				1.96 (***monoclinic****)	*119* (***monoclinic***)	*444*
Tantalum	***Ta***	*73*	*181*	*16.6*	*3,000*	*5,420*
Technetium	***Tc***	*43*	*99*	*11.5*	*2,200*	*3,500*
Tellurium	***Te***	*52*	*128*	*6.2*	*450*	*990*
Terbium	***Tb***	*65*	*159*	*8.27*	*1,360*	*2,800*
Thallium	***Tl***	*81*	*204*	*11.8*	*304*	*1,460*
Thorium	***Th***	*90*	*232*	*11.7*	*1,750*	*3,850*
Thulium	***Tm***	*69*	*169*	*9.33*	*1,540*	*1,730*
Tin	***Sn***	*50*	*119*	*7.3*	*232*	*2,270*
Titanium	***Ti***	*22*	*48*	*4.54*	*1,675*	*3,260*
Tungsten	***W***	*74*	*184*	*19.3*	*3,410*	*5,930*
Uranium	***U***	*92*	*238*	*19.1*	*1,130*	*3,820*
Vanadium	***V***	*23*	*51*	*5.96*	*1,900*	*3,000*
Xenon	***Xe***	*54*	*131*	*3.52 †*	*–112*	*–108*
Ytterbium	***Yb***	*70*	*173*	*6.98*	*824*	*1,430*
Yttrium	***Y***	*39*	*89*	*4.34*	*1,500*	*2,930*
Zinc	***Zn***	*30*	*65*	*7.1*	*420*	*907*
Zirconium	***Zr***	*40*	*91*	*6.49*	*1,850*	*3,580*

* **Atomic number**, 127; **Monoclinic sulfur**, 184; **Red phosphorus**, 182 (**Phosphorus**);
Relative atomic mass, 138; **Rhombic sulfur**, 184; **White phosphorus**, 182 (**Phosphorus**).

NAMING SIMPLE ORGANIC COMPOUNDS

Simple **organic compounds*** (those with one or no **functional group***) can be named by following Stages 1 and 2.

Chart showing prefixes used to denote the number of carbon atoms in a chain

Number of carbon atoms in chain	*Prefix used*
One →	*meth-*
Two →	*eth-*
Three →	*prop-*
Four →	*but-*
Five →	*pent-*
Six →	*hex-*
Seven →	*hept-*
Eight →	*oct-*

Stage 1

Choose the sentence from a) to i) which describes the unidentified molecule, then go to the Stage 2 number indicated.

a) The molecule contains only carbon and hydrogen atoms and ***single bonds****. — Go to 1

b) The molecule contains only carbon and hydrogen atoms and a ***double bond****. — Go to 2

c) The molecule contains only carbon and hydrogen atoms and a ***triple bond****. — Go to 3

d) The molecule contains carbon, hydrogen and a ***hydroxyl group*** *(–****OH****).* — Go to 4

*e) The molecule contains carbon, hydrogen and a –****CHO group*** *at one end.* — Go to 5

f) The molecule contains carbon, hydrogen and a ***carbonyl group*** *(–****CO****–) between two carbons in the carbon chain.* — Go to 6

g) The molecule contains carbon, hydrogen and ***carboxyl group*** *(–****COOH****).* — Go to 7

h) The molecule contains only carbon and hydrogen, but has a ***side chain****. — Go to 8

i) The molecule contains carbon, hydrogen and one or more ***halogen**** *atoms.* — Go to 9

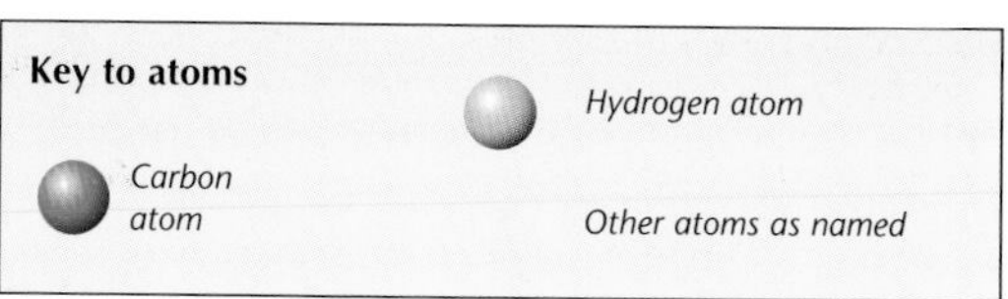
Key to atoms
Hydrogen atom
Carbon atom
Other atoms as named

Stage 2

1*. The name of a molecule that contains only carbon and hydrogen atoms joined by* ***single bonds**** *begins with the prefix for the number of carbons (see prefix chart, left) and ends in* ***-ane****.*
For example:

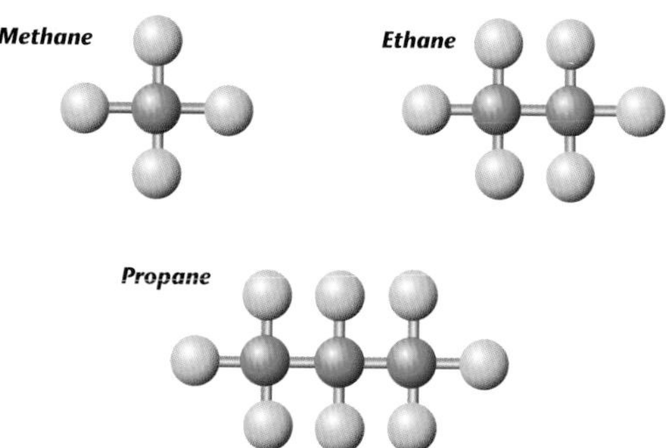
Methane
Ethane
Propane

These molecules are all ***alkanes****.

2*. The name of a molecule that contains only carbon and hydrogen atoms and has one* ***double bond**** *begins with the prefix for the number of carbons (see prefix chart, left) and ends in* ***-ene****.*
For example:

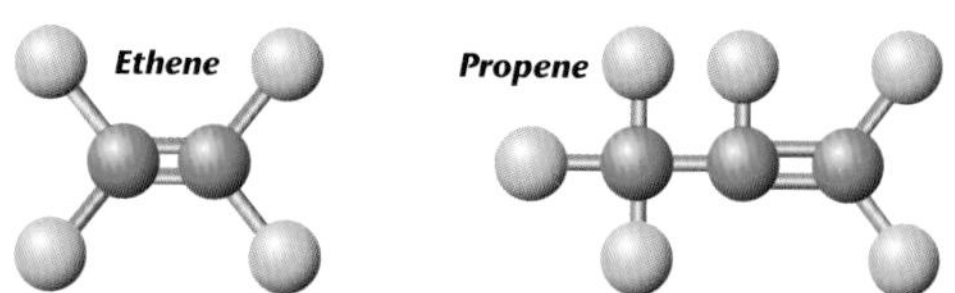
Ethene
Propene

These molecules are all ***alkenes****.

3*. The name of a molecule that contains only carbon and hydrogen atoms and has one* ***triple bond**** *begins with the prefix for the number of carbons (see prefix chart, left) and ends in* ***-yne****.*
For example:

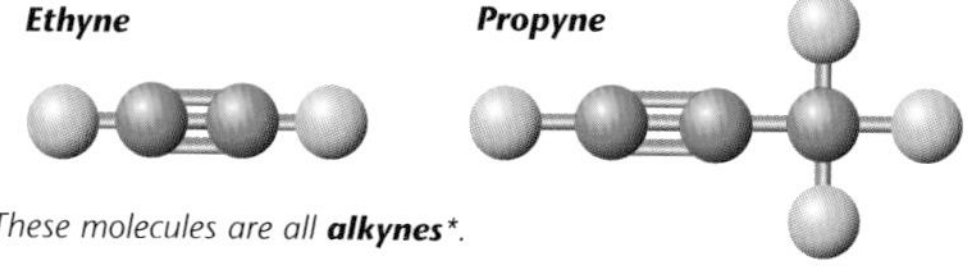
Ethyne
Propyne

These molecules are all ***alkynes****.

4a*. The name of a molecule that contains only carbon and hydrogen atoms and one* ***hydroxyl group*** *(–****OH****) begins with the prefix for the number of carbons (see prefix chart, left) and ends in* ***-ol****.*
For example:

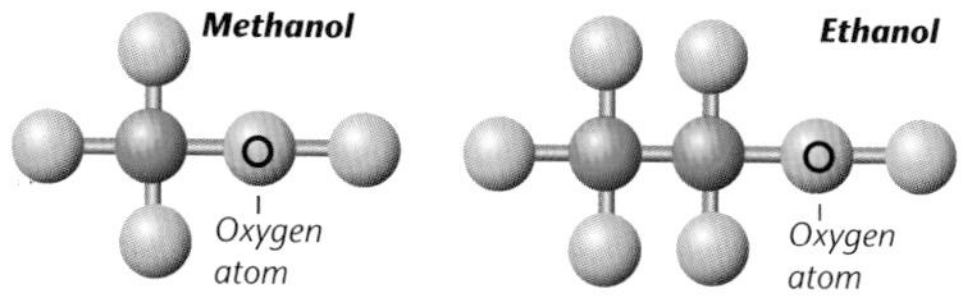
Methanol
O
Oxygen atom
Ethanol
O
Oxygen atom

* **Alkanes**, 192; **Alkenes**, 193; **Alkynes**, 194; **Double bond**, 132; **Functional group**, 190; **Halogens**, 186; **Organic compounds**, **Side chain**, 190; **Single bond**, **Triple bond**, 132.

***4b**. If the **–OH group** is not at one end of the molecule, the number of the carbon to which it is attached is given in front of the name. The carbon atoms are always numbered from the end of the molecule closest to the –OH group. For example:*

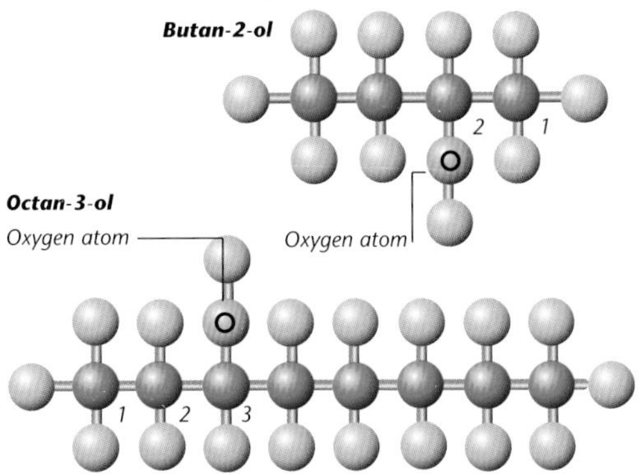
Butan-2-ol
2
1
Octan-3-ol
Oxygen atom
Oxygen atom
O
O
1
2
3

*All molecules in sections **4a** and **4b** are **alcohols***.*

***5**. The name of a molecule that contains only carbon and hydrogen atoms, and has a **–CHO group** ending the chain, begins with the prefix for the number of carbons (see prefix chart, page 214) and ends in **-al**. For example:*

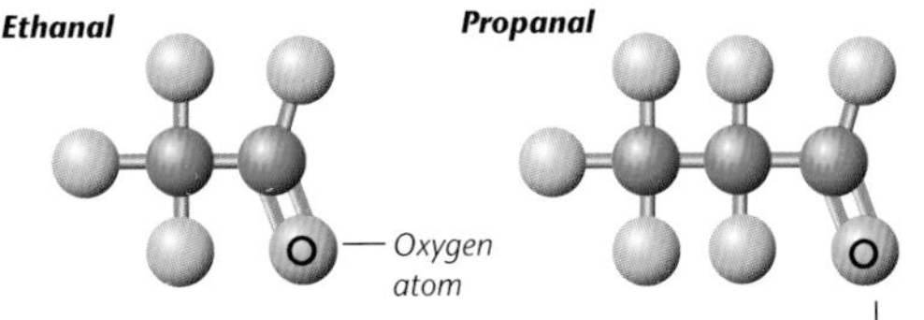
Ethanal
Propanal
O
Oxygen atom
O
Oxygen atom

*These molecules are all **aldehydes***.*

***6**. The name of a molecule that contains only carbon and hydrogen atoms, and has a **carbonyl group** (–**CO**–) between the ends of the carbon chain, begins with the prefix for the number of carbons (see prefix chart, page 214) and ends in **-one**. For example:*

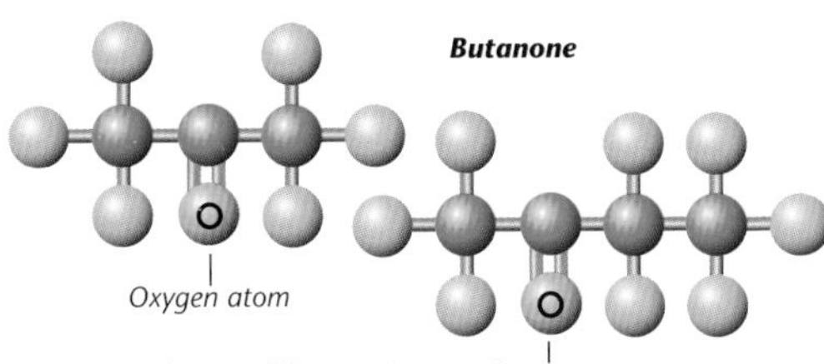
Propanone
Butanone
O
Oxygen atom
O
Oxygen atom

*These molecules are all **ketones***.*

***7**. The name of a molecule that contains only carbon and hydrogen atoms and one **carboxyl group** (–**COOH**) begins with the prefix for the number of carbons (see prefix chart, page 214) and ends in **-oic acid**. For example:*

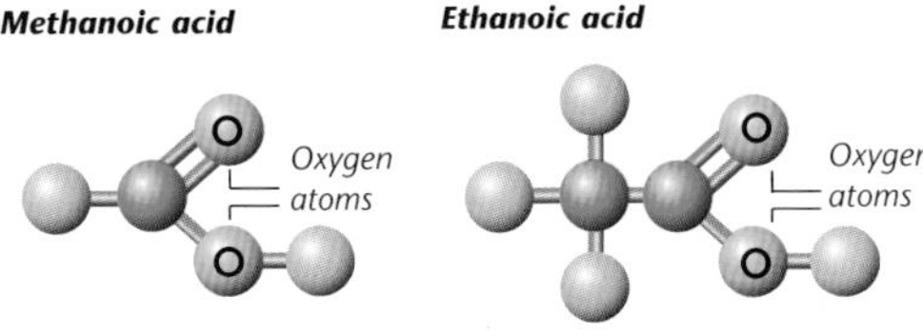
Methanoic acid
Ethanoic acid
O
O
Oxygen atoms
O
O
Oxygen atoms

*All molecules in section **7** are **carboxylic acids***.*

8**. The name of a branched molecule begins with the name of the branch (**side chain). If this has only carbon and hydrogen atoms, its name begins with the prefix for the number of carbons in its chain (see prefix chart, page 214) and ends in **-yl**. The main chain is named afterward in the normal way (see 1). For example:*

*This **side chain*** has only one carbon atom, so it is called a **methyl group**. It is also an example of an **alkyl group**. Alkyl groups are any groups of carbon and hydrogen atoms that have a **general formula*** of C_nH_{2n+1}.*

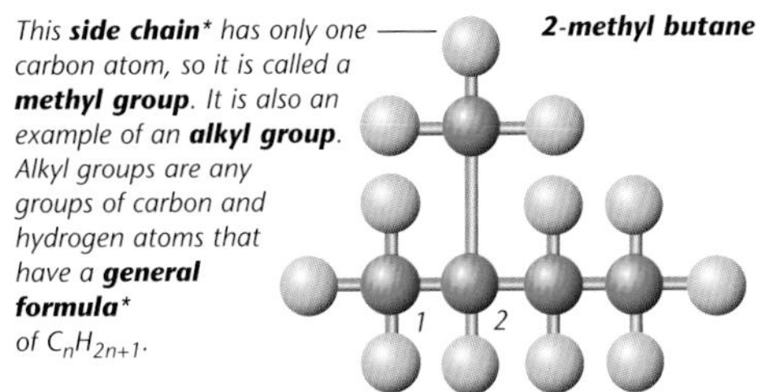
2-methyl butane
1
2

The figure at the beginning of the name gives the number of the carbon atom to which the side chain is joined. The carbon atoms are always numbered from the ends of the chain closest to the branch.

9**. The name of a molecule that contains carbon and hydrogen atoms and one or more **halogens begins with the abbreviation for the halogen(s). (They are listed in alphabetical order if more than one.) The abbreviations for bromine, chlorine, fluorine and iodine are **bromo**, **chloro**, **fluoro** and **iodo** respectively.*

Chloromethane — Chlorine atom (Cl)

Bromoethane — Bromine atom (Br)

The end of the name is that which the molecule would have had if all the halogen atoms had been replaced by hydrogen atoms (see 1). With molecules of three carbon atoms or more, the name includes the number of the carbon atom to which the halogen is attached. The carbon atoms are always numbered from the end of the chain closest to the halogen(s). For example:

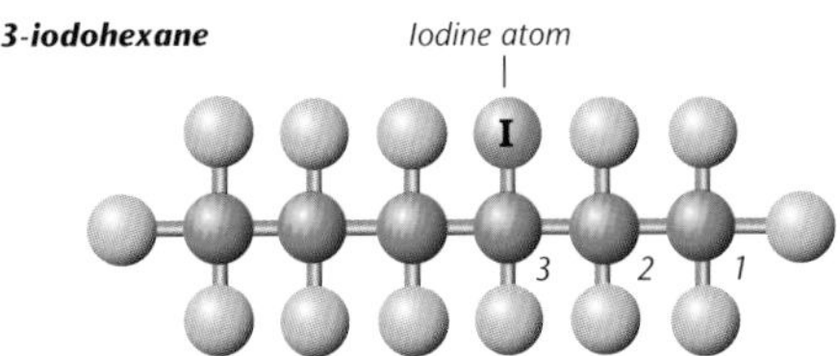
3-iodohexane
Iodine atom
I
3
2
1

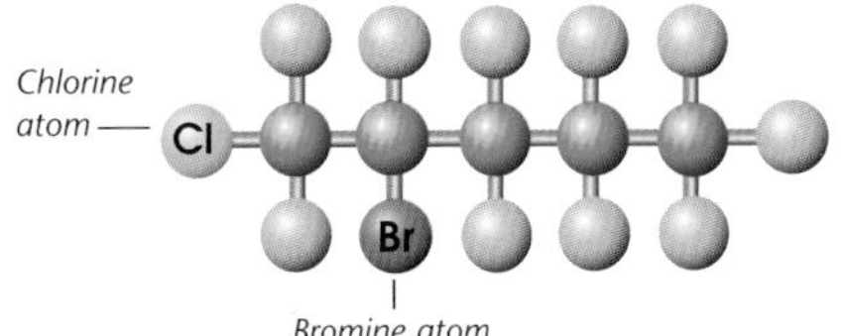
2-bromo,1-chloropentane
Chlorine atom
Cl
Br
Bromine atom

*All molecules in section **9** are **halogenoalkanes***.*

* **Alcohols**, 196; **Aldehydes**, 194; **Carboxylic acids**, 195; **General formula**, 191 (**Homologous series**); **Halogenoalkanes**, 195; **Halogens**, 186; **Ketones**, 194; **Side chain**, 190.

THE LABORATORY PREPARATION OF SIX COMMON GASES

Methods for preparing six gases – **carbon dioxide**, **chlorine**, **ethene**, **hydrogen**, **nitrogen** and **oxygen** – are described below.

Carbon dioxide (see page 179) is obtained from the reaction of hydrochloric acid with calcium carbonate (marble chips). A gas jar filled with water is placed on the beehive shelf over the mouth of the delivery tube. Gas produced by the reaction comes out of the delivery tube and displaces the water in the gas jar. This method of collecting a gas is called collecting gas **over water**.

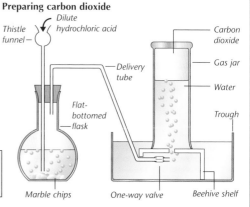

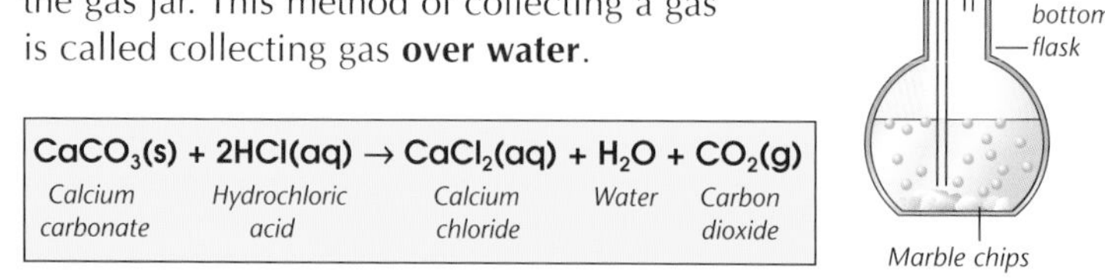

Preparing carbon dioxide
Thistle funnel
Dilute hydrochloric acid
Delivery tube
Flat-bottomed flask
Carbon dioxide
Gas jar
Water
Trough
Marble chips
One-way valve
Beehive shelf

$$CaCO_3(s) + 2HCl(aq) \rightarrow CaCl_2(aq) + H_2O + CO_2(g)$$

Calcium carbonate | Hydrochloric acid | Calcium chloride | Water | Carbon dioxide

Chlorine (see page 187) is prepared by **oxidizing*** concentrated hydrochloric acid using manganese(IV) oxide. This reaction is always done in a **fume cupboard***. The gas produced by the reaction contains some hydrogen chloride and water. The hydrogen chloride is removed by passing the stream of gas through water, and the water is removed by passing the gas through concentrated sulfuric acid. Finally the chlorine is collected in a gas jar. It displaces air from the gas jar as it is heavier. This method of gas collection is called collecting a gas by **upward displacement of air**.

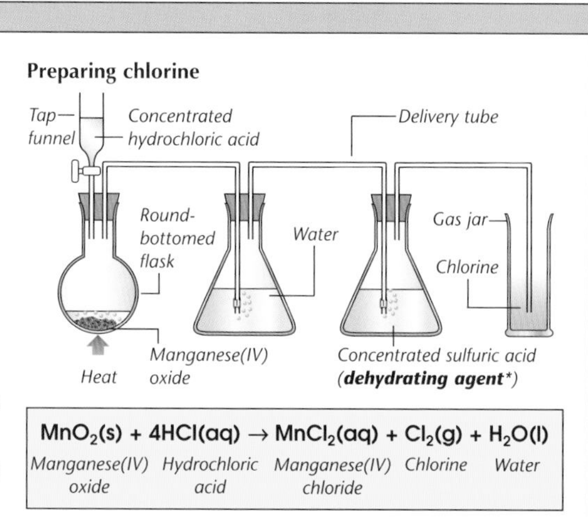

Preparing chlorine
Tap funnel
Concentrated hydrochloric acid
Delivery tube
Round-bottomed flask
Water
Gas jar
Chlorine
Heat
Manganese(IV) oxide
Concentrated sulfuric acid (**dehydrating agent***)

$$MnO_2(s) + 4HCl(aq) \rightarrow MnCl_2(aq) + Cl_2(g) + H_2O(l)$$

Manganese(IV) oxide | Hydrochloric acid | Manganese(IV) chloride | Chlorine | Water

Ethene (see page 193) is prepared by dehydrating (removing water from) ethanol by reacting it with concentrated sulfuric acid. Aluminum sulfate is added to reduce frothing. The buffer flask ensures that any sodium hydroxide sucking back out of its flask does not mix with the acid. The sodium hydroxide removes acid fumes from the gas. Ethene is collected **over water** (see **carbon dioxide**, above).

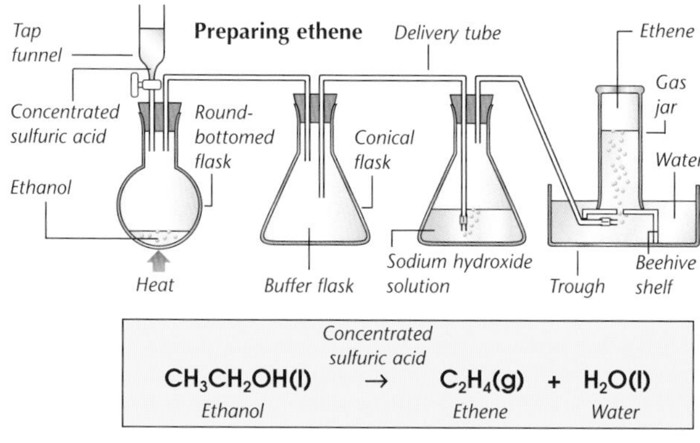

Tap funnel
Preparing ethene
Delivery tube
Ethene
Gas jar
Concentrated sulfuric acid
Round-bottomed flask
Conical flask
Water
Ethanol
Heat
Buffer flask
Sodium hydroxide solution
Trough
Beehive shelf

$$CH_3CH_2OH(l) \xrightarrow{\text{Concentrated sulfuric acid}} C_2H_4(g) + H_2O(l)$$

Ethanol | Ethene | Water

* **Dehydrating agent**, 344; **Fume cupboard**, 224; **Oxidation**, 148.

Hydrogen (see page 167) is obtained from the reaction of hydrochloric acid with granulated zinc. A little copper(II) sulfate is usually added to speed up the reaction. The hydrogen is collected **over water** (see **carbon dioxide**, page 216) unless dry hydrogen is needed, in which case it is passed through concentrated sulfuric acid and is collected by the **downward displacement of air** (it pushes the air down out of the gas jar as it is lighter than air).

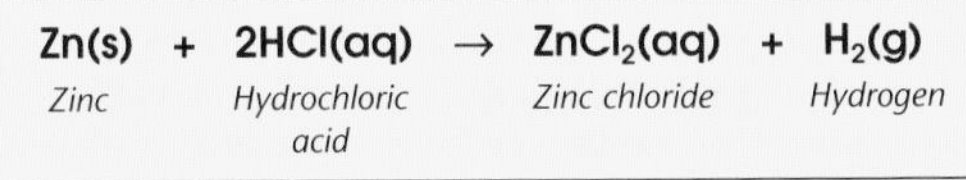

$$Zn(s) + 2HCl(aq) \rightarrow ZnCl_2(aq) + H_2(g)$$

Zinc — *Hydrochloric acid* — *Zinc chloride* — *Hydrogen*

Preparing hydrogen

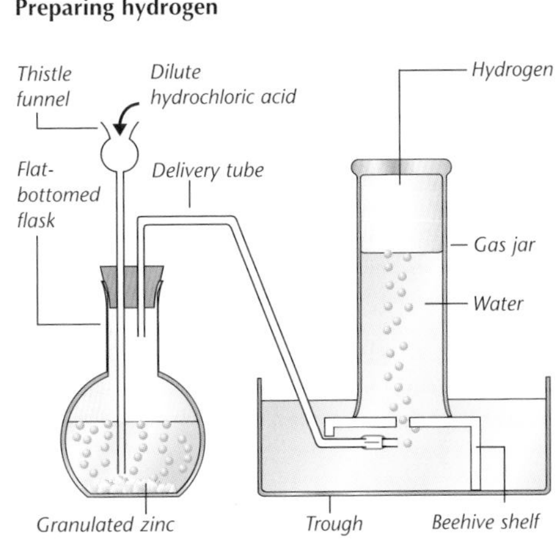
Thistle funnel
Dilute hydrochloric acid
Hydrogen
Flat-bottomed flask
Delivery tube
Gas jar
Water
Granulated zinc
Trough
Beehive shelf

Nitrogen (see page 180) is prepared by removing the carbon dioxide and oxygen from air. The carbon dioxide is removed by passing the air through sodium hydroxide solution. The oxygen is removed by passing the air over heated copper. The nitrogen is collected **over water** (see **carbon dioxide**, page 216). A residue of **noble gases*** remains in the nitrogen.

Preparing nitrogen

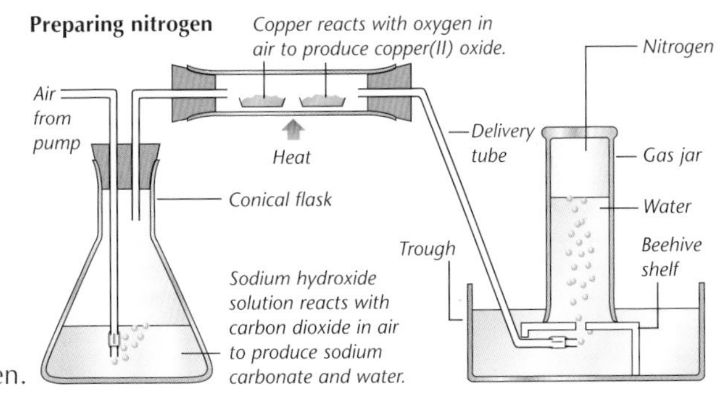
Copper reacts with oxygen in air to produce copper(II) oxide.
Nitrogen
Air from pump
Heat
Delivery tube
Gas jar
Conical flask
Water
Trough
Beehive shelf
Sodium hydroxide solution reacts with carbon dioxide in air to produce sodium carbonate and water.

$$CO_2(g) + 2NaOH(aq) \rightarrow Na_2CO_3(aq) + H_2O(l)$$

Carbon dioxide — *Sodium hydroxide* — *Sodium carbonate* — *Water*

$$O_2(g) + 2Cu(s) \rightarrow 2CuO(s)$$

Oxygen — *Copper* — *Copper(II) oxide*

Oxygen (see page 183) is produced when hydrogen peroxide decomposes. Manganese(IV) oxide is used as a **catalyst*** to speed up this reaction. The gas is collected **over water** (see **carbon dioxide**, page 216) unless it must be dry, in which case it is passed through concentrated sulfuric acid and is collected by the **upward displacement of air** (see **chlorine**, page 216).

$$2H_2O_2(aq) \xrightarrow{\text{Manganese(IV) oxide}} 2H_2O(l) + O_2(g)$$

Hydrogen peroxide — *Water* — *Oxygen*

Preparing oxygen

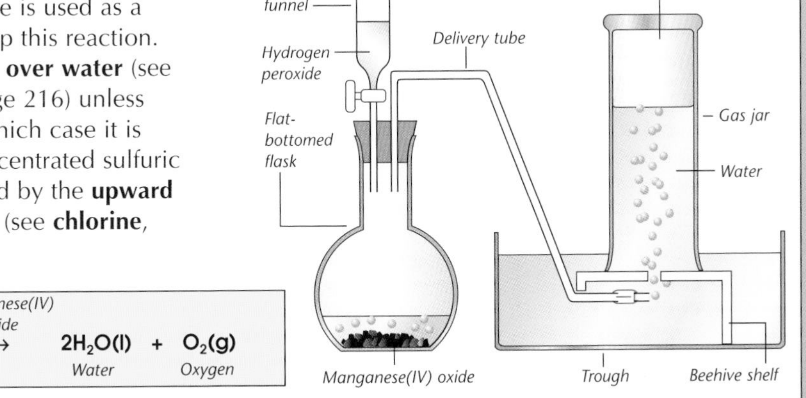
Tap funnel
Oxygen
Hydrogen peroxide
Delivery tube
Flat-bottomed flask
Gas jar
Water
Manganese(IV) oxide
Trough
Beehive shelf

* **Catalyst**, 161; **Noble gases**, 189.

LABORATORY TESTS

Various tests are used to identify substances. Some of the tests involve advanced machinery, others are simple laboratory tests and all are known collectively as **qualitative analysis**. Some of the more advanced tests are shown on page 222; these two pages cover simple laboratory tests leading to the identification of water, common gases, a selection of **anions*** and **cations*** (i.e. components of compounds) and some metals. The appearance or smell of a substance often gives clues to its identity – these can be confirmed by testing. If there are no such clues, then it is a matter of progressing through the tests, gradually eliminating possibilities (it is often a good idea to start with a **flame test**). Often more than one test is needed to identify an ion (anion or cation), as only one particular combination of results can confirm its presence (compare the tests and results for **lead**, **zinc** and **magnesium**).

Tests for water (H_2O)

Test	Results
*Add to **anhydrous*** copper(II) sulfate.*	*White copper(II) sulfate powder turns blue.*
*Add to **anhydrous*** cobalt(II) chloride.*	*Blue cobalt(II) chloride turns pink.*

Tests to identify gases

Gas	Symbol	Test	Results
Carbon dioxide	CO_2	*Pass into **limewater** (calcium hydroxide solution).*	*Turns limewater cloudy.*
Hydrogen	H_2	*Put a lighted splint into a sample of the gas.*	*Burns with a "popping" noise.*
Oxygen	O_2	*Put a glowing splint into a sample of the gas.*	*Splint relights.*

Tests for anions*

These tests are used to identify some of the **anions*** found in compounds.

Anion	Symbol	Test	Results
Bromide	Br^-	*Add silver nitrate solution to a solution of substance in dilute nitric acid.*	*Pale yellow precipitate that dissolves slightly in ammonia solution.*
Carbonate	CO_3^{2-}	*a) Add dilute hydrochloric acid to the substance.* *b) Try to dissolve the substance in water containing **universal indicator*** solution.*	*a) Carbon dioxide gas given off.* *b) If soluble, turns the indicator purple (compare **bicarbonate** test).*
Chloride	Cl^-	*Add silver nitrate solution to a solution of substance in dilute nitric acid.*	*Thick, white precipitate (which is soluble in ammonia solution).*
Hydrogencarbonate	HCO_3^-	*a) Add dilute hydrochloric acid to the substance.* *b) Try to dissolve the substance in water containing **universal indicator***.*	*a) Carbon dioxide gas evolved.* *b) Dissolves and turns indicator solution purple when boiled.*
Iodide	I^-	*Add silver nitrate solution to a solution of substance in dilute nitric acid.*	*Yellow precipitate that does not dissolve in ammonia solution.*
Nitrate	NO_3^-	*Add iron(II) sulfate solution followed by concentrated sulfuric acid to the solution.*	*Brown ring forms at the junction of the two liquids.*
Sulfate	SO_4^{2-}	*Add barium chloride solution to the solution.*	*White precipitate that does not dissolve in dilute hydrochloric acid.*
Sulfite	SO_3^{2-}	*Add barium chloride solution to the solution.*	*White precipitate that dissolves in dilute hydrochloric acid.*
Sulfide	S^{2-}	*Add lead(II) ethanoate solution to the solution.*	*Black precipitate.*

* **Anhydrous**, 154 (**Anhydrate**); **Anion**, **Cation**, 130;
Universal indicator, 152.

Tests for cations*

Most **cations*** in compounds can be identified by the same **flame tests** as those used to identify pure metals (see page 222 for how to carry out a flame test). The chart on the right gives a selection of flame test results. Cations can also be identified by the results of certain reactions. A number of these reactions are listed in the chart below. They cannot be used to identify pure metals, since many metals are insoluble in water and hence cannot form solutions.

Flame tests

Metal	Symbol	Flame color
Barium	***Ba***	*Yellow-green*
Calcium	***Ca***	*Brick red*
Copper	***Cu***	*Blue-green*
Lead	***Pb***	*Blue*
Lithium	***Li***	*Crimson*
Potassium	***K***	*Lilac*
Sodium	***Na***	*Orange-yellow*

Cation	Symbol	Test	Results
Aluminum	Al^{3+}	*a) Add dilute sodium hydroxide solution to a solution of the substance.* *b) Add dilute ammonia solution to a solution of the substance.* *c) Compare with **lead** (see tests below).*	*a) White precipitate that dissolves as more sodium hydroxide solution is added.* *b) White precipitate that does not dissolve as more ammonia solution is added.* *c) –*
Ammonium	NH_4^+	*Add sodium hydroxide solution to a solution of the substance and heat gently.*	*Ammonia gas is given off. It has a distinctive choking smell.*
Calcium	Ca^{2+}	*a) See **flame test**.* *b) Add dilute sulfuric acid to a solution of the substance.*	*a) –* *b) White precipitate formed.*
Copper(II)	Cu^{2+}	*a) See **flame test**.* *b) Add dilute sodium hydroxide solution to a solution of the substance.* *c) Add dilute ammonia solution to a solution of the substance.*	*a) –* *b) Pale blue precipitate that dissolves as more sodium hydroxide is added.* *c) Pale blue precipitate, changing to deep blue solution as more ammonia solution is added.*
Iron(II)	Fe^{2+}	*a) Add dilute sodium hydroxide solution to a solution of the substance.* *b) Add dilute ammonia solution to a solution of the substance.*	*a) Pale green precipitate formed.* *b) Pale green precipitate formed.*
Iron(III)	Fe^{3+}	*a) Add dilute sodium hydroxide solution to a solution of the substance.* *b) Add dilute ammonia solution to a solution of the substance.*	*a) Red-brown precipitate formed.* *b) Red-brown precipitate formed.*
Lead(II)	Pb^{2+}	*a) Add dilute sodium hydroxide solution to a solution of the substance.* *b) Add dilute ammonia solution to a solution of the substance.* *c) See also **flame test** to distinguish between lead and **aluminum**.*	*a) White precipitate that dissolves as more sodium hydroxide solution is added.* *b) White precipitate that does not dissolve as more ammonia solution is added.* *c) –*
Magnesium	Mg^{2+}	*a) Add dilute sodium hydroxide solution to a solution of the substance.* *b) Add dilute ammonia solution to a solution of the substance.*	*a) White precipitate that does not dissolve as more sodium hydroxide solution is added.* *b) White precipitate that does not dissolve as more ammonia solution is added.*
Zinc	Zn^{2+}	*a) Add dilute sodium hydroxide solution to a solution of the substance.* *b) Add dilute ammonia solution to a solution of the substance.*	*a) White precipitate that dissolves as more sodium hydroxide solution is added.* *b) White precipitate that dissolves as more ammonia solution is added.*

* **Cation**, 130.

INVESTIGATING SUBSTANCES

The investigation of chemical substances involves a variety of different techniques. The first step is often to obtain a pure sample of a substance (impurities affect experimental results). Some of the separating and purifying techniques used to achieve this are explained on these two pages. A variety of different methods are then used to find out the chemical composition and the chemical and physical properties of the substance (**qualitative analysis**), and how much of it is present (**quantitative analysis**). For more information, see also pages 218-219 and 222.

Decanting

The process of separating a liquid from a solid that has settled, by pouring the liquid carefully out of the container.

Beaker
Liquid
Settled solid

Filtering

The process of separating a liquid and a solid by pouring the mixture through a fine mesh. The mesh (usually filter paper) only lets liquid through.

Two methods of filtering

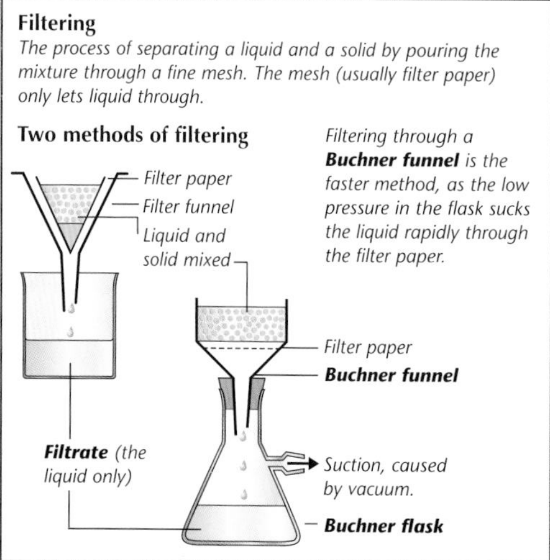
Filter paper
Filter funnel
Liquid and solid mixed
Filtering through a Buchner funnel is the faster method, as the low pressure in the flask sucks the liquid rapidly through the filter paper.
Filter paper
Buchner funnel
Suction, caused by vacuum.
Buchner flask
Filtrate (the liquid only)

Centrifuging

*The process of separating different substances mixed in a liquid by spinning the test tube containing the liquid at high speed in a **centrifuge** (see picture below). Particles of different masses collect at different places in the test tube, the heaviest substance collecting at the bottom.*

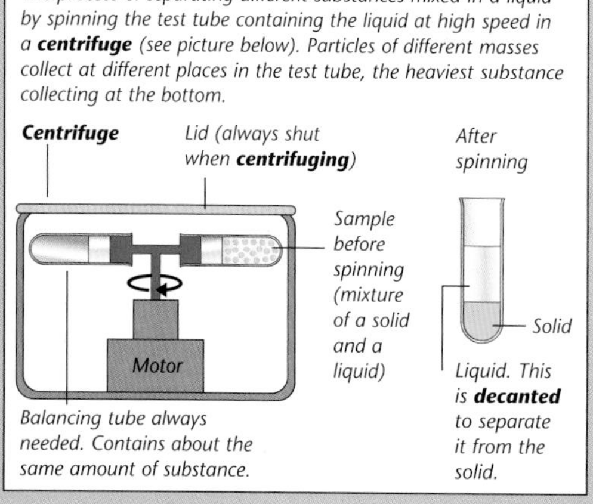
Centrifuge
Lid (always shut when centrifuging)
After spinning
Sample before spinning (mixture of a solid and a liquid)
Motor
Solid
Liquid. This is decanted to separate it from the solid.
Balancing tube always needed. Contains about the same amount of substance.

Distillation

*The process of separating a mixture of liquids, or a liquid from an impurity, by heating. The vapor of the liquid with the lowest boiling point comes off first and is condensed back to a liquid in a **Liebig condenser** (see picture below).*

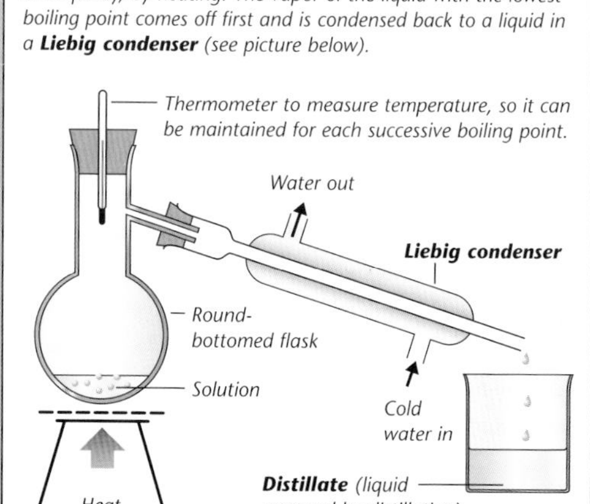
Thermometer to measure temperature, so it can be maintained for each successive boiling point.
Water out
Liebig condenser
Round-bottomed flask
Solution
Cold water in
Heat
Distillate (liquid removed by distillation)

Fractional distillation

*A **distillation** process which separates two or more liquids with close boiling points, using a **fractionating column**. The vapor of the liquid with the lowest boiling point reaches the top of the column first. Small columns are used in laboratories (see picture below). Other columns are much larger and have many points at which different vapors are condensed and collected (see also pages 183 and 198).*

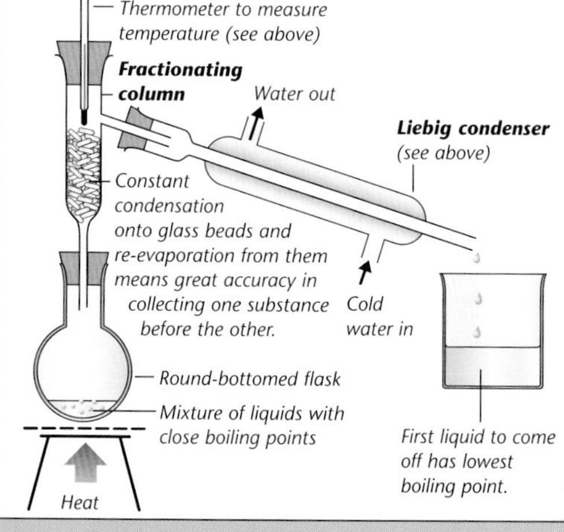
Thermometer to measure temperature (see above)
Fractionating column
Water out
Liebig condenser (see above)
Constant condensation onto glass beads and re-evaporation from them means great accuracy in collecting one substance before the other.
Cold water in
Round-bottomed flask
Mixture of liquids with close boiling points
First liquid to come off has lowest boiling point.
Heat

Solvent extraction

The process of obtaining a ***solute**** *by transferring it from its original* ***solvent**** *to one in which it is more soluble, and from which it can be easily removed. It is a method of separation often used when the solute cannot be heated, and makes use of a particular property of the solvents, i.e. whether they are* ***polar*** *or* ***non-polar solvents*. Ether extraction*** *is an example.*

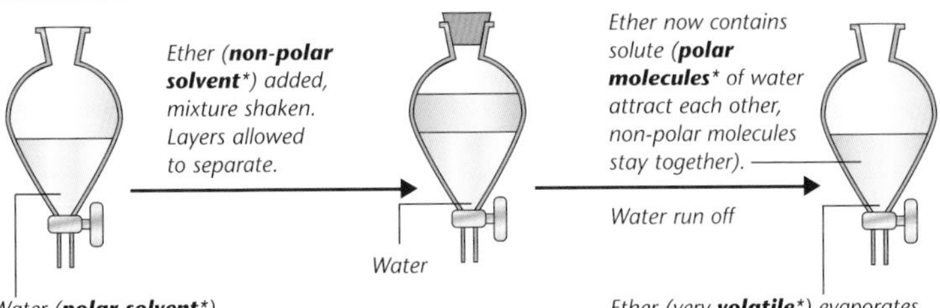
Ether (non-polar solvent*) added, mixture shaken. Layers allowed to separate.
Ether now contains solute (polar molecules* of water attract each other, non-polar molecules stay together).
Water run off
Water
Water (polar solvent*) containing solute* with non-polar molecules*.
Ether (very volatile*) evaporates at room temperature, leaving pure sample of solute.

Chromatography

The process of separating small amounts of substances from a mixture by the rates at which they move through or along a medium (the ***stationary phase****, e.g. blotting paper). Most methods of chromatography involve dissolving the mixture in a* ***solvent**** *(the* ***eluent****), though it is vaporized in* ***gas chromatography****. Substances move at different rates because they vary in their* ***solubility**** *and their attraction to the medium.*

Paper chromatography

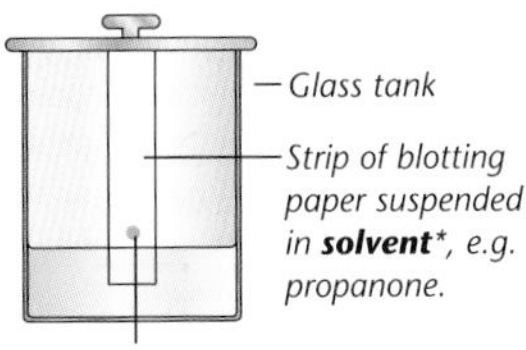
Glass tank
Strip of blotting paper suspended in solvent*, e.g. propanone.
Spot of mixture, e.g. leaf extract

Standard tables identify substances by ***R_f value*** *– distance moved by substance over distance moved by* ***solvent****.*

After removing from tank

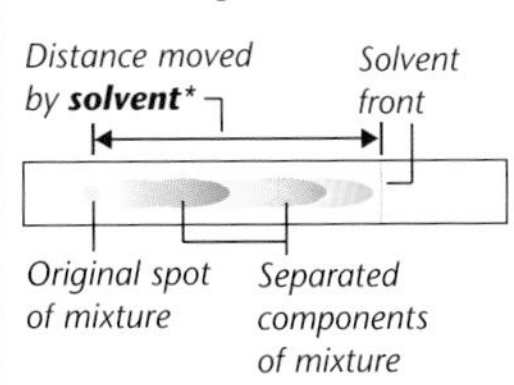
Distance moved by solvent*
Solvent front
Original spot of mixture
Separated components of mixture

There are several methods of chromatography, including ***column chromatography*** *(components in the mixture are separated in a column containing a solvent and a material that attracts molecules) and* ***gas chromatography*** *(vaporized mixture is separated as it passes along a heated column in a stream of gas).*

Crystallization

The process of forming crystals from a solution, which can be used to produce a pure sample of a substance, as the impurities will not form crystals. To make pure crystals, a hot, ***saturated**** *solution of the substance is cooled and the crystals formed on cooling are removed by* ***filtering****.* *See also page 135.*

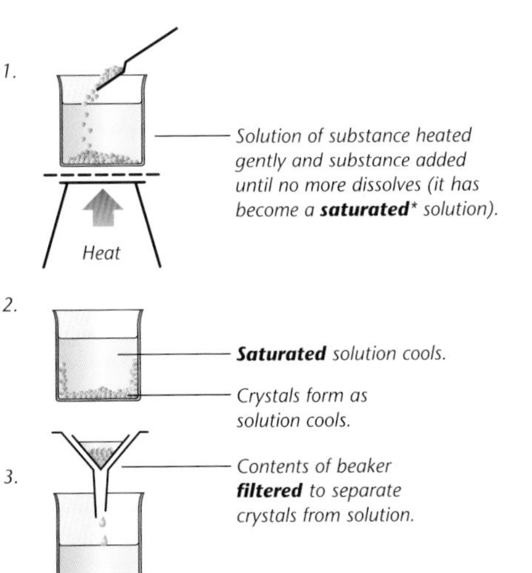
1.
Heat
Solution of substance heated gently and substance added until no more dissolves (it has become a saturated* solution).
2.
Saturated solution cools.
Crystals form as solution cools.
3.
Contents of beaker filtered to separate crystals from solution.

Desiccation

The process of removing water mixed with a substance, or ***water of crystallization**** *from a substance. Solids are often dried in large glass* ***desiccators*** *that contain a* ***drying agent**** *such as silica gel. Water is removed from most gases and liquids by bringing them into direct contact with a drying agent, e.g.* ***anhydrous**** *calcium chloride (which absorbs the water and, in the case of liquids, is then* ***filtered*** *off).*

Desiccator

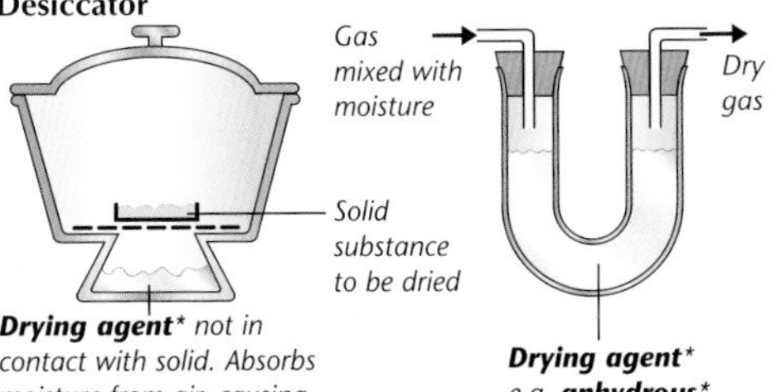
Gas mixed with moisture
Dry gas
Solid substance to be dried
Drying agent* not in contact with solid. Absorbs moisture from air, causing water to evaporate from solid.
Drying agent* e.g. anhydrous* calcium chloride

Melting point and boiling point tests

Tests are used to determine the purity of a sample. A pure sample of a substance has a particular known melting point and boiling point, and any impurities in a sample will alter these measurements.

Measuring the melting point

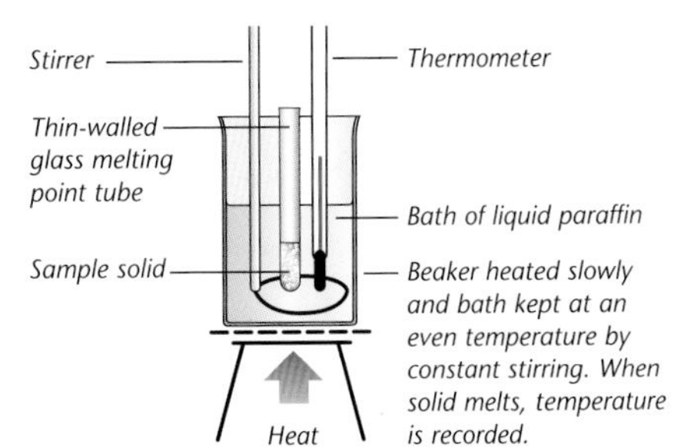
Stirrer
Thermometer
Thin-walled glass melting point tube
Bath of liquid paraffin
Sample solid
Beaker heated slowly and bath kept at an even temperature by constant stirring. When solid melts, temperature is recorded.
Heat

* **Anhydrous**, 154 (**Anhydrate**); **Drying agent**, 344; **Non-polar molecule**, 133 (**Polar molecule**); **Non-polar solvent**, **Polar solvent**, 144; **Saturated**, 144; **Solubility**, 145; **Solute**, **Solvent**, 144; **Volatile**, 345; **Water of crystallization**, 135.

QUALITATIVE AND QUANTITATIVE ANALYSIS

There are two types of analysis to investigate substances: **qualitative analysis** – any method used to study chemical composition – and **quantitative analysis** – any method used to discover how much of a substance is present in a sample. Below are some examples of both types of analysis.

Qualitative analysis

Below are some examples of qualitative analysis. The **flame test** and the tests on pages 218-219 are examples of qualitative analysis used in schools. The other methods described are more advanced.

Flame test

Used to identify metals. A substance is collected on the tip of a clean platinum or nichrome wire. This is held in a flame to observe the color with which the substance burns (see also page 219). Between tests, the wire is cleaned by dipping it in concentrated hydrochloric acid and then heating strongly.

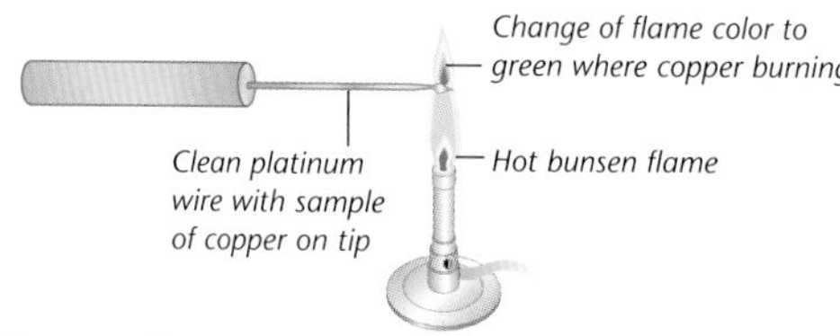

Change of flame color to green where copper burning
Clean platinum wire with sample of copper on tip
Hot bunsen flame

Mass spectroscopy

*A method of investigating the composition of a substance, in particular the **isotopes*** it contains. It is also used as a method of quantitative analysis as it involves measuring the relative proportions of isotopes or molecules in the substance. The apparatus used is called a **mass spectrometer**.*

Mass spectrometer

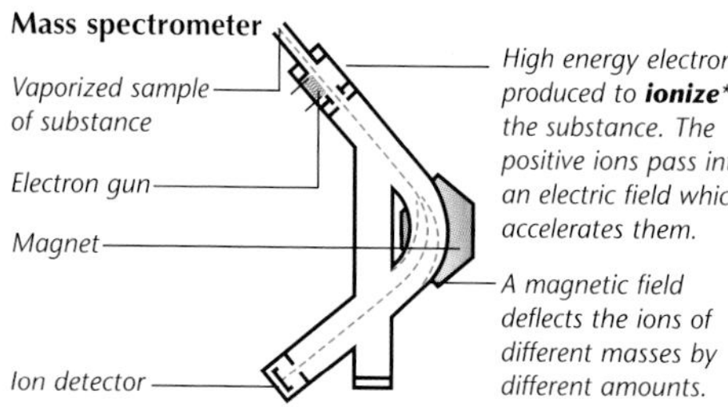

Vaporized sample of substance
Electron gun
Magnet
Ion detector
High energy electrons produced to ionize* the substance. The positive ions pass into an electric field which accelerates them.
A magnetic field deflects the ions of different masses by different amounts.

Nuclear magnetic resonance (n.m.r) spectroscopy

*A method used for investigating the position of atoms in a molecule. Radio waves are passed through a sample of a substance held between the poles of a magnet. The amount of absorption reveals the positions of particular atoms within a molecule. This information is presented on a graph called a **nuclear magnetic resonance (n.m.r.) spectrum**.*

N.m.r. spectrum of ethanol* (CH_3CH_2OH)

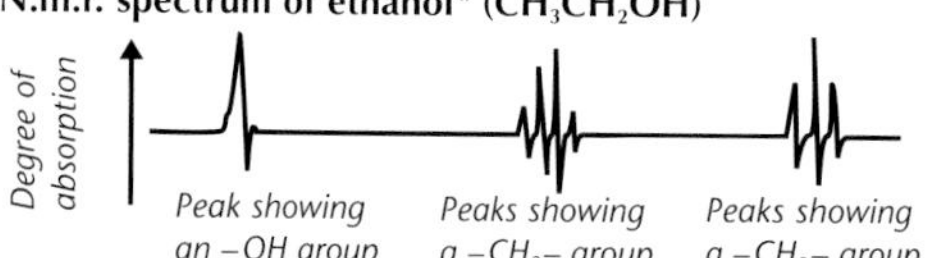

Degree of absorption
Peak showing an –OH group
Peaks showing a $-CH_2-$ group
Peaks showing a $-CH_3-$ group

Quantitative analysis

Below are some examples of quantitative analysis. See also **mass spectroscopy.**

Volumetric analysis

*A method of determining the concentration of a solution using **titration**. This is the addition of one solution into another, using a **burette***. The concentration of one solution is known. The first solution is added from the burette until the **end point**, when all the second solution has reacted. (The end point is detected by using an **indicator***.) The volume of solution from the burette needed to reach the end point is called the **titer**. This, the volume of solution in the flask and the known concentration of one solution are used to calculate the concentration of the second solution.*

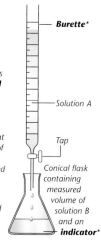

Burette*

Solution A

Tap

*Conical flask containing measured volume of solution B and an **indicator****

*Apparatus used for **titrations***

Gravimetric analysis

A method of determining the amount of a substance present by converting it into another substance of known chemical composition that is easily purified and weighed.

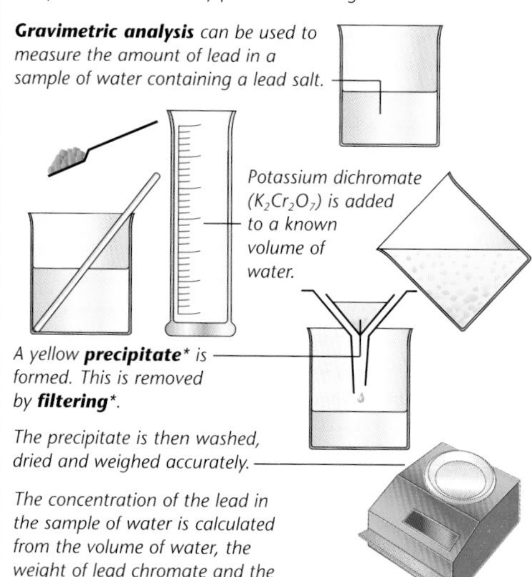

***Gravimetric analysis** can be used to measure the amount of lead in a sample of water containing a lead salt.*

Potassium dichromate ($K_2Cr_2O_7$) is added to a known volume of water.

*A yellow **precipitate*** is formed. This is removed by **filtering***.*

The precipitate is then washed, dried and weighed accurately.

*The concentration of the lead in the sample of water is calculated from the volume of water, the weight of lead chromate and the **relative atomic mass*** of lead.*

* **Burette**, 223; **Ethanol**, 196; **Filtering**, 220; **Ionization**, 130; **Indicator**, 152; **Isotope**, 127; **Precipitate**, 145; **Relative atomic mass**, 138.

APPARATUS

Apparatus is chemical equipment. The most common items are described and illustrated below and on pages 224-225. Simple 2-D diagrams used to represent them are also shown, together with approximate ranges of sizes.

Beaker

Used to hold liquids. Shows approximate volume.

Possible capacities: 5-5,000ml

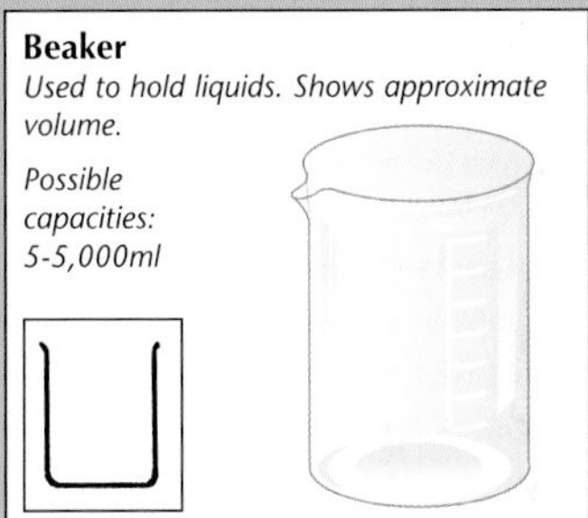

Beehive shelf

*Used to support a **gas jar*** while gas is being collected by the displacement of water. For examples of its use, see pages 216-217.*

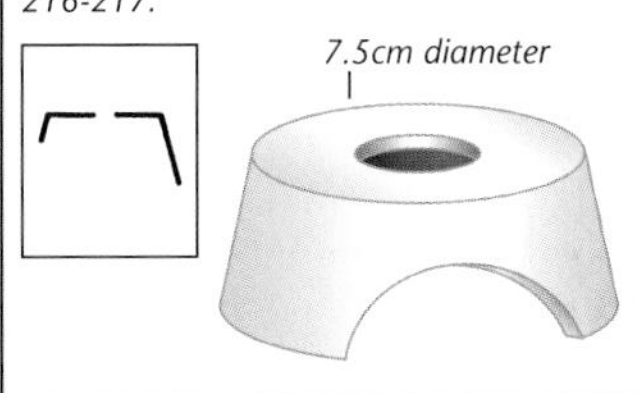
7.5cm diameter

Bunsen burner

Used to provide heat for chemical reactions. Its adjustable air-hole allows some control of the flame temperature. If the hole is closed, the flame is yellow and cooler than the blue flame produced when the hole is open. See picture, page 208.

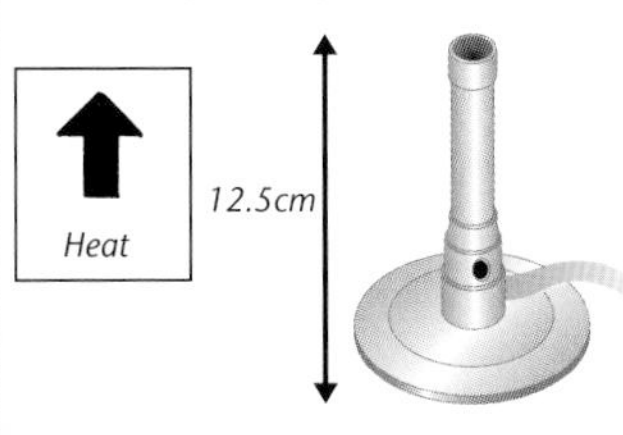
Heat
12.5cm

Burette

*Used to add accurate volumes of liquid during **titrations** (see **volumetric analysis**, page 222).*

Possible capacities: 10-100ml

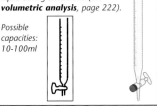

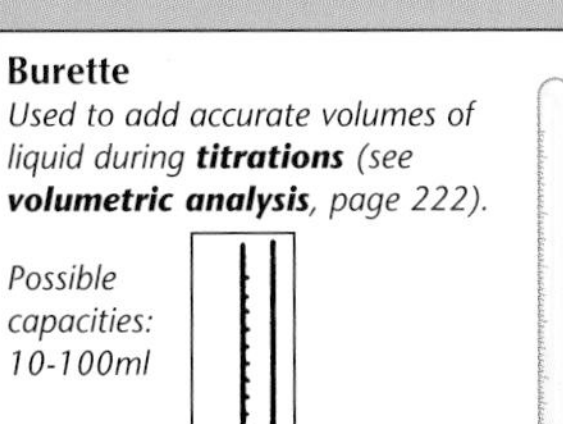

Condensers

Liebig condenser

*Used to condense vapors. Vapor passes through the central channel and is cooled by water flowing through the outer pipe. See **distillation**, page 220.*

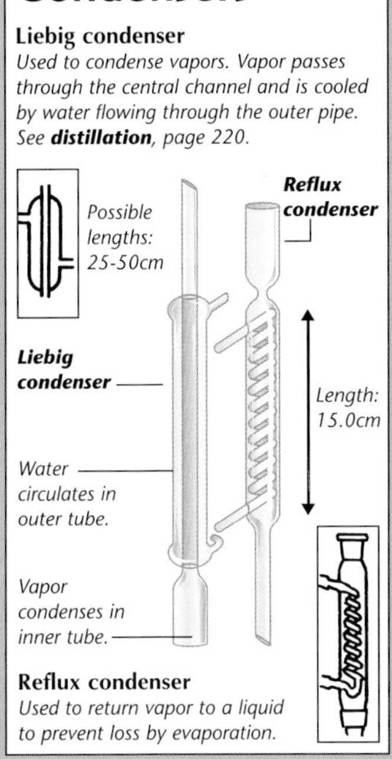
Possible lengths: 25-50cm
Reflux condenser
Liebig condenser
Length: 15.0cm
Water circulates in outer tube.
Vapor condenses in inner tube.

Reflux condenser

Used to return vapor to a liquid to prevent loss by evaporation.

Crucible

*Used to hold small quantities of solids which are being heated strongly, either in a furnace or over a **bunsen burner**. They are made of porcelain, silica, fireclay, nickel or steel.*

Possible diameters: 2.5-5.5cm

Crystallizing dish

Used to hold solutions which are being evaporated to form crystals. The flat bottom helps to form an even layer of crystals.

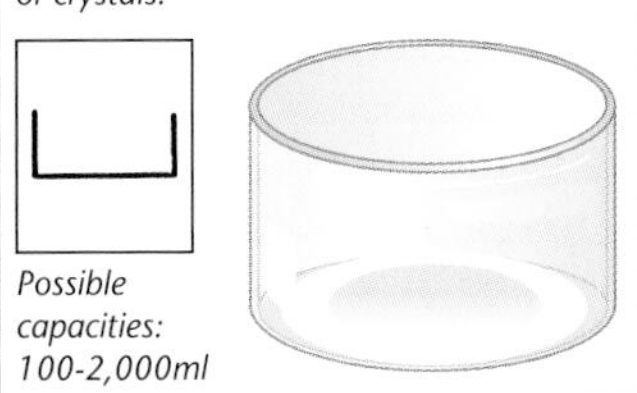

Possible capacities: 100-2,000ml

Delivery tube

A tube used to carry gases.

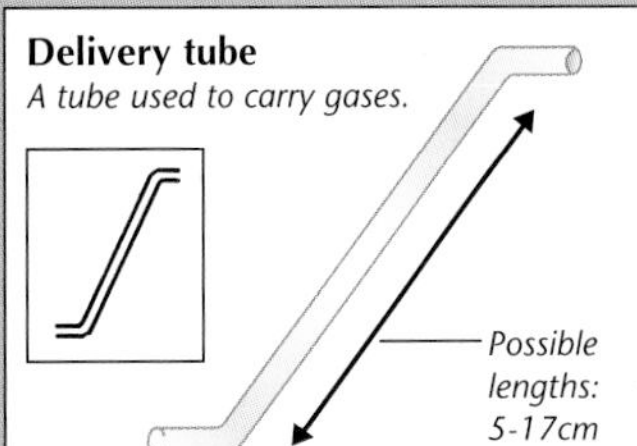
Possible lengths: 5-17cm

Desiccator

*A glass container used to dry solids. It contains a **drying agent***. See **desiccation**, page 221.*

22.0cm diameter

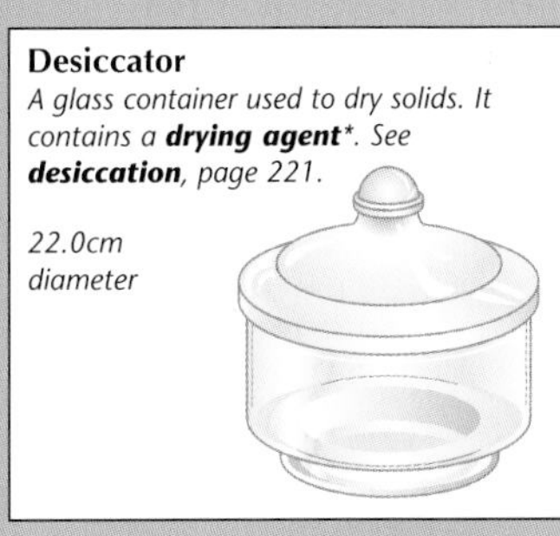

Evaporating basin

*Used to hold a solution whose **solvent*** is being separated from the **solute*** by evaporation (often using heat).*

Possible capacities: 50-500ml

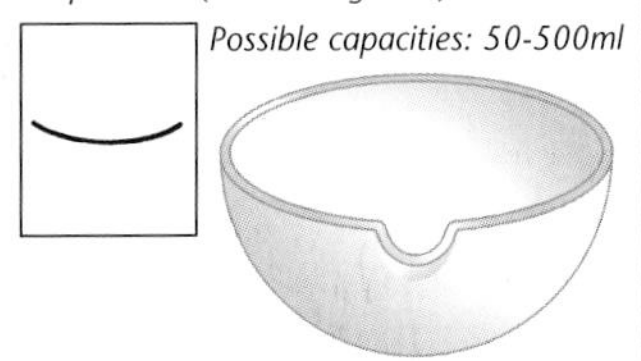

Filter paper

*Paper which acts as a strainer, only allowing liquids through, but no solid matter. Filter paper is graded according to how finely it is meshed, i.e. the size of particle it allows through. It is put in a **filter** or **Buchner funnel*** to give support as the liquid passes through, and the solid settles on the paper. See **filtering**, page 220.*

*Mesh of fine **filter paper**, magnified many times.*

Fiber

*Mesh of coarse **filter paper**, magnified many times.*

Holes between fibers allow tiny particles to pass through.

* **Buchner funnel**, 224; **Drying agent**, 344; **Filter funnel**, **Gas jar**, 224; **Solute**, **Solvent**, 144.

Flasks

Buchner flask

*Used when liquids are filtered by suction. See **filtering**, page 220.*

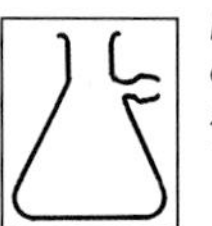

Possible capacities: 250-1,000ml

Conical flask

*Used to hold liquids when carrying out reactions and preparing solutions of known concentration. They are used in preference to beakers when it is necessary to have a container that can be stoppered. They have some volume markings but these are not as accurate as the markings on a **pipette** or **burette***.*

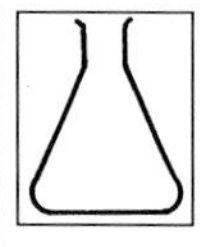

Possible capacities: 25-2,000ml

Flat-bottomed flask

Used to hold liquids when carrying out reactions where heating is not required (the flask stands on the workbench).

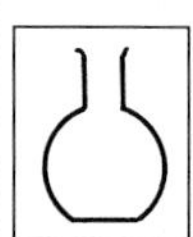

Possible capacities: 100-2,000ml

Round-bottomed flask

Used to hold liquids, especially when even heating is needed. Volume markings are approximate. It is held in position above the flame by a clamp.

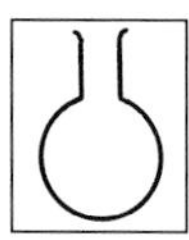

Possible capacities: 100-2,000ml

Volumetric flask

Used when mixing accurate concentrations of solutions. Each flask has a volume marking which is very exact and a stopper so that it can be shaken to mix the solution.

Possible capacities: 10-2,000ml

Fractionating column

*Used to separate components of a mixture by their boiling points. It contains glass balls or rings that provide a large surface area and thus promote condensation and re-evaporation. See **fractional distillation**, page 220.*

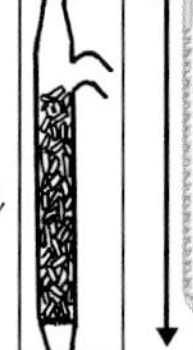

Possible lengths: 15-36cm

Fume cupboard

A glass panelled cupboard that contains an extractor fan and encloses an area of workbench. Dangerous experiments are carried out in a fume cupboard.

Funnels

Buchner funnel

*Used when liquids are filtered by suction. It has a flat, perforated plate, on which **filter paper*** is placed. See **filtering**, page 220.*

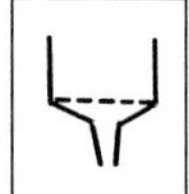

Possible capacities: 50-500ml

Tap funnel

For adding a liquid to a reaction mixture drop by drop. See pages 216-217.

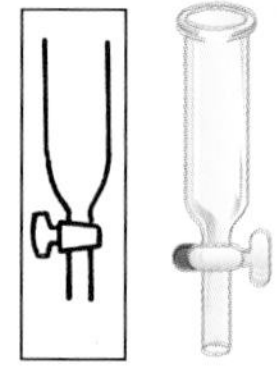

Filter funnel

*Used when separating solids from liquids by **filtering** (see page 220). **Filter paper*** is put inside the funnel.*

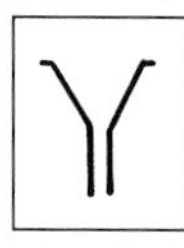

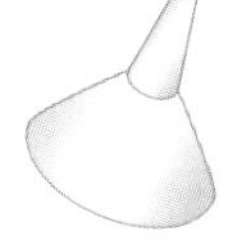

Thistle funnel

Used when adding a liquid to a reaction mixture.

Length: 30cm

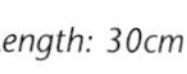

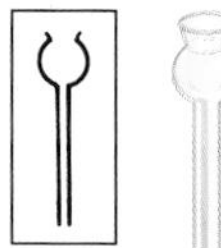

Separating funnel

*Used when separating **immiscible*** liquids. First the denser liquid is run off, then the less dense. See **solvent extraction**, page 221.*

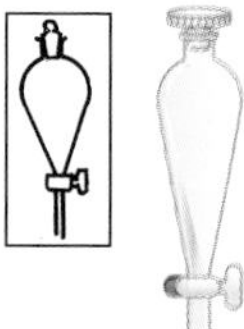

Possible capacities: 50-500ml

Gas jar

Used when collecting and storing gases. The jar can be sealed using a glass lid whose rim is coated with a thin layer of grease. See pages 216-217.

Possible heights: 15-30cm

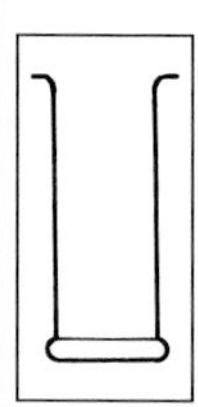

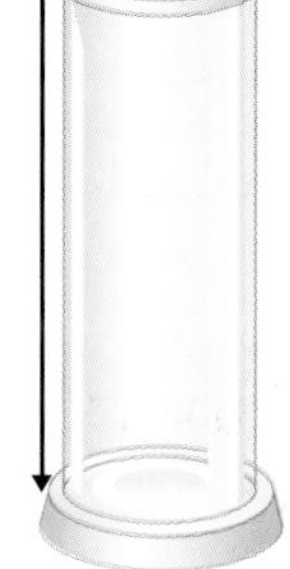

Gas syringe

Used to measure the volume of a gas. It is used both to receive gas and to inject gas into a reaction vessel.

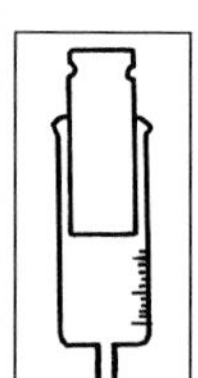

Capacity: 100ml

Gauze

Used to spread the heat from a flame evenly over the base of an object being heated. Made of iron, steel, copper or ceramics.

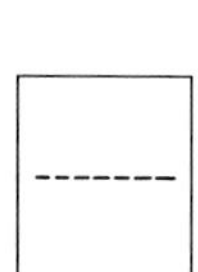

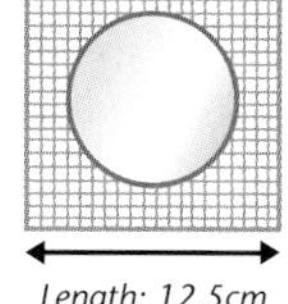

Length: 12.5cm

Measuring cylinder

Used to measure the approximate volume of liquids.

Possible capacities: 5-2,000ml

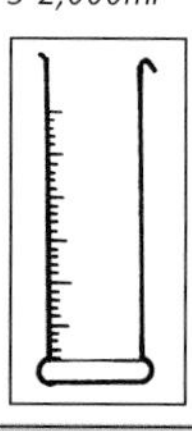

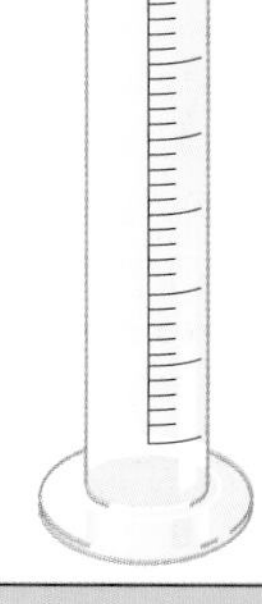

* **Burette**, **Filter paper**, 223; **Immiscible**, 145 (**Miscible**).

Pipeclay triangle
*Used to support **crucibles*** on **tripods** when they are being heated. They are made of iron or nickel-chromium wire enclosed in pipeclay tubes.*

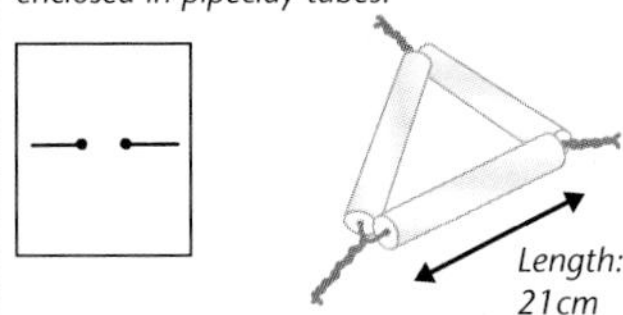
Length:
21cm

Test tube holder
Used to hold a test tube, e.g. when heating it in a flame, creating a chemical reaction within it, or transferring it from one place to another.

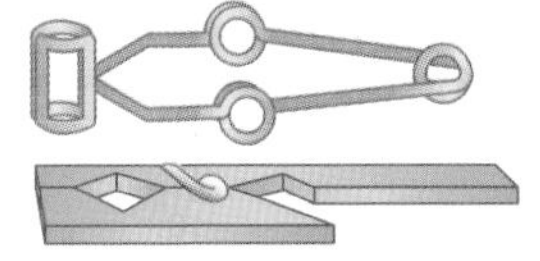

Trough
*Used when collecting gas **over water** (see **carbon dioxide**, page 216). The water contained in a gas jar inverted in the trough is displaced into the trough. Troughs are also used when substances such as potassium are reacted (see picture, page 169). Possible diameters: 20-30cm.*

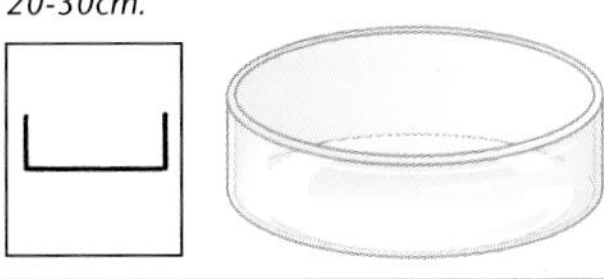

Pipettes

Pipette
Used to dispense accurate volumes of liquid. They come in different sizes for different volumes. The liquid is run out of the pipette until its level has dropped from one volume marking to the next.

Possible capacities: 1-100ml

Dropping pipette or **teat pipette**
Used to dispense small volumes or drops of liquid. It does not provide an accurate measurement.

Possible capacities: 1-2ml

Test tube rack
Used to hold many test tubes upright.

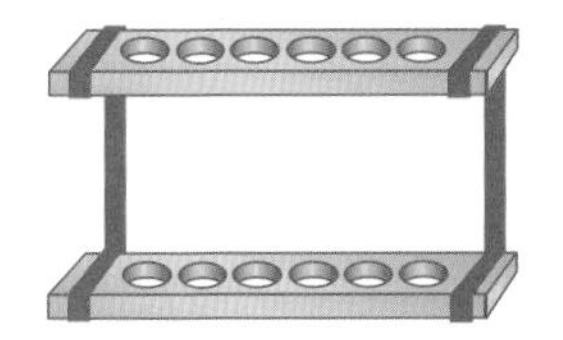

Tripod
*Used with a **pipeclay triangle** or **gauze** when heating **crucibles***, **flasks**, etc.*

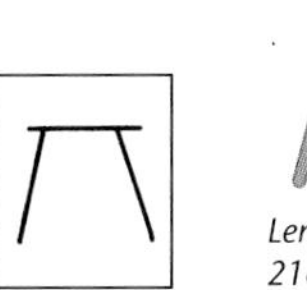

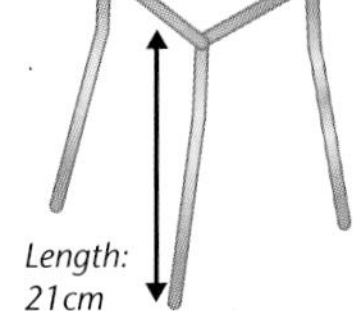
Length:
21cm

Thermometer
Used to measure temperature. They are filled either with alcohol or with mercury, depending on the temperature range for which they are intended.

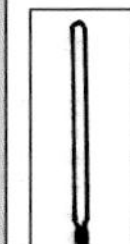

Small temperature range: –10 to 50°C

Large temperature range: –10 to 400°C

Tubes

Boiling tube
A thick-walled tube used to hold substances being heated strongly.

Possible length: 12.5cm

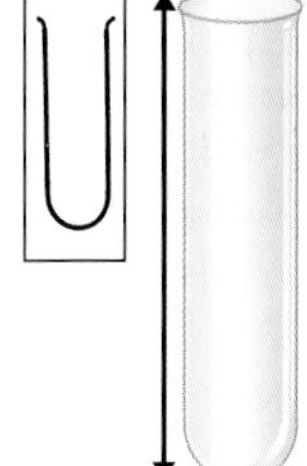

Test tube
A tube used to hold substances for simple chemical reactions not involving strong heating.

Possible length: 7.5cm

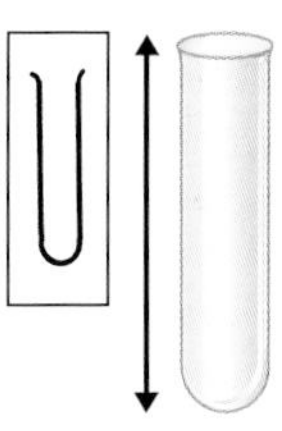

Ignition tube
A disposable tube used to hold small quantities of substances being melted or boiled.

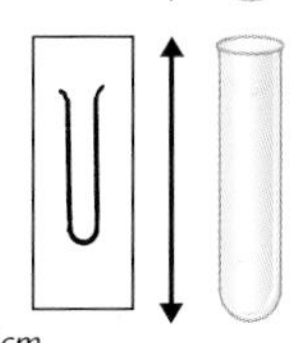

Possible length: 5.0cm

Stands and **clamps**
*Used to hold apparatus, e.g. **round-bottomed flasks**, in position.*

Possible lengths: 50-100cm

Tongs
Used to move hot objects.

Top pan balances
Used for quick, accurate weighing.

Spatula
Used to pick up small quantities of a solid.

Possible lengths: 10-20cm

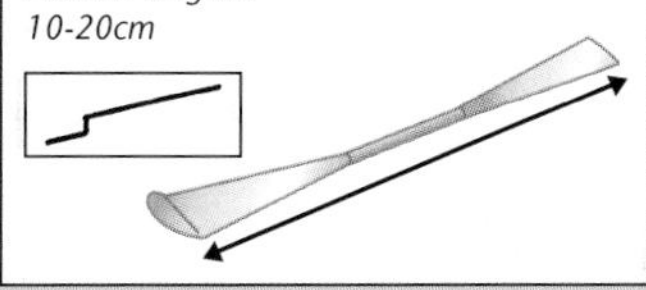

Watch glass
Used when evaporating small quantities. Possible diameters: 5-15cm

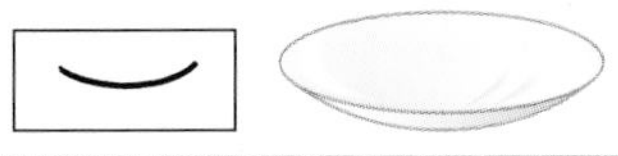

* **Crucible**, 223.

CHART OF SUBSTANCES, SYMBOLS AND FORMULAS

Below is a list of the symbols and formulas used in the chemistry section of this book. Each one is followed by the name of the substance it stands for[†]. Capital letters come alphabetically before small ones, i.e. each element is kept together with its compounds. For example, **CH_3OH** (methanol – a carbon compound) is found in an alphabetical list after **C** (carbon), before the **Ca** (calcium) list begins.

Symbol	Substance
$3Ca_3(PO_4)_2.CaF_2$	Apatite
Ac	Actinium
Ag	Silver
$AgBr$	Silver bromide
$AgCl$	Silver chloride
AgI	Silver iodide
$AgNO_3$	Silver nitrate
Al	Aluminum
$Al(OH)_3$	Aluminum hydroxide
Al_2O_3	Aluminum oxide
$Al_2O_3.2H_2O$	Bauxite
$Al_2(SO_4)_3$	Aluminum sulfate
Am	Americium
Ar	Argon
As	Arsenic
At	Astatine
Au	Gold
B	Boron
B_2O_3	Boron oxide
BCl_3	Boron trichloride
Ba	Barium
$BaCl_2$	Barium chloride
Be	Beryllium
Bi	Bismuth
Bk	Berkelium
Br/Br_2	Bromine
$-Br$	Bromo group
C	Carbon
C_2H_2	Ethyne
C_2H_4	Ethene
C_2H_5Br	Bromoethane
C_2H_5CHO	Propanal
C_2H_5Cl	Chloroethane
C_2H_5COOH	Propanoic acid
C_2H_5OH	Ethanol
C_2H_6	Ethane
C_3H_4	Propyne
C_3H_6	Propene
C_3H_6O	Propanone
C_3H_7OH	Propan-1-ol
C_3H_8	Propane
C_4H_6	But-1-yne
C_4H_8	But-1-ene
C_4H_9OH	Butan-1-ol
C_4H_{10}	Butane
C_5H_{10}	Pent-1-ene
C_5H_{12}	Pentane
$C_6H_8O_6$	Ascorbic acid
$C_6H_{12}O_6$	Glucose
C_6H_{14}	Hexane
C_7H_{16}	Heptane
C_8H_{18}	Octane
C_9H_{20}	Nonane
$C_{12}H_{22}O_{11}$	Sucrose
$C_{17}H_{35}COOH$	Octadecanoic acid
CCl_4	Tetrachloromethane
CH_2BrCH_2Br	1,2-dibromoethane
CH_2CHCl	Vinyl chloride
$-CH_3$	Methyl group
CH_3CCH	Propyne
CH_3CH_2CCH	But-1-yne
$CH_3CH_2CH_2CH_2OH$	Butan-1-ol
$CH_3CH_2CH_2OH$	Propan-1-ol
CH_3CH_2CHO	Propanal
CH_3CH_2Cl	Chloroethane
CH_3CH_2COOH	Propanoic acid
CH_3CH_2OH	Ethanol
CH_3CH_2ONa	Sodium ethoxide
CH_3CHO	Ethanal
$CH_3CHOHCH_3$	Propan-2-ol
CH_3Cl	Chloromethane
$CH_3COCH_2CH_3$	Butanone
CH_3COCH_3	Propanone
$CH_3COOCH_2CH_3$	Ethyl ethanoate
CH_3COOH	Ethanoic acid
CH_3NH_2	Methyl amine
CH_3OCH_3	Methoxymethane
CH_3OH	Methanol
CH_4	Methane
$CHCH$	Ethyne
CO	Carbon monoxide
$-CO-$	Carbonyl group
CO_2	Carbon dioxide
$-COOH$	Carboxyl group
$(COOH)_2$	Ethanedioic acid
$COOH(CH_2)_4COOH$	Hexanedioic acid
Ca	Calcium
$Ca_3(PO_4)_2$	Calcium phosphate
$CaCl_2$	Calcium chloride
$CaCO_3$	Calcium carbonate
$CaCO_3.MgCO_3$	Dolomite
CaF_2	Fluorospar
$Ca(HCO_3)_2$	Calcium hydrogencarbonate
CaO	Calcium oxide
$Ca(OH)_2$	Calcium hydroxide
$CaSiO_3$	Calcium metasilicate
$CaSO_4$	Calcium sulfate
$CaSO_4.2H_2O$	Gypsum
Cd	Cadmium
Ce	Cerium
Cf	Californium
Cl/Cl_2	Chlorine
$-Cl$	Chloro group
Cm	Curium
Co	Cobalt
$CoCl_2$	Cobalt(II) chloride
Cr	Chromium
Cs	Cesium
Cu	Copper
Cu_2O	Copper(I) oxide
$CuCl$	Copper(I) chloride
$CuCl_2$	Copper(II) chloride
$CuCO_3.Cu(OH)_2$	Malachite
$(CuFe)S_2$	Copper pyrites
$(Cu(NH_3)_4)SO_4$	Tetraammine copper(II) sulfate
$Cu(NO_3)_2$	Copper(II) nitrate
CuO	Copper(II) oxide
$CuSO_4$	Copper(II) sulfate
$CuSO_4.3Cu(OH)_2$	Basic copper sulfate
D	Deuterium
D_2O	Deuterium oxide
Dy	Dysprosium
Er	Erbium
Es	Einsteinium
Eu	Europium
F/F_2	Fluorine
$-F$	Fluoro group
Fe	Iron
Fe_2O_3	Haematite
$Fe_2O_3.xH_2O$	Rust
$FeCl_2$	Iron(II) chloride
$FeCl_3$	Iron(III) chloride
$Fe(OH)_3$	Iron(III) hydroxide
FeS	Iron(II) sulfide
$FeSO_4$	Iron(II) sulfate
Fm	Fermium
Fr	Francium
Ga	Gallium

[†] If you know a substance, but not its symbol, use the index (pages 346-381).

Symbol	Substance
Gd	*Gadolinium*
Ge	*Germanium*
H/H_2	*Hydrogen*
H_2CO_3	*Carbonic acid*
H_2O	*Water*
H_2O_2	*Hydrogen peroxide*
H_2S	*Hydrogen sulfide*
$H_2S_2O_7$	*Fuming sulfuric acid*
H_2SO_3	*Sulfurous acid*
H_2SO_4	*Sulfuric acid*
H_3PO_4	*Phosphoric acid*
HBr	*Hydrogen bromide*
HCl	*Hydrogen chloride/ Hydrochloric acid*
HCHO	*Methanal*
HCOOH	*Methanoic acid*
HI	*Hydrogen iodide*
HNO_2	*Nitrous acid*
HNO_3	*Nitric acid*
He	*Helium*
Hf	*Hafnium*
Hg	*Mercury*
HgS	*Cinnabar*
Ho	*Holmium*
I/I_2	*Iodine*
In	*Indium*
Ir	*Iridium*
K	*Potassium*
K_2CO_3	*Potassium carbonate*
$K_2Cr_2O_7$	*Potassium dichromate*
K_2SO_4	*Potassium sulfate*
$K_2SO_4.Al_2(SO_4)_3$	*Aluminum potassium sulfate-12-water*
KBr	*Potassium bromide*
KCl	*Potassium chloride*
KI	*Potassium iodide*
$KMnO_4$	*Potassium permanganate*
KNO_3	*Potassium nitrate*
KOH	*Potassium hydroxide*
Kr	*Krypton*
KrF_2	*Krypton fluoride*
La	*Lanthanum*
La_2O_3	*Lanthanum oxide*
Li	*Lithium*
Li_3N	*Lithium nitride*
LiCl	*Lithium chloride*
LiOH	*Lithium hydroxide*
Lr or *Lw*	*Lawrencium*
Lu	*Lutetium*
Md	*Mendelevium*
Mg	*Magnesium*
$MgCl_2$	*Magnesium chloride*
$MgCO_3$	*Magnesium carbonate*
MgO	*Magnesium oxide*
$Mg(OH)_2$	*Magnesium hydroxide*
$MgSO_4$	*Magnesium sulfate*

Symbol	Substance
Mn	*Manganese*
$MnCl_2$	*Manganese(IV) chloride*
MnO_2	*Pyrolusite/ Manganese(IV) oxide*
Mo	*Molybdenum*
N/N_2	*Nitrogen*
N_2O	*Dinitrogen oxide*
N_2O_4	*Dinitrogen tetraoxide*
$-NH_2$	*Amino group*
$NH_2(CH_2)_6NH_2$	*1,6-diaminohexane*
NH_3	*Ammonia*
$(NH_4)_2SO_4$	*Ammonium sulfate*
NH_4Cl	*Ammonium chloride*
NH_4OH	*Ammonia solution*
NH_4NO_3	*Ammonium nitrate*
NO	*Nitrogen monoxide*
NO_2	*Nitrogen dioxide*
Na	*Sodium*
Na_2CO_3	*Sodium carbonate*
$Na_2CO_3.10H_2O$	*Washing soda*
Na_2SO_3	*Sodium sulfite*
Na_2SO_4	*Sodium sulfate*
Na_3AlF_6	*Cryolite*
$NaAl(OH)_4$	*Sodium aluminate*
NaBr	*Sodium bromide*
NaCl	*Sodium chloride*
$NaClO_3$	*Sodium chlorate*
$NaHCO_3$	*Sodium hydrogencarbonate*
$NaHSO_4$	*Sodium hydrogensulfate*
$NaIO_3$	*Sodium iodate*
$NaNO_2$	*Sodium nitrite*
$NaNO_3$	*Sodium nitrate*
NaOCl	*Sodium hypochlorite*
NaOH	*Sodium hydroxide*
Nb	*Niobium*
Nd	*Neodymium*
Ne	*Neon*
Ni	*Nickel*
NiS	*Nickel sulfide*
No	*Nobelium*
Np	*Neptunium*
O/O_2	*Oxygen*
O_3	*Ozone*
–OH	*Hydroxyl group*
Os	*Osmium*
OsO_4	*Osmium tetroxide*
P	*Phosphorus*
P_2O_5	*Phosphorus pentoxide*
Pa	*Protactinium*
Pb	*Lead*
PbI_2	*Lead(II) iodide*
$Pb(NO_3)_2$	*Lead(II) nitrate*
PbO	*Lead(II) oxide*
PbO_2	*Lead(IV) oxide*

Symbol	Substance
$Pb(OC_2H_5)_4$	*Tetraethyl-lead*
$Pb(OH)_2$	*Lead(II) hydroxide*
PbS	*Galena*
Pd	*Palladium*
Pm	*Promethium*
Po	*Polonium*
Pr	*Praseodymium*
Pt	*Platinum*
Pu	*Plutonium*
Ra	*Radium*
Rb	*Rubidium*
Re	*Rhenium*
Rh	*Rhodium*
Rn	*Radon*
Ru	*Ruthenium*
S	*Sulfur*
SO_2	*Sulfur dioxide*
SO_3	*Sulfur trioxide*
Sb	*Antimony*
Sc	*Scandium*
Se	*Selenium*
Si	*Silicon*
SiO_2	*Silicon dioxide*
Sm	*Samarium*
Sn	*Tin*
Sr	*Strontium*
T	*Tritium*
Ta	*Tantalum*
Tb	*Terbium*
Tc	*Technetium*
Te	*Tellurium*
Th	*Thorium*
Ti	*Titanium*
Tl	*Thallium*
Tm	*Thulium*
U	*Uranium*
V	*Vanadium*
V_2O_5	*Vanadium pentoxide*
W	*Tungsten*
Xe	*Xenon*
$XeFe_4$	*Xenon tetrafluoride*
Y	*Yttrium*
Yb	*Ytterbium*
Zn	*Zinc*
$ZnCl_2$	*Zinc chloride*
$ZnCO_3$	*Calamine*
ZnO	*Zincite/ Zinc oxide*
$Zn(OH)_2$	*Zinc hydroxide*
Zn(OH)Cl	*Basic zinc chloride*
ZnS	*Zinc blende*
$ZnSO_4$	*Zinc sulfate*
Zr	*Zirconium*

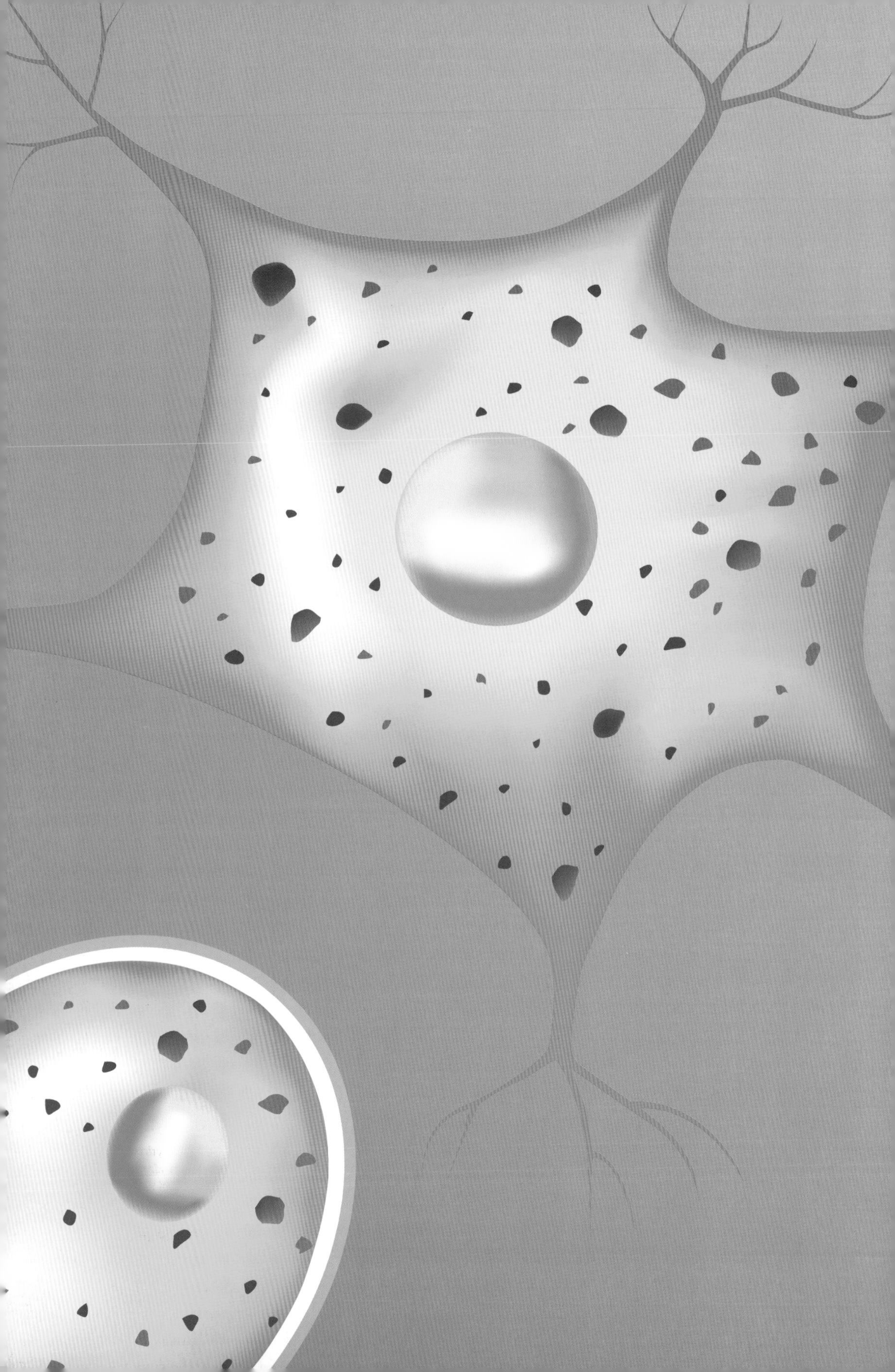

BIOLOGY

ABOUT BIOLOGY

Biology is the study of living things. It examines the structures and internal systems of different organisms and how these operate to sustain individual life, as well as looking at the complex web of relationships between organisms which ensure new life is created and maintained. In this book, biology is divided into six color-coded sections. The areas covered by these sections are explained below.

Ecology and living things

Looks at the complex relationships between all living things, and their basic cellular structure.

Botany

Covers the plant kingdom. Introduces the different types of plants, their main characteristics, internal structures and systems.

Zoology (animals)

Examines the component parts, systems and behavior typical of the major animal groups.

Zoology (humans)

Covers all the major terms of human biology. In many cases, these also apply to the vertebrates in general (see page 341).

Reproduction and genetics

Examines the different types of reproduction and introduces the branch of biology known as genetics.

General biology information

Covers subjects which relate to all living things. Includes tables of general information and classification charts.

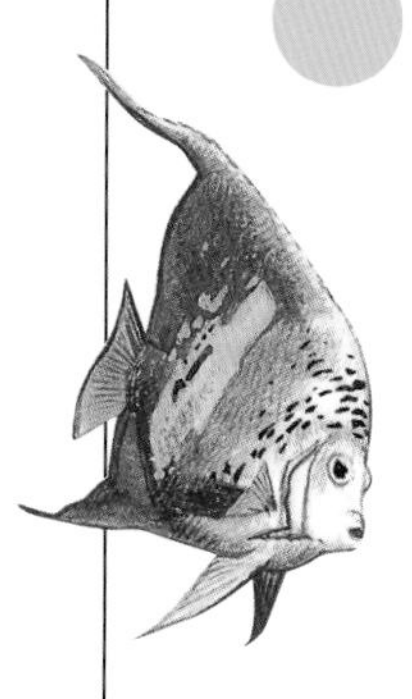

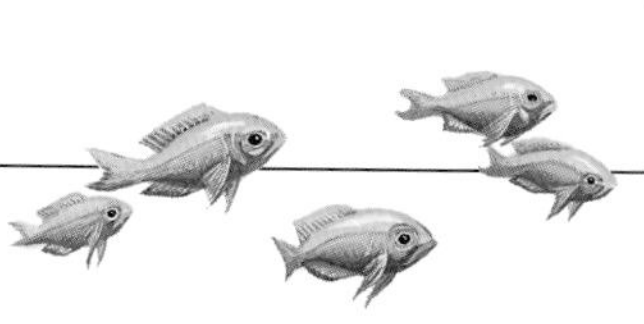

CONTENTS

Ecology and living things

Botany

Zoology (animals)

Zoology (humans)

Reproduction and genetics

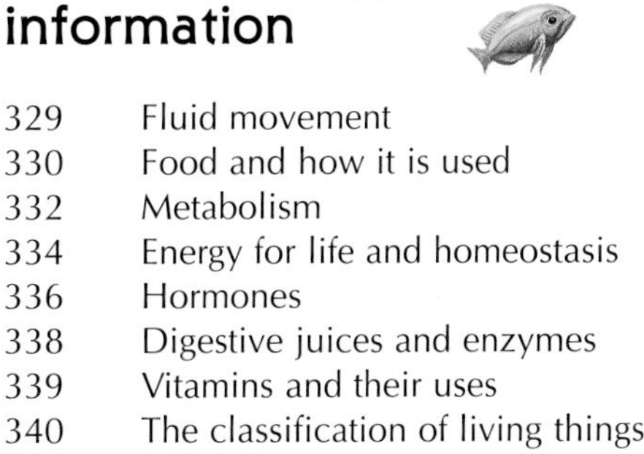

General biology information

LIVING THINGS AND THEIR ENVIRONMENT

The world can be divided into a number of different regions, each with its own characteristic plants and animals. All the plants and animals have become adapted to their own surroundings, or **environment** (see **adaptive radiation**, page 237), and their lives are linked in a complex web of interdependence. The environment is influenced by many different factors, e.g. temperature, water and light (**climatic factors**), the physical and chemical properties of the soil (**edaphic factors**), and the activities of living things (**biotic factors**). The study of the relationships between plants, animals and the environment is called **ecology**.

This tree frog's toes have adapted to help it cling to bark.

Biosphere

The layer of the Earth (including the oceans and the atmosphere) which is inhabited by living things. The biosphere's boundaries are the upper atmosphere (above) and the first layers of uninhabited rock (below).

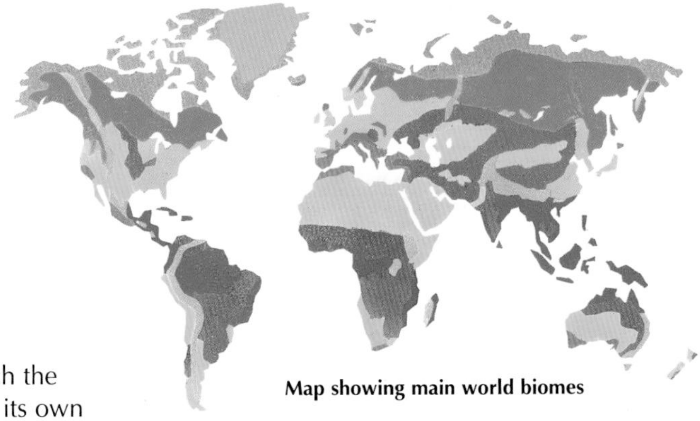

Map showing main world biomes

Biomes

The main ecological regions into which the land surface can be divided. Each has its own characteristic seasons, day length, rainfall pattern and maximum and minimum temperatures. The major biomes (see map, above right) are **tundra**, **coniferous forest**, **deciduous forest**, **tropical forest**, **temperate grassland, savanna** (tropical grassland) and **desert**. Most are named after the dominant vegetation, since this determines all other living things found there. Each biome is a giant **habitat** (**macrohabitat**). Human activity, e.g. deforestation in tropical forests, has begun to have harmful effects on the habitats which exist within many biomes.

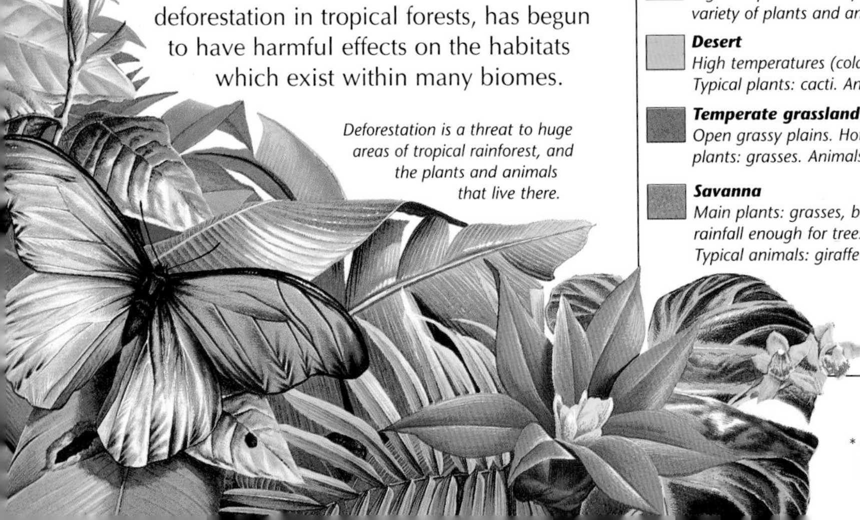

Deforestation is a threat to huge areas of tropical rainforest, and the plants and animals that live there.

Key to biomes on map above

Tundra
Very cold and windy. Most common plants: ***lichens*** ** and small shrubs. Animals include musk ox.*

Coniferous forest
Low temperatures all year. Dominant plants: ***conifers*** **, e.g. spruce. Most common large animals: deer.*

Deciduous forest
Summers warm, winters cold. Dominant plants: ***deciduous*** ** trees, e.g. beech. Many animals, e.g. foxes.*

Tropical forest
High temperatures all year, heavy rainfall. Great variety of plants and animals, e.g. exotic birds.

Desert
High temperatures (cold at night), very low rainfall. Typical plants: cacti. Animals include jerboas, scorpions.

Temperate grassland
Open grassy plains. Hot summers and cold winters. Main plants: grasses. Animals include prairie dogs.

Savanna
Main plants: grasses, but rainfall enough for trees. Typical animals: giraffe.

*Scrubland (**maquis**)*

Mountains

Ice

* **Conifers**, 340; **Deciduous**, 236; **Lichens**, 342 (**Mutualists**).

Habitat

The natural home of a group of living things or a single living thing. Small habitats can be found within large habitats, e.g. a waterhole in the **savanna biome**. Very small specialized habitats are called **microhabitats**, e.g. a rotting acacia tree.

Community

The group of plants and animals found in one **habitat**. They all interact with each other and their environment.

Ecosystem

The **community** of plants and animals in a given **habitat**, together with the non-living parts of the environment (e.g. air or water). An ecosystem is a self-contained unit, i.e. the plants and animals interact to produce all the material they need (see also pages 234-235).

__Ecosystem__ includes environment, e.g. air and water.

The __community__ includes antelopes and ostriches.

Waterhole and acacia tree habitats in savanna

Ecological succession

A process which occurs whenever a new area of land is colonized, e.g. a forest floor after a fire, a farm field which is left uncultivated or a demolition site which remains unused. Over the years, different types of plants (and the animals which go with them) will succeed each other, until a **climax community** is arrived at. This is a very stable **community**, one which will survive without change as long as the same conditions prevail (e.g. the climate).

Ecological succession in a disused field

Pioneer community *(first **community**) of grasses, with insects, field mice, etc.*

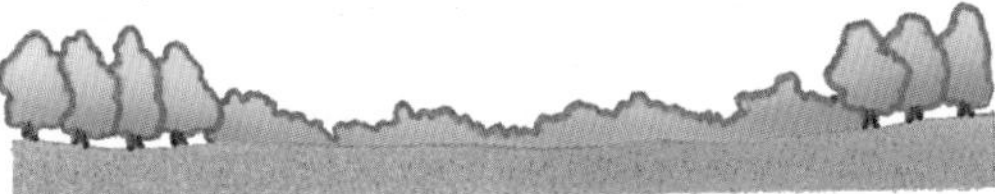

Successional community *(intermediate **community**) of shrubs and bushes, with rabbits, thrushes, etc.*

Climax community *of **deciduous*** trees, e.g. oak and beech, with foxes, badgers, warblers, etc.*

Ecological niche

The place held in an **ecosystem** by a plant or animal, e.g. what it eats and where it lives. **Gause's principle** states that no two species can occupy the same niche at the same time (if they tried, one species would die out or be driven away). For example, in the winter months, both the curlew and the ringed plover can be found living around the estuaries of Britain, and eating small creatures such as worms and snails. However, they actually occupy different niches. Curlews wade in the shallows, probing deep into the mud for food with their long beaks. Ringed plovers, by contrast, pick their food off the surface of the shore (their beaks are too short for probing). Hence both birds can survive in the same general area.

The curlew can probe deep into the mud with its long, curved beak.

The ringed plover can use its short beak to pick food from the surface of the shore.

* **Deciduous**, 236.

WITHIN AN ECOSYSTEM

An **ecosystem** consists of a group (**community***) of animals and plants which interact with each other and with their environment to produce a self-contained ecological unit.

Food web

The complex network of **food chains** in an ecosystem. A food chain is a linked series of living things, each of which is the food for the next in line. Plants make their food from non-living matter by **photosynthesis*** (they are **autotrophic**) and are always the first members of a chain. Animals cannot make their own food (they are **heterotrophic**) and so rely on the food-making activities of plants.

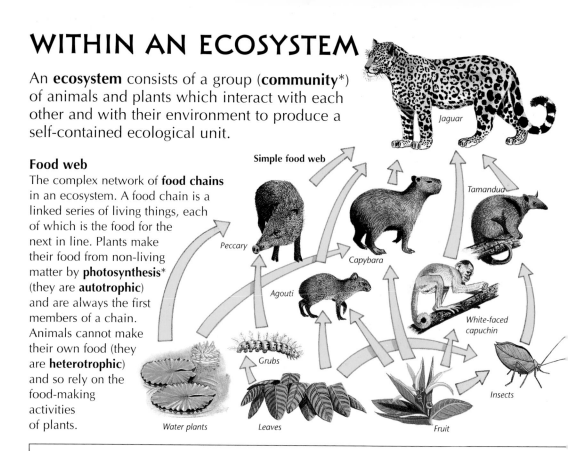

Simple food web

Jaguar
Peccary
Capybara
Tamandua
Agouti
White-faced capuchin
Grubs
Insects
Water plants
Leaves
Fruit

Carbon cycle

The constant circulation of the element carbon through living things and the atmosphere.

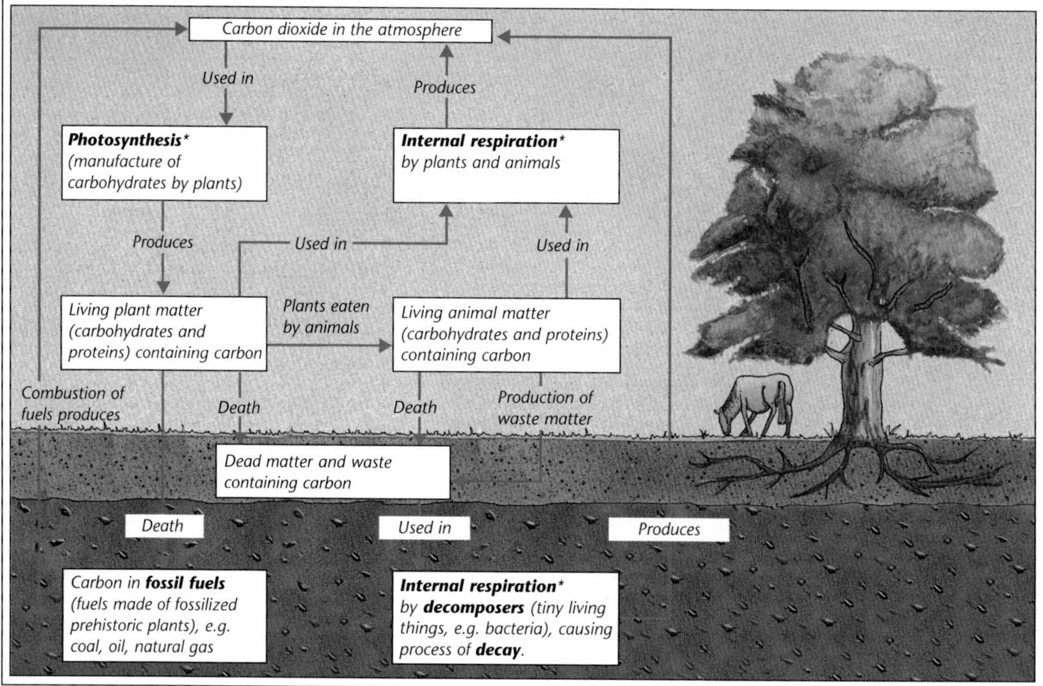

Carbon dioxide in the atmosphere
Used in
Produces
Photosynthesis* (manufacture of carbohydrates by plants)
Internal respiration* by plants and animals
Produces
Used in
Used in
Living plant matter (carbohydrates and proteins) containing carbon
Plants eaten by animals
Living animal matter (carbohydrates and proteins) containing carbon
Combustion of fuels produces
Death
Death
Production of waste matter
Dead matter and waste containing carbon
Death
Used in
Produces
Carbon in fossil fuels (fuels made of fossilized prehistoric plants), e.g. coal, oil, natural gas
Internal respiration* by decomposers (tiny living things, e.g. bacteria), causing process of decay.

* **Community**, 233; **Internal respiration**, 334; **Photosynthesis**, 254.

Trophic level or energy level

The level at which living things are positioned within a **food chain** (see **food web**). At each successive level, a great deal of the energy-giving food matter is lost. For example, a cow will break down well over half of the grass it eats (to provide energy). Hence only a small part of the original energy-giving material can be obtained from eating the cow (the part it used to build its own new tissue). This loss of energy means that the higher the trophic level, the fewer the number of animals, since they must eat progressively larger amounts of food to obtain enough energy. This principle is called the **pyramid of numbers**.

Pyramid of numbers

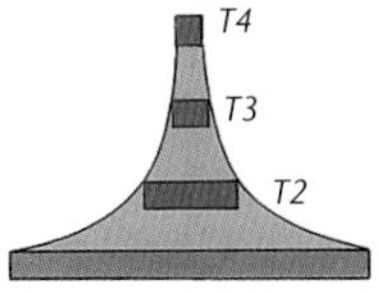

T4
T3
T2
T1

Number of individuals at each ***trophic level***

Pyramid of biomass

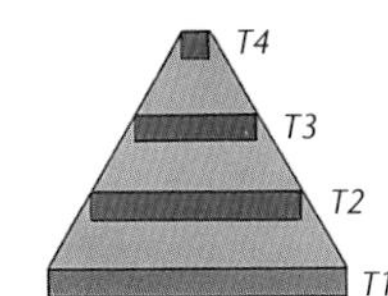

T4
T3
T2
T1

Total mass of individuals at each level (decrease is less extreme than left, since animals at higher levels tend to be larger).

Generalized food chain, showing trophic levels

Producers *– green plants, which make their own food.* ***Trophic level T1****.*

↓

Primary consumers *or* ***first order consumers*** *–* ***herbivores*** *(plant-eating animals), e.g. rabbits. Energy-giving material obtained directly from* ***producers****.* ***Trophic level T2****.*

↓

Secondary consumers *or* ***second order consumers*** *–* ***carnivores*** *(flesh-eating animals), e.g foxes and owls, when they eat herbivores. Energy-giving material obtained from bodies of* ***primary consumers****.* ***Trophic level T3****.*

↓

Tertiary consumers *or* ***third order consumers*** *– carnivores, e.g. foxes and owls, when they eat smaller carnivores. Energy-giving material is obtained by most indirect method – from bodies of secondary consumers, i.e. animals which ate animals which ate* ***producers****.* ***Trophic level T4****.*

Notes:

1. ***Omnivores****, e.g. humans, eat plant and animal matter. They are thus placed on trophic level T2 at some times and on T3 (or T4) at others.*

2. Many carnivores, e.g. foxes, will eat both herbivores and smaller carnivores. They are thus on trophic level T3 at some times and on T4 at others.

Nitrogen cycle

The constant circulation of the element nitrogen through living things, the soil and the atmosphere.

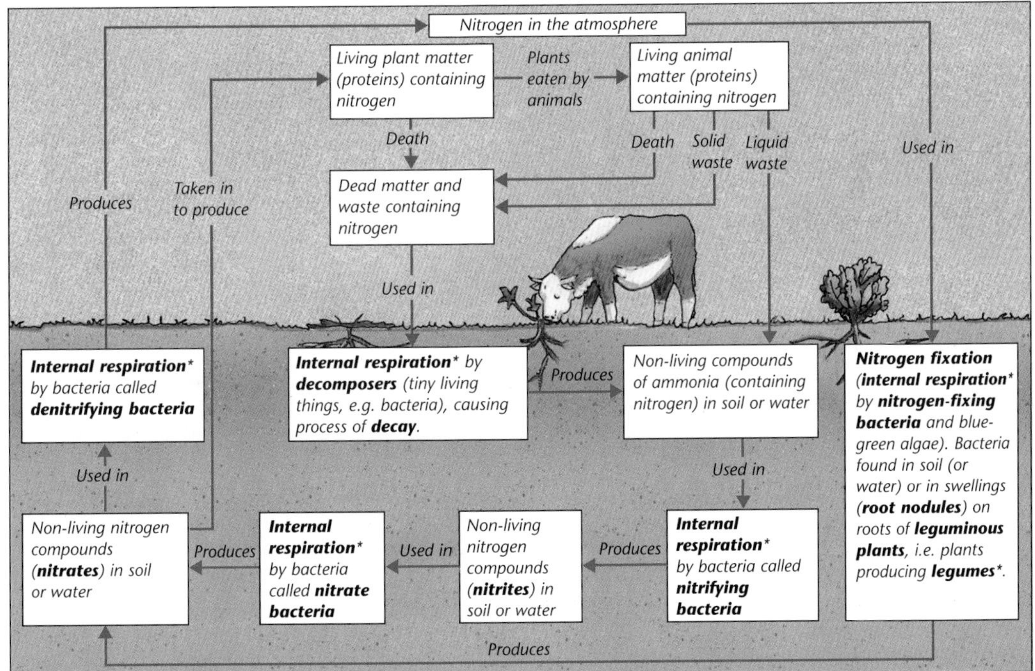

Nitrogen in the atmosphere
Living plant matter (proteins) containing nitrogen
Plants eaten by animals
Living animal matter (proteins) containing nitrogen
Death
Death
Solid waste
Liquid waste
Used in
Produces
Taken in to produce
Dead matter and waste containing nitrogen
Used in
Internal respiration* by bacteria called denitrifying bacteria
Internal respiration* by decomposers (tiny living things, e.g. bacteria), causing process of decay.
Produces
Non-living compounds of ammonia (containing nitrogen) in soil or water
Nitrogen fixation (internal respiration* by nitrogen-fixing bacteria and blue-green algae). Bacteria found in soil (or water) or in swellings (root nodules) on roots of leguminous plants, i.e. plants producing legumes*.
Used in
Used in
Non-living nitrogen compounds (nitrates) in soil or water
Produces
Internal respiration* by bacteria called nitrate bacteria
Used in
Non-living nitrogen compounds (nitrites) in soil or water
Produces
Internal respiration* by bacteria called nitrifying bacteria
Produces

* **Internal respiration**, 334; **Legume**, 262.

LIFE AND LIFE CYCLES

All living things show the same basic **characteristics of life**. These are respiration, feeding, growth, sensitivity (irritability), movement, excretion and reproduction. The **life cycle** of a plant or animal is the progression from its formation to its death, with all the changes this entails. (In some cases, these are drastic – see **metamorphosis**, page 277.) Below are some terms used to group plants and animals together according to their life cycle, or to describe characteristics of certain life cycles.

Perennials

Plants which live for many years. **Herbaceous perennials**, e.g. foxgloves, lose all the parts above ground at the end of each growing season, and grow new shoots at the start of the next. **Woody perennials**, e.g. trees, produce new growth (**secondary tissue***) each year from permanent stems.

*Foxgloves are **perennials**.*

Biennials

Plants which live for two years, e.g. carrots. In the first year, they grow and store up food. In the second, they produce flowers and seeds, and then die.

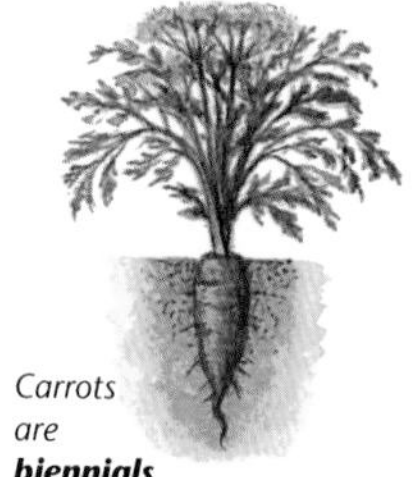

*Carrots are **biennials**.*

Annuals

Plants which live for one year, e.g. lobelias. In this time they grow from seed, produce flowers and seeds, and then die.

*Lobelias are **annuals**.*

Herbaceous

A term describing plants, e.g. phlox, which do not develop **secondary tissue*** above the ground, i.e. they are "like a herb", as distinct from shrubs and trees (**woody perennials**).

*Phlox is a **herbaceous** plant.*

Deciduous

A term describing **perennials** whose leaves lose their **chlorophyll*** and fall off at the end of each growing season, e.g. horse chestnuts.

Horse chestnut

Evergreen

A term describing **perennials** which do not shed their leaves at the end of a growing season, e.g. firs.

Grand fir

Ephemeral

Living for a very short time. Ephemeral plants are found in places which are hot and dry for most of the year (or for many years). The right growing conditions do not exist for long, so they must grow and produce seeds in a very short time. The only truly ephemeral animals are mayflies. Their adult life span is between a few minutes and one day.

Desert plants

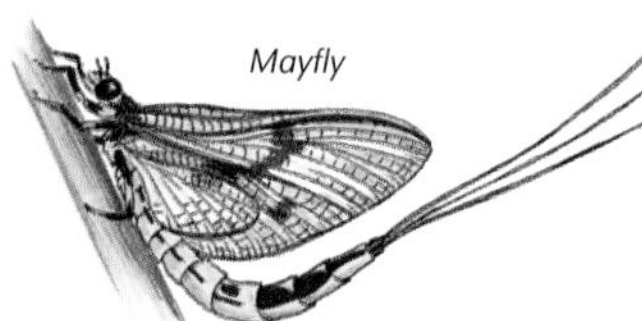

Mayfly

Anadromous

A term describing fish which live in the sea but swim upriver to breed, e.g. salmon. This is a form of **migration**, and the opposite is **catadromous** (going from river to sea).

Salmon swimming upriver

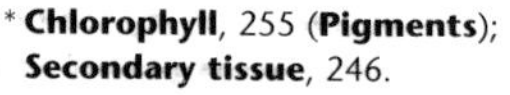

* **Chlorophyll**, 255 (**Pigments**); **Secondary tissue**, 246.

***Migrating** geese*

Migration

Traveling seasonally from one region to another. This normally involves leaving an area in winter to find food elsewhere, and returning in the spring to breed. Migration is part of the life cycle of many animals, especially birds.

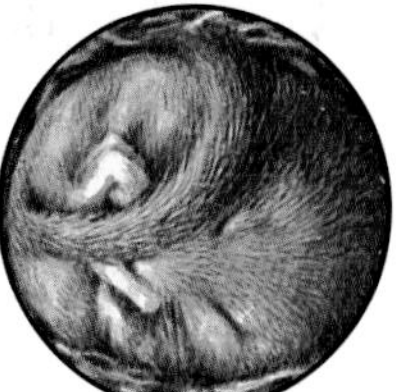

*Dormouse in **hibernation***

Dormancy

A period, or periods, of suspended activity which is a natural part of the life cycle of many plants and animals. Dormancy in plants occurs when conditions are unfavorable for growth (normally in winter). In animals, dormancy usually occurs because of food scarcity, and is either called **hibernation** or **aestivation**. Hibernation is dormancy in the winter (typical of many animals, e.g. some **mammals***), and aestivation is dormancy in drought conditions (occurs mainly in insects).

Life styles

The world has a vast diversity of living things, each one with its own style of life. This situation is a result of **genetic variation**. The living things can be grouped together according to shared characteristics, either by formal classification, which is based mainly on their inferred ancestry (see charts, pages 340-341) or by more informal groupings, based on general characteristics (see list, page 342).

Genetic variation

Birds' wings are shaped for flight.

The span of different forms of life, each of which is a variation and specifically designed to survive its environment. For example, fish and birds have streamlined shapes ideal for swimming and flying.

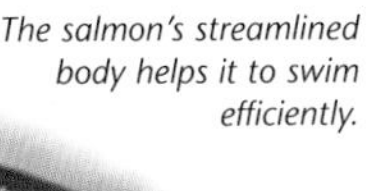

The salmon's streamlined body helps it to swim efficiently.

Thorns on rose stalks

A bee's sting protects it from predators.

Many living things also possess protective measures such as thorns or poison stings. These protective designs become established in successive generations because those creatures with them are the most likely to survive long enough to breed (and perpetuate the designs). This corresponds with Darwin's theory of **natural selection**, (also called **Darwinism**), first expounded in the mid-nineteenth century.

Mimicry

A special type of genetic design, in which a plant or animal (the **mimic**) has a resemblance to another plant or animal (the **model**). This is used especially for protection (e.g. many unprotected insects have the coloring of those which sting), but also for other reasons (bee orchids are mimics for reproduction purposes – see page 259).

Model

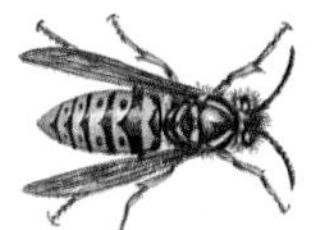

Wasp (protected with stinger)

Mimic

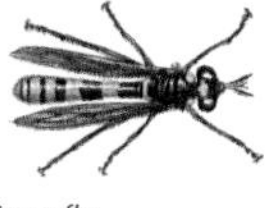

Hoverfly (unprotected)

* **Mammals**, 341.

THE STRUCTURE OF LIVING THINGS

A living thing capable of a separate existence is called an **organism**. All organisms are made up of **cells** – the basic units of life, which carry out all the vital chemical processes. The simplest organisms have just one cell (they are **unicellular** or **acellular**), but very complex ones, e.g. humans, have many billions. They are **multicellular** and their cells are of many different types, each type specially designed for its own particular job. Groups of cells of the same type (together with non-living material) make up the different **tissues** of the organism, e.g. muscle tissue. Several different types of tissue together form an **organ**, e.g. a stomach, and a number of organs together form a **system**, e.g. a digestive system.

*Protozoa and some algae are **unicellular** organisms.*

The parts of a cell

All cells are made up of the same basic parts. Each of these parts has a specific role to play.

Protoplasm
The **cell membrane**, **nucleus** and **cytoplasm**.

Cell membrane
Also called the **plasma membrane** or **plasmalemma**. The outer surface of a cell. It is **semipermeable***, i.e. selective about which substances it allows through.

Cytoplasm
The material where all the chemical reactions vital to life occur (see **organelles**). It generally has a jelly-like outer layer and a more liquid inner one (see **ectoplasm** and **endoplasm** – pictures, page 268).

Animal cell (cut away)

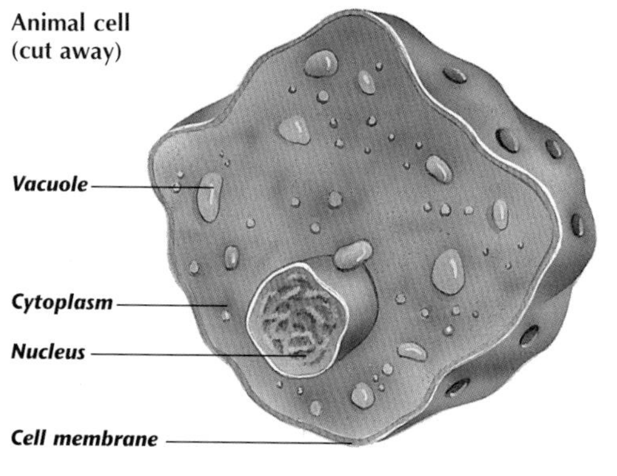
Vacuole
Cytoplasm
Nucleus
Cell membrane

Plant cell (cut away)

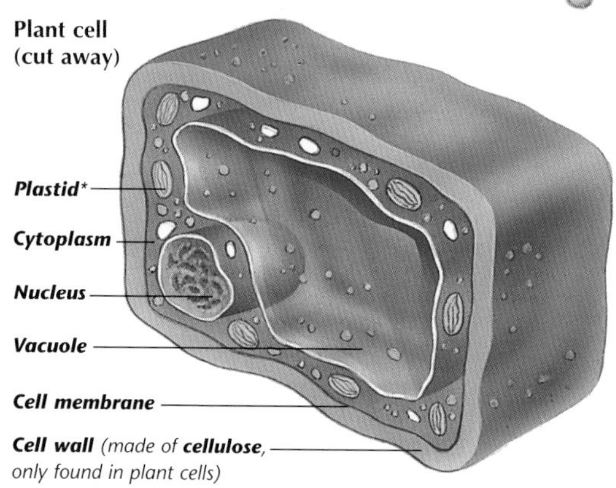
*Plastid**
Cytoplasm
Nucleus
Vacuole
Cell membrane
Cell wall (made of cellulose, only found in plant cells)

Vacuoles
Fluid-filled sacs in the **cytoplasm**. They are small and temporary in animal cells, and either remove substances (see **Golgi complex**) or contain fluid brought in (see **pinocytosis**, page 329). Most plant cells have one large, permanent vacuole, filled with **cell sap** (dissolved minerals and sugars).

Nucleus (pl. nuclei)
The cell's control center. Its double-layered outer surface (**nuclear membrane**) encloses a jelly-like fluid (**nucleoplasm** or **karyolymph**), which contains one or more **nucleoli*** and the genetic material **DNA***. This is held in **chromosomes*** – bodies which form a thread-like mass called **chromatin** when the cell is not dividing.

* **Chromosomes**, 324; **DNA**, 324 (**Nucleic acids**); **Nucleoli**, **Plastids**, 240; **Semipermeable**, 329 (**Diffusion**).

Organelles

The **organelles** are tiny bodies in the **cytoplasm**. Each type (listed below and on page 240) has a vital role to play in the chemical reactions within the cell.

Lysosomes

Round sacs containing powerful **enzymes***. They take in foreign bodies, e.g. bacteria, to be destroyed by the enzymes. Their outer skins do not usually let the enzymes out into the cell (to break down its contents), but if the cell becomes damaged, the skins disappear and the cell digests itself.

Ribosomes

Tiny round particles (most are attached to the **endoplasmic reticulum**). They are involved in building up proteins from amino acids (see page 330). "Coded" information (held by the **DNA** in the **nucleus**) is sent to the ribosomes in strands of a substance called **messenger RNA** (**mRNA**). These pass on the "codes" so that the ribosomes join the amino acids in the correct way to produce the right proteins. **RNA*** is present in at least two other forms in the cells. The ribosomes are made of **ribosomal RNA** (see **nucleoli***), and molecules of **transfer RNA** (**tRNA**) "carry" the amino acids to the ribosomes.

Endoplasmic reticulum or ER

A complex system of flat sacs, folding inward from the **cell membrane** and joining up with the **nuclear membrane** (see **nucleus**). It provides a large surface area for reactions or fluid storage, and a passageway for fluids passing through. ER with **ribosomes** on its surface is **rough ER**. ER with no ribosomes is **smooth ER**.

Golgi complex

Also called a **Golgi apparatus**, **Golgi body** or **dictyosome**. A special area of **smooth ER**. It collects and distributes the substances made in the cell (e.g. proteins and waste from chemical reactions). The substances fill the sacs, which gradually swell up at their outside edges until pieces "pinch off". These pieces (**vacuoles**) then travel out of the cell via the **cytoplasm** and **cell membrane**.

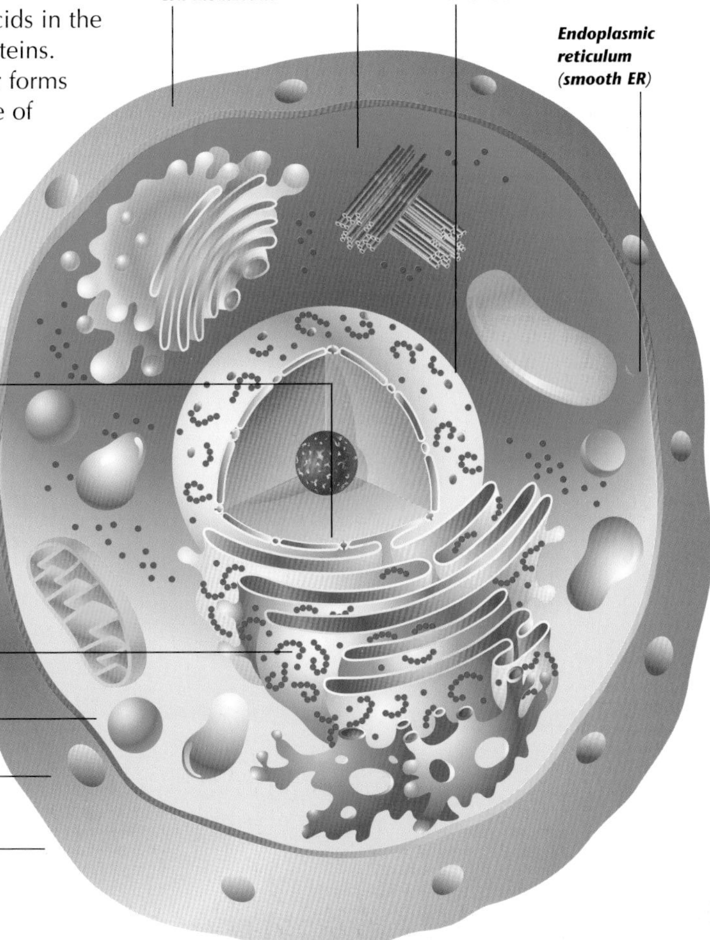

Cell membrane
Vacuole
Centriole
Endoplasmic reticulum (smooth ER)
Nucleus (double membrane cut away). The nucleoplasm and chromosomes are not shown.
Lysosome
Mitochondrion
Nucleolus
Golgi complex
Ribosome
Endoplasmic reticulum (rough ER)

Animal cell showing the organelles in the cytoplasm

* **Enzymes**, 333; **Nucleoli**, 240; **RNA**, 324 (**Nucleic acids**).

Organelles (continued)

Centrioles

Two bodies in animal and primitive plant cells which are vital to **cell division** (see right). In animal cells, they lie just outside the **nucleus***. Each lies in a dense area of **cytoplasm*** (**centrosome**) and is made up of two tiny cylinders, forming an X-shape. Each cylinder is made up of nine sets of three tiny tubes (**microtubules**).

Centriole

Nucleoli (sing. nucleolus)

One or more small, round bodies in the **nucleus***. They produce the component parts of the **ribosomes*** (made of **ribosomal RNA**), which are then transported out of the nucleus and assembled in the **cytoplasm***.

Nucleolus

Mitochondria (sing. mitochondrion) or chondriosomes

Rod-shaped bodies with a double layer of outer skin. The inner layer forms a series of folds (**cristae**, sing. **crista**), providing a large surface area for the vital chemical reactions which go on inside the mitochondria (called the cell's "powerhouses"). They are the places where simple substances taken into the cell are broken down to provide energy. For more about this, see **aerobic respiration**, page 334.

Mitochondrion *Cristae*

Plastids

Tiny bodies in plant cell **cytoplasm***. Some (**leucoplasts**) store starch, oil or proteins. Others – **chloroplasts*** – contain **chlorophyll*** (used in making food).

Plastid (chloroplast)*

Cell division

Cell division is the splitting up of one cell (the **parent cell**) into two identical **daughter cells**. There are two types of cell division, both involving the division of the **nucleus*** (**karyokinesis**) followed by the division of the **cytoplasm*** (**cytokinesis**). The first type of cell division (**binary fission**) is described on these two pages. It produces new cells for growth and also to replace the millions of cells which die each day (from damage, disease or simply because they are "worn out"). It is also the means of **asexual reproduction*** in many single-celled organisms. The second, special type of cell division produces the **gametes*** (sex cells) which will come together to form a new living thing. For more about this, see pages 322-323.

Mitosis

The division of the **nucleus*** when a plant or animal cell divides for growth or repair (**binary fission**). It ensures that the two new nuclei (**daughter nuclei**) are each given the same number of **chromosomes*** (the bodies which carry the "coded" hereditary information). Each receives the same number of chromosomes as were in the original nucleus, called the **diploid number**. Every living thing has its own characteristic diploid number, i.e. all its cells (with the exception of the **gametes***) contain the same, specific number of chromosomes, grouped in identical pairs called **homologous chromosomes**. Humans have 46 chromosomes, in 23 pairs. Although mitosis is a continuous process, it can be divided for convenience sake into four phases. Before mitosis, however, there is always an **interphase**.

Interphase

The periods between cell divisions. Interphases are very active periods, during which the cells are not only carrying out all the processes needed for life, but are also preparing material to produce "copies" of all their components (so both new cells formed after division will have all they need). Just before **mitosis** begins, the **chromatin*** threads in the **nucleus*** also duplicate, so that, after coiling up, each **chromosome*** will consist of two **chromatids** (see **prophase**).

* **Asexual reproduction**, 321; **Chlorophyll**, 255 (**Pigments**); **Chloroplasts**, 254; **Chromatin**, 238 (**Nucleus**); **Chromosomes**, 324; **Cytoplasm**, 238; **Gametes**, 320; **Nucleus**, 238; **Ribosomes**, 239.

Phases of mitosis

1. Prophase

The **nuclear membrane*** begins to break down and the threads of **chromatin*** in the **nucleus*** coil up to form **chromosomes***. Each has already duplicated to form two identical, long coils (**chromatids**), joined by a sphere (**centromere**). The two **centrioles** move to opposite poles (ends) of the cell, as **spindle microtubules** form between them.

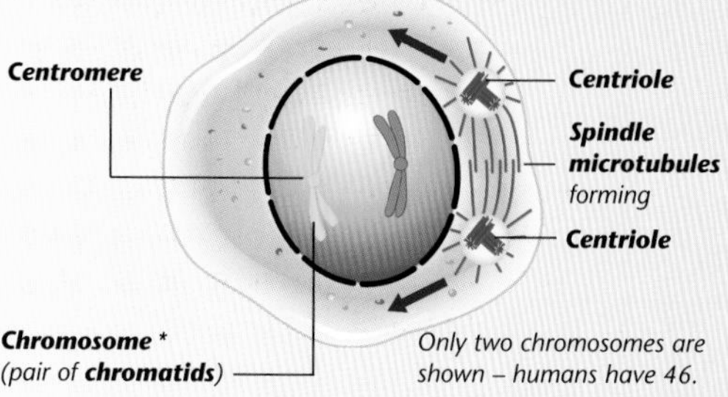

Centromere
Centriole
Spindle microtubules forming
Centriole
Chromosome * (pair of chromatids)
Only two chromosomes are shown – humans have 46.

2. Metaphase

The **nuclear membrane*** disappears and the **spindle microtubules** surround the **chromosomes*** (paired **chromatids**). The chromosomes move towards its equator and become attached by their **centromeres** to the **spindle microtubules**.

Spindle microtubules form a spindle
Centromere
Chromosome * (pair of chromatids)

3. Anaphase

The **centromeres** split and the two **chromatids** from each pair (now called **daughter chromosomes**) move to opposite poles of the **spindle**, seemingly "dragged" there by the contracting **spindle microtubules**.

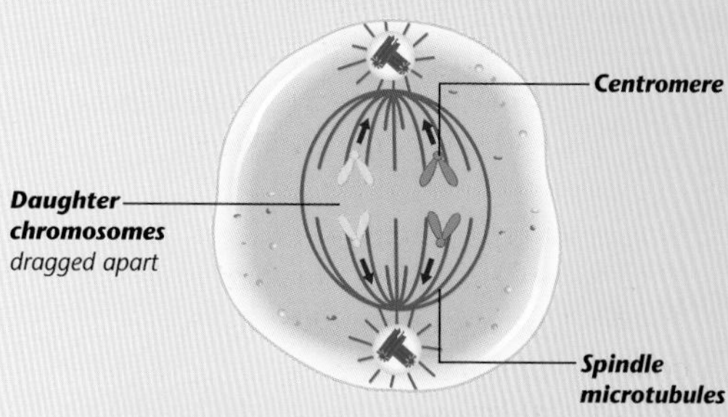

Centromere
Daughter chromosomes dragged apart
Spindle microtubules

4. Telophase

The **spindle microtubules** disappear and a new **nuclear membrane*** forms around each group of **daughter chromosomes**. This creates two new **nuclei*** (**daughter nuclei**), inside which the chromosomes uncoil and once again form a thread-like mass (**chromatin***).

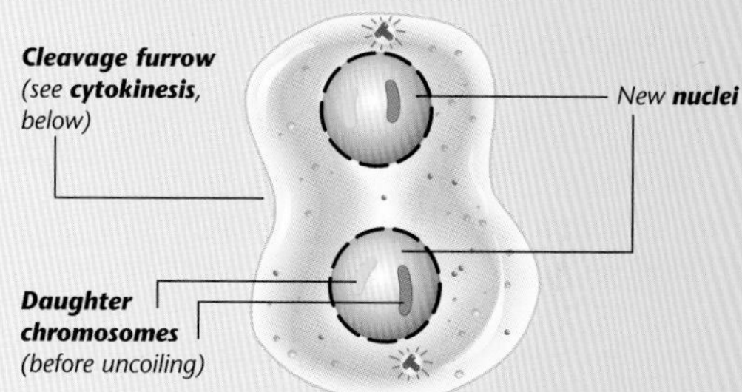

Cleavage furrow (see cytokinesis, below)
New nuclei
Daughter chromosomes (before uncoiling)

Cytokinesis

The division of the **cytoplasm*** of a cell, which forms two new cells around the new **nuclei*** created by **mitosis** (or **meiosis***). In animal cells, a **cleavage furrow** forms around the cell's equator and then constricts as a ring until it cuts completely through the cell. In plant cells, a dividing line called the **cell plate** forms down the centre of the cell, and a new **cell wall*** is built up along each side of it.

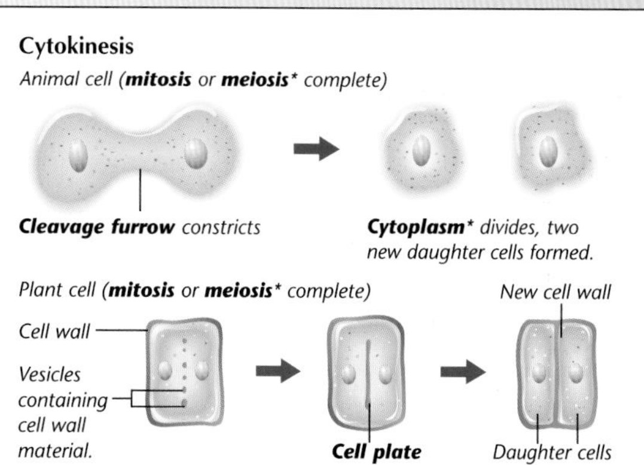

Cytokinesis
Animal cell (mitosis or meiosis* complete)
Cleavage furrow constricts
Cytoplasm* divides, two new daughter cells formed.
Plant cell (mitosis or meiosis* complete)
New cell wall
Cell wall
Vesicles containing cell wall material.
Cell plate
Daughter cells

* **Cell wall**, 238; **Chromatin**, 238 (**Nucleus**); **Chromosomes**, 324; **Cytoplasm**, 238; **Meiosis**, 322; **Nuclear membrane**, 238 (**Nucleus**).

VASCULAR PLANTS

With the exception of simple plants such as algae, fungi, mosses and liverworts (see classification chart, page 340), all plants are **vascular plants**. That is, they all have a complex system of special fluid-carrying tissue called **vascular tissue**. For more about how the fluids travel within the vascular tissue, see pages 252-253.

Vascular tissue

Special tissue which runs throughout a **vascular plant**, carrying fluids and helping to support the plant. In young stems, it is normally arranged in separate units called **vascular bundles**; in older stems, these join up to form a central core (**vascular cylinder***). In young roots, the arrangement of the tissue is slightly different, but a central core is also formed later. For more about the vascular tissue in older plants, see page 246. The vascular tissue is of two different types – **xylem** and **phloem**. They are separated by a layer of tissue called the **cambium**.

Tulips are ***monocotyledons****. Their* ***vascular bundles*** *are irregularly arranged within the stem. In* ***dicotyledons****, by contrast, the bundles are more regular (see root and stem sections, right).*

Cross section of young stem, or young part of a stem (dicotyledon*)

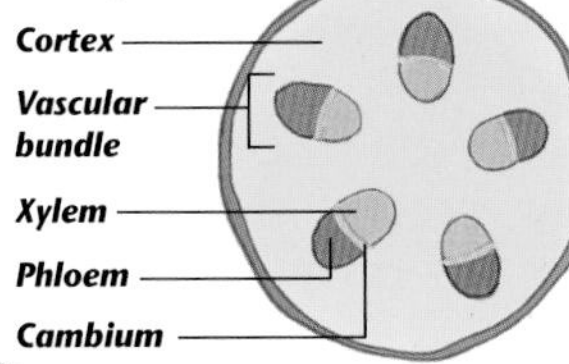
Cortex
Vascular bundle
Xylem
Phloem
Cambium

Cross section of young root, or young part of a root (dicotyledon*)

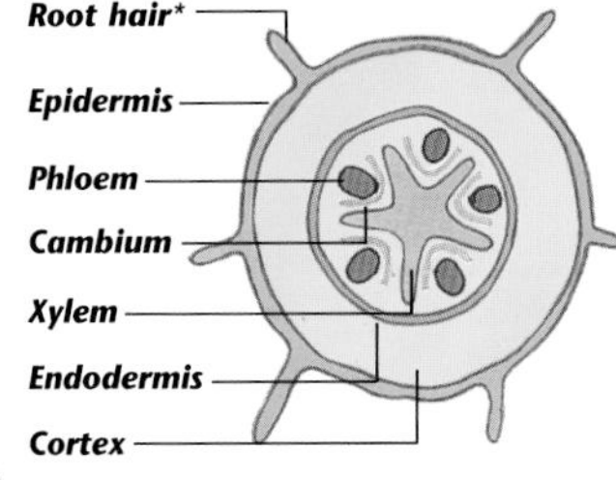
Root hair*
Epidermis
Phloem
Cambium
Xylem
Endodermis
Cortex

Young stem, or young part of a stem (dicotyledon*)

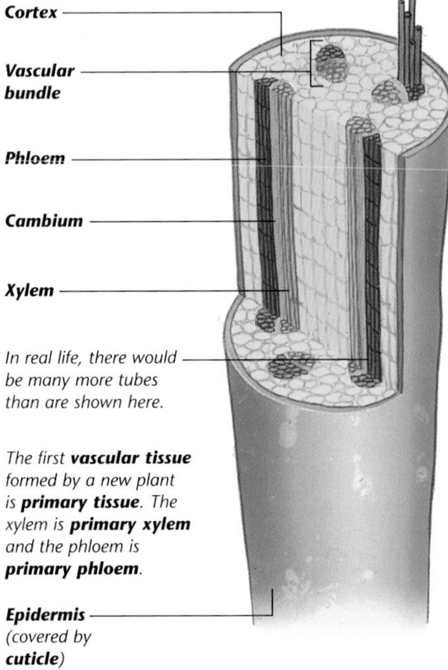
Cortex
Vascular bundle
Phloem
Cambium
Xylem
In real life, there would be many more tubes than are shown here.
Epidermis (covered by cuticle)

The first ***vascular tissue*** *formed by a new plant is* ***primary tissue****. The xylem is* ***primary xylem*** *and the phloem is* ***primary phloem****.*

Longitudinal section of young root, or young part of a root (dicotyledon*)

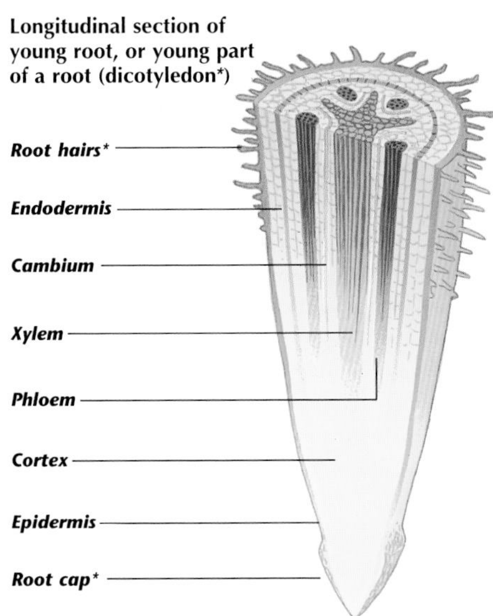
Root hairs*
Endodermis
Cambium
Xylem
Phloem
Cortex
Epidermis
Root cap*

* **Dicotyledon**, **Monocotyledon**, 261 (**Cotyledon**); **Root cap**, **Root hairs**, 245; **Vascular cylinder**, 246.

Constituents of vascular tissue

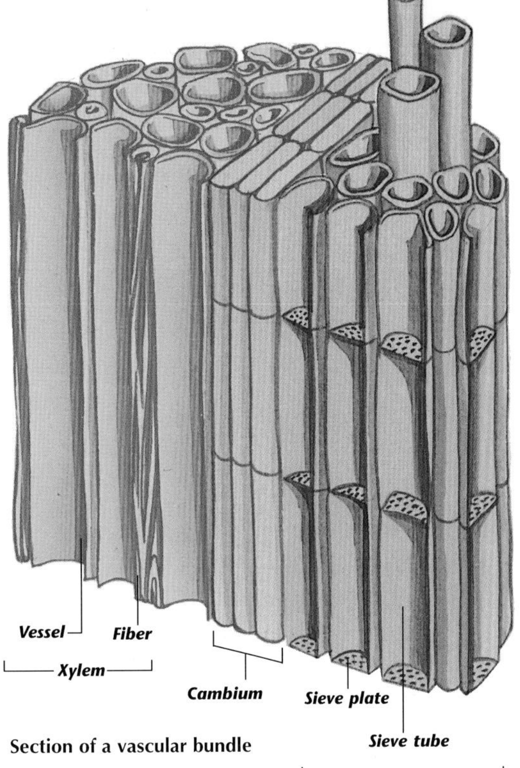
Vessel
Fiber
Xylem
Cambium
Sieve plate
Sieve tube
Phloem
Section of a vascular bundle

Xylem
A tissue which carries water up through a plant. It is made up of **vessels** or **tracheids**, with long, thin cells (**fibers**) providing support between them. In older stems, the central xylem dies away and its vessels become filled in, forming **heartwood***.

Vessels and **tracheids**
Long tubes in the **xylem** which carry water. Their walls are strengthened with a hard substance called **lignin**. They occur as columns of cells whose walls and **protoplasm*** have died. Vessels are shorter and wider than tracheids.

Cambium
A layer of narrow, thin-walled cells between the **xylem** on the inside and the **phloem** on the outside. The cells are able to divide, making more xylem and phloem. Such an area of cells is called a **meristem***.

Phloem
A tissue which distributes the food made in the leaves to all parts of the plant. It consists of **sieve tubes**, with special fluid-carrying **companion cells** running beside them, and other cells packed around them for support.

Sieve tubes
Cells in long columns in the **phloem**. Their **nuclei*** and **protoplasm*** have been lost but their interconnecting walls remain. These are called **sieve plates** and have tiny holes in them to allow substances to pass through.

Other tissues in vascular plants

Epidermis
A thin surface layer of tissue around all parts of a plant. In some areas, especially the leaves, it has many tiny holes, called **stomata***. In older stems, the epidermis is replaced by **phellem***. In older roots, it is replaced by **exodermis*** and then by phellem.

Cortex
A layer of tissue inside the **epidermis** of stems and roots. It consists mainly of **parenchyma**, a type of tissue with large cells and many air spaces. In some plants there is also some **collenchyma**, a type of supporting tissue with long, thick-walled cells. The cortex tends to get compressed and replaced by other tissues as a plant gets older.

Endodermis
The innermost layer of root **cortex**. Fluids which have seeped in between the cortex cells, instead of through them, are directed by its special **passage cells** into the central area of **vascular tissue**.

Pith or **medulla**
A central area of tissue found in stems, but not usually in roots. It is generally only called pith once the stem has developed a **vascular cylinder***. It is made up of **parenchyma** (see **cortex**), and is sometimes used to store food.

Cuticle
A thin outer layer of a waxy substance called **cutin** made by the **epidermis** above ground. It prevents too much water from being lost.

* **Exodermis**, 245 (**Piliferous layer**); **Heartwood**, 247; **Meristem**, 244; **Nucleus**, 238; **Phellem**, 247; **Protoplasm**, 238; **Stomata**, 249; **Vascular cylinder**, 246.

STEMS AND ROOTS

The **stem** and **roots** of a plant are its main supporting structures, as well as being important in transporting fluids (see pages 242-243 and 252-253). Their various parts are listed here. For more about the development of the stem and roots as plants get older, see pages 246-247.

Meristem

Any area in a plant from which new growth arises. The cells of a meristem are able to divide, producing new cells. A meristem found at the tip of the root (the **growing point**) or the stem (part of a **terminal bud**) is known as an **apical meristem**.

Stem attachments

Shoot

A new stem growing out of a seed or off the main stem of a plant.

Bud

A small outgrowth on a stem. It develops either into a new **shoot** or a flower.

Terminal bud

A **bud** growing at the end of a stem or **shoot**.

Axillary bud

Also called a **lateral bud** or **secondary bud**. A **bud** situated in an **axil** – the angle between a **shoot** or leaf stalk and the stem it is growing from.

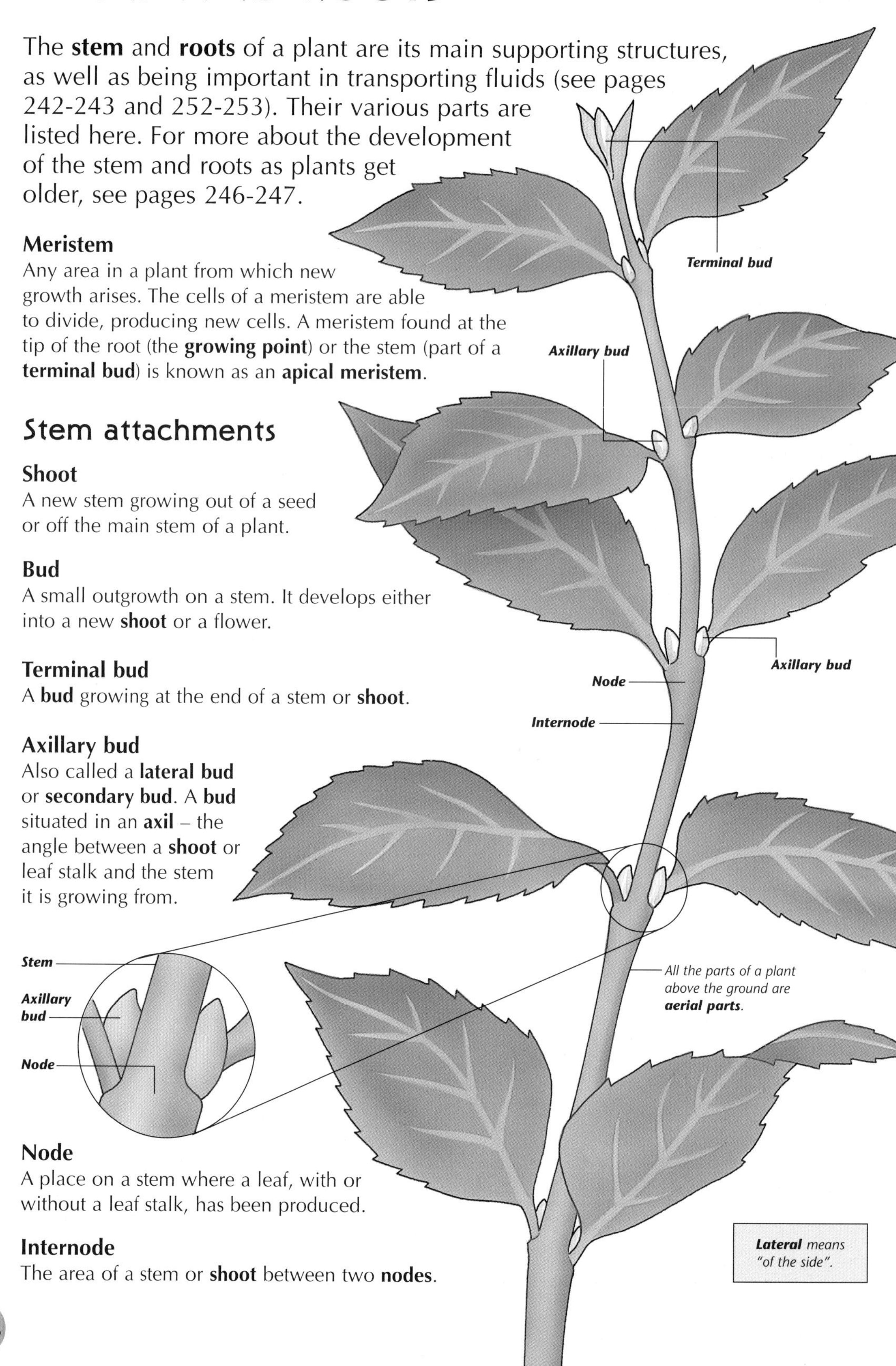

Terminal bud
Axillary bud
Axillary bud
Node
Internode
Stem
Axillary bud
Node
All the parts of a plant above the ground are aerial parts.

Node

A place on a stem where a leaf, with or without a leaf stalk, has been produced.

Internode

The area of a stem or **shoot** between two **nodes**.

Lateral means "of the side".

Parts of a root

Root cap
A layer of cells which protects the root tip as it is pushed down into the ground.

Growing point
An area just behind a root tip where the cells divide to produce new growth.

Zone of elongation
The area of new cells produced by the **growing point**, and located just behind it. The cells stretch lengthwise as they take in water, since their **cell walls*** are not yet hard. This elongation pushes the root tip further down into the soil.

Piliferous layer
The youngest layer of the **epidermis***, or outer skin, of a root. It is the area which produces **root hairs**. It is found just behind the **zone of elongation**. As the walls of the elongating cells harden, the outermost cells become the piliferous layer. The older piliferous layer (higher up the root) is slowly worn away, to be replaced by a layer of hardened cells called the **exodermis** (the outermost layer of the **cortex***).

Root hairs
Long outgrowths from the cells of the **piliferous layer**. They take in water and minerals.

Parts of a root

(See also root section, page 242.)

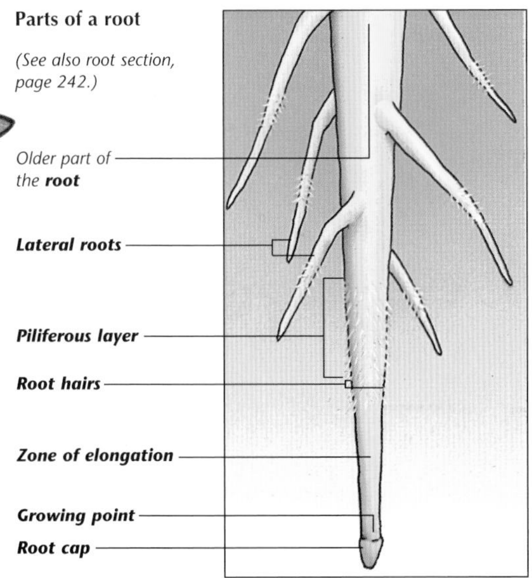

Older part of the root
Lateral roots
Piliferous layer
Root hairs
Zone of elongation
Growing point
Root cap

Types of roots

Tap root
A first root, or **primary root**, which is larger than the small roots, called **lateral roots** or **secondary roots**, which grow out of it. Many vegetables are swollen tap roots.

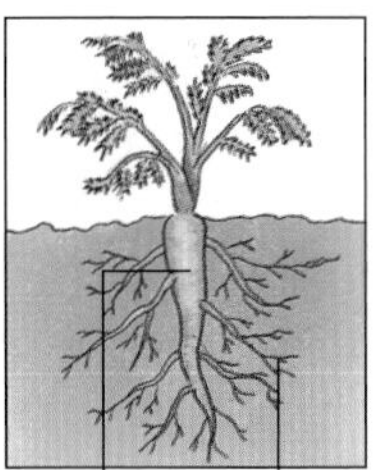

Tap root (carrot)
Lateral root

Fibrous roots
A system made up of a large number of equal-sized roots, all producing smaller **lateral roots**. The first root is not prominent, as it is in a **tap root** system.

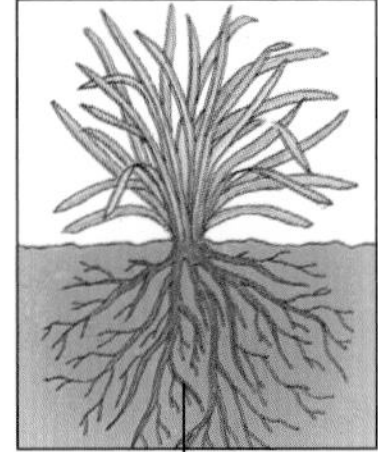

Fibrous roots

Adventitious roots
Roots which grow directly from a stem. Adventitious roots grow out of **bulbs*** (which are special types of stem), or from gardeners' cuttings.

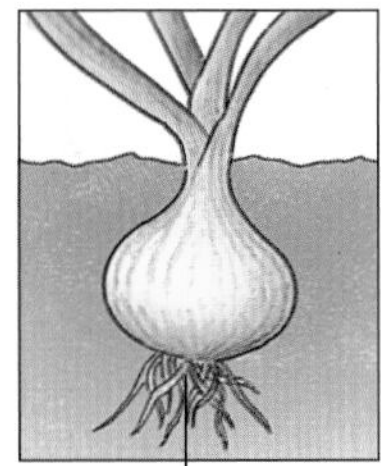

Adventitious roots

Aerial roots
Roots which grow from stems and do not normally grow into the ground. They can be used for climbing, e.g. in an ivy. Many absorb moisture from the air.

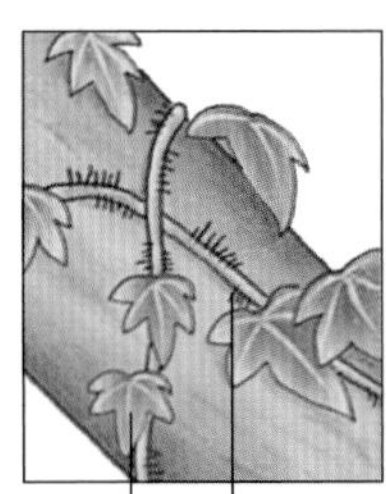

Ivy
Aerial roots

Prop roots
Special types of **aerial root**. They grow out from a stem and then down into the ground, which may be under water. Prop roots support a heavy plant, e.g. a mangrove.

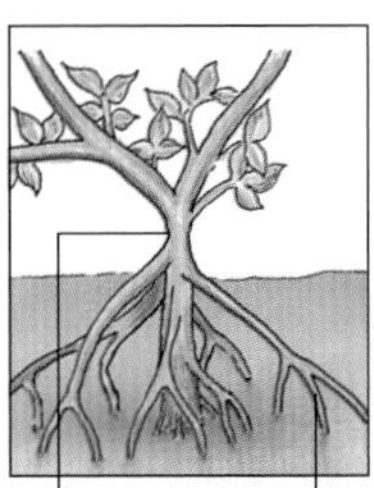

Mangrove
Prop roots

* **Bulb**, 263; **Cell wall**, 238; **Cortex**, **Epidermis**, 243.

INSIDE AN OLDER PLANT

A plant which lives for many years, such as a tree, forms **secondary tissue** as it grows. This consists of new layers of tissue to supplement the original tissue, or **primary tissue***. New supportive and fluid-carrying **vascular tissue*** is formed toward the center of the plant and new protective tissue is produced around the outside. The production of the new vascular tissue is called **secondary thickening**, and results in what is known as a **woody plant**.

New central tissue

Vascular cylinder

A vascular cylinder develops as the first step of **secondary thickening** in stems. More **cambium*** forms between the **vascular bundles***, and this then gives rise to more **xylem*** and **phloem***, forming a continuous cylinder.

Secondary thickening

The year-by-year production of more fluid-carrying **vascular tissue*** in plants which live for many years, resulting in a gradual increase in the diameter of the stem and roots. Each year, new layers of **xylem*** (**secondary xylem**) and **phloem*** (**secondary phloem**) are produced by the dividing cells of the **cambium*** between them. This process differs slightly between stems and roots, but the result throughout the plant is an ever-enlarging core of vascular tissue (which slowly "squeezes out" the **pith*** in stems). Most of this core is xylem, now also known as **wood**. The area of phloem does not widen much at all, because the xylem pushing outward wears it away.

Annual rings

The concentric circles which can be seen in a cross section of an older plant. Each ring is one year's new growth of **xylem***, and has two separate areas – **spring wood** and **summer wood**. Soft **spring wood** (or **early wood**) forms rapidly early in the growing season and has widely-spaced cells. Harder **summer wood** (or **late wood**) is produced later on. Its cells are more densely packed.

The roots and trunk of this tree thicken as it grows.

Secondary thickening in a stem

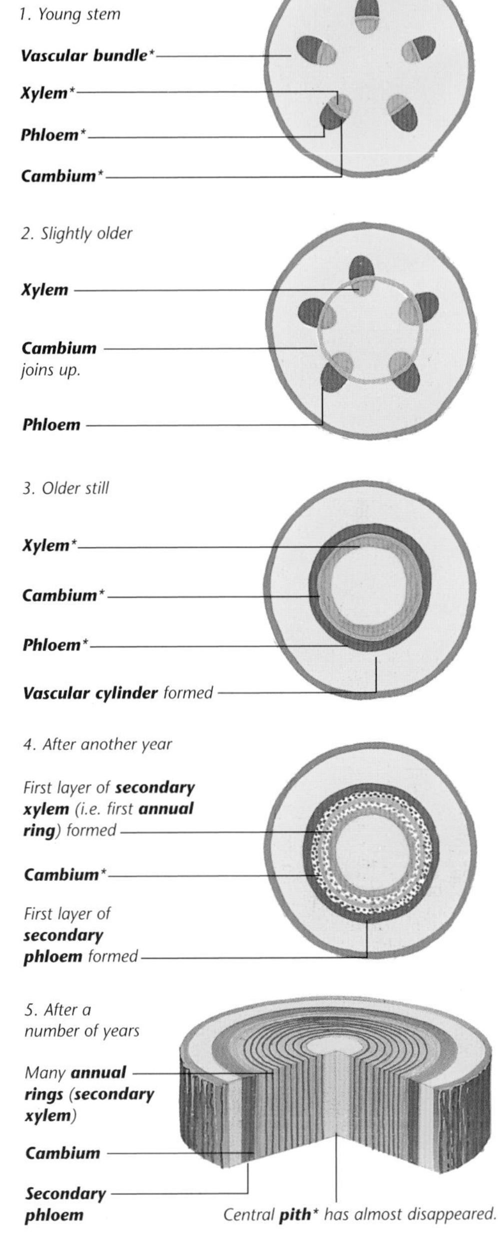

1. Young stem
Vascular bundle*
Xylem*
Phloem*
Cambium*
2. Slightly older
Xylem
Cambium joins up.
Phloem
3. Older still
Xylem*
Cambium*
Phloem*
Vascular cylinder formed
4. After another year
First layer of secondary xylem (i.e. first annual ring) formed
Cambium*
First layer of secondary phloem formed
5. After a number of years
Many annual rings (secondary xylem)
Cambium
Secondary phloem
Central pith* has almost disappeared.

* **Cambium**, 243; **Phloem**, 243; **Pith**, 243; **Primary tissue**, 242; **Vascular bundles**, 242 (**Vascular tissue**); **Xylem**, 243.

New outer tissue

As well as new **vascular tissue***, an older plant also forms extra areas of tissue around its outside to help protect it. These are called **phelloderm**, **phellogen** and **phellem** respectively (working from the inside). The three areas together are known as the **periderm**.

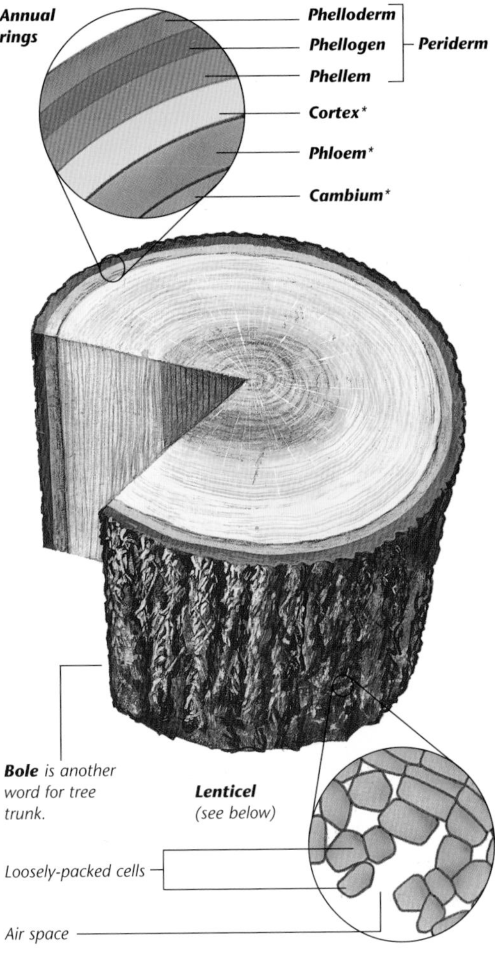
Tree (many years old)
Annual rings
Phelloderm
Phellogen
Phellem
Periderm
Cortex*
Phloem*
Cambium*
Bole is another word for tree trunk.
Lenticel (see below)
Loosely-packed cells
Air space

Phellogen or cork cambium

A cell layer which arises toward the outside of the stem and roots of older plants. It is a **meristem***, i.e. an area of cells which keep on dividing. It produces two new layers – **phelloderm** and **phellem**.

Phelloderm

A new cell layer produced by **phellogen** on its inside. It supplements the **cortex*** and is sometimes called **secondary cortex**.

Phellem or cork

A new cell layer produced by **phellogen** on its outside. The cells undergo **suberization**, i.e. become impregnated with a waxy substance called **suberin**. This makes the outer layer waterproof. The phellem cells slowly die and replace the previous outer cell layer (**epidermis*** in stems and **exodermis*** in roots). Dead phellem cells are called **bark**.

***Bark** stops the tree from drying out and protects it from disease. It cannot grow or stretch, so it splits or peels as the trunk gets wider, and new bark grows underneath.*

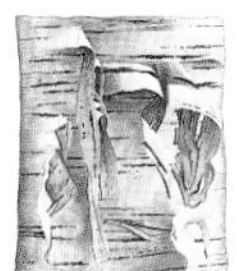
Silver birch bark

English oak bark

Scots pine bark

Beech bark

Lenticels

Tiny raised openings in the **phellem** through which an older plant exchanges oxygen and carbon dioxide. Inside them, a channel of loosely-packed cells allows the gases to move across the outer tissues to or from the **cortex***, which also has air spaces.

Types of wood

Heartwood

The oldest, central part of the **xylem*** in an older plant. The **vessels*** are filled in and no longer carry fluids, but they still provide support.

Heartwood

Sapwood

The outer area of **xylem*** in an older plant, whose **vessels*** still carry fluids. Sapwood also supports the tree and holds the tree's food reserves.

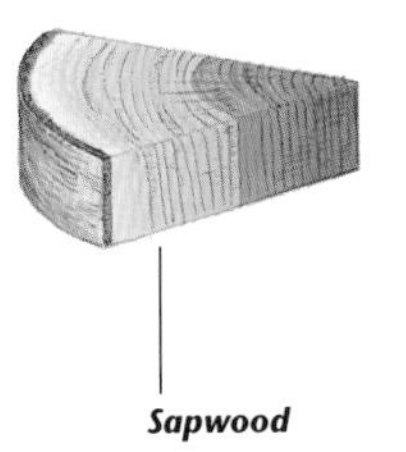
Sapwood

* **Cambium**, **Cortex**, **Epidermis**, 243; **Exodermis**, 245 (**Piliferous layer**); **Phloem**, 243; **Meristem**, 244; **Vascular tissue**, 242; **Vessels**, 243; **Xylem**, 243.

LEAVES

The **leaves** of a plant, collectively known as its **foliage**, are specially adapted to manufacture food. They do this by a process called **photosynthesis**. For more about this, see pages 254-255. There are many different shapes and sizes of leaves, but only two different types. **Simple leaves** consist of a single leaf blade, or **lamina**, and **compound leaves** are made up of small leaf blades called **leaflets**, all growing from the same leaf stalk. You can find out more about some of the different leaf shapes on page 250.

***Simple* leaf** *(holly)*

Compound leaf *(horse chestnut)*

Inside a leaf

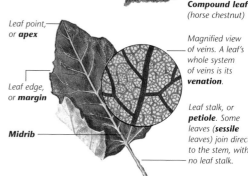

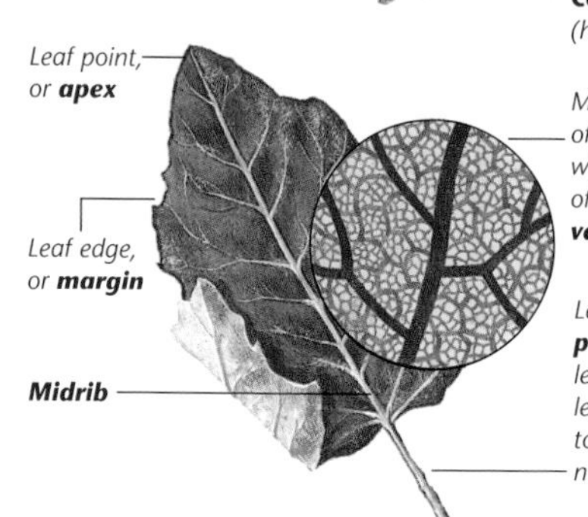
Leaf point, or **apex**
Leaf edge, or **margin**
Midrib
Magnified view of veins. A leaf's whole system of veins is its **venation**.
Leaf stalk, or **petiole**. Some leaves (**sessile** leaves) join directly to the stem, with no leaf stalk.

Veins

Long strips of **vascular tissue*** inside a leaf (see picture, right), supplying it with water and minerals and removing the food made inside it. Some leaves have long, parallel veins, e.g. those of grasses, but most have a central vein inside a **midrib** (an extension of the leaf stalk), with many smaller branching veins.

Spongy layer

A layer of irregular-shaped **spongy cells** and air spaces where gases circulate. The **spongy** and **palisade layers** together are the **mesophyll**.

Palisade layer

A cell layer just below the upper surface of a leaf. It is made up of regular, oblong-shaped **palisade cells**. These contain many **chloroplasts***.

Palisade cell

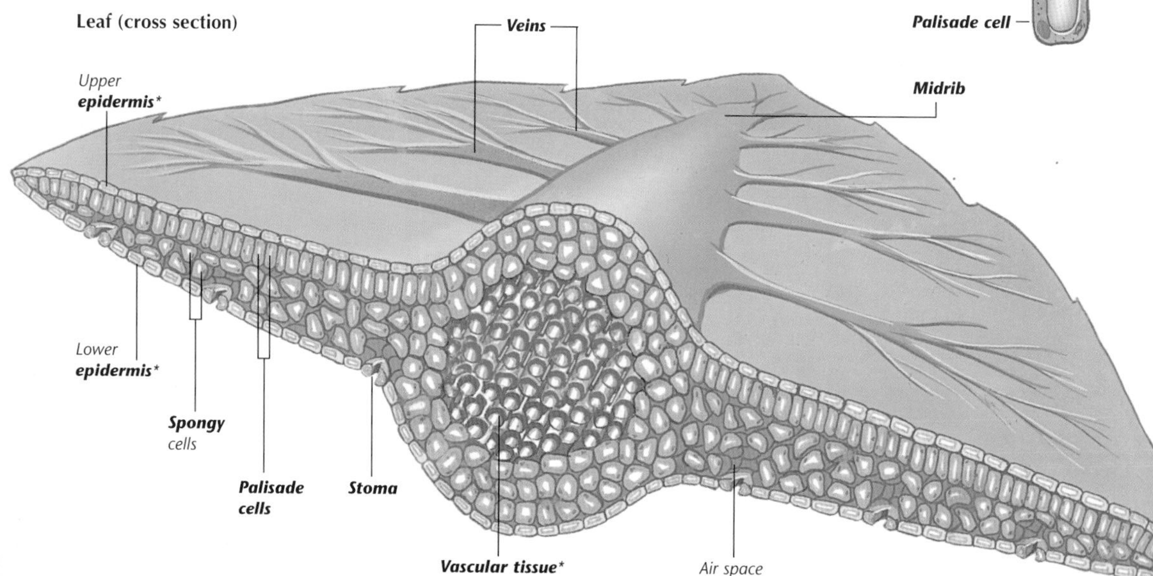
Leaf (cross section)
Veins
Midrib
Upper epidermis*
Lower epidermis*
Spongy cells
Palisade cells
Stoma
Vascular tissue*
Air space

* **Chloroplasts**, 254; **Epidermis**, 243; **Vascular tissue**, 242.

Stomata (sing. stoma)

Tiny openings in the **epidermis*** (outer skin), through which the exchange of water (**transpiration***) and gases takes place. Stomata are mainly found on the underside of leaves.

Guard cells

Pairs of crescent-shaped cells. The members of each pair are found on either side of a **stoma**, which they open and close by changing shape. This controls water and gas exchange. Guard cells are the only surface cells with **chloroplasts***.

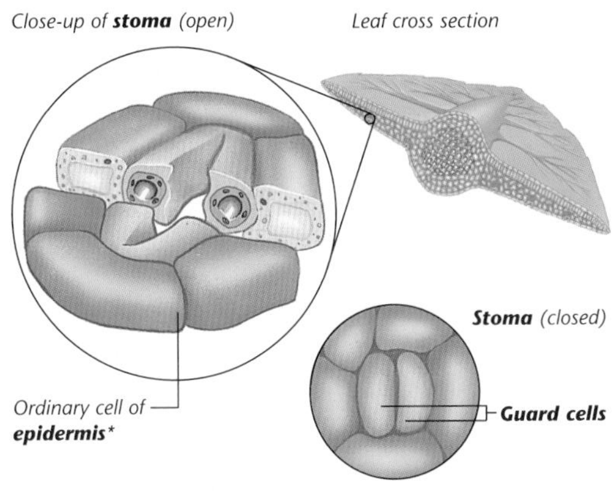

Close-up of stoma (open)
Leaf cross section
Stoma (closed)
Guard cells
Ordinary cell of epidermis*

Leaf trace

An area of **vascular tissue*** which branches off that of a stem to become the central **vein** of a leaf.

Abscission layer

A layer of cells at the base of a leaf stalk which separates from the rest of the plant at a certain time of year (stimulated by a **hormone*** called **abscisic acid**). This makes the leaf fall off, forming a **leaf scar** on the stem.

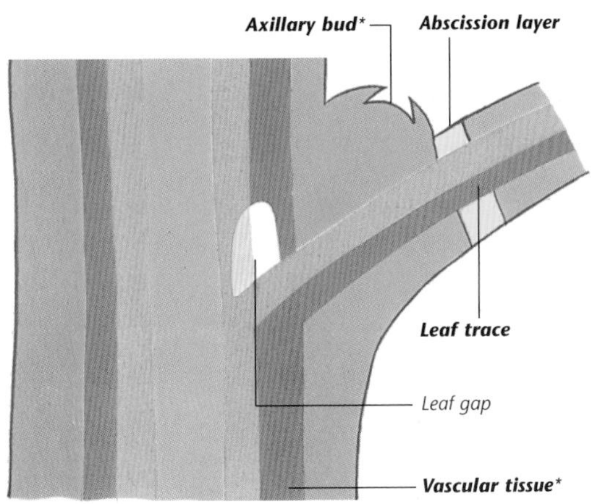

Axillary bud*
Abscission layer
Leaf trace
Leaf gap
Vascular tissue*

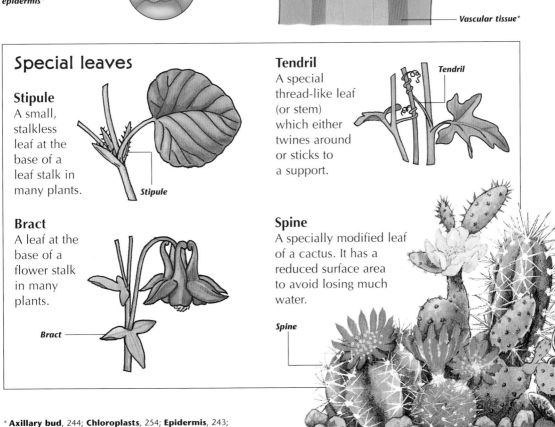

Special leaves

Stipule

A small, stalkless leaf at the base of a leaf stalk in many plants.

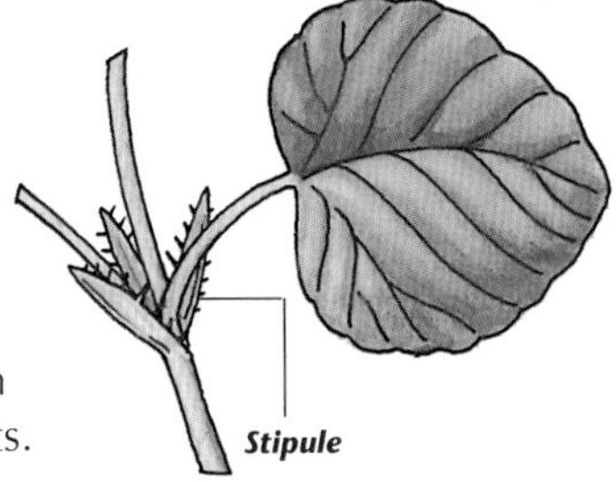

Bract

A leaf at the base of a flower stalk in many plants.

Tendril

A special thread-like leaf (or stem) which either twines around or sticks to a support.

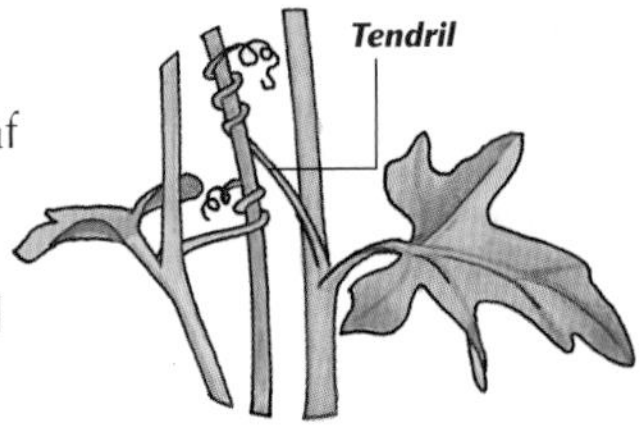

Spine

A specially modified leaf of a cactus. It has a reduced surface area to avoid losing much water.

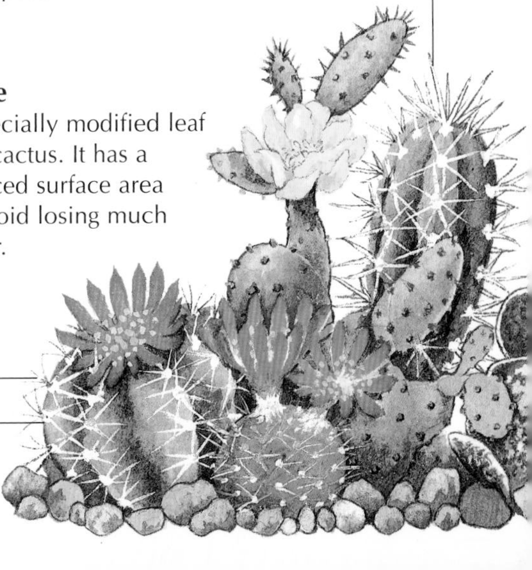

* **Axillary bud**, 244; **Chloroplasts**, 254; **Epidermis**, 243; **Hormones**, 336; **Transpiration**, 252; **Vascular tissue**, 242.

Types of compound leaf

Shown on this page are some types of **compound leaf** (leaves made up of **leaflets***), as well as some common leaf arrangements and leaf edges, or **margins**. The pictures are not to scale.

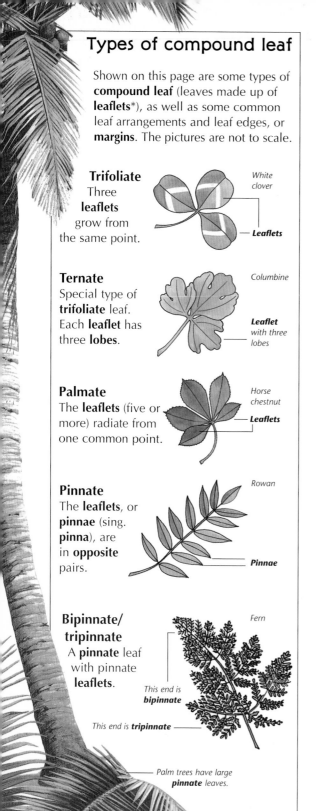

Trifoliate
Three **leaflets** grow from the same point.

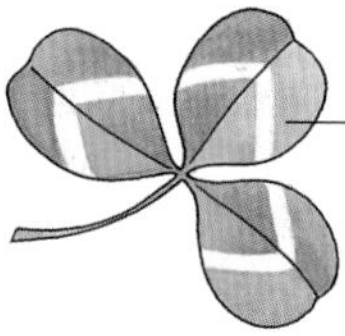

White clover
Leaflets

Ternate
Special type of **trifoliate** leaf. Each **leaflet** has three **lobes**.

Columbine
***Leaflet** with three lobes*

Palmate
The **leaflets** (five or more) radiate from one common point.

Horse chestnut
Leaflets

Pinnate
The **leaflets**, or **pinnae** (sing. **pinna**), are in **opposite** pairs.

Rowan
Pinnae

Bipinnate/ tripinnate
A **pinnate** leaf with pinnate **leaflets**.

Fern
*This end is **bipinnate***
*This end is **tripinnate***

*Palm trees have large **pinnate** leaves.*

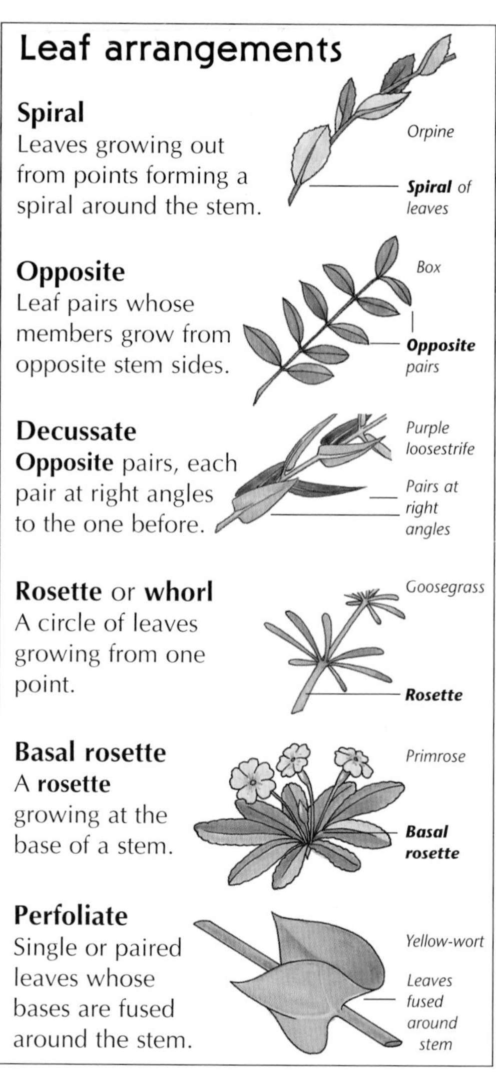

Orpine
Spiral of leaves
Box
Opposite pairs
Purple loosestrife
Pairs at right angles
Goosegrass
Rosette
Primrose
Basal rosette
Yellow-wort
Leaves fused around stem

Leaf arrangements

Spiral
Leaves growing out from points forming a spiral around the stem.

Opposite
Leaf pairs whose members grow from opposite stem sides.

Decussate
Opposite pairs, each pair at right angles to the one before.

Rosette or **whorl**
A circle of leaves growing from one point.

Basal rosette
A **rosette** growing at the base of a stem.

Perfoliate
Single or paired leaves whose bases are fused around the stem.

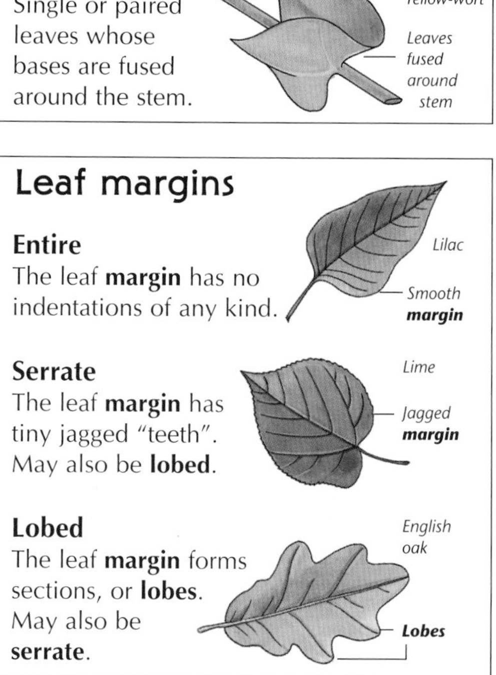

Lilac
Smooth margin
Lime
Jagged margin
English oak
Lobes

Leaf margins

Entire
The leaf **margin** has no indentations of any kind.

Serrate
The leaf **margin** has tiny jagged "teeth". May also be **lobed**.

Lobed
The leaf **margin** forms sections, or **lobes**. May also be **serrate**.

* **Leaflets**, 248.

PLANT SENSITIVITY

Plants have no nervous system, but they do still show **sensitivity**, i.e. they react to certain forms of stimulation. They do this by moving specific parts or by growing. This is called **tropism. Positive tropism** is movement or growth toward the stimulus and **negative tropism** is movement or growth away from it.

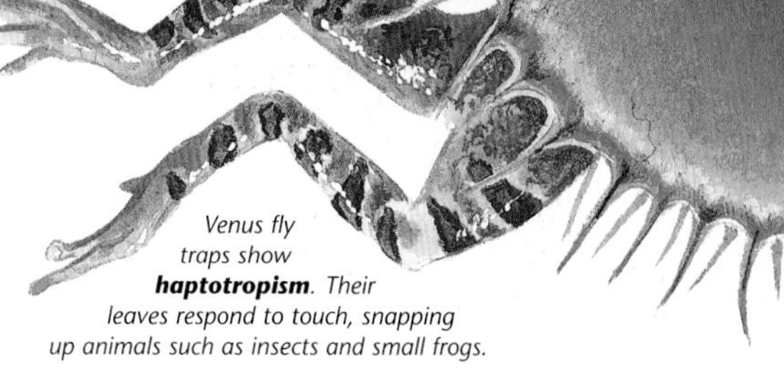

*Venus fly traps show **haptotropism**. Their leaves respond to touch, snapping up animals such as insects and small frogs.*

Hydrotropism
Response to water. For example, some roots may grow out sideways if there is more water in that direction.

Geotropism
Response to the pull of gravity. This is shown by all roots, i.e. they all grow down through the soil.

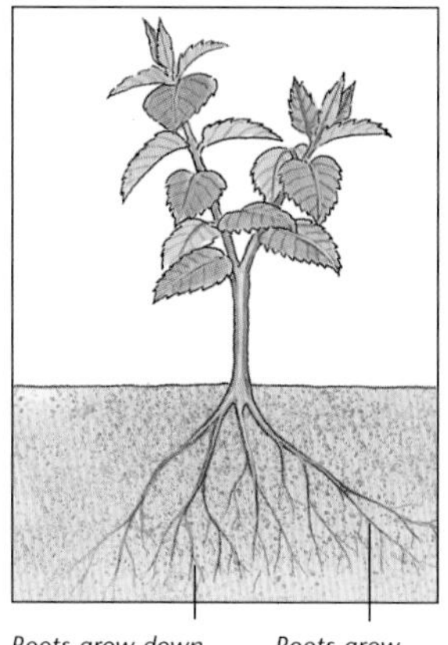

Roots grow down in response to gravity.

Roots grow toward water.

Phototropism
Response to light. When the light is sunlight, the response is called **heliotropism**. Most leaves and stems show this by curving around to grow toward the light.

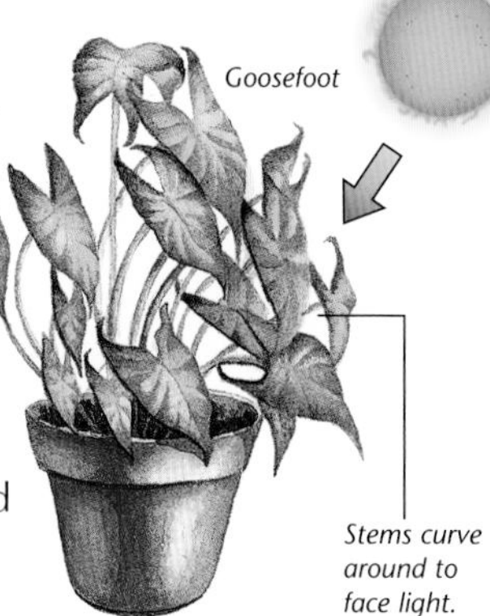
Goosefoot

Stems curve around to face light.

Haptotropism or **thigmotropism**
Response to touch or contact. For example, the sticky hairs of a sundew plant curl around an insect when it comes into contact with them.

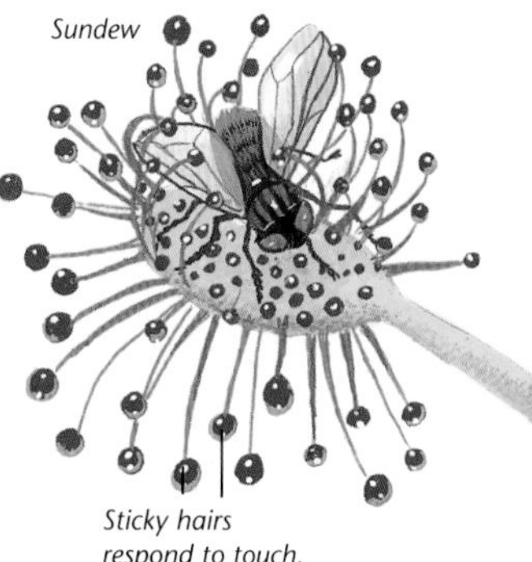
Sundew

Sticky hairs respond to touch.

Photoperiodism
The response of plants to the length of day or night (**photoperiods**), especially with regard to the production of flowers. It depends on a number of things, e.g. the plant's age and the temperature of its environment. **Long-night plants** only produce flowers if the night is longer than a certain length (called its **critical length**), **short-night plants** only if it is shorter. It is thought that a "message" to produce flowers is carried to the relevant area by a **hormone***, produced in the leaves when the conditions are right. This hormone has been called **florigen**. Some plants are **night-neutral plants**, i.e. their flowering does not depend on the length of night (see pictures, below).

*These three plants each produce flowers according to different **photoperiods**.*

*Chrysanthemum (**long-night plant**)*

*Larkspur (**short-night plant**)*

*Snapdragon (**night-neutral plant**)*

Growth hormones or **growth regulators**
Substances which promote and regulate plant growth. They are produced in **meristems*** (areas where cells are constantly dividing). **Auxins**, **cytokinins** and **gibberellins** are types of growth hormone.

* **Hormones**, 336; **Meristem**, 244.

PLANT FLUID TRANSPORTATION

The transportation of fluids in a plant is called **translocation**. The fluids travel within the **vascular tissue***, made up of **xylem*** and **phloem***. The xylem carries water (with dissolved minerals) from the roots to the leaves. The phloem carries food from the leaves to areas where it is needed.

Transpiration

The loss of water by evaporation, mainly through tiny holes called **stomata*** which are found on the underside of leaves.

Transpiration stream

A constant chain of events inside a plant. As the outer leaf cells lose water by **transpiration**, the concentration of minerals and sugars in their **vacuoles*** becomes higher than that of the cells further in. Water then passes outward by **osmosis***, causing more water to be "pulled" up through the tubes of the **xylem*** in the stem and roots (helped by **capillary action**). The roots then take in more water.

Capillary action

The way that fluids travel up narrow tubes (see also page 23). The molecules of the fluid are "pulled" upward by the attraction between them and the molecules of the tube.

Root pressure

A pressure which builds up in the roots of some plants. In all plants, water travels in from the soil and on through the layers of root cells by **osmosis***. In plants which develop root pressure, the pressure of this water movement is enough to force the water some way up into the tubes of the **xylem***. It is then "pulled" on upward by the **transpiration stream**. In other plants, the movement of water through root cells is all due to the "pull" of the transpiration stream.

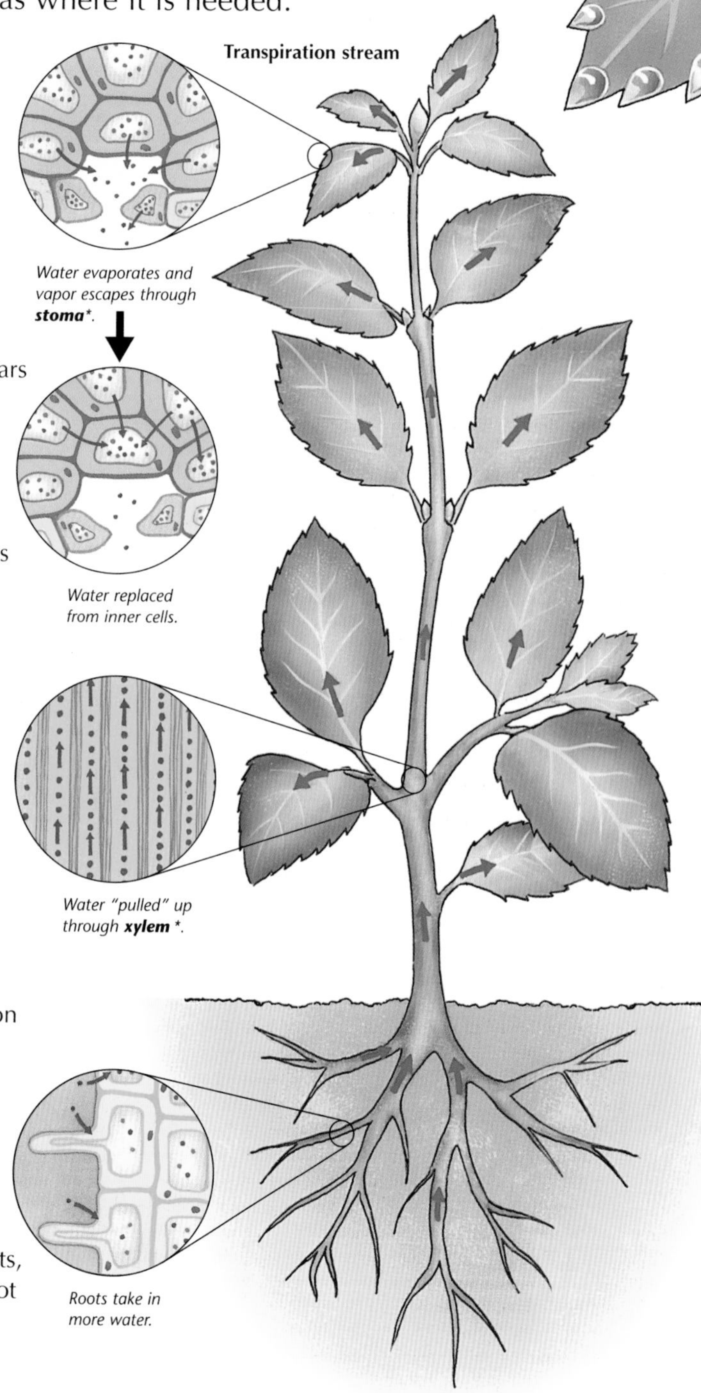

Transpiration stream
*Water evaporates and vapor escapes through **stoma***.*
Water replaced from inner cells.
*Water "pulled" up through **xylem***.*
Roots take in more water.

* **Osmosis**, 329; **Phloem**, 243; **Stomata**, 249; **Vacuoles**, 238; **Vascular tissue**, 242; **Xylem**, 243.

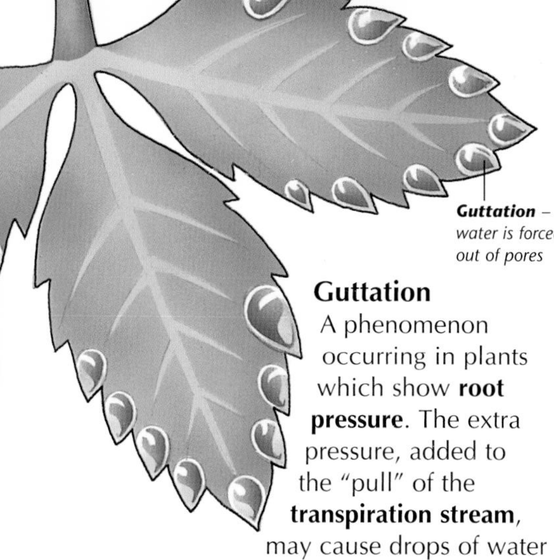
Guttation – water is forced out of pores

Guttation

A phenomenon occurring in plants which show **root pressure**. The extra pressure, added to the "pull" of the **transpiration stream**, may cause drops of water to be forced out of water-secreting areas of cells (**hydathodes**) via tiny pores at the tips or along the edges of the leaves.

Turgor

Healthy plant

The state of the cells in a healthy plant when its cells can take in no more water. Each cell is then said to be **turgid**. This means that water has passed by **osmosis*** into the **cell sap*** (dissolved minerals and sugars) in the cell's large central **vacuole***, and the vacuole has pushed as far out as it can go. The vacuole can push out no further because its outward pressure (called **turgor pressure**) is equalled by the opposing force of the rigid **cell wall*** (**wall pressure**). Turgid cells are important because they enable a plant to stand firm and upright.

Turgor

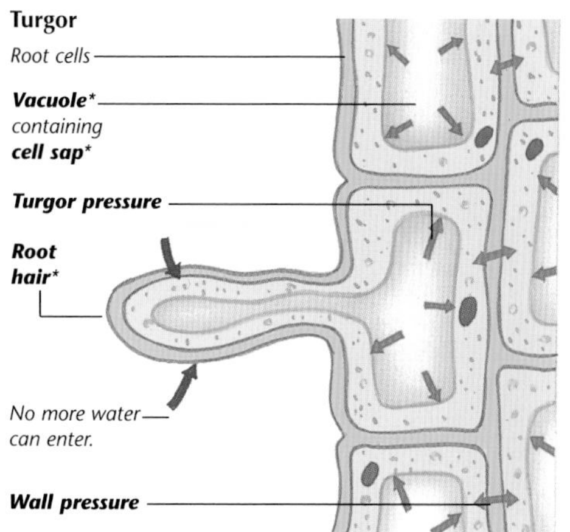
Root cells
Vacuole* containing **cell sap***
Turgor pressure
Root hair*
No more water can enter.
Wall pressure

Wilting

Wilting plant

A state of drooping, found in a plant subjected to certain conditions, such as excess heat. The plant is losing more water (by **transpiration**) than it can take in, and the **turgor pressure** (see **turgor**) of its cell **vacuoles*** drops. The cells become limp and can no longer support the plant, so it will droop.

Wilting

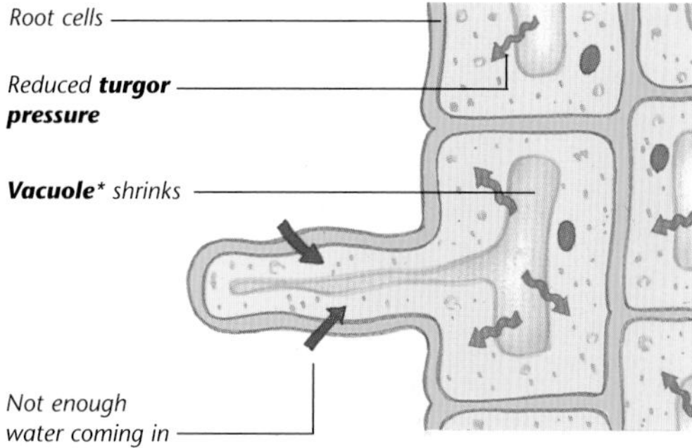
Root cells
Reduced **turgor pressure**
Vacuole* shrinks
Not enough water coming in

Plasmolysis

Dying plant

An extreme state in a plant, which may cause it to die. Such a plant is losing a large amount of water, often not only by **transpiration** in excess heat (see **wilting**), but also by **osmosis*** into very dry soil or soil with a very high concentration of minerals. The **vacuoles*** of the plant cells then shrink so much that they pull the **cytoplasm*** away from the **cell walls***.

Plasmolysis

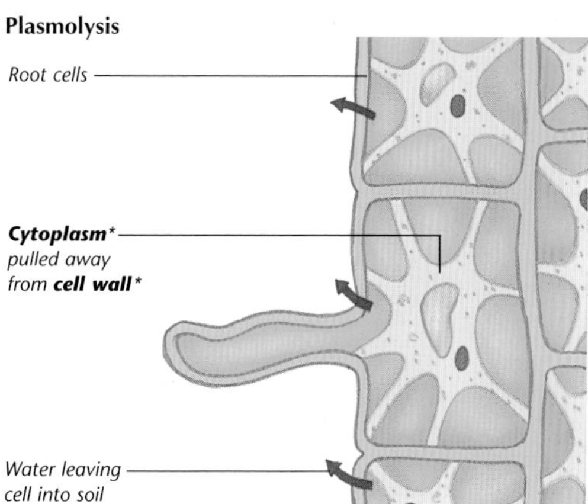
Root cells
Cytoplasm* pulled away from **cell wall***
Water leaving cell into soil

* **Cell sap**, 238 (**Vacuoles**); **Cell wall**, **Cytoplasm**, 238; **Osmosis**, 329; **Root hairs**, 245.

PLANT FOOD PRODUCTION

*Plants need water and carbon dioxide for **photosynthesis**. Lianas have extremely long, twisting stems which carry water to their leaves, where photosynthesis takes place.*

Most plants have the ability to make the food they need for growth and energy (unlike animals, which must take it in). The manufacturing process by which they make their complex food substances from other, simpler substances is called **photosynthesis**.

Photosynthesis

The series of chemical reactions (for basic equation, see page 209) by which green plants make their food. It occurs mainly in the **palisade cells***. Carbon dioxide is combined with water, using energy taken in from sunlight by **chloroplasts**. This produces oxygen as well as the plant's food (see diagram, page 255).

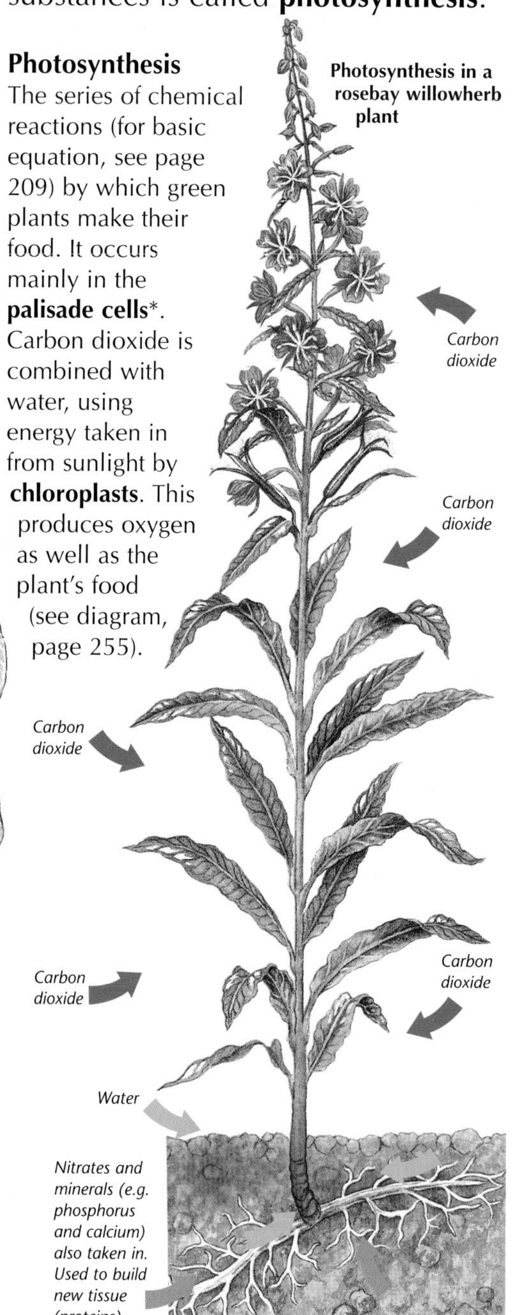
Photosynthesis in a rosebay willowherb plant
Carbon dioxide
Carbon dioxide
Carbon dioxide
Carbon dioxide
Carbon dioxide
Water
Nitrates and minerals (e.g. phosphorus and calcium) also taken in. Used to build new tissue (proteins).

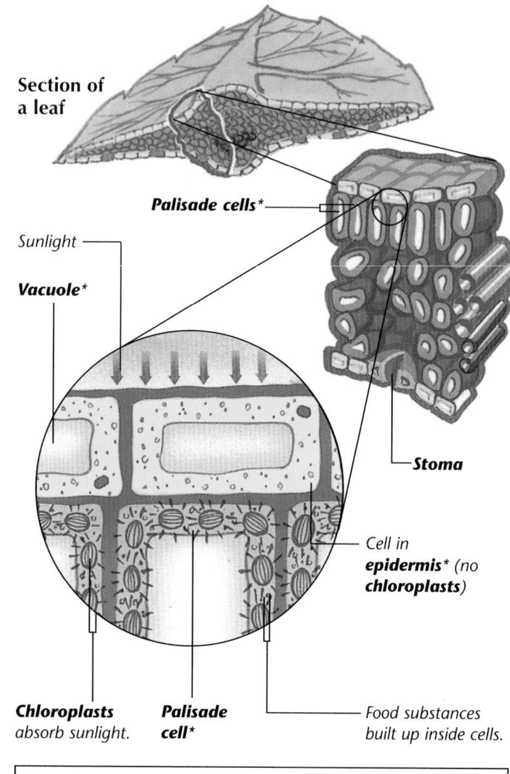
Section of a leaf
Palisade cells*
Sunlight
Vacuole*
Stoma
Cell in epidermis* (no chloroplasts)
Chloroplasts absorb sunlight.
Palisade cell*
Food substances built up inside cells.

Chloroplasts

Tiny bodies in plant cells (mainly in the leaves) which contain a green **pigment** called **chlorophyll**. This absorbs the Sun's light energy and uses it to "power" **photosynthesis**. Chloroplasts can move around inside a cell, according to light intensity and direction. See also page 240.

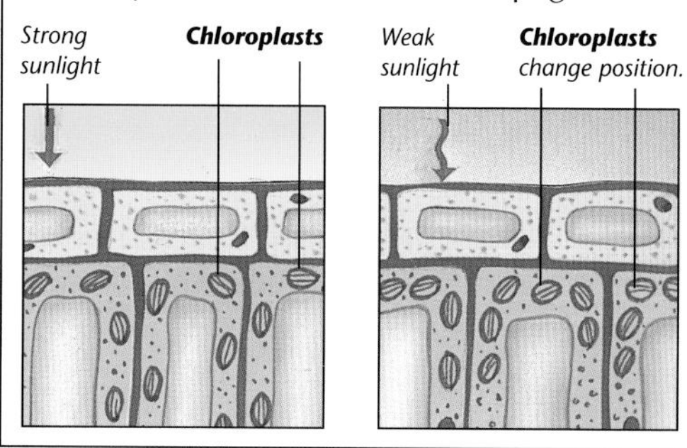
Strong sunlight
Chloroplasts
Weak sunlight
Chloroplasts change position.

* **Epidermis**, 243; **Internal respiration**, 334; **Palisade cells**, 248 (**Palisade layer**); **Vacuoles**, 238.

Products of photosynthesis

The process of photosynthesis works in co-ordination with that of **internal respiration***, the breakdown of food for energy. Photosynthesis produces oxygen and carbohydrates (needed for internal respiration), and internal respiration produces carbon dioxide and water (needed for photosynthesis).

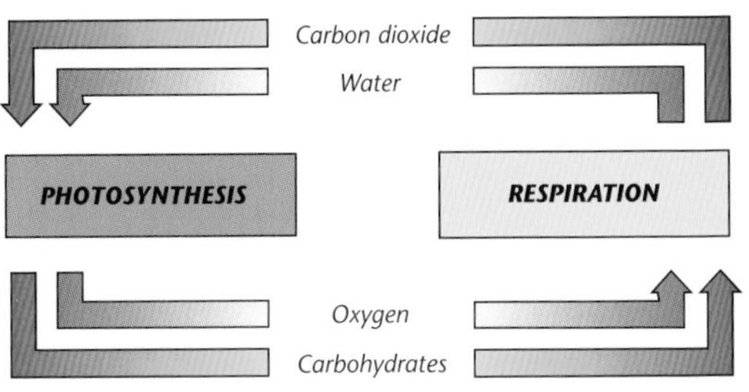

Carbon dioxide
Water
PHOTOSYNTHESIS
RESPIRATION
Oxygen
Carbohydrates

At most times, one of the two processes is occurring at a faster rate than the other. This means that excess amounts of its products are being produced, and not enough of the substances it needs are being made in the plant. In this case, extra amounts must be taken in and excess amounts given off or stored (see pictures 2 and 4 below).

Pigments

Substances which absorb light. White light is actually made up of a spectrum of many different colors. Each pigment absorbs some colors and reflects others.

Chlorophyll is a pigment found in all leaves. It absorbs blue, violet and red light, and reflects green light. This is why leaves look green.

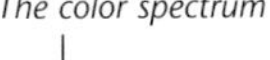

The color spectrum

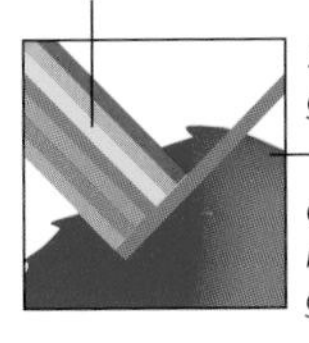

Surface of green leaf
Chlorophyll reflects green light.
The color spectrum
Surface of autumn leaf
Other pigments reflect other colors.

Other pigments, such as **xanthophyll**, **carotene** and **tannin** are also present in leaves. They reflect orange, yellow and red light, but are masked by chlorophyll during the growing season. In autumn, the chlorophyll breaks down, and so the autumn colors appear. Plant pigments are used to give color to many things, e.g. paints and plastics.

Autumn colors appear when **chlorophyll** breaks down.

Compensation points

Two points in a 24-hour period (normally around dawn and around dusk) when the processes of **photosynthesis** and **internal respiration*** (see above) are exactly balanced. Photosynthesis is producing just the right amounts of carbohydrates and oxygen for internal respiration, and this is producing just the right amounts of carbon dioxide and water for photosynthesis.

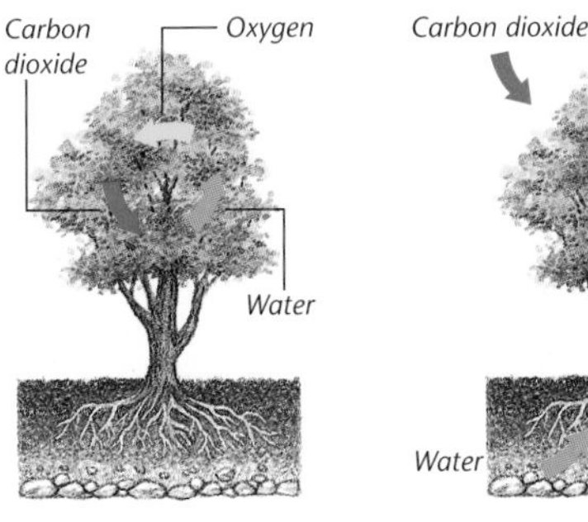

Carbon dioxide
Oxygen
Water

*1. Around dawn (**compensation point**)*

Carbon dioxide
Oxygen
Water

*2. Midday (bright light, so faster **photosynthesis**)*

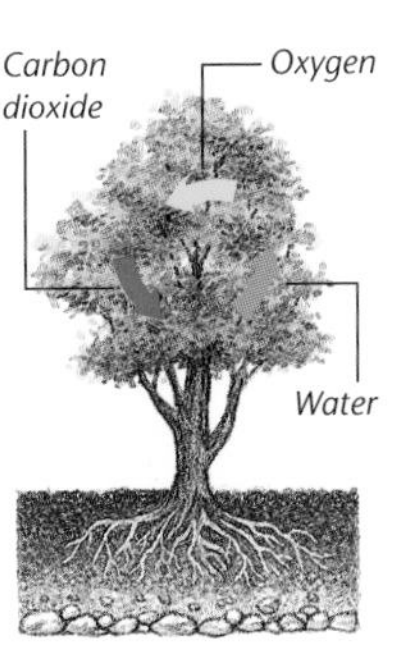

Carbon dioxide
Oxygen
Water

*3. Around dusk (**compensation point**)*

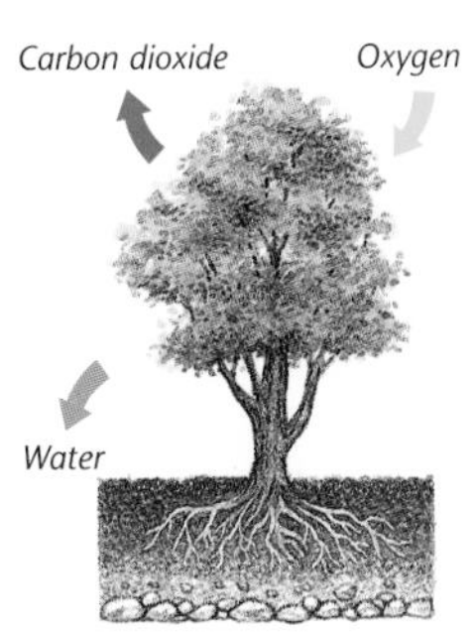

Carbon dioxide
Oxygen
Water

*4. Midnight (no light, so no **photosynthesis**)*

* **Internal respiration**, 334.

FLOWERS

The **flowers** of a plant contain its organs of **reproduction*** (producing new life). In **hermaphrodite** plants, e.g. buttercups and poppies, each flower has both male and female organs. **Monoecious** plants, e.g. corn, have two types of flowers on one plant – **staminate** flowers, which have just male organs, and **pistillate** flowers, which have just female organs. **Dioecious** plants, e.g. holly, have staminate flowers on one plant and pistillate flowers on a separate plant.

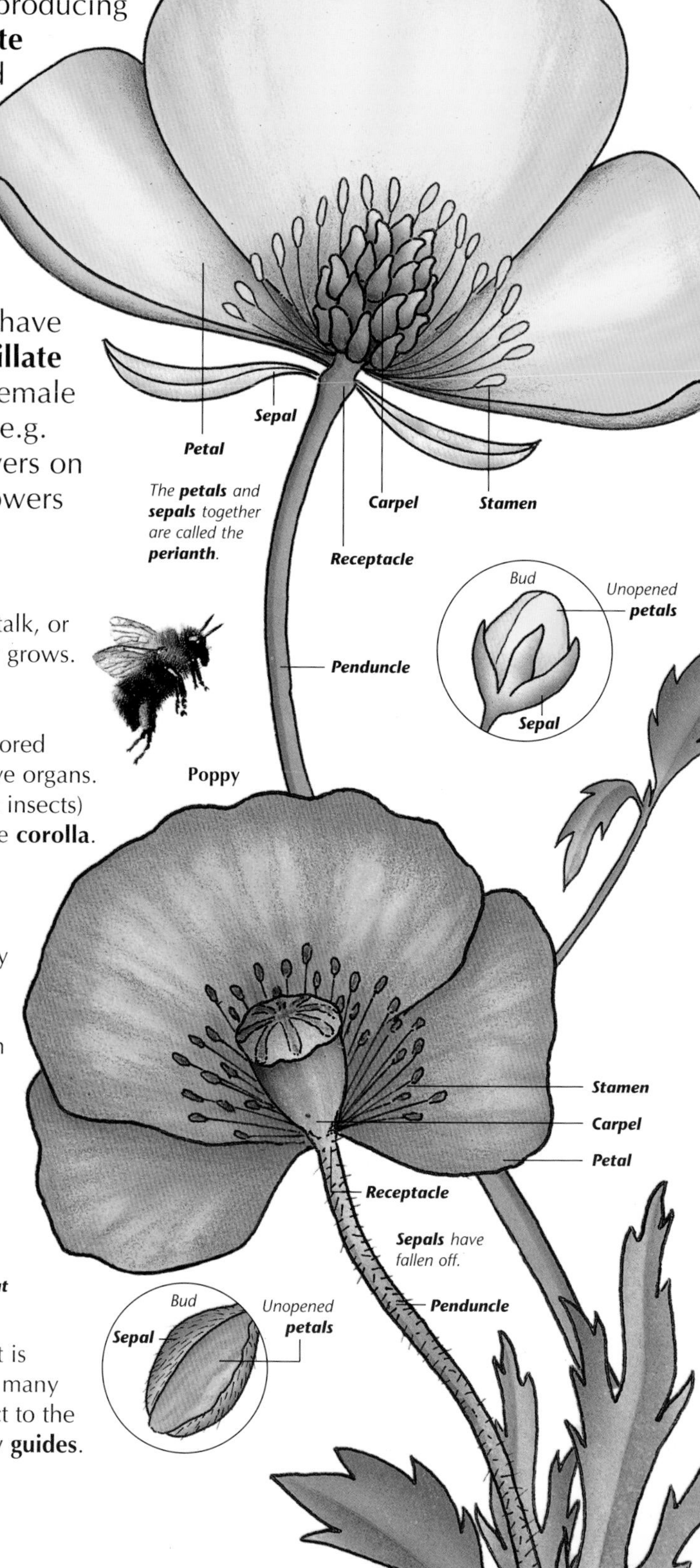

Buttercup
Sepal
Petal
*The **petals** and **sepals** together are called the **perianth**.*
Carpel
Stamen
Receptacle
Bud
Unopened petals
Sepal
Pendunce
Poppy
Stamen
Carpel
Petal
Receptacle
Sepals have fallen off.
Pendunce
Bud
Sepal
Unopened petals
Nectar held at base of petal

Receptacle

The expanded tip of the flower stalk, or **peduncle**, from which the flower grows.

Petals

The delicate, usually brightly colored structures around the reproductive organs. They are often scented (to attract insects) and are known collectively as the **corolla**.

Sepals

The small, leaf-like structures around a bud, known collectively as the **calyx**. In some flowers, e.g. buttercups, they remain as a ring around the opened **petals**; in others, e.g. poppies, they wither and fall off.

Nectaries

Areas of cells at the base of the **petals** which produce a sugary liquid called **nectar**. This attracts insects needed for **pollination***. It is thought that the dark lines down many petals are there to direct an insect to the nectar, and they are called **honey guides**.

* **Pollination**, **Reproduction**, 258.

The female organs

Carpel or **pistil**

A female reproductive organ, consisting of an **ovary**, **stigma** and **style**. Some flowers have only one carpel, others have several clustered together.

Ovaries

Female reproductive structures. Each is the main part of the **carpel** and contains one or more tiny bodies called **ovules***, each of which contains a female sex cell. An ovule is fixed by a stalk (**funicle**) to an area of the ovary's inside wall called the **placenta**. The stalk is attached to the ovule at a point called a **chalaza**.

Stigma

The uppermost part of a **carpel**, with a sticky surface to which grains of **pollen*** become attached during **pollination***.

Style

The part of a **carpel** which joins the **stigma** to the **ovary**. Many flowers have an obvious style, e.g. daffodils, but in others it is very short (e.g. buttercups) or almost non-existent (e.g. poppies).

Gynaecium

The whole female reproductive structure, made up of one or more **carpels**.

Buttercup carpels

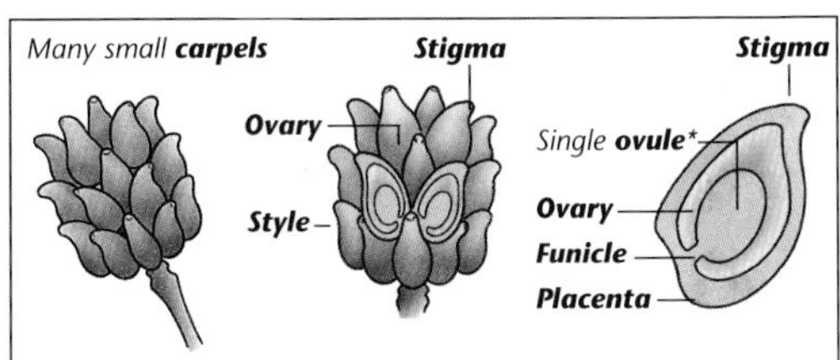
Many small ***carpels***
Stigma
Ovary
Style
Stigma
Single ovule*
Ovary
Funicle
Placenta

Poppy carpel

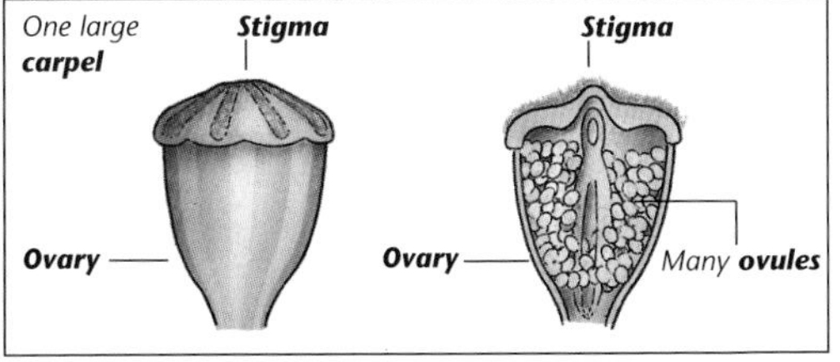
One large ***carpel***
Stigma
Ovary
Stigma
Ovary
Many ovules

* **Ovules**, **Pollen**, **Pollination**, 258.

The male organs

Stamens

The male reproductive organs. Each has a thin stalk, or **filament**, with an **anther** at the tip. Each anther is made up of **pollen sacs**, which contain grains of **pollen***.

Stamens

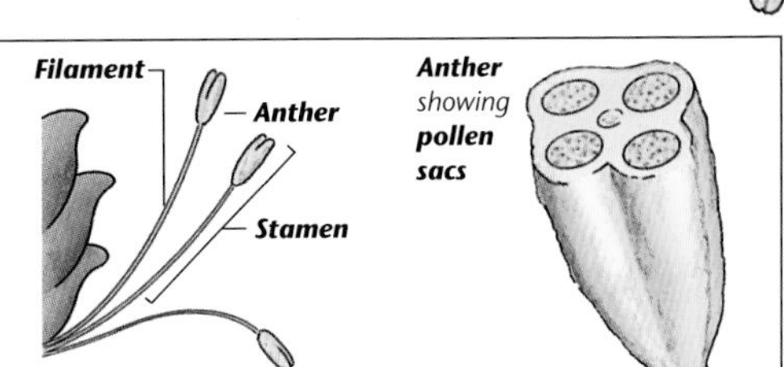
Filament
Anther
Stamen
Anther
showing
pollen
sacs

Androecium

A collective term for all the male parts of a flower, i.e. all the **stamens**.

How the parts are arranged

Hypogynous flower

The **carpel** (or carpels) sit on top of the **receptacle**; all the other parts grow out from around its base. The position of the carpel is described as **superior**.

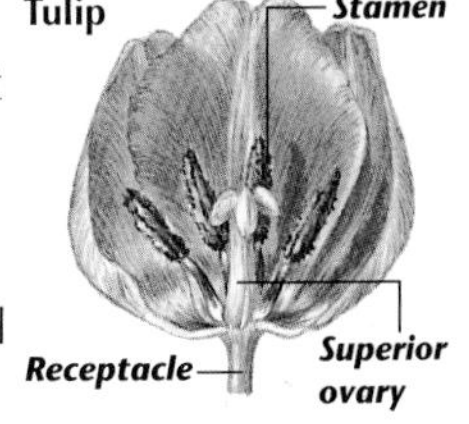
Tulip
Stamen
Receptacle
Superior ovary

Perigynous flower

The **carpel** (or carpels) rest in a cup-shaped **receptacle**; all the other parts grow out from around its rim. The position of the carpel is described as **superior**.

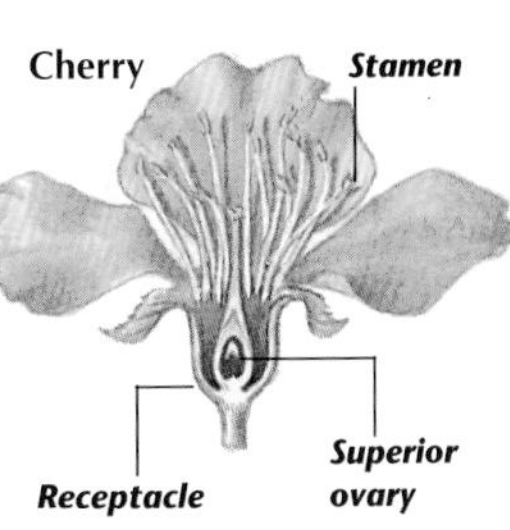
Cherry
Stamen
Receptacle
Superior ovary

Epigynous flower

The flower parts grow from the top of a **receptacle** which completely encloses the **ovary** (or ovaries), but not the **stigma** and **style**. The position of the ovary is described as **inferior**.

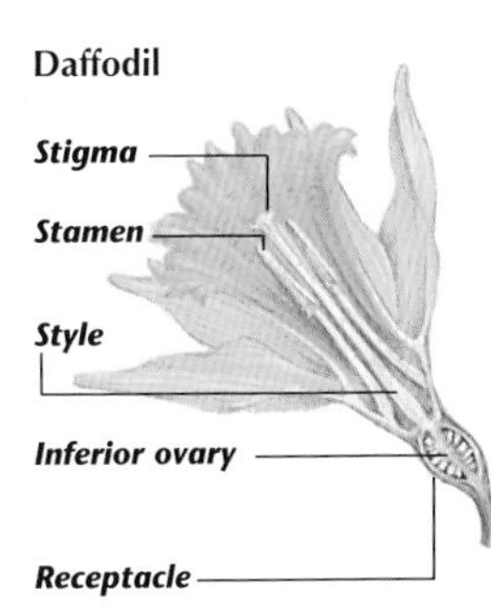
Daffodil
Stigma
Stamen
Style
Inferior ovary
Receptacle

REPRODUCTION IN A FLOWERING PLANT

Reproduction is the creation of new life. All flowering plants reproduce by **sexual reproduction***, when a male **gamete*** (sex cell) joins with a female gamete. In flowering plants, the male gametes (strictly speaking only male **nuclei***) are held in **pollen**, and the female gametes in **ovules**.

*Insects play a major part in the **cross pollination** of some plant species (see page 259).*

Pollen

Tiny grains formed by the **stamens*** (male parts) of flowers (see picture, right). Each grain is a special cell which has two **nuclei***. When a pollen grain lands on an **ovary*** (female body), one nucleus (the **generative nucleus**) divides into two, forming two **male nuclei** (reproductive bodies – see introduction).

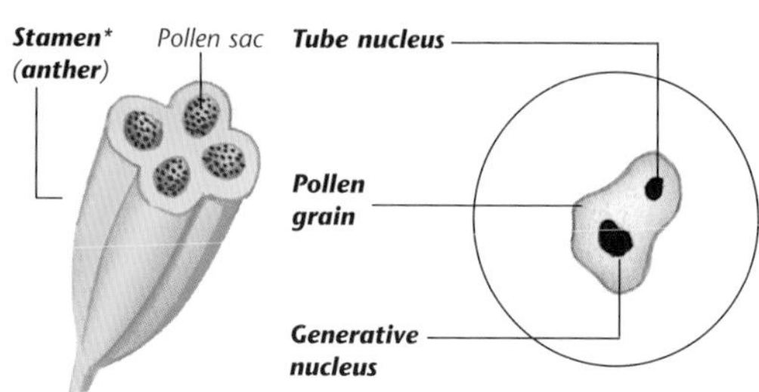

Stamen* (anther)
Pollen sac
Tube nucleus
Pollen grain
Generative nucleus

Ovules

The tiny structures inside a flower's female body, or **ovary***. They become seeds after **fertilization**. Each consists of an oval cell (the **embryo sac**), surrounded by layers of tissue called **integuments**, except at one point where there is a tiny hole (**micropyle**). Before fertilization, the embryo sac **nucleus*** undergoes several divisions (looked at in more detail on page 323 – under **gamete production, female**). This results in a number of new cells (some of which become part of the seed's food store), and two naked nuclei which fuse together. One of the new cells is the female **gamete*** (sex cell), or **egg cell**.

Pollination

The process by which a grain of **pollen** transfers its **male nuclei** (see **pollen**) into the **ovary*** of a flower. The grain lands on the **stigma***, and forms a **pollen tube**, under the control of the **tube nucleus** (the one which did not divide – see **pollen**). The tube grows down through the ovary tissue and enters an **ovule** via its **micropyle**. The two male nuclei then travel along it.

Fertilization

After **pollination**, one **male nucleus** (see **pollen**) fuses with the **egg cell** in the **ovule** to form a **zygote*** (the first cell of a new plant). The other joins with the two fused female nuclei to form a cell which develops into the **endosperm***.

Pollination in a poppy plant

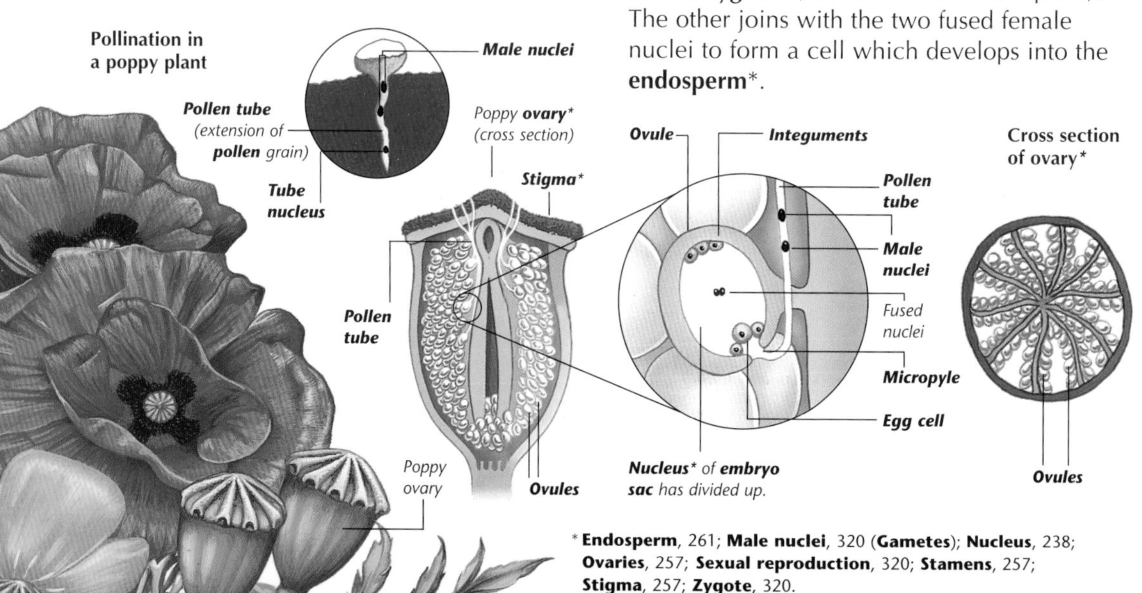

Male nuclei
Pollen tube (extension of pollen grain)
Tube nucleus
Poppy ovary* (cross section)
Stigma*
Pollen tube
Poppy ovary
Ovules
Ovule
Integuments
Pollen tube
Male nuclei
Fused nuclei
Micropyle
Egg cell
Nucleus* of embryo sac has divided up.
Cross section of ovary*
Ovules

* **Endosperm**, 261; **Male nuclei**, 320 (**Gametes**); **Nucleus**, 238; **Ovaries**, 257; **Sexual reproduction**, 320; **Stamens**, 257; **Stigma**, 257; **Zygote**, 320.

Cross pollination

The **pollination** of one plant by **pollen** grains from another plant of the same type. (If the grains land on a different type of plant, they do not develop further, i.e. they do not produce **pollen tubes**.) The pollen may be carried by the wind, or by insects which drink the **nectar***.

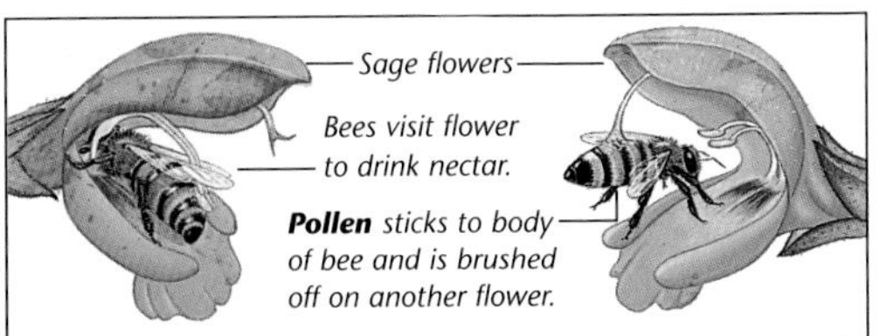
Sage flowers
Bees visit flower to drink nectar.
Pollen sticks to body of bee and is brushed off on another flower.

Self pollination

The **pollination** of a plant by its own **pollen** grains. For example, a bee orchid tries to attract male Eucera bees (for **cross pollination**) by looking and smelling like a female bee. But if it is not visited, its **stamens*** (male parts) bend over and transfer pollen to the **stigma*** of its **ovary*** (female body).

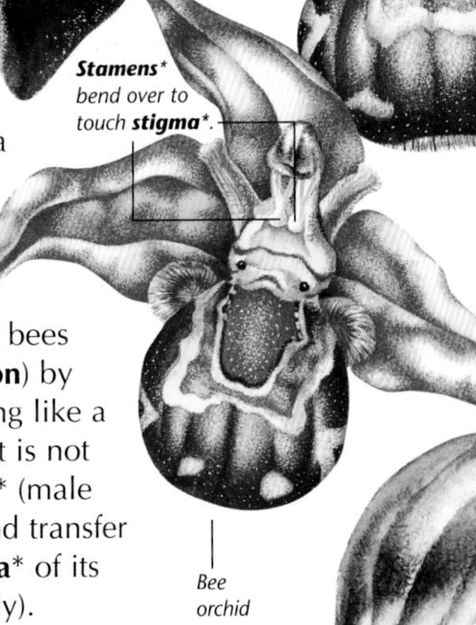
Stamens* bend over to touch **stigma***.
Bee orchid

Types and arrangements of flowers

Inflorescence

A group of flowers or **flowerheads** growing from one point.

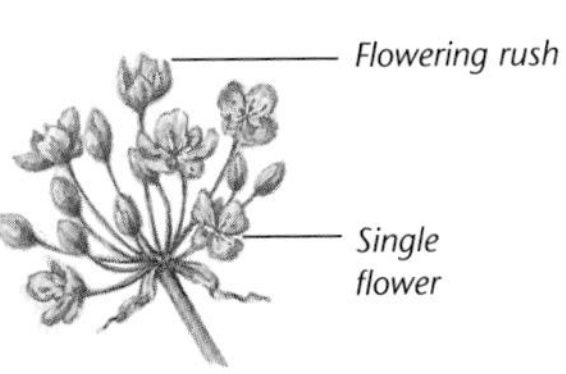
Flowering rush
Single flower

Flowerhead or composite flower

A cluster of tiny flowers, or **florets**.

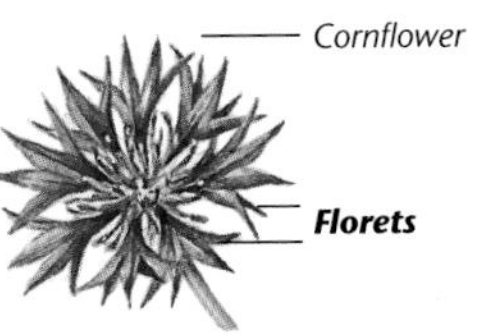
Cornflower
Florets

Umbellifer

An **inflorescence** with umbrella-shaped **flowerheads** (**umbels**).

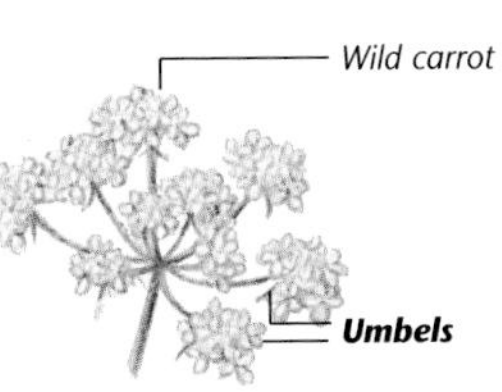
Wild carrot
Umbels

Ray florets

Florets with one long petal.

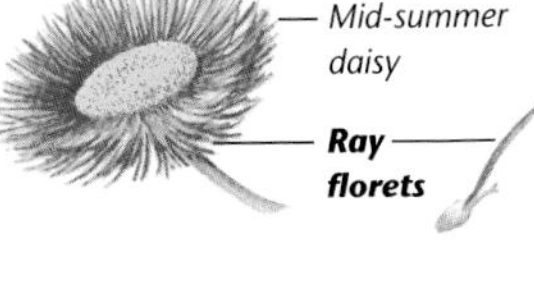
Mid-summer daisy
Ray florets

Disc florets

Florets whose petals are all the same size.

Corn marigold
Disc florets

Bell flower

Also called a **tubular** or **campanulate flower**. Its petals are joined to make a bell shape.

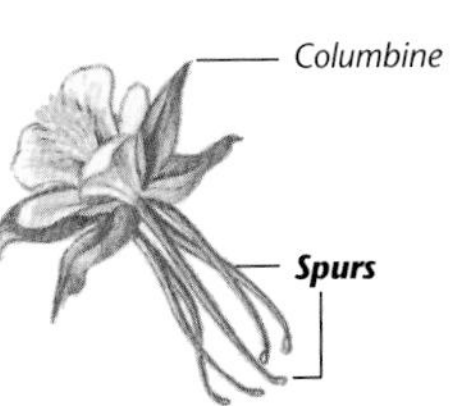
Nettle-leaved bellflower
Bell flower

Spurred flower

A flower with one or more petals extended backward to form **spurs**.

Columbine
Spurs

Lipped flower

A flower with two "lips" – an upper and lower one. The upper one often has a hood.

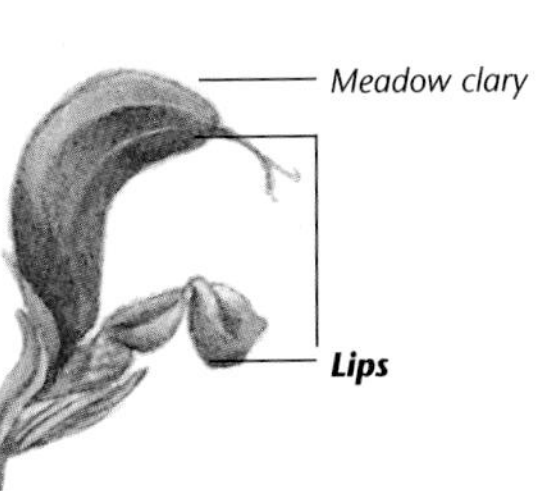
Meadow clary
Lips

Pea flower

A flower with an upper petal (the **standard**), two side petals (**wing petals**) and two lower petals forming the **keel** (which encloses the reproductive parts).

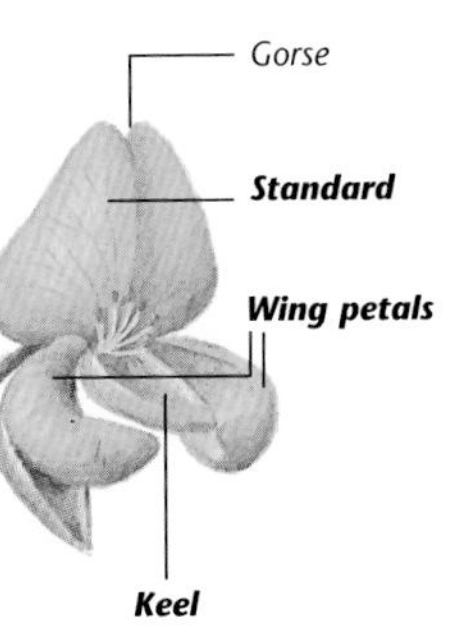
Gorse
Standard
Wing petals
Keel

* **Nectar**, 256 (**Nectaries**); **Ovaries**, 257; **Stamens**, 257; **Stigma**, 257.

SEEDS AND GERMINATION

After **fertilization*** in a flowering plant, an **ovule*** develops into a **seed**. This contains an **embryo**, i.e. a new developing plant, and a store of food. The **ovary*** ripens into a fruit, carrying the seed or seeds. You can find out more about different fruits on page 262.

Rowan berries are ***indehiscent*** *and are eaten by birds.*

Dispersal or dissemination

The shedding of ripe seeds from the fruit of a parent plant. This happens in one of two main ways, depending on whether a fruit is **dehiscent** or **indehiscent**.

Dehiscent

A word describing a fruit from which the seeds are expelled before the fruit itself disintegrates. For example, a poppy capsule has holes in it, and the seeds are shaken out by the wind. Other fruits, e.g. pea pods, open spontaneously and "shoot" the seeds out. In many cases, the seeds may then be carried by wind, water or other means.

Pea pods burst open.

Poppy capsule

Seeds are shaken out.

Seeds

Indehiscent

A word describing a fruit which becomes detached from the plant and disintegrates to free the seeds. For example, the "keys" of sycamores or the "parachutes" of dandelions are carried by the air, and hooked burrs catch on animal fur. The fruit then rots away in the ground to expose the seeds. Edible fruits may be eaten by animals, which then expel the seeds in their droppings.

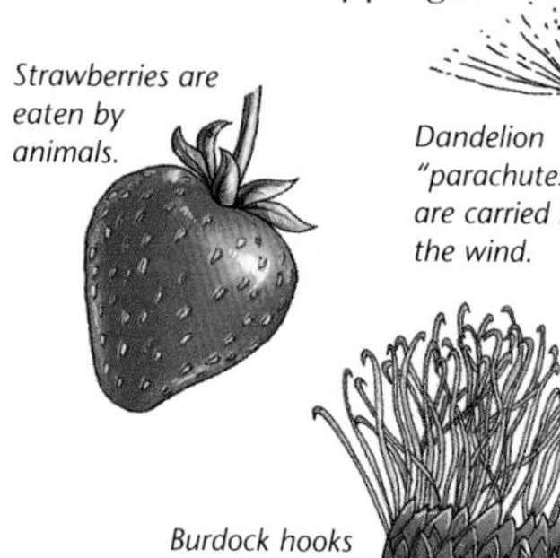

Strawberries are eaten by animals.

Dandelion "parachutes" are carried by the wind.

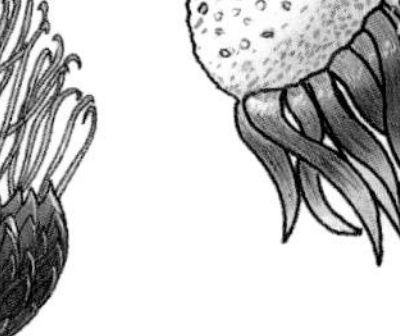

Burdock hooks catch on animals' fur.

Germination

When conditions are right, a seed will **germinate**. The **plumule** and **radicle** emerge from the seed coat, and begin to grow into the new plant, or **seedling**.

Plumule

Seed starting to ***germinate***

Testa

Radicle

Hypogeal

A type of **germination**, e.g. in pea plants, in which the **cotyledons** remain below the ground within the **testa**, and the **plumule** is the only part to come above the ground.

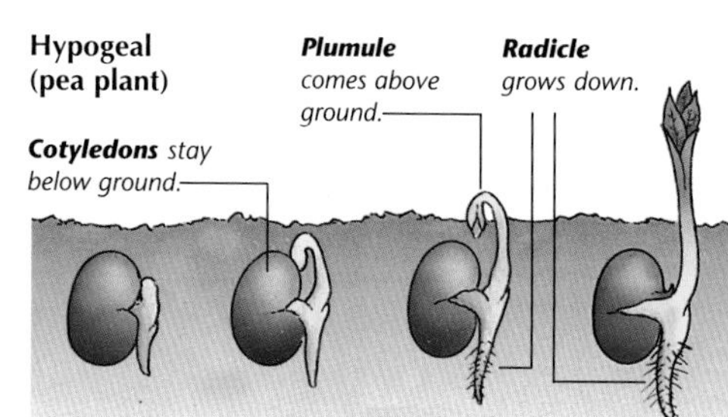
Hypogeal (pea plant)
Plumule *comes above ground.*
Radicle *grows down.*
Cotyledons *stay below ground.*

* **Fertilization**, 258; **Ovaries**, 257; **Ovules**, 258.

Parts of a seed

Hilum
A mark on a seed, showing where the **ovule*** was attached to the **ovary***.

Testa
The seed coat. It develops from the **integuments***.

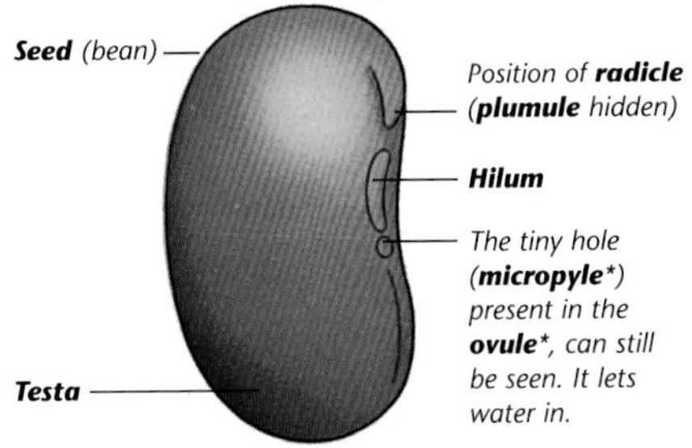

Seed *(bean)*
Position of ***radicle*** *(**plumule** hidden)*
Hilum
*The tiny hole (**micropyle***) present in the **ovule***, can still be seen. It lets water in.*
Testa

Plumule
The first bud, or **primary bud**, formed inside a seed. It will develop into the first shoot of the new plant.

Radicle
The first root, or **primary root**, of a new plant. It is formed inside a seed.

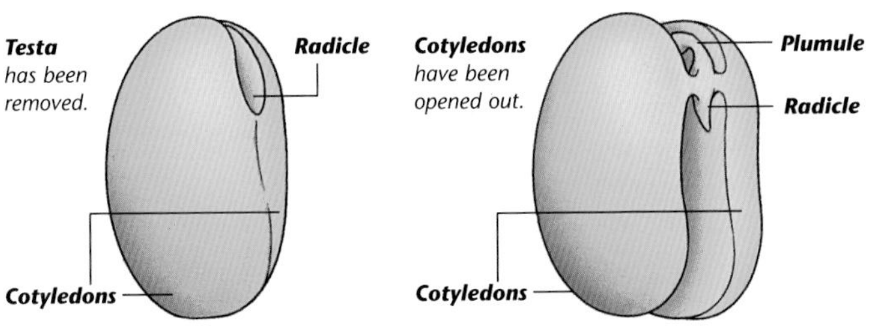

Testa *has been removed.*
Radicle
Cotyledons
Cotyledons *have been opened out.*
Plumule
Radicle
Cotyledons

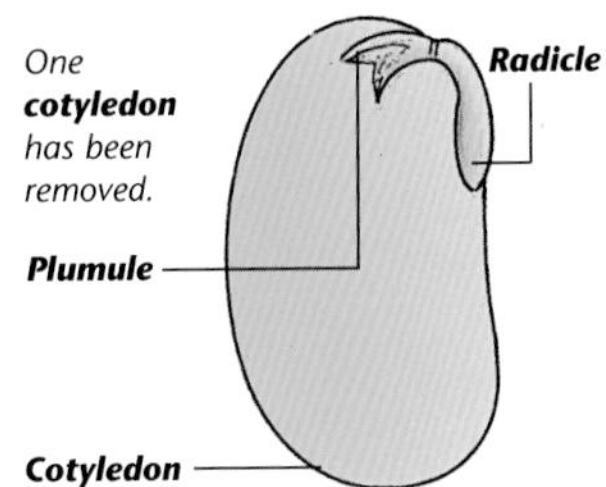

One ***cotyledon*** *has been removed.*
Radicle
Plumule
Cotyledon

Endosperm
A layer of tissue inside a seed which surrounds the developing plant and gives it nourishment. In some plants, e.g. pea, the **cotyledons** absorb and store all the endosperm before the seed is ripe; in others, e.g. grasses, it is not fully absorbed until after the seed **germinates**.

Cross section of a young bean

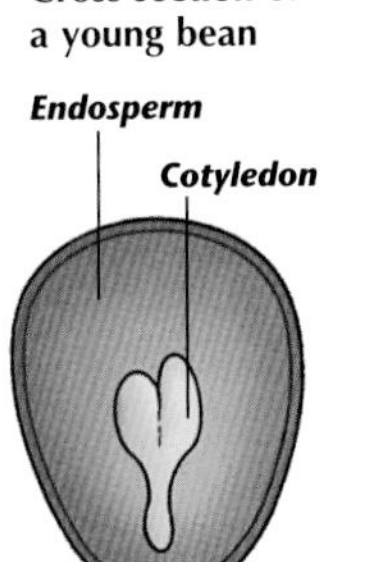

Endosperm
Cotyledon

Cross section of a mature bean

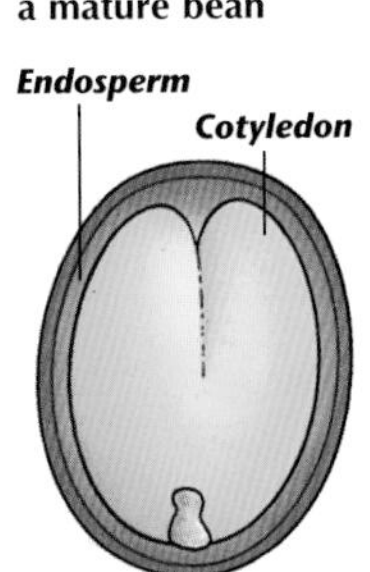

Endosperm
Cotyledon

Cotyledon or seed-leaf
A simple leaf which forms part of the developing plant. In some seeds, e.g. bean seeds, it absorbs and stores all the food from the **endosperm**. **Monocotyledons** are plants with one cotyledon, e.g. grasses; in **dicotyledons**, e.g. peas, there are two.

Epigeal
A type of **germination**, e.g. in bean plants, in which the **cotyledons** appear above the ground, below the first leaves – the true leaves.

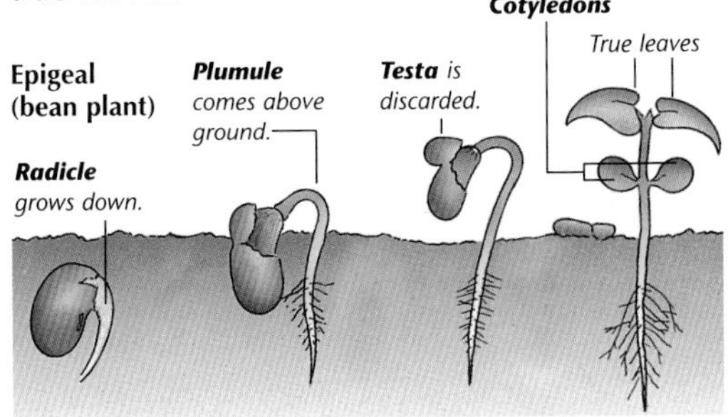

Epigeal (bean plant)
Radicle *grows down.*
Plumule *comes above ground.*
Testa *is discarded.*
Cotyledons
True leaves

Coleoptile
The first leaf of many **monocotyledons** (see **cotyledon**). It protects the first bud, and the first leaves emerge from it.

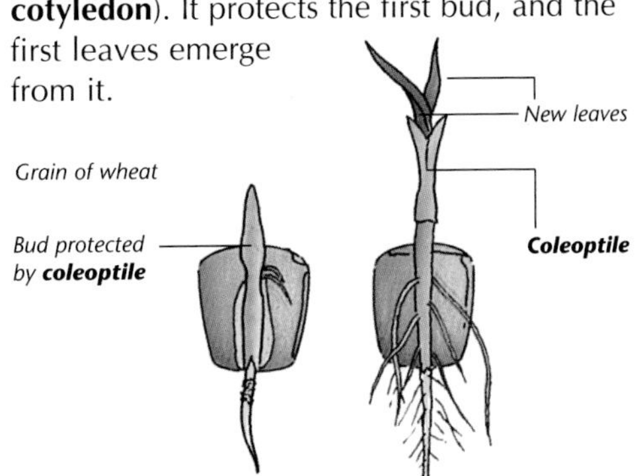

Grain of wheat
Bud protected by ***coleoptile***
New leaves
Coleoptile

* **Integuments**, **Micropyle**, 258 (**Ovules**); **Ovaries**, 257.

FRUIT

A **fruit** contains the seeds of a plant. **True fruit** develop purely from the **ovary***, **false fruit** develop from the **receptacle*** as well (e.g. a strawberry). The outer wall of a fruit is called the **pericarp**. In some fruits, it is divided into an outer skin, or **epicarp**, a fleshy part, or **mesocarp**, and an inner layer, or **endocarp**. Listed below are the main types of fruit.

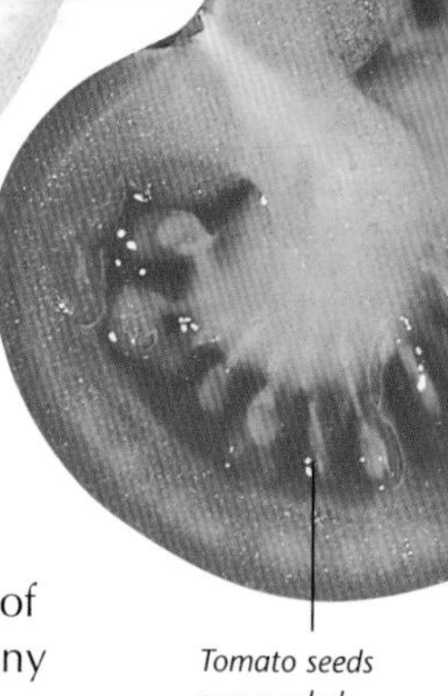
Grapefruit
Seed
Tomato seeds surrounded by juice

Berry
A fleshy fruit which contains many seeds, e.g. a tomato or a grapefruit. The "flesh" of citrus fruits is made up of tiny hairs, each one swollen up and full of juice.

Legume or **pod**
A fruit with seeds attached to its inside wall. It splits along its length to open, e.g. a pea.

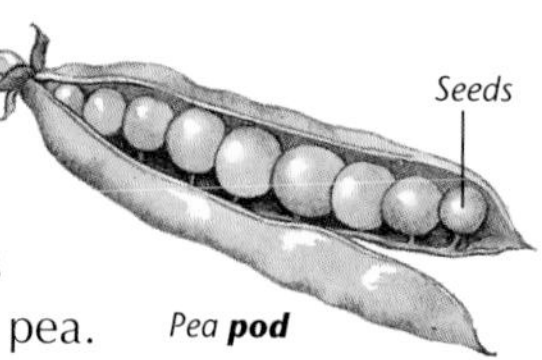
Seeds
Pea **pod**

Grain
Also called a **caryopsis** or **kernel**.
A small fruit whose wall has fused with the seed coat, e.g. wheat.

Grains of wheat

Nut
A dry fruit with a hard shell, which only contains one seed, e.g. a hazelnut or a walnut.

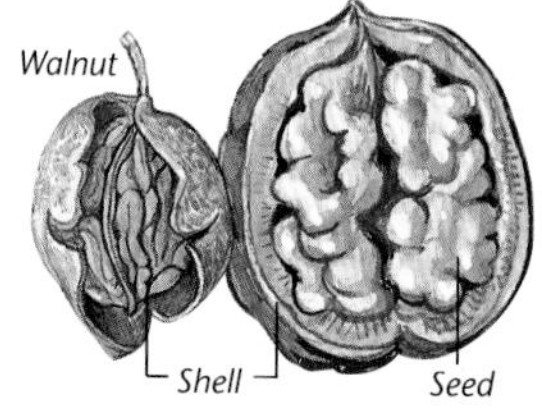
Walnut
Shell
Seed

Pome
A fruit with a thick, fleshy, outer layer and a core, with the seeds enclosed in a capsule, e.g. an apple. Pomes are examples of **false fruits** (see introduction).

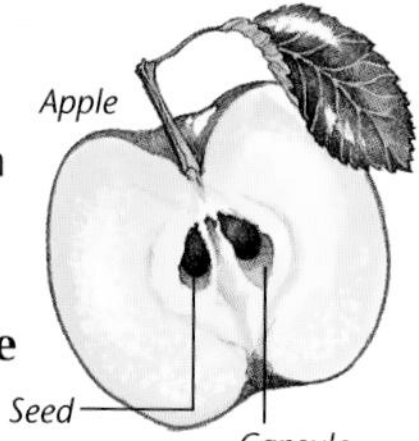
Apple
Seed
Capsule

Drupe
A fleshy fruit with a hard seed in the middle, often known as a "stone", e.g. a plum.

Plum
Seed or "stone"

Achene
A small, dry fruit, with only one seed, e.g. a sycamore or buttercup fruit. A "winged" achene like a sycamore fruit is a **samara** or **key fruit**.

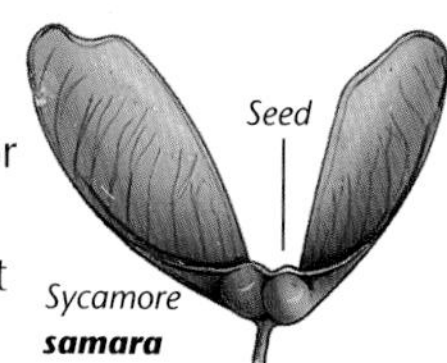
Seed
Sycamore **samara**

Artificial propagation

Artificial propagation is the commercial process, in agriculture and market gardening, which makes use of **vegetative reproduction** (see opposite). The fact that new plants need not always grow from seeds means that many more plants can be produced commercially than would occur naturally.

Plant cutting

Cutting
A process in which a piece of a plant stem (the cutting) is removed from its parent plant and planted in soil, where it grows into a new plant. In some cases, it is first left in water for a while to develop roots.

Taking a cutting

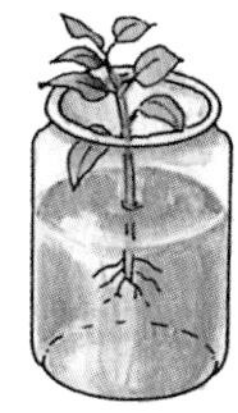
Cutting in water

Cutting replanted

* **Ovaries**, 257; **Receptacle**, 256.

VEGETATIVE REPRODUCTION

As well as producing seeds, some plants have developed a special type of **asexual reproduction***, called **vegetative reproduction** or **vegetative propagation**, in which one part of the plant is able to develop unaided into a new plant.

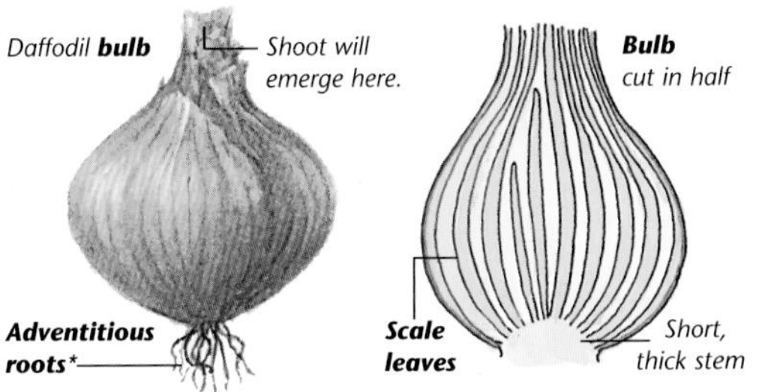
Daffodil bulb
Shoot will emerge here.
Bulb cut in half
Adventitious roots*
Scale leaves
Short, thick stem

Bulb
A short, thick stem surrounded by scaly leaves (**scale leaves**) which contain stored food material. It is formed underground by an old, dying plant, and represents the first, resting, stage of a new plant, which will emerge as a shoot at the start of the next growing season. E.g. a daffodil bulb (see picture above).

Corm
A short, thick stem, similar to a **bulb**, except that the food store is in the stem itself. E.g. a crocus corm.

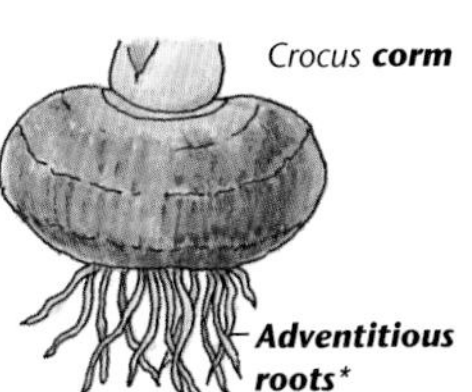
Crocus corm
Adventitious roots*

Rhizome
A thick stem, which has scaly leaves and grows horizontally underground. It produces roots along its length and also buds from which new shoots grow. Many grasses produce rhizomes, as well as other plants, e.g. mint and irises.

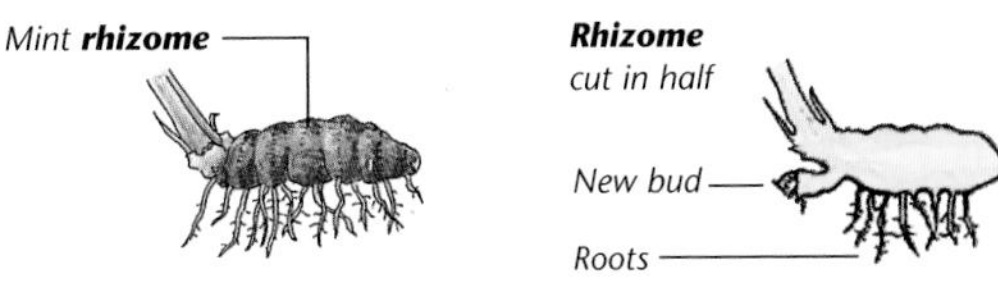
Mint rhizome
Rhizome cut in half
New bud
Roots

Stolon or runner
A stem which grows out horizontally near the base of some plants, e.g. the strawberry. The stolon puts down roots from points at intervals along this stem, and new plants grow at these points.

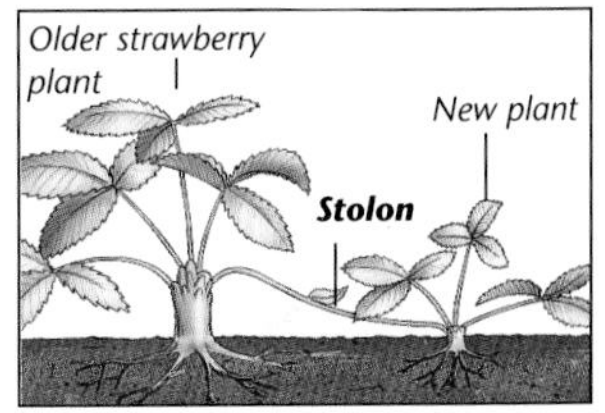
Older strawberry plant
New plant
Stolon

Tuber
A short, swollen, underground stem which contains stored food material and produces buds from which new plants will grow, e.g. a potato.

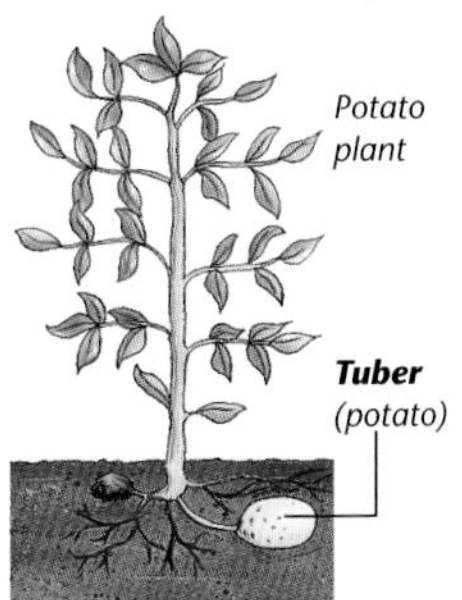
Potato plant
Tuber (potato)

Grafting
The process of removing a piece of a plant stem and re-attaching it elsewhere. The stem piece could be attached to a different part of the same plant (**autografting**), to another plant of the same species (**homografting**), or to a plant of a different species (**heterografting**). The piece removed is called the **scion**, and that to which it is attached is known as the **stock**.

Budding
A type of **grafting** where a bud and its adjacent stem are the parts grafted.

Grafting

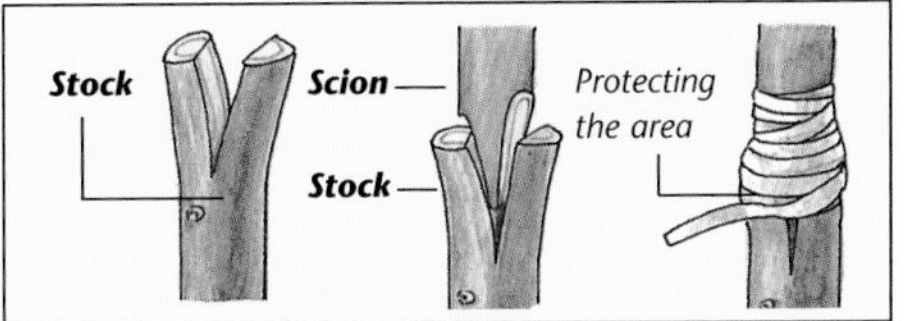
Stock
Scion
Stock
Protecting the area

Budding

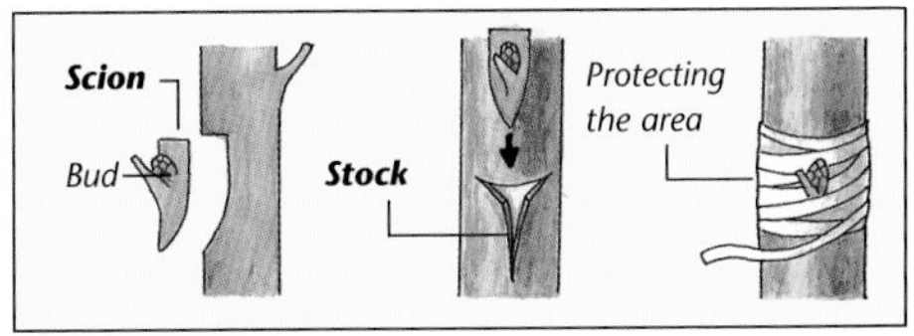
Scion
Bud
Stock
Protecting the area

* **Adventitious roots**, 245; **Asexual reproduction**, 321.

THE BODY STRUCTURE OF ANIMALS

Animals exist in a great variety of forms, from single-celled organisms to complex ones made of thousands of cells. The way they are **classified***, or divided into groups, depends to a large extent on how complex their bodies are. The two terms **higher animal** and **lower animal** are often used in this context. The higher an animal is, the more complex its internal organs are. In general, the distinguishing features of higher animals are **segmentation**, body cavities and some kind of skeleton.

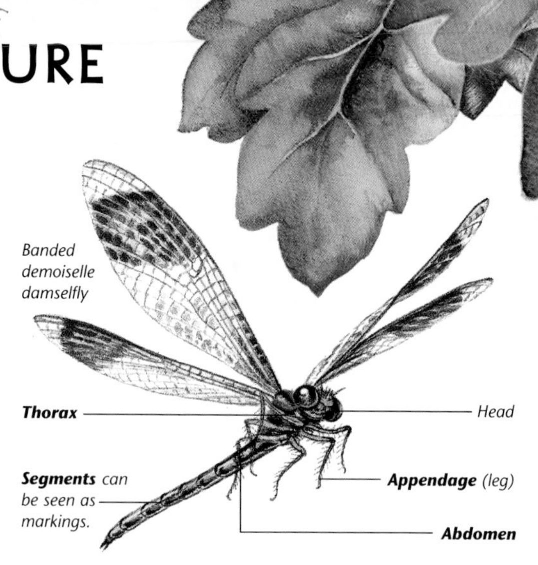

Banded demoiselle damselfly
Thorax
Head
Segments can be seen as markings.
Appendage (leg)
Abdomen

Segmentation

The division of a body into separate areas, or **segments**, a step up in complexity from a simple undivided body. Generally, the more complex the animal, the less obvious its segments are. The most primitive form of segmentation is **metameric segmentation**, or **metamerism**. The segments (**metameres**) are very similar, if not identical. Each contains more or less identical parts of the main internal systems, which join up through the internal walls separating the segments. Such segmentation is found in most worms, for example. More complex segmentation is less obvious. In insects, for example, the body has three main parts – the head, **thorax** (upper body region) and **abdomen** (lower body region). Each of these is in fact a group of segments, called a **tagma** (pl. **tagmata**), but the segments are not divided by internal walls. They are simply visible as external markings.

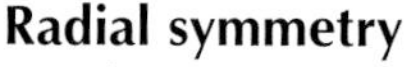

Metameric segmentation *in an earthworm*

Metamere

Appendage

A subordinate body part, i.e. one which projects from the body, such as an arm, leg, fin or wing.

Arrangement of the parts

Bilateral symmetry

An arrangement of body parts in which there is only one possible body division which will produce two mirror-image halves. It is typical of almost all freely-moving animals. The same state in flowers is called **zygomorphy** (e.g. in snapdragons).

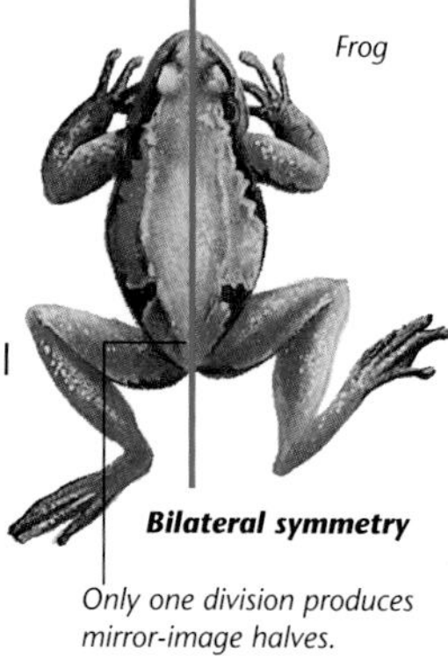

Frog
Bilateral symmetry

Only one division produces mirror-image halves.

Radial symmetry

A radiating arrangement of body parts around a central axis, e.g. in starfish. In such cases, there are two or more possible body divisions (sometimes in different planes) which will produce two mirror-image halves. The same state in flowers is called **actinomorphy** (e.g. in buttercups).

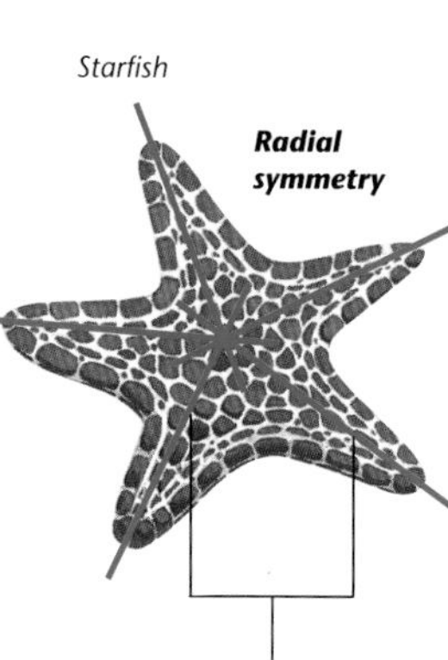

Starfish
Radial symmetry

Several different divisions produce mirror-image halves.

* **Classification**, 340.

Body cavities

Almost all many-celled animals have a main fluid-filled body cavity, or **perivisceral cavity**, to cushion the body organs (very complex animals, e.g. humans, may have other smaller cavities as well). Its exact nature varies, but in most animals it is either a **coelom** or a **hemocoel**. In soft-bodied animals it is vital in movement, providing an incompressible "bag" for their muscles to work against. Such a system is called a **hydrostatic skeleton**.

Simplified cut-away of a peanut worm
(Not all body organs are shown.)

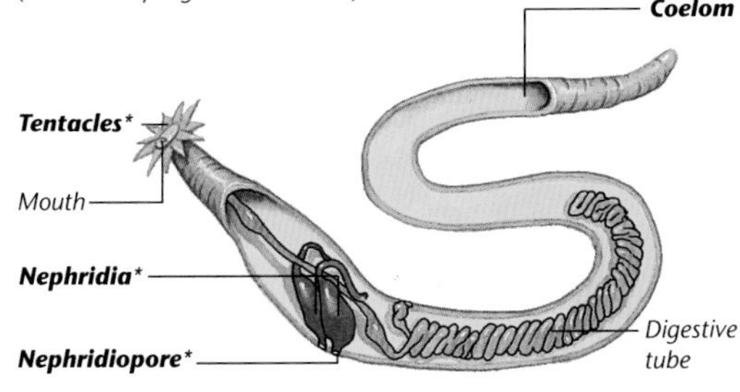
Coelom
Tentacles*
Mouth
Nephridia*
Nephridiopore*
Digestive tube

Coelom

The main body cavity (**perivisceral cavity**) of higher worms, **echinoderms***, e.g. starfish, and **vertebrates***, e.g. birds. It is fluid-filled to cushion the organs and is bounded by the **peritoneum**, a thin membrane which lines the body wall. In lower animals, e.g. many worms, the coelom assists in excretion. Their excretory organs, called **nephridia***, project into the coelom and remove fluid waste which has seeped into it. In higher animals, other more complex organs deal with these functions.

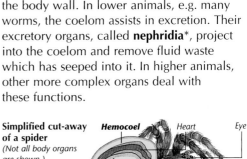

Simplified cut-away of a spider
(Not all body organs are shown.)

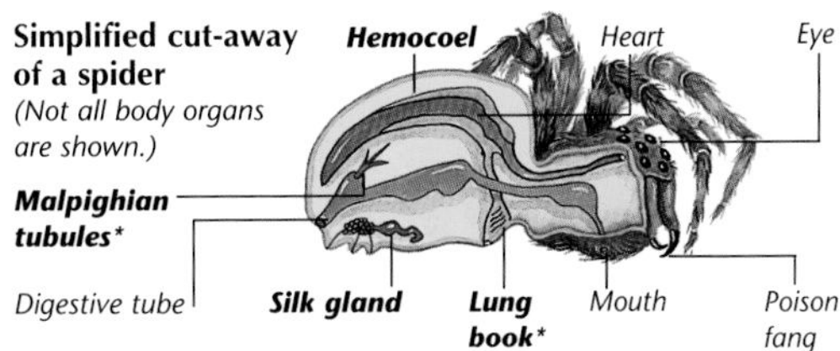
Hemocoel
Heart
Eye
Malpighian tubules*
Digestive tube
Silk gland
Lung book*
Mouth
Poison fang

Hemocoel

The fluid-filled main body cavity (**perivisceral cavity**) of **arthropods***, e.g. insects, and **molluscs***, e.g. snails. In molluscs, it is more of a spongy meshwork of tissue than a true cavity. Unlike a **coelom**, a hemocoel contains blood. It is an expanded part of the blood system, through which blood is circulated. In some animals, the hemocoel plays a part in excretion. In insects, for instance, water and fluid waste seep into it, and are then taken up by the **Malpighian tubules*** projecting into it.

Mantle cavity

A body cavity in shelled **molluscs***, e.g. snails. It lies between the **mantle** (a fold of skin lining the shell) and the rest of the body. Digestive and excretory wastes are passed into it, for removal from the body. In water-living molluscs, it also holds the **gills***; in land-living snails, it acts as a lung.

Simplified cut-away picture of a whelk
(Not all body organs are shown.)

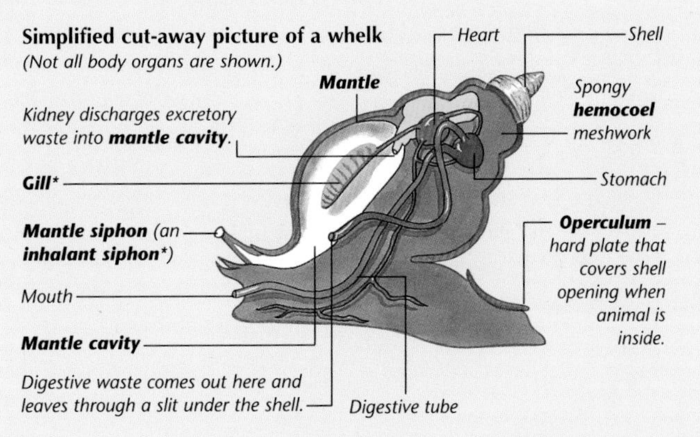
Heart
Shell
Mantle
Spongy hemocoel meshwork
Kidney discharges excretory waste into mantle cavity.
Gill*
Stomach
Mantle siphon (an inhalant siphon*)
Operculum – hard plate that covers shell opening when animal is inside.
Mouth
Mantle cavity
Digestive waste comes out here and leaves through a slit under the shell.
Digestive tube

* **Arthropods**, 341; **Echinoderms**, 341; **Gills**, 272; **Inhalant siphon**, 272 (**Siphon**); **Lung books**, **Malpighian tubules**, 273; **Molluscs**, 341; **Nephridiopore**, 273 (**Nephridia**); **Tentacles**, 274; **Vertebrates**, 341.

ANIMAL BODY COVERINGS

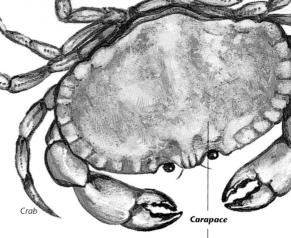

All animals have an enclosing outer layer, or "skin", normally with a further covering of some kind. In many cases, the skin has many layers, like human skin (see pages 310-311), and in most higher animals its covering is soft, e.g. hair, fur or feathers. Hard coverings, e.g. shells, are found in many lower animals and may form their only supporting framework, if they have no internal skeleton (**endoskeleton**). In such cases, the covering is called an **exoskeleton**. Some of the main body coverings are listed here.

Crab

Carapace

Tortoise

Carapace

The shield-like shell of a crab, tortoise or turtle. In tortoises and turtles, it consists of bony plates fused together under a horny skin, but in crabs, it is a hardened **cuticle**.

Cuticle

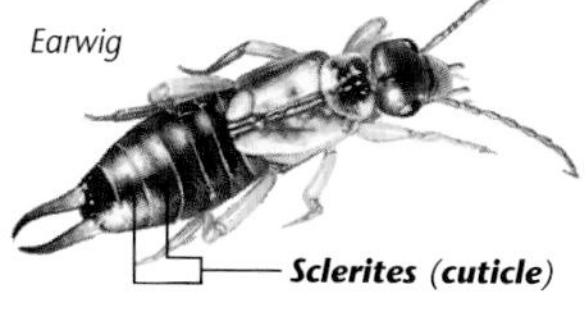
Earwig
Sclerites (cuticle)

A non-living, waterproof, outer layer in many animals, secreted by the skin. In most **arthropods***, it hardens to form a supportive outer skeleton, or **exoskeleton**, e.g. the shells of crabs and the tough outer "coat" of insects. The term cuticle is in fact most often used to describe this insect "coat". It consists of a sugar-based substance (**chitin**) and a tough protein (**sclerotin**). It is often made up of **sclerites** – separate pieces joined by flexible, narrow areas. In other animals, e.g. earthworms, the cuticle remains a soft, waxy covering. (The term cuticle is sometimes used to mean the **stratum corneum*** in humans.)

Denticles or placoid scales

Sharp, backward-pointing plates, covering the bodies of cartilaginous fish, e.g. rays. They are similar to teeth, and stick out from the skin, unlike **scales**.

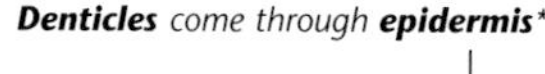
Denticles come through epidermis*.

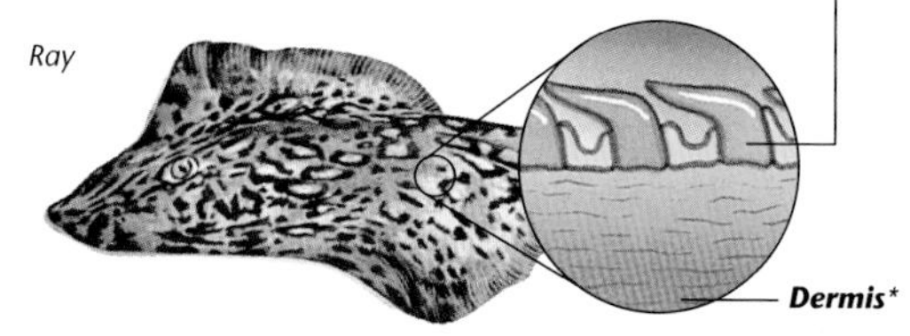
Ray
Dermis*

Scales

There are two different types of scales. Those of bony fish, e.g. carp, are small, often bony plates lying within the skin. Those covering the limbs or whole bodies of many **reptiles*** (e.g. the legs of turtles) are thickened areas of skin.

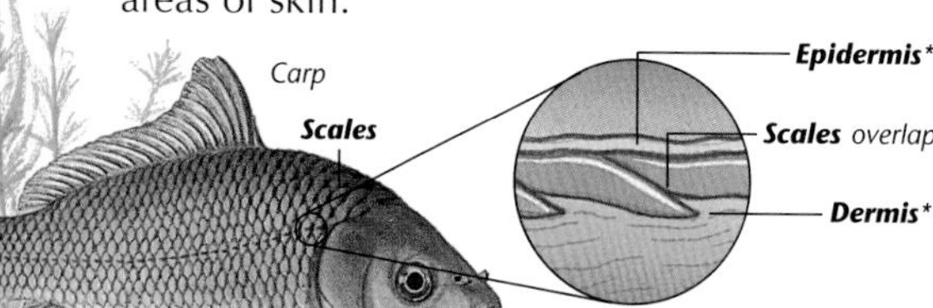
Carp
Scales
Epidermis*
Scales overlap
Dermis*

Elytra (sing. elytron)

The front pair of wings of beetles and some bugs. They are designed to form a tough cover for the back pair of wings, used for flying.

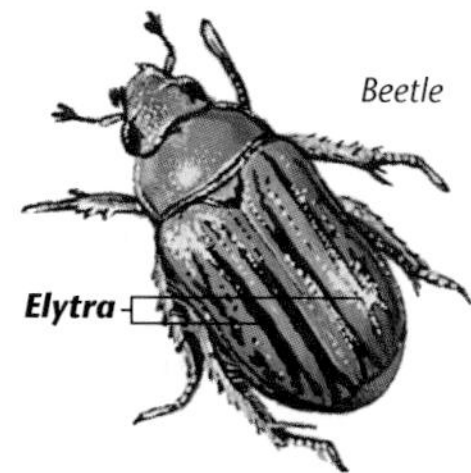
Beetle
Elytra

Scute or scutum (pl. scuta)

Any large, hard, external plate, especially those on the underside of a snake, used in movement.

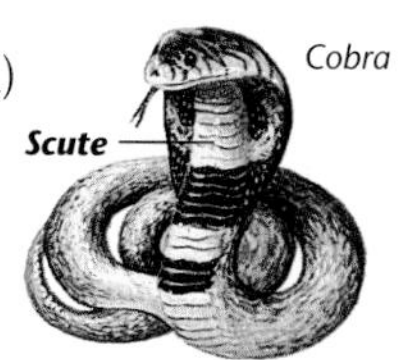
Cobra
Scute

* **Arthropods**, 341; **Dermis**, 310; **Epidermis**, 310; **Reptiles**, 341; **Stratum corneum**, 310.

Feathers

The insulating waterproof layer of a bird's body is made up of **feathers**, together known as its **plumage**. Each feather is a light structure made of a fibrous, horny substance called **keratin**. Each has a central **shaft** (or **rachis**) with thin filaments called **barbs**. The barbs of all **contour feathers**, i.e. all the feathers except the **down feathers**, have tiny filaments called **barbules**. Like body hairs, feathers have nerve endings attached to them, as well as muscles which can fluff them up to conserve heat (see **hair erector muscles**, page 311).

Northern parula warbler

Rectrices *(sing.* ***rectrix****) – tail feathers. They control changes of direction in flight.*

Uropygium *contains* ***uropygial gland****, which secretes an oily fluid used in preening.*

The feathers of the back, shoulders and wings are sometimes called the ***mantle****.*

Mandibles *– upper and lower beak parts*

Coverts *– feathers covering bases of wing and tail feathers*

Primaries *(furthest from the body) – make up end section of wing (****pinion****).*

Secondaries *(nearer the body)*

Birds' feet tend not to be covered in feathers, but are protected by small scales called ***scutella*** *(sing.* ***scutellum****).*

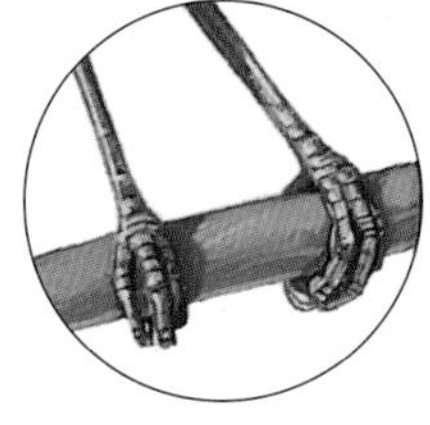

Remiges (sing. remix) or flight feathers

Those feathers of a bird's wings which are used in flight, consisting of the long, strong **primary feathers**, or **primaries**, and the shorter **secondary feathers**, or **secondaries**.

Down feathers or plumules

The fluffy, temporary feathers of all young birds, which have flexible **barbs**, but no true **barbules**. The adults of some types of bird keep some down feathers as an insulating layer close to the skin.

Feather follicles

Tiny pits in a bird's skin. Each one has a feather in it, just like a hair in a **hair follicle***. The cells at the base of the follicle grow up and out to form a feather, and then die away, leaving their hard, tough remains.

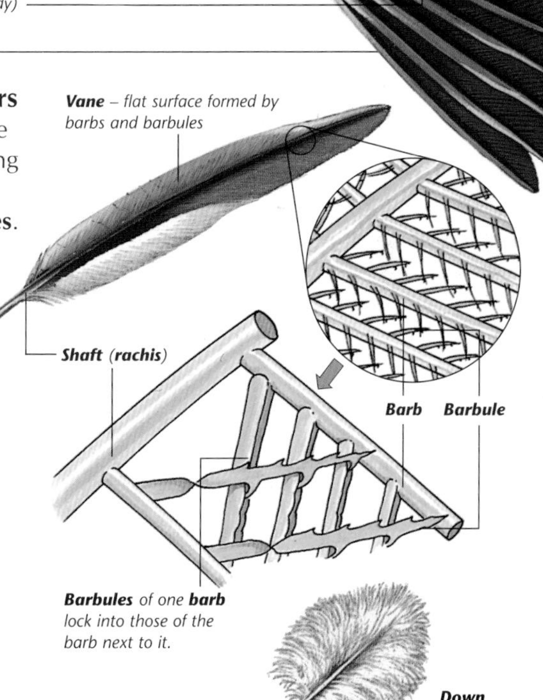
Vane – flat surface formed by barbs and barbules
Shaft (rachis)
Barb
Barbule
Barbules of one barb lock into those of the barb next to it.
Down feather

* **Hair follicles**, 311.

ANIMAL MOVEMENT

Most animals are capable of movement from place to place (**locomotion**) at least at some stage of their life (plants can only move individual parts – see **tropism**, page 251). The moving parts of animals vary greatly. Many animals have a system of bones and muscles similar to humans (see pages 278-283). Some of the parts used in animal movement are shown on these pages.

All fish use ***fins*** *to help them move from one place to another.*

Movement of simple animals

Pseudopodium (pl. pseudopodia)

An extension ("false foot") of the cell matter, or **cytoplasm***, of a single-celled organism. Such extensions are formed either in order for the organism to move or to enable it to engulf a food particle. The latter process is called **phagocytosis**.

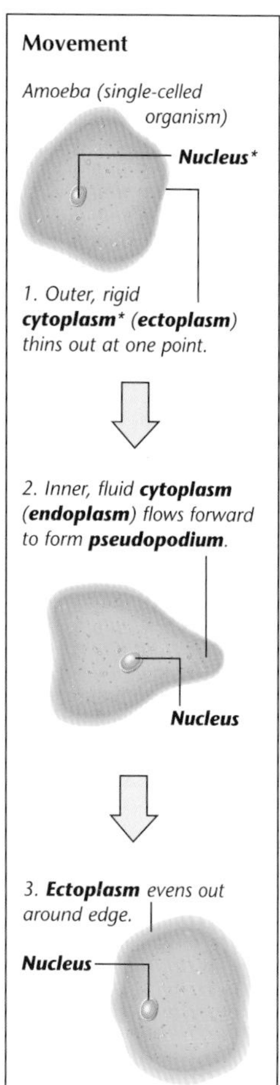
Movement
Amoeba (single-celled organism)
Nucleus*
1. Outer, rigid cytoplasm* (ectoplasm) thins out at one point.
2. Inner, fluid cytoplasm (endoplasm) flows forward to form pseudopodium.
Nucleus
3. Ectoplasm evens out around edge.
Nucleus
Organism has moved.

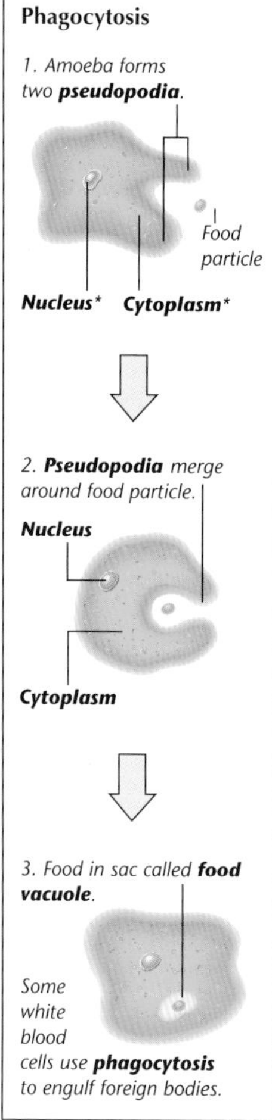
Phagocytosis
1. Amoeba forms two pseudopodia.
Food particle
Nucleus*
Cytoplasm*
2. Pseudopodia merge around food particle.
Nucleus
Cytoplasm
3. Food in sac called food vacuole.
Some white blood cells use phagocytosis to engulf foreign bodies.

Cilia (sing. cilium)

Tiny "hairs" on the outer body surfaces of many small organisms. They flick back and forth to produce movement. Cilia are also found lining the internal passages of more complex animals, e.g. human air passages (where they trap foreign particles).

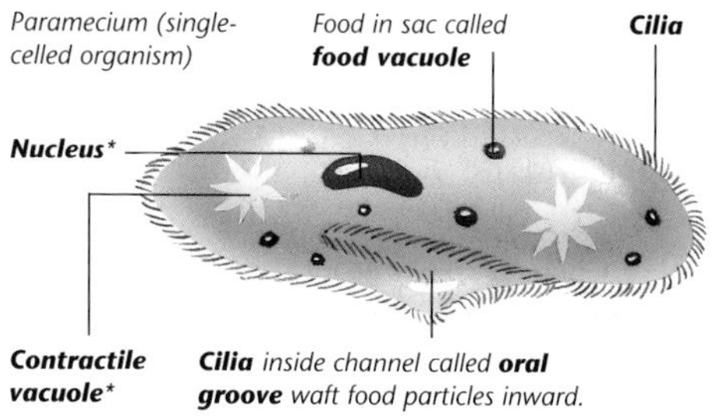
Paramecium (single-celled organism)
Food in sac called food vacuole
Cilia
Nucleus*
Contractile vacuole*
Cilia inside channel called oral groove waft food particles inward.

Flagella (sing. flagellum)

Any long, fine body threads, especially the one or more which project from the surface of many single-celled organisms. These lash backward and forward to produce movement. Organisms with flagella are **flagellate**.

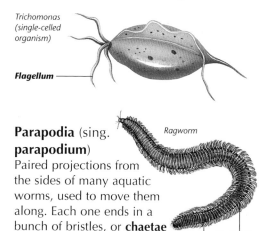

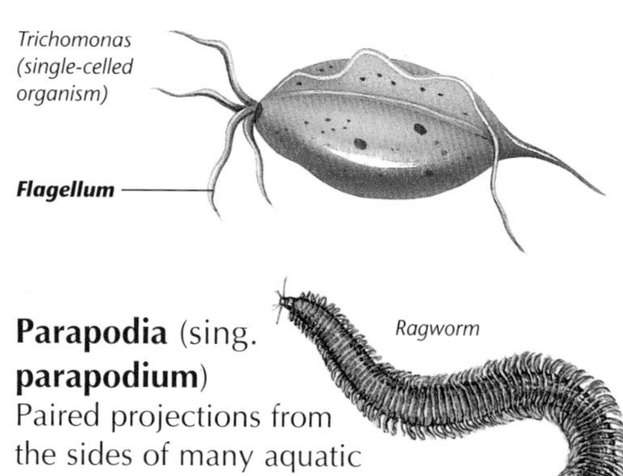
Trichomonas (single-celled organism)
Flagellum

Parapodia (sing. parapodium)

Paired projections from the sides of many aquatic worms, used to move them along. Each one ends in a bunch of bristles, or **chaetae** (sing. **chaeta**), which may also cover the body in some cases.

Ragworm

Parapodium

Chaeta

* **Contractile vacuoles**, 273; **Cytoplasm**, **Nucleus**, 238.

Swimmers

Fins

Projections from the body of a fish, which are used as stabilizers and to change direction. They are supported by **rays** – rods of bone or **cartilage*** (depending on the type of fish) radiating out inside them. Fish have two sets of fins, called **median** and **paired fins**.

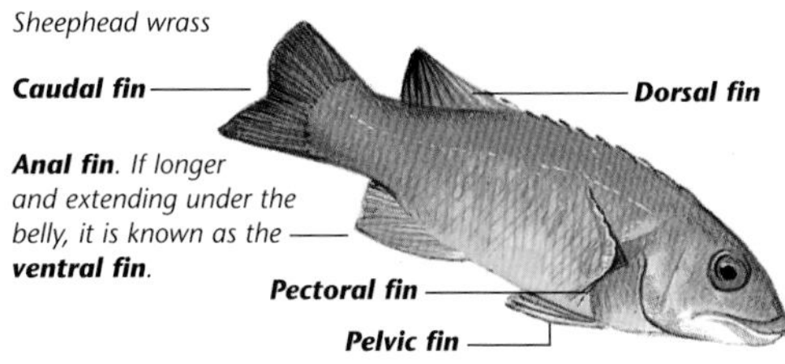

Sheephead wrass
Caudal fin
Dorsal fin
Anal fin. If longer and extending under the belly, it is known as the ventral fin.
Pectoral fin
Pelvic fin

*In many fish, the **pelvic fins** are behind the **pectoral fins**.*

Median fins

The **fins** which run in a line down the center of the back and the belly. In some fish, e.g. eels, they form one long, continuous median fin, but in most they are divided into the **dorsal**, **caudal** (tail) and **anal** (or **ventral**) **fins**. The dorsal fin and the anal fin control changes of direction from side to side. The caudal fin helps to propel the fish through the water.

Paired fins

The **fins** of a fish which stick out from its sides in two pairs: the **pectoral fins** and the **pelvic fins**. They control movement up or down.

Swim bladder or air bladder

A long, air-filled pouch inside most bony fish. The fish alters the amount of air inside the bladder depending on the depth at which it is swimming. This keeps the density of the fish the same as that of the water, so it will not sink if it stops swimming.

Swim bladder

***Median** or **medial** means "lying on the dividing line between the right and left sides".*	***Caudal** means "of the tail or hind part"; **caudate** means "having a tail".*
***Dorsal** means "of the back or top surface".*	***Ventral** means "of the front or lower surface".*

* **Cartilage**, 281; **Digit**, 278 (**Phalanges**); **Habitat**, 233; **Mammals**, 341.

Flyers

Pectoralis muscles

Two large, paired chest muscles, found in many **mammals***, but especially highly developed in birds. Each wing has one **pectoralis major** and one **pectoralis minor**, attached at one end to the **keel**, a large extension of the breastbone. The muscles contract alternately to move the wings.

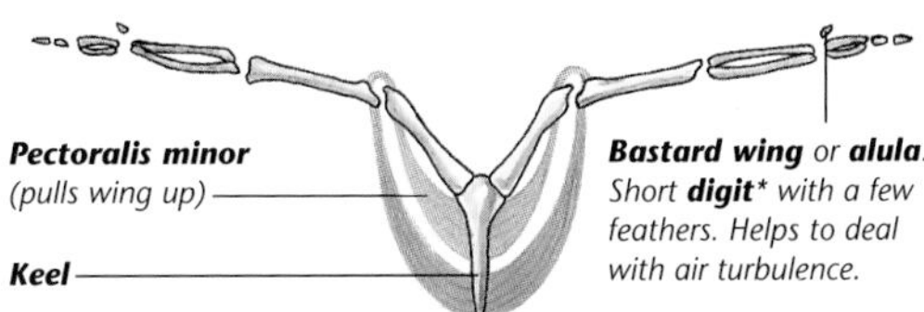

Pectoralis minor (pulls wing up)
Keel
Bastard wing or alula. Short digit* with a few feathers. Helps to deal with air turbulence.

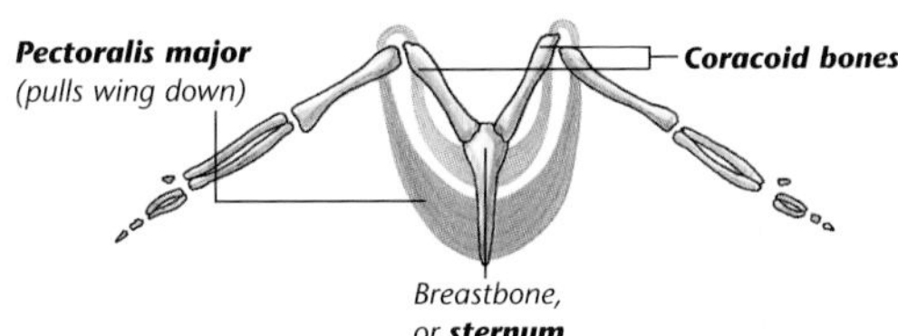

Pectoralis major (pulls wing down)
Coracoid bones
Breastbone, or sternum

Walkers

Unguligrade

Walking on hoofs at the tips of the toes, e.g. horses.

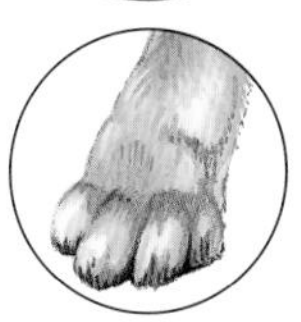

Digitigrade

Walking on the underside of the toes, e.g. dogs and cats.

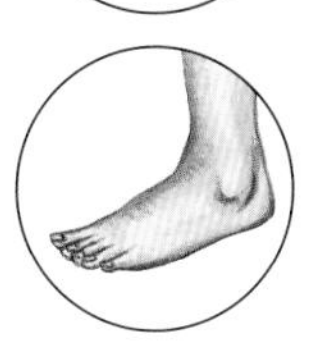

Plantigrade

Walking on the underside of the whole foot, e.g. humans.

*Camels are **unguligrade** animals which are suited to their **habitat***. Their wide, hairy hoofs have a large surface area. This helps to spread out their weight and prevents them from sinking into the fine desert sand.*

ANIMAL FEEDING

Different animals take in their food in many different ways, and with many different body parts. Some also have special internal mechanisms for dealing with the food (others have human-like **digestive systems** – see pages 294-295). Listed here are some of the main animal body parts involved in feeding and digestion.

Sea anemone

Cut-away ***tentacle****

Cnidoblast

Nematocyst *shoots out*

Cnidoblasts or thread cells

Special cells found in large numbers on the **tentacles*** of **cnidarians***, e.g. sea anemones, used for seizing food. Each one contains a **nematocyst** – a long thread coiled inside a tiny sac. When a tentacle touches something, the threads shoot out to stick to it or sting it.

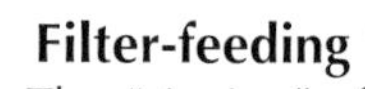

Filter-feeding

The "sieving" of food from water, shown by many aquatic animals. Barnacles, for instance, sieve out microscopic organisms, or **plankton***, with bristly limbs called **cirri** (sing. **cirrus**).

Cirri

Barnacles put out their ***cirri*** *when they are covered with water.*

Some whales use frayed plates of horny **baleen**, or **whalebone**, hanging down from the top jaw. They sieve out small, shrimp-like animals called **krill**.

Krill

Diastema (pl. diastemata)

A gap between the front and back teeth of many plant-eaters. It is especially important in rodents, e.g. mice. They can draw their cheeks in through the gaps, so they do not swallow substances they may be gnawing.

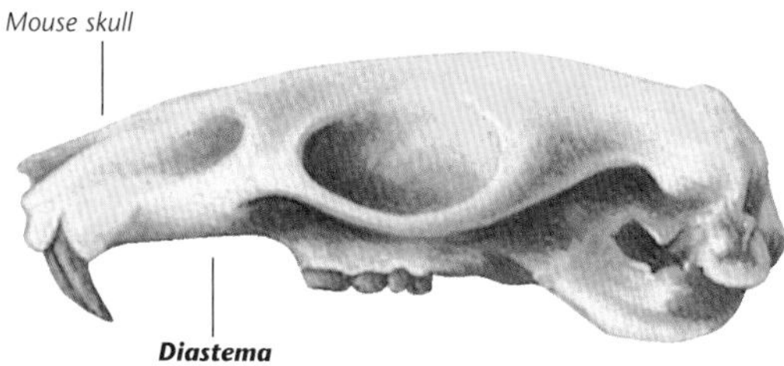
Mouse skull
Diastema

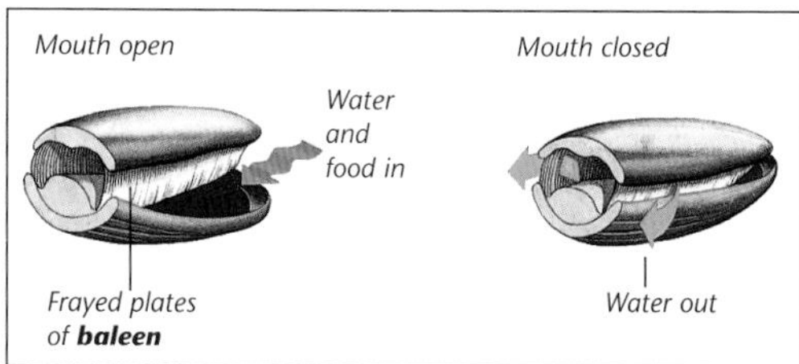
Mouth open
Mouth closed
Water and food in
Frayed plates of baleen
Water out

Carnassial teeth

The specially adapted last upper **premolar*** and first lower **molar*** of carnivorous mammals, used for shearing flesh.

Radula

The horny "tongue" of many **molluscs***, e.g. snails. It is covered by tiny teeth, which rasp off food.

A gray whale filtering sea water through its ***baleen***

* **Cnidarians**, 341; **Molars**, 285; **Molluscs**, 341; **Plankton**, 342; **Premolars**, 285; **Tentacles**, 274.

Arthropod mouthparts

The mouths of **arthropods***, e.g. insects, are made up of a number of different parts. Depending on the animal's feeding method, these may look very different. The basic mouthparts, found in all insects, are the **mandibles**, **maxillae** (sing. **maxilla**), **labrum** and **labium**. The first two are also found in many other arthropods, e.g. crabs and centipedes (some of these other arthropods have two pairs of maxillae).

*The **maxillae** of butterflies, moths and similar insects fit together to make a long sucking tube, or **proboscis**.*

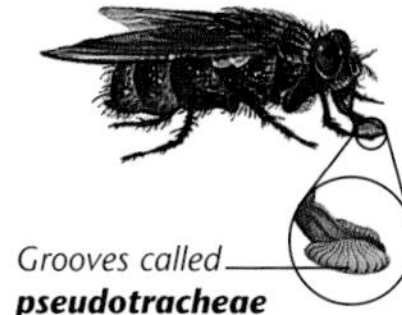

*The **labium** of houseflies is an extended pad-like sucking organ.*

*Grooves called **pseudotracheae** (sing. **pseudotrachea**)*

Typical arrangement of mouthparts (locust)

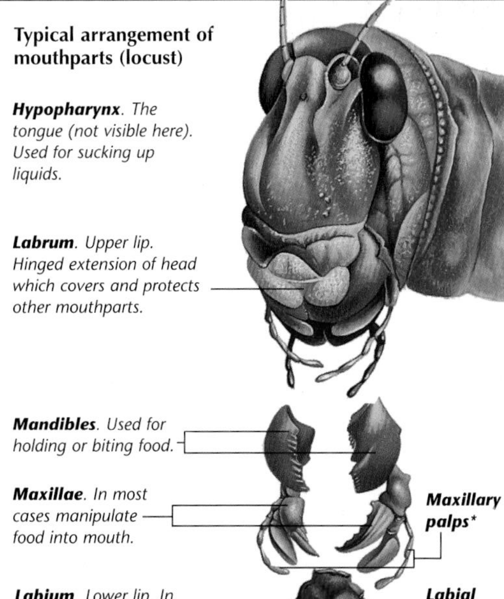
Maxillary palps*
Labial palps*

***Hypopharynx**. The tongue (not visible here). Used for sucking up liquids.*

***Labrum**. Upper lip. Hinged extension of head which covers and protects other mouthparts.*

***Mandibles**. Used for holding or biting food.*

***Maxillae**. In most cases manipulate food into mouth.*

***Labium**. Lower lip. In most cases manipulates food into mouth.*

Digestive structures

Crop

A thin-walled pouch, part of the gullet (**esophagus***) in birds; also a similar structure in some worms, e.g. earthworms, and some insects, e.g. grasshoppers. Food is stored in the crop before it goes into the **gizzard**.

Gizzard

A thick, muscular-walled pouch at the base of the gullet (**esophagus***) in those animals which have **crops**. These animals have no teeth, instead food is ground up in the gizzard. Birds swallow pieces of gravel to act as grindstones; in other animals, the muscular walls of the gizzard, or hard, tooth-like structures attached to these walls, help to grind up their food.

Pigeon

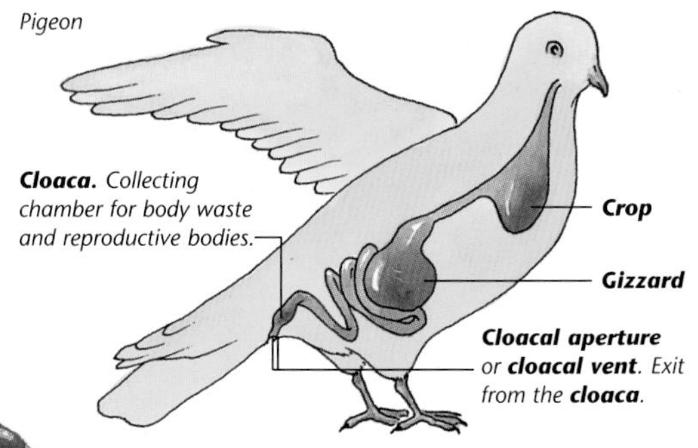
Crop
Gizzard

***Cloaca.** Collecting chamber for body waste and reproductive bodies.*

***Cloacal aperture** or **cloacal vent**. Exit from the **cloaca**.*

Rumen

The large first chamber of the complex "stomach" of some plant-eating **mammals***, e.g. cows, into which food passes unchewed. It contains bacteria which can break down **cellulose***. Other animals pass this substance as waste, but these animals cannot afford to do this, as it makes up the bulk of their food (grass). Partially-digested food from the rumen is digested further in the second chamber, or **reticulum**, and then regurgitated to be chewed, when it is known as the **cud**. When swallowed again, it passes directly to the third and fourth chambers – the **omasum** and the **abomasum** (the true stomach) – for further processing.

*Animals that chew the cud (**ruminate**) are called **ruminants**.*

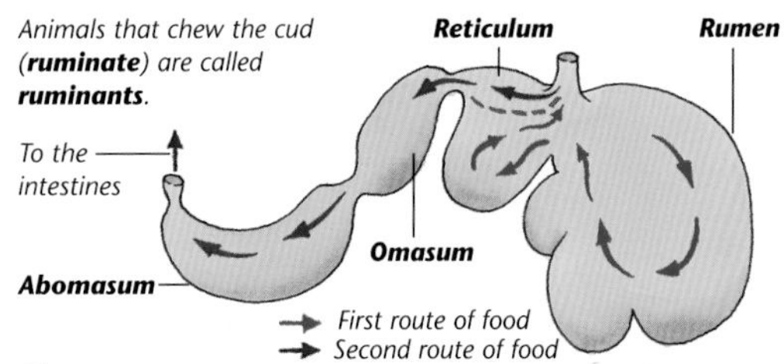
Reticulum
Rumen
To the intestines
Omasum
Abomasum
First route of food
Second route of food

Cecum

Any blind-ended sac inside the body, especially one forming part of a digestive system. In many animals, e.g. rabbits, it is the site of an important stage of digestion (involving bacterial breakdown of **cellulose*** – see **rumen**). In others, e.g. humans (see **large intestine***), it has little use.

* **Arthropods**, 341; **Cellulose**, 238 (**Cell wall**); **Esophagus**, 294; **Mammals**, 341; **Palps**, 274.

ANIMAL RESPIRATION

The complex process of **respiration** consists of a number of stages (see introduction, page 298). Basically, oxygen is taken in and used by body cells in the breakdown of food, and carbon dioxide is expelled from the cells and the body. On these pages are some of the main animal respiratory organs.

*These narrow slits are where water leaves, having passed over the shark's **gills**.*

Gills

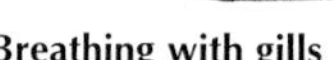

Breathing with gills

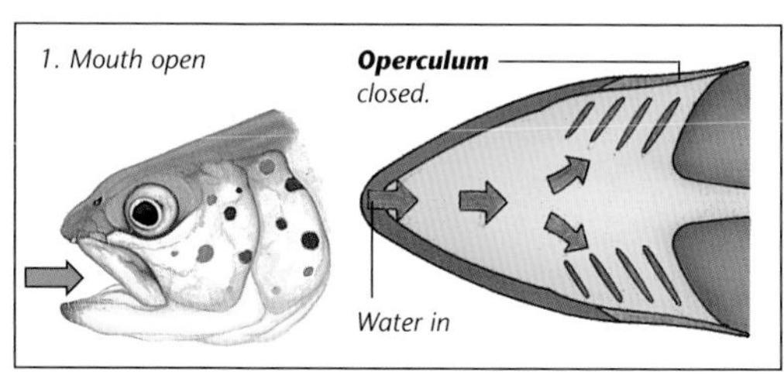

1. Mouth open
Operculum closed.
Water in

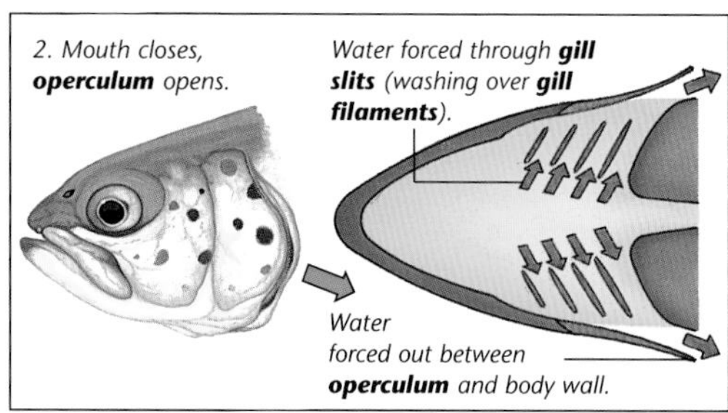

2. Mouth closes, operculum opens.
Water forced through gill slits (washing over gill filaments).
Water forced out between operculum and body wall.

Gills or **branchiae** (sing. **branchia**), are the breathing organs of most aquatic animals, containing many blood vessels. Oxygen is absorbed into the blood from the water passing over the gills. Carbon dioxide passes out the other way. There are two types of gills – **internal** and **external**.

Internal gills

Gills inside the body, found in various forms in all fish, most **molluscs***, e.g. limpets, and most **crustaceans** (a group of **arthropods*** which includes crabs). Most fish have four pairs of gills, with channels between them called **gill slits**. In more advanced fish, e.g. cod, they are covered by a flap called the **operculum**. In more primitive fish, e.g. sharks, they end in narrow openings in the skin on the side of the head. Each gill consists of a curved rod, the **gill bar** or **gill arch**, with many fine **gill filaments**, and even finer **gill lamellae** (sing. **lamella**) radiating from it. These all contain blood vessels.

Branchial means "of the gills."

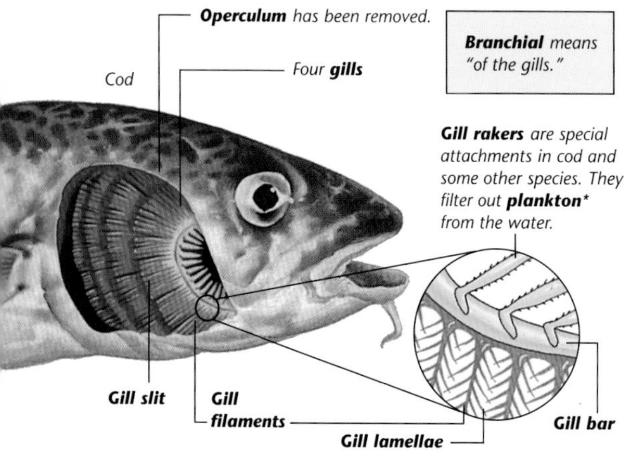

Operculum has been removed.
Cod
Four gills
Gill rakers are special attachments in cod and some other species. They filter out plankton* from the water.
Gill slit
Gill filaments
Gill lamellae
Gill bar

External gills

Gills on the outside of the body, found in the young stages of most fish and **amphibians***, some older amphibians and the young aquatic stages of many insects (e.g. caddisfly **larvae*** and mayfly **nymphs***). Their exact form depends on the type of animal, but in many cases they are "frilly" outgrowths from the head, e.g. in young tadpoles.

Tadpole
External gills are soft and "frilly".

Siphon

A tube carrying water to (**inhalant siphon**) or from (**exhalant siphon**) the **gills** of many lower aquatic animals, e.g. whelks (see picture, page 265). The exhalant siphon of **cephalopods** (**molluscs*** with **tentacles***), e.g. octopuses, is called the **hyponome***.

* **Amphibians**, 341; **Arthropods**, 341; **Hyponome**, 274; **Larva**, 277; **Molluscs**, 341; **Nymph**, 277; **Plankton**, 342; **Tentacles**, 274.

Other respiratory organs

Spiracle

Any body opening through which oxygen and carbon dioxide are exchanged (e.g. a whale's blowhole). The term is used especially for any of the tiny holes (also called **stigmata**, sing. **stigma**) found in many **arthropods***, e.g. insects.

Tracheae (sing. trachea†)

Thin tubes leading in from the **spiracles** of all insects (and the most advanced spiders). They form an inner network, often branching into narrower tubes called **tracheoles**. Oxygen from the air passes through the tube walls to the body cells. Carbon dioxide leaves via the same route.

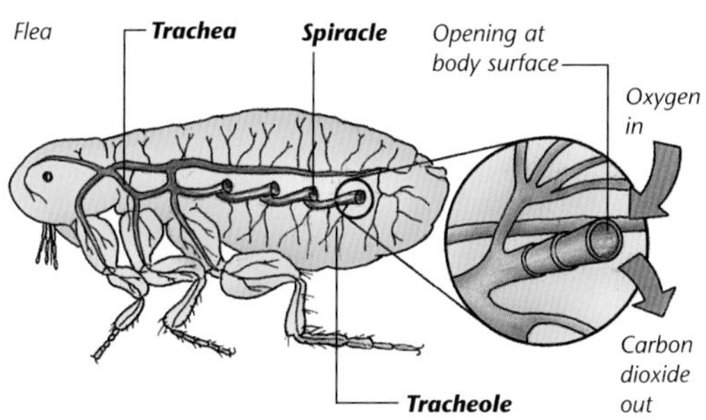
Flea
Trachea
Spiracle
Opening at body surface
Oxygen in
Carbon dioxide out
Tracheole

Lung books or book lungs

Paired breathing organs found in scorpions (which have four pairs) and some (less advanced) spiders (which have one or two). Each one has many blood-filled tissue plates, arranged like book pages. Oxygen comes in through slits (**spiracles**), one by each lung book, and is absorbed into the blood. Carbon dioxide passes out the same way.

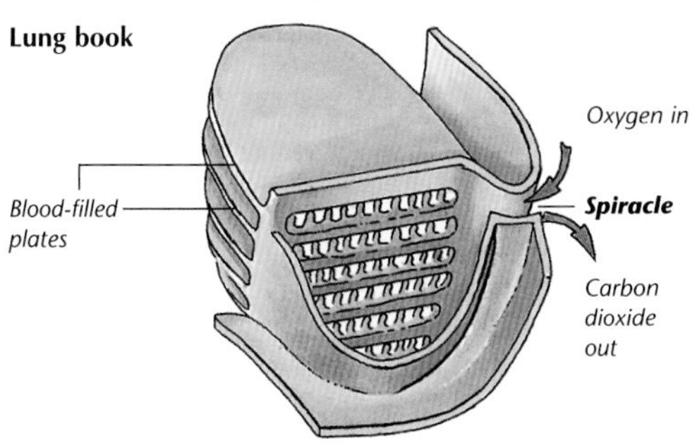
Lung book
Oxygen in
Blood-filled plates
Spiracle
Carbon dioxide out

Animal excretion

Excretion

The expulsion of waste fluid. It is vital to life as it gets rid of harmful substances. It is also vital to the maintenance of a balanced level of body fluids (see **homeostasis**, page 335).

Contractile vacuoles

Tiny sacs used for water-regulation in single-celled freshwater organisms. Excess water enters a vacuole via several canals arranged around it. When fully expanded, it then contracts and bursts, shooting the water out through the outer membrane.

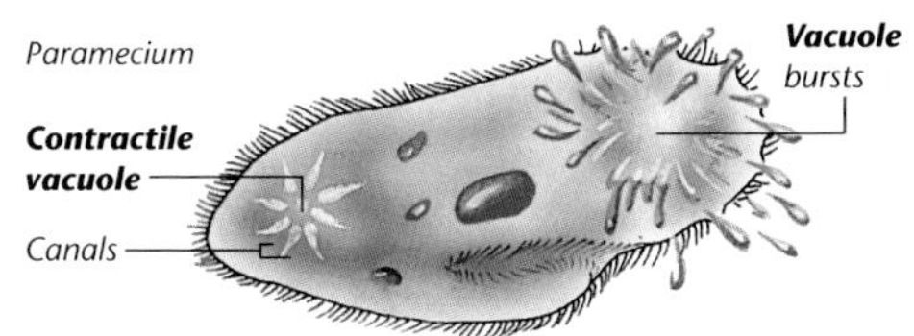
Paramecium
Vacuole bursts
Contractile vacuole
Canals

Nephridia (sing. nephridium)

Waste-collecting tubes in many worms and the **larvae*** of many **molluscs***, e.g. mussels. In higher worms, they collect from the **coelom*** (see picture, page 265). Lower worms and mollusc larvae have more primitive **protonephridia**. The waste fluid enters these via hollow **flame cells** (**solenocytes**), which contain hair-like **cilia***. In both a nephridium and a protonephridium, the waste leaves through a tiny hole, or **nephridiopore**.

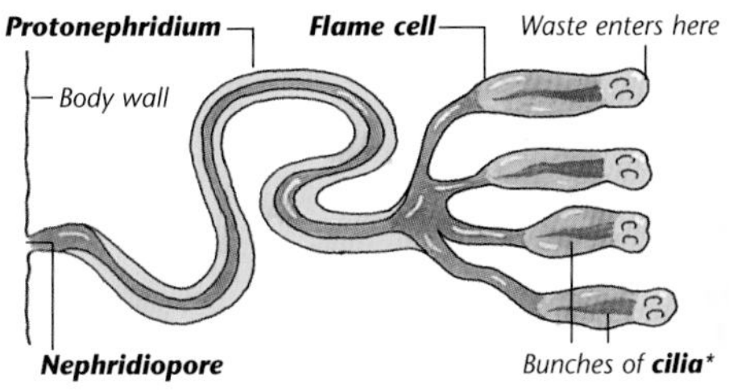
Protonephridium
Flame cell
Waste enters here
Body wall
Nephridiopore
Bunches of cilia*

Malpighian tubules

Long tubes found in many **arthropods***, e.g. insects. They carry dissolved waste from the main body cavity (**hemocoel***) into the rear of the gut. See picture, page 265.

* **Arthropods**, 341; **Cilia**, 268; **Coelom**, 265; **Hemocoel**, 265; **Larva**, 277; **Molluscs**, 341.
† *This is also the word for the human windpipe. See page 298.*

ANIMAL SENSES AND COMMUNICATION

All animals show some **sensitivity** (**irritability**), i.e. response to external stimuli such as light and sound vibrations. Humans have a high overall level of sensory development, but individual senses in other animals may be even better developed, e.g. the acute vision of hawks. Listed here are some of the main animal sense organs (and their parts). Their responding parts send "messages" (nervous impulses) to the brain (or more primitive nerve center), which initiates the response.

Touch, smell and taste

Antennae (sing. antenna)

Whip-like, jointed sense organs on the heads of insects, centipedes and millipedes, and all **crustaceans** (a group of **arthropods*** which includes crabs and prawns). Insects, centipedes and millipedes have one pair, crustaceans have two. They respond to touch, temperature changes and chemicals (giving "smell" or "taste"). Some crustaceans also use them for swimming or to attach themselves to objects or other animals.

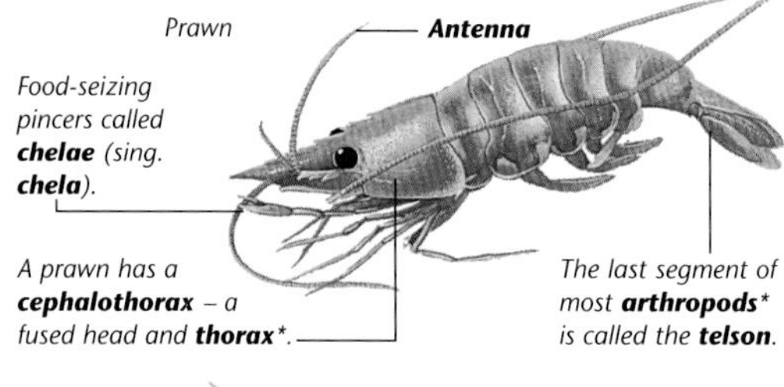
Prawn
Antenna
Food-seizing pincers called chelae (sing. chela).
A prawn has a cephalothorax – a fused head and thorax*.
The last segment of most arthropods* is called the telson.

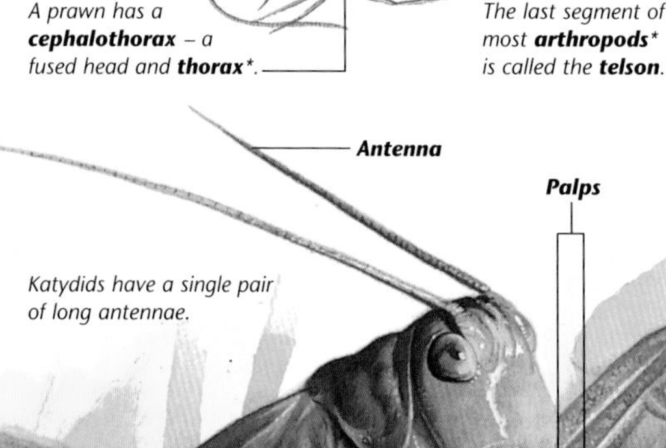
Antenna
Palps
Katydids have a single pair of long antennae.

*The Lion's Mane jellyfish uses its **tentacles** to sting and catch fish. Some large Lion's Mane jellyfish have tentacles that are up to 100ft long.*

Tentacles

Long, flexible body parts, found in many **molluscs***, e.g. octopuses, and **cnidarians***, e.g. jellyfish. In most cases they are used for grasping food or feeling, though the longer of the two pairs found in land snails and slugs have eyes on the end.

Octopus

Tentacles

***Hyponome.** Octopus shoots water out of it to move by "jet propulsion".*

Vibrissae (sing. vibrissa) or whiskers

Stiff hairs standing out from the faces of many **mammals***, e.g. cats, around the nose. They are sensitive to touch.

Palps

Projections of the mouthparts of **arthropods***, e.g. insects (see katydid picture, left). They respond to chemicals (giving "smell" or "taste"). The term is also given to various touch-sensitive organs.

Setae

***Tympanal organ** (see page 275)*

Setae (sing. seta)

Bristles produced by the skin of many **invertebrates***, e.g. insects. Nerves at their bases respond to movements of air or vibrations.

* **Arthropods, Cnidarians, Invertebrates, Mammals, Molluscs**, 341; **Thorax**, 264 (**Segmentation**).

Hearing and balance

Lateral lines

Two water-filled tubes lying along each side of the body, just under the skin. They are found in all fish and those **amphibians*** which spend most of their time in water, e.g. some toads. They enable the animals to detect water currents and pressure changes, and they use this information to find their way around.

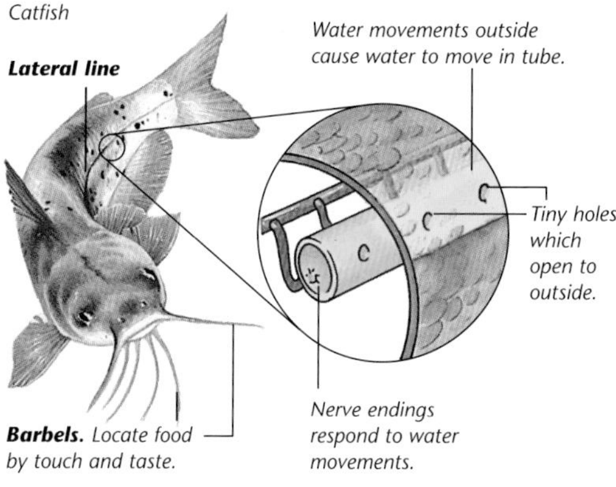

Catfish
Lateral line
Water movements outside cause water to move in tube.
Tiny holes which open to outside.
Barbels. Locate food by touch and taste.
Nerve endings respond to water movements.

Tympanal organs or tympani (sing. tympanum)

Sound detectors found on the lower body or legs in some insects, e.g. katydids, and on the head in some land **vertebrates***, e.g. frogs. Each is an air sac covered by a thin layer of tissue. Sensitive fibers in the organs respond to high-frequency sound vibrations.

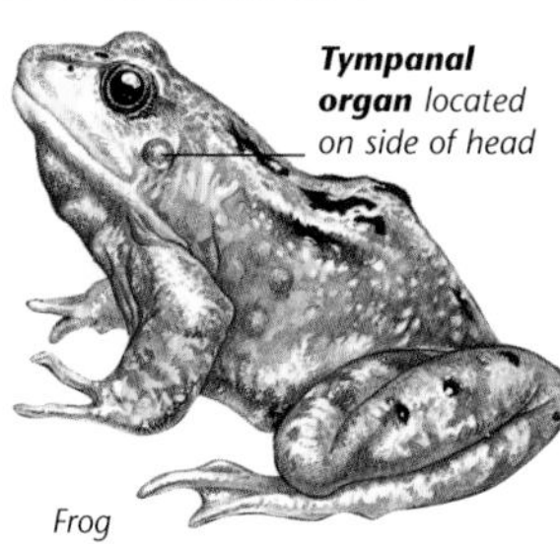

Tympanal organ located on side of head
Frog

Statocysts

Tiny organs of balance, found in many aquatic **invertebrates***, e.g. jellyfish. Each is a sac with tiny particles called **statoliths** inside, e.g. sand grains. When the animal moves, the grains move, stimulating sensitive cells which set off responses.

Haltères

Modified second pair of wings on some insects, which keep balance in flight.

Fly

Haltères

Sight

Compound eyes

The special eyes of many insects and some other **arthropods***, e.g. crabs. Each consists of hundreds of separate visual units called **ommatidia** (sing. **ommatidium**). Each of these has an outer lens system which "bends", or refracts, light onto a **rhabdom**, a transparent rod surrounded by light-responsive cells.

***Compound eye** view of a flower (mosaic image)*

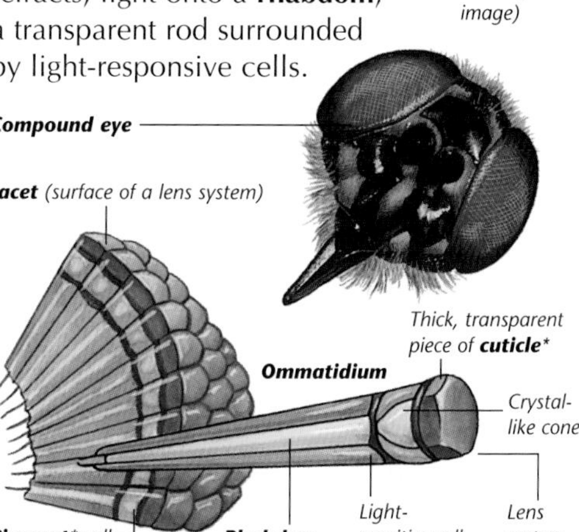

Compound eye
Facet (surface of a lens system)
Thick, transparent piece of cuticle*
Ommatidium
Crystal-like cone
Pigment* cell
Rhabdom
Light-sensitive cell
Lens system

After receiving information from all the ommatidia (each has a slightly different angle of vision so may record different light intensity or color), the brain assembles a complete **mosaic image**. This is enough for the animal's needs, but not as well defined as the image made by the human eye.

Communication

Pheromone

Any chemical made by an animal that causes responses in other members of the species, e.g. sexual attractants produced by many insects.

Stridulation

The rubbing together of body parts to make a shrill noise (often used to attract a mate). Katydids use their wing edges.

Syrinx (pl. syringes)

The vocal organ of birds, similar to the **larynx***, but found at the windpipe's base.

* **Amphibians**, **Arthropods**, 341; **Cuticle**, 266; **Invertebrates**, 341; **Larynx**, 298; **Pigments**, 255; **Vertebrates**, 341.

ANIMAL REPRODUCTION AND DEVELOPMENT

Chick hatching from a **cleidoic egg**

Reproduction is the creation of new life. Most animals reproduce by **sexual reproduction***, the joining of a female sex cell, called an **ovum**, with a male sex cell, or **sperm**. Below are the main terms associated with the reproductive processes of animals.

Viviparous

A term describing animals such as humans, in which both the joining of the male and female sex cells (**fertilization**) and the development of the **embryo*** occur inside the female's body (the fertilization is **internal fertilization**), and the baby is born live.

New-born piglets suckling. Pigs are ***viviparous****.*

Oviparous

A term describing animals in which the development of the **embryo*** occurs in an **egg** which has been laid by the mother. In some cases, e.g. in birds, the male and female sex cells join inside the female's body (**internal fertilization**) and the egg already contains the embryo when laid. In other cases, e.g. in many fish, the many eggs each just contain an **ovum** (female sex cell) when laid, and the male then deposits **sperm** (male sex cells) over them (**external fertilization**).

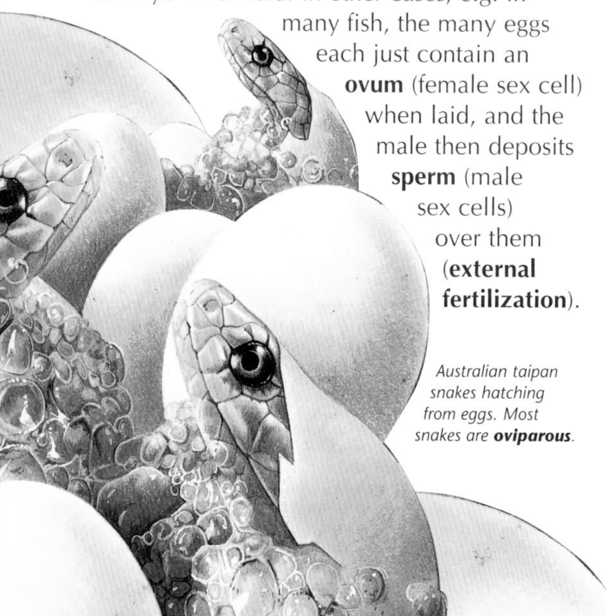
Australian taipan snakes hatching from eggs. Most snakes are ***oviparous****.*

Eggs

There are two main types of egg. **Cleidoic eggs** are produced by most egg-laying animals which live on land, e.g. birds and most **reptiles***, and also by a few aquatic animals, e.g. sharks. Such an egg largely isolates the **embryo*** from its surroundings, allowing only gases to pass through its tough shell (waste matter is stored). It contains enough food (**yolk**) for the complete development of the embryo, and the animal emerges as a tiny version of the adult. The other type of egg, produced by most aquatic animals, e.g. most fish, has a soft outer membrane, through which water and waste matter (as well as gases) can pass. The emerging young are not fully developed.

Cleidoic egg

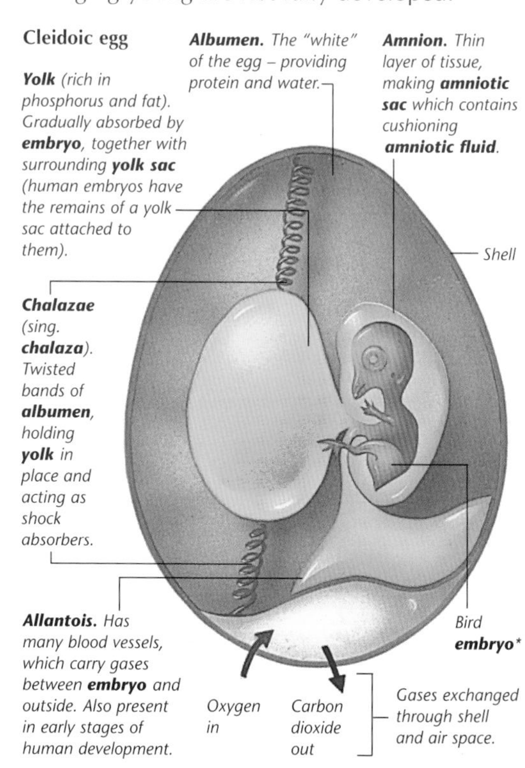
Yolk (rich in phosphorus and fat). Gradually absorbed by **embryo**, together with surrounding **yolk sac** (human embryos have the remains of a yolk sac attached to them).
Albumen. The "white" of the egg – providing protein and water.
Amnion. Thin layer of tissue, making **amniotic sac** which contains cushioning **amniotic fluid**.
Shell
Chalazae (sing. **chalaza**). Twisted bands of **albumen**, holding **yolk** in place and acting as shock absorbers.
Allantois. Has many blood vessels, which carry gases between **embryo** and outside. Also present in early stages of human development.
Oxygen in
Carbon dioxide out
Gases exchanged through shell and air space.
Bird **embryo***

* **Embryo**, 320; **Reptiles**, 341; **Sexual reproduction**, 320.

Oviduct

Any tube in females through which either **eggs** or **ova** (female sex cells) are discharged to the outside. In some animals, e.g. birds, the eggs are **fertilized** on the way out (see **oviparous**).

Ovipositor

An organ extending from the back end of many female insects, through which **eggs** are laid. In many cases, it is long and sharp, and is used to pierce plant or animal tissues before laying.

Spermatheca

A sac for storing **sperm** (male sex cells) in the female of many **invertebrates***, e.g. insects, and some lower **vertebrates***, e.g. newts. The female receives the sperm and stores them until her **ova** (sex cells) are ready to join with them (**fertilization**).

*Some **hermaphrodite** animals (animals with both male and female organs), e.g. earthworms, have **spermathecae**. They "swap" sperm when they mate.*

Metamorphosis

The growth and development of some animals involves intermediate forms which are very different from the adult form. Metamorphosis is a series of such changes, producing a complete or partial transformation from the young form to the adult.

All insects, most marine **invertebrates***, e.g. lobsters, and most **amphibians***, e.g. frogs, undergo some degree of metamorphosis (intermediate larval forms are common, e.g. legless **tadpoles** in frogs and toads). Below are examples of insect metamorphosis (two different kinds – **complete** and **incomplete metamorphosis**).

***Complete metamorphosis** (two different forms between **egg** and adult). The many insects which undergo it, e.g. butterflies, are called **endopterygotes**.*

Male and female spotted fritillary butterflies of southern Europe pair up and mate. Female butterfly lays her eggs on small plant.

Larva** (pl. **larvae**) emerges from egg. Has other names, e.g. **grub** (beetles), **maggot** (houseflies), **caterpillar** (moths and butterflies). Sheds skin several times to allow for growth (process called **ecdysis**, or molting, common to all **arthropods).*

*Final **ecdysis** (see **larva**) results in **pupa** (pl. **pupae**). Called **chrysalis** in butterflies. Outer skin is a hard protective case. The cases surrounding moth pupae have extra protection in the form of a **cocoon** of spun silk.*

*Hard case splits and mature adult (**imago**) emerges. The imago searches for a mate, and the reproductive cycle is then repeated.*

***Incomplete metamorphosis** (gradual development in stages). The insects which undergo it, e.g. locusts, are called **exopterygotes**.*

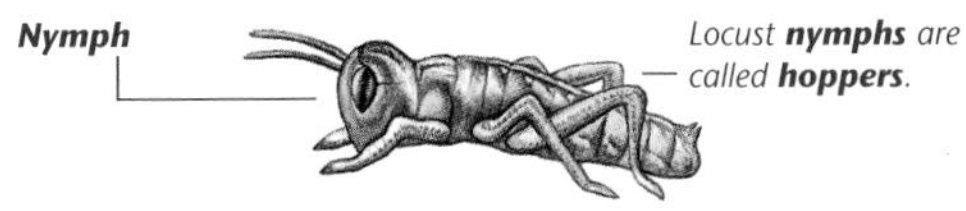
Nymph

*Locust **nymphs** are called **hoppers**.*

***Nymph**. Emerges from egg. "Mini" version of adult insect, but resemblance only superficial, e.g. wings in very early stages of development or non-existent, many inner organs missing.*

*Nymph undergoes several **ecdyses** (see **larva**), with some adult parts emerging each time.*

Old skin

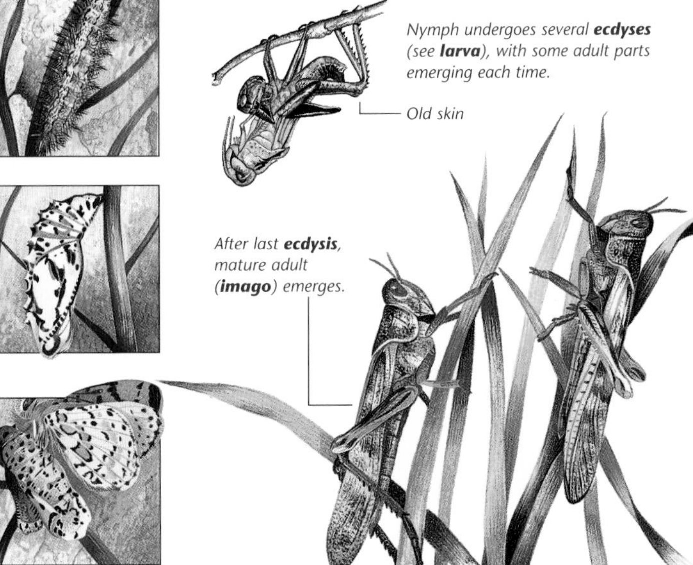

*After last **ecdysis**, mature adult (**imago**) emerges.*

* **Amphibians**, **Arthropods**, **Invertebrates**, **Vertebrates**, 341.

THE SKELETON

The human **skeleton** is a frame of over 200 bones which supports and protects the body organs (the **viscera**) and provides a solid base for the muscles to work against.

Cranium or skull

A case protecting the brain and facial organs. It is made of **cranial** and **facial bones**, fused at lines called **sutures**. The upper jaw, for instance, consists of two fused bones called **maxillae** (sing. **maxilla**).

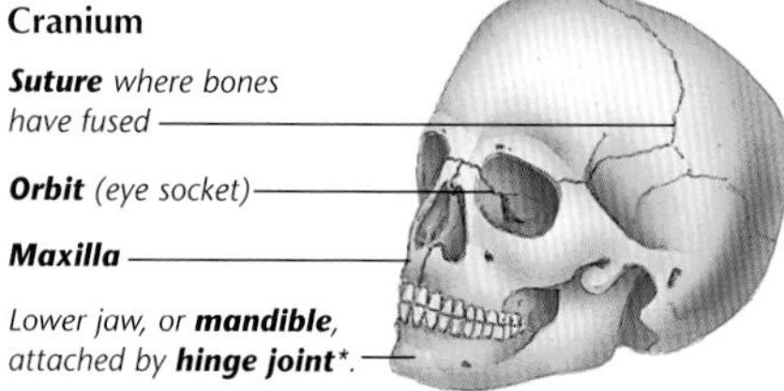
Cranium
Suture where bones have fused
Orbit (eye socket)
Maxilla
Lower jaw, or mandible, attached by hinge joint.*

Rib cage

A cage of bones forming the walls of the **thorax** or chest area. It is made up of 12 pairs of **ribs**, the **thoracic vertebrae** and the **sternum**. The ribs are joined to the sternum by bands of **cartilage*** called **costal cartilage**, but only the first seven pairs join it directly. The last five pairs are **false ribs**. The top three of these join the sternum indirectly – their costal cartilage joins that of the seventh pair. The bottom two pairs are **floating ribs**, only attached to the thoracic vertebrae at the back.

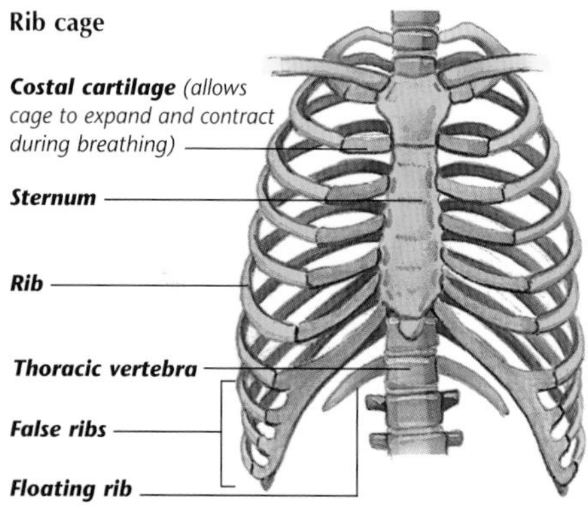
Rib cage
Costal cartilage (allows cage to expand and contract during breathing)
Sternum
Rib
Thoracic vertebra
False ribs
Floating rib

The bones of the skeleton

*Seven **cervical vertebrae** support the neck. The top two are the **atlas** and **axis**.*

Scapula** or **shoulderblade

Sternum** or **breastbone

Ribs

*12 **thoracic vertebrae** support the **ribs**.*

*The five **lumbar vertebrae** are in the lower back (**lumbar**) region.*

***Coccyx**. An area of four fused **coccygeal vertebrae** below the **sacrum**.*

***Pelvis**, **pelvic girdle** or **hip girdle**. Each side is made up of three bones – the **ilium**, **pubis** and **ischium**.*

***Tarsals** (ankle bones), collectively called a **tarsus**.*

***Phalanges** (sing. **phalanx**). The bones of the **digits** – fingers and toes.*

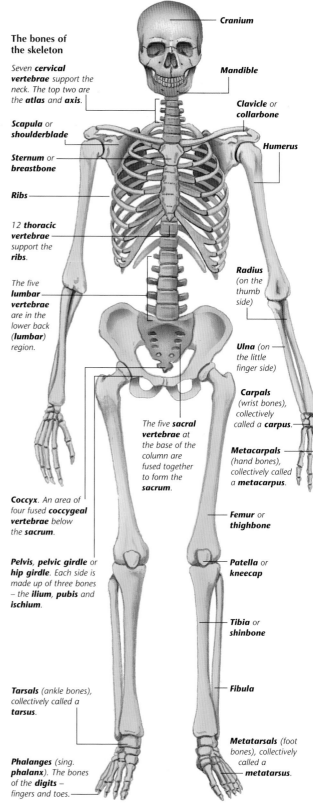

Cranium

Mandible

Clavicle** or **collarbone

Humerus

***Radius** (on the thumb side)*

***Ulna** (on the little finger side)*

***Carpals** (wrist bones), collectively called a **carpus**.*

*The five **sacral vertebrae** at the base of the column are fused together to form the **sacrum**.*

***Metacarpals** (hand bones), collectively called a **metacarpus**.*

Femur** or **thighbone

Patella** or **kneecap

Tibia** or **shinbone

Fibula

***Metatarsals** (foot bones), collectively called a **metatarsus**.*

* **Cartilage**, 281; **Hinge joints**, 280.

Vertebral column

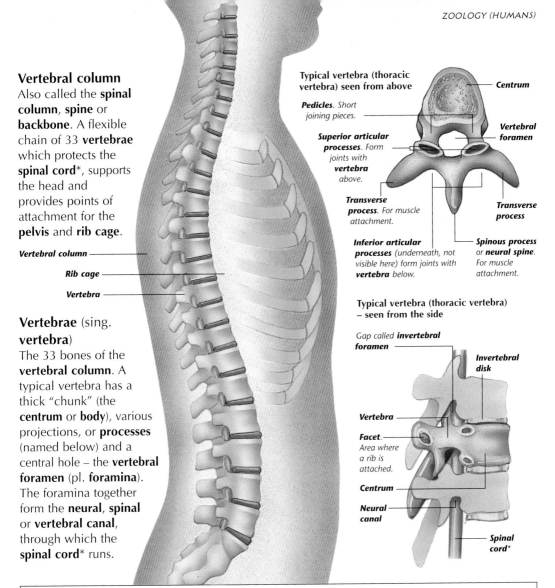

Also called the **spinal column**, **spine** or **backbone**. A flexible chain of 33 **vertebrae** which protects the **spinal cord***, supports the head and provides points of attachment for the **pelvis** and **rib cage**.

Vertebral column

Rib cage

Vertebra

Vertebrae (sing. vertebra)

The 33 bones of the **vertebral column**. A typical vertebra has a thick "chunk" (the **centrum** or **body**), various projections, or **processes** (named below) and a central hole – the **vertebral foramen** (pl. **foramina**). The foramina together form the **neural**, **spinal** or **vertebral canal**, through which the **spinal cord*** runs.

Typical vertebra (thoracic vertebra) seen from above

Centrum

Pedicles*. Short joining pieces.*

Vertebral foramen

Superior articular processes*. Form joints with* ***vertebra*** *above.*

Transverse process*. For muscle attachment.*

Transverse process

Inferior articular processes *(underneath, not visible here) form joints with* ***vertebra*** *below.*

Spinous process *or* ***neural spine****. For muscle attachment.*

Typical vertebra (thoracic vertebra) – seen from the side

Gap called ***invertebral foramen***

Invertebral disk

Vertebra

Facet*. Area where a rib is attached.*

Centrum

Neural canal

Spinal cord*

Vertebral structure

The different vertebrae are named around the skeleton on the opposite page. The top 24 are movable and linked by **invertebral disks** of **cartilage***. The bottom nine are fused together. They all have the typical structure described above right, except for the top two, the **atlas** and **axis**. The atlas (top vertebra) has a special joint with the **skull** which allows the head to nod. The axis has a "peg" (the **dens** or **odontoid process**) which fits into the atlas. This forms a **pivot joint**, a type of joint which allows the head to rotate.

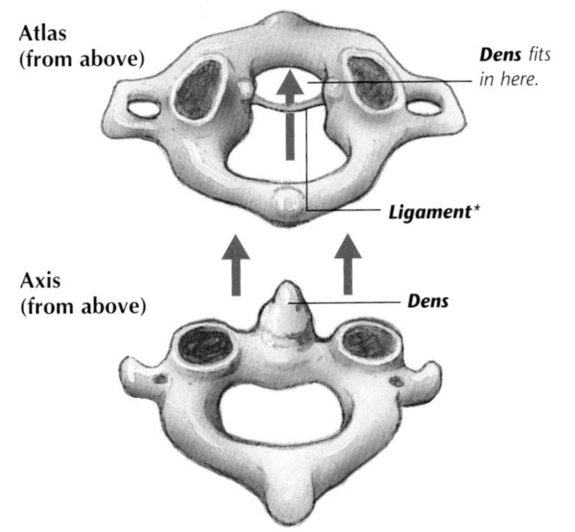
Atlas (from above)
Dens fits in here.
Ligament*
Axis (from above)
Dens

* **Cartilage**, 281; **Ligaments**, 280; **Spinal cord**, 302.

JOINTS AND BONE

The bones of the skeleton meet at many **joints**, or **articulations**. Some are **fixed joints**, allowing no movement, e.g. the **sutures*** of the skull. Most, however, are movable, and they give the body great flexibility. The most common are listed on this page.

Hinge joints

Joints (e.g. the knee joint) which work like any hinge. That is, the movable part (bone) can only move in one plane, i.e. in either of two opposing directions.

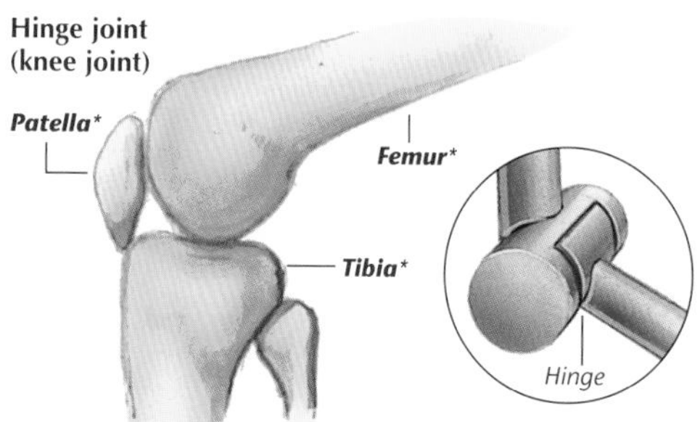
Hinge joint (knee joint)
Patella*
Femur*
Tibia*
Hinge

Gliding joints

Also called **sliding** or **plane joints**. Joints in which one or more flat surfaces glide over each other, e.g. those between the **carpals***. They are more flexible than **hinge joints**.

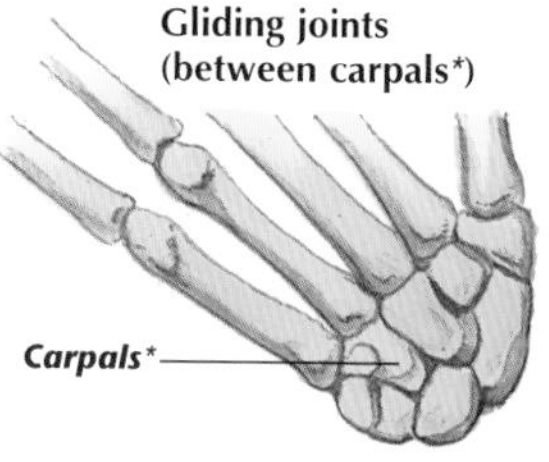
Gliding joints (between carpals*)
Carpals*

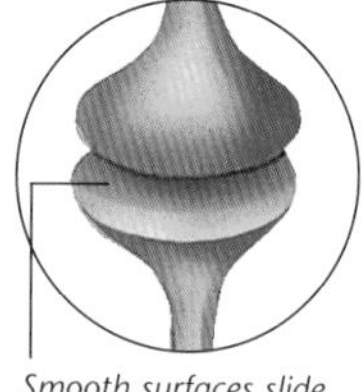
Smooth surfaces slide over each other.

Ball-and-socket joints

The most flexible joints (e.g. the hip joint). The movable bone has a rounded end which fits into a socket in the fixed bone. The movable bone can swivel, or move in many directions.

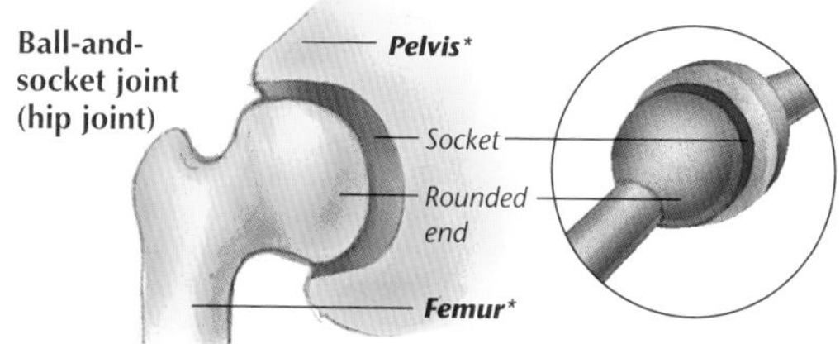
Ball-and-socket joint (hip joint)
Pelvis*
Socket
Rounded end
Femur*

Connective tissue

There are many different types of **connective tissue** in the body. They all protect and connect cells or organs and have a basis of non-living material (the **matrix**) in which living cells are scattered. The difference between them lies in the nature of this material. The various types of tissue found at a joint, including **bone** itself, are all types of connective tissue. They all contain protein fibers and are either tough (containing **collagen** fibers) or elastic (containing **elastin** fibers).

The ease with which different types of tissue grow and repair depends largely on the amount of blood they contain. **Periosteum** is **vascular** (has a blood supply) and repairs itself quickly. **Cartilage** is **avascular** (has no blood supply) so takes longer to repair.

Periosteum

A thin layer of elastic connective tissue. It surrounds all bones, except at the joints (where **cartilage** takes over), and contains **osteoblasts** – cells which make new bone cells, needed for growth and repair.

Ligaments

Bands of connective tissue which hold together the bones of joints (and also hold many organs in place). Most are tough, though some are elastic, e.g. between **vertebrae***.

Synovial sac or synovial capsule

A cushioning "bag" of lubricating fluid (**synovial fluid**), with an outer skin (**synovial membrane**) of elastic connective tissue. Most movable joints, e.g. the knee, have such a sac lying between the bones. They are known as **synovial joints**.

* **Carpals**, **Femur**, **Patella**, **Pelvis**, 278;
Sutures, 278 (**Cranium**); **Tibia**, 278; **Vertebrae**, 279.

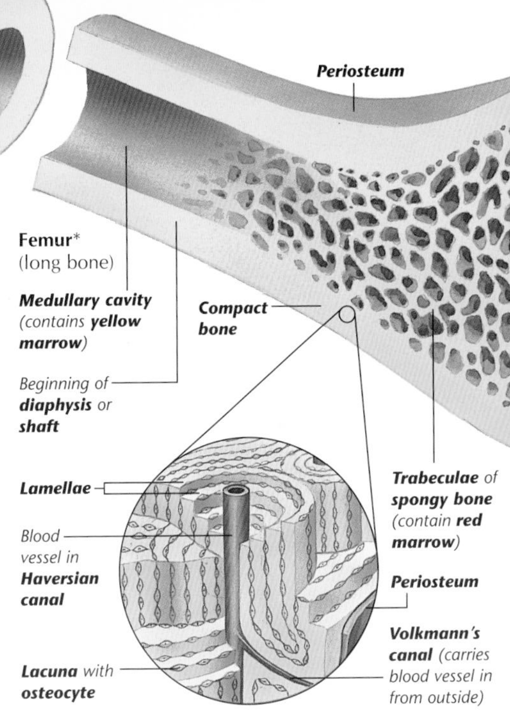
Periosteum
Femur* (long bone)
Medullary cavity (contains yellow marrow)
Compact bone
Beginning of diaphysis or shaft
Lamellae
Blood vessel in Haversian canal
Lacuna with osteocyte
Trabeculae of spongy bone (contain red marrow)
Periosteum
Volkmann's canal (carries blood vessel in from outside)

Spongy bone

A type of **bone** that is found in short and/or flat bones, e.g. the **sternum***, and fills the ends of long bones, e.g. the **femur***. It consists of a criss-cross network of flat plates called **trabeculae** (sing. **trabecula**), with many large spaces between them, filled by **red marrow** (see **bone marrow**).

Compact bone

A type of **bone** that forms the outer layer of all bones. It has far fewer spaces than **spongy bone**, and is laid in concentric layers (**lamellae**, sing. **lamella**) around channels called **Haversian canals**. These link with a complex system of tiny canals carrying blood vessels and nerves to the osteocytes.

Bone or osseous tissue

A type of tough connective tissue, made hard and resilient by large deposits of phosphorus and calcium compounds. The living bone cells, or **osteocytes**, are held in tiny spaces (**lacunae**, sing. **lacuna**) within this non-living material. There are two types of bone: **spongy** and **compact bone**.

Bone marrow

Two types of soft tissue. **Red marrow**, found in **spongy bone** (see **bone**), is where all new red (and some white) blood cells are made. **Yellow marrow** is a fat store, found in hollow areas (**medullary** or **marrow cavities**) in long bone **shafts**.

Tendons or sinews

Bands of tough connective tissue joining muscles to bones. Each is a continuation of the membrane around the muscle, together with the outer membranes of its bundles of fibers.

Cartilage or gristle

A tough connective tissue. In some joints (**cartilaginous joints**) it is the main cushion between the bones (e.g. **vertebrae***). In joints with **synovial sacs**, it covers the ends of the bones and is called **articular cartilage**. The end of the nose and the outer parts of the ears are made of cartilage. Young skeletons are made of cartilage, though these slowly turn to bone as minerals build up (a process called **ossification** or **osteogenesis**).

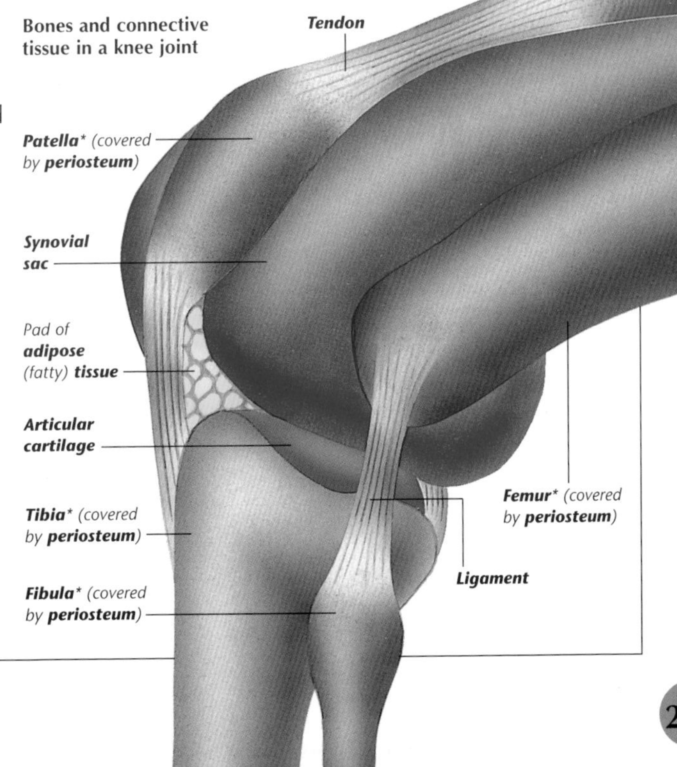
Bones and connective tissue in a knee joint
Tendon
Patella* (covered by periosteum)
Synovial sac
Pad of adipose (fatty) tissue
Articular cartilage
Tibia* (covered by periosteum)
Fibula* (covered by periosteum)
Femur* (covered by periosteum)
Ligament

* **Femur**, **Fibula**, **Patella**, **Sternum**, **Tibia**, 278; **Vertebrae**, 279.

MUSCLES

Muscles are areas of special elastic tissue (**muscle**) found all over the body. They may be either **voluntary muscles** (able to be controlled by conscious action) or **involuntary muscles** (not under conscious control). The main types of muscles are listed on this page.

Antagonistic pairs or opposing pairs

The pairs into which almost all muscles are arranged. The members of each pair produce opposite effects. In any given movement, the muscle which contracts to cause the movement is the **agonist** or **prime mover**. The one which relaxes at the same time is the **antagonist**.

Types of muscles

Skeletal muscles

All the muscles attached to the bones of the skeleton, which contract together or in sequence to move all the body parts. They are all **voluntary muscles** (see introduction) and are made of **striated muscle** tissue (see opposite). Some are named according to their position, shape or size, others are named after the movement they cause, e.g. **flexors** cause **flexion** (the bending of a limb at a joint), **extensors** straighten a limb.

Cardiac muscle

The muscle which makes up almost all of the wall of the heart. It is an **involuntary muscle** (see introduction) and is made of **cardiac muscle** tissue (see opposite).

Visceral muscles

The muscles in the walls of many internal organs, e.g. the intestines and blood vessels. They are all **involuntary muscles** (see introduction) and consist of **smooth muscle** tissue (see opposite).

Example of an antagonistic pair (biceps and triceps)

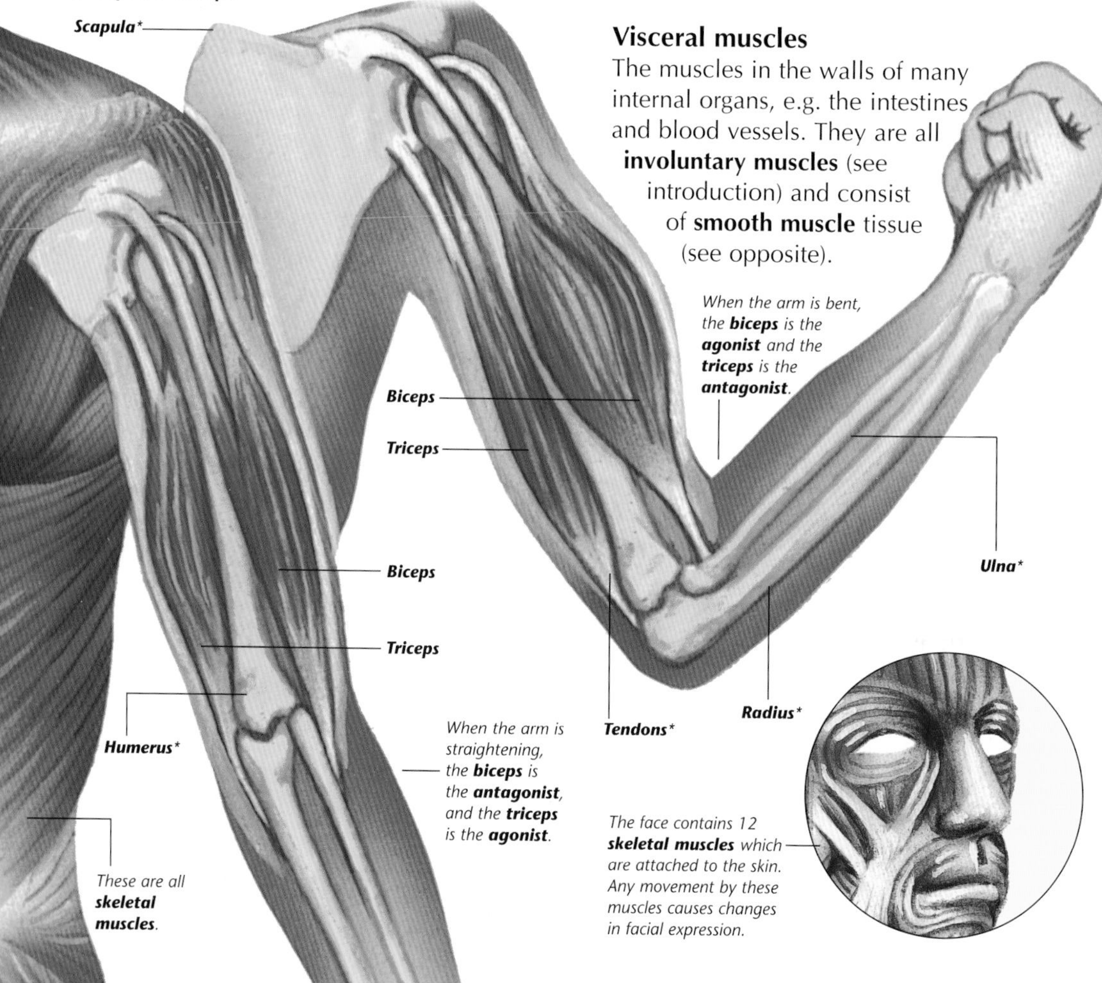

Scapula*
Biceps
Triceps
Biceps
Triceps
Humerus*
When the arm is bent, the biceps is the agonist and the triceps is the antagonist.
Ulna*
Radius*
Tendons*
When the arm is straightening, the biceps is the antagonist, and the triceps is the agonist.
These are all skeletal muscles.
The face contains 12 skeletal muscles which are attached to the skin. Any movement by these muscles causes changes in facial expression.

* **Humerus**, **Radius**, **Scapula**, 278; **Tendons**, 281; **Ulna**, 278.

The structure of muscle tissue

The different muscles in the body are made up of different kinds of muscle tissue (groups of cells of different types). The tissue has many blood vessels, bringing food matter to be broken down for energy, and nerves, which stimulate the muscles to act.

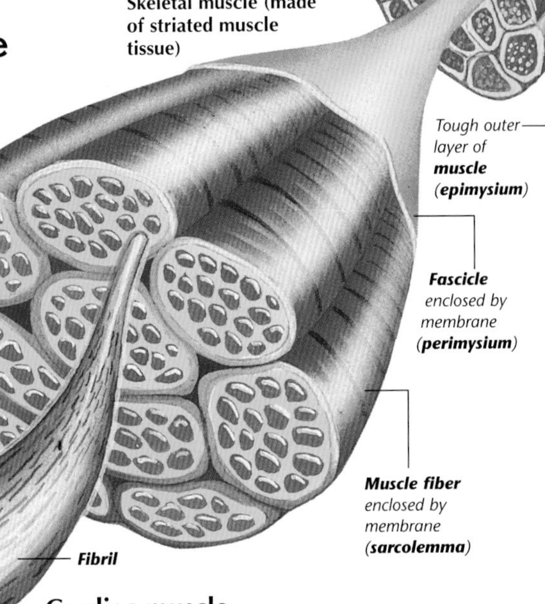

Skeletal muscle (made of striated muscle tissue)
Tough outer layer of **muscle** (**epimysium**)
Fascicle enclosed by membrane (**perimysium**)
Muscle fiber enclosed by membrane (**sarcolemma**)
Fibril
Filaments

Striated or **striped muscle**
The type of muscle tissue which makes up **skeletal muscles**. It consists of long cells called **muscle fibers**, grouped together in bundles called **fascicles**. Each fiber has a striped (**striated**) appearance under a microscope and is made of many smaller cylinders, called **fibrils** or **myofibrils**, which are the parts that contract when a fiber is stimulated by a nerve. The fibrils consist of interlocking **filaments**, or **myofilaments**, of two different types of protein – **actin** (thin filaments) and **myosin** (thicker filaments). These filaments slide past each other as a muscle contracts.

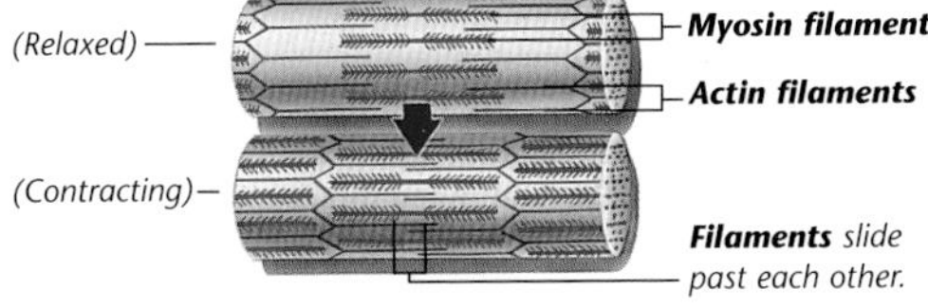

(Relaxed)
Myosin filaments
Actin filaments
(Contracting)
Filaments slide past each other.

Cardiac muscle
A type of **striated muscle** tissue, making up the **cardiac muscle** of the heart. Its constant rhythmical contractions are caused by stimulations from areas of the tissue which produce electrical impulses. Any nervous impulses just increase or decrease this heart rate.

Smooth muscle or **visceral muscle**
The type of muscle tissue which makes up the **visceral muscles**. It consists of short, spindle-shaped cells. The way it contracts is not yet fully understood, but it contains **actin** and **myosin**, and is stimulated by nerves.

Nervous stimulation

Most muscles are stimulated to move by impulses from nerves running through the body. For more about this, see pages 308-309.

Muscle spindle
A group of **muscle fibers** (see **striated muscle**) which has the end fibers of a sensory nerve cell (**sensory neuron***) wrapped around it. The end fibers are part of one main fiber (**dendron***). When the muscle stretches they are stimulated to send impulses to the brain, "telling" it about the new state of tension. The brain can then determine the changes needed for any further action.

Motor end-plate
The point where the end fibers of an "instruction-carrying" nerve cell (**motor neuron***) meet a **muscle fiber** (see **striated muscle**). The end fibers are branches from one main fiber (**axon***). This carries nervous impulses which make the muscle contract. Each impulse is duplicated and sent down each end branch, hence the whole muscle receives a multiplication of each impulse.

Motor end-plate
Axon* of motor neuron*

* **Axon**, 304; **Dendron**, 304 (**Dendrites**); **Motor neurons**, **Sensory neurons**, 305.

TEETH

The **teeth** or **dentes** (sing. **dens**) help to prepare food for digestion by cutting and grinding it up. Each tooth is set into the jaw, which has a soft tissue covering called **gum** (**gingiva**). During their lives, humans have two sets of teeth (**dentitions**) – a temporary set, or **deciduous dentition**, made up of 20 **deciduous teeth** (also called **milk** or **baby teeth**), and a later **permanent dentition** (32 **permanent teeth**).

Parts of a tooth

Crown
The exposed part of a tooth. It is covered by **enamel**. It is the part most subject to damage or tooth decay.

Root
The part of a tooth that is fixed in a socket in the jaw. **Incisors** and **canines** have one root, **premolars** have one or two and **molars** have two or three. Each root is held in place by the tough fibers of a **ligament*** called the **periodontal ligament**. The fibers are fixed to the jawbone at one end, and to the **cement** at the other. They act as shock absorbers.

Dentine or ivory
A yellow substance which forms the second layer inside a tooth. It is not as hard as **enamel** but, like it, has many of the same constituents as bone. It also contains **collagen*** fibers and strands of **cytoplasm***. These run out from the **pulp** cells in the **pulp cavity**.

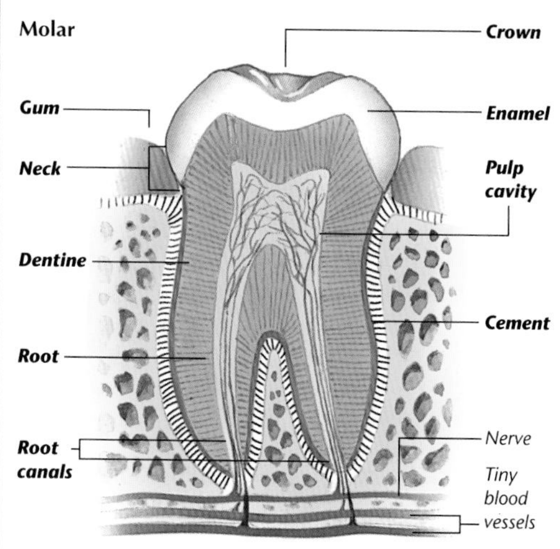

Molar
Crown
Gum
Enamel
Neck
Pulp cavity
Dentine
Cement
Root
Root canals
Nerve
Tiny blood vessels

Neck or cervix
The part of a tooth just below the surface, lying between the **crown** and the **root**.

Enamel
A substance similar to bone, though it is harder (the hardest substance in the body) and has no living cells. It consists of tightly-packed crystals of **apatite**, a mineral which contains calcium, phosphorus and fluorine.

Cement or cementum
A bone-like substance, similar to **enamel** but softer. It forms the thin surface layer of the **root** and is attached to the jaw by the **periodontal ligament** (see **root**).

Pulp cavity
The central area of a tooth, surrounded by **dentine**. It is filled with a soft tissue called **pulp**, which contains blood vessels and nerve fiber endings. These enter at the base of a **root** and run up to the cavity inside **root canals**. The blood vessels supply food and oxygen to the living tissue, and the nerve fiber endings are **pain receptors***.

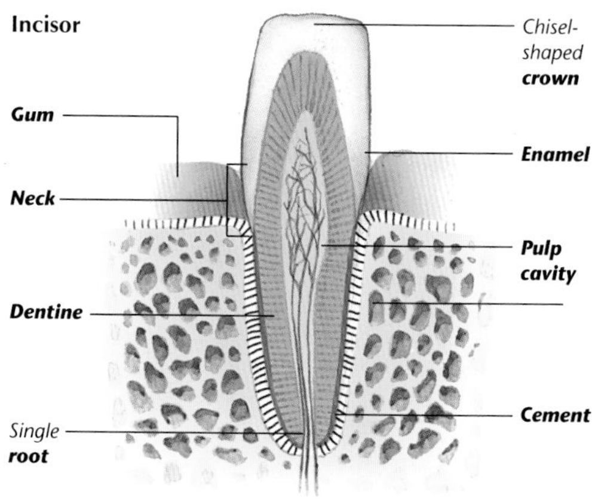

Incisor
Chisel-shaped crown
Gum
Enamel
Neck
Pulp cavity
Dentine
Cement
Single root

* **Collagen**, 280 (**Connective tissue**); **Cytoplasm**, 238; **Ligaments**, 280; **Pain receptors**, 311.

Types of teeth

Incisors
Sharp, chisel-shaped teeth, used for biting and cutting. Each has one root, and there are four in each jaw, set at the front of the mouth.

Canines or cuspids
Cone-shaped teeth (often called **eye** or **dog teeth**), used to tear food. Each has a sharp point (**cusp**) and one **root**. There are two in each jaw, one each side of the **incisors**. In many mammals, they are long and curved.

Premolars or bicuspids
Blunt, broad teeth, used for crushing and grinding (found in the permanent set of teeth only). There are four in each jaw, two behind each **canine**. Each has two sharp ridges (**cusps**) and one **root**, except the upper first premolars, which have two.

Molars
Blunt, broad teeth, similar to **premolars** but with a larger surface area. They are also used for crushing and grinding, and each has four surface points (**cusps**). Lower molars have two **roots** each, and upper ones have three. There are six molars in each jaw, three behind each pair of **premolars**, and the third ones (at the back) are known as **wisdom teeth**.

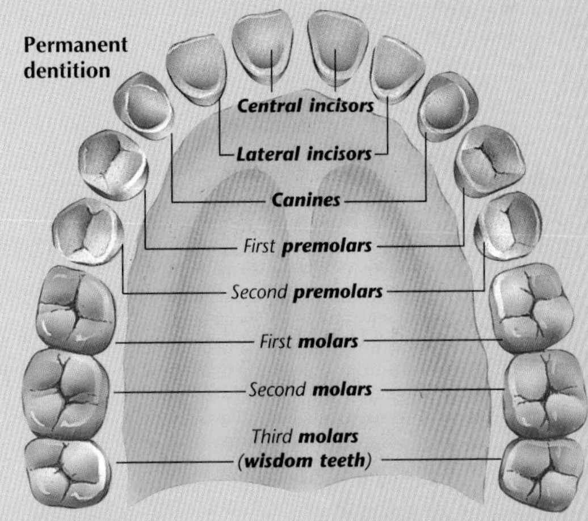

Permanent dentition
Central incisors
Lateral incisors
Canines
First premolars
Second premolars
First molars
Second molars
Third molars (wisdom teeth)

Incisors *(replace eight temporary incisors).*

Premolars *(replace eight temporary molars).*

Canines *(replace four temporary canines).*

Molars *(appear behind* ***premolars*** *and do not replace any deciduous teeth).*

Wisdom teeth
Four **molars** (the third ones in line), lying at the end points of the jaws. They appear last of all, when a person is fully mature (hence their name). Often there is no room for them to come through and they get stuck in the jawbone, or **impacted**. A few people never develop wisdom teeth.

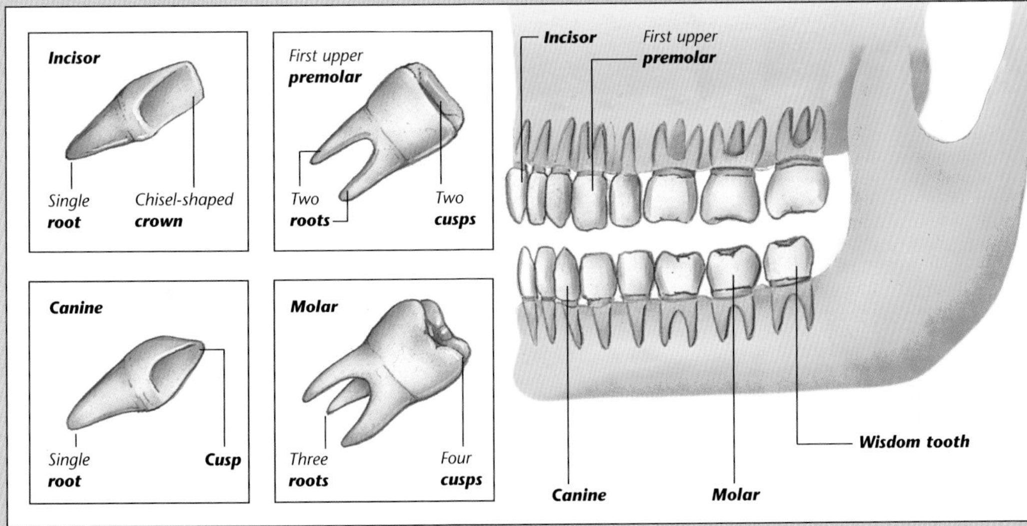

Incisor
Single root
Chisel-shaped crown
First upper premolar
Two roots
Two cusps
Canine
Single root
Cusp
Molar
Three roots
Four cusps
Incisor
First upper premolar
Wisdom tooth
Canine
Molar

BLOOD

Blood is a vital body fluid, consisting of **plasma**, **platelets** and **red** and **white blood cells**. An adult human has about 5.5 liters (9.5 pints), which travel around in the **circulatory system*** – a system of tubes called **blood vessels**. The blood distributes heat and carries many important substances in its plasma. Old, dying blood cells are constantly being replaced by new ones in a process called **hemopoiesis**.

Red blood cells

Blood constituents

Plasma

The pale liquid (about 90% water) which contains the blood cells. It carries dissolved food for the body cells, waste matter and carbon dioxide secreted by them, **antibodies** to combat infection, and **enzymes*** and **hormones*** which control body processes.

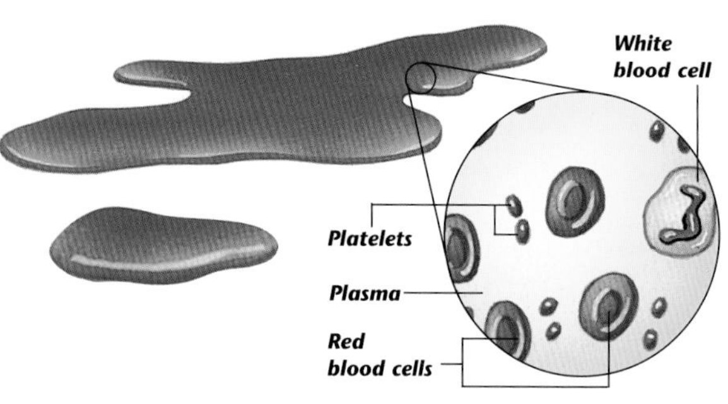
White blood cell
Platelets
Plasma
Red blood cells

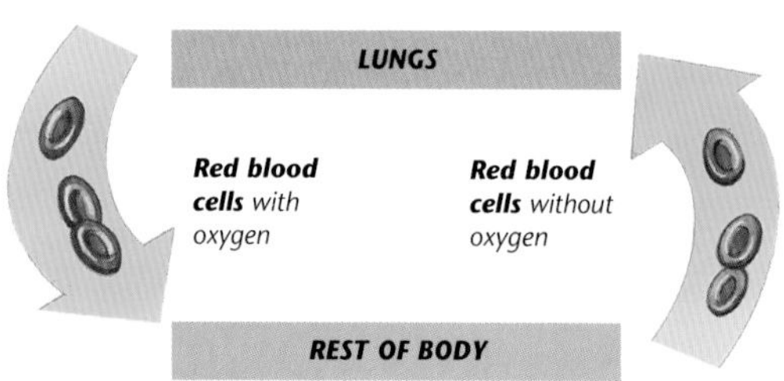
LUNGS
Red blood cells with oxygen
Red blood cells without oxygen
REST OF BODY

Red blood cells

Also called **red corpuscles** or **erythrocytes**. Red, disk-shaped cells with no **nuclei***. They are made in the **bone marrow*** and contain **hemoglobin** (an iron compound which gives blood a dark red color). This combines with oxygen in the lungs to form **oxyhemoglobin**, and the blood becomes bright red. The red cells pass the oxygen to the body cells (by **diffusion***) and then return to the lungs with hemoglobin.

Platelets or thrombocytes

Very small, disk-shaped bodies with no **nuclei***, made in the **bone marrow***. They gather particularly at an injured area, where they are important in the **clotting** of blood.

White blood cells

Also called **white corpuscles** or **leucocytes**. Large, opaque blood cells, important in body defense. There are several types. **Lymphocytes**, for example, are made in **lymphoid tissue*** and are found in the **lymphatic system*** as well as blood. They make **antibodies**. Other white cells – **monocytes** – are made in **bone marrow***. They "swallow up" foreign bodies, e.g. bacteria, in a process called **phagocytosis***. Many of them (called **macrophages**) leave the blood vessels. They either travel around (**wandering macrophages**) or become fixed in an organ, e.g. a **lymph node*** (**fixed macrophages**).

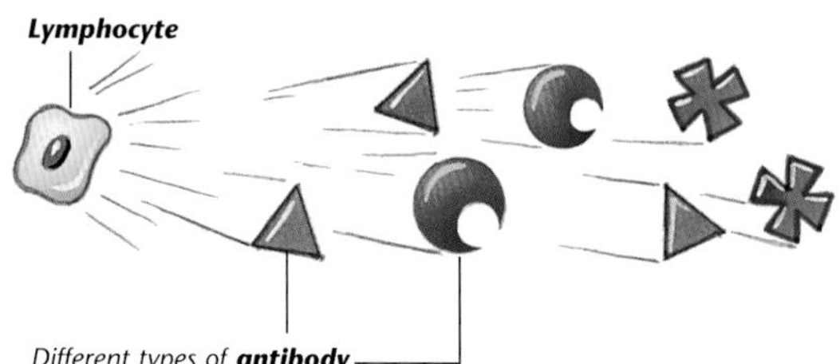
Lymphocyte

*Different types of **antibody***

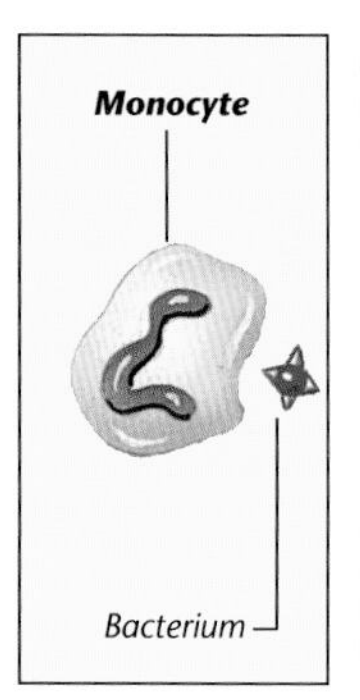
Monocyte
Bacterium

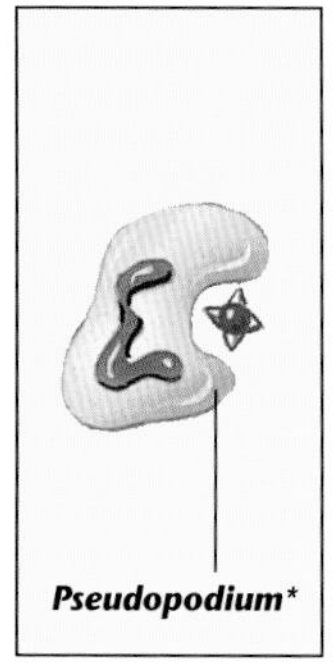
Pseudopodium*

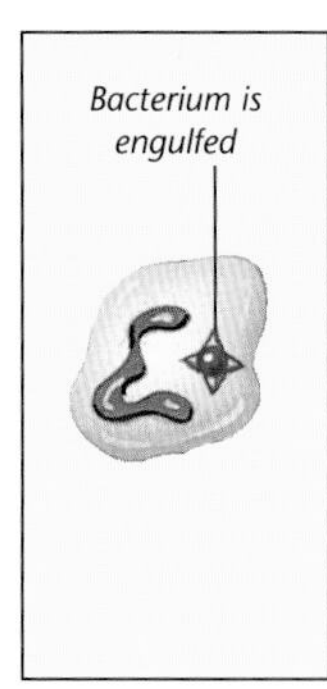
Bacterium is engulfed

* **Bone marrow**, 281; **Circulatory system**, 288; **Diffusion**, 329; **Enzymes**, 333; **Hormones**, 336; **Lymphatic system**, **Lymph nodes**, 293; **Lymphoid tissue**, 293 (**Lymphoid organs**); **Nucleus**, 238; **Phagocytosis**, 268 (**Pseudopodium**).

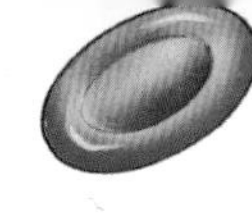

ABO blood groups

The main way of classifying blood. People with group A blood have A **antigen** on their **red blood cells** (and anti-B **antibodies**) and those with group B have B antigen (and anti-A antibodies). People with group AB have both antigens (and neither type of antibody) and those with group O have neither antigen (and both types of antibody).

Rhesus factor or Rh factor

A second way of classifying blood (as well as by **ABO blood group**). People whose **red blood cells** bear the **Rhesus antigen** are said to be **Rhesus positive**. Those without this antigen are **Rhesus negative**. Their blood does not normally contain anti-rhesus **antibodies**, but these would be produced if rhesus positive blood were to enter the body.

Body defense

Antibodies

"Defense" proteins in body fluids, e.g. **plasma**. They are made by **lymphocytes** (see **white blood cells**) to combat **antigens** (see below) in the body. A different antibody is made for each antigen, and they act in different ways. **Anti-toxins** neutralize toxins (poisons). Each one joins with a toxin molecule, making an **antigen-antibody complex**. **Agglutinins** stick the bacteria or viruses together, and **lysins** kill them by dissolving their outer membranes.

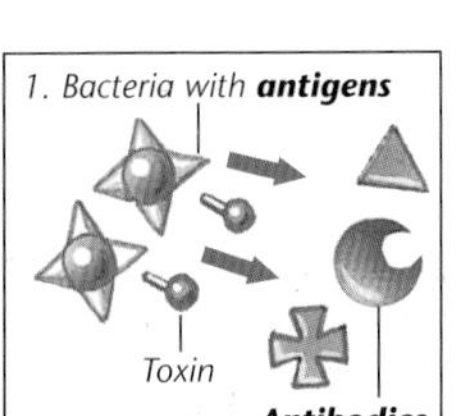
1. Bacteria with **antigens**
Toxin
Antibodies

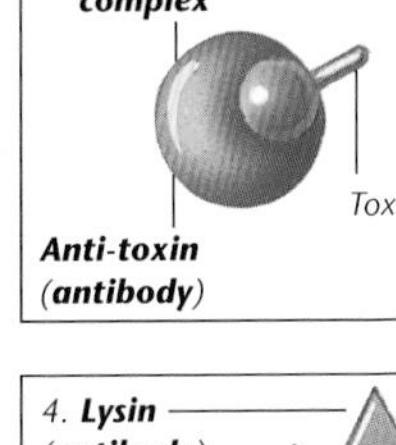
2. **Antigen-antibody complex**
Toxin
Anti-toxin (antibody)

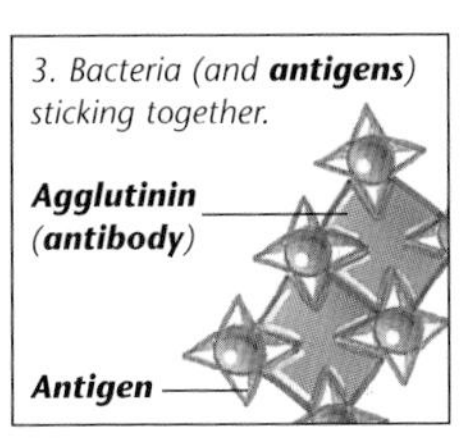
3. Bacteria (and **antigens**) sticking together.
Agglutinin (antibody)
Antigen

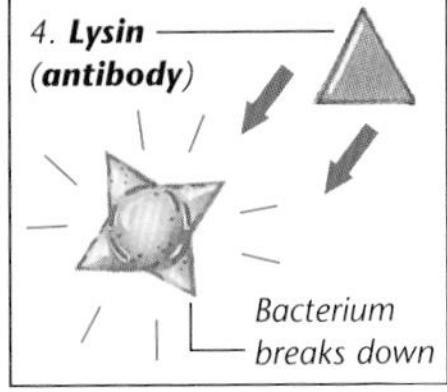
4. **Lysin (antibody)**
Bacterium breaks down

Antigens

Substances, mostly proteins, which cause the production of **antibodies** to combat them and any infection they may cause. They may form part of bacteria or viruses which enter the body, or they may be toxins (poisons) released by them. **ABO blood group** antigens and antibodies (see above) are present in the body from birth, ready to combat foreign blood group antigens.

Clotting or coagulation

The thickening of blood into a mass (**clot**) at the site of a wound. First, disintegrating **platelets** and damaged cells release a chemical called **thromboplastin**. This causes **prothrombin** (a **plasma** protein) to turn into **thrombin** (an **enzyme***). The thrombin then causes **fibrinogen** (another plasma protein) to harden into **fibrin**, a fibrous substance. A network of its fibers makes up the jelly-like clot.

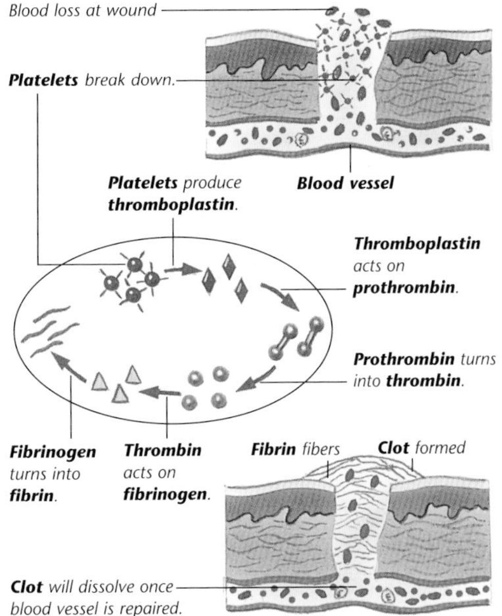
Blood loss at wound
Platelets break down.
Platelets produce **thromboplastin**.
Blood vessel
Thromboplastin acts on **prothrombin**.
Prothrombin turns into **thrombin**.
Fibrinogen turns into **fibrin**.
Thrombin acts on **fibrinogen**.
Fibrin fibers
Clot formed
Clot will dissolve once blood vessel is repaired.

Serum

A yellowy liquid consisting of the parts of the blood left after **clotting**. It contains many **antibodies** (produced to combat infections). When injected into other people, it can give temporary immunity to the infections.

* **Enzymes**, 333.

THE CIRCULATORY SYSTEM

The **circulatory** or **vascular system** is a network of blood-filled tubes, or **blood vessels**, of which there are three main types – **arteries, veins** and **capillaries**. A thin tissue layer called the **endothelium** lines arteries and veins, and is the only layer of capillary walls. Blood is kept flowing one way by the pumping of the heart, by muscles in artery and vein walls and by a decrease in pressure through the system (liquids flow from high to low pressure areas).

Passage of main substances in the circulatory system

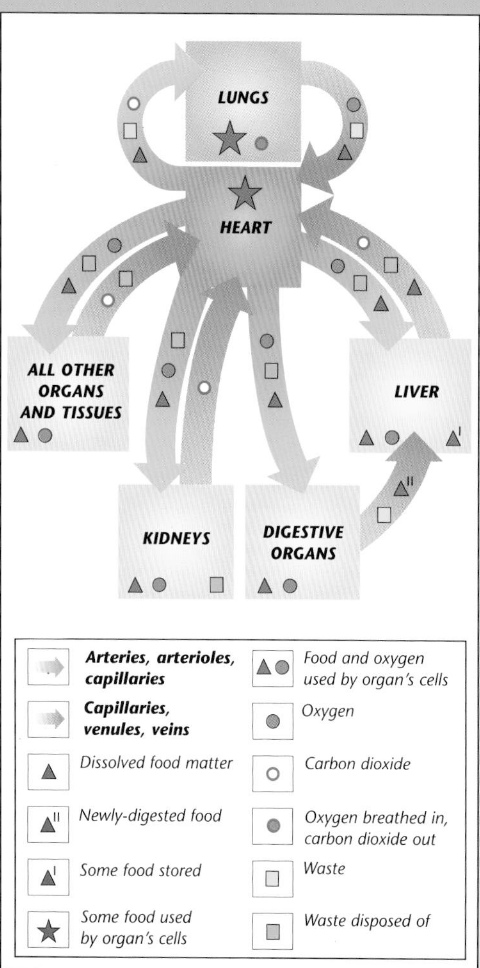

LUNGS
HEART
ALL OTHER ORGANS AND TISSUES
LIVER
KIDNEYS
DIGESTIVE ORGANS
Arteries, arterioles, capillaries
Capillaries, venules, veins
Dissolved food matter
Newly-digested food
Some food stored
Some food used by organ's cells
Food and oxygen used by organ's cells
Oxygen
Carbon dioxide
Oxygen breathed in, carbon dioxide out
Waste
Waste disposed of

Arteries

Wide, thick-walled blood vessels, making up the **arterial system** and carrying blood away from the heart. Smaller arteries (**arterioles**) branch off the main ones, and **capillaries** branch off the arterioles. Except in the **pulmonary arteries***, the blood contains oxygen (which makes it bright red). In all arteries it also carries dissolved food and waste, brought into the heart by **veins**, and there transferred to the arteries. These carry the food to the cells (via arterioles and capillaries) and the waste to the kidneys.

Artery

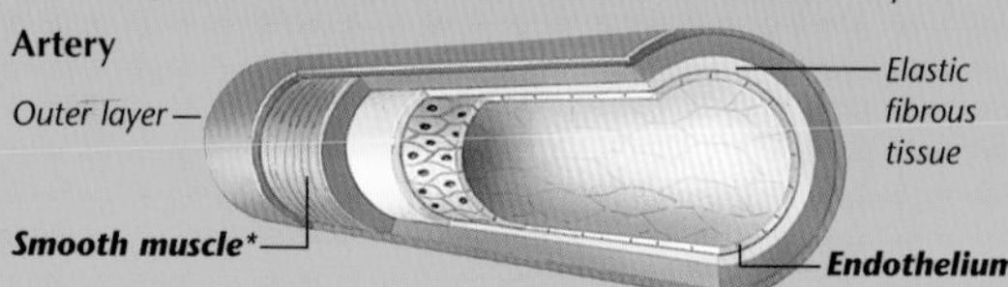

Outer layer
Elastic fibrous tissue
Smooth muscle*
Endothelium

Veins

Wide, thick-walled blood vessels, making up the **venous system** and carrying blood back to the heart. They contain valves to stop blood flowing backward due to gravity, and are formed from merging **venules** (small veins). These are formed in turn from merging **capillaries**. The blood contains carbon dioxide (except in the **pulmonary veins***) and waste matter, both picked up from body cells by the capillaries. The blood in the veins leading from the digestive system and liver also carries dissolved food. This is transferred to the arteries in the heart.

Vein

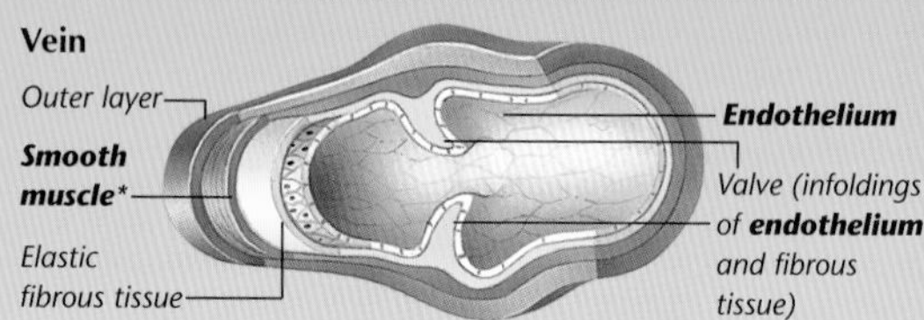

Outer layer
Smooth muscle*
Elastic fibrous tissue
Endothelium
Valve (infoldings of endothelium and fibrous tissue)

Capillaries

Narrow, thin-walled blood vessels, branching off **arterioles** (see **arteries**) to form a complex network. Oxygen and dissolved food pass out through their walls to the body cells, and carbon dioxide and waste pass in (see **tissue fluid**, page 292). The capillaries of the digestive organs and liver also pick up food. Capillaries finally join up again to form small veins (**venules**).

Capillary

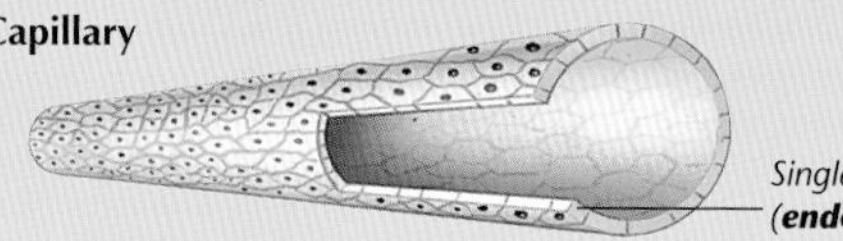

Single layer (endothelium)

* **Hepatic portal vein**, 297 (**Liver**); **Pulmonary arteries**, 291 (**Pulmonary trunk**); **Pulmonary veins**, 291; **Smooth muscle**, 283.

The main arteries and veins

Vascular means "composed of or containing conducting vessels". In the case of animals, it means having a blood supply.

Avascular means "containing no conducting vessels". In the case of animals, it means having no blood supply.

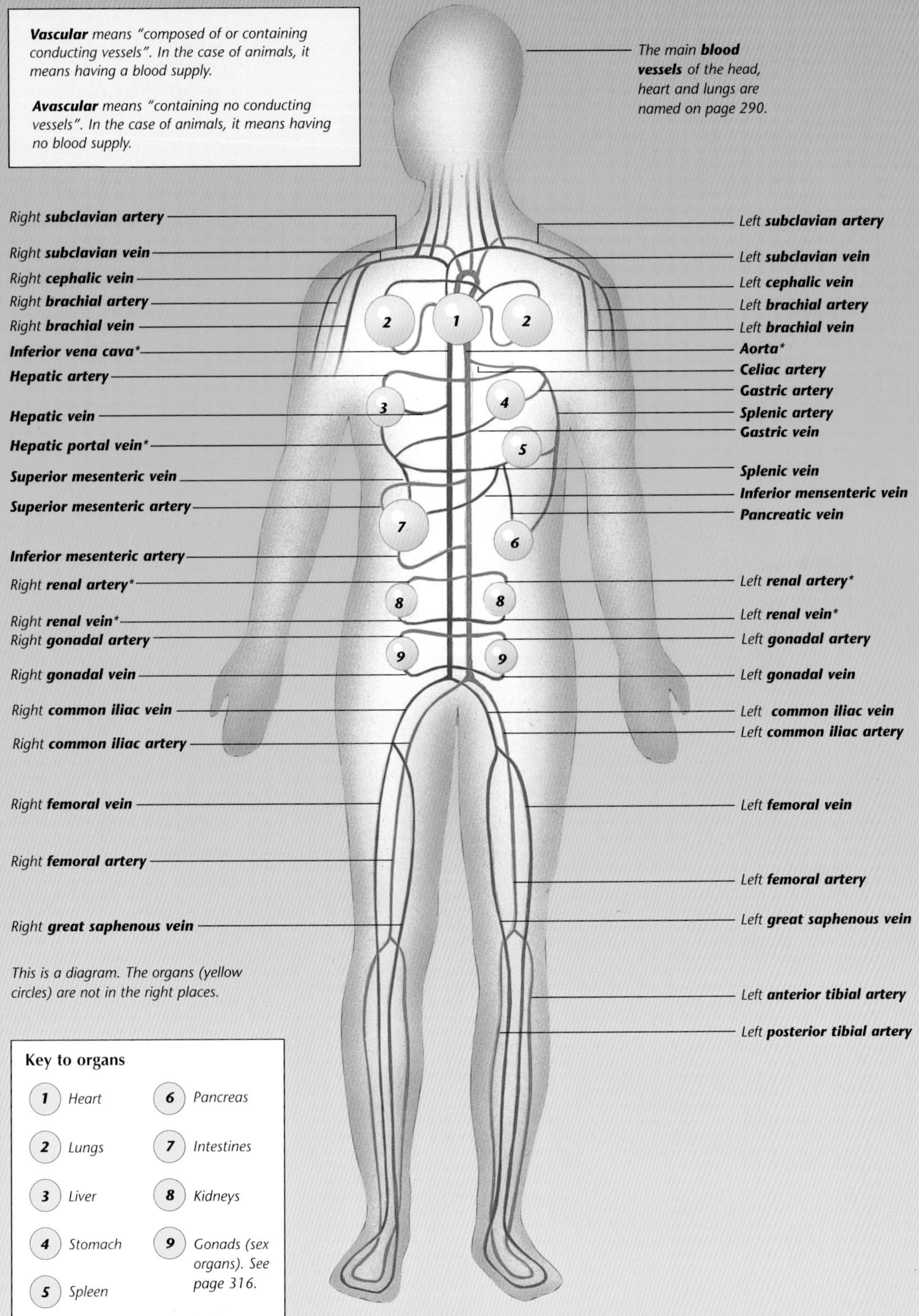
The main **blood vessels** of the head, heart and lungs are named on page 290.
Right **subclavian artery**
Right **subclavian vein**
Right **cephalic vein**
Right **brachial artery**
Right **brachial vein**
Inferior vena cava*
Hepatic artery
Hepatic vein
Hepatic portal vein*
Superior mesenteric vein
Superior mesenteric artery
Inferior mesenteric artery
Right **renal artery***
Right **renal vein***
Right **gonadal artery**
Right **gonadal vein**
Right **common iliac vein**
Right **common iliac artery**
Right **femoral vein**
Right **femoral artery**
Right **great saphenous vein**
Left **subclavian artery**
Left **subclavian vein**
Left **cephalic vein**
Left **brachial artery**
Left **brachial vein**
Aorta*
Celiac artery
Gastric artery
Splenic artery
Gastric vein
Splenic vein
Inferior mensenteric vein
Pancreatic vein
Left **renal artery***
Left **renal vein***
Left **gonadal artery**
Left **gonadal vein**
Left **common iliac vein**
Left **common iliac artery**
Left **femoral vein**
Left **femoral artery**
Left **great saphenous vein**
Left **anterior tibial artery**
Left **posterior tibial artery**
1
2
2
3
4
5
6
7
8
8
9
9

This is a diagram. The organs (yellow circles) are not in the right places.

Key to organs

1 Heart
2 Lungs
3 Liver
4 Stomach
5 Spleen
6 Pancreas
7 Intestines
8 Kidneys
9 Gonads (sex organs). See page 316.

* **Aorta**, 291; **Hepatic portal vein**, 297 (**Liver**); **Inferior vena cava**, 291; **Renal arteries**, **Renal veins**, 300 (**Kidneys**).

THE HEART

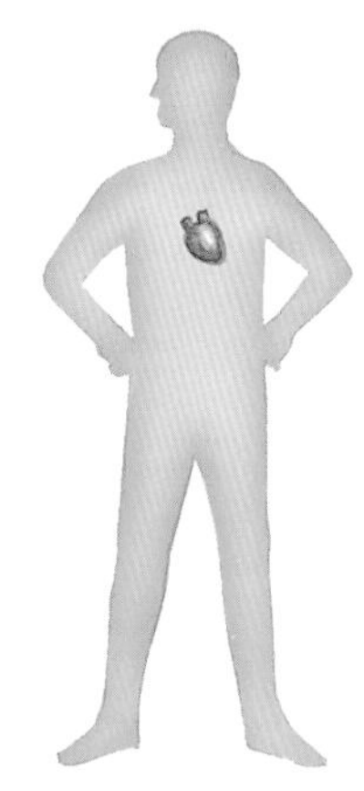

Position of **heart**

The **heart** is a muscular organ which pumps blood around the blood vessels. (The heart and blood vessels together are the **cardiovascular system**.) It is surrounded by the **pericardial sac**. This consists of an outer membrane (the **pericardium**) and the cavity (**pericardial cavity**) between it and the heart. This cavity is filled with a cushioning fluid (**pericardial fluid**). The heart has four chambers – two **atria** and two **ventricles**, all lined by a thin tissue layer called the **endocardium**.

The chambers of the heart

Atria (sing. atrium) or auricles

The two upper chambers. The left atrium receives **oxygenated** blood (blood with fresh oxygen – see also **hemoglobin***) from the lungs via the **pulmonary veins**. The right atrium receives **deoxygenated** blood from the rest of the body via the **superior** and **inferior vena cavae**. This is blood whose oxygen has been used by the cells and replaced by carbon dioxide.

Ventricles

The two lower chambers. The left ventricle receives blood from the left **atrium** and pumps it into the **aorta**. The right ventricle receives blood from the right atrium and pumps it via the **pulmonary trunk** to the lungs.

Key

Oxygenated blood

Deoxygenated blood

Cardiac *means "of or near the heart".*
Pulmonary *means "of the lungs".*

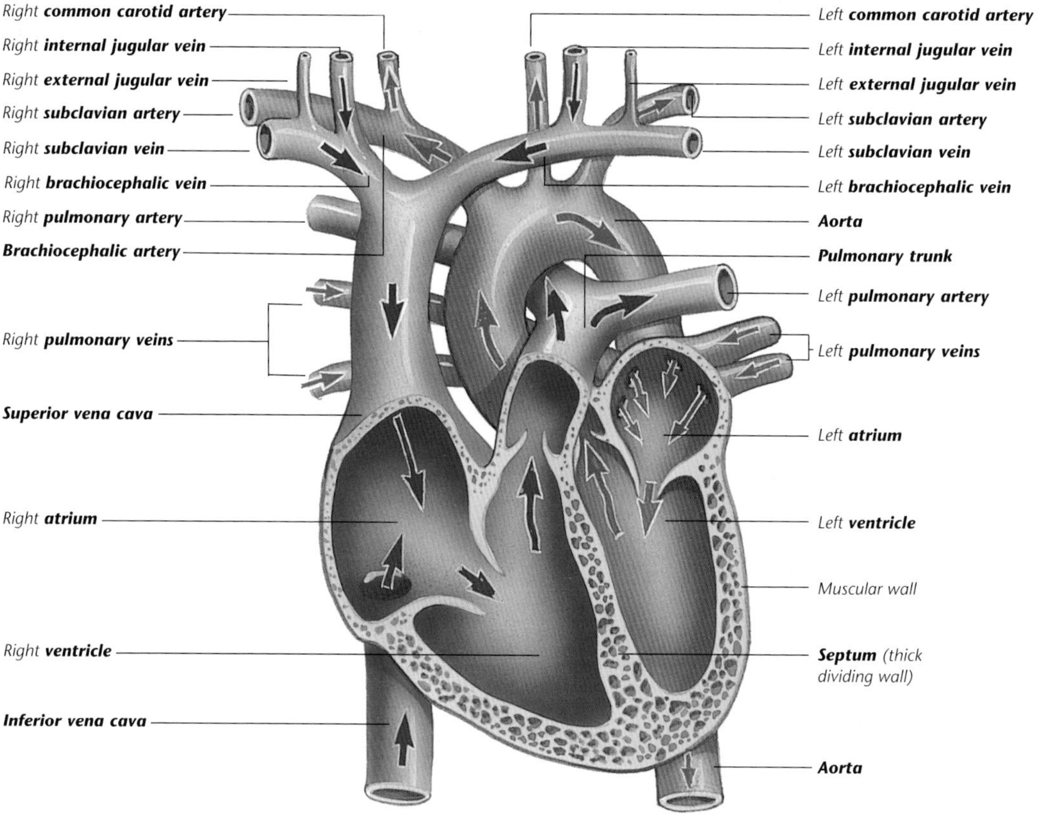

Right **common carotid artery**
Right **internal jugular vein**
Right **external jugular vein**
Right **subclavian artery**
Right **subclavian vein**
Right **brachiocephalic vein**
Right **pulmonary artery**
Brachiocephalic artery
Right **pulmonary veins**
Superior vena cava
Right **atrium**
Right **ventricle**
Inferior vena cava
Left **common carotid artery**
Left **internal jugular vein**
Left **external jugular vein**
Left **subclavian artery**
Left **subclavian vein**
Left **brachiocephalic vein**
Aorta
Pulmonary trunk
Left **pulmonary artery**
Left **pulmonary veins**
Left **atrium**
Left **ventricle**
Muscular wall
Septum (thick dividing wall)
Aorta

* **Hemoglobin**, 286 (**Red blood cells**).

The main arteries and veins

Aorta
The largest **artery*** in the body. It carries blood with fresh oxygen out of the left **ventricle** to begin its journey around the body.

Pulmonary trunk
The **artery*** which carries blood needing fresh oxygen out of the right **ventricle**. After leaving the heart, it splits into the right and left **pulmonary arteries**, one going to each lung.

Superior vena cava
One of the two main **veins***. It carries blood needing fresh oxygen from the upper body to the right **atrium**. All the upper body veins merge into it.

Inferior vena cava
One of the two main **veins***, carrying blood needing fresh oxygen from the lower body to the right **atrium**. All the lower body veins merge into it.

Pulmonary veins
Four **veins*** which carry blood with fresh oxygen to the left **atrium**. Two right pulmonary veins come from the right lung, and two left pulmonary veins come from the left lung.

Semilunar valves
Two valves, so called because they have crescent-shaped flaps. One is the **aortic valve** between the left **ventricle** and the **aorta**. The other is the **pulmonary valve** between the right ventricle and the **pulmonary trunk**.

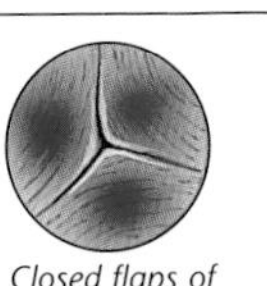

Closed flaps of **pulmonary valve**

Open flaps of **aortic valve**

Atrioventricular valves or AV valves
Two valves, each between an **atrium** and its corresponding **ventricle**. The left AV valve, or **mitral valve**, is a **bicuspid valve**, i.e. it has two movable flaps, or **cusps**. The right AV valve is a **tricuspid valve**, i.e. it has three cusps.

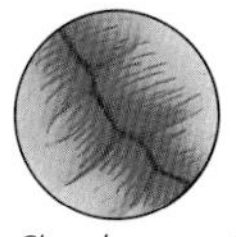

Closed **cusps** of left **AV valve**

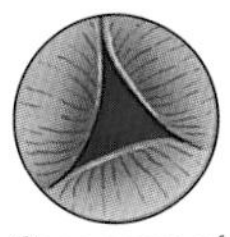

Open **cusps** of right **AV valve**

The cardiac cycle

The **cardiac cycle** is the series of events which make up one complete pumping action of the heart, and which can be heard as the heartbeat (about 70 times a minute). First, both **atria** contract and pump blood into their respective **ventricles**, which relax to receive it. Then the atria relax and take in blood, and the ventricles contract to pump it out. The relaxing phase of a chamber is its **diastole phase**; the contracting phase is its **systole phase**. There is a short pause after the systole phase of the ventricles, during which all chambers are in diastole phase (relaxing). The different **valves** which open and close during the cycle are defined below left.

Cardiac cycle

***1. Atria** in **systole phase**, **ventricles** in **diastole phase**.*

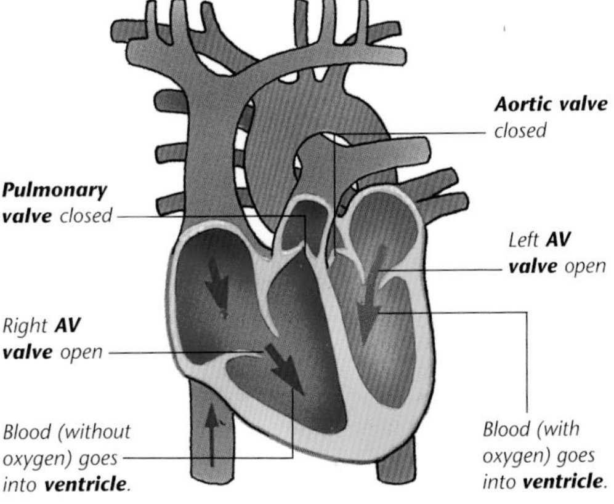
Aortic valve closed
Pulmonary valve closed
Left AV valve open
Right AV valve open
Blood (without oxygen) goes into ventricle.
Blood (with oxygen) goes into ventricle.

***2. Atria** in **diastole phase**, **ventricles** in **systole phase**.*

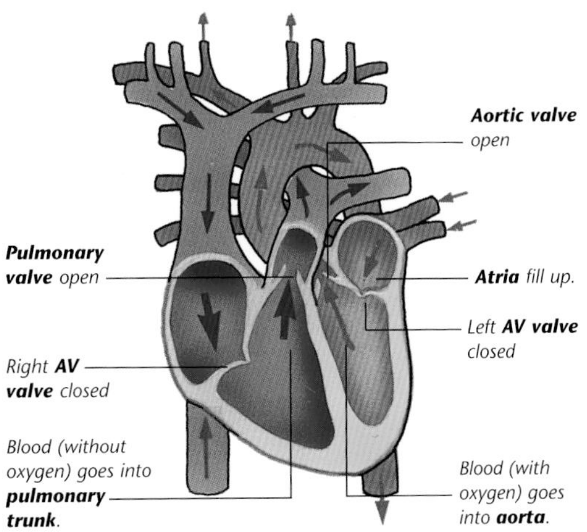
Aortic valve open
Pulmonary valve open
Atria fill up.
Left AV valve closed
Right AV valve closed
Blood (without oxygen) goes into pulmonary trunk.
Blood (with oxygen) goes into aorta.

* **Arteries**, **Veins**, 288.

TISSUE FLUID AND THE LYMPHATIC SYSTEM

The smallest blood vessels, called **capillaries***, are those in the most direct contact with the individual cells of the body, but even they do not touch the cells. The food and oxygen they carry finally reach the cells in **tissue fluid**, a substance which forms the link between the **circulatory system*** and the body's drainage system, known as the **lymphatic system**.

Tissue fluid

Also called **intercellular** or **interstitial fluid**. A fluid which surrounds the body cells. It seeps out from the blood through the walls of **capillaries*** (mainly at their high-pressure ends, after they have branched from **arterioles***) and is essentially **plasma***, though with fewer proteins. It carries oxygen and dissolved food to the body cells, and carbon dioxide and waste matter away from them. These latter substances enter the capillaries (mainly at their low-pressure ends, before they form **venules***).

The protein molecules not needed by the cells are too large to re-enter the capillaries. They pass, with some of the waste, into the **lymph capillaries** (see **lymph vessels**), whose walls are more easily penetrated.

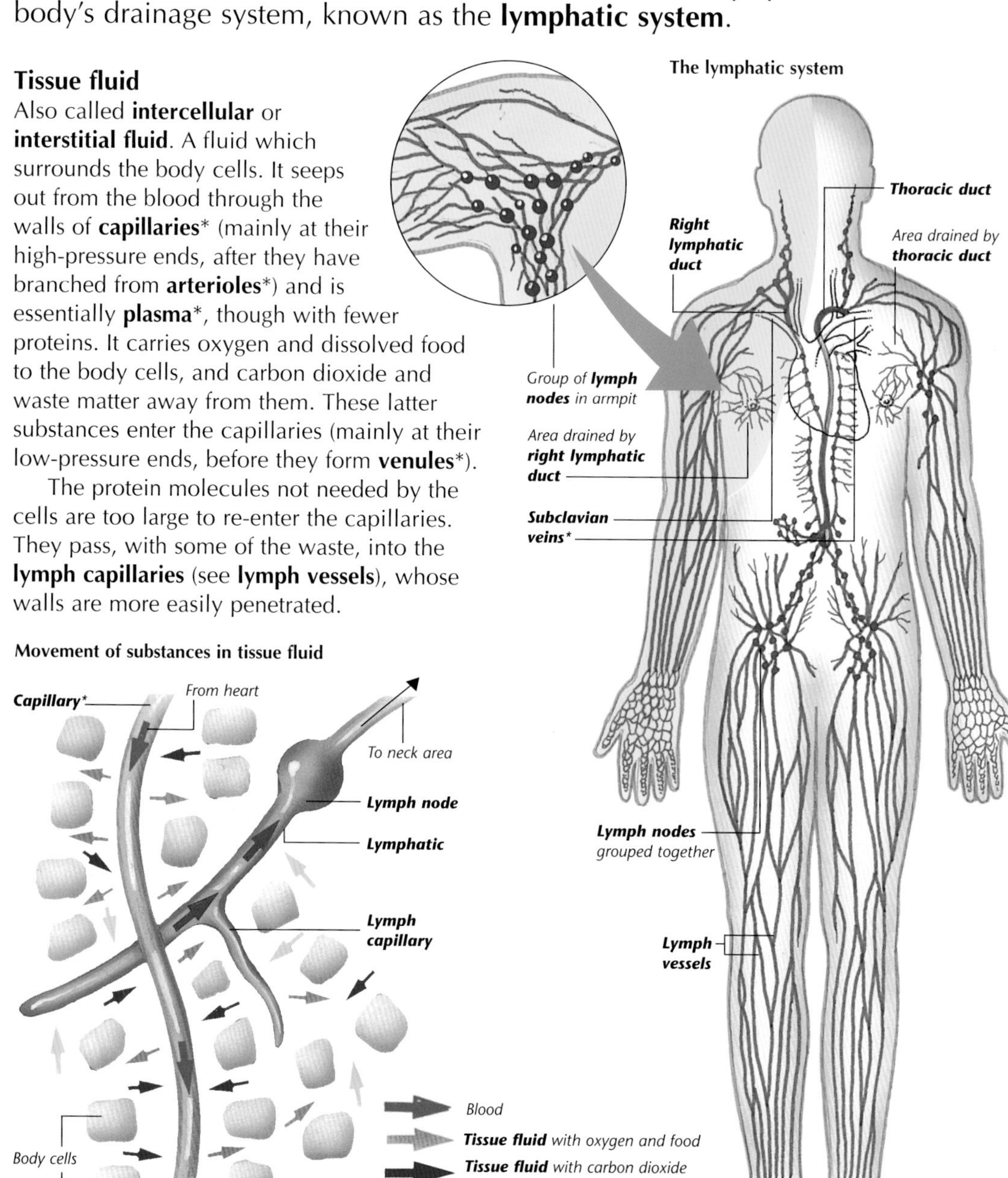

Movement of substances in tissue fluid
Capillary*
From heart
To neck area
Lymph node
Lymphatic
Lymph capillary
Body cells
To heart
Blood
Tissue fluid with oxygen and food
Tissue fluid with carbon dioxide and waste
Proteins and some waste
Lymph
The lymphatic system
Thoracic duct
Area drained by thoracic duct
Right lymphatic duct
Group of lymph nodes in armpit
Area drained by right lymphatic duct
Subclavian veins*
Lymph nodes grouped together
Lymph vessels

* **Arterioles**, 288 (**Arteries**); **Capillaries**, 288; **Circulatory system**, 288; **Plasma**, 286; **Subclavian veins**, 289; **Venules**, 288 (**Veins**).

Lymphatic system
A system of tubes (**lymph vessels**) and small organs (**lymphoid organs**), important in the recycling of body fluids and in the fight against disease. The lymph vessels carry the liquid **lymph** around the body and empty it back into the **veins***, and the lymphoid organs are the source of disease-fighting cells.

Lymph
The liquid in **lymph vessels**. It contains **lymphocytes** (see **lymphoid organs**), some substances picked up from **tissue fluid** (especially proteins such as **hormones*** and **enzymes***) and also fat particles (see **lymph vessels**).

Lymph vessels or lymphatic vessels
Blind-ended tubes carrying **lymph** from all body areas toward the neck, where it is emptied back into the blood. They are lined with **endothelium***, and have valves to stop the lymph from being pulled back by gravity.

The thinnest lymph vessesls are **lymph capillaries**, and include the important **lacteals***, which pick up fat particles (too large to enter the bloodstream directly). The capillaries join to form larger vessels called **lymphatics**, which finally unite to form two tubes – the **right lymphatic duct** (emptying into the right **subclavian vein***) and the **thoracic duct** (emptying into the left **subclavian vein***).

Lymphoid organs

The **lymphoid organs**, or **lymphatic organs**, are bodies connected to the **lymphatic system**. They are all made of the same type of tissue (**lymphoid** or **lymphatic tissue**) and they all produce **lymphocytes*** – disease-fighting white blood cells.

Lymph nodes or lymph glands
Small lymphoid organs found along the course of **lymph vessels**, often in groups, e.g. in the armpits. They are the main sites of **lymphocyte** production (see above) and also contain a filter system which traps bacteria and foreign bodies. These are then engulfed by white blood cells (**fixed macrophages***).

Spleen
The largest lymphoid organ, found just below the **diaphragm*** on the left side of the body. It holds an emergency store of red blood cells and also contains white blood cells (**fixed macrophages***) which destroy foreign bodies, e.g. bacteria, and old blood cells.

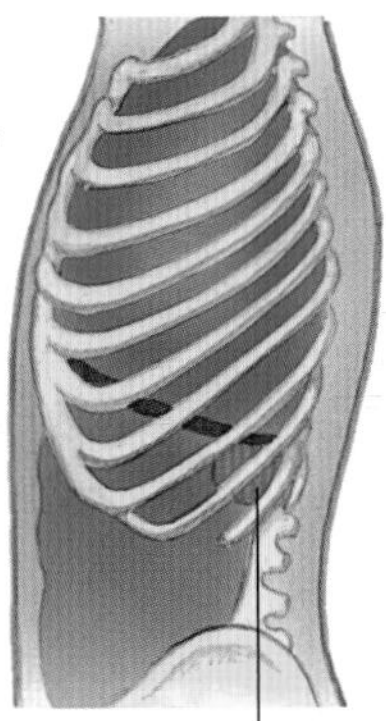

Position of **spleen**

Thymus gland
A lymphoid organ in the upper part of the chest. It is fairly large in children, reaches its maximum size at **puberty*** and then undergoes **atrophy**, i.e. it wastes away.

Tonsils
Four lymphoid organs: one **pharyngeal tonsil** (the **adenoids**) at the back of the nose, one **lingual tonsil** at the base of the tongue and two **palatine tonsils** at the back of the mouth.

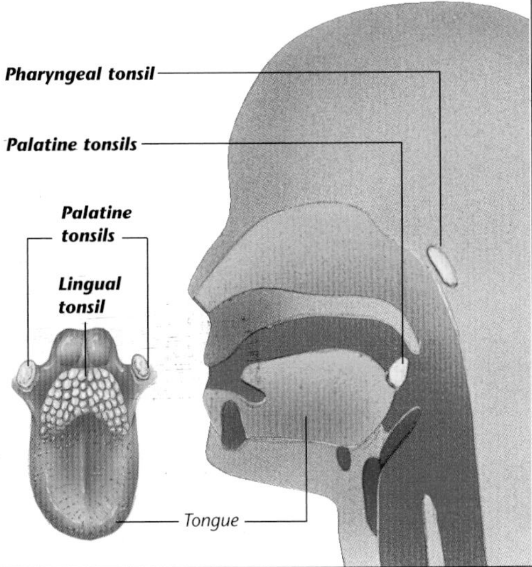
Pharyngeal tonsil
Palatine tonsils
Palatine tonsils
Lingual tonsil
Tongue

* **Diaphragm**, 298; **Endothelium**, 288; **Enzymes**, 333; **Fixed macrophages**, 286 (**White blood cells**); **Hormones**, 336; **Lacteals**, 295 (**Small intestine**); **Lymphocytes**, 286 (**White blood cells**); **Puberty**, 318; **Subclavian veins**, 289; **Veins**, 288.

THE DIGESTIVE SYSTEM

After food is taken in, or **ingested**, it passes through the **digestive system**, gradually being broken down into simple soluble substances by a process called **digestion** (see also pages 338-339). The simple substances are absorbed into the blood vessels around the system and transported to the body cells. Here they are used to provide energy and build new tissue. For more about all these different processes, see pages 330-335. The main parts of the digestive system are listed on these two pages. The pancreas and liver (see page 297) also play a vital part in digestion, forming the two main **digestive glands*** (producing **digestive juices***).

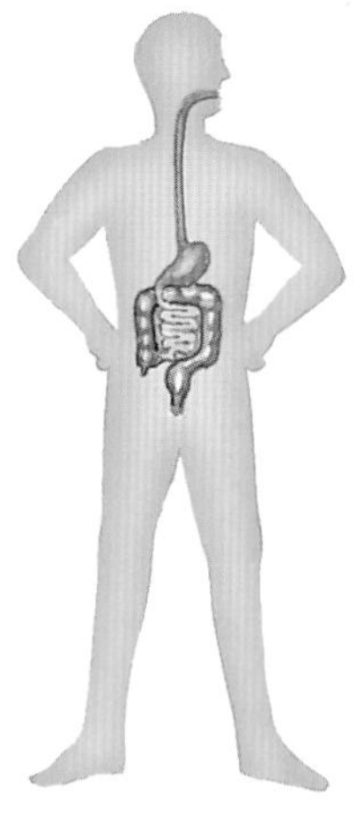

Position of ***digestive system***

Alimentary canal

Also called the **alimentary tract**, **gastrointestinal** (**GI**) **tract**, **enteric canal** or the **gut**. A collective term for all the parts of the digestive system. It is a long tube running from the mouth to the **anus** (see **large intestine**). Most of its parts are in the lower body, or **abdomen**, inside the main body cavity, or **perivisceral cavity***. They are held in place by **mesenteries** – infoldings of the cavity lining (the **peritoneum**).

Pharynx

A cavity at the back of the mouth, where the mouth cavity (**oral** or **buccal cavity**) and the **nasal cavities*** meet. When food is swallowed, the **soft palate** (a tissue flap at the back of the mouth) closes the nasal cavities and the **epiglottis*** closes the **trachea***.

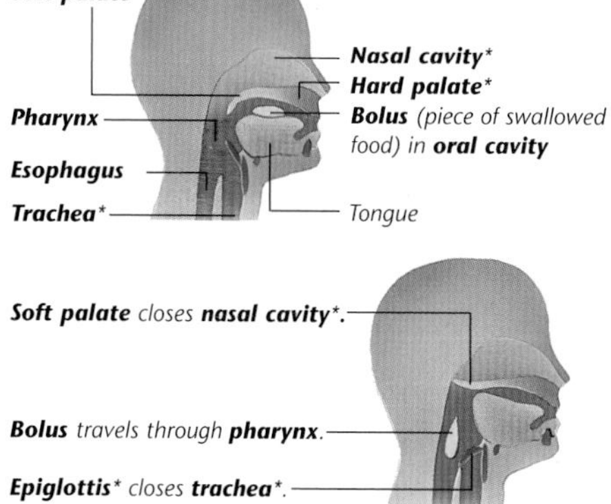

Soft palate
Nasal cavity*
Hard palate*
Pharynx
Bolus (piece of swallowed food) in oral cavity
Esophagus
Trachea*
Tongue
Soft palate closes nasal cavity*.
Bolus travels through pharynx.
Epiglottis* closes trachea*.

Esophagus or gullet

The tube down which food travels to the **stomach**. A piece of swallowed food is a **bolus**.

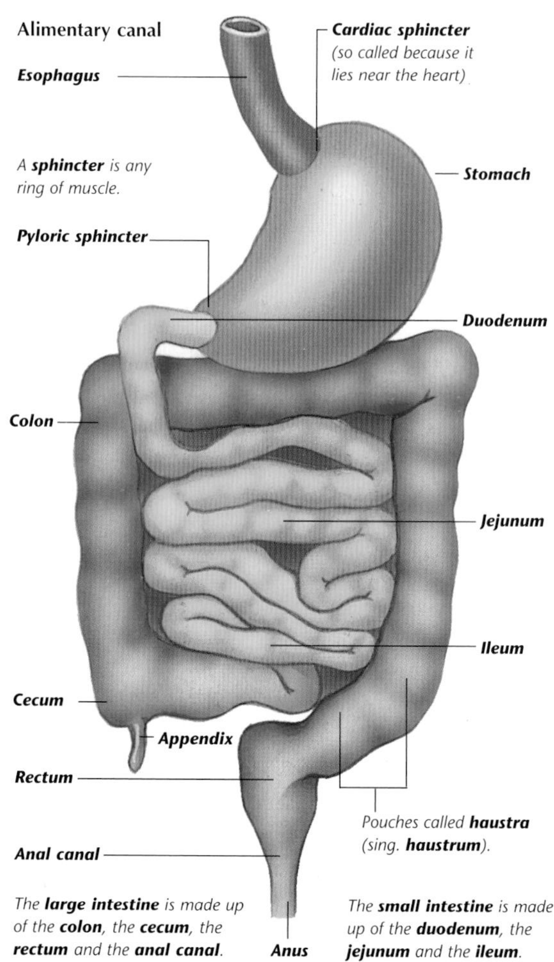

Alimentary canal
Esophagus
Cardiac sphincter (so called because it lies near the heart)
A sphincter is any ring of muscle.
Stomach
Pyloric sphincter
Duodenum
Colon
Jejunum
Ileum
Cecum
Appendix
Rectum
Pouches called haustra (sing. haustrum).
Anal canal
Anus

The ***large intestine*** *is made up of the* ***colon****, the* ***cecum****, the* ***rectum*** *and the* ***anal canal****.*

The ***small intestine*** *is made up of the* ***duodenum****, the* ***jejunum*** *and the* ***ileum****.*

* **Digestive juices**, 296 (**Digestive glands**); **Epiglottis**, 298; **Hard palate**, 307; **Nasal cavities**, 307 (**Nose**); **Perivisceral cavity**, 265; **Trachea**, 298.

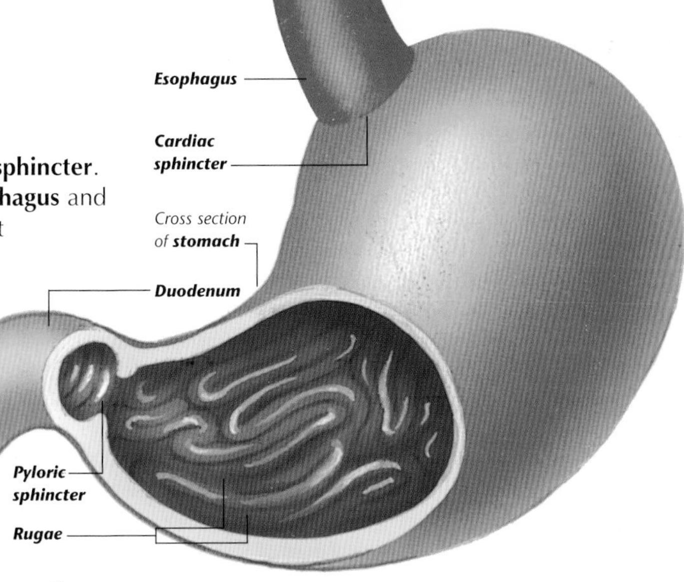
Esophagus
Cardiac sphincter
Cross section of stomach
Duodenum
Pyloric sphincter
Rugae

Cardiac sphincter

Also called the **gastroesophageal sphincter**. A muscular ring between the **esophagus** and **stomach**. It relaxes to open and let food through.

Stomach

A large sac in which the early stages of digestion occur. Its lining has many folds (**rugae**, sing. **ruga**), which flatten out to let it expand. Some substances, e.g. water, pass through its wall into nearby blood vessels, but almost all the semi-digested food (**chyme**) goes into the **small intestine** (**duodenum**).

Pyloric sphincter

Also called the **pyloric valve** or **pylorus**. A muscular ring between the **stomach** and the **small intestine**. It relaxes to let food through only after certain digestive changes have occurred.

Small intestine

A coiled tube with three parts – the **duodenum**, (the main site of digestion), **jejunum** and **ileum**. Many tiny "fingers" called **villi** (sing. **villus**) project inward from its lining. Each contains **capillaries*** (tiny blood vessels) into which most of the food is absorbed, and a **lymph vessel*** called a **lacteal**, which absorbs recombined fat particles (see **fats**, page 330). The remaining semi-liquid waste mixture passes into the **large intestine**.

Cross section of small intestine

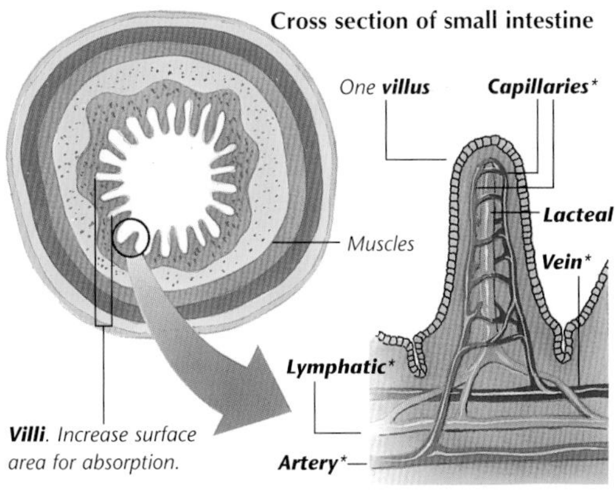
One villus
Capillaries*
Lacteal
Muscles
Vein*
Lymphatic*
Artery*

***Villi**. Increase surface area for absorption.*

Large intestine

A thick tube receiving waste from the **small intestine**. It consists of the **cecum*** (a redundant sac), **colon**, **rectum** and **anal canal**. The colon contains bacteria, which break down any remaining food and make some important vitamins. Most of the water in the waste passes through the colon walls into nearby blood vessels. This leaves a semi-solid mass (**feces**), which is pushed out of the body (**defecation**) via the rectum, anal canal and **anus** – a hole surrounded by a muscular ring (the **anal sphincter**).

Appendix

A small, blind-ended tube off the **cecum** (see **large intestine**).

Mucous membrane or mucosa

A thin layer of tissue lining all digestive passages (also other passages, e.g. the air passages). It is a special type of **epithelium*** (a surface sheet of cells), containing many single-celled **exocrine glands***, called **mucous glands**. These secrete **mucus** – a lubricating fluid which, in the case of the digestive passages, also protects the passage walls against the action of **digestive juices***.

Peristalsis

The waves of contraction, produced by muscles in the walls of organs (especially digestive organs), which move substances along.

* **Arteries**, 288; **Capillaries**, 288; **Cecum**, 271; **Digestive juices**, 296 (**Digestive glands**); **Epithelium**, 310 (**Epidermis**); **Exocrine glands**, 296; **Lymphatic**, 293 (**Lymph vessels**); **Veins**, 288.

GLANDS

Glands are special organs (or sometimes groups of cells or single cells) which produce and secrete a variety of substances vital to life. There are two types of human glands – **exocrine** and **endocrine**.

Exocrine glands

Exocrine glands are glands which secrete substances through tubes, or **ducts**, onto a surface or into a cavity. Most body glands are exocrine, e.g. **sweat glands*** and **digestive glands**.

Digestive glands

Exocrine glands which secrete fluids called **digestive juices** into the digestive organs. The juices contain **enzymes*** which cause the breakdown of food (see chart, pages 338-339). Many of the glands are tiny, and set into the walls of the digestive organs, e.g. **gastric glands** in the stomach and **intestinal glands** (or **crypts of Lieberkühn**) in the small intestine. Others are larger and lie more freely, e.g. **salivary glands**. The largest are the **pancreas** and **liver**.

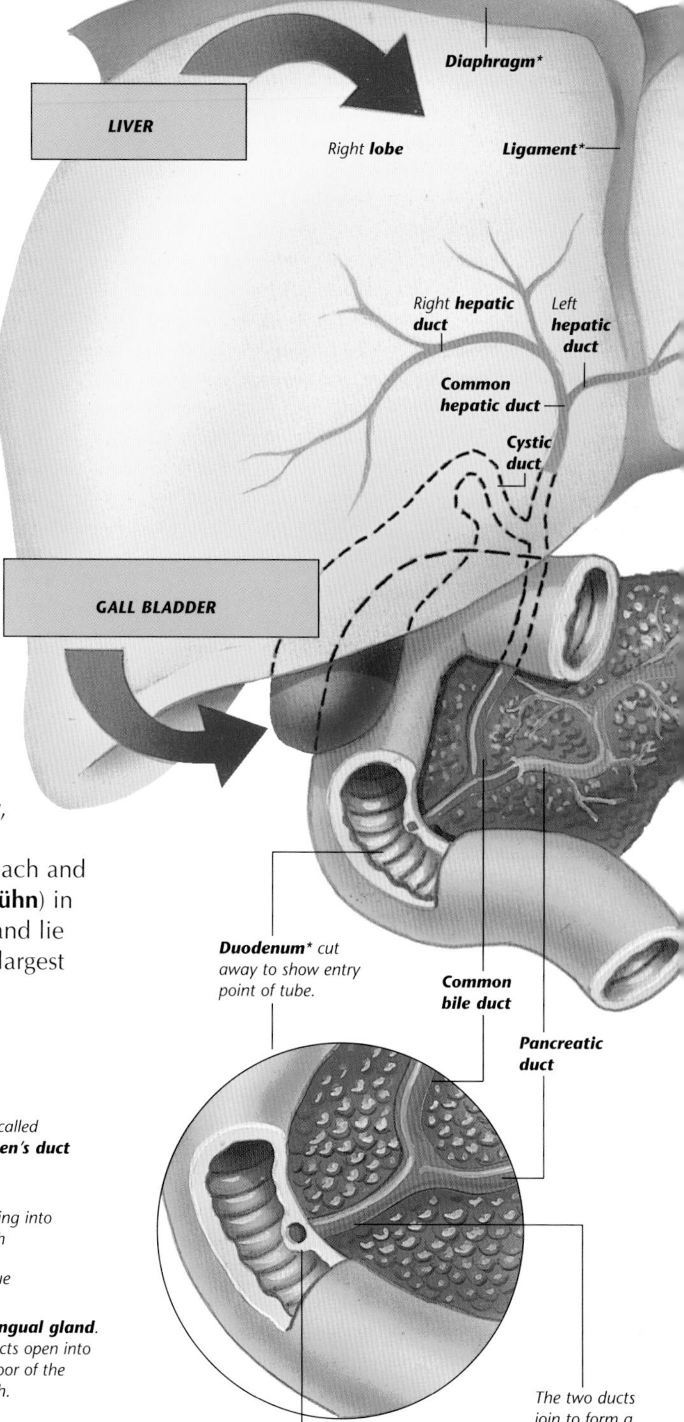

Salivary glands (secrete **saliva*** into mouth)

Only one side is shown – the three glands are duplicated on the other side.

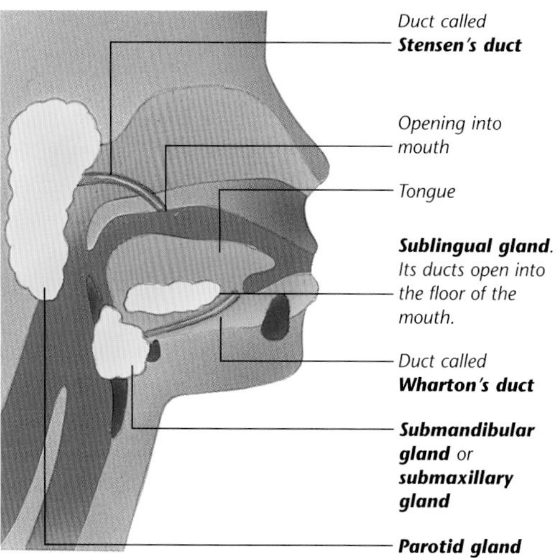

Duct called Stensen's duct
Opening into mouth
Tongue
Sublingual gland. Its ducts open into the floor of the mouth.
Duct called Wharton's duct
Submandibular gland or submaxillary gland
Parotid gland

LIVER

Diaphragm*

Right lobe

Ligament*

Right hepatic duct

Left hepatic duct

Common hepatic duct

Cystic duct

GALL BLADDER

Duodenum cut away to show entry point of tube.*

Common bile duct

Pancreatic duct

*The two ducts join to form a duct called the **ampulla of Vater**.*

*Muscular ring called the **sphincter of Oddi**. If it is closed, **bile** coming from the **liver** is forced back up into the **gall bladder**.*

* **Diaphragm**, 298; **Duodenum**, 295 (**Small intestine**); **Enzymes**, 333; **Ligaments**, 280; **Saliva**, 338; **Sweat glands**, 311.

Left **lobe**

Liver

The largest organ. One of its many roles is that of a **digestive gland**, secreting **bile** (see chart, pages 338-339) along the **common hepatic duct**. Another vital job is the conversion and storage of newly-digested food matter (see diagram, page 331), which it receives along the **hepatic portal vein** (see picture, page 289). In particular, it regulates the amount of glucose in the blood. It also destroys worn-out red blood cells, stores vitamins and iron, and makes important blood proteins.

PANCREAS

Pancreas

A large gland which is both a **digestive gland** and an **endocrine gland**. It produces **pancreatic juice** (see chart, pages 338-339), which it secretes along the **pancreatic duct**, or **duct of Wirsung**. It also contains groups of cells called the **islets of Langerhans**. These make up the endocrine parts of the organ, and produce the **hormones*** **insulin*** and **glucagon***.

Gall bladder

A sac which stores **bile** (made in the **liver**) in a concentrated form until it is needed (i.e. until there is food in the **duodenum***). Its lining has many folds (**rugae**, sing. **ruga**) which flatten out as it expands. When needed, the bile is squeezed along the **cystic duct** and the **common bile duct**.

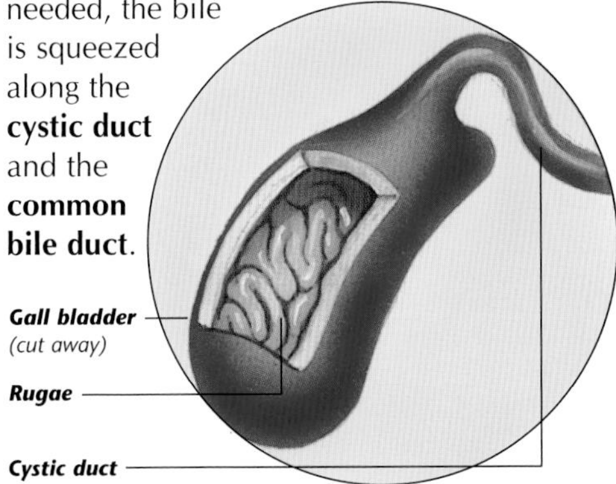

Gall bladder (cut away)
Rugae
Cystic duct

Endocrine glands

Endocrine or **ductless glands** are glands which secrete substances called **hormones** directly into the blood (i.e. blood vessels in the glands). For more about hormones, see pages 336-337. The glands may be separate bodies (e.g. those below) or cells inside organs, e.g. in the sex organs.

Pituitary gland

Also called the **pituitary body** or **hypophysis**. A gland at the base of the brain, directly influenced by the **hypothalamus*** (see also **hormones**, page 336) and made up of an **anterior** (front) **lobe** (**adenohypophysis**) and a **posterior** (back) **lobe** (**neurohypophysis**). Many of its hormones are **tropic hormones**, i.e. they stimulate other glands to secrete hormones. It makes **ACTH**, **TSH**, **STH**, **FSH**, **LH**, **lactogenic hormone**, **oxytocin** and **ADH**.

Thyroid gland

A large gland around the **larynx***. It produces **thyroxin** and **thyrocalcitonin**.

Parathyroid glands

Two pairs of small glands embedded in the **thyroid gland**. They produce **PTH**.

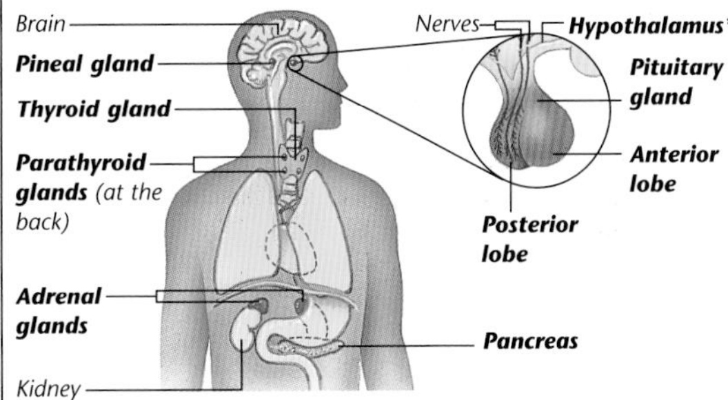

Brain
Pineal gland
Thyroid gland
Parathyroid glands (at the back)
Adrenal glands
Kidney
Nerves
Hypothalamus*
Pituitary gland
Anterior lobe
Posterior lobe
Pancreas

Adrenal glands or suprarenal glands

A pair of glands, one gland lying above each kidney. Each has an outer layer (**cortex**), producing **aldosterone**, **cortisone** and **hydrocortisone**, and an inner layer (**medulla**), producing **adrenalin** and **noradrenalin**.

Pineal gland

Also called the **pineal body**. A small gland at the front of the brain. Its role is not clear, but it is known to secrete **melatonin**, a hormone thought to influence **sex hormone*** production.

* **Duodenum**, 295 (**Small intestine**); **Glucagon**, **Hormones**, 336; **Hypothalamus**, 303; **Insulin**, 336; **Larynx**, 298; **Sex hormones**, 336.

THE RESPIRATORY SYSTEM

The term **respiration** covers three processes: **ventilation**, or breathing (taking in oxygen and expelling carbon dioxide), **external respiration** (the exchange of gases between the **lungs** and the blood – see also **red blood cells**, page 286) and **internal respiration** (food breakdown, using oxygen and producing carbon dioxide – see pages 334-335). Listed here are the component parts of the human **respiratory system**.

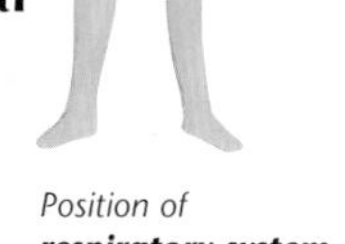

Position of ***respiratory system***

Trachea or **windpipe**

The main tube through which air passes on its way to and from the **lungs**.

Larynx

The "voice box" at the top of the **trachea**. It contains the **vocal cords** – two pieces of tissue folding inward from the trachea lining and attached to plates of **cartilage***. The opening between the cords is called the **glottis**. During speech, muscles pull the cartilage plates (and hence the cords) together, and air passing out through the cords makes them vibrate, producing sounds.

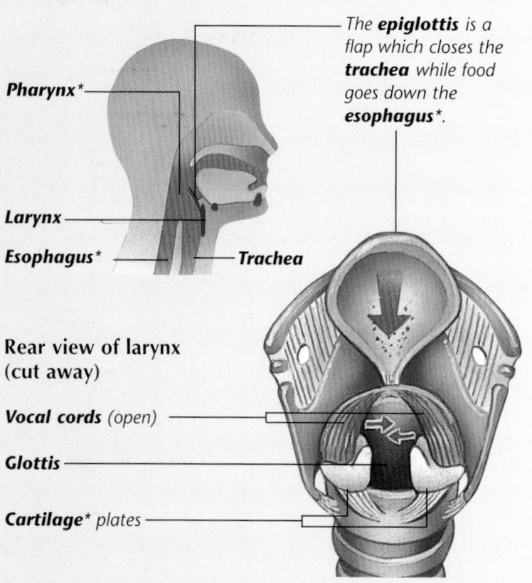

The epiglottis is a flap which closes the trachea while food goes down the esophagus*.
Pharynx*
Larynx
Esophagus*
Trachea
Rear view of larynx (cut away)
Vocal cords (open)
Glottis
Cartilage* plates

Lungs

The two main breathing organs, inside which gases are exchanged. They contain many tubes (**bronchi** and **bronchioles**) and air sacs (**alveoli**).

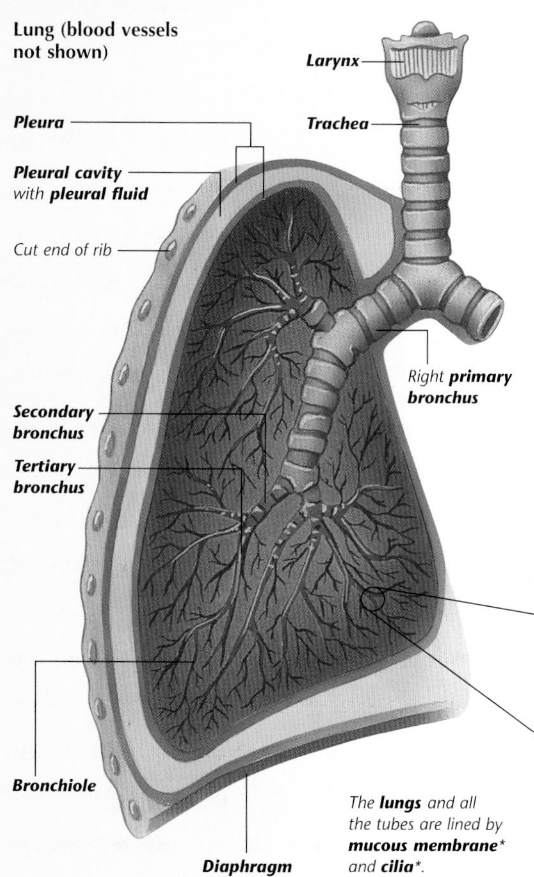

Lung (blood vessels not shown)
Larynx
Trachea
Pleura
Pleural cavity with pleural fluid
Cut end of rib
Right primary bronchus
Secondary bronchus
Tertiary bronchus
Bronchiole
Diaphragm

The ***lungs*** *and all the tubes are lined by* ***mucous membrane**** *and* ***cilia****.

Pleura (sing. **pleuron**) or **pleural membrane**

A layer of tissue surrounding each **lung** and lining the chest cavity (**thorax**). Between the pleura around a lung and the pleura lining the thorax there is a space (**pleural cavity**). This contains **pleural fluid**. The pleura and fluid-filled cavity make up a cushioning **pleural sac**.

Diaphragm or **midriff**

A sheet of muscular tissue which separates the chest from the lower body, or **abdomen**. At rest, it lies in an arched position, forced up by the abdomen wall below it.

* **Cartilage**, 281; **Cilia**, 268; **Esophagus**, 294; **Mucous membrane**, 295; **Pharynx**, 294.

Bronchi (sing. bronchus)

The main tubes into which the **trachea** divides. The first two branches are the right and left **primary bronchi**. Each carries air into a **lung** (via a hole called a **hilum**), alongside a **pulmonary artery*** bringing blood in. They then branch into **secondary bronchi**, **tertiary bronchi** and **bronchioles**, all accompanied by blood vessels, both branching from the pulmonary artery and merging to form **pulmonary veins*** (blood going out).

Bronchioles

The millions of tiny tubes in the **lungs**, all accompanied by blood vessels. They branch off **tertiary bronchi** (see **bronchi**) and have smaller branches called **terminal bronchioles**, each one ending in a cluster of **alveoli**.

Alveoli (sing. alveolus)

The millions of tiny sacs attached to **terminal bronchioles** (see **bronchioles**). They are surrounded by **capillaries*** (tiny blood vessels) whose blood is rich in carbon dioxide. This passes out through the capillary walls, and in through those of the alveoli (to be breathed out). The oxygen which has been breathed into the alveoli passes into the capillaries, which then begin to merge together (eventually forming **pulmonary veins***).

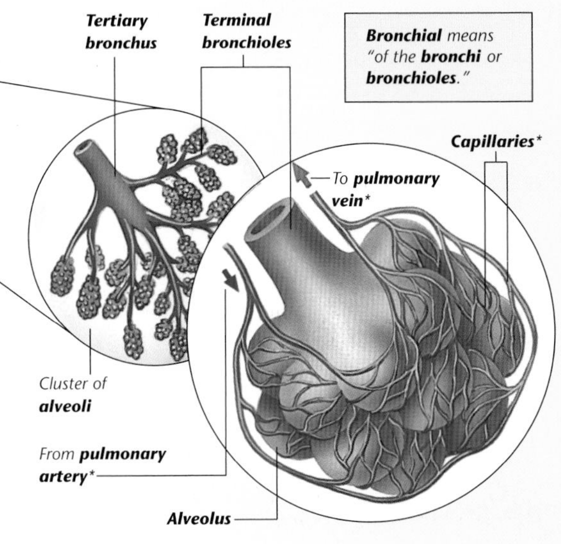
Tertiary bronchus
Terminal bronchioles
Capillaries*
To pulmonary vein*
Cluster of alveoli
From pulmonary artery*
Alveolus

***Bronchial** means "of the **bronchi** or **bronchioles**."*

Breathing

Breathing is made up of **inspiration** (breathing in) and **expiration** (breathing out). Both actions are normally automatic, controlled by nerves from the **respiratory center** in the **medulla*** of the brain. This acts when it detects too high a level of carbon dioxide in the blood.

Inspiration or inhalation

The act of breathing in. The **diaphragm** contracts and flattens, lengthening the chest cavity. The muscles between the ribs (**intercostal muscles**) also contract, pulling the ribs up and outward and widening the cavity. The overall expansion lowers the air pressure in the **lungs**, and air rushes in to fill them (i.e. to equalize internal and external pressure).

Inspiration

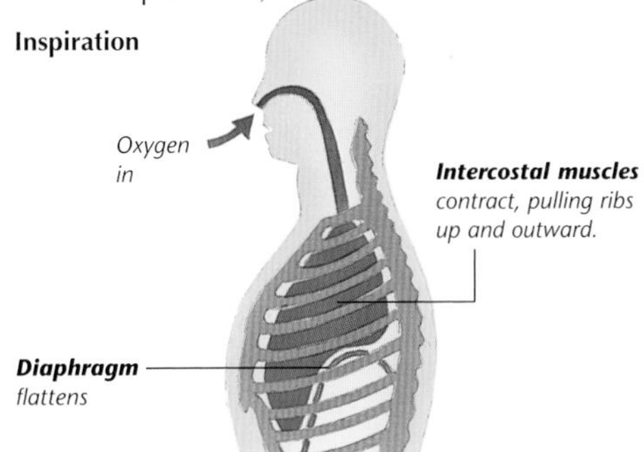
Oxygen in
Intercostal muscles contract, pulling ribs up and outward.
Diaphragm flattens

Expiration or exhalation

The act of breathing out. The **diaphragm** and **intercostal muscles** (see **inspiration**) relax, and air is forced out of the **lungs** as the chest cavity becomes smaller.

Expiration

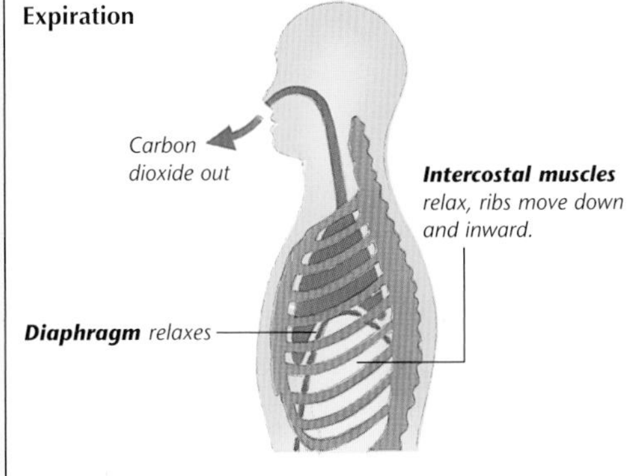
Carbon dioxide out
Intercostal muscles relax, ribs move down and inward.
Diaphragm relaxes

* **Capillaries**, 288; **Medulla**, 303;
Pulmonary arteries, 291 (**Pulmonary trunk**); **Pulmonary veins**, 291.

THE URINARY SYSTEM

The **urinary system** is the main system of body parts involved in **excretion**, which is the expulsion of unwanted substances. The parts are defined below. The lungs and skin are also involved in excretion (expelling carbon dioxide and sweat respectively).

Parts of the urinary system

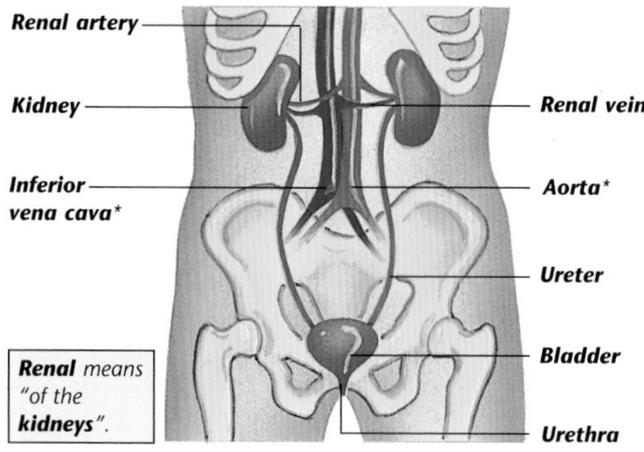

Renal artery
Kidney
Renal vein
Inferior vena cava*
Aorta*
Ureter
Bladder
Urethra

***Renal** means "of the **kidneys**".*

Kidneys

Two organs at the back of the body, just below the ribs. They are the main organs of excretion, filtering out unwanted substances from the blood and regulating the level and contents of body fluids (see also **homeostasis**, page 335). Blood enters a kidney in a **renal artery** and leaves it in a **renal vein**.

Ureters

The two tubes which carry **urine** from the **kidneys** to the **bladder**.

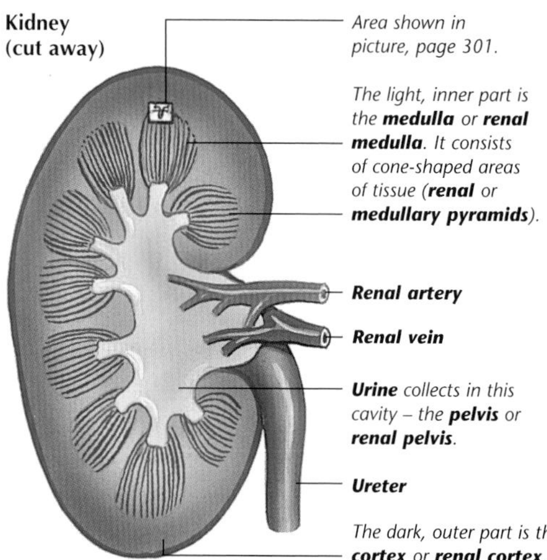

Kidney (cut away)
Area shown in picture, page 301.
The light, inner part is the medulla or renal medulla. It consists of cone-shaped areas of tissue (renal or medullary pyramids).
Renal artery
Renal vein
Urine collects in this cavity – the pelvis or renal pelvis.
Ureter
The dark, outer part is the cortex or renal cortex.

Bladder or urinary bladder

A sac which holds stored **urine**. Its lining has many folds (**rugae**, sing. **ruga**) which flatten out as it fills up, letting it expand. Two muscular rings – the **internal** and **external urinary sphincters** – control the opening from the bladder into the **urethra**. When the volume of urine gets to a certain level, nerves stimulate the internal sphincter to open, but the external sphincter is under conscious control (except in young children), and can be held closed for longer.

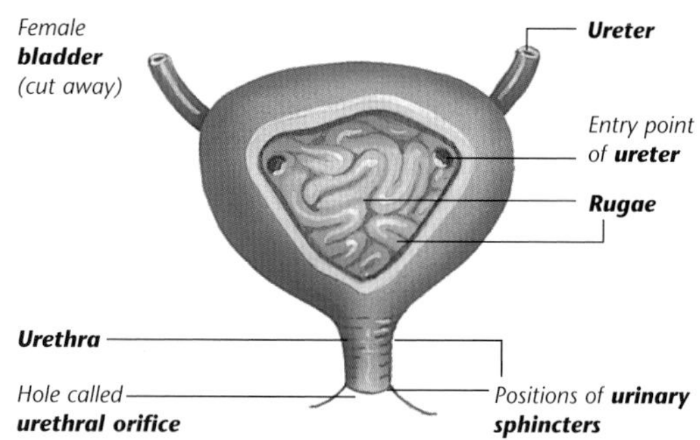

Female bladder (cut away)
Ureter
Entry point of ureter
Rugae
Urethra
Hole called urethral orifice
Positions of urinary sphincters

Urethra

The tube carrying **urine** from the **bladder** out of the body (in men, it also carries **sperm*** – see **penis**, page 316). The expulsion of urine is called **urination** or **micturition**.

Urea

A nitrogen-containing (**nitrogenous**) waste substance which is a product of the breakdown of excess **amino acids*** in the liver. It travels in the blood to the **kidneys**, together with smaller amounts of similar substances, e.g. creatinine.

Urine

The liquid which leaves the **kidneys**. Its main constituents are excess water, **urea** and minerals.

* **Amino acids**, 330 (**Proteins**); **Aorta**, **Inferior vena cava**, 291; **Sperm**, 320 (**Gametes**).

Inside a kidney

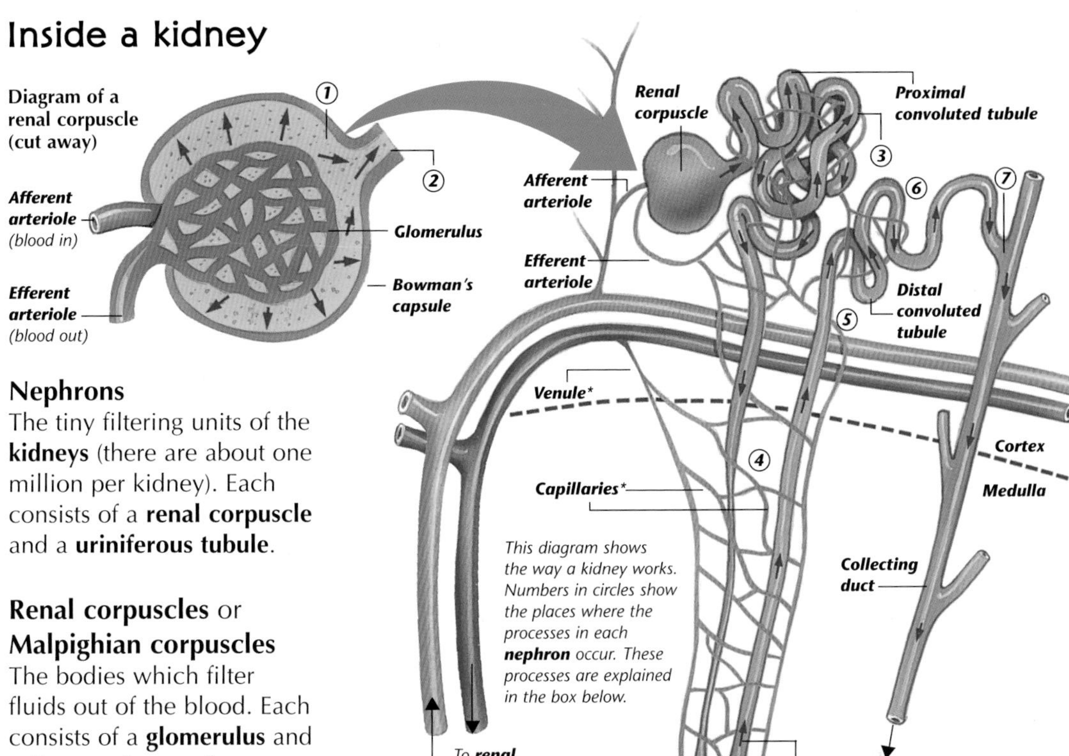
Diagram of a renal corpuscle (cut away)
1
2
Afferent arteriole (blood in)
Glomerulus
Efferent arteriole (blood out)
Bowman's capsule
Renal corpuscle
Proximal convoluted tubule
3
Afferent arteriole
6
7
Efferent arteriole
Distal convoluted tubule
5
Venule*
Cortex
4
Medulla
Capillaries*
This diagram shows the way a kidney works. Numbers in circles show the places where the processes in each nephron occur. These processes are explained in the box below.
Collecting duct
To renal vein
To pelvis
From renal artery
Loop of Henlé

Nephrons

The tiny filtering units of the **kidneys** (there are about one million per kidney). Each consists of a **renal corpuscle** and a **uriniferous tubule**.

Renal corpuscles or Malpighian corpuscles

The bodies which filter fluids out of the blood. Each consists of a **glomerulus** and a **Bowman's capsule**.

Glomerulus

A ball of coiled-up **capillaries*** (tiny blood vessels) at the center of each **renal corpuscle**. The capillaries branch from an **arteriole*** entering the corpuscle (an **afferent arteriole**) and re-unite to leave the corpuscle as an **efferent arteriole**.

Bowman's capsule

The outer part of each **renal corpuscle**. It is a thin-walled sac around the **glomerulus**.

Uriniferous tubules or renal tubules

Long tubes, each one leading from a **Bowman's capsule**. Each has three main parts – the **proximal convoluted tubule**, the **loop of Henlé** and the **distal convoluted tubule** – and has many **capillaries*** (tiny blood vessels) twined around it. These are branches of the **efferent arteriole** (see **glomerulus**) and they re-unite to form larger blood vessels carrying blood from the **kidney**.

Collecting duct or collecting tubule

A tube which carries **urine** from several **uriniferous tubules** into the **pelvis** of a **kidney**.

Key to kidney diagram above

*1. **Glomerular filtration**. As blood squeezes through the **glomerulus**, most of its water, minerals, vitamins, glucose, **amino acids*** and **urea** are forced into the **Bowman's capsule**, forming **glomerular filtrate**.*

*2. **Glomerular filtrate** moves into **proximal convoluted tubule**.*

*3. **Tubular reabsorption**. As **glomerular filtrate** runs through the **uriniferous tubule**, most vitamins, glucose and **amino acids*** are taken back into the blood in the twining **capillaries***.*

*4. Some minerals are also taken back. The **hormone* aldosterone*** controls reabsorption of more if needed.*

*5. Some water is also taken back. The **hormone* ADH*** controls reabsorption of more if needed.*

*6. **Tubular secretion**. Some substances, e.g. ammonia and some drugs, pass from the blood into the **uriniferous tubule**.*

*7. Resulting **urine** passes into **collecting duct**.*

***Distal** means "away from the point of origin or attachment".*

***Proximal** means "near the point of origin or attachment".*

* **ADH**, **Aldosterone**, 336; **Amino acids**, 330 (**Proteins**); **Arteriole**, 288 (**Arteries**); **Capillaries**, 288; **Hormones**, 336; **Venule**, 288 (**Veins**).

THE CENTRAL NERVOUS SYSTEM

The **central nervous system** (**CNS**) is the body's control center. It co-ordinates all its actions, both mechanical and chemical (working with **hormones***) and is made up of the **brain** and **spinal cord**. The millions of nerves in the body carry "messages" (nervous impulses) to and from these central areas (see pages 306-309).

Brain

Brain

The organ which controls most of the body's activities. It is the only organ able to produce "intelligent" action – action based on past experience (stored information), present events and future plans. It is made up of millions of **neurons*** (nerve cells), arranged into **sensory**, **association** and **motor areas**. The sensory areas receive information (nervous impulses) from all body parts and the association areas analyze the impulses and make decisions. The motor areas send impulses (orders) to muscles or glands. The impulses are carried by the fibers of 43 pairs of nerves – 12 pairs of **cranial nerves** serving the head, and 31 pairs of **spinal nerves** (see **spinal cord**).

***Spinal cord** (inside vertebral column*)*

Spinal cord

A long string of nervous tissue running down from the **brain** inside the **vertebral column***. Nervous impulses from all parts of the body pass through it. Some are carried into or away from the brain, some are dealt with in the cord (see **involuntary actions**, page 309). 31 pairs of **spinal nerves** branch out from the cord through the gaps between the **vertebrae***. Each spinal nerve is made up of two groups of fibers: a **dorsal** or **sensory root**, made up of the fibers of **sensory neurons*** (bringing impulses in), and a **ventral** or **motor root**, made up of the fibers of **motor neurons*** (taking impulses out).

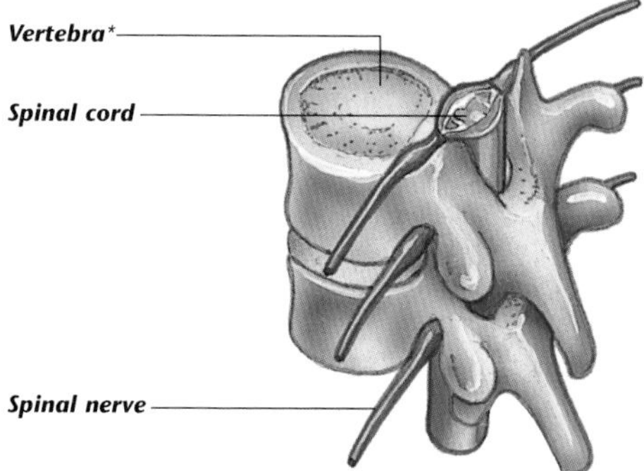
Vertebra*
Spinal cord
Spinal nerve

Neuroglia or glia

Stiffened cells which support and protect the nerve cells (**neurons***) of the central nervous system. Some produce a white, fatty substance called **myelin** (see also **Schwann cells**, page 304). This coats the long fibers found in the connective areas of the **brain** and the outer layer of the **spinal cord**, and leads to these areas being known as **white matter**. **Gray matter**, by contrast, consists mainly of **cell bodies*** and their short fibers, and its neuroglia do not produce myelin.

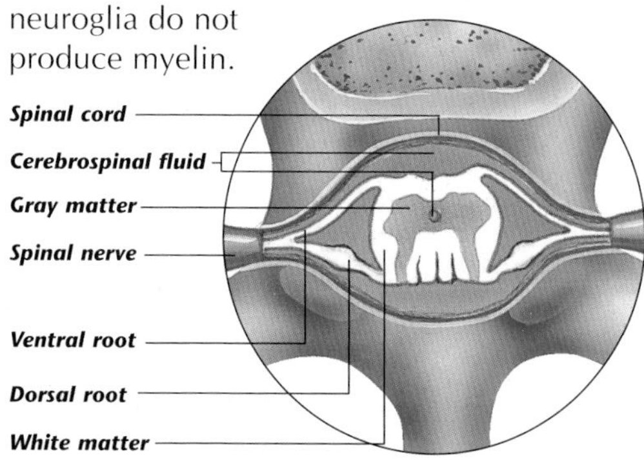
Spinal cord
Cerebrospinal fluid
Gray matter
Spinal nerve
Ventral root
Dorsal root
White matter

* **Cell body**, 304; **Hormones**, 336; **Motor neurons**, 305; **Neurons**, 304; **Sensory neurons**, 305; **Vertebrae**, **Vertebral column**, 279.

The parts of the brain

Cerebrum

The largest, most highly developed area, with many deep folds. It is composed of two **cerebral hemispheres**, joined by the **corpus callosum** (a band of **nerve fibers***), and its outer layer is called the **cerebral cortex**. This contains all the most important **sensory**, **association** and **motor areas** (see **brain**). It controls most physical activities and is the center for mental activities such as decision-making, speech, learning, memory and imagination.

Thalamus

The area which carries out the first, basic sorting of incoming impulses and directs them to different parts of the **cerebrum**. It also directs some outgoing impulses.

Hypothalamus

The master controller of most inner body functions. It controls the **autonomic nervous system*** (the nerve cells causing unconscious action, e.g. food movement through the intestines) and the action of the **pituitary gland***. Its activities are vital to **homeostasis*** – the maintenance of stable internal conditions.

Brain (cut away)

Cerebrum

Thalamus

Cerebellum

Skull

Hypothalamus

Pituitary gland*

Midbrain

Pons

Corpus callosum

Medulla

Ventricles *(spaces). Filled with* ***CSF***.

*Protective membranes (**meninges**, sing. **meninx**). Called (working inward) the **dura mater**, **arachnoid** and **pia mater**.*

Cerebrospinal fluid (CSF) *cushions the **brain** and **spinal cord** and brings dissolved food.*

Spinal cord

Cerebellum

The area which coordinates muscle movement and balance, two things under the overall control of the **cerebrum**.

Diencephalon

A collective term for the **thalamus** and **hypothalamus**.

Midbrain or mesencephalon

An area joining the **diencephalon** to the **pons**. It carries impulses in toward the **thalamus**, and out from the **cerebrum** toward the **spinal cord**.

Pons or pons Varolii

A junction of **nerve fibers*** which forms a link between the parts of the **brain** and the **spinal cord** (via the **medulla**).

Medulla or medulla oblongata

The area which controls the "fine tuning" of many unconscious actions (under the overall control of the **hypothalamus**). Different parts of it control different actions, e.g. the **respiratory center** controls breathing.

Brain stem

A collective term for the **midbrain**, **pons** and **medulla**.

*In general terms, **cerebral** means "of the **brain**".*

***Cephalic** means "of the head".*

Areas of cerebrum

Sensory areas. *Receive incoming impulses.*

1. *General sensory area. Receives impulses from muscles, skin and inner organs.*
2. ***Primary gustatory area**. Impulses from tongue.*
3. ***Primary auditory area**. Impulses from ears.*
4. ***Primary visual area**. Impulses from eyes.*
5. ***Primary olfactory area**. Impulses from nose.*

Motor areas. *Each tiny part sends out impulses to a specific muscle.*

Association areas. *Interpret impulses and make decisions. Some specific ones are:*

6. ***Visual association area**. Produces sight.*
7. ***Auditory association area**. Produces hearing.*

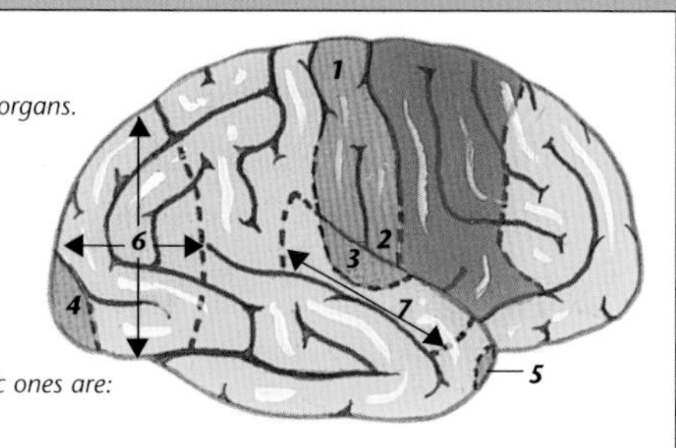
1
2
3
4
5
6
7

* **Autonomic nervous system**, 308; **Homeostasis**, 335; **Nerve fibers**, 304; **Pituitary gland**, 297.

THE UNITS OF THE NERVOUS SYSTEM

The individual units of both the brain and spinal cord (**central nervous system***) and the nerves of the rest of the body (**peripheral nervous system**) are the nerve cells, or **neurons**. They are unique in being able to transmit electrical "messages" (the vital nervous impulses) around the body. Each neuron consists of a **cell body**, an **axon** and one or more **dendrites**, and there are three types of neuron – **sensory**, **association** and **motor neurons**.

An ***association neuron****, found in the brain and spinal cord (see page 305)*

The parts of a neuron

Cell body or perikaryon

The part of a neuron containing its **nucleus*** and most of its **cytoplasm***. The cell bodies of all **association**, some **sensory** and some **motor neurons** lie in the brain and spinal cord. Those of the other sensory neurons are found in masses called **ganglia*** or as part of highly specialized **receptors*** in the nose and eyes. Those of the other motor neurons lie in **autonomic ganglia***.

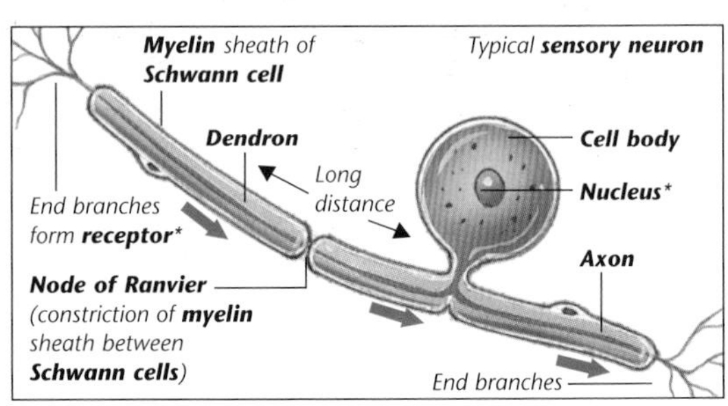

Myelin sheath of Schwann cell
Typical sensory neuron
Dendron
Cell body
Nucleus*
Long distance
End branches form receptor*
Axon
Node of Ranvier (constriction of myelin sheath between Schwann cells)
End branches

Nerve fibers

The fibers (**axon** and **dendrites**) of a neuron. They are extensions of the **cytoplasm*** of the **cell body** and carry the vital nervous impulses. Most of the long nerve fibers which run out round the body (belonging to **sensory** or **motor neurons**) are accompanied by **neuroglial*** cells. These are called **Schwann cells** and they produce a sheath of **myelin*** around each fiber.

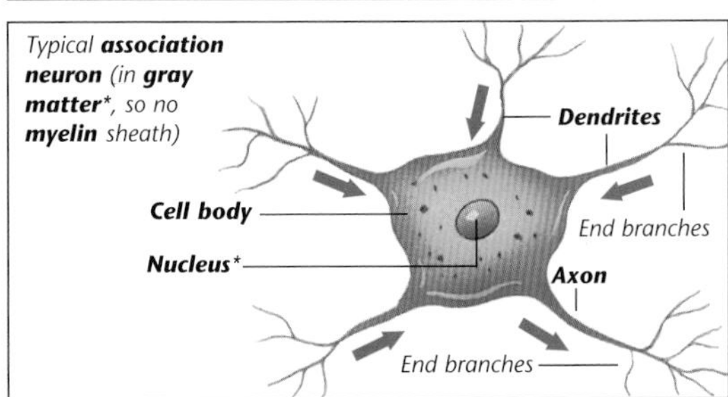

Typical association neuron (in gray matter*, so no myelin sheath)
Dendrites
Cell body
End branches
Nucleus*
Axon
End branches

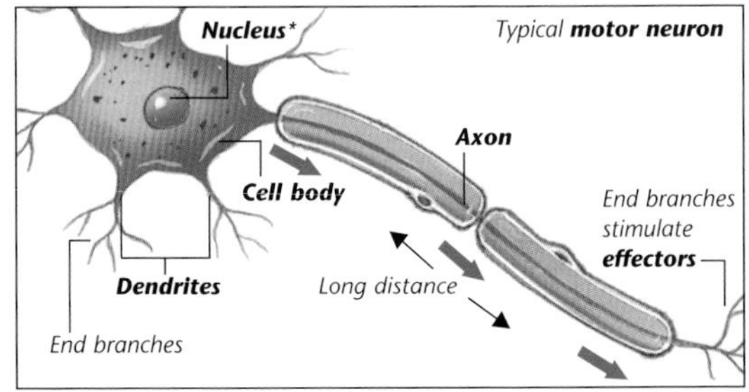

Nucleus*
Typical motor neuron
Axon
Cell body
End branches stimulate effectors
Dendrites
Long distance
End branches

Dendrites

The **nerve fibers** carrying impulses toward a **cell body**. Most neurons have several short dendrites, but one type of **sensory neuron** has just one, elongated dendrite, often called a **dendron**. The endings of these dendrons form **receptors*** all over the body, and the dendrons themselves run inward to the cell bodies (which are found in **ganglia*** just outside the spinal cord).

Axon

The single long **nerve fiber** which carries impulses away from a **cell body**. The axons of all **association** and **sensory neurons** and some **motor neurons** lie in the brain and spinal cord. Those of the other motor neurons run out of the spinal cord to **autonomic ganglia***, or further to **effectors** (see **motor neurons**).

* **Autonomic ganglia**, 309; **Central nervous system**, 302; **Cytoplasm**, 238; **Ganglia**, 306; **Grey matter**, **Myelin**, 302 (**Neuroglia**); **Nucleus**, 238; **Receptors**, 307.

Types of neuron

Sensory neurons or **afferent neurons**

The neurons which carry "information" (nervous impulses) about sensations. The single **dendrites** (**dendrons**) of some sensory neurons run throughout the body, and their endings fire off impulses when stimulated. For more about these endings (**receptors**) and the different sensory neurons, see pages 306-307.

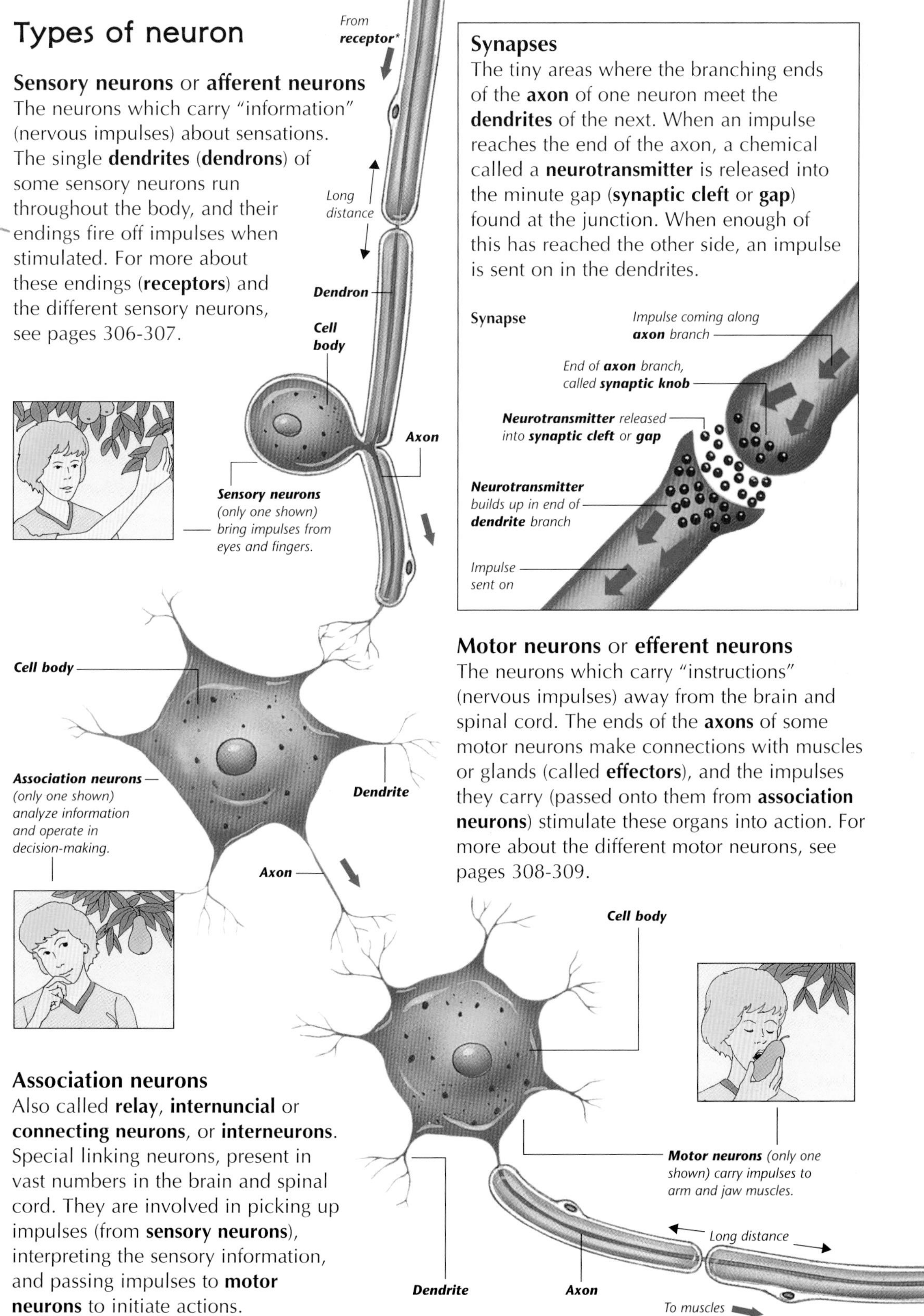

From receptor*
Long distance
Dendron
Cell body
Axon
Sensory neurons (only one shown) bring impulses from eyes and fingers.
Cell body
Association neurons (only one shown) analyze information and operate in decision-making.
Dendrite
Axon
Cell body
Motor neurons (only one shown) carry impulses to arm and jaw muscles.
Long distance
Dendrite
Axon
To muscles
Synapse
Impulse coming along axon branch
End of axon branch, called synaptic knob
Neurotransmitter released into synaptic cleft or gap
Neurotransmitter builds up in end of dendrite branch
Impulse sent on

Synapses

The tiny areas where the branching ends of the **axon** of one neuron meet the **dendrites** of the next. When an impulse reaches the end of the axon, a chemical called a **neurotransmitter** is released into the minute gap (**synaptic cleft** or **gap**) found at the junction. When enough of this has reached the other side, an impulse is sent on in the dendrites.

Motor neurons or **efferent neurons**

The neurons which carry "instructions" (nervous impulses) away from the brain and spinal cord. The ends of the **axons** of some motor neurons make connections with muscles or glands (called **effectors**), and the impulses they carry (passed onto them from **association neurons**) stimulate these organs into action. For more about the different motor neurons, see pages 308-309.

Association neurons

Also called **relay**, **internuncial** or **connecting neurons**, or **interneurons**. Special linking neurons, present in vast numbers in the brain and spinal cord. They are involved in picking up impulses (from **sensory neurons**), interpreting the sensory information, and passing impulses to **motor neurons** to initiate actions.

* **Receptors**, 307.

NERVES AND NERVOUS PATHWAYS

The **sensitivity** (**irritability**) of the body (its ability to respond to stimuli) relies on the transportation of "messages" (nervous impulses) by the fibers of nerve cells (**neurons***). The fibers which bring impulses into the brain and spinal cord are part of the **afferent system**. Those which carry impulses from the brain and cord are part of the **efferent system** (see pages 308-309). The fibers outside the brain and cord make up the **nerves** of the body, known collectively as the **peripheral nervous system** (**PNS**).

Nerves

Bundles of nerve fibers, blood vessels and **connective tissue***. Each nerve consists of several bundles (**fascicles**) of fibers and each fiber is part of a nerve cell (**neuron***). **Sensory nerves** have just the fibers (**dendrons***) of **sensory** (**afferent**) **neurons***, **motor nerves** have just the fibers (**axons***) of **motor** (**efferent**) **neurons***, and **mixed nerves** have both types of fiber.

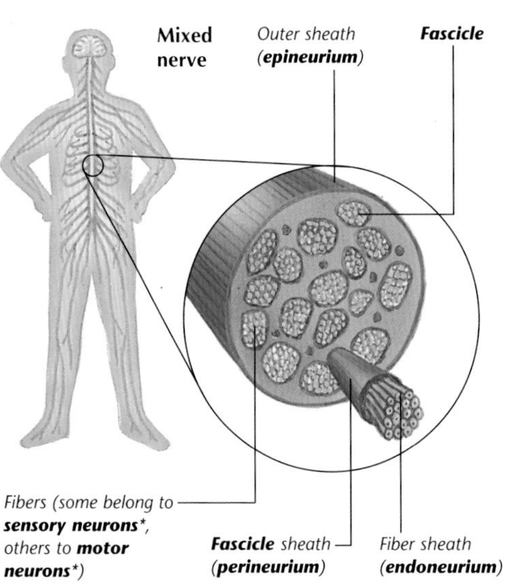
Mixed nerve
Outer sheath ***(epineurium)***
Fascicle
Fibers (some belong to ***sensory neurons****,* *others to* ***motor neurons****)*
Fascicle *sheath* ***(perineurium)***
Fiber sheath ***(endoneurium)***

The afferent system

The **afferent system** is the system of nerve cells (**neurons***) whose fibers carry sensory information (nervous impulses) toward the spinal cord, up inside it and into the brain. The nerve cells involved are all the **sensory** (**afferent**) **neurons*** of the body. The impulses originate in **receptors** and are interpreted by the brain as sensations.

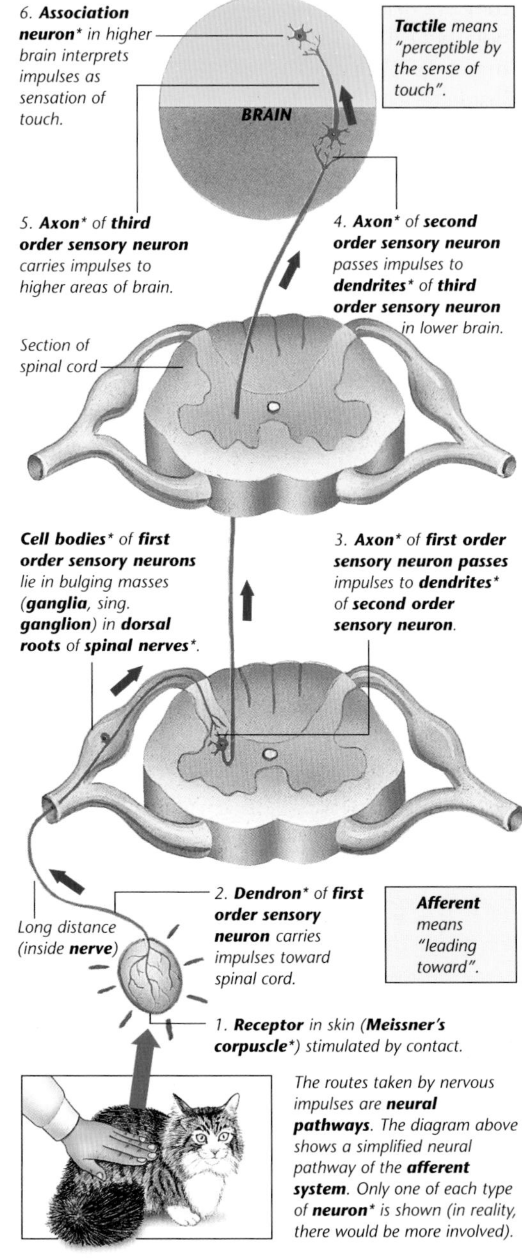
6. ***Association neuron**** *in higher brain interprets impulses as sensation of touch.*
Tactile *means "perceptible by the sense of touch".*
BRAIN
5. ***Axon**** *of* ***third order sensory neuron*** *carries impulses to higher areas of brain.*
4. ***Axon**** *of* ***second order sensory neuron*** *passes impulses to* ***dendrites**** *of* ***third order sensory neuron*** *in lower brain.*
Section of spinal cord
Cell bodies* *of* ***first order sensory neurons*** *lie in bulging masses (****ganglia****, sing.* ***ganglion****) in* ***dorsal roots*** *of* ***spinal nerves****.*
3. ***Axon**** *of* ***first order sensory neuron passes*** *impulses to* ***dendrites**** *of* ***second order sensory neuron****.*
Long distance (inside ***nerve****)*
2. ***Dendron**** *of* ***first order sensory neuron*** *carries impulses toward spinal cord.*
Afferent *means "leading toward".*
1. ***Receptor*** *in skin (****Meissner's corpuscle*****) stimulated by contact.*

The routes taken by nervous impulses are ***neural pathways****. The diagram above shows a simplified neural pathway of the* ***afferent system****. Only one of each type of* ***neuron**** *is shown (in reality, there would be more involved).*

* **Association neurons**, 305; **Axon**, **Cell body**, 304; **Connective tissue**, 280; **Dendron**, 304 (**Dendrites**); **Meissner's corpuscles**, 311; **Motor neurons**, 305; **Neurons**, 304; **Sensory neurons**, 305; **Spinal nerves**, 302 (**Spinal cord**).

Receptors

The parts of the **afferent system** which fire off nervous impulses when they are stimulated. Most are either the single branched ending of the long **dendron*** of a **first order sensory neuron** (see picture) or a group of such endings. They are all embedded in body tissue, and many have some kind of structure formed around them (e.g. a **taste bud** – see **tongue**). They are found all over the body, both near the surface (in the skin, **sense organs**, **skeletal muscles***, etc.) and deeper inside (connected to inner organs, blood vessel walls, etc.).

Sense organs

The highly specialized sensory organs of the body, each with many **receptors**. They are the **nose**, **tongue**, eyes and ears. For more about eyes and ears, see pages 312-315.

Divisions of the afferent system

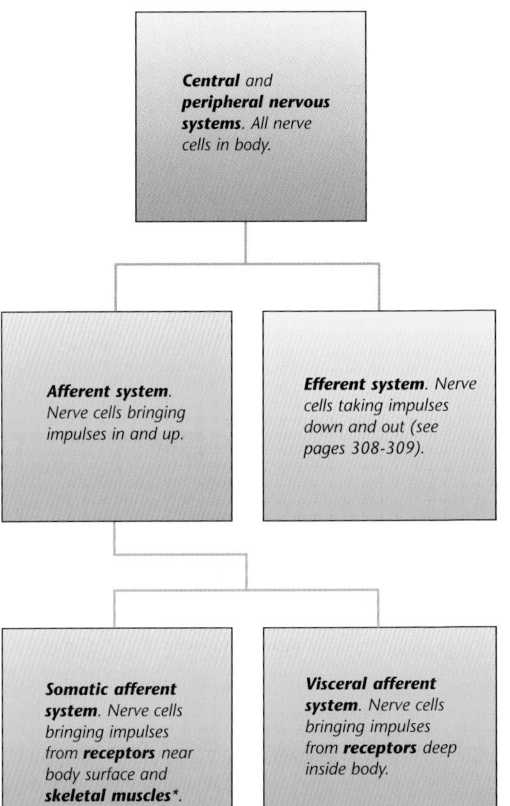

Central and peripheral nervous systems. All nerve cells in body.
Afferent system. Nerve cells bringing impulses in and up.
Efferent system. Nerve cells taking impulses down and out (see pages 308-309).
Somatic afferent system. Nerve cells bringing impulses from receptors near body surface and skeletal muscles*.
Visceral afferent system. Nerve cells bringing impulses from receptors deep inside body.

Nose

The organ of smell. Each of its two nostrils opens out into a **nasal cavity** which is lined with **mucous membrane*** and has many **olfactory hairs** extending from its roof. The hairs are the **dendrites*** of special **sensory neurons*** called **olfactory cells**. These are the **receptors** whose impulses are interpreted by the brain as sensations of smell (**olfactory sensations**).

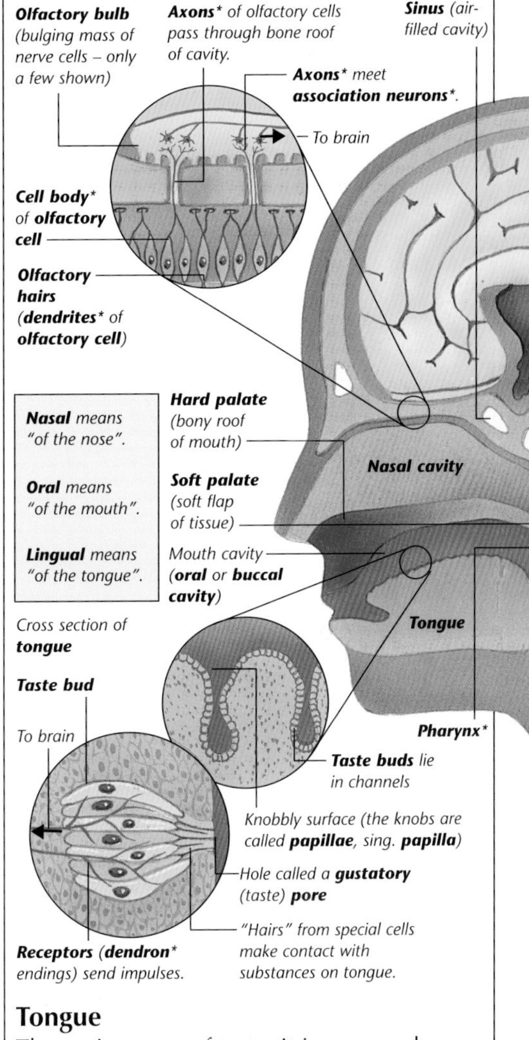

Olfactory bulb (bulging mass of nerve cells – only a few shown)
Axons* of olfactory cells pass through bone roof of cavity.
Sinus (air-filled cavity)
Axons* meet association neurons*.
To brain
Cell body* of olfactory cell
Olfactory hairs (dendrites* of olfactory cell)
Nasal means "of the nose".
Oral means "of the mouth".
Lingual means "of the tongue".
Hard palate (bony roof of mouth)
Soft palate (soft flap of tissue)
Mouth cavity (oral or buccal cavity)
Nasal cavity
Tongue
Cross section of tongue
Taste bud
To brain
Pharynx*
Taste buds lie in channels
Knobbly surface (the knobs are called papillae, sing. papilla)
Hole called a gustatory (taste) pore
"Hairs" from special cells make contact with substances on tongue.
Receptors (dendron* endings) send impulses.

Tongue

The main organ of taste. It is a muscular organ which bears many **taste buds**. These tiny bodies contain the **receptors** whose impulses are interpreted by the brain as taste sensations (**gustatory sensations**).

* **Association neurons**, 305; **Axon**, **Cell body**, 304; **Dendron**, 304 (**Dendrites**); **Mucous membrane**, 295; **Pharynx**, 294; **Sensory neurons**, 305; **Skeletal muscles**, 282.

The efferent system

The **efferent system** is the second system of nerve cells (**neurons***) in the body (see also **afferent system**, pages 306-307). The fibers of its nerve cells carry nervous impulses away from the brain, down through the spinal cord and out around the body. The nerve cells involved are all the **motor** (**efferent**) **neurons*** of the body. The impulses they carry stimulate action in the surface muscles (**skeletal muscles***) or in the glands and internal muscles (in the walls of inner organs and blood vessels). All these organs are known collectively as **effectors**.

Divisions of the efferent system

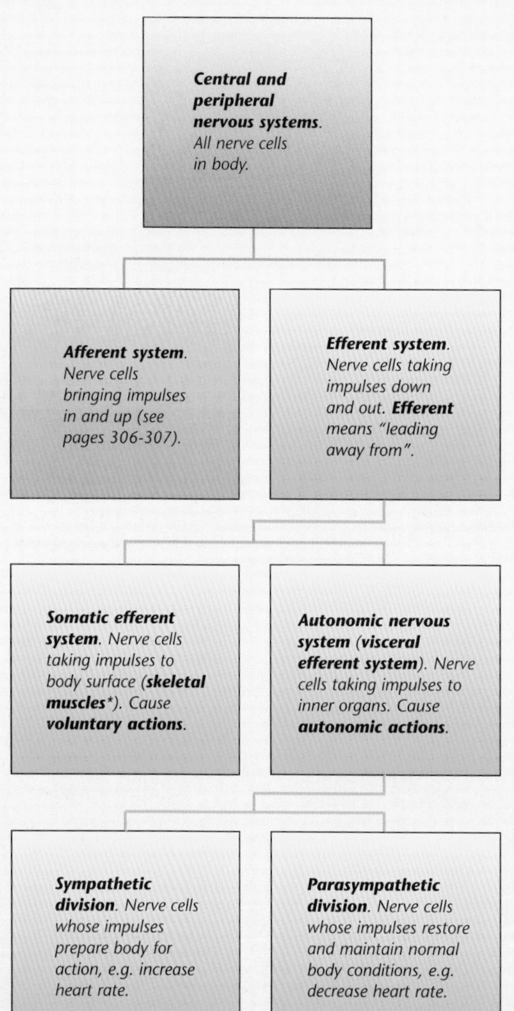

Central and peripheral nervous systems. All nerve cells in body.
Afferent system. Nerve cells bringing impulses in and up (see pages 306-307).
Efferent system. Nerve cells taking impulses down and out. Efferent means "leading away from".
Somatic efferent system. Nerve cells taking impulses to body surface (skeletal muscles*). Cause voluntary actions.
Autonomic nervous system (visceral efferent system). Nerve cells taking impulses to inner organs. Cause autonomic actions.
Sympathetic division. Nerve cells whose impulses prepare body for action, e.g. increase heart rate.
Parasympathetic division. Nerve cells whose impulses restore and maintain normal body conditions, e.g. decrease heart rate.

The different actions

Voluntary actions

Actions which result from conscious activity by the brain, i.e. ones it consciously decides upon, e.g. lifting a cup. We are always aware of these actions, which involve **skeletal muscles*** only. The impulses which cause them originate in higher areas of the brain (especially the **cerebrum***) and are carried by nerve cells of the **somatic efferent system**.

Lifting a cup is a ***voluntary action****.*

Simplified neural pathway* of voluntary action (somatic efferent system)

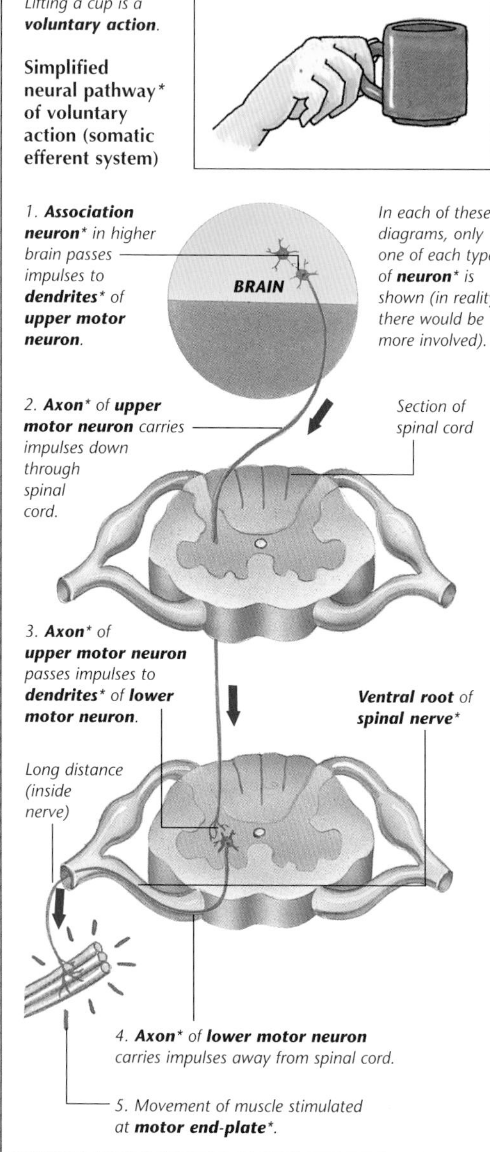

1. Association neuron* in higher brain passes impulses to dendrites* of upper motor neuron.
BRAIN
In each of these diagrams, only one of each type of neuron* is shown (in reality, there would be more involved).
2. Axon* of upper motor neuron carries impulses down through spinal cord.
Section of spinal cord
3. Axon* of upper motor neuron passes impulses to dendrites* of lower motor neuron.
Ventral root of spinal nerve*
Long distance (inside nerve)
4. Axon* of lower motor neuron carries impulses away from spinal cord.
5. Movement of muscle stimulated at motor end-plate*.

* **Association neurons**, 305; **Axon**, 304; **Cerebrum**, 303; **Dendrites**, 304; **Motor end-plate**, 283; **Motor neurons**, 305; **Neural pathways**, 306; **Neurons**, 304; **Skeletal muscles**, 282; **Spinal nerves**, 302 (**Spinal cord**).

Involuntary actions

Automatic actions (ones the brain does not consciously decide upon). There are two types. Firstly, there are the constant actions of inner organs, e.g. the beating of the heart, of which we are not normally aware. The impulses which cause them originate in the lower brain (especially the **hypothalamus***) and are carried by nerve cells of the **autonomic nervous system**. They are called **autonomic actions**. The other involuntary actions are **reflex actions**.

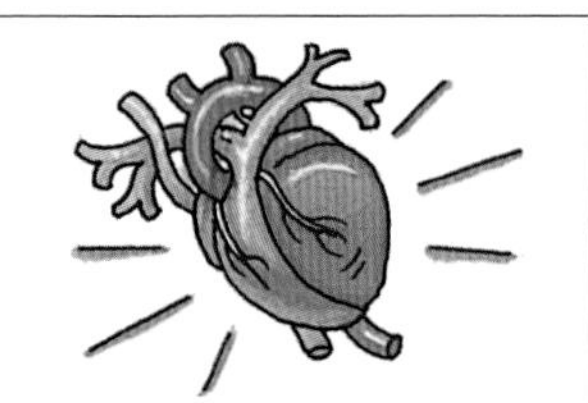

*The heartbeat is an **autonomic action**.*

Simplified neural pathway* of autonomic action (sympathetic division of autonomic nervous system)

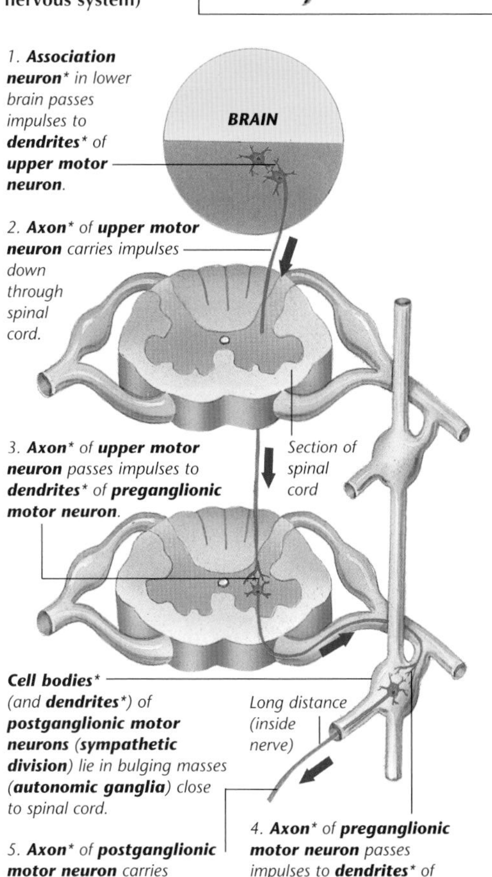
BRAIN
1. **Association neuron*** in lower brain passes impulses to **dendrites*** of **upper motor neuron**.
2. **Axon*** of **upper motor neuron** carries impulses down through spinal cord.
Section of spinal cord
3. **Axon*** of **upper motor neuron** passes impulses to **dendrites*** of **preganglionic motor neuron**.
Cell bodies* (and **dendrites***) of **postganglionic motor neurons** (**sympathetic division**) lie in bulging masses (**autonomic ganglia**) close to spinal cord.
Long distance (inside nerve)
4. **Axon*** of **preganglionic motor neuron** passes impulses to **dendrites*** of **postganglionic motor neuron**.
5. **Axon*** of **postganglionic motor neuron** carries impulses to organ.

Reflex actions

Involuntary actions of which we are aware. The term is most often used to refer to sudden actions of **skeletal muscles***, e.g. snatching the hand away from something hot. The impulses which cause such an action are carried by nerve cells of the **somatic efferent system** and the entire **neural pathway*** is a "short-circuited" one, called a **reflex arc**. In the case of **cranial reflexes** (those of the head, e.g. sneezing), this pathway involves a small part of the brain; with **spinal reflexes** (those of the rest of the body), the brain is not actively involved, only the spinal cord.

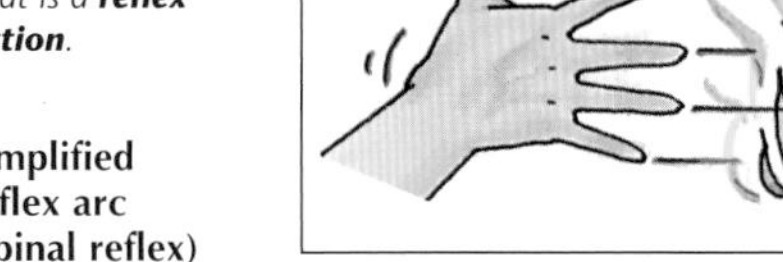

*Pulling your hand away from an intense source of heat is a **reflex action**.*

Simplified reflex arc (spinal reflex)

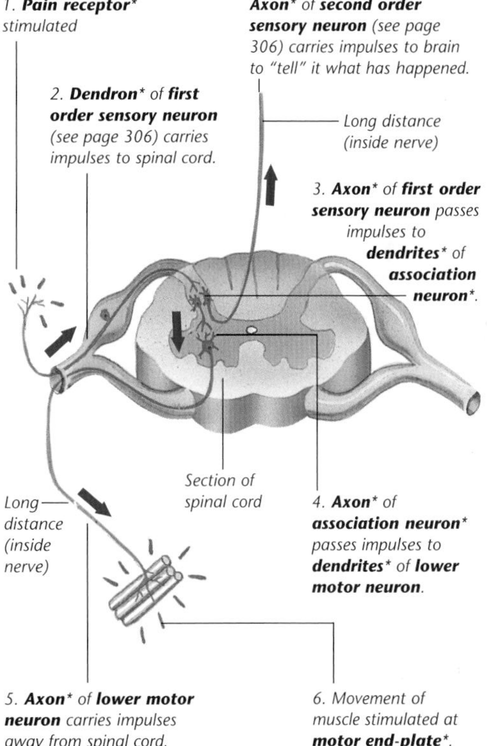
1. **Pain receptor*** stimulated
Axon* of **second order sensory neuron** (see page 306) carries impulses to brain to "tell" it what has happened.
2. **Dendron*** of **first order sensory neuron** (see page 306) carries impulses to spinal cord.
Long distance (inside nerve)
3. **Axon*** of **first order sensory neuron** passes impulses to **dendrites*** of **association neuron***.
Long distance (inside nerve)
Section of spinal cord
4. **Axon*** of **association neuron*** passes impulses to **dendrites*** of **lower motor neuron**.
5. **Axon*** of **lower motor neuron** carries impulses away from spinal cord.
6. Movement of muscle stimulated at **motor end-plate***.

* **Association neurons**, 305; **Axon**, **Cell body**, 304; **Dendron**, 304 (**Dendrites**); **Hypothalamus**, 303; **Motor end-plate**, 283; **Neural pathways**, 306; **Pain receptors**, 311; **Skeletal muscles**, 282.

THE SKIN

The **skin** or **cutis** is the outer body covering, made up of several tissue layers. It registers external stimulation, protects against damage or infection, prevents drying out, helps regulate body temperature, excretes waste (**sweat**), stores fat and makes **vitamin D***. It contains many tiny structures, each type with a different function. The entire skin (tissue layers and structures), is called the **integumentary system**.

The different layers

Epidermis

The thin outer layer of the skin which forms its **epithelium** (a term for any sheet of cells which forms a surface covering or a cavity lining). It is made up of several layers (**strata**, sing. **stratum**), shown in the picture, right.

*1. **Stratum corneum** (**horny** or **cornified layer**). Flat, dead cells filled with **keratin** (a fibrous, waterproofing protein). The cells are continually worn away or shed.*

*2. **Stratum granulosum** (**granular layer**). Flat, granulated cells. They slowly die away (there are no blood vessels in the epidermis to provide food and oxygen) and are pushed up to become part of the **stratum corneum**.*

*3. **Stratum germinativum**. Made up of two layers. The upper one (**stratum spinosum**) consists of new living cells. These push upward (and become part of the **stratum granulosum**) as more cells are made below them by the constantly-dividing cells of the lower layer (**stratum basale** or **Malphigian layer**).*

Epidermal layers

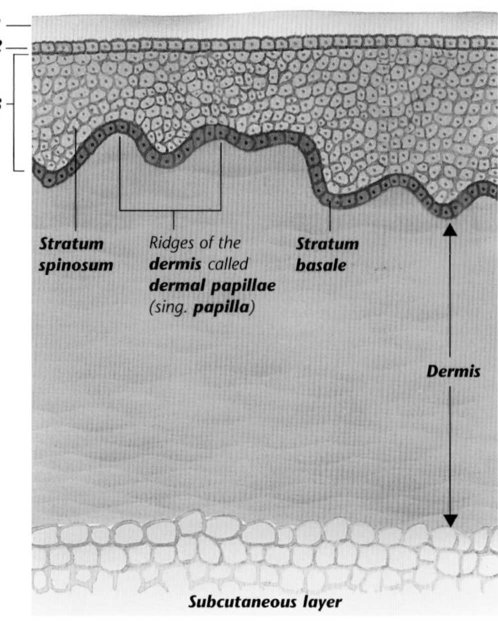

1
2
3
Stratum spinosum
Ridges of the dermis called dermal papillae (sing. papilla)
Stratum basale
Dermis
Subcutaneous layer

Dermis

The thick layer of **connective tissue*** under the **epidermis**, containing most of the embedded structures (see introduction). It also contains many **capillaries*** (tiny blood vessels) which supply food and oxygen.

Subcutaneous layer or superficial fascia

The layer of fatty tissue (**adipose tissue**) below the **dermis** (it is a fat store). Elastic fibers run through it to connect the dermis to the organs below, e.g. muscles. It forms an insulating layer. See also picture, right.

Melanin

A brown **pigment*** which shields against ultraviolet light by absorbing the light energy. It is found in all the layers of the **epidermis** of people from tropical areas, giving them dark skin. Fair-skinned people only have melanin in their lower epidermal layers, but produce more when in direct sunlight, causing a suntan.

*People with **melanin** only in lower layers of the **epidermis** have fair skin.*

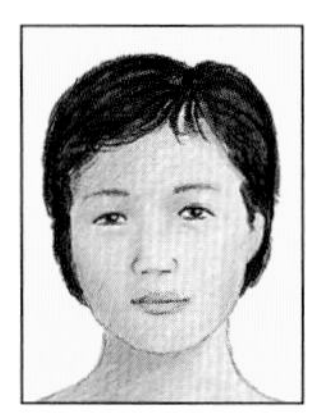

*The **pigment*** **carotene**, together with **melanin**, causes yellow skin.*

*Dark skin is caused by large amounts of **melanin** in all epidermal layers.*

* **Capillaries**, 288; **Connective tissue**, 280; **Pigments**, 255; **Vitamin D**, 339.

Structures in the skin

1. Meissner's corpuscles
Bodies formed around nerve fiber endings. There are especially large numbers on the fingertips and palms. They are touch **receptors***, i.e. they send impulses to the brain when the skin makes contact with an object.

2. Sebaceous glands
Exocrine glands* which open into **hair follicles**. They produce an oil called **sebum** which waterproofs the hairs and **epidermis** and keeps them supple.

3. Hair erector muscles
Special muscles, each attached to a **hair follicle**. When they contract (in the cold), the hairs straighten. This traps more air and improves insulation (especially in animals with lots of hair, feathers or fur). It also causes "goose-pimples".

4. Hair follicles
Long, narrow tubes, each containing a hair. The hair grows as new cells are added to its base from the cells lining the follicle. Its older cells die as **keratin** forms inside them (see **stratum corneum**).

5. Pain receptors
Nerve fiber endings in the tissue of most inner organs and in the skin (in the **epidermis** and the top of the **dermis**). They are the **receptors*** which send impulses when any stimulation (e.g. pressure, heat, touch) becomes excessive. This is what causes a sensation of pain.

6. Hair plexuses or **root hair plexuses**
Special groups of nerve fiber endings. Each forms a network around a **hair follicle** and is a **receptor***, i.e. it sends nervous impulses to the brain, in this case when the hair moves.

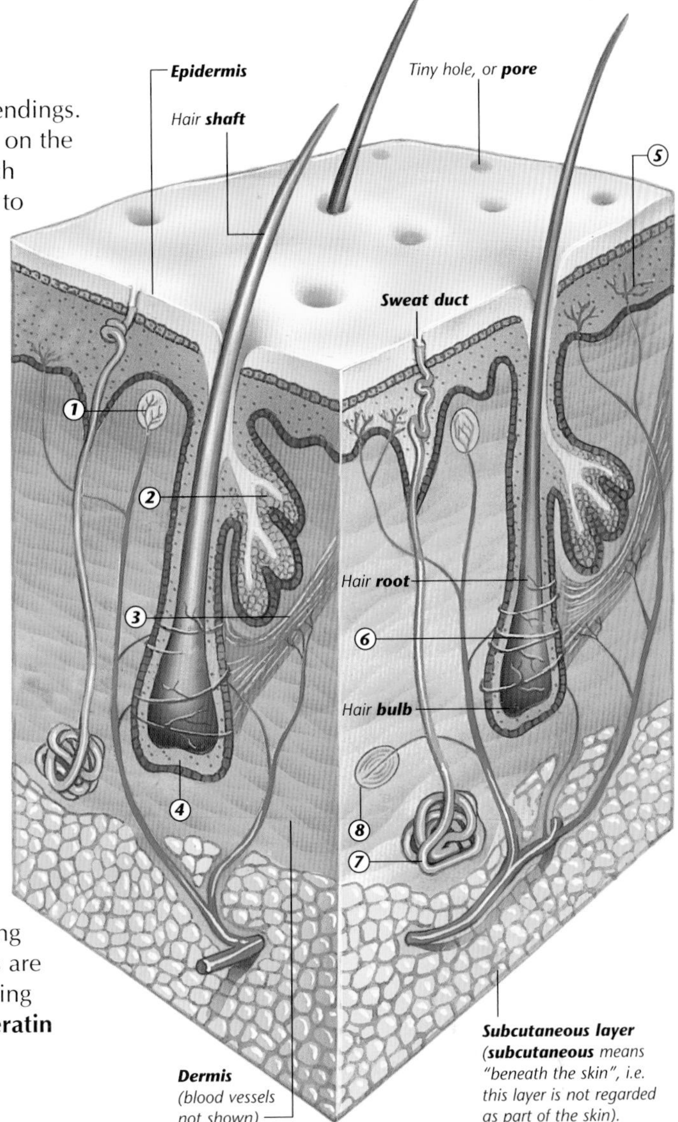
Epidermis
Hair shaft
Tiny hole, or pore
5
Sweat duct
1
2
3
Hair root
6
Hair bulb
4
8
7
Subcutaneous layer (subcutaneous means "beneath the skin", i.e. this layer is not regarded as part of the skin).
Dermis (blood vessels not shown)

7. Sweat glands or **sudoriferous glands**
Coiled **exocrine glands*** which excrete **sweat**. Each has a narrow tube (**sweat duct**) going to the surface. Sweat consists of water, salts and **urea***, which enter the gland from the cells and **capillaries*** (blood vessels).

8. Pacinian corpuscles
Special bodies formed around single nerve fiber endings, lying in the lower skin layers and the walls of inner organs. They are pressure **receptors***, i.e. they send impulses to the brain when the tissue is receiving deep pressure rather than light touch.

* **Capillaries**, 288; **Exocrine glands**, 296; **Receptors**, 307; **Urea**, 300.

THE EYES

The **eyes** are the organs of **sight**, sending nervous impulses to the brain when stimulated by light rays from external objects. The brain interprets the impulses to produce images. Each eye consists of a hollow, spherical capsule (**eyeball**), made up of several layers and structures. It is set into a socket in the skull (an **orbit**), and is protected by eyelids and eyelashes.

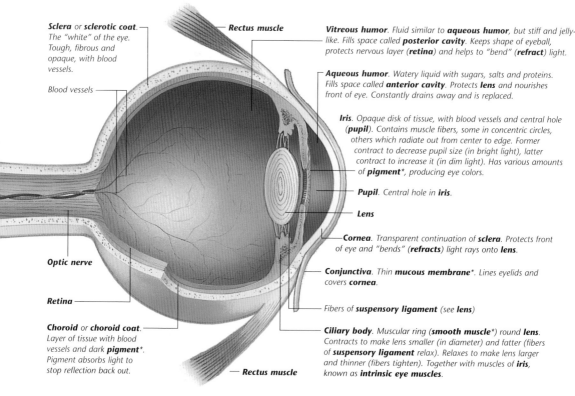

***Sclera** or **sclerotic coat**. The "white" of the eye. Tough, fibrous and opaque, with blood vessels.*

Blood vessels

Rectus muscle

***Vitreous humor**. Fluid similar to **aqueous humor**, but stiff and jelly-like. Fills space called **posterior cavity**. Keeps shape of eyeball, protects nervous layer (**retina**) and helps to "bend" (**refract**) light.*

***Aqueous humor**. Watery liquid with sugars, salts and proteins. Fills space called **anterior cavity**. Protects **lens** and nourishes front of eye. Constantly drains away and is replaced.*

Iris**. Opaque disk of tissue, with blood vessels and central hole (**pupil**). Contains muscle fibers, some in concentric circles, others which radiate out from center to edge. Former contract to decrease pupil size (in bright light), latter contract to increase it (in dim light). Has various amounts of **pigment, producing eye colors.*

***Pupil**. Central hole in **iris**.*

Lens

***Cornea**. Transparent continuation of **sclera**. Protects front of eye and "bends" (**refracts**) light rays onto **lens**.*

Optic nerve

Conjunctiva**. Thin **mucous membrane. Lines eyelids and covers **cornea**.*

Retina

*Fibers of **suspensory ligament** (see **lens**)*

Choroid** or **choroid coat**. Layer of tissue with blood vessels and dark **pigment. Pigment absorbs light to stop reflection back out.*

Ciliary body**. Muscular ring (**smooth muscle) round **lens**. Contracts to make lens smaller (in diameter) and fatter (fibers of **suspensory ligament** relax). Relaxes to make lens larger and thinner (fibers tighten). Together with muscles of **iris**, known as **intrinsic eye muscles**.*

Rectus muscle

Lens

The transparent body whose role, like that of any lens, is to focus the light rays passing through it, i.e. "bend" (**refract**) them so that they come to a point, in this case on the **retina** (for more about lenses and refraction, see pages 50-53). A lens consists of many thin tissue layers and is held in place by the fibers of a **ligament*** called the **suspensory ligament**. These join it to the **ciliary body**, which can alter the lens shape so that light rays are always focused on the retina, whatever the distance of the object being looked at. This is known as **accommodation**. The rays form an upside-down image, but this is corrected by the brain.

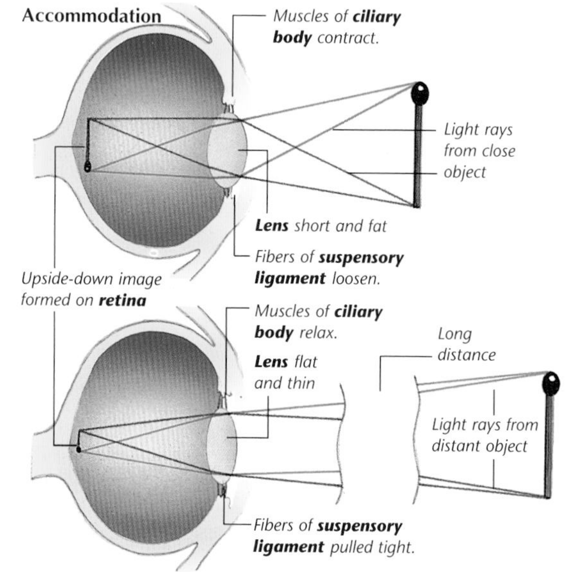
Accommodation
Muscles of ciliary body contract.
Light rays from close object
Lens short and fat
Fibers of suspensory ligament loosen.
Upside-down image formed on retina
Muscles of ciliary body relax.
Lens flat and thin
Long distance
Light rays from distant object
Fibers of suspensory ligament pulled tight.

* **Ligaments**, 280; **Mucous membrane**, 295; **Pigments**, 255; **Smooth muscle**, 283.

The inner nervous layer

Retina

The innermost layer of tissue at the back of the eyeball, made up of a layer of **pigment*** and a nervous layer consisting of millions of sensory nerve cells (**sensory neurons***) and their fibers. These lie in chains and carry nervous impulses to the brain. The first cells in the chains are **receptors***, i.e. their end fibers (**dendrons***) fire off the impulses when they are stimulated (by light rays). These fibers are called **rods** and **cones** because of their shapes. The receptors are **photoreceptors** (i.e. stimulated by light).

Close-up area of retina

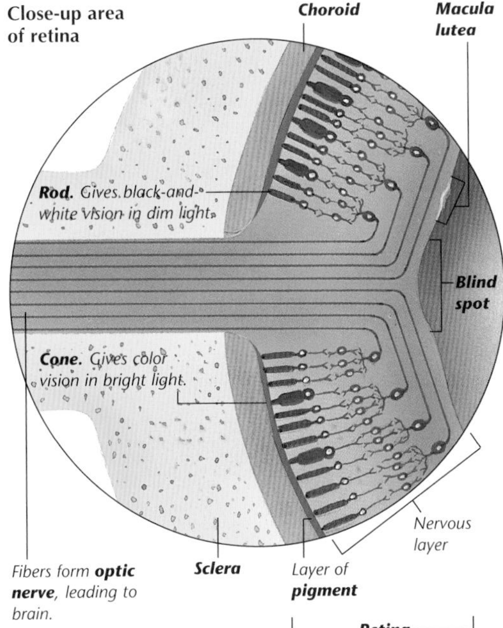
Choroid
Macula lutea
Rod. Gives black-and-white vision in dim light.
Blind spot
Cone. Gives color vision in bright light.
Nervous layer
Fibers form optic nerve, leading to brain.
Sclera
Layer of pigment
Retina

Macula lutea or yellowspot

An area of yellowish tissue in the center of the **retina**. It has a small central dip, called the **fovea** or **fovea centralis**. This has the highest concentration of **cones** (see **retina**) and is the area of acutest vision. If you look directly at a specific object, its light rays are focused on the fovea.

Blind spot or optic disk

The point in the **retina** where the **optic nerve** leaves the eye. It has no **receptors** (see **retina**) and so cannot send any impulses.

Structures around the eyeballs

Extrinsic eye muscles

The three pairs of muscles joining the eyeball to the eye socket (**orbit**). They contract to make the eyeball swivel around.

Extrinsic eye muscles

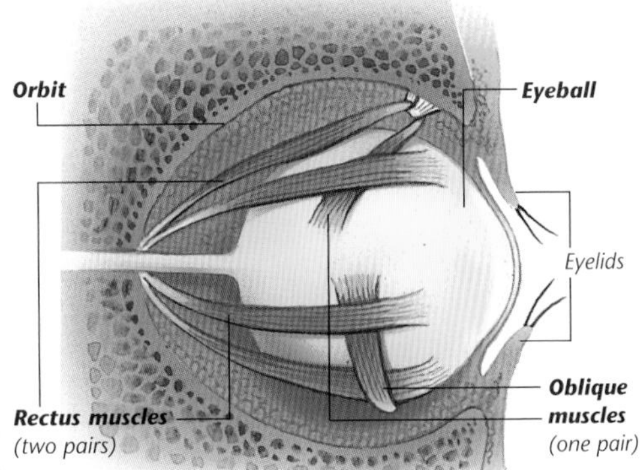
Orbit
Eyeball
Eyelids
Oblique muscles
(one pair)
Rectus muscles
(two pairs)

Lachrymal glands or tear glands

Two **exocrine glands***, one at the top of each eye socket (**orbit**). They secrete a watery fluid onto the lining of the upper eyelids via tubes called **lachrymal ducts**. The fluid contains salts and an anti-bacterial **enzyme***, and it washes over the surface of the eyes, keeping them moist and clean. It drains away via four **lachrymal canals**, two at the inside corner of each eye, which join to form a **nasolachrymal duct**. This empties into a **nasal cavity***.

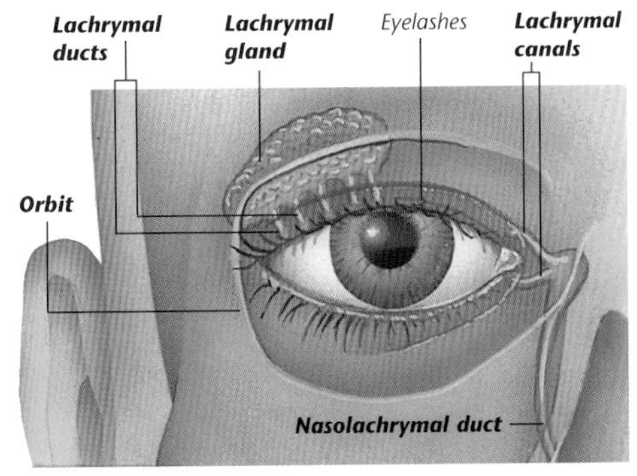
Lachrymal ducts
Lachrymal gland
Eyelashes
Lachrymal canals
Orbit
Nasolachrymal duct

Optic *means "of vision or the eye".*

Visual *means "perceptible by the sense of sight".*

* **Dendron**, 304 (**Dendrites**); **Enzymes**, 333; **Exocrine glands**, 296; **Nasal cavity**, 307 (**Nose**); **Pigments**, 255; **Receptors**, 307; **Sensory neurons**, 305.

THE EARS

The two **ears** are the organs of hearing and balance. Each one is divided into three areas – the **outer ear**, the **middle ear** and the **inner ear**.

Outer ear or external ear

An outer "shell" of skin and **cartilage*** (**pinna** or **auricle**), together with a short tube (**ear canal** or **external auditory canal**). The tube lining contains special **sebaceous glands*** (**ceruminous glands**) which secrete **cerumen** (ear wax).

Middle ear or tympanic cavity

An air-filled cavity which contains a chain of three tiny bones (**ear ossicles** or **auditory ossicles**) called the **malleus** (or **hammer**), **incus** (or **anvil**) and **stapes** (or **stirrup**).

Inner ear or internal ear

A connected series of cavities in the skull, with tubes and sacs inside them. The cavities (**cochlea**, **vestibule** and **semicircular canals**) are called the **bony labyrinth** and are filled with one fluid (**perilymph**). The tubes and sacs are filled with another fluid (**endolymph**) and are called the **membranous labyrinth**. They are the **cochlear duct**, **saccule**, **utricle** and **semicircular ducts**.

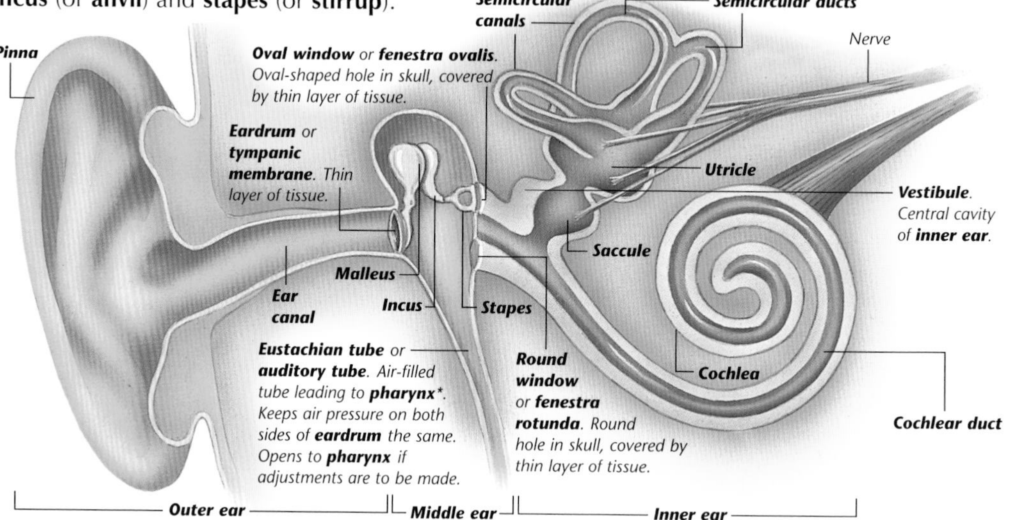
Semicircular canals
Semicircular ducts
Nerve
Pinna
Oval window or fenestra ovalis. Oval-shaped hole in skull, covered by thin layer of tissue.
Eardrum or tympanic membrane. Thin layer of tissue.
Utricle
Vestibule. Central cavity of inner ear.
Saccule
Malleus
Ear canal
Incus
Stapes
Eustachian tube or auditory tube. Air-filled tube leading to pharynx*. Keeps air pressure on both sides of eardrum the same. Opens to pharynx if adjustments are to be made.
Round window or fenestra rotunda. Round hole in skull, covered by thin layer of tissue.
Cochlea
Cochlear duct
Outer ear
Middle ear
Inner ear

The inner ear and hearing

Cochlea

A spiralling tubular cavity, part of the **inner ear**. It contains **perilymph** (see **inner ear**) in two channels (continuous with each other), and also a third channel – the **cochlear duct**.

Cochlear duct

A spiralling tube within the **cochlea**, connected to the **saccule**. It contains **endolymph** (see **inner ear**) and a long body called the **organ of Corti**. This contains special hair cells whose hairs project into the endolymph and touch a shelf-like tissue layer (**tectorial membrane**). The bases of the cells are attached to nerve fibers (**dendron*** endings).

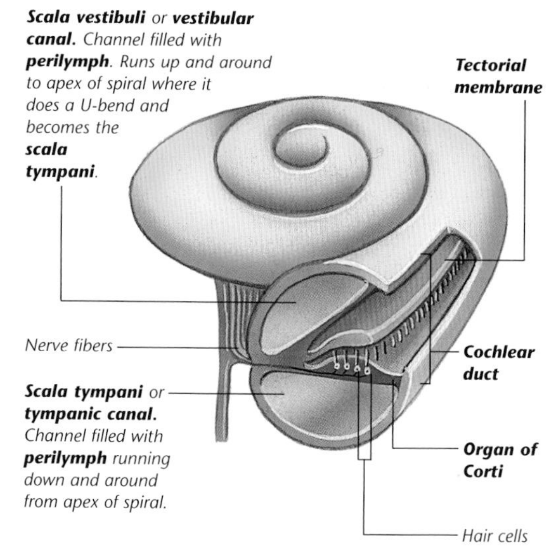
Scala vestibuli or vestibular canal. Channel filled with perilymph. Runs up and around to apex of spiral where it does a U-bend and becomes the scala tympani.
Tectorial membrane
Nerve fibers
Cochlear duct
Scala tympani or tympanic canal. Channel filled with perilymph running down and around from apex of spiral.
Organ of Corti
Hair cells

* **Cartilage**, 281; **Dendron**, 304 (**Dendrites**); **Pharynx**, 294; **Sebaceous glands**, 311.

The inner ear and balance

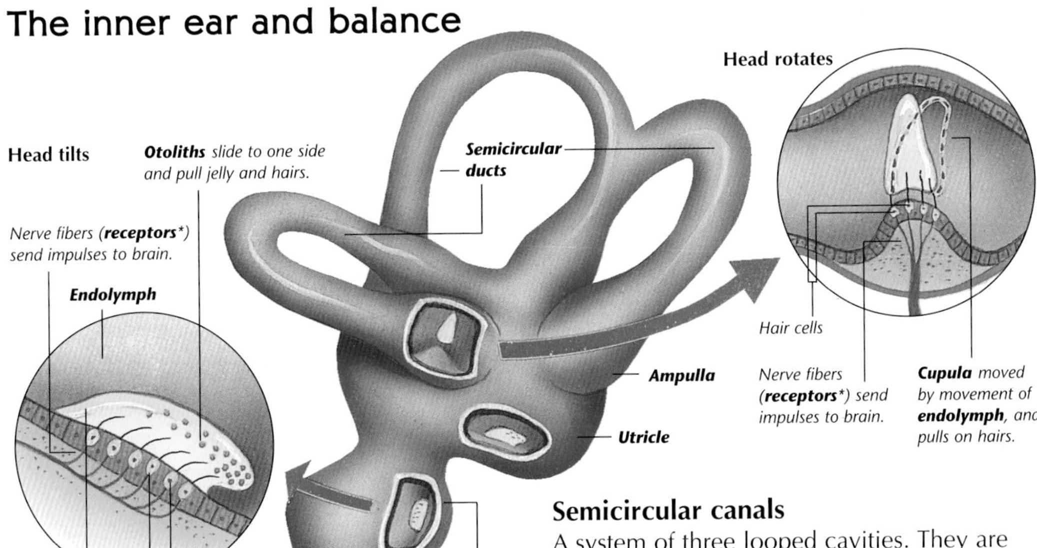
Head tilts
Otoliths slide to one side and pull jelly and hairs.
Nerve fibers (**receptors***) send impulses to brain.
Endolymph
Macula
Hair cells
Semicircular ducts
Ampulla
Utricle
Saccule
Head rotates
Hair cells
Nerve fibers (**receptors***) send impulses to brain.
Cupula moved by movement of **endolymph**, and pulls on hairs.

Saccule (sacculus) and utricle (utriculus)

Two sacs lying between the **semicircular ducts** and the **cochlear duct**. They contain **endolymph** (see **inner ear**) and have special hair cells in patches in their linings. These cells have nerve fibers (**dendron*** endings) attached to them and hairs embedded in a jelly-like mass called a **macula** (pl. **maculae**). This contains grains of calcium carbonate (**otoliths**). The maculae send the brain information about forward, backward, sideways or tilting motion of the head.

Semicircular canals

A system of three looped cavities. They are part of the **inner ear** and are positioned on the three different planes of movement, at right angles to each other.

Semicircular ducts

Three looped tubes inside the **semicircular canals**. Each contains **endolymph** (see **inner ear**) and a special sensory body, which lies across the basal swelling (**ampulla**, pl. **ampullae**) of the duct. The sensory bodies (**cupulae**, sing. **cupula**) work in a very similar way to **maculae** (see **saccule**) – each consists of a jelly-like mass (without **otoliths**) and hair cells. They send the brain information about rotation and tilting of the head.

*a) Sound waves (air vibrations) come in along **ear canal** and make **eardrum** vibrate.*

*b) **Ear ossicles** pick up vibrations and pass them to **oval window** (lever action magnifies vibrations about 20 times).*

*c) Vibrations of **oval window** cause waves in **perilymph** of **vestibule**.*

*d) Waves in **perilymph** of **scala vestibuli** cause waves in **endolymph** of **cochlear duct**.*

*e) Hairs move and cause nerve fibers (**receptors***) to send impulses to brain (which interprets them as sensation of hearing).*

f) Waves gradually fade out.

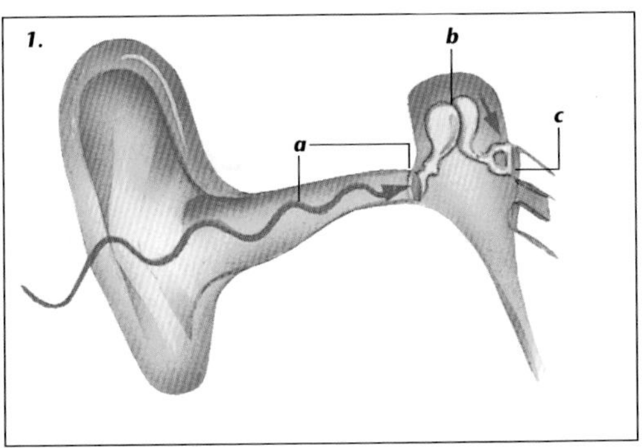
1.
a
b
c

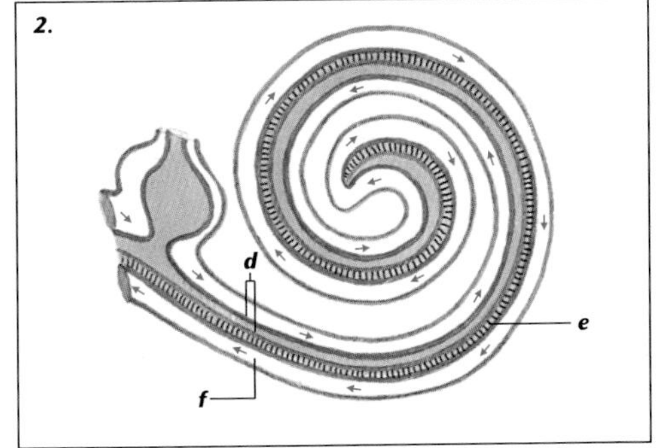
2.
d
e
f

* **Dendron**, 304 (**Dendrites**); **Receptors**, 307.

THE REPRODUCTIVE SYSTEM

Reproduction is the process of producing new life. Humans reproduce by **sexual reproduction*** (described on pages 318-319) and the reproductive organs involved (making up the **reproductive system**) are called the **genital organs** or **genitalia**. They consist of the primary reproductive organs, or **gonads** (two **ovaries** in women, two **testes** in men) and a number of additional organs. In both women and men, cells in the gonads also act as **endocrine glands***, secreting many important **hormones***.

The male reproductive system

Testes (sing. **testis**) or **testicles**
The two male **gonads** (see introduction). They contain tube-like canals called **seminiferous tubules**, inside which the male **gametes*** (sex cells), called **sperm**, are made after **puberty*** (for more about how sperm are made, see pages 322-323). The testes lie in a sac (**scrotum**), which hangs below the abdomen (the temperature for sperm production must be slightly lower than body temperature). They also produce **hormones*** (**androgens** – see pages 336-337) after puberty.

Side view of male organs (only one testis shown)

Sperm duct — ***Bladder****

Urethra*

Penis

Scrotum

Anus*

Testis

Loose skin over ***glans*** *called* ***foreskin*** *or* ***prepuce***

Glans. *Tip of penis (most sensitive part) with many blood vessels.*

Sperm duct *or* ***vas deferens*** *(pl.* ***vasa deferentia****). Continuation of* ***epididymis****, carrying sperm into* ***urethra**** *during* ***ejaculation****.*

Cross section of testis

Epididymis *(pl.* ***epididymides****). Comma-shaped organ enclosing coiled tube where* ***sperm*** *are stored.*

Interstitial cells *(cells between tubules)*

Seminiferous tubule

Ducts and glands (view from behind – testes not shown)

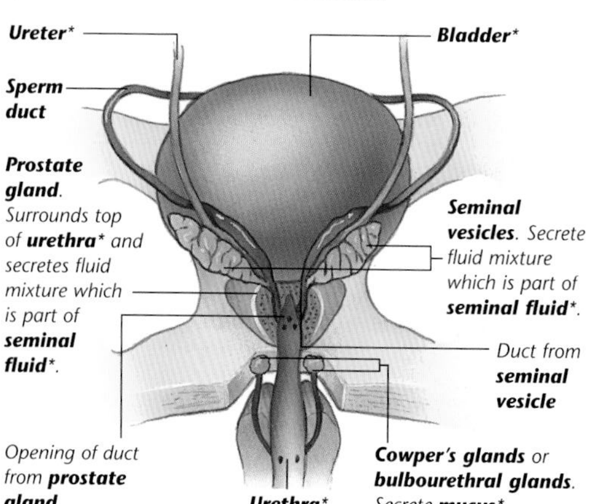

Ureter*
Bladder*
Sperm duct
Prostate gland. Surrounds top of urethra* and secretes fluid mixture which is part of seminal fluid*.
Seminal vesicles. Secrete fluid mixture which is part of seminal fluid*.
Duct from seminal vesicle
Opening of duct from prostate gland
Urethra*
Cowper's glands or bulbourethral glands. Secrete mucus*.

Penis
The organ through which **sperm** (see **testes**) are ejected (via the **urethra***) during **copulation***. It is made of soft, sponge-like **erectile tissue**, which has many spaces (**blood sinuses**), blood vessels and nerve fiber endings (**receptors***). When a man is sexually excited, the sinuses and blood vessels fill with blood (the blood vessels expand). This makes the penis stiff and erect.

* **Anus**, 295 (**Large intestine**); **Bladder**, 300; **Ejaculation**, 319 (**Copulation**); **Endocrine glands**, 297; **Gametes**, 320; **Hormones**, 336; **Mucus**, 295 (**Mucous membrane**); **Puberty**, 318; **Receptors**, 307; **Seminal fluid**, 319 (**Copulation**); **Sexual reproduction**, 320; **Ureters**, 300; **Urethra**, 300.

The female reproductive system

Ovaries

The two female **gonads** (see introduction). They are held in place in the lower abdomen (below the kidneys) by **ligaments***. These attach them to the walls of the pelvis. The female **gametes*** (sex cells), called **ova** (sing. **ovum**), are produced regularly in the ovaries (in **ovarian follicles**) after **puberty***. For more about how ova are made, see pages 322-323.

Vulva or pudendum

A collective term for the outer parts of the female reproductive system – the **labia** and the **clitoris** (see picture, bottom right). The **labia** (**majora** and **minora**) are two folds of skin (one inside the other) which surround the openings from the **vagina** and the **urethra***. The clitoris is the most sensitive part. Like the **penis**, it is made of **erectile tissue** and has many **receptors***.

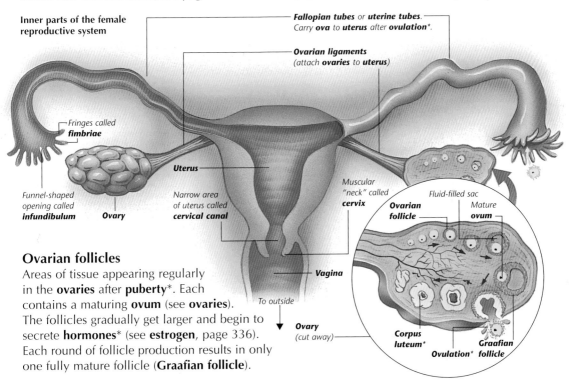

Inner parts of the female reproductive system

Fallopian tubes *or* ***uterine tubes****. Carry* ***ova*** *to* ***uterus*** *after* ***ovulation****.*

Ovarian ligaments *(attach* ***ovaries*** *to* ***uterus****)*

Fringes called ***fimbriae***

Uterus

Funnel-shaped opening called ***infundibulum***

Ovary

Narrow area of uterus called ***cervical canal***

Muscular "neck" called ***cervix***

Fluid-filled sac

Ovarian follicle

Mature ***ovum***

Vagina

To outside

Ovary *(cut away)*

Corpus luteum*

Ovulation*

Graafian follicle

Ovarian follicles

Areas of tissue appearing regularly in the **ovaries** after **puberty***. Each contains a maturing **ovum** (see **ovaries**). The follicles gradually get larger and begin to secrete **hormones*** (see **estrogen**, page 336). Each round of follicle production results in only one fully mature follicle (**Graafian follicle**).

Uterus or womb

The hollow organ, inside which a developing baby (**fetus***) is held, or from which the **ova** (see **ovaries**) are discharged (see **menstrual cycle**, page 318). It has a lining of **mucous membrane*** (the **endometrium**), covering a muscular wall with many blood vessels.

Vagina

The muscular canal leading from the **uterus** out of the body. It carries away the **ova** (see **ovaries**) and **endometrium** (see uterus) during **menstruation***, receives the **penis** during **copulation*** and serves as the birth canal. Its lining produces a lubricating fluid.

Outer parts of the female reproductive system

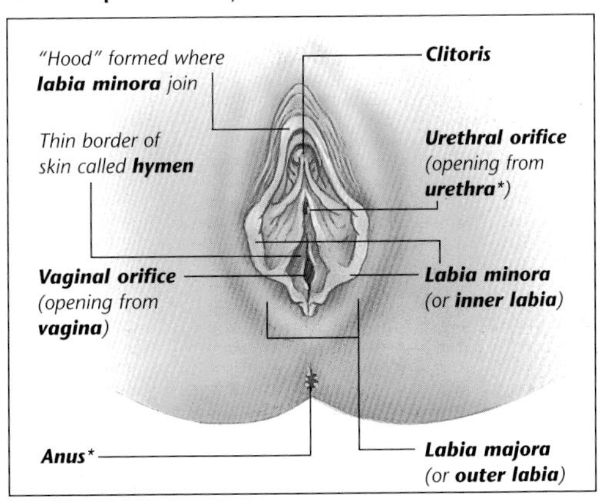
"Hood" formed where labia minora join
Clitoris
Thin border of skin called hymen
Urethral orifice (opening from urethra*)
Vaginal orifice (opening from vagina)
Labia minora (or inner labia)
Anus*
Labia majora (or outer labia)

* **Anus**, 295 (**Large intestine**); **Copulation**, 319; **Corpus luteum**, 318 (**Menstrual cycle**); **Fetus**, 319 (**Pregnancy**); **Gametes**, 320; **Hormones**, 336; **Ligaments**, 280; **Menstruation**, 318 (**Menstrual cycle**); **Mucous membrane**, 295; **Ovulation**, 318 (**Menstrual cycle**); **Puberty**, 318; **Receptors**, 307; **Urethra**, 300.

DEVELOPMENT AND REPRODUCTION

Humans reproduce by **sexual reproduction***. The main processes this involves are described on these two pages, as well as the initial developments which allow it to happen.

Puberty

The point when the reproductive organs mature, and a person becomes capable of reproducing – roughly between the ages of 11 and 15 in girls, and 13 and 15 in boys. It involves a number of significant changes, all stimulated by **hormones*** (see **estrogen** and **androgens**, pages 336-337). All the new resulting features are called **secondary sex characters**, as distinct from the **primary sex characters** – the sex organs present from birth (see pages 316-317).

Changes at puberty

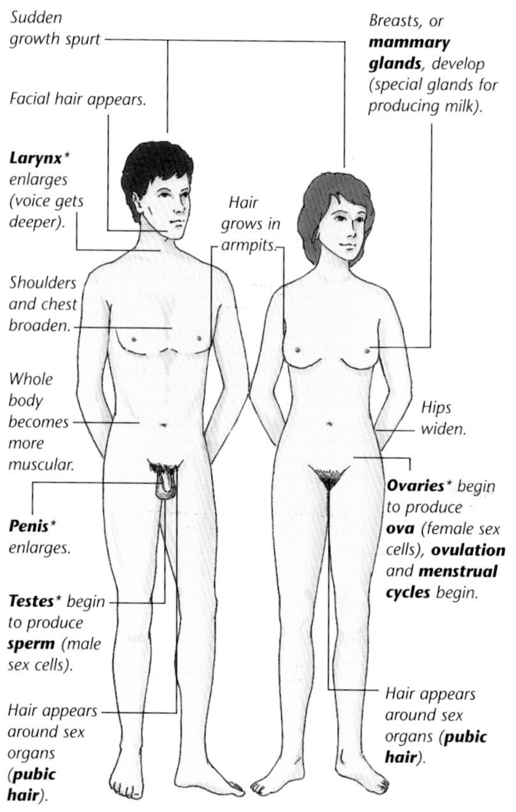
Sudden growth spurt
Facial hair appears.
Larynx* enlarges (voice gets deeper).
Shoulders and chest broaden.
Whole body becomes more muscular.
Penis* enlarges.
Testes* begin to produce sperm (male sex cells).
Hair appears around sex organs (pubic hair).
Breasts, or mammary glands, develop (special glands for producing milk).
Hair grows in armpits.
Hips widen.
Ovaries* begin to produce ova (female sex cells), ovulation and menstrual cycles begin.
Hair appears around sex organs (pubic hair).

Menstrual cycle

A series of preparatory changes in the **uterus*** lining (**endometrium**), in case of **fertilization**. The lining gradually develops a new inner layer rich in blood vessels. If a fertilized **ovum** (female sex cell) does not appear, this new layer breaks down and leaves the body via the **vagina*** (**menstruation**). Each menstrual cycle lasts about 28 days and they occur continuously from **puberty** (usually between the ages of 11 and 15 – see left) to **menopause** (usually between 45 and 50), when ova production ceases. The events of the menstrual cycle run in conjunction with the **ovarian cycle** – the regular maturation of an ovum in an **ovarian follicle***, followed by **ovulation** (the release of the ovum into a **Fallopian tube***), and the breakdown of the **corpus luteum**. This body is formed from the burst **Graafian follicle*** (it does not break down if an ovum is fertilized). Both cycles are controlled by a group of **hormones*** (see pages 336-337).

Menstrual cycle / Ovarian cycle

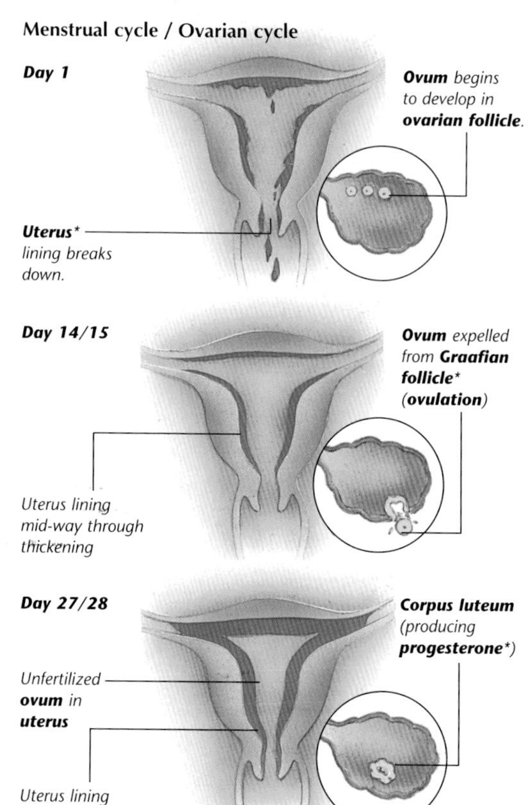
Day 1
Ovum begins to develop in ovarian follicle.
Uterus* lining breaks down.
Day 14/15
Ovum expelled from Graafian follicle* (ovulation)
Uterus lining mid-way through thickening
Day 27/28
Corpus luteum (producing progesterone*)
Unfertilized ovum in uterus
Uterus lining fully thickened

* **Fallopian tubes**, 317; **Graafian follicle**, 317 (**Ovarian follicles**); **Hormones**, 336; **Larynx**, 298; **Ovaries**, 317; **Penis**, 316; **Progesterone**, 336; **Sexual reproduction**, 320; **Testes**, 316; **Uterus**, **Vagina**, 317.

Copulation

Also called **coitus** or **sexual intercourse**. The insertion of the **penis*** into the **vagina***, followed by rhythmical movements of the pelvis in one or both sexes. Its culmination in the male is **ejaculation** – the ejection of **semen** from the **urethra*** (in the penis) into the vagina. Semen consists of **sperm** (male sex cells) and a fluid mixture (**seminal fluid**).

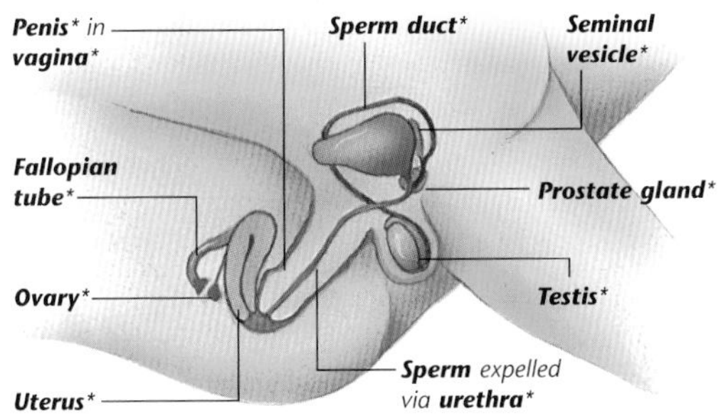

Penis* in vagina*
Sperm duct*
Seminal vesicle*
Fallopian tube*
Prostate gland*
Ovary*
Testis*
Uterus*
Sperm expelled via urethra*

Fertilization

A process which occurs after **ejaculation** if the **sperm** (male sex cells) meet an **ovum** (female sex cell) in a **Fallopian tube***. One sperm penetrates the ovum's outer skin (**zona pellucida**). Its **nucleus*** fuses with that of the ovum, and the first cell of a new baby (**zygote***) is formed. The new cell travels toward the **uterus***, undergoing many cell divisions (**cleavage***) as it does so. The ball of cells formed from these divisions then becomes embedded in the uterus wall (**implantation**), after which it is called an **embryo***.

Zona pellucida

Sperm** penetrates **ovum**. **Nucleus will fuse with ovum nucleus.*

"Tail" is left behind.

Pregnancy

Pregnancy, or **gestation**, is the state of carrying young. The time between **fertilization** and giving birth (**parturition**) is the **gestation period** (about 9 months in humans) and the new developing individual in the **uterus*** is called a **fetus**, a term usually used instead of **embryo*** after about two months of pregnancy. A series of powerful muscular contractions called **labor** occur just before parturition.

Placenta**. "Feeds" **fetus**. Oxygen and food matter pass from mother's **arteries into spaces and then into fetal **vein**. Carbon dioxide and waste pass the other way, to be carried away by mother's **veins***. Placenta also produces **progesterone***.*

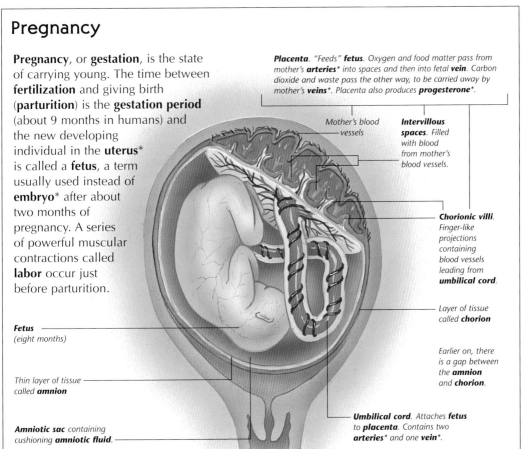

Mother's blood vessels

***Intervillous spaces**. Filled with blood from mother's blood vessels.*

***Chorionic villi**. Finger-like projections containing blood vessels leading from **umbilical cord**.*

*Layer of tissue called **chorion***

*Earlier on, there is a gap between the **amnion** and **chorion**.*

***Fetus** (eight months)*

*Thin layer of tissue called **amnion***

***Amniotic sac** containing cushioning **amniotic fluid**.*

Umbilical cord**. Attaches **fetus** to **placenta**. Contains two **arteries and one **vein***.*

* **Arteries**, 288; **Cleavage**, 320 (**Embryo**); **Fallopian tubes**, 317; **Nucleus**, 238; **Ovaries**, 317; **Penis**, 316; **Progesterone**, 336; **Prostate gland**, **Seminal vesicles**, **Sperm ducts**, **Testes**, 316; **Urethra**, 300; **Uterus**, **Vagina**, 317; **Veins**, 288; **Zygote**, 320.

TYPES OF REPRODUCTION

1.

Reproduction is the creation of new life, a process which occurs in all living things. The two main types are **sexual** and **asexual reproduction**, but there is also a special case called **alternation of generations**.

2.

Sexual reproduction

Sexual reproduction in humans

*1. **Sperm** fertilizes **ovum** to form **zygote**.*
*2. Cell divides in two by **mitosis***.*
3. Cells divide again.

3.

4.

Sexual reproduction is the type of reproduction shown by all flowering plants and most animals. It involves the joining (**fusion**) of two **gametes** (sex cells), one male and one female. This process is called **fertilization**, and is further described on pages 258 (flowering plants), 319 (humans and similar animals) and 276 (other animals). The two gametes each have only half the number of **chromosomes*** (called the **haploid number***) as the plant or animal which produced them. This is achieved by a special kind of cell division (see pages 322-323) and ensures that when the gametes come together, the new individual produced has the correct, original number of chromosomes (called the **diploid number***).

*4. Cells continue to divide, to form a **morula**, then a **blastocyst** which becomes embedded in the wall of the **uterus***.*

Gametes or germ cells

The sex cells which join in **sexual reproduction** to form a new living thing. They are made by a special kind of cell division (see pages 322-323). In animals and simple plants, male gametes are known as **sperm**, short for **spermatozoa** (sing. **spermatozoon**) in animals and **spermatozooids** in simple plants. In flowering plants, they are just **nuclei*** (rather than cells) and are called **male nuclei** (see also pages 258 and 323). Female gametes are called **ova** (sing. **ovum**) or **egg cells** (egg cell is usually used in the case of plants). A sperm is smaller than an ovum and has a "tail" (**flagellum***).

Zygote

The first cell of a new living thing. It is formed when a male and female **gamete** join (see **sexual reproduction**).

Embryo

A new developing individual. It grows from one cell (the **zygote**) by a series of cell divisions (see pages 240-241) called **cleavage**. In humans, this first produces a ball of cells (**morula**) from the one original, and then a larger, hollow ball (**blastocyst**). After **implantation***, this is called the embryo. As it grows, the cells become **differentiated**, i.e. each develops into one kind of cell, e.g. a nerve cell.

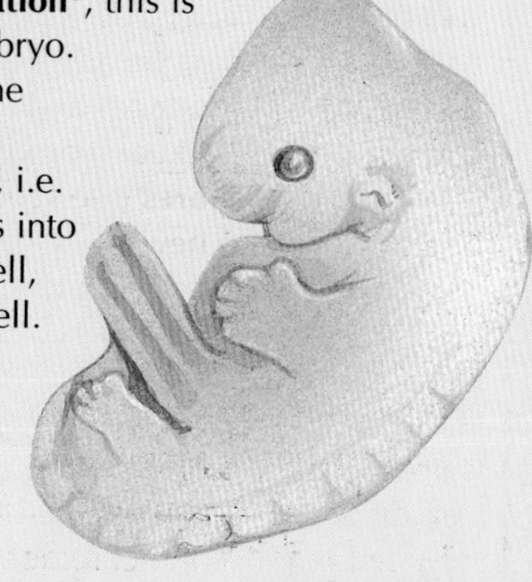

*Human **embryo** (at eight weeks)*

* **Chromosomes**, 324; **Diploid number**, 240 (**Mitosis**); **Flagella**, 268; **Haploid number**, 322 (**Meiosis**); **Implantation**, 319 (**Fertilization**); **Nucleus**, 238; **Uterus**, 317.

Asexual reproduction

Asexual reproduction is the simplest form of reproduction, occurring in many simple plants and animals. There are a number of different types, e.g. **binary fission***, **vegetative reproduction***, **gemmation** and **sporulation**, but they all share two main features. Firstly, only one parent is needed and secondly, the new individual produced is always genetically identical to this parent.

Gemmation

Called **budding** in animals. A type of **asexual reproduction** occurring in many simple plants and animals, e.g. hydra. It involves the formation of a group of cells which grows out of the organism and develops into a new individual. It either breaks away from the parent or (in **colonial*** animals, e.g. corals) it stays attached (though self-contained).

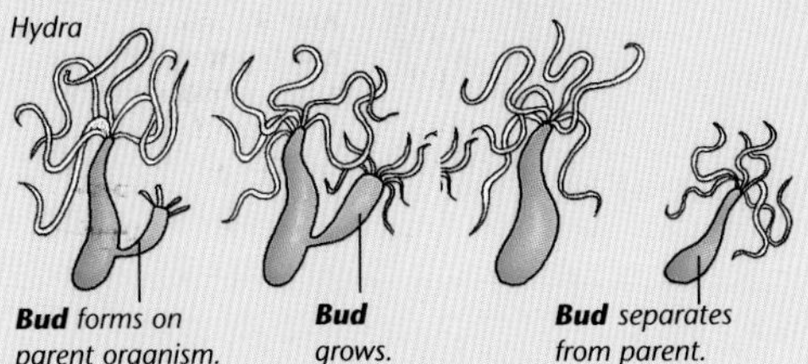
Hydra
Bud forms on parent organism.
Bud grows.
Bud separates from parent.

Sporulation

The production of bodies called **spores** by simple plants, e.g. fungi and mosses. After dispersal by wind or water, these develop into new plants. There are two types of spores. One type is produced (e.g. in complex fungi, mosses and ferns) by a special kind of cell division (see pages 322-323) which is a feature of **sexual reproduction**. The new plants are not the same as the parent (see **alternation of generations**). Another kind of spore, however, is produced in plants such as simple fungi by ordinary cell division (see pages 240-241). The spores develop into plants which are identical to the parent (an important feature of **asexual reproduction**). Although only one parent is needed in both cases, true asexual reproduction really only occurs with the second type.

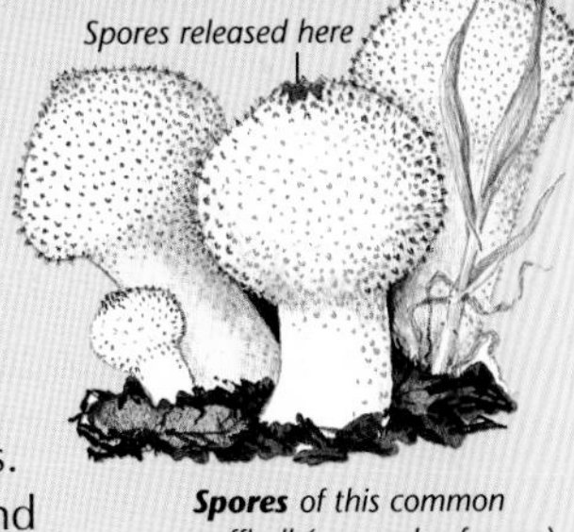
Spores released here

***Spores** of this common puffball (a complex fungus) disperse through a hole that forms in the ball.*

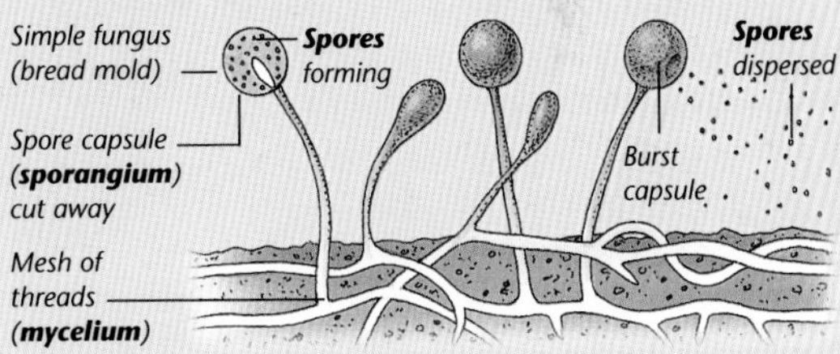
Simple fungus (bread mold)
Spores forming
Spore capsule (**sporangium**) cut away
Mesh of threads (**mycelium**)
Burst capsule
Spores dispersed

Alternation of generations

A reproductive process found in many simple animals and plants, e.g. jellyfish and mosses. In the animals, a form produced by **sexual reproduction** alternates with one produced **asexually**. In the plants, though, the alternation is really between two stages of sexual reproduction. One plant body (**gametophyte**) produces another (**sporophyte**) by sexual reproduction. This then produces **spores** (see **sporulation**) which grow into new gametophytes. However, the spores are made in the same way as **gametes** (see pages 322-323) and they (and the gametophytes) have only half the original number of **chromosomes***. The gametophytes produce gametes by ordinary cell division (see pages 240-241), as there is no need to halve the chromosomes again.

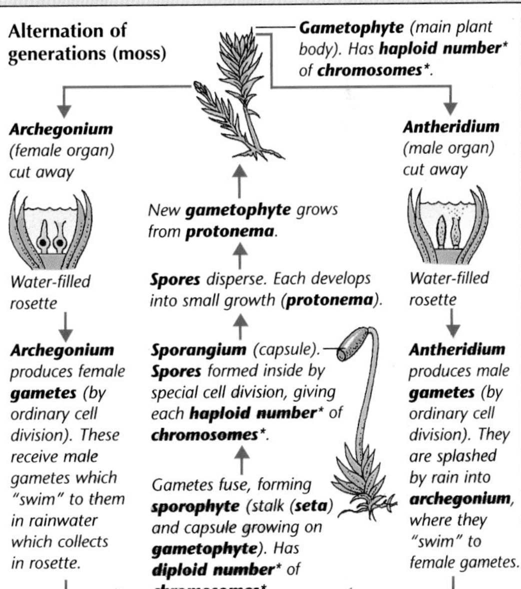
Alternation of generations (moss)
Gametophyte (main plant body). Has **haploid number*** of **chromosomes***.
Archegonium (female organ) cut away
Antheridium (male organ) cut away
New **gametophyte** grows from **protonema**.
Water-filled rosette
Spores disperse. Each develops into small growth (**protonema**).
Water-filled rosette
Archegonium produces female **gametes** (by ordinary cell division). These receive male gametes which "swim" to them in rainwater which collects in rosette.
Sporangium (capsule). **Spores** formed inside by special cell division, giving each **haploid number*** of **chromosomes***.
Gametes fuse, forming **sporophyte** (stalk (**seta**) and capsule growing on **gametophyte**). Has **diploid number*** of **chromosomes***.
Antheridium produces male **gametes** (by ordinary cell division). They are splashed by rain into **archegonium**, where they "swim" to female gametes.

* **Binary fission**, 240 (**Cell division**); **Chromosomes**, 324; **Colonial**, 342; **Diploid number**, 240 (**Mitosis**); **Haploid number**, 322 (**Meiosis**); **Vegetative reproduction**, 263.

CELL DIVISION FOR REPRODUCTION

Many cells within a living thing can divide to produce new cells for growth and repair (see pages 240-241). There is, however, a second type of cell division, which happens specifically to produce the **gametes*** (sex cells) needed for **sexual reproduction*** (and also one of the two types of **spore***). The division of the **nucleus*** in this type of cell division is called **meiosis**. The production of gametes, including both the cell division and the subsequent maturing of the gametes, is called **gametogenesis**.

Meiosis

The division of the **nucleus*** when a cell divides to produce sex cells (see introduction). It can be split into two separate divisions – the **first meiotic division** (or **reduction division**) and the **second meiotic division** (each is followed by division of the **cytoplasm***). These can be divided into different phases (as in **mitosis***). Meiosis in general, and the first meiotic division in particular, ensures that each new **daughter nucleus** receives exactly half the number of **chromosomes*** as the original nucleus. The original number is the **diploid number** (see **mitosis**, page 240); the halved amount is the **haploid number**.

First meiotic division

These pictures show an animal cell, but only four **chromosomes*** are shown.

Prophase (early stage)

*Threads of **chromatin*** in **nucleus*** coil up to form **chromosomes***. Paired chromosomes (**homologous chromosomes**) line up side by side, forming pairs called **bivalents**. Each chromosome duplicates, becoming a pair of **chromatids** (each group of four chromatids now called a **tetrad**). **Centrioles*** move to opposite poles of cell.*

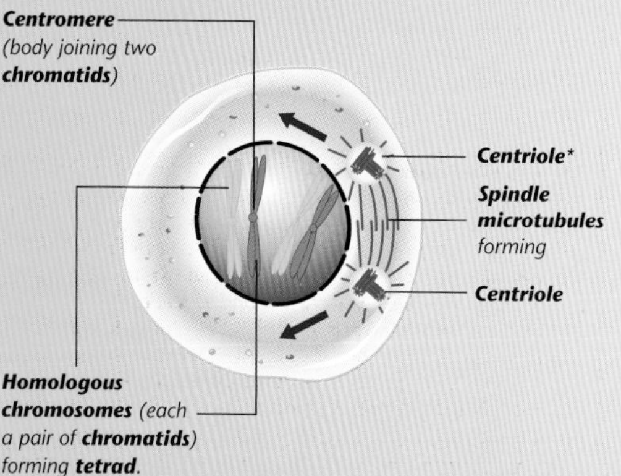
Centromere (body joining two chromatids)
Centriole*
Spindle microtubules forming
Centriole
Homologous chromosomes (each a pair of chromatids) forming tetrad.

Crossing over (occurs in early prophase)

Chromatids** of each **tetrad** cross over each other at places called **chiasmata** (sing. **chiasma**). Two chromatid pieces (one from each pair) break off and swap over. Causes mixing of **genes (helping to ensure new living things are never identical to parents, i.e. always a new variety of types).*

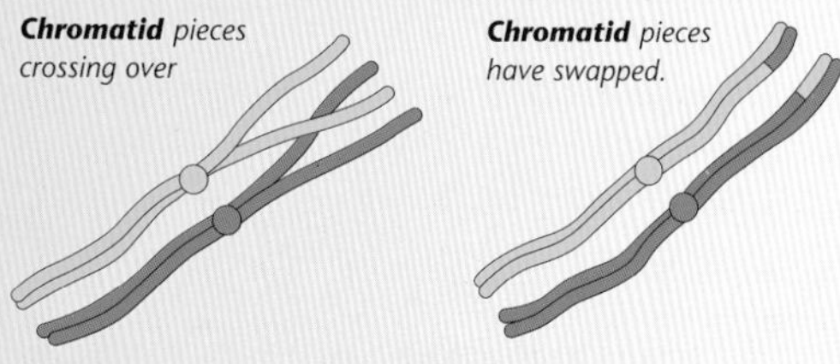
Chromatid pieces crossing over
Chromatid pieces have swapped.

Prophase (later stage)

***Homologous chromosomes** (each a pair of **chromatids**) move together to equator of cell.*

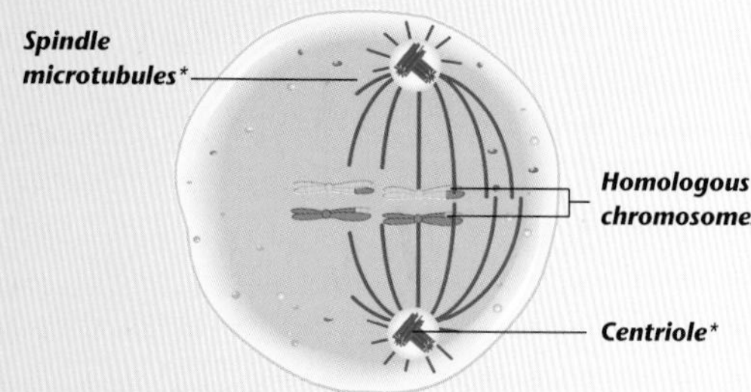
Spindle microtubules*
Homologous chromosomes
Centriole*

Metaphase

Nuclear membrane disappears, two **centrioles*** form a **spindle** (see **metaphase** of **mitosis**, page 241). **Chromosomes*** (pairs of **chromatids**) become attached to spindle by **centromeres**.*

Spindle (made up of microtubules)
Homologous chromosomes
Centromere attached to spindle microtubule
Centriole*

* **Centrioles**, 240; **Chromatin**, 238 (**Nucleus**); **Chromosomes**, 324; **Cytoplasm**, 238; **Gametes**, 320; **Genes**, 325; **Mitosis**, 240; **Nuclear membrane**, 238 (**Nucleus**); **Sexual reproduction**, 320; **Spindle microtubules**, 241; **Spores**, 321 (**Sporulation**).

Anaphase

Homologous chromosomes *(each still a pair of* ***chromatids****) separate (see* ***Law of segregation****, page 326), dragged apart by fibers of* ***spindle****.*

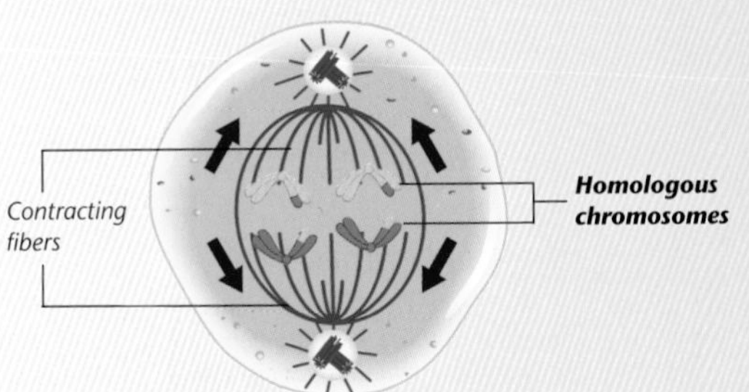
Contracting fibers
Homologous chromosomes

Telophase

Spindle *disappears,* ***centrioles**** *duplicate. Happens in conjunction with* ***cytokinesis*** *(division of* ***cytoplasm*****). Two new cells formed, each with half the original number of* ***chromosomes**** *(each two* ***chromatids****). Brief* ***interphase**** *(intervening period) usually follows, in which case* ***nuclear membranes**** *form and chromosomes uncoil again to form thread-like mass (****chromatin*****).*

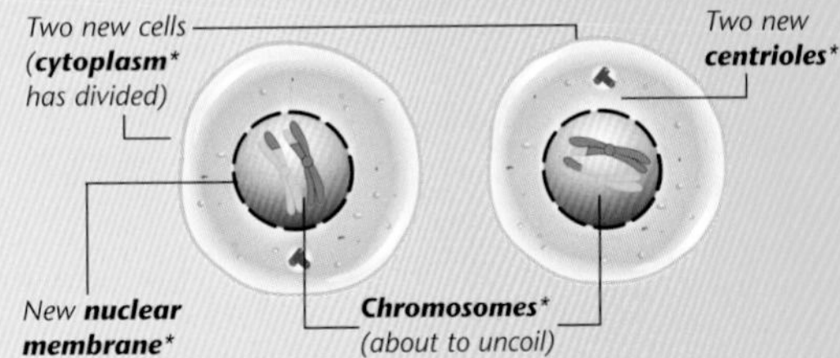
Two new cells (cytoplasm* has divided)
Two new centrioles*
New nuclear membrane*
Chromosomes* (about to uncoil)

Second meiotic division

The **second meiotic division** happens in the cells produced by the **first meiotic division**. It occurs in exactly the same way, and with the same phases, as **mitosis*** (when the **nucleus*** divides as part of cell division for growth and repair) and is followed in the same way by the division of the **cytoplasm***.

The only difference is that each dividing nucleus now has only the **haploid number** of **chromosomes*** (see **meiosis**) so the resulting new sex cells (**gametes***) will also be haploid. The second division differs according to whether male or female gametes are to be produced, and the final maturing of the gametes after the second division is different in animals and plants (see text below).

Gamete production (male)

Two cells formed from ***first meiotic division*** *(****haploid number*** *of* ***chromosomes**** *in* ***nuclei****).*

Four cells result from ***second meiotic division*** *(****spermatids*** *in animals)*

Mature into ***sperm*** *in animals and simple plants*

Two cells formed from ***first meiotic division*** *divide again (see* ***second meiotic division****). In animals, resulting four cells called* ***spermatids*** *and mature into male* ***gametes**** *(sex cells), or* ***sperm****. In simple plants, four cells either develop into sperm or into type of* ***spore**** *involved in* ***alternation of generations*****. In flowering plants,* ***nuclei**** *of four cells each divide again (****mitosis*****). Resulting cells (****pollen**** *grains) each have two nuclei (one later divides again to form two* ***male nuclei*****).*

Gamete production (female)

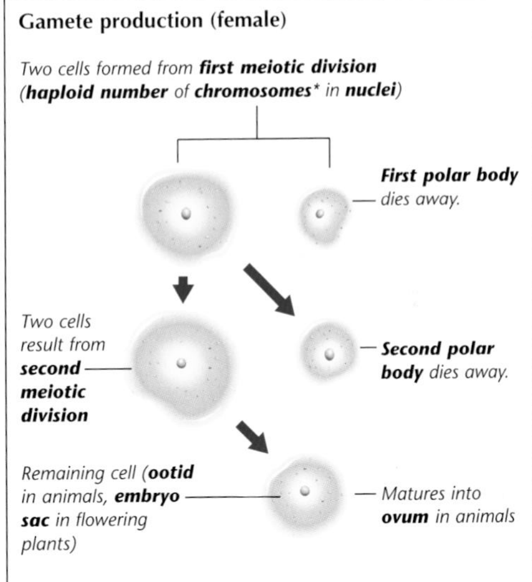
Two cells formed from first meiotic division (haploid number of chromosomes* in nuclei)
First polar body dies away.
Two cells result from second meiotic division
Second polar body dies away.
Remaining cell (ootid in animals, embryo sac in flowering plants)
Matures into ovum in animals

One of two cells formed by ***first meiotic division*** *dies away (called* ***first polar body****). Other divides again (see* ***second meiotic division****). Of two resulting cells, one (****second polar body****) dies away. In animals, other one called* ***ootid*** *and matures into female* ***gamete**** *(sex cell), or* ***ovum****. In flowering plants, other one called* ***embryo sac*** *and its* ***nucleus**** *divides three more times (by* ***mitosis*****). Of eight new nuclei, six have cells form around them, two stay naked. One of six cells is female gamete, or* ***egg cell*** *(see* ***ovule****, page 258). Formation of egg cell in simple plants is very similar.*

* **Alternation of generations**, 321; **Centrioles**, 240; **Chromatin**, 238 (**Nucleus**); **Chromosomes**, 324; **Cytoplasm**, 238; **Gametes**, 320; **Interphase**, 240; **Male nuclei**, 320 (**Gametes**); **Mitosis**, 240; **Nuclear membrane**, 238 (**Nucleus**); **Pollen**, 258; **Spores**, 321 (**Sporulation**).

GENETICS AND HEREDITY

Genetics is a branch of biology. It is the study of **inheritance** – the passing of characteristics from one generation to the next. The bodies which are instrumental in this process are called **chromosomes**. Each chromosome is made up of **genes** – the "coded" instructions for the appearance and constituents of an organism. For more about inheritance, see page 326.

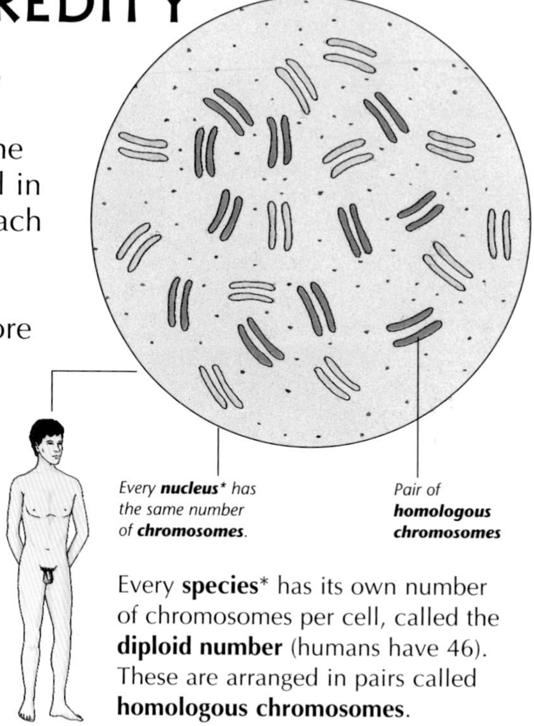

Chromosomes

Structures present at all times in the **nuclei*** of all cells, though they only become independently visible (as thread-like bodies of differing shapes and sizes) when a cell is dividing (and has been stained with a dye). Each one is made with a single molecule of **DNA** (see **nucleic acids**, below), plus proteins called **histones**. The DNA molecule is a chain of many connected **genes**.

*Every **nucleus*** has the same number of **chromosomes**.*

*Pair of **homologous chromosomes***

Every **species*** has its own number of chromosomes per cell, called the **diploid number** (humans have 46). These are arranged in pairs called **homologous chromosomes**.

Nucleic acids

Two different acids, called **DNA** (**deoxyribonucleic acid**) and **RNA** (**ribonucleic acid**). Both are found in the **nuclei*** of all cells, hence their name (RNA is also found in the **cytoplasm*** – see **ribosomes**, page 239).

Each molecule of a nucleic acid is very large, and is composed of many individual units called **nucleotides**. A DNA molecule consists of two chains of nucleotides twisted around each other, forming a shape called a **double helix** (rather like a twisted ladder). An RNA molecule consists of one chain of nucleotides (and looks like a ladder cut in half lengthwise and twisted).

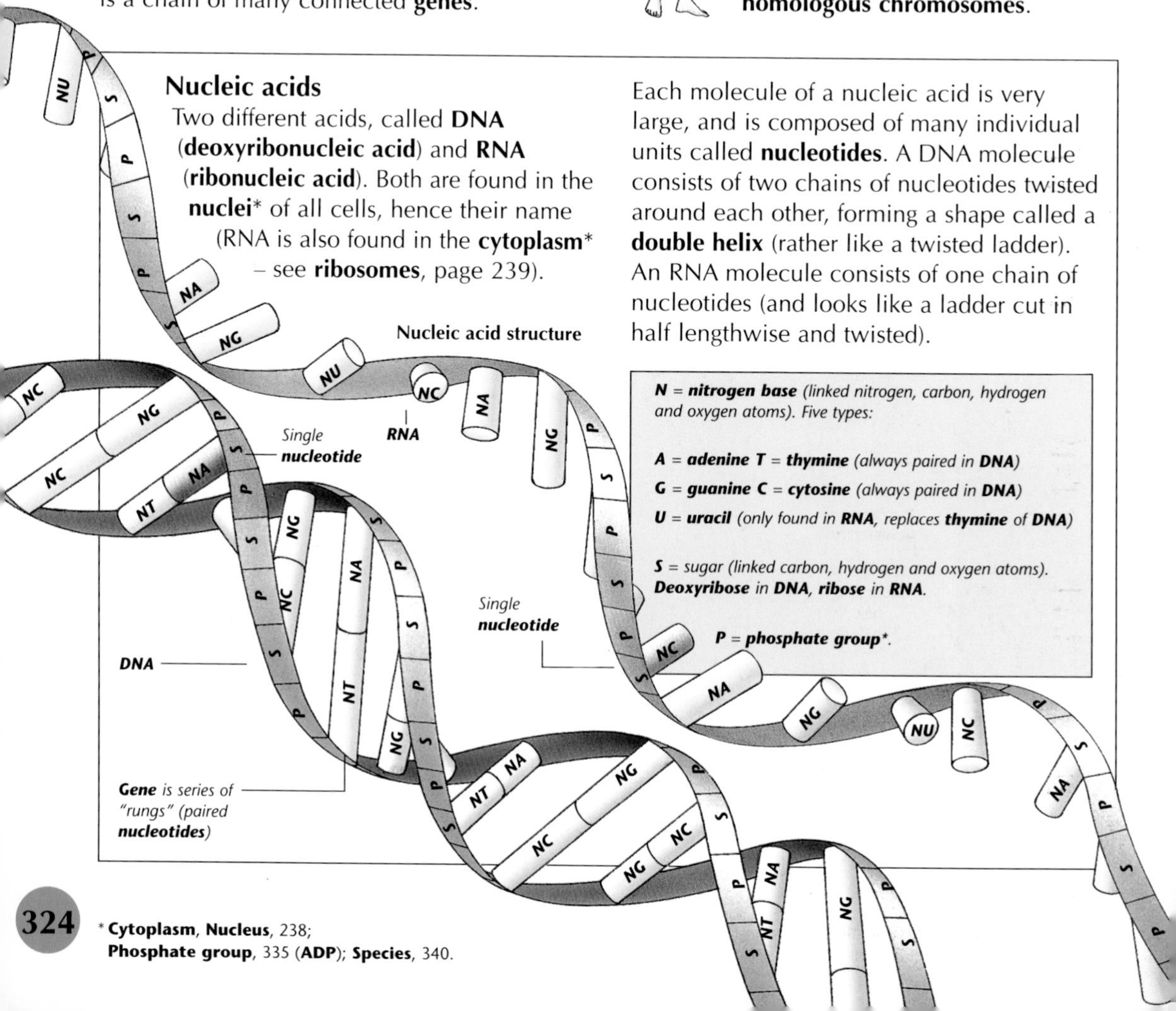

Nucleic acid structure

RNA

*Single **nucleotide***

DNA

*Single **nucleotide***

***Gene** is series of "rungs" (paired **nucleotides**)*

***N** = **nitrogen base** (linked nitrogen, carbon, hydrogen and oxygen atoms). Five types:*

***A** = **adenine** **T** = **thymine** (always paired in **DNA**)*
***G** = **guanine** **C** = **cytosine** (always paired in **DNA**)*
***U** = **uracil** (only found in **RNA**, replaces **thymine** of **DNA**)*

***S** = sugar (linked carbon, hydrogen and oxygen atoms). **Deoxyribose** in **DNA**, **ribose** in **RNA**.*

P** = **phosphate group.*

* **Cytoplasm**, **Nucleus**, 238; **Phosphate group**, 335 (**ADP**); **Species**, 340.

Genes

Sets of "coded" instructions which make up the **DNA** molecule of a **chromosome** (in humans, each DNA molecule is thought to contain about 1,000 genes). Each gene is a connected series of about 250 "rungs" on the DNA "ladder". Since the order of the "rungs" varies, each gene has a different "code", relating to one specific characteristic (**trait**) of the organism, e.g. its **blood group*** or the composition of a **hormone***. With the exception of the **sex chromosomes**, the genes carried on paired **homologous chromosomes** (see **chromosomes**) are also paired, and run down the chromosomes in the same order (one member of each pair on each chromosome). These paired genes control the same characteristic and may give identical instructions. However, their instructions may also be different, in which case the instructions from one gene (the **dominant** gene) will "mask out" those from the other (the **recessive** gene), unless **incomplete dominance** or **codominance** is shown. Two such non-identical genes are called **alleles** or **allelomorphs**.

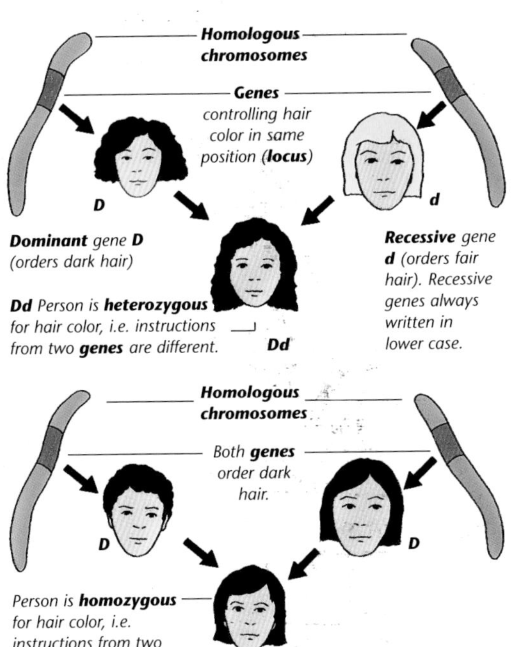
Homologous chromosomes
Genes controlling hair color in same position (locus)
D
d
Dominant gene D (orders dark hair)
Recessive gene d (orders fair hair). Recessive genes always written in lower case.
Dd Person is heterozygous for hair color, i.e. instructions from two genes are different.
Dd
Homologous chromosomes
Both genes order dark hair.
D
D
Person is homozygous for hair color, i.e. instructions from two genes are identical.
DD

*The two examples have different **genotypes** for hair color, i.e. different sets of instructions (**DD** and **Dd**), but are the same **phenotype**, i.e. the resulting characteristic is the same (dark hair).*

Incomplete dominance or blending

A situation where a pair of **genes** which control the same characteristic give different instructions, but neither is **dominant** (see **genes**) or obvious in the result. For example, a lack of dominance between a gene for red color and one for white results in the intermediate roan color of some cows.

***Incomplete dominance** can be used by gardeners to produce flowers of the same species but with a variety of colors. They do this by cross-pollinating flowers of different colors.*

+
=
White camellia
Red camellia
Pink camellia

Codominance

A special situation where a pair of **genes** controlling the same characteristic give different instructions, neither is **dominant** (see **genes**), but both are represented in the result. The human **blood group*** AB, for example, results from equal dominance between a gene for group A and one for group B.

Sex chromosomes

One pair of **homologous chromosomes** (see **chromosomes**) in all cells (all the others are called **autosomes**). There are two different kinds of sex chromosomes, called the **X** and **Y chromosomes**. A male has one X and one Y. The Y chromosome carries the genetic factor (not a **gene** as such) determining maleness, thus all individuals with two X chromosomes are female.

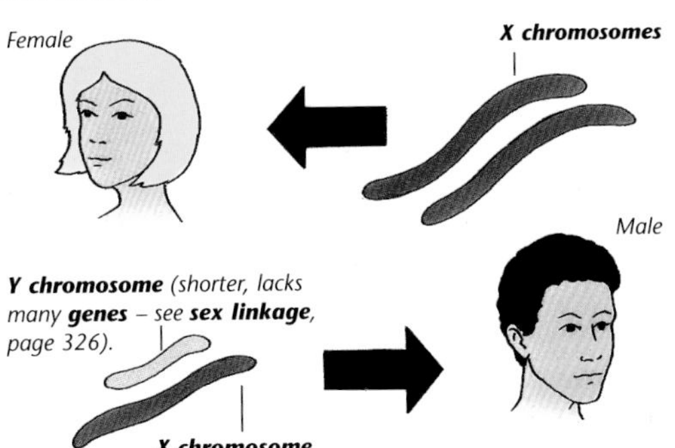
Female
X chromosomes
Male
Y chromosome (shorter, lacks many genes – see sex linkage, page 326).
X chromosome

* **ABO blood groups**, 287; **Hormones**, 336.

Inheriting genes

Every new organism inherits its **chromosomes*** (and **genes***) from its parents. In **sexual reproduction***, the **sperm*** and **ovum*** (sex cells) which come together to form this new individual have only half the normal number of chromosomes (the **haploid number** – see pages 322-323). This ensures that the **zygote*** (first new cell) formed from the two sex cells will have the normal number (see **chromosomes**, page 324). Two laws (**Mendel's laws**) point out genetic factors which are always true when cells divide to produce sex cells.

Law of segregation (Mendel's first law)

Homologous chromosomes* always separate when the **nucleus*** of a cell divides to produce **gametes*** (sex cells – see pages 322-323), hence so too do the paired **genes*** which control the same characteristic. The offspring thus always have paired genes (one member of each pair coming from each parent).

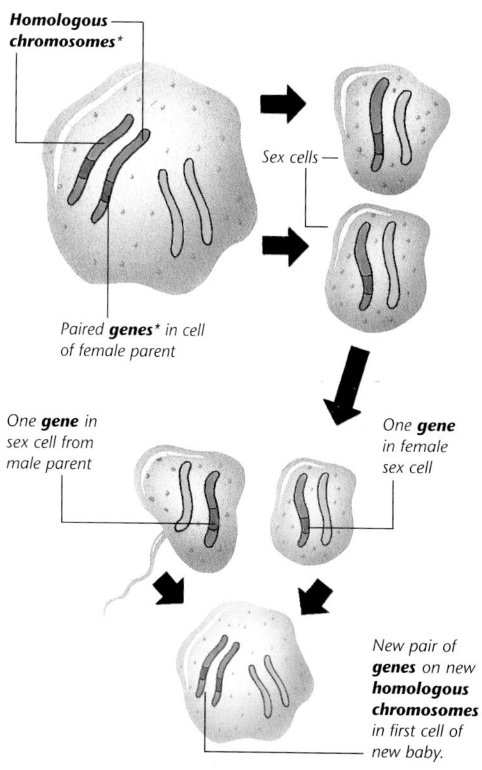

Homologous chromosomes*
Sex cells
Paired genes* in cell of female parent
One gene in sex cell from male parent
One gene in female sex cell
New pair of genes on new homologous chromosomes in first cell of new baby.

Law of independent assortment (Mendel's second law)

Each member of a pair of **genes*** can join with either of the two members of another pair when a cell divides to form **gametes*** (sex cells). Hence all the different mixes are possible in a new individual.

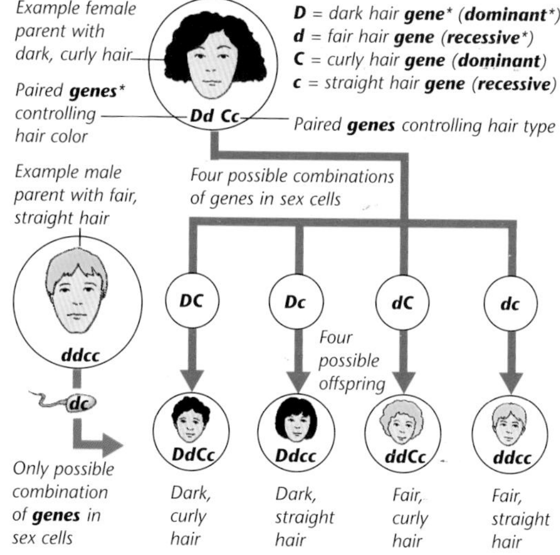

Example female parent with dark, curly hair
D = dark hair gene* (dominant*)
d = fair hair gene (recessive*)
C = curly hair gene (dominant)
c = straight hair gene (recessive)
Paired genes* controlling hair color
Dd Cc
Paired genes controlling hair type
Example male parent with fair, straight hair
Four possible combinations of genes in sex cells
ddcc
DC
Dc
dC
dc
Four possible offspring
dc
Only possible combination of genes in sex cells
DdCc
Ddcc
ddCc
ddcc
Dark, curly hair
Dark, straight hair
Fair, curly hair
Fair, straight hair

Sex linkage

The two **sex (X) chromosomes*** in a female contain many paired **genes*** (like all **chromosomes***), but the **Y chromosome*** in a male lacks partners for most of the genes on its mate (the X). Thus any **recessive*** genes on the X will show up more often in males (see below). The unpaired genes on the X are called **sex-linked genes**.

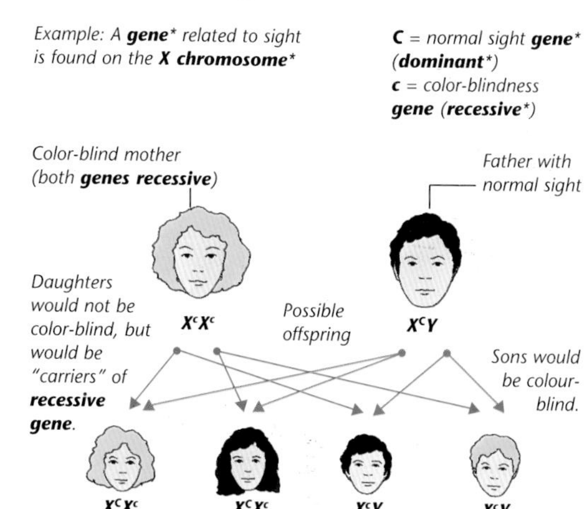

Example: A gene* related to sight is found on the X chromosome*
C = normal sight gene* (dominant*)
c = color-blindness gene (recessive*)
Color-blind mother (both genes recessive)
Father with normal sight
Daughters would not be color-blind, but would be "carriers" of recessive gene.
X^cX^c
Possible offspring
X^CY
Sons would be colour-blind.
X^CX^c
X^CX^c
X^cY
X^cY

* **Dominant**, 325 (**Genes**); **Homologous chromosomes**, 324 (**Chromosomes**); **Nucleus**, 238; **Ovum**, 320 (**Gametes**); **Recessive**, 325 (**Genes**); **Sexual reproduction**, 320; **Sperm**, 320 (**Gametes**); **X** and **Y chromosomes**, 325 (**Sex chromosomes**); **Zygote**, 320.

GENETIC ENGINEERING

Genetic engineering is the deliberate alteration of **DNA*** within a cell **nucleus*** in order to modify an organism or population of organisms. It is used to create new products which are beneficial to science, agriculture, medicine and industry. New uses for genetically engineered organisms are being discovered all the time.

Gene cloning

The main technique of genetic engineering. Desirable **genes*** are duplicated artificially by inserting DNA molecules (containing the genes) into other organisms, such as fast-breeding bacteria, which then reproduce the DNA. Gene cloning is a complex process. The most common method is shown below.

Gene cloning

*1. DNA containing a particular desirable **gene***, known as **target DNA**, is removed from a donor cell.*

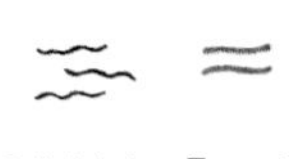
DNA
Donor cell
Cell debris
Target DNA

*2. Some bacteria contain a **plasmid** – a ring of DNA separate from the bacteria's **chromosomes***. Plasmids are capable of inserting themselves into other organisms. Some also give resistance to particular **antibiotics** (drugs that destroy bacteria). Plasmids can be obtained by breaking up bacteria that contain them.*

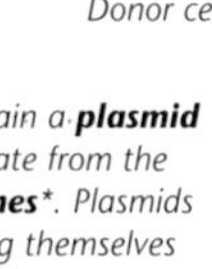

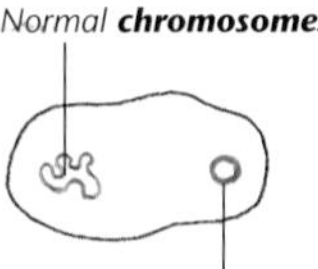
Normal chromosomes
Plasmid carrying antibiotic resistance

*3. The strands of **plasmid** DNA and **target DNA** are treated so that the ends are sticky. When placed together and heated, the plasmid DNA and target DNA join together. This is called **gene splicing**. The new DNA is known as **recombinant DNA**.*

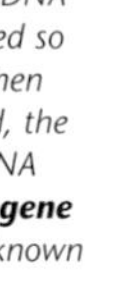
Sticky ends

4. The new plasmids insert themselves into new bacteria not resistant to the antibiotic.

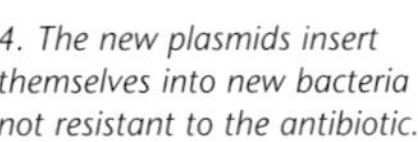

5. As a colony of the bacteria grows, it is treated with this antibiotic. Any bacteria without the new plasmid are destroyed by the antibiotic. Bacteria containing it continue to multiply.

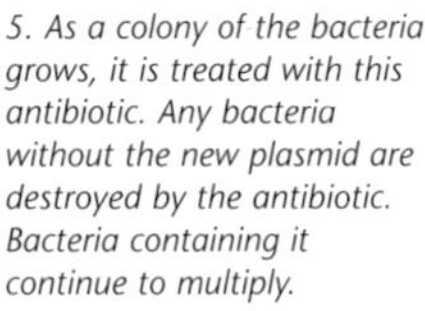

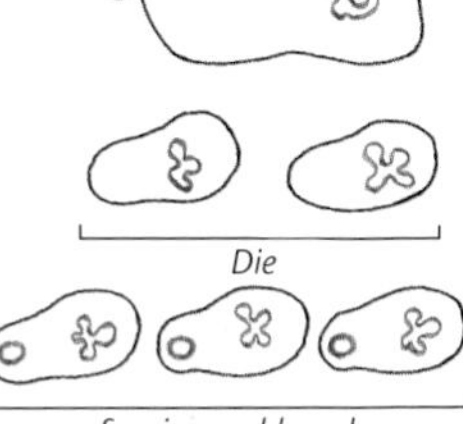
Die
Survive and breed

6. The resultant colony is now made up exclusively of bacteria carrying the antibiotic-resistant plasmids with the target DNA (containing the desired gene). This colony can now be multiplied many times, producing an enormous quantity of the gene.

Uses of genetic engineering

Pharming

The use of plants or animals to produce genetically modified pharmaceutical products. For example, a sheep has been genetically engineered to produce milk which contains **alpha-1 antitrypsin**, a drug which is beneficial to cystic fibrosis patients.

Protein manufacture

The production, in specially-created bacteria "factories", of medically useful proteins such as **insulin*** to help diabetics, and **antihemophilic globulin** to treat people with hemophilia.

Genetically engineered crops

Plants which have been bred with a greater resistance to disease, pesticides and weather, by inserting foreign **genes*** into their **nuclei***. An example of this is shown below.

Some flounders have an antifreeze chemical in their blood, which helps them to survive in freezing water.

*The **gene*** which gives their blood this property can be extracted and introduced into tomato plants. Tomatoes from such plants are now more able to withstand frost and snow. This makes them more readily available at the extremes of their normal growing season.*

* **Chromosomes**, 324; **DNA**, 324 (**Nucleic acids**); **Genes**, 325; **Insulin**, 336; **Nucleus**, 238.

Uses of genetic engineering - continued

Animal cloning

Producing a genetically identical duplicate, or **clone**, of an animal. In 1997, scientists took a cell from a female sheep and placed its **chromosomes*** into another sheep's **ovum***, which had had its own chromosomes removed. The ovum was planted in the second sheep's womb, and five months later, a lamb, known to the world as Dolly, was born. This experiment proved it was possible to produce a complex living organism, without any kind of **sexual reproduction***.

Sheep created by sexual reproduction*

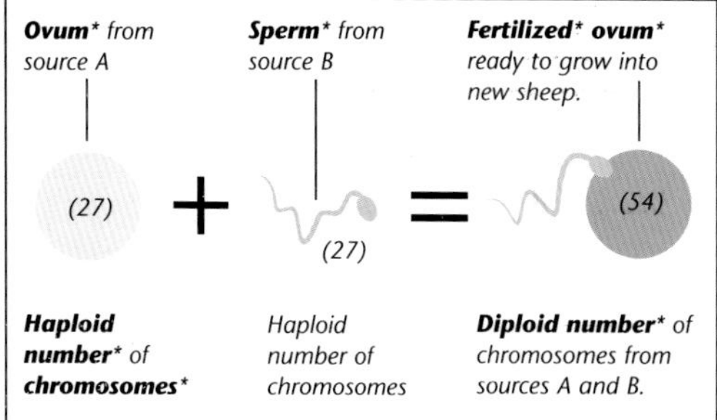

*Ovum** from source A
*Sperm** from source B
Fertilized ovum** ready to grow into new sheep.
(27)
+
(27)
=
(54)
*Haploid number** of *chromosomes**
Haploid number of chromosomes
*Diploid number** of chromosomes from sources A and B.

Sheep created by gene cloning*

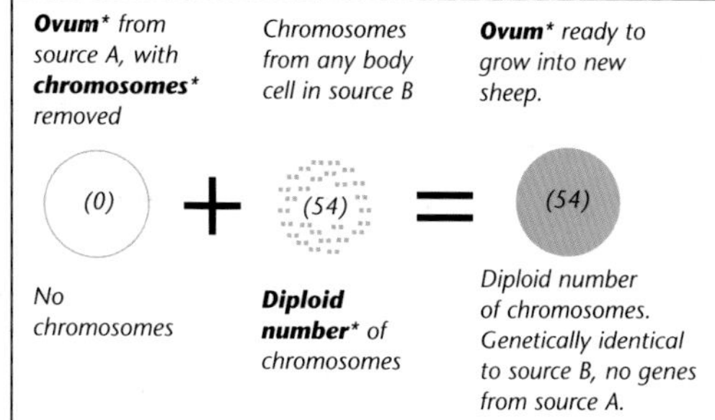

*Ovum** from source A, with *chromosomes** removed
Chromosomes from any body cell in source B
*Ovum** ready to grow into new sheep.
(0)
+
(54)
=
(54)
No chromosomes
*Diploid number** of chromosomes
Diploid number of chromosomes. Genetically identical to source B, no genes from source A.

Genetics and the future

Human cloning

The theoretical creation of human life, using the same method that created Dolly the sheep. Genetic engineering techniques are now so advanced that any one of a human body's 100 million million cells could be used to create a new human. But, just as appearance, character and intellect are slightly different in identical twins, a **clone** of another human being would not be a replica, only a person with identical **genes***. A clone would also be a generation apart in age. Possible uses of this technology include the treatment of **infertile** couples – couples who are not naturally able to have children.

Genome mapping

Making a detailed list of the **nucleotides*** contained in the **genome** (genetic code) of any organism. Scientists have already mapped the genome of a yeast cell, and are currently mapping the three billion nucleotides contained in a human genome. They intend to complete this task early in the twenty-first century. The resulting map will enable them to identify every **gene*** in human **chromosomes*** and understand what each one does.

Genetic diagnosis

The identification of illness by examination of **genes***. Scientists can already identify some genetic disorders, which show up as irregularities in the **nucleotide*** sequence. For example, **Huntingdon's chorea** (an illness which causes gradual physical and mental deterioration) can now be detected in a **fetus***. Such research could also make it possible to identify a gene which makes people more susceptible to some cancers. Once identified, treatment could be applied to prevent the cancer from developing.

Organ modification

Introducing genes which encourage body organs to heal themselves. One new technique encourages the hearts of patients needing bypass surgery to grow new blood vessels themselves.

*When the heart is growing inside an **embryo****, a particular **gene*** instructs it to construct its **arteries****. The instructions cease once the heart is fully grown. Scientists are developing a method of re-introducing this gene into the heart of a patient with blocked arteries. The gene would enable the damaged heart to grow new blood vessels around the constricted artery, so removing the need for a major heart operation.*

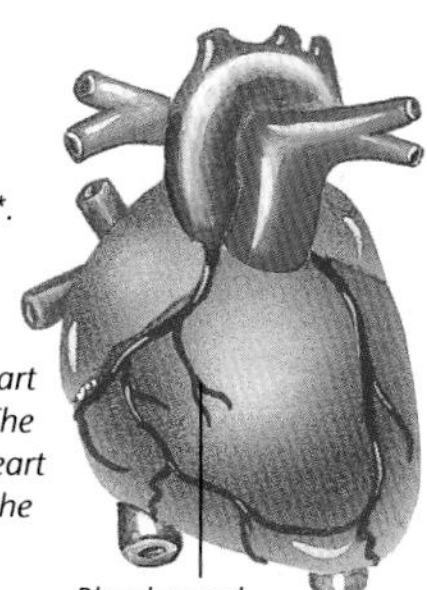

Blood vessel

* **Arteries**, 288; **Chromosomes**, 324; **Diploid number**, 240 (**Mitosis**); **Embryo**, 320; **Fertilization**, 319; **Fetus**, 319 (**Pregnancy**); **Genes**, 325; **Gene cloning**, 327; **Haploid number**, 322 (**Meiosis**); **Nucleotides**, 324 (**Nucleic acids**); **Ovum**, 320 (**Gametes**); **Sexual reproduction**, 320; **Sperm**, 320 (**Gametes**).

FLUID MOVEMENT

The movement of substances around the body, especially their movement in and out of cells, is essential to the life of an organism. Food matter must be able to pass into the cells, and waste and harmful material must be able to move out. Most solids and liquids travel around the body in **solutions**, i.e. they (**solutes**) are dissolved in a fluid (the **solvent** – normally water).

Diffusion

The movement of molecules of a substance from an area where they are in higher concentration to one where their concentration is lower. This is a two-way process (where the concentration of a **solute** is low, that of the **solvent** will be high, so its molecules will move the other way) and it ceases when the molecules are evenly distributed. Many substances, e.g. oxygen and carbon dioxide, diffuse into and out of cells.

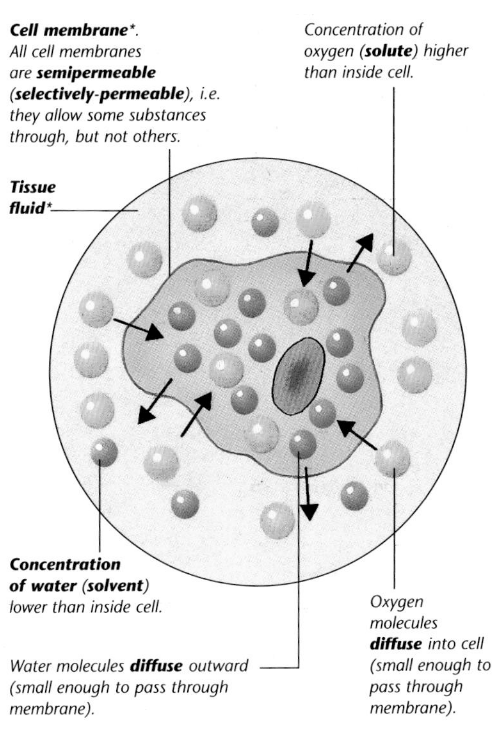

Cell membrane. All cell membranes are semipermeable (selectively-permeable), i.e. they allow some substances through, but not others.*
Concentration of oxygen (solute) higher than inside cell.
*Tissue fluid**
Concentration of water (solvent) lower than inside cell.
Water molecules diffuse outward (small enough to pass through membrane).
Oxygen molecules diffuse into cell (small enough to pass through membrane).

Osmosis

The movement of molecules of a **solvent** through a **semipermeable** membrane (see below, left) which lowers the concentration of a **solute** on the other side of the membrane, and evens out the concentrations either side. This is a one-way type of **diffusion**, occurring when the molecules of the solute cannot pass the other way. **Osmotic pressure** is the pressure which builds up in an enclosed space, e.g. a cell, when a **solvent** enters by osmosis.

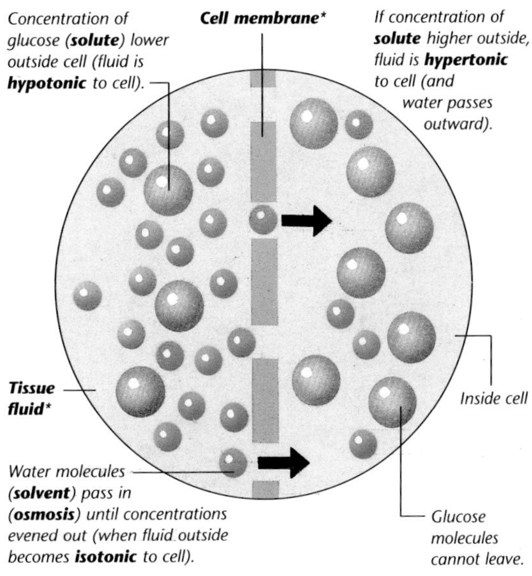

Concentration of glucose (solute) lower outside cell (fluid is hypotonic to cell).
*Cell membrane**
If concentration of solute higher outside, fluid is hypertonic to cell (and water passes outward).
*Tissue fluid**
Inside cell
Water molecules (solvent) pass in (osmosis) until concentrations evened out (when fluid outside becomes isotonic to cell).
Glucose molecules cannot leave.

Active transport

A process which occurs when substances have to be "pumped" in the opposite direction to that in which they would travel by **diffusion** (i.e. from low to high concentration), e.g. when cells take in large amounts of glucose for breakdown. It is not yet fully understood, but it is thought that special "carrier" molecules within the **cell membrane*** pick up molecules of solute, carry them through the membrane and release them. Energy is needed for this action (since it opposes the natural tendency). This is supplied in the form of **ATP***.

Pinocytosis

The taking in of a fluid droplet by inward-folding and separation of a section of **cell membrane*** (forming a **vacuole***). Most cells can do this.

* **ATP**, 335; **Cell membrane**, 238; **Tissue fluid**, 292; **Vacuoles**, 238.

FOOD AND HOW IT IS USED

Food is vital to all organisms, providing all the materials needed to be broken down for energy, to regulate cellular activities and to build and repair tissues (see pages 332-335). Of the various food substances, **carbohydrates**, **proteins** and **fats** are called **nutrients**, and **minerals**, **vitamins** (not needed by plants) and water are **accessory foods**. Plants build their own nutrients (by **photosynthesis***), and take in minerals and water; animals take in all the substances they need and break them down by digestion (see pages 338-339).

Carbohydrates

A group of substances made up of carbon, hydrogen and oxygen, which exist in varying degrees of complexity (see "terms used", page 339 and also page 204). In animals, complex carbohydrates are taken in and broken down by digestion (see page 338) into the simple carbohydrate **glucose**. The breakdown of glucose (**internal respiration***) provides almost all the energy for life's activities. Plants build up glucose from other substances (by **photosynthesis***).

Proteins

A group of substances made up of simpler units called **amino acids**. These contain carbon, hydrogen, oxygen, nitrogen and, in some cases, sulfur. Most protein molecules consist of hundreds, maybe thousands, of amino acids, joined together by links called **peptide links** into one or more chains called **polypeptides***. The many different types of protein each have a different arrangement of amino acids. They include the **structural proteins** (the basic components of new cells) and **catalytic proteins** (**enzymes***), which play a vital role in controlling cell processes.

Plants build up amino acids from the substances they take in (by **photosynthesis***), and then build proteins from them. Animals take in proteins and break them down into single amino acid molecules by digestion (see page 338). These are then transported in the blood to all the body cells and reassembled into the different proteins needed (see **ribosomes**, page 239 and also page 205).

Fats

A group of substances made up of carbon, hydrogen and a small amount of oxygen (see also **lipids**, page 205). Plants build fats from the substances they take in, and their seeds hold most as a store of food. This can be converted to extra **glucose** (see **carbohydrates**) to provide energy for the growing plant. Digestion of fats in animals produces **fatty acids** and **glycerol** (see page 338). If these need to be broken down for energy (as well as glucose), this occurs in the liver. This results in some products which the liver can convert to glucose, but others it cannot. These are instead converted elsewhere to a substance which forms a later stage of glucose breakdown.

Fatty acids and glycerol not needed for energy are immediately recombined to form fat particles and stored in various body areas, e.g. under the skin (see **subcutaneous layer**, page 310).

*Like all animals, humans cannot build thier own **nutrients**, and rely on the food they eat for energy. This comes either from plants, e.g. fruit and vegetables (see picture, left), or animals, e.g. meat and milk.*

* **Enzymes**, 333; **Internal respiration**, 334; **Photosynthesis**, 254; **Polypeptides**, 339.

Roughage or fiber

Bulky, fibrous food, e.g. bran, and pulses such as lentils and beans. Much of it is made up of **cellulose**, a **carbohydrate** found in plant **cell walls***. Unlike most carbohydrates, cellulose cannot be digested by most animals, including humans, because they lack the necessary **digestive enzyme***, called **cellulase**. (Some animals, e.g. snails, do have this enzyme, and others, like cows, who must digest cellulose, do so in another way – see **rumen**, page 271.) The fact that roughage is bulky and coarse means that food can be gripped by intestinal muscles, and so moved on through the digestive system.

Vitamins

A group of substances vital to animals, though only needed in tiny amounts. The most important function of many vitamins is to act as **co-enzymes***, i.e. to help **enzymes*** catalyze chemical reactions. See page 339 for a list of vitamins and their functions.

Minerals

Natural inorganic substances, e.g. phosphorus and calcium. They form a vital part of plant and animal tissue, e.g. in bones and teeth. Many are found in **enzymes*** and **vitamins**. They include **trace elements**, e.g. copper and iodine, present in tiny amounts.

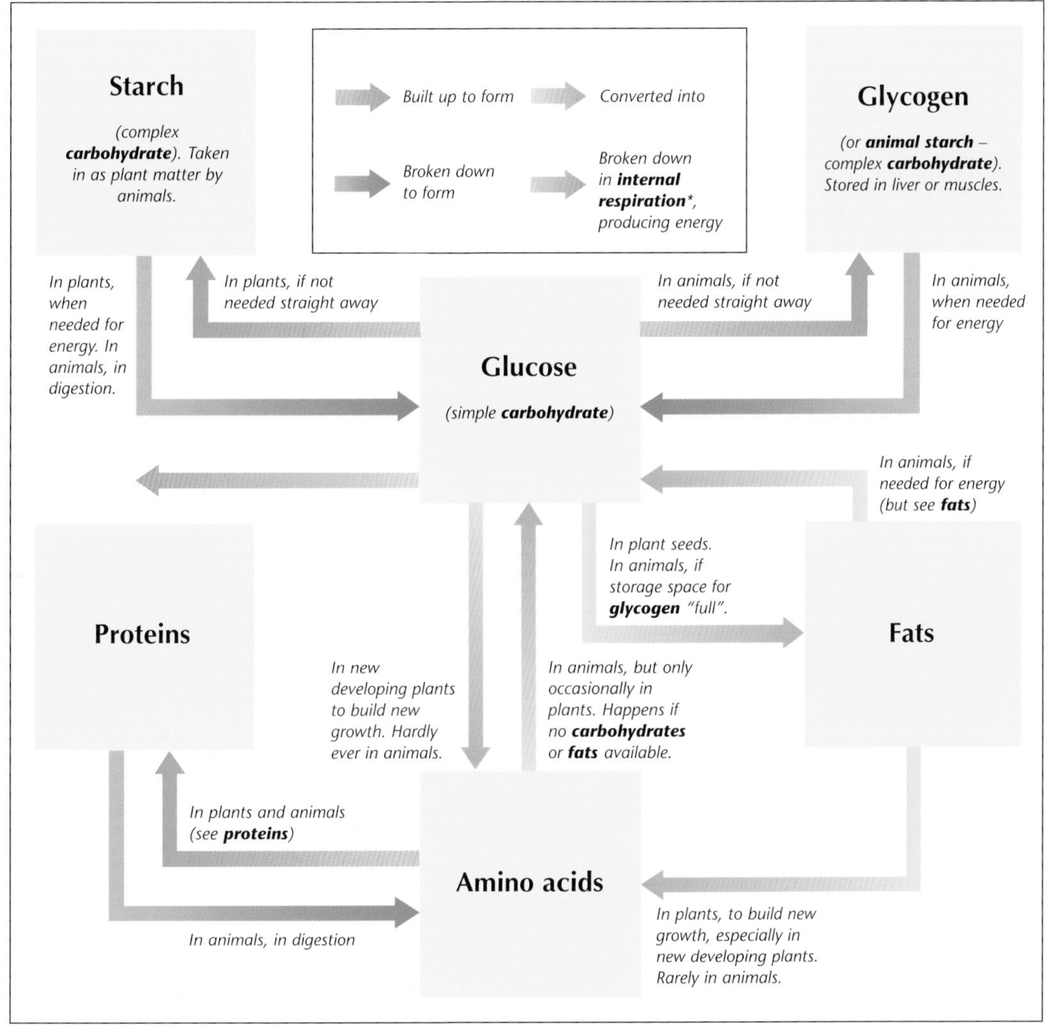
Starch
(complex carbohydrate). Taken in as plant matter by animals.
Built up to form
Converted into
Broken down to form
Broken down in internal respiration*, producing energy
Glycogen
(or animal starch – complex carbohydrate). Stored in liver or muscles.
In plants, when needed for energy. In animals, in digestion.
In plants, if not needed straight away
In animals, if not needed straight away
In animals, when needed for energy
Glucose
(simple carbohydrate)
In animals, if needed for energy (but see fats)
In plant seeds. In animals, if storage space for glycogen "full".
Proteins
Fats
In new developing plants to build new growth. Hardly ever in animals.
In animals, but only occasionally in plants. Happens if no carbohydrates or fats available.
In plants and animals (see proteins)
Amino acids
In animals, in digestion
In plants, to build new growth, especially in new developing plants. Rarely in animals.

* **Cell wall**, 238; **Co-enzymes**, 333 (**Enzymes**); **Digestive enzymes**, 338; **Internal respiration**, 334.

METABOLISM

Metabolism is a collective term for all the complex, closely-coordinated chemical reactions occurring inside an organism. These can be split into two opposing sets of reactions, called **catabolism** and **anabolism**. The rates of the reactions vary in response to variations in the organism's internal and external environments, and they play a major role in keeping internal conditions stable (see **homeostasis**, page 335).

Catabolism

A collective term for all the reactions which break down substances in the body (**decomposition reactions**). One example is digestion in animals, which breaks down complex substances into simpler ones (see chart, page 338). Another is the further breakdown of these simple substances in the cells (**internal respiration***). Catabolism always liberates energy (in digestion, most is lost as heat, but in internal respiration, it is used for the body's activities). This is despite the fact that, as with all chemical reactions, catabolism itself requires energy. The energy needed is taken from the much greater amount of energy produced during the reactions. The rest of this is released, hence the overall result is always an energy "profit".

*Strenuous exercise, such as cycling, can cause the **metabolic rate** to increase to as much as 15 times the **basal metabolic rate**. The heart rate increases, and more oxygen is taken in. These changes enable food to be **catabolized** more quickly to produce the extra energy needed. One side effect is a rise in body temperature, which prompts the body to produce more sweat.*

Anabolism

A collective term for all the reactions which build up substances in the body (**synthesis reactions**). One example is the linking together of amino acids to form proteins (see page 330). Anabolism always needs energy to be taken in, since the small amount produced during the reactions is never enough (i.e. the overall result of anabolism is an energy "loss"). The extra energy is taken from the **catabolism** "profit".

Metabolic rate

The overall rate at which metabolic reactions occur in an individual. In human beings, it varies widely from person to person, and in the same individual under different conditions. It increases under stress, when the body temperature rises and during exercise, hence the true and accurate measurement of a person's metabolic rate is a measurement taken when the subject is resting, has a normal body temperature, and has not recently exercised. This is called the **basal metabolic rate** (**BMR**) and is expressed in **kilojoules** per square meter of body surface per hour (see measuring method and calculations, opposite).

People with high BMR can eat large amounts without putting on weight, because their **catabolism** of food matter (in the cells) happens so fast that not much fat is stored. This fast rate of reactions also often results in "excess" energy (i.e. energy not needed for **anabolism**), so they may appear to have a lot of "nervous energy". People with low BMR put on weight easily and often appear to have little energy.

The metabolic rate is influenced by a number of **hormones***, especially **STH**, **thyroxin**, **adrenalin** and **noradrenalin**. For more about these, see chart on pages 336-337.

* **Hormones**, 336; **Internal respiration**, 334.

Kilojoule

A unit of energy, specifically used in biology when referring to the amount of heat energy produced by the **catabolism** of food, and hence when measuring a person's **basal metabolic rate** (see **metabolic rate**). The calculations involved in measuring BMR combine certain known facts about the number of kilojoules produced by the breakdown of different substances, with a measurement of oxygen consumption obtained under controlled conditions (see below and right).

To determine a person's basal metabolic rate (BMR = kJ m^{-2} hr^{-1})

*1. Facts known (determined using a piece of apparatus called a **calorimeter**):*
a) If 1 liter of oxygen is used to break down carbohydrates, c.21.21kJ are produced (i.e. enough heat energy to heat c.5,050g water by 1°C).
b) With fats, the result from 1 liter oxygen is c.19.74kJ.
c) With proteins, the result from 1 liter oxygen is c.19.32kJ.

2. First calculation: Heat energy generated when food (in general) is broken down using 1 liter of oxygen = the average of the three figures above, i.e. 20.09kJ (provided subject measured has taken in equal amounts of all three foodstuffs).

3. Measure the oxygen used by the subject's body in a fixed time. Done using a spirometer (respirometer) – see picture, right.

Drum rotates

Oxygen in cylinder

The air (minus some oxygen) that is breathed out returns to cylinder.

Soda lime absorbs the carbon dioxide.

The subject breathes in from the cylinder this way.

A trace is drawn as the cylinder moves up and down.

The overall trend of the trace is up (the cylinder moves down as its volume of oxygen decreases).

The subject breathes out to the cylinder this way.

Calculations (example):

1. (Measured) Subject used 1.5 liters oxygen in 5 minutes.

2. Hence he would use 18 liters oxygen in 1 hour (1.5 × 12).

3. (Known) 20.09kJ produced when food broken down by 1 liter oxygen.

4. Hence 361.62kJ produced if food broken down by 18 liters oxygen (20.09 × 18).

5. Hence 361.62kJ produced by breakdown of food in whole of subject's body in 1 hour (he would use 18 liters oxygen per hour – see point 2).

6. But BMR is measured in kJ per square meter of body surface *per hour.*

7. Standard chart used to work out body surface in square meters.

8. 361.62 divided by body surface (e.g. $2m^2$) = 180.81kJ m^{-2} hr^{-1} (BMR).

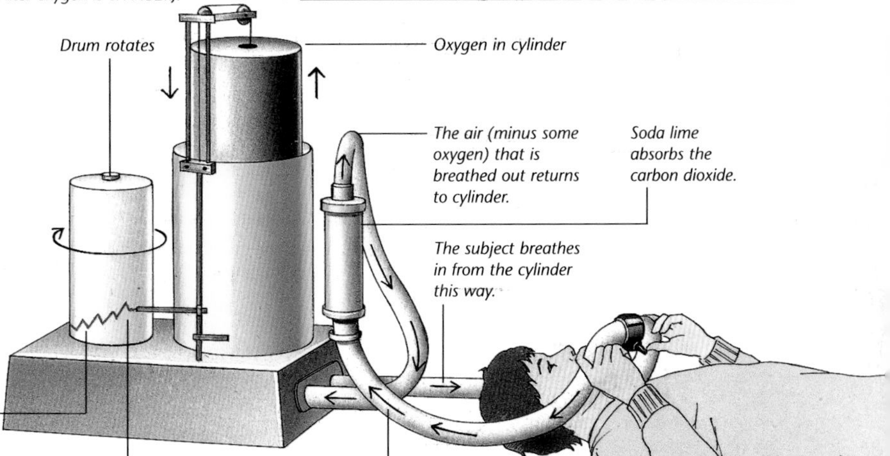

Enzymes

Special proteins (**catalytic proteins**) found in all living things and vital to the chemical reactions of life. They act as **catalysts***, i.e. they speed up reactions without themselves being changed. Many enzymes are aided by other substances, called **co-enzymes**, whose molecules are able to "carry" the products of one reaction (catalyzed by an enzyme) on to the next reaction.

There are many different types of enzyme, e.g. **digestive enzymes**, which control the breakdown of complex food material into simple soluble substances (for more about these, see text and chart, pages 338-339), and **respiratory enzymes**, which control the further breakdown of these simple substances in the cells to liberate energy (i.e. **internal respiration** – see page 334).

* **Catalyst**, 161.

ENERGY FOR LIFE AND HOMEOSTASIS

A living thing needs energy for its activities. This energy comes from a series of chemical reactions inside its cells, known as **internal respiration**, **tissue respiration** or **cellular respiration**. The cells contain various simple food substances, which are the results of digestive breakdown in animals (see pages 338-339) and **photosynthesis*** in plants. These substances all contain stored energy, which is released when internal respiration breaks them down. In almost all cases, glucose is the substance broken down (see **carbohydrates** and diagram, pages 330-331 and also equation, page 209). There are two kinds of respiration – **anaerobic** and **aerobic respiration**.

Anaerobic respiration

A type of **internal respiration** which does not need free oxygen (oxygen taken into the body). It takes place in the cells of all organisms and releases a small amount of energy. In most organisms, it consists of a chain of chemical reactions called **glycolysis**, which break down glucose into **pyruvic acid**. In normal circumstances this is then immediately followed by **aerobic respiration**, which breaks down this poisonous acid in the presence of oxygen. This breakdown releases the bulk of energy. In abnormal conditions, however, it may not be possible for the aerobic stage to follow immediately, in which case a further stage of anaerobic respiration occurs (see **oxygen debt**).

In some microscopic organisms, e.g. yeast and some bacteria, anaerobic respiration always runs through all its stages, providing enough energy for their needs without requiring oxygen.

*In short bursts of physical activity, such as a 100m sprint, cells use up oxygen faster than it can be taken in. This results in the build up of **lactic acid**, which is thought to cause muscle cramps.*

*In longer, less intensive periods of activity, e.g. jogging, cells are able to meet their oxygen need for longer, but **lactic acid** does build up slowly.*

Aerobic respiration

A type of **internal respiration** which can only take place in the presence of free oxygen (oxygen taken into the body). It is the way in which most living things obtain the bulk of their energy and follows a stage of **anaerobic respiration**. Oxygen (brought by the blood) is taken into each cell and reacts in the **mitochondria*** with the **pyruvic acid** produced in anaerobic respiration. Carbon dioxide and water are the final products of the reactions, and chemical energy is released, which is then "stored" as **ATP**.

Aerobic respiration is an example of **oxidation** – the breakdown of a substance in the presence of oxygen.

Summary of aerobic stages of respiration reactions

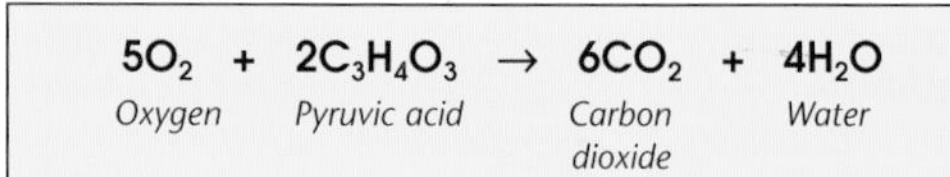

$$5O_2 + 2C_3H_4O_3 \rightarrow 6CO_2 + 4H_2O$$

$5O_2$	+	$2C_3H_4O_3$	→	$6CO_2$	+	$4H_2O$
Oxygen		*Pyruvic acid*		*Carbon dioxide*		*Water*

Oxygen debt

A situation which occurs when extreme physical exercise is undertaken by an organism which shows **aerobic respiration**. Under these circumstances, the oxygen in the organism's cells is used up faster than it can be taken in. This means that there is not enough to break down the poisonous **pyruvic acid** produced in the first, **anaerobic**, stage of respiration. Instead, the acid undergoes further anaerobic reactions to convert it to **lactic acid** (much less harmful). This begins to build up, and the organism is said to have acquired an oxygen debt. This is "paid off" later by taking in oxygen faster than usual to break down the lactic acid, by breathing heavily, for example.

* **Mitochondria**, 240; **Photosynthesis**, 254.

ADP (**adenosine diphosphate**) and **ATP** (**adenosine triphosphate**)

Two substances which consist of a chemical grouping called **adenosine**, combined with two and three **phosphate groups** respectively. These phosphate groups each consist of linked phosphorus, oxygen and hydrogen atoms. A phosphate group can combine with other substances (either by itself or linked with other phosphate groups in a chain).

When **aerobic respiration** occurs, the chemical energy released is involved in reactions which result in a conversion of ADP molecules into ATP molecules (by attachment of a third phosphate group in each case). The energy taken in to effect these reactions can be regarded as being "stored" in the form of ATP. This is a substance which can be easily stored in all cells. It is found in especially large quantities in cells which require a lot of energy, e.g. muscle cells. When the energy is needed, reactions occur which convert ATP back into ADP. These reactions result in an overall release of energy – the "stored" energy. In this way, power is supplied for the cell's activities.

ADP and ATP

Adenine* + *Ribose* = *Adenosine

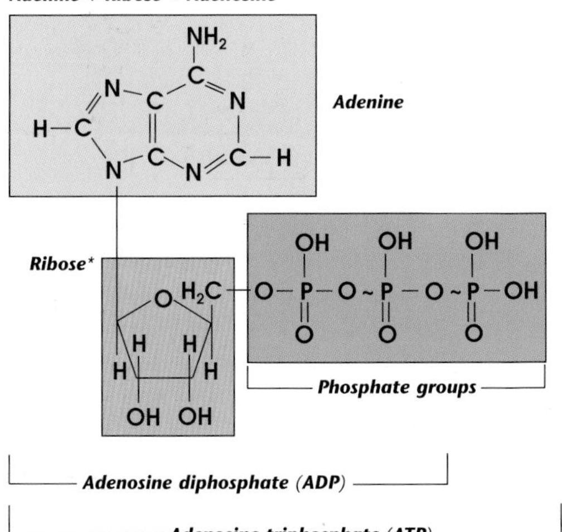
Adenine
Ribose*
Phosphate groups
Adenosine diphosphate (ADP)
Adenosine triphosphate (ATP)

Conversion of ATP into ADP

ATP	⇌	ADP	+	P	+	E
Adenosine triphosphate		***Adenosine diphosphate***		***Phosphate group***		*Energy*

The reaction is ***reversible****.*

Homeostasis

Crocodile gaping to lose heat

Homeostasis is the maintenance, by an organism, of a stable **internal environment**, i.e. a constant temperature, stable composition, level and pressure of body fluids, constant **metabolic rate***, etc. This is vital if the organism is to function properly.

Homeostasis requires the detection of any deviation from the norm (caused by new internal or external factors) and the means to correct such deviations, and is practiced most efficiently in birds and **mammals***, e.g. humans. Their detection of deviations is achieved by the **feedback** of information to controlling organs. The blood glucose level, for example, is constantly being detected by the pancreas (i.e. information is "fed back"). The correction of deviations is achieved by **negative feedback**, i.e. feedback which "tells" of deviations and results in a change of action. If the glucose level gets too high, for example, the pancreas reacts by producing more **insulin*** to reduce it (see also **antagonistic hormones**, page 336).

Most homeostatic actions are, like the insulin example, controlled by hormones, many of which are in turn controlled by the **hypothalamus*** in the brain. An example of the importance of the hypothalamus in homeostasis is the control of body temperature. All birds and mammals, e.g. humans, are **homiothermic** (warm-blooded), i.e. they can keep a constant temperature (about 37°C in humans) regardless of external conditions (the opposite is **poikilothermic**, or cold-blooded). A "thermostat" area of the hypothalamus, called the **preoptic area**, detects any changes in body temperature and sends impulses either to the **heat-losing center** or to the **heat-promoting center** (both also found in the hypothalamus). These areas then send out nervous impulses to cause various heat-losing or heat-promoting actions in the body.

Penguins are ***homiothermic****. They can generate enough heat to keep themselves and their eggs and young warm.*

* **Hypothalamus**, 303; **Insulin**, 336; **Mammals**, 341; **Metabolic rate**, 332; **Reversible reactions**, 162; **Ribose**, 324.

HORMONES

Hormones are special chemical "messengers" which control various activities inside an organism. These pages deal with the hormones produced by humans and their related groups. Plants also produce hormones (**phytohormones**), though these are not yet fully understood (see **abscission layer**, page 249, and **photoperiodism** and **growth hormones**, page 251).

Human hormones are secreted by **endocrine glands***. Some act only on specific body parts (**target cells** or **target organs**), others cause a more general response. The principal controller of hormone production is the **hypothalamus*** (part of the brain). It controls the secretions of many glands, mainly through its control of the **pituitary gland***, which itself controls many other glands. The hypothalamus "tells" the pituitary to produce its hormones by sending **regulating factors** to its **anterior lobe** and nervous impulses to its **posterior lobe**. Hormone secretion is vital to **homeostasis***.

Regulating factors

Special chemicals which control the production of a number of hormones, and hence many vital body functions. They are sent to the **anterior lobe** of the **pituitary gland*** by the **hypothalamus*** (part of the brain). There are two types – **releasing factors**, which make the gland secrete specific hormones, and **inhibiting factors**, which make it stop its secretion. For example, **FSHRF** (**FSH releasing factor**) and **LHRF** (**LH releasing factor**) cause the release of the hormones **FSH** and **LH** (see chart), and hence the onset of **puberty***. Many regulating factors are vital to **homeostasis***.

Antagonistic hormones

Hormones that produce opposite effects. **Glucagon** and **insulin** (see chart) are examples. When the blood glucose level drops too far, the pancreas produces glucagon to raise it again. A high glucose level causes the pancreas to produce insulin to lower the level (see also **homeostasis**, page 335).

Hormones	
ACTH (***adrenocorticotropic hormone***) *or* ***adrenocorticotropin***	
TSH (***thyroid-stimulating hormone***) *or* ***thyrotropin***	
STH (***somatotropic hormone***) *or* ***somatotropin*** *or* ***HGH*** (***human growth hormone***)	
FSH (***follicle-stimulating hormone***)	
LH (***luteinizing hormone***). *Also called* ***luteotropin*** *in women and* ***ICSH*** (***interstitial cell stimulating hormone***) *in men.*	
Lactogenic hormone *or* ***PR*** (***prolactin***)	
Oxytocin	
ADH (***anti-diuretic hormone***) *or* ***vasopressin***	
Thyroxin	
TCT (***thyrocalcitonin***) *or* ***calcitonin***	
PTH (***parathyroid hormone***) *or* ***parathyrin*** *or* ***parathormone***	
Adrenalin *or* ***adrenin*** *or* ***epinephrin*** ***Noradrenalin*** *or* ***norepinephrin***	
Aldosterone	
Cortisone ***Hydrocortisone*** *or* ***cortisol***	
Estrogen (*female* ***sex hormone***) ***Progesterone*** (*female* ***sex hormone***)	
Androgens (*male* ***sex hormones***), *especially* ***testosterone***	
Gastrin	
CCK (***cholecystokinin***)	
Secretin ***PZ*** (***pancreozymin***)	
Enterocrinin	
Insulin	
Glucagon	

* **Endocrine glands**, 297; **Homeostasis**, 335; **Hypothalamus**, 303; **Pituitary gland**, 297; **Puberty**, 318.

Where produced	Effects
Pituitary gland *(page 297) (**anterior lobe**)*	*Stimulates production of hormones in **cortex** of **adrenal glands** (page 297).*
Pituitary gland *(page 297) (**anterior lobe**)*	*Stimulates production of **thyroxin** by **thyroid gland** (page 297).*
Pituitary gland *(page 297) (**anterior lobe**)*	*Stimulates growth by increasing rate at which amino acids are built up to make proteins in cells.*
Pituitary gland *(page 297) (**anterior lobe**)*	*In women, works with **LH** to stimulate development of **ova** in **ovarian follicles** (page 317) and secretion of **estrogen** by follicles in early stages of **menstrual cycle** (page 318). In men, causes formation of **sperm** (page 320).*
Pituitary gland *(page 297) (**anterior lobe**)*	*Stimulates **ovulation** (page 318), formation of **corpus luteum** (page 318) and its secretion of **estrogen** and **progesterone**. Works with **estrogen** and **progesterone** to stimulate thickening of lining of **uterus** (page 317). In men, causes production of **androgens**.*
Pituitary gland *(page 297) (**anterior lobe**)*	*Works with **LH** to cause secretion of hormones by **corpus luteum** (page 318). Causes milk production after giving birth.*
Hypothalamus *(page 303). Builds up in **pituitary gland** (**posterior lobe**)*	*Stimulates contraction of muscles of **uterus** (page 317) during labor and secretion of milk after giving birth.*
Hypothalamus *(page 303). Builds up in **pituitary gland** (**posterior lobe**)*	*Increases amount of water re-absorbed into blood from **uriniferous tubules** (page 301) in kidneys.*
Thyroid gland *(page 297)*	*Increases rate of food breakdown, hence increasing energy and raising body temperature. Works with **STH** in the young to control rate of growth and development. Contains iodine.*
Thyroid gland *(page 297)*	*Decreases level of calcium and phosphorus in blood by reducing their release from bones (where they are stored).*
Parathyroid glands *(page 297)*	*Increases level of calcium in blood by increasing its release from bone (see above). Decreases phosphorus level.*
Adrenal glands *(page 297) (**medulla**). Also at nerve endings. Secreted at times of excitement or danger.*	*Stimulate liver to release more glucose into blood, to be broken down for energy. Stimulate increase in heart rate, faster breathing and blood vessel constriction.*
Adrenal glands *(page 297) (**cortex**)*	*Increases amount of sodium and water in blood by causing re-absorption of more from **uriniferous tubules** (page 301) in kidneys.*
Adrenal glands *(page 297) (**cortex**)*	*Stimulate increase in rate of food breakdown for energy, and thus increase resistance to stress. Lessen inflammation.*
*Mostly in **ovarian follicles** (page 317) and **corpus luteum** (page 318) in **ovaries** (female sex organs, page 317). Also in **placenta** (page 319) during pregnancy.*	*Estrogen activates development of **secondary sex characters** at **puberty** (page 318), e.g. breast growth. Both prepare **mammary** (milk) **glands** for milk production and work with **LH** to cause thickening of lining of **uterus** (page 317). Progesterone dominates toward end of **menstrual cycle** (page 318) and during pregnancy, when it maintains uterus lining and mammary gland readiness.*
*Mostly in **interstitial cells** in **testes** (male sex organs, page 316).*	*Activate development and maintenance of **secondary sex characters** at **puberty** (page 318), e.g. beard growth.*
Cells in stomach	*Stimulates production of **gastric juice** (page 338).*
Cells in small intestine	*Stimulates opening of **sphincter of Oddi**, contraction of **gall bladder** and release of **bile** (all page 297) into **duodenum** (page 295).*
Cells in small intestine	*Stimulate pancreas to produce **pancreatic juice** (page 338) and secrete it into **duodenum** (page 295).*
Cells in small intestine	*Stimulates production of **intestinal juice** (page 338).*
Pancreas, when blood glucose level too high.	*Stimulates liver to convert more glucose to glycogen for storage (page 331). Also speeds up transport of glucose to cells.*
Pancreas, when blood glucose level too low.	*Stimulates faster conversion of glycogen to glucose in liver (page 331), and conversion of fats and proteins to glucose.*

DIGESTIVE JUICES AND ENZYMES

All the **digestive juices*** of the human body (secreted into the intestines by **digestive glands***) contain **enzymes*** which control the breakdown of food into simple soluble substances. These are called **digestive enzymes** and can be divided into three groups. **Amylases** (or **diastases**) promote the breakdown of **carbohydrates*** (the final result being **monosaccharides** – see terms used, right). **Proteinases** (or **peptidases**) promote the breakdown of **proteins** into **amino acids*** by attacking the **peptide links** (see **proteins**, page 330). **Lipases** promote the breakdown of **fats** into **glycerol** and **fatty acids** (see **fats**, page 330). The chart below lists the different digestive juices of the body, together with their enzymes and the action of these enzymes.

Digestive juice: Saliva

Produced by**: **Salivary glands in mouth*

***Digestive enzyme**: **Salivary amylase** (or **ptyalin**)*

***Actions**: Starts breakdown of **carbohydrates* starch** and **glycogen** (**polysaccharides**). See page 331.*

***Products**: Some **dextrin** (shorter **polysaccharide**). See note 1.*

Digestive juice: Bile

Produced by**: Liver. Stored in **gall bladder, secreted into small intestine (see **CCK**, page 336).*

Constituents**: **Bile salts** and **bile acids

Actions**: Break up **fats (and intermediate compounds) into smaller particles, a process called **emulsification**.*

Digestive juice: Gastric juice

Produced by**: **Gastric glands in stomach lining. Secreted into stomach (see **gastrin**, page 336).*

***Digestive enzymes** (and one other constituent):*
*1. **Pepsin** (**proteinase**). See note 2.*
*2. **Rennin** (**proteinase**). Found only in the young.*
*3. **Hydrochloric acid***
*4. **Gastric lipase**. Found mainly in the young.*

***Actions**:*
*1. Starts breakdown of **proteins*** (**polypeptides**).*
*2. Works (with calcium) to curdle milk, i.e. to act on its **protein** (**casein**). See note 3.*
*3. Activates **pepsin** (see note 2), curdles milk in adults (see note 3) and kills bacteria.*
*4. Starts breakdown of **fat*** molecules in milk.*

***Products**:*
*1. Shorter **polypeptides***
*2, 3. **Curds**, i.e. milk solids*
4. Intermediate compounds

Digestive juice: Intestinal juice (or succus entericus)

Produced by**: **Intestinal glands in small intestine lining. Final secretion into small intestine (see **enterocrinin**, page 336).*

***Digestive enzymes**:*
*1. **Maltase** (**amylase**)*
*2. **Sucrase** (or **invertase** or **saccharase**) (**amylase**)*
*3. **Lactase** (**amylase**)*
*4. **Enterokinase**. See note 2.*

***Actions**:*
*1. Breaks down **maltose** (**disaccharide**).*
*2. Breaks down **sucrose** (**disaccharide**).*
*3. Breaks down **lactose** (**disaccharide**).*
*4. Completes breakdown of **proteins*** (**dipeptides**).*

***Products**:*
*1. **Glucose** (or **dextrose**) (**monosaccharide**)*
*2. **Glucose** and **fructose** (**monosaccharides**)*
*3. **Glucose** and **galactose** (**monosaccharides**)*
*4. **Amino acids****

Digestive juice: Pancreatic juice

***Produced by**: Pancreas. Secreted into small intestine (see **secretin** and **PZ**, page 336).*

***Digestive enzymes**:*
*1. **Trypsin** (**proteinase**). See note 2.*
*2. **Chymotrypsin** (**proteinase**). See note 2.*
*3. **Carboxypeptidase** (**proteinase**). See note 2.*
*4. **Pancreatic amylase** (or **amylopsin**)*
*5. **Pancreatic lipase***

***Actions**:*
*1, 2, 3. Continue breakdown of **proteins*** (long and shorter **polypeptides**).*
*4. Continues breakdown of **carbohydrates***.*
*5. Breaks down **fat*** particles.*

***Products**:*
*1, 2, 3. **Dipeptides** and some **amino acids***.*
*4. **Maltose** (**disaccharide**)*
*5. **Glycerol** and **fatty acids** (see **fats**, page 330).*

Notes

*1. Not much **dextrin** is produced at this stage, since food is not in the mouth long enough. Most carbohydrates pass through unchanged.*

*2. **Proteinases** are first secreted in inactive forms, to prevent them from digesting the digestive tube (made of **protein***, like most of the body). Once in the tube (beyond a protective layer of **mucous membrane***), these are converted into active forms. **Hydrochloric acid** changes **pepsinogen** (inactive) into **pepsin**, **enterokinase** changes **trypsinogen** into **trypsin**, and trypsin then changes **chymotrypsinogen** and **procarboxypeptidase** into **chymotrypsin** and **carboxypeptidase**.*

*3. The action of **rennin** and **hydrochloric acid** in curdling milk is vital, since liquid milk would pass through the system too fast to be digested.*

* **Amino acids**, 330 (**Proteins**); **Carbohydrates**, 330; **Digestive juices**, 296 (**Digestive glands**); **Enzymes**, 333; **Fats**, 330; **Gall bladder**, 297; **Gastric glands**, **Intestinal glands**, 296 (**Digestive glands**); **Mucous membrane**, 295; **Proteins**, 330; **Salivary glands**, 296.

Terms used

Polysaccharides
*The most complex **carbohydrates***. Each is a chain of **monosaccharide** molecules. Most carbohydrates taken into the body are polysaccharides, e.g. **starch** (the main polysaccharide in edible plants) and **glycogen** (the main one in animal matter). For more about starch and glycogen, see page 331.*

Disaccharides
*Compounds of two **monosaccharide** molecules, either forming intermediate stages in the breakdown of **polysaccharides** or (in the case of **sucrose** and **lactose**) taken into the body as such. (Sucrose is found in sugar beet and sugar cane, lactose occurs in milk.)*

Monosaccharides
*The simplest **carbohydrates***. Almost all result from **polysaccharide** breakdown, though **fructose** is taken into the body as such (e.g. in fruit juices), as well as resulting from **sucrose** breakdown. **Glucose** is the final result of all action on carbohydrates (fructose and **galactose** are converted to glucose in the liver).*

Polypeptides
*The complex form taken by all **proteins** entering the body. Each is a chain of hundreds (or thousands) of **amino acid*** molecules (see **proteins**, pages 330).*

Dipeptides
*Chains of two **amino acid** molecules, forming intermediate stages in the breakdown of **polypeptides**.*

Vitamins and their uses

Vitamin A (retinol)

Sources**: Liver, kidneys, fish-liver oils, eggs, dairy products, margarine, **pigment (**carotene**) in green and yellow fruit and vegetables, especially tomatoes and carrots (carotene converted to vitamin A in intestines).*

Uses**: Maintains general health of **epithelial cells (lining cells), aids growth, especially bones and teeth. Essential for vision in dim light – involved in formation of light-sensitive **pigment*** (**rhodopsin**), found in **rods** of **retina***. Aids in resistance against infection.*

Vitamin B complex

Group of at least 10 vitamins, usually occurring together. Include:
***Thiamine** (or **aneurin**) (**B1**)*
***Riboflavin** (**B2**)*
***Niacin** (or **nicotinic acid** or **nicotinamide**) (**B3**)*
***Pantothenic acid** (**B5**)*
***Pyridoxine** (**B6**)*
***Cyanocobalamin** (or **cobalamin**) (**B12**)*
***Folic acid** (**Bc** or **M**)*
***Biotin** (sometimes called **vitamin H**)*
***Lecithin**.*

***Sources**: All found in yeast and liver. All except B12 found in wholewheat cereals and bread, wheatgerm and green vegetables, e.g. beans (B12 not found in any vegetable products). B2 and B12 found especially in dairy products. Most also found in eggs, nuts, fish, lean meat, kidneys and potatoes. B6, folic acid and biotin also made by bacteria in intestines.*

Uses:** Most needed for growth and maintenance of healthy tissues, e.g. muscles (B1, B6), nerves (B1, B3, B6, B12), skin (B2, B3, B5, B6, B12) and hair (B2, B5). Several also aid continuous function of body organs (B5, B6, lecithin). All except folic acid, biotin and lecithin are essential **co-enzymes, aiding in breakdown of foods for energy (**internal respiration***). Many (especially B2, B6, B12) also co-enzymes aiding build-up of substances (**proteins***) for growth and regulatory or defence purposes. B12 and folic acid vital to formation of blood cells, B5 and B6 vital to manufacture of nerve chemicals (**neurotransmitters***).*

Vitamin C (ascorbic acid)

***Sources**: Green vegetables, potatoes, tomatoes, citrus fruit, e.g. oranges, grapefruit, lemons.*

Uses**: Needed for growth and maintenance of healthy tissues, especially skin, blood vessels, bones, gums, teeth. Essential **co-enzyme in many metabolic reactions, especially **protein*** breakdown and build-up of **amino acids*** into new proteins (especially **collagen** – see **connective tissue**, page 280). Aids in resistance against infection and healing of wounds.*

Vitamin D (calciferol)

***Sources**: Liver, fish-liver oils, oily fish, dairy products, egg yolk, margarine, special substance (provitamin D3) in skin cells (converted to vitamin D when exposed to sunlight).*

Uses**: Essential for absorption of calcium and phosphorus, and their deposition in bones and teeth. May work with **PTH (**hormone**).*

Vitamin E (tocopherol)

***Sources**: Meat, egg yolk, leafy vegetables, nuts, dairy products, margarine, cereals, wholemeal bread, wheatgerm, seeds, seed and vegetable oils.*

***Uses**: Not yet fully understood. Protects membranes from some molecules which could bind and cause cancer.*

Vitamin K (phylloquinone or menaquinone)

***Sources**: Liver, fruit, nuts, cereals, tomatoes, green vegetables, especially cabbage, cauliflower, spinach. Also made by bacteria in intestines.*

Uses**: Essential for formation of **prothrombin in liver (needed to cause clotting of blood).*

* **Amino acids**, 330 (**Proteins**); **Carbohydrates**, 330; **Co-enzymes**, 333 (**Enzymes**); **DNA**, 324 (**Nucleic acids**); **Epithelium**, 310 (**Epidermis**); **Internal respiration**, 334; **Neurotransmitters**, 305 (**Synapse**); **Pigments**, 255; **Proteins**, 330; **Prothrombin**, 287 (**Clotting**); **PTH**, 336; **Retina**, 313.

THE CLASSIFICATION OF LIVING THINGS

Callicore cyllene

Callicore mengeli

Agrias claudina

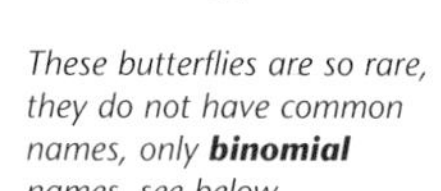

*These butterflies are so rare, they do not have common names, only **binomial** names, see below.*

Classification, also called **taxonomy**, is the grouping together of living things according to the characteristics they share. The main, formal type of classification (**classical taxonomy**) bases its groups primarily on structural characteristics. The resulting classification charts first list the largest groups – **Kingdoms** – and then list the smaller and smaller sub-divisions within these groups.

The first groups after the Kingdoms are called **phyla** (sing. **phylum**) in the case of animals, and **divisions** in the case of plants. After these come **classes**, **orders**, **families**, **genera** (sing. **genus**) and finally **species** – the smallest groupings. A species is defined as a group of interbreeding organisms, reproductively isolated from other groups. If this is impossible to establish, then a species is recognized on a **morphological** basis, i.e. by its external appearance.

Some divisions or phyla, especially those with only a few members, may not have all these groups, so the next group after a phylum may be an order, family, genus or even a species. There are also further "mid-way" groups in some cases, such as **sub-kingdoms**, **sub-phyla** or **sub-classes**.

There are areas which are still under dispute in both plant and animal classification. Most scientists recognize five main Kingdoms (see diagram, page 341), but some prefer to group living things into four Kingdoms: **animals** (including **Protista**), **plants** (including **fungi** and **algae**), **Monera** and **viruses**. The diagram below shows the divisions of the Plant Kingdom.

Nomenclature

The naming of organisms. Names of **species** are given in Latin so that all biologists world-wide can follow the same system. This is necessary as species are often known by various common names in different parts of the world. For example, one type of herring, *Alosa pseudoharengus*, has six different names throughout its geographical range.

Every organism has a two word name. This is called the **binomial system**. The first word is a **generic name** (from the **genus**) and the second identifies the species within that genus. The Latin names are governed by The International Commission for Zoological Nomenclature, at the Natural History Museum in London. Most names make direct reference to specific characteristics of the species, such as size, shape or habitat. The giant anteater, for example, is called *Myrmecophaga tridactyla* (*myrmeco* = ant, *phag* = eat, *tri* = three, and *dactyl* = fingers). This describes the food it eats and the three large digging claws at the end of each foreleg.

Giant anteater

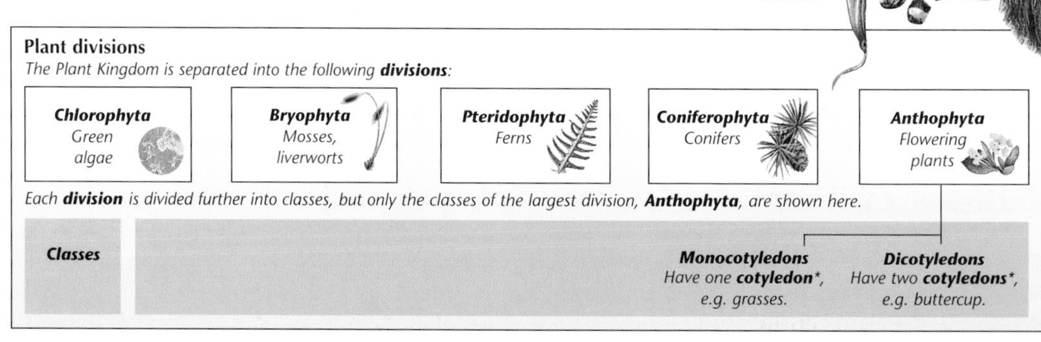

Plant divisions
The Plant Kingdom is separated into the following divisions:
Chlorophyta
Green algae
Bryophyta
Mosses, liverworts
Pteridophyta
Ferns
Coniferophyta
Conifers
Anthophyta
Flowering plants
Each division is divided further into classes, but only the classes of the largest division, Anthophyta, are shown here.
Classes
Monocotyledons
Have one cotyledon*, e.g. grasses.
Dicotyledons
Have two cotyledons*, e.g. buttercup.

* **Cotyledon**, 261.

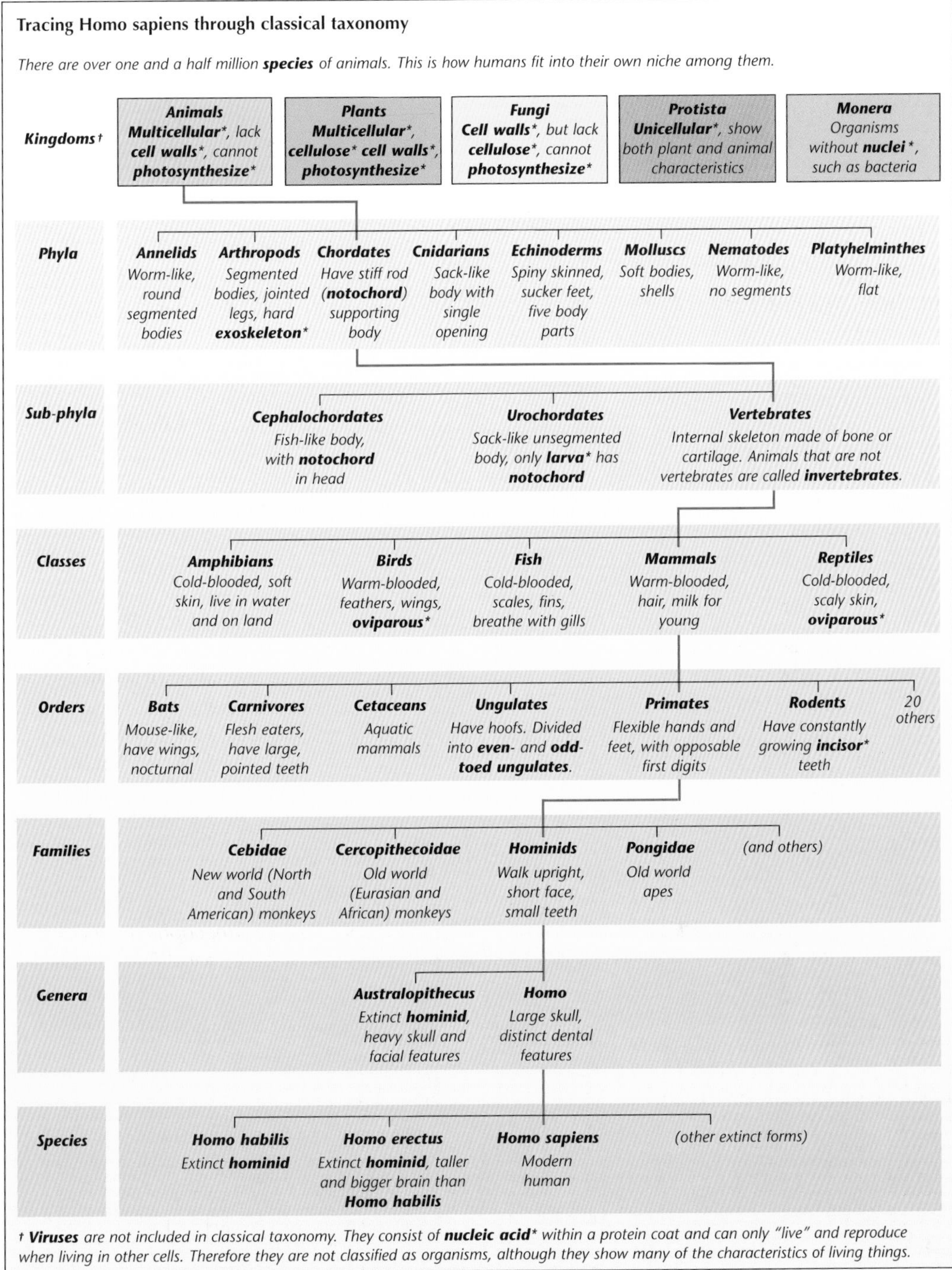
Tracing Homo sapiens through classical taxonomy
There are over one and a half million species of animals. This is how humans fit into their own niche among them.
Kingdoms†
Animals Multicellular*, lack cell walls*, cannot photosynthesize*
Plants Multicellular*, cellulose* cell walls*, photosynthesize*
Fungi Cell walls*, but lack cellulose*, cannot photosynthesize*
Protista Unicellular*, show both plant and animal characteristics
Monera Organisms without nuclei*, such as bacteria
Phyla
Annelids Worm-like, round segmented bodies
Arthropods Segmented bodies, jointed legs, hard exoskeleton*
Chordates Have stiff rod (notochord) supporting body
Cnidarians Sack-like body with single opening
Echinoderms Spiny skinned, sucker feet, five body parts
Molluscs Soft bodies, shells
Nematodes Worm-like, no segments
Platyhelminthes Worm-like, flat
Sub-phyla
Cephalochordates Fish-like body, with notochord in head
Urochordates Sack-like unsegmented body, only larva* has notochord
Vertebrates Internal skeleton made of bone or cartilage. Animals that are not vertebrates are called invertebrates.
Classes
Amphibians Cold-blooded, soft skin, live in water and on land
Birds Warm-blooded, feathers, wings, oviparous*
Fish Cold-blooded, scales, fins, breathe with gills
Mammals Warm-blooded, hair, milk for young
Reptiles Cold-blooded, scaly skin, oviparous*
Orders
Bats Mouse-like, have wings, nocturnal
Carnivores Flesh eaters, have large, pointed teeth
Cetaceans Aquatic mammals
Ungulates Have hoofs. Divided into even- and odd-toed ungulates.
Primates Flexible hands and feet, with opposable first digits
Rodents Have constantly growing incisor* teeth
20 others
Families
Cebidae New world (North and South American) monkeys
Cercopithecoidae Old world (Eurasian and African) monkeys
Hominids Walk upright, short face, small teeth
Pongidae Old world apes
(and others)
Genera
Australopithecus Extinct hominid, heavy skull and facial features
Homo Large skull, distinct dental features
Species
Homo habilis Extinct hominid
Homo erectus Extinct hominid, taller and bigger brain than Homo habilis
Homo sapiens Modern human
(other extinct forms)
† Viruses are not included in classical taxonomy. They consist of nucleic acid* within a protein coat and can only "live" and reproduce when living in other cells. Therefore they are not classified as organisms, although they show many of the characteristics of living things.

Other classification systems

Classical taxonomy is one of several systems used to classify living things. Another significant method is **cladistic classification**.

Cladistic classification

As with classical taxonomy, this system places groups into larger groups (called **clades**) based on shared characteristics. But clades also include the ancestral forms and all their descendants.

* **Cell wall**, 238; **Cellulose**, 331 (**Roughage**); **Exoskeleton**, 266; **Incisors**, 285; **Larva**, 277; **Multicellular**, 238; **Nucleic acids**, 324; **Nucleus**, 238; **Oviparous**, 274; **Photosynthesis**, 254; **Unicellular**, 238.

INFORMAL GROUP TERMS

Listed here are the main terms used to group living things together according to their general life styles (i.e. their ecological similarities – see also page 237). These are informal terms, as opposed to the formal terms of the classification charts (pages 340-341).

Plants

Xerophytes
Plants which can survive long periods of time without water, e.g. cacti.

Hydrophytes
Plants which grow in water or very wet soil, e.g. reeds.

Mesophytes
Plants which grow under average conditions of moisture.

Halophytes
Plants which can withstand very salty conditions, e.g. sea pinks.

Lithophytes
Plants which grow on rock, e.g. some mosses.

Epiphytes
Plants which grow on other plants, but only to use them for support, not to feed off them, e.g. some mosses.

Saprophytes
Plants which live on decaying plants or animals, feed off them, but are not the agents of their death, e.g. some fungi.

Animals

Predators
*Animals which kill and eat other animals (their **prey**), e.g. lions. Bird predators, e.g. hawks, are called **raptors**.*

Detritus feeders
Animals which feed on debris from decayed plant or animal matter, e.g. worms.

Scavengers
*Large **detritus feeders**, e.g. hyenas, which feed only on dead flesh (animal matter).*

Territorial
*Holding and defending a **territory** (an area of land or water) either singly or in groups, e.g. many fish, birds and mammals. This is usually linked with attracting a mate and breeding.*

Abyssal
Living at great depths in the sea, e.g. oarfish and gulper eels.

Demersal
Living at the bottom of a lake or the shallow sea, e.g. angler fish and prawns.

Sedentary
Staying mostly in one place (but not permanently attached), e.g. sea anemone.

Nocturnal
Active at night and sleeping during the day, e.g. owls and bats.

Plants and animals

Insectivores
Specialized organisms which eat mostly insects, e.g. pitcher plants (which trap and digest insects) and hedgehogs.

Parasites
*Plants or animals which live in or on other living plants or animals (the **hosts**), and feed off them, e.g. mistletoe and fleas. Not all are harmful to the host.*

Mutualists
*A pair of living things which associate closely with each other and derive mutual benefit from such close existence (**mutualism**). **Lichens**, normally found on bare rock, are an example. Each is in fact two plants (a fungus and an alga). The alga produces food (by **photosynthesis***) for the fungus (which otherwise could not live on bare rock). The fungus uses its fine threads to hold the moisture the alga needs.*

Commensals
*A pair of living things which associate closely with each other, one deriving benefit without affecting the other. One type of worm, for instance, is very often found in the same shell as a hermit crab. One of the most common examples of **commensalism** is the existence of house mice wherever there are humans.*

Social or **colonial**
*Living together in groups. The two terms are synonymous in the case of plants, and refer to those which grow in clusters. In the case of animals, there is a difference of numbers between the terms. Lions, for example, are social, but their groups (**prides**) are not large enough to be called colonies. With true colonial animals, there is also a great difference in the level of interdependence between colony members. In a gannet colony, for example, this is relatively low (they only live close together because there is safety in numbers). In an ant colony, by contrast, different groups (**castes**) have very different jobs, e.g. gathering food or guarding the colony, so each member relies heavily on others. The highest level of colonial interdependence is shown by the tiny, physically inseparable, single-celled organisms which form one living mass, e.g. a sponge.*

Sessile
In the case of animals, this term refers to those which are not free to move around, i.e. they are permanently fixed to the ground or other solid object, e.g. barnacles. With plants, it describes those without stalks, e.g. stemless thistles.

Pelagic
*Living in the main body of a lake or the sea, as opposed to at the bottom or at great depths. Pelagic creatures range from tiny **plankton** through medium-sized fish and sharks to very large whales. The medium-sized and large ones are all animals, and are called **nekton** (from the Greek for "swimming thing"), as they swim.*

Plankton
*Aquatic animals and plants, vast numbers of which drift in lakes and seas, normally near the surface (plant plankton is **phytoplankton**, and animal plankton is **zooplankton**). Plankton is the food of many fish and whales and is thus vital to the ecological balance (**food chains***) of the sea. Most are small.*

Littoral
Living at the bottom of a lake or the sea near the shore, e.g. crabs and seaweed.

Benthos
*All **abyssal**, **demersal** and **littoral** plants and animals, i.e. all those which live in, on or near the bottom of lakes or seas.*

* **Food chains**, 234 (**Food web**); **Photosynthesis**, 254.

DICTIONARY OF SCIENCE

Glossary and index

GLOSSARY

Abrasive
A material which wears away the surface of another material.

Adhesive
A substance which sticks to one or more other substances (see adhesion, page 23).

Alloy
A mixture of two or more metals, or a metal and a non-metal. It has its own properties (which are metallic), independent of those of its constituents. For example, ***brass**** *is an alloy of copper and zinc, and* ***steel**** *is an alloy of iron and carbon (different mixes give the steel different properties).*

Amalgam
An ***alloy*** *of mercury with other metals. It is usually soft and may even be liquid.*

Antacid
A substance which counteracts excess stomach acidity by ***neutralizing**** *the acid. Examples are aluminum hydroxide and magnesium hydroxide.*

Bleach
A substance used to remove color from a material or solution. Most strong ***oxidizing**** *and* ***reducing agents**** *are good bleaches. The most common household bleach is a solution of sodium hypochlorite (also a highly effective* ***germicide****). The equation below shows the products of the reaction between sodium hypochlorite and a colored material.*

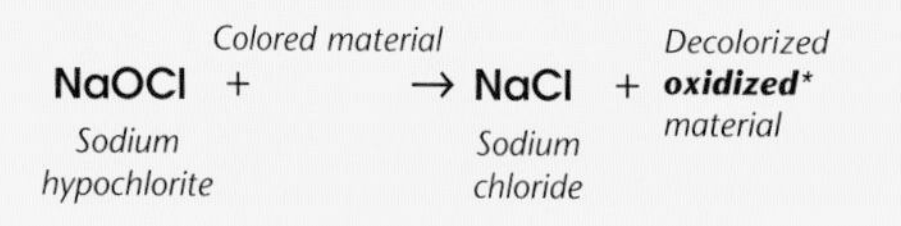

Colored material
Decolorized
NaOCl + → NaCl + oxidized* material
Sodium hypochlorite
Sodium chloride

Calibration
The "setting up" of a measuring instrument so that it gives the correct reading. The instrument is normally adjusted during manufacture so that it reads the correct value when it is measuring a known standard quantity, e.g. a balance would be adjusted to read exactly 1kg when a standard 1kg mass was on it.

Calorimetry
The measurement of heat change during a chemical reaction or event involving heat transfer. For example, measuring the temperature rise of a known mass of a substance when it is heated electrically is used to find ***specific heat capacity****, and the temperature rise of a mass of water can be used to calculate the energy produced by a fuel when it is burned (see* ***bomb calorimeter*** *diagram, page 147).*

Coefficient
A ***constant*** *for a substance, used to calculate quantities related to the substance by multiplying it by other quantities. For example, the force pushing two materials together multiplied by the* ***coefficient of friction**** *for the surfaces gives the* ***frictional force****.*

Constant
A numerical quantity that does not vary. For example, in the equation $E = mc^2$ *(see also page 84), the quantity c (the speed of light in a vacuum) is the constant. E and m are* ***variables*** *because they can change.*

Coolant
A fluid used for cooling in industry or in the home (see also ***refrigerant****). The fluid usually extracts heat from one source and transfers it to another. In a* ***nuclear power station**** *the coolant transfers heat from the nuclear reaction to the steam generator, where the heat is used to produce steam. This turns turbines and generates electricity.*

Cosine (of an angle)
The ratio of the length of the side adjacent to the angle to the length of the hypotenuse (the longest side) in a right-angled triangle. It depends on the angle.

Dehydrating agent
A substance used to absorb moisture from another substance, removing water molecules if present, but also, importantly, hydrogen and oxygen atoms from the molecules of the substance. This leaves a different substance plus water (see also ***drying agent****). Concentrated sulfuric acid is an example:*

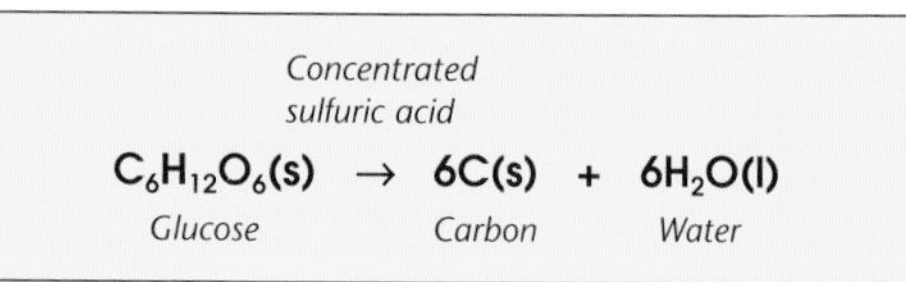

Concentrated sulfuric acid
$C_6H_{12}O_6(s) \rightarrow 6C(s) + 6H_2O(l)$
Glucose
Carbon
Water

Concentrated sulfuric acid can also be used as a drying agent if it does not react with the substance added to it. For example, it is used to dry samples of chlorine gas, i.e. remove surrounding molecules of water vapor (see page 216).

Drying agent
A substance used to absorb moisture from another substance, but which only removes water molecules from in and around the substance, not separate hydrogen and oxygen atoms from its molecules. The substance itself is not changed (see also ***desiccation****, page 221, and* ***dehydrating agent****).* ***Phosphorus pentoxide*** *(*P_2O_5*) is an example:*

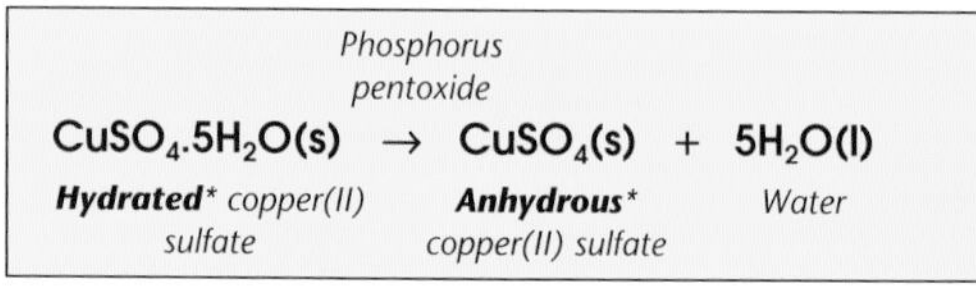

Phosphorus pentoxide
$CuSO_4.5H_2O(s) \rightarrow CuSO_4(s) + 5H_2O(l)$
Hydrated* copper(II) sulfate
Anhydrous* copper(II) sulfate
Water

Ductile
Describes a substance which can be stretched. It is normally used of metals which can be drawn out into thin wire, e.g. copper. Different substances show varying degrees of ***ductility*** *(see page 165). See also* ***yield point****, page 23.*

Fumigation
The killing of pests such as insects by poisonous gas, e.g. sulfur dioxide, or smoke.

Fungicide
A substance used to destroy harmful fungi, e.g. molds and mildews growing on crops.

Germicide
A substance used to destroy bacteria, especially those carrying disease (germs).

* **Anhydrous**, 154 (**Anhydrate**); **Brass**, 112, 175 (**Zinc**); **Coefficient of friction**, **Frictional force**, 7; **Hydrated**, 154 (**Hydrate**); **Neutralization**, 151; **Nuclear power station**, 94; **Oxidation**, **Oxidizing agent**, **Reducing agent**, 148; **Specific heat capacity**, 31; **Steel**, 174.

Graduations
Marks used for measurement, e.g. those on a ***measuring cylinder**** *or a* ***gas syringe****.*

Inert
Describes an unreactive substance, i.e. one which does not easily take part in chemical reactions. Examples are the ***noble*** *(or* ***inert****)* ***gases****.*

Inversely proportional
When applied to two quantities, this means that, for example, if one is doubled, the other is halved.

Latex
A milky fluid produced by plants, particularly that produced by the rubber tree, from which raw natural rubber is extracted (and which also forms the basis of some ***adhesives****). Also certain similar* ***synthetic polymers****.*

Malleable
Describes a substance which can be molded into different shapes. It is normally used of substances which can be hammered out into thin sheets, in particular many metals and ***alloys*** *of metals. Different substances show varying degrees of* ***malleability*** *(see page 165).*

Mean
A synonym for average, i.e. the sum of a collection of values divided by the number of values in the collection.

Medium (pl. **media**)
Any substance through which a physical effect is transmitted, e.g. glass is a medium when light travels through it.

Meniscus
The concave or convex surface of a liquid, e.g. water or mercury. It is caused by the relative attraction of the molecules to each other and to those of the container (see also ***adhesion*** *and* ***cohesion****, page 23 and* ***parallax error****, page 102).*

Ore
A naturally-occurring mineral from which an element (usually a metal) is extracted, e.g. bauxite, which yields aluminum.

Organic solvent
An organic liquid in which substances will dissolve.

Photocell or **photoelectric cell**
A device used for the detection and measurement of light.

Proportional
When applied to two quantities, this means that they have a relationship such that, for example, if one is doubled, so is the other.

Rate
The amount by which one quantity changes with respect to another, e.g. ***acceleration**** *is the rate of change of* ***velocity**** *with time. Note that the second quantity is not necessarily time in all cases. If a graph of Y against X is plotted, the rate of change of Y with respect to X at a point is the gradient at that point.*

Raw material
A material obtained from natural sources for use in industry, e.g. iron ***ore****, coke and limestone are the raw materials used to produce iron (see picture, page 174).*

Reciprocal
The value obtained from a number when one is divided by it, i.e. the reciprocal number of x is $^1/_x$. For example, the reciprocal of 10 is 0.1.

Refrigerant
A type of ***coolant*** *used in refrigerators. It must be a liquid which* ***evaporates**** *at low temperatures. The substances commonly used nowadays are the* ***chlorofluorocarbons****, although ammonia was widely used in the past.*

Resins
Substances used as ***adhesives****. They are often insoluble in water.* ***Natural resins*** *are organic compounds secreted by certain plants and insects.* ***Synthetic resins*** *are plastic materials produced by* ***polymerization****.*

Sine (of an angle)
The ratio of the length of the side opposite to the angle to the length of the hypotenuse (the longest side) in a right-angled triangle. It depends on the angle.

Spectrum (pl. **spectra**)
A particular distribution of wavelengths and frequencies, e.g. the wavelengths in the ***visible light spectrum**** *range from 4×10^{-7}m to 7.5×10^{-7}m.*

Superheated steam
Steam above a temperature of 100°C. It is obtained by heating water under pressure.

System
A set of connected parts which have an effect on each other and form a whole unit, e.g. a ***digestive system**** *or the substances involved in a reaction at* ***chemical equilibrium****.*

Tangent (of an angle)
The ratio of the length of the side opposite to the angle to the length of the side adjacent to it in a right-angled triangle. It depends on the angle.

Tarnish
To lose or partially lose shine due to the formation of a dull surface layer, e.g. silver sulfide on silver or lithium oxide on lithium. Tarnishing is a type of ***corrosion****.*

Variable
A numerical quantity which can take any value. For example, in the equation $E = mc^2$ (see also page 84), E and m are variables since they can take any value (although the value of E depends on the value of m). The quantity c (the speed of light in a vacuum) is a ***constant****.*

Volatile
Describes a liquid that ***evaporates**** *easily, e.g. gasoline, or a solid that* ***sublimes**** *easily, e.g. iodine.*

Volume
A measurement of the space occupied by a body. See page 101 for calculations of volume. The ***SI unit**** *of volume is the cubic meter (m^3).*

Vulcanization
The process of heating raw natural rubber (extracted from ***latex****) with sulfur. Vulcanized rubber is harder, tougher and less temperature-sensitive than raw rubber (the more sulfur used, the greater the difference). This is because the sulfur atoms form cross-links between the chains of rubber molecules (see picture, page 201).*

* **Acceleration**, 11; **Chemical equilibrium**, 163; **Chlorofluorocarbons**, 195; **Corrosion**, 209; **Digestive system**, 294; **Evaporation**, 121; **Gas syringe**, 224; **Measuring cylinder**, 224; **Noble gases**, 189; **Polymerization**, 200; **SI units**, 96; **Sublimation**, 121; **Synthetic polymers**, 201; **Velocity**, 10; **Visible light spectrum**, 54.

INDEX

The page numbers listed in the index are of three different types. Those printed in bold type (e.g. **92**) indicate in each case where the main definition(s) of a word (or words) can be found. Those in lighter type (e.g. 92) refer to supplementary entries. Page numbers printed in italics (e.g. *92*) indicate pages where a word (or words) can be found as a small print label to a picture. If a page number is followed by a word in brackets, it means that the indexed word can be found inside the text of the definition indicated. If it is followed by (**I**), the indexed word can be found in the introductory text on the page given. Bracketed singulars, plurals, symbols and formulas are given where relevant after indexed words. Synonyms are indicated by the word "see", or by an oblique stroke (/) if the synonyms fall together alphabetically.

C

D

E

F

H

I

J

M

N

Q

R

S

T

U

V

X

Y

Z

ACKNOWLEDGEMENTS

Cover designers: Stephen Moncrieff
Additional text by Paul Dowswell
American editor: Carrie A. Seay
Additional design by Chris Scollen, Stephen Wright,
Anne Sharples, Sue Mims and Nerissa Davies.

Additional illustrations by:

Simone Abel, Victor Ambrus, Basil Arm, Dave Ashby, Iain Ashman, Mike Atkinson, Craig Austin (The Garden Studio), Graham Austin, Bob Bampton (The Garden Studio), John Barber, John Barker, Amanda Barlow, Terry Bave, David Baxter, Andrew Beckett, Joyce Bee, Stephen Bennett, Roland Berry, Andrzej Bielecki, Gary Bines, Val Biro, Blue Chip Illustration, Kim Blundell, Derick Bown, Isabel Bowring, Trevor Boyer, Wendy Bramall (Artist Partners), Derek Brazell, John Brettoner, Paul Brooks (John Martin Artists), Fiona Brown, Gerard Browne, Peter Bull, Mark Burgess, Hilary Burn, Andy Burton, Liz Butler, Martin Camm, Lynn Chadwick, Chris Chapman, Peter Chesterton, Paul Cooper, Sydney Cornford, Dan Courtney, Frankie Coventry (Artist Partners), Patrick Cox, Christine Darter, Kate Davies, Sarah De Ath (Linden Artists), Kevin Dean, Peter Dennis, David Downton, Richard Draper, Nick Dupays, Brian Edwards, Michelle Emblem (Middletons), Malcolm English, Caroline Ewen, Sandra Fernandez, James Field, Denise Finney, Dennis Finney, Wayne Ford, Don Forrest, Patience Foster, Sarah Fox-Davies, John Francis, Mark Franklin, Nigel Frey, Judy Friedlander, Peter Froste, Terry Gabby, Sheila Galbraith, Stephen Gardener, Peter Geissler, Nick Gibbard, Tony Gibson, William Giles, Mick Gillah, Victoria Goaman, David Goldston, Peter Goodwin, Victoria Gordon, Jeremy Gower, Terri Gower, Miranda Gray, Phil Green, Terry Hadler, Rys Hajdul, Edwina Hannam, Alan Harris, Brenda Haw, Tim Hayward, Bob Hersey, Nicholas Hewetson, Rosalind Hewitt, Keith Hodgson, Philip Hood, Adam Hook, Shirley Hooper, Chris Howell-Jones, Christine Howes, Carol Hughes (John Martin Artists), Rian Hughes, David Hurrell (Middletons), Gillian Hurry, John Hutchinson, Roy Hutchison (Middletons), Ian Jackson, Tony Jackson, Hans Jenssen, Chris Johnson, Elaine Keenan, Frank Kennard, Roger Kent, Aziz Khan, Colin King, Deborah King, Steven Kirk, Kim Lane, Jonathan Langley, Richard Lewington (The Garden Studio), Jason Lewis, Ken Lilly, Steve Lings (Linden Artists), Mick Loates (The Garden Studio), Rachel Lockwood, Tony Lodge, Kevin Lyles, Chris Lyon, Kevin Maddison, Janos Marffy, Andy Martin, Josephine Martin, Nick May, Rob McCaig, Joseph McEwan, David McGrail, Malcolm McGregor, Doreen McGuinness, Dee McLean (Linden Artists), David Mead, Jamie Medlin, Richard Millington, Annabel Milne, Sean Milne, David More (Linden Artists), Dee Morgan, Robert Morton (Linden Artists), David Mostyn, Paddy Mounter, David Nash, Susan Neale, Louise Nevett, Martin Newton, Barbara Nicholson, Louise Nixon, David Nockels (The Garden Studio), Richard Orr, Steve Page, David Palmer, Patti Pearce, Justine Peek, Liz Pepperell (The Garden Studio), Julia Piper, Gillian Platt (The Garden Studio), Maurice Pledger, Cynthia Pow (Middletons), Russell Punter, David Quinn, Charles Raymond (Virgil Pomfret Agency), Kim Raymond, Barry Raynor, Chris Reed, Phillip Richardson, Jim Robins, Allan Robinson, Michael Roffe, Michelle Ross, Peter Ross, Graham Round, Evie Safarewicz, Mike Saunders (Tudor Art), Jon Sayer, Peter Scanlan, John Scorey, Coral Sealey, John Shackell, Chris Shields (Wilcock Riley), John Sibbick (John Martin Artists), Penny Simon, Gwen Simpson, Chris Smedley, Graham Smith, Annabel Spencerley, Peter Stebbing, Sue Stitt, Roger Stewart, Ralph Stobart, Paul Sullivan, Alan Suttie, John Thompson-Steinkrauss (John Martin Artists), Sam Thompson, Stuart Trotter, Joyce Tuhill, Sally Voke (Middletons), Sue Walliker, Robert Walster, David Watson, Ross Watton, Phil Weare, Chris West, Wigwam Publishing Services, Sean Wilkinson, Adrian Williams, Adam Willis, Roy Wiltshire, Ann Winterbotham, Gerald Wood, James Woods (Middletons), Claire Wright, David Wright (Jillian Burgess), Jo Wright, Nigel Wright, Gordon Wylie, John Yates.

Photograph credits:

Cover (clockwise from top left): © Gusto / Science Photo Library; © Geoff Tompkinson / Science Photo Library; © Sheila Terry / Science Photo Library; © Georgette Douwma / Science Photo Library; © Alfred Pasieka / Science Photo Library; © Dr Mark J. Winter / Science Photo Library
The ultrasound scan on page 40 is reproduced with the kind permission of Charlotte Tomlins.
© Alfred Pasieka / Science Photo Library (45, bottom left); Digital Vision (45, bottom right; 93, bottom right; 206, top right).

This edition first published in 2007 by Usborne Publishing Ltd, Usborne House, 83-85 Saffron Hill, London EC1N 8RT, England. www.usborne.com AE First published in America in 2007. Printed in Dubai.